DISASTER IN THE FAR EAST
1940–1942

DESPATCHES FROM THE FRONT

The Commanding Officers' Reports From the Field and At Sea.

DISASTER IN THE FAR EAST 1940–1942

THE DEFENCE OF MALAYA, JAPANESE CAPTURE OF HONG KONG, AND THE FALL OF SINGAPORE

Introduced and compiled by
Martin Mace and John Grehan
With additional research by
Sara Mitchell

Pen & Sword
MILITARY

First published in Great Britain in 2015 by
Pen & Sword Military
an imprint of
Pen & Sword Books Ltd
47 Church Street
Barnsley
South Yorkshire
S70 2AS

ISBN 978 1 78346 209 4

Printed and bound in England
By CPI Group (UK) Ltd, Croydon, CR0 4YY

Pen & Sword Books Ltd incorporates the Imprints of
Pen & Sword Aviation, Pen & Sword Family History,
Pen & Sword Maritime, Pen & Sword Military, Pen & Sword Discovery,
Pen & Sword Politics, Pen & Sword Atlas, Pen & Sword Archaeology,
Wharncliffe Local History, Wharncliffe True Crime, Wharncliffe Transport,
Pen & Sword Select, Pen & Sword Military Classics, Leo Cooper,
The Praetorian Press, Claymore Press, Remember When,
Seaforth Publishing and Frontline Publishing.

For a complete list of Pen & Sword titles please contact:
PEN & SWORD BOOKS LIMITED
47 Church Street, Barnsley, South Yorkshire, S70 2AS, England
E-mail: enquiries@pen-and-sword.co.uk

Website: www.pen-and-sword.co.uk

CONTENTS

Introduction   vii

List of Illustrations   xi

The Despatches

1. Air Chief Marshal Sir Robert Brooke-Popham's Despatch on   1
   Operations from 17 October 1940 to 27 December 1941.

2. Major-General C.M. Maltby's Despatch on Operations in   91
   Hong Kong, 8 December 1941 to 25 December 1941.

3. Lieutenant General Arthur Percival's Despatch on Operations,   147
   8 December 1941 to 15 February 1942.

4. Air Vice-Marshal Sir Paul Maltby's Despatch on Air Operations   355
   during the campaigns in Malaya and Netherland East Indies,
   8 December 1941 to 12 March 1942.

Abbreviations   505

Index   511

INTRODUCTION

The first officer to have his despatch on operations in the Far East published was Air Chief Marshal Sir Robert Brook-Popham. He took up his post in Singapore on 18 November 1940, with his area of command encompassing Burma, Hong Kong as well as Malaya, and included the Far East Air Command. The Indian, Chinese and the East Indies commands remained outside his authority.

Brook-Popham was directed to avoid war with Japan and was reminded of this fact in March 1941, being informed that, "Avoidance of war with Japan is basis of Far East policy and provocation must be rigidly avoided". This message was reinforced again in September of that year, this time it being stated that "Our policy in the Far East is still to avoid war with Japan".

Brook-Popham was also told that the defence of the United Kingdom, the Battle of the Atlantic and the fighting in North Africa had priority over the Far East. He would simply have to make do with whatever he was given in terms of men and machines. It is interesting to note that Brook-Popham recorded that when he was pushing to bring his forces up to what he described as an irreducible minimum, he was cautioned against over-estimate of the Japanese forces.

Brook-Popham sought to give the impression that the British and Commonwealth forces were so strong that the Japanese would not dare to attack them. As the Japanese showed no fear in attacking the United States, it is evident that, however great a show of force Brook-Popham displayed, it would not have deterred them.

In writing his despatch, Brook-Popham compiled a very thorough explanation of the reasons for the success of the Japanese in the weeks before he relinquished responsibility for the Far East Command. This included an analysis of Japanese tactics and equipment and their use of psychological warfare: "Chinese crackers [were used] and strange cries at night; these tricks, though laughable when one knew about them, had a certain amount of moral effect, especially on young Indian troops."

Another factor which had some effect on morale generally, Brook-Popham explained, was that, strategically, the British forces were on the defensive. All the troops were aware that it was the intention to avoid war with Japan, which meant that the initiative and especially the choice of the moment for opening hostilities rested with the enemy.

That moment came at 01.30 hours on Monday, 8 December 1941, when the Japanese started to land from ships at Kota Bharu on the eastern coast of Malaya. Two large Japanese convoys escorted by warships had been picked up by aerial reconnaissance as early as 14.00 hours on the 6th. Though it seemed fairly obvious that this was the start of the Japanese offensive, because Brook-Popham had been told not to take any provocative action (this had been re-stated as recently as 29 November, just a week before the Japanese attack) he had to wait for the Japanese to open hostilities.

Ridiculous as it may sound, Brook-Popham had to prepare in advance an Order of the Day to communicate to his troops that war had broken out. This had to be written in all the various languages of the people under his command. This also had to be distributed across the thousands of miles which comprised his command so that they could be released on the day war broke out. In order to be able to accomplish this, they had to be sent out the day before the fighting began. So the situation was that Brook-Popham had to issue orders to his troops that war had begun whilst not being permitted to take any action against the enemy.

Thus robbed of the opportunity to attack the Japanese whilst they were still at sea, Brook-Popham had to wait for the enemy to attack wherever and whenever they chose. Little wonder that the Japanese were able to overrun the British lines so rapidly.

Whilst Malaya and Singapore were the main territories Brook-Popham had to defend, he also bore responsibility for Hong Kong and he provided a report on its fall which, given the resources available for its defence, was inevitable. Initially Burma also formed part of the Far East Command but on 15 December this was handed over to the Commander-in-Chief, India. Brook-Popham also reports on the Japanese attack upon Borneo. Allied troops were still fighting in Borneo when, on 27 December 1941, Brook-Popham was relieved by Lieutenant-General Sir Henry Pownall.

A more detailed report on the Japanese attack on Hong Kong is provided in the second despatch reproduced in this volume. It was written by Major General Christopher Maltby, who, like Brook-Popham, was hampered by the reluctance of the British authorities to commit to defensive preparations which might be seen by the Japanese as provocative.

"That war was inevitable seemed clear to me," Maltby declared, "but it was hard to make that definite statement on the information available". As a result he was restrained by his instructions and by the civil authorities of Hong Kong from being able to implement all the defensive measures he believed were essential.

Maltby listed the reasons for this entirely unsatisfactory state of affairs as:

(*a*) The general doubt that Japan would declare war against the Allied powers.

(*b*) The weakness of our intelligence system.

(*c*) The belief that Japan was bluffing and would continue to bluff to the last.

Coupled with this, as Maltby makes very clear, was the absence of modern aircraft, the limited amount of naval support, the absence of radar, and the "paucity" of anti-aircraft guns.

Nevertheless, despite the obvious disadvantages which the British forces had to operate under, they put up a valiant defence. This is presented as a 'War Narrative' which was maintained by Fortress HQ throughout the fighting and probably represents the most comprehensive account of the battle of Hong Kong ever published. Maltby was, of course, taken prisoner when Hong Kong fell, and we are fortunate that the War Narrative survived.

The man who compiled the third despatch was also imprisoned by the Japanese but unlike the information available to Maltby, many documents that would have been of value to Lieutenant General Arthur Percival were lost or destroyed following the fall of Singapore.

Even so, Percival wrote more than 100,000 words and, whilst he obviously sought to justify his decision to surrender to the Japanese, it does provide us with a careful analysis of the British Army's worst ever defeat.

The main reason that Singapore fell so swiftly he attributes to the completely inadequate air defence of the region. He points out that as long ago as 1937 a report was made by the commanding officer at Singapore indicating the problems of aerial defence that Malaya faced should the Japanese attack. This situation was made incalculably more dangerous when, following the fall of France in 1940 and the subsequent occupation of French Indo-China, Japanese air forces were stationed just 400 miles from the Malayan border and 700 miles from Singapore itself. "In the event," Percival wrote, "the Army had to bear practically the whole weight of the Japanese attack with little air or naval support. This was the main cause of defeat."

With regards to his decision to surrender, Percival cites the message he received from the Supreme Commander South-West Pacific on the morning of 15 February 1942: "So long as you are in a position to inflict losses and damage to enemy and your troops are physically capable of doing so you must fight on. Time gained and damage to enemy are of vital importance at this juncture. When you are fully satisfied that this is no longer possible I give you discretion to cease resistance . . . Inform me of intentions. Whatever happens I thank you and all your troops for your gallant efforts of last few days."

Whether or not Percival surrendered too early, when in the opinion of many his troops were still capable of fighting on and inflicting loss and damage to the enemy, is one of continued debate.

The subject of the air defence of Malaya and Singapore is dealt with in the final despatch in this book. Air Vice-Marshal Sir Paul Maltby (the brother of Major General Christopher Maltby), was assistant AOC Far East Command until 10 February 1942, when he was switched by Churchill to take over command of the air forces in Java from where he was expected to continue the fight.

It is surprising to read that Maltby was informed that in the absence of strong naval forces in the region, the primary defence of Singapore and Malaya was in the hands of the air force when, according to Percival, it was the lack of air defence that was the primary reason for the Japanese victory. The simple fact is that Maltby's chief, Air Vice-Marshal C.W. Pulford, was not provided with the means to adequately defend British interests in the Far East.

The tragic defeat in the Far East is neatly summed up by Paul Maltby, and we can do no better that to quote his words: "We lost the first round there because we, as an Empire, were not prepared for war on the scale necessary for the purpose. When war broke out in Europe it absorbed the Empire's resources to such an extent that only a fraction of the strength could be deployed which had been calculated to be necessary for withstanding Japanese aggression in Malaya – navy, army, air force and civil organisation alike being much below the required mark. When Japan attacked she proved to be even more formidable than had been expected, the result being that she swamped our underdeveloped defences before they could be supported."

*

The objective of this book is to reproduce the despatches of Percival, Brooke-Popham and the two Maltby brothers as they first appeared to the general public some seventy years ago. They have not been modified or edited in any way and are therefore the original and unique words of the commanding officers as they saw things at the time. The only change is the manner in which the footnotes are presented, in that they are shown at the end of each despatch rather than at the bottom of the relevant page as they appear in the original despatch. Any grammatical or spelling errors have been left uncorrected to retain the authenticity of the documents.

LIST OF ILLUSTRATIONS

1 A portrait of Air Chief Marshal Sir Robert Brooke-Popham, the author of the first despatch in this volume. (HMP)

2 Part of the preparations for the defence of Singapore – men of the 2nd Battalion Gordon Highlanders demonstrate a Northover Projector to Major General F. Keith Simmons, GOC Singapore Fortress, and other senior officers, 17 October 1941. (IWM; FE15)

3 Australian gunners on the island of Singapore waiting for the Japanese to cross the Johore Strait. Churchill said that if the Japanese broke across the Johore Strait in small boats – which of course they did – it would be "one of the greatest scandals that could possibly be exposed". (HMP)

4 Stocks of rubber, held by a factory on a plantation in Malaya, are burnt during the British retreat to Singapore, December 1941. (HMP)

5 Bristol Blenheim Mk.I, L1134 'PT-F', of 62 Squadron RAF, taxiing in front of a line of Brewster Buffaloes at Sembawang, Singapore, as another section of Buffaloes passes over the airfield, October 1941. It was in L1134 that Squadron Leader Arthur Scarf and his crew single-handedly attacked the Japanese-held airfield at Singora, Thailand, on 9 December 1941 – an action for which Scarf was posthumously awarded the Victoria Cross. (IWM; K662)

6 A line-up of Brewster Buffalos at Sembawang in November 1941. The aircraft nearest the camera is 453 Squadron's Mk.II AN185, TD-V. (RAAF)

7 A Japanese aerial photograph showing HMS *Prince of Wales* (top) and HMS *Repulse* during the early stages of the attack in which they were sunk, 10 December 1941. HMS *Repulse* had just been hit for the first time. (US Naval Historical Center)

8 A group of pilots from 488 Squadron pictured at Singapore in December 1941. (Courtesy of Andy Thomas)

9 Aircraft and vehicles burn during a raid on Kallang during the Japanese offensive. By January 1942, Kallang was the only operational fighter airfield in Singapore, as the other airfields (Tengah, Seletar and Sembawang) were within range of Japanese artillery on the Malay peninsula. (Courtesy of Andy Thomas)

10   Because of the effectiveness of Japanese air strikes, the RAF's ground crews were forced to do much of their work servicing aircraft whilst the latter were dispersed under the trees at Kallang. (Courtesy of Andy Thomas)

11   Deep beneath a Singapore hillside is the "Battle Box", the underground command centre of the British Malaya Command. Comprising twenty-two rooms linked by a corridor, the complex was bomb-proof and capable of recycling its own air supply. Now a tourist attraction, the interior of the "Battle Box" has changed little from as it was in the war. Indeed, this scene, in the actual room used at the time, replicates the dark hours when Lieutenant-General Percival and his staff discussed the impending British surrender. (Courtesy of Roslan Tangah)

12   Lieutenant-General Percival, General Officer Commanding (Malaya), and his party pictured whilst en route to the Ford factory at Bukit Timah, Singapore to surrender the colony to the Japanese, 15 February 1942. Never in the history of the British Army had such a large force laid down its arms to an enemy. (HMP)

13   A captured Japanese photograph, creased by folding, showing Lieutenant-General Arthur E. Percival signing the unconditional surrender of the British and Commonwealth forces at the Ford Works Building near the Bukit Timah Road, Singapore. Lieutenant-General Tomoyuki Yamashita can be seen on the extreme left. (HMP)

14   Japanese officers stand with Lieutenant-General Arthur E. Percival following the surrender of British forces on 15 February 1942. Note the white flag of surrender. At the end of the war, Percival travelled to the Philippines to witness the surrender of the Japanese forces there, which in a twist of fate were commanded by Tomoyuki Yamashita. The Union Flag carried by Brigadier Newbigging on the way to Bukit Timah was also a witness to this reversal of fortunes, being flown when the Japanese formally surrendered Singapore back to the British. (IWM; HU31329)

15   Now a national monument in Singapore, the Ford Works Building still exists. Built in October 1941, it was Ford's first motor car assembly plant in Southeast Asia. During the Malayan campaign, the factory was used to assemble aircraft which has arrived in crates for the RAF. After the surrender, the building was occupied by the Japanese as a military headquarters. Today, the former factory serves as a museum, exhibition gallery and archive.

16   Within Kranji War Cemetery, Singapore, stands the Singapore Memorial. On its walls are the names of over 24,000 casualties of the Commonwealth land and air forces who have no known grave. Many of these have no known date of death and are accorded within our records the date or period from when they were known to be missing or captured. (Courtesy of the Commonwealth War Graves Commission)

1

AIR CHIEF MARSHAL SIR ROBERT BROOKE-POPHAM'S DESPATCH ON OPERATIONS

17 OCTOBER 1940 TO 27 DECEMBER 1941.

The War Office,
January, 1948.

OPERATIONS IN THE FAR EAST, FROM 17TH OCTOBER 1940 TO 27TH DECEMBER 1941

I. – FORMATION OF GENERAL HEADQUARTERS, FAR EAST.

I. This despatch, covers the period from the date of my appointment as Commander-in-Chief, Far East, the 17th October, 1940, to the date on which I handed over to Lieutenant-General Sir Henry Pownall, the 27th December, 1941.

My original staff consisted of seven, exclusive of my personal assistant. Of these seven, the Chief of Staff, Major-General Dewing, the Senior Royal Air Force Staff Officer, Group-Captain Darvall, as well as my personal assistant, travelled out with me.

The Naval Liaison Officer, Captain Back, met me on my arrival at Singapore, and the Army G.S.O.I, Colonel Fawcett, met me in Burma.

Before leaving England I saw the Chief of the Imperial General Staff, Chief of the Air Staff and Major-General Ismay individually, but did not meet the Chiefs of Staff collectively at one of their meetings.

2. I left London on Sunday, the 27th October, and started by air from Plymouth on the 28th October. I spent two clear days in Cairo, three in Delhi and three in Rangoon, arriving at Singapore on Thursday, the 14th November. General Headquarters, Far East, started to operate on Monday, the 18th November, 1940.

During the journey I was able to see the working of the Headquarters of both the Army and Air Force in Cairo, and to consult with the Commander-in-Chief, Sir Archibald Wavell, on the methods of operating his headquarters, and especially why he found such a big expansion from his original staff necessary.

At Delhi I stayed with the Viceroy, and established contact with the Commander-in-Chief, the Air Officer Commanding-in-Chief, and their respective staffs, and with certain civil officials.

At Rangoon I stayed with the Governor, Sir Archibald Cochrane, and reached agreement over the constitutional problems raised by the appointment of a Commander-in-Chief, Far East. I met the General Officer Commanding, Major-General (now Lieutenant-General) Sir K. McLeod, visited various establishments, including the oil refinery at Syriam, and established contact with many of the civil officials.

Instructions and General Policy.

3. My Directive is given in Appendix A.

On my arrival in Singapore it was agreed that, should I become a casualty, the Commander-in-Chief, China Station, should take my place until my successor was appointed.

With reference to paragraph 2 of my Directive, the meaning of the term "operational control" was explained as being higher direction and control as distinct from detailed operational control.

In addition to this Directive, I had two main guides for action: first, that it was the policy of His Majesty's Government to avoid war with Japan, and, secondly, that, until a fleet was available, our policy in the Far East should be to rely primarily on air power in conjunction with such naval forces as could be made available. The first was confirmed during 1941 in many telegrams, *e.g.,* in March, "Avoidance of war with Japan is basis of Far East policy and provocation must be rigidly avoided," and again in September, "Our policy in the Far East is still to avoid war with Japan." The second was laid down by the Chiefs of Staff in August, 1940.

4. It was pointed out to me that the requirements of Home Defence, the Battle of the Atlantic, and the Middle East, must take precedence over those of the Far East; at a later date Russia also took precedence, and, at one time, Iraq and Iran. Realising this, it was obviously our duty to be content with the essential minimum, to consider what we could do without rather than what we would like to have, and to make the fullest use of local resources. But we always regarded the strength of 336 aeroplanes as an irreducible minimum. (*See para.79 below.*) In January, 1941, we were cautioned against over-estimate of the Japanese forces.

I was also informed that the defence organisation in Malaya was apparently not working smoothly or efficiently, and that this would necessitate early investigation and action.

5. To carry out the directions outlined above, it was evident that the following steps were necessary:-

(*a*) To avoid any action that might be deemed provocative by Japan, but at the same time to try and convince her that our strength was too great to be challenged successfully;

(*b*) To strengthen our defences in the Far East, and especially to build up our air forces, not only by obtaining new aircraft but also by making all preparations to ensure mutual reinforcement in the Far East area;

(*c*) To ensure effective co-operation in Malaya, not only between the Royal Navy, the Army and the Air Force but also between them and the civil services;

(*d*) To stiffen the Chinese so that they could contain the maximum Japanese effort (*see paras. 70 and 71 below*); and

(*e*) To establish as close co-operation as possible with the Dutch and Americans, as well as with Australia and New Zealand, the main object being to ensure that, should an attack be made on any part of the Far East area, all the nations concerned would simultaneously enter the war against Japan, thus avoiding the risk of defeat in detail, as had happened in Europe.

6. A very brief study of the area comprised in the Far East Command shows that the defence of the whole area is essentially one single problem. Burma, Siam, Indo-China, Malaya, the Philippines, the Dutch East Indies, Australia and, to a lesser extent, New Zealand, all inter-connect and operations or preparations in any one of these areas affect all the others. In view of the above, I regarded it as one of my principal duties to make personal contacts in these places. During 1941 I visited Australia twice, in February and October, Manila three times and the Netherlands East Indies five times. I also visited Hong Kong in December, 1940, and April, 1941; and Burma in June and September, 1941.

Another point that stands out is that the problem is fundamentally a naval one, and that although the Army and Air Force in combination may defend areas of land and repel an enemy, his definite defeat cannot be brought about unless control of sea communications is obtained. This control will necessitate air superiority.

The Far East is usually examined on a small-scale map, so people are rather apt to get a false idea of distances. From Singapore to Alor Star at the North End of Malaya is a good deal further than from London to Aberdeen. Rangoon to Singapore direct by air is about 1,100 miles; Singapore to Hong Kong, via Manila, is 2,000 miles, about the distance from Gibraltar to Alexandria; and from Singapore to Melbourne about 4,100, which is only slightly less than the distance from London to Aden, via Malta and Cairo.

Size of General Headquarters Staff.

7. Although it was obvious that Singapore was a key position, and therefore that the defence of Malaya was of the greatest importance, it was evident that, apart from my Directive, the size of my Staff rendered it quite impossible to exercise any form of direct operational control, except in the widest sense. I therefore decided that, although the fact of my headquarters happening to be situated at Singapore would naturally involve my dealing with more details in Malaya than elsewhere, the Commands of Hong Kong, Malaya and Burma must be regarded as of equal status. Each General Officer Commanding would have to control the operations in his own area, and the initiative of the Air Officer Commanding, Far East, must not be cramped; the operational control of my headquarters would be limited mainly to the movement of reinforcements, principally air, within my command and to the issue of directives.

The staff of General Headquarters, Far East, was very small for the work it had to carry out, and immediately on its formation in Singapore it was found necessary to add three duty officers of junior rank in order to ensure keeping a twenty-four-hour watch in the office. Requests for an increase in staff at General Headquarters were made on more than one occasion, and finally it was agreed by the Chiefs of Staff, in August, I94I, that the total establishment should be raised to the following:-

> Commander-in-Chief: I.
> Chief of Staff: I.
> Staff Officer, Ist Grade: Navy I; Army 2; R.A.F. 2.
> Staff Officer, 2nd Grade: Navy I; Army 3; R.A.F. 3.
> Staff Officer, 3rd Grade: Navy I.
> Total, I5.

In addition to this, there were:-

> Personal Assistant: I.
> Cipher Officers: 2.
> Signal Officer: I.
> Chief Clerk: I.

Making a total in all of 20. This establishment was not completed by the time war broke out.

The result of the smallness of the Staff was that individuals were overworked, and this, in conjunction with the Malayan climate, led to sickness. The most serious case was that of my Chief of Staff, Major-General Dewing, who went into hospital on the 8th April, and remained there until he started for England in May. General Playfair arrived to take his place on the 2Ist June, but for a period of some ten and a half weeks I was without a Chief of Staff.

This sickness was largely attributed by the medical authorities to the effects of overwork. In addition, Wing-Commander Yarde had to be sent away sick, other officers were in hospital for shorter periods, and when war with Japan broke out

Colonel Scott, who had taken Colonel Fawcett's place as the Army G.S.O.I, was in India on sick leave, having been sent there from hospital.

Intelligence.

8. For intelligence I relied almost entirely on the Far Eastern Combined Bureau, known for short as F.E.C.B. This consisted of branches of Naval, Army and Air Force intelligence, and was under the administrative control of the Admiralty, the officer in charge of the Naval Section acting as head of the Bureau. At the date of the formation of my headquarters, F.E.C.B. was somewhat unbalanced in that attention was mostly concentrated on Naval intelligence, while Army and Air intelligence took a minor place, the latter especially being quite inadequate. This, however, was steadily corrected, and I consider that F.E.C.B. fulfilled its functions and showed that a combined intelligence staff of the three Services is a workable proposition. What was needed, however, was a real chief of F.E.C.B., and not merely one whose main duty was acting as head of his own branch. The difficulty was in finding a really suitable individual, and this we had not succeeded in doing at the time war with Japan broke out.

Attachments to General Headquarters Staff.

9. A branch of the Ministry of Economic Warfare known as the O.M. Section, was started on the arrival of Mr. Killery at Singapore in May, I94I. He and his staff were keen and capable, but they had no experience and very little knowledge of how to set about their work. Further, as in the case of intelligence, this is work that requires a great deal of preparation. In consequence of this, but through no fault of Mr. Killery or his staff, the O.M. activities really never got functioning properly by the time that war with Japan broke out. There was also a curious reluctance on the part of many people to have anything to do with these activities, or to help on the work. This was particularly noticeable in the case of intended activities in Siam.

I0. Colonel Warren arrived in Singapore early in I94I to assist in starting Independent Companies. The obvious disadvantage of these Companies is that they form a drain on infantry units, which were already depleted of many of their best non-commissioned officers and officers owing to the expansion and demands of other organisations. As a result, it was finally decided to limit these Independent Companies to two – one for Burma and one for Malaya.

II. – FACTORS AFFECTING THE DEFENCE OF MALAYA AND BORNEO.

II. Air Vice-Marshal Pulford became Air Officer Commanding, Far East, *vice* Air Vice-Marshal Babington on the 26th April, I94I, and Lieutenant-General Percival took over the duties of General Officer Commanding, Malaya, from Lieutenant-General Bond on the I6th May,I94I.

The strength of the Army and of the Air Force in Malaya in November, 1940, is given in Appendices D and I respectively.

In Malaya, as in Burma and Hong Kong, there was a War Committee, which sat under the Governor.

The main reason for the defence of Malaya was to preserve the facilities of the Naval Base at Singapore. The port and rubber and tin production were also important, but on a different plane from the Naval Base. It was, of course, not sufficient to have a close defence of the area round the Naval Base itself. It was of great importance to keep enemy aircraft as far away from the Base as possible, on account of the danger of bombing; this meant extending the defence right up to the Northern end of Malaya. It may be noted that this was not dependent upon the policy of defending Malaya by means of air power. Had the policy been to defend Malaya by means of Army forces, the dispositions might have been different, but it would still have been essential to hold the greater part of Malaya in order to deny aerodromes or their possible sites to the enemy. Singapore Island was to be provisioned for 180 days.

Communications.

12. The main roads in Malaya are well-metalled, and the railways are single-track metre-gauge. Down the centre of Malaya runs a range of hills rising to some 7,000 feet, and there are no east-to-west communications north of latitude 4, *i.e.,* about the latitude of Kuantan. The central backbone of hills dies away soon after crossing the frontier with Siam, and good lateral communications were available in the neighbourhood of Singora, where, also, there were suitable sites for aerodromes. Generally speaking, communications in the west are good and on the east poor.

The defence of the east coast was simplified by the lack of communications, since it was only necessary to hold those places from which roads ran into the interior. This meant that the key points to hold were Mersing and Kuantan. Kota Bharu in Kelantan was held because of the aerodrome at that place and two others a few miles further south, these being necessary in order to enable us to strike, with aircraft, as far as possible into the Gulf of Siam and into Indo China. (*See para. 52 below.*)

The only existing land communication between Kelantan and the rest of Malaya is the railway, there being no through road. Attempts were made to use the railway for motor transport, but as the rails were spiked and no chairs were available the damage caused to tyres, was so excessive that the project was given up as impracticable. This meant that communications with any force at Kota Bharu were precarious, since everything had to move by the single line of railway, which in many parts was highly vulnerable to bombing. I laid down that the road policy in Kelantan should be not to develop any road on or near the coast, but as soon as practicable to construct an internal road running north and south, following more or less the line of the railway.

The only communication overland with Kuantan was a single road, also very vulnerable in places to air bombing.

Co-operation between the services and with the civil authorities.

13. For some time before November, 1940, the relations between the Army and the Air Force were not happy; there was some jealousy between them, co-operation left a great deal to be desired, and it was some months before this could be considered satisfactory. Every operation should have been looked upon as a combined operation of two, or very often the three, services; for a long time there was a tendency for one of the services to work out a plan on its own and then see how one or both the other services could come in.

A great step in advance was made by getting the headquarters of the Army and Air Force on the same site. This entailed a good deal of building, but before war started there was a single combined Operations Room functioning and the whole of the Army General Staff were located on the same site as Royal Air Force Headquarters. A naval section joined the Operations Room at the start of the war as planned previously.

14. The local tradition of inter-service jealousy had some effect for the first few months on the working of General Headquarters. Personal relations with Army Headquarters were good, but my staff had to be scrupulously careful in dealing with matters that touched on the province of the General Officer Commanding.

Co-operation between the Navy and Air Force was good, and it continually improved between the Navy and the Army, for instance, on such matters as getting advice from naval officers as to the probable sites of landings from the naval point of view.

15. Relations between the Commander-in-Chief, China Station, and myself were close and friendly throughout. Our offices were adjoining after the move of my headquarters to the Naval Base and I had luncheon with him in his house nearly every day.

Relations between the commanders in Malaya and the Governor were good. I always found the Governor ready to help, and our personal relations were very friendly.

As regards the Colonial Service generally, our relations in most cases were satisfactory, and much help was received from many Departments, especially the Survey and the Government Posts and Telegraphs. But, partly owing to the complicated system of government, delays sometimes occurred and on certain matters it was difficult to get full and accurate information. I feel it would be of great value to the Colonial Service if its officers could attend some college on the lines of the Military Staff Colleges at some time in their career.

There was an interchange of liaison officers with the Dutch, first Navy and Air and later Army as well. Observers from the American Army and Navy were also posted to Singapore.

Borneo.

16. Unless we obtained command of the sea, it was impossible to defend British Borneo as a whole with the forces available. But through communications in the

island were practically non-existent; consequently, any defence could be limited to holding the important points. The only place which it was decided to hold was Kuching, the reason for this being not only that there was an aerodrome at that place, but that its occupation by the enemy might give access to the aerodromes in Dutch Borneo at the North-Western end of the island, these aerodromes being only some 350 miles from Singapore, i.e., much nearer than any in South Indo-China.

I informed the Governor of North Borneo that his territory could not be defended, and that the volunteers and police at his disposal were to be utilised for purposes of internal security. No attempt was made to defend Labuan, though it was a cable and wireless station.

The State of Brunei was of some importance owing to the oilfield at Seria in the South, which, in addition to Miri, supplied crude oil to the refineries at Lutong in Sarawak. Although one company of the 2nd/I5th Punjab Regiment less one platoon to Kuching, had been moved to Lutong in December, I940, and two 6-inch guns had been mounted there, it was finally decided that it was useless to attempt to defend the refinery or either of the oilfields. Consequently, a partial denial scheme was carried out before war broke out, whereby the oil output was reduced by some 70 per cent., and only a small number of items were left to complete the denial scheme when war broke out. According to reports, the work was completed satisfactorily.

The 2nd/I5th Punjab Regiment, less the one company referred to above, left Singapore for Kuching on the I0th and IIth May, I94I. Steps were also taken to develop local forces, i.e., volunteers and a body of native troops known as the Sarawak Rangers.

III. – FACTORS AFFECTING THE DEFENCE OF BURMA.

Authorities.

7. Sir Reginald Dorman Smith replaced the Hon. Sir Archibald Cochrane as Governor of Burma on the 6th May, I94I, and Lieut.-General Hutton took over the duties of General Officer Commanding from Lieut.-General McLeod at midnight the 28th-29th December, I94I.

The War Committee in Burma included Burmese Ministers as well as the two British Counsellors and the General Officer Commanding. The Governor was President and the Premier of Burma Vice-President.

Sir R. Dorman Smith established a military liaison officer on his personal staff. There were obvious advantages in this, and it would doubtless have worked well had the facts and figures always been obtained from the responsible authorities. As it was, information was sometimes sought through other channels, with the result that at times inaccurate or incomplete information was given to the Governor, leading to misunderstandings.

Communications.

18. The main factor affecting the defence of Burma was that of communications. The total length of frontier facing Japanese-occupied territory in December, 1941, was nearly 800 miles. There were good roads, as well as railways, running north and south up the valleys of the Sittang and Irrawaddy. Roads in the Tenasserim Peninsula were bad.

Working north from the southern end of the Tenasserim Peninsula, there were only mountain tracks leading eastwards from Siam until reaching the road from Raheng through Mesod towards Moulmein, which crossed the Burma frontier at Myawadi. Even this road was not continuous, and there was a section of fifty miles reported to be not much better than a pack track. From the Japanese point of view, it had the disadvantages that we should be able to operate from close to our railhead at Martaban, and that, so long as we held command of the sea, advance beyond Moulmein by the Japanese would be open to a British flank attack.

Continuing north, there were again only tracks until reaching the road leading from the Bangkok – Chieng Mai railway, through Chieng Rai and thence via Kentung to Taunggyi. On the Siamese side of the frontier this road was good; on our side it was fair-weather only for part of the way.

There were only tracks leading from Burma into Northern Indo-China, and these involved the crossing of the River Mekong. Into China itself there was a fair track from Kentung to Puerhfu, and, secondly, the main road from Lashio to Kunming. A road from Bhamo joined the latter near the frontier.

Westwards, a start had been made on a road communication with India, but this was by no means complete when war broke out.

Landing grounds had been established in the Tenasserim Peninsula with the object of facilitating the movement of aircraft between Burma and Malaya; the main ones were at Tavoy, Mergui and Victoria Point. The last was very isolated, and it was realised that it probably could not be held for long if war with Japan broke out.

19. It was estimated that the total force which the Japanese could bring against Burma, using land communications only, would be about two divisions, of which one division would be on the road running through Chieng Rai. The Chiefs of Staff considered in January 1941 that, although four enemy divisions could be maintained at railhead on the Bangkok – Chieng Mai railway, it was unlikely that even one division could be maintained on the Burma side of the frontier, owing to the limited road communications. The situation would, however, be completely altered should the Japanese get control of sea communications in the Bay of Bengal. In that case, their capture of Mergui, and possibly Tavoy, would only be a question of time. They would be able to outflank our positions at Moulmein, and our line of communication thence with Rangoon; and, should Singapore fall or be invested, would be able to bring by sea against Burma a force much greater than two divisions.

20. Turning to the Chieng Rai line of advance, owing to the indifferent road on our side of the frontier and the shortage of Mechanical Transport, it was impracticable to maintain a big force east of the Salween. The policy, therefore, was to fight

delaying actions as far forward as possible, and to make the Salween the main line of defence.

Owing to the heavy growth of trees along the Japanese lines of advance, conditions were not generally favourable for air reconnaissance. On the other hand, there were certain open defiles against which air bombing would probably have been very effective, and it was hoped that sufficient air force would be available to deter the Japanese advance to a great extent. For this purpose aerodromes were constructed with the object of being able to concentrate either on Central or South Burma, and against either the Mesod road or the Chieng Rai road.

Demolitions were prepared along the enemy lines of advance, especially on the Chieng Rai road.

Engineering Programme.

2I. There was a great shortage of engineers, both civil and military. In planning the engineering programme, priority was given first to aerodrome construction and accommodation for the Royal Air Force; secondly, to road construction for strategical and tactical purposes, including ferries; and then accommodation for troops and stores, including ammunition.

In the time available there was no opportunity to complete elaborate concrete defence lines; all that could be done was to construct field defences on the probable lines of approach. There were limitations even to this: first, the difficulty of working and the prevalence of malaria in the rainy season; secondly, the number of troops available; and thirdly, the lack of Mechanical Transport, until the Autumn of I94I, which severely limited the number of men that could be maintained near, and east of, the Salween River.

Strength of Forces.

22. The composition of the military forces in Burma when war broke out is shown in Appendix G, and the situation regarding Anti-Aircraft guns in Appendix F.

As will be seen, the organisation was somewhat complicated from the desire to make every possible use of local resources. Originally, the Burma Frontier Force had been independent of the General Officer Commanding in peace, and only came under him in time of war. His Excellency Sir Reginald Dorman Smith decided to put the Burma Frontier Force under the General Officer Commanding's control in peace as well, thus simplifying the organisation. The change was effected on the I0th November, I94I.

The Independent Company was abolished before war with Japan broke out, the British portion being used mainly for additional squads for Chinese guerillas, and the Burmese returning to their original units.

23. In the Singapore Conference of October I940 it was recommended that as regards the Army, the force immediately required for the defence of Burma was as follows:-

5 infantry brigades and two additional battalions;

I field regiment and I battery;
2 mountain batteries;
I anti-tank battery;
I heavy A.A. regiment (24 guns);
I light A.A. battery, non-mobile (I6 guns);
I light A.A. battery, mobile; and
I company light tanks.

This was exclusive of the Burma Frontier Force and of the Territorial and Auxiliary forces allotted to internal security duties. It was also stated that an additional requirement for the long-term problem was: one Division, less certain units, which made the fighting portion of this Division as follows:-

2 infantry brigades, each of 3 battalions;
I reconnaissance unit;
I field regiment (24 guns);
I medium regiment (I6 guns);
I light A.A. regiment (48 guns);
I anti-tank battery; and
I machine gun battalion.

In their comments of January I94I, on the Conference, the Chiefs of Staff stated that they considered both the threat of attack, and the demands for land forces, had been overstated.

Comparing the Conference recommendations with the total Army strength available in Burma in December I94I (*see Appendix* G), and omitting the Burma Frontier Force and the Territorial and Auxiliary forces, the shortages were approximately-

3 field batteries;
I anti-tank battery;

and I company light tanks out of the immediate requirements, and the whole of the additional requirement.

Apart from this, up to the outbreak of the war with Japan, Burma remained short of:-
Rifles;
Mechanical transport vehicles;
Officers for the General Officer Commanding's staff and services; and Medical personnel.

24. A Burma Royal Naval Volunteer Reserve under the command of Commander K.S. Lyle, R.N., had been raised in I940. It had two or three patrol boats operating off the Tenasserim Peninsula, and was also responsible for mine-sweeping the Rangoon approaches and for examination services. There were several other craft building at Rangoon, but these had been held up mainly owing to the delay in obtaining engines and fittings from England. The force was under the Commander-

in-Chief, China, for operations, and under the Governor of Burma for administration. It was not under the General Officer Commanding, though co-operation was very satisfactory.

25. In November 1940, air strength in Burma was practically non-existent. The Singapore Conference had recommended the following:-

I general reconnaissance squadron;
2 bomber squadrons; and
I fighter squadron.

No. 60 Squadron, equipped with Blenheim bombers, arrived from India in February 1941; in August 1941, one flight was reorganised as a fighter flight and equipped with Brewster Buffaloes. Later, a complete Buffalo squadron, No. 67, was sent from Malaya in November 1941, and the whole of No. 60 Squadron reverted to bombers. There was a Burma Volunteer Air Unit, but this had not got further than a small training organisation. This merely gave Burma two squadrons, which was admittedly very weak, and, actually, when war broke out, most of the Blenheim squadron, No. 60, was in Malaya for bombing practice.

On the other hand, the American Volunteer Group of the International Air Force started to train in Burma in August 1941, and there was an understanding, amounting practically to an agreement, with General Chiang Kai-shek that, if Burma was attacked, part, or the whole, of this American Volunteer Group would be detailed for the defence of Burma. Actually, two of the American Volunteer Group squadrons were sent to Kunming when war with Japan broke out, and one to Mingaladon, near Rangoon.

It was my opinion that the defence of Burma depended largely upon holding Malaya, and that the defence of the latter must have priority. I also considered it unlikely that the Japanese would attack Burma solely in order to cut the Burma Road to China. They knew that this must involve war with Great Britain, and in all probability with the Dutch and perhaps also the United States. If they were going to face this, they would be much more likely to start attacking Singapore than Burma. Admittedly, we were working on probabilities and not certainties, but, in view of the weakness of our air forces, it was essential to concentrate the maximum effort and not try to be equally strong in two places.

The American Volunteer Group.

26. The American Volunteer Group consisted of three single-seater fighter squadrons which were equipped with Tomahawks up to the time I handed over command.

Doubtless the United States will not forget the help that was freely given to the American Volunteer Group by the Burma Government and by the Royal Air Force. They were given the sole use of the Royal Air Force aerodrome at Toungoo, allowed to use Mingaladon aerodrome, near Rangoon, for testing Tomahawks after erection, and were offered the use of further aerodromes if required. Permission from London was given on the 22nd August, 1941, for the American Volunteer Group to carry out operational training in Burma, and they were given assistance in many other directions.

On the 31st October, 1941, the British Ambassador, Chungking, represented to the Foreign Office that the situation in China was very serious. We were asked what we could do to help, and suggested that we might form a British fighter squadron with volunteers from the Royal Air Force to form part of the International Air Force, and possibly a bomber squadron as well. It was pointed out that this proposal would mean a reduction in our own effective fighting and bombing strength. The suggestion was approved by the Chiefs of Staff, provided I was satisfied they would be able to operate effectively as part of the International Air Force and that I could accept the detachment from the Malaya defences. These squadrons would have been largely dependent on the American Volunteer Group organisation for their maintaintence. Pending a detailed examination of the maintenance arrangements in China, volunteers for these squadrons were not called for and actually they were never formed, but many preliminary steps were taken, including the movement of vehicles, spares and bombs. A telegram to the British liaison mission in Washington, and a personal telegram from me to General MacArthur in Manila, resulted in a very fair stock of spares being received by the American Volunteer Group before war broke out. But for this, it is very doubtful if they could have gone on working for more than two or three weeks.

I found that the pilots of the American Volunteer Group were not satisfied with their Tomahawks when I visited them in September 1941. This was largely corrected before war broke out, partly by giving details of the successes of the Tomahawks in the Middle East, and partly by a test carried out between a Buffalo and a Tomahawk, which showed the latter to be considerably superior in speed, climb and in manoeuvrability over some 10,000 feet.

Aircraft Warning System.

27. There was an air observation corps under General Officer Commanding, organised in five groups, each under an ex-inspector of police, the observers being local Burmans and Anglo-Burmans. This Observer Corps did good work, and, according to later reports, warnings of the attacks on Rangoon were received in time for the fighters to take off and get up. An R.D.F. set at Moulmein was just starting to operate in December 1941.

With regard to A.R.P., the original policy in Rangoon had been evacuation. Sir Reginald Dorman Smith decided to change this, and to construct air raid shelters. There had been no time to complete these shelters before war broke out.

Political Factors.

28. The internal situation in Burma gave rise to much anxiety, and it was realised that in time of war it might become necessary to reinforce the police with military units. There were doubtless many reasons for this potential unrest, but two were particularly evident. The first was the influence of the Buddhist priesthood, especially from

Mandalay. In Burma itself, the priesthood was numerous and powerful; it had been brought largely under the influence of the anti-British political party, and consequently preached the doctrine of Burma for the Burmese and complete independence. Many efforts were being made to counteract this, and were partially successful. Apparently, in the Shan States, the native rulers had kept a tighter control over the Buddhist priests than we did in Burma proper, and had limited their numbers.

The second reason was the anti-Indian feeling. The Indians in Burma were much more clever than the Burmese in business transactions, and, amongst other things, lent money out on mortgage, with the result that they owned a large proportion – about one-half – of the best agricultural land in Burma. We were looked upon to some extent as protectors of the Indians, and consequently attracted to ourselves part of the hatred that was felt by the Burmese for the Indians over this land problem.

Transfer of Command to Commander-in-Chief, India.

29. On the 12th December a telegram was received from the Chiefs of Staff stating that the defence of Burma was to be transferred from Commander-in-Chief, Far East, to Commander-in-Chief, India, including all relations with China. The transfer was effected as from 0630 hours on the 15th December, 1941.

IV. – FACTORS AFFECTING THE DEFENCE OF HONG KONG.

Authorities.

30. In November 1940, General Norton was Acting Governor of Hong Kong. Sir Geoffrey Northcote resumed his post as Governor on the 13th March, 1941, and handed over to his successor, Sir Mark Young, on the 10th September, 1941. Major General Maltby took over the duties of General Officer Commanding from Major-General Grasett on the 19th July, 1941.

General Policy.

31. Hong Kong was regarded officially as an undesirable military commitment, or else as an outpost to be held as long as possible. It must, however, be considered in relation to the whole defence of the Far East, especially China and the Philippines. The withdrawal of our troops from Peking, Tientsin and Shanghai in the summer of 1941 after the collapse of France was recognised by General Chiang Kai-shek and the Chinese as being an inevitable and wise move, but the Chinese interest in the defence of Hong Kong grew as their war developed and their difficulties increased. Hong Kong was very valuable to China as a port of access and had they not been convinced of our determination to stand and fight for its defence, and been taken into our confidence and given opportunities to inspect the defences and discuss plans for defence, the effect on their war effort would in all probability have been serious. A

withdrawal of the troops in Hong Kong coinciding with the closing of the Burma Road might have had a marked effect on Chinese determination to fight on. Our policy for the defence of Hong Kong, therefore, in all probability played an important part at a critical period in China's war effort.

As regards the Philippines, according to information available in Singapore, it was doubtful, at any rate up to the middle of 1941, whether the Americans intended to defend the islands, or whether they did not. It is therefore possible, that had we demilitarised Hong Kong, or announced our intention of not defending it, the Americans might have adopted a similar policy with regard to the Philippines. In this case, they might have ceased to take direct interest in the Far East, and confined themselves to the Eastern half of the Pacific. Should this supposition be correct, then the attempted defence of Hong Kong was justified for this reason alone, even though it did ultimately lead to the loss of six battalions and other troops.

Strength of Defences.

32. The strength of the Hong Kong garrison is given in Appendix H. The official period for which Hong Kong was to be provisioned, both in military stores and food reserves, was 130 days.

The main defence of Hong Kong was on the Island. Whilst the enemy were to be delayed as long as possible in any advance over the leased territory on the mainland, the troops had orders to retire if attacked in force, as they were required for the defence of the Island itself. The Gin Drinkers line was naturally a strong one, and much work had been done on it, but it would have required two divisions or more to hold properly.

Two Canadian battalions arrived in Hong Kong on the 16th November, 1941. This extra force was of greater value than the figures would indicate. Whilst there were only four battalions in Hong Kong, only one could be spared for the Gin Drinkers line, which practically meant merely a thin outpost line. As this battalion was also essential for the defence of Hong Kong Island, it would not have been able to put up any resistance, but would have had to retire before the advance of even a weak force, since heavy casualties would prejudice the defence of the Island, and could not be faced. With the arrival of these two Canadian battalions, three could be put into the Gin Drinkers line, and a far stronger resistance could be put up, not merely because of the increased strength, but because casualties would not cripple the subsequent defence of Hong Kong Island. Even a few days' delay in the occupation of the mainland by the enemy was of great value, enabling steps to be completed which it was impracticable to take before the outbreak of war, for instance, the movement of the fishing fleet and waterborne population out of Hong Kong waters.

33. A great deal of work had been done in preparing the island for defence, and the construction and concealment of pill-boxes and obstacles showed much originality and initiative. Preparations were also made for offensive operations against islands near Hong Kong, should the Japanese seize them, and for "left-behind" parties on the mainland. Every advantage was taken of any local resources available for defence.

34. There were two Walrus amphibians and four Vildebeeste aeroplanes at Hong

Kong, located at Kai Tak aerodrome on the mainland. The former might have been of some value for reconnaissance; in war it had been intended to operate them from Aberdeen Harbour, on the South side of Hong Kong Island, but this was apparently found impracticable. The latter would have had to remain at Kai Tak since no possible site for an aerodrome could be found on the Island itself. It was realised that these aeroplanes could not last for long in time of war, and that the Kai Tak aerodrome would, in fact, be quite unusable unless the Gin Drinkers line could be held.

Civil Population Factors.

35. One of the main problems in the defence of Hong Kong was the large Chinese population. This had nearly doubled during the three years previous to December 1941, owing to the influx from China. The population in April 1941 was-

Hong Kong	709,006
Kowloon	581,000
Water population	154,000
Total	1,444,000

This is exclusive of the population of what is known as the New Territories on the mainland. The great increase above the normal population led to many problems, e.g., civil hospital accommodation and medical staff, police control, supply of water, food and firewood. In addition, this increase, combined with the constant movement taking place between the Island and the mainland, rendered it very difficult to keep complete control of the Chinese, and made it easy for the Japanese to acquire information.

36. The reservoirs on Hong Kong Island were partly filled by rain water and partly by a supply from the mainland. It was, of course, realised that this latter supply might be cut, calculations showed that the rain, added to the capacity of the reservoirs, was normally sufficient to meet the essential requirements of Hong Kong Island, so long as the whole Island remained in our hands. If there was a dry spell during the winter, the supply might have been short in February and March, and there might not have been sufficient to supply water to deal with outbreaks of fire. Although fire engines could draw on sea water, the higher levels of the town of Victoria could not be reached in one lift. This difficulty was largely overcome, however, by the installation of service tanks at medium levels, which it was intended to keep filled with sea water by separate pumps.

37. As regards food, rice was a constant anxiety, since most of it had to be imported from Siam or Burma. In addition, what was known as the rice supplement was a problem, since fish would not be available in case of war, and storage of alternatives over a period of months was difficult. In December 1941 the stocks of food were not much short of that required for the period laid down, *i.e.,* 130 days. The local supply of firewood was insufficent, and some was being imported from North Borneo.

38. The A.R.P. organisation in Hong Kong was good, and some 12,000 A.R.P. workers of one sort or another had been enrolled before war broke out. In addition, tunnels were made into the granite hills behind the town of Victoria; these provided

admirable shelters which should have been proof against any type of bomb. The limitation here was the number of pneumatic drills that could be obtained to enable the necessary blasting to be carried out. It was a slow process but by the time war broke out there was shelter accommodation in the tunnels, concrete splinter-proof shelters and strengthened houses for about 300,000. Provision was made for the movement of the balance to hutments outside the town.

39. Most of the European women and children had been moved away from Hong Kong by July 1941, the total leaving being approximately 1,680 women and children belonging to the Navy, Army or Air Force, and 1,824 civilian. This left about 918 European women and girls in Hong Kong. Of these, 595 were nurses and medical staff, 60 held key duties in A.R.P. and the majority of the remaining 263 were employed in clerical and other duties. The Governor's order for the movement of women and children away from Hong Kong had been disputed, but was upheld in a test case in the courts.

V. – PROBLEMS AND WORK OF GENERAL HEADQUARTERS, FAR EAST.

Site of General Headquarters.

40. General Headquarters started to function at 0800 hours on Monday, the 18th November. The order issued to the three General Officers Commanding and the Air Officer Commanding outlining their relations to General Headquarters is given in Appendix B.

One of the first problems I had to decide was the site of my Headquarters. The Army Headquarters was at Fort Canning and the Air Force Headquarters was in newly-built hutments about five miles away. The Governor and other civil authorities were in Singapore town. The Naval Commander-in-Chief had his Headquarters at the Naval Base, which was some 35 minutes by road from Singapore. It was important for my Headquarters to keep in touch with all these. I hoped at one time that the Commander-in-Chief, China, would move to Singapore, but he felt very strongly that he had to remain in the Naval Base, where the F.E.C.B. was also located. A compromise might have been possible but would have entailed dividing F.E.C.B. After much consideration, I decided that the dominant factors were to ensure close touch with the Commander-in-Chief, China, and to keep the F.E.C.B. intact. Accordingly, my Headquarters moved to the Naval Base in January, 1941, but I continued to reside in Singapore, which enabled me to have interviews with the General Officer Commanding, Air Officer Commanding and the Governor, either before I went to the office or on my return. This was not a perfect solution, but it was the best one in all the circumstances.

Another factor which influenced me in coming to this decision was the danger of my Headquarters becoming intimately involved in the defence of Malaya if I remained at Singapore, to the neglect of the wider problems of the defence of the Far East.

Relations with Commander-in-Chief, China Station.

4I. From about June I94I onwards an intelligence conference was held at ten o'clock every morning, and was attended by the Commander-in-Chief, China, and myself, and our senior staff officers. Generally speaking, the division of responsibilities was clear, and in other cases they were divided up without any difficulty. The Commander-in-Chief, China, had been dealing with Free French problems, and continued to do so after my Headquarters was formed. As our relations with French Indo-China were largely concerned with economics and shipping, he dealt with most of the problems of that country, whilst my Headquarters dealt mainly with Siam. He also agreed to take over responsibility for control of the Press and continued to do so up to the beginning of December, when Sir Tom Phillips arrived and I took over this responsibility.

Other questions, such as food supplies, we dealt with together. In this case also shipping was largely involved, and as the Commander-in-Chief, China, had a representative on the Food Committee, he generally represented our combined views at meetings of the War Committee.

The Commander-in-Chief, China, took over from me the control of the Miri oil denial scheme. This was found more convenient since the problems of oil supply were more closely connected with the Navy than with the Army or Air Force, and the evacuation of both material and personnel from Miri was essentially a Naval matter.

Agreement was reached in regard to surface sea patrols near the coast, and it was decided that the Naval authorities would be responsible for patrolling in the open sea and the Army would be responsible for similar work on the rivers. One or two estuaries were dealt with as special cases, but generally came under the Naval authorities.

Conferences at Singapore.

42. Many conferences were held in Singapore both before and after the formation of General Headquarters, Far East. These were as follows:-

(a) The Franco-British Conference held in June I939. The report of this conference contained some useful observations on the general problems, but the basic assumption of active French collaboration from Indo-China vanished with the collapse of France.

(b) The Singapore Conference of October, I940, with which should be included the Tactical Appreciation dated the I6th October, I940, prepared by the Commander-in-Chief, China Station, the General Officer Commanding, Malaya, and the Air Officer Commanding, Far East. (*See paras.* 79 *and* 90 *below.*)

(*c*) The conversations with the Dutch in December 1940, the principal object being to obtain information and agreement on certain matters raised in Appendix A of the Report of the Singapore Conference.

(*d*) The Conference between British, Dutch and Australian representatives, with United States observers in attendance, held in Singapore in February 1941, resulting, in what is known as the A.D.A. agreement. This agreement included plans for mutual reinforcements, principally of air forces and submarines. (*See para.* 44 *below.*)

(*e*) The Conference between the Americans, Dutch and British, including Australia and New Zealand, together with representatives of India and the East Indies Station. This was held at Singapore in April 1941, and resulted in what is known as the A.D.B. agreement. (*See para.* 45 *below.*) It was followed by a shorter agreement between the British and the Dutch, which dealt almost entirely with Naval matters, and was really a modification of the agreement reached in A.D.A., bringing the latter into line with A.D.B. It was known as B.D.

(*f*) Arising out of A.D.B., a detailed plan for naval and air operations, known as Plenaps was drawn up..

No political commitment was involved by these agreements, and A.D.A. and A.D.B. remained subject to ratification by the respective Governments.

43. In the case of the conference leading to the A.D.A. and A.D.B. agreements, I felt that the representation was somewhat unbalanced. In the former, the Naval representation of the Dominions was weak since the Chief of the Naval Staff in Australia, Admiral Colvin, was unable to come, and New Zealand was represented by Australia. In the A.D.B. Conference, the Naval representation was strong but that of the Dominion Army and Air Force was comparatively weak. Further, in A.D.B. the United States representatives were somewhat junior, and there was no representative of the Pacific Fleet, but only of the Asiatic.

44. In A.D.A. the necessity for collective action was emphasised, it being pointed out that Japanese aggression against any one country would be of vital importance to the others. Agreement was reached on the particular actions by Japan which would necessitate the Naval and Military authorities concerned advising their respective Governments to take active military counter-action. A suggestion was made that Commanders-in-Chief on the spot might be allowed to take measures in such circumstances without prior reference to London.

The principle of mutual reinforcement was agreed, the Dutch undertaking to provide submarines for operation in the South China Sea, as well as one Fighter and three bomber squadrons to reinforce Malaya; whilst it was estimated that four Bomber squadrons would be available from Malaya to reinforce the Netherlands East Indies. Australia was prepared to assist by the provision of Army units, and of an air striking force at Darwin to reinforce Ambon and Koepang. The necessary administrative arrangements to prepare for these land and air reinforcements were to be undertaken at once, and progress reports were to be rendered monthly to G.H.Q., Far East. The principles on which sea communications would be defended were outlined, and emphasis was laid on the importance of making the passage of the Northern line of the Dutch possessions as difficult as possible for the Japanese.

The A.D.A. report was approved generally by the Chiefs of Staff, the main exception being that there could be no prior definition of an act of war and automatic reaction without reference to London.

45. In the A.D.B. report it was stressed that the Atlantic and Europe were the decisive theatres of war, so that the forces employed in other theatres must be reduced to a minimum. Our main strategy in the Far East for the time must, therefore, be defensive, but it was recommended that preparations should be made for air operations against Japanese-occupied territory and against Japan herself, both from China and from Luzon.

The necessity for collective action was reaffirmed as well as the particular actions by Japan which would necessitate the Commanders concerned advising their respective Governments to take active military counter-action. The importance of Luzon, especially from the offensive point of view, was emphasised, and a recommendation made that its defence should be strengthened. It was suggested in this connection that Hong Kong might be of value as a subsidiary base. It was also recommended that the British and U.S.A. should support the Chinese Army, especially with finance and equipment, should assist the guerilla operations in China, and organise subversive activity in Japan and Japanese-occupied territories.

It was recommended that the Commander-in-Chief, China Station, should exercise strategical direction over all Naval forces, excluding those employed solely on local defence or operating under Commander-in-Chief, United States Asiatic Fleet. Similarly, it was recommended that the Commander-in-Chief, Far East, should exercise strategical direction of the air forces in the Far East. The areas of responsibility were defined. The basis of a plan for Naval and air co-operation, both as regards reinforcements and reconnaissance, was laid down. This included the movement of surface vessels of the United States Asiatic Fleet from Manila to Singapore if the former were attacked, and the despatch of two or more Dutch submarines to the South China Sea, all operating under the Commander-in-Chief, China.

For purposes of planning, the air forces available for mutual reinforcement were assumed to be:-

From Malaya: 4 bomber squadrons;

From Netherlands East Indies: 3 bomber and I fighter squadrons;

From Philippines: all available, but in case of evacuation only; and

From Australia: 2 bomber squadrons for the Ambon – Timor Area.

In telegraphic comments by the Commanders-in-Chief, Far East and China, two points were specially stressed: first, the great importance to the defence of the Far East of offensive operations by the United States Pacific Fleet, a point that was deliberately omitted from the report; and, secondly, the importance of strengthening the defences of Luzon.

The A.D.B. report was, with one or two exceptions, approved by the Chiefs of Staff in London. The exceptions were that, whilst they would welcome any strengthening of the Philippines which could be effected otherwise than at the expense of the United States effort in the Atlantic, they were not prepared to press the point in the United States: and that Hong Kong was unlikely to be of much value as an advanced base for operations by United States submarines and naval aircraft against the Japanese sea communications.

But, although signed by the representatives of the United States, the report was objected to in Washington, mainly on the ground that certain political matters had been introduced. An amended A.D.B. agreement, known as A.D.B. 2, was therefore drawn up in London in August I94I, leaving all the main features of A.D.B. practically unchanged, but putting the political matters into an appendix. This, however, did not entirely satisfy the United States authorities in Washington, and eventually it was decided that a further conference should be held in the Far East to draw up a modified A.D.B. This information was conveyed to me on the 25th November, I94I, but was received too late for any action to be taken before war started.

In spite of this, A.D.B. and Plenaps remained the basis on which we were able to work before, and immediately after, the outbreak of war with Japan, both with the Netherlands East Indies and, to a lesser degree, with the Philippines. (*But see para,* III *below.*)

Information from London.

46. I found on arrival in the Far East that there was considerable ignorance of modern war conditions, both in the Army and the Air Force. This could not, of course, be made good entirely by documents; personal experience was essential.

For some months after the formation of my General Headquarters there seemed to be considerable delay in getting information from England with regard to the lessons of recent operations and developments in tactical ideas, both as regards the Army and the Air Force, though A.R.P. pamphlets seemed to arrive regularly soon after issue. The situation improved about July, I94I, but we were always uncertain whether we were being kept up to date. This feeling of being neglected was naturally, intensified by the distance of London from Singapore, and the whole position in this respect would have been greatly improved if visits by liaison officers from the War Office and Air Ministry had been made from time to time. This was actually started in the case of the War Office, and the first liaison officer arrived in Singapore in November, I94I. I believe it was intended to do the same in the case of the Air Ministry. It would have been a great help had this been done twelve months earlier.

Training.

47. As regards training, steps were taken to ensure that troops were thoroughly acquainted with the nature of the country in which they would have to operate. This

was simple in the case of Hong Kong, where units knew exactly the ground over which they were going to fight. It was more difficult in the case of Malaya, as the nature of the country varied considerably, but here special attention was paid to movements through jungle and the acquisition of jungle lore, and many units reached a high stage of proficiency in this. The Volunteers in Malaya were called up for training during February and March 194I.

Apart from minor Staff Exercises, two were carried out under General Headquarters: the first in December, 1940, to test out communications and co-operation between the Army and the Royal Air Force; and the second, a more ambitious one, in March, 194I, to test out all the stages of a change-over from peace to war for the civil authorities as well as for the three Services. This brought out many useful lessons. A very successful exercise based on this second one was held in Burma in July, 194I, and Hong Kong carried out two or three on similar lines.

Defensive Preparations.

48. The question of the best method of defending the important sectors of the East Coast of Malaya gave rise to much discussion. One school of thought argued that, as there were insufficient numbers to defend any great length of beach, the enemy would be able to land outside the defended portion, thus outflanking the defender and possibly cutting them off. The best course of action was, therefore, to fight on a prepared position in rear where the road leading into the interior could be defended. This school also argued that attempts to hold the beaches would result in a purely linear defence with insufficient troops in hand for counter-attack.

The view of General Headquarters, Far East, was that it was essential to hold the beaches, because it was during the period of landing that the enemy would be most vulnerable, and if the beaches were given up he would be fighting on equality with us. Again, it was during this process of landing that our most effective co-operation between the Army and Air, and possibly the Navy as well, could be effected. Admittedly there was a danger of having a purely linear defence, but this was primarily a question of adjustment between the forces retained in reserve and those detailed for holding the beaches themselves.

Another point was that of all-round defence. It was difficult with the forces available to have units in a group of perimeter posts and at the same time to protect an adequate length of beach. Further, the defenders must be prepared to hold on for a period to be reckoned by weeks rather than by days, even if surrounded by the enemy and cut off. There was but little object in this unless adequate reserves were available in rear to attack the enemy and restore the situation. The 22nd Australian Brigade at Mersing found a satisfactory solution to the problem in that they had perimeter defences for units, mutually supporting each other and primarily defending the beaches. But in their case the 27th Australian Brigade was available in Johore for counter-attack on a large scale. The problem was more difficult at Kuantan and Kota Bharu for the reasons indicated above. (*See para.* I2.)

Although it was my policy to allow the General Officers-in-Command as much freedom as possible, I found it necessary in the case of Malaya to issue orders that the first line of our defence was to be the beaches. Previously, except on Singapore Island and Penang, beaches were going to be occupied only by watching posts, and the first lines of defence were sited inland. This change involved a considerable amount of work and preparation of obstacles and defence posts at Mersing, Kuantan and Kota Bharu.

It was found at one period that the work of preparing positions and putting up obstacles was taking up so much time that the training of the troops was being hampered and, in addition, the wire generally required renewing after about six months. Also, I was always on guard against too much reliance upon water obstacles, barbed wire and pill-boxes, in case this should lead to a Maginot Line complex to the detriment of the offensive spirit. Consequently, a division of available hours was drawn up, allowing a proportion for training, a proportion for renewals, and the balance for new work. As far as practicable, troops constructed the actual defences in which they would normally fight. New works carried out included not only defensive preparations, but facilities for making counter-attacks, *e.g.,* preparation of hidden paths fit for Bren Carriers.

Looking back in the light of what actually happened, it is easy to point out that a lot of the preparation was wasted, and that the energy so taken up should have been expended elsewhere; for instance, a great deal of time was spent on the Mersing area, which was never heavily attacked. Mersing, however, was a very important place, and, had the Japanese established themselves here instead of at Kota Bharu, they would have been at once within a short distance of Singapore; and it is possible that, had these defences been less strong, they might have attacked the Mersing area at an early stage in the operations. I feel, however, that steps should have been taken before war broke out to strengthen the defences on the Northern and North-Western sides of Singapore Island.

49. We also had to be prepared for the possibility of a break-through in the Mersing area, which would have isolated Southern and Northern Malaya from Singapore, and this consideration affected the siting of depots for stores and ammunition. Therefore, preparations were made to enable a force to be supplied, if necessary, by a line of communication running through Kuala Lumpur to Penang, so that they would be able to operate quite independently of Singapore.

Another possibility that had to be considered was that of a sudden descent without warning on a part of Singapore Island with the object either of destroying some important place, such as the main wireless station, or of establishing a footing, awaiting subsequent reinforcements. This possibility was met by having a portion of the Singapore garrison ready to come into action and move at very short notice.

Operation "Matador."

50. The importance of the Southern end of the Kra Isthmus, especially the neighbourhood of Singora, has already been referred to (*see paragraph* 12 *above*). The possibility of an advance into this Isthmus, in order to hold a position North of Haad Yai Junction, was considered soon after the formation of General Headquarters, Far East. Detailed plans for carrying out this operation were prepared, and the code

word "Matador" was eventually given to it. It was from the start realised that the essential feature of this operation was forestalling the Japanese on a position near Singora; see, for instance my telegram to the Chiefs of Staff through the War Office, in which it is stated: "The success of this plan would depend on rapidity of execution in order to forestall the Japanese on the Songhla line"; also my telegram from which the following is an extract: "I wish to emphasise the fact that the forestalling of the Japanese in Singora area is essential to the success of 'Matador.' "

This necessitated at least twenty-four hours' start before the Japanese landed, and rapid movement of our force once the order was given. It was realised all along that, if these conditions could not be fulfilled, then the Matador operation would be impracticable. The psychological value of offensive movement at the start of the war and the possibility of thereby upsetting the Japanese plans were fully realised, but had to be weighed against the fact that we should be leaving prepared ground with which the troops were familiar, and that, unless we forestalled the enemy, the fighting would be in the nature of an encounter battle, quite possibly against superior numbers. Further, the attitude of the Siamese was uncertain, and questions of secrecy precluded any attempt to get prior agreement from Bangkok. Orders were issued that, should Matador be ordered, any opposition from the Siamese was to be overcome at once, but we could never be certain in advance how much delay might be caused to our movements by obstacles, destruction of bridges or active resistance. A margin of time was necessary.

A total of thirty officers, two or three at a time, were sent over as visitors to the area in plain clothes in order to collect information, especially on the topography of the country, and to have some individuals familiar with it.

The preparations were completed before the Autumn of 1941 as far as could be foreseen, including maps, arrangements for the distribution of rice to the population, the collection of a quantity of Siamese money, and writing, ready for translation and printing, pamphlets of three varieties to suit the different attitudes which might be adopted by the Siamese Government. For reasons of secrecy, knowledge of the plans was confined to a minimum number of individuals, and for the same reason certain steps could not be taken in advance. For instance, it was considered dangerous to translate or print the pamphlets before the operation was ordered.

5I. Up to the 5th December, Matador was not to be carried out without reference to the War Cabinet, but on that date a telegram was sent to the effect that I could order it without reference to London in either of the following contingencies:-

(*a*) If I had information that the Japanese expedition was advancing with the apparent intention of landing on the Kra Isthmus; or

(*b*) If the Japanese violated any other part of Thailand (Siam).

A few days earlier it had been impressed on me that carrying out Matador if the Japanese intended to make a landing in Southern Siam would almost certainly mean war with Japan, and in view of this I considered it my duty to be scrupulously careful in acting on the telegram of the 5th December.

Aerodrome Policy.

52. The number and location of aerodromes in Malaya was based on the principle of relying mainly on air power for defence. This also applied, though in a somewhat smaller degree to Burma.

It meant, first having a sufficient number of aerodromes to make use of the mobility of aircraft for concentrating a large proportion of our squadrons in any given area; and, secondly, choosing sites as far forward as practicable so as to enable us to reach out the maximum distance both for reconnaissance and for offensive operations. This was particularly important in the case of attacks on Japanese convoys in order to ensure having sufficient time to carry out more than one attack before they reached our coast.

The total number of aerodromes prepared was based on the figure of 336 Initial Equipment aircraft, and since this figure was never reached we had in some areas more aerodromes than we were able to use, the surplus being a liability rather than an asset. The forecasts of development of our air strength were admittedly uncertain, but in view of the long time taken to construct an aerodrome in Malaya we could not afford to wait until we knew definitely that more aircraft were coming. The Army dispositions were largely influenced by the necessity for protecting Royal Air Force aerodromes. As events turned out, owing to the weakness of the Royal Air Force at the time war started, the defence of Malaya devolved largely upon the Army, which meant that sites for aerodromes were not always the most suitable for operations as they were actually carried out. But it was impossible to have foreseen this, since no one could have known in advance when the Japanese would start the war.

In the autumn of I94I, orders were issued that four of the aerodromes in Malaya and two in Burma were to be extended so as to be suitable for the operation of heavy bombers up to the Boeing Fortress type. This meant runways of 2,000 yards with a surface sufficiently strong to bear the weight of these aircraft fully loaded.

Sufficient attention was not always given to the tactical siting of aerodromes from the point of view of their defence. There was rather a tendency at one time to site them solely with reference to their suitability for flying operations; and in one or two cases they were located too near the coast where they were a definite danger so long as the Japanese had command of the sea. This, however, was corrected, and it was laid down that no aerodrome was to be selected or planned except in conjunction with the staff officer of the Army organisation concerned, a principle also applied to the siting of buildings and aircraft pens. The buildings on some of the original aerodromes in Malaya had been laid out entirely on a peace basis, for they were not dispersed and were in straight lines; this was noticeably the case at Alor Star.

53. We learned a lesson from the Dutch as regards the siting of aerodromes. In Borneo, the communications of which were undeveloped, they worked on the principle of locating aerodromes 25 to 50 miles from the coast in jungle country with only one line of access, generally a road, but sometimes a river. This, of course, considerably simplified the problem of defence against overland attacks. It was practicable only to a limited extent in Malaya, but it was laid down that any future aerodromes required in Sarawak and other parts of British Borneo would be sited on this principle.

Aircraft Warning System.

54. There was no air observation system in Malaya when I arrived, and its organisation entailed a large amount of work. The responsibility was at first placed upon the G.O.C. and was later transferred to the A.O.C. Some R.D.F. sets were received during I94I, and before war broke out an air observation system was working well as regards Southern Malaya and Singapore; it was not good up North, partly owing to the lack of depth from the frontier and partly because we had not sufficient R.D.F. sets to install any in the North. Communications were difficult the whole time, as we were short generally of signalling equipment, especially material for the construction of land lines; but the Government Post and Telegraph Service was most helpful, and war experience proved that so long as the Japanese were kept out of Southern Malaya, Singapore could always rely on half-an hour's warning of hostile aircraft. This was, of course, reduced after the Japanese advance had forced us to leave certain R.D.F. stations.

Other Matters that Required Action.

55. Some special camouflage officers having been sent out from England in the late summer of I94I, a Camouflage Committee was set up in Malaya and camouflage classes formed in Malaya for the Far East. Priority in camouflage work was given to the Naval Base and aerodromes, but work was also being done for civilian establishments which were important to the war effort. All this involved a period of years rather than months and was by no means complete when war broke out.

The formation of Army Labour Units in Malaya was a matter that was delayed for various reasons. Finally, however, it was decided to recruit Chinese in Hong Kong, which had the advantage not only of getting labour, but also of reducing the Chinese population of Hong Kong, but, unfortunately, the project was not executed before war broke out.

Arrangements were made for successive variations in the route to be followed by civil aircraft between Australia and India in the event of war with Japan.

56. In December, I940, there was a serious deficiency in ammunition, especially for the 4.5 and 3.7 A.A. guns, and in reserves for ordnance stores which were only sufficient for 90 days instead of I80. Anti-tank weapons and mines, 3-inch mortars and ammunition were also short.

Aircraft bombs at this time were also quite insufficient to allow for the expected expansion, and up to the autumn of I94I, .5 ammunition for the Buffaloes was difficult to obtain in adequate quantity.

By December, I94I, some of these deficiencies had been made good. (*See paragraph* 92 *below.*)

57. Although the Government Post and Telegraph Service was responsible for the communications on the mainland of Malaya, the lines on Singapore Island were mainly in the hands of a private company known as O.T.E.C. This caused some difficulties, *e.g.,* as regards maintenance of stocks of spares. But it was decided that

the situation in 1941 was not suitable for making the big changes that would have been involved had the Government taken over this company.

58. I found the Malayan War Committee was not on a satisfactory basis; though the proceedings were recorded in the relevant files, there were no formal minutes, so it was often difficult at a meeting to find out quickly what had been decided previously or who was responsible for taking action. This was corrected, a new Secretary for Defence was appointed, and three civilians were brought into the War Committee with good results. The Commander-in-Chief, China, and I were not members of this War Committee, but had a permanent invitation from the Governor to attend meetings.

Press Relations.

59. It was realised in the Spring of 1941 that some organisation to deal with the Press would be necessary when war broke out, and, further, that it would be important before war during periods of strained relations with Japan. As a result of a conference attended by all concerned, an organisation was worked out and brought into operation in the middle of May, 1941. The essential feature of it was that the Press relations of all three Services were grouped under one head. As has been stated above (in paragraph 41), Commander-in-Chief, China, agreed to be responsible for Press relations, and a Commander, R.N., who was called up from the Reserve, was put at the head of the Services Press Bureau. I was, and still am, of the opinion that this organisation was workable. Unfortunately, there were some discordant personalities, and, finally, after war broke out, a somewhat different organisation was adopted, with Sir George Sansom at the head.

I always found the Press ready to help when they were asked (*see, for instance, paragraph* 110 *below*) and on many occasions we got good value from them. On the other hand, some representatives of the Press of other countries were difficult and required very tactful handling; and we were undoubtedly hampered in the Far East through lack of officers experienced in dealing with the Press.

Complaints reached the Ministry of Information in London that Press correspondents were not being properly treated; in my reply to one that was passed on to Singapore I stated: "Should be most grateful for any assistance you can give to assure that we get out here officers who have knowledge of the work and can be trusted to work loyally as a team and not for their own individual benefit." I feel that in this matter we should have had more help from England, principally in the way of suitable and experienced personnel from the beginning.

I was reluctant to give Press interviews, but the importance of doing so from time to time was frequently intimated to me. There was one stock question I was frequently asked: "Was I satisfied with the strength of the defences of Malaya or the Far East generally?" I always gave the same reply, that I was never going to be satisfied because defensive preparations could always be improved, and, so far as I could, I was not going to allow any of my subordinates to be satisfied either.

60. One of the steps taken to discourage the Japanese from starting war was to

emphasise the growing strength of our defences in Malaya. (*See paragraph* 5 (*a*) *above.*) The Chiefs of Staff stated in May, 1941, that they saw no objection to this policy and we were aided by directions from the Ministry of Information in London to their representative in Singapore. The method adopted did not consist merely in extensive advertising of any reinforcements; sometimes when these were obvious they were given only a small notice in the papers or broadcast. On the other hand, when reinforcements of Royal Air Force personnel arrived they were merely referred to as Royal Air Force and no mention was made of the fact that no aeroplanes were with them. It is doubtful if the effect was great, but it was probably not negligible.

In interviews with Press correspondents whom I could trust, I made no secret of the fact that the shortage of aeroplanes caused me great anxiety, but warned them that they were on no account to mention it in their papers. A similar attitude was adopted with regard to tanks, of which we had none when war broke out.

Meeting with British Far East Representatives.

61. At the end of September 1941, Sir Earle Page from Australia, the British Ambassador in Chungking Sir A. Clark Kerr, and the British Minister in Bangkok Sir J. Crosby, were all in Singapore. The opportunity was taken to have a combined meeting together with Mr. Duff Cooper and the Governor of Malaya in order that the two Commanders-in-Chief might discuss with them all the situation in the Far East. A report was sent to the Chiefs of Staff.

The meeting agreed generally with the views expressed by the Commander-in-Chief, China, and myself, that Japan's principal asset in the Far East was her foothold in Indo-China, which might be developed as a springboard from which to attack Malaya. Further, that Japan must be anxious to avoid war in the South for the next few months so the time was opportune for bringing pressure to bear on her to withdraw from Indo-China.

The meeting emphasised that, in the absence of a British fleet based at Singapore, there was little doubt that Japan could strike at her selected moment and stressed the propaganda value of even one or two battleships at Singapore. Various steps were recommended, including the following:-

The issue of a co-ordinated announcement by the British, United States and Dutch Governments that they had a combined plan for action in the event of a Japanese move against any of their interests in the Far East;

Urging the United States to reinforce the Philippines, especially with submarines and air forces;

Development of our aid to, and plans for operations in, China; and Liaison with Russian forces in the Far East.

VI. – CIVIL DEFENCE PROBLEMS IN MALAYA.

Food and Water.

62. On my arrival in Singapore I found a large number of Civil Defence matters requiring attention. As regards food supplies, a six months' supply for the whole population, as well as for the Navy, Army and Air Force, had been laid down as the minimum requirement. Rice was a constant source of anxiety. The yield of rice in Malaya was insufficient for the whole population, and so some had to be imported mainly from Burma, and this again was naturally dependent on shipping. As soon as the year's crop was gathered, stocks were plentiful, but the consumption was large and required constant watching. There was difficulty over the storage of rice for more than six months, but this had been solved by the introduction of the method of mixing a small proportion of lime with the rice, which, so far as tests went, preserved it for two years without deterioration. There was also the problem of the distribution of rice, some of the States producing an excess of their own requirements. The custom had been to store this surplus on the spot, and at one time there was some 50,000 tons of rice stored as far North as Alor Star. By the time war broke out, however, distribution was satisfactory.

On two occasions, the War Committee decided that a scheme of food rationing in time of war must be prepared. Committees were formed to carry this out, but on both occasions reported that the difficulties were so great that food rationing was impracticable; and, on one occasion, that if it was necessary from the military point of view, it was up to the military to prepare a scheme. The position was certainly complicated, but I did not believe that the difficulties were insurmountable.

The main source of supply for the water reservoirs on Singapore Island was from the mainland of Johore. It was realised that this might be cut, and the matter was investigated on my arrival. The result of this investigation, showed that the rainfall was sufficient, with certain additional water mains, to supply enough water to meet the requirements of the whole of the anticipated population of the island, except that water-borne sanitation would have to be stopped. The necessary steps were taken. A sea-water fire service already existed for part of Singapore City.

Air Raid Precautions.

63. A.R.P. in Singapore had started, and before war broke out I was satisfied that the organisation, as regards fire precautions, demolition squads, rescue parties and first aid, was good. Up to the time I handed over command, A.R.P. functioned well, with one exception. (*See para.* 99 *below.*) Up-country, progress was somewhat slower.

Black-out in Malaya was difficult. Owing to the construction of most of the houses, complete black-out meant shutting off most of the ventilation, which was extremely disagreeable in Malayan climate. Consequently, when blackout was enforced it meant most people living either in darkness or in physical discomfort. In consequence, a system was introduced of having a "brown-out," a black-out being enforced as soon as warning was received of the actual approach of hostile aircraft. The brown-out allowed a certain amount of light, sufficient with care to read by without closing up the room. In my opinion, this worked satisfactorily.

64. The provision of air raid shelters in Singapore was insufficient for the total population, but the construction of these was not a simple matter. The water-level was near the surface, so that in most places the digging of trenches was not only useless, but dangerous because they soon became filled with water and formed breeding places for mosquitoes. Many of the streets were narrow, and there was little room for the building of shelters. Quite apart from the blocking of traffic, the medical authorities definitely advised against the building of shelters in streets, on the ground that the circulation of air would thereby be stopped, thus leading to epidemics.

On the other hand, many of the streets of Singapore had footpaths covered over by the first floors of the buildings, which were supported by pillars from the outside. Provided the houses were of fairly solid construction, filling up the spaces between the pillars with stone or bricks afforded a good type of air-raid shelter. Where none could be constructed, the policy was to provide accommodation in open spaces outside the town, where it was expected that the population would move as soon as bombing started. Compulsory evacuation was not enforced.

Denial Schemes and Evacuation.

65. A denial scheme was prepared early in 1941 for the event of an invasion of Malaya, and necessary instructions issued. This scheme was directed principally to the destruction or removal of everything that might facilitate the movement of invading forces. It included such things as the removal of food stocks, or their dispersal amongst the villages, the destruction of any form of repair workshop, as well as the demolition of bridges and the removal or destruction of all forms of vehicle or boat. The plan did not envisage a complete "scorched earth" policy. (*See para. 119 below.*) For instance, in the case of tin mines it was only laid down that essential parts of the machinery of dredges were to be removed and brought away. A plan for the denial of British-owned tin mines in the Kra Isthmus was also worked out by the O.M. Section of the Ministry of Economic Warfare, including arrangements with Commander-in-Chief, China, for the evacuation of British personnel by sea after the denial scheme had been carried out.

66. Originally, civil officials were ordered to remain at their posts in the event of invasion. This, however, was modified in December 1941, enabling those who were suitable, physically and otherwise, for service with military units to be withdrawn, so that they could be used for defence. This also applied to a proportion of the civil medical staff.

67. The problem of British families in Singapore and Malaya generally was somewhat involved. In the case of the Navy, families were permitted for those stationed ashore, *i.e.,* officers in the light cruisers were not allowed to bring their families out to Singapore. In the Army and Air Force, families were allowed in those units which were considered to be the permanent garrison in Singapore, which in practice meant the units existing before September 1939. Units which arrived since that date were counted as reinforcements, and families not allowed in their case.

This gave rise to anomalies, because some of the units, *e.g.,* Headquarters, Malaya Command, and the Royal Air Force Depot at Seletar, had expanded very considerably since September 1939, although they were still counted as part of the permanent garrison. In the case of the families of civil officials and civilians there were no restrictions. Apart from 50 W.R.N.S. at the Naval Wireless Station and a number of nurses, many women were employed in the different services for clerical, cipher and other duties, including intelligence work in F.E.C.B. Had all these been sent away, it would have meant a large increase in the number of men absorbed. As it was, we were short of women to fill suitable posts and thus relieve men for the fighting units.

On the other hand, the presence of large numbers of women and children led, in January 1942, to hurried evacuation, with consequent loss of personal belongings and discomfort, and, later, to casualties. (*See para.* 121 *below.*)

Service and Civilian Communities.

68. Relations between the Services and civilian communities were better up-country than in Singapore.

The view held in the Colonial Office was that rubber and tin output was of greater importance than the training of the local forces; for instance, a telegram, dated the 31st December, 1940, to the Governor, states: "The ultimate criterion for exemption should be not what the General Officer Commanding considers practicable, but what you consider essential to maintain the necessary production and efficient labour management."

Attitude of Non-British Population.

69. With regard to the other races in Malaya, the most numerous were the Chinese. Many of them had no particular roots in Malaya. There was difficulty in filling the Chinese companies of the Volunteers up to establishment, nor could we get a sufficient number of Chinese motor drivers. This may have been partly the fault of the British, and there was not sufficient contact between the British and the leading men of the Chinese community. My experience of the Chinese under air bombing was that they were calm, and with no tendency to panic.

There were several thousand Indian labourers in Malaya, mostly Tamils, who worked on the rubber estates. So long as they were kept free from agitators, these Tamils were a law-abiding community.

Some probable fifth columnists were marked down at Kuala Lumpur and rounded up at the start of the war, but there was very little fifth column work or treachery. There was no difficulty in recruiting for the two battalions of the Malay Regiment, and young Malays who had been specially trained in technical schools worked well in the aircraft maintenance unit on Singapore Island, and were not unduly worried by bombing.

VII. – NEIGHBOURING COUNTRIES.

China.

70. The late Major-General Dennys was appointed Military Attaché in Chungking shortly after my arrival in Singapore, with the intention that, when war with Japan broke out, he would become Head of the British Military Mission with the Chinese, this being known as 204 Mission. Chiefly owing to his work, seconded by Wing-Commander Warburton and backed by the Ambassador, Sir A. Clark Kerr, our relations with the Chinese were very satisfactory, and considerable progress was made in plans for co-operation, and, to some degree, in their execution.

Co-operation as regards air consisted mainly in the preparation of aerodrome sites and the dispatch to China of stocks of aviation petrol and, finally, bombs, all for British squadrons which it was hoped to send up later. (*See Para. 26 above.*) The aerodrome sites were in three groups: the first in the area north and west of Kunming, the object of which was largely to protect the Burma Road; the second, an area north of Hong Kong, from which it was hoped to assist in the defence of that place and the third, an area further east, from which it was hoped that one day it might be possible to deliver air attacks on Japan. It was only in the first group that these preparations could be called complete when war broke out. Transport was one of the main difficulties, and it was not until the 13th November, 1941, that permission was given to send up bombs. The petrol and bombs were consigned to the Chinese, who took charge of them.

71. The second form of assistance to China was with their guerillas. It was agreed that fifteen special Chinese guerilla companies should be formed initially, and that each should have a squad of fifteen British and Indian personnel attached to it. These squads would be specially trained in the use of explosives and in carrying out demolitions, and would be kept supplied by us with the necessary material. It was proposed eventually to double the number of guerilla companies, and consequently of the squads. These squads went through a thorough training in Burma, including living under the conditions they would experience when operating with the Chinese guerillas.

72. The whole organisation for the supply to the aerodromes and to the guerilla squads was based on Burma. It was known first as Chi Base and later as Tulip. Lieutenant-Colonel McFeat was in charge; his own headquarters were at Rangoon, the training of guerilla squads was carried out at Maymyo, and stores of all sorts were sent up to Lashio and to Bhamo. A mechanical transport organisation for forwarding stores and supplies was in progress, but by no means complete in vehicles by the 7th December. Signalling and medical facilities were deficient for most of the guerrilla squads. Tulip was directly under my headquarters till war with Japan broke out, when it was transferred, as planned, to General Officer Commanding, Burma.

73. On their part, the Chinese promised not only to help in the defence of Burma with the American Volunteer Group (*see para. 25 above*), but also to send troops to Burma if required, and to threaten the Japanese northern flank should they advance

against Burma via Chieng Rai. They also promised to help in the defence of Hong Kong by an advance towards Canton.

They kept their promises.

74. A Chinese Military Mission visited Burma and Singapore in April and May, 1941, and various Chinese officers also paid visits individually, including General Mow, of the Chinese Air Force, who was in Singapore from the 19th to the 25th June, 1941, and stayed in my house. Certain members of my staff visited Chungking.

Siam and Indo-China.

75. The dominating factor influencing the actions of the Siamese authorities was fear. Our attitude towards the Siamese was governed by the desire to keep on as friendly terms as possible, and to encourage them to resist any encroachment by Japan. The latter was somewhat difficult because it was quite impracticable for us to take any effective military action to prevent Japanese penetration of Siam. Further, as the Siamese quite rightly pointed out, they were very short of equipment, especially aircraft and anti-aircraft, tank and anti-tank, so that, if they could not get help from us or the United States, there was little they could do but to comply with Japanese demands. Definite proposals were made in October, 1941, for giving the Siamese a few weapons, but nothing was actually sent.

It was suggested in March, 1941, that we should adopt a strong line with the Siamese. It is, however, at least doubtful whether, if we had done so, the Siamese would have been willing or able to render any effective aid when the Japanese attacked their country. As events turned out, in spite of statements by the Siamese Prime Minister, the resistance offered by the Siamese for us lasted only a few hours at Battambang on the frontier east of Bangkok, whereas British troops advancing into Southern Siam were opposed by the Siamese after the Japanese had landed.

76. At the time of my arrival in Singapore, the Japanese had troops in Tongking, at the northern end of Indo-China. This in itself was no direct threat to Burma or Malaya. To some extent it was a threat to the Chinese section of the road from Burma to China, but there seemed some reason to believe that the original purpose for which these troops were sent there was to extricate Japanese forces in Kwangsi, who were malaria-ridden and in a difficult position.

77. In the latter part of 1940, Siamese Ministers, possibly encouraged by the Japanese, had stimulated their country to demand the return to Siam of certain areas that had been taken by the French some years before. This eventually led to a mild form of hostilities between the two countries concerned. Endeavours were made at Singapore by the Governor, Commander-in-Chief, China, and myself to bring about a settlement without posing as official mediators, but these endeavours were unsuccessful. By the end of January, 1941, the Japanese had been recognised as the mediators, and thus scored a diplomatic success.

78. We had concluded an economic agreement with the Vichy French authorities in Indo-China, and they professed themselves anxious to develop friendly relations. In spite of this an agreement between them and the Japanese was announced on the 24th July, 1941. Its terms allowed the Japanese to maintain forces in the South of Indo-

China. A Japanese convoy began to arrive at Saigon on the 26th, and by the end of July the Japanese were well established in that town. More important still, this movement gave the Japanese complete control of Camranh Harbour, and they quickly started to make or improve aerodromes to the South and West of Saigon. As was expected, the Japanese did not limit themselves for long to the terms of the agreement, and the French authorities made practically no effort to oppose either the original terms or the successive encroachments. The effect of this expansion on the defence of the Far East is indicated below (*paras.* 93 et seq.).

VIII. – DEVELOPMENT OF THE BRITISH AIR FORCES IN THE FAR EAST.

General Position.

79. In their paper of the I5th August, I940, the Chiefs of Staff estimated the air strength necessary for the Far East as 336 first-line aircraft, to which, of course, had to be added reserves.

In the Singapore Conference of October, I940, the final strength of the Royal Air Force recommended for the Far East was 582 aircraft, an increase of sixteen over that given in the appreciation dated the I6th October, I940 (*see para.* 42 (*b*) *above*). The Chiefs of Staff agreed that 582 aircraft was an ideal, but considered that 336 should give a very fair degree of security. The figure of 566 aircraft given in the appreciation was stated by the Air Ministry to be far beyond the bounds of practical possibility in the light of total resources and vital requirements in active theatres at home and in the Middle East.

The strength of the Air Forces in Malaya in November, I940, is as shown in Appendix I, that in Hong Kong and Ceylon was negligible. Of the total of 88 first-line aircraft, only 48, i.e., the Blenheims and Hudsons, could be counted as modern, and the former suffered from lack of range. The Vildebeestes which we had at the beginning of the war with Japan were considered by the Chiefs of Staff in August, I940, as having become an obsolete type.

The replacement for the Vildebeeste was to be the Beaufort. Manufacture of these had started in Australia and we were to get the first 90. Much of the raw material and certain complete parts of these aeroplanes had to come from England and from the United States, and there was considerable delay in supplying many of the items. The urgency of the matter was represented several times from Australia, and particularly at the beginning of August, when the Prime Minister of Australia sent a special telegram to the Australian High Commissioner in London. In spite, however, of every effort on the part of Australia, Vildebeesltes were still in use in December, I94I (*see para.* 86 *below*).

The flying boats were not only obsolete, but badly in need of complete overhaul, and the Wirraways could only be considered as training aircraft.

But the great weaknesses were the absence of any fighters and the small size of the reserves. This latter even necessitated restrictions on the number of flying hours in squadrons towards the end of 1940, and the first months of 1941. The importance of remedying these weaknesses was emphasised very shortly after my arrival at Singapore, and the aircraft situation was elaborated in a telegram three months later. In this latter telegram I estimated that, at the end of 1941, we should be able to reckon, as an absolute maximum, on a total of only 215 aircraft, including anticipated reinforcements of 39 Dutch aircraft, or 176 exclusive of the Dutch.

80. The general deficiencies in aircraft were also emphasised in many other telegrams.

The following are extracts:-

"This means bluntly that at present not only is our ability to attack shipping deplorably weak, but we have not the staying power to sustain even what we could now do. As our air effort dwindles (as it would if war came now) so will the enemy's chance of landing increase";

and:-

"Nor do I know whether troops or aircraft will be the easier to provide but I have no doubt what our first requirement here is. We want to increase our hitting power against ships, and our capacity to go on hitting."

The need for more aircraft for the attack of shipping had also been emphasised in a previous telegram of the 23rd July, 1941.

81. The Chiefs of Staff fully appreciated my anxiety about the smallness of the air forces at my disposal, but pointed out that they had had to face disappointments in production, had to reinforce the Middle East still further to meet the probable scale of attack in the Spring, and that the necessity for supporting Russia was likely to impose a further strain on British and American resources. Further, that in these circumstances it was clear that neither could the target programme for the Far East be completed, nor, indeed, could any substantial reinforcements be sent before the end of 1941.

82. This Chiefs of Staff's figure of 336 first line aircraft referred to in para. 79 above, was based on the assumption that Borneo would be defended, but took no account of the defence of Burma. Whilst the latter was a greater commitment than the former, I accepted the figure of 336 as the target at which to aim in view of two telegrams from the Chiefs of Staff, in both of which the figure of 336 was confirmed.

Fighters.

83. Single-seater fighter aircraft, known as the Brewster Buffalo, began to arrive in Singapore in cases from the United States in February, 1941, and permission was given by the Air Ministry to form two squadrons in the first instance. These were formed mainly with pilots taken from existing squadrons, who had a good deal of flying experience, and so got up to the operational standard much quicker than the two new squadrons formed later; though not up to establishment, the first two squadrons would have been able to fight by the middle of April, 1941. A total of 167

Buffaloes in all were received in Singapore, and on the 30th May, 1941, permission was given by the Air Ministry to form two further fighter squadrons.

These new squadrons took a long time to become operationally efficient. The majority of the pilots had to be brought from Australia and New Zealand. They all came straight from the Flying Training Schools, and some from New Zealand had never flown anything beyond a Hart, and had no experience of retractable undercarriages, variable-pitch propellors, or flaps. Under these conditions it took over four months from the time that the pilots arrived in Malaya before the squadrons could be considered fit for operations; in fact, they had not been passed as fit when war with Japan broke out. It would have helped a great deal if we could have formed a proper operational training unit in Malaya, but I was informed that neither personnel nor aircraft could be spared for the purpose, and that all the training of pilots would have to be done in the squadrons. As this would have seriously hindered the operational training of squadrons, the nucleus of an O.T.U. was formed from our own resources.

After the formation of the third and fourth Buffalo squadrons had been started, it was found that the re-equipment of the R.A.A.F. Wirraway Squadron was going to be delayed indefinitely, and I was requested by Australia to take any possible steps I could to ensure that this Australian squadron was re-equipped with some form of more modern machine than the Wirraway. The only possible course of action was to re-equip it with Buffaloes. This was sanctioned by the Air Ministry and carried out, but five squadrons were definitely too many for the total number of Buffaloes available, and overstrained the reserves.

84. The Buffalo proved disappointing, at any rate when up against the Japanese Zero fighter. This was due partly to technical reasons and partly to incomplete training of pilots. With regard to the former the performance of the Buffaloes at heights of 10,000 feet and over were relatively poor. (*See Appendix "L"*). Whilst it had been realised that the Buffalo lacked speed, it had been hoped that, with good warning system and the comparatively small area of important objectives, e.g., the Naval Base, it would be able to reach the height necessary before the arrival of enemy aircraft, and that its better armament would enable our squadrons to give a good account of themselves. Whether deliberately or not, the Japanese appear to have sacrificed armour and armament in their Zero fighters in order to save weight, thereby obtaining the advantage of rate of climb and manoeuvrability at heights. In the case of these two particular types, the technical advantage certainly lay with the Japanese. Attempts were made to improve the performance of the Buffalo by substituting .303 for the .5. In addition some trouble was experienced with the valve gear of the Cyclone engine in the Buffalo, and with the interrupter gear of the two fuselage guns. The Buffalo was unsuitable for night flying owing to the exhaust flames, flame dampers would have been essential for night flying but were not available. Actually this was not serious as I had laid down that the Buffalo was to be used for day work only, and that, by night, reliance was to be placed on the A.A. guns assisted by Blenheim fighters.

Pilots have been referred to in paragraph 83 above. What the R.A.F. lacked in

Malaya was a good proportion of pilots with practical war experience. Apart from forming a leaven when operations started, they could have taught the new pilots those niceties of manoeuvre and aiming which just make the difference between missing the enemy and bringing him down, the type of training that can only be given as a result of experience. Again all the Buffalo squadrons were formed in Malaya and there was no squadron with practical war experience to set a standard, and it is possible that in some respects ours was not sufficiently high for modern conditions.

85. Apart from the fighter squadron in Burma, we had in Malaya in December, I94I, a total of four Buffalo squadrons, one Dutch fighter squadron, which arrived on the 9th December, and one Blenheim squadron, the last principally for night fighting. This total was considered adequate both by the Chiefs of Staff and by my own General Headquarters, but results showed that more fighter squadrons were required, largely because the scope of a fighter's duties has widened. One Buffalo squadron was specially trained for Army co-operation, and we really wanted two. I had also agreed with the Commander-in-Chief, Eastern Fleet, that one squadron, which ought to have been a Buffalo, should be trained in the duties of fighter protection for ships. Fighter squadrons are also the most efficient type with which to attack enemy aerodromes. To carry out these functions at all adequately, as well as the normal duties of a fighter, at least seven fighter squadrons were needed in Malaya alone, without allowing for night fighters.

Long-Range Bombers.

86. The need for long-range bombers had been constantly pressed from the time I was first appointed Commander-in-Chief, Far East. At that time I had merely felt that they would be wanted without having any concrete proposals, but as the Japanese advanced into Southern Indo-China, the object for which they would be used became clear and definite. The targets which we wished to reach in Southern Indo-China were just within reach of Blenheim IV's from the Northern end of Malaya, and of Hudsons, but we had too few of the former and the latter were required for overseas reconnaissance.

Six Beauforts were flown from Australia a few days before the war started, but as these aircraft were not operational, and as the crews required considerable operational training in their use, the Air Officer Commanding, with my concurrence, sent all bar one, which was retained in the hope of using it for photographic work, back to Australia in order that they might continue their training under suitable conditions.

Other Requirements.

87. Other requirements which were realised too late were special aircraft for photographic reconnaissance and transport aircraft for facilitating the rapid movement of squadrons. Photographic aircraft were first asked for in August, I94I, after the visit of a special photographic officer. The Dutch were ready to help us in the second requirement, but once war had started were making full use of their transport aircraft for their own purposes, and we felt the lack of having a few of our own available at very short notice.

It was also suggested at one time that a balloon barrage would be valuable for the protection of Singapore, especially the Naval Base. Experiments, however, proved that the climate and meteorology of Malaya were quite unsuitable for the use of kite balloons.

88. The strength and location of the Royal Air Force in the Far East on the 7th December, 1941, are given in Appendix J and a summary of serviceable aircraft in Malaya on different dates in December in Appendix K.

Our most serious deficiency at that time was in reserves, partly of pilots, but principally aircraft. It was not only a stock of reserve aeroplanes we wanted, but also a continuous flow of new aircraft to replace wastage, for aeroplanes must be regarded as expendable material, and there must be a regular, continuous channel of supply. Without these it was impossible to keep the squadrons up to their first-line establishment. Apart from the material weakness, failure to keep up what is commonly known as "a full breakfast table" always has an adverse effect on squadrons' morale.

89. There were several civil flying clubs in Malaya, and the Air Officer Commanding had organised for these an Auxiliary Air Force, which did useful work in communication and assistance to the Army in certain aspects of training.

IX. – ARMY STRENGTH AND REQUIREMENTS, MALAYA.

90. In the appreciation of the situation drawn up by the Commanders in Malaya previous to the Singapore Defence Conference of October, 1940, an estimate was made of the total armed forces required on the supposition that 582 aircraft would be available for the defence of the Far East. The estimate was as follows:-

26 infantry battalions, including 3 for Borneo.
5 field regiments.
3 light tank companies.

In addition anti-tank units, troops for local defence of aerodromes, volunteer units and ancillary troops. This figure of 26 battalions was agreed to by the Chiefs of Staff in January, 1941.

On his arrival, General Percival went thoroughly into the question of the strength of the Army and, in August, 1941, sent his estimate of the strength required, which he summarised as:-

48 Infantry Battalions.
4 Indian Reconnaissance Units.
9 Forward Artillery Regiments.
4 Light A.A. Regiments.
2 Tank Regiments.
3 Anti-Tank Regiments.

2 Mountain Artillery Regiments.

I2 Field Companies.

This was based on my forecast of the strength which our Air Forces would reach by December, I94I, namely I86 first-line aircraft as against the accepted figure of 336. I was asked for observations and my general conclusion was that no drastic reduction in General Percival's estimate was acceptable until the strength of the Royal Air Force was materially increased not only in numbers but in quality of aircraft and in reserves of air crews and aircraft. Also that before General Percival's new target was reached in Malaya, the question of increasing forces in other areas of my command, especially Burma, would have to be considered. The Chiefs of Staff commented: "We accept estimate by General Officer Commanding, Malaya, as reasonable figure for land forces required in present circumstances. Nevertheless, this target cannot be fulfilled in foreseeable future."

9I. In December, I94I, while the actual strength of the Royal Air Force (*see Appendix J*) approached very closely to my forecast, the Army strength (*see Appendix E*) fell far short of the figure which it had been agreed was required to compensate for the deficiency in aircraft.

The main deficiencies were:-

I7 Battalions;

4 Light A.A. Regiments; and

2 Tank Regiments.

The strength in A.A. weapons in the Far Easton the 7th December, I94I, is given in Appendix F.

92. The fact that we were entirely without tanks in Malaya was a serious handicap to any offensive land operations, whether on a small or a large scale. There were also very few armoured cars. Many efforts were made to obtain both tanks and armoured cars from various sources. On the I4th August the War Office offered forty light tanks from the Middle East. These tanks were at the time being employed for aerodrome defence, and they were offered to the Far East on the condition that they would be employed in an operational role, and that we could man them from local resources. Some delay occurred at Singapore in finding the best method of meeting the latter condition. Eventually Australia agreed to provide the necessary men and to train them up to a reasonable standard in Australia, this training to be completed by the Ist January, I942. On the I3th November, I94I, however, Middle East reported to the War Office that they could not provide forty tanks for the Far East except at the expense of operational requirements. After war had broken out, War Office ordered Middle East to send fifty light tanks to India, their subsequent destination to be decided later.

With regard to armoured cars, a model of an armoured vehicle mounted on an American chassis was obtained from the Dutch and six were made in Singapore, chiefly at the Naval Base; drawings were also made and sent to Burma. No more, however, could be made owing to a shortage of boiler plate, which was used for the armouring. By the 24th November, I94I, a total of 84 Marmon-Harrington armoured cars had been shipped from South Africa for Singapore. Some of these arrived a few days before war broke out, and the drivers had not become accustomed to them before they had to go to the front.

The number of anti-tank weapons had improved considerably by the time war broke out, but there was still a shortage of the 0.5 anti-tank rifle in infantry units.

The lack of mobile A.A. weapons was serious, especially in view of the shortage of fighters. A constant anxiety to the General Officer Commanding, also, was the continual drain on the Army for men to protect aerodromes. Indian State troops were brought over to assist, but it would have been a great help if we had had more armoured cars or even tanks of an obsolete pattern for this duty. This would have enabled us to have a mobile defence and to substitute mechanical vehicles for a large proportion of the men required. The reserve of small-arms ammunition was well below the authorised figure. In November, 1941, General Headquarters informed the War Office that, with releases in sight, we should be short of our authorised holding of 150 million rounds by 57 million on the 1st January, 1942. Australia, who were already sending us 3 million rounds per month, agreed to increase this to 8 million.

X. – EVENTS LEADING UP TO THE WAR.

The Problem of Japanese Intentions.

93. As the Japanese spread South into Cambodia and Cochin China, the potential danger to Burma, Malaya, the South China Sea, and even the Philippines, increased; this danger had been realised from the start, and was referred to in a telegram in December, 1940. But it was difficult to judge whether this movement signified definite plans for an offensive against us in the near future, whether it was merely the acquisition of a strategic asset to be used in negotiation, or whether it was the first step towards occupation of Siam. This applied even to the construction of aerodromes, of which we were kept fairly well informed; what we were particularly on the look-out for was any indication of movements of long-distance bombers, or of the Zero-type fighters fitted with detachable petrol tanks. These, of course, could be concentrated on the aerodromes at short notice.

94. Another difficulty in getting any long warning of the Japanese intention was due to the restriction on exports to, and imports from, Japan. So long as Japanese merchant shipping was being employed on its normal work, F.E.C.B. could keep track of every vessel, and should it be found that an unusual number was being kept in home ports for no good reason, it would indicate the possibility, or even probability, that the Japanese were refitting these ships as transports prior to an overseas expedition. The effect of the embargo, however, was to drive all Japanese shipping off the seas for purely economic reasons, and once in Japanese ports they could be altered as required without our being any the wiser. This applied especially to the fast vessels, *i.e.,* round about 18 knots.

In spite of the preparations going on in Southern Indo-China there were some indications – at any rate up to the end of November – that the Japanese did not intend immediate hostilities. The first was a general one, namely, that if the Japanese intended to attack Malaya, they would have been more likely to have done so in 1940, when our forces were far weaker than they were at the end of 1941. Then the winter months, December to February, were less favourable for an expedition against the East coast of Malaya and the Kra Isthmus than other periods of the year owing to the North-East monsoon. (*See also para.* 134 *below.*) Finally, there was the visit of Kurusu to Washington. It seems now probable that Kurusu, though possibly innocent himself, was sent to Washington with the deliberate object of misleading the United States and ourselves as to the Japanese intentions, and keeping us quiet until their own preparations had been finally completed. But at the time it seemed to us in Singapore that this was a genuine attempt on the part of the Japanese to get relaxation of the restrictions that had been imposed, and possibly to drive a wedge between Britain and the United States. I believe the same view was held in England.

95. In the latter part of November information accumulated to show that the Japanese were probably intending an offensive at an early date. Four Mogami class cruisers with a few destroyers had been despatched from the Japanese Combined Fleet to the South China Sea. Two squadrons of long-range Zero fighters arrived in South Indo-China. The number of aircraft in Indo-China rose from a total of 74 at the end of October to 245 at the end of November. The 5th Japanese Division, which was highly trained in landing operations, was reported by the Chinese to have moved to South Indo-China. There were large movements of motor landing craft from Central China, though there was no definite information as to where they had gone. In addition, a telegram was received from the War Office to the effect that the United States Army commanders in the Far East had been informed from Washington that the Kurusu negotiations might break down at any time and offensive operations be started by Japan against Siam, the Netherlands East Indies or the Philippines; up to the receipt of this telegram we had remained completely in the dark on this matter except for Press reports.

Aeroplanes, almost certainly Japanese, occasionally flew over parts of Malaya in the latter part of November and early December, in all probability carrying out photographic reconnaissance, but owing to the speed and height at which they operated we were never able to make contact and obtain definite identification.

In view of the continued Japanese developments in Southern Indo-China, which gave them the facilities needed to attack Malaya, precautionary steps were taken on the 22nd November, and orders were issued for vulnerable points to be guarded, and on the 1st December the Volunteers were mobilised. Certain movements of air forces were carried out, and reconnaissances over the China Sea were instituted.

During this time we felt great need of aircraft capable of doing high-altitude photographic reconnaissance. This applied not only to the aerodromes in Southern Indo-China, but particularly to Camranh Harbour, on which we got no information whatever. We had no aircraft suitable for the purpose since, though a Catalina could have flown the distance, it had neither the speed nor the necessary ceiling. It seemed highly undesirable to aggravate a strained situation by sending over an aeroplane which would in all probability have been intercepted and definitely identified as

British. I asked General MacArthur to carry out a photographic reconnaissance from Manila with one of his Boeing Fortresses, which had the necessary speed and ceiling, but he replied that orders from Washington prevented him from carrying out my request.

96. Near the opposite end of the prospective theatre of operations, the island of Timor was important as being a definite link in the air communications between Australia and the Netherlands East Indies. Its occupation by the Japanese would also be a serious threat to Australia. The importance of Timor was noted in the A.D.A. agreement, and it was referred to in A.D.B. Roughly half the island was Dutch territory and half Portuguese; it was the latter half which gave no small anxiety. The Japanese had a consulate in Dilli, the capital of Portuguese Timor, and by November, I94I, had received permission to run a regular flying-boat service to Dilli, and were gradually getting an economic hold on Portuguese Timor. In November, I94I, a small nucleus of Australian troops was sent to Koepang in Dutch Timor, where there was an aerodrome and a flying-boat base. On the I2th December one infantry battalion, one independent company and a few coast defence troops reached Koepang from Australia. A combined Australian and Dutch force occupied Dilli in the middle of December, I94I. About the 7th December, in accordance with the A.D.A. and A.D.B. agreements, two flights of Hudsons of the Royal Australian Air Force moved to Ambon in the Netherlands East Indies. These were followed later by an infantry battalion.

Order of the Day.

97. The Commander-in-Chief, China, and I had agreed as far back as May, I94I, that it was desirable to prepare an Order of the Day before the war broke out, so that it could reach Burma and Hong Kong in time to be translated into the different languages spoken by the troops in the Far East and be ready for issue on the first day of war. Drafting this Order presented difficulty because it had to appeal to men of varying races and religions, *e.g.,* British sailors and Burmese troops. The main object that I had in view when preparing it was to make an effective appeal to the Indian troops, as I considered it would be necessary to stimulate them rather than the British. Through information that has reached me subsequent to the outbreak of war I believe it had the effect it was meant to. The order is given in Appendix M.

Approach of the First Enemy Expedition.

98. About I400 hours on the 6th December I received information that an air reconnaissance had sighted two Japanese convoys escorted by warships about 80 miles East-South-East of Pulo Obi, an island off the Southern point of Indo-China, steaming West. One convoy consisted of 22 I0,000-ton merchant vessels escorted by one battleship, probably the *Kongoo,* five cruisers and seven destroyers; the other of 2I merchant ships escorted by two cruisers and ten destroyers. Further West, one Japanese cruiser and three I0,000-ton merchant ships had been sighted steering North-West. I consulted with Admiral Sir Geoffrey Layton and Admiral Palliser, Sir Tom

Phillips' Chief of Staff, and we concluded that the probability was that the convoy would not continue its course due West, which would have brought it on to the Kra Isthmus, but that it would follow the first four vessels and round Cambodia Point. It was pointed out that there was a good anchorage on the West Coast of Indo-China at Koh Tron, which they might be making for as the next step towards Siam.

Bearing in mind the policy of avoiding war with Japan if possible – a policy which had been reaffirmed by the Chiefs of Staff as recently as the 29th November – and the situation in the United States with the Kurusu talks still going on in Washington, I decided that I would not be justified in ordering "Matador" on this information, but orders were issued to bring all forces to the first, *i.e.,* the highest, degree of readiness. I also impressed upon the Air Officer Commanding the urgent necessity for maintaining contact with the convoy, a point which he had already realised.

The location of these forces by Hudsons of No. I Royal Australian Air Force Squadron, based on Kota Bharu, was a particularly good piece of work in view of their being at the limit of their patrolling range, over 300 miles from the Malayan Coast. This same factor of distance, however, made it impossible for them to remain in contact until relieved, but a Catalina Flying-boat was despatched to shadow the convoy during the night. The Air Officer Commanding also ordered a reconnaissance by Hudsons starting early on the 7th December, fanning out from Kota Bharu on to the last known bearings of the convoy. No signal was received from the Catalina, and, from information received later, it is almost certain it was shot down. A second Catalina failed to make contact with the convoy. On the morning of the 7th December, visibility East and North-East from Kota Bharu was good. The reconnaissance found no ships in the area between Kota Bharu and the Southern end of Indo-China, thus confirming the supposition that the convoy had rounded Cambodia Point, and had followed the four leading ships North-North-West into the Gulf of Siam. In this Gulf the visibility was very bad and no positive information was received from this area until the evening, when a report was received that a Hudson had seen, through low clouds, three small Japanese ships which were then passing Singora and heading south. This information reached me about 2100 hours. I met General Percival and we proceeded together to the Naval Base; I decided not to order "Matador"; the main reason being that at least 24 hours start was required before the anticipated time of a Japanese landing and this was most unlikely to be available, should the 3 ships seen turn out to be part of a Japanese expedition. Further, the conditions for reconnaissance were bad, on the information then available there could be no certainty that the Japanese were about to open hostilities, and on more than one occasion the British Minister to Thailand had stressed the serious consequences that would ensue should we be the first to break Thai neutrality. (*See also paragraph* 5I *above.*)

It is pertinent to record that, until the Japanese had committed some definite act of hostility against the United States, the Dutch or ourselves, permission had not been given to attack a Japanese expedition at sea.

XI. – THE START OF HOSTILITIES.

The Opening Day.

99. Clear evidence that the Japanese had, in fact, taken the plunge into hostilities was soon forthcoming when, at 0130 hours on Monday, the 8th December, the Japanese started to land from about ten ships at Kota Bharu. I received this news at about 0200 hours in my office at the Naval Base, Singapore, and the necessary steps were at once taken to put everything on a war footing, including the internment of Japanese. Later on, reports were received that the Japanese were landing large forces at Singora and Patani in the Southern part of the Kra Isthmus.

At 0300 hours on the 8th December Singapore was attacked by Japanese bombers, which, in all probability, came from Southern Indo-China. In one case, at any rate, they came over in a formation of nine at a height of between 12,000 and 14,000 feet, without dropping any bombs, apparently with the object of drawing the searchlights and A.A. guns away from a few other aircraft which, flying at 4,000 to 5,000 feet, attacked objectives on Singapore Island, mainly aerodromes, with practically no results. An attack was also made on the Eastern part of Singapore Harbour, possibly in mistake for the aerodrome at Kallang; this attack caused a number of casualties, killing about sixty, mostly Chinese.

The observation system worked satisfactorily, and thirty minutes' warning of the approach of Japanese aircraft was received at my headquarters. For some reason that I never ascertained, the Headquarters of the A.R.P. organisation had not been manned, and it was only a few minutes before bombs were dropping on Singapore that contact was made by Fighter Group Headquarters and the sirens sounded giving the warning for black-out. In my opinion, the absence of black-out had but little effect, since there was a bright full moon, and the coastline and most of Singapore must have shown up very clearly.

Apart from this failure in Civil A.R.P., there was no tactical surprise, since as has been stated above, the troops were all in readiness, and the black-out was carried out at all Naval, Army and Air Force establishments.

100. In the morning of the 8th December the weather was clear over the land and close to the coast, but out to sea there were clouds down to 500 feet. No. I Squadron, Royal Australian Air Force, at Kota Bharu, aided by the Vildebeestes of Nos.. 36 and 100 Squadrons, carried out a vigorous offensive against the Japanese vessels and landing craft. Reports showed that these attacks had a considerable measure of success, many landing craft in the Kota Bharu River being sunk, and a ship reported to have contained tanks being sent to the bottom.

No. 62 Squadron from Alor Star also went out to attack the same target, but, owing probably to being ordered too far from the coast, failed to locate the enemy ships near Kota Bharu and proceeded to the neighbourhood of Patani on the Kra Isthmus. Here it was met by a greatly superior force of Japanese Zero fighters, and though Japanese ships were located there and bombs dropped on them, the attack was probably ineffective.

On the Western side in Kedah reconnaissance forces of the IIth Division crossed the Siam frontier in the afternoon of the 8th December and made contact with the enemy, who were already employing 10 A.F.Vs. After inflicting casualties, our forces withdrew in the afternoon, demolishing bridges on their way to the frontier. Further South a force known as Krohcol also crossed the frontier beyond Kroh in order to take up a position on the Siamese side of the border as originally planned. Both these forces met with some opposition from the Siamese.

Meanwhile, in spite of resistance on the beaches and further back, the enemy had made progress at Kota Bharu, until by 1600 hours the aerodrome was so threatened by Japanese troops that our aircraft had to leave and fly to Kuantan.

101. A feature of the opening day of hostilities was the enemy air attack upon our Northern aerodromes. Gong Kedah, Machang, Penang, Butterworth, Alor Star and Sungei Patani aerodromes were all attacked, the total scale of enemy effort for the day being estimated at some 150 aircraft, of which probably 65 per cent. were fighters. Of these attacks, the most damaging were against Alor Star and Sungei Patani, several aircraft on the ground being rendered unserviceable in both cases and most buildings at Sungei Patani destroyed. Both aerodromes were henceforth unable to operate and had to be vacated.

The attack on Alor Star was made by a formation of 27 twin-engine bombers of the Army type 97, and started about twenty minutes after the return of No. 62 Squadron from their attack at Patani and whilst the aircraft were refuelling. The Japanese attacked from a height of about 13,000 feet and used pattern bombing, the bombs being partly high-explosive, mostly about 150lb., and partly incendiary. The attack was very effective; some ten of our Blenheims were put out of action, four being completely written off. The fuel dump and some buildings were set on fire, and, as the water supply was put out of action, the fires were not extinguished till dusk. Casualties were small, only seven men being killed. Alor Star was defended by four 3-inch 20-cwt. guns, but they failed to bring down any Japanese aircraft, possibly owing to the height at which they were flying.

9th-11th December.

102. Broadly speaking, assaults on our aerodromes, coupled with fresh landings in Siamese territory, continued to be the main feature of the Japanese operations for the first two days of the war. The enemy was greatly helped in them by the prompt use to which he put Siamese aerodromes, our reconnaissances on the 9th and 10th December revealing concentrations of some sixty aircraft at Singora and eighty to a hundred aircraft at Don Muang, Bangkok. On the 9th December eleven Blenheims attacked Singora aerodrome, but they were met by a greatly superior force of enemy fighters and five of our aircraft were brought down; the results of our bombing were not observed. Aircraft of No. 62 Squadron, which had moved back to Butterworth at dawn on the 9th December, were also ordered to attack Singora, starting at 1700 hours the same day. Butterworth was attacked by Japanese aircraft just as ours were about to take off, and, although Buffaloes were up, considerable damage was caused, with the result that only one Blenheim left. The pilot, Flight-Lieutenant Scarf, reached and attacked Singora, but was badly wounded; he flew his aeroplane back, landed at Alor Star and died a few minutes later.

On the 9th December our aircraft were forced to vacate Kuantan owing to enemy bombing, though it was still used for refuelling. Already by this date it was clear that the success of the enemy's attack on our Northern aerodromes would considerably handicap our own air action, and that this in turn would unfavourably prejudice our fortunes in the fighting on land. Interference with Singora landings was made difficult, once our Northern aerodromes had succumbed, by our lack of bombers of adequate range. In a telegram to London from General Headquarters a warning was given that it was unlikely we should find it practicable to maintain the existing air effort for more than two or three weeks.

Dutch air reinforcements arrived in Singapore Island on the 9th; they consisted of three squadrons of Glenn Martin bombers, total 22 aircraft, and one squadron of nine Buffalo fighters. It was found necessary to send eight of the bombers back to the Netherlands East Indies to complete the training of their crews in night flying.

103. The 8th Brigade, defending Kota Bharu, was pressed back on the 9th, demolition being carried out before the aerodrome was evacuated. By the end of the day it was forced back to a line in Kelantan running Peringot – Mulong. The enemy was employing infiltration tactics and working round the flanks of our forces wherever possible. The 8th Brigade had put up a stout resistance round Kota Bharu, and its commander, Brigadier Key, was faced with a difficult problem in deciding when retreat would become necessary.(*See para.* 138 *below.*) The decision having been made, the Brigade was disengaged skilfully.

Japanese Army reinforcements meanwhile arrived on a considerable scale. A large force, consisting of transports escorted by a battleship, three cruisers and eleven destroyers, was sighted by our aircraft between Kota Bharu and the Penhentain Islands on the 9th December. North of Kuantan the Japanese landed in small numbers at Beserah during the night 9th-10th December. These were driven off, and by 0845 on the 10th December all was quiet there. The general situation in regard to Japanese landings was thus that all successful landings took place North of the Malaya – Siam frontier, except that at Kota Bharu, which, as already stated in para. 12 above, had no road communications to Southern Malaya, and depended for reinforcements from the South on the railway alone.

By the 10th December it was evident that the enemy's primary object was the establishment of air superiority in Northern Malaya, whilst at the same time he was testing our defences on a wide front. It was estimated that the Japanese were now employing about 30 Zero-type fighters from Patani and about 70 aircraft, mainly Zero fighters, from Singora. All but about 50 of the Japanese bombers previously based in Southern Indo-China had presumably been moved to Siam.

A complication of the situation which gave some anxiety at this date was that our efforts might be impeded by lack of support, or even actively hostile measures, among native elements. Native labour tended to disappear for days after bombing, and non-British railway employees, including engine-drivers, deserted temporarily on a large scale; the Army was able to replace the drivers to some extent.

104. By the 11th December the 8th Brigade, in Kelantan, retiring along the road which meets the railway at Kuala Krai, was in a position covering Machang. In Kedah

a new threat was opening in the form of enemy infiltration from Siam, especially in the Chaglun area. This advance into Kedah, coupled with the heavy air attacks on Penang, indicated that the Japanese main attack would be down the road communications of Western Malaya. Advanced troops of the IIth Indian Division were in position South, of a line Chaglun – Kodiang, while Krohcol sought to hold off the enemy in this more central region. Some of the demolitions that had been prepared in Northern Kedah failed to be effective; this was not due to any failure to act in time, but to some technical fault either in the fuses or explosives. All our serviceable aircraft had now been withdrawn from Northern Malaya. It was estimated that by the IIth December the Japanese were employing in Malaya at least two divisions, supported by 250-300 aircraft.

H.M.S. *Prince of Wales and Repulse.*

I05. H.M.S. *Prince of Wales* and *Repulse* arrived at Singapore on Tuesday, the 2nd December, I94I, Admiral Sir Tom Phillips having arrived by air two days before. He and I had no opportunity for full consultation over the situation before war broke out, partly because he was taking over from Sir Geoffrey Layton as Commander-in-Chief, Eastern Fleet, and partly because he visited Manila by air to meet Admiral Hart.

H.M.S. *Repulse* left to pay a visit to Port Darwin on the 5th December, and it was agreed she should proceed for the first 48 hours at comparatively slow speed: She was recalled as soon as the air reconnaissance report of the 6th December was received, and arrived back in Singapore on the 7th December. The naval forces at Singapore on the 7th December are given in Appendix C.

I06. Admiral Phillips decided to take action with his two capital ships. So far as my Headquarters was concerned he was put into direct touch with the Air Officer Commanding with regard to the air co-operation required, and asked for three things:-

(*a*) Reconnaissance I00 miles to north of the force from daylight, Tuesday, the 9th December;

(*b*) Reconnaissance to Singora and beyond ten miles from the coast starting at first light on the I0th December; and

(*c*) Fighter protection off Singora at daylight on the I0th December.

The Air Officer Commanding gave tentative replies that he could provide (*a*), hoped to be able to provide (*b*), but could not provide (*c*). It was decided that he should go thoroughly into the problems involved and give definite replies to the Chief of Staff, Eastern Fleet, Rear-Admiral Palliser, who was remaining behind. Air Officer Commanding later confirmed his tentative replies and this information was sent on by signal to Commander-in-Chief, Eastern Fleet, in the evening of the 8th December. The doubt about (*b*) was due to the fact that the reconnaissance would have to be provided by Blenheim IV's based on Kuantan aerodrome, and it was uncertain whether this would be out of action or not. Actually, both the reconnaissances were carried out, though one of the Blenheims doing (*b*) had wireless troubles.

The reason why (*c*) could not be provided was mainly that the northern aerodromes were either untenable or else had been badly damaged by bombing; this meant that the fighters would have to operate from aerodromes at considerable distance from Singora, and, owing to the short endurance of the Buffalo, they would have been able to remain only a very short time over that area before having to return to refuel. The Dutch fighter squadron had not arrived by the 8th; it was uncertain whether it would be available by the 10th and thus there was a shortage of fighter aircraft. These factors meant that a short patrol might possibly have been provided at intervals at Singora, but that it was impossible to guarantee continuous fighter protection.

107. The *Prince of Wales* and *Repulse,* accompanied by four destroyers, left Singapore in the afternoon of Monday, the 8th December. Early on the 10th December a signal was made to Singapore indicating that the ships would return earlier than originally planned. Except for this, no communication was received and their position remained unknown until, shortly after twelve noon on Wednesday, the 10th December, a signal was received from *Repulse* that she was being bombed in a position about 60 miles East-South-East of Kuantan. On receipt of the message a fighter squadron was at once despatched and reached the position of the ships in commendably quick time, but only to see the *Prince of Wales* go down. No enemy aircraft were spotted. Fighter cover, though only a weak one, was provided for the destroyers that picked up the crews from the sunken ships.

108. I had been asked by Rear-Admiral Palliser to give an indication of the strength of the air force that the Japanese might bring against these two ships from Indo-China, and gave an estimate of between 50 and 60 bombers which might be expected to arrive five hours after the ships had been first located by reconnaissance. Whether this information was ever received by the Commander-in-Chief, Eastern Fleet, I do not know.

109. The ships were attacked by high-level bombers and torpedo bombers, the latter being by far the more effective. It is possible that the high-level bombers were used with the object of attracting any of our fighters that might have been with the ships away from the torpedo bombers. The Japanese would probably have expected that such fighters would be flying high, and that they would naturally attack high level bombers in the first instance, thus giving sufficient time for the torpedo bombers to get in their attack before our fighters could get down to them. Admittedly, this is conjecture, but it is on similar lines to the bombing attack carried out on Singapore Island early on the 8th December. It also indicates the value of the dive bomber as a third alternative method of attacking ships, thereby giving greater facilities for surprise.

110. The psychological effect on Malaya of the loss of these two ships was somewhat mitigated by the fact that shortly after they arrived I had summoned a Press conference, and talked to those present on the following lines:-

"The arrival of the two capital ships in no way reduced the need for continuance of every effort being made to improve the defences of Malaya and Singapore; indeed, it enhanced the importance of this effort. Warships must not be tied down to their base; they must be free to operate to the full limit of their range of action and know that they can still return to a safe base when necessary.

These ships would be of value to the Far East as a whole, but must not be regarded in any sense as part of the local defences of Malaya and Singapore. Further, in the same way as these ships had arrived from distant stations, so, if the situation changed and they became needed elsewhere, we had to be prepared for them to be ordered away."

Based on this, the local papers published good leading articles, bringing out the particular points I made. In addition, Mr. Duff Cooper, at my request, gave an excellent broadcast on the evening of I0th December, pointing out that the loss of these ships must not lead to despondency, but merely to a determination to fight all the harder and so avenge their loss.

Japanese Command of the Sea.

III. From the point of view of the defence of the Far East as a whole, what was more serious was the Japanese attack on the United States Pacific Fleet in Pearl Harbour. In appreciations of the situation we had always relied on the deterrent effect of the existence of this Fleet, even if the United States were not in the war from the start. It was expected that this deterrent would prevent the Japanese from allotting more than a limited number of warships for escort duties, which fact would limit the number of convoys sent into the South China Sea, and that it would also stop them from sending an expedition round the East side of the Philippines towards the Netherlands East Indies, especially the Eastern islands.

An indirect result of the Pearl Harbour attack was to prevent the surface ships of the Asiatic Fleet from Manila co-operating with British and Dutch ships in the Java and South China Seas in accordance with the A.D.B. agreement. This Asiatic Fleet was, by orders from Washington, limited to operations between Sourabaya and Port Darwin.

As a final result, the command of the sea acquired by the Japanese was greater than we had ever anticipated. We were, in fact, fighting under conditions of which the British Empire had very little previous experience.

Penang.

II2. Penang Island was of no small importance for three reasons:-

(*a*) Very fair port facilities.

(*b*) Stocks of ammunition and stores.

(*c*) The point of departure of two Overseas cables.

It was decided that the true defence of Penang was on the mainland and that, should the forces in Kedah be driven south, direct defence of Penang would be of no value. This enabled most of the garrison of Penang to be released to reinforce the mainland. One of the great weaknesses of Penang lay in the fact that there were no A.A. guns, which was entirely due to shortage of weapons. It had been laid down that the Naval

Base, Royal Air Force aerodromes, Singapore Harbour and Kuala Lumpur, had to have priority above Penang, and there were not enough to go round.

There was no analogy between Penang and Tobruk.. Even had the garrison of Penang held out for some weeks, it would have been entirely isolated both by land and by sea, and could not have carried out any attacks against the Japanese line of communications except possibly an odd spasmodic raid. Any troops that might have been utilised for a garrison under these conditions would have been more valuable elsewhere.

II3. The first attack on Penang was at II00 hours on the 8th December, when the aerodrome was bombed by Japanese aircraft, the effect generally being small. At I000 hours the IIth December, Georgetown was bombed and heavy casualties caused among the native population; these were due not so much to any inadequacy of A.R.P. as to the fact that the native population turned out into the streets to watch the sight, presumably under the impression that another attack was about to be made on the aerodrome. As a result nearly the whole native population left the town and the labour problem became acute. Next day the military authorities had to take over many civil duties, including burial of the dead, and the naval authorities had to work the ferries between the Island and the mainland.

II4. In view of the situation in Kedah, it was decided to move women and children, other than Malays and Chinese, from Penang on the I3th December. This was intended to apply to Indians as well as Europeans, but owing to some misunderstanding the Sikh Police were not given the opportunity to send their women and children away, and in the end only the Europeans left, the total numbers being about 520.

At 2030 hours, the I5th December, orders were received by the Military Commander at Penang to destroy all military stores, etc., that could not be moved and to come away with the remainder of the garrison and British civilians. About half a dozen British residents were left as they did not wish to move. The native Volunteers were given the option of moving, but most of them decided to remain with their families in Penang; the British personnel of the Volunteers were brought away.

The coast artillery denial scheme was carried out and all 6-inch guns destroyed. Approved armament was withdrawn and most first-line transport. Electrical machinery and the oil fuelling system of the Eastern Smelting Company were smashed, the river house, telephone exchange, cable and wireless station and aerodromes destroyed. The Singapore-Colombo and the Singapore-Madras cables were, however, connected by binding screws and left working in the hope that the Japanese might not discover them – a hope that proved vain. A reserve of food was opened for the civil population, which had suffered some 600 killed and I,I00 wounded in air raids during the last week.

The destruction of material was incomplete, the most notable example being certain vessels that were left intact. Efforts were made by the naval authorities to immobilise these by laying mines in the Southern Channel, the Northern already having been mined by the Japanese. Presumably this was not effective for long.

XII. – THE RETREAT FROM
NORTHERN MALAYA.

12th-18th December.

II5. By the I2th December enemy pressure on the Kedah front was becoming very severe. The Kroh forces were being forced backwards over the frontier, while our right in Northern Kedah was also driven back, necessitating the 6th Indian Infantry Brigade withdrawing on the left to conform and hold a line River Bukit (north of Alor Star) to Penang. Penang was the subject of daily air attacks at this period. Two days of heavy fighting then saw our forces pushed back twenty miles south of Alor Star, the IIth Division taking up a position in the Gurun area. Some of the infantry units in this division reported losses up to 50 per cent., but this included missing, many of whom re-joined later.

The immediate preoccupation on our part at this moment was to co-ordinate the movement of the IIth Division with that of Krohcol. Unless this was done there was serious danger of the Japanese cutting off one of the two forces. Krohcol was now back in Kedah just east of Baling and under the command of the I2th Indian Infantry Brigade, which had been sent up from the south as reinforcements. But on the I6th December the enemy drove in between the Kroh forces and the IIth Division, and counter-attacks by two battalions of the 28th Indian Brigade proved unavailing to restore contact. It was now that the lack of adequate reserves to relieve troops who had been fighting continuously for a week began to be felt. The enemy were pressing home their attacks in spite of heavy losses. Troops from Penang were sent up as reinforcements, while the 6th and I5th Indian Infantry Brigades had been so weakened in the fighting that they were ordered to re-form into one composite Brigade.

The Japanese were now employing Kota Bharu aerodrome, reconnaissance revealing some forty of their fighters on the ground. To attack Kota Bharu, Singora and Patani aerodromes with the object of reducing the scale of Japanese air effort was part of our general air policy at this period, but our bomber effort was painfully limited by our lack of aircraft. Apart from deficiency of adequate A.A. weapons, the defence of our aerodromes was handicapped by lack of adequate warning in the North. (*See para.* 54 *above*.) These formed two causes of our heavy losses of aircraft on the ground. The retention of our main fighter strength for the defence of Singapore (*see para.* I42 *below*) was a contributory cause and also reacted directly on our bombing effort, since it was impracticable to provide fighter escorts.

Two Buffaloes had been specially fitted for photographic reconnaissance. To allow of extra petrol being carried, and at the same time to reduce weight, all guns were taken out. Even then the Buffaloes were inferior in performance to the Japanese Zero fighters. The pilots of these specially fitted aircraft carried out useful work under very difficult conditions.

From the start of hostilities the Dutch submarines had been very active. On the I2th December one of them reported sinking four enemy troop ships at Patani Roads.

II6. The difficulty of combating the Japanese attacks on our aerodromes resulted on the l6th and l7th December in the evacuation and demolition of Butterworth, Taiping and Kuantan aerodromes, and our aircraft were forced further South. Ipoh, too, was now being bombed, and the aerodrome petrol dump was hit.

On land, the enemy, having advanced in Kelantan (as far as the Sungei Nal) and in Kedah, was now also attacking detachments of our troops in Perak round about the Grik area. The 3rd Indian Corps was accordingly authorised to withdraw behind the line of the Perak River to protect the communications of our forces North of Kuala Kangsar. The IIth Indian Division began withdrawing from the line of the River Muda Southwards behind River Krian, linking up with the 28th Indian Infantry Brigade and protected all the time on the right flank by the l2th Indian Infantry Brigade. During this period the Argyll and Sutherland Highlanders made counter-attacks with gallantry and skill. This withdrawal was carried out successfully, the enemy being repulsed with loss at his first attempt to cross the river.

Inter-Allied Conference, 18th December.

II7. On the l8th December a conference of inter-Allied representatives took place at Singapore, in accordance with proposals made by President Roosevelt. Owing to the time factor, China was not represented. Results of the conference were telegraphed to England. The main conclusions were as follows:-

(*a*) The importance of Singapore to the war in the Far East, and to the world war, could not be exaggerated;

(*b*) The immediate plan was to dispose our combined forces then available in the Far East so as to-

(i) Keep the enemy as far North in Malaya as possible and hold him in the Philippines; and

(ii) Prevent the enemy acquiring territory, and particularly aerodromes, which would threaten the arrival of reinforcements;

(*c*) Our urgent and immediate need was for reinforcements, which must be on a scale not only to meet the present scale of attack, but also that likely to be put in the field against us;

(*d*) It was recommended that the United States convoy at present directed to Brisbane should proceed to Sourabaya, where aircraft would be assembled and flown on to destination;

(*e*) It was desirable that the Chinese should be asked to maintain the maximum pressure on the Japanese in order to contain as many divisions as possible, and subsequently to provide bases for long-distance bombing attacks on Japan.

Finally the conference considered that the situation, though serious, need not give rise to undue pessimism provided the necessary reinforcements were supplied in the available time, but time was the essential feature.

Reinforcements.

II8. From the 8th December, I94I, onwards many requests for reinforcements had been made from General Headquarters, Far East. The time factor meant that reinforcements had to come from the Middle East, India and convoys already at sea rather than from the United Kingdom. Complicated quadrangular references between Malaya, India, the Middle East and London were hence entailed, but Commander-in-Chief, India, was most helpful in appreciating the need for diversion to Malaya of forces originally intended for his own command. A sub-committee of the Inter-Allied Conference, having considered all the previous requests for reinforcements, agreed on the following immediate requirements for Malaya to stabilise the situation:-

Air-

> *4 Fighter Squadrons;*
> 4 Bomber Squadrons;
> I Photographic Flight;
> I Transport Flight; and

Reserves at I00 per cent. for fighters and 50 per cent. for bombers, plus aircraft to complete existing squadrons and their reserves.

Land-

> I Brigade Group;
> I Division;
> Reinforcements for 9th and IIth Divisions;
> 3 Light A.A. Regiments;
> 2 Heavy A.A. Regiments;
> I Anti-Tank Regiment;
> 50 Light tanks;
> 350 Anti-tank rifles;
> Bofors ammunition; and
> 500 Tommy guns and ammunition;

Further large forces would be required later in view of probable Japanese reinforcements.

By the 27th December the following had been definitely promised:-

Air-

> 5I Hurricanes. (One fighter squadron ex convoy W.S. I2. Z
> with I8 additional pilots);
> 24 Blenheims. (One squadron from Middle East);
> 52 Hudsons (from United Kingdom);

While measures were in hand aiming at the release of a further 3 fighter squadrons from the Middle East, and for 80 4-engined United States bombers.

Land-

2 Infantry Brigade Groups	}	ex India
Reinforcements for 9th-IIth Divisions	}	
85th Anti-Tank Regiment complete	}	
6th Heavy A.A. Regiment (I6 guns)	}	ex Convoy W.S. I2.Z.
32nd Light A.A. Regiment (24 guns)	}	

Light tank squadron (I7 Light tanks and reserves) ex India;
53rd Infantry Brigade (18th Division), guns and transport of which were to follow after arrival of personnel;

I Machine Gun Battalion and reinforcements for the A.I.F. Brigades ex Australia;

Provision of further tanks was under discussion, while General Headquarters, Far East, was also pressing strongly for the complete I8th Division.

Five Blenheims from the Middle East and four Hudsons from Australia arrived in Singapore on the 23rd December, I94I.

I9th-25th December.

II9. In accordance with instructions from London, a scorched earth policy was ordered at this period instead of the denial scheme referred to in para. 65 above.

The general situation on land by the I9th-2Ist December was that our troops were trying to keep the enemy West of the River Perak, while at the same time preventing him advancing further South than the River Krian. To this end the IIth Indian Division, which it was considered essential to maintain as a fighting formation, was holding a line along the River Kuran with the 28th Indian Infantry Brigade, and also protecting Kuala Kangsar with the I2th Indian Infantry Brigade, a detachment of which was also further North along the Grik road. The Division as a whole was suffering from exhaustion, damaged feet and loss of equipment. The 6th and I5th Indian Infantry Brigades were now re-formed at Ipoh as the composite I5th Infantry Brigade, while a composite battalion of the 2nd/I6th and 3rd/I6th from these two Brigades was in Corps Reserve. The Kelantan forces, 8th Indian Infantry Brigade, 9th Indian Division, had suffered about a hundred casualties in each battalion, and were now along the railway at Manik Orai. Of elements not thus far engaged in the main operations, the 22nd Indian Infantry Brigade (9th Indian Division) was at Kuantan, while the Australian 22nd and 27th Brigades were responsible for Johore, and the Ist and 2nd Malay Infantry Brigades for Singapore Fortress. None of these last four Brigades could be despatched North to relieve the hard-pressed IIth Indian Division, for the reasons given below. (*See para.* I38 *below.*)

I20. Heavy enemy air attack was now falling on Ipoh aerodrome, and our own fighters were driven further South to Kuala Lumpur (Selangor). Attacks on our road and rail communications were becoming an increasing feature of the Japanese air operations. Reconnaissance revealed that the enemy was now making use of Sungei

Patani aerodrome, where thirty fighters were discovered. Our aircraft were making night and dawn attacks on enemy aerodromes, and were very valuable for reconnaissance; reconnaissances were regularly being made-

(*a*) 350 miles N.N.E. of Singapore;

(*b*) along the East coast of Malaya;

(*c*) over the Rhio Archipelago; and

(*d*) to the Miri and Kuching areas – from Sinkawang;

in addition to those over the fighting area.

By the 2Ist-22nd December Kuala Lumpur was coming in for heavy air attack, though little damage was at first inflicted. Against an attack by Ju. 87's on the 2Ist December the Buffaloes were more successful, causing the Japanese bombers to break formation in disorder, but to deal with the Zero fighters it was apparent that only the speedy arrival of Hurricane reinforcements, while we still held sufficient air bases, could turn the tide.

The land situation in the next few days (2Ist-23rd December) witnessed further advances by the enemy in all areas. Pressure along the Grik road was heavy, in spite of severe losses inflicted during a successful clash on the night of the I9th-20th December.

The Japanese floated troops down the Perak River by night, and on the 22nd December the I2th Indian Infantry Brigade was forced back South of Kuala Kangsar. The 28th Indian Infantry Brigade was also pressed in the same direction, small detachments only being left North of Kuala Kangsar and West of the Perak River. Bridges were destroyed as the troops retired. While this was taking place on the Perak front, the Kelantan withdrawal was also continuing, the 8th Indian Infantry Brigade retiring South of Kuala Krai along the railroad. A problem similar to that of Krohcol and the IIth Division referred to above (*see para.* II5) now arose in regard to 8th Indian Infantry Brigade and the main body of III Corps in Perak, and, to a lesser degree, in regard to the force at Kuantan and the 8th Indian Infantry Brigade. It was therefore decided to withdraw this 8th Brigade much further South into Central Malaya, and it took up completely new positions in the Kuala Lipis – Raub area. A small party known as "Macforce" was left with an armoured train at Dabong to withdraw down the railway, demolishing it as they went. The Kuantan force was ordered to prepare to withdraw Westwards at short notice. On the 23rd December all our fighters on the mainland were withdrawn to Singapore, Kuala Lumpur and Port Swettenham being kept as advanced landing grounds. The enemy was also occupying various points down the East coast of Malaya, and had proceeded from Kuala Trengganu to Dungun. By the 25th December it would be true to say that something like one-half of Malaya had passed from our control.

I2I. With the object of maintaining the morale of the civil population of Malaya I held a meeting on the 22nd December, attended by members of the Legislative Council, leading men of the different communities and the Press, the total number being about I20. The main points I stressed were that the available strength had proved inadequate; we had to remember that the aircraft, A.A. guns and tanks that might have come to Malaya were not being wasted, but were being used with great effect in Libya and Russia; that there was every reason for confidence that now the requirements of the Far East had become pressing, those responsible were taking steps to ensure the despatch of adequate reinforcements of men and material; and that it was up to everyone to ensure that no effort was spared to hold up the enemy until the necessary forces arrived.

On the 22nd December, a telegram was sent to Mr. Duff Cooper to the effect that useless mouths were to be evacuated from Singapore without racial discrimination and on a voluntary basis so far as the general population were concerned.

The total number of British women and children evacuated from Malaya from the beginning of the war with Japan to the 31st January, 1942, was as follows:-

7,174	European;
2,305	Indian; and
1,250	Chinese.

According to a Japanese report, the number of British women and children left in Singapore at the time of capitulation was about 200.

XIII. – THE ATTACK ON, AND FALL OF, HONG KONG.

122. On the 8th December, at 0800 hours, hostilities began with the launching of a Japanese air attack on Kowloon. Frontier demolitions were accordingly blown and our troops withdrew according to plan as the Japanese crossed the frontier on a broad front during the course of the morning. It was estimated that the enemy were employing a force of one division, with the possibility of increasing this to two divisions with the troops then in the area.

There was no enemy action from the air or sea during the night of the 8th-9th December, but heavy pressure was exerted against our forward troops along the Taipo Road. During the day of the 9th December these troops were compelled to withdraw within the Gin Drinkers' line in consequence of their left flank being turned. Enemy air attacks during the day, directed mainly against the south coast of the island, did little damage. Leaflets, too, were dropped. The day closed unfortunately, since the Shing Mun Redoubt, held by The Royal Scots, was suddenly captured at 2300 hours – an unexpected blow in view of the difficulty of approach over such country at night. It was considered that local fifth columnists must have guided the Japanese in this attack. One company of Winnipeg Grenadiers was now despatched to reinforce the Kowloon Brigade.

It was soon found necessary, in view of enemy pressure, to readjust the line south-west of the Jubilee Reservoir, where the enemy was making progress, and to vacate Kai Tak aerodrome, after the two remaining aircraft had been demolished. During the morning of the 11th December, however, after the two left Companies (Royal Scots) at Kowloon had been driven in, and reserves (including Winnipeg Grenadiers) had failed to effect more than a temporary halt, it was decided to withdraw from the mainland, with the exception of Devil's Peak. This withdrawal was successfully carried out, beginning at dusk on the IIth, and included howitzers, mechanical transport and armoured cars. Some interference by Kowloon Chinese fifth columnists was experienced. Stonecutter's Island, which had been heavily bombarded and had suffered damage to the military barracks, was also evacuated during the night of the IIth-I2th. Hong Kong Island itself was now also the subject of bombardment, both from the air and by artillery, the main target being the naval dockyard.

123. During the night the I2th-I3th December, troops were withdrawn from Devil's Peak, our last post on the mainland. Coast defence guns were now used landwards for counter-battery work against the Japanese. It was noted that the evacuation of Kowloon had considerably disturbed the morale of the Hong Kong civil population, and defeatist elements came to the fore. It became necessary to organise rice distribution. The Japanese Commander-in-Chief demanded the surrender of Hong Kong, which was refused.

During the I4th December the Japanese shelling of the island increased in severity, and several of our gunposts were hit, as a result of which some Chinese gunners deserted. The enemy was now enjoying the use of Devil's Peak as an observation post. On the same day Aberdeen was bombed from high-level, and the generating station was hit, though not put out of action. Considerable trouble was still being experienced with the civil population, the police were unable to prevent robbery by armed gangs in the A.R.P. tunnels, and rice distribution was a difficulty. Propaganda was accordingly circulated about the proximity of a Chinese advance to relieve Hong Kong; the Chungking Government's representative was most helpful in maintaining order.

During the night of the I4th-I5th December, the Japanese continued their systematic shelling, and gathered together a collection of small craft in Kowloon Bay. The Thracian entered the Bay and sank two river steamers, while a special agent succeeded in blowing up a third ship. The Thracian, however, in view of damage, had to be beached and dismantled the following day.

On the I6th December, Aberdeen was heavily bombed, eight times in all, with resulting loss of one Motor Torpedo Boat and damage to the dock. Most of our Auxiliary Patrolling Vessels were now useless in view of desertion by Chinese crews. The enemy landed parties on Lamma Island, and started concentrations of troops on the mainland at Customs Pass and Waterloo Road, but these were dispersed by our artillery. During the night of the I6th-I7th mortar fire damaged some of our machine guns along the water-front.

On the I7th December, Hong Kong Island was twice raided by fourteen Army light bombers, coinciding with heavy bombardment by artillery. After this raid the Japanese again came across with proposals of surrender, which were rejected.

124. The night of the I7th-I8th was very quiet, but on the I8th decisive events took place. The North face of the Island was subjected to continuous artillery, mortar and dive-bombing attack, some of our infantry defence posts being struck three or four times. Hospitals were badly hit and much damage was done to water mains, roads,

cables and signal communications, also rice stores. Stanley and Murray Barracks were bombed in two raids by nine and six bombers, roughly 100 bombs being dropped – the largest number to that date. Much of the transport of the 2nd Battalion Royal Scots was destroyed, and C Battery Plotting Room O was demolished by a direct hit. The civil Government centre was also dive-bombed. It was following this intense activity that, after dusk, the Japanese effected landings at Quarry Bay and at Lyemun in the north-eastern corner of the island.

The following day the Japanese infiltrated over the hill to the Wong Nei Cheong and Tytam Gaps with pack artillery and mortars. Our artillery from the Collinson and D'Aguilar areas (east and south-east of the Island) were successfully withdrawn to Stanley (south of the Island), but were compelled to destroy their heavy guns and equipment. Our line ran now from Stanley Mound northwards, Stanley Mound itself being held by one battalion of Canadians, two companies of Indian infantry and some miscellaneous artillery and machine guns.

During the afternoon of the 19th a counter-attack was attempted, with the help of motor torpedo boats, to regain possession of Mount Parker and Mount Butler, but broke down through heavy enemy shelling, failure of intercommunications and the exhaustion of our troops. Our motor torpedo boats were successful in destroying landing craft in Kowloon Bay, but two were lost in the operations.

125. On the 20th our line was still roughly North from Stanley Mound. A communiqué was again issued to inspire civilian morale with belief in near relief by Chinese forces. By the 21st the enemy was attacking strongly across Mount Nicholson through Middle Gap, and our troops were suffering greatly from exhaustion, the wet and cold of the night-time, and isolation from food and ammunition stores. Counter-attacks on the enemy rear by the Royal Rifles of Canada came to nought, and Winnipeg Grenadiers were also unsuccessful in an effort to retake Wong Nei Cheong Gap. The enemy still paid attention from the air to the Dockyard area, and practically all Naval personnel were now ashore and took their place in the land fighting. Japanese naval forces blockading the Island consisted of two cruisers, two destroyers and two torpedo boats.

It was during the 21st that the "Resist to the end" message from the Prime Minister was received, followed by instructions from the Admiralty to wreck all oil installations and storages.

The 22nd December witnessed a fresh enemy landing on the north-east coast of the Island. Part of our force was now cut off in Stanley, while various remnants were still holding out in isolated positions. The Japanese were now virtually surrounding Victoria, where a great deal of damage had been inflicted by bombing and shelling. Oil installations were destroyed, but it was found impossible to do so at Lai Chi Kok, since a large hospital would have been endangered. A telegram was received from the Admiralty giving the full text of Mr. Churchill's message, but also leaving to the Governor the discretion of surrender when resistance could no longer be usefully continued.

126. By the 23rd December the principal reservoirs were in the hands of the enemy, and the connections of those that remained under our control were damaged through

shell-fire. Great efforts were made to effect repairs, but, in the absence of any substantial success in this direction, only one day's supply of water remained to the beleaguered city. Food stores, too, were greatly depleted. Our troops had become more or less exhausted, though Royal Marines managed to recapture ground on Mount Cameron (protecting the South of Victoria), which had been heavily bombarded by the Japanese, and the Middlesex Regiment beat off an attack on Leighton Hill. The enemy, however, penetrated through the A.R.P. tunnels and street fighting began at Wanchai. The conduct of the civil population, which had thus far suffered some 4,000 casualties (I,000 killed), was, however, good and had become increasingly so since the first depression after the evacuation of the mainland.

On the same day the forces isolated in the South of the Island made an effort to counter-attack towards Stanley Mound, but to no avail.

On the 24th December the Royal Scots, following heavy enemy attacks, were driven off the top of Mount Cameron, and Leighton Hill was captured after bombardment. The position in the South of the Island was unchanged.

On the 25th December, in the early hours of the morning, street fighting took place as the enemy fought his way towards the centre of the town, but another Japanese demand for surrender was refused. Two hours later, however, the Governor was advised by the Military and Naval commanders that further effective resistance could not be made, and, after carrying out a series of demolitions, our forces were ordered to lay down their arms. The Chinese kept their word and had endeavoured to assist the defence of Hong Kong by advancing on Canton, but their force was not strong enough to produce any serious effect on the Japanese.

XIV. – OPERATIONS IN BURMA AND SARAWAK.

Burma.

I27. A fresh field of operations opened in Burma on the 9th December, when a landing was reported at Prachuabkhirikun, a clear threat to Mergui and the Tenasserim Peninsula.

On the IIth December, Tavoy was bombed. A further enemy landing at Chumporn (Siam) gave access to the southernmost tip of Burma, and an advance on Victoria Point threatened. In the next two or three days the Japanese advance materialised and coincided with raids on Mergui by about fifty aircraft, propaganda leaflets being dropped as well as bombs. An effort was made to cut off the Japanese advance southwards by crossing the Siam frontier to demolish the railway a few miles south of Prachuabkhirikun, but the strength of the opposition and the heavy rains proved too great for the success of this expedition. The situation was still in an undeveloped stage, but with a clear threat to Southern Burma, when on the I5th December Burma reverted to the province of the Commander-in-Chief, India. (*See para. 29 above.*)

Sarawak.

I28. The general problem of the defence of Borneo was indicated in para. I6 above. The oil denial scheme was put into operation at the outbreak of war and completed by the IIth December. The landing ground at Miri was also demolished and the forces at Lutong evacuated by sea to Kuching in H.M.S. *Lipis*.

The Company of 2/I5 Punjab Regiment re-joined the rest of its Battalion, which formed the regular garrison of Kuching and the remaining individuals – from the 2nd Loyals and S.S. Police – were brought on to Singapore.

Considerable anxiety and uneasiness was felt by the authorities in Kuching owing to the absence of Naval and Air Forces. It was pointed out to them, however, that many places in England had stood up to bombing without any direct defence, and that they would be expected to do the same. It was evident, however, that the morale of the population of Kuching was in a bad way. This, in my opinion, was partly due to the fact that the ruler, Rajah Brooke, was absent – actually in Australia. He had a great deal of influence with the natives, and in view of the situation he should have returned to his country immediately on the outbreak of war, if not before. As it was, the Sarawak Rangers proved quite unreliable, and the 2/I5 Punjab Regiment were left to carry out the defence by themselves.

The complete control of the South China Sea exercised by the Japanese reduced the problem of the capture of Kuching to a mere calculation of the strength necessary to overcome the resistance that they would probably meet. They appear to have attacked it with the equivalent of one Brigade Group.

I29. Japanese naval forces were not long in appearing in strength before Miri. By the I6th December, some ten warships had been sighted in company with a tanker off Miri and Lutong, and these ships became the object of our attacks. On the I7th December, 6 Glenn Martins and 5 Buffaloes of the Netherlands East Indies Air Force delivered an attack from Sinkawang, but scored neither hits nor near misses. The same day, Dutch bombers from Samiuwkoa located and attacked this force, a Dutch navy Dornier scoring a direct hit on a destroyer. Encounters between Dutch Buffaloes and the Navy Zero fighters revealed the clear superiority of the Japanese aircraft. Reports of a Japanese landing at Lutong and Baram Point were received, and on the I8th December renewed attacks on enemy shipping in this area were made, without success, by a mixed force. Eight Glenn Martins from Sinkawang had to return without delivering their attack owing to the bad weather. The following day 6 Netherlands East Indies Glen Martins claimed a hit on a cruiser and some near misses. The I9th December, however, was also marked by Japanese air attacks, Kuching aerodrome and town being bombed by about I5 heavy bombers and one seaplane. Civilians suffered approximately I00 casualties, while the main material damage was the destruction of the Borneo Company Benzine Stores. The air war was also carried to Dutch Territory by a heavy attack on Pontianak, much of the city being destroyed.

An expedition clearly aimed at Kuching was then sighted on the 23rd December, and 5 Blenheim IVs, attacking this on the 24th December, scored one hit on a transport and some near misses. Air support from Sinkawang was no longer possible in view of the damage to the aerodrome from a Japanese attack, and the Dutch aircraft were withdrawn to Palembang. The 2/I5 Punjab Regiment carried out demolitions on the aerodromes, held up the Japanese for a time, and eventually moved in accordance with orders, along a jungle path, to join up with the Dutch, though this necessitated abandoning practically the whole of their equipment.

It was noteworthy that Malay labour at Kuching disappeared as the course of operations approached the area.

According to later reports, some 800 of the 2/I5 Punjab Regiment joined the Dutch and were still fighting with them at the end of January, I942.

XV. – SPECIAL FEATURES OF THE OPERATIONS.

Changes in Commands.

I30. A large number of changes took place shortly before or shortly after the war with Japan started. These were as follows:-

(*a*) Admiral Sir Tom Phillips replaced Admiral Sir Geoffrey Layton on the 6th December.

(*b*) On the I0th December, after Sir Tom Phillips had gone down with the *Prince of Wales,* Sir Geoffrey Layton – who was then actually on board his ship about to start for Australia on his way home – resumed command.

(*c*) On the 6th November I was informed that "owing to recent developments in the Far East, it had been decided that the duties of Commander-in-Chief should be entrusted to an Army officer with up-to-date experience." My successor was to be Lieutenant-General Paget. This prospective change became generally known in the Army and Air Force in Malaya by the end of November.

(*d*) On the 29th November a signal was received from Whitehall to the effect that General Pownall had been substituted for General Paget.

(*e*) On the I5th December the responsibility of the defence of Burma was transferred from the Commander-in-Chief, Far East, to Commander-in-Chief, India.

(*f*) On the 29th December General McLeod was replaced by General Hutton as General Officer Commanding, Burma.

(*g*) On the I0th December Mr. Duff Cooper was appointed as Cabinet representative in the Far East, and instructions were received by him that a War Council was to be formed under his leadership.

These changes may have been inevitable, and it could not, of course, have been foreseen that they would coincide so closely with the start of the war, but they did add to the difficulties of the situation.

War Council.

I3I. The composition of the War Council, the formation of which was started on the I0th December, was as follows:-

Mr. Duff Cooper, *Chairman*;
H.E. the Governor of Malaya;
C.-in-C., Far East;
C.-in-C., Eastern Fleet;
G.O.C. Malaya;
A.O.C. Far East;

and later, Sir George Sansom, as being responsible for Propaganda and Press control.

The War Council did useful work in several directions, but as it was not formed until after the war began there had been no time to work out its correct functions. Actually, the composition led to its dealing rather too much with the details of what was happening in Malaya, whilst it would have been more useful if it had concentrated on the wider problems.

On the I6th December a Civil Defence Committee was set up to review and deal with all measures affecting the defence of Singapore other than those of a purely military character.

Its composition was:-

Mr. Duff Cooper, *Chairman*;
Fortress Commander;
Inspector-General of Police; and
One civilian.

Intelligence.

I32. Turning to intelligence, perhaps the most serious error was one involving the broadest aspect, namely, the intention of the Japanese Government. From the tactical point of view in Malaya there was no surprise, but from the wider point of view there was. Whilst in General Headquarters we always realised the possibility of the extreme military party in Japan forcing their country into war, we did not believe, till the end of November, that Japan might be actually on the verge of starting war. (*See paras.* 6I *and* 94 above.)

As indicated in paragraph 75 above, there was also some error regarding the intentions of the Siamese Government.

I33. As regards the more local intelligence, the forces that the Japanese would have at the beginning for an attack on Malaya were estimated with a fair degree of accuracy, but there was an under-estimate of the power of the Japanese to attack several places simultaneously. Before the war it was considered that the Japanese might attack in force either the Philippines (with or without Hong Kong), or Malaya or the Netherlands East Indies. It was not anticipated that they would attack in force both the Philippines and Malaya simultaneously; still less that they would also attack Pearl Harbour. So far as I could gather from telegrams, this opinion was also held in

England, at any rate up to the last few days before war started, though I believe the Embassy in Tokio held a more correct view of the Japanese power to attack several places simultaneously.

134. There was also an under-estimate of the efficiency of the Japanese Army and Air Force, particularly in the following points:-

(*a*) Their disregard of weather conditions, especially their ability to land on beaches in bad weather. Also they appear to have been but little hampered by the flooded state of the country in the Southern end of the Kra Isthmus;

(*b*) Their mobility. This was due to several causes. The Japanese Army seemed generally to depend less on mechanism than ours and to be content with a smaller proportion of artillery. The men needed only simple food and were able to live largely on the country and apparently required nothing in the way of comforts. In some cases they used lighter weapons including a mortar that was lighter than our 2-inch mortar. As a result the Japanese Army was able to operate with less mechanical transport than ours and so was less dependent upon roads. The whole organisation could be kept less complicated than ours and more flexible;

(*c*) The individual initiative of the Japanese soldier;

(*d*) The performance of the naval single-seater fighter known as the Zero type. This had a detachable petrol tank under the fuselage and the Japanese got much value from the long range thus given to it. In spite of this complication, its speed and manoeuvrability at heights of 10,000 feet and over were remarkably good; and

(*e*) The rapidity with which repairs were carried out, in particular of bridges and aerodromes. This last affected the strength of the Japanese air force in the Singora area at the South end of the Kra Isthmus in the early days of the war.

These under-estimates were not attributable solely to errors on the part of F.E.C.B., but also to those of other bodies, including my own General Headquarters.

Japanese Army Tactics and Training.

135. With regard to tactics, in general the Japanese endeavoured to infiltrate or outflank. They made use of certain novelties such as:-

(*a*) A type of light infantry screen acting in advance of their main body. The men were very lightly clad, had but little equipment and were armed with a light automatic weapon, the calibre of which was something under 0.3; they carried only about forty rounds of ammunition and a few hand grenades. These light infantry parties used to work individually, would get round to the rear of our advance troops, and resorted to such expedients as climbing trees from which to fire their automatic or throw hand grenades. Our men frequently mistook these light troops for Malays or Chinese, but it is doubtful if the Japanese soldiers were deliberately disguised as Malayan natives;

(*b*) The use of noise, including Chinese crackers and strange cries at night; these tricks, though laughable when one knew about them, had a certain amount of moral effect, especially on young Indian troops at the commencement of the campaign; and

(*c*) Inflatable rubber belts to enable men to cross creeks and small rivers.

To combat these tactics the General Officer Commanding, Malaya, stressed the importance for alertness and cunning on the part of the individual, and that the way to defeat the enemy was to attack or counter-attack him on every possible occasion. "Essentially war of movement and attack, and too much digging creates defence complex."

I36. An anti-white campaign had started in Japan in I936, and it was evident that for long before the commencement of the war the spirit of hatred of Europeans, particularly the British, had constantly been inculcated into the Japanese soldiers. They appear to have been taught that the killing of Europeans by any method was a patriotic action.

It is possible that had we adopted the same course some men might have fought harder at the start, but it is difficult to inculcate the spirit of hatred into the Englishman. This is partly due to his peculiar faculty of seeing a jest in the most depressing circumstances, and partly to the fact that hatred is ultimately based on fear, which is not a natural characteristic of our race.

Factors affecting Morale of our Forces.

I37. The majority of the Indian regiments laboured under some disability on account of the inexperience of most of their British officers. As a rule, there would be two or three senior officers, with fifteen or more years' experience, then a gap until we came to officers who had joined after September, I939. Somewhere about half these officers had experience in India and could talk the language, but having only from one to two and a half years' service they did not carry the weight which more experienced officers would have done.

In both British and Indian units there was only a small leaven of war-experienced officers and men, and it was under these conditions that young soldiers had to meet the first shock of the Japanese attack.

I38. A factor which had some effect on morale generally was that, strategically, we were on the defensive; everyone knew that it was to our interests to avoid war with Japan, which meant that the initiative and especially choice of moment for opening hostilities rested with them.

As stated above, the Matador plan provided for a tactical offensive, provided adequate warning could be obtained. As events turned out, the execution of Matador was impracticable, and later events confirmed that the decision not to carry out this operation was correct.

Then, owing to the comparative weakness of our forces in Malaya we could neither afford heavy losses up North nor send up there more than limited reinforcements, because of the necessity for retaining a force to defend Southern Johore and in the last resort the island of Singapore itself. This was not the result of a sort of fortress-complex, but because the essential factor was preservation of the repair and other facilities in the Naval Base. The opinion held in London on this point was made perfectly clear in the latter part of December when the Chiefs of Staff telegraphed:

"His Majesty's Government agree your conception that vital issue is to ensure security of Singapore Naval Base. They emphasise that no other consideration must compete with this."

Holding Northern Malaya was not an end in itself; it was with reference to the Naval Base that Northern Malaya acquired its importance. This meant that Commanders in the North had to bear in mind the possibility of withdrawal in the face of superior forces, their action – at any rate until Johore was reached – being mainly a delaying one to gain time for the arrival of reinforcements from overseas. This applied particularly to the Kelantan area, and to a lesser extent, to Kuantan, since in both cases (as stated in para. l2 above) the line of communication was a single one and vulnerable to air bombing.

l39. It is easy to talk of the lack of an offensive spirit and of a "retreat complex," but under the conditions described above withdrawals from the North were necessary; and the adverse effect induced by having to carry out a continuous retreat over some hundreds of miles starting from the early days of the campaign must be attributed to the general situation rather than to any fault in the original morale of the troops themselves.

It is possible however, that the need for offensive action even during a retreat had not been so stressed during the training of officers and men as to become a second nature. For instance, there appeared to be a tendency to use reserves for supporting a weak portion of a defensive position rather than retaining them at all costs for bringing about a counter-attack. Again, up to the time I handed over command, there was a tendency to use the Independent Company in Malaya as a reinforcement and not to carry out the functions for which it was specially intended. Further, officers and men must be taught that occasions will arise when some parties have got to hold on to the last man, even though the main body of the force may be moving back.

Royal Air Force problems.

l40. With regard to the Air Force, reference has already been made in paras. 79 and 88 above to the obsolescence of our Vildebeeste aircraft and to the effect of lack of reserves. Apart from this, the necessity for rapid evacuation of the Northern aerodromes had some effect on the ground personnel, many of whom were young and inexperienced. There were insufficient rifles or Thompson guns to equip all Air Force personnel, but they must be prepared to fight, and, if necessary, sacrifice themselves in the same way as the infantry; and further, must spare no effort to ensure that all material than can possibly be moved is despatched, or in the last resort destroyed, to prevent its being of value to the enemy.

l4l. The Royal Air Force suffered from lack of staff. It was not so much that more officers were required at headquarters as that sufficient should have been available to form another Group Headquarters. A Fighter Headquarters had been formed and operated well, but the rest of the operations had to be carried out direct by Royal Air Force Headquarters, with the result that practically all the headquarters air staff officers had to be employed in the operations room, and, including the Air Officer Commanding, were fully occupied in working out details of bombing and reconnaissance, leaving no one to plan and think ahead. This condition would have been improved had it been possible to form another group to operate the bombing squadrons, or, possibly, naval co-operation and overseas reconnaissance as well as all bombing.

I42. As aerodromes in Northern Malaya became untenable there was a danger of those in the South becoming too few to allow of adequate dispersal of the Royal Air Force Squadrons. The possibility of this had also been foreseen some months before war broke out and it had been decided in such an eventuality to move the bombing squadrons to Dutch aerodromes in Sumatra, retaining most of the fighter squadrons on Singapore Island. Up to the time that war broke out this remained little more than a project owing to the Royal Air Force staff being fully occupied with other work. At the end of December, however, the plans were well advanced, not only for the move of these squadrons but also for the possible establishment of an erecting depot in Java.

I43. The need for preserving an adequate force for the protection of the Naval Base (*see para.* I38 *above*) applied especially to the Royal Air Force. This accounts for the comparative weakness of the fighter strength in Northern Malaya at the start of the war and for fighter escorts not being available for our bombers. From the last week in December air protection for reinforcement convoys absorbed most of our fighter strength.

Defence and Denial of Aerodromes.

I44. As indicated in para. I03 above, the primary object of the Japanese appears to have been to get command of the air, principally by the attack on our aerodromes by aircraft, or by their capture. The weakness of our aerodrome defence is referred to in para. II5 above. In regard to A.A. weapons, as a result of the experiences in Crete, I laid down that the defence of aerodromes was to take precedence over everything else except the A.A. defence of the Naval Base. It was decided that the full scale of the defence would be eight heavy and eight light A.A. guns; this was altered after war broke out to four heavy and twelve light, a scale that was hardly every approached.

I45. When our aerodromes had to be abandoned, steps were naturally taken to render them useless to the enemy, particularly by explosives in runways and other parts of the landing area. The effect of this action was generally of disappointingly short duration. The Japanese were certainly quick in carrying out repairs, but, even allowing for that, the results of many of the demolitions as carried out seem hardly to have repaid the energy expended and the adverse moral effect on troops of hearing explosions behind them. A system of delay-action mines would probably have been effective provided they could have been properly concealed; preparations would have been necessary for this at the time the aerodromes were constructed. A heavy tractor drawing some form of deep plough or scarifier and working in between craters would have been a very useful addition; it could not have gone on working to the last moment, unless it was intended to abandon the tractor, since these could only move very slowly and were likely to block roads if left to the last.

At aerodromes located in wet or low-lying areas, mines should be located with reference to the drainage system with the object of dislocating it and so putting the aerodrome out of action for a long period. Aerodromes in our possession were occasionally rendered unserviceable for about twenty-four hours by Japanese bombing of runways; this would have been much more effective had delay-action bombs been used.

Left-Behind Parties.

I46. An attempt was made to organise left-behind parties in Northern Malaya with the object of obtaining information and carrying out sabotage of all sorts in the enemy's rear. This duty was entrusted to the O.M. Section of the Ministry of Economic Warfare under Mr. Killery. It was, however, started too late and there was no time to organise it thoroughly. This was in no way the fault of the O.M., but was due to the factors mentioned in para. 9 above.

Question of a Military Governor.

I47. The appointment of a Military Governor might have been desirable for Singapore Island during the later stages, but I was of the opinion that such an appointment for the whole of Malaya at the start of the war was not a practicable proposition. The main reason was that the organisation of the Colony, with the Federated and the Unfederated States, was very complicated and that it was not a practical proposition for anyone to take it over at short notice. It would have been found far more practicable for Hong Kong.

Australia's Assistance.

I48. The Australian Government fully realised the importance of Singapore to the defence of the Far East and especially to Australia and did everything in their power to help. In November, I940, there were three squadrons of the Royal Australian Air Force in Malaya. In December, I940, the Australian War Minister visited Singapore. Largely as a result of his representations, the Australian Government despatched the 22nd Brigade, Australian Imperial Forces, to Singapore in February. The 27th Brigade followed later, and arrived on the 20th August. Besides these valuable reinforcements, Australia supplied officers for the Royal Air Force Volunteer Reserve for administrative work on aerodromes, men for two reserve mechanical transport units in the spring of I94I and for the forty tanks which we had hoped to get from the Middle East. The situation regarding Beaufort aircraft has been mentioned in para. 79 above, and small arms ammunition in para. 92. In addition to this, Australia also supplied many items of signalling equipment and special radio sets for coast defence guns. After the war started four Hudsons from Australia reached Singapore on the 23rd December and Army reinforcements were promised. (*See para.* II8 *above.*)

The Dutch.

I49. The Dutch in the Netherlands East Indies faithfully executed their share of the agreements and, indeed, went beyond them, and co-operated wholeheartedly with us in every way. They sent three bomber squadrons and one fighter squadron in the early days of the war in Malaya, although, owing to technical troubles they were having at the time with their engines, the bomber squadrons consisted of only six aircraft, the whole three, therefore, being equivalent to little more than one British bomber squadron. Their submarines operated with great gallantry in the Gulf of Siam. They also gave me three of their reserve flying boats to make good our losses, and sent over a guerilla band to Northern Malaya to operate in the Japanese rear.

At a later stage in the operations I believe they were somewhat critical of the amount of assistance we were able to send to the Netherlands East Indies, and of the length of time before it arrived; should this give rise to any acrimony in the future, I hope that the prompt and whole-hearted assistance they rendered to us will not be forgotten.

Work of General Headquarters.

I50. In Malaya the operations of my own Headquarters were limited to the issue of certain directives to the General Officer Commanding and Air Officer Commanding. These laid down such matters as the withdrawal from Kelantan and Kuantan, and priority of tasks for the Royal Air Force. Apart from that, the main work was to secure the proper co-ordination of air operations with the Dutch and Australians.

A great deal of the time of my small staff was taken up at the beginning by the drafting of Sitreps telegrams and communiqués, as well as preparing appreciations demanded from England. One of the problems regarding the two former was the fact that they had to be sent to Australia as well as to England; their timing was, therefore, a matter of fine adjustment, since it was necessary to ensure, for instance, that a communiqué should not be printed in Australian newspapers before the Sitreps telegrams arrived in England. Eventually, it was found simpler to hand over most of this work to the combined Army and Air Force operations room, in so far as Malaya itself was concerned, and General Headquarters Sitreps communiqués were confined to the situation as a whole.

Although my General Headquarters operated at the Naval Base at the beginning of the war, it was found that, after the loss of the *Prince of Wales* and *Repulse* and the formation of the War Council, it was more convenient for my Headquarters to be located near the Combined Operations Room. Preparations had been made for this some months before, and the necessary accommodation was available. The move was carried out about the I5th December.

I5I. After the transfer of the defence of Burma to Commander-in-Chief, India, and the fall of Hong Kong, it was felt that the location of General Headquarters should no longer be in Malaya, since to keep it there would not only hamper its own work but cramp the initiative of the General Officer Commanding and Air Officer Commanding and make the organisation in Singapore too top-heavy. It was decided before I left that the correct location of General Headquarters would be in Java, preferably near Bandoeng, and steps were already in hand to effect this move. The possibility of a move away from Singapore becoming necessary had been foreseen many months before.

152. The results of the campaign in the Far East naturally gave rise to some speculation as to the advisability of forming what may be called Strategic Headquarters, devoid of all responsibility for direct operational control or administration. Commander-in-Chief, Middle East, at the time I passed through Cairo in November, 1940, stated that, in his opinion, such a General Headquarters was impracticable. My view is that, under special conditions such as existed in the Far East, a strategic General Headquarters was a workable proposition, provided its limitations are fully recognized.

In para. 5 above were indicated the measures which it was expected to achieve by the creation of a General Headquarters, Far East. We failed to convince the Japanese that our strength was too great to be challenged with success; the limitation of the forces, especially aircraft, that could be sent to the Far East was imposed by prior requirements elsewhere.

Co-operation in Malaya and co-ordination of effort with neighbouring countries, including plans for mutual reinforcement, were achieved.

Farewell Order.

153. I handed over Command of the Far East to Lt.-General Sir Henry Pownall on the 27th December, 1941, and left Singapore, in accordance with instructions, on the 31st December. I end with my farewell order which was published on the 28th December, 1941.

TO ALL RANKS OF THE ARMY AND AIR FORCE, MALAYA.

On relinquishing the Far East Command I send to you all in the Army and Air Force in Malaya a message of farewell, of admiration for the way you have faced danger, fatigue and hardship, and of all good wishes for 1942.

I know my successor well, and I turn over the command to good hands.

Remember that upon the issue of this war depends the welfare of the whole world, including our own families. Their eyes are upon you. Do your Duty unflinchingly, knowing that the resources of the Empire and of our Allies are behind you, confident that, however hard the struggle now, our cause will triumph in the end.

R. BROOKE-POPHAM,
Air Chief Marshal.

APPENDICES

A. –   Directive to the Commander-in-Chief, Far East.

B. –   Instructions issued to General Officers Commanding and Air Officer Commanding, Far East.

C. –   His Majesty's Ships based at Singapore and Hong Kong, December 7, 1941.

D. –   Summary of Army Strength, Malaya, November, 1940.

E. –   Order of Battle, Malaya, December 7, 1941, and Summary.

F. –   Anti-Aircraft Position, December, 7, 1941.

G. –   Order of Battle, Burma, December 7, 1941, and Summary.

H. –   Order of Battle, Hong Kong, December 8, 1941.

I. –   Strength of Air Force in Malaya, November, 1940.

J. –   Strength and Dispositions of the Royal Air Force, December 7, 1941.

K. –   Summary of Operationally Serviceable I.E. Aircraft in Malaya.

L. –   Performance of the Buffalo Single-Seater.

M. –   Order of the Day issued December 8, 1941.

APPENDIX A.

DIRECTIVE TO THE COMMANDER-IN-CHIEF, FAR EAST.

I. You are appointed Commander-in-Chief, Far East.

2. You will be responsible to the Chiefs of Staff for the operational control and general direction of training of all British land and air forces in Malaya,[1] Burma and Hong Kong, and for the co-ordination of plans for the defence of these territories.

You will also be responsible for the operational control and general direction of training of British Air Forces in Ceylon and of the general reconnaissance Squadrons of the Royal Air Force which it is proposed to station in the Indian Ocean and Bay of Bengal for ocean reconnaissance in those areas.

3. For these purposes, the following will be under your command:-

General Officer Commanding, Malaya.
General Officer Commanding, Burma.
General Officer Commanding, Hong Kong.
Air Officer Commanding, Far East.

4. It is intended that you should deal, primarily with matters of major military policy and strategy. It is not the intention that you should assume administrative or financial responsibilities or the normal day-to-day functions at present exercised by the General Officers Commanding and Air Officer Commanding.

These Officers will continue to correspond as at present with the War Office, Air Ministry, Colonial Office and Burma Office, on all matters on which they have hitherto dealt with these departments, to the fullest extent possible consistent with the exercise of your Command; keeping you informed as and when you wish.

5. Your staff will consist of the following only, and no expansion of this staff is contemplated:-

A Chief of Staff (an army officer of the rank of Major-General),
A Senior Royal Air Force Staff Officer,
A Naval Liaison Officer,
An Army Officer of the rank of General Staff Officer, Ist Grade,
An officer from each Service of the equivalent rank of General Staff Officer,
2nd Grade, together with the necessary clerical and cypher staff.

6. You will, where appropriate, consult and co-operate with the Commander-in-Chief,

China, the Commander-in-Chief, East Indies, and the Commander-in-Chief in India. You will also communicate direct with the Defence Departments of the Governments of the Commonwealth of Australia and New Zealand on all routine matters of interest to them, but on matters of major policy you will communicate to these Dominion Governments through the appropriate Service Department of His Majesty's Government.

7. You will keep the Governor of the Straits Settlements and High Commissioner for the Malay States, the Governor of Burma and the Governor of Hong Kong closely and constantly informed and will consult them as appropriate.

8. The General and Air Officers mentioned in paragraph 3 above remain, subject to your general direction and supervision, in touch with the Governor of the Straits Settlements and High Commissioner for the Malay States, the Governor of Burma and the Governor of Hong Kong. In the case of Burma you will ensure that the constitutional relations between the Governor and the General Officer Commanding are not affected. This is of particular importance with regard to any movement of troops which might affect internal security.

9. You will, where appropriate, maintain touch with His Majesty's, representatives in Japan, China, the United States of America and Thailand, and with His Majesty's Consuls-General in the Netherlands East Indies and Indo-China. The maintenance of touch with His Majesty's representatives and Consuls-General in these countries will rest with you exclusively and not with the General and Air Officers referred to in paragraph 3.

I0. The Far East Combined Intelligence Bureau, in addition to keeping you informed of current intelligence, will be charged with the duty of collecting such special intelligence as you may require. The Bureau will remain under the control of the Admiralty.

II. You will normally communicate as necessary with the Chiefs of Staff, the Air Ministry being used as a channel of communication for telegrams, and letters being addressed to the Secretary, Chiefs of Staff Committee; but you have the right to correspond direct with an individual Chief of Staff on matters particularly affecting his Service.

APPENDIX B.

INSTRUCTIONS ISSUED TO GENERAL OFFICERS COMMANDING AND AIR OFFICER COMMANDING, FAR EAST.

Headquarters of Commander-in-Chief, Far East, will open at Singapore at 0800 hours on the 18th November.

(2) A prime function of staff of Commander-in-Chief, Far East, will be to prepare, in conjunction with Staff of Commander-in-Chief, China, all joint plans that may be required either by Chiefs of Staff organisation in London or by strategic situation in Far East. The Authority for such plans will be either Chiefs of Staffs in London or two Commanders-in-Chief.

(3) There will be no alteration in channels by which you correspond War Office, Air Ministry, Colonial Office or Burma Office on any matters other than questions of policy affecting strategy or operations. On these questions of policy you will correspond direct with this Headquarters, sending copies of your communications to appropriate Governor. Similarly, all communications from Commander-in-Chief, Far East, to you on these questions will be repeated to appropriate Governor.

On other questions you will repeat to Commander-in-Chief, Far East, such of your communications to War Office, &c., as you judge of sufficient importance.

(4) You will ensure that intimate touch now existing between yourself and Governor in your command is maintained.

(5) You will submit to Commander-in-Chief copies of your most recent appreciations and plans which are now in operation and will keep him fully informed of any changes in situation by signal if of immediate importance, otherwise by periodical liaison letter.

(6) You will submit location statement showing present location of all forces within your command. You will subsequently report major changes in location as they occur.

(7) The Commander-in-Chief requires to be kept informed of general administrative conditions of forces under your command, including position in respect of reserves of essential commodities. Any major administrative difficulties which you may now be experiencing, or which arise subsequently, will be reported at once, in order that both extent to which they may affect operations or policy may

be accurately gauged, and that representations may be made direct by him to higher authority, if such a course appears to be required.

(8) You will submit short report of present state of training of units under your command and your programme of training for coming months. Further instructions will be issued on method by which Commander-in-Chief is to be kept informed of progress of training.

(9) Chiefs of Staff have made Commander-in-Chief, Far East, responsible for maintaining touch with His Majesty's representatives in Japan, China and Thailand, and with His Majesty's Consuls-General in Netherlands East Indies and Indo-China. Your direct touch with His Majesty's representatives or Consuls-General in these countries should therefore be restricted to matters immediately affecting your commands.

APPENDIX C.

H.M. SHIPS BASED AT SINGAPORE AND HONG KONG ON 7TH DECEMBER, 1941.

Singapore-

Capital Ships-
Prince of Wales.
Repulse.

Cruisers-
Danae.
Dragon.
Durban.

Destroyers-
Jupiter.
Electra.
Encounter.
Express.
Tenedos.
Thanet.
Scout.
Stronghold.

Ships from other Stations refitting at Singapore.

Cruiser-
Mauritius *(E.I. Station).*

Destroyers-
Isis (Mediterranean Station).
H.M.A.S. *Vampire* (Australian Station).
H.M.A.S. *Vendetta* (Australian Station).

Submarine-
Rover (Mediterranean Station).

Hong Kong-

Destroyer-
Thracian.

This list does not include auxiliary minesweepers, patrol vessels and small craft.

APPENDIX D.

SUMMARY OF ARMY STRENGTH, MALAYA, NOVEMBER, I940.

Infantry-

I7 Battalions, viz.-

British	6 (including I M.G. Battalion).
Indian	I0
Malay	I

Mobile Artillery-

I Mountain Regiment, R.A.

APPENDIX E.

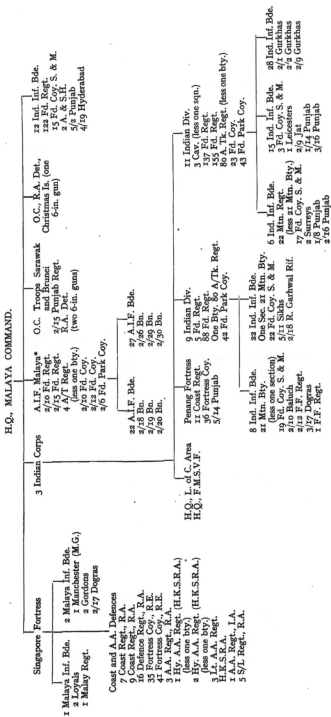

MALAYA COMMAND.

Order of Battle—December 7, 1941.

H.Q., MALAYA COMMAND.

* The Australian Units of the A.I.F. Malaya shown here formed part of the 8th Australian Division.

Summary of Strength of Army in Malaya, December 7, 1941.

(Royal Engineers, Mechanical Transport, Signals and Ancillary Units not included.)

Infantry Battalions-

British	6 (including I M.G. Btn.).
Indian	I8
Australian	6
Malay	I
Total	**3I**

Volunteer Battalions	I0
Johore Military Forces	I
Indian State Forces	5

Artillery-

Field Regiments	7 (5 of 24 guns; 2 of I6 guns).
Mountain Regiments	I (24 guns).
Anti-Tank Regiments	2 (I of 48 guns; I of 36 guns).
Anti-Tank Batteries	2 (I of 8 Breda guns; I of 6 2-pounders).

Total Strength-

Regulars-

British	I9,39I
Australian	I5,279
Indian	37,I9I
Asiatic	4,482
Total	**76,343**

Volunteers-

British	2,430
Indian	727
Asiatic	7,395
Total	**I0,552**
Grand Total	**86,895**

APPENDIX F.

FAR EAST.
Anti-Aircraft Position, December 7, 1941.

	Approved Scale.	Holdings.	En route.	Allocated but not shipped
Malaya –				
Heavy	176	70	12	20 } (b)
Light	100 (plus 144 field force)	78	28	52 }
3-in. Naval	Nil	24	Nil	
Burma –				
Heavy	24	8 } (a)	8	
Light	68	16 }	8	
Hong Kong –				
Heavy	32	14	4	
Light	30	2	8	
3-in. Naval	Nil	2		

(*a*) Of these 4 heavy and 8 light had only just reached Rangoon and had not been installed.

(*b*) A proportion was to be allocated to Burma by Commander-in-Chief, Far East.

APPENDIX G.

BURMA.
Order of Battle at Commencement of Hostilities.

(1) Ist Burma Division-

   consisting of-

Maymyo Brigade	2nd K.O.Y.L.I.
Ist Burma Rifles.	
6th Burma Rifles.	
7th Burma Rifles.	
I2th Mountain Battery.	
56th Field Company (S. and M.).	
Tenasserim Brigade	2nd Burma Rifles.
4th Burma Rifles.	
5th Burma Rifles.	
8th Burma Rifles.	
2nd Mountain Battery.	
Sec. Field Company.	
I3th Indian Infantry Brigade	5th/Ist Punjab.
2nd/7th Rajputs.	
Ist/I8th R. Garh Rifles.	
23rd Mountain Battery.	
5th Field Battery R.A., B.A.F.	

(2) Rangoon Brigade	Ist Gloucesters.
3rd Burma Rifles.	
Coast Defence Battery.	

(3) I6th Indian Infantry Brigade	Ist/9th Jat.
4th/I2th F.F. Regiment.	
Ist/7th Gurkha Regiment.	
5th Mountain Battery.	
Headquarters, 27th Mountain Regiment.	
50th Field Company (S. and M.).	

(4) Burma Frontier Force	Bhama Battalion.
Chin Hills Battalion.	
Myitkyina Battalion.	
Northern Shan States Battalion.	

Southern Shan States Battalion.
Kokine Battalion.
Reserve Battalion.

(5) Garrison Companies	Ist Garrison Company.
2nd Garrison Company.	
3rd Garrison Company.	
4th Garrison Company.	
5th Garrison Company.	

(6) Burma Rifles (Territorials)	IIth Burma Rifles.
I2th Burma Rifles.	
I3th Southern Shan States Battalion Burma Rifles.	
I4th Burma Rifles (forming).	

(7) Burma Auxiliary Force	Rangoon Battalion.
Upper Burma Battalion.	
Burma Railways Battalion.	
Tenasserim Battalion.	
I A.A. Regiment (forming).	

(8) Burma Rifles	9th and I0th Battalions (forming).
Six Anti-Tank Troops.	
One Field Battery.	

(9) Field Company	Forming.

(I0) Armed Police	Three Battalions.

SUMMARY OF STRENGTH OF ARMY IN BURMA, DECEMBER 7, I94I.

Infantry-

British	2 battalions.
Indian	6 battalions.
Burma Rifles (Regulars)	8 battalions (4 of these just formed).
Burma Rifles (Territorials)	4 battalions.
Garrison Company	5 battalions.
Burma Auxiliary Force	4 battalions.
Burma Frontier Force	6 battalions,
I reserve battalion.	

Artillery-

Indian Mountain Batteries	3
Burma Auxiliary Force	I field battery, I8-pounders.
Five mobile detachments Burma Frontier Force.	

APPENDIX H.

HONG KONG.
Order of Battle at Outbreak of War.

At the outbreak of hostilities on the 8th December, I94I, the garrison comprised:-

Hong Kong Infantry Brigade-	*Arrived.*
Ist Battalion Middlesex Regiment (M.G.)	August, I937.
Ist Battalion The Winnipeg Grenadiers	November, I94I.
Ist Battalion The Royal Rifles of Canada	November, I94I.

Kowloon Infantry Brigade-	
2nd Battalion The Royal Scots	January, I938.
2nd I4th Punjab Regiment	November, I940.
5th 7th Rajputana Rifles	June, I937.

Headquarters Fortress, R.E.-
I E. and M. Company.
I Field Company (3 British, I Chinese section).
I Bomb Disposal section.
I Medium Regiment, H.K.S.R.A.
8th Coast Regiment, R.A.
I2th Coast Regiment, R.A.
5th A.A. Regiment, R.A.
Ancillary Units.
Hong Kong Volunteer Defence Corps (strength about 2,000).
A Chinese machine-gun battalion was in process of being formed, but had not progressed beyond the cadre stage.

Appropriate strengths of all personnel mobilised at the 8th December, I94I, were:-

British	3,652
Canadian	I,982
Indian	2,254
Local Colonial	2,428
Hong Kong Volunteer Defence Corps	2,000
Auxiliary Defence Units	2,II2
Nursing Detachment	I36
Total	**I4,564**

APPENDIX I.

STRENGTH OF AIR FORCE IN MALAYA.
November, 1940.

Bombers: 2 squadrons Blenheim I –	24 aircraft.
Reconnaissance: 2 squadrons Hudsons (R.A.A.F.) –	24 aircraft.
Torpedo Bombers: 2 squadrons Vildebeestes –	24 aircraft.
General Purpose: I squadron Wirraways (R.A.A.F.) –	I2 aircraft.
Flying Boats: I squadron Singapores –	4 aircraft.
Total:	**88 first-line aircraft.**

APPENDIX J.

STRENGTH AND DISPOSITIONS OF THE R.A.F., *DECEMBER* 7, I94I.

Malaya.

Aerodrome.	Squadron No.	Type.	Strength in Aircraft.
Alor Star	62	Blenheim I (B)	II
Sungei Patani	2I (R.A.A.F.)	Buffalo	I2
Sungei Patani	27	Blenheim I (F)	I2
Kota Bharu	I (R.A.A.F.)	Hudson	I2
Kota Bharu	36	Vildebeeste	6
Gong Kedah	I00	Vildebeeste	6
Kuantan	60 (*a*)	Blenheim I (B)	8
Kuantan	8 (R.A.A.F.)	Hudson	8
Kuantan	36	Vildebeeste	6
Tengah	34	Blenheim IV	I6
Kallang	243 and 488	Buffalo	32
Sembawang	8 (R.A.A.F.)	Hudson	4
Sembawang	453	Buffalo	I6
Seletar	I00	Vildebeeste	6
Seletar	205	Catalina	3

I58

(*a*) No. 60 Squadron had arived from Burma for Bombing practice, and was retained in Malaya on the start of the war with Japan. About the middle of December the personnel were sent back to Burma by sea, the aeroplanes being retained in Malaya to replace wastage in other squadrons.

There were two maintenance units, No. I5I at Seletar and No. I53 at Kuala Lumpur.

Reserve Aircraft.

Blenheim I and IV	I5
Buffalo	52 (*b*)
Hudson	7
Vildebeeste	I2
Catalina	2
Total	**88**

(*b*) Of these, 2I were temporarily out of action owing to trouble with the engine valve gear on a new mark of engine.

Burma.

Aerodrome.	Squadron No.	Type.	Strength in Aircraft.
Mingaladon	60	Blenheim I (B)	4
Mingaladon	67	Buffalo	I6

Reserve Aircraft.

Blenheim I	Nil
Buffalo	I6

Of the total of 32 Buffaloes in Burma, 24 were temporarily out of action owing to trouble with the engine valve gear on a new mark of engine.

Ceylon.

Catalina	2

Total in Far East.

Initial Equipment	I80
Reserves	I04
Total	**284**

Of these aircraft, the Vildebeestes were obsolete, and if these are deducted the figures become:-

Initial Equipment	I56
Reserves	92
Total	**248**

Requirements as laid down by the Chiefs of Staff were 336 Initial Equipment. Reserves for these on the basis of 50 per cent. for flying-boats and I00 per cent. for all other aircraft should have amounted to 327, a total of 663.

Omitting the Vildebeestes, the total deficiency in aircraft was 4I5.

The Dutch sent over a total of 22 bombers and 9 fighters. If these are included, the net deficiency becomes 384.

The figure of I00 per cent. for reserves of land-based aircraft was laid down in an Air Ministry telegram of the 23rd February, I94I.

APPENDIX K.

SUMMARY OF OPERATIONALLY SERVICEABLE I.E. AIRCRAFT IN MALAYA.

	Dec. 7.	Dec. I2.	Dec. I7.	Dec. I9.	Dec. 22.	Dec. 24.
Bombers (including Torpedo Bombers)	59	45	59	58	49	6I
Fighters	72	53	58	53	45	50
Reconnaissance	24	7	I2	II	I2	I3
Flying Boats	3	3	4	4	3	3
Total	**I58**	**I08**	**I33**	**I26**	**I09**	**I27**

The above figures do not include Dutch aircraft in N. Sumatra or in Borneo, which were stationed North of the Equator and thus came under the command of the Air Officer Commanding, Far East, under the terms of the A.D.B. Agreement. Nor do the figures include Immediate Reserves with Squadrons, Reserves in the Maintenance Units nor Aircraft in the A.A.C.U.

APPENDIX L.

PERFORMANCE OF THE BUFFALO SINGLE SEATER.

A report on the tests of a Buffalo was sent in from the A. & A.E.E., Boscombe Down, dated the 3rd July, 1941. Comparison of this with the official intelligence figures of the Japanese Naval fighter, Zero type, showed that the Buffalo was much inferior at heights of 10,000 feet, and over, viz.:-

	Zero Fighter.	*Buffalo.*
Rate of climb to 13,000 feet	4.3 minutes	6.1 minutes
Speed at 10,000 feet	315	270 (Approx.)

At 20,000 feet the performance, as indicated by the official figures, is more nearly equal, *i.e.:-*

	Zero Fighter.	*Buffalo.*
Speed at 20,000 feet	295	292

Actual experience in Malaya, however, showed that this speed of 292 for the Buffalo could not be obtained. Whether this was due to the aeroplane, to the climate or to the pilots I cannot say.

APPENDIX M.

MALAYA.
Order of the Day issued December 8, 1941.

Japan's action to-day gives the signal for the Empire Naval, Army and Air Forces, and those of their Allies, to go into action with a common aim and common ideals.

We are ready. We have had plenty of warning and our preparations are made and tested.

We do not forget at this moment the years of patience and forbearance in which we have borne, with dignity and discipline, the petty insults and insolences inflicted on us by the Japanese in the Far East. We know that those things were only done because Japan thought she could take advantage of our supposed weakness. Now, when Japan herself has decided to put the matter to a sterner test, she will find out that she has made a grievous mistake.

We are confident. Our defences are strong and our weapons efficient. Whatever our race, and whether we are now in our native land or have come thousands of miles, we have one aim and one only. It is to defend these shores, to destroy such of our enemies as may set foot on our soil, and then, finally, to cripple the power of the enemy to endanger our ideals, our possessions and our peace.

What of the enemy? We see before us a Japan drained for years by the exhausting claims of her wanton onslaught on China. We see a Japan whose trade and industry have been so dislocated by these years of reckless adventure that, in a mood of desperation, her Government has flung her into war under the delusion that, by stabbing a friendly nation in the back, she can gain her end. Let her look at Italy and what has happened since that nation tried a similar base action.

Let us all remember that we here in the Far East form part of the great campaign for the preservation in the world of truth and justice and freedom; confidence, resolution, enterprise and devotion to the cause must and will inspire every one of us in the fighting services, while from the civilian population, Malay, Chinese, Indian, or Burmese, we expect that patience, endurance and serenity which is the great virtue of the East and which will go far to assist the fighting men to gain final and complete victory.

R. BROOKE-POPHAM, *Air Chief Marshal,*
Commander-in-Chief, Far East.
G. LAYTON, Vice-Admiral,
Commander-in-Chief, China.

Footnotes

I Including the Straits Settlements, the Federated and Unfederated Malay States, Brunei, Sarawak and North Borneo.

2

MAJOR-GENERAL C. M. MALTBY'S DESPATCH ON OPERATIONS IN HONG KONG

8 DECEMBER 1941 TO 25 DECEMBER 1941

The War Office,
January, 1948.

OPERATIONS IN HONG KONG FROM 8TH TO 25TH DECEMBER, 1941

The following Despatch was submitted to the Secretary of State for War, on 21st *November* 1945, *by MAJOR-GENERAL C.M. MALTBY, M.C., late G.O.C., British Troops in China.*

SIR,

I have the honour to address you on the subject of the operations in Hong Kong in December, 1941, and to forward herewith an account of the operations which took place at Hong Kong between 8th and 25th December, 1941.

2. In normal circumstances this despatch would have been submitted through Headquarters, Far East, but in the circumstances in which I am now placed I consider that it would be better, after this long lapse of time, to submit it to you direct.

3. Before beginning my account of the operations themselves, I feel it to be my duty, both to myself and the forces under my command, to place on record certain points. Of these you will be fully cognizant, but to compilers of history they may not be so obvious.

4. The defences of this Colony were on a limited scale, with the object of denying the harbour to an enemy rather than retaining the harbour for the use of our fleet.

This object, combined with the forces available, necessitated a plan to defend the Island of Hong Kong only. The arrival of two Canadian battalions on the I6th November, I94I, caused me to alter my plan to a certain degree. I placed one brigade, with a proportion of mobile artillery under command, on the mainland to prepare and defend the so-called "Gindrinkers' Line," with the hope that, given a certain amount of time and if the enemy did not launch a major offensive there, Kowloon, the harbour and the northern portion of the island would not be subjected to artillery fire directed from the land. Time was also of vital importance to complete demolitions of fuel stores, power houses, docks, wharves, etc., on the mainland; to clear certain food stocks and vital necessities from the mainland to the island; to sink shipping and lighters and to clear the harbour of thousands of junks and sampans. It will be appreciated that to take such irrevocable and expensive steps as mentioned in the foregoing sentence was impossible until it was definitely known that war with Japan was inevitable.

5. That war was inevitable seemed clear to me. I had all my forces deployed in their battle positions in ample time, but it was hard to make that definite statement on the information available, with the result that the civil authorities felt that they were not in a position to put into full force all the numerous measures required during the preliminary or the precautionary period of the Civil Defence plan. For this state of affairs I must blame three factors:-

(*a*) The general doubt that Japan would declare war against the Allied powers.

(*b*) The weakness of our intelligence system.

(*c*) The belief that Japan was bluffing and would continue to bluff to the last. The true gravity of the state of affairs was not reflected in the embassy despatches from Tokyo.

6. That these full Civil Defence measures were not put into effect in time had definite reactions on the subsequent powers of defence and were of assistance to the enemy, e.g., small craft and sampans were available to assist the landings on the island, and supplies were to be found in Kowloon although the roads available to the enemy had been destroyed and were kept under harassing fire. These were not large items in themselves, perhaps, but were cumulative against us.

7. In fairness to the civil authorities I must state that I did say that unless the Japanese launched a major offensive against the "Gindrinkers' Line"' I saw no reason why the period between their crossing of the frontier and the evacuation of the mainland by my forces should not extend to a period of seven days or more. I gave no guarantee and still maintain that this was a fair estimate and might well have been accomplished had not the key to our position on the mainland been captured by surprise by the enemy.

8. The forces under my command had many limitations and amongst these must be enumerated:-

(*a*) Absence of modern air power.

(*b*) The weakness of the naval units.

(*c*) The paucity of anti-aircraft guns, both light and heavy.

(*d*) The lack of any radar equipment.

(*e*) The necessary dilution, in order to economise manpower in the arms of the service, by Chinese personnel of unknown reliability in time of war.

(*f*) The lack of regular transport driven by disciplined drivers.

Reference 8(*a*) above, the aircraft here were no match for the enemy fighters, and I gave orders that they were not to be employed unless the opportunity occurred either at first light or at dusk for a torpedo attack on any enemy capital ship or large cruiser. In any case, all were put out of action in the first raid made by the enemy, though precautions such as dispersal had been taken. The lack of reconnaissance both landwards and seawards was naturally a serious handicap. Study of the past history of Japanese operations had led me to believe that they were past masters in combined operations, and throughout the period of the siege I always anticipated a landing on the Southern shores of the island; and lack of distant seaward reconnaissance was for me a distinct handicap. Similarly I know that the lack of opposition to the incessant enemy air raids had a somewhat depressing effect towards the end on the troops, and definitely increased the accuracy of the enemy bombing and the material damage done. For similar reasons the enemy's counter battery tasks were very much simplified.

Reference 8(*b*) above, the forces available carried out their duties in very difficult circumstances with the utmost gallantry and in the true tradition of the Royal Navy. I have nothing but praise for their gallant conduct, and the Commodore R.N. will be submitting his own despatch.

Reference 8(*c*) above, these few detachments fought with great gallantry and can claim five enemy aircraft shot down, and three others probably never reached their base.

Reference 8(*d*) above, the survey for these equipments had been made but their installation had not begun when the war started.

Reference 8(*f*) above, although the R.A.S.C. performed wonders in organising improvised transport and the few regular drivers were never off the road for days and nights on end, the general desertion of local enlisted Chinese drivers (usually after putting their vehicles out of action) was a very serious factor both from the tactical and maintenance aspects.

9. I wish now to make it perfectly clear that I fully appreciate that the demands of Empire strategy made it impossible at the time for full provision to be made for my forces, and I only make these points so that those who may be writing history or wish to criticise the conduct of my forces may be in full possession of the true facts.

Further, I submit that although I and my forces may have been a hostage to fortune, we were a detachment that deflected from more important objectives, such as the Philippines, Singapore, or perhaps even Australia, an enemy force that consisted of two first line divisions, one reserve division, corps artillery, about eighty aircraft and a considerable naval blockade force. Strategically we gambled and lost, but it was a worth while gamble.

I0. *Appendix A.*
In this Appendix will be found the full account of the events. It was prepared shortly after our capitulation under considerable difficulties. The war diary and messages to and from Battle Headquarters were naturally all destroyed before and after capitulation; Japanese interest in all written matter necessitated various methods of subterfuge to retain anything, and the main credit for whatever has been compiled must go to my G.S.O.I. – the late Colonel L.A. Newnham, G.C., M.C. – who took the most meticulous care to make this account tally with the true events. There are naturally a few blanks owing to the fog of war and the inability to gain contact with all the survivors, but with more information that will become available from formation and unit war diaries it is to be hoped that finally there will be little left for the imagination to fill in.

II. Although this Appendix gives a very full account of events, I would like to comment on several points.

Japanese Tactics.

The salient points of the Japanese tactics were:-

(a) *Nightwork.*
The division which made the initial advance over the frontier and those troops that first landed on the island had reached a high standard of efficiency in nightwork. All were provided with rubber soled boots that made movement very silent, systematically they used the smallest of paths and avoided all the more obvious lines of advance, and their patrols were very boldly handled.

(b) *Rapidity of Advance.*
The pace of the advance was surprisingly fast, the troops were lightly equipped and must have been very fit to accomplish the marches undertaken.

(c) *Agents and Spies.*
It was obvious from all sources that agents and spies had been placed both on the mainland and the island well beforehand. Spies led the leading elements on the mainland, disguised as innocent labourers or coolies. Their patrols advanced by paths which could have been known only to locals or from detailed reconnaissance. Armed agents in Kowloon and Hong Kong systematically fired during the hours of darkness on troops, sentries, cars and despatch riders, but little damage was done thereby beyond straining the nerves of a number of the men. After the landing on the island had been effected, penetration to cut the island in half was assisted by local guides who led the columns by most difficult

routes. The possession of these agents and guides with such intimate knowledge counteracted the first great advantage the defence normally has over the attack, i.e., familiarity with the ground.

(d) *Intelligence.*
It was obvious that the enemy system of intelligence was most complete. Marked maps found on dead officers gave a surprising amount of exact detail, which included our defences and much of our wire. Every officer seemed to be in possession of such a map, which was a lithographed reduction of our own I/20,000 map. They seemed to be in possession of a very full Order of Battle and knew the names of most of the senior and commanding officers.

(e) *Artillery Concentration.*
Artillery and heavy mortar concentrations were very heavy and correctly placed. Those fired before landing on the island and for the capture of Leighton Hill were as heavy as any experienced in France during the war of 1914/18. The range of the heavy mortar must have been about 1300 yards as they fired across the harbour with accuracy and effect. The blast and noise of the bursting bomb was considerable, but the killing power was not high. On occasions artillery fire was most accurate, e.g., all the pillboxes on the north shore, where the landing was effected, were systematically destroyed.

(f) *Maintenance of the Objective.*
This principle seems to have been well understood by their junior leaders. The advance to cut the island in two was carried out regardless of cost to life.

(g) *Air Force.*
The efficiency of the enemy air force was probably the greatest surprise to me. Their opening attack on Kai Tak aerodrome by low level attack down to sixty feet was carried out with skill and marked boldness. Subsequent high level bombing proved to be most accurate, and they confined their attention to military objectives with marked results, such as the naval base at Aberdeen and the island water supply mains. Their evasive tactics and use of low cloud displayed a high standard of training. My general impression at the time was that either the Japanese pilots had reached a surprisingly high standard of training, or that German pilots were leading their flights.

12. *Appendix B – Summary of Casualties.*
An approximate summary of casualties has been compiled by me as far as possible. This is, however, by no means complete, and, owing to the facts that the survivors of this force were divided up from the beginning and that no communication was permitted between camps, the full casualty list cannot be known until all figures have been compiled by the Casualty Bureau. Since capitulation, a number have died from wounds and disease, and many drowned, with the result that it is feared that final and correct figures will take a long time to compile, and the fates of many will never be known.

13. *Conduct of the Troops.*

For the sake of clarity I have confined myself to the bare statement of military facts. I feel it to be my duty, however, to bring to notice the conduct of my troops during this period of hostilities

(a) 2 *Royal Scots.* – It was unfortunate that the enemy captured by surprise the most important Shingmun Redoubt and occupied the Golden Hill position. These two incidents were the direct cause of the hasty withdrawal to the mainland. The gallant action of their D Company (Capt. Pinkerton) on the extreme right flank of the Golden Hill position, the later gallant efforts of the whole battalion to recapture the Wong Nei Chong Gap, and their stubborn fighting in the Mount Nicholson and Mount Cameron areas accomplished much to retrieve their prestige. They commenced the siege with a high incidence of sickness, mainly from malaria, and suffered severe casualties during the operations.

(b) *Royal Rifles of Canada and Winnipeg Grenadiers.* – These two battalions proved to be inadequately trained for modern war under the conditions existing in Hong Kong. They had very recently arrived in Hong Kong after a long sea voyage, and such time as was available had been devoted to the completion of the south shore defences and making themselves au fait with and practising the problems of countering a south shore landing. In this role they were never employed and, instead, they found themselves counter-attacking on steep hill sides covered with scrub, over strange country, and as a result they rapidly became exhausted. Many individual acts of gallantry were performed, their stubborn defensive fighting at the Wong Nei Chong Gap and in the area of Mounts Cameron and Nicholson was marked, and the losses they incurred were heavy and are deeply regretted.

(c) *5th Bn. 7th Rajput Regt.* – This battalion fought well on the mainland and their repulse of the enemy attack on the Devils Peak was entirely successful. The full force of the enemy's initial attack on the island fell on this battalion and they fought gallantly until they had suffered heavy casualties (100 per cent. British Officers and most senior Indian Officers being lost) and were over-run.

(d) Of the remainder of my force I wish to say little except to express my tribute to them all for the gallant part they played during a period of intensive fighting against overwhelming odds, with no rest, little sleep, and often short of water and hot meals. Whether Royal Navy, Royal Air Force, Royal Artillery, Royal Engineers, Royal Signals, Infantry or members of the ancillary services, one and all played their part fully in the true traditions of the services.

The casualties suffered and those inflicted on the enemy speak for themselves.

In closing my despatch I wish to pay a special tribute to the Hong Kong Volunteer Defence Corps. They proved themselves to be a valuable portion of the garrison. In peace they had surrendered a great deal of their leisure to training, their mobilization was completed smoothly and quickly, and in action they proved themselves stubborn and gallant soldiers. To quote examples seems almost invidious but I should like to place on record the superb gallantry of No. 3 (Eurasian) Company at Wong Nei Chong Gap and of No. I Battery who undertook infantry defence in the Stanley area, while the efficiency and gallantry of their Signal section and despatch riders were outstanding.

My thanks and deep appreciation are also due to H.E. The Governor who was a tower of strength to me in our trying ordeal; and similarly I must place on record my admiration for all the members of his civil defence services who displayed magnificent fortitude and energy in their multitudinous activities.

APPENDIX A.

WAR NARRATIVE.

This War Narrative of the defence of Hong Kong is built up on the detailed record of Battle (Fortress) HQ kept at the time, minute by minute.

In some cases, where subsequent knowledge of facts has made it possible to insert items to make a clearer picture, this has been done in the text, but care has been taken not to include anything which would have a bearing on possible decisions which might have been taken. Frequently subsequent knowledge has been included in footnote form only. This despatch was compiled in a Prisoner of War Camp under constant fear of observation or search and with no clerical facilities. All maps, plans, schemes, orders, etc., were destroyed on capitulation and the officers and men marched to Shamshuipo, a distance of 5 miles, and were permitted to take only what they could carry on the person. The Fortress HQ War Diary was concealed and brought away. Cross checking has taken place where possible with survivors, but the Canadian troops were moved early to another camp and no visiting was allowed to hospitals, hospital camps or Indian camps. The timings are based on Hong Kong winter time then in force.

PART I.

Own Forces – Before the outbreak of war with Japan.

I. On the outbreak of war with Germany the garrison consisted of three infantry battalions and one machine gun battalion which permitted the employment of only one infantry battalion on the mainland; its role was to cover a comprehensive scheme of demolitions and to act as a delaying force.

With the arrival on 16th November, 1941, of two Canadian battalions a new defence plan was brought in which had been originally outlined in 1937. It had never been fully practised, as troops had never been available in sufficient numbers. It employed three infantry battalions on the mainland on a front of 10½ miles – the so called "Gindrinkers Line" sited on very commanding country but with certain inherent weaknesses. It had necessarily little depth, which in two localities was particularly dangerous, viz., Customs Pass and the Pass between Golden Hill and Laichikok Peninsula.

2. Owing to the extensive front, each battalion's layout consisted of a line of

platoon localities, the gaps between which were covered by fire by day and by patrolling at night. One company only of each battalion could be kept in reserve and this was normally located in a prepared position covering the most dangerous line of enemy approach. The reserve company of the centre battalion (2/14 Punjab Regt.) was employed initially as "Forward Troops" on the Taipo Road to cover the demolitions and to delay the enemy's initial advance.

3. Directly the news arrived of reinforcement by two Canadian battalions, reconnaissance was carried out by commanding officers only, in order to maintain secrecy. The existing garrison carried out detailed reconnaissances down to platoons later, and worked out the exact defence plan for holding the Gindrinkers Line. A considerable amount of work was found to be necessary, for (except for the centre sector) the line was in its partially completed form of three years previously, when the general policy of defence was altered and the Gindrinkers Line abandoned.

4. A few days before the Canadian battalions arrived large working parties were found by the mainland battalions and a little later the three battalions occupied their sectors permanently to push on the work faster.[1] It was in these battle positions that the 5/7 Rajput Regt. (Right battalion), the 2/14 Punjab Regt. (Centre battalion) and the 2 Royal Scots (Left battalion) were located when war against Japan broke out.

The time was too short, however, for either of the (new) flank battalions to be practised properly in their defence roles by a series of four day exercises which had been the custom in the past. These battalions, therefore, were not familiar with the successive rear defence positions. It was indeed unfortunate that the timing of events occurred in such a way that the Japanese attack developed when of the six battalions in the garrison, only two knew their roles in exact and practised detail. (The I Middlesex Regt. throughout had retained its role of beach defence and the 2/14 Punjab Regt. had been "Mainland battalion" centred on the Taipo Road.)

This Island Defence Plan had been developed in great detail in co-operation with the Royal Navy over a period of years. It needed extremely careful study to get full value from every man in the extensive defence sectors (especially in the South East and South West), and it needed careful rehearsals, as had been done in the past. The date of attack, however, forestalled combined training with the Canadian troops.

The change over to holding the Gindrinkers Line necessitated a change of policy re deployment of artillery. Previously it was too risky to deploy any of the Hong Kong Regiment H.K.S.R.A., i.e., the mobile artillery, on the mainland, when the one battalion only could not hope to cause more than 48 hours delay if the enemy attacked in strength.

The new plan deployed the following on the mainland:-

One Troop 6 in. Howitzers – 4 guns (2 Scammels for haulage).
One Troop 4.5 in. Howitzers – 4 guns (hired vehicles).
Two Troops 3.7 Howitzers – 8 guns, one troop only had mule transport.
Troops were sited for support as follows:-
One 3.7 in. Troop to cover the Right battalion.
One 3.7 in. Troop and the 4.5 in. Battery to cover the Centre and Left battalions.

The 6 in. Troop was to cover from the centre of the Right battalion to the extreme left on the Castle Peak Road. Additional support could be given to the Right battalion by two Sections of 6 in. Howitzers on the island.

5. The infantry organisation was also changed. Brigadier C. Wallis was appointed Mainland Commander, and the Island Commander (the two Canadian battalions and the I Middlesex Regt.) was Brigadier J.K. Lawson.

6. The evacuation of the mainland battalion under the former plan was the task of the Royal Navy ("Operation W/M"). It was not easy and had been practised three times. There was obviously no opportunity to work out full detail and to practise the new withdrawal operation. It was to the credit of all concerned that the eventual withdrawal from the mainland was carried out without any loss of guns and with less than forty men being cut off and captured.

Communications.

7. The change over to three battalions to hold the Gindrinkers Line necessitated complete reorganisation of the mainland communications and the carrying on of buried routes from the partially completed system that existed. Contracts were not completed when war came, in spite of the best endeavours of the Royal Corps of Signals which did excellent work.

8. It was unfortunate that the equipment situation in other theatres of war had not permitted earlier despatch of the garrison's infantry mortars and ammunition. For instance, the worst case, the 2/14 Punjab Regt. had had one 3 in. mortar demonstration, of a few rounds only, but ammunition in any appreciable quantity did not arrive until November and then only 70 rounds per battalion both for war and for practice. Hence these mortars were fired and registered for the first time in their battle positions and twelve hours later were in action against the enemy.

The 2 in. mortar situation was worse, for there had been no receipt even of dummies, consequently the men had had no instruction in detonating. There had been no preliminary shooting and the 2 in. mortar ammunition was delivered actually in battle.

For 3 in. mortar there was neither pack mule nor carrying equipment for the men, consequently everything, including ammunition, had to be manhandled.

PART II.

Enemy Forces.

9. Appreciations of the situation at varying times during the preceding two years estimated two to four divisions of Japanese as available for the attack on Hong Kong.

On the evening of 6th December Chinese reports showed the arrival of three Japanese divisions at To Kat 8 miles from the frontier, on the previous day.

Information from the Far East Combined Bureau Singapore showed that attack was likely by one division, with another division in reserve. This I believe to be incorrect, as a Japanese Staff Officer informed me after the capitulation that two divisions had been deployed on the island and a third was held in reserve.

10. Three to four weeks before the outbreak of war all intelligence sources pointed to very unusual activity in Canton and Bocca Tigris, but the best efforts could not ascertain the contents of the shipping employed – the activities being equally explainable by either:-

(*a*) a concentration for an advance North West from Canton on to Kunming, or,

(*b*) development of a base of supply and staging depot for attack on Thailand.

The shipping was not universally fully laden towards Canton, and empty outwards. Information also showed that the Japanese defence lines round Canton had been drawn in so as to encircle the city more closely. It is clear that the Field Security Police of the Japanese Army had a high degree of efficiency.

Available information led to the following conclusions. That the:-

(*a*) Japanese night work was poor.

(*b*) Japanese preferred stereotyped methods and fixed plans.

(*c*) Japanese light automatics were not as numerous as ours nor so up to date.

(*d*) Japanese "Combined Operations" were thorough and that they had excellent boats and equipment but that their successes against the Chinese were flattering as there had never been real opposition.

(e) Japanese Air Force was not up to first class European standards, that their bombing was poor, and that they would not go in for night bombing.

(*f*) Japanese fifth column activities would be encountered, though no actual proof of such organisations existed. The proximity of Formosa, with its mixed population of Japanese and Chinese Formosans, and Canton, furnished the enemy with admirable intelligence bases.

II. About Ist November a Japanese deserter came across the frontier and gave himself up at a civil police post. He gave a certain amount of detail about the Japanese forces, which definitely indicated preparations for the concentration of troops North of the frontier, and the presence of large calibre-artillery, indicating that of a Corps.

I2. From Tokyo, ambassadorial cablegrams did not indicate immediate impending hostilities, in fact the telegrams from there were extremely moderately phrased in comparison with those of June, I940. Consular reports also were not particularly disturbing.

I3. Such intercepts of enemy aircraft movements as were received during the weeks previous to hostilities showed no abnormal activity. Intercepts from other sources showed normality.

PART III.

I4. During the early days of December as the situation progressively deteriorated so were more and more troops deployed, until on the evening of 7th December all were in their battle positions. By evening very definite reports were received of concentrations of Japanese forces in the villages bordering the frontier. The company of 2 /I4 Punjab Regt at Fanling had been in position for some days with constant watch maintained from the frontier observation posts.

At 0445 hours 8th December intelligence sources reported hearing on a Tokyo broadcast code instructions to their nationals that war with Great Britain and U.S.A. was imminent at any moment. His Excellency the Governor was immediately warned and the message was passed on to all concerned. The frontier company (Major Gray, 2/I4 Punjab Regt.) was telephoned and orders were issued for the forward demolitions to be blown, i.e., to the East and North of Fanling. Subsequent events showed that all these forward demolitions were blown successfully.

By 0645 hours the garrison had been informed that the British Empire and Japan were at war.

Command HQ had moved into the underground Battle HQ.

At 0800 hours Japanese aircraft dive attacked Kai Tak aerodrome (down to 60 feet, showing first class standard) and destroyed and damaged the following grounded planes:-

R.A.F. – 3 destroyed, I seriously damaged and I slightly damaged.

Civil – I Clipper and 7 others (D.C. 23 Condors, etc.).

Shamshuipo barracks were also attacked and bombed but very few casualties were caused, owing to full deployment.

By 0900 hours Fortress Engineers and administrative services were on the move to their dispersal areas in accordance with plans. Japanese machines on to Kai Tak and over Kowloon numbered respectively 36 Fighters and I2 Bombers. During the day subversive pamphlets, addressed mainly to Indian troops, were dropped. They were poorly drawn up and carried no weight either with British or Indian troops.

I5. *Action of Forward Troops* on the Taipo Road, commanded by Major G.E. Gray, 2/I4 Punjab Regt.

At 0800 hours 8th December the Japanese began bridging at Lo Wu and our observation posts reported hundreds of Japanese crossing into Laffans Plain. This was later estimated to be a battalion and it seems fairly certain that a two battalion front was adopted – the other battalion going later straight down the Taipo Road. The tactics were almost invariably to push a strong body up the nearest hill and round a flank directly any line of approach was found to be blocked. The threat of a battalion moving round his right flank was a constant menace, and necessitated Major Gray's decision to make sure of the big demolitions No. 73I and R 94 one mile North of Taipo and not to attempt any real delaying action forward of this. It was thus I500 hours when the first enemy attacks developed in this area and were beaten off by fire.

Outflanking movements developed immediately, necessitating withdrawal to South of the causeway, Taipo.

A platoon had been posted wide on the West flank as left flank guard. A Japanese detachment headed by three women (Chinese) attacked here at 1830 hours. All were shot.

At 1930 hours the mechanised portion of Forward Troops, composed of two armoured cars and four Bren carriers, co-operated most effectively in ambushing a Japanese platoon in close formation. It was virtually wiped out by machine gun and light automatic fire from one hundred yards range. The enemy never relaxed his pressure during the bright moonlight night. It was obvious that his small columns, using cross country tracks, were led by guides who knew the ground intimately, thus enabling the attack to develop quicker than had been thought possible, especially as this was combined with a high standard of night training. I was subsequently informed by a Japanese Staff officer (Major Nishiyama) that a month had been spent on concentrated night training for the attack on Hong Kong. At midnight Forward Troops withdrew to Taipo Mei where an important demolition was duly blown, followed by another withdrawal an hour later to Fo Tan Valley, this being necessitated by small parties of the enemy having reached positions on the road behind the Forward Troops' dispositions.

16. By 0330 hours 9th December all demolitions were successfully blown except one at Taipo where Japanese forward patrols were extremely quick in following up and cutting the leads to the abutments after the withdrawal of the final covering party. The safety fuze used for the piers, however, had burned too far for interruption and these piers were successfully destroyed.

At dawn Forward Troops were on Monastery Ridge just forward of the Gindrinkers Line, where they maintained themselves all day, withdrawing by order at dusk. During the day many excellent artillery targets offered themselves and were engaged with success. The Forward Troops had fulfilled their role admirably, and had inflicted some 100 casualties to the Japanese at no real cost to themselves.

17. On the other main line of approach, viz.: Castle Peak Road, late in the evening 8th December enemy transport was seen banking up at the road bridge North of Au Tau, showing the success of the demolition there. 5.9 in. guns were seen to be tractor drawn up to the bridge and then manhandled into a village to the East. This battery fired at intervals during the next fifty-six hours on Hong Kong Island and was calculated by the Royal Artillery to be on Kam Tin aerodrome. Several shells passed over the main ridge of the island and landed near Aberdeen Reservoir; the firing was at too long a range to be taken seriously and in any case was out of range of our artillery.

At 1340 hours on 8th December a large formation of Japanese planes carried out another raid, this time on Stanley, dropping a few bombs. Little material damage was done.

18. (*a*) At 0600 hours 9th December I ordered Mainland Infantry Brigade to move the reserve company of 5/7 Rajput Regt. across to fill the gap East of Smugglers Pass,

previously only patrolled until the direction of the main enemy thrust should be disclosed.

(*b*) Enemy action during the day was chiefly confined to patrol action. 2 Royal Scots had strong patrols on the tracks leading South East from the Kam Tin area which confirmed the use of Chinese guides by Japanese advanced troops. Later information from the Chinese member of "Z Force" was to the effect that these Chinese guides were drawn from the village of Tsun Wan Wai which he said was largely pro-Wang Ching Wei. "Z Force" was a band of local volunteers which had been trained beforehand for work behind the Japanese lines and was led by Mr. Kendall. Dumps of arms, supplies, medical stores, etc., had been made beforehand at three points in the new territories.

(*c*) It transpired at this time that the Japanese scouts and snipers were highly trained and extremely difficult to detect. Their uniform consisting of quilted material with cross stitching was particularly adapted to the insertion of twigs, grass, etc., obtained locally – thus blending perfectly with the surroundings. Others encountered later on the island had a camouflage net rolled up and carried high on the back, from which position it could be quickly drawn over head and shoulders.

(*d*) The demolitions on Castle Peak Road were blown successfully, except the one at the Dairy Farm, where the leads were cut by a saboteur who slipped in immediately the last sentry was withdrawn. He moved to the next demolition, close by, and was blown up and killed whilst standing on top of it.

(*e*) During the night 9th/10th arrangements were made with the police to evacuate the villagers from places where the front line posts ran through or too near to villages – a matter of great difficulty owing to the trip wires of anti-personnel mines which had been put out to supplement the thinly held front.

19. At 2200 hours the CNAC planes left for Free China. In one was despatched Lt.-Colonel H.O. Hughes (HKVDC) who was to act as our liaison officer with 7th Chinese Army.

20. At about 2300 hours on the night of 9th/10th December a report was received from the Company Commander 5/7 Rajput Regt. (whose company had been moved across from being reserve company in the Right battalion Sector) that he could hear enemy moving in the Shingmun Valley on his immediate front, and later the nearest 2 Royal Scots Company ("A" Company) reported hearing explosions from one of the pillboxes constituting "Shingmun Redoubt." Within the hour it was clear that Shingmun Redoubt had fallen, including the artillery observation post and the HQ of "A" Company 2 Royal Scots.

The capture by surprise of this key position, which dominated a large portion of the left flank and the importance of which had been so frequently stressed beforehand, directly and gravely affected subsequent events and prejudiced Naval, Military and Civil defence arrangements. The possibility of mounting an immediate counter attack that night was considered with Commander Mainland Brigade but was ruled out as the nearest troops were a mile away, the ground precipitous and broken, and the exact situation round the Redoubt very obscure.

At about 0315 hours an artillery concentration was put down on the area of the western portion of the Redoubt and this was heard to take toll of the enemy.

21. At midnight 9th/10th December I decided to move the reserve company of the Winnipeg Grenadiers across from Hong Kong Island. It was placed at the disposal of Brigadier Mainland Brigade and arrived at his HQ at 0400 hours. Confused fighting took place South of Shingmun Redoubt, and a further enemy advance next morning was stopped by artillery support and by the vigorous action taken by Captain H.R. Newton, commanding the 5/7 Rajput Company there. About one enemy company attacked and was driven back into Shingmun Redoubt which was then shelled by 6 .in. Howitzers. Captain Newton was confident that severe casualties had been inflicted upon the enemy.

A counter attack by Captain Newton's Company was considered, but this would have caused a serious gap between the 2/14 Punjab Regt. and Shingmun, where the enemy had already made attempts to effect penetration. The enemy success, however, caused dangerous exposure of the centre ("B") and left ("C")Companies of 2 Royal Scots, and at 1530 hours I sanctioned their withdrawal from the Pineapple Road[2] and Texaco Peninsula positions (a mile in front now, and with an open flank) to the strong Golden Hill line which reached the sea at the Laichikok Peninsula. This withdrawal was carried out without incident at dusk – though the two companies required a certain amount of adjustment before dawn.

22. 10th December. – During that day I ordered the R.A.F. to evacuate Kai Tak aerodrome and to destroy machines and equipment. I had at no time contemplated the serious use of obsolete 100 m.p.h. aircraft which would have been shot down immediately by modern fighters, but in any case by this time only one machine was fit to operate. Demolitions there were practically completed, and were finished later by No. 1 Company HKVDC allotted for aerodrome ground and air defence (together with 4 Bren carriers). This company under Captain A.H. Penn performed its duties very well. The aerodrome was left obstructed by using concrete sections of drains, railings from the "surrounds" and derelict M.T. Enemy air activity was spasmodic, but our first A.A. success, confirmed from three sources, was recorded; an enemy plane over Causeway Bay was hit and fell into the sea in Tide Cove.

23. By now the special warning system was in operation and proved most satisfactory. The arrival of enemy aircraft was forecast and known to within a couple of minutes.

An intense shelling of Stonecutters Island began during the day. At first the fire was inaccurate but later became extremely accurate and the attack was also taken up from the air. Much damage was caused by 5.9 in. fire in particular, one round landing between the two 60 pounders which had been moved over to Stonecutters a week previously for firing in enfilade down the Taipo Road, which they had been doing very successfully during the past thirty-six hours.

During the day a fair amount of movement seawards was observed – Japanese torpedo boats, minesweepers and one destroyer. Later three more destroyers and a cruiser were observed. H.M.S. "Cicala" had been covering the left flank of the 2 Royal Scots on the Castle Peak Road during the last three days, and on this day (10th December) discovered a Japanese working party clearing demolitions at Brothers Point. Fire was opened with 6 in. guns and direct hits obtained. Several Japanese attacks from the air were beaten off but eventually the ship received a direct hit which necessitated docking for repair.

At 1742 hours the last of the Eastern Telegraph Company cables between Hong Kong and the outside world was cut by enemy action. Orders were now issued to put in hand, starting with a "Priority A" group, the laying by Royal Engineers of anti-personnel minefields on beaches, etc., on the southern shores of the island.

24. 10th/11th December. – Intermittent shelling of both mainland and island continued throughout the night, and before dawn the Bowen Road Hospital was hit four times. The first air raid of the day took place at 0800 hours.

25. 11th December. – On the mainland at dawn the enemy opened up mortar fire and then attacked the left flank of the 2 Royal Scots[3], driving them back in disorder and exposing the junction of the Castle Peak and Taipo Roads, thus seriously endangering the withdrawal of all the troops based on the Taipo Road (2/14 Punjab Regt., one company 5/7 Rajput Regt., troop 4.5 in. Howitzers, troop 3.7 in. Howitzers). The situation was critical but the company of the 1 Winnipeg Grenadiers and the Bren carriers from Kai Tak aerodrome defences were moved into position covering the gap.

At midday 11th December I ordered withdrawal from the mainland under cover of darkness – except for 5/7 Rajput Regt. detailed under the scheme of defence for occupation of Devils Peak Peninsula. The withdrawal called for a difficult operation by the 2/14 Punjab Regt. – a move by night across the whole front, along the line of the passes (Kowloon Pass, Shatin Pass, Grasscutters Pass) and down the Devils Peak Peninsula – a move not practised beforehand. Brigade Headquarters, 2 Royal Scots and various administrative detachments were to cross from embarkation points on the East side of Kowloon Peninsula. The West side of the Peninsula was free[4] for evacuation of civilians, civil stores of the food in the Godowns, etc. The notice I could give was regrettably short but unavoidable owing to the rapidity with which the situation had deteriorated. In spite of the short notice the Royal Signals personnel successfully evacuated 49 miles of D8 cable and 20 tons of buried type cable.

26. At 1000 hours 11th December the enemy was reported to be landing on Lamma Island, and guns of Aberdeen and Jubilee Batteries were brought into action. This was followed at 1300 hours by a report that an enemy party in Chinese sampans was attempting a landing at Aberdeen Island. This was driven off by machine gun fire.

Again during the afternoon the Japanese were reported to be concentrating about one hundred junks off Lamma, which our artillery engaged.

27. *Stonecutters Island.* – Enemy bombardment of Stonecutters continued throughout the day, West Fort having forty direct hits before midday. Much material damage generally was caused, chiefly to buildings. Telephone communications were continually cut. In the afternoon, to conform to the withdrawal from the mainland, I ordered the withdrawal from this island and the destruction of guns and all immovable

stores, according to a detailed plan previously prepared. This was successfully carried out.

28. During the day IIth December fifth column activities developed in Kowloon. Some of the fifth columnists were armed,[5] and rioting and looting occurred in the streets. A large number of launch crews and lorry and car drivers deserted, throwing a heavy handicap on the shoulders of the administrative services – civil, naval and military – particularly in view of the large and hurried evacuation for that evening and night.

Throughout the day IIth December Hong Kong was subjected to bombing and spasmodic artillery fire. The R.N. Dockyard, R.A.S.C. Camber and the R.A.O.C. Depot all suffered some damage, though casualties were few. The civilian population in Hong Kong remained calm, though naturally the news of early evacuation of the mainland came as a considerable shock.

29. *Withdrawal of troops from the mainland* (II/12th *December*). – (*a*) Careful plans had been drawn up by Brigadier Mainland Infantry Brigade, and all troops were employed on successive positions.

The operation was well carried out. However, HQ details of 2/14 Punjab Regt. and some others came down on to Kai Tak aerodrome by mistake in the darkness and became involved in street fighting in the outskirts of Kowloon City. A launch was sent over at about 0100 hours but could not gain contact with them. The bulk of the Company, however, were taken off at Star Ferry pier at dawn, breaking off a running fight with the enemy as they actually cast off from the pier side.

(*b*) Battalion HQ of the 2/14 Punjab Regt. and two Companies had been unable to maintain the timed programme during the night owing to enemy action, and at dawn they were withdrawing down the West side of Devils Peak Peninsula. They stayed that day dispersed in the foothills at the southern end, whilst two companies of 5/7 Rajput Regt. held the Ma Lau Tong line as planned, with one company on the rear position Hai Wan.

(*c*) The personnel of both Indian battalions were in good heart but somewhat exhausted after four days of continuous day and night vigilance and long night carries, over rough tracks and coolie paths, of many machine guns, light automatics and mortars. Owing to the simultaneous withdrawals of all three battalions, the 5/7 Rajput Regiment's transport had not been augmented by mules from the other battalions as planned, and this emphasised the shortage of mule transport which had always been apparent on peace exercises. It will be realised that units were on an improvised scale of trucks, lorries, and mules, as pooling of the inadequate "Colonial" establishments had been found to be necessary. The transport situation had become much worse with the arrival of the two Canadian battalions, for their transport had been shipped in a different vessel, diverted via. Australia, and had not arrived before war with Japan broke out.

(*d*) At midnight 11/12th December the Hong Kong Telephone Company cut all communications between the island and the mainland.

(*e*) One troop of 3-7-in. Howitzers remained at the southern end of Devils Peak in support of the Ma Lau Tong position. Mainland Infantry Brigade HQ also remained on the Peninsula pending further developments.[6] Most of the Bren carriers and all the armoured cars were safely evacuated from the mainland.

(*f*) At 0600 hours 12th December military cables to Kowloon were cut at the R N. Yard cable hut.

(*g*) At dawn 2 Royal Scots temporarily took over the North East sector of the island defences, this being largely a precautionary measure only, as the occupation of the Devils Peak Peninsula by the 5/7 Rajput Regt. covered this sector effectively. This North East sector had previously been manned in skeleton form by some HQ personnel of I Middlesex Regt. plus a platoon of No. 3 Company HKVDC. In the North West sector was "Z" Company I Middlesex Regt., consisting of spare men of machine gun companies plus battalion cooks, storemen, bandsmen, etc., manning forty machine guns from Fortress reserve stocks. This Company constituted a valuable fighting force enabling *inter alia* the I Middlesex Regt. to man the pill boxes on the entire perimeter of the island from 11th to 13th December.

30. Air raids and shelling of the island continued throughout the day 12th December. The North shore Dockyard was badly damaged and also the R.A.O.C. Depot, which was hit on five occasions. Aberdeen and Green Island cables were both cut. By now many coast defence guns, especially 6-in., were being used for landward firing, calculations to hit one hundred points having been worked out in peace time. Harassing fire by night, and counter battery fire and the engagement of observed targets by day, was carried out.

The allowance of 25 rounds per gun for such landward firing was greatly exceeded. High explosive Mk XIIIA shell of 1918 manufacture was faulty, several bursting immediately in front of the muzzle.

31. *A.A.* – There were insufficient guns to give adequate gun density at any point. More 3.7-in. guns were expected shortly and also more Bofors (the garrison had but two), for "release telegrams" had been received from HQ Far East. The A.A. defences were well known to be inadequate, but I realised that the call for the European and Mediterranean theatres of war had prevented reinforcements. Targets were numerous (12th December) but the A.A. positions extremely few owing to the mountainous nature of the country of Hong Kong Island. The enemy, with such good observation from Kowloon, was very quick on to any A.A. section opening up, and I consider that Lt.-Colonel F.D. Field fought his command very well. The scarcity both of transport and roads severely handicapped the mobility of the guns and also the ammunition supply and administration of the sections. The shortage of British officers was very much felt. During the night one of the A.A. searchlights on Green Island acted as a sentry beam on receipt of a report that the enemy were landing near West Point.

At this juncture Wing Commander H.G. Sullivan, the Officer Commanding R.A.F., offered the services of one officer and 16 N.C.Os. for wireless and telephone duties, which I gladly accepted. They were incorporated with Royal Signals.

The morale of the civilian population had been considerably shaken, and fifth columnists became more active. Rice distribution and the monetary situation caused anxiety and necessitated urgent measures.

32. During the afternoon 12th December the enemy was reported to be occupying George Island (off Lamma) and there was considerable activity seawards.

33. In the late afternoon a strong enemy attack (about one battalion) developed against the left company of 5/7 Rajput Regt. on the Ma Lau Tong line but was successfully beaten off, assisted by quick support provided by the Royal Artillery. Heavy casualties on the enemy were observed. The 5/7 Rajput Regt. was subjected to dive bombing and heavy mortar fire throughout the day. In view of the weight of the Japanese attack, the rapid development of their heavy mortar fire, the contricted passage across the Lyemun Strait, the shortage of launch crews, and as we now had no footing on the mainland except at Devils Peak Peninsula, I gave orders to Commander Mainland Infantry Brigade that the Ma Lau Tong line should be evacuated during the night.

The first task was to be the evacuation of HQ and two companies of 2/14 Punjab Regt. which had been previously arranged. This was to be followed by the withdrawal of the 3.7-in. Howitzer troop R.A. The second and the shorter of the Devils Peak Lines (Hai Wan) was to be held by HQ 5/7 Rajput Regt. and two companies, the remainder of that battalion being evacuated last. The first withdrawal was timed for 1930 hours.

34. Shell fire died down at dusk (12th December) but the water transport difficulties were serious. Chinese crews deserted in the darkness from the W.D. fleet, though covered by rifles, engineers were deficient, and some launches were found to be in a sinking condition. Administrative officers had been sent out from my HQ to accelerate matters and took personal charge and operated what boats they could, but serious delays occurred. It was not until 0130 hours that the 2/14 Punjab Regt., some 300 men, were all across.

At 0400 hours the bulk of the first troop R.A. (less mules) and one company of 5/7 Rajput Regt. were across, but the Mule Corps was still to come. It was clear that the situation was critical if daylight crossings were to be avoided and I called on the Royal Navy to assist. Their response was prompt. Three motor torpedo boats were despatched from Aberdeen and one more was recalled from patrol in Junk Bay where it had been covering the right flank of the 5/7 Rajput Regt. from possible enemy attack in sampans from Hang Hau area (an operation which had been attempted by night during peace training and found feasible).

The destroyer HMS "Thracian" was also ordered round from Aberdeen but could not be expected to arrive before 0600 hours, 13th December.

I ordered Brigadier Wallis to give full priority to personnel, and that there was to be no question of evacuating the 120 mules and further risking the operation. In any case the mule lighter crew had deserted, and the handling of this craft in the dark by personnel unaccustomed to it was a dubious proposition, and moreover she was badly holed by enemy fire and had to be abandoned in a sinking condition. Meanwhile the W.D.V. "Victoria" had been slowly and steadily evacuating personnel and equipment under Major A.J. Dewar and Captain C.G. Turner. When the torpedo boats arrived at the small pier on the Devils Peak Peninsula it was found that the state of the tide did not permit them to "lie close to" – a risk that had been foreseen and accepted. This meant more delay and ferrying by sampans. Ferry trips were, however, made by the torpedo boats directly H.M.S. "Thracian" arrived, the tide having risen slightly.

35. At about 0400 hours I3th December I discussed with Brigadier Wallis the advisability of also including in the withdrawal the two companies of 5/7 Rajput Regt. holding the rear position. The enemy were in constant though light contact throughout, and after their severe handling would be temporarily disinclined to follow up. The water transport situation had already become more than precarious, it was extremely doubtful if any W.D. vessel, except perhaps the "Victoria" would be available next night, and I thus foresaw the greatest difficulties and even the impossibility of maintaining the 5/7 Rajput Regt. with ammunition and supplies in their isolated position. I decided that the risk was too great, and I also urgently required them to relieve and man the North East sector then held by 2 Royal Scots. This latter battalion was not in good shape, as they had lost many of their best officers killed or wounded, and I judged it to be necessary to withdraw them into reserve so that they could obtain a short respite in which to rest and re-equip. In addition they were unfamiliar with the ground, their previous sector having been the South West. One company of 5/7 Rajput Regt. was therefore ordered to cover the withdrawal of the remainder and then themselves embark in the last flights. Daylight had arrived by then, but they accomplished the evacuation without casualties, covered by artillery fire from various island positions.

36. It was not until 0920 hours that the last contingent of 5/7 Rajput Regt. from the mainland reached Aberdeen. The whole battalion was collected in the Tytam Gap area by noon and given twenty-four hours to rest and re-equip before taking over the North East sector from 2 Royal Scots. The 2/I4 Punjab Regt. took over the North West sector. During the night (I2/I3th December), at the urgent request of the civil authorities, arrangements were made with the Harbour Master to pass 9 tons of dynamite from Green Island to the Star Ferry for collection and distribution.

On its return, loaded, it left Green Island two hours ahead of schedule, with the result that it reached the Vehicular Ferry (not Star Ferry) unexpectedly, and the N.C.O. commanding the pill box there gave the order to fire, as no lights or distinguishing marks were visible. The launch blew up and all on board thus unfortunately lost their lives.

37. At 0900 hours I3th December a launch bearing a flag of truce was seen to put off from Kowloon. It arrived at Victoria Pier with a Staff Officer of the General commanding the Japanese Forces (Lt.-General Sakai) bearing a letter addressed to H.E. The Governor. The letter demanded the surrender of the Colony and threatened severe artillery fire and aerial bombardment in the event of refusal. The demand was tantamount to unconditional surrender and was rejected categorically.

38. During the morning the Japanese were observed to be collecting launches in Kowloon Bay and concentrating them mainly at Bailey's Shipyard near the cement works. The situation as I saw it was that the enemy, if he attacked from the mainland, might direct his attack on to:-

(*a*) Lyemun – Quarry Point area	}	From
(*b*) Northpoint Bowrington area	}	Kowloon
(*c*) Victoria	}	Peninsula.
(*d*) Kennedy Town	}	

(*b*) or (*c*) seemed most probable in view of the short distance across, the easy support by artillery and mortars and the possible combination with Wang Ching Wei factions and others in the congested area of the town. The number of derelict craft in the area of (*a*) lessened the likelihood of attack there.

Any attack from the mainland might well be in combination with an attack on the South shore. My available reserves were:-

(i)   2 Royal Scots, after relief and move from North East sector to the Wanchai Gap – Filter Beds area, but temporarily unfit until they could be thoroughly rested and reorganised.

(ii) Two companies 5/7 Rajput Regt. North East sector.

(iii) One company Winnipeg Grenadiers in South West sector.

(iv) Two companies 2/I4 Punjab Regt. in North West sector.

(v)   "Z" Coy. I Middlesex Regt. including one mobile machine gun platoon.

39. *A.A.* – In the early afternoon I3th December our A.A. guns brought down a large seaplane which crashed into the sea about 3000 yards West of Lamma (confirmed later by the Japanese).

40. During the day the enemy artillery fire increased in intensity (up to 9-in. calibre), one 9.2-in. gun at Mount Davis was knocked out by a direct hit, and at dusk Belchers Fort was heavily shelled and set on fire. Other serious fires were started at West Point and Kennedy Town.

Fifth columnists[7] had been active during the day and a large number of army transport drivers deserted, some of them taking their lorries with them. Police dealt with these in due course. The civilian population showed signs of strain, and food queues in some districts became disorderly. The question of rice distribution presented a grave problem in the overcrowded quarters.

4I. At 0200 hours I4th December great anxiety was caused by the speed of the fires at Belchers and Kennedy Town. The civil fire brigades had been fighting the fires for many hours and asked for military assistance. At various times three parties were accordingly sent but on each occasion were returned without any work having been performed on demolitions (a detailed series of "fire lanes" had been worked out and calculations completed before the war broke out). On the fourth occasion, however, some houses were blown down. Fires were under control by midday. Elements of the civil population made these disasters an occasion for disorderly conduct; fifth columnists became more active and great care was necessary in checking telephone calls. The civil police found difficulty in maintaining guards over vulnerable points, and negotiated with the Chungking Government secret societies for assistance.

42. Certain movements of enemy warships were observed during the day (I4th December), steaming on far distant courses.

43. (*a*) There was a marked increase in the intensity and accuracy of hostile shelling on the I4th December. Two 4.7-in. guns at Belchers had been hit and put out of action, and one 9.2-in. at Mount Davis had its communications cut for two hours. Also at Mount Davis, one 3-in. A.A. gun was hit and permanently disabled, causing about 30 per cent. casualties to the A.A. personnel. Many Chinese gunners deserted as a result.

(*b*) Pak Sha Wan Battery (Chinese volunteers) came in for particular attention, being both shelled and mortared. Its Battery Command Post and all internal communications were destroyed and the Battery Commander was wounded and evacuated. The guns were reduced to independent autosight control. At this juncture owing to an imperfectly conveyed message and an error of judgment of the junior officer left in acting command, the personnel were given the option of going to Stanley. All but two Chinese left; seventeen British and Portuguese stayed. A few regular British gunners were later sent up as reinforcements.

(*c*) A very heavy concentration on Magazine Gap cut eight main cables involving I95 circuits, severing communications between Fortress Headquarters and all terminals to the South of that Gap. Within 20 hours the Royal Corps of Signals, working magnificently, restored all lines.

44. *Civil Population.* – The civil police found their hands more than full in maintaining order in the city but had the situation generally under control except in the A.R.P. tunnels, where in certain cases armed gangs of robbers were operating. Pamphlets were dropped by the Japanese.

45. H.M.S. *"Thracian"* carried out an excellent operation during the night (I5/I6th December) making her way past Green Island, across the Japanese front on the Kowloon Peninsula, and then sinking two ferryboats at anchor full of enemy troops one thousand yards East of the Electric Power Station, Kowloon.

46. By now the new organisation of the island defences had been carried out viz.: division into two brigade areas – East Infantry Brigade (Brigadier Wallis) and West Infantry Brigade (Brigadier J.K. Lawson). The North-South dividing line approximated closely to the former dividing line between the easterly and westerly island sectors. At the northern extremity, however, it was placed further East to increase the front held by the 2/I4 Punjab Regt. now considered a safer sector owing to the "anti-boat fence" or boom which was in position from Sheung Wan to Green Island. The continuation towards Kellett Island had been prevented by the desertion

of Chinese crews and there had been no opportunity of carrying the complete scheme through, i.e., a third portion constructed across to Kowloon Point.

I Middlesex Regt. was given a small but important sector based on Leighton Hill Ridge – Causeway Bay area. No preparations, however had been possible on the Ridge before hostilities, except a little wiring and three shell-slits, as the property was Government owned and housed many Government officials who could not be dispossessed or inconvenienced before the "precautionary period" of the Defence Scheme (which actually was never declared owing to the rapid development of full war conditions).

I Middlesex Regt. came directly under command of Fortress as "Corps Troops" for defence purposes. This eased the situation for Brigadier Wallis, who had the larger half of the island to command, and for Brigadier Lawson who was unfamiliar with the ground.

During the night I4/I5th December the 5/7 Rajput Regt. relieved the 2 Royal Scots in the North East sector. The latter moved later to the area Wanchai Gap – Filter Beds to refit and re-organise, but one company took over a narrow front just West of the naval hospital.

47. During the early hours I5th December a broadcast from Kowloon could be heard of European songs and music; the talks, however, were not clear. They were probably from loud speakers on vans in the streets, as the radio transmitting station in Kowloon had been destroyed before evacuation. Several traitors, with lamps of primitive design operated from a dry battery, with a small but adequate mirror, were reported signalling from the island to the mainland. When these operators were intercepted they were shot.

48. (*a*) There was a systematic shelling of pill boxes along the North shore during the morning I5th December: three were knocked out and one badly damaged. One had forty holes drilled right through by a high velocity gun of small calibre located on Kowloon Peninsula, firing from a concealed position inside a water front "Godown." The provision of alternative emplacements for the pill boxes of the North shore defences had already been taken up and some ten to twelve were completed. They should of course have been completed in peace time but it would have meant requisitioning valuable "Godown" and office properties, and requisitioning had not been sanctioned by Government until the proposed "Precautionary Period."

(*b*) By nightfall all military and civil telephone routes in the North East sector, including those to pill boxes Nos. 40 to 53 were severely interrupted. Night repair work was at once put in hand.

(*c*) Aberdeen Island and the A.A. positions at Lyemun (Saiwan Hill) were heavily shelled, one gun being put out of action temporarily.

(*d*) At noon I5th December the enemy was observed preparing sandbagged positions on the water front by the Kowloon Godowns, probably for mortars. Later, mortar fire fell in the vicinity of the R.N. Dockyard, Command H.Q., and Lower Peak Tramway Terminus.

(*e*) By now a "Command Observation Post" with direct lines to Fortress H.Q. was operating well from the Peak, manned by HKVDC, and also two special observation posts (pill box 69 and Kennedy Rd.) manned by 2/I4 Punjab Regt.[8]

(*f*) Enemy was observed collecting small craft in Kowloon Bay – possibly for a raid; special arrangements were made to counter this viz.: a concentration was fired by 6-in. Howitzers and two craft were set alight. Orders were also issued from Fortress HQ to the A.A. searchlights at Saiwan and Braemar to cease their normal role at any time if they heard continuous machine gun fire on the North shore and to turn their lights down to illuminate the harbour.

49. At 2I00 hours, I5th December, an attempted landing was reported by the Pak Sha Wan Battery (HKVDC). It was ascertained later from several sources that a very bold attempt was made by the enemy who, with small rubber boats and petrol tin rafts for equipment, swam across in fair strength – estimates varied from one to three Companies. All were shot in the water, the depleted battery (see para. 43 (b)) contributing stout defence.

50. (*a*) For four hours on I5th December Pinewood A.A. Battery was shelled by calibres up to 9-in. One gun was smashed irreparably and the other so badly damaged that it was out of action for the remainder of the battle. All instruments were rendered useless. Casualties to personnel were not numerous and men not hit were employed on salvage, and in an infantry role with 2/I4 Punjab Regiment. We claimed two hits on enemy aircraft during the day.

(*b*) The general impression of Japanese artillery fire was that their gunners were extremely accurate on targets which were obviously well known from our peace time dispositions and under direct observation, but inaccurate in picking up new targets needing predicted fire, in spite of abundant air reconnaissance. About 30 per cent. of the ammunition burst defectively and of the heavier natures at times 50 per cent. failed to explode.

5I. During this day (I5th December) the last of the "Priority A" anti-personnel minefields was completed by Fortress R.E.

The morale of the civilian population remained shaky, chiefly due to rice distribution difficulties. The Chungking Government representatives had been most helpful in assisting in the maintenance of order.

52. News was received from the Chinese General Staff of the advance of Chinese forces towards Hong Kong. This fitted in with the plans which I had previously received via Chungking of the proposed attack of General Yu Han Mou's 7th Army. However, the information now was modified by the statement that effective assistance could not be available until early January. Information of intended help from Chinese forces from the North was circulated to formations and units.

53. At daybreak I6th December observation revealed no enemy movements along the mainland waterfront between Kai Tak and the Kowloon Star Ferry, but launch activity in Kowloon Bay continued.

54. Bombing and shelling by the enemy were now showing a higher standard of

accuracy and increasing in intensity, being confined mainly to military objectives. The first air raid occurred at 0900 hours and lasted thirty-five minutes.

In the afternoon, l6th December, seventeen enemy planes bombed Mount Davis, which was also heavily and accurately shelled: an unexploded 9-in. shell entered the Fortress Plotting Room and damaged the instruments. A bomb dropped in Shaukiwan caused l50 civilian casualties. Shek O, Lyemun and Aberdeen were also bombed; some casualties to Royal Navy personnel and damage being caused at the last named.

By the end of the day more than half of the pill boxes along North shore from Lyemun to Bowrington had been knocked out. Moves to alternative positions were carried out during the night (sixteen were now prepared but were not yet on the telephone system). The maintenance of communications to the North shore pill boxes, and on other subsidiary routes there, was proving extremely difficult on account of repeated breaks from hostile fire.

55. One enemy plane was seen at 0930 hours l6th December to crash into the sea (three sources confirmed) near Tatong, hit by the 3.7-in section at Wong Nei Chong.

At l030 hours a fighter-bomber was hit by the Brick Hill 3.7-in. gun and crashed in a gulley (two sources corroborated).

56. Civilian morale improved somewhat.

The arrest this day of a prominent Chinese merchant for defeatist talk was expected to have a salutary effect – which in fact it did.

Fifth columnists were still active. Their methods consisted of shining lights to bring shell fire to bear on concentrations of transport, etc., sniping, spreading false rumours, inducing desertion from "essential services" and inciting to riot. They also again attacked the isolated A.A. searchlight position at Shaukiwan.

57. During the hours of darkness and early hours of l7th December mortar fire from Kowloon Peninsula continued on to the North shore pillboxes.

A force of l4 Army light bombers made two separate attacks at about 0930 hours l7th December – the first on Shaukiwan and Wanchai, and the second on the Peak Wireless Station, Garden Road, and Central District in Victoria. These were followed by a short but relatively severe artillery and mortar bombardment on Central District.

Shortly afterwards two Japanese launches flying a white flag crossed the harbour. The delegation brought written proposals for surrender, similar to those of l3th December. It was thought that the Japanese supposed our morale to be shaken. The proposals were signed by Lt.-General Sakai and the Naval C.-in-C. Vice-Admiral Niimi. The envoys appeared genuinely surprised and disconcerted when the proposals were again summarily rejected. They left with the hint that future bombardments might not be so discriminate.

This second delegation coming within four days of the first suggested that either (a) they disliked the prospect of attacking across the water or (b) that the Chinese threat in their rear was taking effect, or (c) that it was an attempt to undermine our morale by thoughts of peace and quiet. The Japanese delegation announced on arrival that there would be no hostilities until l600 hours by which time they expected a reply. Advantage was taken of this very welcome lull to repair communications, etc.

Considerable activity seawards was reported during the afternoon of the l7th

December, including a 2,000 ton freighter operating in the shelter, westward of Lamma. On the mainland there was activity round Kai Tak aerodrome, both launch and motor transport and at Bailey's yard the following were seen – three ferry vessels, three barges, one large water boat, one steam tug, one motor boat.

During the I7th December our artillery suffered no damage or casualties for the first time for many days. Our counter battery fire silenced hostile artillery on Devil's Peak, Gun Club Mill, and also three mortars on the Kowloon waterfront.

58. Aircraft identified to date were of the following types; Navy Reconnaissance Flying Boat, type 94 – Heavy Navy Bomber, type 96 – Army light Bomber, type 98 – Army Fighter, type 97, unidentified fighter, now known to be the Navy O. Heaviest bomb dropped, identified, 250 lbs. – but from deduction (fuze caps, size of crater, etc.) it was considered that some of 500 lbs. were also dropped.

59. Morale of civilian population continued to improve and the rice distribution was getting better.

60. At 2I00 hours I7th December hostile artillery fire started a severe fire at the large paint works at Braemar, causing a heavy smoke pall. Owing to its proximity the ammunition of the I8-pounder Beach Defence section nearby had to be moved to an alternative position, and at about midnight the guns themselves were forced to follow to the same position behind the Police station in that vicinity.

The shelling of the North East sector was particularly heavy and lines were being constantly cut and repaired. At 2000 hours many pill boxes were still out of touch and field cable had to be substituted for the buried system that night.

At about 0I00 hours Aberdeen came under shell fire from seawards and the Industrial School (HQ of the Aberdeen portion of the R.N. Dockyard) was hit.

6I. (*a*) At first light I8th December a Japanese destroyer was sighted sixteen miles South of Aberdeen.

(*b*) A considerable movement of small craft between the Kowloon wharves and piers was observed.

(*c*) In the early hours a 60-pounder gun which had been brought up into the North Point under cover of darkness (Lt. J.S. Vintner commanding) attempted to sink three freighters in Kowloon Bay suspected of being used as observation posts or being prepared as "jumping off places" for an attack. Only shrapnel was available but by obtaining hits on the water line one 4000 ton ship was holed and settled down.

62. At I000 hours an air raid of considerable intensity developed on the Central District Victoria. The Anglo-Persian Company's petrol and oil storage tanks at North Point were set on fire and subsequently shelled at intervals throughout the day. The attack seemed to be directed particularly against the Government Offices, where the Secretariat was hit, and many casualties were caused in the neighbourhood. During the early afternoon Causeway Bay area was very heavily shelled, the water front from that place to Lyemun now becoming a tangle of fallen tramwires and standards and almost impassable for vehicles and despatch riders.

At noon 18th December the Braemar beach defence gun position (para. 60) was shelled, received several direct hits, and the two 18 pounders destroyed beyond repair.

Further air raids occurred from 1500 hours onwards and the Saiwan artillery observation post was dive bombed and also shelled.

Between 1700 and 1800 hours a party of about two hundred enemy was seen working down from Haiwan to Devil's Peak pier and were engaged by our artillery. Just before and after dusk an extremely heavy bombardment by artillery and mortars on Lyemun Peninsula was carried out.

At night fall it was reported that the North Point fixed beam (across to Kowloon Point) could not function owing to the intensity of the heat and the dense smoke arising from the burning Anglo-Persian Company's oil installations. This fire continued for days and was a severe handicap to observed fire.

63. Landing on Hong Kong Island. – (*a*) At 1900 hours 18th December three armoured cars of the HKVDC were sent to Tytam Gap to be a mobile reserve in the hands of the Commander East Infantry Brigade at his HQ there, and two other cars remained in hand at Leighton Hill close to 1 Middlesex HQ.

(*b*) At 1930 hours a report was received that the Saiwan A.A. position and Old Redoubt had been under heavy shell fire (9-in.Howitzer) for half an hour, that the whole fort was badly damaged and that the structure would not stand up to further shelling.

(*c*) At 2000 hours pillboxes 41 and 42 (Shaukiwan) and also the narrow 2 Royal Scots front at Bowrington were bombarded.

(*d*) At 2130 hours the Officer Commanding 5/7 Rajput Regt. reported difficulty in getting in touch with the Lyemun fixed beam and asked for illumination in area Quarry Bay – Aldrich Bay. The Braemar A.A. searchlight was ordered to come down on to a shore defence role but (not known till later) the telephone lines to its position were knocked out by shell fire and the motor cyclist despatch rider sent in lieu was badly wounded and never got through. The communications to the fixed beam at Lyemun had been giving difficulty throughout the evening, owing to breaks from shell fire, and Captain C.E. Otway, R.E., had finally been sent to take personal charge there.

At about 2130 hours 18th December the Officer Commanding 5/7 Rajput Regt. moved a reserve company from the area South of his HQ[9] to a forward area closer to him. The remaining company (B) in battalion reserve was in the Tai Hang Road area, but communications to it had again been cut. Verey lights were seen going up from North Point and Lyemun, and shelling and machine gun fire was heard in considerable volume along the North shore water front, and in the area of the Electric Power Station and the Anglo-Persian Company installation.[10]

(*e*) It was learnt later that at 2200 hours Captain Otway observed sampans lighting smoke flares in the harbour, and motor boats and small craft plying between Devils Peak and Lyemun pier. His light was twice attacked by an enemy patrol with hand grenades and after beating off a third attack he left the light exposed, locked the doors, and at about 2330 hours withdrew his six men through the Japanese lines to join the nearest infantry in the defence of the Saiwan 6-in. Howitzer position in Lyemun Gap. When he left, the Japanese were shooting straight down the beam with an "Infantry gun," 50 per cent. of the shots hitting the concrete surround of the light.

(*f*) The landing of the enemy between Lyemun and North Point appears to have been simultaneous, for at 2200 hours night I8th-I9th December pillbox N. 4 at Taikoo was reported in the hands of the enemy and a little later 5/7 Rajput Regt. was overheard reporting the occupation of the Sugar Factory by the enemy.

At 2205 hours I Middlesex Regt was ordered to send a mobile machine gun platoon to North Point to form a defensive flank from pillbox 49 (Power Station) to join up with the 5/7 Rajput Company in that area ("D" Company). An armoured car was also sent. Defensive artillery fire was promptly put down on Taikoo Dockyard and the Sugar Factory, and the Commanding Officer of 5/7 Rajput Regt. on the spot reported that the results were most effective.

(*g*) At 2242 hours pillbox 55 crew in Causeway Bay reported that the alternative position in which they were located was being shelled and also sniped at from their right flank.

(*h*) At 2330 hours Brigadier Wallis reported that the Officer Commanding 5/7 Rajput Regt. was still at Taikoo HQ and that on the other flank the intention was to recapture Saiwan Redoubt with the bayonet. The 6-in. Howitzer Section on Mount Parker was still in action.

(*i*) At midnight I8-I9th December, B. Company (battalion reserve) of the 5/7 Rajput Regt. was now moving to the area of pillbox 53, a machine gun platoon of I Middlesex Regt. was in area of pillbox 50 and one platoon of B Company 5/7 Rajput Regt was still holding out in North Point area. The Power Station itself was held by a force known as the "Hughesiliers", under the Hon. Major J.J. Paterson, which was formed before the outbreak of war from men of 55 and over who felt the call to duty though they themselves were outside the terms of the Compulsory Service Act. It contained many prominent men of considerable standing in the colony and their role was the prevention of sabotage to the electric plant. It was reinforced about the I6th December by 45 Hong Kong Electric Company employees (HKVDC), China Light and Power Company employees, from Kowloon (numbering 30) plus two officers and seven other "Free French." The two officers were Captains Ega and Jacosta. This force was instrumental in holding the Power Station this night and fought in the streets next day until the late afternoon when the house-to-house fighting and mopping up by the Japanese caused their surrender by encirclement, except for a few who escaped.

The delay the force imposed was very valuable to me.

(*j*) Just after midnight it was reported that the armoured car sent to reconnoitre towards the Power Station had been knocked out by mobile anti-tank gun.[II] It is clear from reports since made that at that time the Japanese were in possession of the ridge overlooking and dominating the Power station and the approach along King's Road from the West. It was from this direction that the reinforcing platoon of I Middlesex Regt came, as it was judged that the road nearer the water front was impassable owing to the flames from the Anglo-Persian Company's installations. The platoon ran straight into the same anti-tank and machine gun fire, the Platoon Sergeant-Major and others were killed and the remainder got into action in the vicinity of the Power Station where they fought excellently. When the bulk of the Hughesiliers withdrew, three I Middlesex N.C.O.s rallied and collected a mixed party of Regulars and Volunteers, nine strong, and fought till 1400 hours in the main office building of the Power Station.

(*k*) At about 2200 hours 18th December the Royal Artillery at Lyemun Gap reported that propaganda from a loud speaker from Saiwan Redoubt was being broadcast – "We Japanese have captured Saiwan Hill," "It is useless to resist," etc. The area was promptly put under small arms fire.

At about 0100 hours it was reported that a counter attack by one platoon of Canadians had been carried out on Saiwan Redoubt, organised and led by an Artillery officer. The counter-attack did not succeed, as was discovered subsequently. This officer then took a Tommy gun and carried out active local defence on his own, round the 6-in. Howitzer position at Lyemun Gap, in a most gallant manner.

(*l*) At 0145 hours the Hughesiliers (see sub-para, (i) above) reported the Power Station surrounded, but were ordered to hold on at all costs as other posts were holding out near them and it was hoped that B Company 5/7 Rajput Regt. (Captain R.G. Course) would at any moment make its presence felt.

(*m*) At 0200 hours 19th December Officer Commanding I Middlesex Regt. reported that B Company 5/7 Rajput Regt. was back in his vicinity South of Leighton Hill – the reason given being that the Company had gone forward into the Braemar reservoir area but had been unable to locate D Company 5/7 Rajput Regt. holding that sector. I Middlesex Regt. was still holding pill boxes 53 and 54 (Causeway Bay) and had sent officer reconnaissance patrols forward to North Point where the Hughesiliers had again reported that they were hard pressed.

(*n*) At 0300 hours R.A. (East) reported two Canadian platoons had tried to capture the Saiwan position about midnight under an accurate barrage on the hill top but that this counter attack was a failure.

The fighting here in the dark was very confused. Later Major Fielden, R.A., reported the road junction at Shaukiwan held by armoured cars and that he was trying to work round West of Saiwan observation post (on the top of the redoubt); he had thirty men covering the 6-in. Howitzer position in Lyemun Gap and he said that pill box 40 was still firing.

(*o*) Between 0400 and 0600 hours I9th December reinforcing platoons of the Royal Rifles of Canada were sent forward on to the Mount Parker high ground.

(*p*) To give increased defence in Victoria against possible landing on that water front which, supplemented by fifth columnists, would constitute a grave danger from the West and perhaps overrun Government House area, a company of 2/I4 Punjab Regt. had been deployed on a line running from pill box 63 southwards past and including the Central Police Station. The situation now developing on the East of Victoria was judged to be serious enough, however, to warrant taking risks in the Victoria area, and so this company (about 0400 hours) was called in from its positions to be in hand at HQ of 2/I4 Punjab Regt. at Garden Road. "A" Company Winnipeg Grenadiers was already in hand at Wong Nei Chong Gap for emergency use.

(*q*) Captain R.S. Cole, 5/7 Rajput Regt., during the early hours was waiting for troops of his battalion on the track from Braemar to Mount Butler when a party of Japanese, headed by three Chinese with rifles approached. They were dressed in uniform and obviously acted as guides. He challenged, shot the Chinese, and dispersed the party. This incident corroborates others, accounting for the speed with which the Japanese troops covered country, supposedly unfamiliar, in the dark.

(*r*) At 0400 hours I9th December I arranged with the Chief Engineer for the despatch of an R.E. party for an infantry fighting role, viz.: to reinforce the Wong Nei Chong Gap area and to come under orders of Commander West Infantry Brigade on arrival there. Seventy British and Chinese was the eventual composition of this party.

(*s*) Shortly after 0400 hours the Officer Commanding I Middlesex Regt. reported the enemy working round the hills by Tai Hang village and going East, that D Company 5/7 Rajput Regt. was still near the Reservoir, that Causeway Bay area was securely held, and that there was no signs of enemy action down the road from Taikoo. At this time I ordered 2/I4 Punjab Regt. to send a company forward to help fill the gap between the Winnipeg Grenadiers and I Middlesex Regt.

(*t*) At 0430 hours Major E. de V. Hunt, R.A., reported the situation to be well in hand at Lyemun Gap.

(*u*) At 0500 hours a small party of enemy was encountered at the Filter Beds. This showed with what vigour the enemy was pressing the attack.

(*v*) At 0600 hours personnel of Fortress R.E.(see sub-para, (r) above) left, and (so it transpired later) arrived in the vicinity of Wong Nei Chong Gap, only to find West Infantry Brigade HQ under heavy enemy machine gun and mortar fire. Three mortar positions were located in folds of the ground but the Royal Engineers had no suitable weapons with which to reach such dead ground. Access to Brigade HQ shelters was out of the question and the Royal Engineers took up a position nearby.

(*w*) 0650 hours 19th December. I had previously consulted with the Commodore R.N. with a view to active participation by the Royal Navy in the land fighting. He now informed me that arrangements had been completed for the Royal Navy to take over infantry posts in the area Aberdeen – Little Hong Kong. This released A Company Winnipeg Grenadiers[12] from the Little Hong Kong Sub Sector, and it moved off at 0500 hours. The Royal Navy however did not take over these infantry posts, for the bulk of the naval party was used in an attempt to reinforce Wong Nei Chong Gap from the South.

(*x*) At daylight laden junks, barges, motor launches and ferries were observed crossing to the vicinity of North Point, but the exact area of landing was not under observation as "low level" observation posts had been over-run, and buildings, etc., obscured the foreshore from the view of the upper observation posts.

(*y*) Between 0800 and 0900 hours small parties of enemy were observed on Jardines Lookout, coming down on to Wong Nei Chong Gap. In this area confused fighting was taking place, troops of various units participating, as well as the Canadian Brigade H.Q. staff. Brigadier J.K. Lawson (about 1000 hours) reported that the H.Q. shelters were over-run, firing into them was actually taking place at point blank range and that he was going outside to fight it out, after destroying telephone exchanges, etc. He did so, and I regret to say was killed, together with his Brigade Major. Major Temple and personnel of H.Q. West Group, R.A. were also killed. During the next thirty-six hours the groups of shelters here changed hands several times, but in spite of every effort the enemy secured a definite lodgment.[13] Part of the enemy attack came on to Stanley Gap and involved the 3.7-in. A.A. Section there. The Royal Artillery of the nearest 3.7-in. Howitzer positions were called on to assist, and leaving their gun position were drawn into the fighting with their small arms. Unfortunately, as it was thought that a temporary counter attack only was involved, steps were not taken to remove small essential parts, e.g., locks, or firing levers, and these guns together with ammunition later fell into enemy hands and were used against us.[14]

64. The Officer Commanding R.A.F. had some time previously requested that his officers and men should be used for ground defence, and at this time the Royal Air Force were taking up positions with the Royal Navy in the Aberdeen area, where they assisted materially in the subsequent fighting.

65. (*a*) It now became necessary to form a new West Group R.A. This was done at Wanchai Gap, and communications readjusted by 1500 hours, Major Duncan being appointed Commander. This small group of artillery gave admirable support during

the next few days, being continuously in action though repeatedly shelled and dive bombed. Such counter battery work as remained possible was undertaken by R.A. HQ at Fortress HQ.

(b) At 0845 hours, 19th December, the Mount Parker 6-in. Howitzer Section 600 yards North of Tytam Gap was firing with one of its howitzers straight down the road towards Lyemun Gap.

66. At 0730 hours six motor torpedo boats were sent to the vicinity of Green Island to be ready to attack enemy vessels ferrying troops from the mainland to the island. On the arrival at the rendezvous they were ordered direct by the Commodore to attack in pairs. The first attack by M.T.Bs. 07 and 09 was successful and sank one enemy landing craft set another on fire and forced a third to turn back (each held about forty troops). Whilst returning 07 was hit and damaged, and was towed in by 09. The second pair of motor torpedo boats had already been ordered to attack, but by the time of their arrival ferrying across the harbour had ceased. Whilst returning M.T.B. 12 was badly hit and ran ashore out of control in Kowloon Dock area. The third pair were ordered not to attack, but by mischance (or deliberately) M.T.B. 26 did so and was sunk with all hands in the middle of the harbour. During these operations these craft came under fire from both sides of the harbour, and in the final stages enemy fighter aircraft joined in both attacking them with light bombs and with machine gun fire. Our casualties amounted to 50 per cent. It was not considered that adequate results would accrue from further attacks by day or by night, the harbour being full of wrecked shipping and underwater obstacles.

67. At 1000 hours, 19th December, Lieut Colonel J.L. Willcocks (who as previously arranged, was commanding the Defence Force around Stanley Prison of which he was Superintendent) reported that the Stanley platoon of prison officers was in its prepared position on Stanley Peninsula, covering the batteries.

68. At this juncture I conferred with Brigadier Wallis about the stabilisation of the position. The situation was that at 0800 hours the Royal Rifles of Canada were finding it difficult to maintain their positions on Mount Parker and they were attempting to hold the 6-in. Howitzer positions in that area, together with the R.A. personnel who had taken up local defence dispositions. Some of the R.A. personnel consisted of those from the .6-in Howitzer Section at Lyemun Gap which had been over-run. No British officer was available for this latter section. Owing to the lack of mobilization transport and the 40 ft. haul up to the road by winch, the guns had been abandoned and small parts removed.

These defensive positions round the Mount Parker 6-in. Howitzer position were obviously not adequate to act as a serious "stop" to the enemy. They had been hastily improvised, Mount Parker not being held by us, they were overlooked by high ground on two sides, and were only six hundred yards in front of the Combined Headquarters of East Infantry Brigade, the infantry battalion in the South East Sector, and R.A East Group. Infantry available for reinforcing in this area had been employed towards Mount Parker and were now out of touch. There was thus the grave danger if the enemy staged a serious attack here, of the loss of all these Headquarters and the cutting off of all the troops in the area Collins Battery – d'Aguilar Peninsula – Obelisk (illegible) included in which were the wireless personnel of the Civil Government at d'Aguilar Wireless Station. Accordingly I authorised Brigadier Wallis to withdraw his HQ to the Stonehill Company HQ and to time his withdrawal so that the last troops left the Tytam Gap area at I300 hours.

At II45 hours I9th December his HQ there closed down.

There was the possibility of carrying out offensive operations from the area of Red Hill and the Tytam Reservoirs and connecting up with Wong Nei Chong Gap when cleared. This would involve capture of the important features Mount Butler and Jardines Lookout. The enemy, so far as could be ascertained, was distributed in small groups on that line of high ground and it seemed to me doubtful if their total strength on the island was more than two battalions. It was realised that the alternative might be necessary, viz.: to operate via Repulse Bay area in order to link up with West Infantry Brigade. Shortly after noon a message was received from the Officer Commanding 2 Royal Scots that one company in a counter-attack had reached a point 200 yards northwards of Wong Nei Chong Gap shelters, where they were holding out with only thirteen effectives left. At this time the 3.7-in. Howitzer section at the Gauge Basin was engaging the enemy over open sights, which it continued to do until small arms fire prevented the service of the guns. One gun was brought away.

69. At II00 hours I ordered Lt.-Colonel G.R. Kidd to counter attack with two companies ("A"[15] and "D"[16] Companies) in an easterly direction from Leighton Hill to link up with "D" Company 5/7 Rajput Regt. and enable it to withdraw for more active employment. At the same time such an attack would cut in at the enemy's rear, thus limiting his exploitation and obstructing further landings and movements in and from the North Point area.

70. At II30 hours I9th December I was visited by H.E. The Governor and C.-in-C. who stressed the importance of fighting it out to the end however bad the military outlook might be. Every day gained was a direct help to the Empire war effort.

7I. At I300 hours a force of R.A.S.C. and details collected in the Pokfulum area, seventy strong, was moved to Bennets Hill to take up an emergency defensive position in case further exploitation by the enemy was attempted: then to move forward to the close support of the Winnipeg Grenadiers at Wong Nei Chong Gap. At I330 hours I issued orders for a general advance eastwards at I500 hours to reach as a first objective Middle Spur – Wong Nei Chong Reservoir – Clementis Ride and then to join up with the objective reached by the 2/I4 Punjab Regiment's counter attack already referred to in para. 69. The 2/I4 Punjab Regt. was to co-operate by exploiting Northwards to relieve the "Hughesiliers"[17] and others in the Power Station. The central axis of attack was to be Middle Gap – Wong Nei Chong Reservoir – Gauge Basin. 2 Royal Scots were to include Jardines Lookout. Only eight field guns were available to support this advance.

At about I630 hours I9th December I Middlesex Regt. reported that Leighton Hill was being heavily shelled, that "B" Company 5/7 Rajput Regt. was forward on their right and that Major Kampta Prasad's "B" Company 2/I4 Punjab Regt. was further to the right.[18] R.A. reported enemy in the Police Station at Wong Nei Chong Gap, on the ridge just to the North, and moving South of Wong Nei Chong Reservoir. From other reports it became clear that the general advance had not been successful and that the enemy was in greater strength than had been believed.

72. (*a*) At 1820 hours it became necessary to withdraw the crew from pillbox 53 at Causeway Bay (North East end) as it was isolated much in advance of the general line. The pillbox itself had been destroyed, the officer had been killed, and 50 per cent. of the crew had become casualties.

(*b*) Enemy transport vessels were still crossing the harbour and artillery action was taken.

73. (*a*) At 1900 hours the R.A.S.C. personnel at the transport pool at Repulse Bay were ordered to hold on to and defend their transport area and not to withdraw.

(*b*) At 2000 hours the party of R.A.S.C. moved forward from Bennets Hill. Its numbers had now been increased to about 150. The party, being unable to reach Wong Nei Chong Gap, joined the R.A.O.C. party at the Ridge.

(*c*) At 2000 hours 19th December it was reported that some of No. 3 Company HKVDC who had been surrounded in Jardines Lookout pillboxes, had managed to escape, after fighting all day, to the Blue Pool area. They were ordered to join 1 Middlesex Regt. at Leighton Hill which they did at 0800 hours next morning.

(*d*) At 2100 hours heavy mortar bombardment of the China Fleet Club area took place.

74. Just before midnight 19-20th December the Commissioner of Police reported that reliable secret information pointed to the likelihood of enemy landings in the Central District and Kennedy Town, and that Police patrols had been sent out. All military units concerned were warned.

75. The troops had now been in action eleven days with no respite. Owing to the shortage of hot food and sleep, and the impossibility of providing reliefs because of the lack of troops, signs of strain were beginning to appear. My A A resources were now very reduced – luckily only three raids of any intensity were carried out by the enemy during the day of the 19th, but the last raid on Stanley was very severe. Two Bofors guns were still in action but were powerless to prevent the enemy bombing selected targets. His bombing throughout was confined to day bombing and my A.A. searchlight detachments were never employed in their true role.

76. At 0135 hours the armoured cars of HKVDC at Wong Nei Chong Gap reported that they were in difficulties and had arranged for help from 2 Royal Scots, who had two companies in the close vicinity. In the meantime the Hong Kong Regt., HKSRA, reported that the enemy had been cleared from Wong Nei Chong Police Station.

At 0400 hours 20th December 2 Royal Scots estimated the enemy to be one battalion strong in the vicinity of Jardines Lookout.

North of Wong Nei Chong Gap the situation was as before, viz., a company of

2/I4 Punjab Regt. then "B" Company 5/7 Rajput Regt. then I Middlesex Regt. on Leighton Hill.

At 07I5 hours the Officer Commanding the Winnipeg Grenadiers reported that he was withdrawing troops from the Mount Nicholson area, as two companies[19] were distributed in many small units and needed reorganising for further employment, especially as they were much mixed up with 2 Royal Scots. He proposed to reorganise on the line held on the day before, viz , Middle Gap, thence South West to Cable Hill.

At 0745 hours it was learnt that the enemy had occupied the large garage at the Repulse Bay Hotel.

At 0800 hours 20th December the Royal Artillery reported two companies 2 Royal Scots digging in on North East slopes of Mount Nicholson.

The Commissioner of Police now reported that a party of enemy had discarded their uniform and had collected in houses in Happy Valley for, he thought, fifth column work. He proposed to round them up.

At about I000 hours the Officer Commanding I Middlesex Regt. reported that the crews of pillboxes I2, I3, and I5, which had been withdrawn to stiffen up the landward defences, were opposing an enemy advance on to Bennets Hill and that the enemy on Brick Hill were moving on Aberdeen. He reported that all pillboxes from Deepwater Bay to Repulse Bay were intact. The Officer Commanding the Winnipeg Grenadiers was authorised to withdraw his platoon from Aberdeen Island to assist in the main defensive positions.

77. At about I000 hours 20th December orders were issued to 2/I4 Punjab Regt. to send a company ("A" Company) to operate through Aberdeen and along Island Road to clear the enemy (estimated at thirty strong) from the Repulse Bay Hotel garage and to relieve the personnel there.

78. Repulse Bay Hotel. – At about 0930 hours Lt. Grounds, I Middlesex Regt., rang upon a civil telephone and reported that the Japanese had surrounded the Hotel. He was ordered to put the women and children on the lowest floor space and to make them lie down, to organise the defence himself and to take full charge with Lt. Tresidder, R.A.S.C., to assist. With him were two or three Royal Navy personnel[20], and his own Middlesex machine gunners. Lt Grounds did excellently until he was unfortunately killed whilst organising an attack on the isolated Hotel garage with the object of driving out a strong enemy party and rescuing HKVDC officers and others imprisoned there.

The area round the Hotel was not finally cleared till the afternoon, "A" Company Royal Rifles of Canada having arrived from the direction of Stone Hill and co-operating in the action. The enemy lost one officer and 25 men killed.

At about II00 hours 20th December a message was received that "A" Company 2/I4 Punjab Regt. had reached Aberdeen and was moving towards Shouson Hill, but during the day they could make no progress, as the enemy were in strength around that position, and the company itself numbered under thirty.

79. At I200 hours Fortress R.E. were re-organised into three sections – two covering Wanchai Gap, the third in reserve. They were ordered to support the Winnipeg Grenadiers in every way possible.

A Japanese monoplane flying over Stanley was hit, was obviously in trouble, lost height and was last seen low behind Lamma Island, and not re-appearing, may be presumed to be a casualty, giving a total of five enemy aircraft shot down during the battle.

80. At 1300 hours the Chinese crew deserted the A.A searchlight on Aberdeen Island. The five remaining British other ranks temporarily joined the nearest infantry unit.

81. – (i) During the morning several eye witnesses stated that Chinese planes had bombed Kowloon.

> (ii) Admiral Chan reported that General Yu Han Mou had wirelessed that 60,000 troops were at Sham Chun on the frontier and were about to attack.[21]

82. During the midday period 20th December the enemy continued pouring troops and material across the harbour in every type of craft. The North Point area and other likely points were accordingly engaged by our artillery.

In the morning Colonel H.B. Rose, M.C., Commanding HKVDC, was nominated as Commander West Brigade. Its role remained as heretofore – to clear the enemy from Wong Nei Chong Gap and to establish itself on the A.A. position on Stanley Gap high ground.

1400-1500 hours. The enemy were active behind the Repulse Bay Hotel, at Shouson and Bennets Hill, and along the road between Tytam Reservoir and the Gauge Basin. An enemy battery and two platoons deployed near Stanley Mound.

During the day Brigadier Wallis from his HQ at Stone Hill was continuously forward along the Repulse Bay Road endeavouring with Lieut-Colonel W.J. Home to force a way either West via Middle Spur or North via the gap to join up with the West Infantry Brigade. It was not known till later that the attempts were unsuccessful owing to the strength of the enemy.

At about 1700 hours the enemy was reported to have surrounded the civilian food stores (Little Hong Kong) and to be attacking again at Wong Nei Chong Gap, driving out a company of 2 Royal Scots and some Winnipeg Grenadiers. Some of the enemy moved up towards the high ground, Mount Nicholson.[22]

83. At about 1930 hours, 20th December, a counter attack, about which I had previously instructed Lieut.-Colonel J.L.R. Sutcliffe and planned for 1900 hours, was launched by a company of Winnipeg Grenadiers from Wanchai Gap, via Blacks Link to achieve the objects set out in para. 82 above, and to collect considerable numbers of wounded known to be at Wong Nei Chong Gap. Artillery support had been arranged but nothing was achieved, nor was the preliminary clearing of Mount Nicholson effected.

84. (a) Major C. Manners (retired R.A.) telephoned at about 1900 hours from Repulse Bay Hotel reporting that Canadian troops had arrived.

(b) At 1930 hours East Infantry Brigade was ordered to hold Repulse Bay Hotel at all costs, and Major Young, Royal Rifles of Canada, the Company

Commander there, was ordered direct from Fortress HQ to pay particular attention to strong patrolling that night. The company was 140 strong.

85. At 2000 hours, 20th December, the Senior Naval Officer Aberdeen reported that "A" Company 2/14 Punjab Regt. was still tied to the ground North of Brick Hill and that Major C.R. Boxer had been wounded – making the third General Staff Officer wounded in that locality that day. It was apparent that there was little chance of getting through to Repulse Bay from the Aberdeen side. (It was afterwards established that "A" Company2/14 Punjab Regt., only 25 strong, had tried every method of clearing the enemy from the strong pocket in which they were established with at least one machine gun and a light mortar.)

86. Serious fires were now reported in the Central District of Victoria and the Civil Fire Brigade asked for the assistance of troops which under the circumstances I was unable to provide.

87. (a) At 2230 hours I discussed the situation with Brigadier Wallis. A special reconnaissance patrol under Lieut. Bompas, R.A., had located two companies of enemy infantry working their way towards Repulse Bay Hotel, along the catchment from the East, during the afternoon. The road from Stanley to Repulse Bay was overlooked from the high ground Violet Hill and Middle Spur, with two hundred enemy in position, making the road unsafe. The Canadians could not get to Wong Nei Chong Gap by the routes tried this day. Brigadier Wallis considered the enemy to be in too great strength in the Hotel area to be turned out without proper artillery support, now a matter of great difficulty. He believed the enemy were not so strong in the Gauge Basin area and that another plan should be tried, but it was pouring with rain, visibility very bad, the men tired out and they had had little food. I ordered him

    (i) to hold what he had got,

    (ii) to press on to Wong Nei Chong Gap via Gauge Basin and

    (iii) to use Bren carriers boldly in reconnaissance.

(*b*) By midnight 20th-21st December two 3.7-in. Howitzers had been positioned near Stanley Prison with an observation post on the hill behind, i.e., to the South. These, together with one 18 pounder from a Beach Defence role (which had to be man-handled and could only fire over open sights from road locations), were the only remaining field pieces in East Infantry Brigade Commander's hands.

(*c*) Later Commander East Infantry Brigade said that the earliest his attack could be staged was 0900 hours. Contributing factors were.-

    (i) lack of transport and administrative facilities and

    (ii) delay caused by a virtual breakdown of unit communications. He was unable to help in the last mentioned item, for the Brigade reserve of signals equipment had already been used to replace this unit's signal equipment, lost on the previous night's positions.

88. The company of 2 Royal Scots – see foot note to para. 82 – was driven back in the early morning, exposing the flank of "B" Company 2/I4 Punjab Regt.

89. Commander West Infantry Brigade arranged for a fresh attack at 0700 hours by the Winnipeg Grenadiers to recapture Wong Nei Chong Gap "C" Company of that regiment was in position at 0300 hours at Middle Gap, though they reported that they had encountered a party of enemy whilst moving up, and had suffered a few casualties. The attack did not succeed.

90. At about 0700 hours 2Ist December Major Manners (see para. 84 (*a*)) rang up again from Repulse Bay Hotel. He said the defences appeared to be quite inadequate, and with the women and children in the Hotel helpless, he viewed the situation with extreme pessimism.

At 0725 hours Major Young at Repulse Bay Hotel was ordered to organise two strong patrols, to reconnoitre Westwards from the Hotel and to clear up the situation at the junction of Island Road with the road to Hong Kong, where some troops who were coming down from "The Ridge" Advance Ordnance Depot had been ambushed over-night.

At 0800 hours a review of the situation was received from Lt. Tresidder at Repulse Bay Hotel:-

Enemy estimated 450 strong on Stanley Mound and over-looking Repulse Bay with HQ at Wong Nei Chong Gap: they had three machine guns and a heavy mortar they had British and Chinese prisoners with them some of the enemy were Koreans.

9I. At about 0600 hours I Middlesex Regt. reported enemy attacking near pillbox I4 and on Brick Hill H.M.S "Cicala" (gunboat) was ordered to assist land operations in the Deepwater Bay area. Valuable close co-operation resulted.

This ship entered the bay and shelled enemy mortars and artillery, scoring hits. Unfortunately strong air action developed against her, and having been badly holed she withdrew and sank later in the Lamma channel.

92. Meanwhile (see para. 85) "A" Company of 2/I4 Punjab Regt had still made no head way and I ordered a senior officer to be sent at once from the battalion in Victoria. Lt.-Colonel Kidd elected to go himself and collected a few naval ratings in Aberdeen en route, but he was most regrettably killed when putting his own men in to the attack on Shouson Hill in order to clear that area. The attack failed with twenty-one casualties (out of a strength of twenty-five).

At 0900 hours 2Ist December Major H. Marsh reported from his machine gun company H.Q. at Little Hong Kong that the enemy could be seen moving from Wong Nei Chong Gap along the crest of the hill westwards. That matters in that area had not progressed favourably was evident when at I025 hours I learnt that out troops were being pushed back North of Blacks Link[23] and Mount Cameron. The Winnipeg Grenadiers now in positions on Mount Cameron were ordered to hold on at all costs.

93. A second air raid on the Peak District developed at 0950 hours and a bomb of 500 lbs. was dropped, amongst others, just below Jardines Corner, entirely blocking the road and cutting off communications with Volunteer HQ except by telephone, by which means the Observation Post Commander reported that forty steam launches in line, with steam up, were assembled two hundred yards off shore by Kai Tak

aerodrome. Unfortunately, at this time Royal Artillery communications to observation posts were destroyed except the one to High West, and from this observation post the target was invisible.

94. At I000 hours 2Ist December 2/I4 Punjab Regt. in the Garden Road – Kennedy Road area were ordered to re-orientate themselves to face South East to cover a possible break through from the Wanchai Gap direction. A section of machine guns was sent at once to connect up by fire with the Wanchai Gap dispositions, at which place were located the HQ of both West Infantry Brigade and the Winnipeg Grenadiers. At the same time all garrisons of 2/I4 Punjab pillboxes on the North shore were to be withdrawn to Battalion HQ – I had now to take considerable risks on other portions of the island defences in view of the direct menace from the Mount Cameron area.

95. By II00 hours the enemy had brought a heavy mortar into action just off King's Road near the Power Station, with which they bombarded the R.N. Yard. They also bombed Repulse Bay area and carried out a ground attack on the Little Hong Kong area from the direction of Aberdeen, thus threatening encirclement, at any rate temporarily, of that important area in which was located the new R.A.O.C. Magazine and the main bulk of the remaining ammunition stock. The enemy had landed some troops near Causeway Bay, and the housetops in that area were reported "crowded with them." At noon they were pressing down King's Road and had mounted a gun at No. I63. At this time all the guns, at the R.N. Yard were out of action, following a heavy bombardment.

96. (*a*) At midday 2Ist December our "line" ran from Little Hong Kong area to the Southern slopes of Mount Cameron. In the former area were located two parties under Major H. Marsh, I Middlesex Regt., and Major A.J. Dewar, R.A.S.C., respectively. Major Marsh had one officer (plus a R.A.M.C. officer), eighteen other ranks I Middlesex Regt., five men of the Winnipeg Grenadiers and fourteen Chinese of the Medium Detachment of the HKVDC, and was located in the "Combined Company HQ" of the defence sub sector – one company of the Winnipeg Grenadiers having been withdrawn for the Wong Nei Chong Gap counter attacks. Major A.J. Dewar, with twenty naval ratings, placed himself under the command of Major Marsh and was posted on the high ground (Shouson Hill private houses) covering the East flank. This "Island" of defence resisted all attacks from 20th December to the afternoon of 25th December and fought very gallantly, as did also a similar isolated detachment, viz , the administrative details on "The Ridge" under Lt.-Colonel R.A.P. Macpherson.

(*b*) During the course of the morning I had issued instructions to withdraw the Middlesex machine guns from the pillboxes between Sandy Bay and Aberdeen, and to put them on a mobile basis as far as possible: a platoon at a time could be "ferried," even though the transport situation was acute. The South West sector of the island defence was therefore completely denuded – another undesirable but necessary risk. A section of machine guns was now sent to supplement the defences in the Aberdeen – Bennets Hill area, under Commander H.C. Millet, R.N. (retd.). A platoon was also sent to the Officer Commanding I Middlesex Regt., for the Leighton Hill defences.

97. (*a*) Mortaring of North shore defences continued at 1300 hours 21st December, and pillboxes were subjected to accurate high velocity shell fire from both Kowloon and positions on their flank on the island. Pillbox 59, for instance received thirty direct hits, but the Middlesex sergeant in command personally upheld the defence, though withdrawing the crew temporarily.

(*b*) Enemy craft were still ferrying backwards and forwards between Kowloon and the Sugar Factory – North Point area.

(*c*) In the morning a motor torpedo boat had evacuated from Stanley the Commanding Officer of 5/7 Rajput Regt. and the remnants of his battle HQ, and he now took over command of the troops of 5/7 Rajput Regt. who were fighting alongside I Middlesex Regt.

98. *HKVDC.* (*a*) A report was received that No. I Company had had heavy casualties in the Stanley Mound area and had lost all their officers. The remains of the company had rallied at Stanley.

(*b*) The A.A. Lewis gun post of No. 6 Company (Portuguese) at "Watson's," Causeway Bay, reported that they had been captured by Japanese, disarmed, and told to make off towards our lines. They did so and rejoined for duty.

99. 1330 hours. A Japanese destroyer, escorting two merchant vessels, was sighted South of Cheung Chau Island, heading for Hong Kong.

100. 1430 hours. (*a*) Two companies of enemy occupied the whole length of Mount Nicholson, and brought up a small gun.

(*b*) A report was received from "A" Company Royal Rifles of Canada that the whole company had moved. One platoon had reached the "Ridge" and another platoon was on Middle Spur though the enemy were still firing from it. The situation at Repulse Bay being so unsatisfactory, I ordered a senior officer to be sent to take local command there. Major C.R. Templar, R.A. was selected. On arrival he collected two trucks, filled them with Canadian troops and went up towards Wong Nei Chong Gap.

101. At 1600 hours 21st December a telegram was received from the Military Attache, Chungking, that the main Chinese attack could not start before 1st January but "it was hoped that" twenty bombers would operate at once against Japanese aerodromes.

102. The question of the women and children at Repulse Bay Hotel now arose. It was difficult to give a satisfactory answer but I decided that the safest course would be to leave them there for the night. The situation was extremely "fluid," both in this area and the Little Hong Kong area.

103. After dark enemy landing craft operating near the R.N. Yard were fired on from pillboxes and passed West down the harbour, but no actual landing was attempted. Strong Police patrols were sent out in the Central and Western Districts for special reconnaissance to confirm this.

104. (*a*) During the day 21st December The Royal Rifles of Canada had been trying to force their way north-eastwards as planned – one company and carriers, with No

I Company Volunteer Machine Gunners in support, up the Tytam Road; a second Company directed across country on to Bridge Hill. These companies made a great effort, in spite of handicaps, but by the late afternoon could get no further forward than Red Hill – Bridge Hill, owing to considerable resistance by the enemy. Volunteer machine-gunners (Nos I and 2 Companies) rendered valuable forward support on this occasion.

(*b*) At 2030 hours 2Ist December Major C.R. Templar reported an unsuccessful attack on Wong Nei Chong Gap and that there were still about one hundred R.A.S.C. and R.A.O.C. on "The Ridge," with fifty Canadians in Altamira House. Further, that sixty to seventy Canadians were in Repulse Bay Hotel, round which sniping was continuing.

I05. At about midnight a cable was received from the War Office emphasising the need to destroy all oil installations. This was carried out by artillery fire on the next day (22nd). The Texaco tanks at Tsun Wan Wai, the Shell tanks at Tai Kok Tsui (next to Cosmopolitan Dock), and the R.N. tanks a mile to the South thereof, were all set well alight, but the Socony tanks[24] at Laichikok could not be shelled as they were close to the hospital establishment in the women's prison.

I06. (*a*) In the evening (2Ist December) the decision was taken to evacuate "The Ridge," and at about 2230 hours 8 officers and I20 other ranks left, trying at the same time to clear the catchwater in a southerly direction. This, however, failed under enemy machine gun fire. They sheltered for the night in "Overbays", a private house on the edge of Deepwater Bay.

(*b*) During the evening some Japanese managed to penetrate into the Repulse Bay Hotel but were evicted by prompt action initiated by Major Templar.

I07. Night 2I/22nd December. Enemy launches kept the North shore defences on the alert, but there were no attempted landings. Sniping occurred from houses round the Race Course and also in Victoria. The civil population observed the curfew well.

I08. In the morning the enemy opened heavy fire from Middle Spur and resumed operations on the high ground North of the Repulse Bay Hotel, and at I000 hours he was reported in possession of two large houses overlooking Deepwater Bay. At I030 hours 22nd December I placed Stanley Garrison under the direct orders of Brigadier Wallis. By now the intention of linking up East Infantry Brigade with West Infantry Brigade by moving westwards had perforce to be abandoned.

It may be noted that at this time the 3 7-in Howitzers at Stanley had only 45 rounds left in all. This was supplemented later when the provisioning of Stanley garrison was carried out by motor torpedo boats from Aberdeen.

In the meantime the enemy had cut off the water supply in Stanley by the capture of the Tytam Reservoir area machinery. For the forces in the Repulse area there was now only two days' supply of food and water. The evacuation of the civilians was still quite impracticable either by road or by water though I went into the question most carefully.

I09 (*a*) I030 hours 22nd December – Commander West Infantry Brigade reported that the Canadian troops in the Mount Cameron area were being heavily dive-bombed and mortared. They had no tools with which to dig in (although the rocky ground made this in any case almost impossible), no 3-in. mortars or bombs, there was no shelter, and there was nothing to do except stick it out with small arms fire from behind the rocks. These conditions applied in general to the subsequent fighting on the important high ground there.

Morale now had been seriously affected by the feeling that it was futile to continue resistance with insufficient equipment, with insufficient mobile artillery support, and without both air support and air observation.

(*b*) At this time, too, 2 Royal Scots were being heavily mortared from the ground near Jardines Lookout. The enemy seemed to have no difficulty in keeping up his ammunition supply across country from North Shore: and evidence was afterwards forthcoming that local Chinese were forcibly impressed as carriers. Much of the Japanese mortar ammunition, too, was of a much lighter nature than the British: one variety was 95 per cent. H.E., thus causing great moral effect, particularly valuable on un-seasoned troops in the opening phases of battle. The Japanese handling of mortars was extremely good. They were very quick into action; were quickly ranged, and accurate concentrations were put down at short notice at ranges of I,500 yards.

(*c*) By the early afternoon 22nd December the enemy was consolidating his positions on the northern lower slopes of Mount Nicholson within one hundred yards of the 2 Royal Scots forward defended localities.

(*d*) The Japanese air force at this time was extremely accurate.

II0. I400 hours. The enemy gradually advanced in the Repulse Bay area. An I8 pounder here, over open sights, knocked out some enemy mortars on Violet Hill. In addition the enemy was infiltrating southwards from the high ground "The Twins" and Notting Hill. The Royal Rifles of Canada's positions on Sugar Loaf and Stanley Mound were precarious.

Commander East Infantry Brigade telephoned that he was hoping to arrange the evacuation of the civilians from the Hotel this night.[25]

III. (*a*) During the morning I suggested to the Officer Commanding I Middlesex Regt. that he could not long hope to exercise control from so forward a position as Leighton Hill. At I600 hours very heavy mortar fire developed on this area. HQ I Middlesex Regt. accordingly withdrew and established itself in Hennessey Road, Wanchai – the densely populated area West of Mount Parish.

(*b*) The enemy launch traffic to North Shore, which had been going on all day, increased during the afternoon.

II2. In the afternoon 22nd December, Commander West Infantry Brigade considered from the information available that the enemy was concentrating between Little Hong Kong and Mount Cameron with a view to attacking North-West on Wanchai Gap. Counter measures were accordingly ordered by him.

II3. Meanwhile I had agreed to an adjustment of the line in the area of the Filter Beds. A gap existed between the right flank of the company of 2/I4 Punjab Regt. and the left of 2 Royal Scots, thus giving the enemy a line of attack towards the Race Course, in which area he was already active with fifth columnists. Such an attack would envelop the whole Leighton Hill area, turn the left flank of the 2 Royal Scots and cut straight in to Wanchai, and I had insufficient troops in hand to meet such a contingency. This adjustment was carried out without incident and the company of 2/I4 Punjab Regt. (only thirty-five strong) thus freed moved to the area South-East end of the Race Course, thus linking up with the 2 Royal Scots West of Mount Nicholson Camp. The Company Commander on arrival had, however, only eight men with two Light Automatics at his disposal, owing to casualties and dispersal of his men from enemy shelling in the darkness. The enemy attacked the company of 5/7 Rajput Regt. which remained in the area South-East end of the Race Course. Although this company was of a composite nature only – two platoons formed from the remains of "B" and "D" Companies – it held its ground successfully.

II4. During the day 22nd December Stanley Mound and Stanley Prison had been shelled and mortared, and at midnight I received news of the enemy capture of the Stanley Mound feature.

II5. The isolated troops at "Overbays" (see para. I06) had been in close contact with the enemy throughout the day and at about I930 hours the place was evacuated in an endeavour to join up at Repulse Bay Hotel. The majority succeeded in getting past the Japanese. A Warrant Officer of the R.A.O.C., however, telephoned to Fortress HQ at 2000 hours to say that he and four wounded were alone in the house. He was instructed to surrender. There was in point of fact (though this was unknown at the time) a party of thirty others upstairs. This party attempted to surrender at 0800 hours the following day (23rd December) but were hand-grenaded in their rooms and a number were bayoneted. Corporal Jeffery and six men escaped, leaving twenty-eight dead, including four Japanese, in the room. The Warrant Officer and the wounded on the ground floor were not seen alive after 2300 hours on the 22nd, and they were not amongst the eventual Prisoners of War. It can only be assumed that they were burned to death when the Japanese later fired the house.

II6. A serious report concerning the water supply came from the Director of Public Works at 0I00 hours. No water was coming from Tytam Reservoir, the Aberdeen supply was out of action for at least two days, and only a trickle was coming from Pokfulam. "The town (of Victoria) was now helpless." The fighting troops were also feeling the shortage of water.

II7. At about 0I30 hours Commander West Infantry Brigade reported the loss of Mount Cameron, that troops were coming back in disorder, and that an effort was being made to rally them at Magazine Gap and Mount Gough. Wanchai Gap was still held.

At 0345 hours 23rd December the Royal Engineers reported their rear party still in position on Mount Kellett and that the Winnipeg Grenadiers were being re-organised in the Gough Hill Police Station area.

At 0430 hours the Royal Engineers and 4 and 7 Companies H.K.V.D.C. were still in position, the Volunteers holding their original line in the area Magazine Gap which they had taken up three days previously.

A new R.A. (West) H.Q. was being established at Victoria Gap. At this critical time the Royal Navy offered valuable help – I officer and 40 men of the Royal Marines – who were ordered to Magazine Gap to report to the senior officer there (Lt.-Colonel F.D. Field, R.A.) for the purpose of clearing up the situation at Wanchai Gap, now out of touch.

At about 0600 hours it was reported that three platoons of the Royal Navy from Aberdeen had already moved forward to Bennets Hill to reinforce the machine gunners of I Middlesex Regt. already in position there.

By 0800 hours 23rd December Lt.-Colonel F.D. Field reported that he had got into touch with 2 Royal Scots at Wanchai Gap and he was instructed to send a fighting patrol to Mount Cameron to ascertain the situation there. It was learnt from him that "A" Company 2 Royal Scots was still in position near St. Albert's Convent, which had been occupied by us as a military hospital.

From now onwards until II00 hours many conflicting reports were received concerning Mount Cameron, but it was apparent that the crest of this commanding and important feature remained in enemy hands. Information indicated that the enemy's local HQ and organising centre was at Wong Nei Chong Gap, but owing to the configuration of the ground it was not possible to shell this over the top of Mount Nicholson, for the remaining sections of mobile artillery were in positions in the area Victoria Peak – Mount Gough – Mount Kellett. However I am confident that heavy casualties were inflicted on the enemy on the stretch of Blacks Link between Wong Nei Chong Gap and Middle Gap, for a 9.2-in. gun from Stanley had been engaging enemy in this area for the last two days with immediate observation from Shoushon Hill nearby. In addition Major H. Marsh had expended some 20,000 rounds from his medium machine guns on very good targets at ideal ranges. It was now learnt that two small ammunition convoys had got through to Little Hong Kong during the previous night and had returned successfully with much needed supplies. At this time Stanley was being supplied with ammunition by motor torpedo boat.

II8. Meanwhile the situation to the North was causing me considerable anxiety. The composite company of 5/7 Rajput Regt. much reduced in numbers and short of ammunition and food, had been forced to withdraw at about 0800 hours, exposing the right flank of the Middlesex Leighton Hill position held by Captain C.M. Man's "Z" Company. At 0922 hours he was holding on, though the enemy was infiltrating into the houses and streets around him. He had only forty men, with six machine guns. At I000 hours the enemy attacked him strongly, and heavily shelled the Bowrington area.

At II00 hours the bombardment again intensified and the positions of one machine gun platoon were completely destroyed. The guns, however, moved into the Lee Theatre to hold the North flank. At Fortress H.Q. fifty Royal Artillery and 2 Royal Scots personnel were collected and sent to reinforce I Middlesex Regt.

II9. At I000 hours 23rd December Commander East Infantry Brigade reported that a counter-attack on Stanley Mound had failed. The Royal Rifles of Canada had had heavy losses, the enemy were infiltrating and the Commanding Officer felt he must fall back. The Infantry Brigade was in the process of reconnoitring and organising three defensive positions in depth which were to be held to the last, the most northerly being well forward of Stanley Village. The Canadians felt that they could put up a better resistance on flatter ground, and on a narrower front, where communications would be simpler. The loss of the tactically important high ground was fully realised and very regrettable.

I20. At I000 hours the enemy were attacking Bennets Hill and bombing Aberdeen Dockyard, also A.A. positions in Victoria City.

I2I. At II30 hours HQ I Middlesex Regt. was forced to withdraw to a prepared position. At noon the line ran: – South-east corner Race Course to (exclusive) Leighton Hill (sixty men of 5/7 Rajput Regt.) – Leighton Hill and northwards (by I Middlesex Regt) to pillbox 55.

At about I500 hours the enemy attacked, but was beaten off.

I22. At I330 hours 23rd December communication was re-established with HQ West Infantry Brigade at Magazine Gap and it was learnt that about 250 enemy were round St. Albert's Convent, that our troops on the Northern slopes of Mount Cameron were withdrawing[26] and that Magazine Gap and Wanchai Gap were being heavily bombed. The positions at every "gap" were unenviable, for the nature of the country was such that local defence was bound to be restricted and confined to the gap itself, thus providing an excellent target for the enemy air force, which did not fail to take due advantage of the opportunity. These positions were originally prepared for limiting any enemy exploitation after a South shore landing.

At I430 hours our line ran from Bennets Hill to Wanchai Gap, and a patrol of 2 Royal Scots was going out to Mount Cameron.

I23. At I645 hours 23rd December the last Army W/T set was knocked out by shell fire, and communications with the United Kingdom and Singapore ceased except that military messages could be and were transmitted by Royal Navy W/T.

I24. At I730 hours communication was re-opened at HQ 2 Royal Scots at Wanchai Gap, who reported that they were holding the western slopes of Mount Cameron.

I25. With difficulty eight ammunition lorries had been collected and organised, and during the night six of these managed, with the help of an armoured car of the HKVDC, to get to the Ordnance Depot at Little Hong Kong and obtain some badly wanted gun and mortar ammunition. There were unfortunately no hand grenades there (they were in the other Reserve Depot at The Ridge), for these were now urgently needed in the street fighting which was developing in the area North of the Race Course.

I26. Morning (23/24th December) dispositions of West Infantry Brigade were – Brigade HQ Magazine Gap, HQ 2 Royal Scots and Winnipeg Grenadiers at Wanchai Gap, 2 Royal Scots still holding the West slopes of Mount Cameron and patrolling forward, Winnipeg Grenadiers holding down to Aberdeen Reservoir, Little Hong Kong area still holding out, 4 and 7 Companies HKVDC on the new line to which they had been moved (Mount Kellett to Mount Gough).

I27. – (*a*) At about 0400 hours 24th December the Royal Rifles of Canada were back on a line across Stanley Peninsula from near pillbox 27 on Tytam Bay, through St Stephens College buildings to West Bay, but the battalion required regrouping. A forward line had been formed through the Police Station manned by "B" and "D" companies I Middlesex Regiment, some H K.V.D.C., prison warders (enlisted as volunteers), and a few other personnel. The I Middlesex crews from the pillboxes in the area of Repulse Bay had been ordered to withdraw and had joined the Stanley Forces with all their machine guns, equipment and most of the small arms ammunition – a timely reinforcement and an excellent achievement.

(*b*) Brigadier Wallis assured me that Stanley Force were in good heart and that he was confident that if the enemy attacked his three lines of defence they would suffer heavily. He confirmed that he had enough food, water and ammunition, and I ordered him to fight on and not to surrender as long as these conditions prevailed.

I28. Information was received in the morning that the enemy held the central and southern portions of Mount Cameron, and that the Royal Scots were on the northern extremity.

At 09I5 hours the enemy had reinforced the northern portion of Mount Cameron where he was about 300 strong. The small party of Royal Marines (q.v. para II7) was now patrolling the spurs South of Mount Parish in touch with the 5/7 Rajput Regt. who had collected hospital discharges, etc , and formed a third platoon which had been positioned on the Mount Parish spur.

I29. Noon. – (*a*) One of the 6-in. Howitzers at Mount Austin was put out of action by bombing.

(*b*) Two enemy launches on the West side of the Kowloon Peninsula were set on fire by our artillery.

I30. At I400 hours 24th December about 200 enemy were seen working North West, and an attack developed at about I500 hours on Leighton Hill after a severe artillery and mortar bombardment, in addition to dive bombing. Attacked from three sides, the garrison was being rapidly surrounded when at I645 hours it was authorised to escape, if it could, through the streets leading North West to Canal Road. The two officers and 40 other ranks did so, losing 25 per cent. casualties. A most determined and valuable resistance had been put up on this position (and q.v. para. II8). These troops withdrew into and assisted the defensive area between Lee Theatre and the Canal Road, already occupied by the reinforcements mentioned in para. II8.

I3I. This evening a convoy plus an armoured car was again formed to obtain ammunition and bombs from Little Hong Kong. Accompanying the convoy were two trucks with reinforcements from 2 Royal Scots and I Middlesex Regt., plus two machine guns. It succeeded, though shot at repeatedly.

I32. I730 hours 24th December. – The patrol of the Royal Marines ascertained that no enemy was on the road North East of Wanchai Gap, and that 2 Royal Scots were at the Gap. Posts were to be established on the spur.

I33. At I800 hours Morrison Hill was heavily shelled. Holding this feature were detachments of I Middlesex Regt. with seven machine guns. All guns were reported knocked out but the majority of the crews escaped, having been withdrawn to nearby cover ready to repel an attack.

At I900 hours a party of thirty clerks, spare signallers, military police, etc, was formed at Fortress H.Q. and went under Major R.E. Moody, D.A.A.G., to assist the Officer Commanding I Middlesex Regt. This party, with a few others collected on the spot, held Morrison Hill until the afternoon of 25th December.

The enemy now had three guns in action on the water front near the Peninsular Hotel, Kowloon, and another battery at Tai Hang. At about I900 hours a large fire broke out on the water front near the China Fleet Club, hindering certain forward movements.

I34. At about 2200 hours reports from Aberdeen and Shouson Hill indicated a general move of the enemy from Mount Nicholson/Mount Cameron area northwards towards the Race Course. A possible intention, I considered, might be to turn West and join in the drive along the North face of the island, possibly with the left flank along the line of the "gaps" and the right flank just clear of Wanchai. This would strike a weak place where I had only the Royal Marines patrolling. In hand were less than a dozen men at H.Q of 2/I4 Punjab Regt. unless I drew on the two companies in positions covering Government House, Command H.Q., R.N Yard, Military Hospital, i.e., our last stand.

I35. Night 24/25th December. – Between 2200 and 2300 hours the Central District of Victoria came under a 3-in. Mortar bombardment – including the R.N. Yard, Victoria Barracks, and Fortress H.Q. Communications were not affected. The direction of the enemy advance on Wanchai made it possible that the enemy might use the A.R.P. tunnels for infiltration, and wardens were warned accordingly. The most important tunnels concerned were those under Mount Parish.

I36. At 2300 hours all units were sent such seasonal greetings as were possible from H.E. The Governor and from Fortress H.Q.

I37. Around midnight the enemy attacked in the area South of Wanchai Gap and effected a slight penetration.

I38. At 0I00 hours on Christmas Day Commander East Infantry Brigade reported a series of attacks on his positions at Stanley. The enemy had succeeded in getting behind some of the forward defended localities and were mopping up parties of H.K.V.D.C. at Stanley Police Station. I again instructed him to hold out till the last.

I39. The enemy continued pressure North of Aberdeen, reached the North slopes of Bennets Hill, and "dug in" there, at 0300 hours he was reported to be advancing again. At this time only one of the two 4.5-in. Howitzers at the "Sanatorium" remained in action.

I40. *Wanchai* – Before dawn 25th December a successful retaliation to the enemies' light infantry gun[27] was carried out. A Bofors A.A. gun was taken to a position just South of Morrison Hill and vigorous short range fire silenced the enemy activity in the sports pavilions immediately South of Canal Road. Many calls had been made on the Bofors detachments during the last few days. Besides their continuous day role they had also performed night roles, e.g., beach defence, replacing equipments disabled or knocked out, such as at Belchers Fort, in which area the infantry beach defences had been weakened by 95 per cent. in order to find troops for counter-attack.

By 0700 hours anti-tank mines had been laid in the main approaches to Wanchai from the East but enemy house to house infiltrations continued to be reported even as far West as the China Fleet Club. This report I discounted, but awkward fighting was developing, for I was unable to employ suitably the available artillery in this street fighting, apart from the desire to escape causing innumerable civilian casualties in such a congested area. The Japanese on the other hand, with their overwhelming superiority of artillery and noted carelessness for loss of life, had no hesitation in putting down in such areas heavy concentrations, with mortars super-imposed, lasting half an hour, and with a rate of fire comparable to those of the Great War.

At 0800 hours the enemy were on a front from the South end of Canal Road to the West arm of Causeway Bay, with snipers in houses further forward.

At 0830 hours, 25th December, the Royal Navy contributed a further small reinforcement which was placed at the disposal of the Officer Commanding I Middlesex Regt. (Lieut-Colonel H.W.M. Stewart, O.B.E., M.C.) who thereupon put in hand the building up of a second line running North from the Mount Parish area – Wanchai Market, O'Brien Street – to the water front ("O'Brien Street Line").

I4I. At daylight our troops were still holding the eastern slopes of Bennets Hill.

I42. At 0900 hours Major C.M. Manners (q.v. paras. 84 and 90) and Mr. A.L. Shields came across from the Japanese lines under a white flag. They had been told that they could talk freely. They informed me of their march with civilians of both sexes from Repulse Bay Hotel via Wong Nei Chong Gap to North point, of the "incredible" number of guns and troops seen during the last half of their "trek" and (in their opinion, *not* put forward by the Japanese) the uselessness of continuing the struggle.

A special defence meeting was immediately called, where it was decided that there could be no talk of surrender.

The Japanese Commander sent one message – that their forces would not initiate active hostilities for three hours. I conformed, including regretfully closing down on a promising counter-attack by Canadian troops on a large enemy "pocket" North-West of Bennets Hill. This impromptu "truce" was difficult to stage, for Japanese planes, operating from Canton, did not conform and bombed Stanley, Aberdeen and Mount Gough. Stanley was also shelled. A constant service of launches was maintained over Kowloon Bay and Japanese artillery continued bombarding the Gaps.

I43. At I030 hours the Royal Marines patrol (q.v. para. I32) reported having established contact with 2 Royal Scots at Wanchai Gap. This patrol had meanwhile been increased by thirty all ranks of Fortress R.E. who were reserved for a minor operation that night, i.e., the mopping up of an enemy post on Stubbs Road. At mid-day Japanese artillery opened up punctually on a large scale, and later hand to hand fighting was reported by 5/7 Rajput Regt. on Mount Parish, where a platoon was surrounded. Shortly afterwards Mount Parish fell into the enemy's hands, and an advance along Kennedy Road was threatened. This put Fortress HQ area, which had a garrison of only one platoon of 2/I4 Punjab Regt., in jeopardy. More road blocks and anti-tank mines were put out.

By I300 hours, 25th December, the 2nd ("O'Brien Street") line was established, held by some 60-70 men of I Middlesex Regt., including small parties of Royal Navy, Royal Engineers, and 5/7 Rajput Regt. The enemy was now in the Wanchai A.R.P. tunnels (q.v. para. I35) but about noon an I8 pounder gun had arrived there, which, mounted in the main street, covered several of the exits. A number of rounds were fired at these exits, more as a deterrent than anything else. No casualties were observed to have been caused, and no enemy emerged.

I44. Communications were increasingly difficult to maintain: between I100 and I200 hours there were none to Stanley area, Wanchai Gap and Magazine Gap, nor to the 2 Royal Scots.

I45. There were, at noon, only six guns of the mobile artillery left in action, with an average of I60 rounds per gun available.

I46. At I430 hours two officers and fifty other ranks of 2/I4 Punjab Regt. reached the Officer Commanding I Middlesex Regt., who had given warnings several times that his men, though in good heart, were being slowly but surely overwhelmed. A further withdrawal was enforced from the Canal Road area, and the "O'Brien Street line" became the forward active line of defence. HQ I Middlesex Regt. withdrew to Murray Barracks.

I47. Very heavy dive-bombing attacks were made in the Wanchai Gap area between I400 and I430 hours, and shortly afterwards this Gap was reported lost.

Magazine Gap was similarly attacked and incendiaries were dropped – most effectively, for the hillside was set on fire and field cables were burnt. A little later the Gap itself came under mortar and small arms fire, and Commander, West Infantry Brigade, reported that the area could not in his opinion be held for more than 24 hours at the most against a determined attack.

I48. At I450 hours the Officer Commanding I Middlesex Regt. reported that his forward positions were being shelled from both Kowloon and North Point and that Captain C.M. Man, the Officer Commanding "Z" Company, had telephoned "the line is breaking." Lt.-Colonel Stewart said he would try to form yet another line East of the R.N. Yard if necessary, i.e., just below, and to the North of, Fortress HQ. The "O'Brien Street line," if seriously attacked, could not hold out long – perhaps half an hour.

I49. I had no communications with East Infantry Brigade HQ at Stanley and consequently had no information.

As far as it was known, the force surrounded in Little Hong Kong Magazine area, was still holding out.

Bennets Hill had been heavily attacked, had been completely surrounded and by I500 hours had been forced to surrender. The Canadian line north of Bennets Hill had been forced to give ground.

I50. This advance by the enemy along the line of Gaps, the possession of these Gaps by him, thus giving him an open line of advance to the Central District, the fall of Bennets Hill, the isolation of the forces in Stanley, the deployment by the enemy of such superior forces and armament, the exhaustion after sixteen days of continuous battle with no reliefs for any individuals, our vulnerability to unlimited air attack, the impossibility of obtaining more ammunition for the few mobile guns I had remaining, the serious water famine immediately impending – these were the factors which led to the inevitable conclusion, namely, that further fighting meant the useless slaughter of the remainder of the garrison, risked severe retaliation on the large civilian population and could not affect the final outcome. The enemy drive along the North shore was decisive.

I asked Lt.-Colonel Stewart, the Officer Commanding I Middlesex Regt. how much longer in his considered opinion the men could hold the line now occupied. He replied "one hour."

The Commodore agreed with my conclusion.

At 1515 hours I advised H.E. The Governor and C.-in-C. that no further useful military resistance was possible and I then ordered all Commanding Officers to break off the fighting and to capitulate to the nearest Japanese Commander, as and when the enemy advanced and opportunity offered.

APPENDIX "B".

A SUMMARY OF APPROXIMATE CASUALTIES.

Officers.

Unit or Formation.	Killed or Died of Wounds	Missing.	Wounded.	Total Strength.
H.Q. China Command	2	2	3	33
H.Q. R.A.	-	I	-	6
8 Coast Regt R.A.	-	-	3	I9
I2 Coast Regt R.A.	I	I	I	I6
5 A.A. Regt R.A.	-	8	I	23
I Hong Kong Regt H.K.S.R.A.	3	7	3	24
965 Def Bty R.A.	-	-	I	3
22 Field Coy R.E.	-	I	-	7
40 Field Coy. R.E.	2	-	-	7
R.E. Services	-	I	I	I8
2 Royal Scots	I2	4	II	35
I Middlesex Regt	I0	2	4	36
Canadian Staff	2	4	3	I4
Winnipeg Grenadiers	6	8	I2	42
Royal Rifles of Canada	6	8	4	4I
5/7 Rajput Regt	6	4	7	I7
2/I4 Punjab Regt	3	-	5	I5
Royal Corps of Signals	I	-	-	7
R.A.O.C.	3	2	I	I5
R.A.S.C.	2	-	3	24
R.A.V.C.	-	-	-	2
R.A.M.C.	2	I	-	28
Royal Army Dental Corps	-	-	-	4
R.A.P.C.	-	-	-	5
Hong Kong Mule Corps	-	-	I	3
Indian Medical Services	-	I	-	5
H.K.V.D.C.	I3	6	I3	89
	74	6I	77	538
Total battle casualties	2I2			39.5 per cent.

British Other Ranks.

Unit or Formation.	Killed or Died of Wounds	Missing.	Wounded.	Total Strength.
8 Coast Regt. R.A.	I9	2	23	285
I2 Coast Regt R.A.	I5	2	24	200
5 A.A. Regt. R.A.	I6	II	I0	23I
I Hong Kong Regt H.K.S.R.A.	2	2	I0	30
965 Def. Bty R.A.	2	4	8	58
22 Field Coy. R.E.	8	20	9	2I3
40 Field Coy R.E.	2	7	I	220
R.E. Services	2	5	I	54
2 Royal Scots	96	45	I88	734
I Middlesex Regt.	94	25	II0	728
Canadian Staff	6	I0	5	78
Winnipeg Grenadiers	28	222	60	869
Royal Rifles of Canada	42	I57	I60	963
Royal Corps of Signals	I6	5	I4	I77
R.A.O.C.	I3	26	4	II7
R.A.S.C.	23	I0	II	I83
R.A.V.C.	2	-	-	3
R.A.M.C.	I3	3	3	I46
Royal Army Dental Corps	-	-	-	6
R.A.P.C.	-	-	2	25
Military Provost Staff Corps	-	I	-	3
Corps of Military Police	-	-	-	I8
Army Education Corps	-	-	-	8
H.K.V.D.C.	I96	I39	I35	1,296
	595	696	778	6,645
Total battle casualties	2,069			3I per cent

Indian Other ranks.

Unit or Formation.	Killed or Died of Wounds	Missing.	Total Wounded.	Strength.
8 Coast Regt. R.A.	-	I	4	233
I2 Coast Regt R.A.	3	-	3	I87
5 A.A. Regt. R.A.	24	80	I5	332
I Hong Kong Regt H.K.S.R.A.	I44	45	I03	830
965 Def. Bty. R.A.	2	-	4	86
5/7 Rajput Regt	I50	I09	I86	875
2/I4 Punjab Regt	52	69	I56	932
R.I.A.S.C.	-	-	I	I3
Hong Kong Mule Corps	I	5	5	250
I.M.D. and I.H.C.-	-	2	-	55
	376	3II	477	3,893
Total battle casualties	1,16			30 per cent.

NOTES

I. All figures are approximate as accurate information can only be obtained when the Casualty Bureau has all facts and figures.

2. The wounded does not include lightly, or returned for duty, wounded. The total wounded shown is I,332 but A.D.M.S. states that 2,000 wounded men passed through our hospitals alone, and many of the wounded of the 5/7 Rajput Regt. fell into Japanese hands and have not been recorded.

The final figures will probably be approximately-

	Killed or Died of Wounds	Missing	Wounded
Imperial Officers	74	595	
Imperial Other Ranks	6I	696	
Indian Other Ranks	376	3II	
	I,045	I,068	2,300

3. It has been impossible to collect any reliable data regarding the casualties suffered by the 450 locally enlisted Chinese.

4. Regarding Japanese casualties-

A local paper reported a Memorial Service held at Kai Tak Aerodrome to I,995 Japanese who fell in the attack on Hong Kong. That figure is certain to be an under rather than an over statement.

A Japanese Medical Major told me early in January I942, when I was appealing for assistance for my sick and wounded, that he had 9,000 wounded on his hands in Kowloon and on the Island.

Taking the wounded figure to be correct, and remembering that many must have been drowned on the assault on the Island, the averages of the last war should give about 3,000 and NOT I,995 killed.

The Japanese admitted in broadcasts and in conversation to me that they had suffered severe casualties.

The Chinese have stated that I0,000 were killed, but this is undoubtedly an oriental exaggeration.

True figures will never be known, but from the above a fair estimate can be made-

Killed	3,000
Wounded	9,000
Total	I2,000

And many of the latter died of their wounds, for funeral pyres near their hospitals were observed regularly for some months.

Footnotes

[1] The urgent necessity for speed called for this to be done in spite of it being a malarial time of the year. The 2 Royal Scots were in an area which was highly malarial and they had many cases. This weakened them considerably and, the hospital being full, many were sent back without the normal ten days convalescence. The battalion was 77I strong but only 600 effectives.

[2] Running North East from Tsun Wan Wai to Pineapple Pass.

[3] Killing both the Company Commanders concerned.

[4] Except that the Vehicular Ferry gave priority to all military vehicles and guns.

[5] At noon in Prince Edward Road an ammunition convoy of 2 Royal Scots was attacked; fifth columnists were in dark grey uniform and armed with rifles.

[6] Owing to shortness of time communications in the Devils Peak area were incomplete, but excellent work by Royal Signals provided efficient field cable circuits in time.

[7] Fifth columnists attacked the A.A. searchlight position at Sau Ki Wan this night.

[8] The Peak Observation Post was forced to move three times, for each location quickly came under heavy and accurate artillery fire in spite of every precaution for concealment. Treachery was certain but the source could not be ascertained.

[9] Near the Police Station, Braemar.

[10] It was subsequently ascertained that the Saiwan A.A. position was heavily shelled at 2I45 hours and Japanese troops rushed it at 2200 hours.

[11] Lieut. Carruthers was the sole survivor (HKVDC).

[12] No evidence has been obtained as to what happened to this company. It is believed to have reached Wong Nei Chong Gap at first light and to have been ambushed by superior Japanese forces, all remaining personnel being captured.

[13] After the capitulation a Japanese Staff Officer informed me that the Japanese had suffered very heavy casualties in this area.

[14] Lt. Gen. Kitajamma three weeks after the capitulation informed my Commander, Royal Artillery, of this fact. Our defences in the Mount Cameron area also noticed that at one period the enemy artillery fire seemed far more efficient, every round going off, and no "blinds" as customary. A map of artillery dispositions was also shown to the Commander, Royal Artillery, with three regimental artillery areas marked, indicating the employment of the artillery of three divisions.

[15] The "University Company" less a proportion of pillbox crews, total 45.

[16] Kennedy Road – China Fleet Club Company.

[17] It was afterwards ascertained that these orders did not reach Colonel Kidd and the two companies which at this time were still operating in the area East of Tai Hang. The spur was captured and occupied for some time but no trace of "D" Company 5/7 Rajput Regt. could be found.

[18] This was the company referred to in para. 63 (s). It was confirmed later that this company had earlier in the morning reached its objective successfully.

[19] One company had lost one platoon in a counter attack.

[20] These R.N. personnel had been manning the mine control station at Chung Am Kok.

[21] The following message was issued to all units – "There are indications that Chinese forces are advancing towards the frontier to our aid. All ranks must therefore hold their positions at all costs and look forward to only a few more days of strain."

[22] Nevertheless later in the evening this company of Royal Scots moved forward from the northern end of Mount Nicholson and occupied a position on the right of "B" Company 2/14 Punjab Regt. – q.v. paras. 71 and 76.

[23] Blacks Link – the track leading from Wong Nei Chong Gap to Wanchai Gap.

[24] A demolition scheme had been fully prepared, but the area was over-run too quickly on the morning of 11th December. Luckily this Depot was only half full.

[25] It was not practicable. The women and children fell into the hands of the Japanese when the troops evacuated at midnight on 23/24th December.

[26] It was not till some time later that this statement re withdrawal was found to be untrue.

[27] This was mounted on balloon type tyres, was about 3" calibre, was very boldly handled, and produced most effective results, both material and moral. Each battalion had two.

3

LIEUTENANT GENERAL ARTHUR PERCIVAL'S DESPATCH ON OPERATIONS

8 DECEMBER 1941 TO 15 FEBRUARY 1942

The War Office, 1948 .

OPERATIONS OF MALAYA COMMAND, FROM 8TH DECEMBER, 1941 TO 15TH FEBRUARY, 1942.

The following Despatch was submitted to the Secretary of State for War on 25th April, 1946, by LIEUT.-GENERAL A.E. PERCIVAL, C.B., D.S.O, O.B E., M.C., formerly General Officer Commanding Malaya.

FOREWORD

The preparation of this Despatch on the Operations in Malaya which took place between the 8th December, 1941, and the 15th February, 1942, has been influenced by the fact that since the conclusion of those operations a great deal of literature has appeared on the subject. Statements have been made and opinions expressed by writers, many of whom had but a cursory knowledge of Malayan conditions or of the factors which influenced decisions. Often these statements and opinions have been based on false or incomplete information. It has therefore become necessary, in the interests both of those who made the preparations for the campaign and of those who took part in it, that a full and comprehensive account should be given both of the operations themselves and of the events which led up to them. A knowledge of events in Malaya prior to the outbreak of hostilities in the Far East is also essential for a proper understanding of the conduct of the operations because the initial dispositions for the defence of Malaya were to a large extent dictated by those events. The Despatch therefore is more detailed than would otherwise have been the case.

2. The Malayan campaign had two novel features (*a*) It was the first large-scale campaign for a very long time to be fought within British or British-protected territory, and (*b*) It was our first experience of a campaign fought with modern weapons in jungle warfare conditions. Many lessons were learned from this campaign under both these headings and many more have been learned since in other theatres of war. In reading this Despatch it should be borne in mind that the knowledge which now exists was not at that time available to those responsible for the conduct of the operations, whose task it was in consequence to attempt to solve many new and novel problems.

3. The preparation of this Despatch after a period of four years has naturally presented certain difficulties, especially as some of the relevant documents were lost either by destruction at the time of the capitulation of Singapore or at sea or from other causes. Every possible endeavour has, however, been made to ensure accuracy by reference to such documents as are in existence, to individuals, and by other means. In particular I have had the advantage of being able to refer to such War Diaries as reached Home safely and also to a very detailed narrative of the operations compiled under my instructions by the late Lt.-Col. F.R.N. Cobley, the Loyal Regiment, while a prisoner-of-war in 1942 when memories were still fresh.

I believe, therefore, that the facts as presented are substantially correct.

PART I.

THE PERIOD PRIOR TO THE OUTBREAK OF HOSTILITIES WITH JAPAN.

SECTION I. – TOPOGRAPHY AND CLIMATE.

I. Malaya is some 400 miles long as the crow flies. The length of the main road and the west coast railway from Singapore to the Malaya – Thailand frontier is approximately 600 miles. The width of the country varies from about 200 miles in the widest part to about 60 miles in the narrowest. Singapore Island lies at the southern end of the peninsula and is separated from it by the narrow Straits of Johore. Malaya is bounded on all sides, except on the North, by sea.

The area of Malaya is approximately equal to that of England and Wales excluding the western Welsh counties and the Devon – Cornwall Peninsula. The Island of Singapore corresponds approximately in size and position to the Isle of Wight. The distance from Singapore to the Thai border is much the same as that from the Isle of Wight to the Tweed.

An extensive mountain range forms a backbone to the peninsula separating the western and eastern areas. There are only a few communications between West and East. Apart from this mountain range the country is for the most part low-lying and rather featureless except for a few small hills on Singapore Island.

2. Malaya is thickly covered with vegetation. Where the country has not been brought under cultivation it is covered with jungle. This jungle is of varying types. Some of it is dense and difficult to penetrate while in other parts it consists of heavy timber and, while providing cover from view, is little or no obstacle to the passage of animals or men. Of the cultivated areas the greatest part is planted with rubber. Rubber plantations, while providing good cover from the air, can easily be traversed by men on foot, by animals and in most places by light tracked vehicles. There are also coco-nut and other plantations. Rice is grown in the north of the peninsula, which is generally more open, and also in certain areas on the west Coast. In the centre and parts of the north there are rich tin-mining deposits, the working of which has resulted in more open areas. Except for the rice and tin-mining areas visibility is almost everywhere restricted to a hundred yards or even less.

The west coast area is much more developed and more thickly populated than is the east. Through it run the main road and rail communications linking Singapore with the North. There are also a coastal road, a number of lateral roads, especially in the central area, and branch railway lines linking the main line with coastal centres. The east coast railway branches from the main line at Gemas and, running east of the mountain range, strikes the coast in the State of Kelantan in north-east Malaya and then, running parallel to the coast, rejoins the main line at Haad-yai in Thailand. There are very few roads in the east coast area, the only ones of importance being those constructed to connect the ports of Mersing, Endau and Kuantan with the interior and the internal road system of the State of Kelantan. The only land communications between this latter State and the rest of Malaya are a single line railway and a fine-weather coastal track.

On the east coast there are good sandy beaches almost throughout. There are also some good stretches of sandy beach on the west coast, but a great deal of this coast line is covered by mangrove swamps.

Numerous rivers and streams, rising in the mountain range, traverse the coastal areas before reaching the sea. The largest of these is the River Perak in the northern part of the west coast area.

The Island of Penang lies off the west coast of Malaya some 350 miles as the crow flies, from Singapore.

To sum up, the country generally tends to restrict the power of artillery and of Armoured Fighting Vehicles. It places a premium on the skill and endurance of infantry. As is true of most types of close country, it favours the attacker.

3. The climate throughout Malaya is humid and enervating, though not unhealthy for normal people. The temperature, which is not excessive, varies little throughout the year. Similarly the rainfall, which comes mostly in tropical storms, is fairly evenly distributed throughout the year. Between April and September the wind blows from the south-west, and between October and March it blows from the north-east. During the latter period rough seas are at times encountered on the east coast.

The efficiency of Europeans who work at high pressure for long periods is liable to be affected unless periodical visits to places where the climate is more invigorating are possible. Malaya is a country where troops must be hard and acclimatized and where strict hygiene discipline must be observed if heavy casualties from exhaustion and sickness are to be avoided.

SECTION II. – THE FORM OF GOVERNMENT.

4. The form of government of Malaya was probably more complicated and less suited to war conditions than that of any other part of the British Empire. This resulted in the main from the way in which it had grown up. Broadly, it was divided into three parts, i.e.

(*a*) The Straits Settlements of Singapore, Malacca and Penang with Province Wellesley. These formed a British Colony and were administered from Singapore by the Governor acting through the Government of the Straits Settlements;

(*b*) The Federated Malay States of Perak, Selangor, Negri Sembilan and Pahang. These States were Malay territory and were governed by their own Sultans assisted by British Residents. They were federated for certain centralized services which were administered by a Federal Government at Kuala Lumpur. The Governor of the Straits Settlements was also High Commissioner for the Federated Malay States.

(*c*) The Unfederated Malay States of Johore, Trengganu, Kelantan, Kedah and Perlis. These States also were Malay territory, incorporated in the British Empire by separate treaties. They were governed by their own Sultans with each of whom was a British Adviser. The Governor of the Straits Settlements was also High Commissioner for these States, with each of which he communicated direct through a Secretary for the Unfederated Malay States.

In pan-Malayan matters the High Commissioner could not deal with the four Federated States as one entity. He had to consult each, either direct or through the Federal Secretariat. More often than not, he had to deal with ten separate bodies, i.e. the Colony plus the nine States, and sometimes with the Federal Government as well, making eleven. This naturally tended to cause delay when subjects affecting Malaya as a whole were under discussion.

5. The British Government had by various treaties promised to afford protection against external aggression to most, if not all, of these Malay States. This was a factor which had to be borne in mind in the conduct of the operations. In a country where there was so little national unity, it was natural that the Sultans should be inclined to consider the security of their own territory as of primary importance.

SECTION III. – THE HIGHER ORGANISATION FOR WAR.

6. Prior to the outbreak of World War II there was a Defence Committee Malaya, modelled on the Committee of Imperial Defence at Home. The Governor was chairman of the Central Committee, while the members were the Heads of the Fighting Services and the leading Civil Officials. The Secretary was at first an officer of the Malaya Command Headquarters. Later joint secretaries were appointed, one military and one civil.

There were a number of sub-committees. The members of these sub-committees were as a rule partly military and partly civil. In some cases, the secretary of the Central Committee acted also as secretary to these sub-committees; in other cases independent secretaries were appointed. A great deal of useful planning work, which was invaluable when war came, was done by these sub-committees.

7. On the outbreak of World War II the Defence Committee Malaya and its sub-committees were dissolved by order of the Governor and High Commissioner. In place of the Defence Committee was set up a War Committee, the chairman and members of which were practically the same as those of the Defence Committee. At a later date, however, some of the leading Unofficials also became members of this

War Committee. In 1941 meetings of this Committee were summoned by the Governor and High Commissioner as and when required. The Sub-Committees of the Defence Committee Malaya were replaced by controllers appointed by the Governor and High Commissioner.

A Secretary for Defence was appointed, responsible direct to the Governor and High Commissioner. Mr. Dawson, who held this appointment at the outbreak of war with Japan, had the confidence and respect of all.

8. Up to November 1940 the three Fighting Services worked independently, the commanders of the Army and Air Force being responsible direct to their own Ministries. The Senior Naval Officer at Singapore was originally responsible only for the sea defences of Singapore Island and for the local defence of the adjoining waters. Later he became, as Rear-Admiral, Malaya, responsible for all the coasts of Malaya. From July 1940 onwards, however, the Naval Commander-in-Chief, China Station, flew his flag on shore at Singapore and assumed responsibility for all the waters off the coasts of Malaya, except that the responsibility for those off Singapore Island was still delegated to the Rear-Admiral.

9. In October 1940 a Commander-in-Chief Far East was appointed, the position being filled by Air Chief Marshal Sir Robert Brooke-Popham. G.H.Q. Far East opened on the 18th November, 1940.

The C.-in-C. Far East was responsible to the Chiefs of Staff for operational control in Malaya, Burma and Hong Kong, and for the co-ordination of plans for the defence of these territories. He was informed that the two main principles to guide his actions were (*a*) It was the Government's policy to avoid war with Japan, (*b*) Reliance for the defence of the Far East was to be placed on Air Power until the fleet was available. He was further instructed that the G.O.C. Malaya was to continue to correspond with the War Office, on all matters on which he had hitherto dealt with it, to the fullest extent possible consistent with the exercise of his command.

The C.-in-C. Far East had no control over any naval forces nor did he have any administrative responsibility, the various Commands continuing to deal with their respective Ministries in this respect. The C.-in-C. Far East, therefore, had only a small operational staff and no administrative staff.

In conformity with the above instructions, the C.-in-C. Far East on assuming command issued the following instructions to his subordinate commanders:-

> "You will correspond direct with Headquarters Far East on questions of policy affecting strategy or operations. On other questions you will repeat to the C.-in-C. Far East such of your communications to the War Office etc. as you judge of sufficient importance."

10. On the 16th May 1941 I assumed the duties of G.O.C. Malaya Command. I had previously served as Chief of Staff Malaya Command (General Staff Officer 1st Grade) in 1936 and 1937. On taking over command I was informed of the general policy and of the instructions of the C.-in-C. Far East as recorded above.

At that time the Air Officer Commanding Far East was Air Vice-Marshal C.W.B. Pulford. He had taken over command only a short time previously.

The Commander-in-Chief China was Vice-Admiral Sir Geoffrey Layton. Rear-Admiral Drew was Rear-Admiral Malaya but was shortly afterwards succeeded by Rear-Admiral Spooner.

SECTION IV – THE LOCATION OF HEADQUARTERS.

II. The location of headquarters of the two Commanders-in-Chief and of the Fighting Services was a problem which received a great amount of attention but which was never satisfactorily settled. Probably there was no satisfactory solution.

In I936 the headquarters of the Naval Commander were in Singapore City. The Army headquarters were at Fort Canning, also in Singapore City, but those of the Royal Air Force were at Seletar on the north side of the Island. In order to improve co-operation, the then A.O.C. moved his headquarters into Singapore City, but about the same time the Naval headquarters were moved to the Naval Base on the north side of the island, to enable the commander to supervise better the rapid developments which were taking place there.

In order to ensure co-operation in war a bomb-proof battle headquarters was constructed at Fort Canning, where it was intended that the Combined Operations Staff of the three Services should work. This headquarters, however, was already too small by the time it was completed and, although it was occupied during the operations, it was never actually used for the purpose intended.

Shortly before the outbreak of war with Japan a new headquarters for the Royal Air Force was completed at Sime Road, near the Singapore Golf Club in the centre of the island. When war broke out a temporary Army headquarters was under construction on an adjoining site with a Combined Operations Room between the two. Here the Operations and Intelligence Staffs of Headquarters Malaya Command worked during the campaign except for the last few days. The Administrative Staff, partly because the temporary accommodation was not finished, and partly to be in closer touch with the Civil Government, remained at Fort Canning.

The Commander-in-Chief China, after moving to Singapore, established his headquarters at the Naval Base.

I2. When the Commander-in-Chief Far East was appointed, the problem of the location of headquarters again came to the front. If his headquarters had been located in the Singapore City area they would have been close to those of the Army and Air Force and of the Civil Government, but would have been separated from those of the Commander-in-Chief China with whom much preliminary planning had to be done. Also the Far East Combined Bureau (Intelligence) which came under the Commander-in-Chief China was located at the Naval Base. The Commander-in-Chief Far East was largely dependent on this bureau for his intelligence. He therefore decided to establish his headquarters at the Naval Base with the intention of moving to the Sime Road area should operations develop in Malaya. This is what actually happened.

I3. It will be seen that when hostilities started the headquarters of the Army, the

Royal Air Force and the Civil Government were grouped in one area, while those of the two Commanders-in-Chief and of the Rear-Admiral Malaya were grouped in another, some I0 miles or more apart. This was far from an ideal solution, but possibly the best under the circumstances.

This problem of the location of headquarters has been discussed at some length as showing the difficulties of reconciling the requirements of independent Services. Had there been at that time a Supreme Commander with an integrated staff probably many of these difficulties would have disappeared.

SECTION V – HEADQUARTERS MALAYA COMMAND.

I4. With the increase in the garrison as the defences developed and relations with Japan became more strained, so there was an increase in the strength of Headquarters Malaya Command. The senior General Staff Officer, who had been a 2nd Grade Staff Officer in I935, became a Brigadier in I940. The senior Administrative Staff Officer was a Brigadier i/c. Administration who, as is customary, was responsible to the War Office for control of expenditure on the administrative side. With the expansion of the Command in I94I, the "A" and "Q" Branches were separated, a Deputy Adjutant General being appointed as Head of the "A" Branch, while the Brigadier i/c Administration remained responsible for the "Q" Branch.

I5. After the outbreak of war with Germany the filling of vacancies on the staff became more and more difficult as the supply of trained staff officers in the Far East became exhausted. Regular units serving in Malaya were called upon to supply officers with qualifications for staff work until it became dangerous to weaken them any further, and selected officers were sent for a short course of training at Quetta. The supply of trained staff officers from Home was naturally limited by non-availability and by the difficulties of transportation. At the same time, even before war broke out with Japan, the work at Headquarters Malaya Command was particularly heavy, including as it did war plans and the preparation of a country for war in addition to the training and administration of a rapidly increasing garrison. In addition, the Command was responsible for placing orders to bring up to the approved scale the reserves of all supplies and stores, except as regards weapons and ammunition. In fact, Headquarters Malaya Command combined the functions of a local War Office and those of a Headquarters of a Field Force.

The Staff of Headquarters Malaya Command was a loyal and conscientious body of men who worked long hours under trying conditions.

I6. Authority for the raising of new units and for all increases in establishments had to be obtained from the War Office. With the pressure of war-time business it will be appreciated that delays occurred, some of which had serious consequences. An instance of this was the delay in connection with the raising of two additional Labour Companies which, owing to the shortage of labour in Malaya, became desirable in the autumn of I94I. All arrangements had been made for the raising of these companies at Hong Kong, but, as a result of delay in obtaining sanction, the outbreak of hostilities with Japan intervened and the project was rendered void. Their presence in Malaya during the campaign would have been of very great value.

In I94I sea voyages from the United Kingdom were taking 2-3 months so that there was a long delay in filling staff vacancies from Home even after approval had been given. In consequence, the strength of Headquarters Malaya Command was usually much below establishment. When war with Japan broke out there were less than 70 officers at Headquarters Malay Command, including the Headquarters of the Services. This is about the war-time establishment of the Headquarters of a Corps. Our resources were thus strained to the limit.

I7. It should be realized that the G.O.C. Malaya did not have a free hand in developing the defences of Malaya. In principle, the defences were developed in accordance with a War Office plan which was modified from time to time in accordance with recommendations made by the G.O.C.

By the beginning of I94I the overall estimated cost of the War Office scheme had amounted to slightly over £5 million, and actual expenditure to 3Ist March, I94I, was over £4 million. Although originally the defence items were mainly in respect of coast artillery and fixed defences the scheme was later expanded to include services on landward defences. Such expansions of the main scheme had to receive War Office and Treasury approval and though they were submitted as major services, this entailed delay. On the IIth December, I94I, when Malaya became an active theatre of operations, the War Office gave the G.O.C. Malaya a free hand with regard to such expenditure.

In circumstances such as those which existed after the outbreak of World War II it is recommended that very much wider powers should be delegated to General Officers Commanding in important potential theatres, who would naturally act in consultation with their Financial Advisers.

SECTION VI – THE DEFENCE PLAN.

I8. It cannot be too strongly stressed that the object of the defence was the protection of the Naval Base, and later of the Air Bases also, at Singapore.

I9. *The Initial Plan of Defence* – When in I92I it was decided to build a Naval Base at Singapore, it was considered that the security of that base depended ultimately on the ability of the British Fleet to control sea communications in the approaches to Singapore. This it would doubtless have been able to do as soon as it had been concentrated in the Far East. For success, therefore, the Japanese would have had to depend on a "coup-de-main" attack direct on to the Island of Singapore. At that time the range of military aircraft was limited and it was considered that the only area suitable for the operation of shore-based aircraft against Singapore was a strip of land in the vicinity of Mersing on the East coast of Johore. Further, the long sea voyage from Japanese territory would both have limited the size of the expedition and greatly prejudiced the chances of obtaining surprise. It was against this type of attack that the defences were initially laid out. The problem was one mainly of the defence of

Singapore Island and the adjoining waters. For this a comparatively small garrison only was required.

20. *The Influence of Air Power.* – The rapid development of Air Power greatly affected the problem of defence. Singapore became exposed to attack by carrier-borne and shore-based aircraft operating from much greater distances than had previously been considered possible. Similarly our own defence aircraft were able to reconnoitre and strike at the enemy at a much greater distance from our own shores.

In May, 1932, the Sub-Committee of the Committee of Imperial Defence, after considering the relative merits of the gun and of aircraft for the defence of fortresses, laid down:

(*a*) Coast defences should be organized on the basis of co-operation between the three Defence Services, the gun retaining its place as the main deterrent against naval attack.

(*b*) The first stage of the plan of defence for the Naval Base at Singapore, modified in the light of the latest developments in coast artillery, should be proceeded with. . . . The second stage should await a further recommendation by the Committee of Imperial Defence.

(*c*) The Royal Air Force should continue to co-operate in the defence of Singapore with such forces as might from time to time be considered desirable. Such co-operation should extend to all branches of the defence, including A.A. Defence (Fighters) and offensive operations against aircraft carriers, capital ships and other forms of attack by sea, land and air.

In April, 1933, as a result of Japan's withdrawal from the League of Nations, the Cabinet decided that immediate steps should be taken to increase the defences of Singapore.

As a result of these decisions the question of the location of aerodromes arose. At that time the only Royal Air Force aerodrome was at Seletar on Singapore Island. The construction of two further aerodromes on Singapore Island was immediately taken in hand. Further, in order to obtain the greatest possible value from the range of aircraft, it was urged that new aerodromes should be constructed on the east coast, an area which it had up till then been the policy to leave as undeveloped as possible, consistent with civil requirements, so as to present the enemy with difficult transportation problems should he land on that coast. It was obvious from the start that these aerodromes, if constructed on the east coast, would present the Army with fresh commitments for their defence – commitments which the existing garrison would be quite unable to meet. The danger of constructing aerodromes in an area where the defence forces might not be strong enough to prevent them falling into the hands of the enemy was also obvious. The Army urged that the policy of the development of air facilities on the east coast, with all the military difficulties which it involved, should only be accepted if a guarantee could be given that, in the event of an attack on Malaya, sufficient modern aircraft would be available to operate from those aerodromes. To ensure this, it was felt that there should in any case be a strong

Air Force cadre permanently established in the Far East, and that it was unsafe to rely on the mobility of aircraft to concentrate adequate strength there from other parts of the Empire when danger threatened. On the other hand, the siting of the aerodromes was complicated by the fact that the aircraft at that time available in Malaya had a very limited range, and also by the fact that weather conditions sometimes made it difficult to fly over the central mountain range, so that it was undesirable to rely on aircraft based on the west coast for operations off the east coast. The result of this was that, when war with Japan broke out, three aerodromes had been constructed in the State of Kelantan and a further one at Kuantan, and a landing ground at Kahang in Eastern Johore. Although these were strategically well placed for air operations, they were quite inadequately defended either by land or air forces.

In 1936 it was decided to fortify the Island of Penang, though the approved scale of equipment was not immediately available.

21. *The Influence of World Politics.* – In 1937 the defence policy was still based on the fundamental assumption that the British fleet would sail from Home waters immediately on the outbreak of war with Japan and would arrive at Singapore within a maximum of 70 days. It was further assumed that the arrival of the fleet in the Far East would automatically put an end to any danger of the capture of Singapore. It followed from these assumptions that the defence plan only had to provide against such types of operations as the Japanese might hope to complete successfully within 70 days and that the role of the garrison was confined to holding out for that period.

In November, 1937, having, as G.S.O.I. Malaya, made a careful study of the problem of the defence of Singapore, I prepared on the instructions of the General Officer Commanding (Major-General, now Lieut.-General Sir W.G.S. Dobbie) an appreciation and plan for an attack on that place from the point of view of the Japanese. In this appreciation it was pointed out (*a*) that, as a result of the political situation in Europe, it was unlikely that the British Fleet would be able to reach Singapore in 70 days, (*b*) that in consequence, a more deliberate form of attack could be undertaken. The plan recommended consisted of preliminary operations to seize the aerodromes in South Thailand and in Kelantan, the Island of Penang and the naval and air facilities in Borneo, followed by the main operation to capture Singapore itself. From this appreciation deductions were made as to the main points in the defence plan which required attention. These deductions stressed the probability of the Japanese making use of territory in South Thailand, the increased importance of the defence of North Malaya and of Johore, the urgent need for the strengthening of our Air Forces and Local Naval Craft, and for more infantry, and the unsatisfactory situation as regards food stocks. A copy of the deductions made is attached as Appendix A to this Despatch. The Appreciation and deductions were forwarded by the G.O.C. to the War Office.

In May, 1938, General Dobbie in another appreciation of the defence problem wrote:

"It is an attack from the northward that I regard as the greatest potential danger to the fortress. Such attack could be carried out during the period of the north-east monsoon. The jungle is not in most places impassable for infantry."

He further stated that defensive positions were being reconnoitred on the general line Johore River – Kota Tinggi – Kulai – Pulai River. Subsequently defences were constructed on the west bank of the river north and south of Kota Tinggi.

22. *Development of the Defence Plan.* – Up to the summer of 1939 the defence policy continued to be based on the assumption that the British Fleet would sail from Home waters immediately on the outbreak of war with Japan whatever the situation in Europe might be. It was then, however, officially recognized that this might not be possible. The "Period before Relief" was increased from 70 to 180 days and authority given for reserves to be built up on that scale. In August, 1939, the 12th Indian Infantry Brigade Group, which had been held in readiness for this purpose, was, in view of the threatening political situation, despatched from India to Malaya.

23. In April, 1940, the G.O.C., (Lt.-Gen. Sir Lionel Bond) submitted a new appreciation in the light of the new situation and especially of the increase of the period before relief from 70 to 180 days. In it he pointed out that the Japanese could now afford to establish their base at a much greater distance from Singapore and possibly in South Thailand. He considered therefore that the northern frontier might have to be held against a considerable force for several months. He estimated that the forces now required for the defence of Malaya were of the order of 40 battalions (say 4 divisions) with 3 machine gun battalions and 2 tank regiments. He realised that it would be impossible at that time to provide this force, and suggested, as an alternative, that the Royal Air Force "could and should be made absolutely responsible, if not for the detection and destruction of a Japanese expedition before it landed, at least for ensuring that no base can be maintained and no line of communication can be operated within striking distance of our aerodromes." If this could be done, he estimated that the land forces then required would be in the nature of 25 battalions with supporting arms, which should include 3 anti-tank batteries and one company of armoured cars or tanks.

It was at this time that the problem, which had hitherto remained one of the defence of Singapore Island and of a portion of Johore, developed, as had appeared inevitable as early as 1937, into one of the defence of the whole of Malaya. The G.O.C. asked for official confirmation of this. The problem was further complicated by the collapse of France in June, 1940, the immediate result of which was that Malaya was exposed to a greatly increased scale of attack.

24. In August, 1940, the Chiefs of Staff, in their Far East Appreciation, officially recognised that both the fundamental assumptions of the C.I.D. 1937 Appreciation had broken down because it was now impossible to send the Fleet to the Far East, and the Japanese advance southward, the development of communications and of aerodromes in Thailand, and the increased range of aircraft, had all contributed to the development of the overland threat to Malaya. The necessity for holding the whole of Malaya, with reliance primarily on Air Power, was now recognised. It was laid down that the role of the land forces was to be (*a*) The close defence of the naval and air bases, (*b*) Internal security, (*c*) To deal with any enemy land forces which might succeed in gaining a footing despite the action of the Air Force. Until the necessary air forces could be provided, their absence must be made up for as far as possible by

the provision of additional land forces. It was estimated that a minimum of 336 Ist Line aircraft would be required for the defence of Malaya and British Borneo, and for trade protection in the north east half of the Indian Ocean. It was laid down that the aim should be to complete this programme by the end of 1941. It was considered that, when this target was reached, the total land garrison required would be the equivalent of 6 brigades with ancillary troops. Meanwhile approximately three divisions would be necessary. It is to be noted that this appreciation was made before the entry of the Japanese into Indo-China. The Commanders in Singapore were instructed to make a tactical appreciation based on the Chiefs of Staff strategical appreciation.

25. In September, 1940, the Japanese occupied the northern portion of Indo-China, thereby greatly increasing the threat to Singapore. In fact, the whole conception of the defence problem had again been changed because a Japanese invading force, instead of having to be transported all the way from Japan, could now be concentrated and prepared within close striking distance of Malaya.

26. The tactical appreciation asked for was prepared by the Commander-in-Chief, China, General Officer Commanding, Malaya, and Air Officer Commanding, Far East. It was reviewed and endorsed by the Singapore Defence Conference held in October, 1940, attended by representatives of Australia, New Zealand, India and Burma, and by one American observer. It was estimated that 566 Ist Line aircraft would now be required and that, when this target was reached, the strength of the land forces should be 26 battalions with supporting arms, ancillary services, etc. The Army estimate was accepted by the Chiefs of Staff who, however, declined to increase the previously approved air scale. The general situation and war plans were further discussed at staff conversations with officers from the Dutch East Indies on 25-29th November, 1940,at a conference with Dutch and Australian representatives and United States observers in February, 1941 ("A.D.A. Conference"), and at a full conference with American and Dutch (as well as Dominion) representatives in April, 1941 ("A.D.B. Conference").

27. Further reinforcements now began to arrive in Malaya. In August, 1940, two British battalions arrived from Shanghai on the evacuation of the latter place and in October and November, 1940, the 6 and 8 Indian Infantry Brigades, both of the II Indian Division (Major-General Murray Lyon) reached Malaya. In February, 1941, the first contingent of the Australian Imperial Force arrived. It consisted of the Headquarters and Services of the 8 Australian Division (Major-General Gordon Bennett) with the 22 Australian Infantry Brigade Group. In March, 1941, the 15 Indian Infantry Brigade and the Ist Echelon of the 9 Indian Division (Major-General Barstow) arrived from India and one Field Regiment from the U.K., followed in April by the 22 Indian Infantry Brigade also of the 9 Indian Division. In May the Ist Echelon of Headquarters 3 Indian Corps (Lt.-Gen. Sir Lewis Heath) arrived and was located at Kuala Lumpur. It took over the 9 and II Indian Divisions, the Penang Fortress and the F.M.S. Volunteers. Some readjustment of formations in the two Indian Divisions had previously been made.

28. *The Disposition of Troops, May,* 1941. – The disposition of the troops at the end of May, 1941, shortly after I took over the Command, was as under:-

(*a*) Northern Area: – 3 Indian Corps, distributed as under:-

East Coast Sub-Area: 9 Indian Division (of two Brigade Groups only) less one Infantry battalion. In the Kelantan area was 8 Indian Infantry Brigade with attached troops (Brigadier Key) and in the Kuantan Area 22 Indian Infantry Brigade (less one battalion) with attached troops (Brigadier Painter).

Northern Sub-Area: II Indian Division (of two Brigade Groups only). Headquarters and 15 Brigade Group (Brigadier Garrett) were at Sungei Patani in South Kedah, the 6 Brigade Group (Brigadier Lay) less one Infantry battalion was at Tanjong Pau Camp in North Kedah, and there was one Infantry battalion each in Perlis, Penang and at Kroh on the Thailand frontier in North Perak.

Penang: The Penang Garrison (Brigadier Lyon) consisted of one Infantry Volunteer battalion, two 6-in. batteries with searchlights, some Royal Engineer and administrative units. The remaining equipment for the Fixed Defences had not arrived and there were no Anti-Aircraft defences.

Lines of Communication: The L. of C. Area consisted of that part of the west coast area which lay south of the River Perak. The Commander was Brigadier Moir, who was also Commandant of the Federated Malay States Volunteer Force.

Corps Reserve: In Corps Reserve was one Infantry battalion situated at Mantin Camp south of Kuala Lumpur.

Federated Malay States Volunteer Force. – This force, which consisted of four Infantry battalions and some supporting units, was not yet mobilized.

The Commander 3 Indian Corps was responsible for the whole of Malaya north of Johore and Malacca and for the Island of Penang.

(*b*) *Singapore Island and Eastern Johore.* – The Singapore Fortress Troops (Major-

General Keith Simmons) consisted of:-

The Fixed Defences (Brigadier Curtis) which were divided into two Fire Commands, i.e The Changi Fire Command which covered the approaches to the Naval Base, and the Faber Fire Command which covered the approaches to Keppel Harbour and to the western channel of the Johore Straits. In each Fire Command was one 15 in. and one 9.2 in. battery and a number of 6 in. batteries; also searchlights and smaller equipments.

The Anti-Aircraft Defences (Brigadier Wildey). – These Defences, which included both guns and searchlights, had been built up over a number of years under War Office direction. Most of the guns were of the static type but a few tractors were available. The defences had been sited on Singapore Island and in Southern Johore to protect the Naval Base and other important installations in the Singapore Fortress area. There were three Anti-Aircraft Regiments, one Light Anti-Aircraft Regiment, and one Searchlight Regiment.

Field Troops. – There were three Infantry Brigades, one Field Regiment and one Field Company, etc. The I Malaya Infantry Brigade (Brigadier Williams) of two battalions only and the 2 Malaya Infantry Brigade (Brigadier Fraser) were responsible for the defence of the beaches on the south coast of Singapore Island and at Pengerang in Southern Johore. The I2 Indian Brigade Group was responsible for the defence of the east coast of Johore.

Fortress Troops. – There were also a number of Fortress units, i.e. Fortress Companies, Royal Engineers, etc.

Straits Settlement Volunteer Force (less the Penang Bn.) – This Force, strength about a weak Brigade Group, was not yet mobilized. It was allotted a role in the defence of Singapore Town.

Command Headquarters and Base Units. – In addition to the troops directly under his command, the Commander Singapore Fortress was responsible for the administration of the Command Headquarters and Base units located in the Singapore Island area.

(c) Malaya Command Reserve. – The A.I.F. (8 Australian Division less two Infantry brigade groups) was in Command Reserve. It was located in the Malacca/Negri Sembilan area with Headquarters at Kuala Lumpur. It was to be prepared to operate anywhere in Malaya, and for this purpose officers of the A.I.F. were ordered to carry out reconnaissances of the areas where operations were most likely to take place.

(*d*) Borneo. – One Infantry Battalion (less one company at Miri), with some Local Forces and administrative units attached, was stationed at Kuching in the State of Sarawak. Its task was to protect the aerodrome under construction there for the use of our Air Force and to deny it to the enemy.

There was also a small infantry and engineer detachment at Miri, where two 6 in. guns had been installed. Its task was to destroy the oil fields and installations, if necessary to prevent them falling into the hands of the enemy.

(*e*) Christmas Island. – There was a small coast artillery detachment at Christmas Island, whose task was to protect the phosphate deposits there.

(*f*) Indian State Forces Units. – There were also in Malaya several State Forces units from the Indian States. They varied greatly in training, strength and efficiency. Being without transport and more suitable for a static role, they were employed principally on aerodrome defence, coming under the commanders of the areas in which they were situated.

The above dispositions were in accordance with the role of the land forces as laid down in the Chiefs of Staff Appreciation of August 1940 already referred to. The commanders of the various forces were given written instructions as to their role and the action to be taken in certain eventualities.

29. *The Advance into Thailand.* – Before leaving London I discussed on broad lines a proposal which was then under consideration to advance into South Thailand if a favourable opportunity presented itself. Immediately after taking over command I was instructed by the C.-in-C. Far East to give this matter my further detailed consideration. It was also discussed on several occasions at conferences. The operation was known as MATADOR. I was informed that it could not be carried out without reference to London since MATADOR could only be put into effect if and when it became clear beyond all reasonable doubt that an enemy expedition was approaching the shores of Thailand. As time would then be the essence of the problem it appeared almost certain that, by the time permission had been asked for and obtained, the favourable opportunity would have passed.

The military advantages of the occupation of South Thailand, or of part of it, were great. It would enable us to meet the enemy on the beaches instead of allowing him to land and establish himself unopposed, it would provide our Air Force with additional aerodromes and, by denying these aerodromes to the enemy, it would make it far more difficult for his Air Force to interfere with our sea communications in the Malacca Straits. It was a question, however, whether it was a sound operation with the meagre resources available. No troops could be spared for the operation other than the II Indian Division, strengthened by some administrative units. The proposal to occupy the narrow neck of the Kra Isthmus was rejected as being too ambitious and the discussions centred round the occupation and denial to the enemy of the Port of Singora and the aerodromes at Singora and Patani.

The following factors, among others, had to be considered:

(*a*) The Thai Government had stated publicly that it would defend its territory against the invasion of any foreign troops. Therefore opposition, even if slight, was to be expected.

(*b*) All the main bridges on the road between the Thailand frontier and Haad 'yai Junction were in process of reconstruction. Therefore time and material might be required for their repair.

(*c*) Large quantities of M.T. would be required to mechanize the road parties of the force and to keep it supplied.

(*d*) The psychological effect of offensive action would be considerable, but this had to be weighed against the possibilities of an encounter battle and the loss of prepared ground.

(*e*) An enemy landing would certainly be supported by tanks, of which we had none. It was noted also that during the period of the North-East Monsoon, i.e. October-March, the country on the east coast is wet, and therefore, less suited to tank action, while on the, west coast it is comparatively dry.

After careful examination of the problem, it was decided:

(*a*) That, provided a favourable opportunity presented itself, the operation MATADOR would be put into effect during the period October-March.

(*b*) That it would take the form of (i) an advance by road and rail to capture Singora and hold a defensive position north of Haad 'yai Junction, and (ii) an advance from Kroh to a defensive position, known as The Ledge position, on the Kroh – Patani road some 35-40 miles on the Thailand side of the frontier. The reason for this limited objective on the Kroh front was lack of resources, both operational and administrative.

(*c*) That at least 24 hours start was required before the anticipated time of a Japanese landing.

Detailed plans were worked out and preparations made for this operation. Maps were printed, money in Thai currency was made available and pamphlets for distribution to the Thais were drafted though, to preserve secrecy, the printing of them was deferred till the last minute.

By a special arrangement made by the C.-in-C. Far East, authority was obtained for a limited number of officers in plain clothes to carry out reconnaissances in South Thailand. In all 30 officers, including some of the most senior officers, were able to visit Thailand in this way. They frequently met Japanese officers who were presumably on a similar mission.

On the 5th December, 194I, I was informed by the C.-in-C. Far East that, in accordance with the terms of a telegram just received from London, MATADOR could thenceforward be put into effect without reference to London (*a*) if the C.-in-C. Far East had information that a Japanese expedition was advancing with the apparent intention of landing on the Kra Isthmus, or (*b*) if the Japanese violated any other part of Thailand.

30. *The Northern Frontier.* – One of the first problems to which I turned my attention was the defence of the Northern frontier. Excluding the Kelantan frontier, which will be referred to later, the Malaya – Thailand frontier was crossed by only two roads and one railway, but there were in addition a number of bush tracks. The main road from Alor Star in Kedah to Haad 'yai in South Thailand and thence to Singora crossed the frontier a few miles north of Changlun. A secondary road, running eastward through Province Wellesley and South Kedah, crossed the frontier at Kroh and then continued via Yala to Patani in South Thailand, an unbridged river being crossed by a ferry. The west coast railway, passing through Alor Star, crossed the frontier in the small State of Perlis and then forked at Haad 'yai Junction, the main line continuing to Bangkok with a branch to Singora.

3I. The C.-in-C. Far East having issued an order that the main road approaches from Thailand were to be put into a state of defence, the problem was studied by senior officers of 3 Indian Corps. The primary role of the troops in this area was to cover the aerodrome at Alor Star and those further south in Kedah and Province Wellesley. The position selected therefore had to be sufficiently north of the Alor Star aerodrome for this purpose. The frontier area itself was found to be unsuitable both for tactical reasons and because it was known to be very malarial. Ultimately a position was selected in front of the small village of Jitra, which lies at the junction of the main road with the branch road to Perlis, some 18 miles south of the frontier. This position had, however, obvious disadvantages, chief of which was the weakness of the left flank in dry weather, for between it and the sea was a stretch of some 12 miles of open or semi-open country, intersected by small canals and ditches. The main defences were, therefore, concentrated astride the two roads, reliance being placed on a skeleton pill-box defence combined with a maximum use of natural obstacles for the protection of the left flank. Plans were made to flood an area astride the railway, which seemed to be a probable line of enemy advance. On the main front anti-tank ditches were dug where there were no natural obstacles and defended localities were constructed, though later preparations and training for MATADOR interfered to some extent with the development of these defences.

32. On the Kroh – Patani road, intelligence reports pointed to the fact that the most suitable place for a defensive position was a locality known as "The Ledge", some 35-40miles on the Thailand side of the frontier. Here the road had been cut out of a steep hillside and it seemed probable that it would be comparatively easy to block it by demolitions, though it was of course impossible to make any preparations in peace-time. Another defensive position was prepared west of the frontier upon which to fall back in case of need.

Although no large bodies could cross the frontier by bush tracks in North Perak, it was nevertheless possible for small parties to do so. Such small parties, by guerilla activities against our communications, could at least develop a nuisance value. In order to watch these tracks a special platoon of local men was formed and incorporated in the Perak Volunteer Battalion.

33. *The East Coast.* – Throughout the whole length of the east coast of Malaya there are numerous beaches very suitable for landing operations. For the greater part of the year the sea is comparatively calm off this coast. The exception is the period of the north-east monsoon. It had, however, been determined, as a result of a staff ride held in 1937, that even during this monsoon landings were possible though it was thought they might be interfered with for two or three days at a time when the storms were at their height. In consequence, it was thought that the enemy would be unlikely to choose the period December-February if he could avoid it.

It has already been explained (see Sections I and VI) that there are large undeveloped areas in the eastern part of Malaya and that communications are scarce; also that the original policy had been to avoid, as far as possible, further development of these communications with a view to reducing military commitments in this part of Malaya. By 1941, however, the Army had been obliged to undertake the defence of three areas on the east coast i.e the Kelantan area, the Kuantan area and the East

Johore area. The primary role of the Army in the first two of these, both of which were situated at the end of very long and vulnerable communications, was the defence of the aerodromes which had been constructed there. In both cases the forces which could be made available were inadequate for their task.

34. The State of Kelantan is divided into two parts by the Kelantan River which flows roughly South to North and reaches the sea near Kota Bharu. The river is wide and unbridged for road traffic which makes communication from one bank to the other difficult and slow. The railway crosses the river west of Machang and then running west of it crosses the frontier into Thailand a few miles from the coast. There are no road communications across the frontier though, as in Perak, the frontier is crossed by tracks and, in the more mountainous sections, by rivers navigable by small craft.

There were three modern aerodromes in Kelantan – one at Kota Bharu completed and in use, one at Gong Kedah some 30 miles down the coast, serviceable and nearly completed, and one at Machang on the Krai – Kota Bharu road under construction. All these were east of the Kelantan River.

The Commander of the Kelantan Force of one brigade group, which had only begun to move into position at the end of 1940, was instructed that his primary task was to secure the aerodromes for the use of our Air Force and to deny them to the enemy. He was also instructed that in order to carry out his task, he was to endeavour to prevent an enemy landing and that, for this purpose, pill-boxes were to be built and beach defences, both anti-personnel and anti-tank, were to be constructed as far as resources would admit. He decided to keep his force east of the Kelantan River with the exception of small mobile detachments whose task was to watch the frontier and, in face of an enemy's advance in force, to fall back across the Kelantan River. Arrangements were made to destroy the railway bridges near the frontier. The bulk of the force was therefore concentrated about the aerodromes at Kota Bharu and Gong Kedah, with beach defence troops on the most likely landing beaches. Reserves were held at Chondong and Peringat. Headquarters were in the Kota Bharu area in touch with the Sultan and British Adviser. Railhead was at Krai where the main reserves of supplies, stores, etc. were held. I approved these dispositions when I visited the area in company with the A.O.C. in July, 1941.

35. At Kuantan the small cantonment lies a mile or so from the sea in the bend of the Kuantan River. North of the river are some 12 miles of beach suitable for landing. South of the river mouth there are also good landing beaches but a tributary of the Kuantan River blocks the deployment from these beaches northwards. The road from Jerantut (100 miles distant) crosses the Kuantan River by a ferry west of the cantonment. The aerodrome was situated near this road some 7 miles west of the ferry.

The Commander of the Kuantan Force of one weak brigade group which had only moved into position in April, 1941, was instructed that his primary task was to secure the aerodrome for the use of our Air Force and to deny it to the enemy. The beaches were far too long to hold in strength, but if the enemy was allowed to land unopposed he could concentrate a large force for an attack on the aerodrome. Moreover, the slow ferry crossing of the Kuanton River was a source of great weakness. The plan, which I approved, was to deploy one battalion on the beaches, where material defences were constructed, and to hold one battalion for the defence of the river lines and of the aerodrome. I also authorised the construction of a swinging pontoon bridge across the river which, however, owing to difficulty in getting suitable material was not finished in time. Communication with Kuantan was by military wireless and by a civil land line. Both these channels of communication were subject to frequent interruption.

36. By far the greater part of the East Johore area is undeveloped forest. There are, however, two small towns of strategical importance, Mersing and Endau, situated about 20 miles apart. Mersing is 90 miles from Singapore and connected to it by a motor road. There are good landing beaches both north and south of the town but the water off-shore is shallow so that ocean-going steamers have to lie a long way out. Mersing is also connected to Kluang in the centre of Johore and thence to Batu Pahat on the west coast by a lateral road which branches from the Mersing – Singapore road at Jemaluang. Endau, a smaller town than Mersing, is connected to it by a motor road. It lies at the mouth of the Endau River on which at Bukit Langkap, some 20 miles from Endau, was situated an important Japanese owned iron ore mine.

From this mine large quantities of iron ore were shipped to Japan annually, being brought down river in a fleet of Japanese-owned barges and loaded into Japanese steamers which lay off the mouth of the Endau River. From the mine there was also water communication with the Jemaluang – Kluang road. The whole of this area was therefore well known to the Japanese.

On the coast south of Mersing there are a number of water-ways in which a small force could be landed within striking distance of the Singapore road.

The Jemaluang road junction was clearly vital to the defence of this area. It was essential, therefore, that the main operations should take place in front of this junction. There were three contingencies to be provided for (*a*) an attempt by the enemy to land in the Endau area with the object of either moving on Mersing or via the Bukit Langkap iron ore mine to the Kluang road and the Kahang aerodrome situated close to it; (*b*) a landing in force in the Mersing area; (*c*) landings of small forces further south with a view to cutting communications with Singapore.

In May 1941, when I took over command, the responsibility for the defence of this area rested on the Commander, Singapore Fortress, who had allotted for this purpose the 12 Indian Brigade Group, one battalion group of which only was actually accommodated at Mersing. The general plan was to hold in force the Mersing area and the beaches to the south with a detachment at Endau and a reserve in a prepared position north of the Jemaluang road junction; other detachments watched the communications to Singapore. The beach defences in this area were more advanced than those further north. I approved this plan during a visit to the East Johore area in June 1941.

Some small minefields were laid off the East Johore coast by the Royal Navy but, owing to the limited supply of mines, it was not possible to lay them off other parts of the east coast.

In view of the possibility of enemy landings on the east coast detailed arrangements had been made with the civil authorities for the removal or destruction of all boats and other surface craft on this coast on receipt of specified code words.

37. *Air Defence* – Prior to the outbreak of World War II, Air Defence in Malaya had been, for all practical purposes, limited to the anti-aircraft defence of selected areas on Singapore Island, though plans had also been made for the defence of Penang. With the extension of the defence problem, however, to embrace the whole of Malaya and the more imminent danger of active operations in the Far East, the plans for active air defence underwent rapid expansion, and passive air defence was organized.

38. As regards the Anti-Aircraft Artillery, the defences of Singapore had been developed in accordance with the War Office plan of 1936 as amended and extended by the plan approved by the Chiefs of Staff Committee in 1940. They were laid out for the defence of the Naval Base and of other vulnerable installations, for which an order of priority was laid down. In May 1941 there were three Heavy Anti-Aircraft Regiments, one Light Anti-Aircraft Regiment and one Searchlight Regiment in the Singapore area. In the autumn of that year the I Indian Heavy Anti-Aircraft Regiment arrived. A very large proportion of the men of this Regiment were still in the recruit stage and none of them had had any training on guns. When hostilities opened there were 60 Heavy Anti-Aircraft guns in the Singapore area out of the 104 which had been authorised. These consisted of two 4.5 in., thirty-eight 3.7 in. and twenty 3 in., the majority of which were static. Every effort had, however, been made to make as many as possible mobile and to train in mobile operations. Outside Singapore Island, authority had been received for the preparation of positions for the defence of Penang and of the aerodromes at Alor Star, Sungei Patani, Kota Bharu and Kuantan, but only those at Sungei Patani had been completed when hostilities opened. Temporary positions were, however, occupied by such 3 in. guns as could be made available for defence of the Alor Star and Kota Bharu aerodromes. One battery of the Light Anti-Aircraft Regiment from Singapore, on a mobile basis, was placed under orders of the Commander, 3 Indian Corps, for expected operations in North Malaya and was located at Alor Star. There were no guns available for the defence of cities on the mainland such as Kuala Lumpur and Ipoh.

At the time of my arrival in Malaya the anti-aircraft artillery was under the orders of the Commander, Singapore Fortress. Having in view, however, the increase in the scale of anti-aircraft defence and its extension to other parts of Malaya, I decided to bring the anti-aircraft artillery directly under my own command, except for purposes of administration, and to reorganize it under the Commander, Anti-Aircraft Artillery, into two brigades, one for Singapore and one for North Malaya. This reorganization had not been completed when war broke out. Command of the Anti-Aircraft Artillery in North Malaya was delegated to the Commander, 3 Indian Corps.

39. In 1940 the Active Air Defence was strengthened by the arrival of fighter aircraft. A proportion of these was always retained at the Singapore bases for defence of the important objectives in that area, the remainder being allotted to the northern area, which appeared to be the most vulnerable to attack.

40. With the arrival in Malaya in the summer of 1941 of Group Captain Rice, who had had much experience, in connection with the Air Defence of Great Britain, the task of building up a co-ordinated Air Defence scheme for Malaya was energetically pushed forward. The fighters allotted to the defence of the Singapore area were placed under the command of Group Captain Rice. This officer was also authorised, as regards the Singapore area, to co-ordinate the action of the fighters and the anti-aircraft artillery and, during hostile attacks, to issue orders direct to these two formations. A control station was established near the Kallang aerodrome.

41. As part of this Air Defence scheme an efficient Warning System was essential. An organization of civilian watchers had already been started. Efforts were now made to extend this organization and provide it with better equipment. There were two main difficulties. Firstly, there was the difficulty of finding suitable people in the less developed parts of Malaya to complete the chain of watchers. Secondly, and more important still, was the paucity of communications. The civil telephone system in Malaya consisted only of a few trunk lines, which followed the main arteries of communication, and local lines in the populated areas. This was quite inadequate for a really efficient Warning System, as it was impossible to allot separate lines for this purpose. A plan was worked out, in conjunction with the civil authorities, for the duplication of this system and for extensions where required. A start was made with the limited amount of cable available but only small progress had been made when war broke out. There were a few radar sets available but efforts to supplement the system with wireless communication met with only partial success owing to the unreliability of wireless in the difficult climatic conditions of Malaya. Nevertheless, in spite of these difficulties, an organization was built up which proved of great value during the subsequent operations, though it should be pointed out that it covered South Malaya and the Singapore area only, and that there was no adequate Warning System for North Malaya.

The organization of Passive Air Defence will be explained later when dealing with Civil Defence.

42. *Defence of Aerodromes.* – As a result of experience in Europe, and especially in Crete, the C.-in-C. Far East laid down that the defence of aerodromes was to take precedence, as regards A.A. weapons, over everything else except the defence of the Naval Base. A scale of Heavy and Light A.A. Guns for each aerodrome was laid down but, owing to lack of resources, it was never approached. Such guns as were available, however, were allotted for this purpose. In addition, small infantry garrisons, drawn from Malayan Volunteer units or Indian State Force units, were provided. There were also a few heavy armoured lorries specially constructed for this purpose. In no case, however, was the strength of the garrison really adequate for the defence of the aerodromes, the perimeters of which varied between 3 and 5 miles.

43. *Borneo.* – The large Island of Borneo, partly British and partly Dutch, was clearly of great strategical importance, lying as it did between the main routes linking Japan with Malaya and Sumatra on the one hand and Java and the Southern Areas on the other, and containing large supplies of oil and other raw materials. Unfortunately neither the British nor the Dutch were able to find adequate garrisons for this island.

The British portion of Borneo consisted of:-

British North Borneo *a territory controlled by the British North Borneo Company, whose headquarters were in London. The Governor and officials of British North Borneo were in the employ of that Company.*

Labuan Island. *– A British Colony administered by a Resident.*

Brunei. *– A British Protected State with its own Sultan.*

Sarawak. *– A Malay State which had for many years been governed by members of the Brooke family. In September 1941, however, the ruling Rajah made over much of his responsibility to a Council. He then left Sarawak for a holiday and was in Australia when hostilities broke out. His efforts to return to Sarawak were unsuccessful.*

There had for some time been a project to open up air facilities in British Borneo. Aerodrome sites had been selected and surveyed. Ultimately, however, as there was no immediate prospect of British aeroplanes being available to use the aerodromes, the project was postponed except as regards an air landing ground at Kuching in Sarawak and a landing strip at Miri.

44. In British North Borneo there were several excellent natural harbours which were undefended. There was a small but efficient local Volunteer Force but, owing to lack of resources, it was not possible to provide any regular troops for the defence of this territory. The Governor of British North Borneo was therefore informed by the C.-in-C. Far East that his territory could not be defended and that the role of his local forces should be the maintenance of internal security.

45. In West Brunei and East Sarawak were situated the important Sena and Miri Oil Fields and the Lutong Refinery. It was the policy of the British Admiralty, in the event of war breaking out in the Far East, to do such damage to the wells and plant that they would be of no use to the enemy. This work was the responsibility of the Army, and for this purpose a demolition party with an infantry escort of about a company (partly Indian and partly British) was stationed there. There was also a 6 in. battery. A partial denial scheme was put into effect before hostilities broke out.

46. The town of Kuching, the capital of Sarawak, is situated some 8 miles from the coast and is approached only by waterways. The intervening country is mostly bush-covered or marshy. The town itself lies on both sides of the Bintawa River. The air landing ground is situated some 7 miles south of the town to which it is connected by a metalled road. The only land communication between Sarawak and Dutch West Borneo was a bush track unfit for wheeled transport.

The O.C. Troops Sarawak and Brunei (Lt.-Col. Lane) was instructed that his primary object was to secure the air landing ground for the use of our Air Force and to deny it to the enemy; also that if, owing to overwhelming forces, this object could no longer be attained, then he should act in the interests of the defence of West Borneo as a whole, his line of withdrawal being by the bush track into Dutch West Borneo. This defence problem was not an easy one. If the plan envisaged only the close defence of the landing ground, then the enemy would be free to move unopposed up the waterways where he would be most vulnerable. Moreover, the people of Kuching Town would be left entirely unprotected. On the other hand any attempt to defend Kuching itself would lead to great dispersion.

The O.C. Troops had at his disposal the 2/15 Punjab Regt. (less one weak company to Lutong), the Sarawak Rangers, some local volunteers trained chiefly for administrative duties and some regular administrative detachments. The Sarawak Rangers, which had previously been disbanded, had recently been reformed but owing to lack of weapons were only partially armed. There was no artillery, except some field guns manned by the infantry, and no engineers.

Under the defence scheme prepared by the O.C. Troops, the Sarawak Rangers were employed as scouts north of Kuching and detachments of regular troops were pushed forward to block the waterways. The remainder of the 2/15 Punjab Regt. was held in reserve at the landing ground, where defensive positions were under construction. I approved this plan during a visit to Kuching at the end of November 1941. I was informed at the same time that there were large Japanese plantations in the area immediately east of Kuching.

47. *Review of Strength Required.* – Shortly after taking over command I was instructed to review the Army strength required for the defence of Malaya. Before doing so I personally visited all the main defence areas and also arranged for a strategical examination of the defence problem by a joint staff committee. In the course of that examination I asked to be informed what damage the Air Force at its existing strength might be expected to inflict on a hostile sea-borne expedition before it reached the shores of Malaya. I based my estimate of the Army strength required on the figure given. In the event, unfortunately, the damage done fell far below this figure. I have no record to show, and I do not wish to infer, that this figure was given by the A.O.C.

I pointed out the serious deficiencies in the strength of the Air Force, the obsolescence of many of the aircraft, the weakness of our naval forces and the greatly increased threat from the Japanese occupation of Indo-China which had then been extended to the southern portions of that country.

On the 2nd August, 1941, I gave my estimate of the Army strength required in a telegram to the War Office. This estimate was not examined in detail by the C-in-C Far East but the despatch of the cable was approved by him as a definition of the target. Summarized, it asked for:-

48 Infantry Battalions.
4 Indian Reconnaissance Units
9 Field Artillery Regiments.
4 Light Anti-Aircraft Regiments
2 Tank Regiments.
3 Anti-Tank Regiments.
2 Mountain Artillery Regiments.
12 Field Companies.

with the necessary administrative units. This was exclusive of the Volunteers, the infantry anti-aircraft and tank units required for aerodrome defence, and also of the Anti-Aircraft units required for the defence of localities including the Naval Base. In a Tactical Appreciation forwarded by telegram in September 1941 two Heavy Anti-Aircraft Regiments for the Field Force were asked for while the Anti-Aircraft Guns required for the defence of Singapore were estimated at 212 Heavy and 124 Light.

The main difference in the above estimate over those which had been submitted previously was that it made provision for a 3rd Corps Reserve in North Malaya of one complete Divison and certain Corps Troops units, for a complete division instead of two brigade groups in the Kelantan – Trengganu – Pahang area, for two regular infantry battalions for Penang and for a brigade group instead of one battalion in Borneo.

This estimate was accepted by the Chiefs of Staff, but it was recognised that the target could not, in the existing circumstances, be fulfilled in the foreseeable future. A working target was subsequently approved by the War Office.

48. *Further Re-inforcements.* – On the 15th August 1941, the second contingent of the Australian Imperial Force arrived in Malaya. It consisted of the 27 Australian Infantry Brigade with attached troops. As the commander of this Brigade had been prevented on medical grounds from accompanying it, Lt.-Col. Maxwell was, on the recommendation of the Commander, A I.F., appointed by the Australian authorities to command it. The Brigade Group had had the advantage of a period of training in Australia but had had no experience of bush warfare. It was accommodated temporarily on Singapore Island pending the completion of hutted accommodation in West Johore and Malacca.

In September the 28 Indian Infantry Brigade disembarked at Port Swettenham. It was composed of three Gurkha battalions which, like other Indian units, had lost a large proportion of their leaders and trained personnel under the expansion scheme. It joined the 3 Indian Corps and was accommodated in the Ipoh area, being earmarked for operations under II Indian Division.

In November-December 1941 two field regiments and one anti-tank regiment arrived from the U.K. and one field regiment and one reconnaissance regiment (3 Cavalry) from India. These were all placed under orders of 3 Indian Corps. The artillery regiments consisted of excellent material but were lacking in experience and had had no training in bush warfare. The Indian reconnaissance unit had only recently been mechanised and arrived without its armoured vehicles. It was so untrained that drivers had to be borrowed for some of the trucks which were issued to it.

49. *Re-adjustment of the Defence Plan.* – On arrival of the 2nd Contingent of the A.I.F. I decided to make certain alterations in the Plan of Defence. I ordered the A.I.F. to take over responsibility for Johore and Malacca and brought into Command Reserve for operational purposes the 12 Indian Brigade Group, leaving it under the Commander Singapore Fortress for training and administration. My reasons for this step were as under:-

(*a*) I considered the dual task imposed upon the Commander Singapore Fortress of defending both Singapore Fortress and East Johore to be unsound as he might well be attacked simultaneously in both areas. Similarly some of the Fortress troops had alternative roles in the two areas.

(*b*) I was anxious to give the 22 Australian Brigade Group, which had now had six months' training in Malaya, a rôle which involved responsibility.

(*c*) There was a greater probability under the new arrangement that the A.I.F. would be able to operate as a formation under its own commanders instead of being split up. The advantages of this need no explanation. In this connection I had enquired on taking over command whether there were any special instructions with regard to the status and the handling of the A.I.F. I had been informed that there were none.

The responsibility for the defence of Johore and Malacca passed to the Commander A.I.F. at 1200 hrs. on the 29th August, 1941.

In September the Kelantan garrison was strengthened by the addition of the infantry battalion which had previously been held in 3 Corps Reserve, an Indian State Forces battalion from the South for aerodrome defence, and some supporting units.

50. *Dispositions on Outbreak of War with Japan.* – As a result of the above changes the disposition of troops in the Malaya Command (Lt.-Gen. A.E. Percival) on the outbreak of war with Japan was as under:

(*a*) *Northern Area* – 3 Indian Corps (Lt.-Gen. Sir Lewis Heath). Responsible for the defence of that part of Malaya which lies north of Johore and Malacca, including the Island of Penang, and for the conduct of Operation MATADOR should it be decided to put it into effect.

Troops-

9 Indian Division of two Brigade Groups, East Coast Area.

II Indian Division, Northern Sub Area.

Penang Fortress.

Lines of Communication Area.

The Federated Malay States Volunteer Force and, for operational purposes, the Penang and Province Wellesley battalion of the Straits Settlements Volunteer Force. Corps Troops.

(*b*) *Johore and Malacca* – The A.I.F. (Maj.-Gen. Gordon Bennett). Responsible for the defence of the States of Johore and Malacca except the Pengerang area of Johore.

Troops-

The A.I.F. of two Brigade Groups.

The Johore Military Forces.

The Johore Volunteer Forces.

The Johore Volunteer Engineers (an European unit).

(*c*) *The Singapore Fortress.* – (Maj.-Gen.F. Keith Simmons). Responsible for the defence of Singapore and adjoining islands and of the Pengerang area in South Johore.

Troops-

The Fixed Defences of two Fire Commands.

Field troops of two Infantry Brigades etc. to man the beach defences.

Fortress units i.e. Fortress Companies Royal Engineers etc.

The Straits Settlements Volunteer Force (Less for operational purposes the Penang and Province Wellesley battalion).

The I2 Indian Infantry Brigade Group (for training and administration only).

Command Headquarters, Base and other units (for administration only).

(*d*) *The Anti-Aircraft Defences* (Brig. A.W.G. Wildey). Responsible, in co-operation with other arms, for the defence of selected targets in the Singapore area against hostile air attack.

Troops-

Four Heavy Anti-Aircraft Regiments.

One Light Anti-Aircraft Regiment (less one battery under 3 Indian Corps).

One Searchlight Regiment.

(*e*) *The Command Reserve.* – (Brig. A.C. Paris). To be prepared to operate anywhere in Malaya. Under Singapore Fortress for training and administration.

Troops-

I2 Indian Infantry Brigade Group.

The Commander 3 Indian Corps was informed that, in the event of an advance into Thailand, this Brigade Group would immediately be moved North and placed under his orders. The Commanders 3 Indian Corps and A.I.F. were instructed that, in the event of this Infantry Brigade Group being committed to operations, they must be prepared to replace it with another infantry brigade group if called upon to do so.

(*f*) *Borneo.* – (i) *Kuching (Sarawak) Detachment.* – (Lt.-Col. C.W. Lane). Responsible for the defence of the Kuching air landing ground.

Troops-

One Indian Infantry Battalion (less one company).

The Sarawak Rangers.

The Sarawak Volunteers.

Administrative detachments.

(ii) Miri Detachment. – Responsible for the denial, in case of necessity, of the Miri and Sena Oilfields and of the Lutong Refinery, to prevent them falling in a serviceable condition into the hands of the enemy.

(iii) British North Borneo, Labuan Island, Brunei. – In these States no regular military forces were maintained, though in British North Borneo there was a small Volunteer Force. The Senior Civil Officials were responsible for internal security.

(*g)* Christmas Island.

Troops. – A Coast Artillery detachment manning a section of 6 in. guns. Responsible for the protection of the phosphate deposits.

(*h*) Command Troops-

Base and Other Administrative Units.

Command Troops units and a number of Base and other units, for the maintenance of all troops in the Malaya Command, were located in the Singapore area and elsewhere in Malaya.

The Order of Battle of Malaya Command on the 8th Dec. 1941, is given in detail in Appendix B attached to this Despatch.

The Plan for the Defence of Malaya was contained in the Malaya Defence Scheme, which was supplemented as necessary by special instructions for the conduct of the defence in the various areas. In view of the wide area covered by the Malaya Command and the possibility of operations developing simultaneously in different parts of that area I considered it advisable to decentralise responsibility for the control of operations as far as possible. Every effort, therefore, was made to ensure that the Defence Scheme and pre-war Instructions should be as comprehensive as possible, so that subordinate formation commanders would be in a position to conduct operations with only such supplementary and amending orders and instructions from higher authority as the development of the situation might demand.

51. Special Operations.

(*a*) Early in 1941 an Independent Company, with a strength of about 300 partly British and partly Indian, was formed. It was accommodated first at Kuantan and then in Kedah, and was trained under Headquarters Malaya Command in amphibious operations and for special operations in enemy territory.

(*b*) In the summer of 1941 a Branch of the Ministry of Economic Warfare was started in Singapore. It suffered from an excess of secrecy and from a lack of knowledge on the part of the gentlemen responsible as to how to set about the work. Thus valuable time was lost. Later, however, some very useful work was done by this organization.

SECTION VII. – TRAINING.

52. Apart from the garrison of Singapore Fortress and the Command Reserve, of which most units had been in Malaya for some time, there were in 1941 very few trained units in Malaya. Practically all the Indian Army units had suffered severely from the rapid expansion of that Army which had only been commenced a year after the outbreak of the war. Officers and N.C.O.s had been withdrawn to meet the needs of this expansion until the lack of leaders, and even of potential leaders, reached a dangerously low level. Few units had more than two or three senior officers with experience of handling Indian troops and of the junior officers only a proportion had had Indian experience. The great majority of the troops were young and inexperienced.

The Australian units were composed of excellent material but suffered from a lack of leaders with a knowledge of modern warfare. The same applied in some degree to the British units in which there were few men with previous war experience.

No units had had any training in bush warfare before reaching Malaya. Several of the units had in fact been specially trained for desert warfare.

53. In June, 1941, the C.-in-C. Far East, in addition to ordering the construction of defences to cover the main road to Thailand, laid down a scale for the material defences on all defended beaches, to include anti-boat, anti-tank and anti-personnel defences. As an early outbreak of hostilities then appeared probable, he issued instructions that these defences were to be completed as early as possible. On the east coast a great deal of work remained to be done.

54. A balance, therefore, had to be struck between the employment of troops on defence work and their field training. I decided that the proper course was to build up a foundation of good individual and sub-unit training, which could be done concurrently with the construction of defences. If hostilities did not break out in the autumn I hoped that we might then expect a period of three months (December/February) during which we could concentrate on higher training.

I therefore issued instructions that individual, sub-unit and unit training was to be carried out during the period July/November, when possible in bush country, under the direction of formation and unit commanders and that formation exercises would be held during the period December/February. During the latter period I also arranged for two exercises without troops to be held to study problems connected with the defence of Malaya as a whole. In the event, the political tension which existed in August and September prevented much training being done by units in the forward areas. The Ist Contingent of the A.I.F. and the Command Reserve, however, carried out some very profitable training in bush warfare conditions. Some units of the latter were still in the Port Dickson training area when war with Japan broke out.

Towards the end of September, the defences having made good progress, I directed that an increased proportion of time should be allotted to training.

55. An exercise with troops arranged by the Commander 3 Indian Corps to study the problems of a withdrawal from Kedah southwards was scheduled to take place early in December, but had to be cancelled when war appeared imminent.

56. During the tenure of office of my predecessor a handbook on bush warfare had been issued by Headquarters Malaya Command. A similar manual had been received from India, while all the War Office training manuals were available in limited numbers. Directives were issued to supplement these manuals as necessary.

57. As regards Courses, Schools of Instruction etc. a balance had to be struck between the requirements of co-ordinating instruction and the desirability of leaving officers and N.C.Os. as far as possible with their units to lay the foundations of field training. Accordingly, I decided as a policy that Command Courses would be held for those subjects in which technical knowledge was required, while courses in other subjects would be held under formation or unit arrangements. In accordance with this policy Command Courses were held in Physical Training, Chemical Warfare, Intelligence and Camouflage. In addition, there was an Officers Cadet Training Unit at Singapore where men from all parts of the Far East were trained for commissions.

58. Profiting by the lessons of Crete, a great deal of attention was paid to the defence of aerodromes, special exercises being held in several areas to study this problem.

Exercises were also held to study the movement of troops by M.T. and the handling of mechanized columns. As in other theatres, a tendency on the part of the troops to become road-minded was apparent. The effects of this were perhaps more serious in Malaya, where the essence of success is familiarity with the jungle, than elsewhere.

During this period both the Fixed and Anti-Aircraft Defences of Singapore Fortress reached a high standard of training.

59. To summarize, the troops in North Malaya were, for reasons given, less well trained when war broke out than those in the South. Had we been allowed a few more months for training, there is reason to suppose that great progress would have been made. Throughout the Army there was a serious lack of experienced leaders, the effect of which was accentuated by the inexperience of the troops.

SECTION VIII. – THE INTELLIGENCE ORGANISATION.

60. In Malaya were a number of Intelligence Organizations all of which had an interest in varying degrees in the local Malayan scene and in the affairs of other countries in the Far East which had an influence on it.

In 1941 the Far East Combined Bureau (F.E.C.B.) was primarily responsible for the collection and collation of intelligence from the Far East outside Malaya. This bureau was located at the Naval Base and was under the control of the Commander-in-Chief China. It was staffed by officers of the three Services, the senior of whom was a naval officer. It held daily meetings, which were attended by a staff officer of Headquarters Malaya Command, and published weekly summaries. It also interested itself in Malayan matters and demanded the closest co-operation of the Malayan Civil organization.

61. At Headquarters Malaya Command there was an Intelligence Branch of the General Staff, which dealt with operational intelligence immediately affecting Malaya

and British Borneo. Its establishment was small and much of its time was taken up with matters affecting the Press, censorship, distinguished visitors, police liaison, the map production programme etc. So heavy were these day to day requirements that they absorbed much time that would have been better spent on broader issues more directly affecting operations. In 1941 I recommended a considerable increase in the establishment of the Intelligence Branch but this had not taken place when war broke out.

62. For Intelligence within Malaya the Services were naturally dependent to a great extent on the Civil Police Intelligence Branch. The Inspector General of Police was Chairman of the Defence Security Committee, of which representatives of the Services and of the Civil Police were members. This Committee examined and made recommendations upon all matters affecting security in Malaya in whatever form.

63. The constitutional organization of Malaya necessitated multiple separate Police Forces and Police Intelligence Services, but the Inspector General of Police Straits Settlements was also Civil Security Officer for the whole of Malaya. Shortly before the outbreak of war the Malayan Security Service was set up to co-ordinate the work of the various Police organizations in the Peninsula, to establish a central control and uniform legislation for aliens, to provide security control of the northern border and pan-Malayan direction from a central office in all police civil security affairs, which covered a very wide field. Malayan Security was in its infancy but showed promising results and did much to overcome the difficulties inherent in the excessively complicated lay-out of the Peninsula.

64. It must be recorded that Headquarters Malaya Command was not well supplied with information either as to the intentions of the Japanese or as to the efficiency of their Fighting Services. At a Senior Military Commanders' Conference held at my Headquarters as late as the end of October 1941 to survey the defence arrangements and to consider the Far East situation as it affected Malaya at that time, a representative of the F.E.C.B. painted a very indecisive picture of the Japanese intentions. Flights of Japanese aircraft over Malayan territory, orders to their nationals to leave Malaya and other indications, however, gave us sufficient warning of the coming attack. As regards the Japanese Fighting Services, it was known that their troops were intrepid fighters and that they were experts in Combined Operations, but their efficiency in night operations, their ability to overcome difficulties, and the efficiency of their Air Force had all been underestimated.

65. Information of Thailand's attitude was similarly lacking even up to within a few days of war. It is difficult to say whether the Thai officers who came on official visits to Malaya were sent with the intention of misleading us or not, but there can be no doubt that there was at least an advanced degree of co-operation between some of the most responsible authorities in Thailand and the Japanese, and that the preparations made in South Thailand by the Japanese for their landing there and for their attack on Malaya were made with the connivance, if not with the actual assistance, of those Thai authorities.

SECTION IX. – ADMINISTRATION.

66. The scale of reserve stocks to be held in Malaya was based on the "Period before Relief" which, as has been stated, stood in 1941 at 180 days. Initially these reserve stocks had been held entirely on Singapore Island, where special bomb-proof magazines had been constructed for the ammunition. With the increase in the garrison, however, and the extension of the defence to cover the whole of Malaya new problems were presented. These problems were akin to those connected with the defence of the United Kingdom in 1940 i.e. the base at Singapore, except that it was more heavily defended, was equally as exposed to attack as were the more forward areas elsewhere in Malaya. It was therefore necessary to distribute some of the reserve stocks throughout the country instead of holding them all in one area. In this way transportation problems would during active operations be reduced and all areas would be to some extent self-contained. Operation MATADOR was another factor in the problem. To meet the requirements of this, should it be put into effect, it was necessary to hold certain reserves well forward. I therefore decided that the main reserve stocks should be held on Singapore Island, that reserves on a scale to be fixed in each case should be held in the forward areas and that the balance should be held in advanced depots in Central Malaya. In accordance with this policy it was decided:-

(*a*) That the full 180 days for the garrisons of Singapore and Penang should be kept in those islands.

(*b*) That 60 days for all the troops, except the Penang garrison, north of Singapore should be kept in Singapore.

(*c*) That on the west coast 60 days should be kept north of the Perak River, and on the east coast 90 days in Kelantan and 60 days in Kuantan.

(*d*) That the balance of the 180 days for the troops in 3 Indian Corps area should be kept in the Kuala Lumpur, Ipoh and Jerantut areas.

In the Singapore Island area a policy of dispersal was adopted. This was due partly to the congestion in the Town area where depot space was difficult to obtain and partly to the desire to avoid heavy loss from air attack. The administrative situation at the outset of hostilities was approximately as under:-

67. *Weapons.* – Early in 1941 the scale of armament had been dangerously low. In particular all Indian formations and units arrived in Malaya with a very low scale of weapons. After March, however a steady and increasing flow came in Malaya, but it was not until November that formations received the higher scale of weapons and were issued with 25-pounder guns for the artillery. Even then many units, i.e. Artillery, Signals, R.A.S.C., were below establishment in light automatics and rifles and there were never more than a few of these weapons in reserve. Requests for weapons from the Sarawak Rangers, the British North Borneo Volunteers and other units had to be refused either in whole or in part, while the lack of weapons also rendered the further expansion of local forces impossible.

68. *Ammunition.* – It had been difficult to keep pace with the increase in the

"Period before Relief" and the great increase in the garrison. Nevertheless, when hostilities started, the situation in most categories was satisfactory though in some, such as those for Light Anti-Aircraft and 25-pounders, there were shortages.

69. *Petrol.* – With an almost unlimited supply in the Netherlands East Indies it had been possible to build up large reserve stocks. The Army stocks were held chiefly in large 60-gallon drums. The Air Force stocks were held dispersed as in the case of the Army, but the main Air Force petrol reserve was held in specially constructed underground tanks at Woodlands on Singapore Island a little south of the Causeway.

The Asiatic Petroleum Company held large reserve stocks for civil use both on Singapore Island and at certain places on the west coast.

70. *Food.* – The food problem was complicated with the Australian ration differing from the British ration and with the Indian and other Asiatic troops having their own specialized rations. Nevertheless, approximately 180 days reserve stocks of all types had been accumulated before hostilities broke out. Cold storage accommodation for frozen meat existed at Singapore and Penang and a few vans were available for distribution to troops on the mainland.

In order to build up reserves the meat ration of British troops (though not of the Australian troops) was reduced in the autumn of 1941 and replaced by other commodities, the full meat ration not being so necessary in the climate of Malaya as it is elsewhere.

The food supply for the civil population of Malaya was a complicated problem. It had been studied for some years by a sub-committee of the Defence Committee, Malaya, and, on the outbreak of World War II, a Food Controller was appointed. In peace-time only the rice-growing areas of Malaya are self-supporting. To all other areas, and especially to Singapore Island, rice has to be imported. Malaya had to import annually from Thailand and Burma two tons of rice for every ton grown. The annual consumption was about 900,000 tons. In Singapore and other large cities stocks for both European and Asiatics were held, while in each State rice stocks were accumulated under State arrangements. In addition, a number of cattle on the hoof were brought from Bali in the Netherlands East Indies. It is probable that, when hostilities broke out, a minimum of 180 days reserves were held in the more important commodities, though in some of the others the reserves were on a smaller scale.

The question of a rationing scheme had been under consideration by the Civil Government for some years but by the summer of 1941 no result had been achieved. Committees appointed to examine the problem reported that the difficulties in producing a rationing scheme for the Asiatic population were so great that they could not put forward a satisfactory solution. As a result, when hostilities broke out only a modified and limited scheme existed. In the light of subsequent experience it appears that it should have been possible to produce a workable scheme, though it is true that during the campaign there was no shortage of foodstuffs for the civil population.

71. *Water.* – It is only necessary here to explain the water supply in the Singapore Island area. In other parts of Malaya there was little or no danger of a water shortage. Singapore Island was dependent upon two main sources of supply (*a*) reservoirs at Gunong Pulai in Johore (10 miles west of Johore Bahru) and (*b*) rainwater catchment

areas and open-air reservoirs on Singapore Island i.e. the Seletar, Peirce and MacRitchie Reservoirs. From the former water was brought by above-ground pipe line to Singapore Town where it filled two high-level covered reservoirs at Pearls Hill and Fort Canning. Branches from the Johore pipe-line supplied the Naval Base and Army and Air Force barracks in that area.

The Peirce Reservoir fed by gravity into the MacRitchie Reservoir whence water was pumped into the distribution mains serving the Singapore and Changi areas against the Johore water coming via the Pearls Hill and Fort Canning Reservoirs. The supply from the Seletar, Peirce and MacRitchie Reservoirs was ample to give a restricted supply indefinitely even if the population was increased by refugees, provided the control of these reservoirs remained in our hands and the machinery for distribution continued to operate.

72. *Medical.* – The hospital accommodation which had been prepared in peacetime was of course quite inadequate for the increased garrison The A.I F. had their own Base Hospital which was housed in one wing of the new civil hospital at Malacca. The Base Hospital for other Europeans of all three Services was at the Alexandra Military Hospital on Singapore Island. The Indian Base Hospital was in hutted accommodation also on Singapore Island. On the mainland forward hospitals were established – often in schools taken over for the purpose. There were also convalescent camps and "change of air" camps for both Europeans and Indians, and steps were being taken for the construction of a large "change of air" station at Cameron Highlands.

Large reserves of medical supplies were held in the Tanglin (Singapore) area.

With a view to increasing the hospital accommodation in the Singapore area in the event of active operations arrangements had been made with the owners of certain large houses for a portion of them to be used, if required, as overflow convalescent hospitals.

The Civil Medical Services were well developed. There were excellent modern hospitals and a plentiful supply of medical stores. The standard of efficiency of the medical officers was high and there were some exceptionally clever specialists.

73. *Red Cross.* – There were Red Cross organizations working for both British and Indian troops. The Australian Red Cross was responsible for all the British troops.

74. *N.A.A.F.I.* – The N.A.A.F I. organisation, which had been established in prewar days, was expanded to supply the needs of the British troops. By special arrangements with the Government of India it also in I94I undertook responsibility for the Indian troops. This branch of its activities was, however, never fully developed, partly owing to the time required to bring in the additional supplies and partly also to the difficulty in finding suitable men to act as branch managers

75. *Accommodation.* – In Malaya, as in other Eastern countries, the problem of accommodation for troops differs widely from that in European countries. There are no farms, large empty houses, or village halls, while billeting on the civil population, mostly Asiatic, has obvious objections. In most places there are good schools and these were made available, when the emergency demanded, by the civil authorities. A limited amount of tentage was also available. A great deal of new construction,

however, became necessary. This took the form of wooden hutments erected by civil contractors. Water supplies and eventually electric light had to be laid on. Delays were caused by the shortage of materials, some of which had to be brought from overseas. The R.E. Works Services received valuable help from the Public Works Department in the preparation of these camps.

Sites for the camps were selected in accordance with tactical requirements. Some of those in the North had been erected before my arrival in rubber plantations with a view to providing them with cover from air observation. From a health point of view, however, these camps were definitely unsatisfactory and caused me much uneasiness. The thick rubber tree-tops prevented the sun and light from penetrating to the camps, which in consequence were damp and depressing. This had an adverse physical and mental effect on the troops, some of whom were in consequence not as fighting fit at the end of 1941 as they otherwise would have been. I attempted to improve conditions by thinning the tree-tops and also by organising "change of air" camps on Penang Island and elsewhere to which troops could be sent in turn for short periods.

76. *Recreation.* – Everything was done to provide recreational facilities, both outdoors and indoors, for the troops. In some places, however, the nature of the country did not lend itself to outdoor recreation grounds. Clubs for the troops were organized and special buildings erected in Singapore and other of the larger towns. In this connection many of the civilians were both hospitable and generous in their help.

77. *Married Families.* – In peace-time married families accompanied the troops to Malaya. After the outbreak of World War II, however, no married families of the Army or the Air Force were allowed to enter Malaya, but those already there remained there. The same policy applied to officers' families. The families of officers coming to Malaya from China were sent to Australia, where living was very expensive as it was also in India. In consequence, a number of officers of both the British and Indian Service, especially those who had children in the United Kingdom, became financially embarrassed. On the other hand, women were urgently required in Malaya as V.A.D.s, car drivers, for work in offices, and for other war work. For these reasons I recommended to the War Office at the request of the C.-in-C. Far East that officers' families should be allowed to enter Malaya at my discretion. This request was refused though they were allowed to visit Malaya for limited periods.

78. *Furlough.* – In peace-time the normal period of service in Malaya was limited to three years. By 1941 many officers and men had already exceeded that period, some by a considerable margin. In order to avoid, as far as possible, deterioration in efficiency I authorised, with the approval of the C.-in-C. Far East, leave ex-Malaya for all ranks for limited periods and provided that no more than a fixed proportion of each unit was absent at any given time. Unfortunately, owing to expense and difficulties of travel, only a few were able to avail themselves of this privilege.

79 *Administrative Inspection.* – In September, 1941, I made an administrative tour lasting eight days of the principal depots, hospitals and other installations in Malaya. Questions of policy were settled and contacts established with the civil authorities. I was satisfied that, as far as lay within our power, everything possible was being done

to ensure the maintenance of the essential administrative services should hostilities break out.

SECTION X. – CIVIL DEFENCE.

The Civil Population.

80. European. *– The European Civilians in Malaya fell into two main categories, the Officials and the Unofficials. Most of them were men of energy and ability but there were some who, after many prosperous years in Malaya, especially during and after World War I, had lapsed into an easier routine. To this the climate partly contributed. This class was gradually disappearing, their place at the beginning of World War II being taken by a splendid type of young man who came out to join the Civil Service or to take up other appointments in civil life.*

The picture, so often portrayed, of the "whisky-swilling planter" was a gross misrepresentation of the conditions under which Europeans in Malaya lived at the time of World War II. That the consumption of alcoholic liquor was fairly high is not to be denied, any more than it can be denied in other tropical countries, but there was little drunkenness and the vast majority of Europeans lived very normal lives. The standard of living, however, as a result of the natural wealth of the country and of the climatic conditions, was exceptionally high – possibly too high for the maintenance of a virile European population.

I felt that in some quarters long years of freedom from strife had bred a feeling of security. This frame of mind was voiced in one of the local newspapers which wrote, when the decision to defend Penang was first announced: "There are not a few who view with concern the disturbance of the restful and placid atmosphere of Penang which will result from the military invasion." Even in 1941 there were those who found it difficult to believe that an attack on Malaya was within the bounds of practical politics. It should be stated, however, that most of the Unofficial Europeans were engaged, directly or indirectly, in the rubber and tin industries which, by order of the Home Government, were working at maximum pressure. Bearing this fact in mind, the European community of Malaya, taken as a whole, shouldered its responsibilities as war approached in the same loyal spirit as was evident elsewhere in the Commonwealth.

81. *Asiatic.* – The bulk of the Asiatic population consisted of Malays and Chinese in approximately equal proportions. In general, the Chinese were to be found in the towns and larger villages while the Malays inhabited the country districts and the sea-boards. The reason for this was that the Chinese, being more industrious by nature and more commercially minded, had gained control of a great deal of the business of the country while the Malays, a more easy-going and less ambitious race, were content to live on the natural products of the soil.

82. The Chinese themselves were of two categories – those who were and those

who were not British subjects. For practical purposes the political sympathies of the Chinese population could be divided into four groups:-

(*a*) The pro-Kuomintang. This was probably the most powerful group.

(*b*) The pro-Wang Ching Wei, i.e., those who were in sympathy with Japanese aims. A small and not dangerous group.

(*c*) The pro-Communists, predominantly Chinese of the working classes. The most active and vocal group.

(*d*) The pro-British and Independents, the former being genuinely loyal adherents of the British Empire, and the latter those who wished to be left alone in the pursuit of fortune and their own self-interest. This group formed the large majority but unfortunately was only too prone to dragooning by (*a*) and (*c*) above.

The temporary reconciliation between the Kuomintang and the China Communist Party following the invasion of Russia by Germany resulted in the formation in Malaya of a "United Front" which, on the outbreak of war with Japan, absorbed all Chinese with the exception of Group (*b*).

As will be readily understood from the above summary, the Chinese population taken as a whole lacked homogenity and centralized leadership.

83. The Malays were divided into four classes, i.e. the Ruling class of Malay Nobles, the "Intelligentsia", the artisan and clerical class, and the peasant.

The Ruling Classes naturally felt that there should be an ever-widening control by the Sultans. Among the "Intelligentsia" were signs of a movement towards Nationalism. The other two classes were not in the broad sense politically minded.

The remainder of the Asiatic populations, totalling less than 20 per cent. of the whole, consisted of Indians, Eurasians, Japanese, etc.

84. The Indians, the great majority of whom were Hindu by religion with an active proportion of Sikhs, were divided politically into-

(*a*) Indian Nationalists who, through the Central Indian Association of Malaya, were bidding for control of the Indian population of the country on a strongly Nationalist basis.

(*b*) The general mass of Indians, normally a peaceful but ignorant section of the population which was mainly interested in the quiet pursuit of its livelihood but was becoming an easy prey to the agitator.

(*c*) Indians who were whole-heartedly British in their loyalty, found largely in the better type of Indian trader and in the clerical classes and professions.

(*d*) The Sikh Community, strongly organized within itself and very susceptible to the anti-British propaganda emanating from overseas.

The Eurasians were to be found mainly in the Colony and particularly in Singapore.

The community as a whole was loyal and presented no political problem. It was not politically active.

85. There were a number of Japanese in Malaya and, as all foreigners were treated alike, no special restrictions had up to 1941 been imposed on their activities. They were located mainly-

(*a*) In Singapore City, where there were large business houses, stores, hairdressing and photographic establishments, etc.

(*b*) In Johore, where they owned rubber and other estates and iron ore mines.

(*c*) In Trengganu and Kelantan where they owned large iron ore mines.

(*d*) In Penang where they carried on similar activities to those in Singapore.

Although access to the defence areas was forbidden to the Public and restrictions were imposed on photography and similar activities, it was quite impossible to maintain secrecy as regards the location and the general nature of the defences being constructed. Moreover, with such a cosmopolitan population, a Foreign Power could have little difficulty in obtaining most of the information it might require, topographical or otherwise, about Malaya.

86. To sum up, the majority of the Asiatic population were enjoying the benefits which British occupation had brought to Malaya. They had so long been immune from danger that, even when that danger threatened, they found difficulty in appreciating its reality and in bringing themselves to believe that the even tenor of their lives might in fact be disturbed.

87. As will be appreciated from this brief review of the civil population of Malaya, the sense of citizenship was not strong nor, when it came to the test, was the feeling that this was a war for home and country. Perhaps more might have been done by the Government in pre-war days to develop a sense of responsibility for service to the State in return for the benefits received from membership of the British Empire.

88. *Contribution to Imperial Defence.* – The Colony of the Straits Settlements was one of those which made an annual contribution to Imperial Defence. In addition to this, the Straits Settlements, the Federated Malay States and the Unfederated States of Johore, Kedah and Kelantan each maintained Local Volunteer Forces. The Federated Malay States also maintained the Malay Regiment and the State of Johore maintained the Johore Military Forces. There were also Naval and Air Volunteer Forces. Among the gifts to Imperial Defence were the battleship "Malaya" given by the Federated Malay States, the 15 in. Johore Battery given by the Sultan of Johore and some armed coastal patrol craft given by the Straits Settlements.

89. *Malaya's War Role.* – Prior to the outbreak of war with Japan Malaya had been given a charter for its participation in World War II. It was to produce the greatest possible quantities of rubber and tin for the use of the Allies. This was a factor which had considerable influence on its preparations for war.

The Governor and High Comissioner had wide powers to enact legislation by orders in Council.

90. *Manpower.* – The subject of the proper utilization of the available man-power

had been carefully examined in peace-time by a sub-committee of the Defence Committee Malaya. It was clear that in time of war as in peace the Government of the country must be carried on and that many of the business concerns must continue to operate. Special war-time officials would also be required. There was no leisured or retired class in Malaya which could be called upon for war-time expansion.

Soon after the outbreak of World War II the Governor and High Commissioner, under the powers conferred upon him, ordered that all European males resident in Malaya should between certain ages be liable for service in one of the local volunteer corps. At Singapore a Controller of Man-Power was appointed in place of the Man-Power Sub-Committee and in each Colony and State Man-Power Boards, on which both civil and military interests were represented, were set up to consider and give decisions on claims for exemption. Many exemptions had to be granted, even after allowing for the fact that in many cases Government and business could be carried on temporarily with reduced staffs.

No liability to military service was imposed upon the Asiatic population. Many of the Asiatics were of a type unsuitable for training as soldiers and the difficulties of nationality of registration and of selection would have been great. Moreover, as already stated, there were no rifles or other arms available with which to equip Asiatic units. There was, however, great difficulty in filling the Chinese sub-units in the existing Volunteer organization. This was in no way due to lack of available material or to lack of effort on the part of the military authorities. It was due chiefly to the lack of unity and of forceful leadership which existed among the Chinese population.

Early in 1941 half the Volunteers were for the first time called out for a period of two months continuous training. It was unfortunate that in April-May labour troubles, involving the calling out of troops, developed on some of the estates in the Selangor and Negri Sembilan area and at the Batu Arang coal mines. This was imputed in some quarters to the absence of European officials at the training camps. At the instance of Government the calling out of the remainder of the Volunteers was postponed to a later date. It never in fact took place.

In Singapore and other large cities Local Defence Corps were formed. They were trained in the use of small arms, but, their role was primarily to assist the Civil Police. They were not incorporated in the military organization but came directly under the Civil Government.

91. *Labour.* – The question of the conscription of labour in time of war had been considered and in accordance with the advice of those best acquainted with labour conditions in Malaya, rejected as unworkable. The question of the control of labour in time of war had, however, been the subject of frequent discussions and tentative schemes had been worked out.

Although the grave labour problems which developed after the outbreak of hostilities had admittedly not been fully foreseen, some of the trouble could in my opinion have been avoided had the problems of war-time control of civil labour been tackled more energetically in time of peace.

The Singapore Harbour Board and the Municipality, independent bodies operating in co-operation with the Government and carrying out its policy, had their own labour forces.

92. *Passive Air Defence.* – The steps taken by the Civil Government as regards reserve stocks of essential commodities, medical services etc. have already been described in Section IX. The general organization of Passive Air Defence was based on the Home organization. Warning sirens were installed at all the main centres and the P.A.D. organizations included First Aid and Salvage detachments, Medical Auxiliary Services, Fire Services etc. As a rule the detachments were led by Europeans, the members being composed of both Europeans and Asiatics.

A few blast walls to important buildings were built. Only very few air raid shelters were constructed for the civil population. As regards Singapore itself this was partly due to the difficulty of constructing underground shelters, and partly due to the advice of the civil medical authorities, who were of the opinion that to obstruct the circulation of air by building surface shelters in the streets might well lead to epidemics. A number of slit trenches had been dug but these soon became waterlogged and bred mosquitoes.

In Singapore the general policy was to rely rather on dispersal to camps constructed outside the town area. Apart from members of the Fighting Services gas masks were provided only for those persons, such as members of salvage squads, whose duties might compel them to work in gassed areas. This decision was made by the War Committee after consultation with gas experts, on the grounds that the danger from gas bombing was not great in the climatic conditions of Malaya.

Generally speaking, it may be said that the arrangements for Passive Air Defence were in 1941 on too small a scale and inadequate to deal with anything but sporadic air raids. Realising this, arrangements were made in October and November of that year for a series of lectures to be given at the main centres of Malaya by Brigadier I. Simson, the Chief Engineer Malaya Command, who had recently had experience of Passive Air Defence both in London and in Scotland. These lectures were attended by both military and civil officials, but there was little time before war broke out for the instruction given in them to be put into effect.

93. *Evacuations.* – Careful plans were worked out jointly by the military and civil authorities for the evacuation, in case of need, of the civil population from the South Coast of Singapore Island and from other exposed areas. Some areas in East Johore were actually cleared of civilians before war broke out.

94. *Hospitality.* – The civil population, following the example set by the Governor and High Commissioner, were generous in their hospitality to the troops. Clubs were built, equipped and operated by civilians for their benefit. Many civilians invited troops to their houses and entertained them in other ways. A debt of gratitude specially is due to the women of Malaya, many of whom worked untiringly in that enervating climate in the interests of the troops.

95. *General.* – Nevertheless, an atmosphere of unreality hung over Malaya. In the restaurants, clubs and places of entertainment peace-time conditions prevailed. There was no restriction on the consumption of foodstuffs. A measure to restrict the hours during which intoxicating liquor could be sold was not passed into law after long

delays until November, 1941. Long immunity from war had made it difficult to face realities.

SECTION XI. – RELATIONS WITH THE SERVICES AND THE CIVIL GOVERNMENT.

96. Throughout the summer and autumn of 1941 the co-operation between the Services was good, commanders and staffs working together on friendly and intimate terms. This was true both in the higher and the lower formations.

Relations with the Civil Government also showed a marked improvement. Generally speaking, officials throughout the country co-operated willingly with the military commanders.

I feel bound to record, however, that in my experience of Malaya there was a lack of the team spirit between the Service Departments on the one side and the Civil Government on the other in tackling problems of common interest. The vital importance of attaining the common object, i.e., the security of Malaya, was at times overshadowed by local interests, aggravated by the insistence of the Home Government on the maximum production of tin and rubber. The task of balancing the requirements of a country of vital strategical importance to the Empire with those of a wealthy and prosperous commercial community was a difficult one requiring great tact and patience. Clashes of interests naturally occurred followed very often by long delays due in part to the complicated form of government. Other delays, as has so often happened before in our history, resulted from discussions as to the relative financial responsibility of the Home and Malayan Governments on matters of defence. There was also a difficulty in getting full and accurate information as to civil defence measures.

These difficulties and delays could to some extent have been overcome if there had been more regular meetings of the Defence Committee Malaya, and later of the War Committee. Both the Services and the Civil Government were represented on these committees and problems affecting the defence, both military and civil, could have been discussed frankly and more expeditiously than by ordinary routine methods. Similarly, reports on the work of the various sub-committees and controllers could have been made and the information could thus have been disseminated to all concerned.

SECTION XII. – INFORMATION, PRESS AND CENSORSHIP.

97. *Information.* – At Singapore were established the Ministry of Information Far East and the Malayan Information Bureau. It was through these channels, among other duties, that official propaganda was disseminated.

98. *Press and Censorship.* – The Local Press in Malaya was divided into two categories, i.e. the English Press and the vernacular Press in which each Asiatic

community had its own paper or papers. In addition there were the war correspondents whose numbers increased rapidly as the situation worsened. For liaison between the Press and the Services a Public Relations Officer was appointed. The holder of this appointment was a retired naval officer who came directly under the Commander-in-Chief China until the beginning of December, 1941, and then under the Commander-in-Chief Far East. Under him were officers representative of the three Services, who acted as conducting officers, advisers to the censors, etc.

In the same building as the Public Relations Officer was the Chief Censor with his staff of subordinates, i.e. press censors, cable censors, mail censors, etc.

With permission of the C.-in-C. Far East I agreed to receive all Press correspondents for interviews at stated intervals. Similar interviews were given by other commanders. We considered that it would be better to give the Press some official data to work on rather than that they should publish statements and views, often harmful, based on false information or misunderstandings. Towards the end of 1941 I had regretfully to discontinue these interviews on instructions of the C.-in-C. Far East who had, I understand, received instructions from Home to this effect.

Visits to troops in all parts of Malaya were arranged, when desired, for the war correspondents.

In the summer of 1941 there was a tendency in certain sections of the Press to give the Overseas troops very much more publicity than was given to the British Troops. This was damaging to good "esprit de Corps" and I had occasion to include the matter in the agenda for one of my Press conferences. I made it clear that my policy was to treat all troops alike and asked that the Press should do the same. This they agreed to do.

SECTION XIII. – THE POLITICAL SITUATION.

99. During 1941 the tension with Japan increased and there were various signs that she was preparing for hostilities in the Western Pacific. Towards the end of July she occupied the Southern part of Indo-China, where she increased her concentrations. She also increased her political activities in Thailand. The attitude of the Thais was uncertain. On two occasions Thai military officers paid official visits to Singapore, where they protested their friendship for Britain. One of them was actually there when war broke out. On the other hand, there is no doubt that the Japanese were permitted to make preparations in advance for their occupation of South Thailand, for our officers, carrying out reconnaissances in that area, frequently met Japanese there and one of them, though too late, found large petrol dumps on the Patani aerodrome which had been made ready for the occupation. In the autumn many Japanese nationals received orders from their Government to leave Malaya, and Japanese reconnaissance aircraft flew over Malaya and Sarawak. As a result of these activities varying degrees of readiness were from time to time ordered by the C.-in-C. Far East. On the 1st Dec., 1941, the 2nd Degree of Readiness was ordered and a

State of Emergency was declared. On the same date the Volunteer Forces were mobilized.

SECTION XIV. – THE NAVAL SITUATION.

I00. On the outbreak of World War II the greater part of the China Fleet had of necessity to be withdrawn for operations elsewhere. The Flag of the Commander-in-Chief, China Station, was transferred from Hong Kong to Singapore at the end of June, I940. He brought with him, however, only a few light cruisers and destroyers as additions to the very inadequate fleet of local naval craft which existed there. We no longer had control over sea communications in the Far East.

On the evacuation of Shanghai in August, I940, three river gunboats from the Yangtze were transferred to Singapore, while a few days before the outbreak of war with Japan the "Prince of Wales" and "Repulse" with some attendant destroyers arrived. There were, however, still no aircraft carriers, heavy cruisers or submarines, so that there was nothing in the nature of a balanced fleet. With the arrival of the "Prince of Wales" and the "Repulse" on 2nd December, Admiral Sir Tom Phillips as Commander-in-Chief, Eastern Fleet, took over command of all Fleet operations, leaving local Naval defence in the hands of Vice-Admiral Sir Geoffrey Layton, then Commander in Chief, China. The Commander-in-Chief, Eastern Fleet, immediately left Singapore by flying-boat for Manila to confer with the American Naval Commander-in-Chief, Asiatic Fleet, with whom contact had been previously established by Commander-in-Chief, China, and did not return to Singapore till 7th December. On the outbreak of hostilities with Japan, the appointment of Commander-in-Chief, China Station, lapsed.

Naval Headquarters remained at the Naval Base.

By December, I94I, the seaward approaches to the Naval Base and to Keppel Harbour were strongly defended by mine-fields, booms, submarine nets, detector loops, etc.

The following ships were at Singapore on the 8th December, I94I:-

Battleship	I
Battle Cruiser	I
"D" Class Cruisers	3
Destroyers (including 2 "S" Class)	7
Gunboats	3
Auxiliary Anti-Submarine Vessels	I3
Minesweeping Vessels	4
Auxiliary Minesweepers	I2 (and 5 at Penang).
Auxiliary Patrol Vessels	5
Motor Launches	II
Boom defence, tugs and depot ships	6

SECTION XV. – THE AIR SITUATION.

I0I. The Air Officer Commanding Far East, Air Vice-Marshal Pulford, on taking over command at Singapore on the 26th April, I94I, was faced with tremendous difficulties. The aircraft at his disposal were still very deficient in numbers and few of them were of modern types.

I02. The bulk of the fighters were the American built Brewster Buffalos, comparatively slow machines with poor manoeuvrability. The device by which the .5 in. machine guns with which they were equipped fired through the propeller was faulty and caused a lot of trouble. A large number of the machines were also temporarily unserviceable when war started. There was also a squadron of Blenheim night-fighters. None of these machines could be classified as modern fighters. For these fighters only a limited number of trained pilots were sent from the United Kingdom. The remainder had to be found from pilots, mostly New Zealanders, who arrived in Malaya with a minimum of flying training and no fighter training, or by transferring pilots from other types of aircraft.

I03. The bombers consisted of two squadrons of Hudson General Reconnaissance machines and two squadrons of Blenheims. Some of these squadrons were below strength. There were no heavy bombers in Malaya.

I04. There were two squadrons of Torpedo bombers of the Vildebeeste type. These machines were obsolete. They had a very limited range, and a speed of less than I00 miles per hour.

I05. There was one Flying-boat squadron of Catalina machines, which had also become deficient in numbers owing to casualties and lack of reserves.

I06. There were no special Army Co-operation aircraft in Malaya. I arranged, however, with the A.O.C. Far East for some of the fighters to be made available for training in Army co-operation work. It was only possible, in the short time available and owing to lack of resources, for the most elementary training to be carried out.

There were no transport or dive-bomber aircraft in Malaya.

I07. There was a great shortage of spare parts, reserve aircraft, and reserve pilots. For this reason and in order to conserve resources flying was from May, I94I, onwards greatly restricted. In order to assist the Air Force, Army Officers, when travelling about by air, usually used light machines belonging to the Civil Transport Line or to the Volunteer Air Force.

The Air Force in Malaya was drained of trained personnel to supply shortages in the Middle East. Trained personnel were also withdrawn from the Australian squadrons to act as instructors in Australia.

The restrictions on flying and the shortage of trained personnel militated greatly against efficiency.

I08. When war broke out with Japan, the total of operationally serviceable I.E. aircraft in Malaya was as under:-

Hudson General Reconnaissance land-based	I5
Blenheim I Bombers	I7 including 8 from Burma
Blenheim IV Bombers	I7 including 8 from Burma
Vildebeeste Torpedo-Bombers	27
Buffalo Fighters	43
Blenheim I Night Fighters	I0
Swordfish (for co-operation with Fixed Defences)	4
Shark (for target-towing, recce, and bombing)	5
Catalinas	3 (of which I in Indian Ocean).
Total	**I4I**

This contrasted with the 566 Ist Line aircraft which had been asked for.

In addition to the above, there were a few Light Aircraft (Moths etc.) manned by the Volunteer Air Force.

I09. This was the Air Force with which we started the war. There was in fact no really effective Air Striking Force in Malaya and the fighters were incapable of giving effective support to such bombers as there were or of taking their proper place in the defence.

The A.O.C. was fully alive to the weakness of the force at his disposal. He frequently discussed this subject with me and I know that he repeatedly represented the situation to higher authority.

II0. In order to facilitate co-operation between the Army and the Air Force in North Malaya should hostilities break out, an air organization known as Norgroup was prepared and a commander appointed. The functions of the commander were:-

(*a*) to command such air forces as Air Headquarters might allot to him from time to time;

(*b*) to act as air adviser to G.O.C. 3 Indian Corps and to command such air forces as might be placed under the Corps Commander.

SECTION XVI. – SUMMARY OF THE SITUATION ON THE OUTBREAK OF WAR WITH JAPAN.

III. When war broke out with Japan on the I8th December, I94I, there were some glaring weaknesses in the arrangements for the defence of Malaya.

II2. The Navy no longer controlled the sea approaches to Malaya and there was a great shortage of craft suitable for coastal defence.

II3. The Air Force, in place of a force of 566 Ist Line Aircraft asked for by the A.O.C. Far East or of 336 approved by the Chiefs of Staff, had a force of only I4I operationally serviceable aircraft, very few of which were of the most modern types and some of which were even obsolete. There were no modern torpedo-bombers and no dive-bombers, the two types required for offensive action against an approaching sea-borne expedition, and no transport aircraft, the type essentially required for the maintenance of forward troops in jungle warfare. In addition, there were for reasons already stated comparatively few trained pilots and there was a great shortage of spare parts.

II4. The Army dispositions are most easily explained by comparing Malaya again to England and Wales (see Section I). It may further be assumed that an enemy with a superior fleet is in occupation of Norway and that Scotland is a neutral State, whose territory may not be entered unless the enemy is advancing with the obvious intention of landing in the South of Scotland or has violated any part of that country.

In Cumberland, Westmorland and Lancashire, then, there is one Division watching the main road and railway approaches from Scotland. On the east coast there is a strong brigade group in Northumberland and a weak brigade group at Hull. The Headquarters of this northern area are at Crewe. In the South of England there is one Division consisting of two brigade groups only. One of these is on the east coast about the mouth of the Thames, while the other is about the Oxford area. The Isle of Wight, where the Army Headquarters is situated, is strongly defended on the seaward side and has reasonably strong anti-aircraft defences.

The Command Reserve, which consists of one brigade group only, is situated partly on the Isle of Wight and partly in the area of the Cotswolds where it has recently been carrying out training.

The object of the defence is to protect the Naval Base of Portsmouth which, for purposes of the comparison, it must be assumed is situated on the north coast of the Isle of Wight.

II5. The dispersion of the land forces and the lack of reserves needs no stressing. The dispositions on the mainland had been designed primarily to afford protection to the aerodromes, most of which had been sited without proper regard to their security. The situation was aggravated by the fact that there was no adequate Air Force to operate from them. It is true that, even without this commitment, it would have been necessary, in order to protect the Naval Base, to hold at least most of Malaya but, had it not been for the aerodromes, better and more concentrated dispositions could have been adopted.

II6. As soon as the threat to Malaya developed in the summer of 1940 everything possible was done, both at Home and in Malaya, to strengthen the land defences. The fact that more could not be done was no doubt due to our Imperial commitments elsewhere. The time proved too short to put a country almost the size of England and Wales, in which there was no surplus labour, into a satisfactory state of defence. The financial control also had a restrictive effect.

II7. As regards the Army itself, the troops generally were inexperienced and far too large a proportion of them were only partially trained. There was a shortage of experienced leaders, especially in the Indian and Australian units.

Instead of the 48 infantry battalions and supporting arms (excluding the Volunteer Forces and troops required for aerodrome defence) which had been asked for, we had only 32 infantry battalions and supporting arms. There were no tanks which, as the operations developed, proved a very serious handicap.

II8. Nevertheless, there was throughout the Fighting Services, in spite of these weaknesses, a firm resolve to do our best, with the limited means at our disposal, to ensure the security of the great Naval Base. The Japanese did not gain either strategical or tactical surprise. Our forces were deployed and ready for the attack.

II9. As regards Civil Defence, much had been done but, viewed as a whole, the preparations were on too small a scale. There were many who responded nobly as soon as the call came but it cannot be said that the people of Malaya were fully prepared for the part they were to play in a total war.

PART II.

THE OPERATIONS ON THE MAINLAND OF MALAYA.

SECTION XVII. – THE OPENING OF HOSTILITIES 6-8TH DECEMBER, 1941

120. At about 1130 hrs. on the 6th December, 1941, the morning air reconnaissance, which was watching the approaches to the Gulf of Thailand, reported having sighted Japanese convoys consisting of warships and transports approximately 150 miles S.E. of Pt. Camo (South Indo-China) steaming westward. Information that there were two separate convoys was received at 1400 hrs. The position of these convoys was about 80 miles E.S.E. of Pul Obi. At that time I was at Kuala Lumpur, whither I had gone by civil air line that morning to confer with the Commander 3 Indian Corps. I received the information by telephone at about 1500 hours. At 1515 hrs. I ordered the Commander 3 Indian Corps to assume the First Degree of Readiness, and, anticipating that Operation MATADOR might be ordered, to instruct the Commander 11 Indian Division to be ready to move at short notice.

121. On returning to my Headquarters at Singapore at 1830 hrs. that evening I was informed that the C.-in-C. Far East appreciated that the Japanese convoys had probably turned North West with a view to demonstrating against and bringing pressure to bear on Thailand; that in consequence he had decided not as yet to order Operation MATADOR, also that one convoy consisted of twenty-two 10,000 ton ships escorted by one battleship, five cruisers and seven destroyers, and the other of twenty-one ships escorted by two cruisers and ten destroyers. Two Hudson reconnaissance aircraft had been sent out at 1600 hrs. to shadow the convoys until relieved by a Catalina flying boat which would continue the shadowing throughout the night. These Hudsons failed to make contact owing to bad weather, which prohibited relief Hudsons being sent.

122. The Combined Army and Air Force Operational Headquarters had already been opened at Sime Road. The Administrative Branch of Headquarters Malaya Command and the Headquarters of the Services remained at Fort Canning, partly because their accommodation at Sime Road was not complete and partly because it was desirable for them to remain in close contact with Government Departments.

During the evening I called on the Governor and the C.-in-C. Far East, to whom I reported that the First Degree of Readiness had been assumed by all troops under my command.

123. The first Catalina sent out failed to make contact during the night 6-7th December. A second was despatched early on the 7th December and instructed that, if no contact was established, a search was to be made from 10 miles off the west coast of Indo-China as G.H.Q. anticipated that the convoys might be concentrating in the Koh Kong area where there was a suitable anchorage. No reports were received from this Catalina and, from information subsequently received, it would appear that this boat was shot down by the Japanese. Three Hudson aircraft sent out on the same morning similarly failed to make contact, owing to bad weather conditions which forced two of them to abandon the search. Further Hudson reconnaissances were sent but only single merchant vessels were sighted in the Gulf of Siam at 1345 hours and 1545 hours respectively. These Hudsons were then sent on a diverging search off the Siamese Coast, and at 1750 hours one merchant vessel and one cruiser were sighted steaming 340°. The cruiser opened fire on the reconnaissance aircraft. At 1848 hours under conditions of very bad visibility, four Japanese vessels, perhaps destroyers, were seen off Singora steaming south.

It will thus be seen that for a period of nearly 30 hours after the first sighting the air reconnaissance sent out had failed to make contact with the main invasion forces, owing to bad weather.

If the report of the Catalina flying boat having been shot down by Japanese aircraft on the morning of 7th December, 1941, is correct, then this was the first act of war in the Malaya area between Japan and the British Empire. If not, then the first act was the firing on the Hudson reconnaissance aircraft by a Japanese ship on the evening of the 7th December.

124. An appreciation of the situation showed that the enemy convoy, if it was bound for Singora, could reach there about midnight 7-8th December, whereas if MATADOR was put into operation, it was unlikely that our leading troops, even if they met with no opposition or obstacles on the way, would arrive there before about 0200 hrs. 8th December. An encounter battle with our small force and lack of reserves would have been very risky, especially as the enemy was expected to include tanks in his force. There was also the complication of part of our force having, owing to the lack of M.T., to move forward by rail and subsequently be linked up with its transport in the forward area. For these reasons I informed the C.-in-C. Far East at a Conference held at Sime Road that I considered Operation MATADOR in the existing circumstances to be unsound. Subsequently at a Conference held at the Naval Base at about 2230 hrs. that night, at which both the C.-in-C. Far East and the C.-in-C. Eastern Fleet (who had just returned from Manila) were present, it was decided not to order MATADOR that night. At 2320 hrs. the Commander 3 Indian Corps was informed of this decision and was instructed to be ready to put MATADOR into effect at dawn on the 8th December if ordered to do so.

125. On the Kelantan front the probable landing beaches had been heavily wired with three belts of double apron or triple dannert wire and concrete pill-boxes had been built. In addition, large numbers of anti-personnel and anti-tank mines had been laid; but the two forward Battalions had to watch a front of over 30 miles and the average company front was over 8,000 yds.

At about 2345 hrs. on the 7th December the Beach Defence troops on Badang and Sabak beaches, the point of junction of which at the Kuala Pa'amat was about one and a half miles N.E of the Kota Bharu aerodrome, reported ships anchoring off the coast. Shortly afterwards our beach defence artillery opened fire and the enemy ships started shelling the beaches. At about 0025 hrs. on the 8th December the leading Japanese troops landed at the junction of the Badang and Sabak beaches and by 0100 hrs. after heavy fighting had succeeded in capturing the adjacent pill-boxes manned by troops of the 3/17 Dogras. The garrisons of the latter inflicted very heavy casualties on the enemy before being themselves wiped out almost to a man. Hudson aircraft between midnight and dawn pressed home numerous attacks in the face of heavy A.A. fire from warships and transports. One of the transports which is believed to have contained tanks and artillery was set on fire, either by air attack or gunfire, or perhaps both, and prevented from discharging its cargo. As soon as the first landing took place the 2/12 Frontier Force Regt. (less one coy. West of the Kelantan River) and 73 Field Battery were ordered up from Chon-Dong with orders to prevent any penetration towards the aerodrome with a view to a subsequent counter-attack.

In the meantime I had informed C.-in-C. Far East and the Governor that hostilities had broken out.

126. At about 0430 hrs. 8th December a Japanese air formation raided Singapore area. It had presumably come from French Indo-China, a distance of about 700 miles. The air raid alarm was sounded but Singapore was not completely blacked out when the aircraft arrived. Bombs were dropped on the Seletar and Tengah aerodromes and in the City area, but damage was slight. This was the first indication the citizens of Singapore had that war had broken out in the Far East.

127. The A.O.C. Far East, in consultation with myself, decided that the task of the Air Striking Force was to co-operate with the Army in repelling the attack on Kelantan. Accordingly the Squadrons based on the Kedah, Kuantan and Tengah aerodromes were ordered to attack the enemy ships lying off Kota Bharu at dawn. Upon arrival at Kota Bharu these aircraft were unable to find the Japanese transports, which had by then withdrawn behind the Perintian Islands some 15 miles off the Kelantan Coast. One squadron went on to Parana, where other Japanese transports were seen and attacked, but owing to fighter opposition it is doubtful if results were obtained. From now on the absence of modern escorting fighters was keenly felt. On return to the aerodromes in Kedah some of our aircraft were attacked by Japanese bombers and fighters while re-fuelling and considerable losses were sustained. The aerodromes at Alor Star, Sungei Patani, Butterworth, Penang, Kota Bharu, Gong Kedah and Machang were all attacked on this day. The performance of the Japanese aircraft of all types and the accuracy of their high level bombing had come as an unpleasant surprise. Our own air force had already been seriously weakened.

128. At 0820 hrs. 8th December G.H.Q. Far East reported that Operation MATADOR had been approved by the Chiefs of Staff if the Japanese attacked Kota Bharu but G.H.Q. added "Do not act". Air reconnaissance sent to Singora and Patani at dawn reported that enemy forces had landed at those places, that there were a number of ships lying off the coast and that the Singora aerodrome was in use. It was

clearly too late now to put Operation MATADOR into effect, so I authorised the Commander 3 Indian Corps to start harassing activities and to lay demolition charges on the roads and railways.

At 1000 hrs. the Straits Settlements Legislative Council, in accordance with previous arrangements, met at Singapore. I took the opportunity to report the situation to it.

At about 1100 hrs. 8th December, sanction to enter Thailand then having been obtained from the C.-in-C. Far East, orders were issued to the Commander 3 Indian Corps to occupy the defensive positions on both the Singora and Kroh – Patani roads, and to send a mobile covering force across the frontier towards Singora to make contact with the enemy and to harass and delay him.

129. This change from an anticipated offensive, for which the II Indian Division had been energetically preparing for some weeks, to the defensive had undoubtedly had a considerable psychological effect on the troops. It was aggravated by the fact that on the 7th December certain preparatory moves had been carried out within the division in preparation for MATADOR, including the moves of two battalions of the 15 Indian Infantry Brigade to Anak Bukit Station to entrain. The Division was thus caught to some extent on the wrong foot for the defensive operations which were to follow. It had, however, always been realised that the chances of being able to put Operation MATADOR into effect were not great in view of the political restrictions and Commanders had been instructed to prepare for either alternative. Possibly the defensive preparations had been to some extent sacrificed in favour of the offensive.

130. It was originally intended that the column operating on the Kroh – Patani road, known as Krohcol and commanded by Lt.-Colonel Moorhead, should consist of the 3/16 Punjab Regt., the 5/14 Punjab Regt. From Penang, one coy. sappers and miners, one field ambulance and a light battery of the F.M.S.V.F. The F.M.S.V.F. battery had, however, been unable to mobilise in time, and was replaced later by the 10 Mountain Battery from the North Kedah front. The 5/14 Punjab Regt. was moved up to Kroh on the 8th December leaving one company in Penang but had not arrived when operations started. Responsibility for operations on the Kroh front was on 8th December delegated by Commander 3 Indian Corps to Commander II Indian Division.

At 1330 hrs. on the 8th December the Commander Krohcol received orders to occupy the Ledge position some 35-40 miles beyond the frontier. It was hoped that the Thais would at worst be passively neutral. These hopes were speedily disillusioned. As the vanguard crossed the frontier at 1500 hrs. they were immediately engaged by a light automatic post manned by Thais. Throughout the afternoon the advance was disputed by snipers assisted by road blocks, the enemy fighting skilfully. By nightfall our troops had cleared only 3 miles of the road and then they halted for the night. The enemy were all Thais, some of whom were armed with Japanese rifles.

131. On the North Kedah front, a mechanised column consisting of two companies and the carriers of the 1/8 Punjab Regt. with some anti-tank guns and engineers attached, crossed the frontier at 1730 hrs. 8th December and moved towards Singora to harass and delay the enemy. Concurrently an armoured train, with a detachment

of 2/I6 Punjab Regt. and some engineers, advanced into Thailand from Padang Besar in Perlis. The Singora column reached Ban Sadao, I0 miles North of the frontier at dusk, where it halted and took up a position north of the village. Here, at about 2I30 hrs. it made contact with a Japanese mechanised column, headed by tanks and moving in close formation with full headlights. The two leading tanks were knocked out by the anti-tank guns, but the Japanese infantry quickly debussed and started an enveloping movement. Our column was then withdrawn through the outpost position at Kampong Imam, destroying two bridges and partially destroying a third on the way back. Meanwhile the armoured train party had reached Klong Gnea, in Thailand and successfully destroyed a large bridge before withdrawing to Padang Besar.

I32. To return to the Kelantan front, as soon as it had become clear from the dawn reconnaissance that there were no ships off the coast further south, the Commander Kelantan force moved up his reserve battalion, the I/I3 Frontier Force Rifles, with some anti-tank guns attached, from Peringat with a view to counter-attacking the enemy who had landed. Some local counter attacks had already been put in and progress made. At I030 hrs. the 2/I2 Frontier Force Regiment (less two coys.) was ordered to counter attack from the south and the I/I3 Frontier Force Rifles from the north. Owing chiefly to the difficulties of the thick waterlogged country and the impassable creeks which lay behind the beaches, these attacks failed to close the gap and by I700 hrs. the advance of our troops was stopped.

At about I630 hrs. the R.A.F. Station Commander decided that Kota Bharu aerodrome was no longer fit to operate aircraft and obtained permission from the A.O.C. Far East to evacuate the aerodrome. All serviceable aircraft were flown away and the ground staff was evacuated by road to rail-head. No offensive or reconnaissance aircraft were then available in that area. By I900 hrs. more ships were reported off the Sabang beach and the Japanese had started to infiltrate between the beach posts in the Kota Bharu area. The Commander Kelantan force therefore decided to shorten his line and ordered a withdrawal during the night to a line east of Kota Bharu. It was pouring with rain and pitch dark and communications had been reduced for the most part to Liaison officers. It was therefore not surprising that some of the orders went astray. As a result part of the I/I3 Frontier Force Rifles were left behind.

Mention should be made of the splendid work throughout a very trying day of the anti-aircraft detachment of the Hong Kong and Singapore Royal Artillery defending Kota Bharu aerodrome.

An important railway bridge on the Thailand side of the frontier was attacked by Hudsons of No. I Squadron (R.A.F.) prior to their withdrawal. Reports on this attack indicate that although the permanent track was damaged the bridge was not.

I33. Thus within 24 hrs. of the start of the campaign the Japanese had gained their first major objective, but at considerable cost. It is believed that the forces landed in Kelantan consisted of rather less than one Japanese division. This force lost its accompanying tank formation and many of its guns before it got ashore and subsequent reports indicated that the Japanese suffered some of their heaviest losses during the first day's fighting in Kelantan.

I34. A midday air reconnaissance reported 2 cruisers and I5 destroyers moving towards Besut, 6 transports lying off Patani and 25 transports off Singora.

At about II30 hrs. 8th December I placed one Battalion of the Command reserve, the 4/I9 Hyderabads which was then in the Negri Sembilan area on the conclusion of brigade training, under the command of 3 Indian Corps for duty in Kelantan. It was moved up at once by rail.

In the 3 Indian Corps area the 28 Indian Infantry Brigade was ordered on the 8th December to move forward from Ipoh and Taiping to the area of the Alor Star aerodrome and to come under orders of the commander II Indian Division.

SECTION XVIII. – THE FAR EAST WAR COUNCIL.

I35. On the I0th December I94I, in accordance with instructions received from the Home Government, the Far East War Council was formed at Singapore. Its composition was as under:-

Chairman.-
The Rt. Hon. A. Duff Cooper, Cabinet representative in the Far East.

Members.-
The Governor and High Commissioner Malaya.
The Commander-in-Chief Far East.
The Commander-in-Chief Eastern Fleet.
The General Officer Commanding Malaya.
The Air Officer Commanding Far East.
Mr. Bowden representing Australia and later
Sir George Sansom, as being responsible for propaganda and Press control.

Secretary.-
Major Robertson, the Argyll & Sutherland Highlanders (staff officer to the Cabinet representative in the Far East).

In addition to the above, Major-General Gordon Bennett, commanding the A.I.F., was told that he was at liberty to attend meetings if and when he wished to do so, and that he would be informed if and when matters particularly affecting Australia were on the agenda.

The Council met at Sime Road at 0900 hrs daily. The meetings usually lasted nearly two hours. The Secretary circulated minutes after each meeting.

If any of the members were unable to attend they were usually represented by deputies.

In January, after the departure from Singaport of Mr. Duff Cooper and Sir George Sansom, the Governor and High Commissioner became Chairman, Mr. Scott took Sir George Sansom's place and Mr. Dawson became Secretary. Later Brigadier Simson, as Director General of Civil Defence, joined the Council.

SECTION XIX. – OPERATIONS 9-11TH DECEMBER, 1941.

136. *The Kedah Front.* – The plan for the defence of the Jitra position was to hold it with two brigades forward, the 15 Indian Infantry Brigade on the right and the 6 Indian Infantry Brigade on the left. Of the two forward battalions of the 15 Brigade the 2/9 Jats extended from the hills on the right flank of the position to a point exclusive of the main road. On their left were the 1 Leicesters whose front included both the main and Perlis roads. West of the latter they linked up with the 2 East Surreys, the right battalion of the 6 Brigade whose position included the wooded Pisang salient forward of the Alor Changlih Canal. On their left the 2/16 Punjab Regt. was responsible for the whole front from the railway to the sea. It had permanent positions on the railway and coast only and patrolled the several miles of padi and marsh which intervened. The remaining battalion of the 15 Brigade had the role of delaying the enemy between the frontier and Asun and of occupying an outpost position at Asun, subsequently coming into brigade reserve. The outpost position of the 6 Brigade at Kampong Imam was to be held by the reserve battalion, the 1/8 Punjab Regt. less two companies. The 28 Indian Infantry Brigade less one battalion was to come into Divisional Reserve on arrival in the Alor Star aerodrome area. Its detached battalion had the role of L. of C. and anti-paratroop protection between Alor Star and Sungei Patani. The Divisional Artillery consisted of 155 Field Regiment of two batteries each of eight 4-5-in. Howitzers, the 22 Mountain Regiment, less one battery in Kelantan, armed with a mixed assortment of weapons, the 80 Anti-Tank Regiment, less one battery in Kelantan, with thirty-six 2-pounders, the 16 Light A.A. Battery with sixteen Bofors and, on its way up, the 137 Field Regiment with twenty-four 25-pounders. The 3 Indian Cavalry was on paper the Divisional Reconnaissance Regiment. It had recently arrived in Malaya without its armoured vehicles, having only recently handed over its horses. It consisted of three squadrons of dismounted men, many of them recruits who had had little training. It had very few trained drivers and was equipped in Malaya with a few unarmoured trucks. It was totally unfit for its role of divisional reconnaissance unit.

The defences in the Jitra position, although well advanced, were not complete. In addition, most of the posts had become waterlogged after a week's heavy rain, which still continued for the next few days. It was in these conditions that the troops set to work to complete the defences. The rain also had a serious effect on the demolitions, all of which were charged on the 8th December but several of which subsequently failed to operate.

137. On the Singora road the advance of the enemy column was delayed by the engagement at Ban Sadao and by demolished bridges and it was not until 0430 hours 10th December that contact was again made about the frontier a few miles north of Changlun. Our forward troops withdrew and the 1/14 Punjab Regt., with some artillery and engineers attached, took up a position behind a stream a little south of Changlun Cross Roads. The Commander 15 Brigade was told by the divisional commander that he must hold the enemy north of Asun at least until the morning of 11th December.

He asked for an additional battalion and was given the 2/I Gurkha Rifles from the 28 Brigade. This battalion took over the Asun outpost position.

I38. During the I0th December the covering troops of 6 Brigade withdrew to Kodiang without incident, carrying out important demolitions on the railway before they went. This withdrawal entailed the evacuation of the State of Perlis, as a result of which Britain was accused by one of the Perlis Ministers of State of violating her treaty by abandoning the State.

I39. At about 0800 hours IIth December the I/I4 Punjab Regt. was attacked in the Changlun position but succeeded in driving the enemy back. By midday, however, the enemy attacking from the right flank had penetrated into the middle of our position and the Commander of the Covering Force decided to withdraw behind the Asun outpost position, calculating that he would be able to reach there before the enemy tanks could negotiate the damaged bridges. At I430 hours, however, he was ordered by the divisional commander to occupy a position 1½ miles north of Asun with a view to imposing further delay on the enemy. At about I630 hours, when the force was moving back, covered by a rearguard, occurred the first of many incidents which showed the influence of the tank on the modern battlefield, especially against inexperienced troops. Suddenly with little warning twelve Japanese medium tanks followed by infantry in lorries and other light tanks attacked the rear of the column. Few of the troops had ever seen a tank before. The tanks advanced through the column inflicting casualties and causing much confusion and approached the bridge in front of the Asun outpost position. The demolition exploder failed but the leading tank was knocked out by anti-tank rifle fire and blocked the road. The blitz was temporarily stopped, but at considerable cost in men and material. Some 200 men of the I/I4 Punjab Regt. With the Brigadier, all of whom had been cut off, rejoined the following day, but the battalion was temporarily rendered ineffective.

I40. By I830 hours the tanks, followed by infantry, had come on again and broken into the outpost position held by the 2/I Gurkha Rifles. Shortly afterwards the Battalion Commander decided to withdraw all his three companies. But communications had been broken and of the forward companies only 20 survivors ever rejoined. The losses of the battalion in this action were over 500.

I4I. On the Perlis road, as may often happen with inexperienced troops, a demolition was prematurely exploded behind the covering and outpost troops. For various reasons it was not repaired in time although there was no contact on this front and all the transport, guns and carriers of the covering and outpost troops and seven anti-tank guns in the main Jitra position were lost.

I42. Withdrawals are admitted to be among the most difficult operations of war even for seasoned troops and the above incidents, which have been described in some detail, serve to illustrate the great difficulty of conducting them successfully with inexperienced troops. They had a profound influence on the Battle of Jitra. At the same time I am of the opinion that some of the trouble might have been avoided had the commanders reacted more swiftly to the problems created by the appearance of tanks on the battlefield.

I43. *The Kroh Front.* – The advance was continued early on the 9th December.

Our column was still opposed by the detachment of the Thailand Armed Constabulary which was now some 300 strong and which adopted guerilla tactics. As the leading troops approached Betong, however, in the afternoon all opposition ceased. Here the column stopped for the night.

144. At first light on the 10th December Krohcol embussed in the 2/3 Australian Reserve M.T. Coy. and moved forward towards the Ledge position. When about 4 miles short of its objective the advanced guard came under fire from Japanese troops. It continued to advance rapidly for 1½ miles and then was held up. An encounter battle developed in which there was heavy fighting with considerable casualties on both sides, but again the issue was decided by Japanese tanks which made a surprise appearance on this front. The 3/16 Punjab Regt. fought splendidly in this engagement as it did also the following day. The 10 Mountain Battery and 5/14 Punjab Regt. (less one Company) had now arrived at Kroh and the Commander Krohcol ordered them up to a position about 10 miles north of Betong. He also reported the situation to the Commander II Indian Division saying that he might have to withdraw. The latter in his reply imposed on him the rôle of stopping, and not merely delaying, the enemy.

145. During the afternoon of the 11th December the enemy made repeated attacks on the forward troops of Krohcol but were repulsed with heavy losses. The battalion casualties, however, after three days' and nights' fighting were past the 200 mark. The commander Krohcol estimated that he was opposed by four enemy battalions and reported accordingly to Headquarters II Indian Division. It was the night after the affair at Asun recorded above and in reply the Commander II Indian Division sent a personal message to the effect that the object of Krohcol must now be to ensure the safety of the whole division by preventing the enemy from debouching on to the L. of C. about Sungei Patani. The Commander Krohcol was given full permission to withdraw as necessary to the Kroh position, where his stand must be final.

A detachment of anti-tank guns was sent to this front.

146. *The Kelantan Front.* – Civil plans during the first day of war had gone smoothly under the capable direction of Mr. Kidd, the British Adviser. During the 8th December all European women and children were withdrawn to Kuala Krai and thence out of the State, and plans for the denial of sea and river craft to the enemy were put into effect. The few remaining Japanese civilians were rounded up for internment. Many of the Japanese civilians had left before the outbreak of war. The Sultan of Kelantan and his household left for his residence near Kuala Krai. The few Asiatic civilians who wished to leave did so under control and there was no refugee problem.

147. During the night 8th-9th December heavy fighting went on at the Kota Bharu aerodrome. At dawn the Japanese put in a heavy attack astride the aerodrome road and the Commander, Kelantan Force, decided to withdraw to a position with a good field of fire South of Kota Bharu. Eventually the line was stabilized at the new position and a large number of troops who had been cut off in the withdrawal rejoined their units. In the afternoon the 4/19 Hyderabad Regt. arrived from the Command Reserve and was ordered to take up a position some 12 miles South of Kota Bharu covering the camp at Chondong. In the meantime, the troops in the north half of the

right sector of the beach defences had been ordered back from the beaches to cover the road Kota Bharu – Pasir Puteh. The troops on the main road were withdrawn through the Hyderabads and night positions were established north of Chongdong.

148. On the I0th December units were reorganized. The strength of each of the battalions which had been heavily engaged was now up to 600 or more. As so often happened later in the campaign our casualties did not prove to be so heavy as at first reported. Several attacks made by the enemy were beaten off.

149. Having in view the threat to his communications should the enemy make fresh landings further south on the coast of Kelantan, the Commander, Kelantan Force, decided on the morning of the IIth December to give up the Gong Kedah and Machang aerodromes, which were no longer required by our Air Force, and to concentrate his force south of Machang to cover his communications. This movement was carried out during the day and a good position occupied. Unfortunately the runways at both the Gong Kedah and Machang aerodromes had to be left intact, for at neither had the demolition arrangements been completed. Orders were given for the demolition of the Guillemard Bridge over the Kelantan River, the longest railway bridge in Malaya.

Information was received that the Japanese had on the I0th December landed another force at Besut in South Kelantan.

150. *The Kuantan Front.* – On the 9th December Japanese aircraft attacked the Kuantan aerodrome They were engaged by small arms fire, there being no anti-aircraft guns available for the defence of this aerodrome. In the afternoon the aerodrome was abandoned as being unserviceable. Subsequently the greater part of the aerodrome was cratered by Army engineers, one runway only being left for emergency use.

Early on the night 9th-I0th December reports were received from the northern part of the beach defences that enemy ships were approaching the beaches. Defensive fire was opened and spread southwards and at about 0400 hrs torpedobombers attacked three ships off this coast. No landing took place but subsequently some boats with Japanese equipment were found on the beach south of Kuantan. This incident had a great influence on the movements of the "Prince of Wales" and "Repulse" which will be recorded later.

151. *Naval Operations.* – In accordance with pre-war plans, submarines of the Royal Netherlands Navy operated off the east coast of Malaya and in the approaches to the Gulf of Thailand during this period. They reported sinking 4 Japanese transports off Patani on the I2th December, and a merchant ship and a laden oil tanker off Kota Bharu on the I2th and I3th December.

Towards dark on the 8th December, Admiral Sir Tom Phillips put to sea with the battleship "Prince of Wales" and the battlecruiser "Repulse" to attack the Japanese ships in the Gulf of Thailand. They were escorted by 4 destroyers. The decision to take the fleet to sea was made by the Commander-in-Chief, Eastern Fleet, after discussing the situation with the Commander-in-Chief, Far East.

On the evening of the 9th December the British Fleet was sighted by a Japanese submarine and also by Japanese reconnaissance aircraft. The Japanese air striking forces, which were being held in readiness, probably in South Indo-China, for this purpose, set off for a night attack on the Fleet but ran into thick weather and were forced to return to their base.

The Commander-in-Chief, Eastern Fleet, realising from his having sighted Japanese aircraft that his movements had been seen, and that the element of surprise had been lost, decided to abandon the project and return to Singapore. During the night 9th-10th December, however, he was informed by his shore Headquarters at Singapore that a landing had been reported at Kuantan. Reconnaissance aircraft were flown off and the Fleet closed the shore in order to clear up the situation before returning to Singapore. Shortly after daylight the Fleet was again located by Japanese reconnaissance aircraft and their striking force was again despatched. At about 1115 it attacked the "Prince of Wales" and "Repulse" when about 60 miles off Kuantan, and by 1320 both these ships had been sunk. Fighter aircraft from Singapore were despatched as soon as the attack on the ships was reported, but only arrived in time to see them go down. 2,185 survivors were picked up by the destroyers and brought to Singapore. The Commander-in-Chief, Eastern Fleet, was lost and was succeeded by Vice-Admiral Sir Geoffrey Layton.

With the sinking of these two ships the Japanese again obtained undisputed control of the sea communications east of Malaya and the whole of the east coast became exposed to attack. I wish to pay tribute to the gallant manner in which the C.-in-C. Eastern Fleet endeavoured to assist the land and air forces by attacking the enemy's sea communications.

152. *Air Operations.* – Early on the 9th December our Air Force attacked targets in the Singora area. Owing to lack of fighter support 5 out of 11 of our aircraft were lost. During the morning Alor Star aerodrome was again heavily bombed and was evacuated later in the day, the buildings being set on fire. The sound of the explosions and the sight of the burning buildings had a considerable psychological effect on the troops of the 11 Indian Division who had been told that their task was to secure this aerodrome for the use of our Air Force. Further attacks were carried out on Sungei Patani and Butterworth aerodromes and, again owing to the lack of light anti-aircraft and fighter defence, casualties were inflicted on the aircraft grounded there. On the 10th Dec. our aerodromes on the Kedah front were again heavily attacked. Sungei Patani aerodrome was evacuated during the day. On this day also the first of a series of heavy Japanese air attacks on Penang Island took place. It was carried out by 70 enemy bombers and Georgetown was the target. There were no anti-aircraft defences, except small arms fire, and few shelters. The inhabitants thronged the streets to watch the attack. The casualties from this raid ran into thousands. A large part of the population left Georgetown and moved to the hills in the centre of the Island, but the A.R.P. and the Medical and the Nursing Services stood firm. The small garrison, in addition to manning the defences, was called upon to assist the Civil Administration by taking the place of labourers and of the personnel of essential municipal services. It also had to assist in burying the dead. On the following day Georgetown was again raided by 25 aircraft and the experiences of the previous day were repeated on a smaller scale.

On the east coast front the enemy during this period concentrated his air attacks on our aerodromes, all of which in the States of Kelantan and Pahang became unserviceable. Valuable photographic reconnaissances were carried out during this period, as they were throughout the campaign, by two pilots flying Buffalo aircraft.

153 *Borneo.* – In accordance with pre-war plans the denials of the Miri and Seria Oilfields and Installations in Sarawak and Brunei were completed, as far as could be done, as soon as hostilities broke out. The refinery at Lutong was also demolished on the 9th Dec.

154. *Command Reserve.* – On the 10th Dec., in view of the threat to Kuantan, the weak strength of the garrison there and the danger to the communications of the Kelantan Force, I moved one battalion of the Command Reserve (2 Bn. The Argyll and Sutherland Highlanders) from the Port Dickson area to the Jerantut area on the east coast railway and placed it under orders of the Commander 3 Indian Corps for duty in that area only.

155. *Summary.* – Since the outbreak of hostilities the general situation had changed greatly to our disadvantage. The Japanese had established complete air superiority over North Malaya and had gained full control of the sea communications east of Malaya. As a result of this the whole of the east coast of Malaya and Singapore Island itself lay open to attack and, to meet attack, reliance would have to be placed almost entirely on the land forces. As regards the land situation the Japanese had established strong forces both in South Thailand and in Kelantan, and nothing could now prevent them from bringing in reinforcements as far as their resources would admit. To make matters worse they had, as far as could be ascertained, landed these forces with the loss of only 7 ships, of which 6 had been sunk by Dutch submarines, in place of the considerable losses which it had been hoped that our Air Force would inflict and which had formed the basis of my estimate of the Army strength required (See Part I, Section VI). Our own forces were weak everywhere and we could not expect any reinforcements until at least the following month, though it was certain that every endeavour would be made to send us such reinforcements as could be made available as early as possible. Further, it had been established that the Japanese force included tanks while we had none.

It was apparent that the safe arrival of reinforcements was of paramount importance and, if we were to attain our object of securing the Naval Base, it was essential that they should arrive in time to take part in operations on the mainland. To enable them to do this, it was necessary that we should impose the maximum delay on the enemy but that at the same time we should avoid having our forces destroyed in detail. If the latter should happen in any area, it might open the way for a rapid advance by the enemy which with our lack of reserves we might find it impossible to stop.

156. *Special Order of the Day.* – On the 10th December I issued the following Special Order of the Day:-

"In this hour of trial the General Officer Commanding calls upon all ranks Malaya Command for a determined and sustained effort to safeguard Malaya and the adjoining British territories. The eyes of the Empire are upon us. Our whole position in the Far East is at stake. The struggle may be long and grim but let all resolve to stand fast come what may and to prove ourselves worthy of the great trust which has been placed in us."

SECTION XX. – THE AIR SITUATION IITH DECEMBER, I94I.

I57. Photographs taken of the aerodromes in South Thailand showed that the Japanese were already operating large numbers of aircraft from them. On Singora aerodrome alone there were upwards of I00 aircraft with comparatively little anti-aircraft gun protection – a wonderful target had we had an adequate and balanced Air Striking Force. The enemy were of course also operating their longer range types of aircraft from their bases in Indo-China and possibly also from aircraft carriers. It is probable that they were operating some 300 modern aircraft at this time. Their bombers were of the Navy 96, the Army 97 and the Junkers 88 types, all twin-engined machines. Their dive-bomber was the Junkers 87B. Their torpedo-bombers were Navy 97's and their fighters were Navy "O" (or Zero) machines. A wide use of auxiliary petrol tanks for the fighters gave them increased range.

In face of this attack the losses suffered by our small Air Force in North Malaya had been comparatively heavy. They had been heavier than they otherwise would have been owing to the inability, due to lack of resources, to provide adequate fighters in North Malaya for the defence of aerodromes and the protection of the bombers, and also owing to the lack of ground defence against low-flying aircraft.

I58. On the 9th and I0th December, Dutch air reinforcements arrived in Malaya from the Netherlands East Indies. They consisted of three squadrons of Glenn Martin Bombers totalling 22 aircraft and one squadron of nine Buffalo fighters. Unfortunately the Dutch bomber pilots were not fully trained in night flying or in advanced navigation over the sea, so that it was necessary for them to return, a squadron at a time, to the Netherlands East Indies for further training in these subjects. Nevertheless, the Netherlands East Indies had shown a most co-operative spirit in sending these aircraft, as well as submarines, so promptly to our assistance.

I59. On the morning of the IIth December, I94I, rather more than I00 aircraft were available for operations disposed as under:-

Seletar.
Vickers Vildebeeste Torpedo-Bombers	I8
Catalina Flying Boats	I
Sharks	5
Swordfish	4

Sembawang.
Hudson General Reconnaissance	4
Buffalo Fighters	I7
Glenn Martin Bombers (N.E.I.)	I3

Tengah.
Blenheim IV Bombers   8

Kallang.
Buffalo Fighters   26

Taiping.
The surviving aircraft from the Northern aerodromes reinforced by a few from the South.

I60. On the IIth December it was decided that the air policy should be as follows:-

(*a*) Bombing, except in special circumstances, to be confined to night. This was made necessary by the enemy's fighter superiority.

(*b*) The primary tasks of the fighters would be the defence of the Singapore Base and the protection of convoys bringing land and air reinforcements to Malaya. The reason for this was that we could not hope to regain superiority without powerful reinforcements. The safe arrival of such reinforcements was therefore the first essential in our air strategy.

As a result of this policy it was clear that the Army would suffer from lack of air support and of close co-operation in the fighting on the mainland, though some seaward reconnaissance would still be possible. I accepted this situation.

SECTION XXI. – THE WITHDRAWAL FROM KELANTAN.

I6I. On the I2th December I94I the Commander, 3 Indian Corps, visited Command Headquarters to discuss the policy as regards the Kelantan Force.

It will be recalled that the task of the Kelantan Force had been the protection of the three aerodromes in that State for the use of our Air Force and the denial of them to the enemy. In view of the situation some fresh instructions were clearly necessary. The alternatives were either to leave the force in Kelantan or to withdraw it for employment elsewhere. The factors in favour of the former course were:-

(*a*) It might still be possible to prevent the enemy making full use of the three aerodromes.

(*b*) The presence of our force in Kelantan would contain a proportion of the enemy's force in that State.

(*c*) The moral effect of the withdrawal both on the civil population and on our own troops would not be good.

(*d*) We should probably lose some material and equipment in the withdrawal.

In favour of a withdrawal were the following factors:-

(*a*) The aerodromes were no longer required by our Air Force and there seemed to be no probability of them being required within a reasonable period of time.

(*b*) It seemed probable that the main threat would develop on the west coast, where we had inadequate resources with which to meet it.

(*c*) The communications of the Kelantan Force, which now consisted of only a single line railway with a number of bridges, were precarious, especially having in view the enemy's great air superiority.

(*d*) In view of (*c*) above and of the superiority on land which the enemy was likely to develop, it seemed probable that we should lose the force if it remained in Kelantan.

After full consideration I decided, with a view to conserving our resources and concentrating them for the main battle which would probably develop on the west coast, to withdraw the Kelantan Force as soon as rolling stock could be made available. This decision was submitted to the C.-in-C., Far East, the same afternoon and approved by him. Orders were issued immediately and the evacuation of surplus stores started at once.

I62. On the I2th December the enemy became very active and attacked in strength, but the 2/I0 Baluch Regt. counter-attacked, coming to close grips with the enemy and inflicting casualties.

On the I3th December the 2/I0 Baluch Regt. again inflicted casualties on the enemy who were trying to advance round their flank.

I63. During the next few days the withdrawal continued systematically, the enemy being made to fight for each position, with comparatively little loss to the defenders. By the I6th December all surplus stores and equipment had been evacuated and the withdrawal of the troops by rail began. The 4/I9 Hyderabads were the first to leave so that they could rejoin their own brigade on the west coast. On the I9th December the railhead at Kuala Krai was evacuated. The rearmost troops withdrew from Kuala Krai on foot as the large railway bridges a little south of that place had by then been destroyed. Practically all the stores and all the vehicles, except about 80 for which no railway flats were available, were successfully evacuated. A rearguard under Lt.-Col. McKellar, known as Macforce, was left behind to watch the railway and prevent the repair of the bridges. It included troops of the Pahang Volunteers and the Malay Regiment and carried out its duties most efficiently.

On completion of the withdrawal on the 22nd December the 8 Indian Infantry Brigade concentrated in the Kuala Lipis/Jerantut area except for the 2/I2 Frontier Force Regt. which rejoined its brigade at Kuantan.

I64. The casualties suffered in the Kelantan fighting had been fairly heavy but not excessive. The conduct of the operations generally and especially of the withdrawal reflected great credit on the Commander of the Force (Brigadier B.W. Key) and his staff.

SECTION XXII. – WEST COAST OPERATIONS I2-I7TH DECEMBER, I94I.

165. *The Battle of Jitra.* – In the absence of the commander of the I5 Indian Infantry Brigade who had, as stated in Section XIX, been cut off as a result of the action in the outpost position, the commander of the 28 Indian Infantry Brigade (Brigadier Carpendale) temporarily took over command of the I5 Brigade as well as his own and held it until the return of Brigadier Garrett, the following day.

166. Shortly after midnight II/I2th December the Japanese attacked the left forward company of the 2/9 Jats east of the Singora road. Two Hours later the frontage had been extended to involve the right forward companies of the 2/9 Jats and the I Leicesters. By 0400 hrs. the right rear company of the Jats had also been attacked but had repulsed the enemy. At dawn the Japanese infantry made a determined frontal attack on the Jats and Leicesters and suffered heavy losses but by midday had penetrated deep into the area held by the Jats. The Leicesters formed a defensive flank to their right. In the meantime the Commander I5 Brigade had called upon the Commander 6 Brigade for assistance and had been given 1½ battalions which he used to protect his right flank.

167. At about 0830 hrs. the Commander II Indian Division asked Headquarters 3 Indian Corps for permission to withdraw his division to Gurun, some 30 miles to the south, and possibly later to the Krian River. The Commander 3 Indian Corps was at that time on his way to Singapore to confer on the Kelantan policy (see Section XXI), so the message was telephoned direct to me. Such a long withdrawal had not been considered in our pre-war discussions of war plans and it would immediately have prejudiced our chances of denying the west coast aerodromes to the enemy. Moreover I felt that such a withdrawal would have a most demoralising effect on both the troops and on the civil population. This view was endorsed by the War Council which was sitting at the time. I therefore replied to the effect that pending further orders the battle was to be fought out on the Jitra position. At that time the Jats were, in point of fact, the only battalion which had incurred serious losses although two battalions had, as already recorded, been rendered ineffective on the previous day.

168. During the morning two counter-attacks were made by the I/8 Punjab Regt. on the enemy who had penetrated east of the road and, although unsuccessful in re-capturing the lost ground, were effective in stopping the enemy's advance for the time being.

In the early afternoon the enemy infantry resumed their advance on the right and attacked the 2/2 Gurkha Rifles holding the line of the Bata River. The left of this battalion was at the iron bridge on the main road and between it and the right of the Leicesters further north was a gap of 1½ miles. The Leicesters were now ordered to withdraw from their prepared position and to take up a new position with their right on the iron bridge, their centre on Jitra village and their left at Rimba. This gave them a front of over two miles with a pronounced salient in the middle.

Later in the afternoon the road south of Jitra came under close range enemy fire. The traffic on it at the time was heavy and some confusion developed. The Divisional

Commander, fearing the enemy would move round our right flank, ordered two companies of the East Surreys to move back by rail to guard the vital bridges at Kepala Batas.

I69. At about I930 hrs. the Commander II Indian Division again asked for permission to withdraw. The request was telephoned to me at Headquarters Malaya Command where I was still in conference with the Commander 3 Indian Corps. After consultation I authorised the latter to despatch the following message to the Commander II Indian Division:-

> "After consultation it is decided that your task is to fight for the security of North Kedah. Estimated that you are only opposed by one Japanese division at most. Consider best solution may be to hold up advance enemy tanks on good obstacle and dispose your forces to obtain considerable depth on both roads and to obtain scope for your superior artillery. Reserves for employment in divisional area are being expedited."

I70. The divisional orders for the withdrawal were sent out at 2I00 hrs. The plan in outline was that the 28 Brigade, reconstituted under Brigadier Carpendale and with one battalion of the I5 Brigade under its command, should hold a position between Langgar and the south bank of the River Kedah at Alor Star. This meant a withdrawal of some I0 miles. The remainder of I5 Brigade was to be in reserve. The 6 Brigade was to occupy a position 7 miles further back at Simpang Empat. A small composite force was to hold the line of the River Padang Terap until the I5 Brigade had passed through.

This withdrawal would have been difficult under the most favourable conditions. With units mixed as a result of the day's fighting, communications broken and the night dark, it was inevitable that orders would be delayed and in some cases would not reach the addressees. This was what in fact occurred. Some units and sub-units withdrew without incident. Others, finding themselves unable to use the only road, had to make their way as best they could across country. Some parties reached the coast and, taking boats, rejoined further south. Some again were still in position the following morning.

I7I. On the day after the battle the strength of the I5 Brigade was only about 600 and it was temporarily unfit for further fighting. The 6 Brigade, though still a fighting formation, had also had serious losses. In the 28 Brigade the 2/I Gurkha Rifles, except for one intact company, had been almost wiped out. The other two battalions had suffered about I00 casualties between them. Several guns had been lost. The majority had either been caught on the wrong side of demolitions, or become inextricably bogged in their gun positions or been cut off by enemy penetration, it being impossible in most places to move them across country. A large number of vehicles were lost for similar reasons. The loss of carriers, small arms weapons, signalling equipment etc. had also been very heavy. These were serious losses as in many cases there were not sufficient reserves in Malaya to replace them.

The II Indian Division needed to be relieved, rested and reorganised before being again called upon to fight, but there were no troops available to relieve it.

I72. It is unlikely that the Japanese employed more than one division during the battle of Jitra. Their success was won primarily by bold and skilful infantry tactics and by the use of tanks. They employed no artillery heavier than the infantry gun and in this action they made little use of aircraft in support of ground forces. They exploited the moral value of noise behind the defences. They also appear to have had an organized "fifth column" plan which had at least a partial success by spreading false rumours.

I73. It is probably true to say that the battle of Jitra was half lost before it began. The change from an anticipated offensive to a strategical defensive had, as has been stated, an adverse moral effect on the troops. The temporary loss of two battalions on the previous day had left serious gaps in the reserves on the right flank. In consequence, when the enemy broke into the defences, the reserves were not strong enough to prevent the enemy getting control of the one vital artery of communications. Veteran troops would have found these conditions trying enough. They were in some cases too trying for the young and inexperienced troops of which the II Indian Division was composed. Finally, the eventual withdrawal, carried out in very difficult circumstances, was too complicated and too long for troops who were already exhausted and considerably disorganised.

I74. *The Command Reserve.* – On the I2th December I placed the Command Reserve (I2 Indian Brigade Group), with the exception of headquarters and one battery of the I22 Field Regiment, at the disposal of the Commander 3 Indian Corps for employment on the west coast. With the exception of the 4/I9 Hyderabad Regiment, which had to be withdrawn from Kelantan, the Brigade Group began to move forward immediately by road and rail

I75 *The Kroh Front.* – Early on the morning of the I2th December (the day of the Jitra battle) the enemy again attacked the 3/I6 Punjab Regiment but was driven back. An outflanking movement, however, forced the Punjabs to withdraw with heavy casualties to one of their forward companies. Eventually the 3/I6 Punjab Regiment withdrew through the 5/I4 Punjab Regiment to Kroh. Their strength, including 50 reinforcements, was now about 400. They destroyed three bridges on the road to Klian Intan and Grik and moved into a prepared position 2 or 3 miles west of Kroh The orders given to the Commanding Officer of the 5/I4 Punjab Regt. were that he was to delay the enemy but not become inextricably involved.

Two Japanese companies attacking at dawn on the I3th December were practically annihilated by the fire of our light automatics. Enemy enveloping movements round both flanks, however, forced a withdrawal and the 5/I4 Punjab Regt. with attached troops fell back to Betong, where the battalion embussed, and by dusk the whole force was in occupation of the position west of Kroh.

At midnight I2/I3th December the Commander 3 Indian Corps took over direct command of Krohcol from the Commander II Indian Division.

At midday on the I4th December the Commander I2 Indian Infantry Brigade took over command of Krohcol and moved it to the Baling area some 9 miles west of Kroh. Krohcol, as an independent force, was then dissolved.

The withdrawal of Krohcol to the position west of Kroh left uncovered the jungle road through Klian Intan to Grik and thence the metalled road to Kuala Kangsar and Ipoh. Reports on this road had indicated that as far as Grik it was passable only for light M.T. in dry weather. We were soon to learn that these reports were optimistic. To meet the threat a company of the 2 Argyll & Sutherland Highlanders with a detachment of the F.M S.V.F. Armoured Cars was ordered to Grik.

176. *Headquarters 3 Indian Corps.* – On the night 13/14th December the Commander 3 Indian Corps moved up to Bukit Mertajam in Province Wellesley where he established an advanced headquarters.

177. *The Battle of Gurun.* – At dawn on the 13th December there were only three companies in position on the south bank of the Kedah River with one company at Langgar. The large road bridge south of Alor Star was destroyed, but an attempt to destroy the railway bridge was less successful. The enemy made only one attempt to cross during the day and, after getting a footing on the south bank, was driven back. During the night 13/14th December and the morning of the 14th all troops of II Indian Division were withdrawn to the Gurun position. Here, where the plain merges into the rolling thickly wooded rubber country of South Kedah, was perhaps the best natural defensive position in Malaya. It had previously been reconnoitred and was again reconnoitred as soon as the Japanese advance began. A large labour force had been ordered to assemble but failed to appear and no work had been done on the position when the division arrived.

178. The Gurun position was occupied with the 28 Indian Infantry Brigade on the right and the 6 Indian Infantry Brigade on the left with the weak 15 Indian Infantry Brigade in reserve. On the afternoon of the 14th December the enemy attacked down the mam road with tanks followed by infantry in lorries and supported by aircraft. Some penetration took place but the enemy were stopped by local counter-attacks. During the night, however, the enemy effected a deep penetration down the road and at 0700 hrs. attacked the Headquarters of the 6 Brigade. All the officers except the Brigadier himself were killed. There was a large gap now between the main road and Kedah peak. East of the road, however, our forward troops were still in position, but they were now moved to block the main road down which the enemy was advancing. By the afternoon the division was again in confusion and the 28 Brigade was the only one which could for the time being be relied upon. The Divisional Commander decided to withdraw his force behind the River Muda during the following night covered by the only fresh troops which were available i.e. the Independent Company which had just arrived from Penang and one squadron of 3 Indian Cavalry. Units of the 28 Brigade and the 2 East Surrey Regt. did some splendid work in covering the withdrawal. As had happened before, the premature demolition of bridges was the cause of losses of many vehicles and carriers.

179. By the morning of 16th December the Division was south of the River Muda and had passed into Province Wellesley. The 12 Indian Brigade Group (less one battalion) had moved into position on its right with one battalion (the 5/2 Punjab Regt.) at Batu Pekaka, an important bridge over the River Muda, and the Argylls at Baling.

180. The Division was in no fit state for further operations. Most of the men were

tired and dispirited. They badly needed time to reorganise and refit. There had been a further heavy loss of vehicles and weapons. Some of these it was now impossible to replace. The tanks had again played their part in the battle of Gurun, but the enemy should not have been allowed to penetrate as he did down the main road. Later, lack of communications made it difficult for formation commanders to control the battle. The Divisional Commander courageously tried to control the battle from a carrier, but the thickly wooded country was against him. All the infantry brigade Commanders had become casualties.

181. On the 15th December the R.A.F. evacuated Butterworth aerodrome The 16 Light A.A. Battery had done some good work in defence of this aerodrome, claiming 4 enemy aircraft certain and 6 other probables brought down.

182. *Penang.* – Although the Island of Penang had been since 1936 (see Part I Section VI) officially a fortress, it was in fact in December, 1941, far from being one. The garrison on the 12th December, 1941, consisted of:-

Fortress Headquarters and Signals.
11 Coast Regt. Hong Kong and Singapore Royal Artillery (two 6-m. batteries).
36 Fortress Company Royal Engineers (manning searchlights).
One Company 5/14 Punjab Regt.
1 Independent Company.
Detachment of 3 Indian Cavalry.
The 3 (Penang and Province Wellesley) Battalion S.S.V.F.
A Mixed Reinforcement Camp.
Administrative Detachments.

There were no anti-aircraft defences as the guns and searchlights had not yet arrived from the U.K. The civil airport was too small for normal R.A.F. requirements. The only fighter defence was provided by five Buffalo Fighters which were able to operate for one day only from the Butterworth aerodrome.

In addition to the Island the Commander Penang Fortress (Brig. Lyon) was responsible also for a part of the Prai-Butterworth area on the mainland and for the Lines of Communication area (North).

183. The original object of fortifying the Island of Penang was to secure the anchorage which lies between the Island and the mainland from sea and air attack, as the Royal Navy contemplated using it both for warships and as a convoy collecting port.

184. The pre-war instructions to the Commander 3 Indian Corps were to the effect that II Indian Division, if driven back, would fall back on the axis of the main road and railway communication arteries, leaving on Penang Island, which would be held, up to two additional infantry battalions with supporting troops.

185. The effects of the first air attacks on Penang on the 10th and 11th December have already been described in Section XIX. On the 13th December 50 Naval Ratings, survivors from the "Prince of Wales" and "Repulse" arrived to operate the ferries, the crews of which had disappeared.

On the 12th December at a meeting between the Fortress Commander and the

Resident Counsellor it was decided to evacuate on the following night all European Service families and the Resident Counsellor was asked to arrange for the evacuation of all civilian European women and children. This decision was taken as a normal measure to evacuate "bouches inutiles". The evacuation of the sick and wounded from the military hospital was also ordered.

186. On the 13th December the policy as regards the defence of Penang had to be reviewed in the light of the situation on the mainland which has been described earlier in this Section. There was a very real danger that the II Indian Division, which at this time was in an exhausted and very disorganized condition, would be overrun and cease to exist as a fighting formation. There was also the danger that the threat from Kroh, which was now much greater than we had anticipated, would cut the communications of the II Indian Division in the Kuala Kangsar area. If either of these things had happened, the enemy would have had a clear run down the west coast, for there were no other troops with which to oppose him north of Johore, and by doing so he would have cut the communications of 9 Indian Division on the east coast. That was the situation we had to face and we had the choice of trying to fight the enemy both on the mainland and on Penang Island or of concentrating the whole of our resources for the battle on the mainland. The anchorage was no longer of any use.

187. The matter was of such importance that I brought it before the Far East War Council on the morning of 14th December. The pros, and cons, were discussed and carefully considered. It was decided that our ability to hold Penang must depend upon the result of the battle upon the mainland, and that we should concentrate on averting the calamity which threatened; further, that if we failed to stop the enemy upon the mainland the policy would be to evacuate what remained of the garrison from Penang rather than leave the population exposed to unrestricted air attack against which we could provide them with no defence.

In accordance with the above decision, I caused the following telegram to be despatched to the Commander, 3 Indian Corps at 1125 hrs. 14th December:-

"Importance of covering Penang is increased by fact that bulk of remaining cables to U.K. and India pass through that Island. Considered that ability to hold Penang depends upon result of Kedah battle. You are at liberty, therefore to use any part of the garrison of Penang that can be made available to take part in Kedah operations, particularly Independent Company. Should it become impossible to cover Penang from mainland, policy will be to evacuate Penang removing by sea the garrison and such essential stores as possible and destroying remainder. Preliminary arrangements should be made as necessary but to avoid causing alarm it is of utmost importance that such arrangements should be kept secret. Resident Counsellor Penang is being given similar instructions. Acknowledge."

188. On the 14th December the Municipal Commissioners of Georgetown presented a memorandum to the Fortress Commander stating that the Civil Administration had broken down and pointing out the danger of outbreaks of cholera and typhoid owing to the fouling of the water catchment area and the breakdown of the sanitary and

conservancy services.

189. At II00 hrs. I5th December, following a warning the previous evening, the Fortress Commander received an order from the Commander 3 Indian Corps that the evacuation, which was to take place by sea, would be completed on the night I6th-I7th December. Shipping had to be found locally. Most of the troops were moved to the mainland but the remainder and all Europeans, except a few who remained behind at their own request, were evacuated. Asiatics serving in the Volunteers were given the option of being evacuated or of staying. The majority decided to stay to protect their families. Lack of transport would have made it quite out of the question to evacuate large numbers of Asiatics. Moreover it was undesirable at that stage to increase the population of Singapore.

190. A great deal of denial work was done at Penang. The Fixed Defences were effectively destroyed and the smaller weapons were withdrawn. At least most of the ammunition in the magazines was destroyed, as also was much of the oil and petrol. Denial schemes were similarly carried out at many of the civil establishments. But it was hardly to be expected in the circumstances that the destruction would be complete and there were two unfortunate omissions which had a very considerable effect on subsequent events. One was the failure to destroy the Penang Broadcasting Station from which during the rest of the campaign a stream of anti-British propaganda was sent out and the other was the failure to remove or scuttle all the small vessels and barges in the harbour. The latter was probably due, at least in part, to the masters and crews having disappeared. The Japanese later made great use of them in developing their threats to our communications from the west coast. When this omission was discovered a destroyer was sent by night to mine the southern exit from the harbour, but this could not have been entirely effective.

19I. *Province Wellesley Operations.* – On the I6th December heavy fighting developed at the Batu Pekaka Bridge on the right of the River Muda position where the 5/2 Punjab Regt. was attacked by enemy troops led by an European. Late in the afternoon the enemy succeeded in getting a footing south of the river but were ejected by counter-attack. The Argylls were withdrawn from Baling to Titi Karangan.

During the day the units of II Indian Division were being reformed in Province Wellesley covered by a weak rear-guard which consisted of one platoon and the armoured train on the railway bridge, the Independent Company and a company of Leicesters at the two main road bridges and a squadron of 3 Indian Cavalry at the ferry to the west of them. The I37 Field Regt. was in support.

The Commander 3 Indian Corps, in consultation with the Commander II Indian Division, decided to withdraw the division behind the River Krian, the main bridges over which were at that time being held by personnel from the Penang Reinforcements Camp. The 28 Brigade moved by road and rail to Simpang Lima and the next morning took over the defence of the River Krian from the railway bridge at Nibong Tebal to the sea. Fifteen miles to their right at Selama was the 3/I6 Punjab Regt. from Kroh.

During the I7th December the troops on the Muda River and in the Bukit Mertajam area were withdrawn to the Taiping area where they came into reserve to the Krian defences. The I2 Brigade Group fought a rear-guard action from the Batu Pekaka Bridge to the Terap – Selama area. By the I8th December all troops were south of the River Krian.

192. *The Grik Road.* – On the Grik Road contact was made a little north of Grik during the night I6th-I7th December. Our small force, which consisted only of one company of the Argylls and a detachment of F.M.S.V.F. Armoured Cars was hard pressed on the I7th and fell back to the area South of Sumpitan. It was reinforced by two platoons of the Perak Battalion F M.S.V.F. It now became clear that the enemy had directed the main body of his Patani Force down this road, difficult as it was for wheeled transport, and was endeavouring to cut off the II Indian Division by reaching the main road at Kuala Kangsar. Indeed, reports from Japanese sources have subsequently indicated that this was a strong attack and that their grand strategy was to cut off and annihilate the whole of the troops in Kedah and Province Wellesley.

193. On the evening of the I7th December the Commander 3 Indian Corps decided that the I2 Brigade Group which he had intended to withdraw into reserve at Taiping, should go straight through to Kuala Kangsar and that the I Independent Company should leave Taiping at first light on the I8th December for Lenggong on the Grik Road.

194. *Future Operations.* – On the evening I7th December I authorised the Commander 3 Indian Corps to withdraw to the line of the River Perak if he thought such a withdrawal absolutely necessary. I also instructed him to arrange for reconnaissances to be carried out of the Slim River Line in South Perak and placed at his disposal officer teams from the Officers Cadet Training Unit to assist in carrying out rearward reconnaissances.

I now foresaw that, if the Japanese advanced into Perak, their communications would become very vulnerable to raids from the sea coast. I therefore arranged for a small force of about 50 picked Australians to be organized for seaborne raids on the enemy's communications, using Port Swettenham as a base.

SECTION XXIII. – THE STRATEGICAL SITUATION, I7TH-23RD DECEMBER, I94I.

195. *Naval.* – Following the loss of the "Prince of Wales" and "Repulse" the seagoing naval forces based on Singapore consisted only of a few light cruisers and half a dozen destroyers and sloops. Most of these were employed on escort work, leaving only three destroyers and a number of auxiliary vessels and small craft for local defence.

On the I7th December the Perak Flotilla, which consisted of H.M.S. "Scout" and some light craft, was formed to deny to all enemy craft the approaches to the West Coast between the River Krian and the River Bernam (south of Telok Anson).

The submarines of the Royal Dutch Navy, which during the first few days had operated successfully in the waters east of Malaya, had had losses and only a very few now remained.

The Japanese Navy had so far confined its activities to protection of its convoys. Although it held undisputed control of the waters east of Malaya it had as yet made no attempt to interfere with our communications south or west of Malaya either by naval or air action.

196. *Air.* – The main concern of the Japanese Air Force was obviously to confirm and extend the superiority which it had already established. Apart therefore from the heavy attacks on Penang and a few attacks on targets in the battle area, its activities continued to be directed against our aerodromes.

The strength of our Air Force, including the Dutch reinforcements, was now a little over 100 – probably about one quarter of the Japanese strength.

In accordance with the agreed policy, the bulk of the fighters were retained on the Singapore aerodromes for defence of the Singapore Base and for convoy protection work. The balance were under command of Norgroup for operations in the 3 Corps area.

The Dutch bombers were, for reasons already given, being used principally for reconnaissance work. The torpedo-bombers, with their limited radius of action, were retained for attack on any naval force which might approach Singapore or the east coast of Johore. As regards the possibility of reinforcements, the Japanese had cut the established air route between Singapore and India. It now became necessary to use the Dutch aerodrome at Sabang, an island off the northern tip of Sumatra, as a link in the air route, but this could only be used by the longer range type of aircraft. Fighters could only be brought by sea.

In order to provide accommodation for the large number of aircraft which it was hoped would shortly concentrate in the Singapore area, the construction of new aerodrome strips was put in hand, both in South Johore and on Singapore Island.

I felt that the recovery of air superiority was so vital that I agreed to give priority to the Air Force so far as labour was concerned for the construction of these new air strips and for the maintenance of the existing aerodromes.

There was no way of regaining air superiority unless and until a sufficient number of modern fighters, superior to the Japanese fighters, could be brought to Malaya and until their pilots could have time to develop full fighting efficiency in conditions that would be strange to them. The first of these fighter aircraft could not be expected to reach Malaya in much under four weeks.

197. *Army.* – Our troops who had been in contact with the enemy had suffered severe losses both in men and material. Our strength on the west coast, apart from the Volunteer units, was now barely one division, including the 12 Indian Brigade Group and 1st Line Reinforcements. Against this the Japanese probably had in the front line one division moving on the axis of the main road and one division on the Grik road. Behind these we estimated that they had in reserve and already landed further forces at least equal to those in the front line.

On the east coast the enemy had landed one division in the Kelantan area.

In Indo-China he undoubtedly held reserves, which he could either use to reinforce those formations which had already landed or for fresh enterprises.

The striking power of his field force was greatly increased by the inclusion of a component of modern tanks of which we had none.

198. On our side we knew that every endeavour would be made to send reinforcements to Malaya, but we also knew that no reinforcements could arrive before some time in the first half of January. The comparison of forces as above showed clearly that we must make every endeavour to ensure the safe arrival of these reinforcements, for it was only with their assistance that we could hope to turn the scales on land. One of the chief dangers to which convoys bringing reinforcements would be exposed was from attack by Japanese aircraft as they were approaching Singapore. If the Japanese could establish their fighters on the aerodromes in Central Malaya they would be able to give their bombers much more effective support and thus render their attacks more dangerous. It was clear therefore that we should make every endeavour to deny these aerodromes to them for as long as possible.

199. On the west coast the terrain in the State of Perak was, generally speaking, more suitable for delaying action than was that in the States of Selangor and Negri Sembilan further south. In the latter States were many more roads to facilitate the enemy's movements, while the vast rubber estates rendered movement off the roads easy for infantry and at the same time provided good cover for the attacker. The States of Perak and Selangor also were the centre of the tin-mining industry which was at that time of such vital importance to the Allied war effort. There were also vast rubber estates in this area.

The weakness of the Perak area from the defence point of view lay in the fact that the long road and rail communications lay roughly parallel to the River Perak. Consequently if enemy detachments could get a footing on the left bank of that river they would be able to harass and temporarily to interrupt our communications.

200. It was necessary also to take into consideration the condition of the troops of II Indian Division. Though their morale was not broken, it could not be regarded as being as high as one would have wished. They were undoubtedly very exhausted by almost continuous fighting and movement both by day and night. Moreover, the superiority which the Japanese possessed in the air coupled with the complete absence of tanks on our side could not but have the most adverse effect upon the trust reposed by the Indian troops in the might of the British Empire. It is not too much to say that the Indian troops were dismayed to find the British so outclassed in these two essentials of modern war.

201. As regards the enemy's course of action, it was now clear that he intended to continue his advance down the west coast with a view to attacking Singapore from the North. Combined with this, his forces in Kelantan might move southward by the coastal route or he might deliver sea-borne attacks against the Kuantan and/or East Johore areas with a view to cutting our communications with our forces in the North, or he might deliver a sea-borne attack against Singapore direct. There remained also the possibility of an air-borne attack directed against our aerodromes.

202. I was informed by the C.-in-C. Far East that the policy was to keep the enemy as far north in Malaya as possible in order to prevent him acquiring territory and particularly aerodromes which would threaten the arrival of reinforcements.

203. I considered the possibility of moving up all or part of the A.I.F. in relief of troops of II Indian Division but rejected the idea for the following reasons:-

(*a*) The relief could not be carried out without temporarily leaving the Johore defences very weak;

(*b*) It was undesirable to break up the A.I.F. organization;

(*c*) On the other hand, if the whole of the A.I.F. was sent, the relief would necessarily take a long time and ultimately the vital Johore area would be held by tired troops with no previous experience of that part of Malaya.

204. I decided to go to Ipoh to discuss the situation with the Commander 3 Indian Corps and left Singapore late on the 17th December.

After a reconnaissance of the area and a visit to some of the forward troops on the 18th December the following decisions were made:-

(*a*) While adhering to the general policy of withdrawal behind the River Perak, the enemy would be held west of the river as long as possible without permitting our forces to become inextricably committed.

(*b*) The Commander 3 Indian Corps would select and have prepared a series of positions between Ipoh and Tanjong Malim.

(*c*) The immediate role of 9 Indian Division would be (i) to continue to deny the Kuantan aerodrome to the enemy, (ii) to secure the II Indian Division and its communications against attack from the east coast.

(*d*) As soon as the withdrawal across the River Perak had taken place, the best area for the operations of the sea-borne raiding force (to be known as "Rose Force") would be that part of the state of Perak which lies west of the river and south of the railway.

(*e*) Arrangements were to be made for land raiding parties and for "left behind" parties to harass the enemy's communications.

(*f*) A liaison officer was appointed to co-ordinate the action of the military and civil authorities in the west coast theatre of operations.

(*g*) The 6 and I5 Indian Infantry Brigades were to be amalgamated and to be known as the 6/I5 Indian Infantry Brigade. Certain units were to be amalgamated, notably the East Surreys and Leicesters which became known as the British Battalion. The I2 Indian Brigade Group was to be incorporated into the II Indian Division.

(*h*) The Commander 3 Indian Corps was to consider the question of the command of II Indian Division. It was felt that an officer with the widest possible experience of bush warfare was required. A few days later Brigadier Paris, the Commander I2 Indian Infantry Brigade, who had been in Malaya for 2½ years, was appointed to succeed Major-General Murray Lyon.

As all the infantry brigade commanders of the division had become casualties, Lt.-Col. Moorhead was appointed to command the 6/15 Brigade, Lt.-Col. Stewart the 12 Brigade and Lt.-Col. Selby the 28 Brigade.

(*j*) All troops were to be given a minimum period of 48 hours rest as soon as this could be arranged. Defence in depth astride the main road after crossing the River Perak seemed to be the only way to make this possible.

(*k*) It was now clear that we were faced by an enemy who had made a special study of bush warfare on a grand scale and whose troops had been specially trained in those tactics. He relied in the main on outflanking movements and on infiltration by small parties into and behind our lines.

For support of his forward troops he relied on the mortar and the infantry gun rather than on longer range weapons. His snipers operated from trees. He exploited the use of fireworks. For mobility he made a wide use of civilian bicycles seized in the country. His tanks he had up to date operated mainly on the roads. His infantry had displayed an ability to cross obstacles – rivers, swamps, jungles, etc. – more rapidly than had previously been thought possible. Finally, speed was obviously of vital importance to him and he was prepared to press his attacks without elaborate preparations.

To meet these tactics, it was agreed that brigade groups should be echeloned in depth astride the main arteries of communication and that in selecting defensive positions special regard should be had to tank obstacles and cover from air, in both of which arms the enemy were well equipped while we were entirely deficient.

205. On return to Singapore I circulated an Instruction on the tactics to be employed, the main points of which were as follows:-

(i) Enemy outflanking and infiltration tactics must not lead to withdrawals which should take place only on order of higher authority.

(ii) Immediate counter-attacks should be exploited. These should, whenever possible, be planned beforehand and, owing to the necessity for speed, should usually be carried out by small bodies of a company on the initiative of local commanders.

(iii) It was suggested that the defences should consist of a holding group dug in astride the main communications, with striking forces forward on the flanks which should attack as soon as the enemy made contact with the holding groups.

(iv) The spreading of rumours must be suppressed.

(v) The enemy could not be defeated by sitting in prepared positions and letting him walk round us. We must play him at his own game and attack on every occasion. The efficiency, cunning and alertness of the individual were of primary importance.

Arrangements were made for the evacuation of as much as possible of the reserve stores from the Ipoh area. There was not, however, sufficient M.T. available to move the petrol, which was stored in 60-gallon drams. Arrangements were made for these to be destroyed by puncturing the drums.

I returned to Singapore on the morning of the 20th December.

206. The importance of the lateral road Jerantut – Kuala Lipis – Raub – Kuala Kubu, which was the main communication between East and West Malaya, now became apparent. If our forces on the west coast were driven back beyond Kuala Kubu, the enemy would be able to cut the only road communication of our forces on the east coast.

I discussed this situation with the C.-in-C. Far East and the A.O.C. It was agreed as a general policy that we should withdraw the Kuantan garrison at a time to be decided later in accordance with the development of the situation.

I also thought it desirable to take preliminary steps for the defence of North Johore and of Singapore Island itself against attack from the North.

On the 23rd December I caused to be issued Malaya Command Order No. 28, an extract from which is attached to this Despatch as Appendix "C".

207. The Commander A.I.F. delegated responsibility for the defence of North Johore to the 27 Australian Brigade Group in A.I.F. Malaya Operation Instruction No. II dated 24th December 1941 from which the following is an extract:-

"The 27 Brigade Group is made responsible for holding delaying positions towards the Johore – Malacca boundary. Requisition for local labour is to be submitted to the C.R.E."

"The Bde. Gp. is to be disposed as under:-

(i) Gemas – Segamat, one Bn. Gp. plus one Coy.

(ii) Muar, one Bn. (less two Coys.) with attached troops.

(iii) Reserve (in Kluang – Ayer – Hitam area) one Bn. Gp."

SECTION XXIV. – WEST COAST OPERATIONS, 18TH-30TH DECEMBER, 1941.

208. *The Grik Road.* – On the 19th December our troops, who had now been reinforced, moved forward to recapture Sumpitan, led by the Independent Company. An encounter battle took place in the village, where our troops fought gallantly and were only withdrawn in face of a strong counter-attack. That night they fell back to Lenggong. On the 20th the Argylls were heavily engaged all day and had to drive off by counter-attack an enemy force which had moved down the river on rafts and reached Kota Tampan in their rear. On the 21st the Argylls held the Kota Tampan area against renewed enemy attacks, while the 5/2 Punjab Regt. occupied positions west of Chenderoh Lake. Some enemy rafts were sunk on the lake. At about 1800 hrs. the Argylls disengaged and withdrew through the 5/2 Punjab Regt. and the enemy following up were stopped at the Causeway.

The river approach through the Chenderoh Lake now gave the Japanese the opportunity of by-passing Kuala Kangsar and of threatening the main road and railway bridges over the River Perak and the communications east of them. To meet this threat the 4/19 Hyderabad Regt., which had now arrived from Kelantan, was concentrated east of the River Perak.

The enemy were now only some 12 miles from Lawin, where the Grik road joins the trunk road, and the situation demanded the speedy withdrawal of the 28 Brigade Group before it could be cut off in its positions north of Taiping.

209. *The Krian River Front.* – On the 19th and 20th December there was some activity on the right of the Krian River position and, to avoid being outflanked on the right, the 28 Brigade Group fell back to Ulu Sapetang and Bagan Serai. The bridges over the River Krian were demolished.

210. *The Tactical Situation.* – On the evening of 21st December all troops west of the River Perak, including those on the Grik road, were placed directly under the Commander II Indian Division. He decided that, in view of the situation on the Grik road, an immediate withdrawal behind the River Perak was necessary. He realised the importance of covering the Blanja Pontoon Bridge over the River Perak which gave direct access to the Ipoh area and the communications south of it.

The withdrawal of the 28 Brigade Group commenced at 2000 hrs. 21st December, the units being disposed as far as possible to meet all possible threats.

On the 22nd December there was further fighting on the Grik Road and that night the 12 Brigade Group withdrew across the Perak River covered by troops of the 28 Brigade Group. By the morning of the 23rd December all troops, except for a bridgehead at Blanja, were east of the river. The Blanja bridgehead was withdrawn on the night 23rd–24th December.

A gap was successfully blown in the Iskander Bridge, the fine main road bridge over the River Perak. A portion of the pontoon bridge at Blanja was swung to the eastern shore and the pontoons sunk.

On withdrawal the 12 Brigade Group bivouacked in the Salak North area and the 28 Brigade Group concentrated in the Siputeh area with a detachment watching the River Perak at Blanja.

211. *Summary.* – After sixteen days of continuous and exhausting operations our troops on the west coast were back behind the River Perak. What would have happened had Operation MATADOR been put into effect in good time is a matter for speculation. It is almost certain that it would have eased the air situation by denying to the enemy some of its fighter bases. On the other hand, had we been unable to hold the strong enemy thrust on the Kroh front our communications to North Malaya and subsequently to East Malaya would have been severed and our whole structure of defence undermined. For the frustration of the enemy's plan to destroy our forces in this way we are indebted particularly to the fine fighting of the troops on the Kroh and Grik roads and to the quick reaction of all commanders to the very real threat which the enemy's thrust on this front constituted.

212. *Operations in the Ipoh area.* – On the 22nd December the Commander 3 Indian Corps decided to hold the areas south of Ipoh as under:-

One Brigade Group between Kg. Sahum and Tapah.

One Brigade Group covering road and railway north of Kampar.

One Brigade Group covering road and railway north of Bidor with a battalion at Ct.

Jong and the Independent Company at Telok Anson.

On the 23rd December the Commander 3 Indian Corps issued instructions to the Commander II Indian Division, the gist of which were as under:-

(*a*) The Commander II Indian Division would assume control of all combatant troops north of the Rivers Slim and Bernam.

(*b*) The enemy was to be delayed for as long as possible west of the River Kinta.

(*c*) The positions at Kg. Sahum – Kampar – Tapah and Bidor must be held until the strategic situation demanded that the Division be withdrawn. A rear position was being prepared in the neighbourhood of the River Slim.

(*d*) Local offensive operations were advocated.

(*e*) In case communications should be cut, each battalion was to hold I0 days' supplies and ammunition.

(*f*) Fighting patrols were to be employed to watch the flanks which could never be secure.

(*g*) Civil labour was being engaged and handled by the Europeans of the Perak Volunteer Force.

The 6/I5 Indian Infantry Brigade had now been rested and reorganised. Three days in the Ipoh area had worked wonders. All units had been partly, but far from completely, re-equipped. The outlook was very much brighter. The Kampar position was rapidly put into a state of defence.

2I3. On the 26th and 27th December the I2 Brigade Group fought a delaying action north of Chemor (I0 miles north of Ipoh) inflicting heavy casualties on the enemy, whose units moved forward in close formation. The 5/2 Punjab Regiment, upon which the brunt of the fighting fell, distinguished itself though it suffered fairly heavy losses.

During these two days the 28 Brigade Group continued to watch the line of the River Perak in the Blanja area.

By the 26th all troops remaining in Ipoh had moved south. Among the last to leave their posts were the Chinese and Eurasian girl operators of the telephone exchange who were handling military traffic and who continued to do so in the face of bombing and the approach of the enemy until ordered to leave. They deserve the highest praise.

The withdrawal of the I2 and 28 Brigade Groups began at I900 hrs. on the 27th December and continued throughout the night. The I2 Brigade Group, to which had been allotted the task of delaying the enemy's approach to the Kampar position north of Dipang, occupied a position south of Gopeng, while the 28 Brigade Group took up positions astride the defile road which protected the right flank of the Kampar position, with one battalion in the Tapah area.

The newly formed Kedah Armoured Car Company, manned by European Volunteers, acquitted itself well during and following the withdrawal. It now became apparent, however, that the enemy were using an armour-piercing bullet against which the armour of the Marmon-Harrington armoured cars was not proof. Many casualties were suffered by the crews of these cars during the subsequent operations.

2I4. On the 29th December the I2 Brigade, Group was early in contact with the enemy who attacked at I000 hrs. The attack was repulsed but, realising that the enemy was now in strength, the divisional commander ordered the brigade to withdraw that evening through the Kampar position and come into reserve at Bidor. The enemy followed up the withdrawal closely and again tanks produced a demoralizing effect on the tired troops. The situation was saved by some excellent work on the part of the I37 Field Regt. and the 80 A/Tk. Regt. The large bridge over the River Kampar at Dipang was destroyed after several abortive attempts.

The I2 Brigade Group had had a gruelling time. Since the battle of Gurun it had borne the brunt of the fighting, and in its doggedly fought rearguard actions between Batu Pekaka and Selama, on the Grik road and in the Ipoh area it had gained time for the re-organization of the remainder of the II Indian Division and the occupation of the Kampar position and had inflicted delay and heavy casualties on the enemy. It had, however, suffered severely itself.

2I5. In order to protect the long and vulnerable communications the I Independent Company had been sent to the Telok Anson area on the lower reaches of the River Perak. From here distant boat and cycle patrols were sent out. It was supported by one infantry battalion at Ct. Jong.

2I6. *Operations of Rose Force.* – Towards the end of December a successful raid was carried out by Rose Force, strength about 40 men, against the enemy's communications west of the River Perak. The party was landed from the sea on the Perak coast but was unfortunately weakened by the breakdown of one of the troop-carrying launches. A M.T. column was ambushed and some lorries and two staff cars containing high-ranking officers destroyed. The party was then withdrawn to Port Swettenham. With a little more persistence even greater results might perhaps have been obtained.

2I7. It was hoped to repeat and develop this enterprise which undoubtedly offered great possibilities. That it was not found possible to do so was due to the lack of sea transport which resulted in the main from losses suffered as a result of the aerial supremacy which the enemy had established on this coast. The last hope disappeared when on the Ist January five "Eureka"' fast coastal vessels which the Army had purchased from America and handed over to the Navy to operate were attacked by aircraft on their way north to Port Swettenham and either sunk or driven ashore. On the 30th December also H.M.S. "Kudat", the base depot ship for this force, was bombed and sunk in the harbour of Port Swettenham.

2I8. *Air Operations.* – The 23rd December was the first day of intensive air action against our troops in the forward areas. Up till then the enemy's air effort had been concentrated chiefly against our aerodromes. On that day heavy attacks were made against troops in bivouac areas and on the move and against Ipoh railway station. These attacks continued for the rest of the month. Our own troops were almost entirely without air support as all the remaining fighters except for a few which operated from Kuala Lampur had by now been withdrawn to the Singapore area.

Air attacks against the Singapore area were not renewed until the 29th December when the first of a succession of night attacks took place.

Our own Air Striking Force, which seldom consisted of more than half a dozen machines, carried out night attacks against enemy occupied aerodromes. The Sungei Patani Aerodrome in particular, where over 100 Japanese aircraft had been located, was attacked on several occasions. In addition, aerial reconnaissances were carried out daily off both the east and west coasts as far as the availability of aircraft permitted.

The C.-in-C. Far East laid down as a policy that convoy protection work must in the future take precedence over all other calls on the Air Force.

219. *Strategy.* – In a telephone conversation which I had with the Commander 3 Indian Corps at 1100 hrs. 29th December it was agreed that it would be better to fight the enemy in the positions then occupied rather than carry out any rearward movements in the immediate future, although this in no way altered the general instructions.

On the same day I informed the Commanders 3 Indian Corps and A.I.F. that I had arranged with the Director of Public Works to form Works Groups in selected areas under State engineers who would report to them for orders. The object of this was to prepare a series of obstacles, especially anti-tank obstacles, in great depth on the probable line of the enemy's advance. The idea was that the officers of the Public Works Department should be given outline instructions and be left to carry out the work themselves with civil labour.

On the 28th December the Commander Singapore Fortress was ordered to prepare schemes for the destruction of the Causeway which connected Singapore Island with the mainland.

SECTION XXV. – THE BORNEO AND CHRISTMAS ISLAND OPERATIONS.

220. *Sarawak and Brunei.* – On the 13th December the Miri detachment, having completed its task, left for Kuching in H.M.S. "Lipis".

At 0330 hrs. on the 16th December Japanese troops landed at Seria. Some of them proceeded by road to Belait. Early on the 22nd they reached Danau.

On the 19th and 20th December Japanese aircraft attacked the aerodrome at Kuching and also dropped bombs on and machine-gunned the town. Many of the inhabitants evacuated. On the 23rd December the O.C. Troops reported that there had been a complete break in civil labour.

221. On the evening of the 23rd December two Japanese cruisers and seven transports arrived off the mouth of the River Santubong near Kuching and landings were made during the night. Before arrival the convoy had been attacked by submarines of the Royal Dutch Navy and three transports and one tanker were reported to have been sunk or disabled. The Japanese troops advanced in landing craft up the waterways leading to Kuching and were engaged by our forward troops at Pending and elsewhere. Later in the day, the situation having become confused, the forward troops were withdrawn to the vicinity of the aerodrome. In the meantime, in accordance with the instructions received from Singapore, the denial scheme on the aerodrome had been put into operation.

222. At 1305 hrs. 24th December I received a wireless message from O.C. Troops Sarawak and Brunei to the effect that, as the aerodrome was no longer required by our Air Force, he presumed that he was at liberty to withdraw his force into Dutch West Borneo. I replied to the effect that he should fight the enemy for as long as possible, and that subsequently he should act in the best interest of West Borneo as a whole, withdrawing if necessary into Dutch territory.

223. On the evening of the 24th December the enemy ships off Kuching were attacked by a small force of Blenheim Bombers.

After some sharp fighting in the vicinity of the aerodrome on the 25th December contact was broken off in the evening and withdrawal to Dutch West Borneo via the 50 mile jungle path was effected. All wheeled transport had to be abandoned. The force arrived at Sanggau in Dutch Borneo on the 29th December and came under orders of the local Dutch commander. Arrangements were made by Headquarters Malaya Command to drop supplies and ammunition on the aerodrome at Sinkawang for this force.

224. *The Japanese arrived at the Sarawak* – Dutch West Borneo frontier on the 7th January, 1942, but were held there by the 2/15 Punjab Regt. until the 18th January. Much bitter fighting took place here in the endeavour to prevent the enemy reaching the large Dutch aerodrome at Sanggau. Eventually the aerodrome, installations and bomb stores were successfully demolished. A rearguard action was then carried out to Nyabang, where contact with the enemy was lost.

225. Subsequently it was decided to move to the South Coast of Borneo in two columns, one making for Sampit in the centre of the south coast and the other for Pankalang Boen 120 miles to the West. It was hoped to find sea transport which would take the columns to Java. The columns left early in February and arrived at their destinations simultaneously. On arrival at Sampit the eastern column found a Japanese force there which it engaged. It then joined the western column by marching on a compass bearing through dense jungle for six days. The distance covered by the eastern column from Kuching to Sampit was over 800 miles, the major portion on foot through jungle. On the 3rd April the whole force, which was in an exhausted state after its long march, became prisoners of war. A high standard of discipline had been maintained by the troops who had covered hundreds of miles carrying their light automatics and ammunition with no transport through some of the worst country in the world.

226. *Labuan.* – On the 3rd January, 1942, a small Japanese force took possession of the Island of Labuan, which was not defended.

227. *British North Borneo.* – The State of British North Borneo was organized into two Administrative Divisions, the east and west coast Residencies. The seat of Government was at Sandakan.

On the 3rd January a small detachment from the Japanese force which had landed at Labuan proceeded in a captured motor vessel to Mempakul on the coast of British North Borneo and from there to Weston, a small port at the mouth of the River Padar. At Weston the detachment commandeered a train and proceeded to Beaufort 20 miles distant. The detachment at Beaufort was reinforced on the evening 3rd January. On the 6th January Japanese forces entered Jesselton by rail from Beaufort (56 miles). All the west coast area was now under Japanese control and the Governor (Mr. C.R. Smith) severed all connection between the east and west coast Residencies.

On the 19th January a Japanese force, estimated at 600 strong, arrived at Sandakan, British North Borneo, having assembled at Banggi Island off the north coast of North Borneo two days earlier. It came in two coastal vessels captured in Brunei waters and twelve Japanese motor fishing vessels. The troops from the latter landed in two creeks to the north of the Sandakan area and reached Sandakan by land at about 0900 hrs. The two coastal vessels entered Sandakan harbour at about 0930 hrs. The Governor surrendered the whole State at 0900 hrs. 19th January and refused to carry on the administration under Japanese control. He and his staff were interned.

Tawau, situated on the east coast near the N.E.I. border, was occupied by the Japanese on the 24th January and Lahad Datu, between Tawau and Sandakan, on the 26th or 27th January. Kudat on the north coast was occupied about the 1st February and the whole State then came under Japanese control.

A great deal of denial damage was done under the Governor's orders in accordance with plans carefully prepared beforehand. In particular, coastal vessels and local craft, including a number of Japanese craft, were sunk. The Japanese occupying forces were much incensed at the damage done, especially at Sandakan and Tawau.

228. *Christmas Island.* – On the 20th January our Coast Defence Artillery at Christmas Island engaged an enemy submarine which had torpedoed a Norwegian vessel.

SECTION XXVI. – THE HIGHER COMMAND.

229. On 5th January, Vice-Admiral Sir Geoffrey Layton, Commander-in-Chief, Eastern Fleet, moved his headquarters from Singapore to Batavia.

This move was decided on primarily because of the now vital necessity of taking every possible step to ensure the safe and timely arrival of troop convoys at Singapore. This necessitated close co-operation with the American and Dutch Commanders, which could only be achieved at Batavia.

Moreover, by this date it had become apparent that Singapore would shortly be exposed to heavy air attack by bombers escorted by fighters and therefore would be of little value in the immediate future as a base for heavy surface ships. The Rear-Admiral Malaya (Rear-Admiral Spooner) became Senior Naval Officer at Singapore, and resumed responsibility for the whole of the local naval defence of Malaya.

230. On the 23rd December, 1941, Lt.-Gen. Sir Henry Pownall arrived to succeed Air Chief Marshal Sir Robert Brooke Popham as Commander-in-Chief Far East in accordance with a decision which had been made before the outbreak of hostilities. He immediately went North to the 3 Indian Corps area, visiting the 11 Indian Division on the 25th Dec. and the 9 Indian Division on the 26th Dec. On the 7th Jan., 1942, General Sir Archibald Wavell (now Field-Marshal Earl Wavell) arrived at Singapore to assume the appointment of Supreme Commander South West Pacific Command. After visiting Headquarters 3 Indian Corps and troops of the 11 Indian Division on the 8th Jan. General Wavell left Singapore for Java. The Far East Combined Bureau accompanied him except for a few officers who were left to strengthen the Intelligence Branches of the Service Staffs at Singapore. On the establishment of Headquarters South West Pacific Command, the appointment of Commander-in-Chief Far East lapsed.

231. Mr. Duff Cooper, the Cabinet representative in the Far East, also left Singapore early in January.

232. It was generally agreed that these rapid changes in the Higher Command, necessary though they may have been, had an unsettling effect and did not make for continuity.

SECTION XXVII. – THE SCORCHED EARTH POLICY.

233. Early in 1941 a denial scheme for the event of the invasion of Malaya had been prepared and necessary instructions issued. This scheme was directed principally to the destruction or removal of everything that might facilitate the movement of invading forces, i.e., the destruction of any form of repair workshop, the demolition of bridges and the removal or destruction of all forms of vehicle or boat. The plan did not envisage a complete Scorched Earth Policy.

About the middle of December, 1941, the Cabinet Representative in the Far East informed the War Council that he had received instructions to the effect that, as our troops withdrew, an unrestricted Scorched Earth Policy was to be applied throughout Malaya. It was at once apparent that our problem differed in some important respects from that which had a few months previously confronted the Russians. This was due in the main to the fact that, whereas their armies were withdrawing through a country inhabited by their own people, our forces were withdrawing through a country inhabited by Asiatic peoples to whom we had by treaty promised our protection. If we deprived these people of the necessities of life such as food, water, etc., or destroyed the symbols of modern civilisation, such as the power supplies of their hospitals, they would claim that we were not treating them in accordance with our promises and they would become fertile ground for the seeds of the enemy's propaganda. On the other hand the machinery, most of which was owned by British firms and individuals, and the rubber stocks could quite properly be destroyed. Of greater importance from the military point of view was the destruction of road and railway bridges. This was obviously essential if we were to succeed in our efforts to delay the enemy and it had in fact been done since the beginning of the operations.

234. Two other aspects of the problem which received consideration were the practicability of applying a Scorched Earth Policy and the moral effect it would have, if applied, on both soldiers and civilians.

As regards the former, widespread destruction of property is not an operation which can be carried out effectively at the last minute. To be effective it must be both prepared and put into execution in advance of the final withdrawal. In that case, however, the explosions and fires give to the enemy a sure indication of the intention to withdraw. It was impossible also for the military authorities to carry out or supervise the destruction in so large an area. The best that could be done was to appoint officers to tour the country to see that adequate preparations had been made. The executive work had to be left to the owners or agents on receipt of orders from a central authority.

235. The moral effect on both soldiers and civilians would be, it was anticipated, extremely adverse. At a time when we were doing our utmost to raise the morale of our troops we feared that the noise of explosions and the sight of smoke in their rear would have the opposite effect. As regards the civilians, we wanted all the help we could get from the Asiatic population but, as is well known, Asiatics tend to take the side of the more powerful and we feared that the sight of destruction being carried out well behind our lines would induce them to help the enemy rather than ourselves.

236. With these considerations in mind the Far East War Council, after referring the matter to London, issued instructions that a scorched earth policy would be enforced, but that it would not apply to foodstuffs already distributed to the civil population, to water supplies or to power plants.

SECTION XXVIII. – WOMEN AND CHILDREN.

237. The situation as regards Army Families at the outbreak of hostilities has already been explained in Part I, Section IX, "Married Families." A similar situation existed in the Royal Air Force. There were also in Malaya a number of families of naval personnel who had shore appointments. On the civil side no restrictions had been imposed on the entry of families into Malaya, so that there were some thousands of women and children, the families of both officials and unofficials. Many of these had made their home in Malaya for a number of years.

238. In December, on instructions from Home, the question of the evacuation of women and children from Malaya came before the War Council. It was at once apparent that important issues were involved. In the first place many of the European women were engaged in essential war work – either in offices or in hospitals or in the Passive Air Defence Organization. In many cases it would be difficult to release them without weakening the organization. Moreover, many of them, especially in the

Passive Air Defence Services, were working side by side with Eurasian and Asiatic women. It was in fact the European women who had in many cases taken the lead in building up the local organizations. If these women were to be withdrawn now that war had broken out and there was work to be done, the effect on the Eurasian and Asiatic population would clearly be little short of disastrous and a severe blow would be dealt to British prestige. Again, if European women were to be evacuated, why should not those Eurasian, Chinese, Indian and other Asiatic women, who were not natives of Malaya, also be evacuated if they wished to go? Although Japan's policy was to try to rally all Asiatics to her flag with the cry of "Asia for the 'Asiatics'" our political object was clearly to hold Malaya for the British Empire. It was not to gain a victory of Europeans over Asiatics. If, therefore, we evacuated immediately all European women, leaving the Eurasian and Asiatic women to do their work, we should, it seemed, be playing into the hands of the Japanese and provide a fertile ground for the seeds of their propaganda.

239. An analysis of the European women in Malaya showed that they could be divided broadly into the following categories:-

(*a*) *Married Families of Service Personnel. – (Rank and File).*

Not very many of these were employed on essential war work. Moreover, many of them were occupying Government accommodation which would shortly be required for reinforcements. They were for the most part "bouches inutiles." Their evacuation was therefore both possible and desirable.

(*b*) *Families of Officers and Civilians who wished to leave.*

It was considered undesirable to force these to stay against their will.

(*c*) *Families of Officers and Civilians who did not wish to leave but who were not engaged in essential war work.*

These could be ordered to leave on the grounds that they constituted "bouches inutiles."

(*d*) *Families of Officers and Civilians who did not wish to leave and who were engaged in essential war work.*

There were a large number in this category. For reasons given above there were strong objections to their evacuation.

The Far East War Council, after full consideration of the factors involved, issued instructions that evacuation should start forthwith and that all available accommodation in ships returning to suitable destinations should be used. A Joint Service and Civil Committee was set up to allot accommodation. In providing passage accommodation for those civilians who wished to leave Singapore the civil Government ordered that all nationalities should receive absolutely equal and impartial treatment. A Committee was set up with a Judge of the Supreme Court as Chairman to decide on priority of claims. The implementation of the policy will be dealt with later in this despatch.

240. This was one of the most difficult problems we had to solve. It is a problem upon which there will be many and varied opinions. It was complicated by the known

characteristics of our adversary, and by considerations for the care of children. I do feel, however, that women who stick to their posts in these conditions so long as the commander allows them to do so are making a very valuable contribution to the general war effort and especially to the maintenance of morale.

SECTION XXIX. – CIVIL DEFENCE.

24I. It had become apparent very soon after the outbreak of hostilities that the pre-war civil defence arrangements were in many respects inadequate for the situation which was developing. This did not apply so much to the Passive Air Defence Services which were for the most part operating efficiently in the area which had been bombed, though they required strengthening especially as regards the Fire Fighting Services whose work was invaluable. It applied chiefly to the material protection of important buildings and to the control of labour and transport.

242. *Martial Law.* – Towards the end of December I94I Martial Law was, at the instigation of the Cabinet Representative in the Far East, declared in the Colony of Singapore. The Commander Singapore Fortress was appointed Administrator. The Commander 3 Indian Corps and the Commander A.I.F. were authorised to declare Martial Law in the Federated Malay States and in Johore and Malacca respectively at their discretion. They did not find it necessary to do so.

243. *The Civil Defence Committee.* – In an endeavour to develop and bring up-to-date the Civil Defence arrangements for Singapore the Cabinet Representative in the Far East set up on the I6th December a Civil Defence Committee to review and deal with all measures affecting the defence of Singapore other than those of a purely military character. Its composition was as under:-

Chairman.-
The Cabinet Representative in the Far East. (The Rt. Hon. A. Duff Cooper).

Members.-
The Commander Singapore Fortress (Maj.-Gen. Keith Simmons).
The Inspector General S.S. Police (Mr. A.H. Dickinson).
Mr. Denham.
The Defence Security Officer (Col. Johnson).
The Committee was dissolved early in January.

244. *The Directorate of Civil Defence.* – Towards the end of December the Cabinet Representative in the Far East proposed the formation of a Directorate of Civil Defence under a Director General. I was asked if I would be willing to make my Chief Engineer, Brigadier I. Simson, available for the appointment of Director-General. Although I was loath to lose the services of so important an officer at this juncture, I agreed to make Brigadier Simson available provided he retained concurrently the appointment of Chief Engineer. This provision was made in his own interests and for financial reasons. In sending my reply I expressed the opinion that the organization which would result from the proposed new Directorate was faulty

because it cut across the existing organization and would lead to a clash of responsibility between the Director General of Civil Defence and the Secretary for Defence. Nevertheless, the Directorate was created on the 3Ist December, Brigadier Simson being appointed Director-General and Mr. F.D. Bisseker, the General Manager of the Penang Smelting Works and the Senior Unofficial Member of the Legislative Council, Deputy Director-General. Mr. Bisseker, was also appointed Director of Labour and Transport.

The Minister gave the D.G.C.D. plenary powers on all matters pertaining to Civil Defence in Singapore Island and Johore, subject only to reference to the War Council through the Minister where considered necessary. A letter to this effect, signed by the Minister, was addressed to certain Heads of Government Departments, Public Bodies and Civil Firms, with copies to the Governor and the Service Chiefs.

On the Ist January I942, under amended terms of reference issued by the Governor, Johore was excluded, so that the Directorate of Civil Defence actually operated in Singapore Island only.

On or about the 23rd January, the D.G.C.D. became a member of the Far East War Council.

245. As the campaign progressed the activities of the Directorate of Civil Defence increased rapidly, but it was an impromptu organization and suffered from lack of staff and normal office facilities. Also the extent of its functions were never clearly defined or understood. The Director-General and his Staff worked untiringly, but I remain convinced that the organization was fundamentally unsound. There was already a Secretary for Defence and there was a Permanent Labour Committee. Plans had also been made for transport in wartime to be handled by the Registrar of Vehicles and his staff. It is true that at this time strong action was required for the rapid development of some of the Civil Defence arrangements but, by making the Director-General of Civil Defence responsible through the Minister to the Far East War Council, the Governor and his subordinates were presumably deprived of some at least of what should have been their responsibility. It would, in my opinion, have been better to build on the existing organization, strengthening it as necessary by the introduction of men of character and experience.

SECTION XXX. – LABOUR.

246. War experience soon showed that, while the organized military labour units worked on the whole satisfactorily, this was far from being the case with civil labour. Trouble first broke out in Kedah, where civil labour disappeared as soon as the operations started. At Penang, during the heavy air raids, the majority of the Asiatic municipal employees disappeared leaving the troops to carry on their functions, an experience which was to be repeated later in Singapore. On the railway, after the spasmodic enemy air attacks on the stations, many of the non-European officials and labourers absented themselves. These included such key men as engine-drivers, stokers, signalmen, plate-layers etc. As a result there was a real danger that railway

traffic would come to a standstill. The danger was averted, firstly by the Volunteer Railway Unit and secondly by seconding for work on the railways military personnel with previous railway experience. The conduct of the senior railway officials throughout was, however, exemplary.

247. In the Singapore area the trouble first appeared on the aerodromes. It had from the first become obvious that a secure base from which our aircraft, and especially our fighter aircraft, could operate was essential for the successful development of the campaign. I therefore agreed to the maintenance of the existing Singapore aerodromes and the construction of new air strips taking priority over other military work. Large labour gangs were required to fill in the craters caused by enemy bombing and for work on the new air strips. After each raid, however, the greater part of these gangs disappeared and after a time it became difficult to get labourers to work on the aerodromes at all. To ease the situation I had to arrange for working parties to be found, whenever available, from the Army Reinforcement Camps for work on the aerodromes, even though this meant that little or no labour was available for work on the beach defences of Singapore Island. The trouble soon spread to the Naval Dockyard where, after one or two air attacks, many of the permanent civil staff absented themselves, with the result that the repair of local naval craft and other work was seriously delayed. Later the Dock workers, employed by the Singapore Harbour Board, similarly disappeared when the Docks became the main target for enemy air attacks. Here also military personnel had to be called in to unload the ships.

248. In the Army, War Office authority had been received shortly before war broke out to form up to six labour companies, but for some time the War Office refused to agree to increase the fixed rate of 45 cents per day for coolies. As the current rate in Singapore at that time was in the region of one dollar per day plus free rations and accommodation, it was not surprising that, in spite of strenuous recruiting efforts, these companies could not be formed. By the 7th January only one additional company had been formed.

249. Early in January efforts were made to solve the grave labour problem. Mr. Bisseker was appointed Director of Labour under the Director-General of Civil Defence. He worked through the Chinese Chamber of Commerce and through influential representatives of the other communities. The Services applied to him for their requirements.

250. On the 8th January a Director of Army Labour was appointed. He took over control both of the existing labour companies and of the labour supplied by contractors. Many of the latter were of a very poor quality and it had become apparent that the only satisfactory solution was to recruit as many labourers as possible into the labour companies; also that it was essential that they should be handled by officers and N.C.Os. who understood them and that accommodation should be provided as near as possible to their work. By arrangement the Governor cabled to the Colonial Office requesting that the Services should be given authority to accept decisions by the D.G.C.D. as regards conditions of service reached after consultation with interested departments. No authority was received, but the War Office was informed that in view of the urgency the labour scheme agreed upon locally was accepted.

25I. We continued to be hampered by the lack of centralized leadership among the Chinese in Singapore, from whom the bulk of the labourers were drawn. The coolies understood little of the war and many of them were quite content to hide in their villages unpaid. There were few who would go among them and lead them. The situation was to some extent aggravated by the distribution of rice to each Asiatic household to be held as a reserve, a measure taken by the Government in order to disperse food reserves but which had the effect of making it unnecessary for the labourers to earn their subsistence.

252. There were those who urged that compulsion should be applied but those best acquainted with the Asiatics, and especially with the Chinese, were opposed to it. They considered that better results would be obtained by trying to find, and get the co-operation of Asiatic leaders. I supported this view. It was only when this had failed to produce the required results that a measure was passed on the 20th January to introduce compulsion, but it came too late for its value to be disclosed.

253. The shortage of civil labour remained a great source of weakness throughout the campaign. It is right to add, however, that many of the senior officials, both European and Asiatic, performed their duties loyally and well. This was particularly the case in the Railway and in the Posts and Telegraphs Departments which were kept working in spite of very great difficulties.

SECTION XXXI. – THE STRATEGICAL SITUATION, 30TH DECEMBER, I94I – 2ND JANUARY, I942.

254. Our object remained as before, i.e. the Defence of the Naval Base.

There had been no change recently in the Naval situation.

The Air situation has been described in Section XXIV. The safe arrival of 50 Hurricane Fighters, due to reach Singapore by sea about the I3th-I5th January, appeared to be of paramount importance as this was still the only chance of re-establishing any measure of air superiority.

255. As regards the relative strength of the Land Forces, we knew from air reconnaissance that Japanese ships had been steadily discharging at Singora and other ports, but the general situation as regards the strength of the forces on both sides remained as stated in Section XXIII.

We had, however, now been informed that we might expect substantial reinforcements during the month of January, the principal of which were as under:-

(*a*) *During the first few days of January.* – One Indian Infantry Brigade with attached troops.

(*b*) *About* I3*th*-I5*th January.* – One Brigade Group of the I8 British Division with certain artillery units. These troops were coming in large American liners, the safe arrival and despatch of which were of the utmost importance.

(*c*) *Later in January.* – The I8 British Division (less one Brigade Group), one Indian Infantry Brigade, some Australian and Indian Reinforcements and certain other units.

256. The Hurricane Fighters were coming in the same convoy as (*b*) above. This was therefore a most valuable convoy, the chief danger to which lay in air attack from bases either in West Borneo, in Malaya or in South Thailand, or from aircraft carriers. The scale of air attack which the enemy could deliver would be much increased if he could, before the arrival of the convoy, establish his aircraft on the Kuantan and Kuala Lumpur aerodromes.

257. In the west coast area the situation appeared to be slightly improved. The new 6/15 Indian Infantry Brigade had had 10 days in which to reorganize and to occupy the Kampar position. The 28 Indian Infantry Brigade, though on continuous front line duty, had had no heavy fighting for the last 10 days and was now also in position. The 12 Brigade Group had, it is true, been continuously in action since its arrival in the North and was tired. A defensive position, to which to fall back, was being prepared north of Tanjong Mahm. The chief danger lay in the threat to the left flank and rearward communications from enemy forces which might either cross the lower reaches of the River Perak or be landed, from coastal craft. It seemed, however, that the strength of such forces must be limited.

258. On the east coast the Kelantan Force was resting in the area Kuala Lipis – Jerantut – Raub covered on the North by Macforce which was still operating on the railway north of Kuala Lipis and on the South by detachments watching the approaches through Pahang. In the Kuantan area patrols had made contact towards the end of December with enemy troops moving South by the coast road in Trengganu and the Kuantan Force had, in accordance with instructions received from Higher Authority, been re-disposed with the bulk of the force, material and transport west of the River Kuantan and with light mobile forces only operating east of the river.

259. It was clear that the enemy intended to continue his advance down the west coast as rapidly as he could. He might also be expected to attempt landings of small forces on the west coast from the sea. On the east coast a combined sea and land attack against Kuantan seemed possible, while the enemy might also deliver a seaborne attack against East Johore or against Singapore Island direct. In this connection a special landing-craft carrying ship had been seen lying off Singora by our reconnaissance aircraft. There remained also the possibility of an airborne attack directed against our aerodromes.

260. As regards our own course of action, the governing consideration was the safe arrival of land and air reinforcements and time to deploy them. An early withdrawal would enable the enemy to establish his aircraft on the aerodromes at Kuantan and Kuala Lumpur before the arrival of the mid-January convoys. In consequence, it would make the task of bringing in these convoys much more difficult.

To achieve our object of protecting the Naval Base it was necessary to fight the main battle on the mainland and it was hoped to be able to deploy all the reinforcements due to arrive in January for that purpose. Therefore the longer we could delay the enemy in Central Malaya the better.

Further, there was a great deal of machinery and large quantities of stores, both military and civil, in the Kuala Lumpur area. Time for the evacuation of these was required.

I hoped to be able to hold the Kuantan aerodrome for another 10 days or so, which would make it impossible for the enemy to repair and organize the aerodrome before the middle of January. Allowing time for the Kuantan garrison to withdraw and cross the Jerantut ferry, this would mean that the west coast force would have to hold the enemy north of the Kuala Kubu Road Junction until about the middle of January. That would mean that it would have a depth of about 70 miles in which to manoeuvre for 15 days.

With the above considerations in mind I went north on the 30th December to discuss with the Commander 3 Indian Corps and his Divisional Commanders the details of the strategy to be pursued.

261. Accompanied by the Commander 3 Indian Corps I visited the Headquarters 11 Indian Division at Tapah on the 31st December. The Divisional Commander reported that the position at Kampar was satisfactory. As regards future strategy, he expressed confidence in his ability to hold the enemy north of the Kuala Kubu Road Junction until at least the 14th January. He was therefore instructed that he was not without permission to withdraw his force beyond that road junction before the 14th January, and that he was to continue to impose the maximum delay on the enemy's advance. I impressed upon all commanders the importance of taking adequate measures to prevent penetration by enemy tanks down the main road – a danger which I considered a very real one in view of our complete lack of tanks with which to counter it.

262. On the 1st January we visited the Headquarters 9 Indian Division at Raub. The Divisional Commander reported that he had instructed the Commander Kuantan Force that he should hold the Kuantan aerodrome for as long as possible, provided he did not thereby jeopardise his force. He had indicated that the aerodrome should be held for 5 more days if possible. Communication with Kuantan had broken down and an officer sent to ascertain the situation had not yet returned. After discussion it was decided that the Commander Kuantan Force should be instructed to hold the aerodrome until the 10th January.

263. Late on the 1st January the Commander 11 Indian Division reported that an enemy force had landed at Ulu Melintang near the mouth of the River Bernam (a little south of the mouth of the River Perak) and that he had moved the 12 Brigade Group to meet this threat. He further said that he thought he could continue to hold the Kampar position, where a strong attack had already been repulsed, for several days but that, if he did so, his ability to hold the enemy north of the Kuala Kubu Road Junction might, in view of the threat to his communications, be prejudiced. He asked for authority to withdraw his force from Kampar at his discretion. This was granted.

264. The Commander 3 Indian Corps was already having reconnaissances carried out of lines on which to co-ordinate the withdrawal as far back as North Johore. With a view to co-ordinating future defence plans I arranged to hold a conference at Segamat in North Johore on the 5th January at which both the Commanders 3 Indian Corps and A.I.F. should attend.

265. After visiting Port Swettenham and Port Dickson, I returned to Singapore late on the 2nd January.

266. During this tour the following matters, in addition to those reported above, were discussed:-

(*a*) Measures to harass the enemy's communications. "Left behind" parties, consisting for the most part of Chinese led by Europeans, were being rapidly trained at Singapore. It was planned to send these parties up to the 3 Indian Corps area as soon as ready. In addition, an offer had been received and accepted from the N.E.I. Military Authorities for a detachment of Marechaussees, specially trained in guerrilla warfare in the jungle, to be sent to Malaya.

(*b*) The preparation of special news sheets for distribution among the Indian troops to counter Japanese propaganda.

(*c*) Methods of anti-tank defence. In this connection, a very large number of concrete cylindrical blocks were being manufactured both at Singapore and at Kuala Lumpur and some were now ready for distribution.

(*d*) Policy as regards the Federated Malay States Volunteer Force. – This Force consisted partly of European and partly of Asiatic personnel. It was organized on a State basis and maintained out of Federated Malay State funds. In practically all cases the families of the Asiatic personnel were resident in the State and would remain there after withdrawal. Faced with the prospect of moving into South Malaya and leaving their families behind, some of the Asiatic Volunteers began to show discontent and desertions had taken place. We were faced with the alternative of continuing to enforce service with the Colours at the expense, almost certainly, of weak and discontented units or of releasing those who wished to leave. We decided on the latter course. Thereafter, when a unit was to be withdrawn from its State every Asiatic member was given the option of remaining with it or of handing in his arms and equipment and going to his home. In almost every case the latter course was chosen. The arms and equipment were re-issued to units requiring them as there were few or none at that time in reserve.

267. On return to Singapore I circulated a letter on Tactics. A copy of this letter is attached as Appendix "D" to this despatch.

SECTION XXXII. – THE KUANTAN OPERATIONS.

268. The Kuantan area was very isolated. As already stated, it was over 100 miles, through desolate jungle country, from Jerantut on the east coast railway, and it was 160 miles from the Headquarters of the 9 Indian Division at Raub. These are big distances when there are no aircraft available for inter-communication. Its military

importance lay solely in the R.A.F. aerodrome, 9 miles inland from the town and on the other side of the Kuantan River.

Kuantan was garrisoned by the 22 Indian Brigade Group under command of Brigadier Painter.

269. Since the 9th December when the aerodrome had been evacuated, Japanese aircraft had been daily active over the Kuantan area, reconnoitring, bombing and machine-gunning, but little damage had been done. It appears that the enemy had intended to make landings on the coast of Trengganu but had been prevented from doing so by his losses, especially of landing craft, in the Kelantan operations.

Between the 20th and 24th December our long distance patrols were in contact with Japanese troops moving southward in M.T. on the coast of Trengganu. On the 27th the enemy were engaged by our artillery near the Trengganu/Pahang frontier.

270. It was now apparent that the threat against the Kuantan area was developing from the North, though it might still be accompanied by a sea-borne landing. It will be recollected that we had by that time had heavy losses of material on the west coast and that our reserves had been depleted. We could not afford to have further heavy losses. The situation at Kuantan was particularly hazardous owing to most of the material being east of the River Kuantan which was crossed only by a single ferry. In consequence of this and of the situation which was developing on the left flank instructions were issued to the Commander Kuantan Force that he should concentrate the bulk of his force, material and transport, west of the River Kuantan, holding the area east of the river with light mobile forces only.

27I. This readjustment of the position was going on when, on the morning of the 30th December the Japanese advanced via the Jabor Valley in greater strength than they had previously shown. They were engaged by our artillery and small arms fire and confused fighting continued throughout the day. The ferry, which had been split into two working halves, was bombed during the day and one half only remained in action.

272. By the morning of the 3Ist December the enemy were attacking the ferry, but a bridgehead was maintained during the day. During the night 3Ist December/Ist January the rearguard was withdrawn across the river and the ferry destroyed. At that time, however, the River Kuantan was fordable in its upper reaches, a most unusual occurrence at that time of year. This seriously weakened the defence.

273. In the meantime the Commander Kuantan Force had been ordered to hold the aerodrome till the 5th January (see Section XXXI) and this had been later extended to the I0th January. On the 2nd January, however, events on the west coast and the serious threat to our communications there forced the Commander 3 Indian Corps to expedite the programme and early on the morning of the 3rd January the Commander Kuantan Force received orders to withdraw his force to Jerantut forthwith. During the day the enemy closed in on the aerodrome and at about I745 hours, as the withdrawal was taking place, a strong attack developed and very heavy fighting took place. It was during this action that Lt.-Col. Cummings, commanding the 2/I2 Frontier Force Regt., won the Victoria Cross. During the withdrawal the

rearguard was twice ambushed on the main road by a Japanese force, which had passed by bush tracks west of the aerodrome, and suffered heavy casualties.

274. The withdrawal was continued on the following days, the rearguard crossing the ferry at Jerantut on the night 6th/7th January. The Kuantan Force then moved to the area Raub – Tras – Tranum. One Infantry battalion (5/II Sikhs) was still nearly at full strength. The strength of the other two battalions combined was rather less than one battalion. The losses in the supporting arms and administrative units had been comparatively small.

275. The Kuantan Force, like many other forces in Malaya, had had a difficult task to perform, because it had been greatly influenced by events elsewhere. It can be claimed, however, that by denying the aerodrome to the enemy for a month it had greatly decreased the scale of air attack which the enemy was able to develop against the Singapore area. That this was so was proved by the rapid increase in the scale of that attack during the month of January. It has also been ascertained from Japanese sources that heavy casualties were inflicted on them during these operations – especially by our artillery when the enemy concentrated his troops in the Kuantan township. There is little doubt that these casualties were considerably in excess of those suffered by our own troops.

SECTION XXXIII. – WEST COAST OPERATIONS, 31ST DECEMBER, 1941 – 8TH JANUARY, 1942.

276. *The Battle of Kampar.* – The Kampar position was the strongest of any occupied in Malaya. The main position was semi-circular covering the township of Kampar on a frontage of about four miles. The eastern flank rested against a limestone mountain 4,000 feet high with its steep sides and summit covered with thick jungle. Close under its western slopes ran the main road. To the North, West and South lay an extensive, open, tin-mining area, broken only to the south-west by a large rubber plantation. Fields of fire for small arms, except in the rubber plantation, extended up to 1,200 yards and more. There was excellent artillery observation from forward O.P.s on the mountain slopes. The newly organized 6/15 Indian Brigade Group was made responsible for the main position.

On the eastern flank the mountain was circled by a loop road which, leaving the trunk road at Kuala Dipang, passed through Sahum and Chenderiang and rejoined the trunk road a little north of Tapah. On this road, covering, Sahum, a position subsidiary to, but independent of, the Kampar position was occupied by the 28 Indian Brigade Group. The 12 Indian Brigade Group was in reserve in the Bidor area.

277. On the 31st December the Japanese increased the pressure which had commenced the previous day on the 28 Brigade Group but made no headway. The Gurkhas, who were fighting in country suited to their well-known qualities, proved themselves superior to the Japanese and, ably supported by the 155 Field Regiment, inflicted heavy losses on the enemy.

278. At 0700 hrs. on the 1st January the enemy started a determined attack on the

Kampar position and heavy fighting continued throughout the day, particularly on the right flank where the British battalion was located. The garrisons of the defended localities held on grimly and localities lost were immediately recaptured by counter-attack. At the end of the day all positions were intact.

279. On the following day the enemy renewed his attacks east of the main road where fierce fighting took place. The British battalion under the inspiring leadership of their Commanding Officer (Lt.-Col. Morrison) fought desperately. Late in the afternoon the enemy were driven out of a vital position, which they had captured, by the Sikh Company of the I/8Punjab Regt. magnificently led by the Company Commander (Capt. Graham) and the situation was again restored.

280. The influence of events elsewhere, however, again predominated though it is doubtful whether in any case the position could have been held much longer and at 2100 hrs., under orders from the divisional commander, the 6/I5 Brigade Group started to withdraw. The withdrawal was closely followed up but, covered by the 28 Brigade Group, the 6/15th eventually disengaged and moved to the Tapah Bidor area.

28I. The Battle of Kampar, where our troops fought extremely well, showed that trained British troops are at least the equal of the best Japanese troops. The infantry were splendidly supported by the artillery, the 88 Field Regt. on the Kampar front doing some particularly good work.

It is worth recording that during their stay at Kampar the British battalion lost over I00 officers and men evacuated with malaria – the result no doubt of operations further north.

282. *West Coast Operations.* – As recorded in Section XXIV the I Independent Company had been sent to the Telok Anson area to watch the seaward approaches. Here it was joined by a squadron of the 3 Indian Cavalry. Supporting units were moved to the Changkat Jong area on the Telok – Anson/Bidor road, where work on defensive positions was begun.

283. On the 28th December long distance reconnaissance patrols reported Japanese troops at Lumut and at Sitiawan. At the latter place repairs were being carried out to the air landing strip. On the 3Ist December, air reconnaissance reported small steamers with barges in tow moving down the Perak coast. At 0900 hrs., Ist January, a motor launch patrol located a tug with four barges in tow stationary at the mouth of the River Perak. It was clear that the tug was stuck on a sandbank. Naval and Air action were requested, but the Japanese air cover proved too strong and nothing could be effected.

284. On the afternoon of the Ist January six small steamers accompanied by other craft were reported anchored at the mouth of the River Bernam, which flows into the sea a few miles south of the River Perak. The River Bernam is navigable for launches to Rantau Panjang, whence tracks lead to the main road, so that the threat to our communications was obvious. At I930 hrs. some enemy troops landed at Ulan Melintang on the River Bernam. To meet this threat the I2 Brigade Group was moved from its rest area at Bidor to the Changkat Jong area.

285. At dawn on the 2nd January an enemy force, strength about one battalion, landed at Telok Anson. It had come down the river Perak in boats. The instructions

given to the I Independent Company and the Squadron 3 Cavalry were to the effect that they were to delay any landing and cover the occupation of the Changkat Jong position. Accordingly, after some fighting in the outskirts of the town, these troops withdrew and passed through the I2 Brigade Group. The enemy followed up closely and by I400 hrs. were in contact with the forward troops of this brigade which fell back fighting. By the evening the Commander I2 Brigade Group estimated that he was being attacked by at least a regiment and reported that he could not guarantee to keep the main road open for more than 24 hours. It was as a result of this report that the withdrawal from Kampar was ordered.

286. On the 3rd January the enemy again attacked strongly in the Changkat Jong area supported by their Air Force but were repulsed. In the evening the I2 Brigade Group withdrew to the Trolak sector of the Slim position. The 6/I5 Brigade Group followed them to a covering position at Sungkai. The28 Brigade Group moved to the Slim River Village area.

287. South of Perak the Commander of the L. of C. Area (Brigadier Moir) was responsible for the defence of the west coast. He came directly under the orders of the Commander 3 Indian Corps. Immediately the threat to the west coast developed the forces at his disposal were strengthened by the temporary transfer of an infantry battalion from the 9 Indian Division and of another infantry battalion, the 3 Cavalry and some artillery from the II Indian Division which was later itself reinforced by another battalion drawn from the 9 Indian Division.

288. Late on the 2nd January two small steamers and about a dozen motor landing craft or barges approached the coast at Kuala Selangor a small village a little south of the Perak frontier. One of the steamers was sunk by artillery fire and the remainder withdrew. On the afternoon of the 3rd January a number of small craft were sighted off Kuala Selangor but out of artillery range. About midday on the 4th, however, patrols of 3 Indian Cavalry made contact with an enemy force moving south down the road from 8th Mile Village north of Kuala Selangor. This enemy force, driving back the cavalry patrols, advanced eastwards along the River Selangor, exercising a direct threat to the main road communications at Rawang. A sharp engagement took place at the bridge east of Batang Berjuntai. To meet this threat the 6/I5 Brigade Group, recently withdrawn from the Kampar position, was moved to Rawang and thence to the Batang Berjuntai area which it reached on the 6th January. It took up a defensive position south of the River Selangor. Orders were given for the Denial Scheme to be put into force at the Batu Arang coal mines – the only coal mines in Malaya – which are situated in this district.

One destroyer (H.M.S. "Scout") and naval patrol craft operated against enemy craft off the west coast.

289. *Reinforcements.* – On the 3rd January the 45 Indian Infantry Brigade with attached troops arrived at Singapore. This was a comparatively newly formed brigade which was only semi-trained. It had been intended for operations in the Middle East and had had no experience of jungle warfare. It was commanded by Brigadier Duncan. It was accompanied by an Indian Pioneer battalion – a non-combatant labour

unit. On disembarkation the Brigade and the Pioneer battalion concentrated in the Segamat – Malacca area.

290. *Plans for the Defence of Johore.* – On the 4th January the Commander A.I.F. informed me that, if 3 Indian Corps fell back to Johore, he would like to be allowed to exercise operational control over all troops in Johore. If this was impossible, then he would prefer that the A.I.F. should be responsible for the West area and the 3 Indian Corps for the East area.

I replied that I could not agree to this for the following reasons:-

(*a*) The fusion of the 3 Indian Corps and A.I.F. must lead to Command and Administrative difficulties.

(*b*) The proposal to transfer the A.I.F. as a whole from East to West Johore was not practical owing to the complicated moves that would become necessary in the middle of active operations and the weakening of the east coast defences.

I informed him that the only practical solution at that time seemed to be for the A.I.F. to be responsible for the East area and the 3 Indian Corps for the West area, but that I would be guided by events.

291. At II00 hrs. 5th January I held a conference at Segamat in North Johore as previously arranged (see Section XXXI) to discuss plans for the withdrawal and the defence of Johore. It was attended by the Commanders 3 Indian Corps and A.I.F. with members of their staffs, and by staff officers of Headquarters Malaya Command.

292. As a result of this conference, orders were issued for the withdrawal to and defence of Johore, the main points of which were as under:-

(*a*) *Intention.* – The intention was to continue to ensure the security of the Singapore Naval Base.

(*b*) *Policy.* – The broad policy was to continue opposition on the mainland to cover the arrival of reinforcements.

(*c*) There was to be no withdrawal without my permission south of the line Endau (later amended to read Mersing) – Batu Anam (N.W. of Segamat) – Muar.

(*d*) North of the line given above the 3 Indian Corps would continue to fight the enemy in areas selected by the Corps Commander. No withdrawal from one area to another would take place until necessitated by enemy action. The enemy should be attacked in flank and rear. It was of the utmost importance for strategical reasons to deny to the enemy the use of the Kuala Lumpur and Port Swettenham aerodromes for as long as possible, but at least until the I4th January.

(*e*) In view of possible enemy attempts to land on the west coast of Singapore Island, the Commander Singapore Fortress should pay particular attention to the defence of that area.

(*f*) After withdrawal the 3 Indian Corps would be responsible for the defence of the West area of Johore and the A.I.F. for that of the East area.

(*g*) The Main Line of resistance to be on the general line Mersing – Batu Anam – Muar.

(*h*) The 45 Indian Infantry Brigade with attached troops to come under orders 3 Indian Corps at once and the Pioneer Battalion from midday 7th January.

(*j*) 3 Indian Corps to take over immediately from A.I.F. Malaya operational control of the area north of the line G. Besar – Labis – Semarah all inclusive to 3 Indian Corps.

(*k*) The State of Johore and Settlement of Malacca to be formed at once into an administrative area to be known as Johore/Malacca area.

293. *The Slim River Battle.* – At dawn on 4th Jan. the I2 Brigade Group was moving into the Trolak sector and the 28 Brigade Group into harbours near Slim River Village ready to man its positions in that area when ordered. No battalion could now muster more than the equivalent in men of three poorly armed companies. No battalion had more than two anti-tank rifles. Some had none.

The Trolak sector of the Slim River position extended for three miles forward from Trolak village and was divided into three battalion sub-sectors. The terrain in the two forward sub-sectors consisted of thick jungle through which the road and railway ran in narrow parallel corridors about 400 yards apart. This jungle was impassable for A.F.Vs. It was also a poor country for artillery support. To block the road against tanks a supply of large concrete cylinders had been sent up. Owing to the constant presence of enemy aircraft which flew up and down the road bombing and machine-gunning all day, work on the defences had to be done under cover of darkness. On the afternoon of the 5th Jan. an enemy attack down the railway was repulsed with heavy loss.

294. At 0345 hours 7th Jan. the enemy attacked the forward troops frontally in bright moonlight. They succeeded in clearing the tank blocks and I5 tanks followed by infantry advanced down the road. On reaching the second sub-sector the leading tank struck a mine and some 30 tanks piled up behind it in close formation. The attack was held up for some two hours in this sub-sector during which seven tanks were destroyed. Then they cleared the obstacles and continued their advance closely followed by infantry. The news of this tank break-through had, partly owing to lack of telephone cable, not reached the troops in rear who were in turn taken completely by surprise. Two battalions were overtaken by the tanks while marching along the road to occupy their position and were badly cut up. Artillery units were similarly surprised. It was not until the tanks had reached a point two miles south of Slim and I5 miles from their starting point that they were stopped by a 4.5-in. howitzer of the I55 Field Regt. There was practically nothing between them and Kuala Lumpur.

The effect of this break-through was disastrous. The enemy tanks were now in control of the bridge at Slim and all our wheeled transport was on the further side of it. The enemy infantry had followed up quickly and there was considerable fighting during the day in the forward areas. In the afternoon the brigade commanders issued orders for a withdrawal down the railway line to Tanjong Malim 17 miles away.

295. Our losses from this battle were very heavy. The three battalions of the 12 Brigade mustered only the equivalent of about a company each. One battalion of the 28 Brigade had been obliterated while the remaining two had a total strength of less than one battalion. In the artillery, the engineers and the administrative units, the losses were on the same scale. A large number of guns and wheeled vehicles had been lost. The II Indian Division had temporarily ceased to exist as an effective fighting formation.

296. On the 8th January the Supreme Commander South-West Pacific, who had visited 3 Corps area on taking over command, initiated a plan to withdraw what remained of 3 Indian Corps into Johore without delay.

297. It would be easy, but unprofitable, to attribute the defeat at the Slim River Battle to the inadequacy of the anti-tank defences, the failure to blow the bridges or to a variety of other causes. The real cause lay in the utter weariness of the troops, both officers and men. They had been fighting and moving by day and by night for a month, and few of them had had any proper rest or relief. In the exhausting and enervating climatic and topographical conditions of Malaya this is far too long. The enemy's troops also no doubt suffered from the local conditions which were no more natural to them than to the majority of ours. But the enemy, with the initiative conferred by the offensive and by the freedom of the sea and air and with the ability to concentrate the whole of their forces against portions of ours in detail, could always relieve their tired troops or ease the pace whenever they found it necessary. Without reserves we were able to do neither. Had we had at this time the reserve division, which had been asked for, in 3 Indian Corps area, the story might have been very different.

298. *Air Operations.* – During this period the enemy gave continuous air support to his troops in the forward areas and also to his craft moving down the West Coast. He also made a series of attacks on the Kluang aerodrome in Central Johore and of night attacks against objectives in the Singapore area. Our own air strength during this period fell to a very low level. Our forward troops were entirely without air support. A large proportion of the available aircraft were employed on the defence of Singapore, on convoy protection duties and on seaward reconnaissances.

SECTION XXXIV. – THE WITHDRAWAL TO NORTH JOHORE, 9TH-14TH JANUARY, 1942.

299. *Orders for the Withdrawal and Defence of Johore.* – On the 9th January, in accordance with instructions received from the Supreme Commander, South West Pacific, I issued outline orders for the withdrawal to Johore, and the defence of that State. The main points of these orders were as under:-

(*a*) Commander A.I.F. to concentrate one Brigade Group, A.I.F., in the Segamat area as soon as possible.

(*b*) 45 Indian Brigade Group to come under command of A.I.F. Malaya immediately.

(*c*) 3 Indian Corps to withdraw from present positions into Johore covered by maximum possible demolitions. Withdrawal to be carried out by rail and by M.T. as ordered by Corps Commander.

(*d*) Withdrawal to be covered by rearguards on the demolitions.

(*e*) On entering Johore 9 Indian Division to come under command of A.I.F.

(*f*) 3 Indian Corps, less 9 Indian Division, to take over operational responsibility for South Johore up to and inclusive of the line Endau – G. Beremban – Kluang – Batu Pahat on a date to be fixed later.

A copy of Malaya Command Operation Instruction No. 33 is attached as Appendix "E" to this Despatch.

300. To the best of my belief these orders were in accordance with the instructions received from the Supreme Commander, South-West Pacific. He has since stated that he directed that the Australian Brigade Group in the Mersing area should be moved as soon as possible to join the remainder of the A.I.F. I have no record or recollection of such instructions, though it was my intention, if opportunity offered at a later date, to relieve this brigade group by a newly arrived formation.

The Supreme Commander, South-West Pacific has also stated that he directed that the 9 Indian Division should be employed in the southern portion (i.e. Muar Sector) of the position to be occupied. I have equally no record or recollection of this instruction.

30I. At II00 hours, I0th January, I held a conference at Segamat. It was attended by the Commanders 3 Indian Corps and A.I.F. with their staff officers and staff officers of Headquarters, Malaya Command. At this conference the orders already issued on the 9th January were supplemented as under:-

(*a*) The troops in Johore would be reorganised into two forces, the one under Maj.-Gen. Gordon Bennett to be known as Westforce, and the other under Lt.-Gen. Sir Lewis Heath to be known as 3 Indian Corps. This did not include troops under command Singapore Fortress or directly under Headquarters, Malaya Command.

(*b*) The composition of Westforce to be as under:-
9 Indian Division.
A.I.F. less 22 Australian Brigade Group.
45 Indian Brigade Group.
2 Battalion The Loyal Regt. less one company (from Singapore Fortress).
Artillery, Engineer and Administrative units not included in formations.
The Indian Pioneer Battalion.

The task of Westforce was to hold the North-West portion of Johore, the main line of resistance to be on the general line, Batu Anam – Muar. There was to be no withdrawal behind the line Segamat – Muar without my permission.

(*c*) The composition of 3 Indian Corps to be as under:-

II Indian Division.

22 Australian Brigade Group with attached troops, which included 2/17 Dogra Battalion from Singapore Fortress, to be known as Eastforce (Brigadier Taylor).

3 Corps Troops, which included Artillery, Engineer and Administrative units.

The task of 3 Indian Corps was the defence of Johore south of and inclusive of the line Endau – G. Beremban – Kluang – Batu Pahat except the Pengerang area, for which Singapore Fortress was responsible.

(*d*) The II Indian Division, less I2 Indian Infantry Brigade, to be accommodated in areas where it could be rested and re-organised. The I2 Indian Infantry Brigade to be withdrawn direct to Singapore.

302. After the conference we reconnoitred in detail the positions to be occupied. I approved a plan for a major ambush on the road west of Gemas.

303. On the morning of I2th January, after a visit to troops of 9 and II Indian Divisions, I held a co-ordinating conference at which the Commanders A.I.F. and 9 Indian Division were present. At this conference the tactics to be adopted were discussed and I approved the following plan:-

(*a*) *Segamat area.* – The crossings over the Rivers Muar and Segamat, which were vital to the defence, to be held strongly against all forms of ground and air attacks.

West of River Muar localities to be held as focal points with striking forces available on the flanks to attack the enemy when he tried to move round them.

An ambush force to be located west of Gemas.

(*b*) *Coastal area.* – On the west coast flank the 45 Indian Brigade Group to cover the main coast road at Muar south of the river with detachments and patrols watching the river and exits south from it over the front Kg. Lenga to Muar.

(*c*) *Anti-Tank Defence.* – Forward field guns to be used for anti-tank and anti-personnel roles. The necessity for a physical obstacle, to be covered by fire, wherever it was intended to stop tanks was stressed.

304. *Commanders.* – At the request of the Commander 3 Indian Corps I appointed Brigadier Key to command the II Indian Division in place of Major-General Paris. The reason for this was that we considered that an Indian Army Officer was now required to pull together and re-establish confidence in what remained of the II Indian Division. Brigadier Lay, who had now returned to duty, was appointed to command the 8 Indian Infantry Brigade and Col. Challen took over command of the 6/15 Indian Infantry Brigade in lieu of Brigadier Moorhead.

305. *The Withdrawal of 3 Indian Corps.* – At 0600 hrs., 9th January, the I/I4 Punjab Regiment on the right of the Batang Berjuntai position was suddenly attacked and suffered considerable losses. In the afternoon the 6/I5 Brigade Group fell back to the Batu Arang area. On the West Coast road our troops after some skirmishing fell back to a position about three miles north of Klang. On the main road the 28 Brigade Group occupied a position at Serendah without being pressed.

306. For the withdrawal of 3 Indian Corps there were in the West Coast area two main roads available, i.e., the main trunk road Kuala Lumpur – Seremban – Tampin – Gemas – Segamat, and the coastal road Klang – Morib – Port Dickson – Malacca. The 9 Indian Division had the tortuous and little-used road Bentong – Durian Tipus, thence either via Kuala Pilah or Bahau to join the main trunk road two miles south of Tampin.

In the States of Selangor and Negri Sembilan and the Settlement of Malacca through which the withdrawal was to take place the roads are much more numerous than they are in the States of Perak and Pahang. The beaches also are sandy and more suitable for landings. These facilities conferred on the enemy greater freedom of action and made our task more difficult.

307. The plan was for the II Indian Division and L. of C. Troops to occupy two delaying positions during the withdrawal, the one covering Seremban and Port Dickson and the other covering Tampin and Malacca. The existence of the lateral road Kuala Pilah – Seremban and the convergence of the two divisional routes at Tampin made it necessary that the 9 Division should be clear of Kuala Pilah and Tampin respectively before the first and second delaying positions were vacated by the II Division.

308. Soon after dawn on the I0th January the enemy attacked the 28 Brigade Group at Serendah and, adopting his usual tactics, quickly enveloped both flanks. Some fierce fighting went on during the day, our troops gradually falling back to Sungei Choh Village, which they found already in possession of an enemy force which had come from the West. They managed to force their way through, however, though suffering severe losses, and late in the afternoon embussed for Tampin leaving behind a party to cover the engineers working on road demolitions.

The 6/I5 Brigade Group, which had been withdrawn the previous night from the Batu Arang area, followed the 28 Brigade Group through Kuala Lumpur. The last bridge in the Federal Capital was blown at 0430 hrs. IIth January and the Brigade, leaving a small force to cover further demolitions, moved to the Labu area west of Seremban.

309. The I2 Indian Infantry Brigade, now only some 600-700 strong, was already in position guarding the Mantin (Setul) Pass, a narrow hilly defile a few miles north of Seremban. A battalion of the newly arrived 45 Indian Infantry Brigade had also been sent forward with requisitioned transport (it's own having not yet arrived) to the Sepang area.

3I0. On the coastal road Port Swettenham was evacuated on the afternoon on the I0th January and the big bridge at Klang was rather ineffectively blown at 2030 hrs.

that night. After some local engagements with the enemy, all troops were withdrawn during the night I0th/IIth January to positions covering Port Dickson.

3II. During the IIth and I2th January there was no contact on the front, though the Japanese aircraft were active on both days reconnoitring and bombing. On the night I2th/I3th January the 6/I5 Brigade withdrew to the Alor Gajah area and the remnants of the I2 Brigade entrained at Gemas for Singapore. On the coast road the L. of C. troops fell back to a position covering Malacca. The 9 Indian Division moved in conformity.

3I2. On the evening of the I3th January, the final stage of the long withdrawal started. As there is only a ferry crossing over the broad river at Muar, all wheeled transport had to pass through Segamat which thus became a bad bottleneck. By the I4th January, however, all troops of 3 Indian Corps were clear and the command of the forward area passed to the Comdr. Westforce. The Commander 3 Indian Corps assumed responsibility for South Johore at 2000 hrs. I4th January.

3I3. During the withdrawal demolitions were carried out on all roads. In particular gaps were blown in all bridges over what might constitute an anti-tank obstacle.

3I4. On completion of the withdrawal the formations of 3 Indian Corps were disposed as under:-

Headquarters 3 Indian Corps, Johore Bahru.
Headquarters II Indian Division, Rengam.
6/I5 Indian Infantry Brigade and II Divisional Artillery, Kluang.
28 Indian Infantry Brigade, Pontian Kechil.
3 Indian Cavalry, Independent Company and one Company Malay Regiment, Batu Pahat.

3I5. On the I3th January the Supreme Commander South West Pacific visited Malaya. At Segamat he discussed the defence dispositions with the Commander Westforce.

SECTION XXXV. – THE ADMINISTRATIVE SITUATION, I5TH JANUARY, I942.

3I6. As a result of our rapid withdrawal from North and Central Malaya there had naturally been losses in material and reserve stocks. This was particularly the case as regards petrol, which required more transport for its removal than was available. On the whole, however, it had been possible by careful organization to evacuate a good proportion of our reserves. The general policy which I had approved was to create new dumps in South Johore for issue to troops in the Johore area. A large dump a few miles south of Segamat, which had been established in the pre-war period to serve both the East and the West Coast areas, was built up. There was also a dump of Royal Engineer material, established for the same purpose, at Batu Anam. The advantages of this policy were threefold. (i) It avoided further congestion on Singapore Island; (ii) it avoided traffic congestion on the Causeway between Singapore Island and the mainland; (iii) it would reduce the length of the forward carry. Accordingly dumps were formed at Johore Bahru and near the waterways in South-West Johore.

3I7. *Food.* – The general food situation remained on the whole satisfactory in spite of the large increase in the population of Singapore caused by the influx of refugees from the mainland, and in spite of the decrease of military reserves occasioned by the arrival of reinforcing units which usually only brought a limited quantity of foodstuffs with them.

3I8. *Water.* – The water situation also up to this time had given no serious cause for anxiety in spite of a most unusually dry season. After the start of hostilities new wells had been dug round Singapore Town but about the middle of January the digging of them had been stopped at the instigation of the Civil Health Authorities. Measures for strict water economy had also been introduced. The necessity for such economy was constantly kept before the public by publicity in the Press, by posters and by police action.

3I9. *Ammunition.* – There had been heavy expenditure of field and light anti-aircraft ammunition in the series of battles on the mainland. Our stocks in these categories had never been very satisfactory and now began to give rise to some anxiety. Apart from this the situation was satisfactory.

320. *Petrol and Oil.* – As regards petrol and lubricating oils we still had the large dumps on Singapore Island and some smaller ones in Johore. The civil supplies, however, were getting low owing to the loss of their large depots on the mainland.

321. *Transport.* – A considerable amount of civil transport had been requisitioned, especially in the Northern area, to supplement military resources. Vehicles now also became available owing to the enforced closing of business enterprises. In consequence the transport problem at this stage presented no great difficulty.

322. *Medical.* – The need for increased hospital accommodation in the Johore and Singapore areas now began to make itself felt. All the hospitals in North and Central Malaya and the large Australian Base Hospital at Malacca had had to be cleared. The Alexandra Military Hospital was full and some overflow branch hospitals for the less serious cases had been established in private houses under the pre-war scheme. New buildings had to be taken over. Included among these was a wing of the large new civil hospital at Johore Bahru.

323. Sick and wounded, not likely to be fit for duty within two months, were earmarked for evacuation These, except acute cases, and those requiring special or constant nursing, were evacuated to the United Kingdom and India by ordinary passenger ship. Both the War Office and Australia had been approached with a view to provision of hospital ship accommodation, but owing to the needs of other theatres of war, no final arrangements could be made and no ship could be promised. With the help of the Naval authorities, however, the "Wu Sueh", a Yangtze river boat of 3,400 tons and 5 feet draught, had some time previously been bought and re-designed as a hospital ship She was not considered capable of making an ocean voyage (though later she did so) but it was the best that could be done and it would at any rate provide transport to the Dutch East Indies.

324. *Accommodation.* – Accommodation on Singapore Island was becoming very

congested. It was clearly impracticable to prohibit the entry of European civilians from the mainland. It was equally impossible to prohibit the entry of influential Asiatics whose lives would be at stake if they fell into Japanese hands. In consequence, though measures were taken to prevent the mass influx of refugees from Johore, the population of Singapore Island increased very greatly during January.

325. *Railway.* – As a result of the rapid withdrawal, great congestion had occurred on the railway. In particular there were insufficient sidings in the southern section of the railway to accommodate the rolling stock. An effort was made to solve this difficulty by building new sidings in South Johore and on Singapore Island where rolling stock not actually in use could be parked. Unfortunately they were not ready for use in time. Consequently, when the withdrawal through Central Johore took place, thirteen fully laden trains had to be abandoned on the Malacca branch. Efforts to destroy them by air attack were only partially successful. Included in the loads of these trains was a large consignment of maps of Singapore Island which had been printed to a special order by the Malayan Survey at Kuala Lumpur. The lack of these maps was to prove a great handicap at a later date. It is not known what, if any, use the Japanese made of them.

356. *Docks.* – The Japanese Air Force had not yet started bombing the Docks at Singapore and work there was proceeding normally up to the middle of January.

327. *Labour.* – *(See Section XXX).* – There had been little improvement in the situation as regards civil labour. The workers still disappeared as soon as any bombs fell near them and usually remained absent for some days. This applied particularly to the aerodromes upon which the Japanese Air Force was now making daily attacks.

328. *Man-Power.* – A number of European civilians, both official and unofficial, had now become available for duty. Their names were registered with the Controller of Man-Power to whom applications were made both by the Services and by the Civil Departments. Those who had technical knowledge, of whom there were many, were employed as far as possible where their knowledge could be utilized. Some of the older men were employed in Government Departments or in the Passive Air Defence Organization which needed strengthening. A number of the younger men were commissioned in the Services. Some specially selected officers were posted direct to Indian Army Units in spite of their lack of knowledge of the language as it was considered essential to strengthen the European element in those units. Others were attached to combatant units as interpreters and advisers on local conditions.

329. *Supplies in Forward Areas.* – The tactics adopted by the enemy of striking at our communications, coupled with the complete lack of transport aircraft, forced us to modify the general principle of keeping supplies in forward areas mobile. I therefore directed that 7 days' reserve of food, ammunition and other essential stores were to be maintained at all times by forces whose communications might be in danger of attack.

SECTION XXXVI. – REINFORCEMENTS.

330. As has already been stated (Section XXXIII), the 45 Indian Infantry Brigade with attached troops and an Indian Pioneer Battalion had arrived at Singapore on the 3rd January. On the I3th January an important convoy reached Singapore safely bringing the following formations and units:-

53 British Infantry Brigade Group of the I8 British Division.
One Heavy British Anti-Aircraft Regiment.
One Light British Anti-Aircraft Regiment.
One British Anti-Tank Regiment.
50 Hurricane Fighters with their crews.

The transports included several large American liners which were discharged with the utmost despatch and left again without delay.

33I. The reception and protection of this and subsequent convoys were combined operations of considerable magnitude. The Navy was responsible for routeing and docking them and for the provision of naval escort vessels, the Air Force for providing aerial protection from the Banka Straits northwards, and the Army for the provision of ground anti-aircraft protection from the time they reached Singapore till the time they left and for the rapid disembarkation of personnel and discharge of cargoes. Each convoy presented separate problems which had to be carefully studied before plans could be formulated. In all three Services the preservation of the utmost secrecy was insisted upon. It was due to this that commanders in the forward areas were sometimes unable to appreciate the broader aspects of strategical plans. It stands to the credit of all three Services that only one ship in convoy was sunk before reaching Singapore.

332. The 53 Infantry Brigade Group had left the United Kingdom in October bound for the Middle East and had been diverted off the east coast of Africa. The voyage had lasted exactly eleven weeks. On arrival the troops were healthy but soft. In addition, a great deal of new equipment had been issued shortly before embarkation with which there had been no time to train. The Brigade had had no experienceof bush warfare conditions. It arrived without its guns and transport, but it was found possible to replace these temporarily from local reserves. It was accommodated in the first instance on Singapore Island, where I had hoped to be able to give it a short time to become acclimatized, but the swift march of events made this impossible. On the I4th January orders were issued for:-

(*a*) One battalion of the Brigade to move to Jemaluang as soon as ready to relieve a battalion of the 22 Australian Infantry Brigade which would then be at the disposal of Westforce,

(*b*) The remainder of the Brigade to be prepared to move as soon as ready to either (i) Mersing in relief of the 22 Australian Infantry Brigade, or (ii) Labis, to come under orders of Westforce. Reconnaissances of the Mersing area were to be carried out at once.

333. On the I4th and I5th January the detachment of Dutch Marechaussees (See Section XXXI) reached Singapore by air from the Netherlands East Indies. This detachment, the strength of which was about 80 all told, consisted of native troops from the N.E.I. with European officers. They were specially trained in jungle guerilla warfare. Their despatch to Malaya provided another proof of the ready co-operation of our Dutch Allies in this Far Eastern war.

After arrival the Marechausses concentrated in the Labis area of North Johore and, after the Japanese advance, operated against their communications in that district. During the latter half of January they had considerable success killing a number of Japanese and doing material damage. Later, however, they experienced difficulties from lack of food and from the unreliability of some elements of the local population. Rather more than half the detachment eventually made its way to Sumatra.

334. The Hurricane Fighters arrived crated, but were unpacked and assembled with the utmost despatch by the R.A.F. They were in the air within a few days of their arrival. These machines were not the most modern type of Hurricane. Most of the twenty-four pilots had previously seen active service, but had been drawn from several different units.

335. As regards the future, another Indian Infantry Brigade, an Australian Machine Gun Battalion and some Indian and Australian reinforcements were expected within the next ten days and the remainder of the I8 British Division towards the end of the month.

SECTION XXXVII. – THE STRATEGICAL SITUATION, I5TH JANUARY, I942.

336 Our object remained as before, i.e., the Defence of the Naval Base.

337. *Army.* – We knew that on the west coast the enemy had two divisions in front line. From the manner in which they were able to maintain the momentum of the attack we thought that they had the equivalent of two divisions in reserve with which they were able to effect regular reliefs of their front line troops.

There was little evidence of what troops the enemy might have on the East Coast, but we knew it was a minimum of one division.

In addition the enemy was known to have in Indo-China a formation trained in air-borne landings and he was believed to have there at least two divisions in reserve which might be employed in Malaya or elsewhere.

We estimated therefore that the enemy had at his disposal, a minimum of seven divisions with a formation of air-borne troops. His land forces included an armoured component. Our forces were approximately as under:-

Eastforce. – One Brigade Group at full strength.
Westforce. – The equivalent of one strong division.
II *Indian Division.* – The equivalent of about 1½ brigade groups.

Singapore Fortress. – Two weak Infantry Brigades and the Straits Settlements Volunteer Force.

Fixed Defences at full strength.
Anti-Aircraft Defences. – At full strength.
Command Reserve. – One Brigade Group.

This gave a total of approximately three divisions with Fixed and Anti-Aircraft Defences. In addition we might expect to receive by the end of the month the eqivalent of one additional division and a number of reinforcements.

338. *Air.* – Before the arrival of the Hurricanes (See Section XXXVI) our Air resources had sunk to a very low level. It had not been possible to replace the daily losses and, owing to the length and dangers of the route, not more than half of the reinforcing aircraft which had been despatched to Malaya by land route had reached their destination. In consequence, there were seldom a dozen aircraft, and often considerably less, available for attacks on selected targets. The A.O.C. did his utmost with his limited resources to meet the Army requirements but it was practically impossibleto give any effective support to troops in the forward areas.

The Japanese Air Force on the other hand had been able to give continuous support to their troops in the forward areas and to their sea-borne landings on the West Coast. They had also carried out a series of attacks against the Kluang aerodrome in Central Johore. During the first ten days of the month there had been nightly attacks against targets, generally aerodromes, in the Singapore area. From the I0th January onwards these attacks were usually delivered by day as the Japanese were then able to escort their bombers with fighters based presumably on Kuantan. On the I2th January three attacks were made on the Singapore aerodromes by a total of I22 aircraft while on the same day our photographic reconnaissance recorded 200 enemy aircraft on aerodromes in Malaya excluding those in Kelantan.

339. *Naval.* – The enemy continued to exercise complete control of the waters east of Malaya. Off the West Coast his coastal vessels were able to move freely under air protection. We felt, however, that these coastal operations would become more difficult for him as he moved further south and as the length of the coastline to be watched by our forces decreased.

340. *Topographical.* – Broadly speaking, the Western area of Johore is much more developed than are the Central and Eastern areas.

In the eastern area the Mersing and Jemaluang districts are for the most part under rubber plantations, but south of the Jemaluang – Kahang road there is a wide belt of untouched jungle passable only for infantry without wheeled transport. On the east coast there are numerous creeks and waterways which give access to the interior.

In the central area east of the railway the country is broken and hilly and has been less developed. Communications are poor.

The west coast area has, except for a few swamps and patches of jungle, been extensively developed. It is mostly covered by rubber plantations, though there are also cocoanut, pineapple and other plantations. Through it ran the railway, the main trunk road and also a coastal road. The large rivers at Muar and Batu Pahat are crossed by ferry only. Along the coastal belt the country is low-lying and swampy. In the Batu Pahat district there had before the war been extensive Japanese-owned estates.

341. *Communications.* – The greatly increased length of the Japanese communications must without a doubt have complicated their supply and maintenance problems. They had behind them a large number of broken bridges both on the roads and the railway. We also hoped that the guerilla bands which had been organized to attack their communications would soon be having effect. To offset these difficulties, however, the Japanese had control of the sea and of the air and were known to be making use of these elements.

Our own communications were now getting shorter but they were constantly subject to enemy air attack.

342. *Aerodromes.* – The large modern aerodrome at Kluang and the unfinished aerodrome at Kahang would be of great value to the enemy if they fell into his hands. Experience had shown that demolitions could not deny an aerodrome to the enemy for more than a few days. The aerodrome near Batu Pahat was a smaller one and suitable only for light and medium aircraft.

343. *Morale.* – The fighting qualities of some of our troops had naturally been affected by the long and continuous withdrawals and by the enemy's superiority in certain types of modern armament. This was particularly the case with some of the Indian infantry who had up to date borne the brunt of the front line fighting. On the other hand, the A.I.F. were fresh and comparatively well trained and we had two recently arrived brigade groups which had not yet been in action.

344. *Political.* – The State of Johore was an Unfederated Malay State bound to us by treaty. It maintained at its own expense a small military force and had in the past made a generous contribution to Imperial Defence. These factors made it politically desirable that we should do our utmost to hold as much of that State as possible.

345. *The Japanese Course of Action.* – It was clear that the Japanese intended to press on as fast as possible down the West Coast. It seemed probable also that a landing would soon be attempted on the east coast of Johore, probably in the Mersing area, from where the enemy could either develop another thrust towards Singapore or open the lateral road to Kluang. A direct sea-borne attack on Singapore was still, as before, a possibility, though it seemed probable that this, if contemplated, would be deferred until it could be combined with an attack from the landward side. Finally, there was the possibility of an airborne landing either in Johore or direct on to Singapore Island.

346. *Our Own Course of Action.* – In order to attain our object it was necessary that we should continue to fight the enemy on the mainland. In view of the disparity in strength between the Japanese and ourselves the safe arrival of our expected reinforcements remained of primary importance. We estimated that the most important formation, the 18 British Division, could not be disembarked and deployed on the mainland before the end of the first week in February at the earliest, i.e., more than three weeks ahead.

Our problem was greatly influenced by the fact that the road Jemaluang – Kluang – Batu Pahat is the only direct lateral communication in Johore and also by the fact that the newly constructed aerodromes of Kahang and Kluang were situated on this road. It was obviously necessary to fight as long as we could north of this vitally important road.

It was therefore decided to deny to the enemy the line Mersing – Segamat – Muar. An outlineof the plan to put this decision into effect has already been given in Section XXXIV.

SECTION XXXVIII. – THE JOHORE OPERATIONS, I4TH-26TH JANUARY, I942.

347. *The Gemas Ambush.* – North of Segamat the Commander Westforce had disposed the 27 Australian Brigade Group and the 8 Indian Brigade Group astride the main road and railway with one battalion (the 2/30 Australian Bn.) forward in an ambush position west of Gemas. The 22 Indian Brigade Group was similarly disposed in depth astride the Malacca – Segamat road with the forward battalion about the Jementah cross roads. The 2 Loyals, withdrawn from the Singapore garrison, was in reserve and responsible for the local defence of Segamat. Major-General Barstow, the Commander 9 Indian Division, was senior officer on the Segamat front and, under his influence, an excellent spirit of co-operation quickly grew up between British, Australian and Indian troops.

The ambush laid by the 2/30 Bn. (Lieut.-Colonel Gallaghan) was very carefully prepared.The forward company covered 700 yards of road immediately east of the River Gemencheh and was 3 miles in front of the main battalion position. The troops were concealed in thick jungle bordering the road. At I600 hrs on the I4th January the leading enemy troops appeared. By I620 hrs. about 250 cyclists had passed through towards the main position, 500 cyclists were in the ambush and another 500 were seen approaching. At this moment the bridge was blown and fire opened. Some 400/500 of the enemy were killed before the company withdrew. More would have been killed had not the enemy cut the artillery telephone line.

By 1000 hrs. the following morning the enemy were in contact with the main battalion position. Attack and counter-attack went on throughout the day in the course of which more of the enemy troops were killed and 8 or 9 tanks destroyed. Our own losses were under 70. During the night the battalion fell back on to the main position.

The R.A.F. co-operated gallantly in this action. A scratch force – all that was available – of Glen Martins, Wirraways, Vildbeeste and Buffalos attacked enemy columns approaching Gemas and headquarters at Tampin and did some damage.

The ambush of Gemas provides an excellent example of the success that will often attend such tactics in jungle country. But fresh and reasonably well trained troops are required and these in the Malayan campaign were seldom available.

348. *The Battle of Muar.* – The town of Muar (Bandar Maharani on some maps) is situated on the south bank of the Muar River a short distance from its mouth. The River Muar is here about 600 yards wide and is unbridged below the main North/South trunk road. In its long course between the main road and the sea the

river is extremely tortuous, especially in its lower reaches in which it winds through low-lying and swampy country. Along the south bank of the river for some 20 miles inland from Muar there stretches a belt of estates with fairly numerous roads and tracks.The defence of this sector was entrusted to the newly arrived 45 Indian Infantry Brigade, to which was attached a battery of Australian field artillery. The Brigade was disposed with two battalions forward on the line of the river, one between the sea and Jorak and the other between Jorak and Lenga, and one battalion in reserve in the Bakri area with patrols watching the coast at Parit Jawa. The plan envisaged a mobile defence using fighting patrols to attack the enemy. Unfortunately each of the forward battalions was ordered to push forward two companies north of the river to harass and delay the enemy. In view of the weakness of the force available this was undoubtedly a tactical error which resulted in a great dispersion of force.

349. The enemy's air offensive against Muar started on the IIth January. The bombing of the town, as in other places, started a general exodus and among those who left were the ferrymen. Nearly all the Asiatic employees of the waterworks and power station also deserted.

350. By the morning of the I5th the enemy had reached the north bank of the river, though no information of their approach had been received from the forward troops. In the afternoon a number of boats were seen off the mouth of the River Muar and a small party landed on the coast between Muar and Batu Pahat. Early the following morning another small force landed at the lighthouse west of Batu Pahat where it was engaged by our troops.

35I. In order to meet this threat to Westforce communications the boundary between Westforce and 3 Indian Corps was amended to read as follows:-

> "all inclusive 3 Indian Corps Road Kluang – Ayer Hitam – Yong Peng – Batu Pahat" thus making the task of protecting Westforce communications the responsibility of the Commander 3 Indian Corps.

At I655 hrs. on the I6th January after visiting commanders in the forward area, I placed the 53 British Infantry Brigade under orders of the Commander 3 Indian Corps land ordered it to move during the following night to the Ayer Hitam area. The Commander 3 Indian Corps placed this brigade under the II Indian Division. One battalion (6 R. Norfolk) was immediately sent to hold the defile East of Bukit Payong, a dominating feature some II miles west of Yong Peng, with a detachment at Parit Sulong Bridge some 5 miles further on. One battalion (2 Cambridgeshire) was sent to Batu Pahat and one (5 R. Norfolk) was held in reserve at Ayer Hitam.

352. At about 0200 hrs. I6th January the leading Japanese troops crossed the River Muar at a point a few miles up-stream from the town and by 0900 hrs. had reached the road and established a block 2 miles east of Muar. During the morning some sharp fighting took place in this area. At I300 hrs. a further collection of barges or landing craft appeared off Muar, some of which were sunk by our artillery fire. Continuous fighting went on throughout the afternoon in the outskirts of the town. By the evening of the I6th all troops of the 45 Brigade south of the river, except for the right forward battalion, were concentrated in the Bakri area and the Brigade Commander was

planning a counter-attack to recapture Muar.

Early on the 17th January the Commander Westforce withdrew the 2/29 Bn. A.I.F. from the Segamat front and despatched it to Bakri to meet the threat which was now developing. It arrived in the afternoon.

353. The enemy's attack from Muar, though it had not yet been possible to assess the full strength of it, obviously constituted a very real threat to Westforce's communications in the Yong Peng area, for if the enemy could reach the road there the whole of the Segamat force would be cut off. I discussed the situation with the Commander Westforce and the Commander II Indian Division at Rear Headquarters Westforce at 1200 hrs. 17th January. We were loth to order an immediate withdrawal from Segamat which we thought would be damaging to morale and decided to strengthen the Yong Peng – Muar front by every means at our disposal. I arranged to make available immediately the 2/19 Australian Battalion from Jemaluang, relieving it temporarily by the reserve battalion of the 53 Brigade.

354. Early on the morning 18th January the 45 Indian Infantry Brigade, with the 2/29 Australian Battalion attached, was strongly attacked by the enemy in its perimeter position west of Bakri. Nine enemy tanks were destroyed by the Australian anti-tank guns and tank hunting platoons. The enemy cut the road between this force and Brigade Headquarters situated a short distance to the east but with the arrival of the 2/19 Australian Battalion the situation was restored. In the evening the Japanese again attacked heavily but were repulsed.

On the afternoon of the 18th the enemy landed a strong force on the coast a few miles north of Batu Pahat.

355. Our Intelligence Service on this day reported that the Japanese were advancing with two divisions in front line, a Division of the Imperial Guards being in the Muar area and the 5 Division on the main road. The latter was a crack division which was known to have been specially trained in landing operations. The full extent of the threat from Muar now became clear. I felt that our chances of holding up this thrust for any length of time were not great and that a withdrawal from Segamat would sooner or later be forced upon us. I therefore approved a proposal by the Commander Westforce on the evening 18th January for an immediate withdrawal behind the River Segamat as a preparatory step to a further withdrawal should such become necessary.

356. At the same time, by agreement with the Commander Westforce, I placed the whole of the Muar front temporarily under the Commander 3 Indian Corps. My reasons for this were:-

(*a*) I thought it difficult for the Commander Westforce with his small staff to give the close attention to the Muar front which the dangerous situation there demanded as well as controlling the operations on the Segamat front some 70 miles distant.

(*b*) It would obviously be necessary to build up a supporting front west of Yong Peng in order to keep open communications both with the Muar and Segamat forces. This could only be done by troops at that time under command of 3 Indian Corps.

357. On the morning of the 19th January very heavy fighting again developed in the Bakri area. The enemy again struck at our communications destroying some transport which was parked in rear of the defensive position and blocked the road. About midday the right forward battalion of the 45 Brigade (4/9 Jats) which had remained detached was ambushed when rejoining the main force and suffered heavily. Brigade Headquarters was practically wiped out by a bomb.

The Commander 53 British Brigade was now made responsible for the Bukit Payong – Yong Peng area, under II Indian Division, having been relieved of his responsibility for Batu Pahat. The 3/16 Punjab Regt of II Indian Division was placed under his orders.

358. At 1420 hrs. 19th January I held a conference at Yong Peng at which the Commanders 3 Indian Corps, Westforce, II Indian Division and 53 British Infantry Brigade were present. The following orders were issued:-

(*a*) The 53 Brigade Group to hold a position from the bridge at Parit Sulong to the high ground S.E. of the junction of the Yong Peng – Muar and Yong Peng – Batu Pahat roads.

(*b*) The 45 Brigade Group to be ordered to withdraw at once through the 53 Brigade Group to a position west of Yong Peng.

(*c*) The Segamat Force to continue its with-withdrawal.

(*d*) The 22 Indian Infantry Brigade, on its arrival at Yong Peng on the night 20th-21st January from the Segamat front, to be at the disposal of II Indian Division.

359. Events, however, anticipated the implementation of this plan, for on the afternoon of the 19th January an enemy force attacked and captured the defile east of Bukit Payong and later occupied the bridge at Parit Sulong. An attempt the following morning to recapture the defile by counter-attack was only partially successful, and eventually our troops took up a defensive position at the west end of a causeway which crossed a marshy area a little further east.

360. In accordance with the orders to withdraw, sent by W/T from Westforce which was the only means of communication then open, the Muar Force started to concentrate on the evening of 19th January but was attacked from all sides and suffered heavily. Early on the 20th the withdrawal started, the force being organised into seven company groups. The road, which passed through miles of swampy country, had been blocked in many places. Each block had to be cleared in turn and some of the fiercest and most terrific fighting of the whole campaign took place on this day, our troops, harassed on all sides, repeatedly charging with the bayonet, and the Japanese Guards fighting with their traditional fanaticism. It was not till 0600 hrs., 21st January, that the head of the column reached the bridge at Parit Sulong to find it held by the enemy.

36I. Early in the withdrawal the Commander 45 Indian Brigade (Brigadier Duncan) was killed while leading a bayonet charge. He had set a magnificent example of courage and fortitude and can in no way be held responsible for the disaster which overtook his untrained brigade. The command of the force devolved upon Lt.-Col. Anderson A.I.F., who for his fine leadership was awarded the Victoria Cross.

362. At 0833 hrs. 2Ist January I ordered the Commander Westforce to assume command of all troops on the Yong Peng – Muar road at a time to be arranged direct with the Commander II Indian Division. The reasons for this change in command were as under:-

(*a*) The movements of the Segamat and Muar Forces now required very careful co-ordination.

(*b*) The shortening of communications now made it possible for the Commander Westforce to control both forces.

(*c*) The only possibility of communication with the Muar Force was by W/T from Headquarters Westforce.

363. At I230 hrs. 2Ist January I held another conference at Yong Peng. The decisions reached at this conference, which concerned chiefly the organization for future operations, will be recorded later. The Commander Westforce reported, however, that he was organizing a counter-attack with 2 Loyals, withdrawn from the Segamat front, to recapture the Bukit Payong feature with the object subsequently of re-opening communications to the Muar Force. To this project I gave my approval. That it was not subsequently carried out was due partly to delay in the provision of transport for the move forward of the 2 Loyals and partly to the difficulty of providing artillery support. Having studied the problem carefully I am now of the opinion that the chances of a single battalion being able to advance 7 miles through that type of country and relieve the Muar Force in the time available were remote. The remaining infantry in the Yong Peng force were by that time too exhausted to be able to take a useful part in the operation.

364. Throughout the 2Ist January desperate efforts were made by the Muar Force to force the river crossing at Parit Sulong. But the bridge was strongly held and the attacks were repulsed. In the rear a new threat appeared in the shape of heavy tanks, several of which were destroyed by anti-tank guns and tank-hunting parties. By nightfall, however, the position held had become very contracted. The following morning food and medical supplies were dropped by three aircraft from Singapore, but at 0900 hrs. the Commander Muar Force reluctantly gave the order for all guns, vehicles and heavy weapons to be destroyed, for the wounded to be left behind in charge of volunteers and for all who could walk to make their way through the jungle to Yong Peng.

Eventually some 550 Australian troops and some 400 Indian troops rejoined. I regret to have to record that the wounded who were left behind were, almost without exception, subsequently massacred by the Japanese.

365. The 45 Indian Infantry Brigade ceased to exist. Those killed included the

Brigade Commander, every battalion commander and second-in-command and two of the three adjutants. Only one or two of the surviving British officers had more than a few months' service. This brigade had never been fit for employment in a theatre of war. It was not that there was anything wrong with the raw material but simply that it was raw. It was the price of our unpreparedness for war and over-rapid expansion.

366. Throughout the Battle of Muar the Navy and Air Force did their utmost to help us, the former by sending gunboats nightly to bombard the Muar area and the latter by mobilizing all possible resources, however antiquated, to attack the enemy.

367. The Battle of Muar, which lasted six days, was one of the most sanguinary of the Malayan campaign. Our small untried force, in spite of its handicaps, had held at bay a division of the Japanese Imperial Guards and by doing so had saved the Segamat Force which would otherwise inevitably have been lost.

368. *The Withdrawal from Segamat.* – On the afternoon of the 18th January the enemy attacked with tanks near the main road north of Batu Anam but were repulsed. During the night, in accordance with the decision previously recorded, the 9 Indian Division fell back behind the line of the River Muar and the 27 Australian Brigade Group behind the River Segamat.

During the night 19th/20th January the 9 Indian Division was withdrawn south of the River Segamat to the Tenang area. All the big bridges over the Rivers Muar and Segamat were destroyed.

During the night 20th/21st January the 27 Australian Brigade Group was withdrawn by M.T. from the line of the River Segamat and fell back direct to Yong Peng, where it took up portions covering the vital road junction. The 9 Indian Division moved one brigade group to the Labis area and one to Kampong Bahru. On the afternoon of the 21st January the forward troops of the 22 Indian Brigade successfully ambushed the leading Japanese troops moving down the main road. Our troops, having got used to this novel form of warfare, were now displaying more cunning.

During the night 21st/22nd January the 22 Indian Brigade Group less one battalion (R. Garhwal Rifles) moved by M.T. to the Kluang area, the R. Garhwal Rifles marching down the railway to the Paloh area. The 8 Brigade Group was in position astride the main road some 12 miles south of Labis where the enemy made contact early on the 22nd January. Fighting continued on this front throughout the day. During the following night the 8 Brigade Group fell back behind the River Gerchang some 4 miles north of Yong Peng, a strong position where further fighting took place on the 23rd. This day was also remarkable for intense enemy air activity, their reconnaissance and ground-strafing aircraft often flying as low as 100 feet. At midnight 23rd/24th January the rearguards from both the Segamat and Muar fronts passed through Yong Peng.

369. The extrication of the Segamat Force from its perilous position was a matter for considerable satisfaction. The whole of the Segamat – Muar operations required the most careful handling by all commanders and quick compliance with orders by all formations and units. They imposed a great strain on commanders and staffs, in illustration of which I may mention that during the twenty-five days ending 23rd

January I motored over 2,500 miles and held numerous conferences in the forward areas besides attending War Council meetings and working late into the night at my Headquarters at Singapore.

370. *Plans for the Defence of Central Johore.* – At the Conference held south of Yong Peng at I2.30 hrs. 2Ist January (see above) it was decided that, after withdrawal from Yong Peng, our forces would be re-organized as under:-

Eastforce. – *All troops in the Mersing and Kahang area under command of an officer to be detailed by the Commander 3 Indian Corps.*

Role. – *To hold Jemaluang with detachments forward in the Mersing area.*

Westforce. – *9 Indian Division and A.I.F. less 22 Australian Brigade Group under command of Major-General Gordon Bennett.*

Role. – *To hold the area exclusive Yong Peng – inclusive Kluang – Ayer Hitam.*

II Indian Division. – 53 British Brigade Group when released from Westforce.

6/I5 Brigade Group of two battalions etc.

28 Indian Brigade Group, under command of Major-General Key.

Role. – *To hold the Batu Pahat area and operate on the West Coast road.*

37I. At a conference held at Rengam on the morning of the 23rd January I decided that Westforce would come under command of 3 Indian Corps as soon as the last troops had been withdrawn south of the Yong Peng road junction. The Commander 3 Indian Corps would then command all troops in Johore except those anti-aircraft defences and administrative units under Headquarters Malaya command and the Pengerang Defences under Comdr. Singapore Fortress.

I directed that the general line Jemaluang – Kluang – Ayer Hitam – Batu Pahat would be held and that there would be no withdrawal from this line without my permission.

372. In this connection I cabled to the Supreme Commander South-West Pacific on the 24th January as under:-

"I want to be able to hold line of road Kluang – Batu Pahat for another 24 hours at least as positions further south are NOT good .... Hope you will press for continuous attacks by Fortress bombers on Kuala Lumpur and Kuantan aerodromes. I feel that if we can drive back his fighters we can then deal with his bombers."

On the 25th January I received the following telegram from the Supreme Commander South-West Pacific:-

"Recent reports of heavy fighting on the Muar front show what determined resistance your troops are making against odds. You have not much ground behind you and this resistance is necessary and well timed. I have no doubt that troops have inflicted severe casualties on the enemy. Well done."

373. The denial of the line of aerodromes in Central Johore to the enemy until the I8 British Division had safely arrived was now of primary importance. It was clear that the crisis of the campaign had arrived.

A copy of Malaya Command Operation Instruction No. 35 issued on the 23rd January, I942 is attached as Appendix F to this dispatch.

374. *The Batu Pahat Operations.* – Batu Pahat was a small coastal port of the same type as Muar. The town lies on the south bank of an estuary some seven miles from the coast. The estuary was crossed by a road ferry. Batu Pahat is also linked by good roads with Yong Peng to the North, Ayer Hitam (20 miles away) to the East, and Pontian Kechil (46 miles away) to the South. The Air landing-ground was at Koris, 7 miles south of Batu Pahat. South of that the road runs within 2 or 3 miles of the sea. The country bordering the road and between it and the sea consists mostly of mangrove and cocoanut plantations. To an enemy possessing command of the sea this route was accessible at any point and indicated the necessity for holding both Batu Pahat and Pontian Kechil for the protection of the main L. of C. 20 miles inland.

Batu Pahat is dominated by the jungle-covered Bukit Banang which lies to the south of the town. Into this area the Japanese troops who had landed at the lighthouse on the I6th January (see above) had disappeared.

375. By the evening of the I9th January the 6/I5 Infantry Brigade (Brigadier Challen) had taken over responsibility for the Batu Pahat area with the following troops under command:-

The British Battalion
2 Cambridgeshire
One Company 2 Malay Battalion
One battery I55 Field Regt. (4 guns)
II Heavy Anti-Aircraft Battery.
Administrative Units.

Batu Pahat was now also used as a base for the Royal Naval West Coast Flotilla.

The task allotted to the Commander Batu Pahat Force was to hold the town and to keep open the road to Ayer Hitam. To assist in the latter task the 5 R. Norfolk Regt., whose withdrawal from Jemaluang I had authorised, was to co-operate, working from the Ayer Hitam end.

376. During the 22nd and 23rd January skirmishes took place with enemy detachments on the Batu Pahat – Ayer Hitam road, as a result of which the road was finally closed on the evening of the 23rd January. 5 R. Norfolks were then despatched to Batu Pahat by M.T. moving south via Pontian Kechil. They arrived on the morning of the 24th January andcame under orders of the Commander Batu Pahat Force.

In the Bukit Banang area also the enemyhad become active and fighting developed in the gun position area. The enemy troops here were supplied with food and ammunition from the air.

377. On the evening 23rd January the Commander Batu Pahat Force, being unable to communicate with higher authority owing to a breakdown in W/T, commenced to withdraw to Senggarang but later, communications having been restored, he was

instructed to make a further effort to hold Batu Pahat with the aid of 5 R. Norfolks due to arrive the following morning. Throughout the 24th fighting continued in the town, but efforts to clear Hill I27 S.E. of Batu Pahat the following morning were only partially successful. On the morning of the 25th the enemy attacking the town were reinforced by fresh troops who arrived in lorries. The Commander Batu Pahat Force reported the situation, expressing a doubt as to his ability to hold the town much longer.

378. On the same day a determined attempt was made by the Commander II Indian Division to support the Batu Pahat Force with the 53 Brigade Group, now released from Yong Peng. The Group, which now included two weak infantry battalions only, was ordered to occupy Benut, Rengit and Senggarang and pass through a supply column to Batu Pahat. As the Group moved forward enemy troops, who had obviously moved down east of the road, occupied the road at various points. Some of the leading troops got through to join the Batu Pahat Force but by the evening the road between Senggarang and Rengit was held by the enemy while further south the road was under fire at several different places.

379. Before the war the Japanese held large commercial interests in the Batu Pahat area and had a complete and detailed knowledge of the country. They put this knowledge to good use during the operations. There were also demonstrations of pro-Japanese sympathies in Batu Pahat itself.

380. At I5I5 hours 25th January I held a conference at Rear Headquarters Westforce near Kulai. The Commanders 3 Indian Corps, Westforce and II Indian Division were present.The only matter discussed at this conference was the immediate policy for the conduct of operations. All were agreed that an immediate withdrawal from Batu Pahat was necessary and that, as a result of this, the other columns should be withdrawn from the line Jemaluang – Kluang – Ayer Hitam. I instructed the Commander 3 Indian Corps, who was responsible for the whole of these operations, to issue orders accordingly and to co-ordinate the action of the various columns. A copy of the Minutes of this conference are attached as Appendix "G" to this Despatch.

38I. The Batu Pahat Force withdrew during the night 25th/26th January and reached Senggarang at dawn on the 26th where it found the road blocked. Repeated attempts made throughout the day to force the block and open the road were unsuccessful. Here again as elsewhere the exhaustion of the troops after several days and nights continuous operations in conditions to which they were not acclimatized told its tale.

In the meantime, the Commander II Indian Division had organized a mechanized column, including armoured cars and carriers, at Benut and ordered it forward to the relief of the Batu Pahat Force. Many road blocks and ambushes were encountered and the column was brokenup into small parties each fighting on its own. Only one carrier, that of the column commander, eventually got through.

In the evening the Commander Batu Pahat Force decided that there was no longer any possibility of the brigade fighting its way out as a formation and adhering to the time-table which he had been given. He therefore gave orders for units to make their way to Benut on foot by a route on the coastal flank of the road. A chaplain and personnel of the Royal Army Medical Corps voluntarily remained behind with the wounded who on this occasion were not molested by the Japanese.

382. Looked at in retrospect, it seems that, owing largely to the uncertainty of the communications, the authority to withdraw from Batu Pahat was delayed for 24 hours too long. When the authority was given, the Force was given a task which, in the existing circumstances, was beyond its powers.

383. *The Kluang – Ayer Hitam Operations.* – Early on the morning of the 24th January the leading Japanese troops were approaching the aerodrome and town of Kluang, which were then being held by the 22 Indian Brigade Group with the 8 Brigade Group in reserve at Rengam. The Commander 9 Indian Division ordered the 8 Brigade Group to move up and relieve the 22 Brigade Group so as to free the latter for a counter-attack. In accordance with this plan the 5/II Sikhs moved by a circuitous route on the left flank, bivouacked for the night, and the following day fought a highly successful action in the course of which they routed the enemy at the point of the bayonet and killed and wounded several hundreds of them.

During the night 25th/26th January, in accordance with the general plan of withdrawal, the 22 Brigade Group fell back to a position covering Rengam while the 8 Brigade Group remained in the Kluang area.

On the front north of Ayer Hitam the enemy made contact again on the 25th and fighting went on throughout the day. Our leading troops (2 Loyals) held their ground and inflicted heavy casualties on the enemy who again proved their ability to cross what had seemed impassable ground and again offered exceptional targets to our troops by disregarding normal field precautions.

During the following night our troops on this front fell back through the 2 Gordons who were in position at milestone 49. I had relieved this battalion from garrison duties at Penggerang and placed it under orders of the Commander Westforce in replacement of 2 Loyals who were now withdrawn to Singapore.

384. *The East Coast Operations.* – Mersing, 100 miles from Singapore on the N.E. Coast of Johore, had long been regarded as the back-door to Singapore Fortress, particularly since the completion of the road Kota Tinggi – Jemaluang. The beaches in the Mersing area are suitable for landings, though not ideal, since sandbanks and shoals extend for about 3 miles from the coast. The swampy and tortuous courses of the Endau River and its tributaries are navigable by shallow draught vessels as far as the Jemaluang – Kluang road in the vicinity of Kahang, where was situated the modern landing-ground prepared by the R.A.F. Plans for the defence of Mersing, therefore, had to take into account the possibility of being outflanked by enemy penetration up this river system from Endau.

The Mersing area was strongly defended. It was covered by a large number of anti-tank and anti-personnel mines, though the effective life of these in the humid climate of Malaya is limited.

385. On the 14th January, when contact was first made on this front, Eastforce (Brigadier Taylor) was composed of:-

22 Australian Brigade Group.
2/17 Dogras (released from the Singapore Garrison).

Detachments of the Johore Military Forces.

Administrative Units.

It was disposed with two battalions holding the Mersing area with detachments forward at Endau, one battalion at Jemaluang, and one (2/17 Dogras) watching the long and vulnerable communications back to Kota Tinggi. Onthe night 17th/18th January, as has been recorded, the Jemaluang battalion was transferred to the Muar area, but later a weak Indian battalion was placed under command for defence of the Kahang aerodrome, and also an anti-aircraft and an anti-tank troop.

386. On the 14th January contact was made with an enemy force moving down the coast from Kuantan at Pontian north of the River Endau. After some patrol encounters our troops fell back behind the River Endau. The loss of the battalion from Jemaluang on the 17th/18th January caused some re-adjustment of the defences as a result of which the Endau detachment was withdrawn and the road between Endau and Mersing heavily cratered.

387. On the 21st January an enemy force approaching Mersing from the North was ambushed by our fighting patrols and suffered heavy casualties. On that day, in accordance with decisions taken at the Yong Peng Conference (see above) the Commander Eastforce was given the role of holding Jemaluang with detachments forward in the Mersing area. On the 22nd a Japanese attempt to cross the river at Mersing was repulsed with heavy loss. During the night 22nd/23rd January one battalion (2/18 Battalion A.I.F.) with supporting arms was withdrawn to the Nithsdale Estate between Mersing and Jemaluang, the forward troops remaining in the Mersing area.

On the 23rd a naval convoy was sighted between Singgora and Mersing moving south.

388. At 0745 hours on the 26th January our air reconnaissances reported two transports and some smaller craft escorted by two cruisers and twelve destroyers closing the shore at Endau. This convoy was twice attacked during the day by Hudson, Albacores and Vickers Vildebeeste aircraft escorted by Hurricanes and Buffalos. Each time a large force of Japanese Navy Zero fighters operating from Kuantan was met and there was much air fighting. A minimum of 13 enemy fighters were destroyed while we lost 11 Vickers Vildelbeeste, 2 Hurricanes and 1 Buffalo. Both enemy transports were hit, but the landing was not prevented. Our Air Striking Force in Malaya, even such as it was, had now vanished. On the night 26th/27th January H.M. Australian destroyer "Vampire" and H.M.S. "Thanet" were sent to sweep up the coast and attack the Japanese transports. Off Endau they fell in with and engaged three destroyers and a cruiser. The "Thanet" was sunk and a Japanese destroyer severely damaged.

389. The fresh enemy troops advanced rapidly from Endau and at midnight 26th/27th January their leading battalion marched into an ambush which had been prepared for them in the Nithsdale Estate. There was confused and bitter hand-to-hand fighting during the night, in the course of which over 300 of the enemy were killed while our losses in killed, wounded and missing were less than 100. Our ambush troops then fell back through the Jemaluang position.

SECTION XXXIX. – THE WITHDRAWAL TO SINGAPORE ISLAND 27TH-3IST JANUARY, I942.

390. *The Plan.* – On the 27th January I received a telegram from the Supreme Commander South West Pacific giving me discretion to withdraw to Singapore Island if I considered it advisable. On that day the full significance of the dispersal of the Batu Pahat Force and the opening to the enemy of the West Coast road became apparent. Our remaining troops on that road were not strong enough to stop the enemy's advance for long and there were no reserves available. The I8 British Division had not yet arrived. I felt that any further delay might result in the loss of the whole of our forces on the mainland. I therefore decided to authorise a withdrawal to Singapore Island, even though this meant failure to achieve our object of protecting the Naval Base. I accordingly approved a plan which was already being worked out by the Commander 3 Indian Corps for this withdrawal.

39I. In anticipation of such a withdrawal certain preliminary steps had already been taken, among which were the following:-

(*a*) An outline withdrawal plan had been issued on the 24th January.

(*b*) Orders had been given to begin thinning out the Anti-Aircraft guns and searchlights from South Johore.

(*c*) The Rear-Admiral Malaya had been requested to arrange for all craft on the north shores of the Straits of Johore to be either sunk or removed to the south shores of Singapore Island.

(*d*) Arrangements had been made to insert explosives under the Causeway and to destroy the lock at the north end of the Causeway.

(*e*) The organization of the defences of Singapore Island had been planned.

392. The Plan, which was approved at a conference held at Headquarters 3 Indian Corps at Johore Bahru on the 28th January, was in outline as under:-

(*a*) A co-ordinated withdrawal to take place simultaneously on all four routes.

(*b*) The final withdrawal to the Island to be on the night 30th-3Ist January.

(*c*) The final withdrawal through the Johore Bahru area to be carried out rapidly in M.T.

(*d*) All withdrawals to be carried out by night in accordance with a pre-arranged programme.

(*e*) Anti-aircraft defence to be arranged for the protection of all bottle-necks. In particular, the maximum anti-aircraft defence to be concentrated for the protection of troops moving over the Causeway.

(*f*) An Outer and Inner Bridgehead to be organized for the ground defence of the Causeway. Three battalions with supporting arms under Brigadier Taylor were allotted for the defence of the Outer Bridgehead and one battalion (2

Argyll and Sutherland Highlanders) under Lt.-Col. Stewart for the defence of the Inner Bridgehead.

393. *Eastforce.* – The withdrawal of Eastforce was carried out according to plan without enemy interference. The final withdrawal took place in M.T. from Kota Tinggi.

394. II *Indian Divison.* – Of the Batu Pahat Force, one contingent moved east of the road and reached Benut on the night 27th-28th January. The remainder, comprising about 2,000 officers and men, reached the sea at the mouth of the River Ponggor. From here they were evacuated during four successive nights by the Royal Navy and taken to Singapore. The operation was a most difficult one and reflected the greatest credit on all ranks of the Royal Navy engaged in it.

Benut was occupied by the enemy on the morning of the 28th January but our successful demolitions on this road slowed up his advance. In the evening there was contact north of Pontian Besar. On the 29th there were patrol encounters in the Gunong Pulai Reservoir area where a strong position had been prepared. By midnight 30th-31st January the head of the main II Indian Division column was following Eastforce across the Causeway, leaving only Westforce to be withdrawn through the bridgehead.

395. *Westforce.* – On the main road and railway front the enemy followed up our withdrawal energetically and much fighting took place. The withdrawal of the two columns required most careful co-ordination. There was little rest for the troops who were constantly fighting by day and moving back by night. The enemy aircraft were particularly active on this front reconnoitring, bombing and machine-gunning. Our own troops received very little assistance from the air.

Astride the main road a number of local engagements were fought by the 27 Australian Brigade Group with 2 Gordons under command and many casualties were inflicted on the enemy by local counter-attacks.

On the railway front disaster overtook the 9 Indian Division on the 28th January. A wide gap developed in the Layang Layang area between the 22 Indian Infantry Brigade, which was forward, and the 8 Indian Infantry Brigade which was supporting it. Into this gap enemy troops penetrated having moved round the eastern flank by estate roads. The Divisional Commander (Major-General Barstow), while moving up the railway to visit the forward brigade, was ambushed by the enemy and there is little doubt that he was killed. He was a gallant and gifted officer and his loss was a severe blow. The 22 Brigade, in an endeavour to rejoin the division, moved through the jungle west of the railway. Some parties of the enemy were met and dispersed, the 5/11 Sikhs again distinguishing themselves, but the dense jungle proved too much for the troops who were hampered by having to carry a number of wounded. In spite of a continuous march of three days and nights they were unable to catch up and efforts to locate them by ground and air patrols failed. The final withdrawal was postponed as long as possible in an effort to recover this brigade but without success, and arrangements were made to ferry them across the Straits from a point east of Johore Bahru. Eventually only about 100 were saved in this way. The remainder were captured in the neighbourhood of Johore Bahru on the 1st February.

The final withdrawal on the night 30th-31st January was carried out without incident and with little interference from the enemy's Air Force. At 0815 hrs. 31st January all troops had been withdrawn and a gap of 70 feet was blown in the Causeway.

396. The operation of withdrawing the whole force through the bottle-neck of Johore Bahru and over the Causeway with the enemy holding complete control in the air had been an anxious one. In spite of the severe losses which we had suffered on the main-land, the successful accomplishment of this operation was a matter for much satisfaction.

SECTION XL. – AIR OPERATIONS, 14TH-31ST JANUARY, 1942

397. During this period the Japanese Air Striking Force concentrated their attacks chiefly on the aerodromes on Singapore Island. Some attacks also were made on the Naval Base and the Docks area and some bombs fell in the Town area. On several days the civilian casualties ran into several hundreds. The attacks were usually carried out in daylight by formations of 27 Bomber aircraft escorted by fighters. The maximum number of aircraft which attacked the Singapore area in any one day was 127. Our Anti-Aircraft Defence system had naturally been weakened by the loss of the outer part of the area covered by the warning system. Nevertheless, with the aid of the radar sets, it was still found possible in most cases to obtain some warning of attack though rarely enough for our fighters to carry out effective interception. There was much air fighting, especially on the 22nd January when the losses on each side were estimated to be about a dozen.

398. There was unfortunately no improvement as regards the labour conditions on the aerodromes. The civilian workers continued to disappear whenever an air attack took place and usually remained absent for some days. In consequence, one or more of the aerodromes on Singapore Island were almost invariably out of use.

399. In the forward areas, the enemy aircraft co-operated effectively with their ground forces by reconnaissances, by attacks on our troops and transport, and by dropping supplies on isolated parties. On our side, as before, we were able to give our forward troops very little air support, but we were now able to provide increased protection against low-flying attacks with our ground anti-aircraft defences.

400. During this period the Singapore Air Defence Organization was severely tested. On the whole the organization for the control of the Active Air Defence, which had been worked out in the latter part of 1941, worked very satisfactorily. The fire control of the Anti-Aircraft Heavy Artillery also worked smoothly, but the height of not less than 20,000 feet at which the enemy air formations invariably flew tended to decrease the effectiveness of our anti-aircraft fire. Nevertheless, casualties were inflicted on the air formations, though these were difficult to assess, and some of the formations were broken up.

As regards Passive Air Defence, some modifications in the system were introduced to avoid the waste of valuable time which took place during periods of Air Raid Warnings.

401. On our side, great hopes had been placed in the Hurricane Fighters which reached Singapore on the 13th January. (See Section XXXVI). It was hoped that the superior quality of these machines might enable us to regain at least some measure of air superiority over the Japanese. Such, however, did not prove to be the case. In the first place the machines, which were not of the most modern type, did not prove to be superior to the Japanese Navy Zero Fighters. Secondly, the pilots lacked knowledge of the Malayan climatic and geographical conditions. As with the Army reinforcements, there was no time to accustom them to the local conditions. As a result, several of these Hurricanes were lost daily, some being brought down in battle, some accidentally lost, while a few were destroyed or damaged on the ground.

402. Our Bomber and Reconnaissance machines also continued to be a wasting asset. All available aircraft, including the torpedo bombers, were used for daily East and West Coast reconnaissances, for reconnaissance of the roads behind the enemy lines and for attacks on enemy aerodromes and troop concentrations. These attacks, however, were so weak that comparatively little damage could be done. By the 26th January our Air Striking Force in Malaya had, as recorded in Section XXXVIII, to all intents and purposes ceased to exist. A few attacks were made late in January on enemy aerodromes by Blenheims from Sumatra and Flying Fortresses from Java, but they were not heavy enough to affect the scale of the Japanese air effort.

403. I wish here to pay tribute to the gallant air crews who throughout the later stages of the Malayan campaign went unflinchingly to almost certain death in obsolete aircraft which should have been replaced many years before, and also to those members of the Malayan

Volunteer Air Force who, with no protection of any sort, continued to carry out reconnaissances in Moths and other light aircraft with complete disregard for their own safety.

404. On the 26th January I telegraphed to the Supreme Commander South-West Pacific as under:-

"With our depleted strength it is difficult to withstand the enemy's ground pressure combined with continuous and practically unopposed air activity. We are fighting all the way but may be driven back into the island within a week. We shall then be subjected to a very heavy scale of air attack unless we can maintain sufficient fighters on the island and drive enemy from Southern Malaya aerodromes. I know that you are doing everything possible to reduce enemy air strength which is at present the dominating factor."

405. On the 30th January, 1942, it was decided to withdraw the whole of our Air Force, except one fighter squadron, to bases in the Netherlands East Indies. This decision was made by the Supreme Commander South-West Pacific after consultation with the Air Officer Commanding Far East. At my urgent request, one fighter squadron was left at Singapore. Some heavy and light anti-aircraft artillery was also despatched from Singapore to Sumatra. Certain preliminary steps had already been

taken in anticipation of these moves. Unfortunately several ships carrying Air Force equipment were sunk before reaching their destination.

SECTION XLI. – FURTHER REINFORCEMENTS.

406. *Royal Navy.* – It was now known that it was not intended to send any additional naval forces to Malayan waters. It was also known that a small British fleet was assembling at Ceylon for operations in the eastern waters of the Indian Ocean, that a strong American fleet was assembling in the South Pacific with a view to keeping open communications with Australia, and that some British (including Australian) and American ships were concentrating with the Dutch Fleet for the defence of Java, which was already being threatened by a Japanese thrust south of Borneo. Detachments of Royal Marine survivors from H.M.Ss. "Prince of Wales" and "Repulse" had joined up with the Argyll and Sutherland Highlanders.

407. *Army.* – The following reinforcements reached Singapore during the latter half of January.

On or about the 22nd January. – The 44 Indian Infantry Brigade with attached troops and 7,000 Indian reinforcements. The 44 Brigade was a sister brigade to the 45 Brigade which had fought at Muar. It was equally raw and only semi-trained. It was commanded by Brigadier Ballantine. With a view to giving it an opportunity for further training, I decided to retain it on Singapore Island and allotted it accommodation in the south-western area.

The 7,000 Indian reinforcements were extremely raw and untrained and included very few non-commissioned officers or even potential leaders which were so badly needed in our Indian units. After consultation with the Commander 3 Indian Corps I decided that it would be unwise to draft more than a proportion of these to the Indian units. The remainder were retained at the reinforcement camps for further training.

24th January. – An Australian Machine-Gun Battalion and about 2,000 Australian Reinforcements. As the terrain on the mainland was not suitable for machine-guns, the Machine-Gun Battalion was allotted accommodation in the Naval Base area and ordered to prepare machine-gun positions on the north coast of the island.

Many of the 2,000 Australian reinforcements had only had a few weeks' training. They had not been in the Army long enough to learn true discipline.

29th January. – The 18 British Division (Major-General M. Beckwith-Smith) less 53 Infantry Brigade Group and Machine-Gun, Reconnaissance, Anti-Tank and other units. These, with exception of the 53 Brigade Group already arrived, were due in a later convoy. This divisionhad left the United Kingdom theprevious October for the Middle East. It had been diverted off the East Coast of Africa to India where it had spent a fortnight. It was a war division which had not previously been overseas. On arrival it was fit but soft. It was accommodated on Singapore Island. I decided to hold it initially in Command Reserve. It was ordered to carry out reconnaissances of (a) the northern area of Singapore Island in detail (b) communications in the western area.

In the same convoy arrived a Light Tank Squadron from India, the only tanks ever to reach Malaya. The tanks, which were obsolescent, had been collected from training establishments etc. in India. On arrival several ofthem had to be taken into workshops for overhaul before they could take the field.

Apart from the above no other early reinforcements were expected. It was, however, forecast that an Armoured Brigade might arrive in the Far East early in March. In replyto an enquiry from the Supreme Commander, South-West Pacific, I stated that "A Cruiser Regt. might well be required to deal with tanks landed on beaches, besides having a great moral effect" and suggested that the destination of one cruiser regiment should be left for decision at a later date when we should know the situation more clearly.

408. *Air.* – Towards the end of January 48 Hurricane Fighters were flown off an Aircraft Carrier west of Java. Of these one squadron was based on the Singapore aerodromes. The remainder went to the Netherlands East Indies. These were modern aircraft with only a small proportion of trained and experienced pilots.

SECTION XLII. – IMPLEMENTATION OF THE SCORCHED EARTH POLICY.

409. The measures decided on under the Scorched Earth Policy have already been explained in Section XXVII. These measures were carried out as far as circumstances would permit but the rapidity of the withdrawal made it impossible to ensure that all destruction was executed as planned. It would be idle for me to attempt to assess the success of the Scorched Earth Policy other than in general terms, as undoubtedly a great deal more information is now in possession of those who have returned to Malaya than is known to me. It was known, however, that the thoroughness with which denial was carried out varied in different areas, though it is probably true to say that, taken as a whole, the work was carried out as efficiently as might be expected in the prevailing conditions.

4I0. As regards rice stocks, it was impossible to burn them and there was not sufficient transport to remove them. In many districts they were thrown open to the people who were invited to take what they required.

4II. The attempts to remove or destroy coastal craft were only very partially successful. Some owners whose livelihood depended on them preferred to hide them or to sink them temporarily in the creeks and rivers.

4I2. As a means of transport the Japanese troops made great use of bicycles which in peace time are widely used throughout Malaya. The removal or destruction of these presented an insurmountable problem except where ample time was available as on the east coast of Johore.

4I3. Both road and railway bridges were systematically destroyed as the withdrawal continued. It is estimated that some 300 bridges in all were destroyed in varying degree. The rapidity with which the Japanese made temporary repairs was remarkable, even allowing for the fact that in most cases ample material was available near the bridge site.

4I4. About the 20th January I received a telegram from the War Office asking for a personal assurance that, if the worst came to the worst, nothing of military value would be left intact for the enemy on Singapore Island. This was a big problem in view of the military and civil equipment and reserve stocks of all sorts which existed on the island. After careful consideration, it was clear to me that no guarantee could be given. Some of the equipment, such as coast defence guns, could in any case only be destroyed at the last minute. One of the main ammunition depots was within a short distance of the military hospital and nobody could be certain what the effect of the demolition of such a depot would be. Civil equipment and stocks would be required as long as Singapore was being held. I therefore replied to the effect that I would make all possible arrangements to ensure that, in case of necessity, the destruction of everything of military value should be carried out, but that I could not guarantee that this would in fact be done.

4I5. A Committee, comprising representatives of the three Services, was then set up to examine this subject in detail and to draw up plans as far as the Services were concerned. These plans clearly allocated the responsibility for executing each demolition. This work, which proved to be of some magnitude, placed a further burden on the already over-worked staff of Headquarters Malaya Command.

4I6. The Director General of Civil Defence was made responsible for the organization of civil demolitions on Singapore Island. The planning of these demolitions proved to be a difficult and delicate work. The plans were made with the utmost secrecy. Nevertheless, as was almost inevitable, information leaked out. This gave rise to the wildest rumours, including stories of immediate evacuation, which were damaging to morale.

SECTION XLIII. – IMPLEMENTATION OF THE EVACUATION POLICY.

4I7. The policy as regards the evacuation of women and children and the measures taken to carry out this policy have already been explained in Section XXVIII. The arrangements worked smoothly and by the end of January only comparatively few European women and children remained on Singapore Island. The majority of those who did remain were engaged on important war work. Practically all ships returning from Singapore to destinations within the British Empire had carried their complement of women and children. In some cases, as had been foreseen, the departure of European women, especially those engaged in the Civil Defence Services, had given rise to adverse comment on the part of the Eurasians and Asiatics.

In the end some 300 European women were interned in Singapore.

4I8. The difficulty as regards Asiatics was to find a country willing to accept them. There were no sailings to the China coast and ships to India were not very large or frequent at that time. Eventually Australia agreed to accept I,500 Chinese and a number were sent to Ceylon.

4I9. Our task being to protect the Naval Base, there was obviously no question of evacuating the Army even if shipping had been available, which in fact was not the case. I refused to allow any discussion of the question of evacuation.

I approved, however, of secret arrangements being made with the Dutch Authorities for the preparation of a route across Sumatra for the use of individuals or small parties who might for one reason or another be given permission to leave Singapore. I refused, however, to allow information of the arrangements made to be circulated among the troops as I feared that any talk of evacuation would cause a loss of confidence both among the troops and among the civil population.

PART III.

THE BATTLE OF SINGAPORE.

SECTION XLIV. – TOPOGRAPHICAL AND CLIMATIC CONDITIONS

420. The Island of Singapore is oblong in shape with a maximum length from east to west of 27 miles and a maximum width from north to south of I3 miles. It is separated from the mainland of Malaya by the Straits of Johore across which is a causeway I,I00 yards long. The Straits west of the causeway, which are the narrower, vary in width from 600 to 2,000 yards. They are navigable at high water for small medium draught vessels, though the channel is narrow and tortuous. East of the causeway the Straits vary in width from I,I00 to about 5,000 yards and are navigable for the biggest vessels afloat as far as the Naval Base. In the middle of these Straits at their widest point lies the Island of Pulau Ubin, with a length of 4½ miles and a width of I½ miles. This island is marshy in the centre and is developed in a few areas only. To the east of Pulau Ubin is the mouth of the River Johore. This river, which is navigable for light craft as far as Kota Tinggi, gives access to the main Johore Bahru – Mersing road. Covering the mouth of the River Johore is the Island of Tekong. A few miles east of Tekong lies Pengerang Hill at the southern tip of the Johore mainland.

42I. Immediately south of Singapore Island and separated from it by the waters of Keppel Harbour lie the Islands of Blakang Mati and Pulau Brani. The former, 2½ miles in length and I¼ miles in breadth, was a military reserve.

422. Three miles south-west of Blakang Mati lies Pulau Bukum, I¾ miles long by ½ mile wide, where was situated the Asiatic Petroleum Company's main reserves of naval fuel, petrol and lubricating oils. Further to the west and separated from the south-west coast of Singapore Island by only a narrow channel lie the Sembilan Islands, a group of low-lying islands of varying size inhabited only by Malay fishermen.

423. South of Singapore Island, and not very far from it, is the Rhio Archipelago Group of Islands of the Netherlands East Indies, while to the west lies Sumatra. The Island of Singapore is approached by four main channels – the Malacca Straits to the west, the Durian and Rhio Straits to the south, and the main channel between South-East Johore and Dutch territory to the east.

424. The town of Singapore is situated in the south of the Island and extends for some 6 miles along the water front with a depth of about I½ miles. Immediately north

of it is an extensive residential area covering several square miles of country. The town is divided into two portions by the River Singapore, a muddy tidal waterway crossed by fine modern bridges. On either side of this waterway are the public buildings and the main shopping and business centres. Further west lies the extensive Docks area. The population of Singapore Town in peace-time was in the neighbourhood of 550,000 but by the end of January, 1942, it was probably nearer a million.

425. From Singapore Town main roads radiate in all directions. The principal is that known as the Bukit Timah Road which, crossing to the mainland by the causeway, becomes the main artery to the north. Other important roads are the Thomson Road, a narrow winding road running out to the Naval Base, the Serangoon Road, a good broad highway running north-eastwards and eventually leading to the Seletar Air Base, and the road which runs due east to the military cantonment at Changi. In addition to these, good roads follow the coast line for several miles in each direction from Singapore Town.

426. Although the Island is thickly populated there are few places of any size outside Singapore Town itself. The most noteworthy are the townships or large villages of Paya Lebar on the Serangoon Road, Nee Soon on the Thomson Road, and Bukit Timah on the Main (Bukit Timah) Road. These lie at important junctions where lateral roads join or cross the roads mentioned above.

427. The only hill features of importance on Singapore Island are (*a*) The Bukit Timah group of hills which lie just north of the village of that name and from which an extensive view can be obtained over the greater part of the Island, (*b*) Bukit Mandai, some 3 miles north of Bukit Timah, from which a good view can be obtained over the Straits and Johore Bahru, and (*c*) The Pasir Panjang Ridge, 4 miles in length, running from Pasir Panjang Village to the western outskirts of Singapore Town. From this ridge an extensive view can be obtained over the western approaches to Singapore and also over the country to the north. In the west of the Island there are other minor hill features.

428. Apart from the built-up areas, Singapore Island like the rest of Malaya is thickly covered by rubber and other plantations, while on the northern and western coasts there are extensive mangrove swamps. These swamps had of recent years, owing to extensive irrigation works, lost much of their value as a military obstacle.

429. In the centre of the Island lie the important MacRitchie, Peirce and Seletar reservoirs and the Municipal Catchment area, a large jungle area traversed only by a few tracks. To the north the Naval Base reservation covers a large tract of country.

430. Visibility is everywhere restricted. Even from the hill features referred to above little detail can be seen of ground objects.

43I. The climate of Singapore, though not unhealthy for most people once they become acclimatized, is damp and enervating. Seasonal changes are slight, though during the period of the north-east monsoon (October-March) the weather is slightly cooler than during the rest of the year. The excessive moisture, however, prevents high temperatures. Rainfall is normally high and spread fairly evenly throughout the year, mostly in the form of thunder-storms. It seldoms rains at night. During the period of the Malayan campaign, however, the weather in Singapore was exceptionally dry.

SECTION XLV. – THE SINGAPORE FORTRESS.

432. Before explaining the plans for the defence of Singapore Fortress an outline of the organization for defence as it existed before the withdrawal from the mainland must be given.

The Singapore Fortress area, as previously explained, comprised the Island of Singapore, the adjoining islands and the Pengerang area in South Johore. It was not a fortress in the old sense of the term. It was rather a large defended and inhabited area, with a maximum length of about 35 miles and a maximum width of about I5 miles, which included the large town of Singapore.

The organization for defence can be divided broadly into three categories: (*a*) The Fixed Defences, which included both guns and search-lights; (*b*) The Beach Defences, and (*c*) The Anti-Aircraft Defences. The first two categories were under the command of the Commander, Singapore Fortress (Major-General Keith Simmons). The third, for reasons which have already been explained in Section VI, were directly under me through the Commander, Anti-Air craft Defences (Brigadier Wildey), though their action during operations was co-ordinated with that of the fighter aircraft by Group Captain Rice, R.A.F. The Headquarters of Singapore Fortress were at Fort Canning.

433. *The Fixed Defences.* – As stated in Section VI, the Fixed Defences were divided into two Fire Commands, i.e. the Changi Fire Command which covered the approaches to the Naval Base, and the Faber Fire Command which covered the approaches to Keppel Harbour and to the western channel of the Johore Straits. In each Fire Command was one I5 in. and one 9.2 in. battery and a number of 6 in. batteries; also searchlights and smaller equipments.

There was an elaborate system of buried cable communications linking headquarters with batteries and lights. Observation of fire was either from Observation Posts which had been constructed at points of vantage along the coast or from aircraft. An Anti-Aircraft Co-operation Flight was maintained by the Royal Air Force for this purpose.

After the Japanese landed in Malaya arrangements were made by which fire from the fixed armament could be brought to bear quickly on a limited number of localities selected as likely landing places for an enemy force attacking the sea-front of the Fortress of Singapore. This involved little difficulty.

As the Japanese advanced southwards, it became evident that the anti-ship guns must be prepared to engage targets on the land front of Singapore. Such a requirement was not easy to meet. The chief difficulties were-

(*a*) Only a limited number of guns were available, the remainder being ruled out either from lack of range or on account of limited bearing.

(*b*) The guns most likely to be available were the I5 in. guns (Forts Johore and

A portrait of Air Chief Marshal Sir Robert Brooke-Popham, the author of the first despatch in this volume. (HMP)

Part of the preparations for the defence of Singapore – men of the 2nd Battalion Gordon Highlanders demonstrate a Northover Projector to Major General F. Keith Simmons, GOC Singapore Fortress, and other senior officers, 17 October 1941. (IWM; FE15)

Australian gunners on the island of Singapore waiting for the Japanese to cross the Johore Strait. Churchill said that if the Japanese broke across the Johore Strait in small boats – which of course they did – it would be "one of the greatest scandals that could possibly be exposed". (HMP)

Stocks of rubber, held by a factory on a plantation in Malaya, are burnt during the British retreat to Singapore, December 1941. (HMP)

Bristol Blenheim Mk.I, L1134 'PT-F', of 62 Squadron RAF, taxying in front of a line of Brewster Buffaloes at Sembawang, Singapore, as another section of Buffaloes pass over the airfield, October 1941. It was in L1134 that Squadron Leader Arthur Scarf and his crew single-handedly attacked the Japanese-held airfield at Singora, Thailand, on 9 December 1941 – an action for which Scarf was posthumously awarded the Victoria Cross. (IWM; K662)

A line-up of Brewster Buffalos at Sembawang in November 1941. The aircraft nearest the camera is 453 Squadron's Mk.II AN185, TD-V. (RAAF)

A Japanese aerial photograph showing HMS *Prince of Wales* (top) and HMS *Repulse* during the early stages of the attack in which they were sunk, 10 December 1941. HMS *Repulse* had just been hit for the first time. (US Naval Historical Center)

A group of pilots from 488 Squadron pictured at Singapore in December 1941. (Courtesy of Andy Thomas)

Aircraft and vehicles burn during a raid on Kallang during the Japanese offensive. By January 1942, Kallang was the only operational fighter airfield in Singapore, as the other airfields (Tengah, Seletar and Sembawang) were within range of Japanese artillery on the Malay peninsula. (Courtesy of Andy Thomas)

Because of the effectiveness of Japanese air strikes, the RAF's ground crews were forced to do much of their work servicing aircraft whilst the latter were dispersed under the trees at Kallang. (Courtesy of Andy Thomas)

Deep beneath a Singapore hillside is the Battle Box, the underground command centre of the British Malaya Command. Comprising twenty-two rooms linked by a corridor, the complex was bomb-proof and capable of recycling its own air supply. Now a tourist attraction, the interior of the Battle Box has changed little from as it was in the war. Indeed, this scene, in the actual room used at the time, replicates the dark hours when Lieutenant-General Percival and his staff discussed the impending British surrender. (Courtesy of Roslan Tangah)

Lieutenant-General Percival, General Officer Commanding (Malaya), and his party pictured whilst en route to the Ford factory at Bukit Timah, Singapore, to surrender the colony to the Japanese, 15 February 1942. Never in the history of the British Army had such a large force laid down its arms to an enemy. (HMP)

A captured Japanese photograph, creased by folding, showing Lieutenant-General Arthur E. Percival signing the unconditional surrender of the British and Commonwealth forces at the Ford Works Building near the Bukit Timah Road, Singapore. Lieutenant-General Tomoyuki Yamashita can be seen on the extreme left. (HMP)

Japanese officers stand with Lieutenant-General Arthur E. Percival following the surrender of British forces on 15 February 1942. Note the white flag of surrender. At the end of the war, Percival travelled to the Philippines to witness the surrender of the Japanese forces there, which in a twist of fate were commanded by Tomoyuki Yamashita. The Union Flag carried by Brigadier Newbigging on the way to Bukit Timah was also a witness to this reversal of fortunes, being flown when the Japanese formally surrendered Singapore back to the British. (IWM; HU31329)

Now a national monument in Singapore, the Ford Works Building still exists. Built in October 1941, it was Ford's first motor car assembly plant in Southeast Asia. During the Malayan campaign, the factory was used to assemble aircraft which arrived in crates for the RAF. After the surrender, the building was occupied by the Japanese as a military headquarters. Today, the former factory serves as a museum, exhibition gallery and archive.

Within Kranji War Cemetery, Singapore, stands the Singapore Memorial. On its walls are the names of 24,000 casualties of the Commonwealth land and air forces who have no known grave. Many of these have no known date of death and are recorded in the CWGC files by the date or period from when they were known to be missing or captured. (Courtesy of the Commonwealth War Graves Commission)

Buona Vista) and the 9.2 in. guns on Blakang Mati (Fort Connaught), but the 9.2 in. guns only had about 30 rounds each of H.E. ammunition while the I5 in. guns had none at all.

(*c*) Observation of fire was likely to be difficult as the topography was highly unfavourable to ground observation, while air observation would not be available in view of the local superiority of the Japanese Air Force.

Nevertheless, an improvised but workable counter-bombardment organization was built up and fields of fire were cleared. A demand was made for more ammunition suitable for engaging land targets, but it did not arrive in time.

During January the Fixed Defences suffered some casualties from air bombing.

434. *The Beach Defences.* – The Beach Defences were designed to protect the Islands of Singapore and Blakang Mati, Pulau Brani and the Pengerang area in South Johore from a sea-borne attack. On Singapore Island they extended along the South Coast from Pasir Panjang to Changi, a distance of 20 miles. Concrete pill-boxes for machine guns and light automatics had been constructed at intervals of about 600 yards along the beaches. There were also a few I8-pounder field guns. The defences were well equipped with beach lights.

The material defences comprised anti-boat, anti-tank and anti-personnel defences. They included timber-scaffolding, timber tank obstacles, mines and barbed wire.

Two switch lines had been partially prepared to protect the centre of the Island from enemy landings in the east and west of the Island respectively. The eastern line, known as the Serangoon Line, was sited between the Civil Airport at Kallang and Paya Lebar. The western line filled the gap between the Rivers Kranji and Jurong. In addition, the western front of the Changi area had been wired.

435. Prior to the outbreak of hostilities with Japan no defences had been constructed on the northern or western shores of Singapore Island. This has been imputed in some quarters to a lack of foresight on the part of successive General Officers Commanding. It has, however, perhaps not been fully realised that the object of the defence was not to hold Singapore Island, but to protect the Naval Base. To do this it was necessary at least to prevent the enemy bringing that base under observed fire and also, as far as possible, to keep the enemy out of close bombing range. Such resources, financial and material, as had been available had therefore been applied to the preparation of defences at a distance from Singapore, beginning with the Mersing area and subsequently extending further north. On the eastern front defences had been constructed as far back as Kota Tinggi. Major-General Dobbie, the then G.O.C., had intended these defences to be part of an extensive system covering the Naval Base. The estimate of cost was, however, so ruthlessly cut down by the War Office that the defences were never completed. The financial restrictions under which defence work in Malaya was carried out have already been explained in Section V. Finally, all defence works were incorporated in the Defence Scheme Malaya which was subject to approval by the Committee of Imperial Defence and subsequently by the Chiefs of Staff Committee.

436. Not long after the commencement of the Malayan campaign it became

apparent that we might be driven back to Johore or even to Singapore Island. On the 23rd December I therefore issued orders as under to the Commander, Singapore Fortress. (See Appendix 'C'.):-

"The Commander, Singapore Fortress will arrange for reconnaissance of the north shore of Singapore Island to select positions for the defence of possible landing places."

Early in January orders were given that the preparation of the defences of the northern part of Singapore Island was to be undertaken at once as an urgent measure.

Labour difficulties, however, then intervened. All the troops on Singapore Island had their allotted tasks in manning the defences, and the military labour companies, of which for reasons already explained there were only three, were fully employed on administrative work. Civil labour, from the beginning of January onwards, failed to an increasing extent as the bombing became heavier. I had, as previously stated, agreed to give priority to the Air Force for this labour for work on the aerodrome's and new air strips. The Air Force seldom got enough and there was none available for our defence works. In fact, I had to make available men from the Reinforcement camps for work on the aerodromes.

As regards material, priority was given to the forward areas and a great deal of engineer material was lost at Batu Anam, at Kota Tinggi and elsewhere. There was a general shortage at this time of steel rods for making reinforced concrete.

Nevertheless, a great deal of work was done. The defences were planned in skeleton as it was not known what the strength of the garrison would be. Sites for the forward defended localities and for reserves were selected. Artillery observation posts and gun positions were reconnoitred and selected. Locations of formation headquarters were fixed and communications arranged. Machine gun positions were constructed. The 44 Indian Infantry

Brigade worked in its area. Oil obstacles and depth charges were placed in creeks which appeared to be likely landing places. All available spare searchlights and Lyon lights were collected and made available. Anti-tank obstacles were constructed and made available.

437. On the 23rd January I issued a secret letter to formation commanders giving an outline of the plans for the defence of the Island, from which the following is an extract:-

Policy for Defence.-

The northern and western shores of the Island are too intersected with creeks and mangroves for any recognized form of beach defence.

The general plan in each area will therefore include small defended localities to cover known approaches, such as rivers, creeks and roads to the coast or tracks along which vehicles can travel.

These localities will be supported by mobile reserves in suitable assembly areas, from which they can operate against enemy parties seeking to infiltrate near these communications or in the intervening country.

The essential requirements of these assembly positions will be concealment from air and ground observation. Slit trenches, shallow and narrow, will be dug.

The covering positions should, where possible, conform to these requirements but must be sited to cover the approaches with fire.

Preparation of Defence-
The present Fortress Commander, Major-General F. Keith Simmons, will be responsible for developing the above outline plan. For this purpose, a special staff will be appointed under him. The senior officer of this staff will be Brigadier A.C. Paris. Commanders 3 Indian Corps and A.I.F. will each detail a selected senior officer to report to Brigadier A. C. Paris at Fortress Headquarters as soon as possible to work on his staff.

A sketch map was attached which showed formation and unit boundaries, sites selected for foremost defended localities and reserves, etc.

438. *The Anti-Aircraft Defences.* – These defences had been sited in accordance with a War Office Plan which was designed eventually to cover the Naval Base, Keppel Harbour and Seletar and Tengah aerodromes, but the lay-out was not scheduled to be completed earlier than the middle of 1942. It was, moreover, based on a lower density than had been found necessary in the defence of London during the German air raids. Sembawang and Kallang aerodromes were given some measure of protection by the defences of the Naval Base and Keppel Harbour respectively. Similarly, Singapore Town and the Base Supply and Ordnance Depots at Alexandra were partly protected.

Towards the end of January all the guns and searchlights from Johore had been withdrawn on to Singapore Island. One Heavy Anti-Aircraft Regiment (less one battery) and one Light Anti-Aircraft Battery were despatched to Sumatra for the defence of aerodromes. There remained for the defence of the Singapore Fortress area four Heavy Anti-Aircraft Regiments plus one battery, two Light Anti-Aircraft Regiments less one battery, and one Searchlight Regiment.

The Anti-Aircraft Defence Headquarters were at Fort Canning and were linked by telephone to the Fighters Operations Room at Kallang.

With the withdrawal from the mainland the Anti-Aircraft Defences were deprived of the help of the Warning System which had been carefully built up. Their efficiency was thereby reduced though the G.L. sets proved of great benefit.

439. Singapore was not a Fortress. It comprised a large area of land and water with strong anti-ship defences, reasonably strong anti-aircraft defences, but weak infantry defences and no tanks. The coasts facing the Straits of Johore were, when war broke out, completely undefended for reasons which have been explained above. From time to time exaggerated statements had appeared in the Press as to the strength of the Singapore defences. It is probable that, as a result partly of these statements, the public believed the defences to be stronger than they really were. It is certain that the troops retiring from the mainland, many of whom had never seen Singapore before, were disappointed not to find the immensely strong fortress which they had pictured.

SECTION XLVI. – THE ADMINISTRATIVE SITUATION 3IST JANUARY, I942.

440. *Reserve Stocks – General.* – As explained in Section IX, the policy adopted by the Army as regards reserve stocks on Singapore Island had been one of dispersion. This was done partly to minimise the loss from air attack and partly owing to lack of accommodation in the Singapore Town area, a situation which became more and more aggravated as refugees poured in from the north. Some of the biggest dumps and depots outside the Town area were adjacent to the Bukit Timah and Thomson roads, where they were easy of access. This fact had a big influence on the operations which subsequently took place on Singapore Island. The civil stocks, on the other hand, were mostly in the Town area, where some large godowns had been taken over for the purpose. A large stock of rice was, however, stored between the River Kranji and the Causeway.

44I. *Food.* – It is difficult to state with any accuracy what food reserves were available on Singapore Island at the end of January but there was probably not less than three months' supply for both troops and civilians, European and Asiatic.

The Main Military Supply Depot for Malaya had been established on the main road just east of Bukit Timah Village. At the Bukit Timah Racecourse a little further east was a large dump of foodstuffs which had been backloaded from the mainland. Other dumps had been established at Bukit Panjang Village, on the Jurong Road, at Changi, at Alexandra and in the Singapore Town area. A limited supply of fresh meat was held in cold storage at Alexandra and at Bukit Timah. There was a large supply of attah for the Indian troops at Bidadari on the Serangoon road.

The majority of the Civil Government's reserves of rice and other foodstuffs for the Asiatic population was held in the Singapore Town area. For the Europeans fresh meat was held in cold storage in Orchard Road, the main thoroughfare leading from the Town to the residential area. Finally, the Bali cattle, which had been purchased from the Netherlands East Indies and which had been grazed in Johore, had been driven back on to Singapore Island. With a view to dispersing the civil reserves, the population had been allowed to purchase and remove to their own houses limited quantities of rice. A modified form of rationing for certain European foodstuffs was in force.

442. *Water.* – After the Japanese captured the main source of Singapore's water supply at Gunong Pulai in South Johore on the 27th January the Island was dependent on water from the reservoirs. The water level in these reservoirs was rather lower than usual owing to the abnormally dry season. Nevertheless, there was with care an adequate supply even for the greatly increased population of Singapore Island. The measures taken to economise water have already been explained in Section XXXV. The two pumping stations, the one at Woodleigh I½ miles S.W. of Paya Lebar Village on the Serangoon road and the other in Mackenzie road east of Government House, were both working at full pressure. Up to the end of January breaks in the mains due to air bombardment had been successfully dealt with. The civil staff of the Municipal

Water Engineer had been augmented by European Volunteers, most of whom were refugees from the mainland.

The garrisons of Blakang Mati, Tekong and Pengerang were dependent on local supplies.

443. *Ammunition.* – The ammunition situation was on the whole satisfactory except as regards the 25-pounder field guns (for which we had about 1,500 rounds per gun), the Bofors Light Anti-Aircraft and some categories of mortar ammunition.

The two magazines which had been originally constructed were at Changi and at Alexandra (west of Singapore Town). These were bombproof and contained all types of ammunition. There was also a small magazine at Pulau Brani, and one at Fort Canning which contained S.A.A. only. Under the dispersion policy a large shell-proof magazine had been constructed on the east bank of the River Kranji and dumps had been formed in the Nee Soon area, on the Bukit Timah Rifle Range, near the MacRitchie Reservoir, in the Paya Lebar area and elsewhere.

In addition to these reserve stocks, the normal scales of equipment ammunition were of course maintained at the battery positions in the case of the Fixed Defences and with field echelons.

444. *Petrol and Oil.* – As previously stated, it had been found impracticable to backload much of the unconsumed petrol from the mainland owing to lack of transport and the bulkiness of the petrol drams. Nevertheless, there were considerable Army reserves on Singapore Island.

The Main Reserve Depot was near the Bukit Timah Road a little east of the Racecourse. The Reserve Depot was just east of Bukit Timah Village. There were other dumps at Bukit Panjang Village, near the Thomson road, and in the Alexandra area.

The Main Reserve for the Royal Air Force was held in underground tanks at Woodlands just south of the causeway. There were also large reserves at Seletar and at the other aerodromes. There were other small dumps of aviation petrol dispersed about the Island.

The Civil Government held no petrol reserves. Considerable stocks were however held by the Asiatic Petroleum Company at Kranji and at Pasir Panjang. The main reserve stocks of that company were on Pulau Bukum.

445. *Fuel Oil.* – The Naval Fuel Oil Reserves were stored in three groups of large tanks, situated at the Naval Base, at Kranji just west of the Bukit Timah road and at Normanton just west of the Alexandra area. In addition there were very large reserves on Pulau Bukum.

446. *Transport.* – There was now a superfluity of transport, both military and civil, on Singapore Island and serious traffic blocks began to develop. To ease the situation all military transport no longer required was parked on the open spaces, while restrictions were placed on the use of civil transport. These measures had an immediate effect in reducing the number of vehicles on the roads.

447. *Medical.* – Accommodation for all hospitals withdrawn from the mainland had with difficulty been found in the Singapore Town area, where there was naturally much congestion. The Alexandra Military Hospital remained the main hospital for

British troops, as did the Tyersall Park Hospital in the Tanglin area for Indian troops. The Australian Base

Hospital evacuated from Malacca was accommodated in a school on the northern outskirts of Singapore Town. Temporary hospitals were formed at Changi, in St. Patrick's School, in the lower part of the Cathay building and, later on, on the lower floors of the Secretariat and of the Municipal Offices, at the Singapore Club and at the Cricket Club.

There were good reserves of medical stores at Tanglin.

As regards the Civil Medical Services, the Main Civil Hospital and a number of other hospitals in the Singapore area were still in full use.

448. *Ordnance.* – The Main Army Ordnance Depot was at Alexandra, with large Sub-Depots at Nee Soon and in the Singapore Town area. That of the Royal Air Force was at Seletar.

449. *Naval Stores.* – At the Naval Base were held large quantities of stores of all descriptions for the use of the Royal Navy.

450. *Docks.* – As a result of the Japanese air raids on the Singapore Docks, labour difficulties, similar to those which had been experienced elsewhere, developed towards the end of January. The Asiatic labourers, who were in the regular employ of the Singapore Harbour Board and most of whom occupied quarters adjoining the Docks, disappeared as the air raids became more intense, with the result that ships bringing military stores had to be unloaded by military personnel.

SECTION XLVII. – APPRECIATION OF THE SITUATION, 3IST JANUARY, I942.

45I. *Object.* – As the Naval Base was now under observed artillery and small arms fire and within close range of enemy aircraft to which we could offer only limited opposition, we had clearly failed to achieve our object of protecting that base. From now onward our object was to hold Singapore.

452. *Naval.* – On the sea the Japanese retained complete control of the waters east of Malaya. With Borneo in their hands it was probable also that their naval forces would rapidly extend their control westwards and south-westwards towards South Sumatra.

On the west coast of Malaya no Japanese warships had yet penetrated to the Straits of Malacca but their coastal craft could move with impunity under cover of their aircraft. In addition to captured coastal craft it was now clear that the Japanese had succeeded in transferring to the west coast some of their own landing craft.

453. *Air.* – In the air the Japanese enjoyed almost complete supremacy, the only Air Forces we had available in Malaya at this stage being the one squadron of Hurricane Fighters and a small number of Buffaloes.

All the aerodromes, except that at Kallang, were under observed artillery fire and some of them were under small arms fire.

454. *Army.* – It was estimated that the Japanese could probably deploy three

divisions against Singapore Island, i.e., the Guards and 5 Division, or their replacements, from the west coast and one division from the east coast. These, if up to strength, would give a total of about 60,000 men. Behind these it was reasonable to expect that they had local reserves in Malaya and they also probably still had a General Reserve in Indo-China or elsewhere of one or two divisions. It was estimated, therefore, that they probably had available for operations against Singapore a total strength of seven or eight divisions. They were known in addition to have tank units and a formation of air-borne troops.

As regards our own strength, I have no official figures available now, but I believe it to have been in the neighbourhood of 85,000, i.e., the equivalent of four weak divisions with a large number of Base and other administrative troops. Included in this figure were units of non-combatant Corps, i.e., the Royal Army Medical Corps and the Pioneer and Labour Units, and men for whom no arms could be provided. Probably about 70,000 of the total were armed and equipped. A large number of these were very inadequately trained. Some of the reinforcements indeed were so untrained that it had been deemed unwise to draft them to units and they remained in the Reinforcement Camps.

We hoped to get reinforcements totalling about 2,500 early in February.

455. As regards equipment, the enemy had complete superiority in tanks as we still only had a few obsolescent light tanks available. We were, however, reasonably well equipped with anti-tank guns and still had a good number of Bren gun carriers and armoured cars. Our coast artillery was strong and our field artillery was equal if not superior to that of the enemy though our ammunition reserve was limited. The Japanese had a good infantry gun and their troops were well trained in the use of the mortar which was a better weapon than our own. We had two fully equipped machine-gun battalions, but few units even approached establishment in light automatics, mortars or Thompson sub-machine guns owing to heavy losses in the fighting on the mainland. There were comparatively few anti-tank rifles.

456. *Topography.* – The comparative narrowness of the western channel of the Johore Straits and the fact that the main west coast land communications led to that front made it appear probable that the main Japanese attack would develop from the west. There was also the possibility of an approach via the Malacca Straits to the south-west sector of Singapore Island. Another possible avenue of approach which could not be neglected was from Kota Tinggi via the River Johore leading to Tekong Island and the Changi area.

Should the enemy succeed in getting a footing on Singapore Island, the offensive and infiltration tactics which he would certainly adopt would be favoured by the lack of ground observation.

457. *Communications.* – The Japanese land communications were now very long and vulnerable and exposed to the harassing tactics of the various parties which had been left behind on the mainland for that purpose. Many bridges had been destroyed. On the other hand by making use of the sea and by landing troops and material at Mersing or at one of the small west coast ports the enemy could to some extent overcome the difficulties of these long communications.

South of Singapore, our own communications were now very precarious as a result of the Japanese advance towards South Sumatra and Java.

The coast-line of Singapore Island, Blakang Mati and Pulau Brani measured 72 miles. In addition to this there was the Island of Tekong and the Pengerang Defended area. This was a long frontage to defend with the forces at our disposal.

458. *Morale.* – As is usual after all long withdrawals, our troops who had fought on the mainland were suffering from exhaustion and from lack of sleep. Their confidence had been shaken by the enemy's naval and air supremacy and by his great superiority in armoured fighting vehicles.

The fact that the Naval Base had ceased to be of use to us and the evacuation of the Air Force except for one fighter squadron, necessary as it may have been, were factors which had a most adverse effect on the morale both of the troops and of the civil population. It was understandable that some among the troops should begin to think of their own homes overseas, which were now being directly threatened.

459. *Japanese Plan.* – I anticipated that the enemy would be certain to launch an attack against Singapore Island as early as possible in order to free troops and aircraft for operations elsewhere and to open sea communications to the Indian Ocean. He would certainly attack from the mainland but he might also simultaneously with this launch a sea-borne and/or an air-borne attack. I expected the attack to develop from the west, combined perhaps with a sea-borne attack via the Straits of Malacca. I thought it probable that another force would come down the Johore River to attack either Tekong Island or Changi.

If a direct sea-borne attack was undertaken this would probably be directed against the south coast east of Singapore Town, while the objectives of an air-borne attack would probably be the aerodromes.

I estimated that it would take the enemy at least a week to prepare his attack and that we must therefore be ready to meet this attack any time after the first week in February.

460. *Plan of Defence.* – The following two alternatives were, broadly speaking, open to us:-

(*a*) To endeavour to prevent the enemy landing or, if he succeeded in landing, to stop him near the beaches and destroy him or drive him out by counter-attack, or

(*b*) To hold the coast-line thinly and retain large reserves with a view to fighting a battle on Singapore Island.

The disadvantage of (*a*) was that it was not possible with the forces at our disposal, owing to the extent of the coast-line, to build up a really strong coastal, defence. On the other hand, as regards (*b*) there was a lack of depth in which to fight a defensive battle on Singapore Island in front of the vital town area. The Naval and Air Bases, depots, dumps and other installations were dispersed all over the Island and some of them would certainly be lost if the enemy was allowed to get a footing on the Island. Further, the close nature of the country and the short visibility would favour the enemy who would be sure to adopt aggressive tactics. Finally, the moral effect of a successful enemy landing would be bad both on the troops and on the civil population.

For these reasons alternative (*a*) was adopted.

46I. There was then the problem of the Pengerang area and the outlying islands. If the Fixed Defences organization was to be retained in its entirety, and it seemed essential that it should be, it was necessary to hold both the Pengerang area and most of the islands. Pengerang was already garrisoned by an Indian State Forces unit in addition to the personnel of the Fixed Defences located there. The Island of Tekong had become, as has been explained, very vulnerable to attack from the River Johore. If retained, it must be provided with an infantry garrison. Pulau Ubin was not required for the Fixed Defences but it formed a screen behind which the enemy might assemble an attacking force. It was therefore of importance for observation purposes, but its size made it impossible to hold it in strength without greatly weakening the Changi defences behind it. I decided to establish observation posts on it only. The Island of Blakang Mati and Pulau Brani were required for the Fixed Defences. It was necessary to hold Pulau Bukum as long as the large oil reserves on that island remained intact.

The Sembilan Islands presented a difficult problem. They were not required for observation purposes as there was better observation to seaward from the higher ground on Singapore Island behind them. To hold them in strength would involve a dispersion of force which we could not afford. I decided therefore to rely on denying them to the enemy by fire.

462. *Outline Plan.* – The Plan of Defence in outline was therefore as follows:-

(*a*) Every endeavour to be made to prevent the enemy landing or, if he succeeded in landing, to stop him near the beaches and destroy him or drive him out by counter-attack,

(*b*) The defence of Singapore Island, other than the Anti-Aircraft Defences, to be organized into three areas (i) Northern Area (ii) Southern Area corresponding approximately to the South Coast Defences already held by the Singapore Fortress and to include the Fixed Defences (except the Pasir Laba Battery) (iii) Western Area (including the Pasir Laba Battery).

The Anti-Aircraft Defences to remain directly under Headquarters Malaya Command.

(*c*) The G.O.C. Malaya to hold a small central reserve. Each Area Commander to hold a reserve and to be prepared to send one battalion immediately to assist other Areas as required.

(*d*) The action of the artillery to be co-ordinated by a Brigadier Royal Artillery appointed for the purpose.

(*e*) Pengerang area to be held. No change to be made in the garrison.

The Island of Tekong to be held and provided with an infantry garrison of one battalion.

Observation posts with small escorts to be established on Pulau Ubin.

The Island of Blakang Mati and Pulau Brani to be held and to be provided with machine gun defence.

The Island of Pulau Bukum to be held and provided with a small garrison.

All inhabitants to be cleared off the Sembilan Islands, which would then be denied to the enemy by fire from Singapore Island.

(*f*) A belt ½ mile deep on the northern and western coasts of Singapore Island to be cleared of inhabitants.

(*g*) The Royal Navy to patrol the approaches to the Singapore Fortress from seaward and to co-operate with area commanders in the defence of their coast-line.

(*h*) The Royal Air Force to (i) co-operate in the defence of the Fortress and (ii) reconnoitre the land approaches from the mainland.

SECTION XLVIII. – THE DEFENCE PLAN.

463. As a result of the loss of the 22 Indian Infantry Brigade, (see Section XXXIX), the 9 Indian Division, which had never had more than two infantry brigades, now had only one weak infantry brigade, Its Commander also had been lost. In these circumstances it was decided that the II Indian Division should absorb what remained of the 9 Indian Division. In consequence it became necessary to include the I8 British Division in the 3 Indian Corps at once instead of at a later date as had been intended.

464. The Intention was to hold the Singapore Fortress area.

465. The essence of the defence was that the enemy must be prevented from landing or, if he succeeded in landing, that he must be stopped near the beaches and destroyed or driven out by counter-attack.

For this purpose the defences were organized into three areas (Northern, Southern and Western) and the Anti-Aircraft Defences. The boundaries of areas and the garrisons allotted to them were as under:-

Northern Area. – Exclusive Changi – inclusive Paya Lebar Village – exclusive
  Peirce

Reservoir to 76 Grid Line – thence due north to exclusive the Causeway.

Commander. – Lt.-Gen. Sir Lewis Heath, Commander 3 Indian Corps.

Troops. – 3 Indian Corps, now consisting of II Indian and I8 British Divisions
  with Corps troops.

Southern Area. – Inclusive Changi – exclusive Paya Lebar Village – inclusive
  Singapore Town and the coastal area west of it as far as inclusive the River
  Jurong: also Pengerang, the Islands of Tekong and Blakang Mati, Pulau
  Brani and Pulau Bukum.

Commander. – Major-Gen. F. Keith Simmons.

Troops. – Fixed Defences, I and 2 Malaya Infantry Brigades, Straits Settlements
  Volunteer Force, and Fortress Troops.

Western Area. – Inclusive Woodlands – inclusive Bukit Timah Village – inclusive Kg. S. Jurong – exclusive River Jurong.

Commander. – Maj.-Gen. Gordon Bennett, Commander A.I.F.

Troops. – The Australian Imperial Force and the 44 Indian Infantry Brigade, with attached troops.

Reserve Area. – The remainder of Singapore Island.

In Command Reserve. – I2 Indian Infantry Brigade (Brigadier Paris).

At a later date the boundary between Northern and Southern Areas was adjusted to read "The Tampines River inclusive to Northern Area."

Commanders Northern and Western Areas were ordered to hold one infantry battalion at one hour's notice at night to move to the support of other areas as required.

Artillery was allotted and its action co-ordinated by the Acting Brigadier Royal Artillery, Headquarters Malaya Command. The inner line of the Defensive Fire Zone was approximately 200 yards in front of the Foremost Defended Localities. Owing to an anticipated shortage of 25-pounder ammunition, normal harassing fire was restricted but could be increased on application in special circumstances.

The lay-out of the Anti-Aircraft Defences was re-organised by the Commander Anti-Aircraft Defences, special protection now being given to the Docks area.

467. The Pengerang area was garrisoned by the personnel of the Fixed Defences and one Indian State Forces battalion.

The Island of Tekong was garrisoned by the personnel of the Fixed Defences and the 2/I7 Dogras.

The Island of Blakang Mati and Pulau Brani were garrisoned by the personnel of the Fixed Defences and a machine gun unit formed from the European personnel of the Federated Malay States Volunteers.

Pulau Bukum was garrisoned by a detachment of the Independent Company.

On Pulau Ubin Northern and Southern Areas each established observation posts with small infantry escorts. The orders to these escorts were to resist minor enterprises but to withdraw in face of an enemy landing in strength. They were also to obtain information of enemy movements.

The Commander Western Area was responsible for denying the Sembilan Islands to the enemy by fire.

468. The personnel of all combatant administrative units were organized for the defence of their respective establishments under the direction of Brigadier Moir, late Commander F.M.S.V.F.

469. A force of Chinese Irregulars which had been operating on the mainland under command of Lt.-Col. J.D. Dalley was now expanded and became known as Dalforce. Owing to lack of weapons it could only be partially armed. Detachments of this force were placed under orders of Area Commanders with the object of (*a*) patrolling the swampy areas where landings might take place (*b*) acting as a nucleus of fighting patrols sent to operate on the mainland.

470. Orders were issued for officers' patrols to be sent across the Straits regularly into South Johore to reconnoitre the enemy's dispositions and ascertain his intentions.

47I. Work was continued on the Serangoon and Jurong Switch lines (see Section XLV).

472. In view of an anticipated air-borne landing similar to those which had been so effective in Crete special steps were taken for the defence of aerodromes. In particular the Seletar and Sembawang aerodromes were strongly defended. Instructions were issued as to the form such airborne landings might take and the best methods of countering them.

473. The Rear-Admiral Malaya arranged for naval craft to patrol the sea approaches to Singapore Island. Local naval craft were also made available for in-shore patrol work as required by Area Commanders. Naval Liaison officers were attached to the headquarters of each Area.

474. The tasks allotted to the Royal Air Force Fighter Squadron were, firstly, to co-operate with the ground defences in the protection of the Singapore Fortress area against attacks by hostile aircraft and, secondly, to reconnoitre the main arteries of communications in South Johore with a view to ascertaining the area of the enemy's concentrations. This squadron was now based on the Civil Airport at Kallang.

475. On the administrative side, certain changes were made. The duties of Martial Law Administrator passed from the Commander, Singapore Fortress, to the G.O.C., Malaya. All Army field units were ordered to hold seven days' reserve rations in addition to the emergency ration, as a reserve in case they should find themselves cut off from the normal supply. To economise petrol and avoid traffic congestion only those vehicles actually required were to be kept in use. All others were to be parked in the open spaces about Singapore Town.

All ships and small craft under control of the Royal Navy were now based on Singapore Harbour instead of on the Naval Base.

476. The Operational Headquarters Malaya Command remained at Sime Road with Administrative Headquarters at Fort Canning. The Headquarters Royal Navy and Royal Air Force were also at Sime Road.

477. The dispositions adopted by the Area Commanders and their subordinates were in outline as under:-

Northern Area.-

Right. – I8 British Division (Major-Gen. Beckwith Smith) less 53 Brigade
    Group.
This Division had the 54 Infantry Brigade (Brigadier Backhouse) on the right and 55 Infantry Brigade (Brigadier Massy Beresford) on the left.

Left. – II Indian Division (Major-Gen. Key).
This Division had the 6/I5 Indian Infantry Brigade (Lt.-Col. Morrison) on the right, and the 28 Indian Infantry Brigade (Brigadier Selby) on the left. The 8 Indian Infantry Brigade (Brigadier Trott) was in divisional reserve. The 6/I5 Brigade was after a few days relieved by the 53 British Infantry Brigade from Area reserve and went into reserve.

Reserve. – 53 British Infantry Brigade (Brigadier Duke), later relieved by the 6/15 Brigade. To re-equip the 53 Brigade a large number of weapons had to be withdrawn from the remainder of 18 Division as there were now few in reserve.

Southern Area.-

Right. – I Malaya Infantry Brigade (Brigadier Williams) with attached troops.

Centre. – *The Singapore Town Area.* – The Straits Settlements Volunteer Force (Col. Grimwood).

Left. – Exclusive Singapore Civil Airport to inclusive Changi and also including Pengerang Area and Tekong Island, 2 Malaya Infantry Brigade (Brigadier Fraser).

Western Area.-

Right. – 27 Australian Infantry Brigade (Brigadier Maxwell) less one battalion.

Centre. – 22 Australian Infantry Brigade (Brigadier Taylor).

Left. – 44 Indian Infantry Brigade (Brigadier Ballantine).

Reserve. – One battalion 27 Australian Infantry Brigade, plus one machine gun company and detachments from administrative and reinforcement units.

478. *The Spirit of Attack.* – The following is an extract from an Instruction issued to all formation Commanders on the 3rd February:-

"All ranks must be imbued with the spirit of the attack. It is no good waiting for the Japanese to attack first. The endeavour of every soldier must be to locate the enemy and, having located him, to close with him."

SECTION XLIX. – THE PERIOD OF PREPARATION 31ST JANUARY-8TH FEBRUARY, 1942.

479. *Public Announcement.* I published an announcement which stated that the Battle for Malaya had concluded and that the Battle for Singapore was now beginning and called upon all ranks and all civilians to play their part in the defence of Singapore. A copy of this announcement is attached as Appendix "H" to this Despatch.

480. *The Far East War Council.* – The Council, under the chairmanship of the Governor, continued to meet at 0900 hrs. daily at the house of the Secretary, Mr. Dawson.

481. *Withdrawals to the Netherlands East Indies.* – In accordance with instructions received from the Supreme Commander South-West Pacific certain units and individuals were despatched to the Netherlands East Indies. The units included an Australian Motor Transport Company and certain Anti-Aircraft units. Among the individuals were senior officers required for Headquarters South-West Pacific and

technicians no longer required at Singapore. I was also instructed by the Supreme Commander South-West Pacific, in view

of the shortage of trained staff officers both in the N.E.I. and in India, to evacuate to the N.E.I. all staff officers who were no longer required and in particular to consider whether I could now dispense with any of the Indian Army formation headquarters in view of the reduction of the fighting strengths of those formations.

Some mechanical transport destined for Singapore was also retained in the N.E.I. or returned there without being discharged from the ships.

482. *Re-Organization of Formations and Units.* – As a result of two months of almost continuous day and night operations on the mainland, it was only to be expected that a great deal of re-organization had now become necessary in almost all formations. This was especially the case in the 3 Indian Corps which had borne the brunt of the fighting. The absorption of the 9 by the II Indian Division has already been recorded. In addition, the weaker formations and units were now strengthened by the appointment of new Commanders, by the transfer of personnel, by the appointment of newly commissioned officers and by returning junior staff officers to duty. In spite of these measures, the fighting efficiency of many units, as a result of their initial dilution and of the heavy losses which they had suffered, was far from what could have been desired. This was an unpleasant but unavoidable fact which had to be faced.

Lt.-Col. Coates, G.S.O.I. 9 Indian Division, was appointed Commander of the 6/15 Indian Infantry Brigade in place of Brigadier Challen who was missing after the west coast operations. Col. Trott was appointed to command the 8 Indian Infantry Brigade.

As Headquarters Malaya Command was, in the peculiar circumstances prevailing, now dealing direct with divisions in matters concerning Artillery, Supply and Transport, Ordnance and Medical Services, I authorized a reduction of the administrative staff of Headquarters 3 Indian Corps to conform with the new conditions. Unfortunately there was no opportunity for evacuating the surplus personnel before the Japanese attack started.

The Australian units which had suffered such heavy casualties in the Muar area had now been re-organized and brought up to strength with new drafts many of which were, as has been stated, lacking in training and experience.

483. *Preparation of Defences.* – The preparation of the defences could now be continued by the troops who were to occupy them. Most of the work on the forward defences had to be done by night as they were directly under enemy observation by day. In most areas it was found desirable to withdraw the garrisons from the Foremost Defended Localities by day, leaving only observation posts, and to re-occupy them at night.

All civilians, except those employed on work for the Fighting Services, were evacuated from the northern and western coastal belts. In view of the congestion which already existed in other parts of the Island this was no easy problem.

484. *Arrival of Reinforcements.* – Early on the morning of the 5th February a convoy of four ships bringing the Reconnaissance, Machine Gun, Anti-tank and certain administrative units of the 18 Division and some Indian troops approached

the Singapore area, At about II00 hrs., when the leading ships were close to Singapore and the slowest ship, the "Empress of Asia", was south-west of the Sembilan Islands, the convoy was attacked by enemy dive-bombers. The "Empress of Asia" received several direct hits and soon began to sink. All the troops had to take to the water owing to fire on the ship. Some acts of great gallantry were performed, especially by members of the hospital staff. Rescues were quickly effected by the Royal Navy. The loss of life fortunately was small, but nearly all weapons and equipment on board were lost and the ship became a total wreck. Owing to heavy air attacks on the Docks area, some of the vehicles and heavy stores were not discharged from the other ships which left again the following night.

It thus happened that some of these units landed without their equipment. They were re-equipped as far as possible with small arms and fought thereafter as infantry. They joined the I8 Division reserve.

485. *The Scorched Earth Policy.* – Very careful plans were made for the implementation of the Scorched Earth Policy. As far as the fighting Services were concerned, the policy briefly was that the authority responsible for the dump, depot or establishment concerned would be responsible for the preparation and execution of denial schemes. As regards the orders to put the schemes into effect, I reserved to myself the responsibility for giving the order if time permitted, but, to provide against the contingency of this not being possible, I laid down that there must always be on the spot day and night sufficient personnel with a reliable Commander who would in the last resort and failing any orders act on his own initiative to ensure that the policy of His Majesty's Government was carried out.

A copy of the Instructions issued in this connectionis attached as Appendix "J" to this Despatch.

As regards the Naval Base area, it was arranged that the Rear-Admiral, Malaya, should confer direct with the Commander II Indian Division as regards any assistance he might require for the implementation of the Scorched Earth Policy.

The Director General of Civil Defence became responsible for the implementation of the policy as far as civil installations were concerned.

486. *Civil Defence.* – The withdrawal of the Air Force, except for one fighter squadron, and the evacuation of the Naval Base had a bad moral effect on certain sections of the civil population. Rumours were circulated that Singapore was not to be defended. In an endeavour to restore confidence, I published a statement in the Singapore newspapers making our intention clear. (See Appendix "H".) I also gave an interview to representatives of the Press on the 5th February and on the evening of the same day received a deputation of the leading members of the Unofficial European community. At both these interviews I explained the reasons for the withdrawal of the Air Force, stressed the strategical importance of Singapore and made it clear that our intention was to defend it to the best of our ability.

On the 2nd February a Chinese District Watch Force was formed whose duties, among others, were (*a*) to assist in arresting looters, hooligans, etc., (*b*) to assist in calming the populace, (*c*) to advise the populace to resume business after alerts, (*d*) to assist in food distribution. By this time the Communist element was taking a major part in the Chinese war effort.

Civil labour continued to be a great difficulty. The Docks at this time were being worked chiefly by military labour assisted by some civilians. In other areas also labour was disappearing.

487. *Operations.* – The operations during this period consisted chiefly of air attacks and of artillery and patrol activities.

The attacks of the Japanese Air Force were directed mainly against the Singapore Docks and the Kallang aerodrome, but attacks were also made on the Changi area on certain of the Fixed Defences and on the Singapore Town area. Attacks on the Johore I5 in. Battery did little damage. Our ground defences succeeded in preventing the enemy aircraft from flying low, while the fighters attacked them as opportunity offered.

The Japanese artillery adopted harassing tactics, batteries becoming active in the plantations north of Pulau Ubin and on the high ground east and west of Johore Bahru. One battery, with a specially long range of about 24,000 yards, shelled the Government House area from near Johore Bahru. A balloon section was brought forward to the high ground above Johore Bahru to assist in the observation of this artillery fire. Our artillery replied with counter-bombardment and harassing fire within the limits laid down. The observation posts on Pulau Ubin proved of great service but had to be withdrawn when enemy troops occupied the island early on the 8th February.

On all fronts our night patrols crossed the Straits and reconnoitred the enemy dispositions. Two of the A.I.F. patrols which returned on the night 7th-8th February, after being in enemy territory over 24 hours, reported that on the 7th February large enemy reinforcements had arrived in the rubber plantations opposite the western shores of Singapore Island between the Rivers Malayu and Perepat.

488. At 0930 hrs. on the 6th Februaoy our air reconnaissance sent out from Palembang in Sumatra reported one cruiser, four destroyers and four merchant ships at anchor in the Anambas Islands some 250 miles north-east of Singapore. We concluded that this was a seaborne force assembling for an attack either on Singapore or on some objective in the N.E.I.

SECTION L. – COMMENCEMENT OF THE JAPANESE ATTACK ON SINGAPORE ISLAND. 8TH-9TH FEBRUARY, I942.

489. At about I330 hrs. on the 8th February, heavy artillery fire opened on the fronts of the 22 Australian and 44 Indian Brigade Groups following lighter shelling during the morning. Forward defences, headquarters and communications received special attention. After a lull at sunset the bombardment continued with increased intensity It was apparent that the enemy had greatly strengthened his artillery during the previous week, the bombardment being reminiscent of that during the World War I. Casualties to personnel were, however, not heavy owing to the protection afforded

by slit trenches, but cable communications were cut and damage was done to searchlight and other equipment.

490. The 22 Australian Infantry Brigade was disposed on a three battalion front, each battalion finding its own reserves. The Brigade front, which stretched from the River Kranji on the right to the River Berih on the left measured 16,000 yards. In rear of the position there is a comparatively narrow neck of about 3,000 yards where the headwaters of the Rivers Kranji and Berih nearly join. The problem was whether to allow the enemy to land unopposed and to endeavour to stop him on this neck or to hold forward positions near the coast with a view to attacking the enemy when he was most vulnerable, i.e., when he was crossing the Straits and landing on the shores of the Island. In accordance with the general policy laid down by Headquarters Malaya Command the forward positions were occupied.

The 2/20 Battalion A.I.F. with a company of Dalforce attached was on the right on a front of 8,000 yards between the River Kranji and Sarimbun Island. The 2/18 Battalion V.I.F. was in the centre on a front of 4,000 yards between Sarimbun Island and Murai Point. The 2/19 Battalion which had absorbed a large number of reinforcements since its heavy losses at Muar, was on the left on a front of 4,000 yards between Murai Point and the River Berih. There was a machine gun company distributed along the front. The Brigade was covered by Australian Field Artillery, the total number of guns which could bear on this front being about 30.

I have no record of the orders issued by the Commander 22 Australian Infantry Brigade, but it appears they were to the effect that the forward troops if overrun were to fall back successively to company and battalion perimeter positions.

491. The first landings took place at about 2045 hrs. 8th February and very soon the whole of the front between the River Buloh on the right of the 2/20 Battalion and the right company of the 2/19 Battalion was being attacked. Some craft also attempted to enter the mouth of the River Berih but were driven off. The troops which formed the first flight of the attacking force were conveyed across the Straits in special armoured landing craft. Successive flights came in more vulnerable types of craft. These landing craft were available in very large numbers, as many as 40-50 appearing on the front of one of the forward companies in the first flight. Each landing craft carried 40 men. It is now known that two divisions, the 18th right and 5th left, took part in this attack. It has been ascertained from Japanese sources that 13,000 troops landed during the night and a further, 10,000 soon after dawn, so that our defending troops were heavily outnumbered. The landing craft emerged from the rivers opposite the north-western and western shores of Singapore Island. It is now known that the Japanese carried them overland by road from Pontian Kechil on the west coast of Johore. There can be no doubt that preparations for this attack on Singapore Island had been made a long time before the war started.

492. The enemy landing craft in the first flight were in many cases sunk or beaten off by the Forward Defended Localities and the machine guns, but they were quickly followed by others and the enemy succeeded in landing at many points. Very heavy, and, in many areas, fierce hand-to-hand fighting developed. Some of the machine guns continued fighting until their ammunition was practically exhausted.

Unfortunately, it appears that the S.O.S. calls for artillery support were not answered until some time after the attack started. This was due partly to the inadequacy of Verey Light signals in that close country, partly to the severing of cable communications by the enemy's bombardment and partly to a failure to make full use of W/T.When the artillery fire did come down, however, it was maintained, within the limits of the resources available, at a high level throughout the night and must have done considerable damage.

There was also a failure to make proper use of the beach searchlights for reasons which it has not been possible to ascertain. This disadvantage was, however, countered to some extent by the illumination provided by burning ammunition barges.

493. The strongest enemy attack was directed from the west up the banks of the River Murai with Ama Keng Village, the key point lying between the headwaters of the River Kranji and the River Berih, as its objective. In this area a wedge was driven between the 2/18 and 2/19 Battalions A.I.F.

494. At about midnight the commanders of the three battalions, in accordance with their instructions as outlined above, ordered the forward troops to withdraw into battalion perimeters. The 2/20 Battalion on the right concentrated in a position about the Namazie Estate, but the 2/18 Battalion was too closely engaged with the enemy and only a small proportion of them reached their perimeter at Ama Keng Village. A similar fate befell the 2/19 Battalion on the left. At about 0900 hrs. the commander of the 2/20 Battalion ordered a withdrawal to the Ama Keng Village area where he hoped to join up with the 2/18 Battalion, but found it occupied by the enemy.

495. The plan for the forward troops to fall back to battalion perimeter positions was contrary to the policy laid down by Headquarters Malaya Command and, in my opinion, involved an operation which was too difficult in the middle of a night battle which was being fought fiercely at close quarters. As a result of it there was much confusion and disorganization, groups of men becoming detached and lost in the close country. Some were collected and taken back to the Base Depot where they were refitted and reorganized. Others made their way to Singapore Town. The 22 Australian Infantry Brigade, however, did not cease to exist – on the contrary it continued to fight well later on as will be seen – and it would be very wrong to judge the performance of the A.I.F. by these stragglers. The action of these men must be judged in relation to the existing conditions. They were not long-service soldiers and discipline was not deep-rooted. They had volunteered for service and had been sent to Malaya to defend the Naval Base. The Naval Base was no longer of any use, but Australia, their homeland, was being threatened. Many of them belonged to units which, after heavy casualties on the mainland, had been reorganized but had had no time to regain their full fighting efficiency. They had fought well throughout a long night against heavy odds and were exhausted. This is the true picture and should be judged on its merits. Active and effective measures were quickly taken by Headquarters Malaya Command and by Headquarters A.I.F. to deal with the situation by means of reinforced stragglers' posts and officers' patrols in the Town area.

496. Shortly after midnight the Commander Western Area ordered the 2/29 Battalion A.I.F. from Area reserve to move up to the Tengah area and come under

the orders of the Commander 22 Australian Infantry Brigade with a view to a counter-attack. It reached Tengah about 0600 hrs, and preparations for a counter-attack to recapture Ama Keng Village were put in hand. The enemy, however, who had by now been strongly reinforced, anticipated this move by continuing his offensive tactics and by 0800 hrs. he was attacking the Tengah aerodrome.

497. At 0700 hrs. the Pasir Laba 6 in. Coast Defence Battery was attacked by dive-bombers and both guns put out of action, many of the crew being killed and wounded.

498. At 0830 hrs. 9th February, it having by then become apparent that no attack was likely to develop against the Northern area, I ordered the Command Reserve (I2 Indian Infantry Brigade) to move at once to the Bukit Panjang – Keat Hong Village area where it would come under command Western Area. This so-called brigade now consisted only of the 2 Argyll and Sutherland Highlanders, 350 strong, of which, I50 were Royal Marines, and one Indian Battalion 400 strong. On arrival about mid-day it took up a defensive position astride the road just west of Keat Hong Village in the right sector of the Kranji – Jurong Line.

499. At II00 hrs., with a view to forming a new Command Reserve, I ordered the Commander, 3 Indian Corps to put his reserve, the 6/I5 Indian Infantry Brigade, at one hour's notice and not to use it without reference to me.

500. In the middle of the day there was a lull in the fighting which had been focused chiefly round the Tengah aerodrome. Early in the afternoon I discussed the situation with the Commander Western Area at his headquarters near Bukit Timah Village. A decision had to be taken with regard to the 44 Brigade Group which was still holding its positions on the southwest coast of Singapore Island and whose only line of communication along the Jurong road was now being threatened. The possibility of using this brigade to attack the right flank of the enemy's penetration was considered but dismissed as being impracticable owing to the dispersion of the brigade in its defensive positions. The following decisions were then taken:-

(*a*) The 27 Australian Brigade Group should continue to hold the Causeway and maintain its position east of the River Kranji.

(*b*) That we should now concentrate on holding the Kranji – Jurong Switch Line.

(*c*) That to assist in holding this line the 44 Brigade Group should be withdrawn at once from its coast defence positions and take up a defensive position on the left of the line astride the Jurong road.

(*d*) That the 6/I5 Brigade from the Northern Area should be moved as soon as possible to a rendezvous on the Bukit Timah road with its head at the Racecourse where it would come under the orders of the Commander Western Area.

50I. The enemy's thrust now exercised a very serious threat to our depots and dumps along the Bukit Timah road, especially to the large Kranji ammunition magazine and to the vital food and petrol dumps east of Bukit Timah Village and in the Racecourse area. I impressed upon the Commander Western Area the great importance of covering the area in which these depots and dumps were located.

502. It now became necessary to formulate a plan for the eventuality that the enemy's advance down the Bukit Timah road might force us to withdraw our troops from the other parts of Singapore Island. There seemed to be two alternatives, either (*a*) to fall back to the east part of the Island and hold the Changi area or (*b*) to concentrate for the defence of Singapore Town. We were not strong enough to hold both areas. The most important considerations were the location of the water reservoirs, the location of our main dumps and depots and of our hospitals and the fact that the Civil Government and the bulk of the civil population were still in Singapore Town. I decided that, in the eventuality under consideration, we would concentrate on holding a perimeter round the Singapore Town area and the outlying islands, even though that meant the loss of the Changi defences. As regards the Fixed Defences, the experience at Pasir Laba that morning had suggested that these would not long remain in action if the enemy concentrated his dive-bombers on them.

The plan in outline was to hold a perimeter which would include the Kallang aerodrome, the MacRitchie and Peirce Reservoirs and the Bukit Timah depots area. It was given out verbally to the Commanders Northern and Southern Areas on the evening 9th February and issued as a Secret and Personal Instruction to Senior Commanders and Staff Officers at 0050 hrs. l0th February. It was issued in order that responsible senior officers might know my intentions in case the situation developed too rapidly for further orders to be issued. A copy of the Instruction is attached as Appendix K to this Despatch.

503. During the evening 9th February the enemy's artillery concentrated on the area held by 27 Australian Brigade. This brigade, on orders from the Commander Western area, had modified its dispositions to guard against the threat to its left rear. At about 1930 hrs. the enemy attacked on a front between the Causeway and the River Kranji. Again a large number of his landing craft were knocked out by artillery and machine gun fire but again he succeeded in getting a footing. Fighting went on in this area until midnight.

504. At midnight 9th/l0th February after a day of very heavy fighting the position was approximately as under:-

Causeway Sector. – The enemy had effected a landing west of the Causeway and confused fighting was going on.

Kranyi – Jurong Sector. – The I2 Brigade were still astride the road west of Keat Hong Village with troops of the 22 Australian Brigade in front of them near Bulim Village. The 44 Brigade Group was occupying a position astride the Jurong road near the headwaters of the River Jurong, having driven off some Japanese troops who had cut the road east of Jurong Village.

River Jurong Sector. – The 2 Malay Battalion of the I Malaya Infantry Brigade (Southern Area) was on the line of the River Jurong with forward troops west of the river.

Other Fronts. – Except for some artillery harassing fire there had been no activity on the other fronts.

Reserve. – The 6/15 Brigade was assembling in the Racecourse area.

505. Throughout the day the Hurricane fighters had been in the air almost continuously, as had indeed been the case during the whole of the previous week. They had inflicted casualties on the enemy aircraft and sustained some themselves. This one weak squadron fought gallantly against the Japanese Air Force. With the loss of Tengah, the aerodrome at Kallang was the only one now serviceable. The A.O.C. with my consent decided to withdraw what remained of the fighter squadron to a base in the Netherlands East Indies intending to use Kallang as an advanced landing ground only. In the event no British aircraft were seen again over Singapore.

506. Under cover of darkness on the night 9th/10th February a naval force of three fast armed patrol vessels (Fairmiles) entered the western channel of the Johore Straits with the object of disrupting the enemy's communications and sinking some of his landing craft. A few small craft were sunk but no other vessels were seen and the force had to withdraw without further success.

The Far East War Council met on the 9th February but no meetings were held on subsequent days.

SECTION LI. – EVENTS OF THE 10TH FEBRUARY, 1942.

507. Shortly after midnight 9th/10th February, his left battalion having been forced back from the beaches, the Commander 27 Australian Infantry Brigade issued orders for his brigade to withdraw to positions north and south of Bukit Mandai. This movement was successfully carried out before dawn. It had the effect, however, of leaving open the vital position overlooking the Causeway and exposing the left flank of II Indian Division. The enemy was not slow to occupy the hill south of the Causeway.

508. The 6/15 Brigade, the leading battalion of which arrived at its rendezvous on the Bukit Timah Road at about midnight 9th/10th February, was immediately ordered forward by the Commander Western Area to a position north of the Jurong road near the headwaters of the River Jurong and some 4 miles west of Bukit Timah Village. This position it reached and occupied, after a tedious march owing to the congested road, at about 0430 hours.

By dawn the 44 Brigade was in position on the left of the 6/15 Brigade and south of the Jurong road.

509. The 22 Brigade was still in the Bulim area where it had been since mid-day on the 9th and was ordered by the Commander Western Area to fall back at 0600 hours to fill in the gap in the Kranji – Jurong Line between the 12 and 6/15 Brigades. This movement commenced according to plan but, partly owing to the Brigade Commander losing touch with his units, and partly owing to a misunderstanding of an order received by him from the Commander Western Area, the brigade became

scattered and only a part of it took up its allotted position. The remainder occupied a position south of Bukit Timah Village.

5I0. As previously stated the Kranji – Jurong Line had been selected and partially prepared in peace-time as a Switch Line to protect the centre of the Island against an attack from the west. A wide belt had been cleared of trees and undergrowth between the two rivers. It was a naturally strong position but the defences had not been completed.

5II. By 0730 hours a strong attack had developed against the I2 Brigade holding the right of the position and later the attack spread southwards. Our troops were forced back to positions covering Bukit Panjang Village and Bukit Panjang to the south of it and further south to a position astride the Jurong road covering Bukit Timah Village. A wide gap developed between the left of the I2 Brigade and the right of the 6/I5 Brigade.

5I2. On the left of the Northern Area the Commander II Indian Division, finding his left flank exposed, ordered the 8 Brigade from divisional reserve to move westwards and re-occupy the high ground south of the Causeway. This it succeeded in doing by about I000 hours. A little later a battalion of the 8 Brigade attacked and re-captured Hill 95 overlooking the Causeway.

5I3. During the morning I ordered the Commander Northern Area to despatch a force of three infantry battalions as soon as possible from his Area to a rendezvous east of the Racecourse to come under the orders of the Commander Western Area. This force was drawn from the I8 British Division. It was commanded by Lt.-Col. Thomas, Commander of the Machine-Gun Battalion, and became known as "Tom Force." As the I8 Division was still holding a front line sector and at this time had only two brigades under command, it was not possible, regrettable as it was, to send a composite formation.

5I4. After visiting Headquarters 3 Indian Corps and II Indian Division I returned again to Headquarters Western Area at I430 hours and instructed the Area Commander to recapture the Kranji – Jurong Switch Line which I looked upon as vital for the defence of the important Bukit Timah area where so many of our main depots were located.

5I5. The orders issued by the Commander Western Area for the counter-attack provided for an advance in three phases as under:

(*a*) To secure by I800 hours I0th February the Bukit Panjang and Bukit Gombok features.

(*b*) To secure by 0900 hours IIth February a line from a point east of Keat Hong Village to Ulu Pandan.

(*c*) To re-establish by I800 hours IIth February the Kranji – Jurong Switch Line.

The first advance involved only a slight re-adjustment of the line and was effected without difficulty. An enemy attack and penetration during the night, however, prevented the fulfilment of the remainder of the plan, which subsequently had to be cancelled.

516. At the same conference I decided, after consultation with the Commander Western Area, who had no ground communication with the 27 Australian Infantry Brigade, to place that brigade temporarily under command II Indian Division, through whose area its communications now ran.

517. On the front of the I Malaya Brigade, the forward troops of the 2 Malay Battalion were attacked and driven back east of the River Jurong.

518. Early in the afternoon the Commanding Officer of a battalion of the 44 Indian Infantry Brigade, which had been attacked, asked for and obtained permission to make adjustments in his dispositions. Troops of the other battalions, seeing this movement, started moving themselves and, before the Brigade Commander could regain control, the whole brigade had reached the village of Pasir Panjang 4 miles away. Here the brigade was re-assembled and marched back in good order, tired but not demoralized, to a position, one mile south of Bukit Timah Village. This incident is recorded to illustrate the unreliability of semi-trained and inexperienced troops in critical situations such as that which then existed. It was not a question of fear or cowardice. It resulted rather from bewilderment in conditions which were entirely strange to these raw and untried troops. Such incidents, however, make the conduct of a battle difficult if not impossible.

519. On receipt of information that the enemy were approaching Bukit Timah Village I gave orders for the Reserve Petrol Depot, situated just east of the village, to be destroyed at 1800 hours. These orders were duly carried out.

520. By dusk the 12 Brigade was in position astride the main road south of Bukit Panjang Village where at about 2015 hours it was attacked by enemy tanks closely supported by infantry. The tanks broke through and proceeded south towards Bukit Timah Village but were held up for a time by the 2/29 Battalion A.I.F. and other troops. About 40 tanks were used in this attack.

521. One more infantry battalion (5 Bedfs and Herts) was withdrawn from the Northern Area, and at 2200 hours 10th February was placed under orders of the Commander Southern Area with instructions to proceed to a rendezvous designated by him.

522. The Supreme Commander South-West Pacific arrived at Singapore early on 10th February and left late at night. During the day he visited all formation commanders. Before leaving he issued orders to the effect that Singapore must be held to the last. These orders I passed on to all ranks.

523. During this and subsequent days enemy aircraft were very active over the forward areas and over Singapore Town. They were now unopposed except for anti-aircraft and small arms fire.

SECTION LII. – EVENTS OF THE IITH FEBRUARY, 1942.

524. At 0630 hrs. 11th February Tom Force moved forward astride the Bukit Timah Road with orders to re-capture Bukit Timah Village which was then in possession of the enemy. On reaching the line of the railway, however, the leading troops came

under small arms fire and were held up. On the right contact was made in the thick country astride the pipe line east of the Bukit Timah Rifle Range where close-range fighting developed. The front stabilized on this general line for the rest of the morning.

525. During the night there was a great deal of mortar and patrol activity on the Jurong Road front and by 0830 hrs. the enemy was attacking this position in rear from the direction of Bukit Timah Village. The 6/15 Brigade and other troops on this front fell back south-eastwards towards Reformatory Road south of Bukit Timah Village. The orders, however, did not reach one battalion of the 6/15 Brigade which was left behind.

By mid-day the front ran approximately from the hills east of the Bukit Timah Rifle Range on the right, along the line of the railway, then forward to the junction of Ulu Pandan and Reformatory roads and then south to a point on the coast north of Pasir PanjangVillage.

526. By 0700 hrs. it had become clear that a dangerous gap existed between the MacRitchie Reservoir and the Racecourse which was not held by any of our troops. As a temporary measure I ordered a composite unit from the Reinforcement Camp to move up immediately and take up a position at the west end of the Golf Course. Later a troop of our light tanks pushed further west as far as Swiss Rifle Club Hill.

At the same time I ordered the Commander Northern Area to take over responsibility for this sector of the front as far left as a line exclusive Racecourse – Bukit Timah Road, and I ordered the 2 Gordons to move immediately from Changi to the Tanglin area and to come under orders of the Commander Western Area.

527. At 0745 hrs. IIth February Advanced Headquarters Malaya Command closed at Sime Road, which was now closely threatened, and moved to Fort Canning.

528. At about 0800 hrs. the Main Reserve Petrol Depot east of the Racecourse was set on fire by enemy action and destroyed.

529. During the morning a letter from Lieut.-General Yamashita, Commander-in-Chief of the Japanese Army, was dropped from an aeroplane calling upon me to surrender the fortress. I made no reply to this and reported to Headquarters, South-West Pacific Command as under:-

"Have received letter from Commander of Japanese Army asking for surrender of fortress. Letter was dropped by air. Have no means of dropping message so do NOT propose to make reply which would of course in any case be negative."

530. To meet the threat developing from the west, the Commander Northern Area decided to withdraw units from the beaches held by the 18 British Division and organized a force under Brigadier Massy Beresford, known as "Massy Force." It consisted of three infantry battalions, a light tank squadron, a battery of artillery and a detachment of mechanized cavalry. It was given the dual task of (*a*) securing the pumping stations at the eastern ends of the Peirce and MacRitchie Reservoirs, and (*b*) filling the gap between the MacRitchie Reservoir and the right of Tom Force. Later in the day, the second task became the more important, but strong patrols were

maintained between the two reservoirs to prevent infiltration. Units of the force were moved into position as they reached the rendezvous east of MacRitchie Reservoir.

531. During the morning a strong enemy attack developed against the 22 Australian Infantry Brigade, now reduced to a few hundred men only, which was in position north of the junction of the Reformatory and Ulu Pandan roads (about one mile south of Bukit Timah Village). Fierce fighting went on in this area throughout the day during which the brigade held its ground most gallantly in face of infantry attacks supported by aerial bombing, artillery, mortar and small arms fire.

532. Further to the south the enemy penetrated as far as the Buona Vista I5 in. Battery which was destroyed, the crew subsequently fighting as infantry.

533. During the evening IIth February Tom Force, which was on a very extended front, was withdrawn to more concentrated positions astride the Bukit Timah Road with the right battalion in the Racecourse area and the left south of Racecourse Village. The gap between Tom Force and the right of the 22 Brigade was filled by an Australian battalion and later by 2 Gordons.

534. In the Causeway sector there was no change in the situation during the morning. Our artillery succeeded in keeping the gap in the Causeway open and at the same time inflicted numerous casualties on enemy parties trying to repair it.

A project to recapture Bukit Panjang Village with the 27 Australian Brigade Group, in order to ease the pressure on the Bukit Timah front, proved abortive. That Group was at this time too dispersed for any co-ordinated action.

During the day enemy troops penetrated between the 28 and 8 Brigades towards Nee Soon Village and at I600 hrs. the Commander II Indian Division was instructed by the Commander Northern Area that his task now was to protect the left flank of the I8 British Division by holding a line from the River Seletar to Peirce Reservoir. He was to take immediate steps to put this plan into effect.

During the night IIth-I2th February II Indian Division fell back to the line River Simpang – Simpang Village – inclusive Sembawang aerodrome – inclusive Seletar Reservoir.

535. The following inter-formation boundaries were fixed as from 2359 hrs. IIth February:

(*a*) *Between Northern Area and Western Area.* – The River Namly south of the Bukit Timah Road. Tom Force passed from command A.I.F. to command Massy Force.

(*b*) *Between Western Area and Southern Area.* – Inclusive to Western Area the Ulu Pandan Road.

536. During the period 9th-IIth February the Johore I5 in. Battery and the Connaught 9.2 in. Battery had co-operated by shelling the Tengah, Johore Bahru and, later, the Bukit Timah Village areas. The fire, most of which was with A.P. shells, could of course not be observed but from reports subsequently received it is believed that heavy casualties were inflicted on the enemy by these guns.

537. The loss of the food and petrol depots and dumps in the Bukit Timah area, in spite of all our efforts to hold them, was a very serious blow. We now only had about

I4 days' military food supplies in the depots which remained under our control. As regards petrol, so little now remained that I issued an order that no further supplies, either Army, Air Force or Civil, must be destroyed without my permission.

538. The Indian Base Hospital at Tyersall was set on fire by enemy action and practically burnt out. There were a large number of casualties among the patients.

SECTION LIII. – EVENTS OF THE I2TH FEBRUARY, I942.

539. Thursday the I2th February was a day of heavy fighting on the whole front. The enemy, who had now been greatly reinforced, launched strong attacks at several different points.

At about 0900 hrs. the enemy attacked with tanks on the Bukit Timah road front and almost reached the Chinese High School area before they were stopped. As happened so often in Malaya, our commanders experienced great difficulty in controlling their units in the thick country. Strengths underwent rapid changes as sub-units became detached and later rejoined. The Commander Massy Force finally stabilized the front on the general line MacRitchie Reservoir – Adam Road – Farrer Road. To relieve the pressure on this front I ordered the Commander Western Area to organize an attack from the south against the enemy's flank in the Racecourse Village area. The Johore I5 in. Battery also engaged targets on this front.

540. After visiting the front on the Bukit Timah road area I formed the opinion that there was a very real danger that the enemy would break through on that front into Singapore Town. After consultation with the Commander Northern Area I decided that the time had come to organize a close perimeter defence round Singapore Town itself. This defence must, however, include the sources of the vital water supply. This plan involved the withdrawal of all troops from the beach defences on the north side of the Island and also from the Changi area with a consequent loss of the Changi Coast Defences. Accordingly, I instructed the Commander Northern Area to withdraw the II Indian and the remainder of the I8 British Division from the beach defences, to select and occupy a position covering the water supply and linking up on the right with Southern Area north east of the Kallang aerodrome, and to appoint the Commander I8 British Division to take over responsibility for the front now held by Massy Force. I also instructed the Commander Southern Area to make all preparations to withdraw from the Changi area and the beaches east of Kallang as soon as he received orders to do so. I informed the Governor of the dangerous situation which was developing on the Bukit Timah road front. He ordered the destruction of the broadcasting station and took certain steps to reduce the stocks of currency notes held by the Treasury.

54I. At about I000 hrs. the Japanese Imperial Guards made a determined attack, supported by tanks, in the Nee Soon Village area, but were held west of the village by units of the 8 and 28 Brigades. Early in the afternoon the 53 Brigade, on withdrawal from the beaches, took up a position astride Thomson road a little south of Nee Soon Village and later in the day the remainder of the II Indian Division passed through it.

542. Throughout the day the 22 Australian Brigade Group continued to hold its advanced position in the Pandan area in spite of all attempts by the enemy to dislodge it. There was a lot of fighting at close quarters. Towards the evening, however, the enemy effected a deep penetration south of the position held by this brigade. The brigade was withdrawn undercover of darkness to the Holland Village area. It had fought a gallant action for 48 hours and done much to hold up the enemy's advance in this area.

543. Further south the enemy concentrated during the day on the front of the 44 Brigade and the I Malaya Brigade, fresh troops being brought up by M.T. Several enemy attacks were repulsed. After dark the front was adjusted to conform with the situation on the right and ran from the Tanglin Halt area to Pasir Panjang Village.

544. At 2030 hrs., in consequence of information which I had received, I ordered the demolition of all the Changi defences and the withdrawal during the night I2/I3th February of all troops from the Changi area and from the south-east coast to the Singapore defences. These orders were duly executed.

545. The general line of the perimeter defences included Kallang aerodrome – Woodleigh Pumping Station (one mile south-west of Paya Lebar Village) – east end of MacRitchie Reservoir – Adam Road – Farrer Road – Tanglin Halt – The Gap and thence to the sea west of Buona Vista Village. The Commander Northern Area was, however, instructed to delay the withdrawal on the Thomson road front to give time for certain dumps in that area to be cleared.

546. During the day the Japanese aircraft and artillery were both active, an observation balloon being moved to the western end of Singapore Island. The Town area came in for much attention and there were a large number of casualties.

547. The administrative situation now began to cause great anxiety. As a result of the further withdrawals the miltary food reserves under our control were now sufficient for only about seven days' consumption. In addition to this there were the reserves, varying in quantity, held by units and the civil food reserves. We still had adequate ammunition reserves except as regards 25-pounder, Bofors and mortar ammunition. As regards petrol, except for the Asiatic Petroleum Company's reserves on Pulau Bukum, we only had one small dump and what was in vehicle tanks.

Pearl's Hill water reservoir was empty and the Fort Canning Reservoir began to lose water rapidly. In the Town area breaks in the mains from bombing and shelling began to gain steadily over repairs, with the result that from the I2th February pressure failed seriously and water at low pressure was only available at certain street and ground floor levels. Special water carrying parties were organized. On the I2th February Royal Engineer personnel and military transport were called in by the Director General of Civil Defence to assist the civil staff. For some time past certain Royal Engineer Officers, Warrant and Non-Commissioned Officers, had been understudying Public Utility Services so as to be able to assist should need arise.

SECTION LIV. – EVENTS OF THE 13TH FEBRUARY, 1942.

548. The main Japanese offensive during the 13th February developed along the Pasir Panjang Ridge on the left of our position. Here the Japanese 18 Division, which had fought in the Mersing area and later taken part in the initial attack against Singapore Island, came into action. After two hours of heavy shelling and mortaring it attacked the Malay Regiment which was holding this feature. The latter fought magnificently but suffered heavy casualties and by the afternoon the enemy had reached The Gap, a dominating position where the Buona Vista Road crosses the ridge. Further north the enemy also gained a local success. After dark our forward troops fell back under orders to positions covering the important Alexandra area in which was situated the Main Ordnance Depot, the Alexandra Ammunition Magazine, the Military Hospital and other installations.

549. In the Tyersall – Tanglin area the Commander A.I.F. (Western Area) had organized an all-round perimeter defence into which most of the units of the A.I.F., including all surplus personnel of administrative units, had been drawn. There was only minor activity on this front during the day.

550. On the Northern Area front the 53 Brigade Group fell back under pressure during the day along the Thomson road, and by the evening had taken up the position allotted to it north of Braddell road and east of Thomson road. Here it reverted to the command of the 18 British Division which now had its three brigades in line, 53rd on the right, 55th in the centre and 54th on the left. The Division was now on a five mile front and there had been much mixing of units as a result of the piecemeal way in which they had necessarily been withdrawn from the beach defences.

On the right of the 18 British Division was the II Indian Division holding a position astride the Serangoon road south of Paya Lebar and with its right in touch with the Southern Area eastern defences which included the Kallang aerodrome where some pre-war defences had been constructed.

551. Southern Area still held the beach defences in the Singapore Town area, and also Pulau Brani and Pulau Bukum, Blakang Mati, Tekong and the Pengerang Area. I gave orders for the infantry battalion on Tekong Island, which had not been engaged, to be withdrawn during the night 13th-14th February for employment on Singapore Island.

552. On the morning of the 13th February the Rear-Admiral Malaya decided to sail all the remaining ships and sea-going craft to Java during the night 13th-14th February and to leave Singapore himself. There was accommodation on these ships and small craft for about 3,000 persons in all, in addition to the crews. It was the last opportunity that could be foreseen for any organized parties to leave Singapore. At a meeting held by the Rear-Admiral the vacancies were divided between the Services and the Civil Government. One thousand eight hundred vacancies were allotted to the Army.

As a result of the above decision the move of the battalion from Tekong Island to Singapore referred to above had to be cancelled.

553. At 1400 hours I held a conference at Fort Canning. The following were present:-

The Commanders Northern and Southern Areas, A.I.F., II Indian Division and 18 British Division, and Anti-Aircraft Defences.

The Brigadier General Staff Headquarters Malaya Command.

The Brigadier i/c Administration Headquarters Malaya Command.

At this conference the future conduct of the operations was discussed. I indicated that I hoped to organize a counter-attack shortly to relieve the pressure on the defences. All formation commanders were agreed that, owing to the exhaustion of the troops, a counter-attack would have no chance of success at that time. After hearing the views put forward by subordinate commanders I gave orders for the defence of Singapore to be continued.

554. The conference then discussed the allotment of Army vacancies for evacuation the following night. I decided that:-

(*a*) All female members of the Military Nursing Service should be sent. This decision was taken as a result of a report from G.H.Q. South-West Pacific on the treatment of nurses by the Japanese after the capitulation of Hong Kong.

(*b*) Trained staff officers and technicians no longer required at Singapore could be sent at the discretion of formation commanders.The decision as regards trained staff officers was made in accordance with instructions received from G.H.Q. South West Pacific that any surplus were to be evacuated as they were badly needed both in Java and in India. Technicians were evacuated to avoid them falling into the hands of the Japanese who, there was reason to suppose, would have endeavoured to extract information from them.

As time was short vacancies were immediately sub-allotted to formations with instructions that they need not necessarily be filled.

555. As a result of the views put forward at the conference I formed the opinion that the situation was undoubtedly grave but was not hopeless. Our defence was now very fully stretched and it was not possible to relieve the troops in the forward areas who were becoming exhausted as a result of the continual day and night operations. The interests of the civil population, which was estimated at that time to number nearly one million, could not in my view be entirely disregarded. As so many and vast Imperial interests were involved I felt it my duty to report the situation fully and candidly as I saw it to the Supreme Commander South-West Pacific. I believe that in such circumstances it is equally wrong to give an over-optimistic view as it is to give one which is unduly pessimistic. As some misleading statements have been made as to the purport of the telegram which I sent to the Supreme Commander South-West Pacific on that day I quote below the final paragraph:-

"Your instructions of 10th February (see Section LI) are being carried out but in above circumstances would you consider giving me wider discretionary powers."

In his reply the Supreme Commander South-West Pacific made it clear that, while he fully appreciated our situation, continued action was essential and instructed me to continue to inflict the maximum damage on the enemy for as long as possible.

556. Throughout the I3th February both the Japanese aircraft and artillery were active. About midday there was a particularly heavy and accurate air attack on the Orchard road area, the main thoroughfare connecting Singapore Town with the Tanglin area. The Alexandra Ammunition Magazine came under shell and mortar fire and at midnight deliveries had to be temporarily suspended owing to fires. Our own artillery was also active throughout the day. Most of the field artillery was now sited on open spaces in the Singapore Town area. All remaining batteries in the Faber Fire Command of the Fixed Defences came into action and themselves came under enemy artillery fire. A number of enemy planes were shot down by our anti-aircraft defences.

557. On this day the Rear-Admiral Malaya, after consultation with me, gave orders for the destruction of the large oil stocks on Pulau Bukum. These comprised both naval fuel and lubricating oils and the Asiatic Petroleum Company's petrol reserves. I had previously opposed the destruction of these stocks on account of the adverse moral effect which I anticipated it would have on both the troops and the civil population. I now informed the Rear-Admiral Malaya that, though I would do my utmost to prevent the enemy seizing Pulau Bukum, I could no longer guarantee the security of the stocks there. The Rear-Admiral who was personally responsible for the destruction of the naval stocks, felt that he could not risk further delay. The demolition was carried out that afternoon. It was partially, though not entirely, successful.

558. The effect of the collapse of civil labour now began to make itself more and more felt. At the Docks all civil labour had disappeared and the Harbour Board Staff was no longer in control. In the Town area debris from the bombing and shelling remained untouched, the dead remained unburied and water ran to waste from the mains from lack of labour to clear the demolished buildings.

559. In the afternoon the Governor moved his headquarters from Government House to the Singapore Club in the centre of Singapore Town.

560. I regret to have to report that the flotilla of small ships and other light craft which, as stated above, left Singapore on the night I3th-I4th February encountered a Japanese naval force in the approaches to the Banka Straits. It was attacked by light naval craft and by aircraft. Many ships and other craft were sunk or disabled and there was considerable loss of life. Others were wounded or were forced ashore and were subsequently captured.

Included in this flotilla was a patrol boat on which were the Rear-Admiral Malaya and his party and the Air Officer Commanding Far East. This boat was driven ashore on a deserted island by a Japanese destroyer and its engines dismantled. After some weeks on the Island the Rear-Admiral and the Air Officer Commanding Far East both died.

I wish here to pay a special tribute to the loyalty of Air Vice-Marshal Pulford, the Air Officer Commanding Far East. Though at liberty to leave Singapore at any time on or after the 5th February he preferred, from a sense of duty and of personal friendship to myself, to remain there until the 13th February and would have remained longer had I wished him to do so. This gallant officer's self-sacrifice cost him his life.

SECTION LV. – EVENTS OF THE 14TH FEBRUARY, 1942.

561. During the day the Japanese renewed their attacks. Their main thrust was again made against the western front of the Southern Area. Here very heavy fighting at close quarters went on throughout the day in which the Loyal Regt. and the Malay Regt. especially distinguished themselves. By the end of the day our troops had been driven back by the weight of the attack to the line Alexandra – Gillman Barracks – Keppel Golf Course. Further north the enemy reached the Alexandra Hospital area but were prevented from making further progress by the 5 Bedfordshire and Hertfordshire Regt. and a composite Royal Engineer Unit. The 44 Brigade took up a position on the line of the Tanglin road in the Mount Echo area.

Japanese troops entered the Alexandra Military Hospital and attacked some of the staff and patients. Later many of the staff and patients were removed from the hospital by the Japanese and were massacred in cold blood.

562. On the A.I.F. front there was little activity, though some bodies of the enemy moving down the railway were engaged by artillery and small arms fire and dispersed.

563. On the front of the 18 British Division the I Cambridgeshire Regt. continued to hold its position west of Adam road where it had shown great determination in resisting enemy attacks during the last two days. To the right of this battalion the enemy developed a strong attack, supported by artillery and tanks, at about 1800 hrs. and succeeded in advancing nearly a mile until they were held up by defences on the line of the Mount Pleasant road. A deep dent in our line was thus created.

At the junction of Braddell and Thomson roads east of the MacRitchie Reservoir the enemy gained some ground but was driven back again by counter-attack. Further to the right, the left flank of the 53 Brigade was driven back south of Braddell road, but the right flank succeeded in maintaining its positions north of the road.

On the Serangoon road front the enemy attacked strongly from the direction of Paya Lebar Village but was stopped by units of the II Indian Division after advancing to within a few hundred yards of the vital Woodleigh Pumping Station.

564. On the eastern front of the Southern Area there were some local engagements between troops of the I Manchester Regt. and enemy detachments.

565. During the day there was fairly heavy shelling of selected areas by the enemy artillery which now had the advantage of observation from the Bukit Timah hills. Our own field artillery with due regard for ammunition economy, replied whenever suitable targets presented themselves.

566. Several enemy aircraft were again brought down by our anti-aircraft guns but casualties in the Town area were heavy.

567. Early in the morning of the 14th February a new and serious situation developed when the Municipal Water Engineer (Mr. Murnane) reported to the

Director General of Civil Defence that he considered a complete failure of the water supply was imminent. In consequence of this report I held a conference at the Municipal Offices at about 1000 hrs., at which the following were present:-

The Director General of Civil Defence
The Chairman of the Municipality (Mr. Rayman)
The Municipal Water Engineer.

The Municipal Water Engineer reported that, owing to breaks in the water mains and pipes as a result of bombing and shelling, a heavy loss of water was going on; that, though both pumping stations were still working, well over half the water was being lost; that all civil labour had disappeared and that it was difficult to get repairs done. He estimated that the water supply would last for 48 hours at the outside and that it might only last for 24 hours. Various methods of dealing with the situation were considered, but the only practical one seemed to be to effect repairs quicker than the mains and pipes could be broken. I therefore ordered additional Royal Engineer assistance, but this could not be provided till the afternoon owing to the fact that all available Royal Engineer personnel were at that time fighting as combatant troops. I arranged another meeting for the evening.

568. At about 1030 hours I met the Governor at the Singapore Club. The Colonial Secretary (Mr. Fraser) was also present. The Governor stressed the dangers which would result if Singapore with its large population was suddenly deprived of its water supply. I informed the Governor that I intended to go on fighting as long as we could, as I did not consider that the water situation, though undoubtedly serious, had yet rendered the further defence of Singapore impossible. I arranged to visit the Governor again in the evening after a further review of the situation. It was agreed that the Governor would report the situation fully to the Colonial Office and that I would report it to the Supreme Commander South-West Pacific. This I did adding that I was watching the situation and fighting on but that I might find it necessary to take an immediate decision.

569. The Supreme Commander South-West Pacific in his reply said:-

"In all places where sufficiency of water exists for troops they must go on fighting." and in a later telegram he said:- "Your gallant stand is serving purpose and must be continued to limit of endurance."

570. At about 1700 hours, after visiting formation headquarters of the 18 British and 11 Indian Divisions, I held another conference at the Municipal Offices. The same officials were present as at the morning conference. The Municipal Water Engineer reported that the position was very slightly better. I instructed the Director-General of Civil Defence to forward to my Headquarters by 0700 hours the following morning an accurate forecast of the water situationas it appeared at that time.

I subsequently reported the situation to the Governor at the Singapore Club.

571. It may not be out of place here to give some description of the conditions which existed in Singapore Town on the 14th February.

The Secretariat and other Government offices were operating on a skeleton basis only. The only newspaper being published was a Government controlled single sheet newspaper of which free issues were made. Practically all offices, business houses and shops were closed. The lower floor of many of the large buildings, including the Secretariat, the Municipal Offices, the Singapore Club and the Cathay building had been taken over as temporary military hospitals and were already full. The Asiatic population with few exceptions was apathetic. There were few people on the streets and public services were practically at a standstill. The Civil Hospitals were working to capacity. Those on the higher levels, including the General Hospital, were without water on the 14th February and special water-carrying parties had to be organized. This applied also to some ofthe military hospitals. The St. James Electric Power Plant, situated in the Keppel Harbour area, was still working but it was now directly threatened as the enemy were within one mile of it. The Peirce and MacRitchie water reservoirs were in enemy hands although water, whether by design or oversight, continued to flow to the pumping stations. The enemy were within a few hundred yards of the Woodleigh Pumping Station.

SECTION LVI. – EVENTS OF THE I5TH FEBRUARY, I942.

572. During the night I4th-I5th February enemy infantry infiltrated on all sectors of the I8 British Division front and also succeeded in getting a footing on the Mount Pleasant Ridge. The lack of an organized reserve made it difficult to deal with these pockets of penetration. Nevertheless, local counter-attacks were staged which regained some of the lost positions on the Mount Pleasant Ridge.

573. On the extreme left of our position the enemy renewed his attacks with vigour and some bitter fighting ensued on the front of the I Malaya Infantry Brigade. Heavy casualties were inflicted and suffered, the 2 Loyal Regt., which bore the brunt of the fighting, at this time totalling only about I30 fighting men. Eventually the line fell back to the east end of the Alexandra Depots area – Mount Washington – east end of the Keppel Golf Links.

574. The morning report on the water situation from the Director General of Civil Defence (see Section LV) showed a serious deterioration. The D.G.C.D. summed up the situation by saying that he anticipated that the water supply would not last more than another 24 hours. On receipt of this report I instructed him to:-

(*a*) Attend a Commanders' conference which was scheduled to take place at 0930 hrs. that morning.

(*b*) In the meantime, confirm the situation with the officials of the Municipality.

575. At 0930 hrs. the Senior Commanders' Conference met at Fort Canning. The following were present:-

The Commanders Northern and Southern Areas, A.I.F. and Anti-Aircraft Defences.

The Brigadier Royal Artillery.
The Brigadier General Staff, the Brigadier i/c Administration and the Deputy
Adjutant General Headquarters Malaya Command.
The Director General of Civil Defence.
The Inspector General of Police Straits Settlements.
A Staff Officer Northern Area.

The formation Commanders reported verbally on the tactical situation in their
respective areas.

I then gave a summary of the administrative situation in accordance with reports
received that morning. The Director-General of Civil Defence, in reply to enquiry,
repeated that the water position was critical, that the rate of breakage of mains and
pipes exceeded repair, and that the meagre water supply still available could not now
be guaranteed for more than about 24 hours; further, that if total failure took place it
would at the best take several days to obtain pipewater again.

The general situation as regards food was that the military food reserves under our
control had now been reduced to a few days, though there were large reserves in the
Bukit Timah area then under Japanese control. There were also civil supplies.

There were adequate reserves of small arms ammunition, but 25-pounder field
gun ammunition was very short and the reserves of Light Anti-Aircraft (Bofors)
ammunition were almost exhausted. The Alexandra magazine was practically in the
front line and fires had prevented any ammunition being withdrawn from there the
previous day.

As regards petrol, the only petrol which now remained, apart from one small dump,
was what was in vehicle tanks.

576. A discussion on the general situation followed. The danger of the water
situation, particularly as it affected the Indian troops and the vast civil population,
was stressed. There was also the danger of a break-through into the crowded Town
area if the Japanese delivered another determined attack. It was clearly no good
remaining on the defensive as we were. As I viewed the situation, the alternatives
were either (a) to counter-attack immediately to regain control of the reservoirs and
of the military food depots and to drive back the enemy's artillery with a view to
reducing the damage to the water supply system, or (b) to capitulate immediately.
Formation Commanders were unanimously of the opinion that in the existing
circumstances a counter-attack was impracticable.

I could see no immediate solution for the critical water situation and decided to
capitulate. The other members of the conference concurred unanimously with this
decision.

577. A discussion on the method of implementing the decision followed. It was
decided that a joint military and civil deputation should proceed into the Japanese
lines as soon as possible and that it should consist of the Deputy Adjutant General,
the Colonial Secretary and an Interpreter. The deputation was instructed (a) to propose
to the Japanese a cessation of hostilities as from 1600 hrs. 15th February, (b) to invite
a Japanese deputation to visit Singapore to discuss terms. This procedure was in

accordance with an arrangement previously made with the Governor in anticipation of an emergency arising.

578. Orders were issued for the destruction before 1600 hrs. of all secret and technical equipment, ciphers, codes, secret documents and guns. It was deemed inadvisable at this stage to destroy personal weapons in case the Japanese should not agree to a cessation of hostilities or should attack before an agreement had been reached.

579. At about 1145 hrs. I reported to the Governor at the Singapore Club.

580. The following is an extract from a telegram received from the Supreme Commander South-West Pacific on the morning of the 15th February:-

> "So long as you are in a position to inflict losses and damage to enemy and your troops are physically capable of doing so you must fight on. Time gained and damage to enemy are of vital importance at this juncture. When you are fully satisfied that this is no longer possible I give you discretion to cease resistance. . . . Inform me of intentions. Whatever happens I thank you and all your troops for your gallant efforts of last few days."

In reply to the above I notified him of the decision to cease hostilities.

581. In the afternoon the deputation returned with instructions that I was to proceed personally with my staff to a given rendezvous. The meeting with the Japanese Commander (Lt. Gen. Yamashita) took place in the Ford Factory north of Bukit Timah Village. There is not, and never has been, any copy of the terms of surrender in my possession. As far as my recollection goes, only one copy was produced by the Japanese and this was retained by them. Certainly no copy was handed to me. The actual terms of surrender cannot therefore be recorded accurately. The main conditions were, as far as my memory goes, as under:-

(*a*) There must be an unconditional surrender of all Military Forces (Army, Navy and Air Force) in the Singapore area.

(*b*) Hostilities to cease at 2030 hrs. British time, i.e. 2200 hrs. Japanese time.

(*c*) All troops to remain in positions occupied at the time of cessation of hostilities pending further orders.

(*d*) All weapons, military equipment, ships, aeroplanes and secret documents to be handed over to the Japanese Army intact.

(*e*) In order to prevent looting and other disorders in Singapore Town during the temporary withdrawal of all armed forces, a force of 100 British armed men to be left temporarily in the Town area until relieved by the Japanese.

As regards paragraph (*d*) above I informed the Japanese Commander that there were no ships or aeroplanes in the Singapore area, and that the heavier types of weapons and some of the military equipment and all secret documents had already been destroyed under my orders. This he accepted.

582. Orders for the cessation of hostilities were issued to all formation

Commanders soon after 1900 hrs. Hostilities finally ceased at 2030 hrs., 15th February, British time.

583. The general line of our foremost positions at the cessation of hostilities was from right to left as under:-

All inclusive the Kallang Aerodrome (Civil Airport) – The Tarlat Air Strip – The Junction of the Serangoon and Braddell roads – The Junction of Braddell and Thomson roads – The Broadcasting Station – Bukit Brown – Adam road—Raffles College area – Tyersall area – Tanglin area – Mount Echo – The Biscuit Factory – The Alexandra Ammunition Magazine – Mount Washington – The eastern end of the Keppel Golf Links.

We also held Blakang Mati, Pulau Brani, Tekong and the Pengerang area.

584. Japanese troops entered Singapore Town on the morning of the 16th February. There was a military demonstration in which 175 Medium and Light Tanks took part. The majority of the Japanese troops, however, were retained outside the Town area.

585. After the cessation of hostilities it was 5½ days, with engineers and water parties working at full pressure, before water again reached the lower areas of Singapore Town, which had been deprived of it, and the first floor of buildings in the lowest areas. It was 10 days before water again reached the General Hospital and many other buildings on the higher levels.

SECTION LVII. – IMPLEMENTATION OF THE SCORCHED EARTH POLICY ON SINGAPORE ISLAND.

586. The plans for the implementation of the Scorched Earth Policy on Singapore Island have already been explained in Section XLII and Appendix J. It was an operation of war, the planning and execution of which took up much time and required constant attention. To fight and destroy simultaneously is in my opinion one of the most difficult things which commanders and troops can be called upon to do. Hoping, as we did, that we should be able to stop the enemy and make use of our material resources we naturally delayed the demolition work for as long as possible. In this respect the problem differed widely from that in a premeditated withdrawal carried out on a time programme. As stated in Appendix J I reserved to myself the responsibility of ordering the various schemes to be put into effect whenever time permitted. In most cases, though not all, it was possible to do this and it was in fact done. As in the case of the mainland, it would be idle for me to attempt to assess the success of the Scorched Earth Policy on Singapore Island other than in general terms. In some cases the Policy could not for various reasons be implemented. It is natural also that, in the turmoil of operations, demolitions, most of which must necessarily be put into effect at the last minute, should not in all cases be as effective as would otherwise be the case. Nevertheless, a general picture of the implementation of the Scorched Earth Policy may be given.

587. *Army. – Fixed Defences. –* It is believed that all the guns and other vital

equipment of the Fixed Defences were damaged in such a way that it would be impossible for the Japanese to make further use of them.

Anti-Aircraft Defences. – With only a few exceptions the guns and the searchlights were effectively destroyed. Subsequent attempts by the Japanese to obtain assistance for the repair of guns were refused.

Field Armament. – The great majority, though not all, of the field and anti-tank guns were rendered unserviceable. In the case of the small arms, however, it was inadvisable to destroy these before the capitulation had been accepted by the enemy while later it was against the terms agreed upon. In consequence, it is probable that only a proportion of the small arms were rendered unserviceable.

Secret and Technical Equipment, Secret Documents etc. – These were, as far as is known, successfully destroyed.

Ammunition. – There is no doubt that considerable stocks of ammunition fell into the hands of the enemy. The large Alexandra Magazine was left intact for reasons which have already been explained, i.e. that it could not with safety be destroyed owing to its proximity to the Military Hospital. The demolition of the Changi Magazine was partially successful, a second effort being made by the Royal Engineers the day after the evacuation of the area. Other stocks were left intact in dumps which were overrun in the course of the fighting, especially at Kranji, Nee Soon and on the Bukit Timah Rifle Range.

Petrol. – The only petrol which fell into the enemy's hands on Singapore Island was the contents of a few small dumps and what was left in vehicle tanks.

588. *Royal Navy.* – The machinery of the Graving Dock at the Naval Base was destroyed.

The Floating Dock was sunk.

I am not in a position to report on the other installations for which the Royal Navy was responsible except as regards the Normanton Group of Oil Tanks: Owing to the proximity of these tanks to the Alexandra Military Hospital the Rear-Admiral Malaya, after consultation with me, issued orders that only the eight most westerly tanks of the group should be destroyed.

589. *Royal Air Force.* – Owing to the withdrawal of Royal Air Force personnel from Singapore Island the responsibility for destroying many of their scattered dumps devolved upon the Army. Though some small dumps were overrun in the course of the operations and fell into enemy hands, it is believed that the bulk of the aviation petrol was successfully destroyed or otherwise disposed of.

The Main Reserve Dump of aircraft bombs was also destroyed.

590. *Civil.* – The application of the Scorched Earth Policy to property owned by the civil government, by public bodies, and by firms and private individuals was carefully organized by the Director General of Civil Defence who was assisted by selected officers of the Public Works Department. The work on denial of machinery, plant and liquor continued throughout the 24 hours for the last week. The machinery and plant belonging to firms with British managers were, with a few exceptions, effectively destroyed in spite of the reluctance on the part of some firms to acquiesce in the proceedings. Those belonging to Asiatic firms were, however, not destroyed.

All the reserve stocks of spirits and liqueurs were destroyed. All railway engines were rendered unserviceable by the removal of vital parts. The plant and machinery in the modern well-equipped workshops of the Singapore Harbour Board were destroyed.

591. As on the mainland, morale was affected very adversely by the implementation of the Scorched Earth Policy. Fighting and destruction do not go hand-in-hand together. In particular, the effect of burning oil should be recorded. The smoke rises in great black clouds and numberless particles are deposited far and wide over the countryside. These blacken everything with which they come in contact including human beings, who are also blackened from contact with the oil-soaked foliage. A soldier's self-respect and in some cases his morale are adversely affected.

592. To sum up, the Japanese undoubtedly obtained on Singapore Island some war material which was of value to them in their war effort. In view of the large quantities of weapons, military equipment and war stores of all natures concentrated there this was inevitable. Nevertheless, taking into account the difficulties which had to be faced and the strain, both mental and physical, under which all concerned were working, the implementation of the Scorched Earth Policy was, in my opinion, as effective as could reasonably have been expected.

593. In conclusion, it may not be out of place to stress once again the difference between the application of a Scorched Earth Policy in defence of a nation's homeland and its application in a distant land inhabited by Asiatic peoples where the property to be destroyed has been built up laboriously over the years by Government or by private enterprise and where in many cases those responsible for the implementation of the Policy have themselves in the past been the leaders of progress in their respective spheres. In this latter case some account must be taken of human nature.

PART IV.

SUMMARY AND CONCLUSIONS.

SECTION LVIII. – THE DEFENCE PLAN.

594. The object of the defence, in accordance with instructions received, was the protection of the Singapore Naval Base.

595. The tense political atmosphere which prevailed in Europe following the advent of the Hitler regime and the rapidly increasing range and power of air forces were two factors which had profound influences on the problem of defence.

So long as it was certain that a strong and balanced British fleet could, when required, be despatched to the Far East and that it would be able on arrival there to control the sea communications leading to Malaya, the task of the local defence was to ensure the security of the Naval Base for a limited period only. Conversely a Japanese attacking force, if it was to be successful, would have had to capture the base within that limited period. The nearest Japanese base was then I,800 miles from Singapore and the Japanese would not have had time to establish an advanced base from which they could develop deliberate operations.

They would therefore have had to rely on some form of "coup-de-main" attack with forces of limited size.

The effect, however, of the uncertainty as to whether a strong British fleet would in fact be able to sail for the Far East was that the Japanese could, without incurring undue risk, undertake a more deliberate form of operation with very much stronger forces. In other words, they could establish bases in North Malaya and in South Thailand from which they could develop operations by land, sea and air. The Naval Base at Singapore, which is only 400 miles from the Malaya – Thailand frontier, would thus become exposed to a heavy scale of air attack. To avoid this, and also to enable our own air forces to reach out and strike at the approaching enemy convoys as far from the shores of Malaya as possible, it became necessary to hold the whole of Malaya and not only Singapore and the adjoining islands with part of Johore.

596. This change in the problem of defence was fully appreciated by the General Officer Commanding Malaya in I937 and was set forth in a document which, as General Staff Officer Ist Grade Malaya, I personally prepared in accordance with his instructions. This document was sent to the War Office. It asked, among other things, for substantial increases in the air forces and in the local naval craft and for more infantry. It seems, however, that the change in the situation was not as fully

appreciated at Home as it was in Malaya, or it may have been that lack of resources of man-power, material and money, made it impossible to comply with the recommendations made. In any case, it was not until 1940 that official approval was given to the policy of holding the whole of Malaya.

597. The fall of France in 1940 and the subsequent occupation of French Indo-China by the Japanese again altered radically our problem of defence. Our potential enemy was now within easy striking range (400 miles) of North Malaya and within what was at that time comparatively long-distance air striking range (700 miles) of Singapore itself. Moreover, he now had an advanced base at which he could assemble a strong invasion force without interference. Thereafter such reinforcements as could be made available were sent to Malaya but, in view of our commitments elsewhere, these were not as large as were required.

598. In the autumn of 1940, when it had become apparent that we were not in a position to send a fleet to the Far East, the Home authorities laid down that the defence of Malaya must depend primarily on air power but that, until adequate air forces could be provided, the land forces must be strengthened. The policy of relying primarily on air power was in fact never implemented.

599. In consequence of the above policy the Army dispositions were designed primarily to afford protection to the bases from which the air forces when available would operate. In the event, the Army had to bear practically the whole weight of the Japanese attack with little air or naval support. This was the main cause of defeat.

SECTION LIX – COMPARISON OF FORCES.

600. *Navy.* – The Japanese were able to operate with a balanced Fleet based on Camranh Bay in French Indo-China. In the battleship "Prince of Wales" we had a more powerful unit than anything the Japanese possessed but we never had a balanced Fleet. The loss of the "Prince of Wales" and "Repulse" left the Japanese in undisputed possession of the eastern approaches to Malaya.

Malaya had a coast line of 1,000 miles with innumerable creeks. To conduct the attack or defence of such a country actively it is essential to be able to undertake water-borne operations on an appreciable scale. In this form of warfare also the Japanese established a superiority, partly by the introduction of a large number of their special military landing craft, partly by the clever use of local craft, and partly by the degree of air protection which they were able to give to their coast-wise shipping. On our side we had three destroyers, three river gun-goats, a few Fairmile motor launches and some converted motor craft, but the latter were slow, unarmoured, lightly armed and very vulnerable to air attack. Our local craft had little air cover.

601. *Army.* – The initial Japanese landings in South Thailand and Malaya were made by the equivalent of two divisions and one tank regiment. A few days later a division of the Japanese Imperial Guards arrived in South Thailand by train from the north. There are indications that a fourth division may have arrived later in December, while a second tank regiment arrived either in December or January. In the middle

of January two fresh divisions landed at Singora in South Thailand. It appears that it was originally intended to employ these divisions for an attack on the east coast of Johore, but as a result of a change of plan they were moved forward by motor transport to the Kluang area in Central Johore. They were in reserve for the attack on Singapore Island.

It appears, therefore, that the Japanese employed five and perhaps six divisions and two tank regiments for the attack on Malaya. As they kept the same divisions in front line for prolonged periods, during which they were known to have suffered heavy casualties, it is probable also that they filled up these divisions with reinforcements. In addition to the above, they had Army, Base and Lines of Communication units. The establishment of these would no doubt be smaller than in the British Army.

On the basis of 20,000 men per division and 150 tanks per regiment, I estimate that the Japanese employed a minimum of 150,000 men and 300 tanks in the Malayan campaign.

602. Against this we had on the outbreak of hostilities the equivalent of 3½ divisions with Fixed and Anti-Aircraft Defences but no tanks. Later we received as reinforcements about the equivalent of another two divisions and one squadron of obsolescent light tanks. The total number of officers and men who took part in the campaign on the British side was a little over 125,000, though the strength in Malaya at any one time was considerably less than this. This number included a high proportion of Command, Base and Lines of Communication troops, many of whom belonged to non-combatant units or were unarmed owing to shortage of personal weapons.

603. The initial attack on Singapore Island was carried out by three Japanese divisions. There were two and possibly three divisions in reserve. Two of the reserve divisions had recently arrived in Malaya and it may be assumed that they were at full strength. Some of the others may have been at less than full strength. On this basis I estimate that there were at the cessation of hostilities a minimum of 100,000 Japanese troops on Singapore Island or in South Malaya. How many of these had actually crossed to the Island and how many were on the mainland is not known nor is it very material, but there is evidence to show that at least 23,000 crossed on the first day of the attack. There were also a minimum of 175 Japanese medium and light tanks on Singapore Island at the cessation of hostilities.

The total of the British forces in the Singapore Fortress area at the same time was in the neighbourhood of 85,000. This figure included a large number of non-combatant troops, i.e., Medical Services, Pioneer and Labour units, etc., of troops for whom no arms were available owing to a general shortage of personal weapons, and of sick and wounded. Probably about 70,000 of these men were armed and equipped but many of them belonged to Base and other administrative units and were very inadequately trained. There was one squadron of obsolescent light tanks.

The Japanese had an advantage in the fact that a high proportion of their forces in South Malaya and on Singapore Island were fully trained combatant troops, most of their Base and Lines of Communication troops being further north.

604. In official statements made in this country and recently published in the world Press, figures very different from the above have been given. In fairness to the officers and men who fought in Malaya I ask that those statements may now be corrected.

605 *Air.* – There is evidence to show that on the IIth December, I94I, i.e., three days after the outbreak of hostilities, the Japanese had I24 aircraft in Thailand and 280 in Indo-China. It may be assumed that in round numbers about 300 of these were being employed against Malaya. They included twin-engined bombers, dive-bombers, torpedo-bombers and fighters. The range of the fighters had been greatly increased by the use of auxiliary petrol tanks.

Opposed to this our Air Force had on the outbreak of war a total of I4I operationally serviceable I.E. aircraft, with a few light aircraft (Moths, etc.) manned by the Volunteer Air Force. Few of these aircraft were of modern types and a number were obsolescent. There were no long-range bombers or long-range fighters, no dive-bombers, no transport or military communication aircraft and no special army co-operation aircraft. The striking force was weak, the fighters were not of the most modern type, the reconnaissance forces were inadequate and the torpedo-bombers were slow and out-of-date.

During the operations we received reinforcements of 3I aircraft from the Netherlands East Indies, some bomber and reconnaissance aircraft from the U.K. and the Middle East, and the equivalent of three squadrons of Hurricane fighters.

These, however, were never more than sufficient to replace casualties and the strength of our Air Force dwindled progressively throughout the campaign.

What reinforcements the Japanese received is not known but shortly after the cessation of hostilities they were reported to have had 258 aircraft in South Thailand and Malaya and 270 in Indo-China. At the cessation of hostilities there were no British aircraft in Malaya.

SECTION LX. – JAPANESE STRATEGY.

606. The Japanese attack on Malaya was very carefully planned and there is now no doubt that preparations had been going on for a very long time before hostilities actually started. The Japanese themselves admitted that the terrain of Malaya, our battle methods and our equipment were all carefully studied for years before the outbreak of war. The Commander-in-Chief of the 25th Japanese Army detailed for the Malayan campaign had spent six months in Germany before taking over command. He was given the best possible senior staff officers. The Japanese Divisions employed in Malaya are known to have been among the best in the Japanese Army. In particular the Guards Division and the 5 Division, both of which had been very highly trained for the type of warfare to be undertaken in Malaya, had been specially sent from Japan. To give them further experience they took part in April, I94I, in a landing operation on the coast of China followed by a quick thrust inland. They then went to Hainan where they did further training in landing operations

and jungle warfare. The Island of Hainan was for a long time used as a springboard for the southward advance.

607. The Japanese strategy consisted in a continuous land and air offensive pressed with the utmost vigour with the object of advancing into South Malaya and capturing Singapore before our reinforcements could arrive. This offensive was supported by their Navy on the east coast of Malaya. Their Navy also co-operated with coast-wise operations on the west coast as soon as landing craft could be made available. These special craft were originally landed at Singora and transported across the peninsula by road to the west coast in the State of Kedah where they were launched on the 22nd December. These sea-borne operations had good and continued air cover. Had there been available at Singapore some flotillas of fast armoured and properly equipped coastal craft it is certain that the enemy would not have been able to exercise the constant threat to our communications with sea-borne forces which they did in fact succeed in doing.

In carrying out this strategy the Japanese undoubtedly took risks as regards the security of their Lines of Communication and the maintenance of their supplies. They relied to a great extent on the resources of the country.

608. The immediate object of the Japanese at the outset of the operations appears to have been (*a*) to cripple our Air Force and (*b*) to cut off and destroy the whole of our forces in Kedah by a rapid thrust from Patani via Kroh to cut the west coast communications west of the River Perak. In this way they hoped to reach the line of the River Perak in two days.

The campaign opened with intensive air operations in which the Japanese Air Force based on Indo-China made full use of the aerodromes which it had occupied in South Thailand. In the course of the first three days the Japanese succeeded in inflicting serious losses on our Air Force and driving it back off the northern aerodromes. The Japanese, however, did not succeed in cutting off and destroying our forces in Kedah, though we suffered very severe losses both in men and material. For a time the situation was very critical and it was only by a great effort that the Japanese plan was frustrated. It actually took them sixteen days instead of two to reach the line of the River Perak.

The Japanese attack on the State of Kelantan appears to have had the double object of capturing the three aerodromes located there and of providing a base from which land operations against Kuantan could be developed.

609. After crossing the River Perak the Japanese continued their drive down the west coast arteries of communications and supported it by sea-borne operations on the west coast and by a land advance against Kuantan on the east coast. All these operations were closely supported by the Japanese Air Force which attacked our aerodromes in Central Malaya, our troops in the forward areas and columns on the move, as well as providing cover for their sea-borne operations and carrying out strategical and tactical reconnaissances.

During January the Japanese Air Force attacked objectives in the Singapore area, first by night and later, when they were able to support their bombers with fighters based on the Central Malaya aerodromes, by day. The aerodromes continued to be the main target but the Naval Base and, in the later stages, the Singapore Docks were also heavily attacked. There was bombing also, possibly not intentional, of areas in Singapore Town.

Towards the end of January a Japanese force landed at Endau on the east coast of Johore.

6I0. On reaching the Straits of Johore the Japanese, pursuing their previous strategy, attacked Singapore Island with the least possible delay with the results already recorded in Part III of this Despatch. That they were able to assemble their forces, bring forward a large number of special landing craft and launch the attack in little more than a week was without doubt a remarkable performance. The landing craft were transported by road from Pontian Kechil on the west coast of Johore to the rivers which flow into the western branch of the Straits of Johore.

6II. The Japanese, in commenting on the Malayan campaign, have attributed their success to their pre-war preparations, to the fact that this campaign was the centre of interest throughout their whole Army, to the fact that their commanders, senior staff officers and troops were specially selected, and to the fact that their land operations were closely supported by their Navy and by their Army and Navy Air Forces.

Other important factors in their success were undoubtedly:-

(*a*) The great superiority, both as regards the quantity and quality of their machines, of the Japanese Air Force;

(*b*) The freedom of manoeuvre conferred on the Japanese Army, and conversely the crippling effect of the ever present threat to our own communications and bases, resulting from the Japanese strategical naval supremacy off the east coast of Malaya and, to a lesser degree, from their tactical supremacy off the west coast also;

(*c*) The inclusion in the Japanese Army of a strong modern Armoured Component, while we on our side had to rely on armoured cars and Bren gun carriers.

SECTION LXI. – BRITISH STRATEGY.

6I2. The evolution of British pre-war strategy in Malaya has been summarized in Section LVIII and it has been shown that the Army dispositions were dictated primarily by requirements of protection of the Naval Base and of the bases from which large Air Forces, when available, would operate. Looked at from the Army point of view alone these dispositions were faulty because the comparatively small force available had to be widely dispersed. How widely dispersed it can best be understood by comparing Singapore to the Isle of Wight, an island strongly defended against sea-borne and air attacks, and applying the problem of defending Singapore and the mainland of Malaya with the equivalent of 3½ divisions but without an Armoured Component to that of defending England and Wales, a territory only very slightly larger in area, with a similar force against an attack from the east or from the north launched by an enemy with superior naval and air forces.

6I3. The project to move into South Thailand, risky though it was with the small forces available, was nevertheless attractive from the point of view of denying to the enemy the use of the two valuable aerodromes in that area. But it suffered from the danger always inherent in such projects, namely the difficulty of deciding when the time has come to enter neutral territory. It was due to this difficulty, combined with our inability to maintain contact with the Japanese convoys carrying their invasion forces during a vital period, that the project to move forward into South Thailand was not implemented. Had it been implemented, it would undoubtedly have eased the air situation but it might, if we had failed to hold the enemy on the Kroh – Patani road, have led to irreparable and early disaster.

6I4. When, after three days of hostilities, the enemy had succeeded in landing a strong force in South Thailand and North Malaya, intact, except for losses suffered in the attack on Kelantan, had by sinking the "Prince of Wales" and "Repulse" gained full control of the sea communications east of Malaya, and had also established air superiority over North Malaya, our initial dispositions became a source of great danger. It became clear that we had little hope of being able to achieve our object with the small force at that time available and that our best chance of achieving it was by ensuring, as far as lay in our power, the safe arrival of our land and air reinforcements. In order to do this it was necessary to impose the maximum delay on the enemy and to keep his air bases at the greatest possible distance from the vital Singapore area. The strategy adopted, therefore, aimed at a gradual fighting withdrawal with a view to an eventual concentration in South Malaya where it was hoped the main battle would be fought. Our aircraft were concentrated on the aerodromes in Central and South Malaya where they would be safer from enemy attack. Later the fighters were allotted as their primary tasks the defence of the Singapore area and, in co-operation with the other Services, the protection of the reinforcing convoys.

6I5. That our strategy was not successful was due primarily to a lack of strength in all three Services but particularly in the Navy and Air Force. With the enemy in control of sea communications east of Malaya, we were prevented from sending more than very limited reinforcements to the northern and central areas of Malaya, and his sea-borne thrusts continually forced us to make detachments to meet them. This, combined, with the lack of reserves, left our forces on the vital central front too weak, with the result that there was little relief for the front line troops who suffered from extreme exhaustion. This had a big influence on the course of the operations.

6I6. Penang was evacuated in accordance with a decision made by the Far East War Council. Although it had been decided in I936 to fortify Penang it was in I94I far from being a fortress. There was one 6 inch Coast Defence battery with searchlights, some beach defences and a very inadequate garrison. There was no anti-aircraft gun defence and practically no fighter defence. The situation on the mainland was critical. The Council was faced with the alternative of trying to restore the situation on the mainland and at the same time to hold Penang or of concentrating all available forces on the former. It chose the latter course which was, temporarily at any rate, successful.

6I7. Up to the 25th January, when we still had possession of the important chain of aerodromes and landing grounds and the lateral road in Central Johore, there was still a hope, though by then only a slender one, that our strategy might be successful. The loss of the Batu Pahat force, however, forced upon us the necessity of withdrawing into the Singapore Fortress area and of concentrating upon its defence. We had then failed in our object of protecting the Naval Base. Our task thereafter was to hold the Singapore Fortress area.

6I8. The policy for the defence of the Singapore Fortress area was to endeavour to prevent the enemy landing or, if he succeeded in landing, to stop him near the beaches and destroy or drive him out by counter-attack. As a result of the large area to be defended (Singapore Island alone, with Blakang Mati and Pulau Brani, has a perimeter of 72 miles), this necessitated weak forward defences and an inadequate reserve, but we were forced to adopt this policy by the nature of the country, by the lack of depth in the defence, and by the location of the Naval Base and of dumps, depots and other installations. The Japanese on the other hand were able to concentrate their forces for the attack on a selected portion of our defences. By doing so, they effected a landing and made a deep penetration in spite of severe losses. In the later stages exhaustion of the troops, accentuated by the moral effect of the loss of the Naval Base and the enemy's undisputed air supremacy following the withdrawal of our Air Force to the Netherlands East Indies, again influenced the operations. Ultimatelythe decisive factor was the imminent danger of a complete breakdown of the water supply as a result of the damage done to the distribution system by bombing and shelling.

SECTION LXII. – TACTICS.

6I9. The campaign in Malaya probably provided the first instance of operations between forces armed and equipped on modern lines being conducted in a country almost wholly covered with jungle or plantations of various types. There was therefore little previous experience on which to draw as a guide for the conduct of this peculiar type of warfare. It is well-known that such country favours the attacker. It makes the defence of a position a difficult and hazardous operation unless the flanks of that position rest securely on natural obstacles. In Malaya there were in fact no positions, sufficiently narrow to be held by the forces at our disposal, which fulfilled this condition. The positions which approached most nearly to it were those in North Perak and in North Johore, but even these were far too extended. In order to impose the required delay on the enemy, therefore, it was necessary to adopt a more mobile form of defence.

620. The Japanese, in accordance with their strategy of a vigorous offensive, invariably attacked with the least possible delay. They seldom made frontal attacks. Their usual tactics were to probe the front and search for the flanks. Having found

the flanks they would then push mobile forces round to attack our communications which usually followed a single road. They also employed widely infiltration tactics by individuals and small parties of men as a means of creating alarm, the use of trees as fire positions, and the use of noise, i.e., fireworks and crackers resembling machine-guns in action, as a weapon of war. For the mobility of their forward troops they relied chiefly on bicycles commandeered in the country. Supporting fire, until they reached Singapore Island for the attack on which a large amount of field artillery was employed, was provided chiefly by the infantry gun and by mortars. Tanks, although able to traverse rubber plantations in which the trees are normally planted in straight rows, were used for the most part for "blitz" tactics on the roads. In order to keep up a relentless pressure the Japanese staged attacks both by day and by night. It is believed that, in order to maintain the momentum of the attack, they relieved their forward troops regularly at short intervals.

The Japanese displayed an ability to cross natural obstacles, i.e., rivers, swamps, thick jungle, etc., much more rapidly than had been thought possible. Their engineers also showed themselves adept at the quick repair of bridges of which some 300 were destroyed to a greater or less degree, though it should be stated that in most cases there was plenty of material available close to the bridge site. The ability of the Japanese to live on the country for long periods was a great asset to them.

The close co-operation between the Japanese infantry and the supporting arms and the co-operation between the ground troops and the air forces, chiefly by W/T, were of a high order.

621. After our initial reverse at Jitra we adopted a policy of defence in depth astride the main channels of communication combined with local offensives as opportunity offered. We also employed ambush tactics and took steps to harass the enemy's communications. In these offensive operations we had on several occasions, as has been recorded in Part II, a considerable measure of success. That they were not more successful was due to the inability of some of our unseasoned troops to employ successfully tactics which demand the highest degree of skill and training. This inability became more pronounced as exhaustion, accentuated by our lack of reserves, overcame the front line troops.

The most successful ambushes were those where it was possible to combine the action of artillery, engineers and infantry.

The employment by the enemy of tanks as the spearhead of his attack made it essential that any position occupied should be covered by a natural or artificial anti-tank obstacle. The existence of an anti-tank obstacle thus became a primary consideration in the selection of our temporary defensive positions and frequently a great deal of ground which might otherwise have been suitable for delaying action had to be given up to the enemy.

Efforts on the part of forward bodies and detachments whose communications had been cut to fight their way out and efforts to re-open communications to them from behind were seldom successful. This was due chiefly to the lack of strong and fresh reserves with which to make the attacks and also to the lack of tanks to support them.

622. The Japanese troops, especially their reconnaissance parties, were frequently

disguised as local inhabitants. In this they had an advantage over our troops, the majority of whom could not well be mistaken for natives of the country.

There is no evidence to show that there was any extensive fifth column organization in Malaya, but there is no doubt whatever that the Japanese obtained considerable assistance at times from the local inhabitants. On many occasions arrows indicating the position of headquarters or other important air targets were found on the ground. Information as to the dispositions and movements of our troops was undoubtedly passed to the Japanese and guides were provided, possibly sometimes under compulsion. The Japanese also impressed what labour they required and did not hesitate to use ruthless methods to attain their ends.

623. The enervating climate of Malaya, which is unfavourable for long and sustained effort, had a considerable effect on the powers of endurance of our troops, many of whom had not been in the country long enough to become acclimatized before going into action. It is probable that the climate had less, though undoubtedly it had some, effect on the seasoned and more highly trained Japanese troops.

624. Specially selected officers were despatched from Malaya before the close of operations to spread the tactical lessons of the campaign to other theatres of war in the East. Since that time many other lessons have been learned in those theatres. It would be unprofitable, therefore, to discuss the tactical lessons of Malaya at any lengthen in this Despatch, more particularly as the conditions were in many respects abnormal. Nothing, however, occurred to disprove the old axiom that thick country favours the attacker and that therefore the offensive should be seized at the earliest possible moment, but for this fresh and well-trained troops are necessary.

SECTION LXIII. – ORGANIZATION.

625. In view of the more recent experience gained in similar theatres of war it would be superfluous to report in any detail on the short-comings of our organization, which was based on normal British and Indian war establishments, for operations in Malaya. It will be sufficient to comment only on those items which had the greatest influence on the operations.

626. *Armoured Forces.* – The lack of an armoured component was due, not to any weakness in our Army organization, but to inability, owing presumably to lack of resources and commitments elsewhere, to send an armoured component to Malaya when it was asked for.

Whatever the cause, however, the absence of an armoured component had a profound influence on the course of the operations, for while the Japanese had at their disposal medium and light tanks in considerable numbers we had until the last few days only armoured cars and Bren gun carriers. The few light tanks which arrived from India towards the end of January were so obsolescent as to be of little value. Efforts were made to offset our deficiency in tanks by anti-tank weapons and other anti-tank devices. Useful as these proved, yet it remained clear that the tank itself is the only satisfactory counter to the tank.

It is true that armoured forces, which depend for their success primarily on speed, manoeuvrability and invulnerability are not so effective in]ungle and wooded country, where their speed and manoeuvrability are limited, as they are in more open country. Nevertheless it is clear from the Malayan campaign that the influence of armoured forces even in that type of country is very great and that no force is complete without an armoured component.

627. *Bren Gun Carriers.* – Full value was not obtained from the Bren gun carrier whose cross-country performance was much restricted and which was too vulnerable to close range fire from troops in ambush. The numbers of these could be reduced.

628. *Artillery.* – Although our field artillery was at times most effective, it was seldom, owing to difficulties of observation and lack of suitable gun position sites, that full value could be obtained from its fire power. On the other hand artillery equipment tends to block roads which are invariably scarce in jungle types of country. Some reduction in the normal allotment of field artillery could therefore be accepted.

629. *Mortars.* – The Japanese used the mortar with great effect as their chief supporting weapon. Their mortar equipment included telephones and cable for observation purposes. I strongly advocate these methods and recommend that the establishment of mortars for operations in Malayan type of country should be increased.

630. *Engineers.* – The engineers were very fully employed as they are always likely to be in similar conditions. No reduction in that arm is recommended.

631. *Signals.* – The fact that communications in the Malayan campaign were at times uncertain can be ascribed to the long distances over which they had to be maintained, to the limitations of the civil telephone system in a country which had been comparatively recently developed, to a shortage of reserve equipment and to the limitations imposed on wireless in the difficult conditions of Malaya. It is important that adequate reserves of equipment should be maintained in countries which are situated at a distance from the main sources of supply.

632. *Transport.* – As soon as operations started it became apparent that there was a superfluity of transport in the forward areas. Besides being very vulnerable to the encircling tactics adopted by the enemy, it tended to block the roads when mobile operations were in progress. In fact, our organization based on trucks was less suited to the Malayan terrain than was the lighter transport of the Japanese. Steps were taken early to reduce this transport but, for operations in that type of country, establishments should be carefully overhauled to ensure that there is no more transport than is absolutely necessary in the forward areas.

SECTION LXIV. – ADMINISTRATION.

633. There is no doubt that the proportion of administrative personnel to the fighting troops was much greater on the British side than it was on the Japanese. This was due principally to the fact that the Japanese, an Asiatic race, were better able to live on the country and required less in the way of maintenance services. Another reason

was the fact that two of our divisions, the 9 Indian and the 8 Australian, were each short of a brigade group of fighting troops while, in the case of the A.I.F., at least, the administrative services were complete for a full division. A third reason was the fact that there was a certain overlapping of Base Services between the Malaya Command and the A.I.F., due to the latter being organised as a self-contained force. It is for consideration whether, in similar circumstances in the future, some economies in manpower could not be effected by the fusion of some of these Services.

634. In general, the administrative organization described in Part I of this Despatch, which was designed with a view to an advance into Thailand but also to meet the contingency of an enemy attack on any part of the coast of Malaya, worked satisfactorily. Bearing in mind that rapid withdrawals were many times forced upon us the losses on the mainland, though considerable, were not excessive.

635. When the Japanese landed on Singapore Island, many important dumps, depots and other installations quickly fell into their hands. This caused serious embarrassments in the closing stages, but it does not indicate that the siting of these installations was faulty. The sites had been selected in accordance with a carefully considered policy of dispersion to avoid excessive losses from air attack and also to avoid as far as possible the already congested Singapore Town area. Most of these installations had been carefully camouflaged. The comparatively few losses sustained from air attack are a proof of the success of this policy.

636. One of the outstanding administrative lessons of the campaign was that troops in forward areas, if cut off temporarily from the normal supply system, must have sufficient reserves of ammunition, petrol, food, water, medical supplies, etc., to enable them to continue fighting. We were forced to the expedient of ordering units which were in danger of being cut off to hold reserves in excess of the normal field service scale – a wasteful procedure because these reserves could not all be carried in the event of a rapid move.

In this connection we felt very acutely the lack of any proper facilities for air supply. There is no doubt that, as was proved later in Burma and elsewhere, air supply is the only practical solution to this problem.

637. In the years preceding the war care for the welfare of the troops had been increasingly practised throughout the Army. It had perhaps to some extent tended to obscure the greater importance of the ability of the troops to endure hardships in the most trying conditions. In countries like Malaya troops must be able to operate independently of road and rail communications for considerable periods. This involves the ability to live on the country and, if necessary, to exist on short rations and with little water. Japanese columns in the Malayan campaign were frequently despatched into the jungle carrying a week's rations. They made great use of local resources and for long periods were able to dispense with the normal system of supply. It has been proved during this war, both during operations in the field and from the experiences in the prisoner of war camps, that Europeans are capable of enduring hardships under Eastern conditions and of living on Asiatic food to a much greater extent than was previously thought possible. This is a lesson which should not be forgotten. The training of troops to this standard, which was reached during

the later stages of the war, should be maintained at all times.

SECTION LXV. – TRAINING.

638. While it is a fact that the Japanese troops being seasoned veterans were better trained for jungle warfare than were the British troops, it is quite wrong to suppose that no attention had been paid to this form of training in the Malaya Command. It is, however, true to say that the standard of training was uneven.The formations and units which had been in the country longest were on the whole well trained, but the great majority had arrived piece-meal within a few months of the outbreak of war. Many of them arrived with a low scale of weapons and it was only towards the end of I94I that the authorised scale was approached. The 9 and II Indian Divisions only received their field artillery late in that year. This greatly interfered with continuity of training.

639. Most of our troops except those of the permanent garrison were inexperienced and semi-trained on arrival in Malaya. This was due to the rapid expansion of our forces which had taken place after the outbreak of the second World War and, in the case of the Indian units, to the fact that expansion had not started till a year later. Even the regular units had been so diluted as to lose some at least, and in some cases a great deal, of their pre-war efficiency.

In making the above statement I have no wish to blame the military authorities either in the United Kingdom, in India, or in Australia. I would rather thank them for the great efforts they made to help us with the very limited resources at their disposal.

640. Those units which had been longest in Malaya had naturally had most opportunities of training and of becoming accustomed to the novel conditions of warfare, but during the period immediately preceding the outbreak of hostilities opportunities for training had been greatly limited, partly by the construction of defence works and partly by the necessity of assuming from time to time a state of readiness in accordance with the political situation as it deteriorated. What was lacking was the ability to drop the construction of defences and take a formation, complete with all its arms, off into new country and there carry out intensive training. It had, however, as explained in Section VII, been planned to do this during the three months commencing December, I94I, and there is no doubt that, had this been possible, many of the lessons which were learned after the war began would have been learned in time to turn them to good account.

64I. Staff Rides and tactical training with and without troops had enabled the practicability of landing on the east coast during the period of the north east monsoon and also of moving through forest country to be accurately gauged but the ability of the Japanese to traverse swamps and cross water and other obstacles with little delay had not been fully appreciated.

In I940, a Manual of Bush Fighting had been produced and circulated by Headquarters Malaya Command. This was subsequently supplemented by training instructions issued as and when required. But doctrine had not only to be disseminated but practised and it was for this that opportunity was lacking.

642. Successful fighting in jungle country is largely a question of the confidence and self-reliance of the individual. These cannot be acquired without a reasonable period of training in such conditions. Inexperienced troops from the towns and the plains opposed by seasoned troops specially trained in jungle warfare are necessarily at a disadvantage until they have had time to accustom themselves to these conditions.

643. The deduction from the experience of Malaya is that, if any parts of the British Empire, where the terrain is of the jungle type, are subject to attack at short notice by an enemy armed and equipped on modern lines, we should either maintain on the spot or be able to send there immediately when danger threatens a force fully trained and accustomed to these conditions. It is not sufficient to send in at the last minute inexperienced and semi-trained troops.

SECTION LXVI. – MORALE.

644. The lack of training and of experience of the great majority of the troops who formed the Army of Malaya has already been stressed in this Despatch. In this connection Field-Marshal Lord Montgomery has written:-

> "New and untried troops must be introduced to battle carefully and gradually with no failures in the initial ventures. A start should be made with small raids, then big scale raids, leading up gradually to unit and brigade operations. Great and lasting harm can be done to morale by launching new units into operations for which they are not ready or trained and which are therefore likely to end in failure. When new units and formations are introduced to battle there must be no failure."

Those are very true words as all who fought in Malaya will testify. Unfortunately there was no time to put these precepts into practice.

645. The effect of having to fight without tanks and with little air support against an enemy well provided with such essential modern equipment cannot be over-estimated. All troops were affected by this in varying degree but more particularly the Indian soldiers who had always been taught to believe in British might and had difficulty in accustoming themselves to these unexpected conditions. During the later stages also the loss of the Naval Base and the withdrawal of the Air Force to the Netherlands East Indies, necessary as it may have been, affected some, but by no means all, of the troops, especially those whose homes were then directly threatened. Finally there was the effect of extreme physical and mental exhaustion which resulted from continual day and night operations over a long period.

The military commanders did their utmost to improve matters by endeavouring to arrange short periods of rest for all front line troops in rotation. Unfortunately, owing to lack of reserves, this did not always prove practicable. The II Indian Division for example, which bore the brunt of the fighting in the north, was engaged almost continuously for the whole period of the campaign.

646. Those who have had the task of re-organising units which have suffered heavy losses in battle will know that time is required before full fighting efficiency can be regained. In Malaya it was never possible to make time available and units had to be sent into action again and again before they had recovered from their previous efforts. Their efficiency suffered accordingly.

647. In these circumstances, it was hardly to be expected that the inexperienced troops would withstand the trials of the campaign as steadfastly as would regular seasoned troops. Nevertheless, although they became more and more exhausted and were bewildered and often disheartened, their morale was never broken. Throughout the campaign there was a great deal of heavy fighting at short range and often, hand-to-hand, in which our troops fought courageously and well. Such was the case, in particular, in Kelantan, on the Kroh and Grik roads, at Kampar, at Kuantan, at Gemas, at Muar, in the Mersing area and in many places on Singapore Island. Nor should the less spectacular operations of administration, of communication and of command, which were going on steadily day and night, be forgotten. It stands to the credit of all ranks that, in the many critical situations which developed in the course of the long withdrawal down the Peninsula, the enemy, in spite of the great advantages which he enjoyed, was never able to effect a complete break-through – an occurrence which, in view of our lack of reserves with which to meet such a situation, would have spelt immediate and irreparable disaster.

648. In the final analysis, it is necessary that the influence of all the conditions under which this campaign was fought, which have been fully set out in this Despatch, should be carefully weighed.

649. I believe that few of the men who came to Malaya had any wide knowledge of the importance of that country, both strategical and economical, as an integral part of the British Empire. To most of them Singapore was known only as the site of the great Naval Base. They knew little of the geography or problems of the Far East generally. In consequence, they had but a very elementary knowledge of what they were fighting for, and in the case of the majority there was no time to bring this home to them after arrival in Malaya.

I believe that the problems and needs of our Empire should be much more widely taught in our schools and colleges and in the Army itself than was, at any rate, the case before the war.

SECTION LXVII. – THE INTELLIGENCE SERVICE.

650. It must be admitted that both during the period prior to the outbreak of hostilities and also during the operations themselves our information of the Japanese activities and intentions left much to be desired. This can be attributed partly to the extreme secrecy which the Japanese always maintain on military matters and also partly to

our shortage of reconnaissance aircraft. But there were other short-comings which cannot be attributed entirely to either of these two causes.

651. Before the Malayan campaign our knowledge of the potentialities of the Japanese Army and more especially of their Air Force was very lacking. The ease with which their aircraft sank our two capital ships on the I0th December, I94I, following on their successful attack on the American fleet at Pearl Harbour, surprised not only us but the whole world. The ability of the Japanese to apply modern "blitz" tactics to jungle warfare was also greater than had been anticipated.

652. The attitude of Thailand remained uncertain until the last minute, although we knew from our reconnaissances that the Japanese had for some time been very active in that country and it was clear that these activities were being carried on with the connivance, if not with the assistance, of the Thai authorities. When war broke out Thailand immediately sided with the Japanese and opposed our advance into Thai territory.

653. The pro-Japanese propaganda, which had for some years previously been spread throughout the East, had undoubtedly had some effect. The Japanese came to Malaya well equipped with the means of continuing these activities and their stream of propaganda, much of it very crude, had its effect on some at least of the people of Malaya, and at times even on a few of the troops. It must be said, however, that those who served in the fighting forces, whatever their nationality, with very few exceptions disregarded this propaganda and conducted themselves with never failing loyalty.

654. Within Malaya itself the Police intelligence organization was handicapped by the complicated political structure of the country. Although certain Japanese subversive activities were brought to light almost simultaneously with the outbreak of hostilities and although the Japanese undoubtedly received some assistance from the population during the campaign, there is no reason to suppose that there was any widespread pro-Japanese organization in the country.

655. The future organization of intelligence in the Far East requires a separate study. It is sufficient to say in this Despatch that a much stronger organization is required than has existed in the past. It should be built up round a nucleus of men trained professionally in Far Eastern affairs with a knowledge of the peoples and their languages. Unless the problem is tackled thoroughly it will be difficult, as it proved in the past, to keep abreast of the great changes which are constantly taking place in that part of the world.

SECTION LXVIII. – LOCAL FORCES.

656. The local Forces played their part in the Malayan campaign in the Navy, in the Army and in the Air Force. The newly formed Malay Regiment in particular acquitted itself with distinction, as did others of the locally raised units.

657. As in other parts of the Empire, which are peopled by coloured races, the resources of European manpower in Malaya were limited. The problem was to make the best use of these resources. In accordance with the principle that every part of

the Empire should be responsible for its own local defence, as far as its resources permit, Local Forces, mostly on a voluntary basis, were raised and maintained by the Governments of Malaya. In the light of experience, it cannot be said that the best use was made of the material available.

A proportion of the Europeans were of course required to carry on the Government and other essential activities. Others, for various reasons, were not available for military service. It is with the balance, i.e. those who were available for military service, that this report deals. Many of these men were possessed of special qualifications, such as knowledge of the country, of the people and of the language. The problem was to make full use of these qualifications.

658. In the Malayan campaign the reinforcing units suffered much from lack of local knowledge and from their inability to converse with the inhabitants. As the campaign progressed and more of the local Europeans became available, this difficulty was met by attaching them to the reinforcing units, but in the earlier stages most of those available were employed with units of the Local Forces.

I recommend that each reinforcing unit on arrival in Malaya, from whatever part of the Empire it comes, should have attached to it an intelligence platoon of local Asiatics with European or Asiatic leaders and a team of interpreters, either European or Asiatic. These men should be supplied by the Local Forces, a proportion of which should accordingly be specially organized and trained for this purpose.

659. Another activity which might well devolve upon the Local Forces is the provision of commando groups whose role would be, in case of invasion, to harass the enemy's communications and rear installations. This is a task which could suitably be allotted to residents of the country districts who would in many cases be able to organize their commandos from among their own employees.

660. Those of the Local Forces, apart from the regular units, which are not employed in either of the above ways should be either organized and trained as specialist units, i.e. engineers, signals, armoured car units, railway units, dock units, etc., or for coast defence or garrisons of vulnerable localities.

There should be no attempt made to train the Local Volunteer Forces in ordinary mobile operations. They do not normally have the time for such training and in any case they would, in the case of major operations, be only a very small proportion of the total forces engaged.

661. Local Forces may be called upon to take their part in ensuring internal security or in the defence of the country in a major conflict. In the latter eventuality, the defence of Malaya must ultimately depend on troops from outside acting in co-operation with the other Services. They will want all the assistance they can get from the Local Forces who should be trained primarily for this purpose.

SECTION LXIX. – AIR.

662. The experience of modern war shows that superiority in the air is necessary before victory can be gained and at least parity in order that defeat may be averted.

The Malayan campaign was no exception to this rule. From the opening of hostilities the Japanese Air Force was immeasurably superior to our own. The effect of this on our strategy was, as has been shown, disastrous. The reason for this lay primarily in the inferiority of our aircraft both in quality and in quantity and in the complete absence of many types of aircraft required in modern war. The shortage of aircraft as compared with what had been considered necessary has been shown in Sections VI and XV of this Despatch. The responsibility for these shortages definitely did not lie with the Air Officer Commanding Far East at the time of the campaign, the late Air Vice Marshal Pulford. He was, I know, fully alive to the inadequacy of the material at his disposal and did not fail to represent the situation.

663. Plans to reinforce the Air Force in Malaya by the air route from India and the Middle East were partly frustrated by the capture by the Japanese of the Victoria Point aerodrome in South Burma in the early days of the campaign. This made it impossible for fighters to reach Malaya by air, while the longer range machines had to fly via Sumatra. Fighters had to be brought by sea with the resultant delay.

The Dutch carried out the plans for mutual support in spirit and in letter. No praise is too high for their co-operative spirit during those critical days.

664. The influence of the aerodromes on the initial Army dispositions and on the subsequent strategy of the campaign has already been fully explained. It was only in 1941 that a combined Army and Air Force plan for the siting of aerodromes was agreed upon. It is of the utmost importance that the strategical and tactical problems of their defence should be fully considered before sites for aerodromes are finally settled.

During the campaign the aerodromes became a liability rather than an asset progressively from north to south as the enemy advanced. It was found impracticable to deny them to the enemy by demolitions for more than a very few days. We were therefore faced with the problem, not of holding them for the use of our own Air Force, but of holding them to deny their use to the enemy Air Force. The psychological effect on the troops who were ordered first to protect the aerodromes for the use of our Air Force and then, after seeing them evacuated and destroyed, to hold them in order to deny them to the enemy, needs no stressing.

665. It is to be hoped that British troops will never again be asked to fight with so little air support as was the case in Malaya. There had never, even before the war, been a sufficiently strong Air Force either in Malaya or within reasonable reach of it. If in future the defence of so important a part of the Empire is to be entrusted in great part to the Air Arm, as indeed it certainly will be, it is most neeessary that the nucleus at least of an adequate Air Force should be maintained at all times either in Malaya itself or in a strategic reserve held somewhere in the East. Where such vital interests are at stake it is unwise to take risks as regards the provision of such a necessary means of defence.

SECTION LXX. – AIR DEFENCE.

666. Prior to the outbreak of the second World War there were no modern fighter

aircraft in Malaya and there was no warning system. The anti-aircraft gun defence was confined to the immediate defence of the Naval Base and other installations on Singapore Island. It had been built up in accordance with a War Office plan.

667. During the period I939/4I considerable progress was made in the development of the air defences. Fighter aircraft arrived, a warning system which covered Singapore and the most southern part of Malaya was organised, some anti-aircraft guns and searchlights were made available for the mainland and a co-ordinated air defence system was built up. The air defence system was modelled on that of Great Britain but with very much more slender resources it naturally fell far short of the target. The aerodromes on the mainland were inadequately protected and no defence, other than passive defence, was possible for such important centres as Kuala Lumpur, Ipoh, Penang and many others. The defence of the Naval Base was reasonably strong judged by pre-war standards, though the equipment was still considerably short of the approved scale. The warning system suffered from the disadvantages inherent in a country which was still not fully developed and in parts of which the population was sparse.

668. During the years immediately preceding the war the anti-aircraft gun defences had carried out much useful training with the co-operation of the Royal Air Force but the value of the firing practices had been limited by the lack of the most modern target-towing facilities.

669. During the campaign the Air Defence System worked satisfactorily within its limits. In the later stages, however, the Singapore defences were seriously handicapped by the contraction, and eventually by the total loss, of the warning system. The height (over 20,000 feet) at which the Japanese almost invariably flew when attacking the Singapore area in the early stages rendered the 3in. guns ineffective and undoubtedly reduced their own casualties. On the other hand our Light Anti-Aircraft guns had good targets throughout the campaign both on the mainland and in the closing stages on Singapore Island. Figures of aircraft brought down by anti-aircraft gunfire are notoriously difficult to assess accurately but it can be said with confidence that well over a hundred were brought down by this means during the campaign, in addition to many others which were badly damaged.

670. The need for mobility of the gun defences was the outstanding lesson of the campaign. The operations on the mainland were always fluid while even within the area of the Singapore defences the static equipments were at a disadvantage compared with the mobile ones. Had all the units been fully mobile few, if any, guns need have been lost and they could have operated to an even greater advantage than they did.

All the anti-aircraft guns and searchlights allotted for the defence of aerodromes and of the Lines of Communication should be fully mobile, and a high proportion of those in a permanent fortress should also have a good degree of mobility. It is unlikely that a lay-out designed in peace will meet the conditions of war, and mobility provides one means of making rapid adjustments.

67I. The system adopted whereby the action of the fighters and the gun defences in the Singapore area were co-ordinated by a senior Air Force Officer worked smoothly and satisfactorily but the appointment in those conditions of an Air Defence

Commander, who would have under him all means of air defence, would undoubtedly be advantageous.

672. The Passive Air Defence Services throughout Malaya had been carefully worked out and, though they needed strengthening as the campaign progressed, they functioned on the whole very efficiently. The provision of material defence against air attack was, however, inadequate judged by modern standards both for people and for property. In this connection, however, it is only fair to point out that the congestion in some of the principal cities in Malaya combined with the technical difficulties of constructing underground shelters in places like Singapore make it almost impossible to provide air raid shelters on a satisfactory scale.

SECTION LXXI. – LABOUR.

673. The failure of civil Asiatic Labour and, in the closing stages, of some of the military labour also under air attack was one of the most crippling events of the Malayan campaign.

674. Pre-war plans to organise civil labour had never reached finality and efforts made to raise additional Army labour companies had, as previously explained in this Despatch, been frustrated through delay in obtaining official sanction. In consequence, when war broke out, reliance had to be placed initially on the peace-time system of obtaining labour through contractors. This system soon proved to be most unsatisfactory, partly because much of the labour produced was unsuitable for the work in hand, partly because it was undisciplined and partly because the system was wasteful from the point of view of time spent on work. When sanction to raise additional Army Labour companies was received it was impossible to get the men owing to the wide difference between the scale of remuneration authorized and the rates current in Malaya. Early in January endeavours were made to improve matters by the appointment of a Director of Labour working directly under the Director-General of Civil Defence. He was, however, responsible only for labour on Singapore Island. An Army Director of Labour also was appointed. On the 20th January a measure to introduce compulsion was passed but there was no time for its value to be disclosed. The labour problem was never satisfactorily solved. To the end labour continued to disappear under air attack.

675. In the sphere of labour there is no doubt that the present long-range hitting power of the air arm, which can attack back areas equally with those near the front line, has created new and difficult problems. Especially is this the case where, as in Malaya, comparatively few of the people are natives of the country and where in consequence "defence of home" is not a strong compelling force. In such a case a much stronger control of labour is required than was actually in existence.

676. The problem is an intricate one. In Malaya it was complicated by the variety of languages spoken by the labourers and the impossibility of finding a sufficient number of supervisors who spoke those languages. There were also difficulties connected with remuneration, transportation, accommodation and food.

There is no doubt that during the pre-war period the problem was not tackled with sufficient vigour. When the danger of the situation became apparent and efforts were made to improve it, there was insufficient time to solve the many and intricate problems which arose.

677. Experience showed that by far the best results were obtained from properly organized labour companies under military control. The labourers were then subject to military discipline and were handled by their own officers and non-commissioned officers, some at least of whom could speak their language. These companies should have their own transport and should be housed as near as possible to the work in hand. They should be issued with regular rations. In this way only will it be possible in a country like Malaya to keep labour at work under modern war conditions and to get the best value from it.

Each of the Fighting Services should have its own labour force and the nucleus at least of these forces should exist in peace-time so that a rapid expansion can take place when war threatens. In Malaya the finding of additional officers and non-commissioned officers to supplement the permanent staff on mobilization should be another call on the Local Forces.

SECTION LXXII. – CIVIL DEFENCE.

678. It is now generally accepted that success in modern war depends upon the whole-hearted co-operation of all concerned, both in the Fighting Services and among the civil population, striving with a singleness of purpose to attain the common goal. In the Malayan campaign, fought within our own territory, that was of paramount importance. To organize the civil community and to prepare itself for prompt and vigorous action was clearly one of the Government's responsibilities.

679. A great deal of criticism has been levelled at the Civil Administration. Much of it is unjust. His Majesty's Government had laid down that the primary duty of the people of Malaya was to produce as much rubber and tin as possible for war purposes. The Civil Administration had to keep this object in mind while making at the same time preparations against eventual attack. It had also to watch over the interests of a mixed population of Malays, Chinese, Indians and Europeans. In the circumstances, it was inevitable that clashes of interests should occur.

680. When the war came many men and women of all races, both official and unofficial, played a creditable and often an heroic part in the defence of the country. Many of them lost their lives and many of them suffered a long period of imprisonment or internment at the hands of the Japanese. Most of those who survived suffered heavy losses of property. I wish to express my deep appreciation of the loyal assistance and self-sacrifice of these people.

68I. Nevertheless, both during the period before the war and during the campaign itself an artificial and unwarlike atmosphere prevailed throughout Malaya. There seemed to be a lack of a united effort by people determined to repel the common foe at all costs. There were many causes for this – a lack of knowledge of war owing to

Malaya's long immunity from it, an inability in some quarters to realise the real danger which threatened, the lack of common citizenship, and the high standard of living resulting from the wealth of the country's resources.

682. Difficulties arose from the complicated machinery of Government comprising as it did a large number of separate administrations. As this is a matter which is now receiving the consideration of His Majesty's Government, it is sufficient to say here that from a defence point of view it is essential that a simpler and more straightforward organization should be evolved.

683. I feel bound to record as a result of my experiences in Malaya that the Fighting Services throughout suffered from this lack of a strong and centralized administration able and ready to take prompt decisions and vigorous action.

SECTION LXXIII. – THE HIGHER COMMAND.

684. The advantage held by the seasoned Japanese troops as a result of the experience of active operations which many of them had had in China applied also in some degree in the case of the senior commanders. Whereas most of the Japanese commanders had had previous experience in handling large forces in the field in Far East conditions of warfare, few of our commanders had had the benefit of a similar experience. Many of them had had no experience whatever of tank warfare.

The importance of commanders in all parts of the Empire being given opportunities in peace-time of training with forces which they will be called upon to handle in war needs no stressing.

685. The Army of Malaya was composed of troops from many parts of the Empire – from the United Kingdom, India, Australia and Malaya – and comprised many different races. The various contingents varied widely in their characteristics. It was my duty and constant effort to weld these contingents into a homogeneous whole.

Between the two wars great progress had been made, by exchange of officers and by other means, in spreading a common doctrine throughout the armed forces of the Empire. There can be no question of the value of this, especially in theatres of war where, as in Malaya, forces are mixed. I recommend, from my experience in Malaya, that this policy should now be developed and greatly expanded because I believe it to be essential that all senior commanders and staff officers should not only have common ideas on the strategy, tactics and staff work applicable to a major war but that they should also look upon all problems of defence from an Imperial rather than from a local point of view. With increased facilities for air travel it seems possible that this ideal may in the future be capable of attainment.

686. Throughout the campaign, Headquarters Malaya Command had the dual function of controlling forces in the field in quickly moving operations ranging over an area nearly as large as that of England and Wales and of dealing with the many matters, such as business with the Home Authorities and the Civil Government, which are necessarily the responsibility of the Headquarters of a Command overseas. Its strength, when war with Japan broke out, was approximately equivalent to that of

the headquarters of a Corps and its establishment was not suited to its dual role. Although the staff was strengthened as more officers became available, it remained throughout the campaign too weak to fulfil adequately the dual task imposed upon it.

It would in my opinion have been of great assistance if there had been a single commander over all the Fighting Services and the Civil Administration. I and my staff would then have been much freer to concentrate on operations.

687. Reference has already been made in this Despatch to the disturbing effect of the numerous changes which took place in the Higher Command. During the short campaign there were in all five Commanders-in-Chief. Such rapid changes, though largely forced upon us by circumstances, are naturally not calculated to create an atmosphere of confidence.

688. It is not within the province of this Despatch to make concrete recommendations for the future organization of Command in the Far East. The defence of British Borneo and possibly also of Hong Kong must enter into the problem. It is obviously necessary to avoid overweighting the structure with too many headquarters, but I feel that a Supreme Commander in the Far East would be a great advantage both in peace and in war. Wide powers of decision, with considerable financial control, should be delegated to him. It is for consideration also whether in time of war the civil administrations as well as the Fighting Services should not come under his control.

689. As war has become an affair of nations and not only of the Fighting Services, I consider it of the utmost importance for the future that all senior commanders, civil officials and staff officers should be fully trained in the art of making war on a national basis. It must be a study in which all brains are pooled. There must be a corps of civilians and officers of each Service fit to staff and command the forces of the future and to understand the complete integration of civil and military efforts. In addition to what they learn in their own Services and Colleges, I am of the opinion that a course at a Combined Imperial Defence College will be essential. For this purpose I would advocate a considerable expansion of the Imperial Defence College as it existed before the war and that graduation at that College should be an essential qualification for the higher military and civil appointments in the strategically important overseas parts of the British Empire.

SECTION LXXIV. – CONCLUSION.

690. The Retreat from Mons and the Retreat to Dunkirk have been hailed as epics. In the former our Army was able with the help of a powerful ally to turn the tables on the enemy; in the latter our Army was evacuated by the Navy with the loss of all heavy equipment. Each of these retreats lasted approximately three weeks. The Retreat in Malaya lasted ten weeks in far more trying conditions. There was no strong ally to help us and no Navy to evacuate the force, even had it been desirable to do so. It has been hailed as a disaster but perhaps the judgment of history will be that all the

effort and money expended on the defence of Malaya and the sacrifice and subsequent suffering of many of those who fought in the Malaya campaign were not in vain. The gain of ten weeks and the losses inflicted on the enemy may well have had a bigger influence than was realised at the time on the failure of the Japanese to reach even more important parts of our Empire.

69I. An analysis of what has been said in this Despatch shows that a great many of the causes which contributed to our defeat in Malaya had a common origin, namely the lack of readiness of our Empire for war. Our shortage in light naval coastal craft and in modern aircraft, our lack of tanks, the lack of training of most of our troops – especially the reinforcements – the lack of experience of modern war of some of the senior commanders and the weakness of our intelligence service can all be attributed to a failure to prepare for war at the proper time. This unpreparedness is no new experience. It is traditional in the British Empire. But it is becoming more and more expensive and, as the tempo of war increases, more and more dangerous. I submit that the security of the Empire can only be assured by making proper provision for its defence in time of peace. Even if this involves increased financial expenditure, the money will be well spent if it acts as an insurance against war or at least against a repetition of the disasters which befell us in the early stages of this war. If the Malayan campaign, in conjunction with other campaigns, has done anything to bring this fact home to the peoples of our Empire, it will not have been without merit.

A.E. PERCIVAL,
Lieut.-General,
Formerly General Officer Commanding Malaya.

APPENDIX "A".

DEDUCTIONS FROM JAPANESE APPRECIATION OF THE ATTACK ON SINGAPORE 1937.
(See Section VI paragraph 2I).

I. The use of territory in Southern Siam by the Japanese is a contingency which demands our careful study. It would enable them both to cut off our food supplies from Siam and also to establish Air Forces within striking distance of Malaya. Naval and Air Forces of sufficient strength to frustrate such an attempt are necessary. In addition everything possible should be done by diplomatic methods to keep the Siamese friendly to us.

2. The defence of the Northern Area of Malaya and of Johore is assuming increased importance. The scale of landing attacks, which was formerly confined to raids by parties of about 200 men, has now greatly increased. On the other hand, the defence of the Northern Area, as far as the Army is concerned, is still entrusted to the Federated Malay States Volunteer Force, assisted by certain units of the Straits Settlements and of the Unfederated Malay States, while the defence of Johore is entrusted to the Johore Military Forces, assisted by part of the Johore Volunteer Engineers.

None of these forces can be considered adequate in all circumstances for the task in hand. At least one Regular Infantry Bn., with R.A. and R.E. attached, is required for the Penang – Province Wellesley Area, and a similar force must be available to strengthen the forces in Southern Malaya.

3. Within Malaya itself the threat from the enemy within our gates is a very real one and is rapidly increasing. The possibility of attempts at sabotage by enemy nationals resident in Malaya has always been accepted. The number of these nationals compared with the strength of the garrison is now so great that it would be within their powers to do extensive damage unless proper precautions are taken to avoid it.

Recently this threat has been increased by the danger of civil disturbance. Labour in Malaya is being organised and the present return to prosperity provides a fruitful field for paid agitators.

It must be expected that an enemy would take advantage of all these conditions and that military operations would be prefaced by sabotage, and perhaps by labour troubles, on a large scale. In these circumstances, it is quite certain that the Police will be unable to assume the responsibilities under the Defence Scheme which hitherto they have accepted. Further responsibilities would fall on the military for which Infantry would be required. It might not be possible to spare them from the present garrison.

4. The problem of the defence of Singapore, has been greatly affected by the new Combined Operations equipment recently used by the Japanese on the China Coasts – in particular, the special landing craft in large numbers, the landing craft "carriers," the sea tanks, etc. The effect of this is that large numbers of men could be put into landing craft out of range of our fixed defences and thrown in a short space of time on to our beaches. In particular the beaches between Singapore Town and Changi have become more vulnerable than previously.

A strengthening of our Air Forces, of our local defence Naval Vessels and of our Beach Defences is required. In connection with the latter, it is for consideration whether authority should not now be sought to erect permanent defences in peacetime in the Siglap, Ayer Gomureh and Changi Sectors.

5. The Air Forces available in Malaya must be strong enough to deal with the scale of attack indicated in the appreciation and must be certain of being able to prevent the special landing craft "carriers" from closing our shores. They are not at present strong enough.

6. The Local Naval Craft, i.e. destroyers etc., which it is intended to base on Singapore are badly needed. Their arrival should not be delayed.

7. The probable effect of the fixed and A/M.T.B. defences, when completed, will be to act as a deterrent against daylight and M.T.B. attacks. The greater damage is likely to be landing attacks under cover of darkness. To counter this danger more Infantry are required. Singapore cannot be considered safe unless reinforcements are brought in before the attack develops. At least two additional battalions are required in the Island itself.

Further, the efficiency of the Volunteer units is still impaired by lack of equipment. It is suggested that a 3-year plan should be worked out, aiming at all requisites being available at the end of that period. If the money cannot be found under the present system, a new system must be adopted.

8. In the light of this appreciation and of recent information, the food supply situation is not satisfactory. The only really satisfactory solution will be to ensure that at any given time the necessary stocks are available within Malaya itself.

A.E.P.

APPENDIX "B"
ORDER OF BATTLE

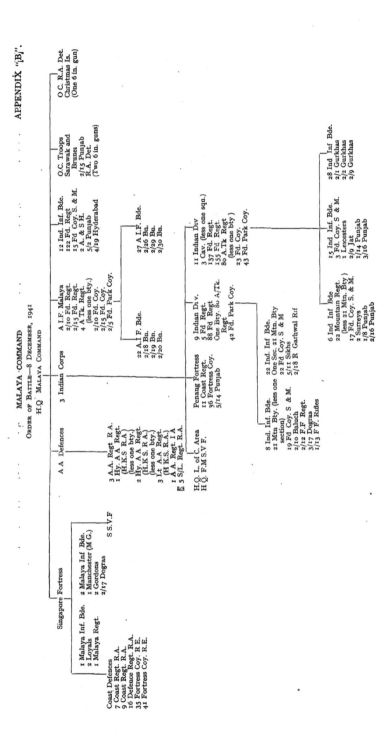

APPENDIX "B".

MALAYA ·COMMAND
ORDER OF BATTLE—8 DECEMBER, 1941
H.Q. MALAYA COMMAND

Singapore Fortress

S.S.V.F
- 2 Malaya Inf. Bde.
  - 1 Manchester (M.G.)
  - 2 Gordons
  - 2/17 Dogras
- 1 Malaya Inf. Bde.
  - 2 Loyals
  - 1 Malaya Regt.

Coast Defences
7 Coast Regt. R.A.
9 Coast Regt. R.A.
16 Defence Regt. R.E.
35 Fortress Coy. R.E.
41 Fortress Coy. R.E.

A A Defences
- 3 A.A. Regt R.A.
- 1 Hy. A.A. Regt. (H.K.S. R.A.) (less one bty.)
- 2 Hy. A.A. Regt. (H.K.S. R.A.) (less one bty.)
- 3 Lt A.A. Regt. (H.K.S. R.A.)
- 1 A.A. Regt. I A
- 5 S/L. Regt. R.A.

H.Q. L. of C. Area
H.Q. F.M.S.V.F.

3 Indian Corps

A.I.F. Malaya
- 2/10 Fd. Regt.
- 2/15 Fd. Regt.
- 4 A.Tk. Regt. (less one bty.)
- 2/10 Fd. Coy.
- 2/15 Fd. Coy.
- 2/5 Fd. Park Coy.

22 A.I.F. Bde.
- 2/18 Bn.
- 2/19 Bn.
- 2/20 Bn.

27 A.I.F. Bde.
- 2/26 Bn.
- 2/29 Bn.
- 2/30 Bn.

12 Ind. Inf. Bde.
- 122 Fd. Regt.
- 15 Fd. Coy. S. & M.
- 2 A. & S.H.
- 5/2 Punjab
- 4/19 Hyderabad

O.C. Troops Sarawak and Brunei
- 2/15 Punjab
- R.A. Det. (Two 6 in. guns)

O.C. R.A. Det.
Christmas Is.
(One 6 in. gun)

Penang Fortress
- 11 Coast Regt.
- 36 Fortress Coy.
- 5/14 Punjab

9 Indian Div.
- 5 Fd. Regt.
- 88 Fd. Regt.
- One Bty. 80 A/Tk. Regt.
- 42 Fd. Park Coy.

11 Indian Div
- 3 Cav. (less one squ.)
- 137 Fd. Regt.
- 155 Fd. Regt.
- 80 A.Tk Regt. (less one bty)
- 23 Fd. Coy.
- 43 Fd. Park Coy.

8 Ind. Inf. Bde.
- 21 Mtn Bty. (less one section)
- 19 Fd Coy. S & M.
- 2/10 Baluch
- 2/12 F.F Regt.
- 3/17 Dogras
- 1/13 F F. Rifles

22 Ind. Inf. Bde.
- One Sec. 21 Mtn. By
- 22 Fd Coy. S & M
- 5/11 Sikhs
- 2/18 R Garhwal Rif

6 Ind Inf Bde
- 22 Mountain Regt. (less 21 Mtn. Bty)
- 17 Fd. Coy. S. & M.
- 2 Surreys
- 1/8 Punjab
- 2/16 Punjab

15 Ind. Inf. Bde.
- 3 Fd. Coy. S & M.
- 1 Leicesters
- 2/9 Jat
- 1/14 Punjab
- 3/16 Punjab

28 Ind Inf Bde.
- 2/1 Gurkhas
- 2/2 Gurkhas
- 2/9 Gurkhas

APPENDIX "C."

23rd December, 1941.

HEADQUARTERS MALAYA COMMAND ORDER No. 28.

The broad policy is to continue opposition to the enemy on the mainland to cover the arrival of our reinforcements.

5. 3 *Indian Corps.* – Will fight the enemy wherever met and will NOT give ground till forced to subject to the condition that the Corps must remain in being as a fighting formation.

It is of importance to cover Kuala Lumpur as long as possible owing to the large amount of material stored in that area.

The lateral road Jerantut – Raub – Kuala Kubu provides the main communication between East and West Malaya. This important factor should be given full consideration in the conduct of the battle.

6. It is the intention to withdraw the Kuantan garrison at a time to be decided later, dependent upon the development of operations elsewhere and upon climatic conditions. Preliminary arrangements will be put in hand forthwith.

7. On completion of the withdrawal of the garrisons from Kelantan and Kuantan, the role of the 9 Indian Division will be:-

(*a*) to protect the Line of Communication Gemas – Kuala Lipis.

(*b*) to prevent the enemy repairing and using the Line of Communication Kuala Lipis – Kuala Krai.

(*c*) to form a reserve in the area Raub –Bentong.

8. The II Indian Division should therefore, if forced to fall back from its present position, fight the enemy in South Perak under instructions to be issued by the Commander, 3 Indian Corps, who will ensure that the operations of the two divisions are co-ordinated.

9. The Commander, 3 Indian Corps, will also be prepared for landings on the west coast of Malaya. For this purpose a small naval flotilla is being formed and will be based on Port Swettenham.

10. *A.I.F.* – While retaining his main forces for the defence of the east coast, the Commander, A.I.F., will at the same time make preliminary arrangements to deal

with (*a*) an enemy advance down the main Kuala Lumpur – Singapore road (*b*) landings by small enemy forces on the west coast of Malaya.

II. *C.A.A.D.* – The C.A.A.D. will be prepared to provide the maximum possible A.A. protection for ships arriving with reinforcements while they are unloading.

I2. *Singapore Fortress.* – The Commander, Singapore Fortress, will arrange for reconnaissance of the north shore of Singapore Island to select positions for the defence of possible landing places.

I4. There must be NO unnecessary withdrawals.

I5. Arrangements are being made by Headquarters Malaya Command to harass the enemy's communications.

Similar arrangements should be made by subordinate formations whenever the opportunity offers.

APPENDIX "D."

Subject:-

TACTICS.

Comd. 3 Ind. Corps.

Comd. A.I.F. Malaya.

Comd. Singapore Fortress.

I. The operations on land in Malaya have developed in a way which probably few of us anticipated to the full before the war started. There have been some normal attacks by formed bodies of the enemy, in which our adversaries have not shown up to any special advantage except that they have shown at times fanatical courage. But the operations have tended to develop more and more on guerrilla lines. The enemy is trying to dislodge us from our positions by flanking and encircling movements and by attacks on our communications. He has the advantage that he is far less dependent on his communications than we are, and also that, being rice eaters, his soldiers are able to live on the country for longer periods than are ours. As I have said before, his Army is an Army of gangsters, relying for success more on weakening the morale of the troops than on any particular skill with his weapons. All reports go to show that, whereas his mortar fire is actually accurate but not very destructive, his small arms fire is generally wild and comparatively ineffective.

2. I believe that our young and inexperienced troops are now getting their second wind. I am confident that, if well led, they will prove their superiority over the enemy. We must play the enemy at his own game. It is developing into a guerrilla war, so let us also adopt guerrilla tactics. Formations should reduce their transport as far as possible by sending all vehicles which are not immediately wanted well to the rear. Every platoon and section should be taught to become both tank hunters and Japanese hunters. The object must be to destroy as many Japanese as possible and also to destroy the morale by constantly attacking him.

To do this we must have a good local intelligence organization. Every unit at least should have attached to it a Malay speaking and if possible Chinese speaking local European who should be able to build up a local intelligence organization. Some of these have already been made available: endeavours will be made to supply others on application.

3. While our policy for the present is to keep our forces in being as fighting formations this does not mean that casualties must always be avoided. Provided

greater losses are inflicted on the enemy, casualties can and should be accepted within reasonable limits. The doctrine to be inculcated into every officer and man is that they must always be looking for a way of getting at the enemy. If they are cut off, they are well placed for attacking the enemy from behind, and should make every effort to do this before seeking to rejoin their own unit.

If on the other hand the enemy succeeds in getting behind us we must turn round and fight him. It is a guerrilla war and must be fought with guerrilla tactics.

A.E. PERCIVAL,
Lieutenant-General,
General Officer Commanding,
Malaya.
6th January, 1942.

APPENDIX "E."

MALAYA COMMAND OPERATION INSTRUCTION No. 33.

Information.
I. Enemy has continued attacks on II Ind Div which has suffered heavily. 9 Ind Div is fresher but weak.

Intention.
2. Malaya Comd, in conjunction with R.N., R.A.F. and civil defence services will continue to ensure security of Singapore Naval Base.

Method.
3. Singapore Fortress will send one regular Ind bn to relieve A.I.F. bn in area Kota Tinggi on I0th January, I942.

4. Comd A.I.F. Malaya will take over from 3 Ind Corps operational control of Settlement of Malacca and that part of Johore north of line G. Besar – Labis – Semerah with effect from receipt of this order.

5. A.I.F. will concentrate one A.I.F. bde gp (less two coys on Kluang and Kahang aerodromes) in area Segamat as soon as possible.

6. 45 Ind Inf Bde Gp will come under comd of A.I.F. Malaya with effect from receipt of this order.

7. 3 Ind Corps will withdraw from present posns into Johore, covered by maximum possible demolitions. Withdrawal will be carried out by rail and by M.T. as ordered by the Corps Comd.

"Withdrawal will be covered by rearguards on the demolitions (.) A.I.F. as soon as it can do so is to send forward mobile detachments into Negri Sembilan to relieve rearguards of 3 Ind Corps and harass and delay the enemy by demolitions."

8. On entering Johore, 9 Ind Div and one twelve gun bty 80 A.Tk Regt will come under comd of Comd A.I.F. Malaya. 3 Ind Corps,will arrange for G and Q staff officers of 9 Ind Div to report to Adv H.Q. A.I.F. Malaya as soon as possible for liaison purposes.

9. 3 Ind Corps less 9 Ind Div and one bty 80 A.Tk Regt will, on withdrawal, take over operational responsibility for Southern Johore up to and incl the line Endau – G. Beremban –Kluang – Batu Pahat. Date on which 3 Ind Corps will assume this responsibility will be fixed later. Until this date is notified, Comd A.I.F. Malaya will be operationally responsible for whole of State of Johore and Settlement of Malacca.

3 Ind Corps will be prepared to provide one bde gp of II Ind Div to take place of A.I.F. tps on rd Kahang – Kluang and to relieve two coys A.I.F. at Kahang and Kluang aerodromes (see para 5 above).

I0. During latter stages of withdrawal, 3 Ind Corps will detail a staff officer to be at Adv H.Q. A.I.F. Malaya to advise as to when rds forward of posns held by tps under Comd A.I.F. Malaya may be demolished.

II. Comd Johore Malacca Area will continue to be responsible for administration of comd depots and units not allotted to formations in State of Johore and Settlement of Malacca.

I2. 3 Ind Corps and A.I.F. Malaya will have equal running rights on all rds in Johore.

Communications.

I3. Adv H.Q. A.I.F. Malaya will be established at Labis. Rear H.Q. A.I.F. Malaya will remain at Johore Bahru. H.Q. 3 Ind. Corps will be established at Johore Bahru after withdrawal.

K.S. TORRANCE,
Brigadier.
General Staff, Malaya Command.
9th January, I942.
I220 hrs.

APPENDIX "F."

MALAYA COMMAND OPERATION INSTRUCTION No. 35.

Information.

I. (a) Enemy. 5 Division (H Q. Labis) operating astride the road Segamat – Ayer Hitam and has Guards Division on the axis Muar – Ayer Hitam.

(b) Own Troops. Our forward troops are holding North and West of Yong Peng road junction. We also hold Batu Pahat.

Intention.

2. Our troops will be withdrawn to-night to positions covering Kluang and Ayer Hitam and including Batu Pahat.

Method.

3. Yong Peng road junction will be held during the withdrawal under arrangements to to be made by Westforce. 53 Brigade Group less Loyals will be withdrawn under orders Westforce clearing Yong Peng road junction by midnight 23-24th January and will come under orders Comd. 3 Indian Corps on passing Ayer Hitam cross roads. Loyals will revert to Comd. Westforce.

Troops of 9 Indian Division operating on road Labis – Ayer Hitam will follow 53 Infantry Brigade under orders issued by Westforce.

4. Westforce will come under command of 3 Indian Corps as soon as last troops have been withdrawn south of Yong Peng road junction.

5. Garrison at Kahang may be withdrawn to Jemaluang area at discretion of Comd. 3 Indian Corps. Comd. Westforce will arrange flanking protection on the road Kluang –Jemaluang.

6. Main L. of C. Batu Pahat will be via west coast road.

Administrative.

7. The Comd. of the Kuang Area will be made responsible that the R.A.F. Petrol Dump at the Kluang Aerodrome which the Army is now using is destroyed if necessary to prevent it falling into the hands of the enemy.

Inter-Communication.

8. H.Q. 3 Indian Corps Johore Bahru. H.Q. Westforce, Rengam Area. H.Q. II Indian Division is moving to Pontian Kechil.

9. Ack.

K.S. TORRANCE,
Brigadier,
General Staff, Malaya Command.

Advance H.Q.M.C.
23rd January, 1942.
T.O.O. 1920.

APPENDIX "G."

MINUTES OF CONFERENCE HELD AT HEADQUARTERS, WESTFORCE.

I5I5 HOURS. 25TH JANUARY, I942.

Present- G.O.C. (Lieut.-General PERCIVAL).

G.O.C. 3 Indian Corps (Lieut.-General Sir LEWIS HEATH).

(Comd. Westforce (Major-General GORDON BENNETT).

Comd. II Indian Division (Major-General KEY).

I. Comd. II Indian Division reported that the force at Batu Pahat had been heavily engaged all the morning and that the coast road had been blocked near Senggarang.

2. Comd. Westforce reported that the situation at Kluang was confused but that we were still holding the Kluang road junction and he believed the counter attack carried out by the Sikhs had been successful.

3. The following decisions were taken:-

(*a*) Order the Batu Pahat Garrison to withdraw at once and link up with 53 Infantry Brigade in the Senggarang area.

(*b*) Westforce to withdraw to-night to the general line S. Sayong Halt – S. Benut. This position to be held until the night 27-28th January at least. Subsequent withdrawals to take place to positions, to be laid down in advance, which would in turn be held for a minimum fixed period and longer if possible.

(*c*) Movement of Eastforce and II Division to conform to that of Westforce, under orders to be issued by 3 Indian Corps.

(*d*) In view of a possible threat to the Pontian Kechil area Comd. Westforce to hold a good battalion in reserve, whenever possible, which could be made available to move rapidly to that flank.

K.S. TORRANCE,
Brigadier,
General Staff, Malaya Command.
Advance H.Q.M.C.
26th January, I942.

APPENDIX "H"

PUBLIC ANNOUNCEMENT BY G.O.C. MALAYA
FEBRUARY, 1942

The battle of Malaya has come to an end and the battle of Singapore has started. For nearly two months our troops have fought an enemy on the mainland who has had the advantage of great air superiority and considerable freedom of movement by sea.

Our task has been both to impose losses on the enemy and to gain time to enable the forces of the Allies to be concentrated for this struggle in the Far East. Today we stand beleaguered in our island fortress.

Our task is to hold this fortress until help can come – as assuredly it will come. This we are determined to do.

In carrying out this task we want the help of every man and woman in the fortress. There is work for all to do. Any enemy who sets foot in our fortress must be dealt with immediately. The enemy within our gates must be ruthlessly weeded out. There must be no more loose talk and rumour-mongering. Our duty is clear. With firm resolve and fixed determination we shall win through.

APPENDIX "J"

LETTER RE IMPLEMENTATION OF SCORCHED EARTH POLICY ON SINGAPORE ISLAND

It is of the utmost importance that no material of military value should be allowed in any circumstances to fall into the hands of the enemy. In the past, mistakes have been made owing to the responsibility for carrying out the destruction when the time comes not being clearly defined.

2. The policy approved by the Chiefs of Staff as regards Singapore is that as much surplus material as possible should be disposed of at once, either by removal or destruction, provided this can be done without destroying public "morale." As regards the rest, every possible preparation must be made at once and detailed schemes drawn up. Destruction by explosion or fire is normally calculated to destroy morale.

3. Responsibility for preparation and execution of schemes will rest on the military authority who is responsible for the dump, depot, or establishment concerned, i.e., Comd. H.Q. (Head of service concerned) will be responsible for Command installations; formation H.Q. for dumps or depots under their control.

4. Food stocks, medical stores, hospital equipment and water supply installations will NOT be destroyed.

5. As regards the orders to put these schemes into effect, if time permits the order will be given by me. It will be readily realised, however, that in the turmoil and confusion of an attack on Singapore it may not be possible to issue any order. Responsible authorities must therefore ensure that there are always on the spot day and night sufficient personnel with a reliable commander who will in the last resort and failing my orders act on his own initiative to ensure that the policy of His Majesty's Government is carried out.

A.E. PERCIVAL,
Lieutenant-General,
General Officer Commanding, Malaya.
Adv. H.Q.M.C.
1st February, 1942.

APPENDIX "K"

MALAYA COMMAND OPERATION INSTRUCTION No. 40
Ref. Map Johore and Singapore I/25,000

I. Enemy attacked Western Area in strength 9th February and succeeded in penetrating to the East of Tengah aerodrome. A party of the enemy is reported to have blocked the road Hong Kah Village 69I7 – road junction 63I3 inrear of 44 Ind. Inf. Bde.

2. A.I.F. Malaya have been ordered to withdraw to and hold the line S. Kranji – BulimVillage 69I9 – S. Jurong. 6/I5 Bde. has been placed under comd. of A.I.F. Malaya.

3. Should it be impossible to hold the enemy on the line mentioned in para. 2 above, G.O.C. Malaya intends to withdraw to an inner position on which the final battle for Singapore will be fought.

4. General line of this inner position will be:-

West Bank of Kallang River in 87II – thence west of the inundated area in 86II, 86I2, and 87I2 to Mt. Vernon 88I4 – north of Pierce Reservoir 8II8 – Hill 58I in 76I6 – west of Bukit Timah Village 75I5 – pt. I05 in 74I2 – Pasir Panjang Village 7409 – thence along the south coast of Singapore Island to west bank of Rochore River in 87I0. Pulau Blakang Mati, Pulau Brani, Pulau Tekong and the defended perimeter of Pengerang will also be held.

5. This position will be divided into three Areas:-

Northern Area – Comd. – Comd. 3 Ind. Corps. Troops – 3 Ind. Corps of II Ind. Div. and I8 Div.

Southern Area – Comd. – Comd. Southern Area (Major-General Keith Simmons). Troops – existing garrison of Southern Area.

Western Area – Comd. – Comd. A.I.F. Malaya.

Note. – Allocation of I2 Ind. Inf. Bde. and 44 Ind. Inf. Bde. will be decided later. At least one of these formations will be in Command Reserve.

6. *Boundaries.* – The defended area defined in para. 4 above will be divided into sectors by boundaries as follows:-

Between 3 *Ind. Corps and A.I.F.* Incl. A.I.F. Electric Transmission Line 77I6 – incl. Swiss Rifle Club 77I5 – incl. road junction 780I43 – incl. Bukit Timah Road – road junction 838II7.

Between 3 Ind. Corps and Southern Area. Incl. 3 Ind. Corps Macpherson Road – Serangoon Road – excl. Farrer Park – road junction 838II7.

Between A.I.F. and Southern Area. Incl. Southern Area track 750I07 – Ayer Raja Road – Alexandra Road – road junction 809092 – incl. road junction 8I2I02 – Grange Road – incl. road junction 827I02 – excl. road junction 829I08 – excl. road junction 838II7.

Comd. Southern Area will be responsible for defence of Pulau Blakang Mati, Pulau Brani, Pulau Tekong and Pengerang.

7. Reconnaissances of Areas will be carried out at once and the plans for the movement of formations into the areas allotted to them will be prepared. Formations will arrange to move back and locate in their new areas units located in their present areas which are under command of H.Q. Malaya Command.

8. C.A.A.D. will remain responsible to G.O.C. Malaya for A.A. Defences.

9. H.Q. of G.O.C. Malaya will be located at Fort Canning (Battle H.Q.) together with H.Q. Southern Area.

I0. Administrative adjustments which can be made now to fit in with the above organization will be put in hand immediately.

II. ACK.

Lieut.-Colonel
for Brigadier,
General Staff, Malaya Command.
Adv. H.Q.M.C.
I0th February, I942.
T.O.O. 0050.

4

SIR PAUL MALTBY'S DESPATCH ON AIR OPERATIONS DURING THE CAMPAIGNS IN MALAYA AND NETHERLAND EAST INDIES

8 DECEMBER 1941 TO 12 MARCH 1942

REPORT ON THE AIR OPERATIONS DURING THE CAMPAIGNS IN MALAYA AND NETHERLAND EAST INDIES FROM 8TH DECEMBER, 1941 TO 12TH MARCH, 1942.

The following report was submitted to the Secretary of State for Air on July 26th, 1947, by Air Vice-Marshal Sir PAUL MALTBY, K.B.E., C.B., D.S.O., A.F.C., Assistant Air Officer Commanding Far East Command, Royal Air Force, from January 12th to February 10th, 1942, and Air Officer Commanding Royal Air Force in Java from February 11th to March 12th, 1942.

FOREWORD.

A report on the operations in Malaya and the N.E.I. would be incomplete without a survey of the situation in the Far East before war broke out there. A convenient date for beginning such a survey is Ist June, I94I, soon after the date, 24th April, I94I, on which the late Air Vice-Marshal C.W. Pulford became Air Officer Commanding R.A.F. Far East Command.

A number of other newly posted Senior Officers also took up their new duties about the same time, the more important amongst them being Lieut.-Gen. A.E. Percival (G.O.C. Malaya - I6th May, I94I), Air Commodore C.O.F. Modin (A.O.A. at A.H.Q. I0.6.4I), Group Captain A.G. Bishop (Group Captain Ops. at A.H.Q. I.6.4I) and the late Group Captain E.B. Rice (Fighter Defence Commander of Singapore and Co-ordinator of Air Defences of Malaya, both newly established appointments, I0.7.4I).

Although Ist June, I94I, has been chosen as the datum line from which to start the survey, full recognition is given to the large amount of preparatory work which was done by the predecessors of the officers whose names are mentioned above. Some reference is necessarily made to matters which occurred during the time they were in office, but in general the survey deals with the period between Ist June, I94I, and the outbreak of war. It indicates the energetic measures which were taken immediately beforehand to prepare the Command for war, and points a picture of the situation as it existed at the outbreak of hostilities.

The narrative contains only brief reference to developments in Hong Kong, Burma and the Indian Ocean, operational control of which passed out of the hands of the A.O.C. Far East Command soon after the Japanese had landed in Malaya. Their presence in the Command during the pre-war period did, however, appreciably divert attention and work from pressing matters of local application, and to this degree affected preparation for war in Malaya.

Some reference is necessary to sources of information on which the report is based.

Official records from the Far East are few and incomplete. Most of those which were maintained there had to be destroyed to prevent their capture by the Japanese. The few which survive consist of brief situation reports and a few files of important signals and correspondence, now with the Air Ministry. To make good the loss of the destroyed documents, reports have since been obtained from a number of officers who held important appointments in the Far East Command. But these are far from authoritative. Most of them were written in December, I945, and January, I946, nearly four years after the events which they describe had taken place, during which years their authors had been prisoners-of-war in Japanese hands, or alternatively had been actively employed in other theatres of war. A number of important individuals who could have given valuable evidence, I regret to report, died in captivity or during subsequent operations. Discrepancies have been slow and difficult to reconcile between sources of information now scattered thoughout the world, despite the ready help I have received from the authors of such reports.

On the other hand valuable information has been freely supplied to me from the Cabinet War Library, the Air Ministry, the War Office, the Colonial Office and by the authors of several other despatches relating to the War in the Far East. To them also I am much indebted.

For the sake of brevity only those matters are mentioned in the report which are necessary for establishing important events, for elucidating the factors which governed action at the time, and for compiling before it is too late a reasonably comprehensive narrative of what happened in the Far East.

Within these limitations every effort has been made to ensure accuracy, and the report, as a whole, is believed to give a reasonably true picture of the campaign from the air aspect - although doubtless it may display inaccuracies of detail brought about by the circumstances in which it has been compiled. It should, however, contain the necessary data from which correct deductions can be drawn. In order, however, that inaccuracies may be corrected, readers are invited to call attention to them through the Air Ministry.

The whole report has been written under my direction, the first two sections on behalf of the late Air Vice-Marshal Pulford who held his command until IIth February, I942, two days before he left Singapore. In my opinion there is nothing in these sections, or in Section V, with which he would not agree.

I myself took over my duties at his headquarters on I2th January, I942, from which date the report is written on my responsibility, and largely with my personal knowledge. This part of the report continues in the third person for the sake of continuity in the narrative.

P.C. MALTBY,
Air Vice-Marshal
Royal Air Force.
London.
July 26th, I947.

LIST OF ABBREVIATIONS USED IN THE REPORT.

G.H.Q. - General Headquarters of the Commander-in-Chief, Far East.

H.Q.M.C. - Headquarters of the General Officer Commanding, Malaya Command.

A.H.Q. - Air Headquarters of the Air Officer Commanding, R.A.F. Far East Command.

Norgroup - Code name for Group H.Q. controlling air operations in Northern Malaya.

Abdacom - Code name for Supreme Allied Headquarters, S.W. Pacific, which formed on I5th January, I942, and absorbed G.H.Q.

Abdair - Code name of the Air Section of Supreme Allied H.Q., S.W. Pacific.

Westgroup - Code name allotted to A.H.Q. on the formation of Supreme Allied H.Q., S.W. Pacific.

Recgroup - Code name for the Allied Air Reconnaissance Group responsible for seaward reconnaissance of whole sphere of Supreme Allied Command, S.W. Pacific.

Britair - Code name for A.H.Q. in Java after the dissolution of Supreme Allied H.Q., S.W. Pacific.

A.A.C.U. - Anti-Aircraft Co-operation Unit.

A.H.K. -   Headquarters of the Dutch Commander-in-Chief at
             Bandoeng, Java.

A.I.F. -   Australian Imperial Forces.

A.L.G. -   Advanced Landing Ground.

A.M.E. Station -   Air Ministry Experimental Station (Radar).

A.O.A. -   Air Officer in charge of Administration.

A.S.P. -   Air Stores Park.

(B) -   Bomber.

D/F -   Radio Direction Finding.

(F) -   Fighter.

(F.B.) -   Flying Boat.

F.E.C.B. -   Far East Combined Bureau - a combined service
             intelligence organisation for obtaining intelligence, under
             Admiralty administration, throughout the Far East.

(G.R.) -   General Reconnaissance.

I.E. -   Initial Equipment.

I.R. -   Immediate Reserve.

M.U. -   Maintenance Unit.

M.V.A.F. -   Malayan Volunteer Air Force.

N.E.I. -   Netherlands East Indies.

[N.F.] -   Night Fighter.

O.T.U. -   Operational Training Unit.

P.R.U. -   Photographic Reconnaissance Unit.

R.T. -   Radio Telephony.

R. & S.U. - Repair and Salvage Unit.

S.A.O. -   Senior Administrative Officer.

S.A.S.O. -   Senior Air Staff Officer.

(T.B.) -   Torpedo Bomber.

V.H.F. -   Very high frequency radio.

SECTION I.

PRE-WAR PREPARATIONS

SCOPE AND FUNCTIONS OF THE ROYAL AIR FORCE, FAR EAST.

By mid-summer 1941 the geographical area of the Far East Command, Royal Air Force, included Hong Kong, Borneo, Malaya and Burma; then, embracing Ceylon, it stretched across the Indian Ocean to Durban and Mombasa.

2. The main functions of the Command were firstly to protect the Naval Base in Singapore, and secondly, in co-operation with the Royal Navy to ensure the security of the trade routes in the Indian Ocean and South China Sea. The Headquarters of the Command was in Singapore.

3. In November 1940, Air Chief Marshal Sir Robert Brooke-Popham was appointed Commander-in-Chief, Far East. He was responsible for operational control and general direction of training of all British land and air forces in Malaya, Burma and Hong Kong, for co-ordinating the defences of those territories; and for similar responsibilities for additional British Air Forces it was proposed to locate later in Ceylon, the Indian Ocean and the Bay of Bengal. He set up his headquarters at the Naval Base in Singapore where he was provided with a small operational staff, but no administrative staff.

4. The formation of G.H.Q. in no way relieved the Air Officer Commanding, Royal Air Force, of his responsibility (which was now within the policy laid down by the Commander-in-Chief) for ensuring the effective co-operation of his Command with the Naval and Military Commands throughout the area, nor did it alter his position vis-à-vis these Commands or the Air Ministry and the several Civil Governments with which he dealt.

THE BASIS OF DEFENCE IN THE FAR EAST.

General Plan.

5. The general defence plan was based on an appreciation written by the Chiefs of Staff in July 1940. Briefly stated, this paper laid down that defence was to rely, in the absence of a Fleet, primarily on air power.

The Chiefs of Staff recognised that, for the defence of the Naval Base, it was no longer sufficient to concentrate upon the defence of Singapore Island but that it had become necessary to hold the whole of Malaya. Their intention now was to replace, by the end of 1941, the existing establishment of 88 obsolete and obsolescent aircraft by an air strength of 336 modern first-line aircraft backed up by adequate reserves and administrative units. This strength was allocated to the defence of Malaya and Borneo and to trade protection in the N.E. half of the Indian Ocean; it did not include aircraft necessary for the defence of Burma.

6. On the basis of this C.O.S. paper, the three Services in Malaya produced a tactical appreciation, which became the agenda of a conference held at Singapore in October 1940 attended by representatives from all Commands in the Far East. This conference recommended that the C.O.S. figure of 336 aircraft should be increased to 582, which it considered the minimum strength of Air Forces required to meet defence commitments in the Far East. The Chiefs of Staffs' reply on this point stated "we agree that 582 aircraft is an ideal, but consider 336 should give a fair degree of security taking into account our experiences in Middle East, Malta, and Air Defence of Great Britain". The conference also recommended that until the additional air forces were provided, the Army in Malaya should be substantially reinforced.

7. Meanwhile, talks had been initiated between the British, U.S.A. and Dutch Staffs with the object of obtaining concerted action in the event of war breaking out with Japan. After the appointment of the Commander-in-Chief, Far East, in November 1940, further Allied conferences were held in Singapore. By April 1941 agreed general plans had been drawn up.

Allied Air Plans.

8. For the purpose of planning, it was assumed that the Japanese would not be able to attack simultaneously at several widely dispersed places in the Far East, in particular that they would not challenge the combined British, American and Dutch might. It was assumed, therefore, that Allied air forces would be able to reinforce one another. Preparations for mutual help were to be made as follows:-

(*a*) For Malaya to reinforce the N.E.I. - 4 Bomber Squadrons, R.A.F.

(*b*) For N.E.I. to reinforce Malaya - 3 Bomber and 1 Fighter Squadrons, Dutch Army Air Service.

(*c*) For the Philippines to reinforce Malaya - All U.S. Army and Navy Air Service Units available, but only if the Philippines were evacuated.

Each service accepted responsibility within its own territory for providing the necessary bases, where stocks of bombs, petrol and lubricants, peculiar to the respective air forces which might use them, were to be laid down.

9. Further matters of importance which were settled at these conferences were:-

(*a*) Responsibility for air reconnaissance over the South China Sea; this was co-ordinated and defined.

(b) Allied cypher and signal procedure.

(*c*) Allied Naval/Air recognition signal procedure.

10. Concurrently with the above, the Far East Command R.A.F. was authorised to provide the means for operating general reconnaissance aircraft in the Bay of Bengal, Ceylon and the Indian Ocean.

Implications of the Plans.

11. Here it is opportune to stress the implications of the expansion programme authorised by the Chiefs of Staff; for the mere statement that the strength was to be raised from 88 obsolete or obsolescent aircraft to 336 modern types conveys no true impression of the extensive preparatory measures required before this force could be accommodated and operated.

12. It should be remembered that until the new policy had been decided by the Chiefs of Staff, defence had been largely confined to the vicinity of Singapore Island: thereafter it included the whole of Malaya.

13. The first step was the construction of bases. Sixteen new ones had to be found and built in Malaya, a country largely covered with secondary jungle remote from human habitations. Of the bases in existence in the colony 5 needed modernisation and 2 reconstruction. Concurrently, construction of new maintenance, repair and storage units was necessary, also throughout the colony.

Fighter defence had to be built up *ab initio;* none whatever had existed hitherto. In addition to bases for fighter squadrons, provision was necessary for an extensive radar system, for a modernised Observer Corps expanded on a primitive one already existing, for communications throughout the colony, and for Fighter Headquarters to control the whole.

At the same time, 8 new bases had to be built in Burma and 3 in Ceylon. Refuelling bases for flying boats were needed at numerous islands in the Indian Ocean from the Andamans to the coast of Africa.

14. The second step was to provide the authorised increase - the new units, the new aircraft; the ancillary services and the staffs for operating them on modern lines; and finally the modern equipment, supplies and local reserves for all.

15. The third step was to train the whole Command in conjunction with the Navy, Army and Civil Defences under the circumstances existing in the Far East, and concurrently to introduce up-to-date methods of operating.

16. The whole presented a truly formidable expansion programme, made still more formidable by the fact that time was short. The end of 1941 was the date by which the Chiefs of Staff planned for the expanded force to be ready for war. A combination of circumstances was, however, to result in realisation falling far short of the mark, dominating all being the prior and acute claims of the war in Europe, and the Middle East.

ACTION TAKEN IN MALAYA TO IMPLEMENT PLANS

Development of Air Bases
Problems of construction

I7. The siting of aerodromes in Malaya was mainly influenced by the topography of the country. A rugged, heavily forested mountain chain runs down the centre of the peninsula cutting off the eastern and western coastal belts from each other until Johore is reached at its southern end. Much of both coastal belts is covered by a medley of broken hills; the rest consists of plains planted with rubber and paddy, or of potential mining sites. Rainfall is heavy throughout the year, increasing as the central mountain range is approached. Constant cloud over this range handicaps flight from one side of the peninsula to the other. Consequently, in order to provide reconnaissance over the South China Sea, from which direction the threat to Malaya by sea was greatest, a number of aerodromes had to be sited on the East Coast.

I8. Workable sites were difficult to obtain. Every effort was made throughout I94I to accelerate construction, but progress was not as rapid as had been hoped, despite the fact that, in some cases, sites involving a minimum of work were selected at the sacrifice of operational requirements.

I9. There were II separate provincial government authorities in Malaya concerned with the acquisition of land; negotiations with each had to be separate. In the earlier stages, delay occurred owing to misunderstanding of the land acquisition legislation; later, emergency powers of acquisition were invoked and this source of delay ceased.

20. Mechanical plant was very short. That which was available was in poor condition, whilst, there were few personnel qualified to operate or maintain it, a combination which constituted a primary handicap to progress.

2I. Labour generally throughout Malaya was insufficient to meet the needs of the defence expansion programmes of the three Services, and later of the Civil Government. A permanent Labour Committee existed but its function was, in practice, mainly limited to controlling wages in order to eliminate expensive and wasteful competition between the three fighting Services and Government departments. The powers of this Committee were limited; all labour was voluntary, not conscripted, and no control could be exercised over the rates paid by civilian firms. By mutual agreement, however, it was possible to arrange a certain priority of employment of the labour available; and this was exercised to the benefit of the Royal Air Force in Kelantan State (in N.E. Malaya).

To improve the labour situation, negotiations were opened with the Civil Government in May, I94I, for forming locally enlisted works units to be clothed in uniform and officered by Europeans. Approval was obtained in August, I94I, and the matter was then put to the Air Ministry, but by the time final sanction was given it was too late to be effective. Fortunately an aerodrome construction unit arrived from New Zealand at the end of October, I94I. It did excellent work.

22. Most R.A.F. sites were in remote and sparsely populated spots to which it was

necessary first to build roads. Native labour had to be collected, conveyed to the spot and housed. When this had been done it was still necessary to carry to the area almost all the building material required.

23. Much effort was necessarily diverted to anti-malarial measures, which had to be put in hand concurrently with construction in order to protect labour from epidemic. On completion, drained areas had to be maintained and oiled.

24. Supplies of material fell far short of the total needs of the services and civil departments. A Joint Priorities Committee was established in the Spring of 1941. It sat regularly and allocated supplies in accordance with the priorities decided from time to time. During the latter half of 1941, some shortages became particularly acute. Metalling material for runways was also always particularly short, a serious matter on aerodromes constantly subjected to tropical rainfall, which in itself was a major handicap to rapid construction.

25. It is clear, therefore, that the problems which confronted the Air Ministry Works Department were as numerous and complicated as any encountered in other theatres in wartime. That it did excellent work does not alter the fact that it was severely handicapped in executing quickly a very large and urgent programme of expansion by the absence, particularly during the early stages, of the accelerated administrative procedure which the situation demanded.

State of Construction, 1st December, 1941

26. The locations of R.A.F. Stations and Establishments in Malaya and Singapore Island, together with remarks about their state of completion a few days before war broke out in the Far East, are shown in Appendix "A."

27. Of the occupied bases in Malaya, both Alor Star and Kota Bharu were old civil grounds with little room for dispersal. The buildings at Alor Star had been constructed on the old R.A.F. peace-time layout and were congested and too near the runway. This station was high in the priority list for reconstruction when opportunity offered. Both stations were in the forefront of operations in the first days of the war; their deficiencies proved a great handicap.

28. The old bases, and the first of those built on the new programme, had no form of camouflage. The ground had first been deforested and no attempt had been made to use natural surroundings or irregular outlines to obtain concealment. They stood out stark and bare, against the surrounding country. This was largely due to failure, before 1940 to realise, not only in the Far East but in Europe also, the need for dispersal and camouflage on the scale which war experience proved to be necessary. In later bases, excellent concealment was obtained by retaining natural surroundings, avoiding straight lines and using a type of construction which, amongst the trees, was indistinguishable from the native huts. Financial considerations, however, continued to prevent the acquisition of sufficient land for effective dispersal.

29. Dispersal areas and splinter-proof pens at aerodromes in Malaya were arranged on what was then thought to be an adequate scale based on:-

(*a*) The scale of attack in accordance with the information then available about the Japanese Air Services.

(*b*) The ultimate scale of A.A. defences to be provided at each aerodrome.

(*c*) The development of a fighter defensive system.

By the Ist December, I94I, however, neither time nor resources had permitted satisfactory development of the fighter system, and few anti-aircraft weapons were available. The Commander-in-Chief, Far East, had laid down that each aerodrome was to be protected by eight heavy and eight light A.A. guns. At no aerodrome in Malaya was this scale approached; on the outbreak of war, some aerodromes had no A.A. guns at all (for details see Appendix A, Column 5 (*b*)).

30. Each base was provided with a supply of road metalling and labour for the repair of aerodrome surfaces in the event of damage by enemy attack. The reason for mentioning this apparently trivial point will become clear later.

Ancillary Construction

3I. In addition to aerodromes the following important works were either completed or in hand on the Ist December, I94I:-

(*a*) Combined Army/Air Operations Room: This was completed and occupied by H.Q. R.A.F. Far East Command (A.H.Q.) and H.Q. Malaya Command (H.Q.M.C.) at Sime Road, Singapore.

(*b*) Alternative Combined Army/Air Operations Room: Provided because of the above-ground vulnerable position of the main Combined Operations Room.

(*c*) Fighter Control H.Q. in Singapore: This was ready for occupation. It had an operations room, a filter room, a W.T. station, etc.

(*d*) A.M.E. Stations: The ultimate intention was to have 20 Radar Stations throughout Malaya. Six stations only, all in the vicinity of Singapore Island, were completed by the Ist December, I94I.

(*e*) Radio Installation and Maintenance Unit: This was partially completed at Ponggol, Singapore.

(*f*) Ammunition Park: Construction at Batak Quarry, Singapore; it was occupied although extensions were in progress.

(*g*) Storage of Petrol:

(i) Reserve storage accommodation for 6,500 tons of aviation petrol was under construction at Woodlands North, Singapore.

(ii) Reserve storage accommodation for 7,500 tons of aviation petrol at Port Dickson was more than 50 per cent. complete.

(iii) Reserve storage accommodation for 930 tons at Kuantan was completed.

(*h*) Universal Holding Unit: This was completed and was occupied by I52 M.U. at Bukit Panjang, Singapore; extensions were in progress. This reduced the congestion and concentration of stores held at Seletar.

(*i*) Engine Repair Depot and Universal Holding Unit: This depot was completed at Kuala Lumpur, provided with its own railway siding and occupied by No. I53 M.U. It was designed to service squadrons based in North Malaya and so to reduce further the congestion and concentration which had hitherto persisted at Seletar.

Allied Reinforcement Arrangements
U.S.A. Reinforcements from the Philippines

32. The actual number of aircraft that might be expected in Malaya, should the evacuation of the Philippines occur, was of necessity indefinite; so was the amount of equipment peculiar to the U.S. Naval and Army Air Services which might accompany them.

33. Reconnaissances were carried out and dispersed moorings planned for a total of 20 reinforcing Catalinas of the United States Naval Air Service. A provisional plan for maintaining them was also prepared.

34. The Commander-in-Chief ruled, in September, I94I, that four bases were to be prepared for accommodating B.I7's of the United States Army Air Corps; two in the North and two in the South of Malaya. Gong Kedah and Butterworth in the North, Tebrau and Yong Peng in the South, were selected. Extensions of the runways to 2,000 yards at each were put in hand but only those at Gong Kedah were completed by the time war came.

Dutch Reinforcements from N.E.I.

35. In the mutual reinforcement programme arranged with the Dutch Army Air Service, it was assumed that:-

(*a*) Three Bomber Squadrons (27 Glenn Martins would be based at Sembawang)

(*b*) One Dutch Fighter Squadron (9 Buffaloes) would be based at Kallong: and plans were made accordingly.

36. The Dutch Squadron and Flight Commanders concerned visited these stations, toured Malaya and were given a short course in R.A.F. operational methods. Appropriate stocks of Dutch bombs were procured.

37. The Dutch Naval Air Service had been allotted, in the initial seaward reconnaissance plan, responsibility for the area Kuantan - Great Natunas - Kuching (B. Borneo). To execute this task, it had to base a Group (3 Catalinas) of Flying Boats at Seletar. Provision was made for this; and stocks of petrol and moorings were also laid down at Kuantan. The Group remained under Dutch operational command.

38. Liaison Officers of the Dutch Army Air Service and the Royal Air Force were interchanged and were attached to A.H.Q. in Singapore and at Dutch Army Air H.Q. in Java respectively.

Preparations within R.A.F., Far East Command.

Role of Squadrons in War.

39. In July, 1941, a memorandum was circulated outlining the role of squadrons in war, and training syllabi were issued. Strict supervision was imposed to ensure that the fullest training value was obtained in all exercises and that the maximum number of practices of different kinds was arranged whenever a training flight was undertaken.

Preparation of Initial Reconnaissance Plan.

40. Seaborne invasion from the N.E. constituted the main threat to Malaya. A reconnaissance plan was therefore drawn up to detect its approach at the maximum distance, responsibility for its execution being divided amongst the Allies. R.A.F. Far East Command was allotted responsibility for the area Kota Bahru - Southern tip of Indo-China - Great Natunas - Kuantan. A reconnaissance plan was prepared accordingly. Its execution necessitated the employment of one G.R. (Hudson) Squadron based on Kuantan and one based on Kota Bahru. The use of two Catalinas was superimposed to ensure an overlap with the Dutch area immediately to the South. Squadrons were exercised in this plan from their war stations.

41. When the Japanese occupied Indo-China in July, 1941, A.H.Q. queried the fact that this reconnaissance plan made no provision for searching the Gulf of Siam, but G.H.Q. confirmed that the limited reconnaissance force available must be concentrated initially upon the more likely area of approach.

Concentration of Squadrons in War.

42. In accordance with the principle that squadrons were to be concentrated in the defence of whatever area was threatened, alternative locations for squadrons, dependent on the axis of attack, were prepared.

Transition to a War Footing.

43. In the past, a considerable number of code words had been issued, each governing the action of units in various kinds of emergency. As a whole, they were most confusing and liable to result in unco-ordinated action. To rectify this situation, G.H.Q. instructed all Commands, in May, 1941, to prepare for three "degrees of readiness" and laid down the general principles governing each. A.H.Q. took the opportunity to issue Units with an exact description in detail of the action to be taken

on promulgation of these degrees of readiness. The transition to a full war footing was thereby made smooth and rapid.

Co-ordination of Night Flying Arrangements.

44. Before the autumn of 1941, arrangements for night flying had not been co-ordinated, each Unit employing its own method of laying out a flare path and other lighting. A standardised procedure was drawn up in November, 1941, as it was essential to ensure that all squadrons could operate by night with confidence and could use any aerodrome in the Command.

Establishment of Air Corridors.

45. Air corridors "in" and "out of" Singapore were established and promulgated, whilst a standardised procedure for "approach" to all aerodromes in the Command was issued in July.

Establishment of Operations Rooms.

46. Operations rooms were opened at each base as it became available for use, the ideal aimed at being that squadrons on arrival should find the same layout, information and procedure as that which existed at their parent aerodromes. This was designed to avoid the delay and disorganisation caused by the necessity of transferring material and documents: it speeded up the efficiency of operations.

Mobility of Squadrons.

47. A high degree of mobility, was necessary for squadrons to fulfil their laid-down role as the primary defence of the Far East in general, and of Malaya in particular, But the composition of the forces allotted to the Far East included no transport aircraft; and although A.H.Q. drew attention to the deficiency on several occasions no aircraft could be provided. The Dutch Army Air Service had a fleet of some 20 Lodestars and promised assistance, provided their own circumstances permitted. In the autumn of 1941, some Lodestars were borrowed, and selected squadrons were practised in the organisation required for moving.

48. A shortage of M.T. in Malaya made the position more serious. Orders for the M.T. required were placed in the U.S.A. but they could not be met in time. There was no M.T. unit in the Command nor were there sufficient spare vehicles to form a Command pool. Individual units were themselves below establishment in M.T.

DEVELOPMENTS IN HONG KONG.

49. No Air Forces were allotted for the defence of Hong Kong. There was a station flight at Kai Tak on the mainland for target towing purposes, but apart from local reconnaissance no war role was envisaged or arranged for this flight.

50. In the summer of 1941, an urgent request was received from Hong Kong pressing for some fighter aircraft because of the great support they would give to civilian morale. This request could not be met. In case it should prove possible later to meet the request for fighter aircraft, a Fighter Sector Control room and Radar Stations were sited and plans were prepared for the provision of a fighter defensive system.

DEVELOPMENTS IN BRITISH BORNEO.

51. Facilities for land planes in British Borneo were confined to one aerodrome and one landing ground, at Kuching and Miri respectively. The former was not large enough for bomber aircraft but its extension was in hand when war broke out. Flying boat moorings were also laid in the river nearby. There were no A.A. defences, but a battalion of the Indian Army, with H.Q. in Kuching, was located in Borneo for the protection of the aerodrome and landing ground areas and the Miri oilfields.

DEVELOPMENTS IN BURMA.

52. As a result of the Singapore Conference in the autumn of 1940 (para. 6), the findings of which were generally endorsed by the C.-in-C. Far East on his arrival, the Government of Burma co-operated actively in constructing and developing the eight air bases, and additional satellite strips, considered necessary for air operations from Burma. These bases stretched from Mergui on the Tenasserim Coast in a half circle round the Siamese frontier to Lashio in the Northern Shan states. In anticipation of approval, Flight Lieutenant C.W. Bailey, Inspector of Landing Grounds at A.H.Q., had been sent by A.H.Q. to Burma in November, 1940. He had drawn up plans for extending old, and constructing new, aerodromes. Further, in co-operation with the Government of Burma, arrangements had been made for reorganising the Public Works Department so that it could undertake supervision of construction, which was immediately begun.

53. In March, 1941, H.Q. No. 221 Group (Commander, Group Captain E.R. Manning) was established at Rangoon to develop these bases and to command the Air Forces located in Burma. Although the Group staff was very small, progress was so good that all bases were completed by the end of 1941 with accommodation at each for some 450 all ranks. Facilities for dispersal were reasonable, pens being provided, as were some satellite strips. There was a measure of A.A. protection in the Rangoon area but none elsewhere.

54. Co-operation with the Army in Burma was excellent. Army H.Q. in Burma and No. 221 Group R.A.F. were in close proximity and the G.O.C. and his staff could not have done more to assist the R.A.F. in its preparations. From the outset of planning in November, 1940, the G.O.C. was in the picture of R.A.F. development. The raising

and training of aerodrome defence troops was consequently conducted in parallel with construction.

55. During 1940, an air observer system was developed by the G.O.C. under the active direction of the Postmaster-General. From the outset, its functions were made clear and, despite difficulties of training, it developed and operated usefully on the outbreak of hostilities; control of it passed to the R.A.F. on the formation of 221 Group Headquarters. One Radar Station was completed at Moulmein and two others in the Rangoon area were nearing completion when war broke out. A Fighter Control Operations room was designed and constructed in Rangoon.

56. No. 60 (B) Squadron (Blenheim I's) ex India, was located at Rangoon from February, 1941. G.H.Q. considered it important to ensure some measure of fighter defence at Rangoon; consequently, pending the availability of an established fighter squadron, half of No. 60 was re-equipped with Buffalo fighters for the period August-October, 1941, somewhat handicapping the squadron's operational efficiency. As soon as No. 67 (F) Squadron (Buffaloes) in Malaya was fully trained it was transferred to Rangoon; the transfer took place in October, 1941.

Heavy demands on No. 60 (B) Squadron for communication flights occupied much of its flying effort; and although it had a very high standard of flying in monsoon conditions over Burma, it became desirable to transfer the squadron to Malaya to bring it operationally up-to-date in practice. All its aircraft and crews were therefore sent to Kuantan, the new Air/Armament Station of the Command, where they arrived shortly before the Japanese attacked Malaya.

57. In addition there was a flight of six Moths used for training Burma's Volunteer Air Force. The aircraft of this flight were allotted the role of maintaining communications and carrying out certain limited reconnaissance.

58. A plan was drawn up in co-operation with the Army in Burma, the object of which was to destroy communication facilities in the Siamese Isthmus. Land forces were to advance across the isthmus and conduct a "burn and scuttle" raid on port, rail and air facilities at Prachuab Kirrikand. Their arrival was to synchronise with air attack from Malaya under A.H.Q. arrangements.

59. The question of the Command of the forces in Burma had been raised on more than one occasion. Those who considered it from the angle of India's defence recommended that control should be by India. A.H.Q. supported the opposite view, namely the retention of Burma in the Far East Command, because it considered that effective co-ordination of the air forces operating from Burma and Malaya in defence of the Far East could only be achieved by unified command. This view was accepted. In the actual event, however, the control of Burma had to pass to India seven days after war broke out - at 0630 hours on 15th December, 1941.

60. Finally, reference must be made to the American Volunteer Group under Colonel Chennault, who was given all possible assistance, particularly in relation to maintenance, training and accommodation. R.A.F. Base, Toungoo, the training aerodrome for the Force, was visited by the A.O.C. and Staff Officers from A.H.Q.; officers who had had fighter experience in Europe were sent to lecture and to assist

in training. Excellent work was later done by this Force, in co-operation with the R.A.F., in the defence of Burma.

DEVELOPMENTS IN N.E.I.

Dutch Borneo.

6I. In accordance with the mutual reinforcement plan, the Dutch allocated Sinkawang and Samarinda in Dutch Borneo for use as bases for four R.A.F. bomber squadrons. Each of these bases was to be provided with accommodation for two bomber squadrons and to be stocked in peace with supplies peculiar to the Royal Air Force. Their only method of supply was by means of transport aircraft provided by the Dutch, who deliberately avoided making roads to them through the dense jungle in which they were situated, and which thus remained an undisturbed defence. By December, Sinkawang was ready and had been inspected by the C.O. and Flight Commanders of one of the squadrons allocated to it. Samarinda was not ready.

Sumatra.

62. Permission was also obtained from the Dutch in the summer of I94I, to reconnoitre all aerodromes in Sumatra. This was required because A.H.Q. anticipated that, in the event of war, Sumatra would be required for:

(*a*) An alternative air reinforcement route from India owing to the vulnerability of the old route to Singapore via Burma and N. Malaya once the Japanese had penetrated into Siam.

(*b*) Potential advanced landing grounds for operations against the flank of a Japanese advance down Malaya.

The main preoccupation was therefore with those aerodromes which were situated in the Northern half of Sumatra.

63. As the result of this reconnaissance, extensions to the grounds at Lho'nga and Sabang were put in hand to make them suitable for modern aircraft.

64. Assistance was also given to B.O.A.C. to organise facilities at Sabang for the operation of an alternative seaplane route Rangoon - Port Blair - Sabang instead of the normal one via Bangkok.

Java.

65. Visits were paid to Java by a number of staff officers from A.H.Q. who thus gained useful information about Dutch maintenance establishments and resources generally.

DEVELOPMENTS IN INDIAN OCEAN AND BAY OF BENGAL.

66. A memorandum was prepared about June, I94I, and issued by A.H.Q. detailing the bases to be developed in this area; their status was defined and priority of provisioning was laid down. By December, I94I, the position was as follows:-

Andamans and Nicobars - at Port Blair and Nancowrie, moorings and petrol had been laid, and limited accommodation constructed for operating flying boats. Port Blair was also prepared by B.O.A.C., with R.A.F, assistance, as an alternative to the route Rangoon - Penang.

Ceylon - H.Q. No. 222 Group was established, with a joint Naval/Air Ops. Room, at Colombo.

> *China Bay - one flight of Vildebeeste was located here for target towing and local reconnaissance. This station was being developed as a permanent base for one G.R. Squadron and one F.B. Squadron, the accommodation for which was practically completed.*

> *Ratmalana - Aerodrome was being constructed for one G.R. Squadron.*

> *Koggala - was being developed as the main base for flying boats operating in the Indian Ocean. Accommodation for one Squadron was nearly ready.*

Christmas Island	}	
Cocos Islands (Direction Island)	}	
Maldives (Male)	}	Fuel and moorings had been
Seychelles (Mahe)	}	laid and limited accommodation
Chagos (Diego-Garcia)	}	provided for operating flying
Mauritius	}	boats at each of these places.
Tanganyika (Lindi).	}	
Durban	}	Were being developed as permanent
Mombasa	}	bases for one F.B. Squadron each.

Much credit is due to the Air Ministry Works Department for the great volume of construction which had been carried out in these outlying parts of the Command, as well as for that executed in Malaya, in a relatively short space of time despite many and considerable handicaps.

OPERATIONAL EFFICIENCY OF UNITS IN MALAYA.

Intelligence Organisation.

67. In June, I94I, A.H.Q., had no Intelligence Organisation of its own. All air intelligence personnel and records in the Far East had been centralised in the Combined Intelligence Bureau (F.E.C.B.) which functioned under the control of C.-in-C. China Station. Theoretically it served, inter alia, the needs of A.H.Q. In practice,

however, its means for obtaining air information throughout the Far East was totally inadequate; its staff was insufficient to cope fully even with G.H.Q. Air Intelligence requirements; and although the information it possessed was always available to A.H.Q., F.E.C.B. had not the means of supplanting the missing intelligence machinery at A.H.Q.

Representations were therefore made by A.H.Q. of the need for a thorough intelligence system throughout the Command. About July, a conference was held with G.H.Q., who wished to create a second Combined Intelligence Centre to serve the joint needs of A.H.Q. and H.Q.M.C. A second joint organisation of this nature would not, however, have been suitable for building up the Intelligence organisation required throughout the Command at all levels from A.H.Q. downwards. This view was accepted.

An establishment for an Intelligence organisation for the whole Command was drawn up and submitted to the Air Ministry, and in late autumn, in anticipation of approval, personnel were made available locally and were appointed to H.Q. and Units. The nucleus organisation thus formed was fortunately in being when hostilities broke out, but its development was backward, and in particular the information it had collated for briefing crews was scanty.

68. According to intelligence current in the Command, the efficiency of the Japanese Naval Air Units was known to be good, but that of their Army Air Units was not high despite the fanatical valour of their personnel.

This wrong assessment of their Army Air Units was partly due to the fact that the system for collecting intelligence throughout the Far East was only sufficient to enable F.E.C.B. to obtain incomplete air information, and the reliability of most of this was far from high. And it was partly due to the fact that A.H.Q., stations and squadrons possessed only the embryonic intelligence organisation already referred to: the result was that such intelligence as the Command received was not effectively digested, promulgated or acted upon.

A particular outcome of this state of affairs, which was destined to have far-reaching consequences in Malaya, was that the personnel of the Command remained unaware up to the outbreak of war of the qualities of the Japanese fighter squadrons, whose Zero fighters were to prove superior in performance to our own fighter's. This naturally affected training in our Squadrons, particularly in the tactics to be adopted by our fighters.

The need for an Operational Training Unit.

69. The Air Ministry had been unable to approve requests made during the year to establish an O.T.U. in Malaya. But in September, 1941, owing to the fact that large numbers of personnel required operational training, A.H.Q. established a makeshift O.T.U. at Kluang from the resources available in the Command. Its role was:-

(*a*) To train pilots for Fighter Squadrons who had been, for some time, arriving from New Zealand direct from Service Flying Training Schools, and who therefore lacked operational training.

(*b*) To convert personnel of No. 36 and No. 100 (T.B.) Squadrons from Vildebeestes to twin-engine aircraft in anticipation of their re-equipment with Beauforts.

(*c*) To train pilots from New Zealand on twin-engine aircraft to fill vacancies in Bomber Squadrons.

Training aircraft were provided, from Wirraways thrown up by No. 21 (F) Squadron when it re-armed with Buffaloes, and by Blenheims borrowed from No. 34 (B) Squadron. The Wing Commander Training at A.H.Q. (Wing Commander Wills-Sandford) was appointed Commanding Officer. The Unit had to be disbanded on 8th December, on the outbreak of hostilities, but it had completed most valuable work.

Lack of Armament Training Facilities.

70. Up till October 1941, the only armament training facilities in the Command were on Singapore Island, and at an improvised air range near Penang. Maximum use was made of the Singapore ranges, but they were very insufficient to meet requirements. In October 1941, the new Command Armament Training Station at Kuantan was opened, but there was time for one squadron only to complete a course before the outbreak of war.

71. The air firing situation was particularly unsatisfactory. There was an acute shortage of target towing aircraft, and the few available were slow.

Lack of Transport and Communication Aircraft.

72. The lack of transport and communication aircraft was acutely felt during the pre-war period when training was all important. G.H.Q. and H.Q.M.C. had frequently to ask for communication flights, aircraft for which had necessarily to be found, mainly by G.R. Squadrons. Although such requests were pruned and co-ordinated, flights were nevertheless sufficiently frequent to interfere seriously with the training of squadrons, many of whose vital flying hours were thus expended. Furthermore, visits to subordinate units by A.H.Q. staff had to be correspondingly curtailed.

Fighter Squadrons.

73. In June-July 1941 a Fighter Group Operational Cadre was formed to take over the training and operation of all fighter aircraft in Singapore: the Senior Officer (Group Captain E.B. Rice) at the same time being appointed Air Defence Co-ordinator, Malaya.

74. The following Fighter Squadrons, with an establishment of 16 I.E. and 8 I.R. Buffaloes, were formed on the dates shown:-

No. 67 (F) Squadron, formed at the end of March 1941. The Squadron and two Flight Commanders to be appointed from U.K., the remaining pilots from bomber squadrons within the Command. Establishments were completed with pilots from New Zealand F.T.S.'s. The Squadron was transferred to Burma in

October 1941, shortly after it had been passed as operationally efficient (para. 56).

No. 243 (F) Squadron, formed in April, 1941. Personnel were found as in the case of No. 67 Squadron, but a slightly higher proportion were F.T.S. personnel.

No. 453 (F) Squadron, formed October 1941. The Squadron and two Flight Commanders were appointed from U.K. This was an R.A.F. "infiltration" squadron[1] filled from F.T.S's in Australia. Some of the personnel were not entirely suitable for a Fighter Squadron, and the Squadron Commander was in Australia selecting replacements when war broke out.

No. 488 (F) Squadron, formed in October-November 1941. The Squadron and two Flight Commanders came from U.K. This was an R.N.Z.A.F. infiltration squadron and was filled from F.T.S's in New Zealand with excellent material; but their standard of flying on arrival was backward. This squadron had taken over the aircraft on which No. 67 (F) Squadron had trained, and many of these were in poor condition.

No. 21 (F) Squadron, R.A.A.F., which had formed as a General Purpose Squadron in Australia and moved into the Command in 1940, was in October 1941 re-equipped with Buffaloes and converted into a Fighter Squadron, with 12 I.E. and 6 I.R. aircraft. The Squadron had been previously equipped with 2-seater Wirraways, some of which were returned to Australia, the remainder being retained to assist in training Nos. 453 (F) and 488 (F) Squadrons. It will be observed, therefore, that the pilots of this squadron had not been selected originally for fighter aircraft, and some were not in fact entirely suitable for this role.

75. The main role of the Buffalo Squadrons was "day defence" only, primarily of the Singapore area, but night flying training was instituted to ensure that pilots could take off before dawn and land after nightfall.

76. Except for No. 488 (F) Squadron all the above squadrons were considered operationally trained by the outbreak of war. No.488 (F) Squadron was deficient in squadron and flight training and was not passed as operationally ready until the latter half of December 1941. Training and assessment of operational readiness had, however, been based on an under-estimation of the enemy. The tactics thus taught and practised proved unsuitable and costly against the Japanese Navy "O" fighter, which was greatly superior to the Buffalo in performance. Moreover, advanced training had suffered because, prior to the formation of an O.T.U. in September 1941 (see. para. 69), all pilots had joined their squadrons without having received individual operational training.

77. The standard of gunnery in all squadrons was low because:-

(*a*) Towing aircraft were very slow and there were very few of them,

(*b*) Cine gun equipment was lacking,

(*c*) Continual trouble was experienced with the .5 gun and synchronising gear. This was largely overcome by local modification by October 1941. Nevertheless, pilots were still not confident about their armament when war overtook them.

78. The Buffalo had a disappointing performance. It was heavy and underpowered and had a slow rate of climb. Maintenance was heavy, which meant a low standard of Serviceability. Wastage during training was high, and many of the aircraft in Squadrons suffered from rough handling. The Buffalo had no V.H.F. radio and the maximum range of R.T./W.T. was 9 miles, being frequently less when atmospherics were bad. Intercommunication between aircraft was unreliable.

79. There was one multi-seat fighter squadron in the Command, No. 27, a night fighter squadron equipped with Blenheim I's. Aircraft were old and in poor condition and were thus of limited value in a night-fighting role. Its conversion into a bomber squadron, for which personnel were available, came up for consideration but could not be adopted owing to the need for retaining a night fighter unit.

Observer Corps.

80. In July, 1941, control of an existing Observer Corps system was transferred from the Army to A.H.Q. It had been organised chiefly as part of the civil air raid warning system, and needed a great deal of development for use in an active air defence system. The personnel were enthusiastic, but unfortunately little time was available to train them in their new duties. It was found impossible to establish the necessary Observer Posts in the jungle-clad mountainous country of Central Malaya where there was, therefore, a serious gap in the warning system. Observer Corps Operations Rooms were established at Kuala Lumpur and Singapore, and were linked up to the Dutch system in the Rhio Archipelago to the South, but difficulty was experienced in organising the whole through lack of existing telephone communications in Malaya and to an acute shortage of telephone material and equipment.

Radar Stations.

81. The approved policy of priority for the development of radar facilities was:-

(*a*) Singapore Island.

(*b*) The East Coast of Malaya.

(*c*) Penang and the West Coast.

All Stations were to look seaward with only restricted overland cover behind, the hinterland being covered by the Observer Corps.

82. By December, 1941, four stations were operating - Mersing, Tanah Merah Besar (in East of Singapore Island), Bukit Chunang (S.E. tip of Johore) and Tanjong Kupang (S.W. tip of Johore). A further station, Kota Tingi, in Johore was nearly ready and was being accelerated partly to close the gap down the central portion of Malaya. A sixth, at Kota Bahru, the most northerly point on the East Coast of Malaya, had been built but no radar had yet been installed.

The general position was, therefore, that there was fair cover for Singapore but little elsewhere.

Fighter Operations Room.

83. A Fighter Group Operations Room in Singapore was designed, constructed and occupied by December - almost too late to do more than break the ice of training its staff and fighter squadrons in the intricate art of fighter defence. It had an operational staff only, no administrative branches: it was in fact an offshoot of the Air Staff of A.H.Q.

Fighter considerations in general.

84. Thus an Air Defence system had been organised by the time war came. Whilst it was by no means as efficient as it would have been if the resources, time and equipment had not been so short, yet it provided Singapore with a scale of defensive effort which was by no means insignificant. Great credit is due to those who achieved this result with so short a time for preparation, outstanding amongst whom was the late Group Captain E.B. Rice.

Bomber and G.R. Land-abased Squadrons.

85. There were two light bomber and two landplane G.R. squadrons in Malaya:-

No. 62 Squadron (Blenheim I) - Alor Star.

No. 34 Squadron (Blenheim IV) - Tengah.

No. I (R.A.A F.) Squadron (Hudson II) - Kota Bahru.

No. 8 (R.A.A.F.) Squadron (Hudson II) - Sembawang.

These two types of squadron, Bomber and G.R., are bracketed together because, owing to the small size of the total force, specialisation was impracticable. Although the Hudson squadrons were the main oversea reconnaissance force, the Blenheims had also to be trained in these duties. Similarly, both types of squadron had to be trained in all types of bombing over the sea and over the land, both by day and by night.

86. From May, I940, until the Spring of I94I there had been severe flying restrictions imposed on Blenheim Squadrons owing to the lack of spares in the Command. During this period, hours were restricted to 5 hours flying monthly per I.E. aircraft. In Spring, I94I, selected pilots had to be withdrawn from these squadrons to assist in the formation of the first two fighter squadrons in Malaya.

87. Nos. I and 8 (G.R.) Squadrons R.A.A.F. had reached a higher standard of training, but it was necessary for the Australian Air Board to withdraw crews as they became fully trained and to replace them by untrained crews, the former being required for the further expansion of the R.A.A.F. in Australia.

There was, therefore, in both types of squadron a wide variation between crews in the degree of their training, and especially in their efficiency in night flying, in which a high degree of skill was desirable for operating through the violent tropical thunderstorms which prevail over Malaya at night during the monsoons.

Torpedo/Bomber Squadrons.

88. There were two Torpedo/Bomber Squadrons, Nos. 36 and 100, both based on Seletar, the personnel of which were highly trained and of long experience. But their aircraft, Vildebeestes, which had a speed of 90 knots and an action radius of 180 miles, were obsolete. With modern aircraft these highly trained squadrons would have been invaluable, especially in the first days of the war. But their approved re-armament programme, with Beauforts, had been delayed by technical complications in production in Australia. In their training more emphasis was placed on the torpedo than the bomb, because their main role was to attack enemy convoys well out to sea. Facilities for them to operate with torpedoes from Kota Bahru had been established.

Flying Boat Squadron.

89. There was one Flying Boat Squadron in the Command, No. 205 Squadron, based at Seletar with a detachment in Ceylon.

90. The squadron did not have sufficient trained crews. When its establishment was raised from 4 I.E. Singapore III's to 6 I.E. Catalinas, no additional crews were available. These were therefore trained by the squadron. One or two trained crews were based in Ceylon for work in the Indian Ocean, where, unfortunately, two crews were lost in accidents in September/October, 1941.

Photographic Reconnaissance.

91. Long-range Hurricanes had been requested for photographic purposes but were not available. In November, 1941, a P.R.U. with 2 I.E. (later raised to 4) aircraft was formed in Singapore with Buffaloes drawn from local resources, and personnel were trained in photographic reconnaissance. By stripping all armament and non-essential equipment and providing additional tankage, the Buffaloes range was increased to 1,400 miles. The formation of this flight proved a most valuable asset to the resources of the Command. Concurrently a Photographic Interpretation Unit was formed.

Malayan Volunteer Air Force

92. The Malayan Volunteer Air Force had flights located in Singapore, Kuala Lumpur, Ipoh and Penang. Its miscellaneous collection of about 30 aircraft comprised two Rapides, one Dragonfly, and a number of Moths and Cadets. Flights were organised for transport duties under A.H.Q., and for communication and reconnaissance in affiliation with Army formations. Moths were fitted with 20-lb. bomb racks and pilots were trained in their use, but none of the aircraft could be fitted with defensive armament. The enthusiasm of the unit was most marked and it made excellent progress.

Elementary Flying Training School

93. An E.F.T.S. had been established at Kallang in 1940 from local resources: instructors and technical personnel were obtained from units stationed in Malaya, and from the M.V.A.F., whose club aircraft were made available for its use. It did excellent work. A number of pilots were trained by it, some subsequently serving in other theatres of war and some in Malaya.

Signals Organisation

94. Signals organisation was generally backward. There was a shortage of W/T equipment, particularly of mobile sets.

Teleprinter lines existed between A.H.Q. and aerodromes on Singapore Island, but not between A.H.Q. and aerodromes up the peninsula.

There were two telephone lines from Singapore to N.W. Malaya and one to the N.E. and east. These were quite insufficient for joint needs, Army, Air Force and Civil, and all passed through civil exchanges. Secraphones were very few and were apportioned between the services in a strict order of priority.

There was no V.H.F., which limited the effective control of fighters to about 10 miles; this was still further limited by atmospherics during thunder periods.

Centralisation of Work at A.H.Q.

95. Appendices A and C will show how many, and scattered, were the units in the Far East Command and how varied were their duties by land, sea and air: their administrative problems were correspondingly numerous and varied.

A degree of decentralisation of work from A.H.Q. was achieved by:-

(*a*) forming, in March, 1941, No. 221 Group H.Q., with a small staff in Rangoon, to which all work of formations in Burma was decentralised.

(*b*) forming, in March, 1941, No. 222 Group H.Q. in Ceylon for controlling flying boat operations based on Ceylon: this Group had no administrative staff, so that A.H.Q. continued to administer direct all its bases throughout the Indian Ocean.

(*c*) forming, in August, 1941, No. 224 (Fighter) Group H.Q. in Singapore, for supervising fighter training and air defence arrangements within Singapore Island: this Group also had no administrative staff (*see* para. 83) so that A.H.Q. dealt direct with its stations and units on administrative matters.

But this was the limit of decentralisation. It resulted in a heavy load of centralised work at A.H.Q. This was particularly felt once the expansion programme began to take effect. It fell heavily enough on Air Staff, but still more so on the Administrative Staff and on that of the Air Ministry Works Department.

The need for an A.O.C. Malaya, with an appropriate staff to whom to decentralise local problems in Malaya, became increasingly apparent during 1941, but it was not found possible to meet this need.

This state of affairs was complicated by a shortage of qualified officers - (*see* next paras.) - caused by the demands of the war in Europe.

Supply of Officers for Staff and Administrative Duties

96. Officers for filling vacancies on the staff of the greatly expanded A.H.Q. and at the new stations were largely found by enrolling personnel from Australia and New Zealand. More than 140 were obtained from this source. It was possible to give them only a short disciplinary course combined with a brief survey of their duties. Their average age was 45. They naturally varied much in their qualifications. The remainder, more than 50 in number, were obtained by commissioning local business men in Singapore; most of them just before, but some after the outbreak of war in the Far East. For them no training was practicable. The majority of these officers were willing and able, but their value was limited owing to their unavoidable lack of service knowledge, experience and training.

97. Of the regular officers, there were few with Staff experience; and the brunt of the work consequently fell on the few. The work of A.H.Q. was increased by the inexperience of officers at stations, which needed more "nursing" than is normally the case.

98. The strain fell particularly heavily upon the A.O.C., who despite the great increase of work which was caused by the expansion of his Command, undertook much supervisory staff work which he would have delegated to others in normal circumstances. He did so in order to ensure that it was properly carried out. This reacted unfavourably on his health, which was poor even when he arrived. He overtaxed his strength, and was a tired man when war descended on Malaya.

Equipment Problems

99. The equipment position was bad in many important items. Except for Buffaloes there were no reserve aircraft whatsoever in the Command. There was an acute shortage of spares, especially for Blenheims and even more for Hudsons, and also of all tools. M.T. was very short, with an effect on mobility that has already been noted. Small arms were insufficient to arm more than a proportion of R.A.F. personnel. All these were items which were badly needed during 1941 in Europe and Africa, and the requirements of the Far East had necessarily to take second place.

On the other hand, stocks of petrol and bombs laid in with G.H.Q.'s particular assistance were good.

Personnel Problems.

100. The following major personnel problems affected the efficiency of the Command:-

(i) There were no reserve aircrews.

(ii) The strength of the Command in airmen was doubled during the last six months of 1941, but most of these reinforcements came direct from training establishments in the United Kingdom and needed further training. At the same time, a number of time-expired airmen were relieved, with the result that at the outbreak of war three quarters of the strength was new to Malaya.

(iii) A number of the reinforcements were posted to the Command in anticipation of the completion of the expansion programme. They arrived faster than the expansion programme could absorb them. A surplus was therefore built-up, which was employed partly as infantry guards on Singapore Island to relieve the Army of such duties.

(iv) Special courses were organised in musketry and, in the expectation of the defection of native employees, in cooking and M.T. driving.

Other Measures.

I0I. The following preparatory measures were also put in hand:-

(i) An Air/Sea Rescue Service was organised. It was given six launches, and some light aircraft of the Malayan Volunteer Air Force. It commenced operations in mid-December, I94I, and altogether saved the lives of 24 aircrew. Five of the launches were provided locally.

(ii) A Bomb Disposal Unit was formed in June, I94I, to serve all Services, including Civil Defence.

(iii) Welfare Services were organised. Holiday facilities were provided at Butterworth and Malacca. A fund of 20,000 dollars was raised and used by a central welfare committee. Mobile canteens were made and equipped locally.

(iv) Arrangements were made for hospitalisation and evacuation of R.A.F. sick and wounded; these facilities were provided by the Army everywhere except within the bounds of R.A.F. stations, where they were provided by the R.A.F.M.S.

RELATIONS WITH G.H.Q.

I02. The Commander-in-Chief, Far East (Air Chief Marshal Sir Robert Brooke-Popham) being an Air Force officer naturally took a keen personal interest in the R.A.F.; and relations between G.H.Q. and A.H.Q. were correspondingly close.

I03. But G.H.Q., had no administrative staff, only an operational one. It was felt at A.H.Q. that the lack of the former prevented the latter from fully appreciating the day-to-day impacts of the multitude of administrative problems which arise in the subordinate command during the period of preparation for war. Without this full experience the operational staff must have found it hard to grasp in their full significance the difficulties which faced the subordinate command. This statement is made in no critical spirit of G.H.Q.'s staff, who were sympathetic and helpful about matters which came their way, but merely to disclose the weakness of an organisation which is vested with operational responsibility but which has no administrative branches of its own through which to keep its finger on the pulse of the administrative problems arising at the level of the subordinate command.

I04. The difficulty which G.H.Q. experienced in obtaining full and accurate intelligence about air matters in the Far East has already been referred to (paras. 67 and 68). Its estimation of the Japanese Naval Air Arm was high. Its estimation of the Japanese Army Air Forces was that, although numbers were great and they were known to possess long-range fighters, efficiency was low and that, despite their fanatical bravery, reasonable opposition would turn them from their targets.

I05. To turn to the enemy's probable actions. For most of I94I, G.H.Q. was in doubt about the date and place Japan would challenge the Allied position in the Far East. The chance that she would do so early was reduced when in the late summer of I94I the U.S.A. decided to reinforce the Philippines. Further support for this view came from the Chinese, who, in the early summer of I94I, considered that the next major Japanese effort would be made on the line Hanoi - Kunming to cut the Burma road. Nevertheless, throughout the summer, G.H.Q. stressed the need for pressing on with all preparations necessary for meeting an attack, realising that Japan could strike at her selected moment so long as no British fleet was based on Singapore.

Early in November, I94I, the C.-in-C. re-affirmed the opinion that Japan was unlikely to attack Malaya now that the N.E. monsoon had set in, because the heavy surf, which beats upon the beaches of the East coast of Malaya throughout the season, would make it difficult for assaulting troops to land. It was reckoned that the attack, although possible, was unlikely before February, I942, by which time the monsoon would be over.

By 22nd November, however, the Japanese intention of further aggression had become clear to the C.-in-C. (para. I40).

I06. Meanwhile, during the autumn, preparations were initiated for giving air support to the Chinese, on the assumption that the next Japanese move would probably be towards Kunming. It was the intention to form an International Air Force, consisting of R.A.F. bombers and fighters and of an American Volunteer Group under Col. Chennault, to operate in South China. Administrative preparations were begun, petrol stocks were sent to the Chinese airfields, and bombs and components were prepared for despatch. Early in November, I94I, an R.A.F. Commission was sent from the Far East to investigate operational conditions: it included several senior staff officers of A.H.Q. and the station commander of Tengah, who were still away when the Japanese landed in Malaya. The project was no small commitment for A.H.Q., as G.H.Q. had insufficient staff to undertake all the detailed planning and administration which would normally have been done at the level of the higher command: much of this had necessarily to be done by the staff of A.H.Q., which was already insufficient for dealing with its own work (paras. 96-98).

CO-OPERATION WITH NAVY.

I07. A.H.Q. had advocated a combined Naval/Air Operations Room in Singapore to co-ordinate and control the seaward air operations of the Command with the naval forces of the Commander-in-Chief, China Station, but it was decided that such co-operation would be better conducted on a G.H.Q./C-in-C. China Station level. To ensure liaison, however, a Naval liaison officer was attached to A.H.Q., for some months before war broke out: later a Naval air-maintenance officer was added.

I08. It was recognised that should a full scale Eastern Fleet be based on Singapore, many detailed arrangements for liaison would become necessary. But a full Eastern Fleet staff could not be assembled owing to a shortage of naval officers; indeed, it was considered unwise to assemble one in Singapore before the situation cleared, namely until a fleet arrived in Singapore and its future role could be estimated.

Five days after the outbreak of war, however, a staff of junior Naval officers was provided for watchkeeping in the Army/Air Combined Operations Room, a step made possible when additional officers were thrown up by the loss of H.M.S. Prince of Wales and Repulse. They proved adequate for subsequent needs, but had the Far Eastern Fleet remained in being in Singapore it would have been necessary to strengthen them in order to provide the close co-operation which would have been then essential.

I09. Co-operation with the C.-in-C., East Indies was close, and a Combined Operations Room had been established at Colombo. There was real understanding of the problem facing the R.A.F., particularly the difficulty, owing to shortage of flying boats, of assisting in the control of sea communications in the Indian Ocean. There were never more than two Catalinas, often only one, available in Ceylon for this work.

II0. Invaluable memoranda about Naval/Air matters, obtained by G.H.Q. from Coastal Command and other sources, were available at A.H.Q. These were collated and revised to suit local conditions and a Far East Command handbook was printed. It was issued in August, I94I, to R.A.F. Units and Naval Commands for guidance in carrying out all types of operations over the sea.

CO-OPERATION WITH ARMY IN MALAYA.

Close Support.

III. Co-operation with the Army in Malaya had not been highly developed or exercised in the past. No. 2I Squadron, R.A.A.F., when it was equipped with Wirraways, had been regarded in part as an A.C. Squadron, and had carried out some limited exercises with troops in the field. The methods of co-operation which had been practised were, however, not in line with recent developments in Europe and the Middle East.

II2. There was much material available at A.H.Q. of the experience gained in other

Commands but, owing to lack of staff, the lessons had not been digested. Active steps were taken to remedy this, and instructions for the joint information of Army and Air Force Units to cover the operations of bombers in support of troops were produced and issued in September, I94I, with the concurrence of the G.O.C., Malaya Command. Similarly, instructions were compiled and issued for joint information to cover the operations of fighter aircraft employed on tactical reconnaissance.

II3. Classes were started for training aircrews in Army organisation and tactics. Each bomber and fighter squadron in the Command was affiliated to an Army formation and was allotted so many flying hours per month for combined training. But owing to lack of signals equipment, communications were improvised and primitive, which severely restricted the type of support which could be given.

Aerodrome Defence.

II4. For some years before war broke out, considerable difference of opinion had existed between the Army and the R.A.F. about the siting of aerodromes on the peninsula of Malaya. Until I937 the army's policy had always been to have the East Coast undeveloped as far as possible because insufficient forces were available to defend the long coast-line.

The need then arose for aerodromes on the peninsula well forward of the Naval base at Singapore. Sites for them on the eastern side of the mountainous backbone of the peninsula, hitherto undeveloped, were essential for two reasons. Firstly to obtain maximum air range over the sea to the east, from which direction the threat to Malaya was greatest. Secondly in order to avoid the cloud-covered mountainous backbone which in those days, effectively prevented aircraft based on aerodromes on the west side from operating over the sea on the east, the threatened, side.

Unfortunately there had been insufficient co-operation on the spot in Malaya between the two interests involved, with the result that some of the sites selected were tactically weak to defend. But in the Spring, of I94I the necessary full co-operation was established between the services on the spot, in this important matter of selecting aerodrome sites.

II5. However, those aerodromes that were located in the Singapore fortress area were well sited for defence. They were, furthermore, covered by the fortress A.A. umbrella. Sabotage was regarded as the main threat, particularly during the initial stages of war.

II6. The defence of aerodromes on the mainland was a more difficult problem. There were three areas of major importance:-

(i) *N.E. Malaya* - Kelantan aerodromes.

(ii) *E. Coast Malaya* - Kuantan.

(iii) *N.W. Malaya* - Kedah aerodromes.

It was some of these aerodromes which had been sited in tactically weak positions for the reasons given in para II4. Some were even in exposed positions close to favourable landing beaches. The desirablility, from an administrative view-point, of selecting sites close to existing communications and sources of labour had contributed to this dangerous situation.

It meant that the Field army on the west coast, down which the main enemy thrust on land was expected to develop, had to make large detachments to protect aerodromes on the east coast.

II7. On the east coast, the direct defence of aerodromes was the prime function of the Army. Accordingly, the Brigadiers at Kota Bahru and Kuantan were, by agreement between the A.O.C. and G.O.C., appointed Aerodrome Defence Commanders in their respective areas. The arrangement, with certain safeguards, worked well and resulted in good co-ordination of the resources available for defence.

II8. The training, experience, quality and numbers of the forces manning the defences of the aerodromes other than those at Kota Bahru and Kuantan were much under requirements. They were mostly Indian State troops, who had had little opportunity for training in this specialised work. A further handicap was a general paucity of weapons of all kinds, particularly A.A. guns and their equipment.

II9. Every effort was made to improve the defences of aerodromes against ground attack. Old tanks, armoured cars and any form of weapons were sought from other Commands and from the U.S.A. H.Q.M.C. did its best, but the men and weapons required could not be made available. Assistance was also given by the Naval Base and later by the Dutch. Financial authority was given by the A.O.C. in the autumn to put in hand urgent work on defence schemes of mainland aerodromes without the necessity for prior reference to A.H.Q.

I20. Joint Army and R.A.F. Aerodrome Defence Boards were set up about July, 194I, throughout Malaya to co-ordinate defence schemes; and thereafter care was taken to ensure that the defence aspect was considered at the outset when new aerodrome construction was put in hand.

I2I. Full instructions were prepared and issued to guide local Commanders in preparing denial and destruction schemes, and arrangements were made for obstructing airfields not in use.

I22. The first two major aerodrome defence exercises were held in the late summer in the presence of large numbers of Army spectators for instructional purposes: one was held at Tengah with the co-operation of Fortress troops, and one at Kluang in Johore with the Australian Division.

I23. Finally, in conjunction with A.H.Q. and H.Q.M.C., G.H.Q. produced about this time a handbook on aerodrome defence which detailed the probable scale of attack to which each would be subject, the minimum defences required, and the priority of their provision.

Co-operation with A.A. Defences.

I24. During the latter half of 194I, A.A. equipments rapidly increased in number, in Singapore especially, and demands for air co-operation for the training of A.A. crews multiplied accordingly. Special aircraft for the purpose were few, so A.A. defence exercises were combined with other forms of training in order to make full use of flying hours. Nevertheless, this resulted in many flying hours of operational units, which were all too precious for their own training, being expended on this work; yet the A.A. Defence Commander's requirements were never approached.

Photographic Survey.

I25. Photographic survey of large areas in Malaya for both the Army and the Civil Government was another commitment which had to be met. It necessitated the allotment and training of a special flight.

Joint Army/Air Planning: Operation "Matador".

I26. During July, I94I, a staff conference was held at H.Q. Malaya Command which was attended, it is believed, by representatives of G.H.Q., H.Q.M.C., III (Indian) Corps and A.H.Q. It was called to consider a War Office project for the occupation of the Kra Isthmus by a joint Army/R.A.F. force from Malaya, the object of which was to deny to the Japanese the port and aerodrome facilities in it (which, if exploited, constituted the main threat to Malaya) by meeting and defeating him on the beaches.

I27. It was evident that the development of the aerodromes there by the Siamese could only be linked up with the spread of the Japanese over Indo-China and their increasing influence in Bangkok. It appeared obvious that they would soon contain all the facilities required by Japanese aircraft, particularly fighters, which would then be able to support effectively landings in Southern Siam and Northern Malaya. The A.H.Q. representative was consequently in favour, at the least, of a raid to destroy these facilities.

I28. The conference finally adopted a plan for seizing and holding the Singora area and "The Ledge" position on the Patani Road, but only if:-

(*a*) a minimum of 24 hours' start of the enemy was available;

(*b*) the opportunity occurred during the North-East Monsoon, (October/March), i.e., when the Japanese would not be able to employ tanks off the roads.

This plan was known as "Operation Matador". The A.H.Q. representative was strongly pressed to state definitely what squadrons would be available to take part in it, with particular reference to breaking the railway running south from Bangkok, along which it was presumed a Japanese advance would come concurrently with any attack from seaward. An offer was made of a Singapore III flying boat to carry a demolition party to some suitable stretch of railroad near the Siamese coast, but it was not taken up. Otherwise, no definite allotment could be made because of the meagre air strength in Malaya and its many commitments. The force available would have to depend on the situation at the time and on the priority of tasks allotted by G.H.Q. to the R.A.F. as a whole. From the Army point of view this was a most unsatisfactory reply.

I29. At this conference the chances of executing this operation successfully appeared remote, dependent as it was upon most accurate timing for forestalling the Japanese in the Singora - Patani area and for doing so without precipitating war with Japan or appearing to be the aggressors. Moreover, there seemed some doubt whether sufficient Army resources would be available to carry it out. However, the benefits deriving from it, if it were successful, were held by G.H.Q. to outweigh the risks involved. Careful and comprehensive plans were therefore drawn up with the Army to move elements of the IIIrd (Indian) Corps by road and rail to Siam, with the R.A.F. supporting from aerodromes in Northern Malaya with such units as the situation at the time permitted.

Control of Army/Air Operations.

130. For the control of operations in support of the Army in the north of Malaya A.H.Q. formed a nucleus Operations Group H.Q. It was designated Norgroup. Its functions were:-

(i) to command such air forces as A.H.Q. might allot to it from time to time;

(ii) to advise G.O.C. IIIrd Corps on air matters and to control such air forces as might be allotted to IIIrd Corps. A Combined IIIrd Corps/Norgroup Headquarters was established at Kuala Lumpur with an advanced H.Q. close to Butterworth.

Norgroup Headquarters was formed in July, I94I, was exercised in its functions, and was then disbanded. But it was held in readiness for mobilization when required.

131. On Singapore Island, under G.H.Q. orders, a combined Army/Air Operations Room was constructed alongside A.H.Q. in Sime Road, Singapore. It was ready for use just before war broke out. (As it was very vulnerable the construction of an alternative Operations Room was put in hand.) It functioned at the level of A.H.Q. and H.Q.M.C. Thus G.H.Q. and C.-in-C. China Fleet were not represented in it. Five days after the outbreak of war, however, the latter provided a staff to represent him in it.

SUMMARY OF SITUATION, 22ND NOVEMBER, I94I.

General pre-war situation.

132. Enough has been said to paint a pre-war picture of the Command and, it is hoped, of the vigorous efforts which were made to carry out the expansion programme authorised by the Chiefs of Staff. But the fact remains that by December, I94I, the R.A.F. Far East Command was not yet in a position to fulfil its responsibility of being the primary means of resisting Japanese aggression. The calls of the war in Europe had allowed it to develop only a fraction of the necessary strength.

133. Re-equipment of squadrons had not taken place and was not likely to do so in the near future; Vickers Vildebeestes were still our main striking strength. Buffalo fighters had arrived, it is true, but their performance and armament were disappointing, and inexperienced pilots were still being trained to man them.

134. The aerodromes in Northern Malaya on which so much was to depend,

especially during the early stages of the war, had none of the pre-requisites of secure air bases for occupation in the face of the enemy. The number of fighters available was very inadequate for providing effective fighter cover. Both heavy and light A.A. guns were quite insufficient. Dispersal arrangements for aircraft and their protection from blast were not as complete as was planned. And, in the absence of an adequate air raid warning system the aerodromes were open to surprise attack.

I35. But the role of the Command remained constant. It was not practicable to alter it.

It was:-

(*a*) To find the enemy at sea as far away from Malaya as possible: then

(*b*) to strike hard and often,

(*c*) to continue attacks during the landing operations: and

(*d*) in co-operation with the Army to delay his advance.

While real progress had been made in fitting the Command for its allotted tasks, deficiencies were still apparent in almost every aspect of its functions.

I36. The Army in Malaya was also still weak: its additional interim strength considered necessary to ensure security until such time as the air strength had been built up was not present in the Colony. It was over-extended in its dispositions, a state of affairs forced upon it by its many and widely scattered commitments.

I37. In a country like Malaya it was not difficult for the enemy to obtain information about our forces. He was well served by a long-established system of agents.

I38. For their part the Japanese had already occupied Indo-China. While no certain information could be obtained by F.E.C.B. it was patent that they were building up their forces there and were preparing operational facilities in Siam. Japanese reconnaissance flights over Borneo and Malaya had become so frequent by October I94I that a section of Buffaloes had been stationed at Kota Bahru to curb those over Malaya.

Deterioration of the Political Situation.

I39. During I94I, relations with Japan became increasingly strained. The attitude of the Siamese Government was doubtful. It professed great friendship for Britain and sent two goodwill missions to Singapore to cement this friendship. Nevertheless, the Japanese continued to reconnoitre Siam and to make preparations for utilising that country as a Base: they accelerated the provisioning of the aerodromes at Singora and Patani, which they also extended to make them suitable for modern aircraft. As November I94I progressed, evidence of Japanese activities increased until, on 22nd November, I94I, the information at G.H.Q's disposal was sufficient to indicate that Japan was about to embark upon a further major venture in South-East Asia. The resultant action initiated by G.H.Q. is dealt with in Section II.

SECTION II.

NARRATIVE OF OPERATIONS BASED ON MALAYA.

EVENTS FROM 22ND NOVEMBER TO MIDNIGHT 7-8TH DECEMBER, 1941.

G.H.Q. Appreciation of the Situation - 22nd November, 1941.

140. On 22nd November, 1941, G.H.Q. issued their appreciation of the situation. Briefly, this appreciation considered that any further major action by Japan in the near future would take place from South Indo-China against Siam, rather than from North Indo-China against the Burma road. G.H.Q. did not, however, disregard the possibility of Japan making a "gambler's throw" against Malaya or even against Singapore itself. G.H.Q. concluded that the most likely operation which would be called for on our part in the immediate future would be to the set plan "Matador," namely an advance by our land forces into South-East Siam. A.H.Q. was accordingly instructed to make all preliminary moves and to be ready to support "Matador" at 72 hours' notice, and was informed that this support for "Matador" was to take precedence over the preparations then being made for an International Air Force to operate in South China. A.H.Q. was also warned that the full reconnaissance plan for detecting the approach of a sea expedition against Malaya might be ordered later.

141. The Order of Battle of the Far East Command in Malaya at this stage is shown in Appendix "C".

Action taken by A.H.Q. to implement Operation "Matador".

142. A.H.Q. immediately adopted the following measures for reinforcing N. Malaya.

(*a*) Formed Headquarters Norgroup which assembled on 24th November at Kuala Lumpur alongside Headquarters IIIrd Indian Corps. The Commander appointed was Wing Commander R.G. Forbes, Station Commander, Alor Star, in the absence of the Commander designate, Group Captain A.G. Bishop, who was away in South China.(See para. 106.)

(*b*) Ordered No. 2I (F) Squadron, R.A.A.F., to move to Sungei Patani: move to be completed by 25th November.

(*c*) Put No. 34 (B4) Squadron (Blenheim IV) at short notice to move to Alor Star.

(*d*) Made provisional arrangements for the move of No. 60 (B) Squadron aircraft (7 Blenheims) out of Kuantan to Butterworth. This move would be necessary if the reconnaissance plan were to be brought into force because No. 8 (GR) Squadron, R.A.A.F. would require the accommodation at Kuantan for carrying out that plan.

(*e*) Instituted certain other precautionary measures, including the warning of our fighters at Kota Bahru, Sungei Patani and Singapore of the action they were to take if unidentified aircraft were sighted. Training was allowed to proceed with certain restrictions.

I43. Commander, Norgroup, was informed that the following squadrons would support Operation "Matador":-

(*a*) No. 62 (B) Squadron (Blenheim I) from Alor Star.

(*b*) No. 34 (B) Squadron (Blenheim IV) from Alor Star.

(*c*) No. 2I (F) Squadron, R.A.A.F. (Buffaloes) from Sungei Patani.

(*d*) No. 27 (NF) Squadron (Blenheim I) from Sungei Patani.

Further G.H.Q. Appreciation - 28th November, I94I.

I44. On 28th November, I94I, G.H.Q. informed A.H.Q. of a report received from Saigon that the Japanese intended landing troops in South Siam on Ist December, I94I. G.H.Q. stated that the Japanese had adequate forces to carry out such a move but placed no great credence in the report. They assumed that if such a convoy did leave Saigon it would travel at I5 knots or less and anchor off Nakwan or between Singora and Patani on the S.E. coast of Siam on the morning of either the 30th November or Ist December. G.H.Q. ordered A.H.Q. to despatch air reconnaissances daily with a view to locating this Force, but in view of the danger that the Japanese might, by holding out a bait, induce us to strike the first blow and thus appear to be the aggressors, with consequent loss of American sympathy, stated that "a striking force will not be ordered to attack the convoy if found". From this day until 3rd December, reconnaissances proceeded without event except that on the 3rd December two large cargo boats were sighted.

I45. On 29th November, I94I, the notice for Operation "Matador" was shortened by G.H.Q. from 72 hours to I2 hours.

Assumption of No. 2 Degree of Readiness.

146. On Ist December, I94I, G.H.Q. ordered the Command to be brought to "No 2 degree of readiness". The promulgation of this degree informed the Command that "the international situation was deteriorating" and brought it into a position to operate at short notice. Inter alia it meant that the full air raid warning system was to be brought into being.

Arrival of Naval Reinforcements.

147. On the 2nd December, H.M.S. "Prince of Wales" and H.M.S. "Repulse" arrived in Singapore as a counter-measure to continued Japanese encroachment in the South-West Pacific. The former wore the flag of Admiral Sir Tom Phillips, the new C.-in-C., Eastern Fleet.

Initiation of full Air Reconnaissance Plan.

148. On 3rd December, I94I, orders were issued by G.H.Q. for the full reconnaissance plan to be put into force on the following day. As a result, in the afternoon of the 3rd, a Dutch group of three flying boats arrived at Seletar in accordance with prearranged plans (see para. 37). The reconnaissance areas allotted to the Dutch and British respectively were:-

Dutch: Kuantan - Gr. Natunas - Kuching (British Borneo).

British: Kota Bahru - Southern tip of Indo-China - Gr. Natunas - Kuantan.

An extension of the reconnaissance area into the Gulf of Siam as part of routine reconnaissance was not possible owing to a shortage of aircraft.

The task of executing the British section of the reconnaissance plan was allotted to Nos. I and 8 (GR) Squadrons, R.A.A.F., based on Kota Bahru and Kuantan respectively. Their effort was reinforced by Catalinas of No. 205 (FB) Squadron to fill in gaps and to ensure overlapping the Dutch.

The initiation of the full reconnaissance plan cancelled the special reconnaissance which had been carried out hitherto, and involved the movement of No. 8 (GR) Squadron, R.A.A.F. from Sembawang to Kuantan. Owing to lack of transport aircraft and inadequate land communications, the ground personnel and equipment of this squadron proceeded there by sea.

Reconnaissance period 4th-6th December, I94I.

149. On the 4th December, owing to bad weather, aircraft at Kota Bahru (No. I (GR) Squadron, R.A.A.F.) were unable to operate, but those at Kuantan (No. 8 (GR) Squadron, R.A.A F.) carried out their part in the reconnaissance plan, as did the Dutch, with nothing to report. Reports of the sightings of strange submarines in the reconnaissance area had been received, so a special reconnaissance was carried out by No. 60 (B) Squadron from Kuantan; but it was negative. On this day a Catalina took Admiral Sir Tom Phillips, Commander-in-Chief Eastern Fleet, to Manila.

On 5th December, 1941, bad weather still prevented No. 1 (GR) Squadron, R.A.A.F., at Kota Bahru operating, but again the Dutch Reconnaissance Group and No. 8 (GR) Squadron, R.A.A.F., at Kuantan gave negative reports. On this day a special anti-submarine patrol was maintained by three Vildebeestes ahead of H.M.S. "Repulse" which proceeded at slow speed en route from Singapore to Australia.

On the 6th December, 1941, three crews were despatched to Sourabaya to collect three Catalinas loaned by the Dutch. The anti-submarine patrol in co-operation with H.M.S. "Repulse" was also maintained.

First sighting of Japanese Expedition - 6th December, 1941.

150. On December 6th Kota Bahru aerodrome was serviceable and the full reconnaissance plan was operated. The N.E. monsoon was blowing; its tropical downpours periodically made unaided navigation and accurate ship recognition matters of considerable difficulty.

A Hudson of No. 1 (R.A.A.F.) Squadron, Captain F/Lieut. J.C. Ramshaw, was the first to sight the enemy. He located two approaching convoys:-

(*a*) at 12.12 1 Motor vessel, 1 minelayer and 1 mine sweeper in a position 185 miles, and on a bearing of 52°, from Kota Bahru, steering a course of 310°.

(*b*) at 12.46 1 battleship, 5 cruisers, 7 destroyers and 25 merchant vessels in a position 265 miles, and on a bearing of 86°, from Kota Bahru steering a course of 270°.

Another Hudson of the same squadron shortly afterwards reported another convoy:-

(*c*) at 13.00 2 cruisers, 10 destroyers and 10 merchant vessels in a position 260 miles, and on a bearing of 76°, from Kota Bahru steering 270°.

151. Information about the latter convoy was subsequently amplified to the effect that it contained 21 merchant vessels which were cruising in two lines astern. This amplification was received by telephone at A.H.Q. at 1517 hours.

152. The position of the first of these convoys was such that it had the appearance of having recently rounded Cape Cambodia and was now headed N.W. into the Gulf of Siam. The position of the other two convoys was about 80 miles S.S.E. of Cape Cambodia, the Southern tip of French Indo-China; both were steering west, one slightly ahead of the other. They might, or might not, be following the first small convoy and in turn head N.W. into the Gulf of Siam.

One of the Hudsons had been chased by an enemy aeroplane and there could be no doubt that the Japanese knew that they had been spotted.

153. In the meantime, reports were received of aircraft, apparently Japanese, taking photographs at various points. G.H.Q. confirmed that no offensive action was to be taken by fighters against them, although A.A. defences were given authority to open fire on unidentified aircraft.

154. As a result of the enemy sighting reports, Kota Bahru was instructed to send

Hudsons from No. I (GR) Squadron, R.A.A.F., to shadow the convoys. Catalinas of No. 205 (FB) Squadron from Seletar were ordered to take over this shadowing from the Hudsons, and to maintain it during the night 6/7th December until relieved by Hudsons again in the morning of 7th December.

I55. On receipt of sighting reports, the Command was put by G.H.Q. at "No. I degree of readiness" which meant that it was to be "ready for immediate operations and prepared for enemy attack without prior warning."

Action taken by A.H.Q. on Enemy Sighting.

I56. The following action was taken by A.H.Q. as a result of the reconnaissance reports received:-

(*a*) 7 Vildebeestes of No. 36 (TB) Squadron were despatched from Seletar to Kota Bahru. (9 were ordered but only 7 could proceed). Aircraft were armed with torpedoes on arrival at Kota Bahru.

(*b*) Norgroup was informed that No. 62 (B) Squadron at Alor Star was removed to A.H.Q. control.

(*c*) No. 34 (B) Squadron was retained at Tengah at short notice to move to Alor Star.

(*d*) The one Beaufort[2] still in the Command was moved to Kota Bahru to stand by there for a special photographic reconnaissance required by G.H.Q. (see para. I62).

Attempts to maintain contact with Enemy.

I57. On the afternoon of the 6th December, Hudsons despatched at I620 hours from Kota Bahru to shadow were unable to contact the convoys, and bad weather prohibited relief aircraft being sent. The first Catalina of No. 205 (FB) Squadron left Seletar at I8.30 hours according to programmes to shadow the convoy during the night.

I58. During the late evening of the 6th, scrutiny of reports and records revealed that the Japanese convoys were probably one hour ahead of the positions reported. It was assumed, therefore, that the convoys on rounding Indo-China had turned to the N.W. into the Gulf of Siam, thus passing out of the reconnaissance area (vide para. I52). This, perhaps, appeared at the time to explain why Hudsons despatched to shadow had not contacted the enemy; visibility conditions, however, had been poor.

I59. No reports having been received from the first Catalina despatched to shadow the convoys, orders were issued to a second Catalina, before it took off to relieve the first, that if no contact was established, a search was to be made off the West Coast of Cambodia.

This was done because G.H.Q. considered the convoy had probably anchored at Ko Kong, for which it might be making as the next step towards Siam. The second Catalina left Seletar at 0200 hours on 7th December. After it was airborne it was ordered to keep 10 miles away from the coast of Siam. No report was ever received from this second Catalina, which was afterwards confirmed as having been shot down by the Japanese.

Reconnaissance Plan for 7th December, 1941.

160. For the 7th December, 1941 the Dutch flying boat "Group" and No. 205 (FB) Squadron at Seletar, and No. 8 (GR) Squadron, R.A.A.F., at Kuantan were instructed to continue the set reconnaissance plan covering the more direct line of approach to Singapore in case a further invasion convoy should attack from that direction. Such an attack would have been most dangerous, particularly if it were directed against the beaches in the Mersing/Endau area, where a successful landing would have gravely jeopardised the field army in Northern Malaya and might even have threatened Singapore itself, before the same field army could come to its defence.

But the G.R. Squadron at Kota Bahru was detailed to carry out a special reconnaissance sweep into the Gulf of Siam with the object of re-establishing contact with the Japanese convoys known to be in it.

Vildebeestes were despatched to maintain an anti-submarine patrol ahead of H.M.S. Repulse which had been recalled from Australia.

Events on the 7th December, 1941.

161. Owing to bad weather, it was not until 0645 hours on the 7th that the reconnaissance aircraft from Kota Bahru, of which there were three, were able to take off for a sweep into the Gulf of Siam. Shortly afterwards, owing to rain, low clouds and bad visibility, two of them returned; the third proceeded alone.

162. At 1025 hours the C.-in-C., Far East, visited the Combined Army/Air Operations Room and stated that he:-

(*a*) Wished B.O.A.C. to continue using Bangkok until the last possible moment, and confirmed that flights on the 8th December were to go through Bangkok.

(*b*) Was considering allowing our aircraft to fire at aircraft not established as friendly.

(*c*) Would issue orders shortly for the reconnaissance of Ko Kong anchorage, which he wished the P.R. Beaufort, now at Kota Bahru, to carry out.

163. Shortly afterwards, G.H.Q. issued their orders for the reconnaissance of Ko Kong. The aircraft left Kota Bahru at 1220 hours, but returned at 1445 hours owing to bad weather. During the morning, the Catalina with Admiral Sir Tom Phillips on board returned from Manila.

164. Meanwhile at 1345 hours on the 7th December, A.H.Q. was informed that air reconnaissance from Kota Bahru had sighted a 6,000-8,000 ton cargo vessel in the Gulf of Siam steaming west, and this was followed by a further sighting at 1545 hours,

by a Hudson of No. 8 (R.A.A.F.) Squadron, of one other Japanese merchant vessel steering south. This latter vessel was stated to have a large number of men on deck in khaki.

I65. Two Hudsons from Kota Bahru were immediately directed on a diverging search north of that place and I0 miles off the Siamese coast. At I750 hours one merchant vessel and one cruiser steaming 270° were sighted about II2 miles north of Kota Bahru. The cruiser opened fire on the aircraft. At I848 hours, under conditions of very bad visibility, four Japanese naval vessels, perhaps destroyers, were seen 60 miles north of Patani steaming south.

I66. Owing to subsequent destruction of records, the exact positions of some of the ship sightings mentioned above cannot now be given with any certainty.

Resulting Action.

I67. In consequence of these reports, G.H.Q. decided, late on 7th December, not to put "Operation Matador" into effect that night, and issued orders for B.O.A.C. aircraft to avoid Bangkok and to use the West coast route.

I68. Conditions at midnight 7th-8th December, I94I were therefore:-

(*a*) Contact with the main Japanese convoys located on the 6th had not been re-established.

(*b*) Conditions for air reconnaissance in the Gulf of Siam had been bad, but in the late evening four ships had been sighted off Singora steaming south.

(*c*) "Norgroup," with Nos 2I (F) R.A.A.F., and 27 (NF) Squadrons at Sungei Patani, was standing by in support of IIIrd Corps, but Operation Matador had not been ordered.

(*d*) The following aircraft under the command of the Officer Commanding Kota Bahru were fully armed and ready to take the offensive:-

(i) No. I (GR) Squadron R.A.A.F., and one Section (2) Buffaloes of No. 243 (F) Squadron at Kota Bahru.

(ii) Seven Vildebeestes (No. 36 (TB) Squadron), with torpedoes, at Gong Kedah, to which they had been transferred owing to congestion at Kota Bahru.

(e) The remainder of the squadrons were under A.H.Q. control as follows:-

(i) Reconnaissance:-

No. 8 (R.A.A.F.) Squadron at Kuantan.

No. 205 (F.B.) Squadron at Seletar.

Dutch (F.B.) Group at Seletar.

(ii) Bombers:-

No. 60 (B) Squadron at Kuantan (N. Malaya).

No. 62 (B) Squadron at Alor Star (N. Malaya).

No. 34 (B) Squadron at Tengah (Singapore).

No. I00 (T.B.) Squadron at Seletar (Singapore).

(iii) Fighters:- (decentralised to 224 (F) Group for the direct defence of Singapore).

No. 453 (F) Squadron at Sembawang.

No. 243 (F) Squadron at Kallang.

No. 488 (F) Squadron at Kallang.

The Command was at the fullest degree of readiness, but there was no undue alarm owing to G.H.Q.'s view that the Japanese expedition was directed against Siam.

I69. A.H.Q. decided to send at first light on the 8th December a coastal reconnaissance to the Lakon Roads, north of Singora, to identify whether or not the Japanese had landed in S.E. Siam as forecast in the G.H.Q. appreciation (para. I40).

OPERATIONS FROM 8TH TO 23RD DECEMBER, I94I.

Japanese landing at Kota Bahru.

I70. At midnight 7th-8th December, the weather at Kota Bahru cleared, but the aerodrome surface was extremely boggy owing to heavy rains. About 0030 hours on the 8th, O.C. Kota Bahru rang up A.H.Q. and stated that three ships had been seen by the beach defences. This message was followed by another at 0100 hours confirming the presence of these ships, stating that shelling was taking place and that Brigade H.Q. were being asked to clarify the situation. On this, A.H.Q. ordered the despatch of a single Hudson with flares to see what was happening. Before this could be done, at 0II5 hours definite information came through from Kota Bahru that landing on the beaches by the Japanese had started from 3-5 ships lying three miles offshore.

Orders issued by A.H.Q.

I7I. O.C. Kota Bahru was immediately ordered to take offensive action with all available Hudsons, and to order the Vildebeestes at Gong Kedah to deliver a torpedo attack at first light. It must be remembered that the orders issued to O.C. Kota Bahru as a result of G.H.Q. instructions (para. I44) specifically stated that no offensive action would be taken against the convoy when sighted. He could not, therefore, initiate the first offensive action of the campaign without further orders.

I72. A.H.Q. also issued orders to Nos. 8 (GR), 27 (NF), 34 (B), 60 (B) and 62 (B) Squadrons to take off at first light and attack shipping in the Kota Bahru area whilst No. I00 (TB) Squadron was ordered to proceed to Kuantan on the following morning and standby for orders.

I73. Norgroup was informed that No. 27 (NF) was also to revert to A.H.Q. control, leaving only No. 2I (F) Squadron (R.A.A.F.), for co-operation with IIIrd Corps.

174. The Beaufort at Kota Bahru was instructed to carry out the photographic reconnaissance at first light to Lakon Roads (para. 169)

First Operations against enemy landings at Kota Bahru.

175. At Kota Bahru the first seven Hudson sorties of No. I (GR) Squadron R.A.A.F. had taken off to oppose the landing, and by 0300 hours the two available Buffaloes had been despatched against landing barges entering the river which flows into the sea within the frontage of the beach defences guarding the aerodrome.

176. At 0730 hours on 8th December, the O.C. Kota Bahru gave a resume of the night's operations. 17 Hudson sorties had been carried out, one transport had been destroyed and two others damaged and perhaps sunk. Landing barges en route to the beaches had been attacked and casualties had been inflicted amongst the troops in them. Intensive A.A. fire had been experienced, particularly accurate from a cruiser covering the landing. Two Hudsons had been shot down and a third badly damaged, leaving him still six. One Buffalo had also been hit. The Vildebeestes from Gong Kedah were in the air.

177. Apparently some 8 transports covered by one cruiser and several destroyers had been involved, and O.C. Kota Bahru thought all vessels had now retired to the north. He intended to carry on using the Hudsons for mopping up small craft and beach parties still visible. At 0800 hours, he confirmed that all vessels had retired to the north and that he was mopping up the few small craft left with bomb and machine-gun fire. He added that there had been some infiltration into the Brigade area.

178. Meanwhile the Vildebeestes of No. 36 (TB) Squadron from Gong Kedah, in heavy rain, found the cruiser, delivered an attack with torpedoes which it evaded, and landed at Kota Bahru on their return.

179. Nos. 8 (GR) R.A.A.F., 27 (NF), 34 (B) and 60 (B) Squadrons also arrived on the scene and found little to attack in the area; a signal sent them whilst they were airborne to search further north was not received by all units. One flight of No. 8 (GR) Squadron at least received it but was unable to find the enemy owing to a very heavy rainstorm. Nos. 8 and 60 Squadrons returned to Kuantan, No. 27 to Sungei Patani, whilst No. 34 Squadron landed at Butterworth. All squadrons were ordered to refuel and re-arm.

180. No. 62 (B) Squadron which had also been ordered to attack, not finding any target, proceeded north to Patani to bomb transports there. This squadron (II Blenheim I's) encountered fighter opposition and fairly intensive A.A. fire. It carried out its attack from 8,000 ft. but the results obtained were not seen.

First Air Attack on Singapore.

181. Whilst the first landings had been taking place at Kota Bahru, Singapore had its first air-raid shortly after 0400 hours on the 8th December. Radar detected the approaching raid at a distance of 130-140 miles from Singapore (giving more than 30 minutes warning). Its approach was promulgated from the Fighter Control Operations Room. Unfortunately the staff of this room was unable to obtain any response from

the H.Qs. of the Civil A.R.P. organisation, with the result that the civil population received no effective warning, nor was the Civil Air Defence Scheme put into effective action until it was too late. Some 17 aircraft took part in this raid, the majority of the bombs falling at Seletar and Tengah. At the latter place 3 Blenheims of No. 34 (B) Squadron were damaged and the aerodrome was cratered.

Japanese attacks on Northern Airfields.

182. Between 0730 and 0800 hours, Kota Bahru, Gong Kedah and Machang aerodromes were attacked by bombers and low-flying fighters; except for dummy aircraft, the latter two were unoccupied at the time. These attacks were repeated throughout the day mainly by low-flying fighters, with little effect save in delaying the refuelling and re-armament of aircraft at Kota Bahru.

183. Sungei Patani, Penang and Butterworth in N.W. Malaya were also attacked throughout 8th December by formations of from 27 to 60 bomber aircraft, with serious results. The Japanese used light bombs only, directed against aircraft and personnel; they studiously avoided damaging aerodrome surfaces. Personnel on the spot noted that for the next few days Japanese attacks in this area frequently synchronised with aircraft landing or getting ready to take off. This indicated a leakage of information to the Japanese, but it was never definitely proved that such a leakage actually occurred.

184. There was a particularly serious attack against Alor Star, delivered immediately after No. 62 (B) Squadron had landed after its attack at Patani (para. 180). The aerodrome was first bombed by 27 Japanese aircraft, which then came down low and machine-gunned aircraft on the ground. As a result No. 62 (B) Squadron had only two serviceable aircraft left.

185. Nos. 21 (F) R.A.A.F. and 27 (NF) Squadrons at Sungei Patani also suffered badly and were each reduced to 4 serviceable aircraft; and in consequence of the repeated low attacks on this airfield both squadrons, with their personnel, were withdrawn to Butterworth. It was later learnt that the guns in the Buffaloes had given trouble and were all unserviceable from lack of solenoids. The serviceable Blenheim fighters of No. 27 Squadron had carried out periodic patrols over N.W. Malaya without result. No 34 (B) Squadron at Butterworth was also seriously reduced.

Ground Situation in N.W. Malaya.

186. Aircraft losses from enemy attack thus gravely weakened the air forces available in N.W. Malaya for supporting the army, where the main enemy advance on land was expected to develop. On the 8th there was little enemy air activity against our own ground forces, owing to the enemy's concentration on the bombing of our aerodromes.

187. "Matador" had been cancelled during the morning, and the Army was taking up positions forward of a partially prepared line at Jitra. Covering forces were advancing north and north-east from Kedah province: one to make contact along the line of advance from the Singora area, the other (Krohkol) to occupy what was known

as the Ledge, an important tactical feature, across the Siamese frontier on the Kroh - Patani road, which protected the communications of the force in North Kedah.

The first of these covering forces made contact with the enemy at 2130 hours on the 8th, at Ban Sadao, ten miles inside Siam. The other (Krohcol) reported some opposition from Siamese forces, but continued its advance.

Enemy landings in Singora and Patani area.

188. At 0915 hours on the 8th December the P.R. Beaufort returned from its reconnaissance of the Lakon Roads (para. 174). En route, it had been heavily attacked by fighters and landed in a badly shot up condition, subsequently having to be destroyed. The pilot reported verbally that a large concentration of vessels was landing troops in the Singora - Patani area. His photographs were flown back to Singapore by the remaining Buffalo fighter. Shortly afterwards, Norgroup, under orders from IIIrd Corps, despatched 3 Buffaloes of No. 21 (F) Squadron R.A.A.F. on a tactical reconnaissance to Singora. This reconnaissance confirmed the presence of the main convoy in the Singora area and also revealed a force of about 60 Japanese aircraft, mainly fighters, on Singora aerodrome.

Squadrons driven out of aerodromes in N.E. Malaya on 8th December.

189. It is now necessary to return to the Kota Bahru area. Heavy fighting had been going on on the beaches all day, and reserves had been put in to try and regain the beaches by counter attack. At 1245 news was received at A.H.Q. of the landing of further troops from one transport covered by a cruiser and several destroyers. The Station Commander at Kota Bahru had at 1200 hours despatched 4 Hudsons and 3 Vildebeestes to deal with this threat. It transpired later that the report of this further landing was false, but aircraft continued mopping up barges and machine gunning beaches. At 1530 a Hudson from Kota Bahru bombed the railway bridge across the South Golok River west of Kota Bahru, but with doubtful success; the crew, however, observed that the line itself had been partially destroyed already at a point further eastward.

190. Towards 1600 hours reports received at A.H.Q. indicated that the situation on the ground had become serious. The Station Commander reported that penetration had been made up to the aerodrome boundary, and that aircraft and personnel had come under sporadic fire. On his representation A.H.Q. approved the evacuation of the aerodrome. All aircraft were ordered to Kuantan, personnel and stores to proceed by train, whilst the denial scheme was to be put in operation. This was successfully achieved, and 5 Hudsons and 7 Vildebeestes arrived at Kuantan. This withdrawal as far south as Kuantan was unavoidable because Gong Kedah, the only aerodrome in the Kota Bahru area that might have been used, was virtually undefended and was in a very exposed situation near the coast.

191. During the day, various reports of suspicious vessels off the East coast had been received, necessitating reconnaissances which, however, were all negative.

Summary of situation on the evening of the 8th December, 1941.

192. That night (8th-9th December) the situation was, therefore:-

(*a*) The Japanese expedition to capture the Kota Bahru aerodrome area was succeeding; and the use of aerodromes in this area was now denied to the R.A.F. Our troops in the area were thus without close air support.

(*b*) The Japanese main forces were landing unimpeded in the Singora - Patani area, covered by air operations against our aerodromes in N. Malaya. Their advance towards the north-west frontier of Malaya had already begun, and our forward troops had made contact. The shipping at Singora had not been attacked, partly because the aircraft at Kota Bahru were fully engaged locally by the time it was reported, and partly because heavy Japanese air attacks against our virtually undefended aerodromes in N.W. Malaya had seriously reduced the squadrons available on them.

(*c*) The Japanese Air Force was already operating in strength from Singora aerodrome. From the narrow view point of the Royal Air Force, it was apparent that the cancellation of Operation "Matador" was to have a far-reaching influence on air operations in Northern Malaya.

Air Operations in North West Malaya - 9th December, 1941.

193. In the N.W. aerodrome area, enemy air attacks continued, and early on the 9th No. 62 (B) Squadron was forced to withdraw from Alor Star to Butterworth.

194. To counter these attacks, it was decided to destroy the Japanese fighters based on Singora. Two attacks against this aerodrome were planned. The first was to be made by the aircraft of No. 34 (B) Squadron still located at Tengah, reinforced by No. 60 (B) Squadron, which had by now moved there from Kuantan. No. 34 Squadron was ordered to land at Butterworth, re-arm and take part in the second attack. The second attack was to be made by all available aircraft of Nos. 34 and 62 Squadrons, from Butterworth. A.H.Q. issued orders that both attacks were to be escorted by the maximum strength of Buffaloes from No. 2I (F) Squadron, R.A.A.F.

195. The first attack, consisting of 6 Blenheims of No. 34 (B) Squadron, three of which were manned by crews of 60 (B) Squadron, was made in the early afternoon of the 9th. Heavy fighter opposition was encountered, and 3 of our aircraft were shot down. Results of the attack were not observed, but returning crews claimed that, at least, a congested aerodrome had been hit

196. No fighter escort had been available. No. 2I (F) Squadron, R.A.A.F., had two aircraft serviceable only, which were on tactical reconnaissances for IIIrd Corps. It may be noted here that these aircraft, on the morning of the 9th reported the presence of Japanese light tanks, which were observed at Ban Sadao moving south.

197. The second attack - a mixed force of Blenheim I's and IV's from Nos. 34 (B) and 62 (B) Squadrons - due off from Butterworth at 1700 hours, was never launched.

Just before the time of "take-off," Japanese bombers carried out a high bombing attack followed up by machine-gunning aircraft on the ground. One aircraft only of No. 62 (B) Squadron - Captain, Flight Lieutenant A.S.K. Scarf - took off as the attack was developing; the remaining aircraft on the ground were all rendered unserviceable. Flight Lieutenant Scarf circled the aerodrome until it became apparent that no other aircraft were joining him. He then proceeded to Singora and pressed home his attack. During his approach to the target and subsequent get-away, A.A. fire and heavy fighter opposition were encountered, and Flight Lieutenant Scarf was mortally wounded. This very gallant officer felt unable to make the longer journey back, to Butterworth, but managed to retain consciousness until he reached Alor Star, where he crash-landed without injury to his crew. He died in hospital that evening. He was subsequently awarded the Victoria Cross.

198. As a result of this day's operations against Singora, A.H.Q. decided that no more bombing by day should take place over land until such time as fighter escort could be provided.

Preparations for withdrawal from the N.W.

199. At 0900 hours on the 9th, Adv. H.Q. Norgroup opened at Bukit Martajim (near Butterworth), but it became evident that the evacuation of the N.W. bases could not long be delayed. Up till this time there had been no A.A. defences at Butterworth. Eight Bofors guns arrived on the afternoon of the 9th but their presence was not, of course, any deterrent to high flying bombers.

200. A.H.Q., therefore, issued instructions that all airfields on the mainland to the southward were to be got ready for immediate operational use. At the same time, orders were issued to do everything possible to improve dispersal arrangements at aerodromes on Singapore Island.

Evacuation of Kuantan Aerodrome on 9th December.

201. During the night of the 8-9th there were many reports of further landings on the East coast, fears of which were to persist throughout the brief campaign and cause many hours to be spent on coastal reconnaissance.

202. On the 9th, two pairs of Vildebeestes were sent at 0300 hours to sweep the coast north and south of Kuantan. During the day, 6 Hudsons were employed on similar duties: whilst Catalinas extended the search area into the South China Sea. The remainder of the aircraft at Kuantan stood by to attack whatever might be found. Confirmation was obtained of the large concentration of ships of all natures unloading in the Singora - Patani area, but no threat of further seaborne attack was discovered although 3 Vildebeestes were despatched on a false report to attack a ship 60 miles east of Kuantan.

203. However, with the destruction of aircraft on the ground in N.W. Malaya in mind it became evident to A.H.Q. that a dangerous congestion of aircraft existed at Kuantan, particularly vulnerable because there was no A. A. protection there at all.

Orders were issued to O.C. Kuantan, early on the 9th, to retain I2 Vildebeestes and the I3 Hudsons of Nos. 3 and 8 (GR) Squadrons, R.A.A.F., and to despatch the remainder to Singapore.

204. At noon the expected attack took place, and Kuantan was subjected to its first experience of high bombing, followed up by the bombers flying low and shooting up at will. A.H.Q. thereupon decided to evacuate Kuantan, the surviving I0 Hudsons and 8 Vildebeestes returning to Singapore. The withdrawal of the ground party from Kuantan might have been better controlled. From then on Kuantan was available as an A.L.G. for refuelling only.

Reports of a landing at Kuantan - 9-I0th December, I94I.

205. During the night 9-I0th, reports were received of a landing north of Kuantan. Six Vildebeestes and 3 Hudsons were ordered to attack. The Vildebeestes found 3 small ships and bombed them with doubtful results, but the Hudsons which arrived later found no target although they prolonged their search of the area past daylight. There is reason to believe that the beaches at Kuantan had been fired on during the night, but that the enemy force was only a light reconnaissance to test the defences, and its size had been magnified in the telling.

206. Further bombing of Kuantan aerodrome on the morning of the I0th added to the uncertainty of the situation and all available bombers in Singapore were put at short notice to await developments. Sharks from the target towing flight carried out reconnaissance of the approaches to Singapore, whilst Blenheim IV's from No. 34 (B) Squadron, using Kuantan for refuelling purposes, continued reconnaissance of the east coast up to 50 miles north of Singora, confirming once more the large concentration of shipping off the Siamese coast.

207. The false report of a landing at Kuantan proved to have a vital bearing on the movements of H.M.S. "Prince of Wales" and H.M.S. "Repulse", and it is now necessary to turn to the events leading up to the sinking of these two vessels.

Sinking of H.M.S. "Prince of Wales" and "Repulse" - I0th December, I94I.

208. The C.-in-C. Eastern Fleet, Admiral Sir Tom Phillips, decided to sail on the 8th December, I94I, with H.M.S. "Prince of Wales" and H.M S. "Repulse" accompanied by four destroyers, with the object of attacking the concentration of Japanese transports reported between Singora and Patani. He intended to arrive in the target area at dawn on the I0th December.

209. Before leaving on the 8th December (p.m.) the C.-in-C. asked for the following:-

(*a*) Reconnaissance I00 miles to north of the force from daylight, Tuesday, the 9th December:

(b) Reconnaissance to Singora and beyond, ten miles from the coast, starting at first light on the 10th December:

(c) Fighter protection off Singora at daylight on the 10th December.

The A.O.C. gave tentative replies that he could provide (a), hoped to be able to provide (b), but could not provide (c). It was decided that he should go thoroughly into the problems involved and give definite replies to the Chief of Staff, Eastern Fleet (Rear Admiral Palliser), who remained at the Naval Base in close liaison with G.H.Q.

210. The doubt about the reconnaissance required in (b) above was due to the fact that the reconnaissance would have had to be provided by Blenheim IV's based on Kuantan, and it was uncertain whether this aerodrome would be out of action or not.

211. The reason why the fighter protection asked for in (c) could not be provided was mainly that the northern aerodromes were either untenable or else had been badly damaged by bombers; this meant that the fighters would have to operate from aerodromes at considerable distance from Singora, and, owing to the short endurance of the Buffalo, would have been able to remain only a very short time over the Singora area before having to return to refuel. These factors meant that a short patrol might possibly have been provided at intervals at Singora, but that it was impossible to guarantee appreciable fighter protection.

212. On the evening of the 8th December the A.O.C. confirmed his tentative replies to the Chief of Staff, Eastern Fleet, and this information was passed by the latter to the C.-in-C. The signal as received on board "Prince of Wales" expressly stated that no fighter protection could be provided on 10th December, 1941. The words "off Singora" did not appear in the text of the signal, but were implied in the light of Admiral Phillips' request (para. 209 (c)).

213. The agreed air reconnaissances were carried out on both the 9th and 10th December.

214. In the early hours of 10th December a signal was received at Singapore indicating that the Fleet might return sooner than was originally planned. Apart from this no communication was received from the C.-in-C. and his position was unknown.

215. Suddenly, shortly after 1200 hours on the 10th December, a signal, originating from H.M.S. "Repulse", was received in the Operations Room at A.H.Q. of enemy air attacks on H.M.S. "Prince of Wales" and "Repulse" in a position some 60 miles Eastwards of Kuantan. No. 453 (F) Squadron (11 aircraft), which was standing by specifically to provide protection for these ships in case of their return to Singapore, left six minutes later, only to arrive in the area, 165 miles away, to find destroyers picking up survivors from these two great vessels. For the rest of the day a number of sorties by flying boats and fighters was carried out in connection with the return of these destroyers to Singapore.

216. It subsequently transpired that the Fleet had been located by Japanese reconnaissance p.m. 9th December, and that later the same day the C.-in-C. received news of a landing at Kuantan (in para. 205). These two events must have decided the C.-in-C. to abandon the Singora operation and to close Kuantan on the 10th December.

2I7. Had the C.-in-C. notified his change of plan, it is conceivable that A.H.Q. might have moved No. 453 (F) Squadron to Kuantan where it could have stood by at call: R/T inter-communication between the two ships and the squadron aircraft had already been arranged. Some effective support might then have been given. Actually no call for assistance was sent until the Japanese attack had been pressed home, by which time intervention from Singapore was impossible.

2I8. It also transpired later that the ships had been attacked by a force of high level bombers backed by a large number of torpedo bombers, that both ships had suffered a number of hits by torpedoes and had thus been sunk. The sinking of these two ships was a serious shock to the morale of everybody in the Far East. Their loss, combined with the American losses at Pearl Harbour, gave the Japanese an undisputed command of the sea in Malayan waters. The reactions of this state of affairs upon the subsequent dispositions of air units, with particular reference to the share they were able to take in the land battle, will become clear later in the narrative.

Arrival of Dutch Reinforcements.

2I9. During the morning of 9th December the three Dutch Bomber (22 Glenn Martins) and one Fighter (9 Buffaloes) Squadrons arrived at Sembawang and Kallang respectively in accordance with the mutual reinforcement plan. It was found that the Dutch bomber crews were not trained in night flying, and so one squadron (9 aircraft) was sent back to the N.E.I. to train; the intention being, on its return, to send back the other squadrons in succession for the same purpose. As A.H.Q. had already decided not to use British bomber squadrons in their bombing role by day until fighter escort or cover could be provided (see para. I98), it was obviously essential to apply the decision to the Dutch bomber squadrons, particularly as their Glenn Martins were slower and no better protected than the British Blenheims.

Air Forces driven out of Aerodromes in N.W. Malaya.

220. Meanwhile in Northern Malaya it was evident that the main line of advance by the Japanese Army was from Singora across Malaya to the Alor Star area. The advanced troops of the IIth (Indian) Division were still holding a position near the frontier but the vital Ledge position on the Kroh - Patani road had not yet been secured.

22I. Bombing of our aerodromes in N.W. Malaya continued during the I0th December and A.H.Q. decided that the area must be evacuated. From Butterworth No. 62 (B) Squadron (reduced to 2 aircraft) was evacuated to Taiping: No. 2I (F) Squadron R.A.A.F. (6 repairable aircraft) to Ipoh, where 8 Bofors guns had by now been installed, leaving No. 27 (NF) Squadron (nil serviceability) still at Butterworth. All the unserviceable aircraft of Nos. 27, 34 (B) and 62 (B) Squadrons which were capable of flying were flown to Singapore for repair.

222. The withdrawal of the ground parties was carried out under difficult circumstances.

Units had been subjected to severe and constant bombing and machine gun attacks on scantily defended aerodromes where they saw no effective means of hitting back, and aircraft were remorselessly destroyed on the ground without replacement. The apparent opportuneness of the enemy's attacks (see para.I83) and pernicious rumours of disaster in the land fighting added their influence. There was no senior officer at Butterworth with sufficient weight to take control, and some of the personnel of No. 2I (F) Squadron R.A.A.F. and No. 27 (NF) Squadron R.A.F., both of which had already been driven out of Sungei Patani, did not behave at all steadily. Other units, however, maintained their order.

223. The difficulties of all units was intensified by the wholesale, but understandable, disappearance of unenlisted native followers - cooks, M.T. drivers, sanitary personnel etc. - and only improvised arrangements were possible for replacing them by European personnel at the dislocation of the latter's normal work.

The defection of labour spread to the railway area.

224. Withdrawals were nevertheless effected successfully and, in the case of units other than those mentioned above, in good order. It was due to the untiring energy of a small party headed by Flight Lieutenant R.D.I. Scott, who himself drove a locomotive, that much R.A.F. equipment was removed south.

225. In an endeavour to improve repair and maintenance facilities in N.W. Malaya, an R. & S.U. was formed at this time from No. I5I M.U. at Seletar and was ordered to Taiping; on arrival it detached a Mobile Salvage Section to Butterworth to assist in the work of salving material.

226. Meanwhile, during the commencement of the denial schemes at Alor Star on I0th December, the sight of large fires and the sounds of explosions in their rear had caused some concern amongst our forward troops. Orders were therefore issued to the Commander, Norgroup, that no fires were to be started and no demolitions by explosives carried out. Buildings were to be damaged only, petrol and oil run to waste, and the demolition of aerodromes with the help of explosives was to be left to Corps Royal Engineers to co-ordinate with the operations of our troops.

Scale of Enemy Air Effort.

227. It was computed that on the 8th, 9th and I0th December the Japanese had used a daily average of over I20 aircraft in N. Malaya, mostly against R.A.F. aerodromes. Fighters and some bombers were based on S.E. Siam, the majority of bombers on Indo-China. It was estimated that over I00 aircraft were based in the Singora - Patani area and at least 280 in Indo-China. Types identified were:-

Fighters - Navy "O".
Twin-Engined Bomber - Navy 96 and Army 97.
Dive Bombers - Junkers 87N (Japanese version).

Formation of War Council, Malaya.

228. On the I0th December Mr. Duff Cooper, whose ministerial duties had taken him to Singapore, formed a War Council, the composition of which was as follows:-

Mr. Duff Cooper, Chairman;
H.E. the Governor of the Straits Settlements;
C.-in-C., Far East;
C.-in-C., Eastern Fleet;
G.O.C., Malaya;
A.O.C., Far East;

and later, Sir George Sansom as being responsible for propaganda and Press control, and the late Mr. Bowden as representative of the Australian Government.

This War Council met daily for deliberation, mainly in connection with the conduct of the war in Malaya.

Events on the IIth December, 1941.

229. On IIth December the squadrons in N. Malaya were not in a position to take offensive action. Coastal reconnaissance, however, to the north of Kuantan by sections of Hudsons, continued. Catalinas extended the search into the S. China Sea, whilst P.R. Buffaloes continued to register Japanese activities of the South Siamese coast. Enemy submarine reports necessitated the despatch of sections of Vildebeestes without result.

230. No. 2I (F) Squadron, R.A.A.F. at Ipoh had no aircraft available for tactical reconnaissance for IIIrd Corps, and so A.H.Q. issued orders that the squadron was to be brought up to strength (I6 I.E.) immediately with a proportion of new pilots.

23I. Eighty Japanese aircraft attacked Penang Town; no aircraft were available for its protection.

232. On the ground, in addition to advances in the N.E. and N.W., the Japanese had infiltrated down the east coast as far as Trengannu. In the north-west, where the main Japanese forces were advancing, there was considerable pressure on the IIth (Indian) Division, but no major action had been fought. Attacks from the air on our forward troops increased in weight on the IIth, though the enemy air effort was still being expended chiefly on our aerodromes.

233. To assist in the defence of Borneo the Dutch placed at Sinkawang under A.H.Q. operational control one squadron of (9) Glenn Martins and one flight of (4) Buffaloes.

Consideration of Bomber Policy.

234. On the evening of the IIth December it was decided to attack Singora aerodrome once more, the arrival over the objective to be just before first light on the I2th. Eight aircraft of No. 34 (B) Squadron at Tengah were detailed. The attack was unsuccessful: few aircraft got through the bad weather and others were lost as a result of it.

235. This raid was carried out as part of the current policy for bombing Japanese aerodromes in order to reduce the scale of their air activity against our ground forces.

The Air Staff at A.H.Q., however, favoured the view that the correct employment of air forces, was in the attack of the shipping and troop concentrations in the Singora area, where the main landing had taken place, and through which reinforcements were still entering. They felt that the time had not yet come to concentrate on co-operation with the Army to delay the Japanese advance on the ground. Furthermore, the resources available for the bombing of aerodromes were not sufficient to produce any real effect on the Japanese effort. This was the view of the A.O.C., but he considered that he could not alter the policy which was selected to meet the wishes of the G.O.C., Malaya, who was anxious that action should be designed to reduce the scale of air attack on our troops. The G.O.C. was approached again at about this time, but reiterated that "bomber policy must give immediate relief to his troops" which, in his view, could only be achieved by bombing aerodromes.(See next paragraph.)

236. *Note by Lieut.-General A.E. Percival.*

"I have no recollection of this approach. In any case I am quite certain that there was no strong difference of opinion on the subject between the late Air Vice Marshal Pulford and myself. I would point out that there had been practically no air attacks on the ground troops up to that time, so it was very unlikely that I should press for immediate relief of the troops. At the same time I have always held, and still do, that the first essential in any campaign is to obtain some measure of control in the air. By IIth December the Japanese fighters, most of which were based on Singora aerodrome, had established control of the air over Northern Malaya. As long as they held that control the chances of our aircraft doing damage to Japanese shipping and troop concentrations in the Singora area was remote. Before that could be done it was necessary to regain some measure of air control. The only chance of doing this was to destroy a number of enemy fighters on their congested and weakly defended aerodrome. Therefore, if I did press for an attack on the aerodrome, it would have been for that reason and not to provide immediate relief for the ground troops."

237. The G.O.C.'s point of view was confirmed by G.H.Q. who, on I2th December, issued a War Instruction, the relevant paragraph of which read:-

"For the present, assistance to the IIth Ind. Division is to take precedence over other R.A.F. offensive tasks."

On the I2th December the C.-in-C. visited A.H.Q and re-emphasised the importance of providing support to the Army in the north-west.

Provision of Support for the Army.

238. On the IIth/I2th December the land position in the north-west worsened. The IIth (Indian) Division was attacked in and forced to evacuate the Jitra position, and Krohcol came under heavier attacks. The withdrawal of the latter force would have had grave consequences as it would have exposed the communications of the IIth Indian Division and thus necessitated a general withdrawal out of Kedah province.

239. The only aircraft still available in the area for direct support of the Army were two or three Buffaloes of No. 2I (F) Squadron, R.A.A.F., at Ipoh; the rest of the

squadron was being re-equipped at Singapore. The A.O.C. decided, therefore, to send the aircraft and pilots of No. 453 (F) Squadron from Singapore to Ipoh where they would be serviced by the ground crews of No. 2I Squadron. It was intended to return them to Singapore when the rest of No. 2I Squadron had been re-equipped.

240. No. 453 (F) Squadron arrived at Ipoh on the morning of the I3th and began operating from there, using Butterworth as an advanced landing ground. Connection was established with the Observer Corps Operations Room at Kuala Lumpur in the hope of obtaining at least a short warning of attacks upon the station.

24I. Operations were vigorously undertaken from Ipoh between the I3th and the I5th December. Japanese convoys were attacked on the road Simpang - Alor Star - Kepala Bantas. Tactical reconnaissances were carried out, and enemy bombers and reconnaissance aircraft in the area were engaged with some success, notably on the I3th when five enemy aircraft attacking Penang were claimed by the squadron. As a result, it was reported that the morale of our troops sharply appreciated.

242. On the I5th December No. 2I (F) Squadron, R.A.A.F., left Singapore to reinforce Ipoh, but owing to bad weather five aircraft force-landed and crashed and only six aircraft got through.

243. Operations in support of the Army seriously reduced the serviceability of No.453 (F) Squadron, and further losses were caused by the intensive bombing of Ipoh aerodrome, which now started. In consequence, on the I5th December, G.H.Q. issued an instruction that the role of the Ipoh fighter force was primarily reconnaissance for IIIrd Corps: it was not to be used against ground targets, and wastage was not to be made good at the expense of the squadrons allotted to the defence of Singapore. In practice, the squadrons in the north functioned mainly in the defence of the Ipoh area, carrying out such tactical reconnaissance as was required by IIIrd Corps. They continued in this role at Kuala Lumpur, to which enemy air attacks drove them on the19th December.

Demolition of Aerodromes.

244. The salvage of equipment from aerodromes in north-west Malaya continued. Sungei Patani, Butterworth and Taiping were successively cleared, and all stores and personnel sent back to Kuala Lumpur by road and rail for sorting.

245. Experience was to show that the demolition of aerodrome surfaces had little more than nuisance value, and only slightly retarded the Japanese efforts to bring them into service for their own forces. Speedy repairs were possible because:-

(*a*) large stocks of road-metal had been accumulated on each aerodrome for repairs, and it proved too bulky for removal and denial to the enemy (para. 30);

(*b*) occupation by the Japanese followed demolition so quickly that the heavy rains had no time to take effect;

(*c*) the abundant native labour was forcibly impressed by the enemy for repair work.

Air Forces driven out of North-West Malaya.

246. As early as the 20th December Japanese bombers and fighters were using aerodromes in the north-west, particularly Sungei Patani, and the scale of attack in the Kuala Lumpur area correspondingly increased. By the afternoon of 22nd December these attacks had reduced the combined strength of Nos. 2I (F) R.A.A.F. and 453 (F) Squadrons to four operationally serviceable aircraft.

247. In view of the enemy's great numerical superiority, further attempts to reinforce these squadrons only meant dissipating aircraft from their main role - the defence of Singapore. It was decided, therefore, to withdraw the force to Singapore, and this was done on 23rd December. It meant that operations in support of the Army in the north-west could be undertaken only by using Kuala Lumpur and other airfields to the south of that place as advanced landing grounds.

248. These two fighter squadrons had been forced to operate under very difficult conditions. Maintenance and servicing facilities had been necessarily primitive, whilst the warning system gave little, if any, notice of attack.

249. However, the unexpectedly high calibre of Japanese aircraft and pilots, and the superior numbers of the enemy, had proved too much for them.

250. Nevertheless, the work of these squadrons had had a good effect on the attitude of our troops to the air, although the number of enemy aircraft shot down was only small.

25I. With the withdrawal of the R. A. F. from the north-west, Norgroup was disbanded, and a Liaison Officer was left at H.Q. IIIrd Corps.

Army Situation.

252. While these operations and moves of air forces had been taking place the Army had been compelled to give more ground. On I5th December the Japanese forced the IIth (Indian) Division to evacuate the Gurun position, and threatened to push through the gap between the division and Krohcol. A big withdrawal had therefore to be made out of Kedah province to the Krian river. Penang was thus left isolated and was evacuated on the night of I6th/I7th December.

253. Between the I7th and 26th December our forces fought for the Taiping-Ipoh area,preparatory to taking up positions in theKampar district, which offered the best possibilitiesfor prolonged defence in this part ofMalaya.

254. The prospects of stabilising the situation, however, were not good; and as early as I6th December the sole Command reserve, consisting of a Brigade Group, had been committed to the fighting in the north-west.

255. In the rest of Malaya were:-

(i) A Brigade Group which was in process of being withdrawn from the State of Kelantan.

(ii) A Brigade Group at Kuantan which was already threatened by Japanese infiltration down the Trengganu coast.

(iii) A Division (2 Brigades) of the Australian Imperial Forces in Johore, whose particular role was to guard against landings in the Mersing area on the east coast of Malaya.

(iv) The garrison of Singapore Fortress.

All these formations were either already committed actively or potentially. Adequate reinforcement for the main battle area therefore depended upon the safe arrival of reinforcements from outside Malaya. But before dealing with this aspect it is first necessary to dispose of some other matters.

Preparations for basing squadrons in the N.E.I.

256. The evacuation of the northern aerodromes had been foreseen, and as this would eventually result in congestion of aerodromes on Singapore Island, A.H.Q. issued orders as early as the I4th December for stocks of bombs together with refuelling and re-arming parties to be sent to aerodromes in Sumatra. Shortly afterwards, two staff officers from A.H.Q. and an officer of the A.M.W.D. were ordered to Sumatra to accelerate work in connection with:-

(*a*) providing facilities for the transit of reinforcing aircraft;

(*b*) the operation of bombers from Sumatra, including the selection of a Bomber Group H.Q.

257. For these movements it was possible to call upon an Air Transport service from Singapore - Sumatra - Java which had been instituted by the Dutch Army Air Service. The number and capacity of the transport aircraft were limited, but they enabled the movements to Sumatra to be carried out rapidly. They illustrated the value of transport aircraft. It was considered inadvisable to operate these aircraft in Northern Malaya where little fighter protection could have been provided for them.

258. A warning order was also issued on the 22nd December for moving No. I53 M.U. from Kuala Lumpur to Java. By that date the Japanese had advanced as far south as Taiping, and Kuala Lumpur was threatened. Thus it was felt that the work of the unit could be more satisfactorily carried out in Java.

Japanese Attack on Borneo.

259. It is now necessary to revert to operations off the East coast of Malaya leading up to the Japanese attack on Borneo.

On the I3th December G.H.Q. received information from a reliable source that a large convoy of well over a hundred ships was heading S.S.W. from the direction of Saigon. Its destination was not known for some days. It constituted a serious threat to Malaya, on the east coast of which existed several good landing beaches with little or no defence, where a successful landing would have seriously jeopardised our army formations still closely engaged with the enemy on the western side of the peninsula.

260. Accordingly, reconnaissance activity from Malaya was materially increased, and during the period I3th to 24th December most of the available bombers stood by to attack the enemy convoy in the event of its approach.

26I. An average of 2 Catalina, 6 Hudson and 6 Glenn Martin sorties was sent out daily from Malaya to locate the expedition, whilst Dutch Glenn Martins from Sinkawang in Dutch Borneo were similarly employed. On the I4th, 6 cruisers were reported south of Saigon, and on the afternoon of the I6th a landing was reported at Miri, in British Borneo. The ships in the area were attacked by the Dutch in bad weather on the I7th, I8th and I9th. Hits were claimed on a cruiser and transports, and several near misses against transports.

262. The reconnaissance activity continued, spreading south-east to the Rhio Archipelago, and on the 23rd December an expedition heading towards Kuching was detected. Both Kuching and Sinkawang aerodromes had been attacked by Japanese aircraft on the preceding days, and the former had been "blown". The Dutch aircraft at Sinkawang were withdrawn to Palembang in Sumatra on the 24th, though before they were transferred they were able to carry out a few attacks against the enemy convoy.

263. This same convoy was attacked on the 24th by 3 Hudsons and also by 5 Blenheim IVs of No. 34 (B) Squadron. Several near misses were claimed but no positive sinkings. A Dutch submarine claimed to have sunk 3 transports and I tanker in the area.

Increased Air Reconnaissance activity.

264. Seaward reconnaissance at this time absorbed almost all the G.R. and bomber aircraft in Malaya. In addition to major Japanese expeditions east of Malaya, Japanese forces were still infiltrating southwards down the East coast towards Kuantan; and on the I5th December a flight of M.V.A.F. was established at Kahang to carry out local coastal reconnaissance for the Australian forces in Johore who were responsible for guarding against landings in the Mersing - Endau area. Reconnaissance up the West-coast also became an increasing commitment during the second half of December. Regular reconnaissances were instituted from 22nd December, as the Japanese were already showing signs of infiltrating in small boats by day and night down the West coast behind our Army's left flank. The discovery and attack of these infiltrations was difficult because the boats moved in waters flanked by luxuriant tropical undergrowth. By day the Japanese protected their movements with fighter patrols.

265. The possibility that the Japanese might spread across from Malaya to Sumatra had also to be faced, thus a squadron of Dutch Glenn Martins at Pakenbaroe in Sumatra were employed on reconnaissance to detect any such movement with effect from I5th December.

Minor Reorganisations.

266. Meanwhile, certain reorganisation of squadrons had taken place. One flight of Wirraways (6) was formed at Kluang on the I8th and training in dive-bombing commenced. The aircrews of No. 60 (B) Squadron were sent back to Burma by sea

by B.O.A.C. to join their ground personnel at Rangoon: the squadron's aircraft were taken over by No. 62 (B) Squadron.

Order of Battle - 24th December, 1941.

267. At this stage of the campaign the disposition of squadrons and their approximate strengths in serviceable aircraft were as follows:-

Bomber Squadrons:

Blenheims	No. 34 Squadron	10	Tengah
	No. 62 Squadron	9	Tengah
Dutch Glenn Martins	Two Squadrons	15	Sembawang
Wirraways	One Flight	6	Kluang

T.B. Squadrons:

Vildebeestes	No. 36 Squadron	16	Seletar
	No. 100 Squadron	13	Seletar
Albacores	One Flight	5	Seletar

Fighter Squadrons:

Buffaloes	No. 21 Squadron R.A.A.F. }		reorganising
	No. 453 Squadron }		Sembawang
	No. 243 Squadron	15	Kallang
	No. 488 Squadron	14	Kallang
	Dutch Squadron	9	Kallang
Night Fighter (Blenheims)	No. 27 Squadron	}	reorganising Kallang

G.R. Squadrons:

Hudsons	No. 1 Squadron R.A.A.F.	5	Sembawang
	No. 8 Squadron R.A.A.F.	8	Sembawang
	No. 205 Squadron	4	Seletar

Miscellaneous:

No. 4 A.A.C.U. Swordfish	One Flight	4	Tengah
Sharks	One Flight	4	Tengah
M.V.A.F. (Various)	Recce. Flight	-	Kahang
M.V.A.F. (Various)	Comm. Flight	-	Kahang
Dutch Squadron (Glenn Martins)	One Squadron	9	Pakanbaroe (Sumatra)

Reinforcement Situation

268. From the 8th December onwards many messages had been interchanged between the Air Ministry and the Far East on the subject of reinforcements, which, commencing with a long-range policy of supply, developed, with the steady advance of the Japanese Army, into an emergency arrangement of diverting to the Far East

squadrons from other Commands which it was hoped could arrive in time. By the 25th December, the position as understood by A.H.Q. was:-

Hudson II's - 6 arrived from Australia on 25/12 to reinforce Nos. I and 8 (GR) Squadrons, R.A.A.F.

Hudson III's - 52 to be flown out from England commencing about 20/12.

Blenheim IV's - I2 from Middle East - 7 arrived by 25/I2: remainder en route.

Hurricanes - 5I in crates with 24 pilots en route by sea due on or about 8th January, I942. These had left England as reinforcements for the Middle East but were diverted to Singapore whilst at sea.

Catalinas - 4 en route with 2 spare crews.

The Plan for their disposition was:-

Hudson III's - to (*a*) re-equip No. 62 (B) Squadron: and

(*b*) reinforce Nos. I and

8 (GR) Squadrons R.A.A.F.

Blenheim IV's - to be absorbed into No. 34 (B) Squadron.

Hurricanes - to be used from Kallang and Johore hi defence of Singapore; it was anticipated Buffalo Squadrons would be whittled away by the time these Hurricanes arrived.

Catalinas - One to remain at Ceylon, remainder to reinforce No. 205 (FB) Squadron at Seletar.

Thus some air reinforcements, urgently wanted, were now on their way despite the still critical state of the war in Europe from which they had had to be diverted to Singapore.

NARRATIVE FROM 25TH DECEMBER, I94I, TO 30TH JANUARY, I942

Changes in Higher Command

269. Before proceeding further with the narrative, it is appropriate to mention some changes in the Higher Command in the Far East which were about to take place during the next few weeks.

On 27th December, General Sir Henry Pownall relieved Air Chief Marshal Sir Robert Brooke Popham as Commander-in-Chief, Far East. The former's instructions differed from those of the latter, as described in para. 3. General Pownall was instructed to deal with "matters of major military policy and strategy", but that it was not the intention that he should "assume operational control". These instructions were given before the outbreak of the Japanese war, which occurred however whilst he was en route. As their consequence, the system described in para. 3, under which G.H.Q. was responsible for the control of operations, now came to an end.

270. On Ist January, I942, the small Fighter Control H.Q. in Singapore was expanded, albeit on a restricted scale. It became known as No. 224 (F) Group. Group Captain E.B. Rice remained in command. Circumstances, however, did not permit full administration of its units and stations being transferred to it from A.H.Q.

27I. On 4th January, Air Vice Marshal P.C. Maltby arrived in Singapore as Chief-of-Staff designate to the newly appointed C.-in-C. Far East. He remained in Singapore to assist the A.O.C., being attached to A.H.Q. on I2th January for the purpose.

To resume the narrative of events

Arrival at Singapore of Reinforcement Convoys

272. With effect from the 26th December, arrangements for the reception of reinforcement convoys at Singapore became of overriding importance, not the least factor being the urgent necessity to maintain the secrecy of their arrival. This was successfully accomplished, it is believed.

273. In view of the importance of these convoys to the defence of Malaya, G.H.Q. issued an instruction on the 27th December that "air protection for convoys bringing reinforcements will now take precedence before the other tasks".

274. Reinforcements were, if anything, more important to the Army even than to the R.A.F. All the fighting since the beginning of the campaign had fallen on the IIIrd Corps, particularly the IIth (Indian) Division, and the troops badly needed a rest; and as the reinforcements contained a complete fresh Division (I8th) as well as anti-aircraft regiments, it was vital from the Army point of view that the Air Force in Malaya should do everything in their power to ensure that the convoys got through.

275. Air protection for these convoys was provided by means of widespread reconnaissance sweeps into the S. China Sea, close anti-submarine patrols from the Banka Straits onwards and fighter escort for the final approach to Singapore. An extremely vulnerable part of the route was that which lay through the Banka Straits off E. Sumatra. For the protection of the convoys in this area, the Dutch Fighter Squadron based at Kallang was moved to Palembang on the 29th December, and again on the 9th January. Apart from the fighters, operations for shepherding these convoys, for periods of three days for each convoy, employed at least 2 Catalinas, 6 Hudsons and 4 Glenn Martins daily. In addition, during these 3-day periods, all other available aircraft in the Command were kept at short notice in case the convoys were attacked by enemy naval or air forces. In this situation the absence of effective Naval strength in Malayan waters was aggravated by the insufficiency of air forces to reinforce the Navy, and at the same time to meet the needs of the battle on the land. In these circumstances there was no alternative but to withdraw appreciable numbers of our aircraft, and to make them stand by for the protection of convoys when they might otherwise have been participating in the battle on land.

276. The task was successfully accomplished. The first convoy arrived in Singapore on 3rd January and a second on 13th January. The, latter included the first brigade of the 18th Division to arrive. It also contained 51 crated Hurricanes accompanied by more than 20 Hurricane pilots.

It is difficult here adequately to convey the sense of tension which prevailed as these convoys approached Singapore, and the sense of exultation at their safe arrival. The feeling spread that at least the Japanese were going to be held on the ground if not driven back, whilst many confidently expected that the Hurricanes would sweep the Japanese from the sky.

Withdrawal of the Army to Johore

277. But by the time that the first reinforcements arrived the position of the Army had seriously worsened. On the West coast a withdrawal from the strong Kampar position had been forced upon IIIrd Corps by an out-flanking landing at Telok Anson on the West coast.

278. The forcing of a line on the Slim river and further landings in the Kuala Selangor region led to the evacuation of Kuala Lumpur and Port Swettenham on the 10th January; and by the middle of January the bulk of our forces, were back to the northern frontier of Johore, little more than 100 miles from Singapore.

279. On the East coast, the Brigade that had originally held the Kota Bahru area had fallen back, without serious losses, to Central Malaya. The Brigade Group defending Kuantan, which had been attacked from the north on 30th December, had also to be withdrawn to prevent its communications being cut as the result of the West Coast withdrawal.

280. Thereafter, the Japanese on the East coast began to move steadily down towards Mersing. There had been no attacks in this area up to the middle of January, but a major Japanese landing was expected daily.

281. Thus the progress of the Japanese Army was quicker than had been anticipated, chiefly as the result of its possession of an armoured component, its superiority in jungle warfare, its superiority in the air, and its ability to pass parties in boats down the West coast round the left flank of our Army. Infiltrating Japanese frequently got behind our forward troops and formed road blocks on their lines of communication which proved difficult, and sometimes impossible, to clear. Our own demolitions were swiftly repaired or circumvented by the enemy; and in general the speed and aggression of his follow-up came as a surprise.

Co-operation with the Army on the West coast

282. The heavy commitments of the air forces for reconnaissance, convoy protection and the air defence of Singapore, reduced the number of aircraft available for the direct support of the Army during this period. But, within the limitations thus imposed, air action was carried out on both West and East coasts, increasing in quantity as the battle area came within range of aircraft based on aerodromes in Singapore.

283. In response to requests from H.Q.M.C. and IIIrd Corps, action was taken against Japanese landing parties on the West coast. Daily offensive reconnaissances were carried out by 4 to 6 Glenn Martins or Blenheims, unescorted at first, but later, after 4 aircraft had been shot down in one day, with fighter protection. Five Shark aircraft were moved up to Batu Pahat on 2nd January: they also took part in this type of operation.

284. Barges off Port Swettenham were attacked by Blenheims on the 2nd, 3rd and 4th January: several near misses were observed but no definite sinkings.

285. As Japanese activity against the West coast increased, so, from l5th January, air attacks were made on an increased scale:-

15*th Jan.* - by 6 Hudsons, 6 Glenn Martins and 3 Blenheims escorted by l2 Buffaloes attacked barges in the Linggi River: two barges were sunk and three damaged by the Hudsons.

l6*th Jan.* - l5 Buffaloes attacked transport and movements on the road Tampin/Gemas whilst 9 Blenheims and 6 Glenn Martins followed by 4 Buffaloes attacked barges in the Muar River where further landings were taking place.

l7*th Jan.* - 9 Vildebeestes escorted by 6 Buffaloes continued attacks on barges in the Muar River, whilst fighter cover was provided for a move by road of the A.I.F. in the area.

18*th Jan.* - Attacks on barges in the Muar River and on troop concentrations in the Gemas area continued - a total force of 6 Blenheims, 5 Hudsons and l4 Buffaloes being employed.

286. In addition, tactical reconnaissance by one or two sections of Buffaloes was carried out for IIIrd Corps, chiefly in the Seremban - Tampin - Gemas area. Special bombing attacks were carried out by Blenheims on l0th January to destroy trains full of Army stores, which, owing to the congestion and dislocation of the railway system, had been stranded at Malacca. The attacks were at least partly successful, as were others made on l2th January against some oil tanks which had been left intact at Port Swettenham.

287. Part of our offensive effort continued to be made against Japanese-held aerodromes in order to meet the wishes of G.O.C. Malaya for reducing enemy air action against our forward troops, which had been carried out concurrently with attacks against our aerodromes both in Malaya and on Singapore Island and against our road and rail communications behind the battle front.

288. Daily flights over Northern Malaya by our P.R. Buffaloes revealed that aerodromes "blown" in the withdrawal were quickly repaired and occupied. Gong Kedah was occupied by the enemy on the 3lst December, Ipoh on the 4th January and Kuantan on the 9th January.

289. Consequently our aircraft made attacks on aerodromes in Northern Malaya at frequent intervals during the latter part of December and the first half of January. They entailed long flights by night, often in the face of violent tropical thunderstorms.

Altogether, between 20th December and 15th January, some eighty sorties were carried out against this type of target. Sungei Patani was attacked six times, Gong Kedah twice, Ipoh and Alor Star once. Good results were achieved by Blenheims of No. 34 (B) Squadron at Sungei Patani on 27th/28th December, photographic reconnaissance on the following day confirming that at least 7 fighters had been destroyed and 5 fighters and 3 bombers damaged.

290. Good results were also obtained at Gong Kedah on 1st/2nd January by Catalinas. These aircraft had by this time largely been withdrawn from reconnaissance work, which was instead carried out by Hudsons, owing to the vulnerability of the Catalina to fighter attack. The range and bomb load of the Catalinas proved very useful for night bombing operations. Twice in January they attacked the main enemy base at Singora, a target which by this time was beyond the range of any other aircraft in the Command.

291. In addition, two attempts were made to carry out strong fighter attacks against Kuantan aerodrome; but tropical thunderstorms on each occasion forced our fighters to return.

292. That these operations inflicted losses upon the enemy is certain. It is equally certain that he had more than sufficient reserves to replace his losses without delay.

Air Activity off the East coast.

293. Off the east coast there was considerable reconnaissance and activity. On 27th December, photographic reconnaissance confirmed the arrival of 34 ships at Singora, which were proved subsequently to have brought a reinforcing Division. Further reports of enemy shipping necessitated sweeps by Hudsons to the Natunas on the 3rd and 4th January.

294. Daily East coast reconnaissances to the north from Endau beyond Trengannu occupied at least 6 Glenn Martins or Hudsons, whilst the M.V.A.F. continued close reconnaissance for the A.I.F. in the Endau - Mersing area.

295. On the 8th January, 9 Glenn Martins and 4 Hudsons bombed and scored direct hits on a ship anchored in the South China Sea, believed to be used by the Japanese as a navigational aid for their aircraft. On 9th January, 9 Glenn Martins bombed with success ships unloading at Kuantan.

296. Meanwhile, Kuantan had been occupied by the Japanese on the 9th January. Infiltration down the coast towards Endau and Mersing immediately commenced. By the 13th January A.H.Q. became convinced of the possibility of a landing in this vital area, and a general direction was therefore issued to all squadrons governing their action in such a contingency. A daily reconnaissance by 6 Hudsons was instituted to detect the approach of any convoy from Indo-China; reconnaissance northwards up the east coast, although restricted, was still maintained.

Capture of Borneo.

297. Borneo had been lost by this time. Kuching had been captured on 26th December, and its garrison of one Indian Battalion forced to retreat. It was located

by our reconnaissance as it made its way to Sinkawang, where supplies were dropped for it by three aircraft on 31st December. Apart from a further reconnaissance on 9th January to ascertain the state of Kuching aerodrome, no further air action in the Borneo area was possible.

Japanese air operations against Singapore.

298. During the first half of January the Japanese extended their air attacks to Singapore Island, directing them mainly against its aerodromes, with the evident intention of neutralising our squadrons. Tengah, on which the Blenheim force was based, received particular attention. Night raids were a constant occurrence, but these were mainly of a nuisance value and little damage was done by them. No. 27 (NF) Squadron, which had been reorganised at Kallang, and which now had 5 Blenheim I's serviceable, was used in an endeavour to intercept these attacks, but without success owing to the poor performance of their aircraft.

299. Day raids by the enemy took place with increasing intensity, at first by bombers alone, and later by bombers escorted by fighters. On the 1st January the first serious attack against Tengah took place, as a result of which native labour disappeared. This was to happen at all aerodromes as they became attacked, necessitating the replacement of domestic personnel by Europeans and making it increasingly difficult to repair damage to aerodrome surfaces. At all Stations on the Island dispersed accommodation was provided for personnel normally quartered at them, mobile kitchens were improvised, and, in the case of Seletar, married families were moved to alternative quarters.

300. Tengah was attacked again on the 6thJanuary, 9th January, 12th January, 13th January and 14th January. On the 15th, the naval base was attacked, and on the 16th, aerodromes and the docks. The 17th was a particularly bad day. Attacks on aerodromes were carried out by escorted bombers, and, under their cover, low flying fighters slipped in and attacked Sembawang and Seletar. At Seletar, 2 Catalinas at their moorings were burned out and another 2 damaged. Six Blenheims at Tengah were damaged to a varying degree, whilst at Sembawang 3 Buffaloes on the ground were destroyed and 4 damaged. Attacks were carried out by some 80 bombers, of which 2 were brought down and another 4 damaged. The attack was repeated on the 18th against the naval base and the docks, and again 2 were brought down and possibly 6 damaged for the loss of 8 Buffaloes.

301. The absence of a first-class fighter aircraft prior to the second half of January was a handicap. An attempt was made to improve the performance of the Buffalo by reducing its petrol load and replacing the unsatisfactory .5 guns, which were heavy and possessed faulty interrupter gear, by .303 machine guns, but it remained inferior to the Navy O particularly in "dog-fighting".

302. Moreover, owing to the short warning of enemy raids, our fighters were frequently still climbing to meet the enemy when they were themselves attacked. A warning of at least thirty minutes was required to enable the Buffalo to reach 24,000 feet, which was the height at which the enemy formations often flew. But the successive evacuation of Observer Corps Posts on the mainland as the Japanese

advanced, and the inadequate radar cover available, meant that the period of warning was almost always insufficient.

303. The Dutch Fighter Squadron in Singapore was transferred in the middle of January to Palembang (para 357), leaving only 2 squadrons of Buffaloes - Nos. 243 (F) and 488 (F) -

for the defence of Singapore, because Nos. 2I (F) R.A.A.F. and 453 (F) Squadrons based at Sembawang were used primarily for Army co-operation and for escorting bombers operating by day on the West coast. Apart from other handicaps, therefore, defending fighters were outnumbered in the air by the Japanese fighters in varying degrees between 6-I and I5-I.

304. The A.A. defences of the Island were of limited effect in countering air attacks, Bofors guns gave protection against all but a few surprise low level attacks. But the great majority of the enemy's bombing was carried out from altitudes of over 20,000 feet, where they were well above the effective range of the 3-in. guns which formed one-third of the heavy A.A. defences. At such heights only the 3.7-in. guns, of which there were only 40 for the defence of the many targets on the Island, could reach them.

Further changes in the Higher Command.

305. At the beginning of January it had been decided by the Allied authorities to unify the command of all their forces in the South West Pacific under a Supreme Allied Commander. General Sir Archibald Wavell was appointed to this post. He arrived in Singapore on 7th January and commenced to form his staff, absorbing into it the Commander-in-Chief, Far East, and his staff. On IIth January he moved to the site selected for his Supreme Allied Headquarters, South West Pacific Command, namely to Bandoeng in Java. There on I5th January he assumed command of operations throughout the S.W. Pacific, and G.H.Q. as such ceased to exist. The code name for General Wavell's H.Q. was Abdacom.

306. It is unnecessary for the purpose of this report to describe the organisation of Abdacom. Suffice it to say that it included a department, the code name of which was Abdair, whose head functioned in the dual capacity of Chief-of-the-Air-Staff at General Wavell's H.Q., and of Commander of all the Allied air forces in the S.W. Pacific. This appointment was temporarily filled by Major General Brereton, U.S. Army Air Corps, pending the arrival of Air Chief Marshal Sir Richard Peirse, R.A.F., who was appointed to it and who took up the duty during the last days of January.

307. To facilitate control of air operations within the S.W. Pacific Command, the area was divided by Abdair into six Groups, of which only two need be mentioned in this Narrative:-

(i) *West group* - consisting of R.A.F. Far East Command, including Units in Malaya and those in process of being transferred to the Netherlands East Indies.

(ii) *Recgroup* - consisting of all seaward reconnaissance units in S.W. Pacific Command, British, Dutch and American. Its Headquarters was in Java.

Directive to Air Forces in Malaya.

308. On the 18th January Abdacom stressed the importance of Singora as a target and issued a general directive to govern the operations of the Air Forces in Malaya. This directive stated that "protection of convoys at present takes precedence over action against other Japanese forces. If, however, new expeditions are located threatening the east coast of Malaya or endeavouring to pass south of Singapore, all available air effort should be directed to destroying such targets". The directive also stressed the importance of slowing up the Japanese advance on land by attacking Singora, intervening in the land battle, and of reducing the scale of Japanese air attack.

Relative Strength of Air Forces in Malaya.

309. To carry out efficiently all these tasks was beyond the strength of the Air Forces available. On the afternoon of 18th January, the serviceability state of the Air Forces in Malaya showed 74 bomber and G.R. aircraft and 28 fighters, all based on Singapore with the exception of a small detachment at Kahang. Moreover, many of these aircraft were obsolete or obsolescent. Against these it was estimated that the Japanese were maintaining in Malaya at this time a force of 150 fighters and 250 bombers. Concentration was therefore made, in general, on one task at a time in the order of priority indicated in the directive, but influenced by the situation.

Arrival of Further Convoys and of Air Reinforcements.

310. Special attention, as the directive instructed, continued to be paid to the provision of protection for reinforcing convoys arriving at Singapore. Further convoys came in on 22nd, 24th and 28th January, bringing the remainder of the 18th Division, except for a few units, a Brigade Group from India, two to three thousand troops from Australia, and more anti-aircraft units.

311. Five Hudson sorties were made daily over wide areas around the convoys to detect the approach of Japanese naval forces. One Catalina was maintained on anti-submarine patrol, and during the final approach to Singapore a fighter escort of six aircraft was maintained. All other aircraft were kept at short call as the convoys approached, in case the enemy should attack them.

312. Three reinforcing Catalinas arrived on 7th January and were allotted to No. 205 (FB) Squadron.

313. During the third week in January, the 51 Hurricanes which had arrived on the 13th January (para. 276), were being assembled preparatory to joining Buffaloes in the defence of the Island. Spares were ample but tool kits were scarce.

314. On their arrival they were immediately unloaded, and the majority dispersed to previously selected concealed positions, where they were erected and wheeled to nearby airfields for test; the remainder proceeded direct to No. 151 M.U. for erection at other dispersed points. The speed with which these aircraft were erected was a very remarkable achievement (see Postscript).

315. Twenty-four pilots from Nos. 17, 135 and 136 (F) Squadrons had arrived with them: some had had experience in the Battle of Britain. When A.H.Q. first heard of

their diversion to the Far East, it had been planned to give aircrews a spell before employing them in operations. This spell was obviously desirable, not only because of the length of their sea voyage, but also because of the need for acclimatising pilots to local conditions. However, events had moved too fast and the stake was too high for delay to be acceptable. The Hurricanes had to be used immediately they had been erected and tested. They were in action as a squadron by the 20th January, exactly a week after they had been landed in crates.

316. The aircraft were accompanied by some ground personnel of No. 232 (F) Squadron, deficiencies being made good by personnel from the transit camp. They were based at Seletar and Kallang, and the whole operated as No. 232 (F) Squadron.

317. Sixteen Hudson III's arrived in Singapore from the United Kingdom, the first of them during the third week of January: They were allotted to 62 (B) and No. 8 (GR) R.A.A.F. Squadrons. They came at somewhat scattered intervals, and as long as the air route to the Far East remained open, i.e., until mid-February. The balance of the 52 which had been expected were unable to get through before the enemy cut the air route from India.

318. Two reinforcing bomber squadrons, Nos. 84 (B) and 2II (B) Squadrons, began to arrive on 23rd January from the Middle East. They were diverted to Sumatra, for reasons which will be related in due course. They, too, arrived at scattered intervals and were far from complete when the enemy cut the air route. Their ground crews and equipment were to follow by sea (para. 4I7).

A.H.Q. was notified that a further 48 Hurricanes, over and above those mentioned in para. 3I3, would be flown into Singapore from H.M.S. Indomitable about the end of January, and that 39 more in crates were en route by sea.

Further withdrawal of the Army - to Singapore Island.

3I9. Despite the arrival of reinforcements the position on land continued to develop adversely during the second half of January.

320. On the west coast, the Japanese took full advantage of their command of the sea to land behind the Army positions. Between the I6th and I8th January there was a succession of landings on the Johore coast between Muar and Batu Pahat, which, combined with heavy frontal attacks, forced our troops to withdraw to the line Batu Pahat - Mersing.

32I. On the East coast, the long expected landing in the Mersing - Endau area took place at Endau on 26th January. The lateral communications available in north Johore permitted a junction between the Japanese forces in the east and west of the peninsula, while a Japanese advance from the Endau area threatened the communications of the main British forces in the west.

322. Our losses in the west coast battle and the new threat from the East dictated a general withdrawal of our forces to Singapore Island itself, a decision which was taken on the 27th January. The withdrawal was achieved in good order. Nevertheless it had been hoped that the arrival of reinforcements would permit the holding of a bridgehead in Johore, but this now proved to be impossible.

Air Action against the Japanese Advance.

West Coast.

323. The Japanese exploitation of their superiority at sea led, on the west coast as well as the east, to a number of air reconnaissances and sweeps being undertaken over the left flank of the Army. Attacks against Japanese-held aerodromes in Central Malaya, were also carried out.

324. On the I9th January the situation at Muar was reported to be serious. Twelve Buffaloes carried out an offensive sweep of the area, using surplus ammunition on barges during their return. The latter were also attacked twice during the day by 3 Hudsons escorted by Buffaloes. That night, I9th/20th January, 9 Vildebeestes bombed the aerodrome at Kuala Lumpur, where some twenty fighters had been observed by Buffaloes of No. 488 (F) Squadron.

325. On the 20th January two Blenheims made an offensive reconnaissance against shipping off the coast. Later, 6 Buffaloes carried out an offensive sweep of the Muar - Gemas area where the Army reported heavy dive bombing against troops of IIIrd Corps. They met a formation of 6 Army 97's, destroyed one and forced the others to jettison their loads. That evening, at last light, 7 Blenheims bombed and machine-gunned Kuala Lumpur with great success, claiming the destruction of over 20 fighters. 6 Hudsons attacked Kuantan at the same time. These attacks were followed up that night by 24 Vildebeestes, I2 bombing each aerodrome.

326. From the 2Ist to 24th January, many requests for support of the Army in the Muar area were received, but these were days during which the protection of convoys took precedence, and little was available with which to meet them. On the 2Ist January, 6 Buffaloes carried out sweeps in the morning and afternoon in the Parit Salong - Batu Pahat area; 2 Albacores and 2 Buffaloes attacked small boats near Batu Pahat; and 2 Albacores dropped supplies successfully for troops who had been cut off, and thus assisted them to extricate themselves.

327. On 22nd January the Japanese were infiltrating from Muar to Batu Pahat. This road was attacked by 2 Albacores, I Shark and 6 Buffaloes. More supplies were dropped by Albacores of No. 36 Squadron to troops cut off in the Parit Salong area. That night, 22nd/23rd January, 2I Vildebeestes again bombed Kuala Lumpur.

328. On the 23rd January, 5 Buffaloes patrolled over the withdrawal of troops from the Yong Peng area (N.NE. of Batu Pahat)and engaged I2 Navy 'O' fighters which were harassing them. All available Sharks, Albacores and Wirraways attacked enemy troops on the road leading south from Muar. That night, 23rd/24th, I2 Vildebeestes bombed Kuantan aerodrome.

329. On the 24th January, 6 Vildebeestes attacked troops on the bridge at Labis on the Segamat - Singapore road, whilst 3 others bombed oil tanks left standing at Muar.

330. On the 25th January, I2 Buffaloes carried out sweeps, morning and evening, in the Kluang - Gemas - Batu Pahat area, whilst that night 24 Vildebeestes and 3 Albacores carried out 2 sorties each to cover the sea evacuation of a battalion which had been cut off in the Batu Pahat area. During that day 5 U.S.A. Fortresses from

Java bombed Sungei Patani under Abdair direction. At night, 3 Hudsons attacked Kuala Lumpur.

33I. By the evening of the 25th January, the airfields at Kahang, Kluang and Batu Pahat became untenable and were demolished, as were also the strips which had been prepared in S. Johore. Their loss was a severe blow, as it had been hoped they would be available for the reinforcing Hurricanes; they had been specially prepared and equipped for that purpose. Seletar, which had now to be used instead, was not so well equipped with dispersal points.

Air Action against the Landing at Endau.

332. To turn to the East coast. On the 26th January, at 0930 hours, Hudson reconnaissance sighted 2 cruisers, II destroyers and two I0,000 ton vessels accompanied by barges, I0 miles off the coast approaching Endau. (para 32I). They were being protected by Japanese fighters based on Kuantan.

333. The forces available for opposing them were:-

9 Hudsons of Nos. I and 8 (GR) Squadrons, R.A.A.F.

2I Vildebeestes, 3 Albacores of Nos. 36 and I00 (TB) Squadrons.

334. The attack was organised in two waves. The first wave comprised 9 Hudsons and I2 Vildebeestes and was escorted by I5 Buffaloes and 8 Hurricanes; the second, 3 Albacores and 9 Vildebeestes, escorted by 4 Buffaloes and 8 Hurricanes.

335. Unfortunately, as the Vildebeestes and Albacores of Nos. 36 and I00 (TB) Squadrons had been operating throughout the whole of the previous night (para. 330), the first wave of attack could not be launched until the early afternoon. By this time most of the Japanese troops were probably clear of their transports.

336. However, the first wave, consisting of 9 Hudsons and the Vildebeestes of No. I00 (TB) Squadron, was able to press its attack home, being helped by rather cloudy conditions. 5 Vildebeestes were lost. It was claimed that one cruiser and two destroyers were sunk, both transports were hit (one set on fire), and casualties were caused to troops in barges and on the beaches.

337. With the arrival of the second wave, the Vildebeestes of No. 36 (TB) Squadron, the weather in the area suddenly cleared and enemy fighters intercepted the squadron before it could attack. 6 Vildebeestes and 2 Albacores were shot down and other aircraft damaged and aircrews wounded. Later, 5 Hudsons of No. 62 (B) Squadron from Sumatra arrived in the area and attacked barges.

338. The fighter escort problem had not been easy owing to the slow speed of the T.B. aircraft and the distance of the target from their aerodrome. During these two attacks, I2 Japanese Navy "0" fighters were shot down and 4 damaged for the loss of 2 Hurricanes and I Buffalo, one Hurricane pilot personally accounting for 4 Japanese fighters.

339. No. 36 & I00 (TB) Squadrons suffered very heavily. More than half their aircraft were shot down, including those of both Commanding Officers. The remainder were badly shot about, and a number of aircrews in them were wounded.

Both were withdrawn to Java on 29th/30th January for reorganisation after their very gallant effort.

Sustained Japanese Air Attacks on Singapore

340. During the second half of January the Japanese carried out air attacks on targets on Singapore Island with increasing intensity. Two, and sometimes three, attacks were delivered by formations of 27 to 54 enemy bombers escorted by fighters. The main targets were our aerodromes, but a number of attacks were delivered against Singapore harbour, the naval base and other military objectives. Raids were made in perfect formation despite A.A. fire, and the accuracy of bombing from heights over 20,000 feet was marked.

341. This continual pounding made it difficult to keep aerodrome surfaces serviceable. Kallang was built on reclaimed salt marsh, which oozed up through the bomb craters. The drainage at Tengah had never been satisfactory. Effective repairs were thus difficult. Rainfall at the time was exceptionally heavy, which in itself was a further handicap to repair work.

342. To complicate matters further, all native labour, which had many disabilities to face under air bombardment, disappeared. On the 7th January the Director General of Civil Defence had appointed a Director of Labour who was to organise and control all labour, allotting it to the services in accordance with an arranged priority programme.

There was also an acute shortage of M.T., without which labour, and the material for labour to use, could not be transported to the places where it was needed. The collection and allocation of M.T. was also placed under the Director General of Civil Defence.

Both these measures had become acutely necessary - to provide and organise labour in the face of repeated air raids, and in order to make the best use of limited supplies of motor transport.

343. First priority for what labour there was, was given to the repair of aerodromes. The G.O.C. Malaya diverted some of his reserves, at the expense of the construction of defence work, to reinforce R.A.F. labour parties. Later, parties of 100 sailors, survivors from H.M.S. "Prince of Wales" and "Repulse", were stationed at each of the 4 airfields in the Island.

344. Heavy attacks on our aerodromes on the Island had been anticipated some weeks beforehand by A.H.Q. In order to augment the number of airfields on the Island, six sites for landing strips had been selected, and work on them was put in hand on various dates during the latter half of December. Labour difficulties slowed up their construction, and, as will be narrated later, they had all to be demolished before they could be brought into use.

345. A considerable number of aircraft was destroyed, or rendered unserviceable on the ground largely because dispersal points had not been widely enough scattered in the first instance, whereas, time and labour had not been sufficient afterwards to rectify this shortcoming.

Operations by Fighters in the defence of Singapore

346. During the second half of January our depleted fighter squadrons did their utmost to ward off the enemy's attacks. No. 2I (F) Squadron R.A.A.F. and 453 (F) Squadron were mainly employed in operations in support of the army (paras. 323-330), leaving Nos. 243 and 488 (F) Squadron in a defensive role. To their assistance now came the newly arrived squadron of Hurricanes (paras. 3I4-3I6).

347. The Hurricanes' first day, 20th January, was most successful. Twenty-seven bombers came over unescorted and 8 were shot down without loss. It appeared as if confidence in their decisive influence was to be justified. This was the last occasion, however, on which Japanese bombers came over unescorted. The following day 5 Hurricanes were shot down, including the C.O., S.L. Landells and a Flight Commander, against no loss to the Japanese.

348. From then on the Hurricanes were constantly airborne, carrying out 3 to 5 "scrambles" daily. Owing to their being constantly outnumbered by the escorting fighters, which were well handled, bombers could seldom be attacked. But with the realisation that "dog-fighting" did not pay, the revised "in and out" tactics adopted gradually gave increasing success.

349. The Hurricane pilots had been informed of the characteristics of the Navy "Os" and particularly warned of the inadvisability of getting involved in "dog-fighting" owing to the Navy "O's" small turning circle. Despite this, some of them had become involved in "dog-fights", which led to casualties.

350. The limitations of the warning system for Singapore have already been described (para. 302). Some help was obtained at this stage from Army G.L. sets; but the short time of warning, I0-I5 minutes, remained a great handicap to efficient fighter defence. Operational control remained restricted owing to the lack of V.H.F. and to the unreliability of R/T.

35I. These new aircraft were Hurricane IIs. They were fitted with desert oil filters because their original destination had been the Middle East. These deprived them of some 30 m.p.h. They were not quite so fast as the Navy "O" near the ground, but as height increased the Hurricane gradually overhauled the Navy "O" until at 20,000 feet it had an appreciable advantage in speed and climb. The Hurricane could always dive at higher speeds, but at all heights the Navy "O" was the more manoeuvrable.

352. It must be admitted here that too much had been expected of this handful of Hurricanes. Civilians and the armed forces alike had anticipated that these modern aircraft would carry all before them. That this was not achieved was no fault of the pilots, who under S/L. R.E.P. Brooker, D.F.C., achieved, in the face of overwhelming numbers, results which stand greatly to their credit. Nevertheless the false hopes which had been placed in them reacted keenly when they were not realised.

353. The average daily serviceability of Hurricanes from the 2Ist January to 28th January was I6, and by the latter date the position as regards the 5I crated aircraft was:-

I7 destroyed (some of them at their bases).
2 repairable at Unit.

7 repairable at Depot.

2I available + 4 more in 24 hours.

On the 29th and 30th January, 20 were available.

354. During this period the Buffaloes of Nos. 2I R.A.A.F. and 453 (F) Squadrons were employed mainly on operations in support of the Army. Nos. 243 and 488 (F) Squadrons had continued in their role, in co-operation with the Hurricanes, in the defence of Singapore. By the 30th January, the number of Buffaloes had so dwindled that all (6) were concentrated in No. 453 (F) Squadron. Nos.2I R.A.A.F. and 243 (F) Squadron personnel were evacuated, whilst No. 488 (F) Squadron was retained to service the Hurricanes, together with a few of the pilots of all these squadrons to replace casualties.

Effect of Japanese Advance on R.A.F. dispositions.

Decision to Transfer Units to N.E.I.

355. The advance of the Japanese into Johore meant that our aircraft had to operate from the four aerodromes on Singapore Island. Thus a dangerous congestion of aircraft on the ground had come about. The dangers of congestion increased as enemy air attacks steadily grew in violence during January. When expected aircraft reinforcements should begin to arrive from the United Kingdom and the Middle East during January there were prospects of still greater congestion. Dispersal beyond the confines of Singapore Island would then become imperative.

356. During December, the first preparations had been made for operating R.A.F. Units in the N.E.I. (paras. 256-258). On 4th January No. I53 M.U. was moved to Java, and on I6th January No. 225 (B) Group Headquarters was formed in Singapore and moved to Sumatra two days later in order to make preliminary arrangements for operating bombers from aerodromes in that island.

357. By mid-January it was clear to A.H.Q. that the transfer of Units must be accelerated even though facilities for their operation and maintenance in Sumatra were not yet ready. In accordance with a prior agreement made with the Dutch Army Air Force, that Dutch Units should be moved first, a progressive withdrawal now took place from Singapore:-

I9*th January* - Dutch Buffalo Squadron at Kallang was withdrawn. On arrival in the N.E.I. it reverted to Dutch control. Its main function was to maintain, as requisite, fighter cover required for future convoys through Banka Straits.

22*nd January* - 2 Dutch Glenn Martin Squadrons withdrew to Java and reverted to Dutch control.

23*rd-27th January* - Nos. 27 (NF), 34 (B) and 62 (B) Squadrons, except for small aircraft handling parties, were transferred to Sumatra, as were also the main parties of Nos. I and. 8 (GR) Squadrons, R.A.A.F.

358. Concurrently with the above moves:-

(b) Base Accounts and Record Offices were ordered to Java.

(c) Station H.Q. Sembawang was ordered to Sumatra.

359. Each Unit was instructed to proceed with 30 days' rations, certain barrack stores and 28 days' pack-up of aircraft equipment. All ground personnel proceeded by sea. It will be seen later that, owing to confusion at the Singapore docks caused primarily by bombing, and owing to enemy attacks on shipping en route, the arrangements made for the transfer of our units to the N.E.I. were badly disorganised. Dutch Lodestars helped in these moves. Their assistance was invaluable.

360. When the decision was taken on 27th January that it would be necessary for the army to withdraw to Singapore Island, it became evident at once that one aerodrome only, Kallang, would shortly be available for use. The other three on the Island, Tengah, Sembawang and Seletar, were sited on its northern coastline and would soon be exposed to observed artillery fire from Johore at ranges as close as 1,500-2,000 yards: it would not be practicable to operate aircraft from them for long. Unfortunately Kallang itself was rapidly becoming of limited use. Its surface, a crust of marl laid on a salt marsh, was pock-marked with bomb craters which were most difficult to fill. Extension was impracticable, huddled as it was between the sea and the built-up area of Singapore Town. Consequently, further transfer of squadrons to the N.E.I. now became inevitable.

36I. On the 27th January No. 8 (GR) Squadron, R.A.A.F., was sent to Sumatra, and No. 205 (FB) Squadron on the 28th to Java. The latter on arrival in Java, was placed by Abdair under Dutch control as part of Recgroup. No. 205 Squadron left I Catalina at Seletar until the 30th January in connection with the arrival of a further convoy. On the 29th and 30th January the remaining G.R. Squadron (No. I, R.A.A F.) was transferred also to Sumatra.

362. Thus by the end of the month the whole of the bomber force had been compelled to withdraw to air bases in Southern Sumatra, where they were now organising with the intention of providing air support from that quarter to the army invested in Singapore.

363. On the 3Ist January, apart from fighters, there were left in Singapore only 3 Swordfish. They were still under Army control for coast defence spotting purposes, as H.Q.M.C. at this stage still did not rule out the possibility of a landing from the sea on Singapore Island itself.

Changes in appointments in the Command.

To digress for a moment from the narrative:-

364. With the arrival of reinforcements a reorganisation of senior appointments became practicable in the second half of January.

365. About I7th January Group Captain G.E. Nicholetts replaced Group Captain A.G. Bishop as Group Captain, Operations, at A.H.Q., the latter having been appointed to command the Bomber Group (No. 225) in Sumatra.

366. About 19th January Air Commodore W.E. Staton arrived and began taking the duties of S.A.S.O. from Air Commodore B.J. Silly. His recent and personal experience of air operations over Europe was to prove of great value to the Command.

367. On the 29th January Air Commodores S.F. Vincent and H.J.F. Hunter arrived from the U.K. They had been sent by the Air Ministry as Commanders designate of Fighter and Bomber Groups respectively Air Commodore Hunter was sent to Sumatra on 1st February, to command No. 225 Group which had already formed at Palembang.

368. By the 30th January, owing to the transfer of units to the N.E.I., the A.O.C. decided to make preparations for establishing of a rear A.H.Q., in the N.E.I. Air Commodore Silly was sent to Sumatra as Deputy A.O.C. in order to select its site and begin its organisation.

NARRATIVE - 30TH JANUARY UNTIL THE FALL OF SINGAPORE.

Situation of the Army.

369. It will be remembered that the Army withdrew into Singapore Island on a programme to be completed on 31st January. This was successfully carried out.

Early in February a reinforcing convoy arrived in Singapore. It brought the few remaining units of the 18th Division.

370. But the position of the Army, now invested on the Island, was jeopardised by the presence of four aircraft landing strips which were being constructed to augment the airfields of the Island (para. 344). There was real danger that the Japanese might use them for establishing airborne troops behind the frontal defences of the Island in order to accelerate the reduction of the garrison, a danger which could only be averted so long as they remained serviceable, by means of large detachments of troops who could not be spared for the purpose. On 30th January it was therefore decided to blow them, and also to accelerate the obstruction of other open spaces.

Reduction of the Fighter Force in Singapore.

371. This action restricted our fighters to the four main aerodromes of the Island, and negatived any possibility of their further dispersal. These aerodromes were under constant bombing, and considerable difficulty was being experienced in maintaining serviceable strips upon them. Further, three of them - Tengah, Sembawang and Seletar - were sited on the northern side of the Island and were therefore likely to be usable for a short time only (para. 360).

372. On the 30th January, therefore, Sir Archibald Wavell approved A.H.Q. plans to maintain in Singapore only a fighter strength of 8 Hurricanes reinforced by the remaining Buffaloes. It was agreed that the further reinforcing Hurricanes now arriving in H.M.S. "Indomitable" should be based on Sumatra, and from there not only maintain the strength at Singapore but also reinforce it as opportunity permitted.

373. To implement this policy A.H.Q.:-

(*a*) decided to retain in Singapore for the maintenance of the Fighter Force - an Air Stores Park, a Repair and Salvage Unit and an Ammunition Park.

(*b*) formed No. 226 (F) Group with H.Q. in Palembang and appointed Air Commodore Vincent the Group Commander. The staff for this Group H.Q. was to be provided partly from the reductions now possible in the Staff of the existing Fighter Group in Singapore and the remainder from H.Q. No. 266 (F) Wing, known to be arriving by sea in the N.E.I.

(c) issued orders for the move to Java of No. I5I M.U. less the repair and salvage party referred to in para. 358 (a).

374. Concurrently with this reduction in strength, General Wavell approved the A.O.C.'s proposal that, consequent on the transfer of the bulk of the strength of the Command to the N.E.I., he should proceed himself with the main body of A.H.Q. to the N.E.I. whence it would be possible to control more effectively the conduct of further air operations. It was intended to leave in Singapore a small advanced A.H.Q. to maintain liaison with H.Q.M.C. H.Q. No. 224 (F) Group was also to remain to control fighter operations.

375. A.H.Q. was reduced in accordance with this plan, personnel being despatched to Palembang in Sumatra for attachment to H.Q. No. 225 (B) Group pending the decision about the site for the rear A.H.Q. which Air Commodore Silly had been instructed to find.

376. On 5th February Abdair expressed disapproval of the transfer of A.H.Q. to the N.E.I., being of opinion that A.H.Q. should remain in close contact with the G.O.C. Malaya, to ensure that future air operations were planned in relation to the best means for the defence of Singapore. The A.O.C., after an exchange of signals with Abdair on the subject, cancelled the transfer on 6th February. He decided to remain himself with A.H.Q. in Singapore, despite another signal he had received on 5th February which instructed him to proceed temporarily to Java when it was convenient for him to do so: he was badly in need of a rest. But circumstances moved fast, and he declined to go until the last of his subordinates had been evacuated (para. 394).

377. By the 5th February it had become clear that no suitable site for a Rear H.Q. existed in Sumatra, and so Air Commodore Silly was instructed to proceed to Batavia and take administrative charge there.

378. Not only were personnel and equipment from Singapore now arriving at that port, but also the ground personnel of the reinforcing squadrons. It was also anticipated that the site for a Rear A.H.Q. would best be located in the Batavia area.

Dislocation at Singapore Docks.

379. There was a scarcity of suitable shipping for conveying equipment, particularly M.T., to the N.E.I.: a difficulty aggravated because some vessels had to be loaded at their moorings by means of lighters. Those which did come alongside, of which there were many, deserve great credit. Owing to enemy air bombardment, ships had to be

dispersed, which further delayed loading. Air bombardment also caused dock labour to disappear; its replacement by Service personnel could not be on a scale adequate to meet requirements. Conditions at the docks became confused as the scale and intensity of air attack increased. Plans made for the embarkation of personnel and stores were disorganised. Units became split up and personnel became separated from their equipment. Much equipment, urgently required by the Bomber Force in Sumatra, could not be loaded at all. In some instances, owing to air attack, ships sailed before being fully loaded.

Severe losses were inflicted by the Japanese air attacks on ships en route from Singapore during the final 14 days of evacuation. Considerable quantities of equipment including some 200 M.T. vehicles, were lost, all of it urgently needed in the N.E I.

Final Air Operations from Singapore.

380. Except for a small number of Hudson sorties for convoy protection, and a sweep by Buffaloes over the Batu Pahat area on 28th January to cover the evacuation of troops cut off by the Japanese advance, air operations from Singapore itself from the last days of January to the fall of the Fortress were nearly all carried out by fighters for the defence of the Island. Bomber operations from Sumatra for the support of the defence of Singapore are narrated in Section III.

381. An attack was carried out on the night of 2nd February by the Swordfish flight, released by the Army for the purpose, against the aerodrome at Kluang, where the Japanese had by now established a strong fighter force. Subsequently this Flight had to be destroyed, as its aircraft were in no condition to be flown to Sumatra.

382. The P.R. Buffalo Flight, which had functioned almost daily with outstanding success under the command of Squadron Leader Lewis since the beginning of the campaign, finally lost its aircraft by enemy air attacks on the 7th February. This Flight had carried out over 100 sorties, the majority of which had proceeded as far north as Singora. Aircraft were intercepted by Japanese fighters and hit on numerous occasions, although none was shot down. Throughout, no armour or guns had been carried pilots had relied entirely upon evasion in order to fulfil their missions. The greatest credit is due to them for the valuable work they did.

Final Fighter Operations from Singapore.

383. On the 31st January the fighter strength of Singapore was 8 Hurricanes of No. 232 (F) Squadron and 6 Buffaloes taken over by No. 453 (F) Squadron. The small Buffalo force gradually wasted away and 453 (F) Squadron was evacuated to Java about 4th February. The Hurricanes were maintained from Sumatra at an average daily strength of 10 aircraft. This average was maintained firstly by the arrival on 29th January of No 258 (F) Squadron with 15 Hurricanes. This squadron was one of several which had been convoyed from the Middle East (where they had just arrived as reinforcements from England) to the Far East in H.M.S. Indomitable. They had been "flown off "" south of Java and had proceeded by air via Batavia and Sumatra,

No 258 thence flying on to Seletar. They had had a long and varied passage from England, involving a sea voyage to Sierra Leone, followed by a long flight across the whole breadth of Central Africa to Port Sudan, where they had embarked in H.M.S. Indomitable. They came into action on Ist February after a delay caused by the necessity for removing all guns to clear them of anti-corrosion grease with which they had had to be protected for the journey. This squadron was relieved by 232 (F) Squadron on 3rd February, also ex H.M.S. Indomitable. The latter remained in Singapore until the withdrawal of the last of our aircraft.

384. These fighters were far too few in number to affect materially the scale of enemy attack. But they put up a stout fight, and throughout the first ten days of February they were almost constantly airborne throughout the hours of daylight, attempting to ward off the constant Japanese attacks.

385. Most of their sorties were for the defence of the Island. Fighter cover was provided on 30th January for the final withdrawal of the Army across the Johore causeway; and a few sorties were also flown against aircraft attacking our troop positions on the Island. On 9th February, the day following the Japanese landing on the Island, Hurricanes took off at the request of the Army and engaged enemy dive bombers, shooting down at least one.

386. A number of patrols were made for convoy protection. One convoy reached Singapore on 5th February. It had been shepherded through the Banka Straits, and during its onward passage towards Singapore, by reconnaissance and protective patrols from Sumatra. Fighters from Singapore covered its final approach. The "Empress of Asia" was attacked and set on fire, but that was the only loss incurred by reinforcing convoys. They escaped unscathed partly because of the protection they were given, but partly also because, it must be admitted, the Japanese made no very determined attacks against them. In contrast, many ships leaving Singapore during February were heavily attacked and there were many losses amongst them.

387. The devotion to duty of the fighter pilots and of the ground crews who serviced their aircraft and maintained landing strips during these last few days was exemplary. Warning of attack was short, and on occasion the Japanese bombers had dropped their bombs and were withdrawing before our fighters could reach them. But with experience of the enemy's tactics results steadily improved; and on the final day of operations, (9th February), 6 enemy aircraft were shot down and a further I4 seriously damaged for the loss of 2 Hurricanes and I pilot. It was significant that by 5th February the surviving pilots were mostly experienced men who had had previous battle experience before coming to the Far East.

388. On the 4th and 5th February, Seletar, Sembawang and Tengah came under steady observed shell fire, and all operations had then to be carried out from Kallang. The Japanese bombers concentrated their attack on this station, and the landing area was soon so riddled with craters that only by constant and arduous labour was a landing strip 750 yards long maintained in operation. Even so, by 6th February our pilots experienced very great difficulty in avoiding craters when taking-off and landing.

389. On the I0th February, by which time the Japanese were established in strength

on the Island, all aircraft were withdrawn to Sumatra. G.O.C. Malaya concurred in this decision, which was also endorsed by C.-in-C. South-West Pacific who visited Singapore the same day. A few Buffaloes were left, owing to their condition, and had to be destroyed.

Results of Fighter Operations in Malaya.

390. Total results of the fighting in the air over Singapore are difficult to assess with any accuracy, as definite confirmation of successes was in most cases impossible. Group Captain Rice, who commanded the Fighter Force during the whole of its operations over Malaya, estimated that 183 Japanese aircraft were destroyed, exclusive of others lost by them during our attacks on their aerodromes.

391. It is felt that this claim may be excessive, though, not by much. Reports which have been received from all sources appear to establish that the Buffalo Squadrons shot down a total of 30 Japanese aircraft: others were damaged and a proportion of them probably crashed during their return to base.

It is probable that the Hurricane force destroyed, or so seriously damaged that they failed to return to base, a total of 100 Japanese aircraft. For this total, 45 Hurricanes were lost from all causes, including flying accidents and enemy air bombardment. In view of the odds which were faced these figures speak for themselves.

Final transfer of R.A.F. to Sumatra.

392. On 8th February the Japanese launched their attack on Singapore Island and rapidly obtained a firm foothold. It now became essential to transfer A.H.Q. to Sumatra in order to take control of the Command, whose combatant units were already there, for the purpose of carrying on the fight in the N E.I.

A nucleus staff, including the S.A.S.O. (Air Commodore Staton) proceeded by air to Palembang on 10th February by order of the A.O.C.

Sir Archibald Wavell again visited Singapore the same day, 10th February. He ordered the immediate evacuation to the N.E.I. of all remaining R.A.F. personnel, which was commenced the following day. At the same time he instructed Air Vice Marshal Maltby, hitherto Assistant A.O.C. at A.H.Q., to take charge in the N.E.I. as soon as possible, that officer proceeding there by air the same afternoon accompanied by an addition to the nucleus staff which had preceded him. He was appointed by Abdair A.O.C. Westgroup in the N.E.I. with effect from 11th February.

393. Aerodrome surfaces were ploughed up. Bomb components, large stocks of petrol and much equipment which could not be got away was destroyed or rendered ineffective. But the volume of the whole was so great that neither time nor circumstances permitted its transfer or destruction, particularly a large quantity salved from Malaya which was housed in the town of Singapore where its destruction by fire was impossible. Special action was taken to destroy secret equipment e.g. radar apparatus, signals installations etc. It is believed that little of immediate value to the enemy was left to him.

394. On 13th February Air Vice Marshal Pulford, who had declined to leave until

all R.A.F. personnel, who could be, had been evacuated, left Singapore. He did so at General Percival's instigation. He accompanied a party under the orders of Admiral Spooner, R.A. Malaya. When they sailed they were unaware that the Japanese fleet had interposed itself between Singapore and their destination, which was probably Batavia in Java. They were detected, attacked from the air and their boat was stranded on an island of the Tuju or Seven Islands Group some 30 miles north of Banka Island. There the whole party, some 40 in number, lived as best they could, the fishermen inhabitants having deserted it. It was malarial, unhealthy and contained little food. The party had few stores, practically no medicines and no doctor. After remaining at large for more than two months the survivors were compelled to surrender. By then 18 had died, including Air Vice Marshal Pulford and Rear Admiral Spooner. The remainder were in a bad way. Thus it was that these gallant officers lost their lives and that the former was unable to rejoin his Command in the N.E.I.

Fall of Singapore.

395. On the 15th February Singapore Fortress was compelled to surrender.

SECTION III.

SUMMARY OF OPERATIONS BASED ON SUMATRA.

INTRODUCTION.

396. As has already been narrated in Section II of this Report, by the I6th January, I942, all Air Force units in Malaya had been driven back to Singapore Island. Even with the existing strength, aerodromes on the island were already congested, they would become more congested when reinforcements, now well on their way, arrived. The scale of Japanese air attack against these aerodromes was increasing. It had become imperative to disperse more widely. Extra elbow room was particularly desirable because H.M.S. "Indomitable", with 48 Hurricanes on board, was due to arrive at the end of January. If bomber units could be transferred to Sumatra, not only would they be dispersed more safely, but fighter squadrons could then be distributed to all the aerodromes in Singapore. It was not realised at the time how soon three of those aerodromes - Tengah, Sembawang and Seletar - would become untenable (para. 360).

General Conditions in Sumatra.

397. Sumatra, an island nearly I,000 miles long, lies west of and runs parallel to the west coast of Malaya, but extends far to the southward. Its main features are a mountain range running down the west coast throughout the whole length of the island, and a relatively low-lying belt of country eastward of it, consisting mainly of jungle and swamp, which is intersected by many rivers with a west to east trend. It is developed in scattered areas only. Roads are few, and although there are railway systems in the north and south, they are not connected, and communications are consequently poor. From the Allied point of view the chief economic importance of Sumatra was the oil field and refinery near Palembang, of which the normal outlet is to the east via Palembang river to the sea, though there is a single track railway running to the Port of Oesthaven in the extreme south. There was a radio telephone system inter-connecting the principal towns in Sumatra with an external connection to Java. This telephone system was open and insecure.

398. At the time this Section of the Report opens, the monsoon was still in progress over Sumatra. A feature of this monsoon was the prevalence of torrential thunderstorms, both by day and night. These thunderstorms are very violent indeed, and they completely black out all visibility from aircrews flying through them, whose

skill and endurance they test to the utmost: navigation through them is fraught with great risk. Unfortunately at this season several such thunderstorms were certain to be encountered during the course of every long flight.

State of Aerodromes.

399. Up to this date, 18th January, the policy of A.H.Q. had been to develop aerodromes in Northern Sumatra as refuelling grounds for reinforcements arriving by air from India, and as advanced landing grounds for operational use on the flank of Malaya. In consequence of this policy constructional work on them had been given priority over that at aerodromes in the south, and it was the aerodromes in the south of Sumatra which would now be wanted for our squadrons to use as their main bases. By the middle of January small refuelling and re-arming parties of varying strengths, up to 50, had been established at the following places:-

(*a*) Sabang (also for Flying Boats).

(*b*) Lho'nga.

(*c*) Medan Civil Aerodrome (a large military aerodrome was also being constructed in this area).

(*d*) Pakanbaroe.

(*e*) Padang.

(*f*) Palembang - at the civil aerodrome known as P.I.

(*g*) a secret military aerodrome 20 miles south of Palembang known as P.II.

In addition there was a strip at Lahat, and a field under construction by the Dutch at Oesthaven. Wing Commander Duncan, Squadron Leader Briggs and Squadron Leader Wightwick (A.M.W.D.) were already located at Palembang for liaison with the Dutch in connection with the development of these aerodromes.

DEVELOPMENT OF R.A.F. ORGANISATION IN SUMATRA.

400. A.H.Q. therefore decided, on the 16th January, that the time was becoming imminent when bomber units would have to be transferred to Sumatra. For this reason H.Q. 225 (B) Group was formed at Singapore on this date, and was sent to Palembang in Sumatra on the 18th January 1942. Initial appointments made by A.H.Q. were:-

Group Commander	Group Captain A.G. Bishop.
S.A.S.O.	Wing Commander K. Powell.
S.A.O.	Squadron Leader Briggs.
A.M.W.D.	Squadron Leader Wightwick

Instructions to No. 225 (B) Group.

40I. On formation of the Group Headquarters, the A.O.C. instructed the Group Commander-

(*a*) to establish a Bomber Group H.Q.

(b) to accelerate, to the maximum, arrangements for operating bomber units from Sumatra; such arrangements not only to provide for all bombers then in Singapore but also for the following reinforcements:-

(i) Nos. 84 and 2II (B) Squadrons (Blenheim IV) then en route from Middle East.

(ii) Hudson III's en route from U.K. which were to re-equip in succession No.62 (B) Squadron, and Nos. I and 8 (GR) Squadrons, R.A.A.F.

402. The A.O.C. also decided that, dependent on the situation, when bomber units were located in Sumatra, either Group H.Q. would be responsible for the selection of targets (within the policy laid down by A.H.Q.) and for the briefing of squadrons, or alternatively squadrons would proceed to bases in Singapore and be briefed there under A.H.Q. arrangements. To provide for this latter arrangement, refuelling and re-arming parties for bomber units would be maintained at aerodromes on Singapore Island. At this time it, was fairly confidently anticipated that the situation on the ground in Malaya would be stabilised and that a bridgehead would be held of sufficient area for the deployment of reinforcements preparatory to a counter-offensive being undertaken (para.322). That it would be necessary later to transfer fighter squadrons from Singapore was not at this time "on the cards". *Development by No. 225 (B) Group H.Q.*

403. Group Captain Bishop, on arrival at Palembang on the I8th January, decided to:-

(*a*) Establish Group Headquarters at Palembang.

(*b*) Expand and accelerate the provision of accommodation at P.I and P.II aerodromes, and improve aircraft dispersal at each.

(*c*) Develop Lahat for use by bombers.

(*d*) Reconnoitre the area to the south of Palembang for the selection and development of further landing strips.

At the same time he put in hand reconnaissance for siting an Ammunition Park, an Air Stores Park and an R.S.U., which were to be provided for the maintenance of the Force.

A.H.Q. were informed and approved of these decisions.

404. P.I. was, at that time, a large 'L' shaped aerodrome with two hard runways. It possessed dispersal arrangements which were at once considerably developed by

Dutch Engineers. There was no accommodation for personnel nearer than the town, 8 miles away.

P.II was a huge natural field about I0 miles in perimeter with good natural cover for aircraft. It was not visible from the road, and its construction had been successfully kept secret from the Japanese. Similar clearings in the neighbourhood made it difficult for air crews to locate it from the air, even by those who had been briefed as to its location. Great care was taken to preserve its secrecy and, although at one time more than I00 aircraft were based on it, Japanese reconnaissance, which frequently flew over it by day and night, never located it. Communications between Palembang and P.II were handicapped because there was no bridge over the Palembang river, on the north of which lay Palembang town and P.I, the river had to be crossed by a small ferry which had a limit of 4 to 6 vehicles. The Dutch put in hand the construction of huts for accommodation of personnel at P. II aerodrome.

405. There was a single line telephone linking each aerodrome with Group H.Q's., but instruments and wire were not available for developing an internal telephone system on either aerodrome.

For point to point communication a W/T set was improvised which was able to link up with A.H.Q., and with Sabang and Lho'nga on the air reinforcement route.

406. A civil Dutch Observer system existed at Palembang, consisting of two concentric circles of posts round Palembang, at 50 and I00 kilometers radius. There were a few posts still further out - one on the north end of Banka Island, one at the mouth of the Palembang river and one on Tanjong Pinang Island, just south of Singapore. Posts on the outer circle were unavoidably somewhat widely spaced: most warnings came from the 50 kilometre circle only. Communication between posts and the centre was by W/T or telephone. No radar was available to supplement the observer system, whose volunteer operators were most enthusiastic but unfortunately had had little experience in aircraft recognition. Warnings were consequently erratic.

407. With the most willing and energetic co-operation of the head of the Observer Corps, steps were immediately taken to improve the system. Additional posts were selected, manufacture of W/T sets began and additional personnel were trained. But events moved too fast for these measures to take effect. The original system only was available during the actual events which followed.

408. The Dutch army in the N.E.I. had no A.A. artillery, having been unable to obtain guns from the belligerents in Europe or from the USA. Thus the aerodromes in Sumatra had no A.A. defences. The Dutch had already had aircraft destroyed on the ground at Medan and Pakenbaroe by Japanese low flying fighters.

409. By the end of January, however, Abdacom was able to allot A.A. defences to P.I. and P.II., 6 heavy and 6 Bofors guns to each aerodrome, and 4 of each type to the oil refinery at Palembang. Ships carrying ammunition for these guns were unfortunately sunk and there was little ultimately available. There were two Dutch armoured cars and I50 native Dutch troops allotted to the defence of each aerodrome. With the arrival of R.A.F. ground personnel, aerodrome defence parties were organised to reinforce them.

4I0. There was one Dutch native regiment for the defence of the whole Palembang area, but there were no defences on the river leading to the town. On the 23rd January representations were made both to the Dutch naval and military authorities, and to Abdacom, on the inadequacy of the defences in the Palembang area, but no reinforcements were available. It is thought that plans were in hand to strengthen the defences, as General Sir John Laverack, Commanding Ist Australian Corps, visited Palembang about 25th January and indicated that an Australian division might be expected in the near future. Presumably, owing to the general situation in the Far East, the move was cancelled.

4II. In short, the aerodrome defences were very weak and few troops were available for the defence of the area against invasion.

Arrival of R.A.F. Units from Singapore.

4I2. However, Japanese progress in Malaya was quicker than had been anticipated. The transfer from Singapore had to be accelerated and expanded beyond what had first been contemplated. In the event, all aircraft had to be based on P.I and P.II, although the personnel of one bomber squadron moved to Lahat on I0th February, Group Captain Noble being appointed Station Commander. But events moved too quickly for that aerodrome to come into use.

4I3. This Report has already narrated the plans made by A.H.Q. in Singapore for transferring and re-organising in Sumatra and Java, and how these plans were largely frustrated by the speed of the Japanese advance in Malaya and by the dislocation caused at the docks in Singapore by air attack. These plans were further frustrated by Japanese action against shipping at sea en route to the N.E.I. Many ships were sunk and others re-routed at sea to other ports. The cumulative effect was disastrous. Practically all equipment destined for Sumatra went astray. In particular no M.T. arrived except some light motor cars about the 8th February and a few bomb trailers. There were only three refuellers available. Most important of all on the domestic side, few rations arrived and no tentage and field equipment. On aerodromes which were practically without accommodation, the last was a serious loss during the prevailing monsoon weather.

Aircraft spares were also scarce, particularly those for Blenheims, with which type the two reinforcing squadrons, Nos. 84 and 2II (B) Squadrons, were also equipped.

Three month's anticipated requirements in petrol, oil and lubricants had arrived at each aerodrome. A limited number of bombs also came across and these were distributed to P.I. and P.II.

4I4. Local buses were requisitioned and gradually came into service. An organisation for the local purchase of supplies was set up and contracts already placed for the manufacture of domestic equipment were expedited and expanded.

4I5. By the end of the first week of February personnel were reasonably fed and accommodated. But later when large numbers arrived, many unexpectedly, from Singapore, accommodation had to be found at short notice. Thus I,500 were provided for in P.II, where provision was ready for only 250, whilst 2,500 were housed in schools and cinemas in Palembang town.

Throughout, however, operational and maintenance facilities remained primitive in the extreme. The aerodromes in Sumatra were virtually landing grounds "in the blue".

All the problems which faced the staff and units were tackled with energy and spirit, and the praiseworthy results which were achieved in the face of every handicap are a great credit to both.

The Dutch gave magnificent assistance in all these local preparations, headed by the Resident Palembang, who personally inspired and directed the civil authorities in their efforts.

4I6. From the 22nd January onwards, personnel and aircraft started streaming in. The former were in some disorder owing to loss of kit and a splitting up of units through the confused conditions of embarkation at Singapore. The situation was further aggravated because the arrivals included units destined for Java, which had been re-routed at sea to Palembang. All had to be sorted and re-organised, and units for Java entrained for Oesthaven and shipped thence to Batavia.

4I7. On the 23rd January Blenheim IV's of Nos. 84 and 2II (B) Squadrons began to arrive from the Middle East. Their ground personnel, who came by sea, landed at Oesthaven about I4th February. The arrival of the latter coincided with the Japanese attack on the Palembang area (which will be related in due course), and they had to be re-embarked for Batavia before they could join their squadrons, which thus never had their own ground staffs with them in Sumatra. Each squadron had 24 aircraft when it left the Middle East. Sixteen of No. 84 Squadron arrived at P.I. I8 of No. 2II Squadron arrived on different days between 23rd January and I4th February (para. 3I8). Unfortunately the change of route from Singapore to Palembang resulted in the loss of 3 aircraft of No. 84 Squadron as a result of wrong briefing given to them on leaving Burma about the location of landing grounds in Sumatra.

Dispositions arranged for Units.

4I8. On the 23rd January P.I aerodrome received its first air attack. Twenty-seven unescorted bombers dropped their loads from 22,000 feet with great accuracy, but caused only slight damage to the surface of the aerodrome. The Dutch Buffalo Squadron on the aerodrome established contact with the formation and damaged at least two Japanese bombers without loss to themselves. It was now evident that our aerodromes in southern Sumatra were about to be bombed in their turn, in all probability with increasing severity. It was therefore decided to dispose our squadrons accordingly. Fortunately it was possible to take advantage of Japanese habits which by this time were well known, complete confidence could be placed in the fact that no daylight attack would take place before 0830 hours or after I700 hours. Other factors which were taken into consideration were:-

(*a*) that P.I. was best adapted to the use of fighters, and it was soon realised that part of the Hurricane force, which was known to be arriving in H.M S Indomitable, would want to use it: thus it would be advisable to minimise the number of bombers on it.

(*b*) that P.II was suitable for all types of medium bombers, that its existence was believed to be unknown to the Japanese. Moreover it had good facilities for dispersal, and cover from view in the scrub jungle which surrounded it.

4I9. Squadrons were, therefore, to be disposed on them as follows:-

P.I. M.V.A.F., Nos. 84 and 2II (B) Squadrons, serviceable aircraft moving to P.I during Japanese raid hours.

P.II. Nos. I (GR), 27 (NF), 34 (B) and 62 (B) Squadrons, whose aircraft strength when they arrived from Singapore would be low.

It will be remembered that the ground parties of Nos. 84 and 2II (B) Squadrons had yet to arrive by sea from the Middle East. Provision for servicing them was therefore made from amongst technical personnel who had been evacuated from Singapore. Those surplus to requirements were sorted out and despatched to Java.

420. Aircraft and personnel began to arrive from Singapore earlier than had been anticipated, so Wing Commander Powell, S.A.S.O. of the Group, was appointed Station Commander of P.II until the arrival of Group Captain McCauley on 29th January. The former then took over command of P.I from Wing Commander Duncan, the latter being placed in charge of the refuelling party at Pakenbaroe.

OPERATIONS CARRIED OUT BY No. 225 (B) GROUP.
22nd January-14th February.

42I. No. 225 (B) Group was responsible for reconnaissance northwards from the Sunda Straits to cover several convoys that went through to Singapore during the last week in January and the first in February. During the passage of a convoy through the Banka Straits on the 27th January, Blenheim IV's maintained a fighter escort over it because no fighters were available in Sumatra; the Dutch Buffalo Squadron had by this time been withdrawn to Java. All other available bomber aircraft stood by during these periods in case convoys were attacked by Japanese naval forces. The whole resources of the Group were directed towards the protection of these convoys during the two-day periods each took to traverse the area for which it was responsible.

422. On the 26th January the Endau landing took place (paras. 332-339) and No. 225 (B) Group was ordered to despatch all available aircraft to the scene. A force of 6 Hudsons from No. 62 (B) Squadron and 5 Blenheim I's of the same squadron but manned by No. 84 (B) Squadron aircrews was scraped up. The Hudsons arrived on the scene during the late afternoon, and landed at Sembawang for the night, returning to Palembang on the 27th January. The Blenheims arrived too late to participate, and so were ordered to land at Tengah and await orders from A.H.Q. This force was used on the night 27th-28th January to bomb Kuantan, returning to Palembang on 28th January.

423. On 26th January 6 Blenheim IV's of 34 (B) Squadron and 6 Hudsons of No. 8 (GR) Squadron R.A.A.F. were withdrawn from operations and were sent to Java under orders of A.H.Q. in connection with the arrival of H.M.S. Indomitable with 48

Hurricanes on board. This carrier was met at a point some distance to the Southward of Java by the bombers or G.R. aircraft, on which the Hurricanes were flown off in Squadron formations and were navigated to Java by the former aircraft. Meanwhile a Catalina provided anti-submarine patrols for the carrier's protection. The Hurricanes were again navigated during their onward journey to P.I, one squadron No. 258 (F) Squadron onward again to Singapore. The bombers and G.R. aircraft returned to P.II on 2nd February and became available again for operations.

424. On the 30th January Air Commodore H.J.F. Hunter, who had been appointed by the Air Ministry as Commander designate of a Bomber Group in the Far East, arrived in Sumatra and took over Command, Group Captain Bishop becoming S.A.S.O. of the Group.

425. Incidentally, Air Commodore Silly, Deputy A.O.C., also arrived in Palembang on the 30th January with orders from the A.O.C. to site a Command H.Q. in Sumatra. In this he was unsuccessful and left on 6th February to organise the R.A.F. Base, Batavia.

426. By the 30th January Singapore was clear of all but fighter aircraft. The strengths of
bomber squadrons in Sumatra then were:-

No. I Squadron, R.A.A.F.	I6 Hudson II	Many overdue for inspection and showing signs of wear and tear.
No. 8 Squadron, R.A.F.	6 Hudson III }	
No. 34 Squadron _	6 Blenheim IV }	Not available until 2nd February.
No. 62 Squadron _	I0 Hudson III	
No. 62 Squadron _	5 Blenheim I }	
No. 27 Squadron _	3 Blenheim I }	Particularly poor condition.
No. 84 Squadron _	I0 Blenheim IV }	Most aircraft required inspection and minor repairs, after their long flight from the Middle East.
No. 2II Squadron _	4 Blenheim IV }	
M.V.A.F.	Mixed Flight	

427. From the 30th January-5th February, as convoy duties permitted, the following attacks, were carried out during the nights shown:-

30th January-3Ist January.
6 Blenheims - Ipoh aerodrome - using Pakenbaroe for refuelling.
3Ist January-Ist February.
6 Hudsons - Alor Star aerodrome - using Medan for refuelling. Hits were scored on the runway and aerodrome buildings.
Ist February-2nd February.
5 Blenheims - Penang aerodrome - using Medan for refuelling.

2nd February-3rd February.
7 Blenheims, 3 Hudsons - Singora docks - using Medan for refuelling.
4th Febraary-5th February.
5 Blenheims, 4 Hudsons - Kluang aerodrome - using Singapore for refuelling.
5th February-6th February.
8 Blenheims - proceeded Medan en route Singora: cancelled owing to bad weather.
12th February-13th February.
12 Hudsons - Kluang aerodrome.

The policy was for aircraft to arrive at the advanced landing ground just before dusk, refuel and rest. Then after delivering their attacks aircraft either returned direct to base, or alternatively refuelled again at the appropriate advanced landing ground and returned to base at first light. On account of Japanese fighter patrols, aircraft could not remain on undefended grounds in Northern Sumatra during daylight hours.

428. These long nights in themselves imposed great strain on crews, it was still the wet monsoon season in Sumatra and torrential thunderstorms were prevalent, particularly at night. Not all the crews of reinforcing squadrons were up to the standard of night flying required for such conditions, particularly in the absence of radio aids to navigation: those that were showed outstanding determination and skill, and of them Wing Commander Jeudwine, C.O. of No. 84 (B) Squadron, was pre-eminent. It was only rarely, that results of bombing could be observed in any detail owing to the bad conditions of visibility.

429. Up to the 6th February No. 225 (B) Group had maintained daily reconnaissances across the South China Sea to Borneo to detect any Japanese movement southwards.

On the 6th February there were reports of a Japanese force assembling in the Anambas. This was located by Hudson sorties; it was attacked on the night 7th-8th February by 9 Blenheims in most adverse weather conditions, and again on the 11th-12th February by 10 Blenheims.

430. Throughout this period many transit flights to and from Singapore were carried out by Hudson aircraft either escorting Hurricanes or assisting in the evacuation of personnel.

Serviceability in all units was low.

The M.V.A.F. at Palembang were invaluable throughout in maintaining communications between P.I. and P.II. and Lahat, providing a twice daily reconnaissance of the river approaches, and locating crashed aircraft.

ORGANISATION - No. 226 (F) GROUP.

431. It will be remembered that it had not been the intention until quite a recent date to operate any of our fighters on aerodromes in South Sumatra, but that the unexpectedly rapid Japanese advance right up to the confines of Singapore island had made it impracticable for them to use the aerodromes on the island except

Kallang. It now became necessary, therefore, to make arrangements for them in Sumatra. On the Ist February, I942, Air Commodore Vincent arrived in Palembang and formed H.Q. No. 226 (F) Group. For this purpose he brought with him personnel drawn from No. 224 (F) Group, Singapore, and absorbed those of H.Q 266 (F) Wing which was now arriving in Sumatra from U.K. (para. 373 (*b*)).

432. In anticipation of the formation of a Fighter organisation, and with the energetic co-operation of the Dutch, a Fighter H.Q. Operations Room had already been established at Palembang on the 25th January by H.Q. 225 (B) Group. This Operations Room was connected to a naval transmitter in the docks some distance away, for communicating with aircraft. At first, orders from the Operations Controller had to be relayed to aircraft: later this arrangement was improved and the Controller was connected direct to the transmitter.

Arrangements were made for the Gun Operations Room to be in the same building. It was also connected with the Dutch Civil Observer System, which was in course of being improved (paras. 406 and 407).

433. The role of the Group was:-

(*a*) Defence of the Palembang area.

(*b*) Protection of shipping in the Banka Straits, by means of escort patrols and offensive sweeps.

(*c*) Up till the 9th February I942 maintenance of a token force of fighters in Singapore.

434. V.H.F. was not available, nor was D/F for assisting homing aircraft. The absence of the latter was a serious handicap because intense thunderstorms were frequent and fighter pilots were apt to lose their bearings when negotiating them.

All aircraft of the Fighter Group were based on P.I. aerodrome, the administrative shortcomings of which have already been related. It had a telephone from the Operations Room in Palembang but no instruments were available for dispersal points round the aerodrome, which slowed down the speed with which fighters could get away to intercept an enemy raid.

Strength of Fighter Squadrons.

435. About 50 Hurricanes were available when the Group formed, the majority direct from H.M.S. "Indomitable." The remainder were part of the original consignment which had arrived in crates in Singapore on the I3th January.

436. Forty-eight flew off H.M.S. "Indomitable" on 20th January. All flew off with their guns protected with anti-corrosion grease with which they had been provided for the journey. Fifteen flew via Batavia and P.I. to Singapore, arriving on the 29th January. Their guns were cleaned at Seletar. The remainder remained at P.II to have their guns cleaned before transfer to P.I. Cleaning of these guns was a slow operation owing to lack of all the usual facilities, and considerable delay occurred before squadrons were able to go into action.

437. Pilots were drawn from Nos. 232, 242, 258 and 605 (F) Squadrons and

operated as two composite squadrons - Nos. 232 and 258. Most pilots, with the exception of the Commanding Officers and Flight Commanders, were straight from O.T.U's., and deserve credit for the spirit with which they went straight into action. They had experienced a long sea voyage, but once again no time could be spared for acclimatization or training.

438. When they first arrived their aircraft were serviced by personnel from Buffalo squadrons. From the 6th February onwards however, ground personnel of No. 266 (F) Wing began to arrive via Oesthaven, including advanced parties and stores with an Air Stores Park and an R.S.U. There was a deficiency of Hurricane tool kits, few battery starters for aircraft, and no battery-charging facilities were available at the aerodrome: factors which contributed to a low standard of serviceability.

439 To improve the climb and manoeuvrability of the Hurricane the four outside guns were removed, as it was considered that eight guns were ample against the unarmoured Japanese aircraft.

OPERATIONS CARRIED OUT BY No. 226 (F) GROUP.

440. From the 2nd-5th February many sorties were carried out escorting shipping proceeding north and south through the Banka Straits. On the 3rd February, nine aircraft of No. 258 Squadron left for Singapore to co-operate with a bomber force in a combined attack on Kluang aerodrome, returning the following day. They landed at Tengah, but owing to an error on the part of that Station, the squadron was not ready to take off at the appointed time, and the attack was a failure.

44I. Meanwhile, Japanese reconnaissance was maintained daily over Palembang, and was quick to note our activity. Air attacks on P.I. aerodrome took place on 6th, 7th and 8th February by formations of bombers escorted by fighters.

442. On the 6th February warning was short, and the Hurricanes, caught at a tactical disadvantage, lost four and claimed one Navy "O". No. 232 Squadron were away at Singapore on this day conducting operations from the Island.

443. On the 7th February warning was even shorter, and results were serious. The Japanese combined a high bombing attack with a low attack by fighters. Three Hurricanes were destroyed and II others damaged on the ground, whilst three were shot down in the air. In addition four unserviceable Blenheims on the ground, and one Hudson, which arrived as the attack was in progress, were destroyed. Only one Navy "O" fighter could be claimed.

444. On the 8th and I3th February fresh attacks on the aerodromes took place, but more warning was received: on the 8th an inconclusive interception took place, but on the I3th, three Navy "O" fighters and two Army 97 bombers were shot down for the loss of one Hurricane.

445. On the I2th February the Group was reinforced by Wing Commander Maguire and eight aircraft. These were part of a reinforcing Wing, No. 226 (F) Wing which included 39 Hurricanes, a pool of I5 pilots, and the ground crews of Nos. 232, 258 and 605 Squadrons: it had arrived at Batavia by sea on the 4th February.

446. On the I3th February a further nine aircraft from Batavia arrived at P.I. Unfortunately they did so while the attack on the aerodrome was in progress. They were short of petrol, and in ensuing engagements six were either shot down or crashed.

447. It was quite evident that the Japanese already realised that we were endeavouring to establish our squadrons on P.I. and that they were devoting a very considerable effort, particularly with strong forces of fighters, to prevent it.

It is opportune at this juncture to digress for a moment.

Control of operations in Sumatra assumed by Abdair.

448. It will be realised that A.H.Q. in Singapore had, by the end of January, much depleted its staff in forming the staffs of the two new Groups, Nos. 225 and 226, in Sumatra, which were themselves much under requirements. This depletion particularly affected the signals organisation. Firstly because its numbers were reduced at a time when signals traffic was on the increase consequent upon the splitting up of the Command between Singapore and Sumatra. Secondly because it was just as this time that the trained and experienced lady cypher staff had to be evacuated. The result was acute congestion of, and increasing delays in, signals traffic. This had reached such a pitch on 6th February as to constitute a breakdown between Palembang and A.H.Q. in Singapore. Abdair therefore assumed operational control of all R.A.F. units in Sumatra with effect from 7th February.

Formation of Westgroup H.Q.s in the N.E.I.

449. Air Vice-Marshal P.C. Maltby and Air Commodore W.E Staton arrived in Palembang on the I0th February, and on the following day the former became A.O.C. and the latter S.A.S.O. of Westgroup, which comprised all R.A.F. and R.A.A.F. Units of the Far East Command now located in Sumatra and Java. Whilst in Palembang they picked up a nucleus staff and moved with it on I2th February to Java, having first reconnoitred South Sumatra and ascertained that no suitable site for a H.Q. existed in that area. It was arranged that, pending the establishment of H.Q. Westgroup in Java, Abdair would continue in direct control of all operations carried out by Westgroup Units.

FURTHER OPERATIONS BY 225 (B) GROUP - I2TH TO I4TH FEBRUARY.

450. From the 7th February onwards, all reconnaissance by No. 225 (B) Group had been discontinued under orders from Abdair, who wished to economise air effort by centralising all reconnaissance under the Reconnaissance Group in Java and thereby increasing the size of the striking force available in Sumatra.

45I. On the I3th February, however, the shipping situation as known at H.Q. 225 (B) Group appeared most confused. Reconnaissance reports made by Reconnaissance

Group and received through Abdair showed that Japanese naval forces were in strength south of Singapore. These reports were 5-7 hours old by the time they reached 225 (B) Group owing to bad communications, locations of convoys had by then completely changed. To confuse matters still further, a stream of shipping of all kinds was at the same time passing south from Singapore to Java despite the presence of Japanese forces; friend was difficult to distinguish from foe.

452. By the I3th February (p.m.) it was felt at H.Q. 225 (B) Group that, despite orders to the contrary, a reconnaissance must be carried out to clear the situation and ascertain whether or not there was an immediate threat to Sumatra. One Hudson of No I (GR) Squadron, R.A.A.F., was sent in the afternoon and reported a concentration of Japanese shipping north of Banka Island, which confirmed impressions that a landing at Palembang was imminent. All available Blenheims were immediately despatched to attack the enemy force, but results were difficult to assess owing to darkness and rainstorms.

453. On the I4th February an offensive reconnaissance of 5 Hudsons was despatched so as to be over the area at first light. This located and attacked a convoy consisting of 25-30 transports, heavily escorted by naval vessels, at the northern entrance of the Banka Straits, heading towards the Palembang river. The convoy was protected by fighters believed to be from one or two aircraft carriers which were not, however, located. This was followed up by attacks by all available Hudsons and Blenheims, during which at least 6 transports were sunk or badly damaged. All of these attacks, except the first, were unescorted and carried out in the face of heavy A. A. fire and strong fighter defence. Six to eight of our aircraft were shot down or destroyed on landing in a damaged condition, whilst the majority were hit to a varying degree. Nevertheless, the successes already achieved more than balanced those losses and during the night of the I4th everything possible was done to prepare for further attacks the following morning.

454. The reason why no fighter escort had been available except for the first attack was because the Japanese had, in co-ordination with the approach of their convoy, staged a parachute attack on P.I. aerodrome, on which our fighters were based. It was the only occupied aerodrome which they had located in Sumatra. Presumably by attacking it they hoped to neutralize all air resistance to the convoy. As events will show, their failure to locate P.II and neutralize it as well was to prove costly. However, before proceeding further it is now necessary to turn to describe events at P.I.

Parachute attack on Palembang I Aerodrome - I4th February.

455. On I4th February all serviceable Hurricanes were airborne, escorting 225 Group's bombers which were attacking enemy shipping in Banka Straits. At about 0800 hours the approach of a large hostile formation was reported by the Observer Corps. Attempts to divert our Hurricanes to intercept it failed because they were beyond R/T range.

456. Shortly afterwards P.I. was attacked, first by bombers with light bombs, then

it was well shot up by the large escort of fighters, and finally troop carriers dropped 2 groups of parachutists, each I50-200 strong, at two points 400-800 yards to the S. and W. in the scrub jungle which surrounds the aerodrome. Simultaneously 300 more were dropped on the oil refinery a few miles away near Pladjoe.

457. The aerodrome defences (8 heavy and 8 Bofors British A.A. guns, I50 Dutch infantry with 2 old armoured cars and about 60 R.A.F. ground defence gunners of 258 and 605 (F) Squadrons) warded off an attempt to rush the aerodrome, a number of casualties occurring on both sides.

458. Our absent fighters, now with empty tanks and guns, were diverted to P.II. And were subsequently employed against the main enemy attack in the Palembang river. Some landed at P.I. not having received the diversion order, were refuelled and sent on to P.II.

459. Shortly afterwards the A.A. guns, having by then almost exhausted their small stock of ammunition, were withdrawn to Palembang Town. Wing Commander Maguire organised the withdrawal of unarmed R.A.F. personnel at the same time. He remained himself with about 60 R.A.F. personnel and some Dutch native infantry to deny the aerodrome to the enemy. One paratroop party had, however, reached the road leading to Palembang and ambushed part of the withdrawing parties, subsequently making a road block with overturned vehicles.

460. Two subsequent attempts from Palembang Town to reinforce the aerodrome were driven back at the road block after close quarters fighting. The first, at about II00 hours, was by an R.A.F. party under F.L. Jackson and P.O. Umphelby who pressed their attack with determination: some of the party succeeded in reaching the aerodrome through the scrub and assisted in evacuating some wounded and unarmed personnel. The second, at I6.30 hours, was by a Dutch contingent which also was able to get some small assistance and information to the aerodrome.

46I. Wing Commander Maguire's party, by now much reduced, was running out of ammunition, and had no water or food. Thus, this handful of men was in no position to continue their gallant denial of the aerodrome to the enemy in face of an attack in force which was certain to come at night. He therefore destroyed all material, including some unserviceable aircraft, and withdrew. Being cut off from Palembang Town the party made its way to the West Coast of Sumatra after an arduous trek of seven days, during which they destroyed a number of stocks of petrol and some rubber factories. They there rejoined their units in Java.

462. Our aircraft at P.II meanwhile were too busy dealing with far greater a threat to be in a position to help recover P.I aerodrome, as will now be related.

EVENTS FROM I4TH FEBRUARY (P.M.) - I8TH FEBRUARY.

Attacks on Japanese Convoy off Palembang, I5th February.

463. By I4th February (p.m.) therefore, the total Air Forces located in Sumatra were at P.II aerodrome. The strength assisted of:-

22 Hurricanes.

35 Blenheim I's and IV's - many of whioh were unserviceable.

3 Hudsons (the remainder of the Hudson force was flown to Java for repairs on the I4th February).

The whole was placed under the command of the Station Commander P.II, Group Captain McCauley, who was instructed by the A.O.C. No. 225 (B) Group to continue attacks on the Japanese convoy entering the Palembang River from first light on the I5th (paras. 452-4).

464. Reconnaissance on the I5th pin-pointed the position of transports and barges, and revealed approximately 20 naval vessels and transports steaming through the Banka Straits, whilst other transports and landing craft were in the river mouth.

465. The first attack, off at 0630 hours, was made by 6 Blenheims escorted by Hurricanes. It met strong fighter opposition but pressed home the attack. From then onwards until I530 hours a constant stream of our aircraft proceeded to attack the convoy, and, as all enemy fighter opposition had ceased, Hurricanes were employed in shooting up barges whilst bombers similarly expended their ammunition after dropping their bombs. The limiting factor in the number of attacks was the speed with which re-armament and refuelling could be carried out. The Japanese in barges and transports fought back for a time with A.A. and small arms fire but by II00 hours this opposition ceased. By I530 hours all movement on the river was stopped and surviving barges and landing craft had pulled in to the thick undergrowth. Troops had dispersed onto the river bank, and against them attacks continued.

466. It is difficult to assess the damage done. All pilots reported upon its extent. Thousands of troops in barges were caught in the open by machine gun fire, particularly by the Hurricanes, and very heavy casualties were inflicted upon them. Bombing accounted for many more, whilst in addition, 3 transports were sunk, a number of others were hit and an unknown number of landing craft were also sunk.

467. As a fitting finale to the day, a number of Navy 'O' fighters were located on a strip on the beach on Banka Island and were destroyed by Hurricanes. It is probable that these fighters were those which had been encountered during the initial sorties of this day.

468. Air action thus brought the landing to a standstill. The Japanese were punished heavily for their failure to locate P.II aerodrome. Unfortunately, there were no troops or naval light craft available in the area to take advantage of the situation.

Withdrawal from Sumatra.

469. On the evening of the I4th February, A.O.C. 226 Group returned to Palembang from P.II. Both he and A.O.C. 225 Group were informed by the local Dutch Territorial Commander that the situation was well under control and that he had every hope of eliminating the paratroops. He gave the impression that a drive was to take place that

night to clear the area. Contrary orders evidently were received later by him, because a start was made during the night in burning oil and rubber stocks in the town, and in the destruction of the oil refinery area.

470. When A.O.C.'s. Nos. 225 and 226 Groups saw the Dutch Territorial Commander early on the morning of the I5th, they found that the Dutch H.Q. had closed and that the Territorial Commander himself considered it too late to restore the situation. He was himself about to leave for Lahat in the South.

47I. The Dutch Territorial Commander also stated that the ferries across the river and the railhead facilities would be blown in one hour's time, with the object of embarrassing the Japanese advance towards the South. In consequence, A.O.C. No. 225 Group ordered the immediate evacuation of the town by all remaining R.A.F. personnel. This was effected by road and rail to Oesthaven.

472. A further paratroop landing took place at P.I. later during the morning of the I5th, and the Japanese established themselves in the vicinity of Palembang town. There was thus a distinct possibility that P.II. aerodrome might be over-run during the night I5th/I6th February. Also by I5th February (p.m) stocks of bombs and ammunition at P.II were almost expended, whilst food supplies were cut off.

473. In view of these factors and the lack of any supporting troops, Abdair approved the evacuation back to Java of all R.A.F. units, and this was effected by road and rail on the evening of the I5th via Oesthaven. All flyable aircraft were flown to Java, the remainder destroyed. Aircraft of Nos. 84 and 2II (B) Squadrons, which had borne the brunt of the attacks during the day, finished their last sorties too late to proceed that evening. They remained on the aerodrome, flying to Java on the morning of the I6th February.

474. Personnel at landing grounds in N. and Central Sumatra were instructed to proceed by road to west coast ports for evacuation in accordance with pre-arranged plans.

475. Special mention must be made here of the valuable services rendered by the General Manager, Sumatra Railways Despite orders received from his superior authorities he delayed destruction of rail facilities and personally arranged for the trains required during the night I5th/I6th February. He himself did not leave until after the departure of the last train conveying R.A.F. personnel.

Credit is also due to Group Captain A.G. Bishop for the part he played in Sumatra. He put our squadrons on their feet and organised the staff despite primitive circumstances. He contributed in no small degree to the success of the operations which were conducted in Sumatra, and finally he personally supervised the successful withdrawal of the force from the Palembang area when its position there was no longer tenable.

476. At Oesthaven on the I6th February, it was found that the Dutch had already fired the bazaar and destroyed all military property. At the docks the British Military Embarkation Commandant stated that he had been given orders that all personnel were to be clear by midnight; personnel only were to be evacuated, not M.T. or equipment. As a result, essential and vital aircraft equipment, including that brought from Palembang, was left behind. This was particularly unfortunate because spare

engines and other urgent stores for the Hurricanes which had been landed at Oesthaven with No. 4I Air Stores Park, of No. 266 (F) Wing, were left behind. No. 266 (F) Wing's R.S.U. similarly lost valuable equipment. A.A. guns and ammunition which had been brought to the port from P.I. and P.II aerodromes had also to be abandoned. Section IV of this Report will show that the loss of this R.A.F. and A.A. equipment had serious results during operations conducted later in Java. Fortunately the light tanks were re-embarked, and all personnel, Army and R.A.F., were evacuated.

477. The evacuation of the port was covered by a screen of R.A.F. personnel from No. 84(B) Squadron acting under the command of Group Captain G.E. Nicholetts, who had been appointed R.A.F. Base Control Officer about ten days previously.

478. It was unfortunate that Oesthaven was evacuated so hastily. Two days later Group Captain Nicholetts, with a party of 50 volunteers of No. 605 (F) Squadron, returned from Batavia to Oesthaven by sea in H.M.S. "Ballarat" which was commanded by a Royal Australian Naval Reserve officer specially appointed for the voyage owing to his knowledge of Oesthaven Harbour. On arrival, early on the 18th, twelve hours were spent by the party loading the ship to the gunwales with R.A.F. equipment and some Bofors ammunition. At the same time the railway track was damaged, loaded rolling stock and petrol dumps were fired, and the water by the dockside was obstructed by pushing into the sea abandoned heavy M.T. and other vehicles.

479. That this work of salvage and destruction proceeded unhampered by the enemy must not detract from the spirit shown by both the R.A.F. party and the crew of H.M.S. "Ballarat," who volunteered for the adventure with a full knowledge of the hazards involved.

As it happened, air reconnaissances from Java had made it clear that the casualties and disorganisation caused as a result of our air attacks on the convoy off Palembang during the I4th and I5th February had been so severe that the Japanese were in no state to run through from Palembang to Oesthaven at the speed which had been anticipated when the port was evacuated, but Group Captain Nicholetts and his party were unaware of this fact.

SECTION IV.

SUMMARY OF OPERATIONS BASED ON JAVA.

INTRODUCTION.

Early Days of War in the N.E.I.

480. Before hostilities had broken out in the Far East the Dutch considered that their best interests lay in co-operating with the British from the outset with the object of repelling a Japanese attack in its early stages. They felt confident that, by joint means, an attack could be halted in the north and that war would never reach Java itself.

48I. Dutch air units, therefore, operated from the first day of war in Malaya, Borneo and the northern islands of the N.E.I. There they suffered considerable casualties. Dutch naval units also played an early part and suffered considerably.

482. Early reverses caused apprehension but acted as a spur to Dutch co-operation. Their will to help was most marked although their resources were very limited.

Formation of H.Q. S.W. Pacific Command (Abdacom) in Java.

483. On I5th January, I942, Sir Archibald Wavell arrived in Java to take control of all Allied Forces in the S.W. Pacific and formed his H.Q. (Abdacom) near Bandoeng. Confidence was raised by this and by the news of expected reinforcements - British, Australian and American - and still further by the actual arrival, towards the end of January and early February, of the first of them. More were on the way.

484. Even when the British forces in Malaya were, by 3Ist January, invested on Singapore Island, it was believed that that fortress, the key of the Far East, would hold out for some while. This would provide the necessary time for adequate forces to be built up in the N.E.I. for the successful defence of the rest of the Far East.

Then came a series of unpleasant events.

Effect in the N.E.I. of Japanese Capture of Singapore and Sumatra.

485. On 8th February the Japanese secured a foothold on Singapore Island and within a couple of days its imminent capitulation became evident.

486. On I4th February they attacked and overran South Sumatra, admittedly at heavy cost. The British forces, mainly air units, had to withdraw to Java.

487. Between I2th and I8th February large numbers of personnel, evacuated from Singapore and Sumatra, arrived in considerable confusion in Western Java: amongst

them were approximately I0,000 R.A.F. of all ranks. They augmented considerable numbers of refugees who had preceded them in a steadily growing stream from the same places and from other N.E.I. Islands.

488. At this time, mid-February, Abdacom was still established in Bandoeng, reinforcements were arriving and more were expected. Nevertheless it was evident now that Java would be attacked in the near future. A civilian exodus from Java on a grand scale replaced the small stream which had been leaving for some time through Sourabaya and Batavia.

Congestion in Batavia.

489. At Batavia the exodus became confused with incoming reinforcements and evacuees from Singapore and Sumatra. For several days the harbour of Batavia, and the roadstead outside, were congested with shipping. This unloaded as best it could. The result was that quays, warehouses and the roads leading from them rapidly became blocked with an inextricable confusion of merchandise, equipment, M.T., abandoned cars and goods of every description. The town of Batavia became congested with personnel - outgoing refugees, incoming reinforcements, incoming evacuees and Dutch troops mobilised for defence of the locality.

490. Into this confused area the R.A.F. evacuated from Singapore and Sumatra, arrived, for the most part between 12th and I8th February.

49I. Those from Singapore had embarked there under heavy air attack on shipping of all kinds as it came to hand, and amongst a number of civilian refugees. Units had become much mixed, many personnel were separated from units and many had become separated from their equipment. It had proved impracticable to embark much equipment owing to conditions at Singapore docks, and some of what had been embarked had been lost at sea through enemy action.

492. Units from Sumatra had also suffered loss of their equipment by reason of the hasty withdrawal from aerodromes near Palembang, and still more so by circumstances at the port in South Sumatra, Oesthaven, at which they had embarked: such small amount of equipment as they had possessed in Sumatra, and which they had succeeded in removing to Oesthaven, could not be embarked and brought with them (para. 476).

493. An appreciable number of bombers and fighters had, however, reached aerodromes in the Batavia district, though a high proportion of them were unfit for operations.

494. Such was the situation in Batavia on I6th February. It was from personnel and equipment so placed that a maximum air fighting strength with ancillary services had to be evolved, and surpluses evacuated from Java. Twelve days were destined to be available for this work before the Japanese landed in Java.

R.A.F. RE-ORGANISATION IN JAVA.

Situation on 16th February.

495. On the 16th February, the date of the evacuation of Sumatra, the position in Java was as follows:-

(*a*) *H.Q. Westgroup* (A.O.C. - A.V.M. P.C. Maltby) - A.O.C. and a nucleus staff had arrived at Soekaboemi on 14th February and were organising a H.Q. there; this was still known as Westgroup. Soekaboemi was chosen because it is centrally located in Western Java, where all Westgroup units were being located. Westgroup assumed administrative responsibility for its units on 16th February. As it was not yet ready to take operational control, this was retained by Abdair, which had assumed it on 7th February whilst units were still operating in Sumatra (para. 448).

(*b*) *No. 205 (F.B.) Squadron* - (Wing Commander Councell in Command) had arrived in Batavia on 1st February and was operating as part of the Allied Reconnaissance Group (Recgroup), using anchorages at Batavia and Oesthaven.

(*c*) *Nos. 36 and 100 (T.B.) Squadrons* - (Squadron Leader Wilkins in Command). Aircraft had arrived on 29/30th January from Singapore for re-organisation. After being based on various aerodromes they were rejoined by their ground personnel on 15th February at Tjikampek.

(*d*) *No. 153 M.U.* - (G/Capt. Ridgway in command) had arrived in Java on the 9th January and moved to Djocjacarta, where it was ready to start work on 15th January.

(*e*) *No. 152 M.U* - (Squadron Leader S.G. Aylwin in command) had arrived in Batavia on 14th February and moved on the 17th to Poerbolinggo to form a transit store.

(*f*) *R.A.F. Base, Batavia* (Group Captain Ridgway in command until 18th February 1942 when Air Commodore Silly relieved him). This base had been established in Batavia on the 24th January to organise the reception, sorting and despatch of personnel arriving by sea from Singapore and Sumatra and of air reinforcements from the Middle East and the United Kingdom. It also organised the reception and erecting of a number of boxed Hurricanes. By 18th February this base was administering 5 transit camps in Batavia and one at Buitenzorg. Personnel of all other units not mentioned in (*a*) to (*e*) above passed through this base for reorganisation and disposal, a total of over 12,000 being handled.

(*g*) *Certain A.M.E. Units* were installing radar facilities in the Batavia and Sourabaya areas.

(*h*) Thirty-nine crated Hurricanes had been erected in Batavia during the first ten days of February. Seventeen had proceeded to No. 266 (F) Wing in Sumatra, where a number of them were lost. Twelve were handed over by Abdair to the Dutch Army Air Force. For diplomatic reasons they could not be withdrawn in spite of the losses which our fighter squadrons had just sustained in Sumatra. Thus only 10 were left as replacements for our squadrons.

Allocation of Aerodromes.

496. On the evacuation of Sumatra, on 16th February, Abdair allocated aerodromes as follows:-

(a) All Hudsons to Samplak:

(b) All Blenheims to Kalidjati:

(c) All fighters to Tjililitan.

These aerodromes had not been highly developed, dispersal being limited, aerodrome ground defence weak, internal signals and night flying arrangements lacking. No A.A. defences were available.

497. On the 18th February, in view of the reduced strength of squadrons and the fact that no further bomber reinforcements could be expected, A.O.C. Westgroup decided to concentrate all aircraft by types into selected squadrons as follows:-

(*a*) *Semplak:*
Station Commander - Group Captain Brown, No I (GR) Squadron, R.A.A.F. - Commander, W/Cdr. R.H. Davies. Strength 14 Hudson II's and 12 Hudson III's (about 12 operationally serviceable).

(*b*) *Kalidjati:*
Station Commander - Group Captain Whistondale (pending availability of Group Captain Nicholetts) No. 84 (B) Squadron - Commander, W/Cdr. Jeudwine. Strength 26 Blenheims (about 6 operationally serviceable).

(*c*) *Tjikampek:*
No. 36 (TB) Squadron - Commander, S/Ldr. Wilkins. Strength 9 Vildebeestes and I Albacore. (No torpedo facilities were available in Java.)

(*d*) *Tjililitan:*
No. 232 (F) Squadron - Commander, S/Ldr. Brooker.
No. 605 (F) Squadron - Commander, S/Ldr. Wright.
Total strength of 25 Hurricanes (about 18 operationally serviceable).

The former had been in action since its arrival in the Far East, in Singapore and Sumatra, and had been kept up to strength by absorbing No. 232 (F) Squadron proper which had arrived in H.M.S. Indomitable. It was now very depleted again, and in turn absorbed practically the whole of No. 242 (F) Squadron also from H.M.S. Indomitable - but the original designation of the squadron, No. 232 (F) Squadron, was retained.

No. 605 (F) Squadron had hitherto been mainly employed in erecting Hurricanes for No. 266 (F) Wing. But it was now armed with a small quota of aircraft and came into action on 23rd February.

The decision to retain two fighter squadrons in Java was taken in expectation of the arrival of U.S.S. "Langley," a U.S.A. aircraft carrier, with a consignment of P.40 fighters on board, with which it was hoped to arm one of them, the other retaining Hurricanes. Unfortunately the "Langley" was later sunk when approaching Java and the expectation was never realised.

Re-formation of Bomber and Fighter Groups.

498. On 18th February H.Q. Nos. 225 (B) and 226 (F) Groups were re-formed in skeleton to assist Westgroup in re-establishing their squadrons in Java.

No. 225 (B) Group, under Air Commodore Hunter, re-formed in Bandoeng. Bomber aerodromes were visited and assistance given, in co-operation with the Dutch, to units to solve their acute problems of housing, rationing and transportation. Air Commodore Hunter was absorbed into Abdair on 19th February to act as A.O.A.; the remaining members of Group H.Q. were absorbed into H.Q. Westgroup on its arrival in Bandoeng on the 23rd February.

No. 266 (F) Group, under Air Commodore Vincent, took charge of Nos. 232 (F) and 605 (F) Squadrons, and of a fighter operations room in Batavia and its local warning system. This had made good progress during the preceding few days, thanks largely to the initiative of Wing Commander Bell, previously Station Commander at Kallang, Singapore. Owing to the highly developed nature of communications in Java, efficient operations and filter rooms were quickly connected to the Dutch Observer Corps, the fighter aerodrome, the A.A. defences of Batavia, and Abdair's (later Britair's) operations room in Bandoeng. Two R.D.F. and two G.L. sets were quickly erected in the Batavia district and were also connected with them. The Dutch provided the utmost assistance, including the provision of many volunteer Dutch youths and women to man the filter and operations rooms; their alertness and enthusiasm could hardly have been bettered.

499. To maintain this Force it was decided to retain:-

(*a*) No. 153 M.U. (already organised for work at Djocjacarta).

(*b*) No. 81 R.S.U.

(*c*) No. 41 Air Stores Park for Unit supply.

(*d*) An improvised Air Stores Park for collection and sorting of equipment.

500. Establishments were drawn up and issued; and instructions were given that all personnel surplus to establishment were to be evacuated via the R.A.F. Base, Batavia, as shipping became available and as far as possible with their original units. Preference was to be given in the following order, after women and children evacuees - formed units, aircrews, technical personnel and selected details.

501. Aircraft serviceability for various reasons was low: the Hudson and Blenheim Squadrons had about six serviceable each, the two fighter squadrons not more than 18 in all. For the next few days minor operations only were carried out (under Abdair

orders), and all efforts were directed towards improving the condition of aircraft and to getting ready generally for the serious operations to come.

AIR OPERATIONS I8TH TO 24TH FEBRUARY.

502. While re-organisation described above was progressing under Westgroup direction, the following operations were carried out under the directions of Abdair.

503. On the I8th February, one Hudson reconnoitred the port of Oesthaven and the road to Palembang. No signs of Japanese activity were observed.

504. On the I9th February all available (5) Blenheims attacked shipping at Palembang. On this day a bombing attack was launched by the Japanese against Semplak and 6 Hudsons were destroyed. Semplak had no A.A. defences and dispersal facilities were poor.

505. On the 20th February 4 Hudsons and 3 Blenheims again bombed shipping at Palembang in the face of severe fighter opposition from aircraft based on P.I. The following day 2 Hudsons and 5 Blenheims continued these attacks. On this occasion it was possible to observe results, hits were obtained and one I0,000-ton ship was set on fire.

506. On the 22nd February, Semplak, which had no A.A. defences, sustained low flying attacks by some 20 fighters. Six Hudsons were burnt out and three others damaged beyond repair. As a result of this raid Abdair approved the move of the remains of No. I (G.R.) Squadron R.A.A.F. to Kalidjati where a light battery (8 Bofors) had by 20th February been located as part of the aerodrome defence. Six aircraft were transferred the next day, a rear party being left at Semplak to repair the unserviceable aircraft on the aerodrome and to strip the rest of serviceable parts. Whilst they were there, another attack was sustained on 24th February, and more aircraft, unserviceable, were destroyed.

507. On the 23rd February, 3 Blenheims bombed 4 submarines off the coast and claimed that one had been sunk.

508. On the 24th February, Kalidjati was bombed by the enemy, and again twice on the 26th. The Bofors guns successfully prevented a low flying attack from developing on the latter date.

509. Four Blenheims attacked P.I on the 25th February. By this time there were only 2 Hudsons operationally serviceable, with 9 others repairable: the Blenheim position, however, was slowly improving.

SUPREME ALLIED H.Q. S.W. PACIFIC LEAVES JAVA.

5I0. The enemy's unexpectedly rapid advance had frustrated the hopes, originally entertained, of building up a large Allied strength in the S.W. Pacific under the direction of Abdacom in Java, which was by now under imminent threat of invasion. Being without appropriate forces to handle, Abdacom could serve no useful purpose by remaining in the island: on the contrary such action could only result in the loss of a valuable Allied staff, the capture of which would have given great prestige to the enemy. On 22nd February its withdrawal was ordered.

5II. It was decided that the British forces remaining in the island should in future operate under the Dutch Naval and Army Commanders-in-Chief in the N.E.I. In conformity with this decision H.Q. Westgroup moved on 23rd February from Soekaboemi and took over the H.Q. in Bandoeng vacated by Abdair. It took over operational control of its squadrons from Abdair on 24th February and was renamed Britair. It was placed under the orders of Maj.-Gen. van Oyen, the Dutch A.O.C., whose staff was already installed in Abdair's operations room. Command passed to the Dutch Authorities on 25th February, and personnel of Abdacom left Java on 25th and 26th February.

5I2. Before he left Java Sir Archibald Wavell issued his instructions to the A.O.C. Britair (Air Vice Marshal Maltby). They were to the effect that:-

(*a*) He was to command all R.A.F. units left in Java.

(*b*) He would exercise Command under the orders of General van Oyen, the Dutch A.O.C. in Java, who, in turn, was under Command of the Dutch C.-in-C., General ter Poorten.

(*c*) The British Army troops left in Java were under command of Major-General H.D.W. Sitwell who would receive his orders from General ter Poorten.

(*d*) To co-operate with the Dutch and to go on fighting as long as they continued effective resistance.

(*e*) Thereafter to do the utmost to evacuate remaining personnel.

(*f*) To ensure that no undamaged equipment fell into enemy hands.

(*g*) As senior British Officer in Java to act as signals link between all British forces in the island and their service departments in London, Delhi, Washington and Melbourne.

(*h*) That no help from outside could be expected for a long time.

5I3. Gen. van Oyen issued instructions that the operations room, vacated by Abdair, was to be maintained for the combined use of his H.Q. and of Britair, and that it was to be organised for covering all operations in the S.W. Pacific. This necessitated a last minute augmentation of Britair's staff.

5I4. As the Japanese invasion fleet began its approach to Java, from bases in and around Borneo, on 25th February, energetic action was essential for collecting and organising the necessary personnel and material, and for establishing the contacts with the various Dutch, American and British authorities with whom Britair was now to deal.

5I5. During the following days encouraging messages were received from the Prime Minister, the Secretary of State for Air, and from the Chief of the Air Staff, emphasising the importance of every day which could be gained by resistance in Java These were promulgated.

FORCES AVAILABLE AND DUTCH PLAN FOR DEFENCE OF JAVA.

5I6. Before proceeding further with the narrative of events it is advisable to give a brief description of the outstanding topographical and climatic features of Java, of the Dutch naval, army and air resources, and of the Dutch plan of defence.

Topography and Weather.

5I7. Java is approximately 650 miles long with an average width of 80 miles. Its northern coast, the one most exposed to Japanese attack, affords innumerable landing beaches throughout its length. The western end is dominated by aerodromes in South Sumatra. Highly developed road and rail communications cover the Island, the main arterial lines of which run east to west: these are exposed at many points throughout their length to attack by landings on the northern coast. An outstanding feature of the island is its mountainous southern coast, parallel to which run a series of mountainous massifs along the centre of the island. During the season under consideration, S.W. winds pile up tropical thunderstorms on them from midday until far into the night. Whilst these are raging, aircraft based on aerodromes in the southern (mountainous) half of the island are, for the most part, seriously handicapped by them.

Squadrons based on aerodromes along the northern coastal strip are, on the other hand, not so severely handicapped: although heavy cloud and rain occur throughout the afternoon and night, aircraft can effectively operate at all hours. Mornings are usually bright and cloudless. Aerodromes in the northern coastal strip are, however, sited not far from exposed landing beaches Their occupation was, therefore, not unattended by risk.

Naval, Army and Air Resources.

High Command.

5I8. Bandoeng, in central western Java, was the wartime seat of the Dutch Government, and of Naval and Military Headquarters. The latter was known as A.H.K. (The Dutch have no separate air force - their navy and army having their own air contingents.)

The High Dutch Commanders were-

Governor-General of N.E.I. - Jonkheer Dr. A.W.L. Tjardo van Starkenborgh Stachouwer.

C.-in-C. Royal N.E.I. Navy - Admiral Helfrich.

C.-in-C. Royal N.E.I. Army - Lt.-Gen.ter Poorten.

Navy

5I9. A Combined Allied Fleet was based on Sourabaya, with a subsidiary base at Batavia. It consisted of 8 cruisers (3 British, 2 Australian, I American, 2 Dutch), II destroyers (5 British, 4 American and 2 Dutch) some Dutch submarines and other auxiliary craft, and was commanded by Vice Admiral C.E.L. Helfrich, Royal Netherlands Navy, as Commander of Naval Forces. He had assumed command on the IIth February.

Army.

520. (*a*) The Dutch had approximately 25,000 regular troops, made up of four regiments of infantry (native) with artillery, garrison and ancillary units. They had a few obsolete A.F.V.'s, having been unable to obtain modern tanks from the Allies. Units had been heavily depleted of white personnel for various reasons, from a proportion of one white to five native to a proportion of one to about forty. An attempt to re-arm and to re-organise on modern lines had failed because modern armaments were unobtainable for the new units which had been formed for handling them.

(*b*) In addition there was a Home Guard of about 40,000. They were static in role, and necessarily poorly armed and trained. Those in west Java were reported to be the best, particularly those in the vicinity of Soebang near Kalidjati aerodrome (eventually to be occupied by British bombers) where there were about I,000 men with twelve armoured cars.

(*c*) To the Dutch Army was added a small British force under the direction of Major-General H.D.W. Sitwell. It consisted of a squadron of light tanks, two Australian infantry battalions (one a machine-gun unit without its machine guns) and a number of small administrative units. The whole was organised hastily into a mobile striking force for operation in western Java, and was under the command of Brigadier A.S. Blackburn, V.C. (Australian Imperial Forces). To it were added later an American Field Battalion much under strength, and a contingent of 450 R.A.F. airmen hastily armed and trained as infantry under Wing Commander Alexander. It was called "Blackforce". It co-operated closely with the Dutch troops (under the command of General Schilling) located in western Java for the defence of the Batavia area.

(*d*) Certain British A.A. batteries were concentrated on aerodrome defence in Western Java as follows:-

Tjililitan - I2 Bofors guns soon after I5th February. Also one battalion Australian Infantry relieved on 25th February by I5th Heavy A.A. Battery armed as infantry. The former were relieved from aerodrome defence duties because they were required as part of "Blackforce".

Kalidjati - I0 Bofors guns soon after I5th February. Also some Dutch Infantry relieved on night 28th February/Ist March by I2th Heavy A.A. Battery hastily armed as infantry. The former were wanted for service with the Dutch field army.

Thus there were no Heavy A.A. guns for the defence of these aerodromes. The few available on the island were wanted at more vulnerable places, including the Naval base at Sourabaya.

Air Forces.

52I. (*a*) The Dutch had about 5 Bomber, 3 Fighter and 2 Observation Squadrons in Java, most of which were much depleted as the result of protracted operations in the north. Serviceability of aircraft was low. They and their administrative units operated under Dutch control decentralised from Bandoeng.

(*b*) There were I2 to I5 American heavy bombers (believed to be B.I7's) and a few fighters (P.40's). Whole serviceability was low. These were located under American control in east and central Java.

(*c*) There was also a mixed Dutch, American and British Reconnaissance Group based in Java for seaward reconnaissance, which operated under a Dutch Commander. No. 205 (F.B.) Squadron formed part of it.

(*d*) To this force was to be added the British Air Contingent under Westgroup, alias Britair, whose re-organisation has already been described.

During the time that Abdair remained in Java, all the above air formations acted under its direction, control of the first two being exercised through the Dutch A.O.C., General van Oyen. When Abdair left Java, the latter took command of them all.

Strategy

522. An invasion of Java was considered most likely to approach down the east or west sides of Borneo, or both. The Dutch High Command feared simultaneous landings at both ends of the islands, near Sourabaya in the east and in the Sunda Straits on the west: this was the most difficult form of attack to parry, and it was to be expected that the enemy would adopt it. A landing in central Java was not thought to be likely. The Dutch defence plan was laid accordingly.

Dutch Plan.

523. This was:-

(*a*) To watch, by means of air reconnaissance, as far northwards as possible on both sides of Borneo, and the whole of the Java Sea - this being undertaken by the Reconnaissance Group. Submarines supplemented this watch.

(*b*) An invasion was to be opposed as far out to sea as possible by air action: all bomber and reconnaissance aircraft were to be used for the purpose when occasion arose.

(*c*) A Combined Allied Naval Striking Force of 5 cruisers and 9 destroyers was based at Sourabaya and would engage the main threat when it appeared.

(*d*) Finally, should the enemy land, he was to be resisted on the beaches at certain points only. Suitable landing beaches were so numerous that only a few of the most obvious could be defended. Elsewhere the plan was to keep troops in local reserve and to counter-attack landings with them, the Army falling back if necessary on to previously prepared positions covered by demolitions.

(*e*) As a successful invasion was all too probable it was decided that there should be two centres for a final stand, a decision which was enforced by a shortage of troops and by the great length of the island. The two chosen centres were Malang Plateau in the east and Bandoeng volcanic plateau in the west.

APPROACH OF ENEMY CONVOYS.

524. On the 25th February air reconnaissance on the east side of Borneo reported that shipping, which had been collecting for some time past in ports in the Macassar Straits, was forming up at Balikpapan, evidently in preparation for putting to sea. The invasion of Java was imminent.

525. On 26th February a convoy of more than 50 ships and transports, accompanied by a strong naval escort, was located in the southern end of the Macassar Straits steaming south.

526. On the 27th February it was again located, now in the Java Sea, on a course and speed which would bring it to the north coast, westward of Sourabaya, at midnight 27th/28th February.

527. The Allied Fleet put to sea and fought an engagement with the escort of heavy cruisers and destroyers during the night 27th/28th February. The latter was very superior in numbers, weight and metal. The Allied ships were either sunk or disabled. This gallant action afforded the land defences another 24 hours' grace, because the transports turned away northwards at the beginning of the sea action and steamed towards Borneo during the night.

528. On 28th February the transports were again located steaming south at a speed which would bring them to landing-beaches westward of Sourabaya about midnight 28th February/Ist March.

529. Meanwhile the situation on the west side of Borneo had not developed so clearly. Invasion forces had been suspected in the Natuna or Anambas Islands and possibly at Muntok on Banka Island. Reconnaissances had failed up to 26th February to clarify the situation.

530. On the 27th February, a small convoy with escort was located about 50 miles south of the southern tip of Banka Island steaming slowly on a north-easterly course. This might or might not be part of an invading convoy "marking time" before turning south towards Western Java.

53I. On the 28th February about noon, the situation became clearer. A convoy was sighted at that hour approximately I00 miles north-east of Batavia steaming on an easterly course at high speed. It consisted of II transports; one cruiser and three destroyers were disposed some 30 miles to the south and on a parallel course. Another and larger convoy was located to the north-west: strength, course and speed were not clear. Both were at a distance which would make landings possible at two points in western Java about midnight.

532. The moon was one day past full, wind off shore, ideal conditions for landing. All was evidently set for simultaneous landings - one at the eastern end of Java probably just west of Sourabaya, and two at the western end of Java in the vicinity of Batavia.

BOMBER OPERATIONS 27TH FEBRUARY TO IST MARCH.

533. To revert to the night of 27th/28th February. It then appeared that the major threat would develop against Eastern Java. It was therefore decided to move No. 36 (T.B.) Squadron (9 Vildebeestes and I Albacore) at once to Madioen (near Sourabaya) to co-operate with American B.I7's in resisting it. No. 36 (T.B.) Squadron arrived at Madioen on the afternoon of 28th February, and during the night 28th February/Ist March carried out two sorties per aircraft, the first against transports, the second against landing barges. The first attack entailed a long search because reconnaissance information with which they had been briefed proved inaccurate. A convoy of 28 ships was eventually found 5 miles off the Coast, north of Rembang, some I00 miles west of Sourabaya. Most pilots claimed hits on transports, and execution amongst the barges. Subsequent reports received from American H.Q. in the area stated that attacks had been most successful and that No. 36 (T.B.) Squadron had sunk 8 ships - the Americans themselves claimed 7 others: but it has not been possible to verify this seemingly very high rate of success. On completion of the second attack, No. 36 (T.B.) Squadron returned direct to Tjikampek, less three aircraft which had been shot down including that of the C.O., Squadron Leader J.T. Wilkins, an outstanding leader who was unfortunately killed. Each aircrew of this squadron, operating from a strange aerodrome, thus carried out two night attacks in 24 hours, involving over I5 hours flying in open cockpits - an excellent achievement.

534. In the meantime, during 28th February, the threat to western Java had crystallised (para. 53I) in the form of two Japanese convoys approaching from the north with the evident intention of landing on both sides of Batavia.

535. All available Blenheims and Hudsons were directed against that convoy, which was approaching the beaches eastward of Batavia. During the night 28th February/Ist March, 26 Blenheim and 6 Hudson sorties were carried out against it from Kalidjati. The first attack found it 50 miles north of Eritanwetan, a point on the north coast about 80 miles east of Batavia: it was steaming south at high speed. Weather conditions were bad and by this time only one narrow strip was serviceable on the aerodrome. Not all pilots were sufficiently well trained to cope with the conditions: of those that were, some carried out three sorties each. There is no doubt that attacks were successful and were pressed home from a low level with great determination. When attacks began, I5 ships formed the convoy: early on Ist March, only 7 were seen anchored off the disembarkation beach which was at Eritanwetan.

At least three, perhaps more of its ships, are believed to have been sunk. The larger figure may be an exaggeration, as other Japanese ships were seen on Ist March lying off some miles N.W. of the main convoy.

536. Disembarkation at Eritanwetan began at about 0I00 hours on Ist March and continued during the rest of the night, despite a number of attacks by our aircraft while landing was in progress.

537. During the night, the Dutch A.O.C., General van Oyen, advised Air Vice Marshal Maltby that the bomber force at Kalidjati would be more favourably placed for opposing the enemy landings if it remained there than if it were withdrawn to aerodromes further inland amongst the hills. He did not appear to have much confidence in the weak detachments of Dutch Home Guard which were watching the river crossings on the roads leading from the enemy landing at Eritanwetan to Kalidjati, a distance of more than 50 kilometres. But he placed more reliance upon the Home Guard of about I,000 strong, supported by about I0 armoured cars, which were located at Soebang, a town on the road leading to the aerodrome. He also stated that a Dutch battalion at Cheribon had been ordered to counter-attack the landing. The British A.O.C., therefore, decided to keep the bomber force at Kalidjati where it was best placed to resist the enemy.

538. It was decided to "stand down" bombers at Kalidjati at the end of the night's operation because:-

(*a*) Crews had been on a stretch for 36 hours, standing by during much of the night of 27th-28th February, and then operating at high pressure throughout late afternoon and the night of 28th February-Ist March. They had worked splendidly, had achieved good results, and needed a rest.

(*b*) There would be plenty for the crews to do at high pressure for several days to come.

(*c*) Previous experience had shown that Blenheims and Hudsons were particularly vulnerable if employed in the cloudless conditions which prevail during the mornings at this season, because the Japanese normally provided their landings with strong Navy 'O' fighter cover. It was therefore decided to employ bombers daily during the late afternoons (when cloud cover could be relied upon) and under cover of darkness, and to use all available fighters, which could look after themselves, to continue the opposition, during the cloudless mornings.

539. On completion of the night's work, the Station Commander at Kalidjati, Group Captain Whistondale, was instructed at 0700 hours, Ist March, to disperse his aircraft and to prepare them for further operations later in the day.

Shortly after daybreak the Dutch squadrons withdrew from Kalidjati aerodrome, under General van Oyen's orders as it later transpired, although no information that they were going to do so was given to the A.O.C. or his staff. Nor were the latter kept informed that the Dutch counter attack had failed or that the Dutch defences between the beaches and Kalidjati had not been able to put up the resistance it had been understood they would offer. It is probable that this failure was due to the fact that time had been insufficient for the wheels of co-operation of the recently established staffs (see para. 5I4) to get run in, and that there was a similar unestablished close touch between the aerodrome and the local Dutch Commander in Soebang. It had a disastrous sequel.

540. About I030 hours the aerodrome was overrun by Japanese light tanks supported by infantry in lorries - part of the force which had landed at Eritanwetan some hours earlier - and the aerodrome was captured. The whole force of Blenheims, by now reduced to 8 serviceable aircraft, being fully dispersed, was captured. 4 Hudsons which were dispersed on the aerodrome managed to take off under fire of light tanks, which were by now on the aerodrome, and to reach Andir near Bandoeng.

54I. Subsequent inquiry made it clear that the aerodrome defence party, a combination of Army and R.A.F. personnel, put up a stout fight and covered the withdrawal of the ground personnel of the squadrons, the majority of the Bofors guns adopting an anti-tank role. It is believed that there are no British survivors of the aerodrome defence party. The Japanese appear to have given no quarter. Later the Japanese testified to the gallant and protracted defence the aerodrome defences put up, and this was supported by the number of bodies, both British and Japanese, which were found near the aerodrome and in the woods around it by the British salvage parties employed by the Japanese after the capitulation of Java. The Dutch aerodrome defence contingent, although it had been relieved during the night by the newly arrived British defence party, remained to assist in the defence. It located posts on the roads leading to the aerodrome on the N., E., and W., the two former of which were overrun by the enemy's armoured vehicles, to deal with which it had no anti-tank weapons. The number of Dutch bodies which were later found on both sides of the roads along which the Japanese attack came, testify to the opposition it put up.

542. It has been impracticable as yet to obtain a clear picture of what exactly happened at Kalidjati. Surviving British witnesses of consequence are few. Much still remains unsatisfactorily explained. It is hoped that time may reveal the full facts.

543. The captured aerodrome was only a few miles from Tjikampek, the aerodrome on which No. 36 (T.B.) Squadron was also resting after having operated throughout the night (para. 533). The latter aerodrome had no defences whatever and was in considerable danger of being overrun by the same troops which had already captured Kalidjati. The Squadron was, therefore, immediately withdrawn to Andir, and was later moved to Tjikamber in S.W. Java, Group Captain Nicholetts being placed in command of the Station.

FIGHTER OPERATIONS IN BATAVIA AREA - IST FEBRUARY TO 3RD MARCH I942.

Consolidation of Fighter Strength.

544. Before proceeding further it is necessary to turn to earlier operations of the Fighter Force.

545. It will be remembered that Nos. 232 (F) and 605 (F) Squadrons were

operating at Tjililitan under a Sector Control (a skeleton of No. 226 (F) Group) whose operations rooms and warning systems were installed in and around Batavia.

546. From 17th to 27th February this force was continually in action in its role of the air defence of Batavia. Normal odds met in air fighting were in the vicinity of 10-I. Its operations were handicapped, particularly during the earlier part of the period, by insufficient warning of approaching enemy aircraft.

547. A Fighter Group H.Q. became redundant by 27th February, its squadrons and overhead controlling organisation being established by that date. The Group Commander, Air Commodore Vincent, and several members of his staff, were ordered on that date by the A.O.C. to leave Java, which they subsequently did by sea.

548. By noon on 28th February the combined strength of the two fighter squadrons was less than that of one. The U.S. aircraft carrier "Langley" had been sunk by the Japanese when bringing in a full load of P-40 fighters, with some of which it had been hoped to re-arm one of the squadrons. Thus the last prospect of keeping two fighter squadrons at reasonable strength had gone. It was decided to retain No. 232 (F) Squadron which, under Squadron Leader Brooker's leadership, volunteered to remain in Java. Vacancies in it were filled from volunteers in No. 605 (F) Squadron. No. 605 Squadron, except the volunteers who could be employed, was withdrawn for evacuation after it had handed over its remaining aircraft to No. 232 (F) Squadron on the afternoon of 28th February.

Fighter Operations 1st - 3rd March.

549. In accordance with the decision (para. 538 (c)) not to employ bombers during the cloudless mornings, but to oppose the landings during these hours by means of fighters, instructions were issued to No. 232 (F) Squadron to employ all its Hurricanes throughout the forenoon of 1st March, in co-operation with 10 Dutch Kittyhawks and 6 Buffaloes, in attacking two Japanese landings which had occurred simultaneously during the night in Western Java.

550. One of these landings was that which had been made at Eritanwetan (para. 536). Twelve Hurricanes took part in opposing it, and in doing so encountered intense A.A. fire. They pressed home their attacks at low height, inflicting severe casualties amongst troops in landing craft, and set on fire at least six landing craft and three motor vehicles. Several later attacks against the same targets also produced good results.

551. The other landing in Western Java had occurred simultaneously with the foregoing one, but on the extreme western beaches on either side of Merak in the Sunda Straits. It was in greater strength. The remaining Hurricanes of No. 232 (F) Squadron made several sorties against it during the morning at the request of the Dutch Army: they successfully engaged enemy columns, including cavalry and M.T., advancing along the roads from the landing beaches towards Batavia.

552. After the British bombers had been overrun at Kalidjati the fighters continued their attacks against the landing at Eritanwetan. Shortly after midday they brought to

a standstill a cyclist column proceeding westwards towards Batavia. In addition three Japanese flying boats were destroyed on the water.

553. All No. 232 (F) Squadron aircraft suffered damage in varying degree from A.A. fire during these operations, which were all carried out at low level.

554. On 2nd March Tjililitan aerodrome was under constant attack by the enemy, and the squadron was in action all day defending it and carrying out road reconnaissances in western Java for the Dutch Army. The aerodrome was also becoming somewhat exposed to overland attack by Japanese forces which had disembarked at Eritanwetan; these were, by the afternoon, reported to be approaching Poerwokerto and the river crossings thirty miles or so to the north-east of the aerodrome. Withdrawal along the road which passes through those places was already out of the question. Moreover, these places were held by Dutch troops on similar lines to Soebang and the river crossings protecting Kalidjati aerodrome; a repetition of the Kalidjati debacle, involving the only remaining British fighter squadron, was distinctly possible during the night or following morning. The A.O.C. therefore, when visiting the aerodrome on this day, ordered No. 232 (F) Squadron, now 10 Hurricanes, to move back to Andir near Bandoeng, the move of the ground parties and aerodrome defence troops to be completed along the Buitenzorg road by the following day. Group Captain Noble was appointed Station Commander at Andir.

555. In the early morning of 3rd March the squadron returned to Tjililitan from Andir under orders issued by General van Oyen. It was airborne throughout the morning repelling Japanese air attacks. At noon it was finally withdrawn to Andir, en route to which it made a successful attack on Kalidjati aerodrome destroying several enemy aircraft. A running fight took place with Japanese fighters from Kalidjati to Bandoeng.

Withdrawal from Batavia.

556. As the Dutch announced on 3rd March their intention of declaring Batavia an "open" town, the operations and filter rooms; together with the radar stations in the vicinity, were destroyed, and their staffs were ordered to Bandoeng on the 3rd March.

OPERATIONS BY No. 205 (F.B.) SQUADRON - 1ST FEBRUARY TO 3RD MARCH.

557. No. 205 (F.B.) Squadron during the whole of its stay in Java operated as a unit of the Allied Reconnaissance Group which was responsible for all seaward reconnaissance throughout the S.W. Pacific Command. This Group, under Dutch Command, took its orders first from Abdair and then, after Abdair left Java, from General van Oyen, the Dutch A.O.C. Britair was responsible for administration only of 205 (F.B.) Squadron.

558. Based on Batavia and Oesthaven, 205 (B) Squadron carried out

reconnaissances between Borneo and Sumatra, and also undertook anti-submarine patrols in the Sunda Straits.

559. When the Japanese descended upon the Batavia area on Ist March it was ordered to transfer its base to Tjilitjap, an unserviceable flying boat having to be destroyed when it left. The Squadron operated from Tjilitjap on anti-submarine patrols until 3rd March, by which time it could no longer be usefully employed. The squadron was then ordered out of the island, two boats going to Ceylon and one, with a damaged air-screw, to Australia.

FINAL AIR OPERATIONS - 4TH MARCH TO 8TH MARCH I942.

560. The position on the morning of 4th March was:-

(*a*) H.Q. Britair - Bandoeng.

(*b*) No. I (GR) Squadron, R.A.A.F., 7 Hudsons (3 serviceable) - Andir.

(*c*) No. 232 (F) Squadron, I0 Hurricanes (all in dubious condition) - Andir.

(*d*) No. 36 (T.B.) Squadron, 5 Vildebeestes (4 just serviceable) - Tjikamber.

(*e*) About 450 armed R.A.F. personnel under Wing Commander Alexander operating as infantry with "Blackforce" in the Buitenzorg area.

(*f*) About I,900 unarmed personnel awaiting evacuation near the port of Tjilitjap, and a further 600 at Djojacarta; many other personnel now surplus to squadron requirements were under orders to move to the area as accommodation became available near the port.

56I. The Army situation on 4th March was:-

Eastern Java: The enemy had made a successful landing on Ist March west of Sourabaya and was pressing the Dutch forces in two directions - those originally in the Sourabaya district towards the S.E. extremity of the island, and those in central Java westwards towards Poerwokerto.

Western Java: The enemy after landing at Eritanwetan had captured Kalidjati aerodrome, on which strong Japanese fighter forces were by now well established. The enemy had repulsed Dutch attempts on 2nd March to recapture Soebang (from the direction of which the enemy was by now pressing towards Bandoeng) and on 3rd March to recapture Kalidjati aerodrome.

The enemy force, which had landed in the Sunda Straits, had forced the evacuation of Batavia, and the Dutch garrison of extreme western Java was in the Buitenzorg - Soekaboemi vicinity, falling back on the final Bandoeng "stronghold."

562. *No. 36 (T.B.) Squadron* based at Tjikamber attacked Kalidjati aerodrome, now full of enemy aircraft, on the nights of 2nd-3rd and 3rd-4th March. On 4th March it

was moved to Tasik Malaja because of reports (subsequently proved to be false) of landings in S.W. Java which threatened the aerodrome, and because the rapid advance, authentic, of the enemy towards Soekaboemi threatened to cut the only road available for withdrawal from it.

563. From Tasik Malaja the squadron continued attacks on Kalidjati during the nights of 4th-5th and 5th-6th March, doing two sorties per aircraft on the former night. Large fires were caused and considerable damage was done.

564. On 6th March, by which date an early capitulation had been forecast by General ter Poorten (See para. 577), two aircraft only remained serviceable, and orders were given for these to be flown north in an endeavour to reach Burma. They left on the 7th March but unfortunately both crashed in Sumatra and the crews were either killed or captured.

565. *No. I (G.R.) Squadron, R.A.A.F.,* was ordered to fly its three remaining flyable Hudsons to Australia carrying operational records and as many spare aircrews as possible. The first left on the night 4th-5th, the others on the nights of 5th-6th and 6th-7th - all reaching Australia.

566. *No. 232 (F) Squadron,* now at Andir, was given the role of carrying out periodic offensive sweeps against Kalidjati aerodrome. It was instructed also to take advantage of any particularly favourable targets presented by the Japanese Army attacking Bandoeng from the north. For the latter purpose the squadron established a liaison officer at the Dutch H.Q. responsible for defences on that front.

567. By this time no warning of impending attack could be obtained, and the aerodrome was subjected to almost continuous attack throughout each day. The squadron was repeatedly in action and considerable success was achieved.

568. By the 7th March the squadron was reduced to 5 aircraft. On this day it was transferred to Tasik Malaja, and by the evening only two aircraft remained. These two carried out a tactical road reconnaissance on the morning of the 8th March, and on completion of this they were destroyed under orders from Britair.

Operations of No. 266 (F) Wing.

569. Whilst No. 266 (F) Wing was in action in Sumatra and Java it is believed to have inflicted the following losses on the enemy:-

In Sumatra, 2nd-I6th February.
About 8 enemy aircraft were shot down. In co-operation with the bombers of No. 225 (B) Group, very heavy casualties were inflicted on troops in boats and barges moving up the Palembang river on I5th February.

In Java, I7th February-8th March.
About 32 enemy aircraft were shot down (8 by No. 605 Squadron and 24 by 232 Squadron) of which about I5 were destroyed during the closing days in Java, 2nd to 8th March. Heavy casualties were also inflicted on enemy troops which landed on Java at Eritanwetan and Merak, particularly the former.

During the combined periods about 60 Hurricanes were lost, chiefly on the ground, by enemy attacks on our inadequately defended aerodromes.

PROGRESS OF EVACUATION.

570. Throughout the period under review, evacuation of surplus R.A.F. personnel proceeded as fast as shipping permitted. Units were concentrated for evacuation as they became surplus to requirements. They were kept together as units as far as possible, and as shipping accommodation allowed. Towards the end, when accommodation became extremely limited, priority was given to aircrews and technical personnel whose value in other theatres of war was greatest.

57I. On the 23rd February, owing to enemy action, Batavia was closed as a port and the R.A.F. Base, Batavia, with its ancillary transit camps, was progressively transferred to Poerwokerto, adjacent to Tjilitjap in South Java, the sole port still open. Tjilitjap was also subjected to air bombardment, and ships leaving it to attack by Japanese light naval forces. On the 27th February, S.S. "City of Manchester" was torpedoed off Tjilitjap whilst approaching the port to assist in the evacuation.

572. From the Ist March onwards, little movement from the port took place. It was finally closed on the 5th March leaving on the island about 2,500 R.A.F. personnel whom it had been intended to evacuate, but for whom no shipping was made available.

573. On 5th and 6th March about 8 seats were allotted to the R.A.F. in Dutch Lodestars; the Dutch had been using these aircraft to evacuate personnel to Australia. The Lodestar service ceased on the 6th March, thus closing the last evacuation channel from Java.

574. A handicap experienced throughout the evacuation of surplus R.A.F. personnel was the difficulty which many of the Dutch had in understanding the necessity for sending out of the island, at a time when it was about to be invaded, personnel who appeared to them to be soldiers: they could not realise that our airmen were untrained as such and were of great value in their real role as airmen for prosecution of the war elsewhere. Informed Dutch authorities appreciated the matter, but many failed to grasp its truth. This is said in no critical spirit; the Dutch outlook is easily understood. But it must be stated in part explanation of the loss in Java of a number of surplus airmen.

575. During the period I8th February onwards, nearly 7,000 R.A.F. personnel were evacuated, leaving a total of about 5,000 in Java.

EVENTS LEADING UP TO SURRENDER OF JAVA.

576. *Conference at Dutch Headquarters.* At I800 hours on the 5th March, the Dutch Commander-in-Chief, Lieut.-Gen. ter Poorten, convened a conference at his H.Q., A.H.K. in Bandoeng. The Air Officer Commanding, Britair, and the General Officer

Commanding British Military Forces in Java, Major-General H.D.W. Sitwell, and representatives of their staffs, were summoned to this conference. It was also attended by senior officers of the Dutch C.-in-C's. staff.

577. At this conference the Dutch Commander-in-Chief stated:-

(*a*) That the situation was grave: the enemy had practically overcome the northern defences of Bandoeng and was also rapidly closing in from the west.

(*b*) That morale was at a low ebb and that it was possible Bandoeng might fall very soon. When the enemy penetrated the outer defences, the C.-in-C. did not propose to defend that town, which would be declared an open city. It was full of refugees and could not in any case hold out for long.

(*c*) That no guerilla warfare was possible or would be attempted by the Dutch. There was great hostility amongst the native population towards the whites, and without the help of the natives guerilla warfare could not possibly be successful. All his staff were emphatically agreed that such warfare was out of the question.

(*d*) That owing to difficulties of communication, Dutch G.H.Q. could operate only from Bandoeng. They could not exercise control from elsewhere and so would not move from Bandoeng.

(*e*) That resistance was to be carried on elsewhere under the direction of local commanders if possible and in accordance with an order issued by Queen Wilhelmina of Holland that there should be no surrender to the Japanese. He then added an unexpected rider - that he had instructed his troops to disregard any order that he might subsequently issue to them to cease fighting: they were to disobey it and to go on fighting.

578. In subsequent discussion the Commander-in-Chief was informed by General Sitwell that the British would certainly continue to fight on as long as any of the Dutch did so. When Dutch resistance ceased, then he must reserve to himself the right to decide his actions in accordance with the circumstances at the time. The Commander-in-Chief also informed the A.O.C. that A.H.Q. and Andir aerodrome in Bandoeng must not be defended in the event of the Japanese entering the town. The Commander-in-Chief was then asked to allot an area in the hills in which the British Forces could concentrate and continue resistance. After some discussion he allotted an area near Santoso to the southward of Bandoeng. Its choice appeared to be influenced more as a means of escape to the south coast than as a stronghold; emphasis had to be laid on the fact that it was wanted for the latter purpose.

British move into the Hills.

579. In consequence the G.O.C. and the A.O.C. British Forces went to Santosa at first light on the 6th March to reconnoitre. The remainder of A.H.Q. and other Army and R.A.F. personnel in the area of Bandoeng, except the ground party at Andir, were moved to Tasik Malaja the same day.

580. The distribution of Air Force personnel on the 6th March (p.m.) was:-

(*a*) Tasik Malaja, preparing for defence, with Army Units also ordered there
900

(*b*) Contingent with "Blackforce"   450

(*c*) Andir area, aerodrome staff and units   850

(*d*) Poerwokerto area awaiting evacuation, under
Air Commodore Silly's orders   2,500

(*e*) Detached from units, stragglers, escape parties, etc.,
in south central Java   400

Total   5,100

58I. The orders issued to the various contingents on the 6th March were:-

(*a*) The Andir contingent was to surrender because Bandoeng was being declared an "open" town, and on that day there was no transport to move them.

(*b*) The Poerwokerto contingent was to place itself under the orders of the local Dutch Commander, stand fast and surrender. There was no alternative as the men were unarmed and had very slender rations and other resources. They would have been an embarrassment to a final stand in the hills, yet would have had to share its hardships and any retribution which might be meted out. They were therefore less likely to come to harm if they were not associated with further resistance.

(*c*) The Tasik Malaja contingent was to defend to the last the aerodrome area, where the G.O.C. and A.O.C. would rejoin them if a better place for continuing the fight was not found.

582. Reconnaissance of the Santosa area on 6th March drew a blank. Not only was the terrain unsuited for defence by a small force, but the local Dutch had no defence plan, obviously did not want fighting to occur there, and were only too ready to assist the British to the coast.

583. As the result of a suggestion from General Schilling, who was most helpful to the British in their wish to continue resistance, the area south of Tjikadjang was reconnoitred on 7th March. It was found more suitable for protracted defence. It was therefore decided to concentrate all army units and all armed R.A.F. personnel in the defence of that area.

584. In conformity with this decision orders were issued to the following to move to the area on 8th March:-

(*a*) The Andir contingent, for whom transport was now available; and

(*b*) the Tasik Malaja contingent.

Both of these contingents were armed. In addition, "Blackforce" and all other British

Army Units in Java were also ordered to the area. The total combined force was about 8,000 strong.

585. At the same time it was confirmed that the remainder of the personnel, who were unarmed, were to stand fast and surrender. The Dutch G.O.C. of the Poerwokerto area, under whose direction Air Commodore Silly had placed the Poerwokerto contingent in accordance with his instructions, ordered them to move further west because unarmed forces would be an embarrassment in a locality where he intended to resist the Japanese advance. This was done under his arrangements and the contingent arrived at Tasik Malaja on 8th March (p.m.). It had suffered severe casualties owing to its rail convoy having been ambushed en route.

586. On 7th March (p.m.) A.H.K. declared Bandoeng, Tasik Malaja and Garoet "open" towns. This action had been anticipated for Bandoeng but in respect of the other two it came as a complete surprise, and it did not assist the concentration of the British Forces in the hills, which was by now in progress.

587. Early on 8th March moves to the concentration area in the hills began. A combined Army/Air H.Q. was established at Tjikadjang with W/T station alongside to communicate with the Air Ministry, etc.

Order to Surrender received from Dutch H.Q.

588. At about 0900 hours 8th March, a rough translation of a broadcast by the Dutch C.-in-C. was received at British H.Q. at Tjikadjang. It had been promulgated in the name of all the Allied Forces in Java as well as in that of the Dutch. At about 1030 hours it was telephoned through in English by, it is believed, Colonel Gulik the Dutch Air Staff Officer at A.H.K., who had come for the purpose to Garoet at the foot of the hills. It was to the effect that "all organised resistance" in Java had ceased and that troops were to offer no further resistance to the Japanese. Colonel Gulik said that the Dutch C.-in-C. had cancelled his instructions about disregarding surrender orders and that he intended this order to be obeyed. The last was quite unexpected.

589. The A.O.C. received this message and, in the absence of the G.O.C., who was reconnoitring the area and allocating defence positions, he first sent a despatch rider to inform the G.O.C., and then, feeling that further clarification was desirable, went himself to Garoet to make further enquiries.

590. At Garoet the Dutch Resident, Heer Koffman (the District Civil Administrator) who had on the previous day, 7th March, strongly emphasised the difficulties of local supplies and accommodation, and had been apprehensive about the prospects of a "massacre of whites" if guerilla warfare was attempted particularly amongst the difficult natives of the Garoet district, now on 8th March re-emphasised his belief in the dangers of a native rising if fighting in the hills was attempted. He called in other authorities to support his opinion - amongst them the District Regent (Native District Administrator).

591. The A.O.C. rang up A.H.K. and spoke (it is believed) to Colonel Gulik who confirmed that the Dutch C.-in-C. had cancelled his order, and that he intended his latest instruction, namely for fighting to stop, to be obeyed. He said that all Dutch

troops were complying. The A.O.C. then telephoned to several other Dutch centres and found this to be so in each instance.

592. Whilst he was so engaged, A.H.K. again rang him up at the Resident's House. The Staff Officer doing so specifically enquired whether the British were going to fight, whether General Sitwell had full control of "Blackforce", and whether the last could be persuaded to stop fighting. To these questions he was given non-committal answers except an assurance that "Blackforce" would definitely obey any orders General Sitwell might issue. The A.O.C. was given a further urgent message from the Dutch C.-in-C., which it is understood was telephoned through from Kalidjati, where at that time the Dutch C.-in-C. was negotiating terms with the Japanese C.-in-C. The message pressed for action to be taken to stop "Blackforce" blowing up any more bridges to cover their withdrawal to the hills, as this action was handicapping the negotiations. It is not known how the information about blowing the bridges south-east of Bandoeng reached the Japanese at Kalidjati many miles to the north. This information made it clear that the Japanese already knew our intention and whither we were withdrawing into the hills.

593. The A.O.C. then returned to Tjikadjang where he met the G.O.C. and Brigadier Blackburn at I330 hours, when the situation was as follows:-

(*a*) Troops were arriving in the concentration area, the last being due during the night. They possessed small arms and ammunition and a few Bofors guns, but as had been expected, no mortars, aircraft or artillery. Although personnel were tired and many were poorly clad and kitted, particularly R.A.F. personnel evacuated from Singapore, morale appeared on the whole good.

(*b*) Administrative arrangements were, however, grave. Only 3 days' rations had so far accompanied the force. Army convoys had experienced considerable obstruction when collecting stores, and the dump in Bandoeng was reputed to be destroyed (news later to prove false). There might be time to collect some more, but this was not certain. Petrol was limited to what vehicles had in their tanks. The combined British/Australian Field Hospital in Bandoeng could not be moved to the hills because it was already overloaded with patients. Hospitalisation was therefore totally impracticable, and medical supplies limited to those carried by units, which were few and of a first aid nature only. Water was everywhere polluted by reason of native habits, water carts were few and effective sterilization was impracticable. Stomach troubles were already in evidence.

594. Given local co-operation and time these handicaps could have been overcome, but there appeared to be prospect of neither. The Dutch had ceased fighting everywhere and, to say the least, were not being helpful. The natives might, or might not, turn against the whites: warning about them had been received, and in any case they were unlikely to assist. And time had suddenly become unexpectedly short now that the Japanese knew about the movement. Much had still to be done in reorganising, in preparing positions for defence and in solving administrative difficulties. Time was now particularly short for training the R.A.F. contingent, which

comprised about one-third of the force, in its new and future role, namely in infantry fighting about which it knew nothing, particularly of jungle fighting. Indeed, many A.A. gunners recently rearmed as infantry were in little better case.

595. Yet something might have been done but for the quandary in which the British had now been placed by reason of the Dutch C.-in-C's. broadcast (para. 588). This had been promulgated on behalf of the British forces, as well as on that of the Dutch, but without consultation with the A.O.C. or G.O.C. and although the British intention to continue resistance was well known to the Dutch C.-in-C. The broadcast contained the phrase "All organised resistance having now ceased." This phrase had an important bearing. It was believed to have the effect in international law of placing those who continued to resist outside the protection of belligerent rights and subject to summary execution if captured. The Japanese were likely to exercise their rights in the matter. The problem which now faced the A.O.C. and G.O.C. was how to sort out the force, now in a state of movement over a wide area, into those who were willing to face such consequences and those who were not. The latter could not be given legal orders to continue fighting under such conditions as bandits against their will. The next problem was to reorganise the former into a fighting force well clear of the latter and of the 2,900 unarmed R.A.F. contingent which had by now moved unpleasantly close, although still in the plains (para. 585). One alternative was to send the "bouches inutiles" down to the plains to surrender and for the former to fight where they were. But Japanese revenge on those who submitted themselves under such circumstances was already too well known to permit adoption of such a course. The other alternative was for the volunteer contingent to move to, and reorganise in, a new defence area. But this was impracticable. The Japanese already occupied Bandoeng, through which led all roads to the hill country in the S.W. extremity of Java, where lay the only other remote spots which might be suitable for guerilla resistance: the country elsewhere was too highly developed and too well served by numerous roads. The Japanese quite clearly knew where the British had withdrawn and their intention, and were free to follow up quickly, as was their habit. It was thus impracticable by now to reorganise anything effective.

596. In these circumstances the A.O.C. and G.O.C., regretfully decided that they must comply with the order to surrender. The order as received from A.H.K. was accordingly issued to units about 1430 hours.

Orders were also issued:-

(*a*) To destroy arms and warlike stores likely to be of value to the enemy, except a limited amount of transport.

(*b*) For all ranks to observe absolute reticence if questioned for military information by the enemy.

A signal was sent to the R.A.F. H.Q. Signal Section for transmission to the Air Ministry to the effect that the orders to surrender were being complied with. The reasons why this signal did not get through are contained in paras. 610-613.

Escape Organisation.

597. Col. van der Post, a British officer believed to be of South African Dutch descent, had remained in Java in order to organise a means of escape after the foreseen occupation of the island by the Japanese. He initiated plans for assembly points in the mountains to the southward of Batavia and tried to organise shipping and boats for surreptitious evacuation from the mountainous S.W. coast. Lack of time prevented his plans maturing. Great credit is due to this officer for his activities, attended as they were by considerable personal risk at the hands of the enemy, a fact of which he was well aware. In anticipation of Col. van der Post's plans succeeding, authority was given by the A.O.C. for the issue from public funds of 2,000 guelders to each of twenty individuals to finance the attempt; action was to be taken by Air Commodore Staton to select them.

598. Despite the necessity for abandoning the organised escape scheme, many still wished to make an attempt to leave Java. The hazards involved by the doubtful attitude of the natives and the malarial nature of the country were pointed out; if nevertheless they wished to persevere in their attempts they were assisted by advice and the advance of money from the funds already drawn for the organised escape scheme.

POST-CAPITULATION PERIOD, 8TH - 30TH MARCH, 1942.

8th - 10th March.

599. By 2200 hours 8th March the concentration in the hills, as ordered, was complete. Distribution of Royal Air Force personnel was:-

In Tjikadjang area, in the hills, armed	2,200 (approx.)
Tasik Malaja and other areas, in the plains, unarmed	2,500 (,,)
Stragglers, detached and in hospital in Bandoeng	400 (,,)
	5,100 (,,)

600. On 9th March a second order was received from A.H.K., containing instructions to collect arms, to display white flags and to make surrender arrangements with the nearest Japanese General. The A.O.C. accordingly went to Bandoeng on 9th March and on 10th March contacted Lieut. General Maruyama, the Japanese Commander in the Bandoeng district. From him were received instructions about collecting arms and troops and handing them over to Japanese representatives. Accommodation and promises to help with supplies were also obtained. He forbade communication with outside countries, but implied when pressed, without committing himself fully, that prisoners would be treated in accordance with the Geneva Convention of 1929.

60I. On IIth March the four Senior Officers (British A.O.C. and G.O.C.: Australian - Brigadier Blackburn: American - Col. Searle) were summoned to Garoet. They were conducted during the night from there to Bandoeng. The true reason was not told them. After being kept waiting all night they were assembled at 0730 hours I2th March for the formal signing of the surrender terms before General Maruyama.

602. In front of a number of Japanese witnesses General Maruyama undertook that prisoners would be treated in accordance with the terms of the Geneva Convention of I929, an undertaking which was recorded in writing.

603. An undertaking that the British and American troops would obey all orders of the Japanese was also included. An attempt to introduce the word "lawful" before the word "orders" was refused by General Maruyama who stated that it was unnecessary since he was giving P.O.W's. the protection of the Geneva Convention, under which no unlawful orders by the Japanese Army would be possible. It was evident that further insistence on the inclusion of the word "lawful" might lose the grant of the terms of the Geneva Convention. It was, therefore, erased from the original Instrument of Surrender, which was retained by General Maruyama.

604. Arms and equipment were subsequently surrendered at Garoet, all equipment and weapons in possession of the R.A.F. except some M.T., a number of rifles and bayonets, some field glasses and minor equipment, having been destroyed. Some difficulty arose about this, but an explanation that it was a point of honour with the British not to let arms fall undamaged into the enemy's hands was accepted.

605. On I7th March all senior officers were summoned to Garoet for the first cross-examination by the Japanese Intelligence Staff: a few other officers who happened to be nearby also became involved. So far as the G.O.C. and A.O.C. were concerned, it was conducted entirely correctly. Refusals to answer questions, based on the Geneva Convention of I929, were generally accepted.

606. Brigadier S.R. Pearson was, however, faced by a firing party but, on still refusing to speak, was pardoned. Pilot Officer R.L. Cicurel was threatened with mutilation but, still refusing, was also pardoned.

607. On 20th March occurred a further deliberate and flagrant violation of the Geneva Convention. General H.D.W. Sitwell, Air Commodore W.E. Staton, Brigadier S.R. Pearson, Group Captain A.G. Bishop and Colonel A.E. Searle, U.S. Army, went to Bandoeng ostensibly to attend a conference. They were, instead, subjected to interrogation for military information by Major Saitu, an Intelligence Staff Officer. The first four were subjected to a month's rigorous imprisonment, which in Japanese hands is truly rigorous, for refusing to answer questions, after which they were released. Whether or not representations made by the Dutch Representative of the International Red Cross in Bandoeng and by Col. E.E. Dunlop, C.O. of the Australian Hospital in Bandoeng, to General Maruyama's H.Q. had any effect in bringing about

their release will never be known; but there is reason to believe that this may have been the case, because these events coincided in time.

608. The Japanese subsequently endeavoured to extract information from aircrews of Nos. 232 (F) Squadron and No. I (G.R.) Squadron, R.A.A.F., and from other individual officers and airmen, with almost complete lack of success, in spite of protracted brutal treatment in many cases. They then gave up all attempts to obtain it. More than once, their Intelligence Officers afterwards stated that the British had proved obstinate and stupid about the matter and had suffered accordingly. Credit is due to the above named individuals, who were the first to set an example of compliance with orders to observe complete reticence in spite of brutal treatment, as it is due to those who subsequently followed their lead.

609. The later treatment of P.O.W.'s, with little regard to the terms of the Geneva Convention of I929 which had been accorded to them on surrendering, is too well known to need further elaboration in this report.

Breakdown of Signals Communication with Air Ministry.

6I0. The original site chosen on 7th March (p.m.) for the Signals Station near Tjikadjang proved unsuitable for communication with outside countries, screened as it was by the surrounding mountains. It was, therefore, moved about noon 8th March towards the coast, in an attempt to find a suitable position.

6II. A technical breakdown, caused by contamination of the Diesel fuel of the T. I087 high power transmitter, followed by a road accident which damaged the transmitter itself, presented this set being used again.

6I2. Attempts were made that evening to come into action with another, a low power, set were at first forbidden by the Commander of the Dutch troops into whose area the station had by now moved, and who by this time, was strictly obeying the terms of surrender. These orders forbade further communication with the outside world. Despite them a T. I082/R. I083 Vanette set was brought into action but it failed to establish communication with Melbourne, Ambala or Air Ministry. Several signals were broadcast by this means for three hours on the morning of 9th March in the hope that they would be picked up. Amongst them was the signal which informed the Air Ministry that the orders to surrender were being complied with (para. 596).

It subsequently transpired that these signals were not picked up although at the time the operator believed that they had been.

6I3. Subsequent attempts by the Signal Station to contact H.Q. and reciprocal attempts by H.Q. to find the new position of the station, failed to establish touch before the staff of this station had to destroy their equipment because:-

(*a*) It was believed that the last signals for despatch had been sent:

(*b*) Current reports of the imminent arrival of Japanese troops (subsequently proved to be false) made it necessary to destroy compromising documents and the set itself, to avoid capture in accordance with strict instructions which the A.O.C. had issued a few days previously on the subject of preventing the capture of cyphers and secret equipment.

These were the circumstances in which the report of the final surrender of the British troops in Java was not received by their respective Governments.

REFLECTIONS ON THE FAR EAST CAMPAIGN, DECEMBER, 1941, TO MARCH, 1942.

SCOPE OF REPORT.

614. This paper reports on only one aspect of the campaign of 1941/42 in the Far East - the air aspect. Weaknesses are admitted where they are believed to have existed. The air aspect was, however, only one of several. An account which discloses its weaknesses, but not those of the other aspects, is liable to leave an impression that the air was primarily responsible for the downfall of Malaya. This was not the case.

615. In order to counteract this tendency it is necessary, therefore, to refer to weaknesses elsewhere which played their part. This is done hereunder in no carping spirit, but in recognition of their causes and of the efforts made by those who endeavoured to overcome them. It is done for one reason only - to counterbalance a one-sided examination and to throw the whole into perspective. Weaknesses lay in many places. Failure in Malaya was a combined failure brought about firstly by the unpreparedness of the Empire as a whole for war, and then, when war came, by the needs of far more vital theatres of war on the other side of the world and in the seas which served them.

WEAKNESSES IN THE FIGHTING SERVICES.

616. In Malaya, the old policy of restricting the defence of Singapore to the immediate vicinity of the Island had been replaced by one of defending the whole of Malaya. In conformity with this policy the Chiefs of Staff had authorised large army and air force increases. In the absence of the Fleet, defence of the Far East was to depend primarily on a mobile air defence. Pending provision of the increased air strength, the army needed additional interim strength, over and above its ultimate total, to ensure security in the meantime.

617. The Japanese attacked whilst this policy was being implemented. The air force and the army had by then received only a part of the modern equipment and reinforcements which had been estimated to be necessary. The vital and pressing needs of the war in Europe and the Middle East, which had passed through a long and very critical period, had proved of overriding importance. The result was that the forces in the Far East were attacked in positions which could only have been defended if the full strength planned by the Chiefs of Staff had been available.

Mutual Naval and R.A.F. Support.

6I8. The Air Force in Malaya was not yet in a position to deny the waters off Malaya to a seaborne invasion. It possessed, neither the necessary aircraft nor secure aerodromes, and the enemy proved altogether too strong in the air once he had obtained a footing in South Siam and North Malaya.

6I9. The "Prince of Wales" and "Repulse" were lost in a gallant attempt to help the army and air force in their predicament in North Malaya. The attempt was made in the face of a strong shore-based Japanese Air Force but without the corresponding air support, either carrier-borne or shore-based. Thereafter it was progressively impracticable for the Navy, other than the lightest units, to remain in Malayan waters, particularly in the absence of such support.

620. The freedom of the seas which the enemy gained by his use of air power both at Pearl Harbour and off the coast of Malaya, was such that he was virtually free thereafter to hit when and where he liked. The consequences to the army and air force dispositions and operations in Malaya were profound. No criticism is levelled, the war against Germany and Italy had stretched our resources as never before. The small forces which were available in the Far East were faced with overwhelming circumstances and were too weak to overcome the advantages which the enemy gained in the first and most vital days of the campaign. In short, neither the Air Force nor the Navy was in a position to support the other.

Mutual Army/Air Support.

62I. The enemy army proved to be more effective than had been expected: our army had a number of shortcomings. It is not for this paper to say what they were or to expand upon them: it is appropriate only to say that they existed and that the army, in consequence, was unable to play its part adequately in the provision of secure air bases for our air forces. The root cause was the same, namely the overriding calls of the war in Europe and the Middle East.

622. When war came, the construction of aerodromes in Malaya had outstripped the provision of air forces to occupy them. But the aerodromes had had to be defended - a factor, amongst others considerably more important, which led to the army adopting a forward policy. The army had insufficient troops for the purpose, particularly in the absence of the additional interim strength it required pending full Air Force expansion. It became widely scattered in trying to meet all its commitments, and was defeated in detail.

623. The R.A.F., although inadequate for the task, had to occupy these forward and ineffectively defended aerodromes. There it suffered severe losses which could not be replaced, and it was driven out.

624. Thereafter the army had to fight in northern and central Malaya without any air support, and to face an enemy whose air support was constant and strong. It was not until the Japanese advance brought the land battle within effective range of aerodromes on Singapore island, that our army could be supported from the air. Even then this support fell far short of the scale demanded by the situation, although it was

the maximum available. The enemy's air support remained undiminished. Neither service was in a position to support the other or to fulfil its commitments: both suffered severely in attempting to do both.

Mutual Support between Japanese Forces.

625. The Japanese, on the other hand, had sufficient forces to support one another. Their naval and air forces were adequate to cover the initial landings of their army, and to give its subsequent expeditions virtual freedom of action to strike where and when they liked. Their army was strong enough to hold the countryside as it was overrun, and in particular to defend the aerodromes it captured. Their air forces were able to fill those aerodromes with aircraft, maintain them there at full strength, and from them gain and fully exploit the advantages of air superiority in the land, sea and air battles.

They possessed what we had not - balanced harmony by land, sea and air, their forces in which elements were strong enough to play their respective parts and to support one another fully.

Joint Navy/Army/Air Co-operation.

626. Two lessons emerge from the foregoing factors:-

Firstly, that only by full co-ordination of the fighting services - in strength, organisation and methods of operating - can success be achieved.

Secondly, that the issue of a modern war largely depends on the struggle for secure air bases, which all three fighting services have a joint responsibility for obtaining, defending and maintaining.

That side which is successful, and which denies its opponent the advantage of secure air bases, dominates the whole theatre of war within air striking range. It has then every prospect of success, while its opponent has but little.

THE CIVIL COMMUNITY.

Shortages of Labour and Material.

627. Civil interests and the fighting services competed keenly for labour, M.T., constructional material and equipment, all of which were in short supply (see paras 2I and 24). Before war came it was difficult to obtain access to land for the construction of aerodromes and other installations (see para. I9), particularly if its acquisition affected the production of rubber or tin, which were Malaya's most important contribution to the war in Europe and which her administrators had been enjoined to raise to a maximum.

628. The complicated administrative machinery in Malaya, which comprised numerous states with varying constitutions, was slow to produce results. Speed was

further handicapped by the multiplicity of nationalities - Chinese, Malay, Indian and European - who populated Malaya and whose interests and outlook varied widely.

Native Labour.

629. Experience confirmed the unreliability of unenlisted natives employed as domestics, as M.T. drivers and for construction and repairing damage to aerodromes. They disappeared en bloc, as did many native employees of the railways, whenever bombing started or the siren sounded. At critical moments dislocation occurred to the domestic life of R.A.F. stations, and to road and rail movements.

630. It is imperative in these days of air warfare to enlist all native personnel on whom dependence is to be placed in war. If enlisted, and officered by trained leaders, the natives in the Far East proved to be most reliable. This was demonstrated by the R.A.F. Special Technical Corps of enlisted Chinese, Malays and Indians, whose service in Malaya and Java during the war was exemplary.

Outlook in Malaya Towards War.

63I. A word on this subject is necessary because it had its effect upon preparation for war in the Far East. Considerable criticism, much of it unjust, has been levelled against the civil population of Malaya, although, unfortunately, there was justification for much of it. But it must be remembered that Malaya had been enjoined to spare no effort to raise business output to a maximum in support of the war in Europe, particularly of rubber, tin and of dollars for financing foreign exchange. It was thus natural that many in Malaya should have felt that Malaya's best contribution to the war in general lay in this direction - and no one will deny that the response they gave was a great contribution to the war in Europe.

Nevertheless their efforts in this direction had its effect on Malaya's preparations for her own defence, because the calls of the latter could only be met by diverting effort from the former. It must have been most difficult at times for those in responsible positions, in administrative and business circles alike, to hold the correct balance between these diametrically opposed interests.

In short, the calls of the war in Europe had its effect upon the civilian side of preparation for war in Malaya as it had on the fighting services.

632. Despite these difficulties much was done on the civil side towards preparing for war. Yet much remained to be done when war came. Shortages of equipment and still more important, lack of thorough training resulted in voluntary organisations not being ready, some more some less, when war broke out. Credit is due to those who volunteered to play their part and who, when war overtook them, played it despite many a handicap. But it is unfortunate to have to state that there were appreciable sections of the community, particularly amongst its Asiatic element, which might have been more interested and might have done more towards putting Malaya's defences on a sound footing.

In this respect a belief was widely held that Singapore defences were in reasonably good order, and that war was not imminent in any case. More than one official pronouncement on the subject had the unintentional effect of fostering a false sense of security and of supporting the view that business output came first, despite other official pronouncements which were made with the express object of combating complacency. Again that statement is made in no critical spirit. The former pronouncements were made for very good reasons. But they must be mentioned because of their effect on civilian and service personnel alike. The general atmosphere inevitably affected the latter, who had to live in it from day to day. Only the more informed and imaginative of both communities could be expected to foresee the future with accuracy and to remain unaffected. Nevertheless there were many, amongst the civil community as well as in the services, who foresaw the danger and who strove to accelerate readiness for war. To them the greatest credit is due. But despite their efforts the general atmosphere militated against the progress of which they aimed and had a grave effect upon preparations for war.

633. Two lessons were learned:-

Firstly, the most drastic and comprehensive measures are necessary to shake up a community which has long lived in peace into a realisation of the dangers of war and of the need to take timely action to prepare for it. This is particularly true if a community is of such a complex political and economic structure as that which existed in Malaya.

Secondly, the success of the fighting services is largely dependent upon the wholehearted, thoroughly organised and, where necessary, trained support of the civil community.

UNITY OF COMMAND.

634. In the Far East the Higher Direction of War, and of preparation for it, was not unified until the formation, in January, 1942, more than a month after war had broken out, of H.Q. Supreme Command, S.W. Pacific, under General Sir Archibald Wavell.

635. Before this date many and complicated channels of control had existed between Ministries and the Chiefs of Staff in the United Kingdom on the one hand, and, on the other,

the Civil Government and Service Commanders in Malaya. They varied in degree. G.H.Q. had operational but not administrative responsibility for the army and the air forces; while in the case of the navy its responsibility was limited to co-operation with the naval C.-in-C. in the Far East. G.H.Q. had no administrative staff, which handicapped its operational staff in appreciating in full detail the true state of affairs in the subordinate commands (para. I03). The situation was further involved by additional channels of communication with the Australian and Dutch Governments, and by varying control of the forces which they contributed to the defence of Malaya.

636. Such complicated machinery is unlikely to work efficiently during times of emergency when speed in preparing for war is paramount. It has even less chance of success in war itself.

637. From this emerges the lesson that responsibility for the defence of any region which is exposed to attack is better centralised in a Higher Command, both during the preparatory period before war and during war itself. This Higher Command should have full operational and administrative authority over the three fighting services, and also strong representation in all matters affecting the civil population.

638. In short, control should be comprehensive, and, in particular, administrative responsibility should not be divorced from operational responsibility. The outcome of war is likely to be in proportion to the observance of this lesson. Unity of Command enhances the prospect of success: lack of it invites failure.

POLITICAL CONSIDERATIONS BEFORE OUTBREAK OF WAR.

Handicap imposed on Air Striking Force.

639. At the outbreak of war, political circumstances, which made it imperative for us to avoid any action that might precipitate war, or that might make us appear to be the aggressors, were partly responsible (but only partly - see paras. 64I and 67I) for preventing the small air striking force that was available in Malaya being used in the role for which it had been primarily trained - to hit the enemy convoys at sea, as far away and as often as possible. The consequence was that the enemy was able to establish himself firmly ashore in a neutral country before action could be taken against his convoys.

Operation Matador.

640. The political factor was also partly responsible for preventing the initiation of the planned British advance into Siam. The consequences were far-reaching: those affecting the Air Force were immediate. The enemy was able to establish his squadrons in strength in Siam within easy striking distance of our virtually defenceless aerodromes in northern Malaya. Many of our aircraft were thus destroyed with little accomplished, and our squadrons were driven out. Thereafter they were unable to give air support to the army in its battles in northern and central Malaya.

64I. In passing, it is legitimate to reflect that had the reconnaissance into the Gulf of Siam been greater on 6th December after the Japanese convoys had been sighted, and on 7th December (paras. I50-I69 and 67I), and had the object of the Japanese expedition been disclosed thereby, it might well have had an influence on the decision to initiate operation "Matador", or brought about its cancellation earlier than was the case.

Japanese Action.

642. The Japanese, on the other hand, chose the moment for attack that was most opportune for themselves. In doing so they brushed aside political hindrances - as

indeed they had done whenever it suited them during their successive encroachments into the South-Western Pacific.

Lesson.

643. The lesson which emerges is that when the initiative lies in the hands of a prospective enemy, as it did in the Far East, it is highly dangerous to depend upon a plan of defence which may be frustrated by political considerations.

WEAKNESS OF ALLIED INTELLIGENCE.

Under-estimation of Japanese Strength.

644. Put bluntly, the enemy's true value was much under-estimated. Although he was known to possess some good military (the word is used in its widest sense) qualities, conspicuous amongst which was a fanatical valour, it was believed that he would display weaknesses, hitherto undisclosed, when he came face to face with the modern forces of the British Empire and the U.S.A.

645. There is reason to believe, from the experience of those who underwent military interrogation as prisoners-of-war in Japanese hands, that the enemy took deliberate steps in peace-time to mislead her potential enemies into under-estimating her fighting forces. They themselves on the other hand were not deluded about our true value: they were too well informed by a long-established organisation of agents.

Japanese Air Forces.

646. The qualities of the Japanese Air Force came as a complete surprise - in numbers, performance and quality of equipment, training and experience of its personnel, and in its mobility. Its fighters displayed unexpected all-round qualities. They and the Japanese medium bombers had ranges of 1,500 to 1,600 miles which enabled them to operate from bases out of our reach. Their normal operational height was 20,000-24,000 feet where they were immune from any of our A.A. gun defences. Japanese torpedo-bombers proved to be unexpectedly effective.

647. It is difficult to assess the precise air strength the enemy deployed against Malaya. At the time, it was thought that he had 700 first line aircraft based in South-Indo-China, with adequate immediate reserves, as against our 158 obsolete and obsolescent types with practically no reserves.

Japanese Army and Naval Forces.

648. It is not for this paper to explain the extent to which these were under-estimated, except to say that his army proved to be more effective than it was believed to be, and that the Japanese ability to strike so strongly and simultaneously in several directions in the Pacific had not been anticipated.

Need for an Intelligence Corps.

649. It is therefore appropriate to suggest here that our mistakes can only be attributed to lack of an adequate Intelligence organisation. True, a combined services intelligence organisation was in existence for obtaining naval, military and air information throughout the Far East (F.E.C.B. - see para 67) but it was inadequate for the purpose. In the East an Intelligence system of any real value takes years to build up and requires considerable funds at its disposal. That it should be a combined organisation to serve the needs of all the defence Services goes without saying. It is suggested that a specialised Intelligence Corps will be essential in the future: that only by this means can continuity of knowledge, experience and contact be maintained: and that the appointment of individuals, as an incident of their service careers, can no longer be relied upon to fulfil requirements.

WEAKNESS OF JOINT ARMY/AIR FORCE INTEREST.

Army/Air Force relations.

650. There has been much exaggerated talk about the poor relations which existed between the Army and R.A.F. in Malaya. That there was foundation for it in limited quarters is unfortunately true during the time immediately before the arrival of the late Air Vice-Marshal Pulford and Lieut.-General A.E. Percival, who quickly took steps to put matters right. Unfortunately, honestly held differences of opinion about defence matters between their predecessors had led to weaknesses which had not been fully rectified by the time war came. The two chief matters are hereunder (paras. 65I and 652).

Army/Air Support.

65I. Organisation of, and training in air support for the army was in a primitive state of development in both services. There was a marked lack of specialised equipment for the purpose, and there were but few persons in both services who had had appreciable experience in co-operation between air and ground forces, particularly modern experience. The result was that neither party in Malaya knew much about the technique of co-operating with the other when war came.

Siting of Aerodromes in N. Malaya.

652. Unfortunately the selection of several aerodrome sites in Malaya had been made with insufficient regard to the needs of their tactical defence. Until the middle of I94I, sites had been chosen without sufficient consultation between the army and air force authorities concerned. Sited as they were, in positions tactically difficult to defend, these aerodromes imposed an unnecessary strain on the army in the ultimate event. It is only fair to point out, however, that they were strategically necessary if the R.A.F. was to fulfil its allotted role in the defence of Malaya.

Insecurity of Aerodromes.

653. Our aerodromes, particularly in N. Malaya, were far from being the secure air bases which could properly be occupied in the face of a strong enemy. There were neither the fighter aircraft, nor sufficient A.A. defences, nor an effective warning system to ensure reasonable defence against air attack. The enemy could, and did, destroy our aircraft on the ground in N. Malaya almost at will, and our squadrons were driven out of the aerodromes there within a matter of days.

654. These same aerodromes were invaluable to the enemy. He had the necessary air forces to occupy them as they were captured, and he had the means of defending them from all forms of attack.

655. From this emerges the lesson that aerodromes may be a liability rather than an asset unless there are sufficient forces, both air and ground, available to prevent the enemy capturing and using them. In other words - provision of defences must go hand in hand with aerodrome construction.

WEAKNESSES IN AIR FORCE MATTERS.

Over-centralisation in A.H.Q.

656. A.H.Q. had to deal directly with eight superior and collateral authorities. The area it controlled stretched from Durban to Hong Kong. The majority of its units were located in Malaya. (See Appendices A and C).

657. When war came in 1941 the formations in Burma and the Indian Ocean were transferred to another Command. Nevertheless, A.H.Q. still had to handle a large number of units with many different functions, and to do so simultaneously in a land battle, in seaward operations and in air defence. It had to administer direct the operational units engaged in them as well as a large number of administrative units, many of which were unexpectedly involved in mobile operations for which they were not fully prepared. It had no intervening bomber, coastal or administrative groups to which to decentralise in Malaya.

658. Even if the staff had contained an adequate number of experienced staff officers, such a high degree of centralisation would have been difficult to exercise efficiently. But most of the staff were inexperienced, although they were willing and many were able men. The load had consequently to be carried by a few able and experienced officers whose numbers were quite inadequate to cope with the situation - either before war broke out or after. Here again the war in Europe had its effect: its urgent needs absorbed all but a few experienced officers.

659. These faults demonstrated the weakness of an over-centralised organisation and of a Command which lacks a sufficient percentage of trained staff officers. A Headquarters which suffers from either fault cannot withstand the strain of war.

Allied Air Forces.

660. The British air striking force which was available in the Far East was in numbers far below that which the Chiefs of Staff considered necessary to ensure a reasonable degree of security, even against the calculated Japanese strength which, as already shown, was under-estimated.

66I. In quality our aircraft were obsolescent or obsolete. Squadrons had not been modernised. Their signals and navigational aids were primitive or out of date. Radar warning was limited to the immediate vicinity of Singapore. Their armament was in some respects poor.

662. Several fighter squadrons had formed shortly before the war broke out and were not adequately trained. Others had recently re-armed and were still unfamiliar with their aircraft. A high proportion of fighter pilots had joined their squadrons straight from F.T.S.'s without O.T.U. training.

All were troubles which would have been put right but for the war in Europe.

Change of Personnel.

663. A sweeping change of personnel by posting and drafting occurred during the summer and autumn of I94I. Those who were relieved had been over-long in the Far East and it was time they went. A high proportion of those who replaced them came straight from training establishments without having had unit experience. No criticism of those responsible is intended: it was assumed that there would be time for them to settle down before war broke out. When war unexpectedly came the Command contained a high percentage of personnel who had much to learn about the application of what they had been taught or about their new duties in service units. Many were new to the tropics. Much credit is due to them for the manner in which they strove to play their part. It is unfortunate that circumstances in Europe had prevented the change being spread over a longer period by being started sooner.

Inadequate Training.

664. Personnel were willing, but the means for training them were inadequate because the demands elsewhere had drained resources. Many courses of instruction were improvised locally, during the summer and autumn preceding the war, to make good short-comings in training of aircrews, administrative and other personnel of all ranks, but they were too late to produce the results required.

665. In particular there were weaknesses in the training of fighter squadrons which had been based on the assumption that the enemy was of poor quality.

666. The imperative necessity for personnel to be fully trained in their duties before they have to face a trained enemy needs no further emphasis.

Reserves.

667. Reserves of aircrews and aircraft were inadequate; even the first casualties could not be fully replaced. Spare parts, for engines, airframes, armament, and M.T. in

particular were short. Squadron strengths consequently became abnormally low at the outset and remained so.

The need for adequate reserves in a theatre of war cannot be over-emphasised. Unfortunately it had been impossible to build up reserves in Malaya because supplies had been absorbed in supplying critical theatres in Europe, particularly in the Middle East and Russia.

Morale.

668. As perhaps is liable to happen when a force is confronted by an unexpectedly superior enemy, there was a loss of morale by a small section of the Command in the early days of the war. Trials had been severe, and had come before those concerned had had time to adjust themselves to their unpleasant and unforeseen circumstances. Lack of sufficient experienced officers undoubtedly contributed to the trouble, many of whom were newly commissioned and were not versed in their responsibilities.

Such incidents were few, and should not be exaggerated. But they serve to emphasise the need for giving all ranks that vital training which alone enables inexperienced troops to withstand their first novel shock of war. Such incidents also serve to enhance the credit of those who did maintain their morale, and who did their duty as was expected of them, and they comprised the great bulk of the force.

Mobility.

669. Few units were properly organised for mobile warfare. M.T. was very scarce and there were no transport aircraft. Each move involved appreciable interruption in operations, caused loss of valuable equipment and subsequent reduction of efficiency. The lack of transport aircraft was particularly felt when squadrons had to be transferred from Malaya to Sumatra, and thence later to Java: they suffered considerable loss and disorganisation during the enforced sea passage in the face of the enemy and without naval cover, the provision of which was quite impossible at the time.

670. The lesson was demonstrated that ability to take part in mobile operations, without loss of operational efficiency, is dependent on correct organisation and provision of suitable transport. A liberal scale of air transport is essential in those cases where long distances, sea crossings or other natural obstacles are involved.

INCIDENTS DURING THE CAMPAIGN.

Air Reconnaissance of approaching Japanese Convoy, 7th/8th December.

67I. Contact with the Japanese expedition at sea was lost on 6th December and was not regained, except for a few ships sighted on the afternoon of 7th December. Admittedly weather conditions were bad in the Gulf of Siam during this vital period.

Nevertheless only a small air reconnaissance effort was made for re-establishing contact. No. 8 (R.A.A.F.) Squadron at Kuantan had to be directed to continue its initial role of searching in an area far to the south and eastward of the probable position of the lost Japanese expedition for fear of a still more dangerous but possible attack, namely one directed against southern Malaya where a successful landing, particularly on the Endau/Mersing beaches, would have been very dangerous indeed. It is impossible to resist the inference that reconnaissance dispositions were strongly influenced by a conclusion at the time that the lost Japanese expedition might be proceeding against the Bangkok area of Siam. It is easy to be wise after the event, but the reconnaissance effort which was directed into the Gulf of Siam appears to have been small, bearing in mind its great area and the possible courses open to the Japanese convoys which were known to be in it.

Initial Action at Kota Bahru.

672. Only those who have given insufficient thought to the matter could venture to criticise the station commander at Kota Bahru for not having launched his aircraft to the attack on receipt of the news, at 0030 hours on 8th December, 1941, that ships were lying off the coast. It is equally easy to criticise the A.O.C. for ordering away only a reconnaissance to clear up the situation. But that both were correct in doing as they did, in the circumstances which existed at that particular moment, is beyond doubt. War had not broken out: Pearl Harbour had not been attacked and the U.S.A. was still neutral: there was grave risk that the Japanese might stage a bait in order to induce us to strike the first blow, and by doing so reinforce that section of the American Public which was then strongly opposed to America entering the war, a danger against which all in Malaya had been warned emphatically by G.H.Q. Admittedly 45 minutes were lost before the first air action was taken, but it is merely academic to conjecture what might have happened if it had been taken at once.

Main Japanese Landing at Singora not attacked.

673. It may fairly be asked why the initial Japanese landing at Singora was not attacked on 8th December, as this was the best target for our air striking force. The answer is that it was not realised, until too late, that it was in fact the enemy's main effort, although Singora had long been recognised as the area in which a Japanese expedition against Malaya was likely to be landed. The enemy, moreover, achieved a tactical surprise because our air reconnaissance failed to maintain contact with the main Japanese convoy, which was not found again until landings at Singora were well under way. By the time that the situation was fully realised, all our available aircraft had been launched against the Kota Bahru subsidiary attack. Before their objective could be changed to Singora, our own aerodromes in Northern Malaya were undergoing so heavy a scale of air attack that another effective force for opposing the Singora landing could not be launched from them.

Attempt to Neutralise Enemy Air Bases.

674. As soon as our Squadrons had been driven out of the aerodromes in Northern Malaya, our army was in turn subjected to heavy air attack. Its A.A. protection was quite inadequate and it had no fighter cover. Our own aircraft were therefore employed in the early stages of the campaign against enemy aerodromes, in an effort to give immediate relief to our troops. This was not successful. The enemy's reserves were sufficient to replace at once the small casualties which our attenuated squadrons could inflict. Moreover, he had the means to repair rapidly the damage our squadrons inflicted on his aerodromes.

675. The lesson was again learnt that little relief can be obtained by attacking the aerodromes of an enemy who has the means for replacing or repairing damage, particularly if such attacks are of little weight.

Reinforcements.

676. The reinforcements which the R.A.F. received arrived too late to save the situation. By the middle of January, when the first few came on the scene, the aerodromes which they had to use in Singapore were already under constant and heavy bombing. Reinforcements which came later had to use aerodromes in Sumatra which were little more than clearances in the jungle, for by this time, namely late January and early February, the enemy was in possession of the whole of the mainland of Malaya, and three out of the four aerodromes on the Island of Singapore were under observed artillery fire.

677. Hurricane reinforcements arrived in batches at intervals, and had to be thrown into the battle against greatly superior numbers and at tactical disadvantage caused by the lack of effective warning or efficient R/T control. The great majority of their pilots had never been in action before, and some had been at sea for as long as three months.

678. About half the bomber reinforcements that were despatched reached Malaya. They arrived in driblets of two and three aircraft at a time - the result of circumstances along a lengthy and insufficiently developed air reinforcement route. They had to be used piecemeal, without their own ground crews, and not as complete units. No time could be allowed for acclimatising and training them in local conditions. Extremes of weather caused navigational difficulties to which crews were strange. Adequate ground and radio aids, to which many were accustomed, were lacking.

679. The very important lessons were demonstrated that reinforcements must, in order to be effective, arrive as complete units, with aircraft, aircrews, specialised equipment, servicing crews and sufficient stocks and reserves. They are merely frittered rapidly away if they arrive piecemeal. They must have adequate bases from which to work, and they gain much if they are given time to obtain experience of local conditions before being engaged in battle. In short, the more orderly and methodical their arrival and their preparation for battle, the greater their chances of success - and vice versa.

POSTSCRIPT.

The Army in Malaya.

680. I wish to pay a tribute to the help which the R.A.F. received from the army in Malaya. Despite its own acute needs and shortages it gave ungrudging help - in defence of aerodromes at cost to its vulnerable points; in working parties and native labour to repair aerodromes at cost to the construction of military defences; in maintaining signals communications and in many other ways. In particular, thanks are due to Lieutenant-General A.E. Percival for all that he did, in conjunction with the late Air Vice-Marshal Pulford, during the months immediately before war broke out, to re-establish good relations between the two services. Had the latter officer survived I know how strongly he would have expressed these views.

The Royal Navy in Malaya.

68I. The R.A.F. owes much to the Royal Navy also. Nothing that was requested was refused if it was available; frequently it was given at cost to itself - working parties for aerodrome repair, for replacing stevedores and labour which had deserted the docks under bombing: facilities in the dockyard workshops, and in many other ways. Thanks are particularly due to the late Rear Admiral Spooner, R.N., who lost his life in attempting to escape with the late Air Vice-Marshal Pulford, and whom the latter would wish to commend to your notice for all that he and his subordinates did for the R.A.F. in Malaya.

The Merchant Navy.

682. Much credit is due to the Merchant Navy. It rendered the R.A.F. devoted service in bringing into Singapore reinforcements and supplies at a critical time, in transferring units to the N.E.I., and in evacuating several thousands of personnel from Singapore and later from the N.E.I. This work was done at great hazard in waters exposed to surface, submarine and air attack. A number of ships and seamen were lost in the doing of it. I wish to record our deep appreciation to the masters and crews who did so much for us at such cost to themselves.

Civilians in Malaya.

683. A tribute is also due to the civilians, men and women, who put themselves and their means at the disposal of the R.A.F. Of them there were many - nurses, business men, clerical staffs, tradesmen, welfare workers, contributors of material and money, and others. Their assistance and good-will were invaluable at a most difficult time. To them the R.A.F. owes a real debt of gratitude.

The Dutch in the Far East.

684. It must be remembered that the Dutch pinned their faith to collective Allied resistance in the Far East, and that they lost part of their Air Force and of their Navy

to the common cause before the Japanese reached Java at all. When their hopes of successful resistance disappeared, and only a small British force remained to replace the forces the Dutch themselves had sacrificed, their isolated position came home forcibly to them.

685. Moreover, everything that the Dutch community possessed was in the N.E.I. Towards the end it was obvious to them that the whole of it, including their families, must inevitably fall into the hands of the Japanese. They had already experienced incidents of Japanese savagery in Borneo. They were consequently reluctant to continue guerilla resistance in Java in the circumstances in which they finally found themselves. It was only then, when the British wanted to go on fighting after the general capitulation in Java, that differences arose as to the best line to pursue.

686. Nevertheless, I want to express my thanks to the Dutch. Their wish to help was unbounded. They fulfilled their planned undertakings to the full. Special recognition is due to those of them who, as a result lost their lives in Malaya's defence. When arrangements had to be made to transfer the R.A.F. to the N.E.I., their Army, Air Force and Civil Administration placed everything at our disposal. As a community the Dutch refused the British nothing - labour, materials, money and help of every kind were ungrudgingly given - frequently at considerable sacrifice. The devotion of their doctors and nurses to our sick and wounded was outstanding. The Royal Air Force owes a debt of gratitude to these people.

Recommendations for meritorious service.

687. I have already reported to the appropriate branch of the Air Ministry the names of those whose services were particularly meritorious, and whom I recommend for honours, awards and mention in despatches. But I want to bring to your notice here the units mentioned hereunder, and also to name a few individuals who rendered particularly meritorious service but who, I regret to report, are no longer alive.

Air Vice-Marshal C.W. Pulford, C.B., O.B.E., A.F.C.

688. This officer, despite ill health, worked unceasingly and uncomplainingly to overcome the many difficulties with which he was faced when preparing his Command for war and after hostilities had broken out. He never flinched from meeting an overwhelming situation with very inadequate means. No man could have striven more wholeheartedly to carry a burden which was far beyond one man's capacity. All his decisions were reached with complete disregard for self and entirely in the interests of what he felt to be his duty according to the situation and to his instructions.

689. He refused to leave Singapore himself until all his men had been evacuated. He lost his life in a last minute attempt to follow his Command to the N.E.I. (see para. 394). His selfless devotion to duty and his loyalty to all those around him, both senior and junior, were an inspiration to all.

Personnel of the R.A.F. Far East Command.

690. I am confident that the late Air Vice-Marshal Pulford would wish me to place on record the praiseworthy manner in which the personnel, of all ranks, under his Command carried out their duties. I know how deeply he appreciated the loyal support they gave him.

Aircrews.

691. The aircrews of our squadrons, of the Royal Air Force, Royal Australian Air Force and Royal New Zealand Air Force alike, consistently met the calls that were made upon them despite the enemy's great superiority in numbers and equipment, especially in the matter of fighters. Their own aircraft, on the other hand, were many of them obsolete and old, and were difficult to maintain owing to technical shortages and poor facilities for over-haul work. Their aerodromes possessed little protection against air attack, sometimes none at all. They flew long distances by night over jungle-clad country in the face of violent tropical thunderstorms with the help of only rudimentary navigational aids; towards the end with none at all. It is difficult to overstate the cumulative effect of the hazards which they faced. They deserve the very greatest praise for the way in which they consistently carried out their missions despite these hazards and despite casualties.

692. At the risk of selecting examples which may prove invidious to other units, against whom no reflection is intended, I would particularly mention the following:-

Fighter Defences of Singapore.

693. Credit is due to the spirited leadership of the late Group Captain E.B. Rice, Fighter Defence Commander of Singapore, and of the late Wing Commander R.A. Chignell, his Chief Air Staff Officer. Both were outstanding in their selfless devotion to duty. They were primarily responsible for the good morale which the small fighter force at Kallang maintained throughout the campaign in the face of a numerous and better armed enemy. The steadiness of the ground personnel of this fighter station is also worthy of mention.

No. 4 Photographic Reconnaissance Unit.

694. This flight, flying unarmed and unarmoured Buffaloes, unfailingly carried out their photographic missions deep into enemy territory dominated by a very superior enemy fighter force. Its service throughout the Malayan campaign was most valuable.

No. 232 (F) Squadron.

695. This unit, under the leadership of the late Squadron Leader R.E.P. Brooker D.S.O., D.F.C., who volunteered to take command at a critical moment, was in constant action from the time it arrived in Singapore in mid-January 1942 until fighting ceased in Java. It inflicted severe casualties on the enemy in the air, in landing craft and on the ground. It volunteered to remain in Java as the last fighter squadron.

Great credit is due to all ranks of a magnificent squadron, drawn as they were from the ranks of several different fighter units.

Nos. 36 and 100 (TB) Squadrons.

696. These two squadrons attacked the enemy landing at Endau on 26th January, 1942, covered as it was by numerous Zero fighters, whereas their own fighter escort was unavoidably small. They pressed home their attacks on their obsolete Vildebeeste torpedo-bombers regardless of casualties, amongst whom I regret to report were lost the Commanding Officers of both squadrons, the late Squadron Leaders R.F.C. Markham and I.T.B. Rowland. After being reorganised into a composite squadron in Java, and after having patched up their old aircraft, they again pressed home attacks against the enemy convoys which were invading that island, this time at night, again suffering casualties and the loss of their squadron commander, the late Squadron Leader J.T. Wilkins. Such gallant conduct speaks for itself.

No. 84 (B) Squadron.

697. This unit arrived as a reinforcement much strung out after a long flight from the Middle East. Its crews set a fine example of throwing themselves into the fight at once under many handicaps. Particular credit is due to the Commanding Officer, the late Wing Commander J.R. Jeudwine D.S.O., O.B.E., D.F.C., whose leadership and courage were a great inspiration to others. He led a small party which escaped from Java in an open boat across the 1000 mile crossing of the Timor Sea to Australia, a typical example of his spirit.

M.V.A.F.

698. At a critical time of the fighting in Southern Malaya, a number of successful reconnaissances were carried out by this unit to locate bodies of our troops who had been cut off by the enemy, and to locate the enemy's infiltrating forces. These reconnaissances were performed in unarmed Moth aircraft (originally the property of Malaya's flying clubs) at tree top height over a battle field dominated by Japanese Zero fighters. Their value was great to the Army, then closely engaged with the enemy. Pre-eminent in this work was the late Flight Lieutenant Henry Dane, M.V.A.F., whose qualities as a leader and a man were a byword amongst those who knew him. His example was largely responsible for the excellent work done throughout by the M.V.A.F.

Technical Personnel.

699. A word of recognition is due to the Technical Personnel of the Command.

700. Before war broke out they handled great quantities of stores and equipment which arrived in Malaya greatly in excess of the new stations' power, and that of the Command's backward maintenance organisation, to absorb them. Many aircraft were

erected and rapidly passed into commission and many others were overhauled during the period of the Command's expansion.

70I. During the war itself, technical personnel worked untiringly in most difficult circumstances. Aircraft and equipment had to be dispersed as a protection against bombing, mostly to improvised dispersal points in rubber plantations or scrub. There they were erected, overhauled and serviced with little or no protection against tropical downpours.

702. An example of such work was the erection of the first 50 Hurricanes which arrived in Singapore in mid January I942; it was a particularly fine feat. Within a few days all were ready to take the air, the first in under 48 hours: during that time they had been unloaded in crates at the docks, conveyed many miles by road to scattered hide-outs in rubber plantations, and there rapidly erected despite tropical rain, blackout conditions at night and a great shortage of specialised tools.

703. It would be invidious to select any particular unit for special mention. Suffice it to say that most meritorious technical work of all kinds was performed by units throughout the command at all stages of the operations in Malaya and the N.E.I. under very severe conditions. Not least of these handicaps was an almost complete breakdown of the backward maintenance organisation of the command which was brought about by circumstances that first overloaded and then disrupted it.

704. I will mention only one name, that of the late Wing Commander E.B. Steedman, whose unflagging efforts did much to inspire others to overcome their difficulties. He subsequently lost his life as a prisoner of war for refusing, it is believed, to divulge technical information about Spitfires. His spirit remained unbroken to the end.

Personnel in the N.E.I.

705. Those who landed in unavoidable disorganisation in the N.E.I. were required to reorganise into a fighting force within a few days with very limited resources indeed. I wish to express my gratitude to them for the very loyal manner in which they gave their best services, in particular to our squadrons who had to face a well organised enemy in overwhelming numbers. Their behaviour is particularly creditable, coming as it did after many reverses, and was in the best tradition of the Service.

Finally, I am indebted to all those who, at the end, were willing, despite shortage of arms, lack of training, and lack of most essentials, to fight in the hills in a form of warfare about which they knew nothing, namely in infantry warfare and in the jungle at that, and to do so against an enemy whom they knew to be well-equipped and highly trained in this form of fighting. That they were unable to put their willingness to the test was no fault of theirs. I wish to place on record my gratitude for the loyal response they gave to the call made upon them. Their conduct deserves the highest praise.

SUMMARY.

706. One can summarise in a few words the reason for the initial reverses in the Far East.

707. We lost the first round there because we, as an Empire, were not prepared for war on the scale necessary for the purpose. When war broke out in Europe it absorbed the Empire's resources to such an extent that only a fraction of the strength could be deployed which had been calculated to be necessary for withstanding Japanese aggression in Malaya - navy, army, air force and civil organisation alike being much below the required mark. When Japan attacked she proved to be even more formidable than had been expected, the result being that she swamped our underdeveloped defences before they could be supported.

708. Mistakes undoubtedly occurred, as they always do in war when the unexpected happens on the scale that it did in the Far East. But credit should be given to those on the spot who did their best to take the first brunt of the enemy's overwhelming strength with inadequate means, and who gained thereby the necessary time for other forces to be collected to prevent his further advance towards Australia and India.

P.C. MALTBY,
Air Vice-Marshal.
London,
26th July, 1947.

APPENDIX "A"

To Report on R.A.F. Operations in Malaya and N.E.I. 1941-2.

SITUATION AT R.A.F. STATIONS IN MALAYA - 8TH DECEMBER, 1941.

Location	(a) Peace Scale of Accommodation (b) Concentration Scale of Accommodation	Runways	(a) Aircraft Shelters State of Accommodation	Defences (b) A.A. Guns (c) Troops	Bombs (Approx weight)
North-West Malaya					
Alor Star	(a) I B Squadron	Hard I-I 400 yds	I Squadron	(a) Yes. (b) 4-3" guns. (c) I Coy. Infantry (Bahawalpur).	250 tons.
Butterworth	(a) I GR Squadron	Hard I-1,600 yds, being ex tended to 2,000 yds. 2nd in hand.	Hutted 2 Squadrons. Occupied.	(a) Yes Incomplete. (b) None until I0.I2.4I. Then 8 Bofors. (c) Bahawalput Inf. Btn (less 2 Coys).	250 tons.
Jabi	(b) I B Squadron	Hard I,400 yds Graded but not Surfaced.	I Squadron only, Just commenced.	(a) – (b) – (c) –	Nil.
Kuala Ketil	Satellite for Sungei Patani.	Tarmac I,400 yds	Guard Room; Petrol, oil and bomb stores.	(a) Nil. (b) Nil. (c) I Coy. Bahawalpur Inf.	Nil

Location	Squadron	Landing ground	Accommodation	Defences	Reserve
Lubok Kiap	(a) I B Squadron	Hard 1-1.600 yds 1-1,200 yds partly graded.	Hutted – 2 Squadron nearing completion. Partly occupied.	(a) – (a) – (b) Nil. (c) Nil.	Nil. Nil.
Malakoff	Satellite for Lubok Kiap.	600 yds Grading not complete	No buildings completed.	Nil.	Nil.
Panang Sungei Bakap	Civil Airfield Satellite for Butterworth.	Limited grass Airfield. 2,000 yds (1,400 yds soled but not surfaced)	Nil. No buildings completed.	Nil.	Nil.
Sungei Patani	(a) 2 F Squadrons	Grass 1-1,400 yds 1-1,200 yds	Hutted : 2 Squadrons. Partly occupied.	(a) Not quite finished. (b) 7-3.7" guns. (c) Btn HQ and I Coy. Indian State Troops.	250 tons.
North-East Malaya Gong Kedah	(b) I B Squadron	Hard 1-2,000 yds	Hutted I Squadron Ready and partly occupied	(a) Yes nearly 100%. (b) 2-3". (c) I.Pltn Mysore Inf.	250 tons.
Kota Bahru	(a) I B Squadron	Grass 1-1,600 yds Being extended	Hutted 2 Squadrons. Being extended.	(a) Yes nearly 100%. (b) 4-3" guns. (c) I Btn Inf (less I Coy).	250 tons.
Machang	(b) I F Squadron	Hard 1-1,600 yds 1-1,200 yds in hand.	Hutted 2 Squadrons partly completed.	(a) Just started. (b) Nil. (c) 2 Coys Mysore Inf	50 tons.
East Malaya Kuantan	(b) I B Squadron I GR Squadron	Grass 1-1,500 yds. 1-1,200 yds	Hutted 2 Squadrons Complete.	(a) In hand. (b) Nil. (c) 3 Coys 5th Sikhs.	100 tons.
Central Malaya Ipoh	(b) I B Squadron	Grass plus tarmac 1-1,400 yds	Hutted 2 Squadrons Nearly completed. Partly occupied	(a) Nil. (b) Nil. (c) I Coy Indian State Troops. I M.G. Platoon.	Nil.

Sitiawan	Civil Airfield	Grass 1-1,000 yds. 1-800 yds	Guard Room only.	(a) Nil. (b) Nil. (c) I Coy (less I Pltm) Indian State Troops.	Nil.
Taiping	Satellite for Ipoh	Grass plus tarmac 1-1,400 yds	Requisitioned cottages. Hutments in hand	(a) Yes. (b) Nil. (c) I Coy and I M.G. Pltm Indian State Troops.	Nil.
South Malaya Batu Pahat	Civil Airfield Satellite for Kluang	Grass 1-1,400yds	Petrol and oil stores Only	(a) Nil. (b) Nil. (c) I Pltm A.I.F. Inf.	50 tons.
Bekok (Labis)	(a) I Squadron	2,000 yds 1,400 yds Surveyed only	Nil	Nil	Nil
Kuala Lumpur	Civil Airfield	Grass 1,315 yds	Completed Occupied by 153 M.U.	(a) Nil. (b) Nil. (c) I Coy Indian State Troops I M.G. Pltm.	50 tons.
Kluang	(a) 2 F Squadrons, I F Squadron (Dutch).	Grass 1-1,200 yds 1-1,600 yds. Hard runway Commenced	Hutted. 2 Squadron Nearing completion Mostly occupied.	(a) Nil. (b) Nil. (c) I Btn (less I Coy and I Pltm) and Johore Military Forces Details	50 tons.
Kahang	(b) I GR Squadron	Grass 1-1,400 yds. 1-1,300 yds	Hutted. 2 Squadrons. In hand.	(a) In Hand. (b) Nil. (c) I Coy A.I. F. and Johore Military Forces Details.	50 tons
Port Swettenham	Civil Airfield	Grass (tarmac in centre). 1-1,000 yds.	Nil	(a) Nil. (b) Nil. (c) I Coy and I M.G. Pltm Indian State Troops.	10tons.

Station	Squadrons to be based	Runway	Squadrons allotted	Defences	P.O.L.
Tebrau		Hard 1-1,200yds. 1-2,000 yds. in hand	1 Squadron only. 2nd Squadron in Hand.	(a) In hand. (b) Nil. (c) A. I. F. Infantry in Vicinity.	Nil.
Singapore Island Kallang	(a) 1 B Squadron	Complete (Civil Airfield) Grass 1,400 yds	2 Squadrons	(a) Yes. (b) Under cover of A. A. defences Singapore Town (c) 1 Coy Jind Inf.	10 tons (plus ammunition).
Seletar	(a) 2 TB Squadron	Complete. Grass 1,400 yds	3 Squadrons and M.U. Dispersed Hutted accommodation partly completed.	(a) Yes. (b) 8 Bofors. Within defended zone of Naval Base A.A. cover. (c) 1 Btn. (less 1 Coy) Kapurtala Inf.	500 tons.
Sembawang	(a) 2 B Squadrons	Grass 1,380 yds Construction of 2 hard runways deferred.	2 Squadrons F.A.A. adjacent	(a) Yes (b) Nil. Within defended zone of Naval Base A. A. cover. (c) 1 Coy Kapurtala Inf.	1,000 tons.
Tengah	(a) 3 B Squadrons 2 GR Squadrons (for Borneo).	Grass L G 1-1,400 yds Concrete runway.	2 Squadrons	(a) Partly finished. (b) Nil. Under extended A.A. cover of Island Defences. (c) 1 Btn Jind Inf.	750 tons.

NOTE

1. Aerodrome Operational Equipment - serious shortages existed at Stations in North and Central Malaya, other than Alor Star and Kota Bahru, despite local manufacture and purchase.

2. Adequate stocks of P.O.L. were in position at the Stations where required.

RADAR UNITS - FAR EAST COMMAND - 8TH DECEMBER, 1941

Location (1)	Unit No. (2)	Type (3)	Degree of Completion on 8th December, 1941 (4)	
MALAYA EAST COAST.				
Kota Bahru		C.O.L.	Not technically complete.	
Kota Bahru		T.R.U.	Some construction done.	
Kuantan			Under construction.	
Endau			Under construction.	
Mersing	243	M R U	Operational.	
Bukit Chunang	511	C.O L	Operational.	
Ayer Besar		T.R.U	Under construction.	
MALAYA WEST COAST				
Penang			Three stations. One partly complete.	
Batu Phat	512	C.O.L.	Partly completed.	
Tanjong Kupang		C.O.L.	Operational.	
MALAYA JOHORE				
Kota Tinggi	518	C.O.L.	Operational late December, 1941	} Over-run by
Bukit Dinding			Crews on site. Not quite complete Did not function.	} Enemy.
Sungei Kahang			Work nearing completion	
SINGAPORE ISLAND				
Seletar	243	R.I.M.U.	Operational.	
Tuas	250	T.R U.	Operational 15. I. 42.	
Tanah Merah Besar	308	M.R.U.	Operational.	
Serangoon		T.R U.	Operational December, 1941	
Changi Jail		LD/CHL	Operational December, 1941	
JAVA WEST				
Batavia (East)		T.R.U.	Operational February, 1942.	
Batavia (West)		T.R.U.	Operational February, 1942.	

Angelor	Army G.L	Operational February, 1942.
Lebuan	Army G.L	Operational February, 1942.
Tanara	Army G.L	Operational February, 1942.
JAVA EAST		
Modong	American G.L.	Operational 22. 2. 42.
Parmakassen	American G.L.	Operational 22. 2. 42.
Sitoebondo	American G.L.	Operational 22. 2. 42.

APPENDIX "C"

to Report on R.A.F. Operations in Malaya and N.E.I. 1941-2
R.A.F. ORDER OF BATTLE IN MALAYA
22nd November, 1941
AIR HEADQUARTERS, SINGAPORE
A. OPERATIONAL UNITS

SINGAPORE ISLAND

1. *Seletar* Station Commander - Group Captain H.M.K Brown.

   (*a*) No. 36 (TB) Squadron - Commander - Wing Commander R.N. McKern - 12 Vildebeestes.

   (*b*) No 100 (TB) Squadron - Commander - Wing Commander A.W.D. Miller - 15 Vildebeestes.

   (*c*) No 205 (GR) Squadron - Commander - Wing Commander L.W. Burgess - 3 Catalinas.

   (*d*) P R Flight - Commander - Squadron Leader C.G.R Lewis - 2 Buffaloes.

2. *Sembawang* Station Commander - Group Captain J.P.J. McCauley (R.A.A.F.).

   (*a*) No 8 (GR) Squadron, R.A.A.F. - Commander - Wing Commander F.N. Wright - 8 Hudson II.

   (*b*) No 21 (F) Squadron, R.A.A.F. - Commander - Squadron Leader W.F. Alshorn. - 10 Buffaloes.

   (*c*) No 453 (F) Squadron - Commander - Squadron Leader W.J. Harper - 12 Buffaloes.

3. *Tengah* Station Commander - Group Captain F.E. Watts.

   (*a*) No 34 (B) Squadron - Commander - Wing Commander G.P. Longfield - 17 Blenheim IV.

   (*b*) No 4 A.A.C.U. - Commander - Squadron Leader N.W. Wright - 5 Sharks, 5 Swordfish, 2 Blenheim I.

4. *Kallang* Station Commander - Wing Commander R.A. Chignell.

   (*a*) No 243 (F) Squadron - Commander - Wing Commander G.B.M. Bell - 12 Buffaloes.

(*b*) No 488 (F) Squadron - Commander - Squadron Leader W.G. Clouston - 9 Buffaloes.

5. *Fighter Control* in Singapore - Group Captain E.B. Rice.

MAINLAND OF MALAYA

6. *Kota Bahru* Station Commander - Wing Commander C.H. Noble.

No. I (GR) Squadron, R.A.A.F. - Commander - Wing Commander R.H. Davis - 7 Hudson II.

7. *Kuantan* Station Commander - Wing Commander R.B. Councell.

No 60 (B) Squadron - Commander - Wing Commander R.L. Vivian (From Rangoon for training at Armament Practice Camp) - 7 Blenheim I.

8. *Alor Star* Station Commander - Wing Commander R.G. Forbes.

No. 62 (6) Squadron - Commander - Wing Commander J. Duncan - I0 Blenheim I.

9 *Sungei Patam* Station Commander - Squadron Leader F.R.C. Fowle.

No 27 (NF) Squadron - Commander - Squadron Leader F.R.C. Fowle - I0 Blenheim I.

I0. *Butterworth* - Care and Maintenance - i/c - Flight Lieutenant R.D.I. Scott.

II. *Kluang* Station Commander - Wing Commander W.R. Wills-Sandford - Improvised O.T.U.

I2. *Kuala Lumpur* Norgroup H.Qs - Wing Commander R.G. Forbes.

NOTES.

(*a*) Aircraft shown are those serviceable as at 22nd November, I94I.

(*b*) A further 40 Buffaloes were repairable within I4 days.

(c) For other Squadrons, there was an average of 2 or 3 aircraft per Squadron repairable within I4 days.

B. MAINTENANCE UNITS.

I3. No I5I M.U.	*Seletar.*	Group Captain C.T. Walkington.
I4. No. I52 M.U.	*Bukit Panjang, Singapore*	Squadron Leader S.G. Aylwin.
I5. No. I53 M.U.	*Kuala Lumpur*	Group Captain M.W.C. Ridgway.
I6. No. 8I R. & S.U.	*Kluang*	Wing Commander H. Stanton.
I7. "Z" M.U.	*Batak Quarry, Singapore*	Flight Lieutenant J.H. Cocks.
I8. R.I.M.U.	*Seletar.*	Squadron Leader T.C. Carter.

C. MISCELLANEOUS UNITS

I9. Radar Units (Four operational)	Wing Commander N. Cave.
20. R.N.Z.A.F. Aerodrome Construction Unit	Squadron Leader Smart.
2I. Transit Camp, Singapore	Squadron Leader O.G. Gregson.
22. S.S. "Tung Song"	Pilot Officer G.T. Broadhurst.
23. S.S. "Shenking"	Pilot Officer C.E. Jackson.

Footnote

I i.e. - an R.A.F. as distinct from a Dominion squadron but manned by Dominions personnel.

2 6 Beauforts had recently been delivered, but 5 were sent back to Australia owing to "teething" troubles with the aircraft. Nos 36 (TB) and I00 (TB) Squadrons were due to be rearmed with this type.

ABBREVIATIONS

A&AEE	Aeroplane and Armament Experimental Establishment
A/MTB	Anti-Motor Torpedo Boat
A/T	Anti-Tank
A/TK	Anti-Tank
AA	Anti-Aircraft
AACU	Anti-Aircraft Co-operation Unit
Abdacom	Code-name for the Supreme Allied Headquarters, S.W. Pacific, which formed on 15 January, 1942, and absorbed GHQ
Abdair	Codename of the Air Section of Supreme Allied H.Q., S.W. Pacific ADA Anglo, Dutch and Australian (agreement)
ADB	American, Dutch and British (agreement)
ADC	Aide-De-Camp
ADMS	Assistant Director Medical Services
Adv	Advanced
AFC	Air Force Cross
AFV	Armed Fighting Vehicle
AHK	Headquarters of the Dutch Commander-in-Chief at Bandoeng, Java
AHQ	Air Headquarters
AIF	Australian Imperial Forces
ALG	Advanced Landing Ground
AME	Air Ministry Experimental (station – Radar)
AOA	Air Officer in charge of Administration
AOC	Air Officer Commanding
AP	Armour Piercing
ARP	Air Raid Precautions

ASP	Air Stores Park
(B)	Bomber
BAF	Burma Auxiliary Force
Bde	Brigade
BFF	Burma Frontier Force
Bn, Btn	Battalion
Britair	Code-name for AHQ in Java after the dissolution of Supreme Allied HQ, S.W. Pacific
Bty	Battery
CAAD	Commander, Anti-Aircraft Defence
CB	Companion of the Order of Bath
CBE	Commander of the Most Excellent Order of the British Empire
Cdr	Commander
C-in-C	Commander-in-Chief
CMG	Companion of the Most Distinguished Order of Saint Michael and Saint George
CNAC	China National Aviation Corporation
CO	Commanding Officer
Comd	Command
COS	Chiefs of Staff
CRE	Commander Royal Engineers
CSF	Commander, Singapore Fortress
DAAG	Deputy Assistant Adjutant General
D/F	Direction Finding (Radar)
DFC	Distinguished Flying Cross
DGCD	Director General of Civil Defence
Def.	Defence
Div	Division
DSC	Distinguished Service Cross
DSO	Distinguished Service Order

(F)	Fighter
(FB)	Fighter Boat
FDC	Fighter Defence Commander
FECB	Far East Combined Bureau (a combined service intelligence organisation for obtaining intelligence, under Admiralty administration, throughout the Far East)
FFR	Frontier Force Rifles
FMS	Federated Malay States
FMSVF	Federated Malay States Volunteer Force
GC	George Cross
GCVO	Knight Grand Cross of The Royal Victorian Order
GHQ	General Headquarters
GL	Ground Locating/Gun Locating
GOC	General Officer Commanding
GSO	General Staff Officer
gp	group
(GR)	General Reconnaissance
GSOI	General Staff Officer, Intelligence
HAA	Heavy Anti-Aircraft
HE	High Explosive, His Excellency
HKSRA	Hong Kong and Singapore Royal Artillery
HKVDC	Hong Kong Volunteer Defence Corps
HMAS	His Majesty's Australian Ship
HMS	His Majesty's Ship
HQ	Headquarters
HQMC	Headquarters of the General Officer Commanding, Malaya Command
i/c	in command
IE	Initial Equipment
in	inch(es)
inc, incl	included

Ind	Independent
IR	Immediate Reserve
KBE	Knight Commander of the Most Excellent Order of the British Empire
KCB	Knight Commander of the Most Honourable Order of the Bath
KOYLI	King's Own Yorkshire Light Infantry
LNC	Local Naval Craft
MC	Military Cross
MG	Machine Gun
mph	miles per hour
MRNVR	Malayan Royal Navy Volunteer Reserve
MT	Motor Transport
MTB	Motor Torpedo Boat
MU	Maintenance Unit
MVAF	Malayan Volunteer Air Force
MVO	Member of the Royal Victorian Order
NAAFI	Navy, Army and Air Force Institutes
NCO	Non Commissioned Officer
NEI	Netherlands East Indies
(NF)	Night Fighter
NLO	Naval Liaison Officer
Norgroup	Code-name for Group HQ controlling air operations in Northern Malaya
OBE	Officer of the Most Excellent Order of the British Empire
OC	Officer Commanding
Op, Ops.	Operation(s)
OTU	Operational Training Unit
PAD	Passive Air Defence
posns	positions
PRU	Photographic Reconnaissance Unit

RA	Royal Artillery
RAAF	Royal Australian Air Force
RAF	Royal Air Force
RAMC	Royal Army Medical Corps
RAN	Royal Australian Navy
RAOC	Royal Army Ordnance Corps
RAPC	Royal Army Pay Corps
RASC	Royal Army Service Corps
RAVC	Royal Army Veterinary Corps
rd/rds	round(s)
RDF	Radio Direction Finding (Radar)
RE	Royal Engineers
Recgroup	Code-name for the Allied Air Reconnaissance Group responsible for seaward reconnaissance of whole sphere of Supreme Allied Command, S.W. Pacific
Regt	Regiment
RN	Royal Navy
RSU, R&SU	Repair and Salvage Unit
RT, R/T	Receiver-Transmitter/Radio Transmitter/Radio Telephony
SAA	Small Arms Ammunition
SAO	Senior Administrative Officer
SASO	Senior Air Staff Officer
Sitrep	Situation Report(s)
SL	Squadron Leader
SS	Steam Ship/Straits Settlements
SSVF	Straits Settlements Volunteer Force
(TB)	Torpedo Bomber
tp, tps	troop(s)
TK	Tank
UMS	Un-federated Malay States
US	United States

USN	United States Navy
VAD	Voluntary Aid Detachment
VC	Victoria Cross
VHF	Very High Frequency
WD	War Department
WDV	Wreck Dispersal Vessel
Westgroup	Code-name allotted to AHQ on the formation of Supreme Allied H.Q., S.W. Pacific

INDEX OF NAVAL, MILITARY AND AIR FORCE UNITS

American Volunteer Group, 12–13, 32, 369, 381

Australian Army:

Australian Imperial Force, 54, 78, 159, 161, 171–3, 175, 199, 219, 221, 225, 231, 236, 242–3, 245–6, 254, 257, 259, 261, 265, 279, 287, 292–4, 299, 301, 304–305, 307, 309, 326, 342, 344, 346–7, 353–4, 408, 415, 498–9

1st Corps, 437

8th Division, 159, 161, 326

22nd Brigade, 54, 67, 159, 172, 245–6, 251, 261, 264, 267, 289, 292–5, 301, 303

27th Brigade, 54, 67, 171, 221, 255, 260, 289, 295–7, 299, 301

2/18 Battalion, 265, 293–4

2/19 Battalion, 257, 293–4

2/20 Battalion, 293–4

2/29 Battalion, 257, 294, 299

2/30 Battalion, 255

2/3 Australian Reserve Motor Transport Company, 202

Australian Red Cross, 180

British Army:

Royal Army Medical Corps, 129, 141–2, 264, 283

Royal Army Ordnance Corps, 107–108, 124, 129, 131, 133, 141

Royal Army Service Corps, 93, 107, 123–5, 129, 131, 141, 178

Royal Artillery, 82, 96, 109, 119–23, 127, 130, 134, 141–3, 339, 432

6th Heavy Anti-Aircraft Regiment, 54

10th Mountain Battery, 202

11th Heavy Anti-Aircraft Battery, 262

16th Light Anti-Aircraft Battery, 200

22th Mountain Regiment, 200

32nd Light Anti-Aircraft Regiment, 54

80th Anti-Tank Regiment, 200, 224

85th Anti-Tank Regiment, 54

122nd Field Regiment, 211

137th Field Regiment, 200, 215, 224

155th Field Regiment, 200, 239, 243, 262

Royal Corps of Signals, 96, 100, 106, 109, 112, 127, 141–2, 144, 178, 213, 325, 378

Royal Engineers, 82, 96, 106, 114, 117, 120–1, 125, 133, 137–9, 141–2, 161, 173, 181, 213, 221, 239, 313, 405

18th Division, 54, 234, 251–2, 254, 262, 266, 270, 286, 288, 290–1, 298, 300–302, 304–305, 307–309, 353

53rd Infantry Brigade, 54, 251, 256, 258, 261, 270, 288–9, 304, 348

54th Infantry Brigade, 288

55th Infantry Brigade, 288

Argyll and Sutherland Highlanders, 52, 205, 267, 270, 295

Bedfordshire and Hertfordshire Regiment, 299, 307

Cambridgeshire Regiment, 256, 262, 307

East Surrey Regiment, 200, 210, 212, 219

Gloucestershire Regiment, 80

Gordon Highlanders, 264, 267, 300–301

King's Own Yorkshire Light Infantry, 80

Leicestershire Regiment, 200, 209, 215
Loyal Regiment (North Lancashire), 60,
    148, 245, 255, 259, 264, 307, 309,
    348
Manchester Regiment, 307
Middlesex Regiment, 59, 82,
    99–100, 108, 111, 113, 117–20, 123–
    5, 128–30, 132, 134–42
Royal Norfolk Regiment, 262–3, 256
Royal Scots Regiment, 56, 58–9, 82, 96,
    99, 104–6, 108, 110–11, 113, 117,
    123–6, 128, 132–6, 138–9, 141,
    144–5
Burma Naval Royal Volunteer Reserve, 11

Canadian Army:
Royal Rifles of Canada, 58, 82, 96, 120,
    122, 125–6, 130, 132,
    134–5, 141
Winnipeg Grenadiers, 56–8, 82, 96,
    105–106, 112, 120–1, 123, 125–6,
    128–9, 133, 135, 141

Gurkha Regiment/Rifles, 80, 171, 201,
    209–10, 239

Hong Kong Regiment, 124, 142–3

Indian Army:
3rd Corps, 52, 55, 159–60, 164, 167,
    171, 191, 194–5, 197, 199–10,
    205–206, 209–16, 219, 222–3, 225,
    228, 231, 236–48, 256–8, 261, 263,
    266, 270, 279, 286, 290, 295, 298,
    342, 346–8, 350, 353–4, 386, 388,
    394–5, 398–9, 405, 407–408,
    413–5, 421
9th Division, 53–4, 159–60, 172, 214,
    219, 228, 236–7, 241,
    245–8, 255, 260–1, 264, 267, 277,
    290, 326–7, 342, 346, 348
11th Division, 44–5, 47, 51–4, 159, 160,
    162, 171, 194, 197, 199, 202, 204,
    209–16, 218–19, 222–4, 228, 236,
    241–2, 246–8, 252, 256, 258–9, 261,
    267, 286, 288, 290–1, 297–8,
    301–305, 307–308, 328–9, 342,
    346–7, 348, 350, 353
6th Infantry Brigade, 51, 54, 80, 159–
    60, 200, 212

6/15th Infantry Brigade, 219–20, 223,
    235, 239–41, 246–8, 261–2, 288–9,
    295, 297–8, 300, 353
8th Infantry Brigade, 46, 54–5,
    159–60, 208, 246, 255, 267, 288,
    290, 298, 301
12th Infantry Brigade, 51–2, 54–5, 158,
    161, 166, 171, 173, 211–12, 216–17,
    219, 222–4, 235–6, 239–41, 243–4,
    246–8, 287, 295–6, 298–9, 353
13th Infantry Brigade, 80
15th Infantry Brigade, 51, 54, 159, 197,
    200, 209, 212, 219, 223, 235, 239,
    246, 248, 288, 290, 295
16th Infantry Brigade, 80
22nd Infantry Brigade, 54–5
27th Infantry Brigade, 54, 67
28th Infantry Brigade, 51–2, 54–5,
    199–201, 209–10, 212, 215, 220,
    222–4, 235, 239–41, 244,
    247–8, 261, 288, 302
44th Infantry Brigade, 270, 278, 287,
    289, 292, 299, 353
45th Infantry Brigade, 241, 243, 245–7,
    251, 256–7, 259, 346
Baluch Regiment, 208
Dogra Regiment, 246
1 Heavy Anti-Aircraft Regiment, 167
Hyderabad Regiment, 199, 202–203,
    208, 211, 222
Jat Regiment, 209, 258
1st Punjab Regiment, 80
2nd Punjab Regiment, 212, 215, 221,
    223
8th Punjab Regiment, 197, 200, 209,
    240
14th Punjab Regiment, 82, 99–100, 102,
    105–107, 109–14, 120, 124–5,
    127–33, 137, 139, 141, 143, 145,
    197, 200–202, 211, 213, 247
15th Punjab Regiment, 8, 60–1, 170,
    226
16th Punjab Regiment, 54, 197–8, 200,
    202, 211, 215, 258
7th Rajputana Rifles, 72, 80, 96, 99,
    103–25, 130, 133–9, 141, 143, 145
11th Sikh Regiment, 239, 264, 267, 350
Frontier Force, 10–11, 80–1, 196, 198,
    208, 238, 506

1st Burma Division, 80
Burma Auxiliary Force, 81
Burma Rifles, 81
Maymyo Brigade, 80
Rangoon Brigade, 80
Tenasserim Brigade, 80

International Air Force, 12–13, 381, 388

Japanese Army:
   25th Army, 318
   Imperial Guard, 257, 260, 302, 316, 318
   5th Division, 41, 257, 318

Kelantan Force, 54, 165, 198, 202–203,
   205, 207–208, 235

Malay Infantry Brigades, 54, 161, 289, 296,
   299
   Malay Regiment, 31, 184, 208, 248,
     304, 330
   2 Malay Battalion, 262, 296, 299
Federated Malay States Volunteer Force
   (FMSVF), 160, 172, 197, 216, 237, 287,
   339
Straits Settlements Volunteer Force
   (SSVF), 72, 90, 150–1, 172–3, 177, 184,
   253, 286, 289, 339

Netherlands East Indies Air Force, 60, 206,
   318

Observer Corps, 13, 361, 375, 407, 417,
   436, 445, 454

Royal Air Force, 65–8, 70–1, 96, 121, 153–
   4, 156, 158, 229, 276, 281–2, 286, 288,
   313, 333, 354–504
   221 Group, 368–9, 378
   222 Group, 371
   224 Group, 378, 395, 413, 428, 442
   225 Group, 426, 428, 435, 441–2, 444
   226 Group, 428, 441–4, 447–8, 454, 464
   266 Wing, 428, 442–3, 449, 452, 454,
     467–8
   21 Squadron, 373–4
   27 Squadron, 375, 389, 394, 396–7,
     403–404, 411, 417, 425, 439–40
   34 Squadron, 373, 376, 389, 392, 395–7,
     399, 401, 405, 410–12, 416, 440
   36 Squadron, 373, 377, 392, 394, 396,

     411, 421–2, 439, 452–3, 461, 463,
     466
   60 Squadron, 12, 84–5, 369, 389, 394,
     396, 399, 410
   62 Squadron, 376, 389, 392, 394, 396–7,
     399–400, 403, 411–12, 420, 422,
     425, 435, 439–40
   67 Squadron, 12, 85, 374, 369,
     373–4, 381
   84 Squadron, 420, 435, 437–41, 448–9
   100 Squadron, 373, 377, 395, 411, 422,
     452
   135 Squadron, 419
   136 Squadron, 419
   205 Squadron, 377, 390, 392, 394, 411–
     12, 426, 452, 465
   211 Squadron, 420, 435, 437–40, 448
   232 Squadron, 420, 430, 442–3, 453–4,
     463–7, 476
   242 Squadron, 442, 453
   243 Squadron, 374, 394–5, 411, 418,
     424
   258 Squadron, 440, 442–3
   453 Squadron, 374, 395, 403, 407–408,
     411, 418, 424–5, 429
   488 Squadron, 374, 395, 411, 418, 421,
     424–5
   605 Squadron, 442–3, 449, 453, 463–4,
     467
Royal Australian Air Force, 36, 42, 67, 83–
   4, 190, 374, 376, 382, 389–99, 401,
   403–408, 411–12, 418, 420, 422, 424–6,
   435, 439–40, 444–5, 453, 455, 466–7,
   476, 488, 492, 502–503
   1 Squadron, 43–4, 84, 376, 390–2, 394,
     396, 412, 422, 425–6, 435, 440, 445,
     453, 455, 466–7, 476, 503
   3 Squadron, 401
   8 Squadron, 84, 376, 389–91,
     393–6, 401, 411–12, 420, 422, 425–
     6, 435, 439–40, 488, 502
   21 Squadron, 84, 374, 382, 389, 394–5,
     397–9, 403–408, 411, 418, 424–5,
     502
Royal Australian Navy:
   Vessels,
     Vampire, 75, 265
     Vendetta, 75
Royal Marines, 59, 134, 136–8, 295

Royal Navy, 315
  Royal Navy West Coast Flotilla, 262
  Vessels,
    Ballarat, 449
    Cicala, 106, 128
    Danae, 75
    Dragon, 75
    Durban, 75
    Electra, 75
    Encounter, 75
    Express, 75
    Indomitable, 420, 427, 438, 442
    Jupiter, 75
    Kudat, 224
    Lipis, 60, 225
    Malaya, 184
    Mauritius, 75
    Prince of Wales, 47–8, 61, 68, 75,
      189, 203–204, 213, 216, 270, 316,
      321, 382, 390, 401–402, 423, 478
    Repulse, 47–8, 68, 75, 189,
      203–204, 213, 216, 270, 316, 321,
      382, 390–1, 393, 401–402, 423,
      478
    Rover, 75
    Scout, 75
    Stronghold, 75
    Tenedos, 75
    Thanet, 75, 265
    Thracian, 57, 75, 109–10, 112

Sarawak Rangers, 8, 60, 170, 173, 178
Straits Settlements Volunteer Force, 161,
  172–3, 253, 286, 289, 339

United States Navy Pacific Fleet, 19, 21, 49

Alexander, Wing Commander, 458, 466

INDEX OF PERSONS

Anderson, Lieutenant Colonel Charles
  Groves Wright VC, 259

Babington, Air Commodore John
  Tremayne, 5
Back, Captain, 1
Backhouse, Brigadier Edward Henry
  Walford, 288
Ballantine, Brigadier George Cecil, 270,
  289
Barstow, Major-General Arthur Edward,
  159, 255, 267
Beckwith-Smith, Major-General Merton,
  270, 288
Bennett, Lieutenant General Henry Gordon,
  159, 172, 199, 245, 261, 287, 350
Bishop, Group Captain A.G., 355, 388,
  426, 434–5, 440, 448, 475
Blackburn, Brigadier Arthur Seaforth VC,
  458, 472, 475
Bond, Lieutenant General Sir Lionel, 5, 158

Brooke-Popham, Air Chief Marshal Sir
  Robert, 1–90, 152, 228, 359, 380, 412,
  507–509

Carpendale, Brigadier W. St. John, 209–10
Chiang Kai-Shek, 12, 14
Churchill, Winston, 58, 456
Cobley, Lieutenant Colonel Frank Reginald
  Newnum, 148
Cochrane, the Honourable Sir Archibald, 2,
  8
Cooper, The Right Honourable Alfred Duff,
  28, 49, 56, 61–2, 199, 228, 231, 405
Cummings, Brigadier Arthur Edward VC,
  238

Dalley, Lieutenant Colonel John D., 287
Dannys, Major-General, 32
Darvall, Group Captain Sir Lawrence, 1
Dewing, Major-General Richard Henry, 1,
  4
Dobbie, Lieutenant General Sir William

George Shedden, 157, 277

Drew, Rear]-Admiral T.B., 153

Duke, Brigadier Cecil Leonard Basil, 289

Duncan, Brigadier Herbert Cecil, 241, 259

Fawcett, Colonel, 1, 5

Field, Lieutenant Colonel F.D., 134

Fieldon, Major, 119

Fraser, Brigadier F.H., 161, 289

Galleghan, Major-General Sir Frederick
 Gallagher, 255

Garrett, Brigadier Kenneth Alfred, 160, 209

Graset, Major-General, 14

Hart, Admiral Thomas Charles, 47

Heath, Lieutenant General Sir Lewis, 159,
 172, 245, 286, 350

Hunt, Major E. de V., 120

Hunter, Air Commodore H.J.F., 427, 440,
 454

Hutton, Lieutenant General Sir Thomas
 Jacomb, 8, 61

Jeudwine, Wing Commander John
 Raymond, 441, 453, 493

Kerr, Sir A. Clark, 28, 32

Key, Major-General Berthold Wells, 46,
 160, 208, 288, 350

Kitajamma, Lieutenant General, 145

Lawson, Brigadier John Kelburne, 100,
 112–13, 121

Laverack, General Sir John, 437

Lay, Brigadier William Oswald, 160, 246

Layton, Vice-Admiral Sir Geoffrey, 42, 47,
 61, 89, 153, 189, 204, 227

Lyle, Commander K.S., 11

Lyon, Major-General Murray, 219

MacArthur, General Douglas, 13, 42

Maguire, Wing Commander H.J., 443, 446

Maltby, Major-General Christopher
 Michael, 14, 91–146

Maltby, Air Vice-Marshal Sir Paul
 Copeland, 354–504

Manning, Group Captain E.R., 368

Maruyama, Lieutenant General Masao,
 474–5

Massy-Beresford, Brigadier Tristram Hugh,
 288, 300

McFeat, Lieutenant Colonel, 32

McLeod, Lieutenant General Sir K., 2, 8,
 61

Modin, Air Commodore Charles O.F., 355

Moir, Brigadier R.G., 160, 241, 287

Moorhead, Lieutenant Colonel H.D., 209,
 220, 246

Morrison, Lieutenant Colonel C. Esmond,
 240, 288

Newnham, Colonel L.A., 94

Nicholetts, Group Captain G.E., 426, 449,
 453, 463

Niini, Vice-Admiral, 115

Nishiyama, Major, 104

Northcote, Sir Geoffrey, 14

Oyen, General van Hendrik Ludolph, 456,
 459, 462, 465

Page, Sir Earle, 28

Paget, General Sir Bernard Charles Tolver,
 61

Palliser, Rear-Admiral, 42, 47–8, 402

Paris, Brigadier Archibald Charles Melvill,
 173, 219, 246, 279, 287

Percival, Lieutenant General Arthur Ernest,
 5, 38–9, 43, 147–355, 406, 432, 484,
 490

Phillips, Admiral Sir Thomas, 18, 42–3, 47,
 61, 189, 203, 390, 393, 401–402

Playfair, General Ian Stanley Ord, 4

Pownall, Lieutenant General Sir Henry, 1,
 61, 69, 228, 412

Pulford, Air Vice-Marshall Conway Walter,
 5, 152, 190, 306, 332, 355, 357, 406,
 431–2, 484, 490–2

Rice, Group Captain E.B., 168, 276, 355–6,
 373, 376, 413, 431, 492, 503

Ridgeway, Group Captain M.W.C., 452,
 503

Roosevelt, Franklin D., 52

Sakai, Lieutenant General Takashi, 110,
 115

Scarf, Flight Lieutenant Arthur Stewart
 King VC, 400

Searle, Colonel A.E., 475

Selby, Lieutenant Colonel William Ray, 220, 288

Silly, Air Commodore Benjamin James, 427–8, 440, 452, 470–1

Simmons, Major-General Frank Keith, 173, 231, 276, 279, 286, 353

Simson, Brigadier I., 186, 199, 231–2

Sitwell, Major-General Hervey D.W., 456, 458, 469, 472, 475

Smith, Sir Reginald Dorman, 8, 10, 13, 227

Spooner, Rear-Admiral Ernest John, 153, 228, 432, 490

Staton, Air Commodore William Ernest, 427, 431, 444, 474–5

Steedman, Wing Commander Edward Blakeway, 494

Stewart, Lieutenant Colonel H.W.M., 138, 140, 220, 267

Taylor, Brigadier Harold Burfield, 246, 264, 266, 289

Templer, Major C.R., 130–1

Trott, Brigadier, 288, 290

Vincent, Air Vice-Marshal Sir Stanley Flamank, 427–8, 442, 454, 464

Wallis, Brigadier C., 100, 109–10, 112–13, 118, 122–3, 126–7, 131, 136

Warren, Colonel, 5

Wavell, Field-Marshal Sir Archibald, 2, 228, 418, 427–8, 431, 450, 456, 481

Wildey, Brigadier Alec Warren Greenlaw, 161, 173, 276

Wills-Sandford, Wing Commander W.R., 373, 503

Willcocks, Lieutenant Colonel J.L., 123

Williams, Brigadier G.C.R., 161, 289

Yamashita, Lieutenant General Tomoyuki, 300

Yarde, Wing Commander Brian Courtenay, 4

Young, Sir Mark, 14

ENCYCLOPEDIA OF
HUMAN
NUTRITION

SECOND EDITION

ENCYCLOPEDIA OF
HUMAN
NUTRITION

SECOND EDITION

Editor-in-Chief
BENJAMIN CABALLERO

Editors
LINDSAY ALLEN
ANDREW PRENTICE

ELSEVIER
ACADEMIC
PRESS

Amsterdam   Boston   Heidelberg   London   New York   Oxford
Paris   San Diego   San Francisco   Singapore   Sydney   Tokyo

Elsevier Ltd., The Boulevard, Langford Lane, Kidlington, Oxford, OX5 1GB, UK

Second edition 2005

Library of Congress Control Number: 2004113614

A catalogue record for this book is available from the British Library

ISBN 0-12-150110-8 (set)

This book is printed on acid-free paper
Printed and bound in Spain

EDITORIAL ADVISORY BOARD

FOREWORD

Why an encyclopedia? The original Greek word means 'the circle of arts and sciences essential for a liberal education', and such a book was intended to embrace all knowledge. That was the aim of the famous Encyclopedie produced by Diderot and d'Alembert in the middle of the 18th century, which contributed so much to what has been called the Enlightenment. It is recorded that after all the authors had corrected the proofs of their contributions, the printer secretly cut out whatever he thought might give offence to the king, mutilated most of the best articles and burnt the manuscripts! Later, and less controversially, the word 'encyclopedia' came to be used for an exhaustive repertory of information on some particular department of knowledge. It is in this class that the present work falls.

In recent years the scope of Human Nutrition as a scientific discipline has expanded enormously. I used to think of it as an applied subject, relying on the basic sciences of physiology and biochemistry in much the same way that engineering relies on physics. That traditional relationship remains and is fundamental, but the field is now much wider. At one end of the spectrum epidemiological studies and the techniques on which they depend have played a major part in establishing the relationships between diet, nutritional status and health, and there is greater recognition of the importance of social factors. At the other end of the spectrum we are becoming increasingly aware of the genetic determinants of ways in which the body handles food and is able to resist adverse influences of the environment. Nutritionists are thus beginning to explore the mechanisms by which nutrients influence the expression of genes in the knowledge that nutrients are among the most powerful of all influences on gene expression. This has brought nutrition to the centre of the new 'post-genome' challenge of understanding the effects on human health of gene-environment interactions.

In parallel with this widening of the subject there has been an increase in opportunities for training and research in nutrition, with new departments and new courses being developed in universities, medical schools and schools of public health, along with a greater involvement of schoolchildren and their teachers. Public interest in nutrition is intense and needs to be guided by sound science. Governments are realizing more and more the role that nutrition plays in the prevention of disease and the maintenance of good health, and the need to develop a nutrition policy that is integrated with policies for food production.

The first edition of the Encyclopaedia of Human Nutrition established it as one of the major reference works in our discipline. The second edition has been completely revised to take account of new knowledge in our rapidly advancing field. This new edition is as comprehensive as the present state of knowledge allows, but is not overly technical and is well supplied with suggestions for further reading. All the articles have been carefully reviewed and although some of the subjects are controversial and sensitive, the publishers have not exerted the kind of political censorship that so infuriated Diderot.

John Waterlow.

J.C. Waterlow
Emeritus Professor of Human Nutrition
London School of Hygiene and Tropical Medicine
February 2005

INTRODUCTION

T he science of human nutrition and its applications to health promotion continue to gain momentum. In the relatively short time since the release of the first edition of this Encyclopedia, a few landmark discoveries have had a dramatic multiplying effect over nutrition science: the mapping of the human genome, the links between molecular bioenergetics and lifespan, the influence of nutrients on viral mutation, to name a few.

But perhaps the strongest evidence of the importance of nutrition for human health comes from the fact that almost 60% of the diseases that kill humans are related to diet and lifestyle (including smoking and physical activity). These are all modifiable risk factors. As individuals and organizations intensify their efforts to reduce disease risks, the need for multidisciplinary work becomes more apparent. Today, an effective research or program team is likely to include several professionals from fields other than nutrition. For both nutrition and non-nutrition scientists, keeping up to date on the concepts and interrelationships between nutrient needs, dietary intake and health outcomes is essential. The new edition of the Encyclopedia of Human Nutrition hopes to address these needs. While rigorously scientific and up to date, EHN provides concise and easily understandable summaries on a wide variety of topics. The nutrition scientist will find that the Encyclopedia is an effective tool to "fill the void" of information in areas beyond his/her field of expertise. Professionals from other fields will appreciate the ease of alphabetical listing of topics, and the presentation of information in a rigorous but concise way, with generous aid from graphs and diagrams.

For a work that involved more than 340 authors requires, coordination and attention to detail is critical. The editors were fortunate to have the support of an excellent team from Elsevier's Major Reference Works division. Sara Gorman and Paula O'Connell initiated the project, and Tracey Mills and Samuel Coleman saw it to its successful completion.

We trust that this Encyclopedia will be a useful addition to the knowledge base of professionals involved in research, patient care, and health promotion around the globe.

Benjamin Caballero, Lindsay Allen and Andrew Prentice
Editors
April 2005

GUIDE TO USE OF THE ENCYCLOPEDIA

Structure of the Encyclopedia

The material in the Encyclopedia is arranged as a series of entries in alphabetical order. Most entries consist of several articles that deal with various aspects of a topic and are arranged in a logical sequence within an entry. Some entries comprise a single article.

To help you realize the full potential of the material in the Encyclopedia we have provided three features to help you find the topic of your choice: a Contents List, Cross-References and an Index.

1. Contents List

Your first point of reference will probably be the contents list. The complete contents lists, which appears at the front of each volume will provide you with both the volume number and the page number of the entry. On the opening page of an entry a contents list is provided so that the full details of the articles within the entry are immediately available.

Alternatively you may choose to browse through a volume using the alphabetical order of the entries as your guide. To assist you in identifying your location within the Encyclopedia a running headline indicates the current entry and the current article within that entry.

You will find 'dummy entries' where obvious synonyms exist for entries or where we have grouped together related topics. Dummy entries appear in both the contents lists and the body of the text.

Example
If you were attempting to locate material on food intake measurement via the contents list:

FOOD INTAKE *see* DIETARY INTAKE MEASUREMENT: Methodology; Validation. DIETARY SURVEYS. MEAL SIZE AND FREQUENCY

The dummy entry directs you to the Methodology article, in The Dietary Intake Measurement entry. At the appropriate location in the contents list, the page numbers for articles under Dietary Intake Measurement are given.

If you were trying to locate the material by browsing through the text and you looked up Food intake then the following information would be provided in the dummy entry:

Food Intake *see* Dietary Intake Measurement: Methodology; Validation. **Dietary Surveys. Meal Size and Frequency**

Alternatively, if you were looking up Dietary Intake Measurement the following information would be provided:

DIETARY INTAKE MEASUREMENT

Contents

Methodology

Validation

2. Cross-References

All of the articles in the Encyclopedia have been extensively cross-referenced.

The cross-references, which appear at the end of an article, serve three different functions. For example, at the end of the ADOLESCENTS/Nutritional Problems article, cross-references are used:

i. To indicate if a topic is discussed in greater detail elsewhere.

> *See also*: **Adolescents**: Nutritional Requirements of Adolescents. **Anemia**: Iron-Deficiency Anemia. **Calcium**: Physiology. **Eating Disorders**: Anorexia Nervosa; Bulimia Nervosa; Binge Eating. **Folic Acid**: Physiology, Dietary Sources, and Requirements. **Iron**: Physiology, Dietary Sources, and Requirements. **Obesity**: Definition, Aetiology, and Assessment. **Osteoporosis**: Nutritional Factors. **Zinc**: Physiology.

ii. To draw the reader's attention to parallel discussions in other articles.

> *See also*: **Adolescents**: Nutritional Requirements of Adolescents. **Anemia**: Iron-Deficiency Anemia. **Calcium**: Physiology. **Eating Disorders**: Anorexia Nervosa; Bulimia Nervosa; Binge Eating. **Folic Acid**: Physiology, Dietary Sources, and Requirements. **Iron**: Physiology, Dietary Sources, and Requirements. **Obesity**: Definition, Aetiology, and Assessment. **Osteoporosis**: Nutritional Factors **Zinc**: Physiology.

iii. To indicate material that broadens the discussion.

> *See also*: **Adolescents**: Nutritional Requirements of Adolescents. **Anemia**: Iron-Deficiency Anemia. **Calcium**: Physiology. **Eating Disorders**: Anorexia Nervosa; Bulimia Nervosa; Binge Eating. **Follic Acid**: Physiology, Dietary Sources, and Requirements. **Iron**: Physiology, Dietary Sources, and Requirements. **Obesity**: Definition, Aetiology, and Assessment. **Osteoporosis**: Nutritional Factors. **Zinc**: Physiology.

3. Index

The index will provide you with the page number where the material is located, and the index entries differentiate between material that is a whole article, is part of an article or is data presented in a figure or table. Detailed notes are provided on the opening page of the index.

4. Contributors

A full list of contributors appears at the beginning of each volume.

CONTRIBUTORS

E Abalos
Centro Rosarino de Estudios Perinatales
Rosario, Argentina

A Abi-Hanna
Johns Hopkins School of Medicine
Baltimore, MD, USA

L S Adair
University of North Carolina
Chapel Hill, NC, USA

A Ahmed
Obetech Obesity Research Center
Richmond, VA, USA

B Ahrén
Lund University
Lund, Sweden

J Akré
World Health Organization, Geneva, Switzerland

A J Alberg
Johns Hopkins Bloomberg School of Public Health
Baltimore, MD, USA

L H Allen
University of California at Davis
Davis, CA, USA

D Anderson
University of Bradford
Bradford, UK

J J B Anderson
University of North Carolina
Chapel Hill, NC, USA

R A Anderson
US Department of Agriculture
Beltsville, MD, USA

L J Appel
Johns Hopkins University
Baltimore, MD, USA

A Ariño
University of Zaragoza
Zaragoza, Spain

M J Arnaud
Nestle S.A.
Vevey, Switzerland

E W Askew
University of Utah
Salt Lake City, UT, USA

R L Atkinson
Obetech Obesity Research Center
Richmond, VA, USA

S A Atkinson
McMaster University
Hamilton, ON, Canada

L S A Augustin
University of Toronto
Toronto, ON, Canada

D J Baer
US Department of Agriculture
Beltsville, MD, USA

A Baqui
Johns Hopkins Bloomberg School of Public Health
Baltimore, MD, USA

Y Barnett
Nottingham Trent University
Nottingham, UK

G E Bartley
Agricultural Research Service
Albany, CA, USA

C J Bates
MRC Human Nutrition Research
Cambridge, UK

J A Beltrán
University of Zaragoza
Zaragoza, Spain

A E Bender
Leatherhead, UK

D A Bender
University College London
London, UK

I F F Benzie
The Hong Kong Polytechnic University
Hong Kong SAR, China

C D Berdanier
University of Georgia
Athens, GA, USA

R Bhatia
United Nations World Food Programme
Rome, Italy

Z A Bhutta
The Aga Khan University
Karachi, Pakistan

J E Bines
University of Melbourne
Melbourne, VIC, Australia

J Binkley
Vanderbilt Center for Human Nutrition
Nashville, TN, USA

R Black
Johns Hopkins Bloomberg School of Public Health
Baltimore, MD, USA

J E Blundell
University of Leeds
Leeds, UK

A T Borchers
University of California at Davis
Davis, CA, USA

C Boreham
University of Ulster at Jordanstown
Jordanstown, UK

F Branca
Istituto Nazionale di Ricerca per gli Alimenti e la Nutrizione
Rome, Italy

J Brand-Miller
University of Sydney
Sydney, NSW, Australia

A Briend
Institut de Recherche pour le Développement
Paris, France

P Browne
St James's Hospital
Dublin, Ireland

I A Brownlee
University of Newcastle
Newcastle-upon-Tyne, UK

H Brunner
Centre Hospitalier Universitaire Vaudois
Lausanne, Switzerland

A J Buckley
University of Cambridge
Cambridge, UK

H H Butchko
Exponent, Inc.
Wood Dale, IL, USA

J Buttriss
British Nutrition Foundation
London, UK

B Caballero
Johns Hopkins Bloomberg School of Public Health and
  Johns Hopkins University
Baltimore, MD, USA

E A Carrey
Institute of Child Health
London, UK

A Cassidy
School of Medicine
University of East Anglia
Norwich, UK

G E Caughey
Royal Adelaide Hospital
Adelaide, SA, Australia

J P Cegielski
Centers for Disease Control and Prevention
Atlanta, GA, USA

C M Champagne
Pennington Biomedical Research Center
Baton Rouge, LA, USA

S C Chen
US Department of Agriculture
Beltsville, MD, USA

L Cheskin
Johns Hopkins University
Baltimore, MD, USA

S Chung
Columbia University
New York, NY, USA

L G Cleland
Royal Adelaide Hospital
Adelaide, SA, Australia

L Cobiac
CSIRO Health Sciences and Nutrition
Adelaide, SA, Australia

G A Colditz
Harvard Medical School
Boston, MA, USA

T J Cole
Institute of Child Health
London, UK

L A Coleman
Marshfield Clinic Research Foundation
Marshfield, WI, USA

S Collier
Children's Hospital, Boston, Harvard Medical School,
   and Harvard School of Public Health
Boston, MA, USA

M Collins
Muckamore Abbey Hospital
Antrim, UK

K G Conner
Johns Hopkins Hospital
Baltimore, MD, USA

K C Costas
Children's Hospital Boston
Boston, MA, USA

R C Cottrell
The Sugar Bureau
London, UK

W A Coward
MRC Human Nutrition Research
Cambridge, UK

J M Cox
Johns Hopkins Hospital
Baltimore, MD, USA

S Cox
London School of Hygiene and Tropical Medicine
London, UK

P D'Acapito
Istituto Nazionale di Ricerca per gli Alimenti e la Nutrizione
Rome, Italy

S Daniell
Vanderbilt Center for Human Nutrition
Nashville, TN, USA

O Dary
The MOST Project
Arlington, VA, USA

T J David
University of Manchester
Manchester, UK

C P G M de Groot
Wageningen University
Wageningen, The Netherlands

M de Onis
World Health Organization
Geneva, Switzerland

M C de Souza
Universidad de Mogi das Cruzes
São Paulo, Brazil

R de Souza
University of Toronto
Toronto, ON, Canada

C H C Dejong
University Hospital Maastricht
Maastricht, The Netherlands

L Demeshlaira
Emory University
Atlanta, GA, USA

K G Dewey
University of California at Davis
Davis, CA, USA

H L Dewraj
The Aga Khan University
Karachi, Pakistan

C Doherty
MRC Keneba
The Gambia

C M Donangelo
Universidade Federal do Rio de Janeiro
Rio de Janeiro, Brazil

A Dornhorst
Imperial College at Hammersmith Hospital
London, UK

E Dowler
University of Warwick
Coventry, UK

J Dowsett
St Vincent's University Hospital
Dublin, Ireland

A K Draper
University of Westminster
London, UK

M L Dreyfuss
Johns Hopkins Bloomberg School of Public Health
Baltimore, MD, USA

R D'Souza
Queen Mary's, University of London
London, UK

C Duggan
Harvard Medical School
Boston, MA, USA

A G Dulloo
University of Fribourg
Fribourg, Switzerland

E B Duly
Ulster Hospital
Belfast, UK

J L Dupont
Florida State University
Tallahassee, FL, USA

J Dwyer
Tufts University
Boston, MA, USA

J Eaton–Evans
University of Ulster
Coleraine, UK

C A Edwards
University of Glasgow
Glasgow, UK

M Elia
University of Southampton
Southampton, UK

P W Emery
King's College London
London, UK

J L Ensunsa
University of California at Davis
Davis, CA, USA

C Feillet-Coudray
National Institute for Agricultural Research
Clermont-Ferrand, France

J D Fernstrom
University of Pittsburgh
Pittsburgh, PA, USA

M H Fernstrom
University of Pittsburgh
Pittsburgh, PA, USA

F Fidanza
University of Rome Tor Vergata
Rome, Italy

P Fieldhouse
The University of Manitoba
Winnipeg, MB, Canada

N Finer
Luton and Dunstable Hospital NHS Trust
Luton, UK

J Fiore
University of Westminster
London, UK

H C Freake
University of Connecticut
Storrs, CT, USA

J Freitas
Tufts University
Boston, MA, USA

R E Frisch
Harvard Center for Population and Development Studies
Cambridge, MA, USA

G Frost
Imperial College at Hammersmith Hospital
London, UK

G Frühbeck
Universidad de Navarra
Pamplona, Spain

D Gallagher
Columbia University
New York, NY, USA

L Galland
Applied Nutrition Inc.
New York, NY, USA

C Geissler
King's College London
London, UK

M E Gershwin
University of California at Davis
Davis, CA, USA

H Ghattas
London School of Hygiene and Tropical Medicine
London, UK

E L Gibson
University College London
London, UK

T P Gill
University of Sydney
Sydney, NSW, Australia

W Gilmore
University of Ulster
Coleraine, UK

G R Goldberg
MRC Human Nutrition Research
Cambridge, UK

J Gómez-Ambrosi
Universidad de Navarra
Pamplona, Spain

J M Graham
University of California at Davis
Davis, CA, USA

J Gray
Guildford, UK

J P Greaves
London, UK

M W Green
Aston University
Birmingham, UK

R Green
University of California
Davis, CA, USA

R F Grimble
University of Southampton
Southampton, UK

M Grønbæk
National Institute of Public Health
Copenhagen, Denmark

J D Groopman
Johns Hopkins University
Baltimore MD, USA

S M Grundy
University of Texas Southwestern Medical Center
Dallas, TX, USA

M A Grusak
Baylor College of Medicine
Houston, TX, USA

M Gueimonde
University of Turku
Turku, Finland

C S Gulotta
Johns Hopkins University and Kennedy
 Krieger Institute
Baltimore, MD, USA

P Haggarty
Rowett Research Institute
Aberdeen, UK

J C G Halford
University of Liverpool
Liverpool, UK

C H Halsted
University of California at Davis
Davis, CA, USA

J Hampsey
Johns Hopkins School of Medicine
Baltimore, MD, USA

E D Harris
Texas A&M University
College Station, TX, USA

Z L Harris
Johns Hopkins Hospital and School of Medicine
Baltimore, MD, USA

P J Havel
University of California at Davis
Davis, CA, USA

W W Hay Jr
University of Colorado Health Sciences Center
Aurora, CO, USA

R G Heine
University of Melbourne
Melbourne, VIC, Australia

R Heinzen
Johns Hopkins Bloomberg School of Public Health
Baltimore, MD, USA

A Herrera
University of Zaragoza
Zaragoza, Spain

B S Hetzel
Women's and Children's Hospital
North Adelaide, SA, Australia

A J Hill
University of Leeds
Leeds, UK

S A Hill
Southampton General Hospital
Southampton, UK

G A Hitman
Queen Mary's, University of London
London, UK

J M Hodgson
University of Western Australia
Perth, WA, Australia

M F Holick
Boston University Medical Center
Boston, MA, USA

C Hotz
National Institute of Public Health
Morelos, Mexico

R Houston
Emory University
Atlanta, GA, USA

H-Y Huang
Johns Hopkins University
Baltimore, MD, USA

J R Hunt
USDA-ARS Grand Forks Human Nutrition Research Center
Grand Forks, ND, USA

R Hunter
King's College London
London, UK

P Hyland
Nottingham Trent University
Nottingham, UK

B K Ishida
Agricultural Research Service
Albany, CA, USA

J Jacquet
University of Geneva
Geneva, Switzerland

M J James
Royal Adelaide Hospital
Adelaide, SA, Australia

W P T James
International Association for the Study of Obesity/
   International Obesity Task Force Offices
London, UK

A G Jardine
University of Glasgow
Glasgow, UK

S A Jebb
MRC Human Nutrition Research
Cambridge, UK

K N Jeejeebhoy
University of Toronto
Toronto, ON, Canada

D J A Jenkins
University of Toronto
Toronto, ON, Canada

G L Jensen
Vanderbilt Center for Human Nutrition
Nashville, TN, USA

I T Johnson
Institute of Food Research
Norwich, UK

P A Judd
University of Central Lancashire
Preston, UK

M A Kalarchian
University of Pittsburgh
Pittsburgh, PA, USA

R M Katz
Johns Hopkins University School of Medicine and Mount
    Washington Pediatric Hospital
Baltimore, MD, USA

C L Keen
University of California at Davis
Davis, CA, USA

N L Keim
US Department of Agriculture
Davis, CA, USA

E Kelly
Harvard Medical School
Boston, MA, USA

C W C Kendall
University of Toronto
Toronto, ON, Canada

T W Kensler
Johns Hopkins University
Baltimore, MD, USA

J E Kerstetter
University of Connecticut
Storrs, CT, USA

M Kiely
University College Cork
Cork, Ireland

P Kirk
University of Ulster
Coleraine, UK

S F L Kirk
University of Leeds
Leeds, UK

P N Kirke
The Health Research Board
Dublin, Ireland

G L Klein
University of Texas Medical Branch at Galveston
Galveston TX, USA

R D W Klemm
Johns Hopkins University
Baltimore, MD, USA

D M Klurfeld
US Department of Agriculture
Beltville, MD, USA

P G Kopelman
Queen Mary's, University of London
London, UK

J Krick
Kennedy–Krieger Institute
Baltimore, MD, USA

D Kritchevsky
Wistar Institute
Philadelphia, PA, USA

R Lang
University of Teeside
Middlesbrough, UK

A Laurentin
Universidad Central de Venezuela
Caracas, Venezuela

A Laverty
Muckamore Abbey Hospital
Antrim, UK

M Lawson
Institute of Child Health
London, UK

F E Leahy
University of Auckland
Auckland, New Zealand

A R Leeds
King's College London
London, UK

J Leiper
University of Aberdeen
Aberdeen, UK

M D Levine
University of Pittsburgh
Pittsburgh, PA, USA

A H Lichtenstein
Tufts University
Boston MA, USA

E Lin
Emory University
Atlanta, GA, USA

L Lissner
Sahlgrenska Academy at Göteborg University
Göteborg, Sweden

C Lo
Children's Hospital, Boston, Harvard Medical School, and
   Harvard School of Public Health
Boston, MA, USA

P A Lofgren
Oak Park, IL, USA

B Lönnerdal
University of California at Davis
Davis, CA, USA

M J Luetkemeier
Alma College
Alma, MI, USA

Y C Luiking
University Hospital Maastricht
Maastricht, The Netherlands

P G Lunn
University of Cambridge
Cambridge, UK

C K Lutter
Pan American Health Organization
Washington, DC, USA

A MacDonald
The Children's Hospital
Birmingham, UK

A Maqbool
The Children's Hospital of Philadelphia
Philadelphia, PA, USA

M D Marcus
University of Pittsburgh
Pittsburgh, PA, USA

E Marietta
The Mayo Clinic College of Medicine
Rochester, MN, USA

P B Mark
University of Glasgow
Glasgow, UK

V Marks
University of Surrey
Guildford, UK

D L Marsden
Children's Hospital Boston
Boston, MA, USA

R J Maughan
Loughborough University
Loughborough, UK

K C McCowen
Beth Israel Deaconess Medical Center and Harvard
   Medical School
Boston, MA, USA

S S McDonald
Raleigh, NC, USA

S McLaren
London South Bank University
London, UK

J L McManaman
University of Colorado
Denver, CO, USA

D N McMurray
Texas A&M University
College Station, TX, USA

D J McNamara
Egg Nutrition Center
Washington, DC, USA

J McPartlin
Trinity College
Dublin, Ireland

R P Mensink
Maastricht University
Maastricht, The Netherlands

M Merialdi
World Health Organization
Geneva, Switzerland

A R Michell
St Bartholomew's Hospital
London, UK

J W Miller
UC Davis Medical Center
Sacramento, CA, USA

P Miller
Kennedy–Krieger Institute
Baltimore, MD, USA

D J Millward
University of Surrey
Guildford, UK

D M Mock
University of Arkansas for Medical Sciences
Little Rock, AR, USA

N Moore
John Hopkins School of Medicine
Baltimore, MD, USA

J O Mora
The MOST Project
Arlington, VA, USA

T Morgan
University of Melbourne
Melbourne, VIC, Australia

T A Mori
University of Western Australia
Perth, WA, Australia

J E Morley
St Louis University
St Louis, MO, USA

P A Morrissey
University College Cork
Cork, Ireland

M H Murphy
University of Ulster at Jordanstown
Jordanstown, UK

S P Murphy
University of Hawaii
Honolulu, HI, USA

J Murray
The Mayo Clinic College of Medicine
Rochester, MN, USA

R Nalubola
Center for Food Safety and Applied Nutrition,
US Food and Drug Administration, MD, USA

J L Napoli
University of California
Berkeley, CA, USA

V Nehra
The Mayo Clinic College of Medicine
Rochester, MN, USA

B Nejadnik
Johns Hopkins University
Baltimore, MD, USA

M Nelson
King's College London
London, UK

P Nestel
International Food Policy Research Institute
Washington, DC, USA

L M Neufeld
National Institute of Public Health
Cuernavaca, Mexico

M C Neville
University of Colorado
Denver, CO, USA

F Nielsen
Grand Forks Human Nutrition Research Center
Grand Forks, ND, USA

N Noah
London School of Hygiene and Tropical Medicine
London, UK

K O O'Brien
Johns Hopkins University
Baltimore, MD, USA

S H Oh
Johns Hopkins General Clinical Research Center
Baltimore, MD, USA

J M Ordovas
Tufts University
Boston, MA, USA

S E Ozanne
University of Cambridge
Cambridge, UK

D M Paige
Johns Hopkins Bloomberg School of Public Health
Baltimore, MD, USA

J P Pearson
University of Newcastle
Newcastle-upon-Tyne, UK

S S Percival
University of Florida
Gainesville, FL, USA

T Peters
King's College Hospital
London, UK

B J Petersen
Exponent, Inc.
Washington DC, USA

J C Phillips
BIBRA International Ltd
Carshalton, UK

M F Picciano
National Institutes of Health
Bethesda, MD, USA

A Pietrobelli
Verona University Medical School
Verona, Italy

S Pin
Johns Hopkins Hospital and School of Medicine
Baltimore, MD, USA

B M Popkin
University of North Carolina
Chapel Hill, NC, USA

E M E Poskitt
London School of Hygiene and Tropical Medicine
London, UK

A D Postle
University of Southampton
Southampton, UK

J Powell-Tuck
Queen Mary's, University of London
London, UK

V Preedy
King's College London
London, UK

N D Priest
Middlesex University
London, UK

R Rajendram
King's College London
London, UK

A Raman
University of Wisconsin–Madison
Madison, WI, USA

H A Raynor
Brown University
Providence, RI, USA

Y Rayssiguier
National Institute for Agricultural Research
Clermont-Ferrand, France

L N Richardson
United Nations World Food Programme
Rome, Italy

F J Rohr
Children's Hospital Boston
Boston, MA, USA

A R Rolla
Harvard Medical School
Boston, MA, USA

P Roncalés
University of Zaragoza
Zaragoza, Spain

A C Ross
The Pennsylvania State University
University Park, PA, USA

R Roubenoff
Millennium Pharmaceuticals, Inc.
Cambridge, MA, USA and Tufts University
Boston, MA, USA

D Rumsey
University of Sheffield
Sheffield, UK

C H S Ruxton
Nutrition Communications
Cupar, UK

J M Saavedra
John Hopkins School of Medicine
Baltimore, MD, USA

J E Sable
University of California at Davis
Davis, CA, USA

M J Sadler
MJSR Associates
Ashford, UK

N R Sahyoun
University of Maryland
College Park, MD, USA

S Salminen
University of Turku
Turku, Finland

M Saltmarsh
Alton, UK

J M Samet
Johns Hopkins Bloomberg School of Public Health
Baltimore, MD, USA

C P Sánchez-Castillo
National Institute of Medical Sciences and Nutrition
Salvador Zubirán, Tlalpan, Mexico

M Santosham
Johns Hopkins Bloomberg School of Public Health
Baltimore, MD, USA

C D Saudek
Johns Hopkins School of Medicine
Baltimore, MD, USA

A O Scheimann
Johns Hopkins School of Medicine
Baltimore, MD, USA

B Schneeman
University of California at Davis
Davis, CA, USA

D A Schoeller
University of Wisconsin–Madison
Madison, WI, USA

L Schuberth
Kennedy Krieger Institute
Baltimore, MD, USA

K J Schulze
Johns Hopkins Bloomberg School of Public Health
Baltimore, MD, USA

Y Schutz
University of Lausanne
Lausanne, Switzerland

K B Schwarz
Johns Hopkins School of Medicine
Baltimore, MD, USA

J M Scott
Trinity College Dublin
Dublin, Ireland

C Shaw
Royal Marsden NHS Foundation Trust
London, UK

J Shedlock
Johns Hopkins Hospital and School of Medicine
Baltimore, MD, USA

S M Shirreffs
Loughborough University
Loughborough, UK

R Shrimpton
Institute of Child Health
London, UK

H A Simmonds
Guy's Hospital
London, UK

A P Simopoulos
The Center for Genetics, Nutrition and Health
Washington, DC, USA

R J Smith
Brown Medical School
Providence, RI, USA

P B Soeters
University Hospital Maastricht
Maastricht, The Netherlands

N Solomons
Center for Studies of Sensory Impairment, Aging and
  Metabolism (CeSSIAM)
Guatemala City, Guatemala

J A Solon
MRC Laboratories Gambia
Banjul, The Gambia

K Srinath Reddy
All India Institute of Medical Sciences
New Delhi, India

S Stanner
British Nutrition Foundation
London, UK

J Stevens
University of North Carolina at Chapel Hill
Chapel Hill, NC, USA

J J Strain
University of Ulster
Coleraine, UK

R J Stratton
University of Southampton
Southampton, UK

R J Stubbs
The Rowett Research Institute
Aberdeen, UK

C L Stylianopoulos
Johns Hopkins University
Baltimore, MD, USA

A W Subudhi
University of Colorado at Colorado
Colorado Springs, CO, USA

J Sudagani
Queen Mary's, University of London
London, UK

S A Tanumihardjo
University of Wisconsin-Madison
Madison, WI, USA

J A Tayek
Harbor–UCLA Medical Center
Torrance, CA, USA

E H M Temme
University of Leuven
Leuven, Belgium

H S Thesmar
Egg Nutrition Center
Washington, DC, USA

B M Thomson
Rowett Research Institute
Aberdeen, UK

D I Thurnham
University of Ulster
Coleraine, UK

L Tolentino
National Institute of Public Health
Cuernavaca, Mexico

D L Topping
CSIRO Health Sciences and Nutrition
Adelaide, SA, Australia

B Torun
Center for Research and Teaching in Latin
  America (CIDAL)
Guatemala City, Guatemala

M G Traber
Oregon State University
Corvallis, OR, USA

T R Trinick
Ulster Hospital
Belfast, UK

K P Truesdale
University of North Carolina at Chapel Hill
Chapel Hill, NC, USA

N M F Trugo
Universidade Federal do Rio de Janeiro
Rio de Janeiro, Brazil

P M Tsai
Harvard Medical School
Boston, MA, USA

K L Tucker
Tufts University
Boston, MA, USA

O Tully
St Vincent's University Hospital
Dublin, Ireland

E C Uchegbu
Royal Hallamshire Hospital
Sheffield, UK

M C G van de Poll
University Hospital Maastricht
Maastricht, The Netherlands

W A van Staveren
Wageningen University
Wageningen, The Netherlands

J Villar
World Health Organization
Geneva, Switzerland

M L Wahlqvist
Monash University
Victoria, VIC, Australia

A F Walker
The University of Reading
Reading, UK

P A Watkins
Kennedy Krieger Institute and Johns Hopkins
    University School of Medicine
Baltimore, MD, USA

A A Welch
University of Cambridge
Cambridge, UK

R W Welch
University of Ulster
Coleraine, UK

K P West Jr
Johns Hopkins University
Baltimore, MD, USA

S Whybrow
The Rowett Research Institute
Aberdeen, UK

D H Williamson
Radcliffe Infirmary
Oxford, UK

M-M G Wilson
St Louis University
St Louis, MO, USA

R R Wing
Brown University
Providence, RI, USA

C K Winter
University of California at Davis
Davis, CA, USA

H Wiseman
King's College London
London, UK

M Wolraich
Vanderbilt University
Nashville, TN, USA

R J Wood
Tufts University
Boston, MA, USA

X Xu
Johns Hopkins Hospital and School of Medicine
Baltimore, MD, USA

Z Yang
University of Wisconsin-Madison
Madison, WI, USA

A A Yates
ENVIRON Health Sciences
Arlington, VA, USA

S H Zeisel
University of North Carolina at Chapel Hill
Chapel Hill, NC, USA

X Zhu
University of North Carolina at Chapel Hill
Chapel Hill, NC, USA

S Zidenberg-Cherr
University of California at Davis
Davis, CA, USA

T R Ziegler
Emory University
Atlanta, GA, USA

CONTENTS

VOLUME 1

A

ACIDS *see* ELECTROLYTES: Acid-Base Balance

ADIPOSE TISSUE   *G Frühbeck and J Gómez-Ambrosi*   1

ADOLESCENTS

Nutritional Requirements   *C H S Ruxton and J Fiore*   15

Nutritional Problems   *C Lo*   26

AGING   *P Hyland and Y Barnett*   40

ALCOHOL

Absorption, Metabolism and Physiological Effects   *R Rajendram, R Hunter, V Preedy and T Peters*   48

Disease Risk and Beneficial Effects   *M Grønbæk*   57

Effects of Consumption on Diet and Nutritional Status   *C H Halsted*   62

ALUMINUM   *N D Priest*   69

AMINO ACIDS

Chemistry and Classification   *P W Emery*   76

Metabolism   *P W Emery*   84

Specific Functions   *M C G van de Poll, Y C Luiking, C H C Dejong and P B Soeters*   92

ANEMIA

Iron-Deficiency Anemia   *K J Schulze and M L Dreyfuss*   101

Megaloblastic Anemia   *J M Scott and P Browne*   109

ANTIOXIDANTS

Diet and Antioxidant Defense   *I F F Benzie and J J Strain*   117

Observational Studies   *I F F Benzie*   131

Intervention Studies   *S Stanner*   138

APPETITE

Physiological and Neurobiological Aspects   *J C G Halford and J E Blundell*   147

Psychobiological and Behavioral Aspects   *R J Stubbs, S Whybrow and J E Blundell*   154

ARTHRITIS   *L A Coleman and R Roubenoff*   163

ASCORBIC ACID

Physiology, Dietary Sources and Requirements   *D A Bender*   169

Deficiency States   *C J Bates*   176

ATHEROSCLEROSIS *see* CHOLESTEROL: Sources, Absorption, Function and Metabolism. CORONARY HEART DISEASE: Prevention

B

B VITAMINS *see* COBALAMINS. NIACIN. PANTOTHENIC ACID. RIBOFLAVIN. THIAMIN: Physiology; Beriberi. VITAMIN B_6

BACTERIA *see* INFECTION: Nutritional Interactions; Nutritional Management in Adults

BASES *see* ELECTROLYTES: Acid-Base Balance

BEER *see* ALCOHOL: Absorption, Metabolism and Physiological Effects; Disease Risk and Beneficial Effects; Effects of Consumption on Diet and Nutritional Status

BEHAVIOR   *E L Gibson and M W Green*   183

BERIBERI *see* THIAMIN: Beriberi

BEVERAGES *see* ALCOHOL: Absorption, Metabolism and Physiological Effects; Disease Risk and Beneficial Effects; Effects of Consumption on Diet and Nutritional Status. TEA

BIOAVAILABILITY   *R J Wood*   195

BIOTIN   *D M Mock*   201

BLOOD LIPIDS/FATS *see* HYPERLIPIDEMIA: Overview. LIPOPROTEINS

BLOOD PRESSURE *see* HYPERTENSION: Etiology

BODY COMPOSITION   *D Gallagher and S Chung*   210

BONE   *B M Thomson*   220

BRAIN AND NERVOUS SYSTEM   *J D Fernstrom and M H Fernstrom*   225

BREAST FEEDING   *C K Lutter*   232

BURNS PATIENTS   *S A Hill*   238

C

CAFFEINE   *M J Arnaud*   247

CALCIUM   *L H Allen and J E Kerstetter*   253

CALORIES *see* ENERGY: Balance; Requirements. ENERGY EXPENDITURE: Indirect Calorimetry; Doubly Labeled Water

CANCER

Epidemiology and Associations Between Diet and Cancer   *G A Colditz*   260

Epidemiology of Gastrointestinal Cancers Other Than Colorectal Cancers   *H-Y Huang*   266

Epidemiology of Lung Cancer   *A J Alberg and J M Samet*   272

Dietary Management   *C Shaw*   284

Effects on Nutritional Status   *C Shaw*   289

Carcinogenic Substances in Food   *D Anderson and J C Phillips*   295

CARBOHYDRATES

Chemistry and Classification   *C L Stylianopoulos*   303

Regulation of Metabolism   *C L Stylianopoulos*   309

Requirements and Dietary Importance   *C L Stylianopoulos*   316

Resistant Starch and Oligosaccharides   *A Laurentin and C A Edwards*   322

CARCINOGENS *see* CANCER: Carcinogenic Substances in Food

CAROTENOIDS

Chemistry, Sources and Physiology   *B K Ishida and G E Bartley*   330

Epidemiology of Health Effects   *S A Tanumihardjo and Z Yang*   339

CEREAL GRAINS   *R W Welch*   346

CHEESE *see* DAIRY PRODUCTS

CHILDREN

Nutritional Requirements   *M Lawson*   357

Nutritional Problems   *E M E Poskitt*   370

CHOLECALCIFEROL *see* VITAMIN D: Physiology, Dietary Sources and Requirements; Rickets and Osteomalacia

CHOLESTEROL

Sources, Absorption, Function and Metabolism   *D J McNamara*   379

Factors Determining Blood Levels   *S M Grundy*   385

CHOLINE AND PHOSPHATIDYLCHOLINE   *X Zhu and S H Zeisel*   392

CHROMIUM   *R A Anderson*   396

COBALAMINS   *R Green*   401

CELIAC DISEASE   *V Nehra, E Marietta and J Murray*   407

COFACTORS

Inorganic   *E D Harris*   418

Organic   *E D Harris*   427

COFFEE *see* CAFFEINE

COLON

Structure and Function   *A Maqbool*   439

Disorders   *A Maqbool*   448

Nutritional Management of Disorders   *D M Klurfeld*   460

COMPLEMENTARY FEEDING   *K G Dewey*   465

COPPER   *X Xu, S Pin, J Shedlock and Z L Harris*   471

CORONARY HEART DISEASE

Hemostatic Factors   *W Gilmore*   476

Lipid Theory   *D Kritchevsky*   482

Prevention   *K Srinath Reddy*   487

CYSTIC FIBROSIS   *J Dowsett and O Tully*   494

CYTOKINES   *R F Grimble*   501

D

DAIRY PRODUCTS   *J Buttriss*   511

DEHYDRATION   *A W Subudhi, E W Askew and M J Luetkemeier*   518

DENTAL DISEASE   *R C Cottrell*   527

DIABETES MELLITUS

Etiology and Epidemiology   *J Sudagani and G A Hitman*   535

Classification and Chemical Pathology   *K C McCowen and R J Smith*   543

Dietary Management   *C D Saudek and S H Oh*   551

DIARRHEAL DISEASES   *A Baqui, R Heinzen, M Santosham and R Black*   565

DIETARY FIBER

Physiological Effects and Effects on Absorption   *I T Johnson*   572

Potential Role in Etiology of Disease   *D L Topping and L Cobiac*   578

Role in Nutritional Management of Disease   *A R Leeds*   586

VOLUME 2

DIETARY GUIDELINES, INTERNATIONAL PERSPECTIVES   *B Schneeman*   1

DIETARY INTAKE MEASUREMENT

Methodology   *A A Welch*   7

Validation   *M Nelson*   16

DIETARY SURVEYS   *K L Tucker*   27

DIETETICS   *P A Judd*   32
DIGESTIBILITY *see* BIOAVAILABILITY
DRUG–NUTRIENT INTERACTIONS   *K G Conner*   38

E
EARLY ORIGINS OF DISEASE
   Fetal   *A J Buckley and S E Ozanne*   51
   Non-Fetal   *L S Adair*   59
EATING BEHAVIOR *see* MEAL SIZE AND FREQUENCY
EATING DISORDERS
   Anorexia Nervosa   *A R Rolla*   66
   Bulimia Nervosa   *A J Hill and S F L Kirk*   74
   Binge Eating   *M D Marcus, M A Kalarchian and M D Levine*   80
EGGS   *D J McNamara and H S Thesmar*   86
EICOSANOIDS *see* PROSTAGLANDINS AND LEUKOTRIENES
ELECTROLYTES
   Acid-Base Balance   *A G Jardine and P B Mark*   93
   Water–Electrolyte Balance   *S M Shirreffs and R J Maughan*   100
ENERGY
   Metabolism   *S Cox*   106
   Balance   *Y Schutz*   115
   Requirements   *W P T James*   125
   Adaptation   *A G Dulloo and J Jacquet*   131
ENERGY EXPENDITURE
   Indirect Calorimetry   *A Raman and D A Schoeller*   139
   Doubly Labeled Water   *W A Coward*   145
EXERCISE
   Beneficial Effects   *C Boreham and M H Murphy*   154
   Diet and Exercise   *R J Maughan*   162

F
FAMINE   *K P West Jr*   169
FAT-SOLUBLE VITAMINS *see* VITAMIN A: Biochemistry and Physiological Role. VITAMIN D: Physiology,
   Dietary Sources and Requirements; Rickets and Osteomalacia. VITAMIN E: Metabolism and
   Requirements. VITAMIN K
FAT STORES *see* ADIPOSE TISSUE
FATS *see* FATTY ACIDS: Metabolism; Monounsaturated; Omega-3 Polyunsaturated; Omega-6
   Polyunsaturated; Saturated; *Trans* Fatty Acids. LIPIDS: Chemistry and Classification; Composition and
   Role of Phospholipids
FATS AND OILS   *A H Lichtenstein*   177
FATTY ACIDS
   Metabolism   *P A Watkins*   186
   Monounsaturated   *P Kirk*   198
   Omega-3 Polyunsaturated   *A P Simopoulos*   205
   Omega-6 Polyunsaturated   *J M Hodgson, T A Mori and M L Wahlqvist*   219
   Saturated   *R P Mensink and E H M Temme*   225
   Trans Fatty Acids   *M J Sadler*   230

FERTILITY   *R E Frisch*   237

FETAL ORIGINS OF DISEASE *see* EARLY ORIGINS OF DISEASE: Fetal; Non-Fetal

FIBER *see* DIETARY FIBER: Physiological Effects and Effects on Absorption; Potential Role in Etiology of
   Disease; Role in Nutritional Management of Disease

FISH   *A Ariño, J A Beltrán, A Herrera and P Roncalés*   247

FLAVONOIDS *see* PHYTOCHEMICALS: Classification and Occurrence; Epidemiological Factors

FOLATE *see* FOLIC ACID

FOLIC ACID   *J McPartlin*   257

FOOD ALLERGIES

   Etiology   *T J David*   265

   Diagnosis and Management   *T J David*   270

FOOD CHOICE, INFLUENCING FACTORS   *A K Draper*   277

FOOD COMPOSITION DATA   *S P Murphy*   282

FOOD FOLKLORE   *J Dwyer and J Freitas*   289

FOOD FORTIFICATION

   Developed Countries   *R Nalubola*   295

   Developing Countries   *O Dary and J O Mora*   302

FOOD INTAKE *see* DIETARY INTAKE MEASUREMENT: Methodology; Validation. DIETARY SURVEYS.
   MEAL SIZE AND FREQUENCY

FOOD INTOLERANCE   *T J David*   309

FOOD SAFETY

   Mycotoxins   *J D Groopman and T W Kensler*   317

   Pesticides   *M Saltmarsh*   323

   Bacterial Contamination   *N Noah*   329

   Other Contaminants   *C K Winter*   340

   Heavy Metals   *G L Klein*   344

FORTIFICATION *see* FOOD FORTIFICATION: Developed Countries; Developing Countries

FRUCTOSE   *N L Keim and P J Havel*   351

FRUITS AND VEGETABLES   *A E Bender*   356

FUNCTIONAL FOODS

   Health Effects and Clinical Applications   *L Galland*   360

   Regulatory Aspects   *H H Butchko and B J Petersen*   366

G

GALACTOSE   *A Abi-Hanna and J M Saavedra*   377

GALL BLADDER DISORDERS   *B Nejadnik and L Cheskin*   384

GERIATRIC NUTRITION *see* OLDER PEOPLE: Physiological Changes; Nutritional Requirements;
   Nutrition-Related Problems; Nutritional Management of Geriatric Patients

GLUCOSE

   Chemistry and Dietary Sources   *D J A Jenkins, R de Souza, L S A Augustin and C W C Kendall*   390

   Metabolism and Maintenance of Blood Glucose Level   *V Marks*   398

   Glucose Tolerance   *B Ahrén*   405

GLYCEMIC INDEX   *G Frost and A Dornhorst*   413

GOITRE *see* IODINE: Deficiency Disorders

GOUT   *L A Coleman and R Roubenoff*   419

GRAINS *see* CEREAL GRAINS

GROWTH AND DEVELOPMENT, PHYSIOLOGICAL ASPECTS   *W W Hay Jr*   423

GROWTH MONITORING   *T J Cole*   433

GUT FLORA *see* MICROBIOTA OF THE INTESTINE: Probiotics; Prebiotics

H

HANDICAP

    Down's Syndrome   *M Collins and A Laverty*   443

    Prader–Willi Syndrome   *A O Scheimann*   449

    Cerebral Palsy   *J Krick and P Miller*   452

HEART DISEASE *see* CORONARY HEART DISEASE: Hemostatic Factors; Lipid Theory;

    Prevention

HEIGHT *see* NUTRITIONAL ASSESSMENT: Anthropometry

HOMOCYSTEINE   *J W Miller*   462

HUNGER   *J C G Halford, A J Hill and J E Blundell*   469

HYPERACTIVITY   *M Wolraich*   475

HYPERLIPIDEMIA

    Overview   *T R Trinick and E B Duly*   479

    Nutritional Management   *A H Lichtenstein*   491

HYPERTENSION

    Etiology   *T Morgan and H Brunner*   499

    Dietary Factors   *L J Appel*   506

    Nutritional Management   *C M Champagne*   513

HYPOGLYCEMIA   *V Marks*   523

VOLUME 3

I

IMMUNE SYSTEM *see* IMMUNITY: Physiological Aspects; Effects of Iron and Zinc

IMMUNITY

    Physiological Aspects   *A T Borchers, C L Keen and M E Gershwin*   1

    Effects of Iron and Zinc   *C Doherty*   7

INBORN ERRORS OF METABOLISM

    Classification and Biochemical Aspects   *D L Marsden*   13

    Nutritional Management of Phenylketonuria   *D L Marsden, F J Rohr and K C Costas*   22

INFANTS

    Nutritional Requirements   *S A Atkinson*   28

    Feeding Problems   *R M Katz, L Schuberth and C S Gulotta*   42

INFECTION

    Nutritional Interactions   *H Ghattas*   47

    Nutritional Management in Adults   *J A Tayek*   54

INTESTINE *see* SMALL INTESTINE: Structure and Function; Disorders; MICROBIOTA OF THE INTESTINE:

    Probiotics; Prebiotics

IODINE

    Physiology, Dietary Sources and Requirements   *R Houston*   66

    Deficiency Disorders   *B S Hetzel*   74

IRON   *J R Hunt*   82

ISCHEMIC HEART DISEASE *see* CORONARY HEART DISEASE: Lipid Theory

K

KESHAN DISEASE *see* SELENIUM

KETOSIS   *D H Williamson*   91

L

LACTATION

    Physiology   *J L McManaman and M C Neville*   99

    Dietary Requirements   *N M F Trugo and C M Donangelo*   106

LACTOSE INTOLERANCE   *D M Paige*   113

LEGUMES   *M A Grusak*   120

LIPIDS

    Chemistry and Classification   *J L Dupont*   126

    Composition and Role of Phospholipids   *A D Postle*   132

LIPOPROTEINS   *J M Ordovas*   143

LIVER DISORDERS   *J Hampsey and K B Schwarz*   150

LOW BIRTHWEIGHT AND PRETERM INFANTS

    Causes, Prevalence and Prevention   *M Merialdi and M de Onis*   161

    Nutritional Management   *J M Cox*   168

LUNG DISEASES   *A MacDonald*   175

LYCOPENES AND RELATED COMPOUNDS   *C J Bates*   184

M

MAGNESIUM   *C Feillet-Coudray and Y Rayssiguier*   191

MALABSORPTION SYNDROMES   *P M Tsai and C Duggan*   196

MALNUTRITION

    Primary, Causes Epidemiology and Prevention   *A Briend and P Nestel*   203

    Secondary, Diagnosis and Management   *N Solomons*   212

MANGANESE   *C L Keen, J L Ensunsa, B Lönnerdal and S Zidenberg-Cherr*   217

MEAL SIZE AND FREQUENCY   *F E Leahy*   225

MEAT, POULTRY AND MEAT PRODUCTS   *P A Lofgren*   230

MENKES SYNDROME *see* COPPER

MICROBIOTA OF THE INTESTINE

    Prebiotics   *J M Saavedra and N Moore*   237

    Probiotics   *M Gueimonde and S Salminen*   244

MILK *see* DAIRY PRODUCTS

MINERALS *see* CALCIUM. MAGNESIUM. PHOSPHORUS. POTASSIUM. SODIUM: Physiology

MOLYBDENUM *see* ULTRATRACE ELEMENTS

MONOSATURATED FAT *see* FATTY ACIDS: Monounsaturated

MYCOTOXINS *see* FOOD SAFETY: Mycotoxins

N

NIACIN   *C J Bates*   253

NITROGEN *see* AMINO ACIDS: Chemistry and Classification; Metabolism. PROTEIN: Digestion and Bioavailability; Quality and Sources; Requirements and Role in Diet; Deficiency

NUCLEIC ACIDS   *E A Carrey and H A Simmonds*   260

NUTRIENT–GENE INTERACTIONS

Molecular Aspects   *C D Berdanier and H C Freake*   269

Health Implications   *C D Berdanier and H C Freake*   276

NUTRIENT REQUIREMENTS, INTERNATIONAL PERSPECTIVES   *A A Yates*   282

NUTRITION POLICIES IN DEVELOPING AND DEVELOPED COUNTRIES   *C Geissler*   293

NUTRITION TRANSITION, DIET CHANGE AND ITS IMPLICATIONS   *B M Popkin*   301

NUTRITIONAL ASSESSMENT

Anthropometry   *J Eaton–Evans*   311

Biochemical Indices   *F Fidanza*   318

Clinical Examination   *B Caballero*   329

NUTRITIONAL SUPPORT

In the Home Setting   *M Elia and R J Stratton*   332

Adults, Enteral   *K N Jeejeebhoy*   342

Adults, Parenteral   *J Binkley, S Daniell and G L Jensen*   349

Infants and Children, Parenteral   *S Collier and C Lo*   357

NUTRITIONAL SURVEILLANCE

Developed Countries   *N R Sahyoun*   363

Developing Countries   *L M Neufeld and L Tolentino*   371

NUTS AND SEEDS   *J Gray*   381

O

OBESITY

Definition, Etiology and Assessment   *A Pietrobelli*   389

Fat Distribution   *J Stevens and K P Truesdale*   392

Childhood Obesity   *E M E Poskitt*   399

Complications   *A Ahmed and R L Atkinson*   406

Prevention   *T P Gill*   413

Treatment   *E C Uchegbu and P G Kopelman*   421

OILS *see* FATS AND OILS

OLDER PEOPLE

Physiological Changes   *N Solomons*   431

Nutritional Requirements   *N Solomons*   437

Nutrition-Related Problems   *C P G M de Groot and W A van Staveren*   444

Nutritional Management of Geriatric Patients   *M-M G Wilson and J E Morley*   449

OSTEOMALACIA *see* VITAMIN D: Rickets and Osteomalacia

OSTEOPOROSIS   *K O O'Brien*   460

OXIDANT DAMAGE *see* ANTIOXIDANTS: Observational Studies; Intervention Studies

P

PANTOTHENIC ACID   *C J Bates*   467

PARASITISM   *P G Lunn*   472

PATHOGENS *see* INFECTION: Nutritional Interactions; Nutritional Management in Adults

PELLAGRA   *C J Bates*   481

PESTICIDES *see* FOOD SAFETY: Pesticides

PHENYLKETONURIA *see* INBORN ERRORS OF METABOLISM: Nutritional Management of Phenylketonuria

PHOSPHATE *see* SMALL INTESTINE: Structure and Function

PHOSPHORUS   *J J B Anderson*   486

PHYSICAL ACTIVITY *see* EXERCISE: Beneficial Effects; Diet and Exercise

PHYTOCHEMICALS

Classification and Occurrence   *A Cassidy*   490

Epidemiological Factors   *H Wiseman*   497

PHYTO-ESTROGENS *see* PHYTOCHEMICALS: Classification and Occurrence;

Epidemiological Factors

POLYUNSATURATED FATTY ACIDS *see* FATTY ACIDS: Omega-3 Polyunsaturated; Omega-6

Polyunsaturated

POTASSIUM   *L J Appel*   509

POULTRY *see* MEAT, POULTRY AND MEAT PRODUCTS

PREGNANCY

Role of Placenta in Nutrient Transfer   *P Haggarty*   513

Nutrient Requirements   *L H Allen*   521

Energy Requirements and Metabolic Adaptations   *G R Goldberg*   528

Weight Gain   *L H Allen and J M Graham*   533

VOLUME 4

PREGNANCY

Safe Diet for Pregnancy   *S Stanner*   1

Dietary Guidelines and Safe Supplement Use   *L H Allen, J M Graham and J E Sabel*   8

Prevention of Neural Tube Defects   *P N Kirke and J M Scott*   15

Pre-eclampsia and Diet   *E Abalos and J Villar*   27

PREMENSTRUAL SYNDROME   *M C de Souza and Ann F Walker*   35

PROSTAGLANDINS AND LEUKOTRIENES   *G E Caughey, M J James and L G Cleland*   42

PROTEIN

Synthesis and Turnover   *D J Millward*   50

Requirements and Role in Diet   *D J Millward*   58

Digestion and Bioavailability   *Z A Bhutta*   66

Quality and Sources   *B Torun*   73

Deficiency   *Z A Bhutta and H L Dewraj*   82

PULSES *see* LEGUMES

PYRIDOXINE *see* VITAMIN B$_6$

R

REFUGEES   *R Bhatia and L N Richardson*   87

RELIGIOUS CUSTOMS, INFLUENCE ON DIET   *P Fieldhouse*   93

RESPIRATORY DISEASES *see* CANCER: Epidemiology of Lung Cancer. LUNG DISEASES

RETINOL *see* VITAMIN A: Biochemistry and Physiological Role; Deficiency and Interventions

RIBOFLAVIN   *C J Bates*   100

RICKETS *see* VITAMIN D: Rickets and Osteomalacia

ROUGHAGE *see* DIETARY FIBER: Physiological Effects and Effects on Absorption; Potential Role in Etiology

of Disease; Role in Nutritional Management of Disease

S

SALT *see* SODIUM: Physiology; Salt Intake and Health

SATIETY *see* APPETITE: Physiological and Neurobiological Aspects

SATURATED FAT *see* FATTY ACIDS: Saturated

SEASONALITY   *F Branca and P D'Acapito*   109

SEEDS *see* NUTS AND SEEDS

SELENIUM   *C J Bates*   118

SENESCENCE *see* AGING

SKINFOLD THICKNESS *see* NUTRITIONAL ASSESSMENT: Anthropometry

SMALL INTESTINE

Structure and Function   *D Rumsey*   126

Disorders   *R D'Souza and J Powell-Tuck*   133

SOCIO-ECONOMIC STATUS   *E Dowler*   140

SODIUM

Physiology   *A R Michell*   150

Salt Intake and Health   *C P Sánchez-Castillo and W P T James*   154

SODIUM CHLORIDE *see* SODIUM: Salt Intake and Health

SPIRITS *see* ALCOHOL: Absorption, Metabolism and Physiological Effects; Disease Risk and Beneficial
Effects; Effects of Consumption on Diet and Nutritional Status

SPORTS NUTRITION   *R J Maughan*   167

STARCH *see* CARBOHYDRATES: Chemistry and Classification; Regulation of Metabolism; Requirements
and Dietary Importance; Resistant Starch and Oligosaccharides

STARVATION AND FASTING   *J E Bines and R G Heine*   173

STOMACH

Structure and Function   *J P Pearson and I A Brownlee*   180

Disorders   *J A Solon*   190

STROKE, NUTRITIONAL MANAGEMENT   *S McLaren*   196

SUCROSE

Nutritional Role, Absorption and Metabolism   *J Brand-Miller*   204

Dietary Sucrose and Disease   *B Caballero*   212

SUGAR *see* CARBOHYDRATES: Chemistry and Classification; Regulation of Metabolism; Requirements and
Dietary Importance; GALACTOSE. GLUCOSE: Chemistry and Dietary Sources; Metabolism and
Maintenance of Blood Glucose Level; Glucose Tolerance. SUCROSE: Nutritional Role, Absorption and
Metabolism; Dietary Sucrose and Disease

SUPPLEMENTATION

Dietary Supplements   *S S Percival*   214

Role of Micronutrient Supplementation   *R D W Klemm*   220

Developing Countries   *R Shrimpton*   227

Developed Countries   *M F Picciano and S S McDonald*   233

SURGERY

Perioperative Feeding   *E Kelly*   241

Long-term Nutritional Management   *E Lin and T R Ziegler*   246

T

TEA   *D J Baer and S C Chen*   257

TEETH *see* DENTAL DISEASE

THIAMIN

Physiology   *D I Thurnham*   263

Beriberi   *D I Thurnham*   269

THIRST   *J Leiper*   278

TOCOPHEROL *see* VITAMIN E: Metabolism and Requirements; Physiology and Health Effects

TRACE ELEMENTS *see* CHROMIUM. COPPER. IMMUNITY: Effects of Iron and Zinc. IODINE:
   Physiology, Dietary Sources and Requirements. IRON. MANGANESE. SELENIUM. ZINC:
   Physiology

TRANS FATTY ACIDS *see* FATTY ACIDS: *Trans* Fatty Acids

TUBERCULOSIS
   Nutrition and Susceptibility   *J P Cegielski and D N McMurray*   287
   Nutritional Management   *J P Cegielski and L Demeshlaira*   294

TUMOR *see* CANCER: Epidemiology and Associations Between Diet and Cancer; Epidemiology of
   Gastrointestinal Cancers Other Than Colorectal Cancers; Epidemiology of Lung Cancer

U

ULTRATRACE ELEMENTS   *F Nielsen*   299

UNITED NATIONS CHILDREN'S FUND   *J P Greaves and R Shrimpton*   311

URBAN NUTRITION   *N Solomons*   317

V

VEGAN DIETS *see* VEGETARIAN DIETS

VEGETABLES *see* FRUITS AND VEGETABLES

VEGETARIAN DIETS   *J Dwyer*   323

VITAMIN A
   Physiology   *A C Ross*   329
   Biochemistry and Physiological Role   *J L Napoli*   339
   Deficiency and Interventions   *K P West Jr*   348

VITAMIN B$_1$ *see* THIAMIN: Physiology; Beriberi

VITAMIN B$_2$ *see* RIBOFLAVIN

VITAMIN B$_6$ *D A Bender*   359

VITAMIN B$_{12}$ *see* COBALAMINS

VITAMIN C *see* ASCORBIC ACID: Physiology, Dietary Sources and Requirements; Deficiency States

VITAMIN D
   Physiology, Dietary Sources and Requirements   *M F Holick*   368
   Rickets and Osteomalacia   *J J B Anderson*   378

VITAMIN E
   Metabolism and Requirements   *M G Traber*   383
   Physiology and Health Effects   *P A Morrissey and M Kiely*   389

VITAMIN K   *C J Bates*   398

W

WATER *see* THIRST

WEIGHT MANAGEMENT
   Approaches   *N Finer*   407
   Weight Maintenance   *H A Raynor and R R Wing*   413
   Weight Cycling   *L Lissner*   421

WHOLE GRAINS   *R Lang and S A Jebb*   427

WILSON'S DISEASE *see* COPPER

WINE *see* ALCOHOL: Absorption, Metabolism and Physiological Effects; Disease Risk and Beneficial Effects; Effects of Consumption on Diet and Nutritional Status

WORLD HEALTH ORGANIZATION *J Akré* 437

Y

YOGURT *see* DAIRY PRODUCTS. FUNCTIONAL FOODS: Health Effects and Clinical Applications; MICROBIOTA OF THE INTESTINE: Probiotics; Prebiotics

Z

ZINC

Physiology *H C Freake* 447

Deficiency in Developing Countries, Intervention Studies *C Hotz* 454

INDEX 463

DIETARY GUIDELINES, INTERNATIONAL PERSPECTIVES

B Schneeman, University of California—Davis, Davis, CA, USA

Introduction

The use of food-based dietary guidelines (FBDG) has emerged as an important food and nutrition policy and education program since the late 1970s and is valuable for addressing issues of both nutrient adequacy and excess. Importantly, FBDG communicate nutritional principles in a manner that is relevant to the population. Most FBDG encourage energy balance, physical activity, a healthful variety of foods including fruits and vegetables, whole-grain products, food sources of protein, calcium, and unsaturated fatty acids, and safe food handling. Cautionary messages focus on excess energy intake, saturated and *trans* fatty acids, added sugars, salt, and alcohol. To develop relevant FBDG, each country must identify local public health issues and appropriate diet-related strategies for the population.

Historical Background

Throughout the ages, religious and philosophical writings have included dietary recommendations, and this is reflected in an oft-quoted line from Hippocrates: 'Let thy food be thy medicine'. In the late 1800s, modern science began to influence the nature of recommendations regarding foods and beverages. The original focus of guidelines developed from Pasteur's discoveries of the disease-causing organisms that could be present in foods such as milk; thus, recommendations emphasized sanitation in food handling. In the early 1900s the discovery of vitamins and minerals led to the realization that foods contain factors that are essential for health. This 'vitamin theory of disease' led to research throughout the first half of the twentieth century to discover these factors and determine their essential functions in the treatment of deficiency diseases. The knowledge that food was important in the prevention of diseases that were major public health problems, such as scurvy, beri-beri, night blindness, and pellagra, led to early efforts to develop and promote dietary recommendations or guidelines, even though the specific curative factors in foods had not been identified. Among the earliest examples, Egyptians were known to promote the use of liver to correct night blindness, the British Navy used lemons or limes to prevent scurvy, and alkali treatment of corn was associated with a lower incidence of pellagra in Mexico. The understanding of the linkage between certain foods and the prevention of disease resulted in the development of food guides or groups illustrating a pattern of food choices that was most likely to prevent deficiency diseases. As the chemical nature of the factors in food that prevented or cured nutritional deficiencies became known, it was possible to determine the specific amount required in the diet to maintain health. These studies led to the development of recommended dietary allowances (RDA), which are numeric recommendations of the nutrient intakes that will meet the needs of the majority of the population. RDA have also been used to evaluate the adequacy of diets in many populations.

By the second half of the twentieth century, it had become clear that in many developed countries the primary causes of disease were shifting from dietary deficiencies to those associated with dietary excess. As noted by the Surgeon General of the USA, by 1988 micronutrient deficiencies were no longer major public health problems in the USA, and diseases associated with excess intakes of energy, saturated fat, total fat, cholesterol, alcohol, and sodium, in conjunction with inadequate fiber intake, were the major causes of death in the USA. The economic transition experienced by many developing countries has led to a similar pattern; this is sometimes referred to as the double burden of disease. While nutritional deficiencies continue to be prevalent in large segments of the population, an increasing proportion of the population is at risk of developing diet-related chronic diseases, such as obesity, cardiovascular disease, cancer, and diabetes. This emerging pattern of disease has resulted in the development of FBDG, which recommend dietary patterns that are adequate in nutrient content and encourage food choices to lower the risk of noncommunicable diet-related diseases.

Types of Guidelines

This section outlines the evolution of three inter-related general types of nutrition recommendations that are developed and used in most areas of the world by national or regional government agencies: technical recommendations, which provide specific numeric criteria for nutrient intake; FBDG, which outline strategies to lower the risk of chronic disease; and food guides, which illustrate dietary patterns or food choices to encourage individuals to meet the recommended nutrient requirements and to follow the advice in dietary guidelines. The more technical quantitative guidelines are typically used by health professionals to develop educational materials and evaluate the adequacy of diets. Food guides and FBDG are important components of educational materials for healthy individuals. Although this section will focus on FBDG, it is important to understand how they are related to the other types of nutritional recommendations, and also that recommendations categorized as FBDG ideally are related to and supportive of other types of nutritional recommendations that are part of national or regional health policy. Frequently, non-governmental groups develop food guides or FBDG to suit a specific purpose (such as weight loss, treatment of cardio-vascular disease, or promotion of a food culture) or a specific population (such as older individuals); however, before accepting these recommendations, it is important to determine how they have been validated in terms of other criteria such as the dietary reference intakes. These non-governmental recommendations do not have the same policy status as recommendations developed by government agencies or through government-sponsored scientific organizations and may be suitable only for a specific targeted function.

In 1992 a recommendation of the International Conference on Nutrition organized by the World Health Organization (WHO) and the Food and Agriculture Organization (FAO) was that each country should to develop nutritional recommendations that included FBDG. To encourage this activity, FAO and WHO convened a group of experts to recommend a process for developing FBDG; their findings are published in a WHO technical report.

The Development of Food-Based Dietary Guidelines

FBDG express the principles of nutrition education in terms of the food and food choices available to the population rather than in terms of specific nutrients or food components. Scientifically, these guidelines are based on the association between dietary patterns and the risk of diet-related diseases and incorporate recommendations that address major diet-related public health issues. In addition to communicating scientific knowledge about the association between food, dietary patterns, and health, development of FBDG provides an opportunity to strengthen consensus among various government and non-government organizations on important nutrition recommendations to be incorporated into educational programs. In addition, by expressing scientific principles in terms of food, FBDG recognize the consumer awareness of food rather than nutrients and emphasize to consumers the importance of meeting nutrient needs with foods. Thus, both the content of the FBDG and the process of development are important.

Researchers often focus their studies on a specific nutrient or food component that may alter the risk of developing a disease. These studies are reviewed in the development of FBDG, but the information must be reorientated from a nutrient-based focus to a food recommendation by addressing the questions in **Table 1**. As indicated by these questions, the process is driven by the identification of diet-related public health issues and the development of food-based strategies that are relevant to the target population.

The process for developing FBDG is based on building consensus among various sectors and groups involved in public health. **Table 2** provides a general outline of the steps in the process, which can be adapted to the specific needs of a country or region. The goal is to have a set of guiding principles for food-based recommendations that lay out the overall policy agreed by various agencies and groups.

The product of the working group is likely to be a document that outlines recommendations and includes background information on the rationale for the guidelines as well as guidance on implementing the recommendations. The guidelines from three countries are shown in **Table 3** as an example of the types of message developed during this process. In all cases, the messages are accompanied by a document containing background information. **Table 4** presents common themes emerging from the FBDG that have been developed in a variety of countries. Based on foods available and cultural practices, the types of fruits, vegetables, and whole grains and the specific types of food that are emphasized as sources of protein, calcium, or unsaturated fatty acids may vary. In

Table 1 Reorientating from nutrients and food components to foods

What are the important public health issues for the population? Do they have diet-related factors?
Health statistics will indicate the major causes of morbidity and mortality in a population. Diet-related diseases include
  nutritional-deficiency diseases and noncommunicable diseases such as obesity, type 2 diabetes, certain types of cancer, and
  cardiovascular disease. It is important to determine whether nutrition is the primary cause of the disease or secondary to some other
  more prevalent problem (e.g., smoking, infectious agents)

What are the target nutrients linked to the major public health issues? Are there related nutrients or other factors?
In many nutrition-related problems several nutrients or food factors may interact to cause the nutritional problem. For example,
  the fat content of the diet affects absorption of fat-soluble vitamins, obesity can be related to either excess energy intake or
  inadequate expenditure, multiple factors contribute to adequate bone formation, folic acid can mask vitamin B_{12} deficiencies,
  etc. Simply increasing the intake of a target nutrient and ignoring these other factors may not address the problem
  adequately

What foods are high in the nutrient(s) or consumed in sufficient quantity to be a significant source of the nutrient(s)?
Using both food-composition databases and food-consumption data, foods that are good sources of the nutrient and foods that are
  consumed in sufficient quantity to meet the target intake can be identified. Likewise, dietary patterns that lower the risk for the public
  health problem and are associated with adequate intake of the nutrient can be identified

What is likely to be acceptable by the target audience?
For nutrition interventions to achieve success, recommendations must target food choices that can be integrated into the diet based on
  cost and acceptability of the foods

How do diet strategies integrate with other food policies?
Economic, agricultural, and trade analysis is useful to determine which diet strategies are sustainable

Table 2 Steps in the development of food-based dietary guidelines

1. Develop support from key government agencies
  The successful implementation of FBDG will depend on support from key ministries such as health, agriculture, education, sports, and
    recreation. Building consensus among these agencies will result in consistent messages regarding diet, health, and lifestyle for the
    public. Examples of support include technical support for data analysis or a Secretariat to maintain and coordinate activities

2. Form a working group of experts
  The working group should include diverse expertise in areas such as public health, nutrition, food science, agriculture, and
    behavioral sciences

3. Solicit public comment and input
  The expert panel needs to gather and evaluate scientific information to determine the guidelines that are most relevant to the target
    population. This information can be obtained from the scientific literature. In addition, professional groups may have important
    information to submit to the panel for consideration. Solicitation of information is consistent with an open process; however, the
    panel is responsible for evaluating the relevance of the information submitted

**4. Review and identify key public health issues and evaluate the diet–health relationships of concern for the population,
  determine the critical health, food, and nutrition issues to be targeted in the FBDG, and define the purpose, target groups,
  and content of the FBDG**
  Even if data are limited, it is important for the working group to identify the key public health issues. This step may be especially
    important in countries in which both under-nutrition and over-nutrition are of concern. Identification of the public health issues
    allows the working group to address the questions in **Table 1**

5. Develop and draft the main messages for the FBDG
  The working group will need to decide whether the draft document will be targeted primarily at health professionals, and hence may
    be more technical, or will be targeted toward the general public. In developing the main messages, they may identify
    consumer-orientated materials, such as a food guide that will be useful in communicating the FBDG to the public

6. Assess the cultural and economic appropriateness and credibility of the messages as perceived by the target groups
  Through focus groups or other types of consumer testing the effectiveness of the FBDG can be assessed. This information can be
    used to revise the guidelines before developing the final draft

7. Release and implement the FBDG
  It is valuable to have government leaders from key ministries involved in the release and implementation of the FBDG so that there is a
    commitment to integrate the guidelines into departmental policies. In addition, the implementation can require development of educational
    materials for different target groups as well as public–private partnerships to aid in dissemination of the messages to the public

8. Monitoring and revision
  Monitoring can be used to assess the impact and implementation of the FBDG. In addition, monitoring data are useful for making
    appropriate revisions and updates to the guidelines on a periodic basis

FBDG, food-based dietary guidelines.

Table 3 Dietary-guideline messages from three countries

USA	China	Thailand
Aim for fitness		
Aim for a healthy weight	Eat a variety of foods, with cereals as the staple	Eat a variety of foods from each of the five food groups, and maintain proper body weight
Be physically active each day	Consume plenty of vegetables, fruits, and tubers	Eat adequate amount of rice or alternative carbohydrate sources
Build a healthy base		
Let the pyramid guide your food choices	Consume milk, beans, or diary or bean products every day	Eat plenty of vegetables and fruits regularly
Choose a variety of grains daily, especially whole grains	Consume appropriate amounts of fish, poultry, eggs, and lean meat; reduce fatty meat and animal fat in the diet	Eat fish, lean meats, eggs, legumes, and pulses regularly
Choose a variety of fruits and vegetables daily		
Keep food safe to eat		
Choose sensibly		
Choose a diet low in saturated fat and cholesterol and moderate in total fat	Balance food intake with physical activity to maintain a healthy body weight	Drink milk in appropriate quality and quantity for one's age
Choose beverages and foods to moderate your intake of sugars	Choose a light diet that is also low in salt	Eat a diet containing the appropriate amounts of fat
If you drink alcoholic beverages, do so in moderation	If you drink alcoholic beverages, do so in limited amounts	Avoid sweet and salty foods
	Avoid unsanitary and spoiled foods	Eat clean and safe food
		Avoid or reduce the consumption of alcoholic beverages

Table 4 Common themes for food-based dietary guidelines

Foods or behaviors that are encouraged	Cautionary messages
Energy balance	Saturated fatty acids and *trans* fatty acids
Includes physical activity	
Encouraging a healthful variety of foods	Energy balance
Fruits and vegetables	Total energy from fat
Use of whole grains	Consumption of foods high in added sugar
Protein-based foods	
Foods that are calcium sources	Use of salt and salty foods
Sources of unsaturated fatty acids	Alcohol
Safe food handling	

all countries concerns about the increasing incidence of obesity have placed greater focus on energy balance, in terms of both food selection and physical activity. As a part of their effort to support the development of FBDG, the FAO launched a public information initiative for consumers entitled 'get the best from your food'. This initiative promoted four simple principles (**Table 5**) that can be adapted for educational programs in a variety of settings.

Most countries that have developed FBDG have also developed a food guide to accompany the messages in the guidelines. The food guide is typically a simple graphic illustration of food choices and dietary patterns. The food guides that accompany the FBDG shown in **Table 4** are illustrated in **Figure 1**. Criteria for a food guide should include representation of foods common to the population, consistency with the FBDG, use of simple graphics that are meaningful to the target population, and developing a food pattern that meets the nutrient requirements of the population. Although a simple graphic is useful for visual communication, it should be clear that proper use of the food guide depends on understanding the more complete information in the FBDG.

Table 5 Food and Agriculture Organization initiative: get the best from your food

	Key concept
Enjoy a variety of food	Recognizing the importance of food in understanding nutrient requirements, nutrient and non-nutrient interactions, and diet–health relationships
Eat to meet your needs	Importance of energy balance and different needs across the life cycle
Protect the quality and safety of your food	Recognizing the importance of food and water sanitation, especially in developing countries
Keep active and stay fit	Importance of physical activity in maintaining well-being

Food-guide pyramid
A guide to daily food choices

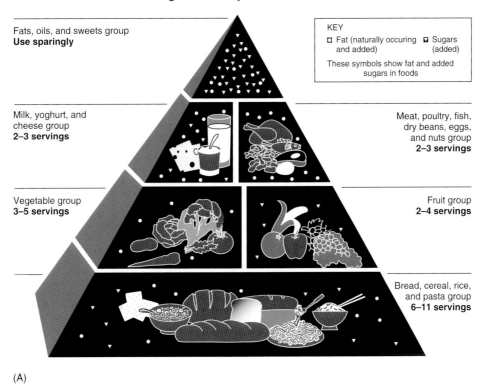

Fats, oils, and sweets group
Use sparingly

KEY
☐ Fat (naturally occuring and added)   ▣ Sugars (added)
These symbols show fat and added sugars in foods

Milk, yoghurt, and cheese group
2–3 servings

Meat, poultry, fish, dry beans, eggs, and nuts group
2–3 servings

Vegetable group
3–5 servings

Fruit group
2–4 servings

Bread, cereal, rice, and pasta group
6–11 servings

(A)

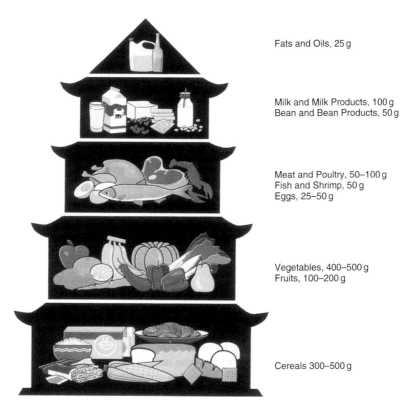

Fats and Oils, 25 g

Milk and Milk Products, 100 g
Bean and Bean Products, 50 g

Meat and Poultry, 50–100 g
Fish and Shrimp, 50 g
Eggs, 25–50 g

Vegetables, 400–500 g
Fruits, 100–200 g

Cereals 300–500 g

(B)

Figure 1   The food guides that accompany the FBDG in (A) the USA, (B) China, and (C) Thailand.

(C)

Figure 1   *Continued.*

Conclusion

The use of food-based dietary guidelines (FBDG) has emerged as an important food and nutrition policy and education program since the late 1970s and is valuable for addressing issues of both nutrient adequacy and excess. Importantly, FBDG communicate nutritional principles in a manner that is relevant to the population. As a policy document, they should be revised periodically so that the information reflects current science on food and nutrition factors that promote health and prevent disease. Additionally, it is important for each country to develop their own set of FBDG so that the recommendations and presentation are relevant to the local population.

See also: **Nutritional Surveillance**: Developed Countries; Developing Countries. **World Health Organization**.

Further Reading

Centers for Disease Control (1999) Achievements in public health, 1900–1999: safer and healthier foods. *MMWR Weekly* 48: 905–913.

Chinese Nutrition Society (1999) Dietary guidelines and the food guide pagoda for Chinese residents: balanced diet, rational nutrition, and health promotion. *Nutrition Today* **34**: 106–115.

Dietary Guidelines Advisory Committee (2000) *2000 Report.* Washington, DC: US Government Printing Office.

Food and Agriculture Organization *Get the Best From Your Food.* Rome: FAO.

Food and Agriculture Organization and World Health Organization (1998) *Preparation and Use of Food-Based Dietary Guidelines.* WHO Technical Report Series 880. Geneva: WHO.

National Research Council (1989) *Diet and Health: Implications for Reducing Chronic Disease.* Washington, DC: National Academy of Sciences Press.

Schneeman BO (2001) Preparation and use of food-based dietary guidelines: lessons from Thailand and the Philippine Islands. *Food, Nutrition and Agriculture* **28**: 55–62.

Schneeman BO and Mendelson R (2002) Dietary guidelines: past experiences and new approaches. *Journal of the American Dietetic Association* **102**: 1498–1500.

Surgeon General (1988) *Surgeon General's Report on Diet and Health* Washington, DC: United States Government Printing Office.

US Department of Agriculture and Department of Health and Human Services (2000) *Nutrition and Your Health: Dietary Guidelines for Americans*, 5th edn. Home and Garden Bulletin 232. Washington, DC: US Government Printing Office.

Welsh S, Davis C, and Shaw A (1992) A brief history of food guides in the United States. *Nutrition Today* Nov/Dec 1992: 6–11.

Working Group on Food-Based Dietary Guideline for Thai *Food Based Dietary Guideline for Thai.* Institute of Nutrition, Mahidol University, and Food and Agriculture Organization.

World Health Organization and Food and Agriculture Organization Expert Consultation (2003) *Diet, Nutrition and the Prevention of Chronic Disease.* WHO Technical Report Series 916. Geneva: WHO.

DIETARY INTAKE MEASUREMENT

Contents
Methodology
Validation

Methodology

A A Welch, University of Cambridge, Cambridge, UK

Introduction

Dietary intake measurements are used to assess food or nutrient intake of individuals, groups, or populations. The purpose of collection of measurements varies from individual assessments in clinical situations (nutrition screening) or the adequacy of intake of population groups (nutrition surveillance) to use in research relating diet to health status, particularly in epidemiology. Measurements are also used to establish exposure to food-borne contaminants, in the evaluation of nutritional intervention programs, and to develop nutritional guidelines for governmental health policy.

This article describes the dietary intake measurements available, issues associated with data collection, conversion to nutrients and food types, measurement error when using dietary intake methods, validation and calibration of dietary methods, and future developments.

Dietary Intake Measurements

Table 1 describes the advantages and limitations of the main types of dietary methods, which are suitable for different purposes.

Of the individual methods weighed records, estimated food records, 24-h recalls (24-h), and dietary histories are more intensive. The quantity of food consumed may be weighed directly or estimated using household measures such as cups and spoons, photographs, standard units, or average portions (see **Table 2**). For all methods the amount consumed can be measured or described either including or excluding wastage material usually discarded during food preparation, e.g., outer leaves and peel from vegetables or bones from cuts of meat.

Some considerations when choosing a dietary method are shown in **Table 3**.

Methods for Measuring Food Consumption at the National Level

Food Balance Sheets

The FAO (Food and Agriculture Organization) publishes food balance sheets (FBSs) for around 200

Table 1 Names and characteristics of dietary methods used for estimating food and nutrient intake

Name of method	Advantages	Limitations
National level		
Food balance sheets	Available for 200 countries; suitable for monitoring change	Per caput not individual intake; intake overestimated as nutrient losses during storage and preparation not accounted for; should not be used to provide estimates of nutritional adequacy of particular regions
Household level		
Food account method	Low respondent burden; relatively inexpensive	No estimates of change in larder stocks; measurements confined to food brought into the home (unless method modified to measure food consumed outside the home, which can be quite large); consumption of confectionery, alcoholic, and soft drinks excluded
Inventory method	Low respondent burden; relatively inexpensive	Consumption of confectionery, alcoholic, and soft drinks excluded
Household record	Suitable for populations with high proportion of home-made foods; useful if literacy levels are low; provides direct measure of food available for consumption	High input from field workers or interviewers
List recall methods	Relatively rapid and inexpensive; only 1 interview required; suitable for populations with higher proportion of purchased than home-produced food	Advance warning of interview may distort food consumption patterns; subject may fail to record items from memory; no record of foods eaten outside the home
Individual level		
Retrospective methods		
24-Hour recall (24-HR) (single or multiple days)	If interviewed, respondent literacy not important; not reliant on long-term memory; providing not forewarned, individuals do not alter food consumption; interview length 20–45 min	Single 24-h should not be used for estimating intake of individuals but can be used for group assessments
Diet history	Respondent literacy not required	Report of past intake is influenced by current diet; trained interviewers required; average interview length 1–1.5 h; high processing costs
Food frequency questionnaire (FFQ) (if includes portion estimates termed semiquantitative FFQ)	Useful for large numbers; relatively straightforward to complete; administration simpler and less costly than other individual methods; more rapid data processing	Needs to be developed for specific population group to ensure important food items are covered and requires updating to accommodate changes to supply of foods; less flexible for later analysis as food lists are fixed; responses governed by cognitive, numeric, and literacy abilities of respondents also by length and complexity of the food list
Current methods		
Weighed food record (weighed inventory technique)	No requirement for memory retrieval as it records current intake; food intake weighed so estimates of quantity consumed not required	Literate, cooperative respondents required as burden is high; possible that respondents change usual eating patterns to simplify the record; high processing costs
Food record with estimated weights	No requirement for memory retrieval as it records current intake	Literate, cooperative respondents required as burden is high; possible that respondents change usual eating patterns to simplify the record; necessary to find values for estimates of quantity of food consumed; high processing costs
Duplicate analysis	Greater accuracy	Highly labor intensive; requires laboratory to do food composition analysis; limited applicability in population studies

In all methods 'foods' refers to consumption of foods, beverages, and snacks both inside and outside of the home.

countries. Food balance sheets present a comprehensive picture of the pattern of a country's food supply during a specified reference period. Food balance sheets may also be termed national food accounts, food moving into consumption, food consumption statistics, food disappearance data, and consumption level estimates, reflecting differences in the method of calculation but providing similar information.

Table 2 Types of portion used for methods using estimated portions

Portion types

Average or small, medium, large portions, weights – available from studies of weighed intake
Photographs (ideally should be 5 or more representing the population range of intake)
Household measures (spoons, cups, mugs, liquid measures)
Standard units (1 apple, 1 banana)
Food models/replicas (three-dimensional models representing foods)

Data should be derived from weighed intakes, government surveys, and research groups in populations similar to the one to be studied.

The supply available during a period is calculated from the total quantity of foodstuffs produced in a country, added to the total quantity imported and modified for any change in stocks that may have occurred. Calculation of quantities used for purposes other than human consumption (exports, livestock, used for seed, nonfood uses) and losses during storage and transportation are made. The per caput supply of each food item available for human consumption is calculated by dividing the total of available food by the number of the population actually consuming it and expressed in terms of quantity and nutrients. Estimates from FBSs include household wastage material, plate waste, and food fed to pets. Nutrient losses during storage, preparation, and cooking are not calculated and so figures for available food are greater than those reported by individual dietary surveys.

Table 3 Factors determining choice or suitability of method

Size and scale of the data collection
Screening, clinical, research, surveillance purposes?
Literacy or numeracy of the population
Age of the individual or population (the very young or very old may need assistance with completion)
Intended or potential use of the data (immediate short-term assessment versus prospective research)
Requirement for group or individual estimates for nutrient intake
Requirements from the data for nutrients, food groups, or phytonutrients
Detail and comprehensiveness of the information to be extracted for analysis (if information only required for particular nutrient or food type, shortened questionnaires may be administered)
Has repeatability of the method been assessed?
Have previous validation studies performed on the method by other researchers in similar population group to be studied?
Availability of resources for interviewers and including training
Availability of suitable coding program (record and recall methods require greater resources than frequency methods but frequency programs are more complex to develop)

Food balance sheets can be used to formulate agricultural policies concerned with production, distribution, and consumption of foods and as a basis for monitoring changes and forecasting food consumption patterns, as well as to provide inter-country comparisons of available supplies.

Methods for Estimating Dietary Intake at the Household Level: Household Budget Surveys

Techniques for estimating intake at the household level include the food account method, the inventory method, the household record, and the list recall method. These methods measure all foods and beverages available for consumption by a household or family group during a specified time period of between 1 and 4 weeks, although some last for 2–3 months. Wastage factors are sometimes applied. Household surveys provide data for per capita consumption of foods or nutrients, not intake for specific individuals. Data are calculated irrespective of the age and gender distribution in the household. These methods provide population data for annual mean food consumption and selection patterns, and are used for analyzing trends in intake. Household budget surveys are used more widely in Europe than elsewhere. As countries may not produce compatible data the Data Food Networking Project (DAFNE) has developed the methodology to allow the data from 11 European countries to be combined and compared.

Food Account Method

A record is made by a respondent of details of all quantities of food entering the household (purchased, home grown, or received over a period), usually over a period of 7 days. Changes in larder stocks are not estimated as on average some households will gain and some will use up stocks. Estimates of losses and wastage during preparation are made. This method is used for the UK Expenditure and Food Survey (until 2001 the National Food Survey), and has included consumption of food, confectionery, soft drinks, and alcohol outside the home since 1992. As consumption outside the home now accounts for a substantial proportion of dietary intake in the UK the method was modified in 2001 to include the use of till receipts and individual 2-week diaries for each household member aged 7 years or older. This method can be used to measure seasonal variation in intake over 1 year.

Inventory Method

The inventory method is similar to the food account method and respondents record all foods coming into the household. A wastage factor is often applied and a larder inventory is included at the beginning and end of the survey period.

Household Record

Foods available for consumption (either raw or processed) are weighed or estimated. Foods for each meal are recorded separately to give a total for the household. Waste is measured directly or estimated. Interviewers visit the household early in the day to determine the quantity of food used to prepare the first meal and the number of individuals who consumed it. The midday meal may be weighed or recorded using estimated measures. A further interview is required later in the day. This method is appropriate for use in pre-industrial societies where literacy is low and units for buying foods not standardized.

List Recall Methods

The respondent is asked by a trained interviewer to recall the amount and cost of food obtained for household use over a period, usually of 1 week. The method takes into account food use, purchases, and acquired food, but not waste. Quantities consumed are weighed or estimated using household measures. The interview can take up to 2.5 h. Response rates are usually high. Information on the age and sex of people in the household and the number of meals eaten both in and outside the home, income, and other socioeconomic characteristics may be collected. It is helpful to notify the respondent in advance so that records of purchases can be kept prior to the interview. This method was used by the United States Department of Agriculture (USDA) National Food Consumption Survey between 1931 and 1988.

Individual Dietary Intake Methods

Many methods are available for estimating individual dietary intake measures and can be divided into two types: retrospective measures of intake such 24-h recalls (24-HR), dietary history or food frequency questionnaires (FFQs), or current measures of intake such as weighed or estimated food records. Qualitative information is available from all methods but quantitative estimates for nutrient consumption are possible only if data for weighed or estimated portion weights are available. Most methods may be either self-completed or completed by a surrogate.

Surrogates may be required if study individuals are too young, old, or infirm but data will be less reliable than when reported directly.

24-HR and FFQs may be self completed or interview administered either face-to-face or by telephone and can be mailed. Data collection costs can be reduced if questionnaires can be self-completed or mailed.

The number of days of report required for adequate measures of nutrients using 24-h recalls, weighed, or estimated records varies depending on the day to day variability of nutrient consumption. The number of days is partly dependent on the variation in nutrient concentration in foodstuffs. The concentration of macronutrients such as protein and carbohydrate in foods varies less than micronutrients such as vitamin C or iron. The number of days required to classify individuals into the correct third of the percentage distribution for usual intake, for 80% of individuals, has been calculated in British and Swedish populations. Up to 7 days of recall would be required for energy, protein, sugars, and calcium. Nutrients with greater variability and requiring between 4 and 14 days of records were alcohol, vitamin C, riboflavin, and iron.

24-Hour Recalls

24-HR determine intake during the preceding 24 h. Interviews can be recorded on paper or using interactive computerized software. Day-to-day variability in nutrient intake is large and a single day will not categorize individuals correctly within a distribution of intake. Therefore, single 24-HR are better used for group assessments than estimates for individuals. However, multiple 24-HR can be used to overcome this problem. The sampling protocol for studies should include an equal proportion of all days of the week and coverage of all four seasons.

Diet History

The diet history consists either of an interview administered 24-HR or establishing usual eating pattern over a 1-week period, followed by a frequency questionnaire to provide additional information. The dietary history provides a representative pattern of usual intake and is interview administered only.

Food Frequency Questionnaires

FFQs consist of a list of specific foods or food types associated with frequency of consumption. They are termed semi-quantitative if portions are included. Most questionnaires specify a frequency response in relation to an average or medium portion but some request records of specific portions. The period of record is usually the previous month or year. FFQs provide an indication of usual intake and can be used to obtain population estimates of frequency of consumption of food types.

FFQs need to be developed for specific population groups otherwise important foods may be missed. FFQs may become outdated if the supply of foodstuffs changes. FFQs consist of a fixed food list, which may be a disadvantage for prospective studies as hypotheses to be tested are limited by the list. Factors that affect the response to FFQs are the literacy and numeracy of respondents as some mathematical ability is necessary to calculate relative frequencies, the length and complexity of the food list, and the influence of current diet. Not all respondents will relate frequency to portion size accurately.

In the US examples of FFQs are the Block and Willett questionnaires. In Europe FFQs were developed for the European Prospective Investigations into Cancer and Nutrition (EPIC) study in the Netherlands, Germany, Greece, Italy, Denmark, France, and the UK.

Weighed Food Record Inventory and Estimated Food Record

For weighed food records (WRs) all food consumed over a period is weighed and recorded with details of food type and method of preparation, on preprinted forms or booklets, to obtain consumption over a period of days. Portable scales need to be supplied. WRs may include some estimated items eaten out of the home. Leftover food should be weighed and deducted. The recommended time period for records is 4–7 days or more, although the number of days depends on the nutrient of interest, study population, and objectives of the study. As some populations have different eating habits at weekends, weekend days should be included proportionately.

For estimated food records all foods consumed over a period are recorded with details of food type, method of preparation, and estimated portions over a period of days (see **Table 2**). If recorded over 7 days, this may be called a '7-day diary'.

Both these methods have a high respondent burden and need cooperative, literate respondents. Respondents require training in the level of detail needed to describe foods. It is also possible that respondents may change usual eating patterns to simplify the process of the record. It is also beneficial to include a review of weighed records during the period of recording either after the first day or at the end.

Duplicate sample technique

Duplicate samples of all foods consumed are made and the nutrient content analyzed. This method is used for metabolic studies and though providing greater accuracy than other methods, its use is not feasible for most purposes.

Further Information

Although nomenclature for dietary methodology is reasonably consistent, care should be taken when reading the literature as methods with the same name may have been applied differently. The final decision over which method to choose will depend on the aims of the study, the population for study, the potential burden on respondents, and the resources available. Household surveys and food balance sheets provide data for per caput but not individual intake. In general, individual and the more intensive methods are associated with higher costs and respondent burden, whereas household methods are more economical and have a lower respondent burden.

Clinical Practice

Dietary methodology for clinical practice requires rapid assessments of nutritional intake in order to prescribe dietary change or to improve nutritional status. Traditionally, 24HR of 'usual' intake or diet histories have been used for this purpose. Food frequency questionnaires and weighed or estimated food records are not generally used due to the more intensive burden on respondents and on the resources required for coding and processing the data.

There is considerable discussion over the optimum method to use for establishing individual dietary intake and studies designed to measure the validity of methods suggest that those that are more intensive and detailed lead to greater measurement precision, justifying the greater cost. Confirmation of these findings is required. Despite these potential benefits if resources are unavailable less intensive methods tend to be used.

Factors Affecting Individual Ability to Report Intake Accurately

Factors governing individual accuracy and quality of reports are respondent's literacy and numeracy skills; preconceived ideas on the purpose of the enquiry and, for list-based methods, the interpretation and meaning of food names. Individuals may make errors when measuring and recording food weights or estimating weights of foods consumed.

There is also respondent variation in the perception of the size of portions represented by photographs.

Interviewers

The aim of using interviewers with dietary methods is to obtain a complete, accurate, and detailed record of what respondents eat. Therefore, it is important for interviewers to be well trained and have an awareness of food composition and preparation techniques. Ideally, interviewers should be educated in nutrition (dietitians or nutritionists), although nonnutritionists can be trained to standardized techniques, and come from the same cultural or ethnic background as the study population. Interviewer protocols should be developed.

Computerized Interview Procedures

Computerized interview systems can aid interviewers by prompting for specific questions to elicit sufficient and specific detail and reduce the burden on interviewers. Examples are the Minnesota Nutrition Data System and the EPIC-SOFT systems, used in the US and a number of European countries. Although computerized interviews have advantages in improving accuracy and standardization, and in saving time and effort when recording and coding data, interviewers do have to be competent with computers and the resources required to develop systems are high.

Using Dietary Methods in Different Populations

Ethnic subpopulations may consume different food types than a main population and baseline surveys will be required to establish what types of foods and method of preparation are common. This information would be required before list-based methods such as the FFQ could be developed.

Recall of Remote Diet

Investigators may wish to recall diet in the remote past, perhaps of many years. However, interpretation of remotely recalled dietary data is complex as recalled diet is heavily influenced by current dietary habit. Some studies have found that the correlations between recalled past diet and current diet were higher than the correlations between actual past diet and recall of past diet. The onset of diseases such as cancer may affect the appetite and dietary intake of study participants and as recall of remote diet is strongly related to current diet, may affect recall of remote diet. As diet prior to the onset of disease is the measure of interest, it is preferable to collect dietary information prospectively, that is before disease onset. Case–control studies in which the diet of cases with disease is compared with controls may be affected by altered perception of recalled diet, particularly by cases.

Reproducibility of Dietary Methods

The reproducibility of a method may also be referred to as reliability, repeatability, or precision and is a measure of the extent to which the same results can be obtained when repeated under the same conditions. Repeated measures provide an estimate of the within-person variability of intake. However, interpretation of the repeatability of measures is difficult as a lack of consistency may be due to genuine change over a time period or a lack of sensitivity or specificity of the method used to measure intake.

Use of Data and Conversion of Reported Intake to Nutrients and Food Types

Qualitative Analysis

Dietary method data can be used qualitatively, for instance during the process of reviewing nutritional intake for the purpose of dietary treatment as in clinical practice. Data on frequency of consumption may also be collected and analyzed by the FFQ method without conversion to nutrient intakes. However, even for qualitative analyses it is likely that paper-based dietary methods will require conversion to an electronic format. The majority of uses of dietary methods are targeted towards quantitative analyses.

Quantitative Analysis

The data collected by dietary methods are converted into food and nutrient consumption by calculating the amount of food eaten and linking this to a database with values for the nutrient composition of foods.

The databases of nutrient composition of foods are provided by the governments of many countries. They consist of nutrient composition data for the average composition of commonly consumed foodstuffs and are usually available as printed publications, computerized databases, or as part of software packages. Values in nutrient composition databases are expressed as either per 100 g of food or per common household measure. Nutrient databases vary in the coverage and comprehensiveness of the foods and nutrients. They are revised periodically to cover newer foods of different nutrient compositions or to modify or extend the nutrient coverage. Some issues concerning the choice of nutrient databases are shown in **Table 4**. It is important to read the

Table 4 Factors to consider when choosing a nutrient database to calculate nutrient intakes

Comprehensiveness of food item and beverage coverage?
Does the database contain entries for important foods consumed by the population to be studied?
How comprehensive is the coverage of nutrients?
Does the database contain data for mixed or multiple ingredient recipes or dishes?
What analytical techniques were used to derive nutrients in the database? (There can be differences in nutrients measured by different techniques)
Are the data officially evaluated?
What compilation methods were used to construct the database?
Which conversion factors are used to calculate metabolizable energy content of foods for protein, fat, carbohydrate, and alcohol?
What proportion of missing values exists within the database? (Missing values are counted as zero in calculations, resulting in systematic underestimates of intake.)
For international studies or comparisons how do the analytical methods for determining nutrient composition and compilation techniques affect the resulting data?

information distributed with the printed or electronic versions of databases to determine the uses and limitations of the data.

Several steps are involved in calculating nutrient intake (also known as coding or processing). The first is to choose an item in the database, which corresponds most closely with the food consumed. If the food consumed is not in the database a suitable alternative can be chosen by considering food type, general characteristics, and likely nutrient profile. Once the food has been chosen the nutrient composition of the food quoted in the database is multiplied by the amount of food eaten, e.g., for 60 g food the nutrients would be multiplied by 0.6 (where nutrients are expressed per 100 g of food).

To calculate daily intake for an individual the contribution of each food is calculated and all the foods for a day summated. If more than one day's data have been collected it is usual to calculate the average of the number of days recorded. Data from FFQs are usually computed to consumption per day but can also be computed per week.

Although it is possible to compute intake by hand, using a calculator and a printed copy of a nutrient database, this is very labor intensive and in practice for most purposes has been superseded by computerization.

Data Processing and Computing Dietary Intake

The same care as that invested in data collection should be applied to data processing as errors of great magnitude may be introduced.

Estimated Food Quantities

To obtain quantitative information for nutrients or food groups, actual or estimated food weights are used. For methods using estimated food weights, values also need to be found for foods described such as standard units, average portions, or household measures. Sources of data are national publications, surveys of weighed dietary intakes, and food manufacturers. Data may also be included in nutrient calculation programs. Portion weights need to be population specific and, if unavailable, studies to establish values will be needed. Intensive methods used for large-scale surveys will require databases of more than 20 000 values for portion weights.

Data Entry and Nutrient Calculation Systems

A number of computerized data entry systems and nutrient calculation programs exist; factors that need to be considered when choosing a system are given in **Table 5**. The features required depend on the intended use of the data but as a minimum should include a list of foods, weights of portions, and a nutrient composition database. Ideally, systems should enable entry of data in sufficient detail to fulfil hypotheses for investigation and include measures to ensure consistent entry by staff such as defaults for inadequately reported foods, portions, or mixed component foods. They should also include a method for entering newer foods with different nutrient composition from the existing nutrient database. This is particularly important, as the range of new foodstuffs and products with different nutritional characteristics is ever increasing.

Computerized systems and nutrient databases become out-dated and for large-scale prospective studies it is desirable to develop systems with a flexible approach to updating by using database technology.

Data Processing Errors

Errors arising during the coding (data entry) and processing of individual dietary methods (24-HR,

Table 5 Factors to consider when choosing a computerized entry or interviewing program

Speed of the assessment
Requirements of the study for detailed or general data
Food composition database used
Food portion database used
Cost of the system
Facilities for organization of data
Ability to extract nutrients or food groups from the system
How up to date are the nutrient composition databases included in the system?
Commercial availability

diet history, weighed and estimated records) need to be avoided. Misclassification can arise due to human error if incorrect foods are chosen during coding, for instance, if milk was consumed in the full-fat form but was coded for skimmed milk. This may also arise where a food has local or alternative food names, which may be unknown to the coder. It is important to have a qualified nutritionist available to develop a protocol for training staff, answering queries, and dealing with ambiguities. Coders should have knowledge of food composition and food preparation techniques. It is difficult to control entry of incorrectly matched foods but careful checking and staff training are crucial in preventing this. Other potential errors are entry of incorrect quantities or multiplication factors for portion weights and missed items, problems that can occur even with structured computer programs. So, systematic post-entry checks to identify extremes of portion weights or nutrient values and the verification and correction of data are necessary.

Issues Associated with Measurement of Dietary Intake

Measurement Error

There is potential for the occurrence of measurement error with the measurement of any exposure such as when using dietary methods to measure nutritional intake. Errors may arise as a result of flaws in the design of the measurement instrument or during data collection or processing. Measurement error may also occur as a result of individual characteristics of participants in studies. Measurement error can be defined as the difference between the measured exposure (or measure of dietary intake) and the true exposure. All measurement of dietary exposures is subject to some degree of measurement error making it difficult to achieve measurements of true intake.

Efforts to reduce measurement error during data collection and processing should be introduced into the protocol of all studies, however, even if preventative measures are taken it is impossible to eliminate it altogether. It is difficult to identify the type and structure of measurement error associated with dietary intake. Measurement error may occur because of inaccurate reporting by respondents. It may also vary according to dietary method, for instance, food items within record methods may be intentionally or unintentionally omitted and with FFQs frequency of consumption may be inaccurately reported. Systematic bias, interviewer bias, recall bias, and social desirability bias have been identified

but there are likely to be other sources of error. (Bias can be defined as the modification of a method of measurement by a factor, which influences the measurement in one or more directions.) Measurement error associated with dietary methods may consist of one or more types of error.

Measurement Error in Data Collection and Processing

Systematic bias Systematic bias is a systematic mismeasurement of data and can occur, for instance, if equipment such as weighing scales under- or overestimates values or if an interviewer consistently fails to use questions to probe for consumption of snacks and additional foods. If systematic bias can be identified solutions can be found, for instance, by calibrating equipment or training and monitoring interviewers.

Interviewer bias The behavior of an interviewer can influence the response of interviewees leading to interviewer bias. The degree of rapport between interviewer and respondent also influences results. Bias may occur if interviewers omit responses or record them incorrectly. Trained interviewers should ask open-ended questions in a neutral or nonleading manner, and not imply that a food or beverage should or should not have been consumed and avoid value judgments.

Social desirability bias Social desirability bias can influence dietary measures as respondents strive to report what they think is required not what was actually consumed, for example, reporting less alcohol consumption than is the case or greater consumption of foods with perceived health benefits such as fish, fruit, or vegetables. This is likely to be the cause of mis-reporting, under-reporting, or low energy reporting, which occurs in certain respondents. It is possible to predict how much energy a respondent should report, as this is the amount required to maintain a stable weight. (Weight will be either gained or lost if more or less energy is consumed than required.) As energy intake should equate to energy expenditure, expenditure effectively measures intake. Techniques for measurement of energy expenditure such as whole body calorimetry and doubly labeled water can be used. Using these techniques those individuals classified as low energy reporters are likely to be older, more overweight, and of lower educational and socioeconomic status than the rest of the population. Low energy reporters tend to have lower consumption of foods in the groups cookies, cakes, puddings, confectionery (candy) and sugary foods and, in some populations, lower consumption of spreads, cooking fats, and potato chips. Interviewers should be aware of low energy reporting, aim to be entirely nonjudgemental, and also request participants make complete records of food intake.

Impact of Measurement Error

As the proportion of error within a measurement increases, the accuracy of the measurement decreases and the results using the measurement will become less interpretable. Hence, greater measurement error reduces the likelihood that the truth has been measured with accuracy and increases the likelihood that analyses relating diet to disease status will tend towards null results. The effect of measurement error is to mis-classify an individual within a range of intake.

Validation of Dietary Methods

Validation is used to quantify the measurement error that occurs when measuring dietary intake exposures. It requires two measures: a main measurement and a second measurement subject to less measurement error than the first. The errors of the two measurements should be independent. Validation is used to estimate the proportion of measurement error within the main method by modeling the differences between the main and the secondary measurement. It had been considered that dietary methods had errors independent of each other and that record methods such as 24-HR could be used, but it is now known that the errors are not independent as individuals report in the same way with different methods. Therefore, it is better to use biological variables measurable in blood or urine (also known as biomarkers) as the second measure for dietary validation. Examples are vitamins, minerals, and individual fatty acids in blood such as vitamin C and carotenoids or urinary excretion over 24-h of nitrogen, potassium, and sodium. Examples of validation studies are those performed within EPIC-Europe and the Observing Protein and Energy Nutrition Study (OPEN) in the US. Work is ongoing to extend the number of biomarkers available and to define further and elicit the structure of measurement error.

Use of Calibration Methods to Adjust for Measurement Error

In contrast to validation, which attempts to identify the type and scale of measurement error, calibration is designed to adjust for systematic over- or underestimation in dietary intakes within populations. It may also be used at the individual level to attempt to correct for attenuation bias (or dilution) in relative risk due to errors in dietary measurements. Calibration of data has been proposed for large multicentre nutritional studies that have used different dietary methods to capture population-specific diets. Calibration studies require a highly standardized second dietary measure to be used in a representative sub-sample from each cohort to form a common reference measurement across populations. An example of this approach has been used by the European EPIC (European Prospective Investigations into Cancer and Nutrition) Study using a computerized, standardized 24-h recall in ten countries.

Future Developments

Future developments in methodology are likely to use computing, digital, and Internet technology, such as videos of food eaten and online programs for self-reported intake. Use of Dictaphones and combinations of weighing and other recording equipment are also possible.

The number of foodstuffs available, particularly of manufactured foods and ready-made meals, will continue to increase, presenting challenges for those attempting to estimate nutrient intake. Nutrient databases will continue to be expanded and updated to incorporate newer food items and nutrient measurements available using improved analytical techniques.

In some populations more than 40% of individuals have been shown to consume supplements and as very few comprehensive databases of vitamin and mineral supplements exist these need to be developed, as supplements can make a major contribution to nutrient intakes.

See also: **Dietary Intake Measurement**: Validation. **Dietary Surveys**. **Food Composition Data**.

Further Reading

Bingham SA (1987) The dietary assessment of individuals; methods, accuracy, new techniques and recommendations. *Nutrition Abstracts and Reviews (Series A)* 57: 705–742.

Cade J, Thompson R, Burley V, and Warm D (2002) Development, validation and utilisation of food-frequency questionnaires – a review. *Public Health Nutrition* 5(4): 567–587.

Cameron ME and Van Staveren WA (1988) *Manual on Methodology for Food Consumption Studies.* Oxford: Oxford University Press.

Feskanich D, Sielaff BH, Chong K, and Buzzard IM (1989) Computerized collection and analysis of dietary intake information. *Computer Methods and Programs in Biomedicine* 30: 47–57.

Freudenheim J (2003) Biomarkers of nutritional exposure and nutritional status. *The Journal of Nutrition* **133** no. 873S–874S.

Gibson RS (1990) *Principles of Nutritional Assessment*. Oxford: Oxford University Press.

Margetts BM and Nelson M (1997) *Design Concepts in Nutritional Epidemiology*, 2nd edn. Oxford: Oxford University Press.

Pao EM and Cypel YS (1996) Estimation of dietary intake. In: Zeigler EH and Filer LJ (eds.) *Present Knowledge in Nutrition*, 7th edn, pp. 498–507. Washington, DC: ILSI Press.

Riboli E, Hunt KJ, Slimani N *et al.* (2002) European Prospective Investigation into Cancer and Nutrition (EPIC): study populations and data collection. *Public Health Nutrition* **5**(6B): 1113–1124.

Slimani N, Deharveng G, Charrondiere RU *et al.* (1999) Structure of the standardized computerized 24-h diet recall interview used as reference method in the 22 centers participating in the EPIC project. Prospective Investigation into Cancer and Nutrition. *Computer Methods and Programs in Biomedicine* **58**: 251–266.

Smith AF (1993) Cognitive psychological issues of relevance to the validity of reports of dietary intake by college men and women. *European Journal of Clinical Nutrition* **47**(supplement 2): S6–S18.

Thompson FE and Byers T (1994) Dietary assessment resource manual. *The Journal of Nutrition* **124** no. 11S.

Welch AA, McTaggart A, Mulligan AA *et al.* (2001) DINER (Data Into Nutrients for Epidemiological Research) – a new data-entry program for nutritional analysis in the EPIC-Norfolk cohort and the 7-day diary method. *Public Health Nutrition* **4**(6): 1253–1265.

Willett W (1998) *Nutritional Epidemiology*, 2nd edn. Oxford: Oxford University Press.

Relevant Websites

http://www.fao.org – INFOODS information for nutrient database compilers and suppliers.

Validation

M Nelson, King's College London, London, UK

Although the basic approaches to dietary assessment have changed little in the past 20 years, there has been a growing awareness of the ways in which errors in dietary assessment may undermine an understanding of diet–disease relationships. There have been two stages in this process: (i) acceptance of the fact that every measure of food consumption is likely to be influenced by the reporting process and (ii) the improvements in the methods for estimating the size of the difference between what is observed and the likely true values for countries, households, or individual subjects. This article examines the techniques for coping with the sources of error in the assessment of diet, particularly through the use of biochemical and statistical techniques that are available to evaluate the quality or enhance the interpretation of dietary data.

Reproducibility and Validity of Dietary Intake Measurements

Reproducibility, Repeatability, and Reliability

'Reproducibility' is the extent to which a tool is capable of producing the same result when used repeatedly in the same circumstances. The terms 'repeatability' and 'reliability' are often used synonymously with 'reproducibility.' All of these terms are equivalent to the word 'precision,' often used by biochemists to describe the variation of a measurement based on repetition of a particular assay using a single piece of equipment.

A measurement may have good reproducibility and yet have poor validity, but a measurement that has good validity cannot have poor reproducibility.

In reality, 'the same circumstances' can never exist in relation to dietary measurements because diet (whether of individuals, households, or countries) varies over time, be it on a daily, weekly, seasonal, or annual basis. In epidemiological studies, the aim is usually to assess 'usual' intake. Part of the variation in any dietary measurement will thus relate to genuine variability of diet. The remaining variation will relate to biases associated with the method. Due consideration must be given to these time-related factors when evaluating the reproducibility and validity of dietary measures, and a well-designed validation study will separate the variability associated with reproducibility (the error in the method) from that associated with genuine biological variation over time.

Validity

Validity is an expression of the degree to which a measurement is a true and accurate measure of what it purports to measure. Establishing validity requires an external reference measure against which the 'test' measurement (the one being used in the main survey or research activity) can be compared. In nutrition, there is no absolute reference measure of the truth. Every measurement of dietary intake includes some element of bias. The best that can be managed is to assess relative or congruent validity of measurements, comparing results obtained with the test instrument with what are believed to be more accurate measures of food or nutrient intake obtained, for example, using a biological marker.

There are two main problems arising from inaccurate measurements:

1. Incorrect positioning of a country, household, or person in relation to an external reference measure (e.g., dietary reference values)
2. incorrect ranking of countries, households, or people in relation to one another

The first type of error can result in inappropriate investigations or actions being taken to remedy an apparent dietary deficit or excess that does not really exist. Alternatively, no action may be taken when some is needed (e.g., a true deficit is not detected because diet is overestimated). The second type of error tends to undermine the ability to assess relationships between diet and health. For example, if someone who properly belongs in the top quarter of the distribution of saturated fat intake (associated with an increased risk of heart disease) is classified in the bottom quarter because he or she underreports his or her true fat intake, the relationship between fat intake and outcome (risk of heart disease) will not be shown. Again, this can lead either to inappropriate recommendations for improving health in the population or, more often, to a failure to take action because the true relationship between diet and health is obscured by measurement error.

Table 1 lists some of the sources of measurement error, their principal effects, some ways of taking errors into account in analysis, and ideas for dealing with them in practice. At the national level, errors in reporting of food production, imports, exports, food moving in and out of stocks, and nonfood uses (e.g., sugar used in the brewing industry) tend to produce overreporting of food and nutrient availability in economically developed countries and underreporting in developing countries. The consequences for between-country comparisons will therefore vary nutrient by nutrient. Where true values are higher in developed countries and lower in developing countries (e.g., energy), a tendency in wealthier countries to overstate consumption and in poorer countries to understate consumption will exaggerate the true differences between countries (**Figure 1**). Where true intakes tend to be higher in developing countries and lower in developed countries (e.g., nonstarch polysaccharides), such biases in measurement will minimize any apparent differences between countries. These types of errors do not lend themselves easily to correction or adjustment. The best solution is to try to improve reporting mechanisms that reduce duplication or omission, although this may be particularly problematic in developing countries, in which a high percentage of the population is engaged in subsistence agriculture.

At the household level, information can be obtained from records of food acquisitions (expenditure and/or amounts), often referred to as household budget surveys. Errors associated with the recording process (omission and misrecording) will contribute to the error of estimates of consumption. Keeping a record of purchases can lead householders to alter their usual purchasing patterns or encourage purchasing in excess of true requirements (especially easily storable items such as flour, sugar, oil, and cooking or spreading fats). Some form of cross-check is necessary—either an internal reference measure such as a cross-check list of foods purchased or used at mealtimes or an external reference measure such as an independent assessment of food consumption by all household members. There are problems related to the estimation of waste and the amount of food given to pets. The true amount of food wasted cannot be known, and direct measures of waste are likely to introduce bias into the measurements. Adjustments for waste range from 4 to 10%, and 6% is a typical value for average waste.

In household budget surveys, the amounts of food eaten away from home (or, more correctly, derived from outside the household food supply) are sometimes measured directly by individual household members who keep records of their food and drink consumption away from home. Alternatively, the amount of food eaten from outside the household food supply can be measured indirectly by asking the main household respondent to record which meals have been consumed from the household food supply and the ages and genders of all people present at those meal, including any visitors. The menu records do not usually include information about snacks between meals. Whether based on the direct or indirect method, household surveys tend to underestimate the amount of food eaten away from home and thus to overestimate the proportion of the diet consumed from the household food supply.

The estimate of the nutrient content of the diet in household-level surveys is based on nutrient conversion factors. These differ from food composition data. Food composition data reflect the chemically determined nutrient content of foods. Nutrient conversion factors modify these values to allow for preparation and cooking losses so that the final estimate of the nutrient content of the diet relates the amount of food initially purchased to the amount of food and nutrient likely to be consumed. There are many assumptions in the determination of the nutrient conversion factors (e.g., the proportion of water-soluble vitamins lost in the cooking process). The result may be an over- or underestimate of

Table 1 Sources of error at different levels of dietary assessment, their effects, ways to adjust for measurement error in analysis, and ways to minimize error in data collection

Level of assessment	Source of error	Effect of error	Statistical adjustment	Ways to minimize
National: Food balance sheets	Inaccurate values of food production, imports, exports, storage, nonfood uses	Over- or underemphasizes apparent differences between countries	Not possible: error likely to vary nonsystematically between countries	Improve reporting mechanisms and estimates of waste and production losses
Household: Household budget surveys, with or without larder inventories	Omission of food items	Underestimation of consumption, especially for certain foods (e.g., sweets)	Inflate estimate of intake to compensate for known underestimation	Cross-check food purchasing list at final interview
	Misrecording of food items	Misrepresentation of true consumption pattern	Not possible: likely to differ between households for different foodstuffs	Cross-check food purchasing list at final interview
	Distortion due to effect of survey (e.g., selection of items believed to be 'healthy')	Misrepresentation of true consumption pattern	Not possible: likely to differ between households for different foodstuffs	Cross-check food purchasing list at final interview
	Overpurchasing stimulated by measurement process	Overestimation of consumption, especially for certain foods (e.g., flour and sugar)	Deflate estimate of intake to compensate for known overestimation	Validate purchasing against reference measure of actual consumption at individual level (for all household members)
	Estimate of amount wasted or given to pets	If amount is underestimated, leads to overestimation of consumption (and vice versa)	Deflate estimate of intake to compensate for known overestimation (or inflate)	Improve estimates of waste through surveys
	Estimate of amounts of food eaten away from home or consumed by visitors, based on menu records	If amount is underestimated, leads to underestimate of total consumption (if overestimated, leads to overestimation)	Inflate estimate of intake to compensate for known underestimation (or deflate)	Household members keep records of amounts eaten away from home (but see problems with records kept by individuals)
	Use of nutrient conversion factors	Unknown biases introduced into calculation of the nutrient content of the diet	Not possible; errors not systematic between foods	Improve estimates of nutrient content and of preparation and cooking losses
Individual: prospective or retrospective methods	Underreporting	Underestimate of usual intake	Calibrate result against valid measure of intake and adjust accordingly	Use more than one measure of intake, including valid reference measure
	Differential misclassification	The error in measurement not consistent between subgroups, making valid comparisons impossible	Identify likely error according to characteristics on which subgroup comparisons are to be based, and adjust accordingly	Undertake appropriate validation studies within subgroups
	Distortion of usual diet (prospective recording or retrospective recall)	Overestimation of intake of some foods and nutrients and underestimation of others	Not possible unless nature of distortion is known for different foods and for different subgroups	Use biomarkers of intake to confirm dietary measures; use more than one measure of intake, including valid reference measure

Adapted from Nelson M (1998) Methods and validity of dietary assessment. In: Garrow J and James WPT (eds.) *Human Nutrition and Dietetics*, 10th edn. London: Churchill Livingstone.

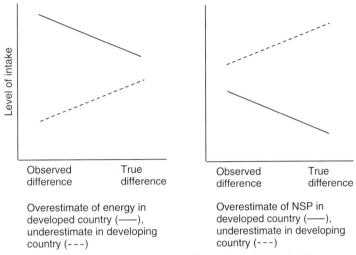

Overestimate of energy in
developed country (——),
underestimate in developing
country (- - -)

Overestimate of NSP in
developed country (——),
underestimate in developing
country (- - -)

Figure 1 Effects of measurement error on between-country comparisons of nutrient availability.

the actual nutrient content of the diet consumed, depending on the nutrient concerned.

At the individual level, the high reproducibility of results using a given technique led researchers for many years to assume that the observed results were valid. Reproducibility was confused with validity. Researchers argued that the results from their chosen technique were correct, but they were unable to explain adequately why measurements of the same diets using different techniques yielded different results. It is now clear that different techniques introduce different types of errors in assessment. Moreover, one can argue that the main sources of error in the assessment of diet at the individual level (e.g., errors in perception of frequency of consumption and of food portion sizes; the desire to increase the reporting of those foods perceived as being 'healthy' or to reduce the reporting of foods perceived as being 'unhealthy'; and items forgotten, intentionally or unintentionally) are not readily amenable to correction.

The most common error in the assessment of diet at the individual level is underreporting. Thus, the mean estimate of energy intake in a group of subjects that includes people who underreport their true consumption is also likely to be an underestimate. Moreover, any comparison of subgroups that include different proportions of underreporters will yield a false picture of the relationships between subgroups. For example, when comparing energy intake based on 7-day weighed records between normal weight and overweight subjects, it is often observed that the overweight subjects (whose energy requirements are higher) will report energy intakes equal to or less than those of the normal weight subjects. This is because overweight subjects show a strong tendency

to underreport their usual consumption levels, particularly of foods with a high proportion of fat. It is worth noting that there is also a small group of subjects who overreport their usual consumption, but their characteristics are less readily defined.

In many validation studies, comparisons are made between methods to establish 'concurrent validity,' often between a new instrument such as a food frequency questionnaire and a more established technique such as a weighed inventory of diet. **Table 2** summarizes the problems associated with the use of specific dietary reference measures. The

Table 2 Limitations of dietary reference methods appropriate for validation of dietary assessment measures

Reference method	Limitations
Weighed records and household measures	Underreporting
	Unrepresentative of 'usual' diet over sufficient number of days
	Distortion of food habits due to recording process
Diet history	Interviewer bias
	Inaccuracy of portion size reporting due to conceptualization and memory errors
	Errors in reporting of frequency, especially overreporting of related foods listed separately (e.g., individual fruits and vegetables)
	Requires regular eating habits
Repeat 24-h recalls	Under- or overreporting of foods due to reporting process (e.g., alcohol underreported and fruit overreported)
	Unrepresentative of 'usual' diet over sufficient number of days
	Inaccuracy of portion size reporting due to conceptualization and memory errors

principal error is likely to be underreporting within certain subgroups, and any validation study needs to address this. Issues regarding distortion of diet are more difficult to identify, however. Work has been carried out to identify some of the errors associated with perception, conceptualization, and memory in relation to assessment of food portion sizes. Agreement between methods is no guarantee of validity. If the two methods are biased in the same way (e.g., using a diet history to validate a short food frequency questionnaire), then the observed level of agreement is likely to overstate the validity of the new method. If the validation is based on repeated measures and the errors in the reference assessment are repeated (e.g., validating a food frequency questionnaire against repeat 24-h recalls), then the level of agreement between the two methods is likely to underestimate the true correlation between the test measure and the truth because the true variance of diet will be underestimated by the reference measure.

Some types of bias may influence reporting in a similar way in all subjects. For example, if a food frequency questionnaire does not ask for sufficient detail about tropical fruit consumption in a survey of West Indian families living in London, then all responses are likely to be biased in the same way. This will result in nondifferential misclassification: Everyone's intake of tropical fruit (and hence vitamin C and carotene intake) is likely to be similarly misclassified. If, on the other hand, the nature of the bias is likely to be related to individual characteristics—for example, West Indian women overreport their tropical fruit consumption compared to West Indian men—then the tropical fruit intake of men and women will be misclassified in different ways in different subgroups. This is known as differential misclassification. If the risks for men and women are being compared in a diet–disease analysis, the errors in the estimates of those risks will not be the same for both groups.

There are many factors in addition to body size or gender that may influence the ability of a dietary measure to estimate accurately the level of food consumption or nutrient intake. **Table 3** lists the potential confounders of good dietary reporting that may affect validation studies. If there is concern about misclassification in one group (e.g., smokers) being different from misclassification in another group (e.g., nonsmokers), then validation must identify the extent of misclassification in the two groups independently so that it can be compensated for in any subsequent analyses. It is therefore important to measure all of the potential confounders that may be a source of misclassification (differential or nondifferential).

Table 3 Factors that may influence the reliability and validity of dietary assessments and that may need to be measured in a validation study

Related to the subject	Related to the measuring process
Age	Portion size
Gender	Interviewer
Height, weight, etc.	Learning effects
Region	Recency effects
Social class	Lag time
Education	Number of foods on an FFQ
Language	Nutrient database
Culture and ethnic background	
Smoking	
Social approval	
Social desirability	

The design of a validation study must also reflect the purpose for which the dietary assessment is being carried out. Most dietary assessments measure current or recent consumption. However, if the aim is to estimate past diet related to the induction of cancer 10 years before the time of the assessment (e.g., in a case–control study), then the validation process should in theory address the relevant time period. In practice, this may be very difficult (i.e., if there is no robust reference measure of diet relating to the relevant time period). In such circumstances, the weaknesses of an unvalidated test measure should not be overlooked nor understated.

Use of Biological Markers to Validate Dietary Intake Measurements

Nutritional biomarkers are those elements or compounds in biological samples capable of reflecting relationships between diet, nutritional status, and disease processes. Not all biomarkers are suitable for use in dietary validation studies. One of the key features of a marker should be its ability to reflect intake over a wide range of intakes.

Figure 2 shows the sequence whereby food or drink containing potential biomarkers (nutrients and nonnutrients) may be ingested, absorbed, distributed, and excreted. The stages in the top of **Figure 2** are not usually amenable to sampling (e.g., taking samples of gastric contents), and it is only in the later stages in which compounds are in circulation, present or stored in tissues, or excreted that they are more readily sampled. The complexity of the relationship between intake and the measured levels of biomarkers in these lower stages, however, may limit the usefulness of certain compounds in validation studies. **Figure 3** illustrates for four nutrients the varying relationships between tissue levels

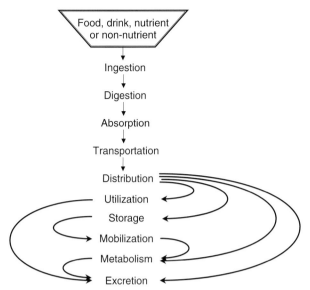

Figure 2 Stages in the pathway between intake and measurement of biomarkers.

and levels in diet. Vitamin E shows a more or less linear relationship between blood and dietary levels across a broad range of intakes. Riboflavin appears in urine only after tissues are saturated and any excess is excreted. An alternative measure to assess riboflavin, erythrocyte glutathione reductase activity coefficient), is a sensitive biomarker of intake only at low levels. Vitamin C in blood is a poor marker at low levels of intake, increases in sensitivity as a marker of intake across the middle range of intakes, and is poor once again at high levels of intake where excess vitamin is excreted in the urine. Retinol is stored in the liver and its level in blood is controlled

homeostatically. It is therefore a poor marker above relatively low intakes. A further problem is the point in time or span of intake reflected by the marker. **Figure 4** shows that some markers relate to intakes days or weeks prior to the sampling point (e.g., energy and doubly labeled water), whereas other may reflect intake over months (iron intake reflected by ferritin) or years (calcium intake reflected by bone mass). The influence of other factors relating marker to intake (e.g., hem versus non-hem iron in the diet, and the influence of vitamin C or dietary fiber on absorption) may undermine the ability to conclude that a low measurement of a marker is necessarily a reflection of low dietary intakes. Thus, the value of markers in assessing the validity of intake measurements is often limited to specific ranges of intake in diets of known composition. This may not be sufficient for epidemiological purposes, where the entire range of intake may be of interest in relation to disease risk.

The two most widespread uses of biomarkers for the assessment of the validity of measures of diet are to identify under- or overreporters and to assess the correctness of ranking of individuals according to their nutrient intake.

Techniques for Identifying Under- and Overreporters

Doubly labeled water The scientific basis that underlies the doubly labeled water method for estimating energy expenditure relies on the differential rates of loss of hydrogen and oxygen from the body at different levels of energy expenditure. Hydrogen is lost primarily in water, whereas oxygen is lost in

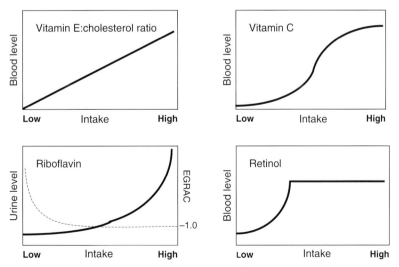

Figure 3 Associations between intake and biomarker over a wide range of intakes: vitamin E:cholesterol ration, vitamin C, riboflavin, and retinol. EGRAC, erythrocyte glutathione reductase activity coefficient. (Adapted from Kohlmeier L (1991) What you should know about your biomarker. In: Kok FJ and van't Veer P (eds.) *Biomarkers of Dietary Exposure.* London: Smith Gordon.)

	Days	Weeks	Months	Years
Energy	Doubly labeled water		Body weight	
Fatty acids	Cholesterol esters	Erythrocyte membranes	Adipose tissue	
Tocopherols	Serum		Adipose tissue	
Retinol			Liver tissue	
Carotenoids	Plasma		Adipose tissue	
Vitamin C	Urine Leucocytes Plasma			
Iron		Hemoglobin	Ferritin	
Calcium	Urine			Bone mass
Selenium	Plasma	Erythrocyte glutathione peroxidase	Toenails	

Figure 4 Time scale over which different biomarkers may reflect the relationship with intake.

both water and carbon dioxide. The relative rates of loss can be used to estimate energy expenditure in free-living subjects over a period of approximately 2 weeks, thereby providing a reference measure for energy intakes over a similar period. Provided the subject is in energy balance (neither gaining nor losing weight due to changes in body composition), the measures of expenditure and intake should agree. The technique allows for identification of both under- and overreporters. The boundaries of acceptability of the test measures (e.g., to within $\pm 10\%$ of habitual energy intake) need to be chosen according to the needs of the study in which the validity of the test measure is being assessed. The level of agreement between test and reference measure will dictate both the precision of the estimate of mean intake for an individual or subgroup and the extent to which subjects will be misclassified when ranked according to level of intake.

The main disadvantage of the doubly labeled water technique is its high cost. In a large-scale study, it is not feasible to use doubly labeled water with every subject in order to assess the completeness of dietary records. The technique is therefore usually used to assess validity of the test measure in a sample of subjects who are taken to be representative of the sample for the main study.

Another disadvantage is that doubly labeled water provides a marker for energy only. The diet recorded could differ substantially from the subject's usual diet but have an energy content in agreement with the estimate of energy expenditure. In the absence of additional information about usual patterns of food consumption, such a record would be regarded as valid. A further problem is that not all food consumption or nutrient intake correlates strongly with

energy intake. For example, fruits and vegetables and their associated nutrients (e.g., vitamin C, beta-carotene, and potassium) may be overreported in a dietary assessment in which energy intake agrees well with energy expenditure, but the overreporting would not be identified. These comments are summarized in **Table 4**.

Urinary nitrogen and potassium excretion A second technique for identifying under- or overreporters is to collect 24-h urine samples and compare the amounts of nitrogen and potassium excreted with the amount ingested. Allowing for incomplete absorption and losses of nitrogen from the gastrointestinal tract (digestive juices and shed epithelial cells), hair, skin, and sweat, the amount of nitrogen excreted should be approximately 81% of the nitrogen ingested. Allowing for daily variations in intake and excretion, if daily recorded intake of nitrogen is less than 70% of the corresponding urinary nitrogen excretion over the following 24 h, the respondent is likely to have underreported his or her usual consumption; anyone whose recorded intake of nitrogen is more than 100% of their excretion is likely to have overreported their consumption. The more days of intake and excretion data that are collected, the better the agreement over the recording period should be for subjects who are in nitrogen balance. If urinary nitrogen is to be used as a marker for the completeness of dietary recording, it is helpful to have at least 4 days' worth of data (diet and urine). For potassium, the expected urinary excretion is 95% of the intake, with limits of 80 and 110% for 'good' reporting.

As with doubly labeled water, it is assumed that the subject is in balance, neither losing nor gaining body nitrogen or potassium.

Table 4 Limitations of biological reference methods appropriate for validation of dietary assessment measures

Reference method	Limitations
Doubly labeled water	Energy only
	Assumptions of model regarding water partitioning may not apply in cases of gross obesity, high alcohol intake, or use of diuretics
	Very expensive
	Analysis technically demanding
Urinary nitrogen: completeness of samples confirmed using PABA	Protein only
	PABA analysis affected by paracetamol and related products
Urinary nitrogen only	Protein only
	Danger of incomplete samples
Biochemical measurements of nutrients in blood or other tissues	Complex relationship with intake mediated by digestion, absorption, uptake, utilization, metabolism, excretion, and homeostatic mechanisms
	Cost and precision of assays
	Invasive
Energy intake:BMR ratio	Imprecision of estimate of BMR based on body weight and regression equations
	Single cutoff point (e.g., EI:BMR <1.1) will not identify low-energy reporters with higher habitual energy expenditures
	Higher estimates of cutoff (e.g., EI:BMR <1.2) captures more true low energy reporters but also more good reporters

It is important to ensure that the urine collections are complete. This necessitates the use of an inert metabolic marker (para-amino benzoic acid (PABA)), which is rapidly absorbed and excreted. Subjects take a divided dose of 240 mg PABA throughout the day. At least 85% of the PABA should be recovered in the urine in a 24-h collection. If the amount recovered is less than 85%, the urine sample may be regarded as incomplete and therefore not suitable for analysis of nitrogen in order to check the completeness of the dietary record. Because paracetamol and related compounds interfere with the PABA assay, a measure of excretion over 115% of the administered dose would be suspect.

As with doubly labeled water, the principal weakness of urinary nitrogen as a marker for the completeness of dietary records is that many foods contain low levels of nitrogen but may be important sources of other nutrients. Any check for the completeness of dietary records based on nitrogen will not assess the presence or absence of these other foods. Also, the issue of dietary distortion is not addressed. Potassium is more widespread in foods, although the largest contributors are usually fruits and vegetables. Using urinary nitrogen and potassium in combination gives a better assessment of the completeness of the recording than any single marker.

Ratio of energy intake to basal metabolic rate Doubly labeled water and urinary nitrogen excretion are particularly useful for assessing the validity of prospectively recorded diets because the time frame of the test and reference measures can be made to coincide. A third technique for assessing validity can be used with both prospective records and recalls of diet. It is based on energy and thus has the limitations of a validating marker relating to a single dietary factor. It has the advantage, however, of being able to be applied to all subjects in a dietary survey because no external reference measure is needed. It is a biomarker in the sense that it relies on a biological measure (body weight) and is best applied when measures of physical activity at the individual level are also available. The assumption is that there should be reasonable agreement between estimated requirement and estimated intake.

Schofield equations can be used to estimate basal metabolic rate (BMR) based on age, gender, and body weight. An individual whose reported energy intake is below the level of energy expenditure likely to be needed to carry out day-to-day activities has probably underreported his or her diet. A typical cutoff point for an acceptable ratio of the energy intake to BMR ratio in an individual is 1.2, taking into account daily variations in energy intake over a period of 7 days of dietary recording and allowing for the inaccuracies of the estimate of BMR based on the Schofield equations. A cutoff of 1.2 will identify only those subjects who underreport and whose levels of activity are low. For subjects with higher levels of activity (e.g., estimated from questionnaire responses), proportionately higher cutoff points are appropriate. It is also possible to estimate an upper probable level of energy expenditure (e.g., 2.5 times BMR, depending on habitual level of activity) and subjects with reported levels of intake over this value may be regarded as being overreporters.

Statistical Assessment of Validity

There are two broad approaches to establishing validity between test and reference measures: comparison of mean values and correlation. The use of mean values is appropriate where group intakes are to be determined or where an absolute measure of intake is required. This is especially important where a threshold value of intake will be used to make recommendations (e.g., recommending an increase in potassium intake because of its association with lower blood pressure and reduced risk of myocardial infarction—there would be no point in recommending additional consumption of potassium for individuals who were identified as having intakes already above the levels that were seen to be protective). The correlation technique (plotting the observed measure against the reference measure) is appropriate where it is important to classify subjects according to high or low intakes because differences in intake are associated with different levels of disease risk. In relation to disease risk, a steeper or shallower slope of observed intake in relation to true intake will have a profound effect on the relative risk estimates in relation to disease outcome. Moreover, the correlation coefficient describes only one aspect of agreement. In practice, both ranking and absolute levels are important in establishing correct diet–disease relationships.

Mathematically, disease risk can be modeled by the expression

$$R(D|T) = \alpha_0 + \alpha_1 T$$

where $R(D|T)$ is the risk of disease D, T is the unobservable true long-term habitual intake of a given food or nutrient relevant to disease risk, α_0 is the underlying risk of disease in the population independent of dietary exposure, and α_1 is the log relative risk (RR) that may be positive (for predisposing factors) or negative (for protective factors).

Because we cannot measure the true dietary exposure, we approximate it using the dietary test measure that is the focus of the validation process. The expression for describing disease risk then becomes

$$R(D|Q) = \alpha_0 + \alpha^* Q$$

where Q is the observed intake, and α^* is the observed log relative risk. In most circumstances, it can be argued that $\alpha^* = \lambda \alpha_1$, where λ is known as the 'attenuation' factor and is equal to the slope of the regression line of T plotted against Q. In most dietary studies, the value for λ is between 0 and 1, but in cases of differential misclassification it may

also be negative. The consequence is that the estimate of disease risk in relation to diet is likely to be different from the true risk (usually tending toward a relative risk of unity).

For a given individual i, the observed measure Q_i will be given by the expression

$$Q_i = (T_i)B + a + \epsilon_i + e_i$$

where T_i is the true measure, and the attenuation factor λ is a function of B (proportional bias), a (constant bias), ϵ_i (random error within a subject, such that the mean of the random error across all subjects is equal to zero), and e_i (bias in the ith subject, such that the mean of the individual biases across all subjects is not equal to zero—this is the consequence of differential misclassification). In practical terms, the aim of a validation study is to quantify these sources of error (see **Table 3** for the main likely sources) and to estimate the value for λ so that the true relative risk α_1 can be estimated using the expression $\alpha_1 = \alpha^*/\lambda$.

It is probable that both the test measure and the reference measure are positively correlated with the truth. This is represented by r_{QT} and r_{RT} in **Figure 5**. There will also be a relationship between the test and reference measures, r_{QR}, given by the expression

$$r_{QR} = r_{QT} \times r_R$$

The relationship between the test measure and the truth can be estimated by solving for r_{QT}:

$$r_{QT} = r_{QR}/r_{RT}$$

Assuming that the reference measures are unbiased, r_{RT} can be estimated by knowing the relationship between within- and between-subject variance in a group of subjects whose records or measures are assumed to be valid (e.g., from whom

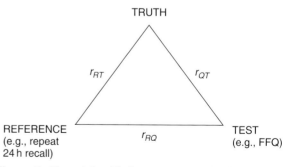

Figure 5 The relationship between test and reference measure and the truth. (Source: Nelson M (1997) The validation of dietary assessments. In: Margetts BM and Nelson M (eds.) *Design Concepts in Nutritional Epidemiology*, 2nd edn. Oxford: Oxford University Press.)

likely under- or overreporters have been excluded) using the expression

$$\sqrt{n/(n + (s_w^2/s_b^2))}$$

where n is the number of repeat observations within one subject, and s_w^2 and s_b^2 are the within- and between-subject variances, respectively. In this way, the likely relationship between the test measure and the truth can be estimated, and the relative risk can be adjusted to account for misclassification of subjects based on the test measure alone.

This approach has two weaknesses. First, if the reference measure is a dietary measure, it does not address the problem of correlation of errors (the tendency for an individual to misreport diet in the same way using the test and reference measures). If errors are correlated between methods, then the observed r_{RQ} is likely to overestimate $r_{RT} \times r_{QT}$; it will appear that the test method is performing better than it actually is performing. If the errors are correlated within methods (e.g., if the same types of within-person bias are occurring from day to day using repeat 24-h recall), then the observed r_{RQ} is likely to underestimate $r_{RT} \times r_{QT}$. The second weakness of this approach is that it does not address the problem of differential misclassification.

A similar technique is the method of triads (**Figure 6**), in which no assumption need be made about the relationships between reference measures and the truth. Instead, the relationships between three measures can be used to estimate values for ρ, which in theory approximate the correlation between each of the measures and the truth. As in the technique described previously, valid estimates of ρ are based on the assumption that the errors in the methods are uncorrelated and that the errors are random and not differentially biased between subjects.

Because the validation process helps to identify subjects who are likely to be misreporting their diet, the temptation may be to exclude from analysis those subjects who have misreported their diet. It may be, however, that the very subjects who are most likely to misreport their food consumption (e.g., people who are overweight) are also those who are at increased risk of disease (e.g., hypertension, heart disease, and colon cancer). In estimating disease risk, therefore, the aim must be to retain all of the subjects in the analysis.

Estimating the components of error and finding appropriate values for λ is the best way to address this issue. A special case is to adjust nutrient intakes to allow for misreporting in some subjects by assuming that true energy intake and true nutrient intake in all subjects are well correlated. Thus, if a subject underreports energy intake, it is assumed that other nutrients will be underreported to a similar extent. By estimating nutrient intake in relation to reported energy intake, subjects can be ranked according to whether, for a given level of energy intake, their nutrient intake was above or below the average. This is known as energy adjustment. To find the energy-adjusted estimate of nutrient intake, the nutrient intakes should be plotted against energy intakes and the regression line and the residual values derived (**Figure 7**). Energy-adjusted nutrient intakes are then computed by adding the residual to the mean nutrient intake. This approach allows all subjects to be included in an analysis, and it provides realistic estimates of intake (unlike computations of nutrient density in which each subject's nutrient intake is divided by his or her energy intake). Like doubly labeled water, however, the

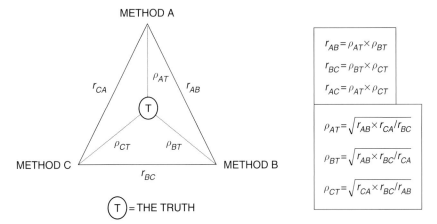

Figure 6 Graphic representation of the method of triads. (Source: Ocké M and Kaaks R (1997) Biochemical markers as additional measurements in dietary validity studies: Application of the method of triads with examples from the European Prospective Investigation into Cancer and Nutrition. *American Journal of Clinical Nutrition* **65**:1240S–1245S.)

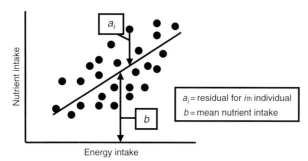

Figure 7 Energy-adjusted nutrient intake for the ith individual $= a_i + b$. (Adapted from Willett WD, Howe GR and Kushi LH (1997) Adjustment for total energy intake in epidemiologic studies. *American Journal of Clinical Nutrition* **65**:1220S–1228S.)

weakness of energy adjustment lies in the fact that not all nutrient intakes are well correlated with energy intake. Overreporting of fruits and vegetables consumption leading to an overestimate of vitamin C intake, for example, would not be appropriately compensated for using energy adjustment if the person was at the same time underreporting his or her fat consumption.

Conclusions

The validation of dietary assessment measures is a necessary part of any dietary investigation. The use of unvalidated instruments is likely to lead to misinterpretation of diet–disease relationships. In most circumstances, unvalidated measures of diet will lead to the conclusion that there is no diet–disease relationship when in reality one exists (bias toward the null). In circumstances in which differential misclassification is at play, it may also lead to the conclusion that there is a relationship when in fact none exists. In order not to waste resources, it is vital to ensure either that dietary assessments are valid or that the errors associated with them are clearly identified and taken into account in the interpretation of diet–disease relationships.

In summary,

- Never take dietary measurements at face value.
- Always include an analysis of errors of dietary data in epidemiological studies.
- Ensure that the validation study sample is representative of the population in the main study.
- Quantify all significant sources of error.
- Obtain measures of within-subject reliability.
- Adjustment of estimates of intake is preferable to excluding misreporters from the diet–disease analysis.

Finally, it is worth noting that virtually all of the discussion in this article relates to nutrient intakes. There is an urgent need to improve our understanding of the validity of measurements of the consumption of foods. Advice on healthy eating is given primarily in terms of foods, not nutrients.

See also: **Dietary Intake Measurement**: Methodology. **Dietary Surveys**. **Energy Expenditure**: Doubly Labeled Water.

Further Reading

Bates CJ, Thurnham DI, Bingham SA *et al.* (1997) Biochemical markers of nutrient intake. In: Margetts BM and Nelson M (eds.) *Design Concepts in Nutritional Epidemiology*, 2nd edn. Oxford: Oxford University Press.

Bingham SA, Cassidy A, Cole T *et al.* (1995) Validation of weighed records and other methods of dietary assessment using the 24 h urine technique and other biological markers. *British Journal of Nutrition* 73: 531–550.

Black AE (2000) Critical evaluation of energy intake using the Goldberg cut-off for energy intake: Basal metabolic rate. A practical guide to its calculation, use and limitations. *International Journal of Obesity* 24: 1119–1130.

Cameron ME and van Staveren WA (eds.) (1988) *Manual on Methodology for Food Consumption Studies*. Oxford: Oxford University Press.

Clayton D and Gill T (1997) Measurement error. In: Margetts BM and Nelson M (eds.) *Design Concepts in Nutritional Epidemiology*, 2nd edn. Oxford: Oxford University Press.

Department of Health (1991) *Report on Health and Social Subjects, 41. Dietary Reference Values for Food Energy and Nutrients for the United Kingdom. Committee on Medical Aspects of Food Policy.* London: HMSO.

Goldberg GR, Black AE, Jebb SA *et al.* (1991) Critical evaluation of energy intake data using fundamental principles of energy physiology: 1. Derivation of cut-off limits to identify underrecording. *European Journal of Nutrition* 45: 569–581.

Kohlmeier L (1991) What you should know about your biomarker. In: Kok FJ and van't Veer P (eds.) *Biomarkers of Dietary Exposure*. London: Smith Gordon.

Margetts BM and Nelson M (1997) *Design Concepts in Nutritional Epidemiology*, 2nd edn. Oxford: Oxford University Press.

Millward DJ (1997) Urine nitrogen as an independent validatory measure of protein intake: Potential errors due to variation in magnitude and type of protein intake. *British Journal of Nutrition* 77: 141–144.

Nelson M (1997) The validation of dietary assessments. In: Margetts BM and Nelson M (eds.) *Design Concepts in Nutritional Epidemiology*, 2nd edn. Oxford: Oxford University Press.

Nelson M, Atkinson M, and Meyer J (1997) *A Photographic Atlas of Food Portion Sizes* London: Ministry of Agriculture, Fisheries and Food.

Prentice AM, Black AE, Coward WA *et al.* (1986) High levels of energy expenditure in obese women. *British Medical Journal* 292: 983–987.

Schatzkin A, Kipnis V, Carroll RJ *et al.* (2003) A comparison of a food frequency questionnaire with a 24-hour recall for use in an epidemiological cohort study: Results from the biomarker-based Observing Protein and Energy Nutrition (OPEN) study. *International Journal of Epidemiology* 32: 1054–1062.

DIETARY SURVEYS

K L Tucker, Tufts University, Boston, MA, USA

Purpose and Design

Dietary surveys are used for multiple purposes and range from measurement of food disappearance at the national level, to food use at the household level, to detailed multiple assessments of individual intake for linkage with health outcomes. Each of these methods has strengths and limitations, depending on the survey purpose (see **Table 1**).

Research Questions and Data Needs

At the national level, information on food use and dietary intake is needed for economic and agricultural policy decision making. For policy makers to advise on food production, food imports, pricing of staple foods, and other factors that affect food availability, they require information on the production, inflow, and outflow of food commodities and products at the national level. Most countries use food balance sheets to measure these flows, and total available nutrients are estimated in relation to the size and composition of the population. These surveys measure overall national food production, imports, and available food stocks, and subtract exports, food used for animals rather than humans, and losses that occur during production, storage, and manufacturing. The FAO has compiled food balance sheets for many countries since 1949, thus allowing useful intercountry comparisons of food availability. However, the aggregate information obtained with food balance sheets does not allow consideration of food distribution within a country and does not quantify food intake or needs of subgroups of the population.

Most countries need more information on household level food use to target food nutrition policies toward groups at need. Household food surveys capture the amounts and types of food that enter a household, and *per capita* intake equivalents are calculated by dividing the total nutrients available in the household from the edible portion of entering foods by the numbers of household members, weighted by specific age and sex. With information on the average *per capita* intake of specific households, it is possible to consider groups at risk of inadequate intake of energy or of specific macro- or micronutrients. For example, these surveys may highlight rural–urban differences, inland–coastal differences, differences by socioeconomic strata, and so on. Such surveys provide critical information within countries for the development and targeting of economic, agricultural, and nutritional policies specific to regions or other subgroups of the population.

Table 1 Advantages and disadvantages of different types of dietary survey

Level	Survey type	Advantages	Disadvantages
National	Food balance sheets	Inexpensive	Crude estimate; no consideration of wastage; does not allow disaggregation to sublevels
Household	Food account method	Inexpensive	Does not account for food consumed away from home, inventories or wastage
	Interviewer-administered list-recall	More detail obtained on foods than in the food account method	List may limit responses; Waste usually not accounted for
	Household diet record	Usually covers one week with great detail; most accurate of household methods	High respondent burden; expensive
Individual	24-h Dietary recall	Detailed information on food intake, good estimate of means by subgroup	Misclassifies individuals; not useful for correlative investigation
	Multiple recalls	Average of multiple days can give good quantitative estimate of usual intake	Expensive
	Food frequency questionnaire	Inexpensive, measures usual intake	Semiquantitative, dependence on food list and recipe assumptions may lead to error in estimation of intake in some subgroups

They do not, however, provide information on individual intakes within the household, and are not useful for understanding age- and sex-specific intakes.

For a detailed understanding of food and nutrient intake by age, sex, and physiologic state, data are needed at the individual level. Surveys of individual dietary intake use methods that range from qualitative food checklists to multiple detailed records of food intake, with quantification of preparation methods and portion sizes. Data at the individual level are used for a variety of purposes and the design of the survey and level of detail utilized will depend on the primary data needs. At the national level, a primary objective is to identify subgroups at risk of inadequate intake of energy or specific nutrients. The important advantage of individual level data is that target age and sex groups may be identified in addition to groups identified by region or other household level characteristics. A further objective is to determine the extent of undernutrition in relation to energy or specific nutrients in the total and subpopulations. This requires consideration of the distribution of intakes in specific age, sex, and physiologic status groups. A more ambitious objective of some national or targeted dietary surveys is to associate aspects of individual dietary intake with the existence of health conditions. This objective requires that survey data be valid and reliable at the individual level and requires the estimation of usual intake by individuals.

Issues in Survey Design

National data on food availability is generally collected with food balance sheets. While not a survey in the formal sense, this is a collection of data from the food sector regarding wholesale distribution. After adjusting for expected losses and wastage, these data are compared to nutrient values and then to the size and composition of the population to calculate *per capita* nutrient availability. Because this is a crude assessment, it generally does not account for all losses or waste and therefore tends to overestimate availability.

In order for a household level survey to be nationally representative, one must carefully consider the sampling design. This is generally done by multilevel selection of regions, then sub-regions, then households, in such a way that the resulting data may be generalized to the national level. In cases where results are required at the regional level, coverage of all regions is necessary, although this will usually increase the cost of the survey. When the objective is more specific than national

description, target areas may be selected, based on risk status or relevance to the question being addressed.

Similarly, for individual level data to be representative of the greater population of individuals, complex sample design is employed to be sure individuals are selected randomly. Decisions on sampling design will generally be a balance between equal opportunity for subject inclusion against logistic and cost considerations of full randomization. For that reason, multi-level complex sampling design is usually employed. This design may be similar to that of the household level survey, with the added step of randomly selecting individuals within households. Although some surveys do select households and then interview all members of the household, this decreases the generalizability of the individual data due to the lack of independence of the observations. Members in the same family, for example, will consume similar foods and therefore will be more like each other than like others in their community. Although this lack of independence can be adjusted in the analysis design, it will require larger total numbers of interviews to achieve representative stability of data estimates and is therefore not usually the most effective design. While the multistage approach of region, subregion, and community also leads to reduced power, this is corrected by consideration of the 'design effect,' which can be calculated by comparing the variation in intake within versus between sampling units at each level. Although the design effect may demand higher overall numbers of surveyed individuals, this is generally considerably less expensive than expanding coverage to all locations.

In addition to the multistage selection of respondents for representation of the general population, many surveys are concerned with subgroups that will not be well represented unless specifically over-sampled. Examples may include pregnant women, ethnic subgroups, or low-income groups. In these cases, individuals that meet the specified characteristic are identified within the existing sampling design, but are then selected in larger numbers than would be representative of the entire population. This allows sufficient sample size to present valid estimates for these groups. When included in measures of the total population, the extent of over-sampling by subgroups can be adjusted using weights that correct for what would otherwise be an over-representation of these groups.

Another design consideration relevant to accurate representation of dietary intake is the timing of the survey. In many countries, intake may vary considerably by season, and it is therefore important that all seasons are represented. Although logistic and cost constraints often limit ideal design planning, it is also optimal if data from all seasons is collected in all survey locations, as opposed to certain regions being collected in the summer and others in the winter. If the latter is the case, comparisons across regions may be compromised. Similarly, intakes are known to differ by day of the week, and overall intakes may be misrepresented if certain days of the week are not included in the data collection plan.

Selection of Dietary Assessment Measure

Household Level

There are several alternative methods of dietary assessment that may be selected to assess intake. At the household level, a commonly used approach may be referred to as the food account method. A person in the household who is responsible for the acquisition and/or use of food is selected to keep a daily record of all the food that enters the household for a specified period – often 1 week. This includes household food purchases, food production, and food received as gifts during that period. This provides a general picture of the food that passes through the household in a given week. There are several limitations to this approach, including the assumption of constant food stores, which may not be the case.

In some locations, it is not feasible for many individuals to record this information accurately. In this case, an interviewer-administered list-recall method is often used. The interviewer asks the responsible household member to recall food purchases, production, or other receipt in the household during a specified period of preceding days, following a list of major foods that are relevant for that country or location. Additional information on age and sex of household members and number of meals each consume at home is collected to calculate adult equivalent *per capita* food availability for the household. Although edible portions of foods are generally considered in quantifying availability, most such surveys do not account for wastage, loss, or use by animals and therefore may overestimate household food use and availability. On the other hand, they do not generally account for food consumed away from the home, thereby underestimating food intake. While useful for economic and food commodity flow information, this type of survey is therefore limited with respect to nutritional intake assessment.

For the purpose of better understanding the dietary intake within households, more elaborate methods are needed. One approach is to use a household diet record. In this case the household respondent is asked not only to report inflows of food, but also to record actual use and preparation of foods in the household over a specified period of time. Food consumed outside the home may also be recorded for each household member as well as the number of individuals, including guests, who are present at each meal. While much more demanding for the respondent, this approach provides a better estimation of the total food consumed by the household than do the inventory methods described above. Estimation of waste is included in some but not all such surveys and is a limitation of most. Because of the heavy respondent burden, nonresponse or incomplete response is also a major problem. With high proportions of nonresponders, the generalizability of the survey is threatened.

Individual Level

A wide variety of methods are available for use at the individual level, and their selection depends on the questions to be addressed balanced with cost considerations. As noted above, major uses of individual intake data from dietary surveys include the description of mean intakes by subgroup, description of the proportions of the population with inadequate intake of specific foods or nutrients, and comparison of dietary intake with individual characteristics, including health status.

For the purpose of describing mean intake of groups and subgroups, the most efficient method is the use of a single 24-h dietary recall per selected individual. For estimating group means, it is most effective to include sufficient numbers of individuals per subgroup to be represented as opposed to completing multiple recalls on a smaller number of individuals. This is the methodology that was, until recently, used in the US National Health and Nutrition Examination Survey (NHANES), providing a good description of average intakes of nutrients by age, sex and ethnic groups. As an aggregate measure, this design has worked very well. However, there are limitations to these estimates and validation against quantified energy expenditure measurements has shown that most people tend to under-report intakes with the 24-h dietary recall method. Further research is needed to better understand whether this tendency to under-report is random or, as some investigations have shown, associated with individual characteristics such as obesity, restrained eating behavior, or social desirability bias in reporting.

The major limitation in the use of single 24-h recalls in a dietary survey is the misclassification of individuals that results from day-to-day variation in individual intake. An individual who on average is a heavy consumer of energy and fat, for example, may on any single day, eat uncharacteristically lightly or vice versa, leading to severe misclassification of individuals in the intake distribution. Although the mean intake is reliable and reasonably valid, the tails of the intake distribution with a single day of intake per person are extended, leading to overestimation of proportions either above or below a specified cut-off point, relative to what is seen when usual intake is assessed as the average of multiple days. The misclassification of individuals relative to their actual usual intake also severely limits the ability to correlate intake data with any individual characteristics, including health status and biomarkers.

Because of the importance of using national or regional survey data to identify the extent of inadequate nutrient intake, there has been considerable discussion on how to assess diet efficiently, yet estimate prevalence of inadequacy. As noted above, the distribution of intake obtained with a single day per individual is extended due to day-to-day variability in intakes. However, with repeated recalls on a representative subset of the population, this day-to-day variability may be quantified and used to adjust the distribution to better represent usual intake. Although they require specialized training to use, statistical methods have been developed to adjust distributions for this purpose. By adjusting the distribution, we are able to pull in the tails and get a more realistic distribution of usual intake and, thereby, a more accurate estimate of the proportion that falls below or above a specified cut-off point.

Because recommended dietary allowances (RDAs) are set as a guideline for nutrient intake that will meet the requirements of most healthy individuals in the population, a cut-off point of two-thirds of the RDA has frequently been used for assessing the proportion with low intake. A more precise way to estimate the relationship between intake and actual requirements was proposed that uses information on the probability that a specific nutrient is inadequate. This method requires information on the requirement distribution for that nutrient, which is then compared with an intake distribution. In actuality, we still have only limited data on the distribution of requirements. In the most current US nutrient intake recommendations, estimated average requirements (EARs) are proposed as well as RDAs. In general, the proportion

of individuals who fall below this EAR, using an intake distribution adjusted for day-to-day variability, are a good estimate of the proportion of the population with inadequate intake.

A third important objective of dietary survey data is to gain a better understanding of the correlates of nutrient intake, but with respect to individual characteristics that may be associated with lower versus higher intake and the extent to which intake is associated with indicators of health. For many nutrients, the day-to-day variation in intake is considerable, and multiple days would be required to achieve stable estimates of intake at the individual level. Without this, the misclassification of individuals in the distribution leads to a weakening in the ability to see associations that may truly be there. An extreme example is vitamin A, which tends to be concentrated in a few foods. If one frequently has liver and carrots, but happened not to on the day of the recall, that individual would be classified as having low vitamin A intake when their usual intake is quite large. Conversely, one who almost never eats these foods, but happened to have liver on the day of the recall would be placed at the upper end of the vitamin A distribution despite the fact that this may have been the only time that year they consumed such a high vitamin A source food. The effect of this is to weaken correlations or regression coefficients so that no association may be seen between intake and outcomes such as plasma retinal or eye health.

There are two ways that this major limitation may be handled in dietary surveys. First, with information from multiple recalls on a subset, it is possible to calculate the ratio of the intra-individual variance, or day-to-day intake variation within individuals, to the inter-individual variance, or difference in intake across individuals. To the extent that intra/inter-individual variance ratios are large, as in the case of vitamin A, the ability to see associations will be severely limited. When inter-individual differences exceed day-to-day variation within subjects, the ability to correlate intakes with other factors is stronger. Unfortunately, in most cases, this variance ratio is sufficiently large that a single day of intake will not allow correlational analyses. The collection and averaging of multiple days of intake will greatly improve this situation. For most nutrients 3 or 4 days are acceptable. However, for some nutrients of interest, including vitamin A and vitamin B_{12}, the variability ratios are so high that an unrealistic number of days is needed for stable estimates. For this reason, many researchers choose to use food frequency questionnaires when correlational analysis is a major objective.

The food frequency questionnaire asks respondents to report the frequency of consumption of a prespecified list of specific foods. Additional questions on portion size and on preparation methods are added in differing ways to different questionnaires. Food frequency questionnaires provide a lower cost alternative to multiple recall days, but also have limitations. Because they rely on a food list, their validity is dependent on the representativeness of that list, and of portion size and recipe assumptions. Most food frequencies in wide use have been developed using data that represent the major sources of nutrient intake in a population. However, individuals with divergent eating patterns will not be well represented using this tool.

When single recalls are available along with information on the variance ratios for each nutrient, another approach to improving correlational estimates is to use what is called 'deattenuation' methods to correct for the effect of day-to-day variability. Because the effect of this variability is assumed to be random in the population, the ratios provide a mathematical basis from which to estimate what the 'true' association between the nutrient intake and correlated indicator may have been, after accounting for this variability.

Data Analysis and Limitations

Whatever dietary assessment measure is used, the utility of the data is dependent on the translation of reported food intake to nutrient intake. This requires detailed and accurate nutrient databases. The US Department of Agriculture has the most extensive nutrient database in the world, allowing for good estimation of dietary intakes in the US. Most other countries have not conducted this level of food composition analysis for their own locations. Therefore, most databases used throughout the world have obtained at least some of their values from the US nutrient database, adding information as possible from locally analyzed products. However, because the nutrient composition of many foods, including fruits, vegetables, and even animal products can vary widely by growing conditions and specific subvariety, most available nutrient databases remain inadequate. Many use extrapolated values from similar foods when chemical analysis has not been completed. Furthermore, it is common for many country-specific databases to include information only on macronutrients and a few selected vitamins and minerals. The continual arrival of new manufactured products also complicates the upkeep and management of food composition databases.

Consequently, considerable database work remains to expand the utility of worldwide dietary surveys.

Once the nutrient data are calculated, data are generally tabulated to present age, sex and, sometimes, ethnic specific mean intakes and standard deviations. Further disaggregation by region, socioeconomic group, or other group characteristic can by very helpful in understanding the macro-distribution of nutrient intake and for targeting specific groups with nutrition intervention programs. If a complex survey design was used, or if systematic nonparticipation was observed, sampling weights must be applied to adjust the means and standard errors.

Using the methods described above, estimates of the population with low intakes of specific nutrients are also calculated. Beyond these descriptive measures, comparison of nutrient intakes with individual characteristics and health measures generally requires multiple regression analysis with appropriate adjustment for potentially confounding variables. Again, when complex survey designs have been used, the inclusion of sample weights and appropriate adjustment of variances is needed. Specialized statistical software for use with survey data is available. In cases where a single recall has been used, substantial weakening, or attenuation, of associations is likely, but use of 'deattenuation' methods can, at a minimum, provide information on the likely extent of this attenuation. When food frequency data are used, it is important to include some validation methods, preferably with comparison to key biomarkers of nutritional status, but at least to multiple recalls on a subset. This is particularly true when a new questionnaire is being used, but is also important over time as the food supply and food habits change in the population.

See also: **Dietary Intake Measurement**: Methodology; Validation. **Nutritional Assessment**: Anthropometry; Biochemical Indices. **Nutritional Surveillance**: Developed Countries; Developing Countries. **Vitamin A**: Biochemistry and Physiological Role.

Further Reading

Briefel RB and Sempos CT (eds.) (1992) *Dietary Methodology Workshop for the Third National Health and Nutrition Examination Survey.* Vital Health Stat 4 (27). Hyattsville, MD: National Center for Health Statistics.

Food and Nutrition Board, Institute of Medicine (2001) *Dietary Reference Intakes: Applications in Dietary Assessment.* Washington, DC: National Academy Press.

Gibson RS (1990) *Principles of Nutritional Assessment.* New York: Oxford University Press.

Interagency Board for Nutrition Monitoring and Related Research (1995) *Third Report on Nutrition Monitoring in the United States*, vol. 2. Washington, DC: US Department of Agriculture.

Murphy SP (2003) Collection and analysis of intake data from the Integrated Survey. *Journal of Nutrition* **133**: 585S–589S.

Subcommittee on Criteria for Dietary Evaluation, National Research Council (1986) *Nutrient Adequacy: Assessment*

Using Food Consumption Surveys. Washington, DC: National Academy Press.

Thompson FE and Byers T (1994) Dietary assessment resource manual. *Journal of Nutrition* **124**: 2245S–2317S.

Willett W (1998) *Nutritional Epidemiology*, 2nd edn. New York: Oxford University Press.

DIETETICS

P A Judd, University of Central Lancashire, Preston, UK

This article briefly relates the history of the development of dietetics, discusses the changing roles of the dietitian, and outlines the current involvement of dietitians in some general and specialist areas of practice.

Definition and History of Dietetics

Dietetics is defined as 'the application of the science of nutrition to the human being in health and disease.' However, the term 'dietitian,' used to describe a practitioner of dietetics, was in use long before the science of nutrition had become an accepted discipline. The first use of the title of dietitian was recorded in 1899 in the United States when the dietitian was described as 'a person working in a hospital who provided nutritious meals to patients.' The earliest dietitians were therefore mainly concerned with provision of food and usually trained as home economists. The role of the dietitian has changed markedly in the past 50 years, and the dietitian is now accepted as the expert in the planning and evaluation of nutritional care for patients requiring therapeutic dietary regimens as well as for the population in general.

The profession of dietetics is a relatively young one, first formalized in the United States in 1917 with the foundation of the American Dietetic Association (ADA). In the United Kingdom, the first dietitians were nurses and the first dietetic department opened in the Edinburgh Royal Infirmary in 1924. The British Dietetic Association (BDA) was established in 1936. The profession developed rapidly in other countries, and in 2004 there were 23 dietetic associations registered with the European Federation of the Association of Dietitians and 36 national dietetic associations registered with the International Committee of Dietetic Associations.

The Role of the Dietitian

The first dietitians (with the exception of those concerned mainly with food service provision) worked mainly in hospitals. Clinical dietetics and the acute hospital service still claim a large proportion of the graduates from dietetics but other areas of work are increasingly becoming more important. In the United Kingdom, changes in the emphasis of health care, particularly the change from acute (hospital) care to care in the primary health care setting, has resulted in a marked increase in the number of dietitians based in primary care.

Dietitians also have many other roles outside the health services. Increasingly practitioners work with government agencies, for example, in dietary surveys of the population, in execution and evaluation of nutrition intervention programs, and advising on the practical application of policy. In industry, they may work as advisors to food companies, wholesale and retail suppliers of food, and with companies producing specialized dietary products. In addition, dietitians are increasingly working independently as consultants, for example, in private practice, journalism, and sports nutrition. The scope of the dietitians' work is illustrated by **Table 1**, which lists the special interest groups for dietitians in the United Kingdom.

Whatever aspect of work a dietitian chooses, one of his or her primary roles will be that of an educator, whether this be in assisting individuals to understand and apply a therapeutic regimen; teaching doctors, nurses, or other health professionals about nutrition and dietetics so that they may carry out their own role more effectively; teaching groups of people about aspects of preventative nutrition; or writing an article for the scientific or lay press. The ability to communicate is therefore central to every dietitian's role.

Table 1 Specialist groups and special interest groups in the British Diatetic Association (2004)

Specialist groups	Special interest groups
Community Nutrition Group	Burns Interest Group
Diabetes Management and Education Group	D – Liver (Dietitians Working in Liver Disease)
Dietitians in HIV and AIDS	
Freelance Dietitians Group	Dietitians in Neurological Therapy
Mental Health Group	
Multicultural Nutrition Group	Dietitians in Sport and Exercise Nutrition Group
Food Counts	
Nutritional Advisory Group for Elderly People	Dietitians Working in Obesity Management (UK)
National Dietetic Managers Group	Gastroenterology Interest Group
Oncology Group	
Pediatric Group	Northern Eating Disorders Dietitians Interest Group
Parenteral and Enteral Nutrition Group	Nutritionists in Industry
Renal Nutrition Group	Pediatric Renal Interest Group
UK Heart and Thoracic Dietitians	UK Dietitians Cystic Fibrosis (CF) Interest Group

The Dietitian's Role in Food Service

In the United States and countries that follow the US model hospital dietitians work in either administrative or clinical (therapeutic) areas. Administrative dietitians manage the provision of food services for all patients and staff. They are responsible for food production and quality control in the delivery of the hospital meal service as well as ensuring their nutritional adequacy. They are also often responsible for budgeting and staffing of the dietary departments and usually relate to other administrators and managers, having little or no direct contact with patients or medical staff. The clinical dietitian is the person who has direct contact with patients and the medical and paramedical staff involved in their care.

In the United Kingdom, very few dietitians have overall responsibility for food service. However, there is usually close liaison between the dietitians and the catering manager in hospital practice to ensure the provision of nutritionally sound selective menus. The dietetic manager will also be consulted on matters of policy, such as the implications of changes in food preparation systems or the introduction of healthy eating policies. It is accepted now that many patients (especially elderly people) are malnourished when they enter

the hospital and that this malnourishment may get worse during the hospital stay. Dietitians are therefore very much involved in attempts to ensure that every patient has a nutritionally adequate diet.

Clinical or Therapeutic Dietetics

The term 'therapeutic dietetics' is used in the United Kingdom to describe the work of the dietitian in his or her direct dealings with patients who require 'special diets' for various reasons. In the United States, the corresponding term is 'medical nutrition therapy' and the importance of this is recognized by its acceptance as allowable treatment by medical insurance companies. Medical nutrition therapy includes nutritional diagnostic, therapeutic, and counselling services provided by a registered dietitian and can

effectively treat and manage disease conditions;
reduce or eliminate the need for prescription drug use;
help reduce complications in patients with disease; and
improve patients' overall health and quality of life.

The role of the clinical dietitian has broadened in the past decade, with respect to both the range of conditions that are encountered and the setting in which the work is done. In the past, the role of the therapeutic dietitian was to calculate, teach, and facilitate compliance to a range of dietary regimens prescribed by medical or surgical practitioners for specific disorders. These functions are still important and are extending as improvements in medicine enable patients who would previously have died in childhood to survive to adulthood with continuing needs for nutritional care. For example, patients with cystic fibrosis require nutritional support as their lungs deteriorate and women with hyperphenylalaninemia need dietary advice in order to help them achieve successful pregnancies. The dietitian is an important member of the multidisciplinary team dealing with many clinical conditions.

In addition to these roles, dietitians are increasingly involved in the assessment and support of patients not traditionally seen as requiring a therapeutic diet. For example, planning and implementing feeding for patients who are nutritionally compromised as a result of aging, trauma, surgery, or chronic illnesses such as cancer or AIDS is now an important part of the workload of the dietitian working in both acute and community settings.

Clinical dietitians are increasingly involved in decisions about the appropriateness of particular dietary regimens or the type of nutritional support required and in many institutions are responsible for prescribing the patients' diet in consultation with the physician or surgeon, who recognises the dietitian as the expert. In acute care a dietitian is an important member of the nutrition support team, working alongside nurses, pharmacists, and medical staff to advise on the feeding of all patients who need nutritional support.

The dietitian must be aware of advances in clinical practice, and many dietitians are now involved both in research on the development of new treatments and in evaluating current practice. In the past decade, the requirement to demonstrate evidence-based practice and satisfy the demands of clinical governance within acute care has increased the need for understanding and contribution to the development of the evidence base. Dietitians are increasingly obtaining research qualifications and initiating their own projects, working alongside experienced investigators and in multidisciplinary teams.

In the United Kingdom, consultant posts for Allied Health Professionals, who are considered to be 'experts in a specialist clinical field, bringing innovation, personal mastery, and influence to clinical leadership and strategic direction,' have recently been introduced. The consultants are expected to have exceptional skills and advanced levels of clinical judgment, knowledge, and experience and be able to enhance quality in areas of assessment, diagnosis, management, and evaluation, improving patient outcomes and extending the dietitian's role. Although in early 2004 there were only two such dietetic posts (in diabetes and oncology), the number will doubtless increase.

In the United Kingdom a shortage of dietitians and the recognition that many of the tasks carried out by dietitians did not require such highly qualified practitioners have resulted in the recent official recognition of the role of assistant practitioner by the BDA. Dietetic assistants (or community nutrition assistants) are now working under the supervision of registered dietitians, carrying out many of the tasks that do not require specialist input. In the United States and some other countries, diet technicians have been undertaking these roles for some years and the American Dietetic Association has recognized training programs for them; such training programs are being developed in the United Kingdom.

Examples of Specialist Roles in Dietetics

Renal Dietetics

Renal dietitians are usually attached to specialized renal units and are an integral part of the team involved in the treatment of people suffering from varying degrees of renal impairment, whether acute or chronic. In the United States, there is a legal requirement related to funding of patient care that states that a qualified dietitian must be part of the professional team that develops long- and short-term care plans for renal patients. The dietitian, together with the nephrologist, has responsibility for nutritional assessment, the diet prescription, and for monitoring responses to treatment. In addition, he or she must be able to devise appropriate individualised dietary plans, taking into account any other ongoing disease processes or conditions (e.g., diabetes mellitus), and will teach the patient and family how to manipulate the diet. The dietitian will also monitor dietary compliance. A thorough knowledge of physiology and the pathological processes involved in the various kidney diseases and an ability to interpret the patient's biochemical data are therefore essential for the renal dietitian.

Some disorders may resolve with treatment, whereas others may become chronic and result in permanent kidney failure. In progressive renal disease, patients may initially be managed using diet and drugs alone but as the kidneys fail will require replacement therapy, such as peritoneal dialysis, hemodialysis, or transplantation. Each of these stages requires different dietary treatment. The dietitian will deal with a variety of patients with different types of disease and at different stages of progression, with different needs with respect to diet, and will also have to teach the patient how to cope with changes in diet that follow as he or she changes from one treatment to another.

Nutritional Support

Nutritional support of patients who are unable to feed themselves adequately by the normal oral route is an important area of practice. The dietitian's involvement will include the assessment of the nutritional status of the patient, decisions about the most suitable method of nutritional support, and advising on provision of appropriate nutrition. This may range from prescribing oral supplements for the patient who cannot eat enough to designing and advising on complete parenteral nutrition regimens for the unconscious patient in intensive care. Between these two extremes will be the patients who need enteral feeds to provide complete or supplementary nutrition for a variety of reasons and for periods varying from a few days to a lifetime.

Patients requiring nutritional support may be acutely ill or may require long-term feeding, sometimes at home. The dietitian must be able to assess the nutritional requirements of each individual and design appropriate feeding regimens in all circumstances. Many patients will be sent home while still being tube fed, either enterally or parenterally, and the community dietitian as well as the dietitian in the acute hospital will both be closely involved in the patient's care and in monitoring progress.

Diabetes Care and Education

Traditionally, the dietitian always had an important role in the treatment of patients with diabetes mellitus (DM), and the radical changes in dietary approaches during the past 15–20 years have emphasized this role. In the latter part of the twentieth century there was a move away from the use of diets low in carbohydrate in the treatment of diabetes and the basis for the treatment of all people with DM, whether young and insulin dependent or older and treated by diet alone or diet and hypoglycemic drugs, tended to rely on the supply of an appropriate amount of energy as a low-fat diet with at least 50% of energy from foods rich in complex carbohydrates and nonstarch polysaccharides. In addition, the recognition that similar amounts of carbohydrate from different foods have different effects on blood glucose levels, and that this response may be further effected by other foods eaten with them, has led to less stress on absolute intakes of carbohydrate and more toward a qualitative approach to the diet.

Many established diabetics found the change in dietary treatment confusing and have needed help in switching to the new regimen, and newly diagnosed patients also need help in learning to manipulate and control this lifelong disorder. Many dietitians have also been involved in the research that has underpinned the progression of dietary treatment and are now evaluating its effects.

HIV and AIDS

The dietetic care of patients with HIV and AIDS has become increasingly important in the past decade. Dietitians may work with people who are HIV positive to help them optimize their nutritional status and resist the opportunistic infections that eventually cause death in patients with frank AIDS. Once the person develops AIDS, the dietitian's role becomes both therapeutic and palliative, devising and implementing with the patient regimens that enable him or her to satisfy nutritional requirements when, for example, disease of the gastrointestinal tract results in multiple malabsorption or cancer results in weight loss and anorexia. The advent of new, multidrug regimens that require careful planning of meals to match their absorption characteristics and that have side effects affecting nutritional status has made the dietitian's role even more important.

Pediatric Dietetics

The pediatric dietitian has a unique role in that they have to combine the metabolic requirements of the disease process or condition with the normal requirements for growth and development. With the advances in early diagnosis of many complex metabolic conditions, children may require complicated diets that are very different from those of the rest of their family and peers, need constant modification as the child grows, and may be lifelong. The dietitian is responsible for modifying the diet as necessary to take account of the patient's metabolic requirements, any feeding difficulties, mechanical or physiological, and the patient's food preferences and dislikes as he or she grows. The dietitian is an essential part of the support system for children with inborn errors of metabolism such as phenylketonuria and cystic fibrosis, conditions such as renal or heart disease, food allergies, diabetes, and many others, being able to tailor the diet to the patient's specific needs and having access to information about special foods and products of which the care provider may be unaware or have difficulty locating.

The increase in overweight and obese children and adolescents and the consequent increase in type 2 diabetes in young people is a new challenge for the pediatric dietitian.

The pediatric dietitian has an important role as an educator, often teaching the child's parents initially and later the child how to cope with the constraints of a special diet both at home and at school. As is the case with adult patients, the dietitian will often be able to put the child and family in contact with support groups in which newly diagnosed patients or parents will be helped by others with firsthand experience of the disease and its treatment.

Other Areas of Specialization

There are many other areas of clinical dietetics in which individuals may specialize, including obesity, oncology, liver disease, gastroenterology, eating disorders, gerontology, and care of the mentally ill or mentally handicapped. Many of the activities in these areas and those described in the previous sections are not confined to the hospital but require input from the dietitian in the community.

Dietetics in the Community

Community dietitians fulfill a variety of roles that may range from working mainly in clinical dietetics in the community setting (e.g., advising a variety of patients in a general practitioner's clinic) to being a public health nutritionist advising the local health or social services on aspects of food policy. In recent years, due to the changing emphasis in health care, the number of community dietitians in the United Kingdom has increased markedly. The main focus of the increase has been in supplying clinical (therapeutic) care to the primary health care setting and approximately 21% of UK community dietitians surveyed in 1997 stated that this was their only role. Approximately half of the respondents to the survey were involved in health promotion activity as well as clinical work, but only 9% worked solely in health promotion.

Many dietitians working in health promotion achieve their objectives by educating other professional groups, such as doctors, nurses, health visitors, and midwives, who will then pass the specific knowledge on to the individual or groups of patients. Prevention of diseases that may be diet related has recently become a much more important issue, and dietitians are working with schools, health education departments, and industry to try to educate the public to consume a healthier diet. Dietitians also work as advisors in government departments and are therefore involved in planning nutrition policies for the country as a whole.

Dietitians in Research and Education

The advances in all areas of nutritional knowledge, both in terms of achieving optimal health and prevention of disease and in therapeutic nutrition, have led to an increasing number of dietitians working in research. The combination of nutritional and medical knowledge and the ability to translate these into terms of foods eaten means that the dietitian has a unique role to play. Dietitians often approach research from a deductive perspective (i.e., in order to understand or solve difficulties observed in practice) and the results of this research will often have practical significance and can be incorporated into treatments. Evaluation of practice can also be considered as part of this deductive process and is essential in the current health care climate, in which increasing reliance is put on measuring effectiveness and the use of evidence-based medicine. In addition, dietitians are increasingly involved in the basic experimental and analytical scientific research that is essential for nutrition and dietetics to advance in both clinical and nonclinical areas. Involvement in research has led to registration for higher degrees and the number of dietitians with masters' degrees or doctorates is now considerable in countries such as the United States, United Kingdom, Canada, and Australia.

Research is also seen as an important part of the role of those dietitians employed in universities and colleges to teach dietetic and other students. In the United Kingdom and other countries, there is a requirement that each dietetic training course has registered dietitians on the staff, and in many cases these people also work in the NHS in order to keep up-to-date with current practice. Dietitians have been involved for many years in the education of other professional groups, including nurses, midwives, and pharmacists. Recently, advances have been made in convincing those in charge of medical education at undergraduate and postgraduate levels of the importance of nutrition in medical education, and this is also seen as an important area in which dietitians should be involved.

Dietetics Education and Training

The following quotation from the introduction of *The Manual of Dietetic Practice* (Thomas, 2001) summarizes some of the skills needed by a dietitian—all of which must be acquired during preregistration and continuing professional development. The emphasis here is on the role of the clinical dietitian; additional skills will be acquired by the dietitian working in public health and policy:

> While principles of care can be standardised, the way in which they are applied has to vary to take account of individual needs, problems, lifestyle, associated health risks, and readiness to change. In order to provide effective care the modern dietitian has to exercise considerable clinical judgement in deciding how a specific set of circumstances may be most appropriately managed. This requires more than just nutritional knowledge. The modern-day dietitian has to make a global risk assessment when setting nutritional goals, have an understanding of human behaviour in order to achieve dietary change, acquire the interviewing and counselling skills necessary for meaningful dialogue between patient and professional, and have the ability to evaluate whether objectives have been achieved.
>
> (page x)

It is now therefore accepted that the practice of dietetics requires a wide range of knowledge and skills that are achieved by both academic study and practice learning. As the scope of dietetic practice has expanded over the years, the preregistration education and training programs have continually adapted to ensure that the practitioner has the current knowledge and skills required. The education and training of a dietitian usually comprises a degree program (either BSc or MSc), based in a university, including or followed by a period of practical training (or internship) based in recognized hospital dietetic departments.

Preregistration programs include coverage of basic and applied sciences (chemistry, biochemistry, physiology, nutrition, and microbiology) as well as social sciences (psychology and sociology). In addition, because dietetics is concerned with feeding people, a knowledge of the food habits of populations together with detailed knowledge of food composition and food preparation is essential. To this basic foundation is added knowledge of medicine, pathology, and the therapeutic uses of dietary treatment and, increasingly emphasized, the development of skills required to communicate with all types of people whether counselling individuals or teaching groups.

During the practical training or internship, the student dietitian learns to apply the theory learned at university with individuals or groups of people. The training covers all aspects of dietetic practice and the students spend time in different settings, including community care and, in some countries, large-scale catering establishments. In order to become a registered practitioner, the students must demonstrate that they have both good theoretical knowledge and are competent practically.

In the United States, United Kingdom, Canada, Australia, New Zealand, South Africa, The Netherlands, and many other countries training programs are regulated by bodies external to the educational establishments and successful completion of such a regulated training allows registration as a dietitian. In the United States, regulation of courses and training programs is carried out by the ADA and in the United Kingdom by the Health Professions's Council (HPC), in conjunction with the Quality Assurance Agency of the Higher Education Funding Council. In the United Kingdom, only registered dietitians may be employed in the National Health Service. The registration body, in each case, produces a statement of conduct that describes the role and responsibilities of the registered dietitian, and failure to work within this statement of conduct may result in disciplinary action and removal from the register. In the United Kingdom, since 2003 this code of conduct has been presented as 'standards of proficiency' and on registration the registered dietitian must sign a document that involves taking responsibility to work only in areas in which he or she is competent to practice.

Registration in one country does not automatically mean that a dietitian can work elsewhere in the world because levels of education and training are not always comparable from country to country. Within Europe, for example, the education level and skills of dietitians vary widely and there is currently a move within the European Federation of Dietitians to develop benchmarks for dietetic qualifications. The registering body will therefore consider applications from dietitians from other countries and suggest further training if appropriate.

Continuing education and demonstration of continuing competence to practice are increasingly being seen as vital in this rapidly changing profession; in the United States there has long been a requirement to demonstrate continuing education, and continuing registration is dependent on this. In the United Kingdom, it will soon become a requirement to demonstrate continued competence to practice for continued registration with the HPC. The BDA, the professional association for dietitians, has well-developed systems for assisting dietitians in both accessing and recording continuous professional development. The provision of validated specialist courses, the development of a Diploma in Advanced Dietetic Practice, which recognizes CPD over a 5-year period, and most recently the support for a Masters Course in Advanced Dietetic Practice are examples of this. In Australia, continuing professional development is recognized by the status of Accredited Practising Dietitian.

See also: **Arthritis**. **Burns Patients**. **Children**: Nutritional Requirements; Nutritional Problems. **Celiac Disease**. **Colon**: Nutritional Management of Disorders. **Cystic Fibrosis**. **Diabetes Mellitus**: Dietary Management. **Food Allergies**: Diagnosis and Management. **Gall Bladder Disorders**. **Gout**. **Handicap**: Down's Syndrome. **Hyperlipidemia**: Nutritional Management. **Hypertension**: Nutritional Management. **Inborn Errors of Metabolism**: Classification and Biochemical Aspects; Nutritional Management of Phenylketonuria. **Infection**: Nutritional Management in Adults. **Low Birthweight and Preterm Infants**: Nutritional Management. **Obesity**: Prevention; Treatment. **Older People**: Nutritional Management of Geriatric Patients. **Stroke, Nutritional Management**. **Surgery**: Long-term Nutritional Management.

Further Reading

American Dietetic Association (1995) Position of the American Dietetic Association: Cost-effectiveness of medical nutrition therapy. *Journal of the American Dietetic Association* 95(1): 88–91.

American Dietetic Association (2003) Position of the American Dietetic Association: Integration of medical nutrition therapy and pharmacotherapy. *Journal of the American Dietetic Association* 100(10): 1363–1370.

Bateman EC (1986) *A History of the British Dietetic Association. The Second Twenty-Five Years 1936–1986*. Sunderland, UK: Edward Thompson.

Council for Professions (2000) *Supplementary to Medicine: Dietitian's Board Pre-registration Education and Training.* London: Council for Professions.

Department of Health (1994) *Targeting Practice: The Contribution of State Registered Dietitians. Health of the Nation.* London: HMSO.

Department of Health (1994) *Nutrition Core Curriculum for Nutrition Education of Health Professionals.* London: HMSO.

Fox C (1999) *Community Dietetics: Supporting the Future.* Birmingham, UK: Community Nutrition Group of the British Dietetic Association.

Judd PA, Butson S, Hunt P *et al.* (1997) Pre-registration training for dietitians—Report of the Dietitians Board/BDA working group on pre-registration training. *Journal of Human Nutrition and Dietetics* **10**: 157–162.

Thomas B (ed.) (2001) *The Manual of Dietetic Practice*, 3rd edn. Oxford: Blackwell Science.

Digestibility *see* **Bioavailability**

DRUG–NUTRIENT INTERACTIONS

K G Conner, Johns Hopkins Hospital, Baltimore, MD, USA

Introduction

Understanding the interactions between dietary constituents and pharmacological compounds is essential to monitor drug therapy correctly and to assess the potential nutritional impact of medications. Most therapeutic agents exhibit some form of interaction that ultimately affects the nutritional status of the host, by altering absorption or utilization of nutrients. Frequently, these changes are not readily identified or may be obscured by the underlying disease.

The interactions between therapeutic agents and nutrients are part of the large number of interactions occurring between nutritional and non-nutritional constituents of the human diet. These constituents include all substances added to the food chain – incidentally or deliberately – during harvesting, processing, packaging, distribution, and preparation of foods. Some examples are pesticides, food additives, antibiotics, hormones, and environmental toxins.

Drug–nutrient interactions operate in two directions: drugs can have a significant impact on nutrient absorption and utilization, and the nutritional status of the host affects the drug's ability to be absorbed and transported and to exert an effect on the target tissues.

Drug–nutrient interactions can be broadly classified into two categories: direct physicochemical interaction and physiological or functional interaction. Drug–nutrient interactions can also be classified according to their site of occurrence: within the food matrix, in the gastrointestinal (GI) tract, or during transport, metabolism, and excretion. The mechanisms and sites of drug–nutrient interactions are listed in **Table 1**.

Table 1 Mechanisms and sites of drug–nutrient interactions

Site	Mechanism	Effect
Food matrix	Binding and chelation	Decreases bioavailability
Gastrointestinal tract	Changes in gastrointestinal motility, binding and chelation, bile-acid concentration, and gastric pH	Increase in transit time reduces absorption, decreases bioavailability, and reduces absorption of fat-soluble nutrients
Circulation	Albumin concentration	Affects absorption of iron, vitamin B_{12}, and other substances
	Competitors for albumin binding	Decreases transport of bound substances; displaces albumin-bound nutrients (fatty acids, tryptophan, etc.)
Target tissues	Antagonistic effects	May increase requirements for antagonized nutrients
	Enzyme activities	Reduced concentration of enzyme product
Excretion	Renal function	Increased excretion may lower nutrient levels, increasing requirements
	Sequestration	As above

Physicochemical Interactions

Physicochemical interactions usually involve some form of molecular interaction between the drug and a nutrient, and occur primarily during digestion and absorption. The usual consequence of this interaction is a reduction in the bioavailability of the drug and/or the nutrient. A well-known example of this is the binding of metals by the antibiotic tetracycline.

Functional Interactions

Functional Interactions in the Gastrointestinal Tract

Functional interactions in the GI tract are particularly significant because alterations in GI function are likely to affect the digestion and absorption both of the drug and of a number of nutrients. The most common GI functional effects are as follows.

Changes in GI motility A reduction in transit time may lead to decreased absorption. There are a large number of drugs that affect gut motility, whether this is their primary therapeutic effect or not. Conversely, food composition also affects motility. Dietary fiber not only increases motility but also may trap other nutrients and drugs and reduce their bioavailability.

Changes in gastric-acid output Reduced production of chloride with a subsequent increase in gastric pH retards gastric emptying and may alter the balance between ionized and nonionized forms of therapeutic agents.

Reduction in the concentration of bile acids A reduction in the concentration of bile acids will affect the absorption of most fat-soluble compounds. Lower bile-acid concentration may result from increased binding and excretion or from decreased production. For example, the antibiotic neomycin binds to bile acids and increases their faecal excretion, thus reducing their luminal concentration and, in this fashion, decreasing the absorption of fat-soluble vitamins. This interaction, like many others, can be used therapeutically to reduce bile-acid turnover in patients with certain liver diseases and to lower cholesterol levels by reducing their reabsorption.

Alterations in the GI microflora Alterations in the GI microflora may affect the availability of nutrients produced by the normal gut flora, such as vitamin B_{12}'. Since many drugs are susceptible to bacterial metabolism, changes in the gut flora may also affect drug bioavailability. In certain cases, drug cleavage by intestinal microorganisms is an expected and

necessary step for adequate drug action. For example, the anti-inflammatory agent 5-aminosalicylic acid is given as its precursor sulfasalazine, which is converted into the active compound by colonic bacteria. An altered colonic flora will affect the production of the active compound. Drugs can also affect nutrient absorption by directly inhibiting protein synthesis in the enterocyte. Since most transport systems require active protein synthesis and turnover, such inhibition results in a decreased rate of nutrient absorption. Furthermore, certain drugs undergo initial metabolism in the enterocyte, before reaching the bloodstream. Alterations in protein synthesis in the enterocyte, or an impaired turnover of the intestinal epithelia, will also affect this process.

Interactions Affecting Transport, Metabolism, and Excretion

Functional Synergism or Antagonism

The biological actions of nutrients and drugs can be synergistic or antagonistic, occur at different times after exposure, and affect a variety of target tissues. Some of the most common mechanisms are as follows.

Alterations in drug transport Drugs circulate in the bloodstream as free compounds or bound to other constituents, usually proteins. Drugs vary greatly in their propensity to bind to circulating proteins, covering virtually the entire spectrum from 0 to 100%. For a given drug, the bound fraction tends to be relatively constant under physiological conditions, but responds to changes in pH, electrolyte balance, and the presence of competing molecules. The major transport protein in plasma is albumin, and its concentration and the presence of other compounds with an affinity for albumin binding will affect the amount of drug that will ultimately be transported by this protein.

Increase in nutrient catabolism Certain drugs stimulate detoxifying systems, such as the cytochrome P-450 pathway. Activation of this system may result in increased catabolism of certain nutrients. In other cases, drugs directly affect nutrient catabolism, as in the case of anticonvulsant drugs, which stimulate vitamin D catabolism in the liver.

Changes in drug metabolism Certain nutrients (such as those found in grapefruit) can inhibit the activity of cytochrome P-450. Cytochrome P-450-3A is the only isoform affected in a clinically significant way. The mucosal cells of the small intestine are affected to a greater degree than the hepatic cytochrome P-450-3A. Certain HMG-CoA reductase inhibitors (statins), simavastin, and lovastatin can have a significant interaction with grapefruit juice.

Biological antagonism Biological antagonism occurs when drug and nutrient have opposite biological actions, as is the case, for example, with vitamin K and salicylates in the coagulation process.

Increased nutrient losses Many drugs directly or indirectly enhance the urinary excretion of nutrients. Examples are the increased urinary losses of electrolytes caused by aminoglycoside antibiotics and amphotericin B antifungals, and the increase in urinary ascorbic acid excretion induced by barbiturates.

Host-related Functional Interactions

Nutrients and nutritional status can also affect drug action and disposition. Perhaps the most significant host-related factor affecting drug disposition is protein synthesis. Altered protein synthesis, usually resulting from insufficient dietary protein intake or severe diseases, will affect absorption, transport, metabolism, and excretion, as these are all protein-dependent processes. The role of plasma albumin in drug transport was discussed above and will certainly be affected by impaired albumin synthesis and/or sequestration in the extravascular space, as seen in protein-energy malnutrition. It should be noted, however, that malnutrition affects many aspects of drug metabolism, not all in the same direction. For example, drug delivery may be reduced by impaired albumin concentration, but the drug concentration in the bloodstream may be increased as a result of impaired clearance, which is also affected by malnutrition.

The plasma amino-acid profile may affect the efficacy of drug entry into the central nervous system. At the blood–brain barrier, certain drugs are transported into the brain by the same transport system that carries the large neutral amino-acids; thus they must compete with them for use of the carrier binding sites. Diet composition, by affecting the postprandial amino-acid profile, may significantly affect the clinical efficacy of drugs such as L-dopa, used in the treatment of Parkinson's disease.

Body composition is also a relevant determinant of drug disposition and action. Although most drug dosages are calculated by total body weight, most drugs act only in the fat-free body mass. Thus, at a given body weight, individuals with more body fat will tend to receive a higher effective dose than those with less body fat. The amount of body fat is also important for drugs that are stored in adipose tissue.

Major Drug–Nutrient Interactions of Clinical Relevance

Table 2 provides information on the major drug–nutrient interactions of clinical relevance. The list reflects well-known interactions of drugs that have been on the market for some time. The US Food and Drug Administration (FDA) maintains an on-line database of recently reported interactions and interactions of new drugs. The database can be assessed at http://www.fda.gov.

Table 2 Major drug–nutrient interactions of clinical relevance

Drug	Class	Food/nutrient	Effect/mechanism
Acarbose	Antidiabetic	Food	Delays carbohydrate breakdown and glucose absorption
		Iron	Decreased iron absorption
Acetaminophen	Analgesic	Food	May delay extended release; high-pectin food delays absorption
		Alcohol	Increased risk of hepatotoxicity
Acetohexamide	Antidiabetic	Glucose	Hypoglycaemia
		Alcohol	Flushing, headache, nausea, vomiting, sweating, tachycardia
		Sodium	Hyponatremia, SIADH
Acyclovir	Antiviral	Food	No effect; may take with meals
Aluminum hydroxide	Antacid	Thiamin	Affects bioavailability, owing to pH
		Iron	Decreased iron absorption
		Phosphorus	Inhibits phosphorus absorption
		Vitamin A	Inhibits vitamin A absorption
Amikacin	Antibiotic	Calcium, potassium, magnesium	Causes renal wasting of these nutrients
Amoxicillin	Antibiotic	Food	Decreased absorption owing to delayed gastric emptying
Amphotericin B	Antifungal	Potassium, magnesium	Causes renal wasting of potassium and magnesium
Ampicillin	Antibiotic	Food	Decreased absorption owing to delayed gastric emptying

Continued

Table 2 Continued

Drug	Class	Food/nutrient	Effect/mechanism
		Potassium	High doses increase urinary potassium losses
Antipyrine		Green vegetables, beef protein	Decreased absorption
Aspirin	Analgesic	Food	Decreased rate of absorption
		Folic acid	Increased excretion of folate
		Amino-acids	Decreased intestinal absorption of amino-acids, increased urinary excretion of tryptophan
		Iron	Chronic high dose 3–4 g day^{-1}, iron deficiency possible
		Alcohol	Gastric irritation, leading to possible gastric bleed
		Curry powder, liquorice, teas, raisins, paprika	Potential salicylate accumulation
		Ascorbic acid, fresh fruits, high vitamin	Increased urinary excretion; decreased concentration in serum and platelets
Astemizole	Antihistamine	Grapefruit juice	May result in cardiotoxicity
		Food	Decreased bioavailability
Atenolol	Antihypertensive	Food	Delayed absorption
Atovaquone	Antibiotic	Food	Bioavailability increased, especially in high-fat foods
Atropine	Anticholinergic	Iron	Delayed absorption
Azithromycin	Antibiotic	Food	Decreased rate and delayed absorption
Bacampicillin	Antibiotic (penicillins)	Food	Decreased absorption
Barbiturates	Anticonvulsants	Alcohol	Enhanced CNS depression
		Calcium, vitamin D	Increased vitamin D requirements, owing to increased metabolism
		Cyanocobalamin	Increased bone resorption
		Folic acid	Decreased serum levels, leading to megaloblastic anemia
		Serum lipids	Decreased CSF folate and erythrocyte concentration; may increase cholesterol, HDL triacylglycerols
Benzodiazepines	Anticonvulsants	Nutrient	Enhanced CNS depression
Clonazedam		Calcium	Increased vitamin D requirements secondary to increased metabolism
Clorazepate dipotassium		Vitamin D	Increased bone resorption
Lopazepam		Cyanocobalamin	Decreased serum levels, leading to megaloblastic anemia
Oxazepam		Folic acid	Decreased CSF folate and erythrocyte concentration
		Serum lipids	May increase cholesterol, HDL triacylglycerols
Buprenorphone HCL	Analgesic Narcotic Agonist–antagonist	Alcohol	Enhanced CNS depression
Butorphanol tartate	Analgesic Narcotic Agonist–antagonist	Alcohol	Enhanced CNS depression
Calcium carbonate	Antacid	Iron	Decreased iron absorption
		Fats	May cause steatorrhea
Captopril	Antihypertensive ACE inhibitor	Food	Reduced absorption
Carbamazpine	Anticonvulsants	Sodium	SIADH
		Food	Enhanced absorption, increased bile production
Carbenicillin iandanyl sodium	Antibiotic	Food	Decreased rate of absorption
Cephalosporins	Antibiotic	Alcohol	Flushing, headache, nausea, vomiting, tachycardia

Continued

Table 2 Continued

Drug	Class	Food/nutrient	Effect/mechanism
Cefadroxil		Food	No effect (may take with food)
Cefpodoxime proxetil		Food	Bioavailability increased with food
Cefuroxim axetil		Food	Bioavailability increased with food
Cefixime		Food	Decreased rate of absorption
Cefachlor		Food	Decreased rate of absorption
Cephalexin		Food	Absorption reduced for suspension, delayed for capsules
Cephradine		Food	Rate of absorption delayed
Ceftibuten		Food	Decreased absorption
Cefamandole		Vitamin K	Decreased vitamin K hypoprothrombinemia
Cefoperazone		Vitamin K	Decreased vitamin K hypoprothrombinemia
Cefotetan		Vitamin K	Decreased vitamin K hypoprothrombinemia
Cetrizine	Antihistamine	Food	Delays time to serum peak; no effect on overall absorption
Chlorambucil	Antineoplastic	Food	Reduced absorption
Chloramphenicol	Antibiotic	Iron	Increased serum level iron; increased total iron-binding capacity
		Folic acid	Antagonist to physiological action; increased requirements of folic acid
		Vitamin B$_{12}$	Increased requirements of vitamin B$_{12}$ can cause peripheral neuropathy
Chlorothiazide	Diuretic	Food	Increased drug absorption owing to delayed gastric emptying
Chloroquine	Antimalarial	Food	Increased bioavailability
Chlorpromazine	Antiemetic	Food	Decreased absorption owing to delayed gastric emptying
Chlorpropamide	Antidiabetic	Glucose	Decreased blood glucose concentration
		Sodium	Hyponatremia, SIADH
		Alcohol	Flushing, headache, nausea, vomiting, tachycardia
Cholchicine	Antigout	Cyanocobalamin	Decreased absorption of cyanocobalamin
Cimetidine	Histamine 2 antagonist	Food	Delays absorption
Ciprofloxacin	Antibiotic (quinolone)	Caffeine	Decreased rate of absorption
		Food	Decreased elimination of caffeine
		Calcium	Calcium can bind quinolones
		Mineral supplement	Absorption of divalent and trivalent cations decreased by binding to quinolones
Cisapride	Motility	Food (grapefruit)	May result in increased cardiotoxicity
Clarithromycin	Antibiotic (macrolide)	Food	Decreased onset of absorption; no change in total amount absorbed
Clonazepam	Anticonvulsants (benzodiazepine)	Nutrient	Enhanced CNS depression
Clorazepate dipotassium		Calcium	Increased vitamin D requirements, owing to increased metabolism
		Vitamin D	Increased bone resorption
		Cyanocobalamin	Decreased serum levels, leading to megaloblastic anemia
		Folic acid	Decreased CSF folate and erythrocyte concentration
		Serum lipid	May increase cholesterol, HDL triacyclglycerols
Clorgyline	Antidepressant (MAO inhibitor)	Tyramine-rich foods (avacado, canned figs, aged cheese, cola beverage, coffee, chocolate, wine, soy sauce, fermented meats, yeast, yoghurts)	May increase blood pressure

Continued

Table 2 Continued

Drug	Class	Food/nutrient	Effect/mechanism
Cloxacillin	Antibiotic (penicillin)	Food	Decreased rate of absorption
Codeine	Narcotic agonist, analgesic	Alcohol	Enhanced CNS effect
		Glucose	Can cause hyperglycemia
Corticosteroids Prednisone Prednisolone Dexamethazone Methylprednisolone Hydrocortisone	Steroids	Calcium, phosphorus, vitamin D	Decreased absorption of calcium and phosphorus; increased urinary excretion; chronic high dose can cause osteomalacia
Corticosteroids	Steroids	Nitrogen	Increased urinary nitrogen losses
		Zinc	Increased urinary excretion and decreased serum levels
		Glucose	Impairs glucose tolerance; increases plasma levels
		Triacylglycerols, cholesterol	Increased serum levels
Co-trimaxazole	Antibiotic	Potassium	Decreased excretion hyperkalemia
		Sodium	Increased excretion hyponatremia
		Folic acid	Potential for folate deficiency
Cyclosporine	Antirejection	Milk, fat, pineapple juice	Increased absorption
Demeclocycline	Antibiotic	Food, calcium, iron	Decreased absorption of dairy products and divalent and trivalent cations
Diazepam Clonazedam Clorazepate dipotassium Lopazepam Oxazepam	Anticonvulsant	Food	Increased absorption with high-fat meals and delayed gastric emptying
Dicumarol	Anticoagulant	Food	Increased absorption with high-fat meals and delayed gastric emptying
Didanosine Tab	Antiviral	Food	Decreased rate and extent of absorption
Oral suspension		Fruit juice or acid liquid	Didanosine unstable in acid
Digoxin	Cardiac	Food	Delayed absorption; adsorbent to high-fiber high-pectin foods
Dirithromycin	Antibiotic (macrocide)	Food	Slightly increased absorption
Divalproex	Anticonvulsant	Food	Decreased rate of absorption; extent of absorption not affected
Doxycycline	Antibiotic	Food	Decreased absorption of food and milk
Erythromycin	Antibiotic (macrocide)	Food	Increased absorption by delayed gastric emptying
Erythromycin stearate		Food	Reduced absorption by delayed gastric emptying
Ethionamide	Antituberculosis	Pyridoxins	Reports of peripheral neuritis and paraesthesia
Etodolac	NSAID	Food (milk)	Decreased total bioavailability of tolmetin; decreased absorption of ibuprofen
		Sodium	Hyponatremia (indomethacin/ketorolac)
		Potassium	Hyperkalemia (indomethacin/ketorolac)
		Food	Increased rate of absorption
Felbamate	Anticonvulsant	Glucose	Hypoglycemia
		Magnesium	Hypomagnesemia
		Phosphorus	Hypophosphatemia
		Potassium	Hypokalemia
		Sodium	Hyponatremia
Fenoprofen	NSAID	Food (milk)	Decreased total bioavailability of tolmetin
Fenoprofen calcium		Sodium	Hyponatremia (indomethacin/ketorolac)
		Potassium	Hyperkalemia (indomethacin/ketorolac)
		Food (milk)	Decreased bioavailability of tolmetin; decreased absorption of ibuprofen

Continued

Table 2 Continued

Drug	Class	Food/nutrient	Effect/mechanism
		Food	Increased rate of absorption
Fluconazole	Antifungal	Potassium	Hypokalemia
Flucytosine	Antifungal	Food	Decreased rate of absorption; no change in extent of absorption
Foscarnet	Antiviral	Calcium	Hypocalcemia; drug chelates; divalent metal ions
		Magnesium	Hypomagnesemia
		Phosphorus	Hypophosphatemia and hyperphosphatemia
		Potassium	Hypokalemia
Furazolidone	Anti-infective	Tyramine-rich foods (avocados, canned figs, aged cheese, cola beverages, coffee, chocolate, wines, soy sauce, fermented meats, yeast preparation, yoghurts)	Prolonged large doses result in increased risk for hypertensive crisis
		Alcohol	Rushing, headache, nausea, vomiting, sweating, tachycardia
Furosemide	Diuretic	Food	Delayed absorption
Ganciclovir	Antiviral	Food	Increased area under curve plasma concentration
Glipizide	Antidiabetic	Food	Delayed absorption
		Alcohol	Flushing, headache, nausea, vomiting, sweating, tachycardia
		Sodium	Hyponatremia, SIADH
Griseofluvin	Antifungal	Alcohol	Can increase alcohol effect, flushing, tachycardia
		High-fat food	Increased drug absorption rate
Hydralazine	Diuretic	Food	Increased absorption
Hydrochlorothiazide	Diuretic	Food	Increased absorption by delayed gastric emptying
HMG-CoA Reductase inhibitors Simvastatin Lovastatin	Antihyperlipidemic	Food (grapefruit)	Increase drug serum concentration; increase area under curve concentration
Ibuprofen	NSAID	Food (milk)	Decreased total bioavailability of tolmetin; decreased absorption of ibuprofen
		Sodium	Hyponatremia (indomethacin/ketorolac)
		Potassium	Hyperkalemia (indomethacin/ketorolac)
		Food	Increased rate of absorption
Indinavir	Antiviral	Food	Decreased absorption of high-calorie, high-fat and protein-rich foods
		Grapefruit juice	Decreased area under curve concentration
Indomethicin	NSAID	Food (milk)	Decreased total bioavailability of tolmetin; decreased absorption of ibuprofen
		Sodium	Hyponatremia (indomethacin/ketorolac)
		Potassium	Hyperkalemia (indomethacin/ketorolac)
		Food	Increased rate of absorption
Iron	Mineral	Ascorbic acid	Increased absorption
		Amino-acids	Increased absorption
		Calcium phosphate	Decreased absorption
		Zinc	Inhibits absorption
		Vitamin A	Vitamin A deficiency inhibits iron utilization and accelerates the development of anemia
		Tea/coffee	Decreased absorption owing to formation of iron tannate

Continued

Table 2 Continued

Drug	Class	Food/nutrient	Effect/mechanism
		Vegetable polyphenols	Binds and insolubilizes iron
Isoniazid	Antituberculosis	Food	Decreased intestinal absorption
		Pyridoxine	Decreased metabolism, antagonism
		Food and histamine, tuna, liver, aubergine, parmesan cheese, tomato, spinach, tyramine-containing foods	Headache, redness, itching of eyes and face, chills, diarrhea, palpitation; potential hypertensive crisis due to monoamine oxidase inhibitor activity
Itraconazole	Antifungal	Food	Increased absorption, increased triacylglycerols
		Potassium	Hypokalemia
Ketoconazole	Antifungal	Alcohol	Flushing, headache, nausea, vomiting, sweating, tachycardia
Lansoprazole	H/K proton-pump inhibitor	Food	Delays absorption
Labetalol	Antihypertensive	Food	Increased absorption
Lamivudone (3TC)	Antiviral	Food	Decreased rate of absorption
Levodopa	Anti-Parkinson's	Food	Decreased absorption; with high-protein meals amino-acids compete for absorption
Lithium	Antimanic	Low-sodium diet	Increased lithium concentrations
		High-sodium diet	Increased lithium clearance
		Food	Increased absorption
Linezolid	Antibiotic	Tyramine-rich foods	May result in blood-pressure changes
Lomefloxacin	Antibiotic (quinolone)	Food	Decreased rate and extent of absorption
Loracarbef	Antibiotic	Food	Decreased rate of absorption
Lovastatin	Antihyperlipidemia	Food	Increased absorption
Mebendazole	Anthelmintic	Food	Increased absorption
Meclofenamate	NSAID	Alcohol	Additive CNS effects; increased prothrombin time
		Food	Decreased bioavailability
Melphalan	Antineoplastic	Food	Reduced absorption
Mercaptopurine	Antineoplastic	Food	Reduced absorption
Methacycline	Antibiotic	Food, calcium, iron	Decreased absorption of dairy products, cereals, divalent and trivalent cations
Methenamine mandelate	Urinary anti-infective	Milk products, citrus fruits	Excessive amounts inhibit drug conversion
Methosuximide	Anticonvulsant	Alcohol, calcium	Additive CNS effects; hypocalcemia
Methotreate	Antineoplastic	Food	Increased absorption
Methyldopa	Antihypertensive	Vitamin B_{12}, folate	In high doses methyldopa can increase vitamin B_{12} and folate losses
		Food	High-protein meals compete for absorption
Metoprolol	Antihypertensive	Food	Increased absorption
Metronidazole	Antibiotic	Alcohol	Flushing, headache, nausea, vomiting, sweating, tachycardia
		Food	Decreased peak serum concentration but total amount of drug absorbed is not affected
Minocycline	Antibiotic	Food, calcium	Decreased absorption
Nafcillin	Antibiotic	Food	Decreased absorption; decreased serum levels due to altered gastric pH
		Potassium	High doses can cause hypokalemia owing to increased urinary losses
Nifedipine	Antihypertensive	Food (grapefruit)	Increases pressor effect of drug
Nitrofurantoin	Antibiotic	Food	Increased absorption by delayed gastric emptying
NSAIDs	NSAID	Food (milk)	Decreased bioavailability of tolmetin
Diclofenl Etodolac		Sodium	Hyponatremia (indomethacin/ketorolac)

Continued

Table 2　Continued

Drug	Class	Food/nutrient	Effect/mechanism
Fenoprofen Ca Ibuprofen		Potassium	Hyperkalemia (indomethacin/ketorolac)
Ketoprofen Ketorolac Naproxn Oxapron Piroxican Sulindac		Food	Decreased absorption of ibuprofen
Tolmetin NA		Food	Increased rate of absorption
Norfloxacin	Antibiotic (quinolone)	Food, dairy products	Decreased rate of absorption
		Multivitamin and mineral supplements	Decreased absorption due to formation of divalent and trivalent cation complexes with quinolones
Nifedepine	Antihypertensive calcium-channel blocker	Grapefruit juice	Increased serum level of nifedepine flavonoids inhibits cytochrome P-450
		Food	Decreased bioavailability, formulation dependent
Ofloxacin	Antibiotic (quinolone)	Dairy products and mineral supplements	Decreased absorption by polyvalent cations
Ondansetron	Antiemetic	Food	Increased extent of absorption
		Potassium	Hypokalemia
Omeprazole	H/K proton-pump inhibitor	Food	Delays absorption
Oral contraceptives		Ascorbic acid	Decreased ascorbic-acid concentration in plasma, platelets, leucocytes
		Vitamin C, folic acid	Decrease in serum levels
		Vitamin B_{12}	Impairs tryptophan metabolism
		Amino-acids, vitamin A, vitamin E, copper	Increase in serum levels
Oxacillin	Antibiotic	Food	Decreased absorption and decreased serum concentration
		Fats	Oxacillin can cause steatorrhea
Paromomycin	Amoebicide	Food	Increased absorption by delayed gastric emptying
		Vitamins A, D, E, K	Malabsorption of fat-soluble vitamins owing to hypocholesterolemia
Penicillamine	Antidote (chelating agent)	Food	Decreased absorption
		Iron, zinc	Decreased absorption 30%–70% of increased zinc absorption; decreased penicillamine absorption
Penicillin G & VK	Antibiotic	Food	Decreased absorption by delayed gastric emptying
		Glucose	Hyperglycemia
Pentamidine	Antibiotic	Calcium, magnesium	Hypomagnesemia, hypocalemia
		Potassium	Hyperkalaemia due to nephrotoxicity
Phenacemide	Anticonvulsant	Fresh fruits and vitamin C	Increased urinary excretion of phenacemide
Phenobarbital	Anticonvulsant (see Barbiturates)	Food	Decreased absorption due to protein binding
		Protein	Low-protein diet increases duration of action of phenobarbitol
		Vitamin D, calcium	Decreased serum vitamin D by cytochrome P-450 hypocalcemia
		Fresh fruits and vitamin C	Increased urinary excretion of phenobarbitol
Phensuximide	Anticonvulsant (succinimides)	Calcium, vitamin D	Decreased serum vitamin D by P-450 cytochrome hypocalcemia

Continued

Table 2 Continued

Drug	Class	Food/nutrient	Effect/mechanism
		Vitamin B$_{12}$, folic acid	Decreased absorption and serum levels of folates; inhibits vitamin B$_{12}$ transport
		Copper	Increased serum levels
Phenytoin	Anticonvulsant (hydantoins)	Fresh fruits and vitamin C	Increased urinary excretion
		Vitamin D, calcium	Decreased serum vitamin D by cytochrome P-450 hypocalcemia
		Enteral feeds	Decreased absorption
		Food	Increased absorption by delayed gastric emptying
Pimozide	Antineruoleptic	Food (grapefruit)	Increased risk of cardiotoxicity
Piroxicam	NSAID	Food	Delayed absorption
Praziquantel	Anthelmintic	Food	Decreased rate and extent of absorption
Primidone	Anticonvulsant	Fresh fruits and vitamin C	Increased urinary excretion of primidone
		Protein	Low-protein diet increases duration of action of primidone
Propantheline	Anticholinergic	Food	Decreased absorption
Propranolol	Antihypertensive	High-protein foods	Increased absorption
Proxyphene	Analgesic	Food	Increased absorption by delayed gastric emptying
Pyrimethamine	Antimalarial	Folic acid	Decreased serum folate concentrations
Quinidine	Antiarrhythmic	Food	Delayed absorption due to protein binding
Riboflavin	Vitamin	Food	Increased absorption by delayed gastric emptying
Rifampin	Antibiotic	Food	Decreased absorption
Ritonavir	Antiviral	Vitamins	Can cause vitamin deficiency
		Potassium	Hyperkalemia and hypokalemia
		Cholesterol	Hypercholesterolemia
		Triacylglycerols	Hypertriacylglycerolemia
Oral solution		Food	Delayed absorption
Capsules		Food	Increased extent of absorption
Salicylates	Analgesics	Iron	Long-term chronic use decreases serum iron
Magnesium salicylate			
Choline salicylate		Vitamin C	Decreases concentration in serum and platelets
Sodium salicylate		Amino-acids	Decreases their intestinal absorption and increases urinary secretion
Saquinavir mesylate	Antiviral	Food	Increased absorption of high-calorie, high-fat foods
		Calcium	Hypercalemia
		Glucose	Hyperglycemia and hypoglycemia
		Phosphorus	Changes in serum phosphorus
		Potassium	Hyperkalaemia and hypokalemia
Spironolactone	Diuretic	Food	Increased absorption by delayed gastric emptying
Sulfonamides	Antibiotic	Food	Delayed with no effect on extent of absorption
Sulfadiazine			
Sulfisoxazole		Folic acid	Decreased intestinal synthesis, absorption, and serum levels
Sulfamethoxazole			
Tetracycline	Antibiotic	Food	Decreased absorption
		Minerals	Inhibits absorption of iron, calcium, zinc, and magnesium; chelation by polyvalent cations
		Fats	Decreases absorption
		Vitamin K	Decreases bioavailability
		Vitamin C	Increases urinary losses; decreases

Continued

Table 2 Continued

Drug	Class	Food/nutrient	Effect/mechanism
Terfenadine	Antihistamine	Food (grapefruit)	Increased risk of cardiotoxicity
Theophylline	Broncodilator	Charbroiled beef	Increased metabolism of theophylline
		High-fat meals	Increased absorption dependent on formulation
Tolazamide	Antidiabetic	Sodium	Hyponatremia and SIADH
Tolbutamide	Antidiabetic	Ethanol	Prolonged hypoglycemia, disulfram reaction
Trimethoprim	Antibiotic	Folic acid	Decreased serum folate levels
Valproic acid Divalproex Sodium valproate Sodium oral solution	Anticonvulsant	Milk, food, carbonated drinks	Delayed absorption but no effect on extent of absorption
Warfarin	Anticoagulant	Alcohol, vitamin K	Inhibits warfarin metabolism; beef liver, pork liver, green tea, leafy green vegetables high in vitamin K inhibit anticoagulant effect
		Vitamin E	Can increase warfarin response
Zalcitabine	Antiviral	Food	Decreases rate and extent of absorption
Zafirlukast	Selective leukotiene antagonist	Food	Delayed absorption
Zidovudine	Antiviral	Food	Decreased rate of absorption

SIADH, Syndrome of inappropriate antidiuretic hormone excretion; CNS, central nervous system; CSF, cerebrospinal fluid; NSAID, nonsteroidal anti-inflammatory drug

Herb–Drug Interactions

Herbal botanicals have been used in many cultures throughout the world for hundreds of years. These products are usually seen as natural; they should not be synonymous with safe.

Possible interactions can involve hepatic cytochrome P-450 and changes in intestinal absorption, distribution, and renal excretion. Herbal interactions with certain drugs are listed in **Table 3**.

Table 3 Herbal–drug interactions

Herbal	Drugs	Effect/mechanism
Echinacea	Methotrexate, aminodarone, ketoconazole, steroids (anabolic)	Increased hepatotoxicity
Feverfew	NSAIDs	Decreased herbal effect
	Anticoagulants	Additive platelet inhibition
Garlic	Aspirin, anticoagulants	Reduced clotting time
Ginkgo biloba	Aspirin, anticoagulants, NSAIDs, tricyclic antidepressants, anticonvulsants	Decreased seizure threshold; increased risk of bleeding
Ginseng	Monoamine oxidase inhibitors	Headache, tremors, mania
	Corticosteroids	Increased steroid toxicity
	Warfarin	Decreased INR
	Digoxin	Increased digoxin levels
Kava kava	Benzodiazepines	Increased CNS depression
Epherda	Antidepressants, CNS stimulants	Increased herbal effect
St John's wort	Antidepressants, CNS stimulants	Additive effects
	Piroxicam, tetracycline	Increased photosensitivity
	Theophylline	Decreased theophylline levels
Saw palmetto	Oestrogen	Increased effect of herbal
Valerian	CNS depressants	Additive CNS depression

CNS, central nervous system; INR, International Normalization Ratio; NSAIDs, nonsteroidal anti-inflammatory drugs.

See also: **Amino Acids**: Metabolism. **Malnutrition**: Primary, Causes Epidemiology and Prevention; Secondary, Diagnosis and Management.

Further Reading

Caballero B (1988) Nutritional implications of dietary interactions: a review. *Food Nutrition Bulletin* **10**: 9–20.

Knapp HR (1996) Nutrient–drug interactions. In: Ziegler FF and Filer LJ (eds.) *Present Knowledge in Nutrition*, pp. 540–546. Washington, DC: ILSI Press.

Neuvonen P (1989) Clinical significance of food–drug interactions. *Medical Journal of Australia* **150**: 36–40.

Roberts J (1988) Age and diet effects on drug action. *Pharmacology and Therapeutics* **37**: 111–149.

Roe DA (1986) Drug–food and drug–nutrient interactions. *Journal of Environmental Pathology, Toxicology and Oncology* **5**: 115–135.

Roe DA (1994) Diet, nutrition and drug reactions. In: Shils ME, Olson JA, and Shike M (eds.) *Modern Nutrition in Health and Disease*, 8th edn, pp. 1399–1416. Philadelphia: Lea & Febiger.

Schmidt LE (2002) Food–drug interactions. *Drugs* **10**: 1481–1502.

Wurtman RJ, Caballero B, and Salzman E (1988) Facilitation of DOPA-induced dyskinesias by dietary carbohydrates. *New England Journal of Medicine* **390**: 1288–1289.

EARLY ORIGINS OF DISEASE

Contents
Fetal
Non-Fetal

Fetal

A J Buckley and S E Ozanne, University of
Cambridge, Cambridge, UK

Introduction

The prevalence of metabolic diseases such as type 2
diabetes and cardiovascular disease is increasing at
an alarming rate. Around one in ten people today
suffer from type 2 diabetes and it is estimated that
by 2010 over 250 million people worldwide will
have this condition. Although the etiology of these
metabolic diseases is considered to be multifactorial, there is now a substantial body of evidence
suggesting that the pathogenic mechanisms underlying these adult-occurring diseases originate from
disturbances experienced during *in utero* and early
life.

The long-term effect of an insult during a critical
period of development has been recognized for
many years. As long as 70 years ago it was recognized that the early environment in which a child
grows could have long-term effects on its health.
This was based on the observations in England,
Scotland, and Sweden that suggested that death
rates in specific age groups at any time depended
upon the year of birth, suggesting that the time of
death was more related to the year the person was
born in rather than the age of the person. Additional evidence supporting the importance of the
early environment came from a study in Norway
investigating the geographical variations in current
death rates from arteriosclerotic heart disease. For-
sdahl and coworkers demonstrated a significant
positive correlation between the current death
rates and geographical variation in past infant mortality rates.

In utero growth and development is an extremely
critical period in one's life. This was first recognized
by Barker and Osmond when they demonstrated a
striking association between adult mortality from
cardiovascular disease and past infant mortality
rates earlier in the century in the same geographical
regions of England and Wales. As infant mortality
was greatest in regions where low birth weight was
also present, it was hypothesized that adverse early
life nutritional influences could result in low birth
weight and lead to an increased predisposition to
cardiovascular disease. Subsequent regional studies
have also demonstrated associations between low
weight both at birth and 1 year of age and high
mortality rates from ischemic heart disease. Mounting support for the role that the early life environmental influences play in establishing the risk for
disease came when this association was found not
to disappear even with an improvement in diet during adult life or with moving to other regions of the
country.

It is thus now well established that poor fetal
growth confers an amplified risk for the development of diseases such as type 2 diabetes, cardiovascular disease, insulin resistance, and obesity.
Metabolic programing, a concept defined as the
process whereby exposure to a stimulus or insult
during a crucial phase of growth and development
results in permanent alterations in the structure or
function of an organ or metabolic action, is involved
in amplifying this risk. Maternal nutrition and the
maternal metabolic milieu during gestation and lactation, as well as the functionality of the placenta,
have been widely recognized as major influential
factors of adverse fetal and early life metabolic
programing.

Birth Weight and Adult Disease

Further evidence for the role that the early life environmental influences play in establishing the risk for disease came in the early 1990s when studies conducted by Barker and colleagues in a large cohort of men and women from Hertford-shire, UK revealed strong correlations between low birth weight and a high prevalence of meta-bolic diseases in later life (**Table 1**). Although not universally accepted, numerous epidemiological studies completed throughout the world, includ-ing other parts of the UK, Europe, US, and India, have found reproducible results in extensive population and ethnic groups and various age ranges.

The Hertfordshire study was a retrospective study that collected the birth records of 15 726 men and women born in Hertfordshire between 1911 and 1930. This study was the first to demonstrate that the incidence of death from coronary heart disease was highest in adults born with a low birth weight. Barker and colleagues replicated this finding in a cohort of 1586 men born in Sheffield, UK between 1907 and 1925. The link between low birth weight and coronary heart disease in adult life again received confirmation from studies involving over 70 000 nurses from the US born between 1921 and 1945. A study in South India demonstrated that in a cohort of 517 men and women born between 1934 and 1954, the prevalence of coronary heart disease rose to 11% when the recorded birth weight was less than 2.5 kg. In those people who had a birth weight of more than 3.1 kg the prevalence of coron-ary heart disease was only 3%. A Swedish study of over 14 000 men and women born in Uppsala, Sweden between 1915 and 1929 was able to clearly identify that the risk of death from cardiovascular disease was associated with being small for gestational age.

In the Hertfordshire study, Hales and Barker demonstrated a strong inverse relationship between birth weight and type 2 diabetes or impaired glucose tolerance in men aged 64 years. Similar findings have been reported in populations of men and

Table 1 Adult health characteristics associated with low birth weight

- Type 2 diabetes
- Coronary heart disease
- Hypertension
- Hypertriglyceridemia
- Impaired glucose tolerance
- Insulin resistance

women in other parts of Europe, Australia, and the US. Further support of the association between low birth weight and the development of metabolic dis-ease comes from studies of monozygotic twins. Two studies have demonstrated that impaired glucose tolerance and type 2 diabetes is more prevalent in the twin with the lower birth weight.

Although initial studies focused on the relation-ship between cardiovascular disease and type 2 dia-betes subsequent studies have reported associations with other conditions. From an early age, children born with a low birth weight demonstrate reduced endothelium-dependent dilation and increased arter-ial stiffness. It has been observed that this endothe-lial dysfunction persists into adult life. The mechanisms behind the association between low birth weight and impaired vascular function remain to be elucidated. Despite this, it has been suggested that endothelial dysfunction is an early feature and precedes the metabolic disorders that develop in low-birth-weight humans.

Whilst the association between low birth weight and high predisposition to disease has been reported quite substantially, it is important to note that a U-shape relationship does occur when investigating the association between birth weight and the devel-opment of metabolic diseases. Babies born large for gestational age are also at an elevated risk of devel-oping diseases such as coronary heart disease and type 2 diabetes.

The etiology of breast cancer has now also been linked to prenatal influences. Investigations in Sweden, Norway, and the US have provided epide-miological data indicating that high birth weight potentially increases the risk of developing breast cancer. The specific biological mechanisms under-lying this association still remain unclear. However, it has been suggested that prenatal exposure to the high level of estrogen that occurs during pregnancy may play a significant role. Other maternal hor-mones and growth factors may also be involved. A U-shape relationship also exists when investiga-ting prenatal influences upon the development of breast cancer. Studies have reported birth weights below 2.5 kg and above 4 kg are significant risk factors for the development of breast cancer in women.

Underlying Mechanisms

The Fetal Insulin Hypothesis

Hattersley and colleagues have suggested that the relationship between birth weight and type 2 diabetes could be mediated by mutations/polymorphisms in genes that influence insulin secretion or insulin sensitivity. Insulin is an important fetal growth factor, thus any defects in its secretion or action would result in both low birth weight and increased risk of diabetes. This is supported by studies of individuals with maturity onset diabetes of the young 2. These individuals who have mutations in the glucokinase gene have a lower birth weight compared to their unaffected siblings. The fetal insulin hypothesis therefore holds true in this rare monogenic form of diabetes.

The Thrifty Phenotype Hypothesis

An alternative hypothesis, termed the thrifty phenotype hypothesis, was proposed by Hales and Barker in 1992. This proposal focused on the role played by the fetal environment. It suggested that the mechanistic basis underlying the observed relationship between poor fetal growth and the future development of metabolic diseases was related to fetal nutrition.

Central to the thrifty phenotype hypothesis is the suggestion that during times of nutritional deprivation, the growing fetus undergoes metabolic adaptations that are beneficial to survival postnatally in similar conditions of poor nutrition. Such adaptations include the essential preservation of brain growth at the expense of the normal development of organs such as the liver, muscle, and the

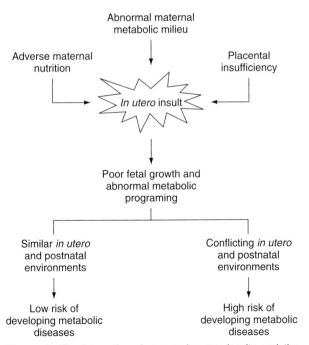

Figure 1 The interactions between *in utero* insults and the subsequent development of metabolic diseases.

pancreas. This has no detrimental effect if the fetus is born into conditions of poor nutrition. Hence in sub-Saharan Africa where there is chronic malnutrition, rates of diabetes are very low. Detrimental consequences of fetal programing arise when the fetus is born into conditions that differ from those experienced *in utero*. The imbalance between the early and adult environments may then conflict with the programing that occurred during fetal life and predispose the offspring to the subsequent development of metabolic diseases in adulthood (**Figure 1**).

Underlying Factors

Glucocorticoids

Maternal glucocorticoids can also influence birth weight of the offspring. Under normal conditions, fetal exposure to glucocorticoids is relatively low due to the presence of placental 11β-hydroxysteroid dehydrogenase 2 (11βHSD2), an enzyme that acts as a placental barrier by inactivating maternal glucocorticoids before they cross into the fetal environment. Maternal glucocorticoid treatment during pregnancy or inhibition of the placental 11βHSD2 can therefore increase the amount of active glucocorticoid crossing the placenta. Excess glucocorticoid exposure has also been implicated in disturbing the normal growth and development of the fetus with consequential effects on the overall health of the adult offspring. There does, however, appear to be a critical window of sensitivity where the developing fetus is particularly sensitive to glucocorticoids. Glucocorticoid overexposure in the 3rd trimester is known to cause reductions in birth weight. Studies in rats have established that glucocorticoid-exposed offspring undergo rapid postnatal catch-up growth, which proves deleterious to their adult health. These studies have demonstrated that excess exposure to glucocorticoids during fetal life is linked to low birth weight, altered functioning of the hypothalamic-pituitary-adrenal (HPA) axis, and the subsequent development of hypertension and impaired glucose tolerance in adulthood.

Increased HPA activity has been demonstrated in low-birth-weight human adult populations. Enhanced responsiveness of plasma cortisol to ACTH and increased urinary cortisol metabolite excretion has been reported in low-birth-weight adult males. Prenatal alteration of the HPA axis may therefore be involved in the subsequent development of cardiovascular disease in low-birth-weight adults.

Leptin

Cord plasma leptin levels have been shown to correlate positively with birth weight and neonatal adiposity. It has been suggested that leptin has a regulatory role in growth and development. Low levels of cord blood leptin have been reported in growth-restricted offspring. These low leptin levels may also predict significant weight gain and catch-up growth, both of which are evident in these growth-restricted offspring. Ong and colleagues hypothesized that there may be a link between *in utero* programing of leptin levels and the predisposition to the development of metabolic diseases.

Maternal Nutrition and Fetal Origins of Adult Metabolic Diseases

Assessing the impact of maternal nutrition on health of the offspring in humans is difficult. However, investigations involving offspring conceived during conditions of famine have provided direct evidence of the effects that maternal nutrition during gestation and lactation has on the overall health of the adult offspring. The Dutch famine, which occurred in the western part of the Netherlands at the end of World War II, only lasted around 5 months from late November 1944 to early May 1945, and was therefore defined as a short period of famine. Prior to the onset of the famine conditions, the affected area of the Netherlands consisted of a reasonably well-nourished population. The occurrence of this abrupt famine therefore granted researchers a unique opportunity to retrospectively study the effect of maternal nutrition during specific stages of gestation on insulin-glucose homeostasis and obesity risk in adult offspring (**Table 2**).

Investigators traced and studied individuals who were born immediately before the famine commenced, those born during the famine, and those born up to 21 months after the famine had ceased. Compared to the offspring not exposed to *in utero* famine conditions, individuals who were *in utero* during the famine had higher plasma glucose levels

Table 2 Effects of famine conditions during the different stages of pregnancy

Maternal exposure to famine during pre-early gestation	Maternal exposure to famine during mid-late gestation
Increased birth weight	Reduced birth weight
Increased birth length	Reduced birth length
Increased obesity	Reduced glucose tolerance
Increased risk of coronary heart disease	Increased risk of type 2 diabetes

2 h after a standard oral glucose tolerance test. These glucose levels were highest in those individuals who had been exposed to the famine during the final trimester of pregnancy and then become obese in adult life. In terms of obesity, individuals who were exposed to the famine during the first half of pregnancy were more obese at age 19 years. In contrast those who were exposed to the famine during the last trimester of pregnancy and in early postnatal life had reduced obesity. This suggests that the critical time windows for increased risk of obesity and type 2 diabetes differ. This study provided direct evidence that poor maternal nutrition leads to increased susceptibility of type 2 diabetes and obesity in offspring. It also supports the hypothesis that the greatest risk of developing metabolic diseases exists when there is a marked conflict between the environmental conditions experienced *in utero* and that experienced in adult life.

As nutritional studies in humans are complex and clouded by multiple confounding factors, a number of animal models of maternal nutritional insults have been developed. Investigations involving these models have significantly contributed to elucidating pathogenic mechanisms underlying the fetal origins of adult metabolic diseases.

Maternal Total Food Intake

Animal models replicating human famine conditions have been developed to enable a more in-depth investigation of maternal calorie restriction throughout pregnancy and the long-term health consequences that this nutritional insult imposes on the developing offspring. Various animal species have been utilized whilst studying the fetal origins of adult metabolic disease in response to maternal feed restriction using dietary insults of up to 70% *ad libitum* food restriction.

Maternal total food restriction (50% of normal food intake) in the rat throughout the gestation period can induce intrauterine growth restriction and result in significantly reduced birth weight. This poor fetal growth is then accompanied by numerous metabolic disturbances in later life. Compared to age-matched control rat offspring, the blood pressure of the maternal food-restriction offspring is significantly elevated and endothelial vascular dysfunction is evident. Insulin resistance, as defined by an elevated fasting plasma insulin level, has also been shown in adult rats exposed *in utero* to the adverse effects of severe maternal food restriction (to only 30% of *ad libitum* intake). In guinea pigs, mild to moderate maternal food restriction (70%–85% *ad libitum* intake) during the pregnancy leads to perturbations in postnatal glucose-insulin homeostasis as well as alterations in the homeostasis of cholesterol metabolism in the male offspring.

Despite the observed significant reduction in birth weight, adult rats exposed to maternal undernutrition (30% of *ad libitum* intake) whilst *in utero* have been shown to develop obesity. Compared to the control offspring, the feed-restricted offspring appear to have been inappropriately programed and display hyperphagia and elevated food consumption as a consequence of *in utero* exposure to an adverse maternal diet. The underlying mechanisms leading to the hyperphagia in these offspring remains to be determined. However, the involvement of leptin resistance has been implied as these offspring also display hyperleptinemia and have significantly elevated fat pad mass as adults.

Even short-term maternal food restriction during the various stages of the gestational period has been demonstrated to provoke perturbations within the metabolic processes of the offspring. Exposure to maternal malnutrition, particularly in the final trimester and during lactation, impairs the programming of β-cell development and induces alterations in the fetal endocrine pancreas that persist into adulthood such that the offspring at 12 months of age display profound insulinopenia and marked glucose intolerance.

Maternal Protein Consumption

In addition to total calorie intake there is also evidence that composition of the maternal diet can have long-term consequences on the metabolism of the offspring. Experimental animal models involving maternal protein restriction have suggested that adequate protein intake is critical in both development of the fetus and its long-term health. They have also provided insight into the possible underlying mechanisms.

Offspring of rat dams fed a low (8%) protein diet throughout the gestational period are consistently smaller at birth than offspring of a control diet containing 20% protein. Initially, the low-protein offspring have significantly improved glucose tolerance than the control offspring. In humans, small-for-gestational-age infants also display increased insulin sensitivity with respect to glucose disposal in early postnatal life. Offspring of dams fed a low-protein diet appear to undergo a greater age-dependent loss of glucose tolerance. By 15 months of age, the male low-protein offspring are considered to have developed glucose intolerance that is

associated with insulin resistance and by 17 months of age this has progressed to type 2 diabetes.

Consistent with the thrifty phenotype hypothesis, the growth restriction of the tissues and organs of the low-protein offspring is not uniform. In the growth-restricted rats, brain growth is spared at the expense of the growth of other developing tissues. In addition to the altered structure and growth patterns, the insulin-sensitive tissues (skeletal muscle and adipose tissue) and organs (liver and pancreas) of the low-protein offspring have been metabolically programed to have altered functionality.

Recently, evidence has been provided suggesting that taurine supplementation to the maternal low-protein diet may benefit the health outcomes of the rat offspring. Maternal taurine supplementation was found to restore and normalize the vascularization of the offspring's endocrine pancreas. Despite these findings, there is little evidence to suggest that a maternal high-protein intake has overall beneficial effects on the metabolic health of the offspring. Some human epidemiological studies and human trials involving high-protein dietary supplementation have in fact demonstrated that the consumption of a high-animal-protein, low-carbohydrate diet throughout late pregnancy can lead to metabolic disturbances in the offspring when they reach adulthood. It has been suggested that these high-protein diets stimulate the hypothalamic-pituitary-adrenal axis and cause maternal cortisol levels to increase. As a result, the developing fetus is presented with the metabolic stress of being exposed to excess cortisol levels. This inappropriate exposure to cortisol during fetal life appears to program lifelong hypercortisolemia and elevated blood pressure. It is likely that the type of protein is also important and this may in part explain some of these apparent discrepancies.

Adverse metabolic disturbances in offspring have therefore been demonstrated as consequential effects of both the *in utero* exposure to either maternal protein restriction or maternal high-protein consumption. The role of the carbohydrate level in these diets still needs to be ascertained. Nevertheless, it is essential that the optimal level of protein intake during pregnancy and lactation be clearly established so as to aid in the normal growth and development of the fetus.

Maternal Iron Restriction

Women, especially pregnant women, in today's society are often diagnosed as being anemic or iron deficient. A rodent model of maternal iron restriction has been developed to determine if metabolic health consequences are observed in the offspring of iron-deficient women. Similar to other restricted maternal diets, iron restriction during pregnancy in rats can lead to disturbances within the events of early life metabolic programing and can induce permanent adaptations of the offspring's physiological and metabolic processes.

Although the mechanisms remain unclear, growth restriction of the offspring of rats fed an iron-deficient diet throughout gestation has been consistently reported. Elevated blood pressure appears to occur in response to maternal iron restriction and persists throughout the life of the offspring. Changes in cardiac size are evident prior to the initiation of hypertension in the offspring of iron-restricted rat dams. Elevated levels of cardiac hypertrophy may therefore contribute to the programed rise in blood pressure documented in these offspring. Renal development is also adversely altered in the offspring of iron-restricted dams. Maternal iron restriction during pregnancy can induce reductions in nephron and glomerular number in the adult rodent offspring. Significant inverse relationships between glomerular number and systolic blood pressure exist in the offspring of iron-restricted dams suggesting that abnormal renal development may also be involved in inducing the hypertensive state in these offspring. The principal mechanisms behind the association of maternal iron restriction during pregnancy with the altered cardiac and renal growth in the offspring and the subsequent induction of permanently elevated blood pressure still need to be further investigated.

Maternal High-Fat Consumption

In today's Western, more affluent society, the *in utero* environment is likely to be influenced by maternal nutritional insults such as excess fat consumption. There is little dispute regarding the deleterious effects of a high-fat diet. It is well documented that a diet high in fat has played a fundamental role in the prevalence of type 2 diabetes, reaching the epidemic proportions that is seen today. Both human epidemiological studies and experimental animal investigations have demonstrated clear associations between the consumption of a high-fat diet and the increasing prevalence of cardiovascular disease, insulin resistance, and type 2 diabetes. In light of this, a high-fat diet can increase the risk of a pregnant woman developing gestational diabetes. As will be discussed later, it is well established that offspring of diabetic mothers are themselves at an increased risk of developing the disease at an early age. Consumption of a high-fat diet may not only therefore cause deleterious effects to the current generation, but may ultimately have

profound consequential effects on future generations. Considering this, the negative impact that a maternal high-fat diet has on the offspring is a topical area of research that requires more detailed attention.

Like any maternal nutritional insult, exposure to an abnormal *in utero* environment, induced by the maternal high-fat diet, can lead to subsequent disturbances in metabolic programing of the developing fetus. To date, investigations studying this nutritional insult have mainly concentrated on the effects of a maternal diet high in saturated fat. Such a diet has led to rat weanlings having increased amounts of body fat, increased liver weight, increased liver triglyceride content, higher blood glucose, and higher blood triglyceride levels. Permanent alterations in the structure and function of the pancreas, vascular dysfunction, and reduced insulin sensitivity have also been documented in rat weanlings and young adult offspring of high-saturated-fat-fed rat dams. Recently, it has emerged that feeding pregnant rats with diets containing a high proportion of animal lard can induce severe endothelial dysfunction in the offspring, along with the subsequent development of increased adiposity, hyperglycemia, insulin secretory deficiency, and insulin resistance. Taken together, these investigations demonstrate profound metabolic derangements in the offspring of fat-fed rats. The underlying mechanistic basis for these observations, however, still requires elucidation. It is also important to note that a high-fat diet is concurrently low in carbohydrate content and it cannot be ruled out that a carbohydrate deficiency in the female rats may account for the metabolic perturbations observed in the offspring of high-fat-fed dams.

Maternal Alcohol Consumption

Several laboratories have investigated the effects of sustained maternal alcohol consumption on the offspring's metabolic health. Alcohol consumption during pregnancy can lead to abnormal fetal development and a subsequent reduction in birth weight. Increased offspring morbidity may also be linked to gestational alcohol consumption. It has been previously documented that female rats fed a gestational diet supplemented with alcohol tended to have a higher number of pups die in early postnatal life. Of those alcohol-exposed offspring that survived, the reduced rate of prenatal growth and development has been linked to abnormalities in the offspring's glucose and insulin homeostasis. Both glucose intolerance and insulin resistance are evident in the rat offspring exposed during *in utero* life to maternal alcohol. Phenotypic abnormalities, commonly associated with insulin resistance and other metabolic diseases, are also evident in the *in utero* alcohol-exposed offspring. The accumulation of triglycerides in nonadipocyte tissue, namely the skeletal muscle and the liver, is commonly observed in both insulin-resistant humans and experimental animal models of insulin resistance. Elevated levels of plasma and nonadipocyte tissue triglycerides have now also been documented in low-birth-weight rats that were exposed to maternal alcohol *in utero*.

Consumption of alcohol is quite common among breast-feeding mothers as studies have shown ethanol to aid in the promotion of lactation. Establishing the harmful effects of alcohol consumption during lactation is therefore important. Newborn rats exposed to maternal alcohol only during the lactation period have also been shown to develop reduced insulin sensitivity despite having normal prenatal growth and development. In early postnatal life some important metabolic processes are still undergoing development. Therefore, it must be considered that early postnatal life is still a vulnerable period of growth and the developing metabolic processes may still be particularly susceptible to adverse effects induced by alcohol consumption by breast-feeding mothers.

Maternal Metabolic Milieu and Fetal Origins of Metabolic Diseases

Over two decades ago it was hypothesized that perturbations in the metabolic milieu of pregnant women can disturb the intrauterine environment and influence long-term health consequences in the offspring. Abnormalities in the maternal metabolic milieu can evoke the adverse transfer of hormones and fuels from the mother to the growing fetus and thereby increase the predisposition to metabolic disease in the offspring's later life.

The effect of a diabetic pregnancy has been thoroughly examined in the Pima Indians of Arizona. The Pima Indian population has the world's highest prevalence and incidence of type 2 diabetes. Metabolic disorders are becoming increasingly common in the younger generation of this population. Consequently, it is possible that these disorders are present in Pima Indian women of childbearing age. In fact, 10–15% of Pima Indian pregnancies are complicated by type 2 diabetes.

Diabetic pregnant women are hyperglycemic, a characteristic of the general diabetic population. Whilst maternal insulin cannot cross the placental barrier, maternal glucose can freely do so. Elevated maternal glucose levels can therefore induce fetal hyperinsulinemia, subsequently promoting excessive growth and adipose tissue accumulation in the offspring. Compared to the offspring of either nondiabetic or prediabetic (those who developed type 2 diabetes after the birth of their offspring) women, the offspring of diabetic females generally have increased birth weights. This obese state then tracks with the offspring throughout life. Interestingly, excessive obesity can also develop in the subset of normal-birth-weight offspring of diabetic women. These findings suggest the offspring of diabetic women are detrimentally programed into developing altered metabolic processes regardless of birth weight.

Exposure to maternal diabetes whilst *in utero* is also largely responsible for the offspring having an increased risk of developing insulin resistance, impaired glucose tolerance, and type 2 diabetes at an early age. These metabolic disorders are significantly more prevalent in the offspring of diabetics than the offspring of nondiabetics and prediabetics. It has been established that more than one-third of Pima Indian children diagnosed with type 2 diabetes in the past decade seem to have developed the disease as a direct programed response to being exposed to an intrauterine diabetic environment.

Metabolic disorders such as type 2 diabetes have been suggested to have a strong genetic component. It has been postulated that diabetes-susceptibility genes are transmitted to the fetus and this then confers an increased risk for the offspring to develop the disease in adulthood. According to this explanation, offspring born either prior to or after the mother's type 2 diabetes diagnosis should carry the same risk of inheriting the diabetes-susceptibility genes. However, it has become evident that this does not appear to be the case. Sibship studies have compared the prevalence of type 2 diabetes and the degree of obesity in Pima Indian siblings either born before or after their mother was diagnosed with type 2 diabetes. Within the same family, offspring born prior to the mother having developed the disease remained relatively unaffected. Conversely, children born after the diagnosis developed obesity at an early age and were at an increased risk for type 2 diabetes. Therefore, these findings confirm that in addition to any genetic effect, direct exposure to the diabetic intrauterine environment is implicated in the offspring having an increased predisposition to the premature development of metabolic disorders.

Placental Insufficiency and Fetal Origins of Metabolic Diseases

Poor fetal growth and development can occur in the offspring of adequately nourished women or women with normal metabolic milieu. It is believed that placental insufficiency may be largely responsible for the growth restriction observed in this subgroup of offspring. Placental transfer of nutrients and metabolites is pivotal to fetal growth and development. Interference within this transfer process can lead to placental insufficiencies and a disruption to fetal nutrition, hence disturbing the normal growth of the developing fetus.

Placental insufficiency has been artificially produced in both rats by uterine artery ligation and in sheep by placental embolization. Both models have demonstrated intrauterine growth restriction to be a direct consequence of functional disturbances within the placental nutrient transfer process. To date, these studies have mainly focused on the detrimental effects present during fetal and early postnatal life. Further investigations are indeed warranted to establish whether metabolic disturbances persist into adult life.

Summary and Conclusions

Studies investigating the fetal origins of metabolic disease have confirmed a pivotal role for the *in utero* environment mediating the relationship between poor fetal growth and the subsequent increased risk of developing metabolic diseases in adult life. Disturbances within the critical *in utero* environment may be induced by maternal nutritional insults, abnormalities within the maternal metabolic milieu, or by placental insufficiencies. Animal models have been developed in an attempt to elucidate the mechanistic basis of this adverse metabolic programing. However, there is still an urgent need to explore further the pathogenic mechanisms involved in order to allow suitable intervention studies to be initiated.

The escalating epidemic of obesity and type 2 diabetes may be a consequence of a vicious cycle (**Figure 2**). Exposure to an abnormal *in utero* environment may predispose the offspring to the premature development of metabolic diseases. Consequently, the female offspring that are programed to develop the metabolic disease at a young age may, when pregnant, perpetuate this cycle. Generation after generation then has the subsequent risk of also prematurely developing metabolic diseases such as obesity and type 2 diabetes.

The ultimate aim in medical research is to prevent human disease. As maternal nutrition and their metabolic milieu status appears to have such a sizeable influence over the correct functioning of the metabolic processes in the offspring, there is an urgent need to establish ideal nutritional recommendations for pregnant and lactating women. Additionally, ways to treat the occurrence of placental insufficiencies successfully need to be identified. It is of utmost importance to optimize the growth, development, and metabolic programing of the offspring during the critical phase of *in utero* and early life. The development of possible prevention and treatment strategies may therefore aid in combating the epidemic prevalence of metabolic diseases such as obesity, coronary heart disease, and type 2 diabetes.

See also: **Alcohol**: Absorption, Metabolism and Physiological Effects; Disease Risk and Beneficial Effects. **Anemia**: Iron-Deficiency Anemia. **Cancer**: Effects on Nutritional Status. **Diabetes Mellitus**: Etiology and Epidemiology; Classification and Chemical Pathology; Dietary Management. **Early Origins of Disease**: Non-Fetal. **Famine. Fats and Oils. Iron. Low Birthweight and Preterm Infants**: Causes, Prevalence and Prevention; Nutritional Management. **Pregnancy**: Nutrient Requirements; Energy Requirements and Metabolic Adaptations. **Protein**: Requirements and Role in Diet.

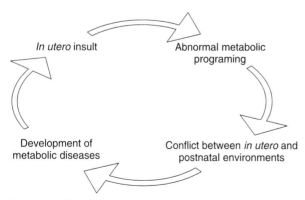

Figure 2 The vicious cycle that may be responsible for the increasing prevalences of metabolic diseases.

Further Reading

Barker DJP (1998) *Mothers, Babies and Disease in Later Life*, 2nd edn. Edinburgh, New York: Churchill Livingstone.

Bauer MK, Harding JE, Bassett NS, Breier BH, Oliver MH, Gallaher BH, Evans PC, Woodall SM, and Gluckman PD (1998) Fetal growth and placental function. *Molecular and Cellular Endocrinology* 140: 115–120.

Bertram CE and Hanson MA (2001) Animal models and programming of the metabolic syndrome. *British Medical Bulletin* 60: 103–121.

Dabelea D, Knowler WC, and Pettitt DJ (2000) Effect of diabetes in pregnancy on offspring: follow-up research in the Pima Indians. *Journal of Maternal-Fetal Medicine* 9: 83–88.

Drake AJ and Walker BR (2004) The intergenerational effects of fetal programming: non-genomic mechanisms for the inheritance of low birth weight and cardiovascular risk. *Journal of Endocrinology* 180: 1–16.

Godfrey KM and Barker DJP (2001) Fetal programming and adult health. *Public Health Nutrition* 4(2B): 611–624.

Hales CN and Ozanne SE (2003) The dangerous road of catch-up growth. *Journal of Physiology* 547(1): 5–10.

Harding JE (2001) The nutritional basis of fetal origins of adult disease. *International Journal of Epidemiology* 30: 15–23.

Holness MJ, Langdown ML, and Sugden MC (2000) Early-life programming of susceptibility to dysregulation of glucose metabolism and the development of type 2 diabetes mellitus. *Biochemical Journal* 349: 657–665.

Khan IY, Lakasing L, Poston L, and Nicolaides KH (2003) Fetal programming for adult disease: where next? *The Journal of Maternal-Fetal and Neonatal Medicine* 13: 292–299.

Newnham JP, Moss TJM, Nitsos I, Sloboda DM, and Challis JRG (2002) Nutrition and the early origins of adult disease. *Asia Pacific Journal of Clinical Nutrition* 11(supplement): S537–S542.

Ong KKL and Dunger DB (2001) Developmental aspects in the pathogenesis of type 2 diabetes. *Molecular and Cellular Endocrinology* 185: 145–149.

Ozanne SE and Hales CN (2002) Early programming of glucose-insulin metabolism. *Trends in Endocrinology and Metabolism* 13(9): 368–373.

Roseboom TJ, van der Meulen JHP, Ravelli ACJ, Osmond O, Barker DJP, and Bleker OP (2001) Effects of prenatal exposure to the Dutch famine on adult disease in later life: an overview. *Molecular and Cellular Endocrinology* 185: 93–98.

Non-Fetal

L S Adair, University of North Carolina, Chapel Hill, NC, USA

Introduction

A substantial body of evidence supports the hypothesis that adult chronic diseases have origins in early life. The basic premise of research in this field is that nutritional insufficiency during sensitive developmental periods results in structural changes or programing of metabolic functions. In the short term, such changes may enhance survival and spare brain growth at the expense of other organs. In the long run, the cost of such adaptive responses may be an increased risk of chronic disease. The main focus of research has been on fetal origins of adult disease, but there remains substantial potential for nutritional programing of later disease risk during infancy and childhood. The young infant has high energy and nutrient needs to support rapid growth and development. Birth weight typically doubles in the first 4–6 months of life, and length increases by about 30% between birth and 6 months. Many organ systems continue to mature after birth, notably the immunologic, gastrointestinal, and renal systems. This combination of rapid growth and continued development make the infant highly susceptible to the effects of environmental exposures and suboptimal nutrition, which might affect the development of disease risk. Differentiating postnatal from fetal origins is challenging, however, owing to the inevitable link between pre- and postnatal growth.

Instances of purely postnatal effects relate primarily to infant feeding or exposure to pathogens or toxins. The potential effects of infant feeding relate to nutritional adequacy, and to exposure or lack of exposure to specific substances in human milk or human milk substitutes. Effects of feeding may occur independently of the infant's nutritional status at birth. This topic is discussed further in a separate section below.

There is also a continuum of fetal and postnatal effects. Intrauterine growth-restricted infants may experience optimal or even excess postnatal nutrition, or they may continue to be exposed to nutritional insufficiency. Their responses to postnatal challenges may be conditioned by their fetal nutritional history, such that there is an interaction or synergism of fetal and postnatal effects.

Prenatal nutritional insufficiency may be thought to result in 'downsizing.' It may produce smaller organs, for example, kidneys with a reduced nephron number, a pancreas with fewer islet cells, or a low skeletal muscle mass. Nutritional insufficiency may also alter metabolic or hormonal regulation, for example, hormone secretion or sensitivity of the hypothalamic-pituitary axis. In either case, the effects may be permanent, or subject to compensatory responses once nutritional or other insults are removed. For example, a permanently reduced nephron number is a hypothesized mechanism through which fetal growth restriction affects later blood pressure. Similarly, a reduced skeletal muscle mass may persist and affect insulin sensitivity in later life associated with a reduced number of insulin receptors. In such cases, the physiological capacity to respond to risk factors encountered later in life (e.g., diets high in sodium or excess calories relative to energy needs) may be compromised.

Alternatively, catch-up or compensatory postnatal growth may occur. Many infants who were underweight for length at birth typically undergo a period of rapid postnatal compensatory growth in weight, while those who are relatively short at birth have larger length increments (see **Figure 1** for an example from a Philippines infant cohort). A central finding in many studies is that chronic disease risk is most likely to be elevated in individuals who were growth restricted *in utero* and thus small at birth, but relatively large at the time health outcomes were measured, leading to the conclusion that excess

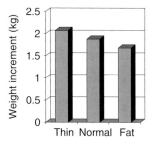 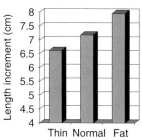

Figure 1 Early growth of Filipino infants is associated with relative weight at birth. Mean growth increments from birth to 2 months of age in children who were relatively thin (BMI < 10th sample percentile) or fat (BMI > 90th sample percentile).

postnatal growth contributes to disease risk. The extent to which rapid postnatal growth itself is a risk factor for the development of chronic disease has been the subject of extensive recent research. The relationship of early growth patterns to later disease risk is discussed in detail in a subsequent section.

Long-Term Effects of Infant Feeding

Much of the literature on the long-term effects of infant feeding is based on comparison of outcomes associated with human milk versus infant formula feeding. Postulated effects relate primarily to the different composition of human milk versus formula and different energy and nutrient intake by infants. The literature does not provide a clear and consistent picture of the long-term effects of feeding. When effects are found, they tend to be modest. Before discussing the results of these studies, it is important to raise several important methodological issues relevant to the interpretation of the literature.

First, breast feeding is a complex behavior chosen by mothers. Women who choose to breast-feed are likely to differ in systematic ways from those who do not. The choice to breast feed and the duration of breast feeding may be related to other short- and long-term health behaviors that affect the ultimate health outcomes of interest. To isolate the effect of infant feeding, it must be assumed that other concurrent and subsequent exposures are not systematically related to feeding history, or such exposures must be taken into account in multivariate analysis. Unfortunately, most studies have insufficient data to adequately control statistically for these other behaviors, particularly since they are often unmeasured or poorly measured.

Second, many studies use historical cohorts in which feeding method is recalled by the mother or based on limited records. While the decision to initiate breast feeding is likely to be accurately recalled, information about breast feeding duration and timing of introduction of other foods may be subject to recall bias.

Third, the composition of proprietary infant formulas has changed since their introduction in the 1920s. For example, sodium levels and fat sources have changed, and new ingredients such as n-3 fatty acids and nucleotides have been added recently. Therefore, results from older versus younger cohorts may differ either because true age-specific effects have emerged or because they were exposed to infant formula of different composition. Furthermore, the effects of breast and formula feeding on infant health are likely to differ depending on the environmental context.

The ideal study design for determining the long-term effects of infant feeding would require randomization to feeding regimens, and frequent follow-up of subjects up to the time when a disease risk factor or outcome is measured. Such designs are rarely ethical or feasible. An exception is a series of studies in the UK conducted by Alan Lucas and colleagues, which assessed long-term outcomes among preterm infants randomized to receive banked human milk or formula, and full-term infants whose mothers chose not to breast-feed randomized to different types of formula. While many of the studies have focused on neurodevelopment, some are now looking at other health outcomes.

Selected Outcomes Related to Infant Feeding

The following are examples of some chronic disease-related outcomes studied in relation to infant feeding. The selected outcomes are intended to be illustrative of a range of effects rather than a comprehensive treatment of all outcomes related to infant feeding.

Serum lipids Based on a systematic review of literature relating infant feeding to blood lipids in infants, adolescents, and adults, total cholesterol was found to be consistently higher in breast-fed infants compared to bottle-fed infants. No consistent differences related to feeding history were found in children and adolescents; and among adults, a majority of studies reported lower mean total cholesterol in those who had been breast-fed. The proposed but unproven mechanism for the protective effect of breast-feeding in adults is downregulation of endogenous cholesterol synthesis.

Blood pressure Differences in the sodium and fat content and composition of breast milk versus formula are thought to be the relevant determinants of long-term effects of infant feeding on blood pressure. In a recent systematic review, data were compiled to compare exclusive breast feeding to formula feeding, with adjustment for current age, sex, height, and body mass index (BMI). The analysis was based on 26 studies of systolic blood pressure and 24 studies of diastolic blood pressure. On average, subjects who were breast-fed had a modestly lower systolic blood pressure than those who had been formula fed, with an average effect of -1.10 mmHg, and no marked differences by age. However, the analysis suggested publication bias since the effect was significantly larger in small studies than large studies. The studies showed no effects of feeding on diastolic blood pressure.

Taking advantage of a 1980 randomized trial to study the effect of a low or normal sodium diet in Dutch infants, a follow-up study at age 15 years found systolic blood pressure to be 3.6 mmHg lower and diastolic to be 2.2 mmHg lower in the low-sodium group. These results suggest that sodium intake in infancy may affect blood pressure later in life.

Further evidence of the effects of diet composition comes from a long-term follow-up of the Barry Caerphilly Growth study cohort. In this study, mothers and their offspring were randomly assigned to receive a milk supplement or usual care. In young adulthood (age 23–27 years), blood pressure was positively associated with dried formula milk supplement consumed in infancy. The effect was attenuated but remained significant after controlling for current BMI, suggesting an effect of diet composition independent of growth.

Reproductive function The relatively high levels of isoflavones in soy-based infant formula have raised concerns about potential effects on endocrine and reproductive function later in life. A recent retrospective cohort study of young adults who as infants had participated in controlled feeding studies during infancy found no differences associated with soy feeding across a large number of outcomes potentially susceptible to estrogenic or antiestrogenic activity of phytoestrogens, including timing of maturation, sexual development, or fertility in adolescents or adults. Another literature review reported no meaningful differences in child growth related to feeding of soy formula. However, data are limited and further randomized controlled trials are needed to provide definitive evidence.

Growth and body composition Mode of feeding may indirectly affect later disease risk through its effects on energy intake or aspects of metabolic regulation that affect growth and body composition.

Numerous studies demonstrate different growth patterns in breast- and formula-fed infants that are hypothesized to reflect differences in nutrient intakes. In fact, evidence of systematic differences in breast- and formula-fed infants has led the World Health Organization to undertake the development of growth charts for breast-fed infants. In one careful study of body composition, total energy intakes and weight velocity from 3 to 6 months of age were higher in formula-fed compared to breast-fed infants. Estimates of fat and fat-free mass also indicate higher adiposity in formula-fed infants, however, none of these differences persisted into the second year of life. Similarly, in a study of nearly 5600 children who participated in the Third National Health and Nutrition Examination Survey, those who had been exclusively breast-fed for 4 months weighed less at 8-11 months than did infants who were fed in other ways, but few other meaningful differences in growth status through age 5 years were associated with early infant feeding.

Longer term effects of infant feeding have been assessed in studies that examined whether breast-feeding protects against later overweight or obesity. A recent review found inconsistent results, with some large cohort studies showing a moderate protective effect, and others showing no effect. The studies were also inconsistent in showing a dose response. An illustrative large study in 3–5-year-old children found that after adjusting for potential confounders, risk of having a BMI > 85th percentile was reduced among exclusively breast-fed children compared with those never breast fed, but there was no reduced risk of having a BMI > 95th percentile.

The findings are typically based on retrospective studies, in which breast-feeding data derive from maternal recall. This makes it difficult, if not impossible, to control for confounding, since a mother's decisions about breast-feeding may relate to subsequent child feeding and other factors associated with overweight. Thus, it is not clear based on the available data whether the effects of infant feeding are causal or whether breast-feeding serves as a marker for other health behaviors that may affect child and adolescent growth. Recent studies among siblings, which allow control for maternal characteristics, show no protective effects of breast-feeding on obesity in adolescents and young adults.

Exposure to antigens and development of autoimmune disease The infant's diet is the main source of exposure to antigens suspected to be related to the development of autoimmune diseases. A likely protective effect of exclusive breast-feeding relates to lack of exposure to food allergens, though some other protective mechanisms related to specific substances in breast milk have been postulated. Exposure to bovine proteins by milk feeding, and to allergenic plant proteins such as those found in wheat is suspected to increase risk of developing diseases such as type 1 diabetes and celiac disease in genetically susceptible individuals.

Type 1 diabetes is one of the most prevalent chronic diseases with childhood onset. It is characterized by autoimmunity to pancreatic islet cells and is associated with a specific human leucocyte antigen (HLA) genotype. Not all individuals with the genotype develop the disease, suggesting an important role for gene–environment interactions. Hypothesized early exposures include infant feeding and enterovirus infections. Early introduction of cows' milk has received a great deal of attention as a potential risk factor. Numerous case–control studies associate increased risk with cows' milk, but a nearly equal number of studies show no effects. These retrospective studies have been criticized as suffering from recall bias and inappropriate control groups, for example, controls without the susceptible genotype. Recent prospective studies of at-risk infants in Australia and Germany found no association of type 1 diabetes with feeding of cows' milk. However, pilot study data from an international primary prevention trial suggests that eliminating cows' milk proteins in at-risk infants reduces risk of developing islet cell autoantibodies. This study also supports a role for early enterviral infections in the etiology of type 1 diabetes in genetically susceptible individuals. In fact, the research team has suggested that the effect of cows' milk may depend on viral exposures.

Recent studies suggest a role for other food antigens. A study of at-risk German children found that feeding of gluten-containing foods before 3 months of age was associated with risk of having pancreatic islet cell autoantibodies. Another study in the US also found an increased risk of islet cell autoimmunity among at-risk children given cereal before 3 months or after 7 months of age. Furthermore, they found that risks associated with cereal introduction were reduced by breast-feeding.

Other aspects of diet may have immunomodulatory effects. Vitamin D and the n-3 fatty acids EPA and DHA are suggested to be protective against immune-modulated diseases. For example, in a case–control study, Norwegian children given cod liver oil, a rich source of EPA and DHA, in the first year of life had significantly reduced risk of type 1 diabetes.

Type 2 diabetes Few studies have assessed the relationship of infant feeding to later development of Type 2 diabetes. Early feeding may affect patterns of insulin secretion in the newborn period, and thereby program subsequent development of metabolic control. Two studies in native American populations, one in Canada and one among Pima Indians, report a protective effect of breast-feeding on later development of Type 2 diabetes. In the Pima study, exclusive breast-feeding in the first 2 months of life was associated with a lower rate of Type 2 diabetes in children and adults. In the Canadian study, breast-feeding for more than 12 months was associated with decreased risk of Type 2 diabetes. Other studies have examined early risk factors related to subsequent development of Type 2 diabetes. For example, in a study of preterm infants randomized to human milk or formula of different composition, 32-33 split proinsulin, a marker of insulin resistance, was elevated in adolescents who had received a nutrient-enriched diet compared to those with a lower nutrient diet.

In sum, infant feeding, through nutritional adequacy, direct exposure to antigens, and protective substances provided in human milk, has the potential to alter response to subsequent exposures and to directly influence the beginning of disease processes.

Postnatal Growth and Later Risk of Disease

Small body size in childhood may reflect nutritional insufficiency that may program adult disease in ways similar to that observed in the fetal period. Independent of birth weight, low weight at 1 year of age has been associated with increased risk of cardiovascular disease in adult men. Similarly, poor childhood growth manifested as short stature has been linked with insulin resistance.

More attention has recently been paid to the effects of rapid childhood growth in height and weight. The observation in much of the fetal programing literature that effects of birth size emerge or are strengthened when current body size (typically represented as BMI) is taken into account suggests an important role for postnatal growth in the origins of adult disease. Individuals who are born small, but who end up relatively large (taller or heavier than their peers) have clearly experienced more rapid growth at some point between birth and when health outcomes and current size are assessed. Whether rapid growth is an independent risk factor or whether it confers increased risk only in individuals with a history of intrauterine growth restriction is a question requiring further research. Moreover, even when strong associations of growth rate and chronic disease risk are found, it is unclear whether the association is causal or whether growth serves as a marker for other underlying causal processes.

Postnatal growth is clearly related to prenatal growth. Some metabolic changes associated with prenatal nutritional sufficiency may affect postnatal physiology and behavior that, in turn, affect growth. In addition, there is intriguing evidence from animal studies that prenatal nutritional restriction alters appetite and induces hyperphagia, and also reduces physical activity in adult animals (see **Figure 2**). If true in humans, this would be an important pathway by which disease risk is affected. Suggestive evidence comes from human infants whose cord blood leptin levels at birth were inversely related to weight gain in the first 4 months of life, independent of birth weight. Leptin may relate to subsequent growth by affecting appetite and energy intake.

Depending on the outcome under study, there are differences in whether linear growth or growth in weight, particularly weight relative to height, matters. Most often, more rapid weight gain is the risk factor, owing to the fact that excess adiposity is an important risk factor for many chronic diseases of adulthood. Another key issue concerns the timing of effects. There is controversy about whether early infancy compensatory growth following intrauterine growth restriction confers risk, or whether it is only later growth that matters.

Where many potential adverse outcomes might be affected by postnatal growth, the following sections focus on adiposity, blood pressure and coronary heart disease, insulin resistance and diabetes, and cancer.

Adiposity and Obesity

Early undernutrition followed by later overnutrition as well as early overfeeding independent of prior growth restriction are thought to increase risk of later obesity. Rapid postnatal weight gain occurs in a significant proportion of infants who are born small for gestational age. Prospective studies in US, South African, and British cohorts show that rapid growth in early infancy increases later risk of overweight. Longitudinal data from the US National Perinatal Collaborative study show that, independent of birth weight, one-third of obesity at age 20 is attributable to rapid weight gain in the first 4 months of life. In a Bristol, UK cohort, nearly one-third of children had an increased weight standard deviation (SD) score of more than 0.67 units from birth to age 2 years, and these children remained fatter, having more central fat distribution at age 5 years compared to children with lower early growth rates. Similarly, data from the South Africa Birth to Ten cohort showed that children with rapid weight gain in infancy were significantly lighter at birth and significantly taller, heavier, and fatter throughout childhood.

Early postnatal growth rates may program insulin-like growth factors, IGF-I and IGF-II. **Figure 3** illustrates this point with data on 5-year-old children from Bristol, UK in whom IGF levels were strongly related to current body size, but also that, independent of current size, children who had experienced catch up growth (change in Z-score >0.67 SD) from birth to age 2 had higher IGF levels. Childhood IGF levels are important as determinants of later linear growth and timing of puberty, and are associated with later risk of hormone-dependent cancers.

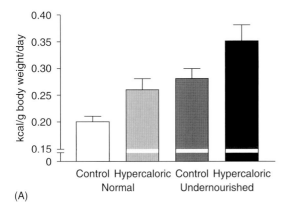

(A)

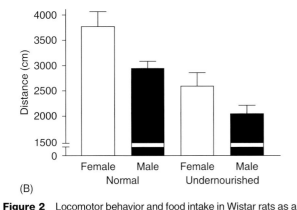

(B)

Figure 2 Locomotor behavior and food intake in Wistar rats as a consequence of a normal or adverse fetal environment ($n = 6$–8/ group). (A) Food intake (kcal per gram body weight per day over a 5-day period) in females at day 145; $P < 0.005$ for effect of fetal programing, $P < 0.05$ for postnatal hypercaloric diet. (B) Locomotor activity at 14 months in males and females; $P < 0.005$ for effect of fetal programing and gender. Data analyzed by factorial ANOVA, and data are shown as means ±SE. (Reproduced from Vickers MH, Breier BH, McCarthy D, and Gluckman PD (2003) Sedentary behavior during postnatal life is determined by the prenatal environment and exacerbated by postnatal hypercaloric nutrition. *American Journal of Physiology. Regulatory Integrative and Comparative Physiology* **285**(1): R271-273 with permission from the American Physiological Society.)

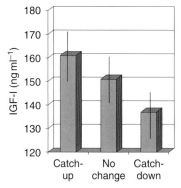
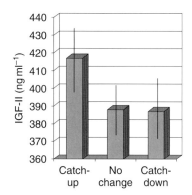

Figure 3   Hormone levels at age 5 years by change in weight Z-score from birth to 2 years of children in the ALSPAC cohort: means and 95% confidence intervals of IGF-I and IGF-II, adjusted for fat mass and fat-free mass. (Drawn from data from Ong K, Kratzsch J, Kiess W, Dunger D, and ALSPAC Study Team (2002) Circulating IGF-I levels in childhood are related to both current body composition and early postnatal growth rate. *Journal of Clinical Endocrinology and Metabolism* **87**(3): 1041–1044.)

Cancer

A large body of literature relates adult height to cancer risk, with the largest volume of evidence on breast, prostate, and colorectal cancers. In each case, risk of disease is increased with taller stature. A role for accelerated childhood growth is inferred, since taller individuals have experienced more linear growth. Possible mechanisms fall into two categories: childhood growth as a marker for other exposures that influence risk (fetal exposures, infections, timing of puberty, and energy intake) or growth as a mediator of risk (effects of growth promoting hormones such as IGF-I and IGF-II).

Few studies have directly addressed the effects of childhood growth, owing to lack of longitudinal data. Based on data from the UK Boyd Orr cohort, a one SD difference in height was associated with a 42% higher risk of overall cancer mortality in later life among males, but no effects were found in females. In another UK birth cohort, risk for breast cancer was elevated among women who were large at birth and tall at age 7. Based on data from the US Nurse's Health Study, rapid adolescent growth was associated with an increased risk of both pre- and postmenopausal breast cancer.

Blood Pressure and Coronary Heart Disease

Blood pressure is the one of the most well-studied outcomes in the context of fetal programing, with fairly consistent findings of a modest inverse relationship of birth weight to adult systolic blood pressure that increases with age. Substantial evidence demonstrates a synergistic relationship of fetal growth restriction with rapid postnatal growth. **Figure 4** presents the classic picture for systolic blood pressure: the highest pressure is found among

adolescent males who were relatively thin at birth, but relatively heavy as adolescents. Current BMI is typically the strongest anthropometric predictor of blood pressure, but at the same BMI, those with a history of fetal growth restriction have higher mean blood systolic pressure and increased risk of having high blood pressure.

Owing to the existence of good longitudinal growth data in Scandinavia, child growth trajectories can be traced for individuals with and without hypertension or other adverse outcomes such as coronary heart disease. As shown in **Figure 5**, though initially smaller, adults with hypertension diverged in their BMI trajectory and were relatively heavier after age 7 compared to those without hypertension.

There remains controversy about the age at which higher growth rates pose risk of later disease. Some studies show elevated blood pressure in association with rapid weight gain in infancy, while other studies show no effect, or a protective effect (infants with larger weight increments have lower blood pressure

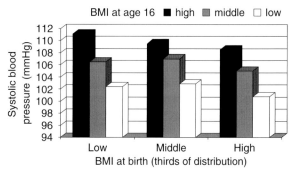

Figure 4   Synergistic effect of BMI at birth and age 16 on systolic blood pressure of Cebu (Philippines) boys: ■ high; ▤ middle; and □ low BMI. Data from the Cebu Longitudinal Health and Nutrition Survey.

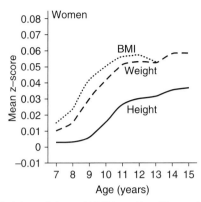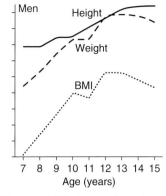

Figure 5 Z-scores for height, weight, and BMI from 7 to 15 years in 975 boys and 983 girls who later developed hypertension. Mean values for all 7086 subjects in cohort are zero. (Reproduced with permission from Eriksson J, Forsen T, Tuomilehto J, Osmond C, and Barker D (2000) Fetal and childhood growth and hypertension in adult life. *Hypertension* **36**(5): 790–794.)

as adults). The degree to which rapid infant growth represents risk may depend on whether it occurs in the context of recovery from fetal growth restriction and results in normalization of body weight versus excess growth leading to infant obesity.

There is more consistent evidence of increased risk associated with rapid weight gain in later childhood. In a Philippines cohort, larger weight increments from age 8 to 15 years increased risk of high blood pressure in boys who were relatively thin at birth. However, higher childhood weight gain in the absence of fetal growth restriction was not a risk factor in this population.

Fetal undernutrition may result in a reduced number of nephrons. Such deficits may not increase disease risk in individuals who remain small, but excess growth may challenge the ability of the kidneys to effectively regulate blood pressure. Catch-up linear growth has not been consistently implicated as a risk factor for later elevated blood pressure. In fact, continued poor linear growth, particularly in association with more rapid weight gain, increases risk of later elevated blood pressure.

Insulin Resistance and Diabetes

Most evidence relates to type 2 diabetes, but one large, population-based case–control study of type 1 diabetes in European populations found that height and weight were higher in cases starting at 1 month after birth, with maximum differences in cases and controls between 1 and 2 years of age. In the case of type 2 diabetes, both continued growth faltering in infancy and more rapid growth are associated with increased risk. Postnatal faltering in length is associated with impaired insulin metabolism.

As was the case for blood pressure, highest risk is associated with the combination of small size at birth and rapid postnatal growth gain. In a well-studied cohort in Finland, men and women who

developed type 2 diabetes had lower birth weight, length, and ponderal index, and accelerated growth in weight and height from age 7 to 15 years. Precursors of diabetes such as insulin resistance have been studied. For example, in a follow-up study of British children who were born preterm, fasting split proinsulin and glucose concentration 30 min after a glucose load were highest in children with the greatest increase in weight centile between birth and time of measurement, regardless of early size.

Extensive studies of early origins of type 2 diabetes have been conducted in India, where rates are rising very rapidly. Indian babies who are small at birth have a deficit in skeletal muscle, but not body fat compared to normal size infants. These infants tend to grow into adults that retain a lower skeletal muscle mass, but have increased abdominal obesity. This body composition is strongly related to increased risk of type 2 diabetes. Prospective studies of Indian children show an interaction between birth weight and subsequent growth. For example, children who were born small but were relatively large at age 4 had higher plasma glucose and insulin concentrations 30 min after an oral glucose load, and greater insulin resistance at age 8.

Higher growth rates in previously growth-restricted individuals may pose excessive demands on systems initially adapted to function in the face of limited resources, leading to increased risk of diseases, particularly those associated with the metabolic syndrome. Rapid growth in weight during infancy and childhood, and in particular, rapid growth following prenatal growth restriction, increases risk of developing obesity, especially abdominal obesity. Factors that contribute to early onset of obesity are therefore important to control, since obesity tracks from early life to adulthood, and is a well-recognized risk factor for diseases such as type 2 diabetes, hypertension, and coronary heart disease.

In sum, the continued vulnerability and responsivity of the developing infant and child suggest the importance of a life course perspective on the development of diseases that are typically thought of as 'adult onset.'

See also: **Breast Feeding. Cancer**: Epidemiology and Associations Between Diet and Cancer. **Coronary Heart Disease**: Hemostatic Factors; Lipid Theory. **Diabetes Mellitus**: Etiology and Epidemiology. **Hyperlipidemia**: Overview; Nutritional Management. **Hypertension**: Dietary Factors. **Infants**: Nutritional Requirements. **Lipids**: Chemistry and Classification.

Further Reading

Cameron N and Demerath EW (2002) Critical periods in human growth and their relationship to diseases of aging. *Yearbook of Physical Anthropology* 45: 159–184.

Dewey KG (2003) Is breast feeding protective against child obesity? *Journal of Human Lactation* 19: 9–18

Huxley RR, Shiell AW, and Law CM (2000) The role of size at birth and postnatal catch-up growth in determining systolic blood pressure: a systematic review of the literature. *Journal of Hypertension* 18: 815–831.

Lucas A (1998) Programming by early nutrition: An experimental approach. *Journal of Nutrition* 128: 401s–406s.

Martorell R, Stein AD, and Schroeder DG (2001) Early nutrition and later adiposity. *Journal of Nutrition* 131: 874s–880s.

Okasha M, Gunnell D, Holly J, and Davey Smith G (2002) Childhood growth and adult cancer. *Best Practice and Research Clinical Endocrinology and Metabolism* 16: 225–241.

Ong KK and Dunger DB (2002) Perinatal growth failure: the road to obesity, insulin resistance and cardiovascular disease in adults. *Best Practice in Research Clinical Endocrinology and Metabolism* 16: 191–207.

Owen CG, Whincup PH, Gilg JA, and Cook DG (2003) Effect of breast feeding in infancy on blood pressure in later life: a systematic review and meta-analysis. *British Medical Journal* 327: 1189–1195.

Owen CG, Whincup PH, Odoki K, Gilg JA, and Cook DG (2002) Infant feeding and blood cholesterol: A study in adolescents and a systematic review. *Pediatrics* 110: 597–608.

Singhal A and Lucas A (2004) Early origins of cardiovascular disease: is there a unifying hypothesis? *Lancet* 15; 363(9421): 1642–5.

Wasmuth HE and Kolb H (2000) Cow's milk and immune-mediated diabetes. *Proceedings of the Nutrition Society* 59: 573–579.

Yajnik CS (2003) Nutrition, growth, and body size in relation to insulin resistance and type 2 diabetes. *Current Diabetes Reports* 2: 108–114.

Eating Behavior *see* **Meal Size and Frequency**

EATING DISORDERS

Contents
Anorexia Nervosa
Bulimia Nervosa
Binge Eating

Anorexia Nervosa

A R Rolla, Harvard Medical School, Boston, MA, USA

The relentless pursuit of thinness and the increasing prevalence of obesity in modern societies are the roots of the present higher prevalence of eating disorders. These eating disorders can be classified according to the interaction between the preoccupation with food and body weight and the self-control of hunger (**Figure 1**).

Classification of Eating Disorders

Obesity

Obesity can be classified as an eating disorder since, primarily or secondarily, obese patients eat

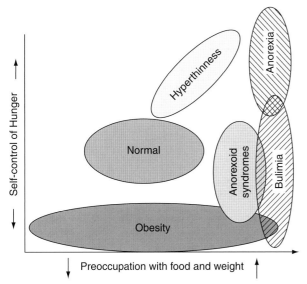

Figure 1   Classification of eating disorders based on the interaction between the preoccupation with food and body weight and the self-control of hunger. © 1999 Academic Press.

inappropriately for their increased weight and because obese individuals tend to suffer also from the other eating disorders.

Anorexia Nervosa

Anorexia nervosa is usually seen in younger women who restrict their food intake and increase exercise, causing a voluntary, stubborn malnutrition.

Bulimia

People who cannot control their hunger over a long period of time tend to have secret binging episodes. This is followed by an overwhelming feeling of guilt and depression, which frequently leads to self-induced vomiting. For this reason, the terms 'bulimia' (which means binge eating) and 'self-induced vomiting' are used interchangeably.

Anorexoid Syndromes

These abnormalities are seen in individuals who can no longer control their weight by dieting and exercising and have to resort to abnormal subterfuges, such as the following:

Self-induced vomiting
Ipecac abuse
Laxative abuse
Diuretic abuse
Anorexic agents abuse
Self-induced glycosuria in patients with insulin-dependent diabetes mellitus

Thyroid hormone abuse
Excessive, compulsive exercising

Professional Hyperthinness

This is a borderline condition, not necessarily pathological, in which individuals, usually with narcissistic tendencies, overvalue personal appearance and thinness as a way of obtaining professional success. It is commonly seen among models, figure skaters, ballerinas, artists, gymnasts, etc. They do not use the 'subterfuges' of the anorexoid patients; they are not socially isolated; their weight loss is not extreme; they have normal psychosexual activity; and they do not see themselves as overweight, unlike people with anorexia nervosa. For them, thinness is a means of obtaining success, not the final goal as in anorexia nervosa.

Anorexia Nervosa

Anorexia nervosa is a serious disease.

Psychological Disturbances

Psychological disturbances are most likely to be the initial event; they result in a complex obsession characterized by the following features:

1. An intrusive body image delusion makes the patients see themselves as being overweight when they are actually severely undernourished. This leads to a pathological fear of fatness (dysmorphophobia), a chronic voluntary starvation, and resistance to any external pressures to gain weight. Anorexic patients hide and dispose of food in the most ingenious ways to avoid eating.
2. An overwhelming sense of personal ineffectiveness makes anorexic patients believe that they cannot control the world around them. They continuously fear that they are going to lose their inner control. They therefore tightly control their world inside and slowly separate themselves from their social surroundings, with growing feelings of alienation and loneliness. There is no psychosexual development or interest, and no dating, unlike patients with bulimia.
3. Depression occurs which may be primary or secondary, obvious or atypical, and may or may not be amenable to treatment with psychotherapy and/or antidepressant medications.
4. Increased physical activity coexists with an apparent lack of hunger and fatigue and is inappropriate for the degree of malnutrition and depression.

Malnutrition

Anorexia nervosa is a self-imposed starvation. The term 'anorexia' is a misnomer since (at least initially) these patients are hungry. Anorexia nervosa is different from other forms of malnutrition because it is voluntary, resistant to nutritional treatments, accompanied by increased physical activity, without an initial organic cause (such as malignancy or surgery), and without associated infections. Because anorexia nervosa is a state of pure malnutrition without associated increased energy expenditure due to fever, immune response, or tissue reconstruction, these patients have a lowered metabolic rate and do not tend to develop opportunistic infections.

The exact mechanism by which these patients are able to control their hunger is unknown. Disturbed brain neurotransmitter activity may be implicated primarily or secondarily.

Endocrine and Metabolic Changes

Amenorrhea, decreased metabolic rate, hypothermia, hypotension, bradycardia, lanugo hair, carotinodermia, leucopenia, osteoporosis, etc. are mostly secondary to the severe malnutrition and are reversible with weight gain.

Other Clinical Characteristics

Anorexia nervosa is more frequent among daughters of white, affluent, achievement-oriented families in developed societies; it is extremely uncommon in areas of the world with poor nutrition. It tends to occur during the last years of high school or at the time of departure to a university or college.

The patients tend to be well-behaved perfectionists with good academic performance. Mothers of anorexic patients have a higher incidence of obsessive–compulsive personalities and preoccupation with diets and weight loss. Anorexic patients have done everything their mothers or families have trained them to do and, when faced with the increasing demands (and choices) of adult life, they exaggerate the only control left in their lives: *hunger*. There is an unconscious wish to revert to childhood, or to a prepubertal state, by means of undernourishing.

The onset of anorexia nervosa is usually subacute, over a period of weeks, not uncommonly after an episode of weight gain or after somebody has made a comment about the patient being overweight. Initially, it appears as an innocent attempt to lose weight, but soon thereafter it starts showing its rebellious and progressive nature. Anorexia nervosa appears in small epidemics in cities and countries, probably owing to social pressures and to imitation behaviors.

In contrast to their poor dietary intake, these patients have a paradoxical enhanced interest in nutrition and cooking. They collect recipes, read nutrition textbooks, plan a career in nutrition or cooking, or find a job in a restaurant (usually waitressing). Anorexic patients enjoy cooking and feeding the rest of the family. They know the precise energy content of all usual food and use their knowledge to select low-energy items.

When forced to eat, anorexic patients will dispose of or hide food. They use their above average intelligence to overcome all efforts to make them gain weight. They can be very resourceful in tampering with scales (adding weights to shoes or clothing, drinking large amounts of water just before weighing, etc.), and they have the most imaginative excuses as to why they are not gaining weight. They are extremely manipulative and master the art of confusing the different members of the treating team and family in their favor and against each other.

As they lose their natural insulation (subcutaneous tissue), it is difficult for anorexic patients to maintain their body temperature. They wear layer upon layer of clothing, which also helps them to hide their malnutrition. Lack of body fat is sensed by the hypothalamus as a sufficiency of stored energy, and therefore the cycling and amplitude of gonadotrophins decrease. This leads to hypothalamic amenorrhea, although approximately 30% of patients stop having menses before there is a significant weight loss. Depression may be another cause of hypothalamic amenorrhea in these patients. Some will remain amenorrheic for several months after regaining normal weight.

In primary or classical anorexia nervosa, patients lose weight by dieting (restrictive) and exercising. These patients tend to be younger, more naive, introverted, and obsessive, and they do not resort to subterfuges to lose weight. Their serum electrolytes, checked at frequent intervals, should be completely normal. Some patients find it impossible to control their hunger and start having binge episodes followed by forced vomiting (bulimia plus anorexia—'bulimarexia'). Others may start abusing laxatives or diuretics as they grow older.

There are patients in whom anorexia is secondary to an underlying, more serious psychiatric disorder, such as depression, schizophrenia, hysteria, or borderline personality disorder. In these cases, the course is longer and depends on the primary condition, as does its treatment. It is very uncommon for men to have anorexia nervosa, in men the condition tends to be associated more often with psychiatric problems and with homosexuality.

Physical Examination

The profound weight loss and cadaveric appearance contrast with the patient's increased physical activity. While hospitalized, if allowed, these patients try to perform some of the nursing chores or even to counsel other patients. Many patients exercise secretly in their rooms and jog or go for long walks when not supervised.

Pubic and axillary hair is preserved, and there is an increase in light, thin hair ('peach fuzz') on the face and neck, back, arms, and thighs (lanugo hair). Patients have low body temperature and poor tolerance to cold exposure because of their malnutrition-induced lowered metabolic rate and the loss of insulation of the diminished subcutaneous tissue. Layers of clothing tend to hide their cachectic appearance. Bradycardia and hypotension are common and secondary to decreased sympathetic drive due to malnutrition.

The skin is dry and has a peculiar bluish erythema over the knuckles and knees. Orange-yellow discoloration of the skin (carotinodermia), seen in palms and soles, is frequently found. It is caused, at least in part, by an increased intake of vegetables, since it may also be seen among vegetarians.

Symptoms

Symptoms are amazingly few. Usually these patients are forced to see a physician by their families. Spontaneous complaints may be amenorrhea, constipation, abdominal pain or distension after eating, 'fluid retention,' and inability to lose weight, for which they may ask to be placed on special diets.

Laboratory Investigations

The following findings are typical:

Mild normochromic, normocytic anemia.
Leucopenia with relative lymphocytosis.
Low sedimentation rates due to low fibrinogen levels.
Serum albumin and transferrin levels are normal, except in severe cases.
Serum carotene and cholesterol levels are normal or slightly elevated, which helps to rule out malabsorption.
Low normal blood glucose levels are found, with low levels of glycohemoglobin.
Electrolyte abnormalities, particularly low serum potassium values, occur only where there is self-induced vomiting or abuse of diuretics or laxatives.

Low serum levels of luteinizing hormone, follicle-stimulating hormone, and estradiol.
Increased growth hormone levels with decreased levels of insulin-like growth factor 1 (somatomedin C) in the serum.
Plasma renin activity and aldosterone levels may be very high in patients who abuse laxatives or diuretics (pseudo-Bartter's syndrome).
Electrocardiography shows sinus bradycardia, flat or inverted T waves, and prolonged QT_c.
Decreased bone density is due to decreased estrogen and progesterone secretion, decreased calcium and vitamin D intake, protein malnutrition, and increased marrow fat content of the bones. The conversion of hematopoietic to fatty marrow is related to the severity of the malnutrition and may be demonstrated with magnetic resonance imaging.

Endocrine Changes

Insulin

Low serum insulin levels occur with increased glucagon concentration. There is a tendency to asymptomatic low blood glucose levels and a low glycohemoglobin concentration. Fasting ketosis may be seen. The number and affinity of insulin receptors in target cells are increased, and abnormal glucose tolerance occurs due to prolonged fasting.

Adipose Tissue Hormones

The adipose tissue secretes different hormones called adipocytokines. Their secretion seems to vary in relation to the amount of adipose tissue accumulated, although the exact mechanism is not known. During profound weight loss, as in anorexia nervosa, there is a marked decrease in the adipose tissue mass with the typical changes in adipocytokines secretion that occur in these circumstances. One of the most studied adipocytokine changes is decreased leptin secretion. Increased fat mass stores are accompanied by an increased leptin secretion; decreased fat mass stores decrease leptin secretion. Low serum levels of leptin reaching the hypothalamus increase the activity of the 'hunger center,' in part by increasing the local activity of neuropeptide Y. Individuals with anorexia nervosa have very low levels of leptin in blood and cerebrospinal fluid, in relation to their decreased adipose tissue. This should cause an increase in hypothalamic neuropeptide Y content and hunger, but this compensatory mechanism to maintain a normal body weight does not seem to be effective in anorexic patients. Another important effect of the serum levels of leptin on the hypothalamus is the modulation of the gonadal axis. Low levels of leptin are associated with decreased activity of the gonadal axis, and this explains the relationship between starvation and hypogonadism. After nutritional rescue and weight regain, the levels of leptin in the serum become normal.

Gonadal Axis

The female hypothalamus needs to 'sense' the presence of approximately 14–18 kg of body fat in order to allow fertility and menstrual cycles. With lesser amounts of fat, there is a progressive regression to the prepubertal state (low, nonspiking serum gonadotrophin levels). The signal from the fat stores to the gonadal hypothalamus seems to be the level of serum leptin. Very low levels of serum leptin, secondary to the decreased fat mass, seem to result in a decrease in luteinizing hormone-releasing hormone (LHRH) secretion. The hypothalamic, hypogonadal state of anorexia nervosa is due to the combined effects of malnutrition and the psychological disturbances on the hypothalamus. Secretion of LHRH and gonadotrophins improves as weight is regained and leptin levels increase; however, in up to one-third of these patients menses do not return immediately after nutritional rescue and weight restoration are accomplished. The decreased estrogen secretion from the ovaries causes a significant loss of bone mass at a critical time, which will subsequently aggravate postmenopausal osteoporosis.

In males, malnutrition seems to have a less important influence on the gonadal axis. Severe weight loss of long duration decreases serum testosterone and gonadotrophin levels, but to a lesser degree than in women.

Thyroid

Thyroid-stimulating hormone levels are normal but there is a delayed response to thyrotrophin-releasing hormone. Serum thyroxine, both total and free, is normal. The level of serum T_3 is low owing to decreased peripheral conversion (euthyroid sick syndrome), and there is a concomitant increase in reverse T_3. The basal metabolic rate is decreased by 20–30% and not fully corrected with T_3 replacement since it is also due to decreased sympathetic activity.

Sympathetic Nervous System

There is decreased peripheral sympathetic activity, with normal adrenomedullary function. This is due to decreased ingestion of energy, and it explains the tendency to bradycardia, postural hypotension, and low basal metabolic rate.

Adrenal Cortex

Serum cortisol levels are slightly raised, without diurnal variation, and may not suppress with dexamethasone overnight. Urinary 17-hydroxy and 17-keto steroids are decreased by 30–50%, but urinary-free cortisol may be increased. Corticotrophin-releasing factor (CRF) stimulation causes a subnormal corticotrophin rise but a normal or supernormal serum cortisol response. Levels of CRF in the cerebrospinal fluid are elevated. These changes in the hypothalamic–pituitary–adrenal axis are very similar to those seen in untreated depression.

Growth Hormone

Basal and pulsatile secretion of growth hormone (GH) is increased, with a peripheral resistance to its effects. Serum GH levels are elevated in 60% of patients, particularly in the most severe cases. This is due to decreased feedback from lowered serum concentrations of insulin-like growth factor 1 (IGF 1) and to increased serum levels of ghrelin. Growth hormone levels do not rise normally after L-dopa or insulin hypoglycemia, but there may be an unexpected rise in GH blood levels after stimulation with thyrotrophin-releasing hormone.

Ghrelin is a recently discovered polypeptide secreted by the stomach that increases in circulation with weight loss. Ghrelin is an activating ligand for the GH secretagogue receptor in the hypothalamus. With starvation and weight loss, the increased serum levels of ghrelin increase the release of GH and hunger. Individuals with anorexia nervosa have high serum levels of ghrelin that return to normal with normalization of body weight.

Vasopressin

There is decreased capacity to concentrate urine due at least in part to sluggish vasopressin secretion in response to osmotic stimuli. Levels of vasopressin in the cerebrospinal fluid are increased.

Inflammatory Cytokines

Inflammatory cytokines have important endocrino-metabolic effects in people with infections and neoplasias, including anorexia and weight loss. In individuals with anorexia nervosa the serum levels of interleukin-1β, interleukin-6, tumor necrosis factor-α, and their soluble receptors are lower than normal, which may be due to decreased adipose production of these cytokines due to the decreased fat mass.

Hypothalamic Control of Hunger in Anorexia Nervosa

In normal individuals fasting and weight loss increase hunger by multiple mechanisms (decreased serum levels of leptin, insulin, and blood glucose and increased levels of ghrelin). At the level of the hypothalamus there is an increase in the potent orexigenic neuropeptide Y and other changes in neurotransmitters secondary to the fasting state. Some of these neurotransmitter changes may be the cause or a mechanism of anorexia nervosa, and for this reason they have received considerable attention in the past several years. It is important to understand that appetite control is a very complex hypothalamic function that involves many local and systemic neuropeptides, amines, and hormones.

Abnormal serotonin activity has been found in the brain of women with anorexia nervosa. An area in the chromosome 1 (p36.3–34.3) that contains genes for the serotonin 1D receptor and for the opioid delta receptor was associated with patients with anorexia nervosa by linkage analysis. One polymorphism in the Agouti related protein (Ala67Thr) has also been found associated with anorexia nervosa. Melanocortin system stimulants in the hypothalamus, such as Agouti related protein, are also involved in appetite and energy regulation. On the other hand, these genetic abnormalities may amount to only a biological tendency and do not explain the relatively short term of the illness during a life time or the changes in prevalence in the past decades.

Bone Density

Decreased estrogen and progesterone secretion; low serum levels of IGF-1; increased levels of serum cortisol; malnutrition with protein, calcium, and vitamin deficiencies; and fatty degeneration of the bone marrow lead to decreased bone density. Increased exercising does not counteract this osteopenic tendency, which affects mostly young women during the years of skeletal growth. The osteopenia of anorexia nervosa is mostly asymptomatic, but some patients may present with stress fractures (diagnosed only with bone scans) related to their increased exercising. Many of these patients do not achieve their peak bone density even after their nutritional recovery and restoration of menses, and they are left with a propensity to fracture bones for the rest of their lives. Treatment with estrogens, calcium, and vitamin D is mildly effective. IGF-1 and DHEA-S have been used with partial success.

Rapid restoration of nutrition seems to be the best management of anorexic osteopenia.

Differential Diagnosis

In the majority of cases the severe and voluntary malnutrition accompanied by the typical delusion of being fat and resistance to gain weight make the diagnosis very clear. Malnutrition due to organic causes in adolescents usually has an obvious reason and the patients want to improve their nutrition. Hypothalamic tumors may rarely present with severe loss of appetite.

The differential diagnosis should include the anorexoid syndromes. In pure anorexia nervosa the weight loss is due only to restrictive eating habits and exercise. Some anorexic patients may start binging and inducing vomiting, in which case their condition is called bulimarexia.

In some cases, anorexia nervosa is secondary to a serious, underlying psychiatric illness, with the weight loss being only an added problem. A particular diagnostic and therapeutic dilemma may occur for young women with personality disorder or chronic schizophrenia and anorexia nervosa.

Treatment

The multifaceted pathogenesis of anorexia nervosa requires an experienced team of psychiatrists, nutritionists, endocrinologists, internists or pediatricians, and nurses. *Each patient should be considered individually* since there are as many variations as there are patients. It is important to maintain communication between the different members of the team in order to present a unified front to the patient. Invariably, the patient will try to find and exploit the most minimal differences of opinion between the members of the team. Ideally, all important decisions should be made by one central team leader. Nurses, aides, and other paramedical personnel should be instructed about how to deal with the patient's behavior and charming search for allies.

There is no specific treatment and the methods reported are, at best, controversial. The etiology of this disorder is unknown, and etiological factors are probably different in each patient. It is therefore important to tailor the therapeutic approach to each patient.

Many cases of established and severe anorexia nervosa require prolonged hospitalization for psychological and nutritional rescue. Separation from parents and home environment is only part of what is to be gained from hospitalization. Administrators and health insurance companies must understand this need.

Hospitalization is indicated for the following:

Severe and rapid weight loss
Serious metabolic or cardiovascular problems (hypokalemia less than $2.5 \, mmol \, l^{-1}$) despite oral replacement, blood urea nitrogen more than $10.6 \, mmol \, l^{-1}$ of urea ($30 \, mg \, dl^{-1}$) in the presence of normal renal function, pulse less than $45 \, min^{-1}$, systolic blood pressure less than $70 \, mmHg$, or a body temperature less than $36 \, °C$
Severe depression and suicide risk
Psychosis
Family crisis

Psychiatric Treatment

From the outset, the entire family should be interviewed to gain insight into the patient's previous behavior and to understand the family dynamics and enlist their help in therapy. Clear, simple contracts with the patient are a form of behavior modification that is simple to carry out. Initially, most daily activities and visits are curtailed and the patient is watched, particularly around mealtimes. As the patient improves, restrictions are lessened and privileges increased. Short-term goals are set from the beginning. Weight gains of 250 g daily or 1.3–1.8 kg per week are acceptable limits. Patients who accomplish these goals are rewarded by increasing levels of activity and autonomy within the hospital as a positive reinforcement.

The general attitude of the team should be one of understanding, concern, and firmness. One should try to build a trusting relationship in which the patients feel understood but without giving them a chance to deceive. The nature and course of the illness should be clearly explained to the patient and the family. This includes the serious complications of malnutrition and the fatal outcome of severe cases. Emphasize that the goal of treatment is not to make the patient fat but to make the patient feel better and to improve self-confidence and eating habits. Weight is only a by-product of the improvement, and 'muscle mass and protein recovery,' not fat, is what has to be gained.

This firm understanding should engage the patient in a *treatment alliance* with the team. Remember that many of these patients are very polite and 'out to please you' at least superficially, and many times their initial acceptance hides deeper feelings of isolation and resentment. Psychotherapy is of help for some patients, usually accompanied by behavior modification and family therapy.

Despite the common use of antidepressants, several double-blind trials have been inconclusive or only slightly favorable. Patients with clear manifestations of depression and the more severe cases seem to benefit more from these medications. Tricyclic antidepressants tend to increase appetite and are more suited for patients with pure anorexia nervosa. Selective serotonin reuptake inhibitors may help decrease binging in patients with associated bulimia. Olanzapine, an atypical antipsychotic medication associated with weight gain, has been shown to be useful in some patients with anorexia nervosa in uncontrolled studies.

Nutritional Treatment

The psychiatric treatment is beneficial only as long as the patient's nutrition is improved. The nutritional rescue breaks down the vicious circle of the psychological consequences of starvation and makes the patient more receptive to psychotherapy. The team should be prepared to deal with the most ingenious ways to deceive. The patient should be told that because of the tendency to deceive frequently found in her illness, close supervision will be necessary at least in the beginning of the treatment. Patients should be weighed fasting in the morning, in nightgown without shoes and with the same scale, daily or at regular intervals by a nurse.

Initially, oral intake should be monitored carefully with a nurse sitting through the eating period and for 30 min thereafter to prevent postprandial vomiting. The tray should be checked for any food not consumed. In this way, a careful energy count is obtained daily. If the energy intake is inadequate or if the patient is not gaining weight, the diet should be supplemented with low-residue, high-energy canned formulae dispensed by the nurse during medication rounds. These diet supplements should be consumed in front of the nurse. Many patients with anorexia nervosa have subclinical vitamin deficiencies and they should receive a multivitamin tablet every day.

It is not infrequent for these patients to complain of gastric distress after sudden increases in food intake; smaller and more frequent feedings and/or administration of metoclopramide or cisapride before meals may be of help. Tube feeding is poorly tolerated by most of these patients; it has connotations of a gastrointestinal 'rape.'

If severe malnutrition is present (low serum albumin and transferrin levels, anergic skin testing), parenteral hyperalimentation should be instituted from the beginning. It is recommended to start with small amounts of hyperalimentation fluid to avoid excessive sodium and water retention (refeeding edema) which is very distressing to patients. The rate of hyperalimentation solution administration should be modified according to the improvement in oral intake and weight. Staff should be continuously aware of the possibility of tampering with the central lines by the patient, with the potential for air embolization, infection, and bleeding. In many patients it is important to curtail all physical activity initially, to the point of confining them to absolute bed rest with only bathroom privileges. As the patient improves, the activities are progressively increased.

Estrogen replacement is indicated to prevent the progressive decrease in bone density but it is poorly tolerated and accepted by these patients. Ideally, a birth control pill with good estrogen content should be administered.

Prognosis

The outcome for patients with anorexia nervosa is variable; a worse outcome is associated with older age of onset, severity and duration of the illness, male sex, and severe associated psychiatric disturbances. In general, 40–60% of patients achieve full nutritional and psychological recovery after 6–12 months. Approximately 20–40% attain a borderline normal weight and existence for the rest of their lives, but with the occurrence of significant stress they may revert to their previous anorexic behavior. There is a mortality rate of 5–30% in the most severe cases due to suicide, electrolyte imbalance, and starvation-induced myocardial damage causing intractable arrhythmias; it is rarely due to infection. Long-term follow-up of these patients has shown an increased later mortality due to alcoholism.

See also: **Adolescents**: Nutritional Requirements. **Eating Disorders**: Bulimia Nervosa. **Malnutrition**: Primary, Causes Epidemiology and Prevention; Secondary, Diagnosis and Management. **Obesity**: Definition, Etiology and Assessment. **Starvation and Fasting**.

Further Reading

Adan RAH, Hillebrand JJG, de Rijke C *et al.* (2003) Melanocortin system and eating disorders. *Annals of the New York Academy of Science* **994**: 267.

Ahima RS, Prabakaran D, Mantzoros C *et al.* (1996) Role of leptin in the neuroendocrine response to fasting. *Nature* **382**: 250.

Audenaert K, van Laere K, Dumont F *et al.* (2003) Decreased 5-HT2a receptor binding in patients with anorexia nervosa. *Journal of Nuclear Medicine* **44**: 163.

Becker AE, Grinspoon SK, Klibanski A *et al.* (1999) Eating disorders. *New England Journal of Medicine* **340**: 1092.

Bergen AW, van den Bree MB, Yeager M *et al.* (2003) Candidate genes for anorexia nervosa in the 1p33–36 linkage region: Serotonin 1 D and delta opioid receptor loci exhibit significant association with anorexia nervosa. *Molecular Psychiatry* **8**: 397.

Brambilla F *et al.* (2001) Plasma concentration of interleukin-1-beta, interleukin-6 and tumor necrosis factor-alpha, and their soluble receptors and antagonists in anorexia nervosa. *Psychiatry Research* **103**: 107.

Fairburn CG and Harrison PJ (2003) Eating disorders. *Lancet* **361**: 407.

Garfinkel PE and Gardner DM (1982) *Anorexia Nervosa, a Multidimensional Perspective.* New York: Brunner/Mazel.

Gordon CM, Grace E, Emans SJ *et al.* (2002) Effects of oral dehydroepiandrosterone on bone density in young women with anorexia nervosa: A randomized trial. *Journal of Clinical Endocrinology and Metabolism* **87**: 4935.

Kaye WH (1997) Persistent alterations in behavior and serotonin activity after recovery from anorexia and bulimia nerviosa. *Annals of the New York Academy of Science* **817**: 162.

Kennedy SH, Kaplan AS, Garfinkel PE *et al.* (1994) Depression in anorexia nervosa and bulimia nervosa: Discriminating depressive symptoms and episodes. *Journal of Psychosomatic Research* **38**: 773.

Klibanski A, Biller BM, Schoenfeld DA *et al.* (1995) The effects of estrogen administration on trabecular bone loss in young women with anorexia nervosa. *Journal of Clinical Endocrinology and Metabolism* **80**: 898.

Mantzoros C, Flier JS, Lesem MD *et al.* (1997) Cerebrospinal fluid leptin in anorexia nervosa: Correlation with nutritional status and potential role in resistance to weight gain. *Journal of Clinical Endocrinology and Metabolism* **82**: 1845.

Pannacciulli N, Vettor R, Milan G *et al.* (2003) Anorexia nervosa is characterized by increased adiponectin plasma levels and reduced nonoxidative glucose metabolsim. *Journal of Clinical Endocrinology and Metabolism* **88**: 1748.

Schwabe AD (moderator) (1981) Anorexia nervosa. *Annals of Internal Medicine* **94**: 371.

Soyka LA, Misra M, Frenchman A *et al.* (2002) Abnormal bone mineral accrual in adolescent girls with anorexia nervosa. *Journal of Clinical Endocrinology and Metabolism* **87**: 4177.

Tolle V, Kadem M, Bluet-Pajon MT *et al.* (2003) Balance in Ghrelin and leptin plasma levels in anorexia nervosa patients and constitutionally thin women. *Journal of Clinical Endocrinology and Metabolism* **88**: 109.

Treasurer J and Hollander AJ (1989) Genertic vulnerability to eating disorders. In: Remschmidt H and Schmidt MW (eds.) *Child and Youth Psychiatry: European Perspectives.* New York: Hogrefe & Hubert.

Vande Berg BC, Malghem J, Lecouvet FE *et al.* (1996) Distribution of serouslike bone marrow changes in the lower limbs of patients with anorexia nervosa: Predominant involvement of the distal extremities. *American Journal of Roentgenology* **166**: 621.

Bulimia Nervosa

A J Hill and S F L Kirk, University of Leeds, Leeds, UK

Episodes of ravenous overeating, referred to as compulsive eating or binge eating, have been recognized clinically since the 1950s. However, the disorder of bulimia nervosa was not formally described until 1979. This relatively recent recognition of the eating disorder has two important implications. First, the clinical picture and understanding of the psychopathology is changing with time. This has led both to a refinement in the diagnostic criteria used to characterize the disorder and to changes in reported prevalence. Second, the research base used to make judgments about development, prevalence, treatment, prognosis, and prevention is smaller than that for anorexia nervosa. Quite simply, there are still many unknowns in the area of bulimia nervosa.

This article focuses on the features used to make a diagnosis of bulimia nervosa, the psychopathology and developmental course of the disorder, and the groups at risk. Specific attention is paid to the nutritional consequences of bulimia nervosa and the ways in which dietary management is used in its treatment. Finally, long-term prognosis is considered.

Diagnostic Criteria

The behavior at the center of the disorder, binge eating, has been progressively redefined. A priority has been to separate binge eating from mere indulgence and everyday overeating. Accordingly, two features of a true binge have been identified: consumption of unusually large amounts of food and an aversive sense of lack of control over eating. The size of binges varies but is typically between 1000–2000 kcal.

Diagnostic schedules (such as DSM-IV and ICD-10) agree on three features that must be present in someone with bulimia nervosa. The first is the presence of binge episodes. Second, the person must use compensatory behavior to control body shape or weight. The most common is self-induced vomiting, but these strategies also include use of laxatives or diuretics, excessive exercise, and extreme dieting or fasting. Third, the person must show overconcern with body weight and shape. Importantly, the person should not be of low body weight, in which case a diagnosis of anorexia nervosa would be made.

The tightening of these formal diagnostic criteria has had the consequence of reducing misdiagnosis and prevalence but has increased the numbers of those with atypical eating disorders. Failing to exhibit one or more of the key diagnostic features, such as an insufficient frequency of binge eating, is classified variously as atypical, partial syndrome or 'eating disorders not otherwise specified' (EDNOS). It is also useful to note that the diagnostic criteria for another eating disorder, binge eating disorder (BED), are included in DSM-IV, albeit for research purposes. The key difference between BED and bulimia nervosa is the absence of the extreme compensatory behaviors that follow the binge. Those with BED are less likely to be restricting their eating but more likely to be overweight and to be older (most presenting between ages 30 and 50).

Psychopathology

The description of body image disturbance that is central to both anorexia and bulimia nervosa has undergone revision. A distinction has been argued for between dissatisfaction with body shape and overvalued ideas about weight and shape. Although body shape dissatisfactions are commonly found in these patients, it is their overvalued ideas about weight and shape that are the necessary diagnostic feature. In other words, concern should go beyond simply feeling fat to a point where a person's life is dominated by their feelings about body weight and shape.

If these overvalued ideas are accepted as the core psychopathology of bulimia nervosa, then the chaotic eating that typifies the condition can be seen as a behavioral consequence. Binges are often interspersed between periods of intense dieting, even fasting, themselves strategies to control weight. Purging always follows a binge and is a way of expelling the food ingested or compensating for the food energy intake. Binges are secretive, planned, often expensive, and emotionally self-destructive. Paired with purging, they are cyclical and self-perpetuating, although their frequency may wax and wane. In addition, this behavior may have a long history before treatment is considered and clinical attention sought.

Bulimic episodes may be triggered by a variety of factors, including anxiety, boredom, tension, or breaking the self-imposed dietary rules necessary to maintain rigid control over eating (see **Figure 1**). Only rarely is hunger identified as precipitating a binge, even though the person may not have eaten for 24 h or more.

Sustained depressive and anxiety symptoms are common and are part of a range of psychological

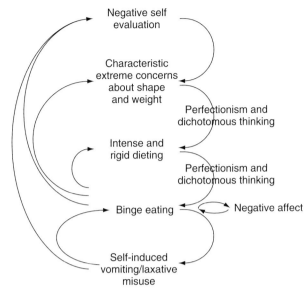

Figure 1 The cognitive behavioral view of the maintenance of bulimia nervosa (adapted from Fairburn & Brownell, 2002).

and social problems characteristic of bulimia nervosa. Impulsivity is also characteristic, with sexual promiscuity, self-harm, drug use, and stealing frequently noted. One suggestion is that impulsivity is a personality trait that favors bingeing over restriction, and so predisposes a person to bulimia nervosa rather than anorexia nervosa.

Etiology

As with anorexia nervosa, the picture of development is complex and multifactorial. There is no single cause of bulimia nervosa. Rather, a variety of psychological, biological, and social factors are involved in the emergence of the disorder. Although etiology is diverse, it has much in common with the forces responsible for anorexia nervosa and is clarified by looking at the groups of people most at risk. Overall, the balance of etiological factors is in favor of psychological and social causes, given that bulimia nervosa is a relatively new condition and has arisen at a time of profound social and cultural change, with little concurrent change in human biology.

The process of the development of eating disorders can be usefully divided into three stages. These conceptually separate the factors that predispose an individual to the disorder, precipitating events that lead to onset, and factors that perpetuate or maintain the disorder once initiated. Any framework drawn up for bulimia nervosa would be very similar to that for anorexia nervosa because the etiology of the two disorders appears to have a lot in common. Indeed, up to a third of patients with bulimia nervosa have a premorbid history of anorexia nervosa.

Although the etiological picture is very similar to that for anorexia nervosa, there are a few clues to differences. Genetic studies suggest the disorder is less heritable than anorexia nervosa, although heritability estimates of 46–71% have been calculated for the key behaviors, binge eating and self-induced vomiting. Evidence from case–control and cohort studies suggests two groupings of factors that contribute independently to the risk of developing bulimia nervosa. First, there is increased exposure to dieting and related risk factors, including parental and childhood obesity, and critical family comments about weight, shape, or eating. Second, a greater number of general risk factors for psychiatric disorder has been observed. These include parental psychiatric disorders such as depression, alcohol and substance abuse during childhood, low parental contact but high parental expectations, neglect, and abuse. Sexual abuse has been reported in 20–25% of patients with bulimia nervosa, a higher level than that found in restricting anorexia nervosa. Although the rate is increased compared to that of matched controls, it is no higher than the rate among young women with other psychiatric disorders. However, women with eating disorders in the context of sexual abuse appear to have higher rates of comorbid psychiatric conditions than other women with eating disorders.

The perspective on the perpetuation of bulimia nervosa is a cognitive one. **Figure 1** shows the vicious circles that maintain binge eating. Four points are emphasized in explaining this to patients. First, although dieting is a response to binge eating, it also maintains binge eating by both biological and psychological mechanisms. Second, compensatory purging encourages bingeing through a belief in its effectiveness at removing food for digestion. In other words, the barriers against overeating are removed since the food will not be absorbed. This is sometimes described as the reason why an individual initiated a binge–purge cycle of behavior. Third, extreme concern about body shape and weight promotes intense and rigid dieting and maintains the eating problem. Fourth, extreme concern about shape and weight is commonly associated with negative self-evaluation such as low self-esteem and long-standing feelings of worthlessness.

Groups at Risk

Like anorexia nervosa, bulimia nervosa is more common in women than in men, with a female:

male ratio around 10:1. The exact prevalence is notoriously difficult to establish for eating disorders, and for bulimia nervosa in particular. Problems in this regard include the recency of the disorder, changing diagnostic criteria, and the secrecy and non-life-threatening nature of the disorder preventing its routine appearance in clinical settings. Studies of US college students in the 1980s revealed up to 20% with bulimic symptoms. However, when such epidemiological studies investigate community samples and use interviews to follow-up questionnaire surveys, the average point prevalence among young women using strict diagnostic criteria is 1000 per 100,000 or 1.0%. In specific groups such as university students, there may be more than twice this level of the disorder. Bulimia nervosa is extremely rare in girls under 14 and the majority of cases are recognized between the ages of 18 and 25. Cases do present clinically in women in their late 20s and 30s, although they may have a long history of disordered eating.

The invisibility of bulimia nervosa is demonstrated by estimates of 1-year-period prevalence rates. These are calculated by adding figures for point prevalence and annual incidence. The 1-year-period prevalence rates for bulimia nervosa per 100,000 young women have been reported as follows:

In the community: 1500
In primary care: 170
In specialist mental health care: 87

These data indicate that only 11% of the community cases of bulimia nervosa are detected, and of these only half are received by specialist services. Since the first clinical description in 1979, there has been a dramatic upsurge in the number of bulimia nervosa cases seen, and much greater than that for anorexia nervosa. Although improved detection may account for some of this increase, there is general agreement that this represents a real increase in the number of women with bulimia nervosa.

Since women are most at risk, it is reasonable to ask why. One reason is that women are far more likely to diet than men. Dieting is itself a behavior that places individuals at risk of developing bulimia nervosa. But the motivations for dieting may be equally important. Women diet more than men for several reasons. These are bound together as a sociocultural perspective on bulimia, an approach that has become a powerful model for explaining who develops bulimia and why. At the heart of this perspective are three issues: the importance of a thin body shape for women, the centrality of appearance in women's gender role, and the importance of appearance for societal success. The arguments and evidence to support this analysis are compelling.

The above information on prevalence indicates that the average age of someone with bulimia nervosa is older than that for anorexia. This may reflect the observation that bulimia nervosa often follows a period of anorexia or at least low weight. Developmental challenges and age-dependent life events are also seen as important. The developmental task of achieving a sense of identity during mid- and late adolescence may be disrupted by relationship problems, peer or family difficulties, or events such as leaving home to go to college. The resultant erosion of self-esteem and perceived control can lead to problems with eating manifest as intensified dieting or periods of overeating and weight gain. The disrupted pattern of eating that follows may be the early stage of the disorder.

Nutritional Findings

A key feature of bulimia nervosa is the extreme dietary restraint that is exhibited in between episodes of binge eating. Such behavior has been described as all or nothing, so that on a good day the sufferer may describe consuming a very low-energy diet, whereas a bad day will consist of several episodes of uncontrolled eating. This will be accompanied by the purging behaviors previously described.

To sustain binge eating episodes, the person with bulimia nervosa may spend hundreds of pounds on food, selecting foods normally avoided during periods of dietary restraint which are easy to eat and subsequently remove from the body. To them, it is this overeating that is seen as the basic problem, not the dietary restraint that precedes it. Yet, it is this dietary restraint that drives the disorder. When not binge eating, it is common for patients to avoid eating for long periods, with 80% reporting consumption of one meal a day or less. While restricting their intake, they will consume reduced energy foods, with a strong tendency to avoid fat and choose energy-reduced foodstuffs.

It is often assumed that people with bulimia nervosa have good nutritional knowledge. Indeed, to the untrained eye, a diet history for a 'good day,' consisting of foods such as wholemeal bread, lots of vegetables and fruit, and skimmed milk, can be interpreted as conforming to healthy eating guidelines. However, this is not the case. Such restrictive behavior may fail to achieve even half the recommended energy intake and consequently may be deficient in micronutrients. The anxiety experienced through consuming diet-breaking, 'unsafe' foods leads to the individual adopting extremely restricted diets between binges. Such intakes have been found to be lower in fat and higher in protein than the intakes of controls. People with bulimia nervosa also report feeling greater anxiety and guilt after eating foods they believed to be fattening.

Purging behaviors begin as a compensatory mechanism to offset episodes of binge eating. Consequently, it is a widely held belief that they are effective methods of weight control. However, the damage done to the body by these methods far exceeds any benefits in terms of weight. Any weight loss experienced is usually related to disruption of fluid balance rather than a loss of fat tissue. Furthermore, if self-induced vomiting is adopted, binges are likely to become more frequent and severe. If vomiting is prevented, the bulimic will consume significantly less food, thus maintaining the cycle previously described. Research has shown that vomiting fails to rid the body of all the food ingested. It has been estimated that only half the contents of the stomach are removed through vomiting, although this is variable and difficult to determine. Similarly, laxatives work on the system *after* food has been digested. One classic experiment looked at the amount of food energy lost through laxative abuse and found that, despite copious diarrhea, the amount of energy lost from the body was less than that found in the average chocolate bar.

What both laxative abuse and vomiting have in common is the depletion of fluid, leading to dehydration and electrolyte disturbances, particularly hypokalemia (low potassium). In some cases, hypoglycemia may develop as a response to fasting or binge eating and vomiting. In extreme cases, death may occur through cardiac arrest or gastrointestinal complications, such as oesophageal or gastric rupture. Vomiting also leads to erosion of dental enamel, resulting in periodontal disease and an increased incidence of dental caries. Other effects of bulimia nervosa include menstrual irregularities, swelling of the salivary glands secondary to vomiting, and reflex constipation, which occurs as a consequence of laxative abuse and dehydration. Laxative abuse has also been found to cause steatorrhea and protein-losing enteropathy in some cases.

People with bulimia nervosa may have lower energy requirements. Using indirect calorimetry, it has been found that patients have a measured resting energy expenditure below that predicted by standard formulas such as the Harris–Benedict equation. They also report consuming fewer kilocalories per kilogram body weight than control subjects. One explanation for this finding is that bingeing and purging may alter energy efficiency. These findings have implications for nutritional management, particularly in relation to the prescription of energy intakes.

Dietary Management

Dietitians and nutritionists are increasingly involved in the treatment of bulimia nervosa. While this is best utilized within a multidisciplinary team, ideally with some form of psychological intervention available, it is not uncommon for dietitians or nutritionists to be the only professional involved. Any professional working with eating disorders should be clear about what they can address and be aware of when it is appropriate to enlist other forms of help. Thus, nutritional intervention should aim to separate food from underlying issues, leaving these to be addressed by professionals more experienced in psychological techniques. Research suggests that nutritional intervention, alongside other psychological therapies, most notably cognitive behavior therapy (CBT), is an important part of treatment. In addition, training in CBT techniques is advized for dietitians and nutritionists involved in bulimia nervosa management.

The aim of dietary management of bulimia nervosa is to break the binge–purge cycle previously described. The individual should be informed of the problems of maintaining this cycle through dieting and should be encouraged to stop dieting in an extreme way. They should also be educated about the damaging effects of vomiting and other purging behaviors. In some cases, this is enough to stop such behaviors. In others, this message should consistently be given to encourage them to work toward stopping these behaviors. An important part of breaking this cycle is to get the individual to monitor his or her intake through completing a food diary. In the example shown (**Table 1**), it can be seen how restricting intake earlier in the day can make the person more vulnerable to overeating later in the day. Food diaries are a powerful cognitive tool that enable the individual to understand his or her eating behavior more fully.

Education is essential to ensure that people understand why they are being asked to abandon what are some of the only coping mechanisms they have. They feel anxious that by giving up the pattern of dieting, binge eating, and purging they will gain excessive amounts of weight. These fears are very real and failure to address them with sensitivity can sabotage any attempt to control the disorder. This is

Table 1 Example of a food diary

Time	Food/drink eaten and amount	Binge/vomit/laxatives	Comment/feelings
Breakfast	Nothing	—	Not hungry.
Midmorning	Cup of black coffee × 2	—	Need something to fill my stomach. Really busy at work so no time to eat.
Midday (1.30 pm)	2 crispbreads, dry Small tub of diet cottage cheese 1 tomato, can of diet pop	—	Very hungry, feel as if I could eat more but mustn't.
Midafternoon	Chocolate eclair	Vomited	Someone's birthday in the office so couldn't refuse. Feel really guilty and had to be sick.
Evening meal	2 dishes of blackcurrant cheesecake, a choc ice, 4 bowls of ice cream, 6 snack-size chocolate bars, 5 cheese biscuits with butter and cheese, 5 slices of toast with butter and peanut butter, 2 packets of chocolate biscuits, 2 bowls of cereal, 1 packet of crisps and 1 chocolate and mint biscuit	Binge!! Vomited and took 10 laxatives	Couldn't decide what to have for tea, so started on cheesecake. Could not stop this binge at any cost. I feel terrible.
During evening	6 glasses of water		
Supper	—	—	Feel so terrible and bloated. Will have to cut back tomorrow.

particularly important when an individual has a history of overweight in the past. A detailed weight history should be carried out to include current, highest, lowest, and ideal weights and it should be stressed that recovery cannot be accomplished if the sufferer is trying to maintain a weight below normal. Thus, those with a premorbid history of obesity may have to accept that they will need to reach a weight that is higher than they would like it to be. Weight stabilisation should be an initial emphasis, particularly for those experiencing weight fluctuations. Initially, weight is likely to fluctuate through rehydration and repletion of glycogen stores. This effect should be explained to the individual to reduce unnecessary anxiety. They should also be discouraged from weighing themselves. If they must get weighed, this should be no more than once a week.

An important goal for nutritional management is to establish the individual on a regular pattern of eating. Often, normal cues for hunger and satiety are disrupted through repeated cycles of binge and restrictive eating so encouraging a regular meal pattern also helps the sufferer to begin to identify hunger and fullness again. They should be encouraged to eat regular meals and snacks and to maintain this pattern of eating even after a binge. Each meal or snack should be based around carbohydrate, with moderate amounts of protein foods and vegetables and fruit. They should be encouraged to include non-diet foods and to include foods containing fat. It is also worth getting them to compile a list of foods normally avoided or associated only with binges and to encourage them to include them within their meal pattern, when they feel able to do so. A system of food exchanges may also be useful (see the sample meal plan in **Table 2**). The amount of food required to meet energy needs is greater than that needed to consume sufficient nutrients. Thus, consumption of some energy dense, less nutritious food should be encouraged. A minimum intake of 6.0 MJ (1500 kcal) is usually an appropriate level to begin with, increasing to an intake corresponding to the estimated average requirement for women as recovery proceeds.

If the bulimic is used to keeping his or her stomach empty, even a normal amount of food may seem excessive and may trigger the urge to vomit. They should be informed that stomach distension is a normal consequence of eating and reassured that they will get used to the feeling in time. Similarly, if someone has been abusing laxatives, he or she may suffer from constipation and should be encouraged to have a reasonable fiber intake along with plenty of fluids.

Although it is important to give positive encouragement and feedback when working with individuals with bulimia nervosa, it should also be explained that relapse is a normal occurrence and should not be viewed so negatively that the individual feels a complete failure. Education on relapse prevention should be an important component of any treatment programme.

Table 2 Sample meal plan[a]

Breakfast:	Glass of fruit juice Bowl of cereal with milk Slice of toast, spread with butter/margarine and marmalade/jam if desired
Midmorning:	**Choose from exchange list**
Snack meal:	Sandwiches made with two large slices of bread, spread with butter/margarine, and filled with lean meat, egg, or cheese or beans on toast, etc.
Midafternoon:	**Choose from exchange list**
Main meal:	Average helping of meat, chicken, fish, or vegetarian alternative Potatoes, boiled rice, or pasta equivalent to two exchanges Vegetables or salad **Option from exchange list**
Supper:	1–2 slices of toast or option from exchange list

Exchange list
  1 large slice of bread or a roll, teacake, or plain bun
  1 small scone
  2 plain biscuits or crackers
  1 chocolate or cream biscuit
  Small bowl of breakfast cereal or porridge
  2 spoons boiled rice or pasta
  1 medium potato
  4 spoons baked beans or tinned spaghetti
  1 piece of fruit (apple, orange, pear, banana, etc.)
  1 carton of yoghurt
  1 glass of milk
  6–8 tablespoons custard or rice pudding
  1 packet crisps or nuts and raisins
  1 average-sized chocolate bar

[a] This plan deliberately does not include specific portion sizes. However, some individuals may need the reassurance of a more detailed plan. The aim is to provide a minimum of 6.25 MJ (1500 kcal). In addition to using the above to exchange foods within the meal plan, some people benefit from having an additional number of exchanges (e.g., five extra) to allow for when they are feeling more hungry and to offset binges. This also ensures an energy intake that conforms to the current EAR for women.

Long-Term Prognosis

Once more, the relative recency of the disorder mitigates against definitive statements. However, the outcome studies conducted so far show that bulimia nervosa is far from being intractable, as was originally suggested. Of the studies with a follow-up of at least 5 years, between a third and a half of those with bulimia nervosa at outset still had an eating disorder, and between 10 and 25% still had bulimia nervosa. There is also considerable flux within samples. For example, in a community sample, each year about a third of patients remitted and a further third relapsed. Studies also report very low rates of spontaneous remission.

In terms of treatment, several psychotherapies have shown their effectiveness in improving the symptoms of bulimia nervosa. Most evidence is available on CBT, and the outcome is generally impressive and replicable. The treatment, usually provided by psychiatrists or clinical psychologists, aims to modify both the disturbed eating habits and the extreme concerns about shape and weight (the core psychopathology). Consequently, it combines psychological and dietetic approaches to patient management. Given a treatment program of around 20 sessions over 5 months, between a half and two-thirds of patients make a full and lasting recovery.

There is still uncertainty regarding prognostic indicators of treatment success. Patients with a less severe form of the disorder appear to do better in treatment. Self-help programs administered on their own or with modest support and encouragement from a nonspecialist therapist (guided self-help) may be of particular assistance to those in whom the disorder is less fully established. Conversely, those with childhood obesity, low self-esteem, or personality disturbance appear to do worse. Importantly, there is no evidence that bulimia nervosa evolves over time into other psychiatric disorders or of any persistent impairment in social functioning.

See also: **Appetite**: Physiological and Neurobiological Aspects; Psychobiological and Behavioral Aspects. **Eating Disorders**: Anorexia Nervosa; Binge Eating. **Hunger**.

Further Reading

Abraham S and Llewellyn-Jones D (2001) *Eating Disorders: The Facts*, 5th edn. Oxford: Oxford University Press.

American Academy of Pediatrics Committee on Adolescence (2003) Identifying and treating eating disorders. *Pediatrics* **111**: 204–211.

American Dietetic Association (2001) Nutrition intervention in the treatment of anorexia nervosa, bulimia nervosa, and eating disorders not otherwise specified (EDNOS). *Journal of the American Dietetic Association* **101**: 810–819.

American Psychiatric Association (2000) Practice guidelines for the treatment of patients with eating disorders. *American Journal of Psychiatry* **157**(supplement 1): 1–39. Available at http://www.psych.org/clin_res/guide.bk-2.cfm.

Fairburn CG (1995) *Overcoming Binge Eating*. New York: Guilford Press.

Fairburn CG and Brownell KD (eds.) (2002) *Eating Disorders and Obesity. A Comprehensive Handbook*, 2nd edn. New York: Guilford Press.

Fairburn CG, Cooper Z, Doll HA, Norman P, and O'Connor M (2000) The natural course of bulimia nervosa and binge eating disorder in young women. *Archives of General Psychiatry* **57**: 659–665.

Fairburn CG, Marcus MD, and Wilson GT (1993) Cognitive-behavioural therapy for binge eating and bulimia nervosa: A comprehensive treatment manual. In: Fairburn CG and

Wilson GT (eds.) *Binge Eating: Nature, Assessment, and Treatment*. New York: Guilford Press.

Fairburn CG, Norman PA, Welch SL *et al.* (1995) A prospective study of outcome in bulimia nervosa and the long-term effects of three psychological treatments. *Archives of General Psychiatry* 52: 304–312.

Gordon RA (2000) *Eating Disorders: Anatomy of a Social Epidemic*, 2nd edn. Oxford: Blackwell.

Hay P and Bacaltchuk J (2002) Bulimia nervosa. *Clinical Evidence* 7: 834–845.

Latner JD and Wilson GT (2000) Cognitive-behavioral therapy and nutritional counseling in the treatment of bulimia nervosa and binge eating. *Eating Behaviors* 1: 3–21.

National Collaborating Centre for Mental Health (2004) Eating Disorders. Core interventions in the treatment and management of anorexia nervosa, bulimia nervosa, and related eating disorders. *National Clinical Practice Guideline CG9*. Leicester: British Psychological Society http://www.bps.org.uk/eatingdisorders/files/ED.pdf.

Polivy J and Herman CP (2002) Causes of eating disorders. *Annual Review of Psychology* 53: 187–213.

Rome ES, Ammerman S, Rosen DS *et al.* (2003) Children and adolescents with eating disorders: The state of the art. *Pediatrics* 111: e98–e108.

Russell GFM (1979) Bulimia nervosa: An ominous variant of anorexia nervosa. *Psychological Medicine* 9: 429–448.

Schmidt U and Treasure J (1997) *Getting Better Bit(e) by Bit(e). A Survival Kit for Sufferers of Bulimia Nervosa and Binge Eating Disorders*. Hove: Psychology Press.

Stice E (1994) Review of the evidence for a sociocultural model of bulimia nervosa and an exploration of the mechanisms of action. *Clinical Psychology Review* 14: 633–661.

Waller G (2002) Treatment of bulimia nervosa. *Psychiatry* 1: 12–16.

Binge Eating

M D Marcus, M A Kalarchian and M D Levine, University of Pittsburgh, Pittsburgh, PA, USA

In 1959, Stunkard noted three patterns of eating behavior in obese patients: night eating, binge eating, and eating without satiation. It was not until the 1980s that binge eating began to receive attention as a distinct clinical syndrome. Spitzer and colleagues proposed diagnostic criteria for binge eating disorder (BED) and subsequently evaluated them in two field trials. These initial investigations led to the inclusion of BED in the *Diagnostic and Statistical Manual of Mental Disorders*, fourth edition (*DSM-IV*), of the American Psychiatric Association as an example of Eating Disorder Not Otherwise Specified (EDNOS) and as a proposed diagnostic category requiring further study. BED is characterized by persistent and recurrent episodes of binge eating without the regular use of inappropriate compensatory behaviors seen in bulimia nervosa (BN). Research on BED is still in an early stage, and the key features of the disorder and its relationship to other eating disorders, especially BN, nonpurging type, continue to be debated in the field.

This article discusses the assessment of BED, prevalence and risk factors, and comorbid conditions associated with BED. In addition, empirically supported treatments are reviewed, including guidelines for choice of treatment approach. Throughout the article, a biopsychosocial framework for understanding aberrant eating behavior is emphasized.

Assessment of Binge Eating

A binge episode is defined as the consumption of a large amount of food within a discrete period of time, accompanied by a sense of loss of control over eating. Researchers and clinicians have agreed that loss of control involves the subjective feeling that one cannot stop eating or control what or how much is being eaten. However, there has been much less agreement about the size and duration of a binge eating episode. Specifically, there is no consensus as to what constitutes a large amount of food, and the duration of binge eating episodes can vary widely, sometimes continuing throughout an entire day. Many individuals have difficulty delineating binges into discrete episodes but can more readily recall whether a binge occurred or not on a given day. Thus, the BED diagnosis is made based on binge 'days' rather than 'episodes.' Similarly, many observers have concluded that the loss of control, rather than the amount of food ingested during a binge (i.e., a 'large' amount), is the hallmark of binge eating. See **Table 1** for the full research criteria for BED.

Several methods can be used to assess BED, including clinical interviews, self-reports such as questionnaires and food diaries, and observation of eating behavior in the laboratory. Currently, a clinical interview by a trained professional is the preferred assessment method. It provides the opportunity to standardize definitions of key concepts such as a 'large amount of food' and 'loss of control.' Although questionnaires are relatively easy to administer, there is high potential for misinterpreting these terms. Interview-based assessments tend to yield ratings of binge eating that are lower, but more precise, than questionnaire-based surveys.

Food diaries involve having individuals keep a daily record of the specifics of eating episodes, including how much food was consumed, whether or not there was loss of control over eating, any use of

Table 1 *DSM-IV-TR* criteria for binge eating disorder

1. Recurrent episodes of binge eating. An episode of binge eating is characterized by both of the following:

   Eating, in a discrete period of time (e.g., within any 2-h period), an amount of food that is definitely larger than most people would eat in a similar period of time under similar circumstances

   A sense of lack of control over eating during the episode (e.g., a feeling that one cannot stop eating or control what or how much one is eating)

2. The binge eating episodes are associated with at least three (or more) of the following:

   Eating much more rapidly than normal

   Eating until feeling uncomfortably full

   Eating large amounts of food when not feeling physically hungry

   Eating alone because of being embarrassed by how much one is eating

   Feeling disgusted with oneself, depressed, or very guilty after overeating

3. Marked distress regarding binge eating is present.

4. The binge eating occurs, on average, at least 2 days a week for 6 months.

5. The binge eating is not associated with the regular use of inappropriate compensatory behaviors (e.g., purging, fasting, and excessive exercise) and does not occur exclusively during the course of anorexia nervosa or bulimia nervosa.

inappropriate compensatory behavior, and the associated context. Food diaries can provide detailed assessment information without introducing the bias of retrospective self-report; however, self-monitoring also has been shown to affect eating behavior and is frequently employed in clinical treatment. Findings from studies that have utilized food diaries indicate that BED patients report higher calorie intakes than non-binge eaters on both 'binge days' and 'non-binge days.'

Observation of binge eating in the laboratory is a specialized technique that is limited to use in research settings, providing the opportunity to document actual eating behavior and measure consumption. Laboratory studies with relatively small samples have shown that, compared to equally overweight patients who do not binge eat, BED patients ingest more calories, both during binges and at 'regular' meals. This difference in eating behavior in binge compared to non-binge eaters supports the validity of BED as a distinct diagnostic category.

Prevalence and Risk Factors

Available research suggests that the prevalence of BED among the general population is approximately 1 or 2% and thus more common than BN. In addition, preliminary findings suggest that the demographic profile of individuals with BED may be more diverse, affecting relatively more men and minority groups than BN or anorexia nervosa. Furthermore, binge eating is more prevalent among obese individuals in both clinical and community samples. It is estimated that up to one-third of individuals who present for treatment in university-based weight control clinics report significant binge eating.

The most comprehensive risk factor study to date suggests that the risk factors for BED may be weaker and more circumscribed than for BN. Fairburn and colleagues interviewed four groups of subjects matched for age and social class: individuals with BED, BN, another psychiatric disorder, and healthy controls. In comparing the BED group to the controls, negative self-evaluation, parental depression, adverse childhood experience, and exposure to repeated negative comments about shape, weight, or eating emerged as risk factors for BED. Further comparing BED patients to other groups with psychiatric diagnoses, childhood obesity and negative comments from family about eating, shape, and weight emerged as risk factors specific to BED. Thus, BED appears to be associated with two classes of risk factor—those that increase the risk of psychiatric disorder in general and factors that increase risk of obesity.

In order to improve our understanding of how multiple factors interact to determine the onset and maintenance of binge eating, prospective risk factor studies including males and females of different racial groups are needed. As suggested previously, biological (e.g., obesity), psychological (e.g., negative self-evaluation), and social (e.g., exposure to repeated negative comments about shape, weight, or eating) factors have been implicated in the pathogenesis of binge eating. Emergent research also has linked binge eating in a small proportion of individuals to a mutation in *MC4R*, a candidate gene for the control of eating behavior. Thus, future research may further elucidate the genetic influences on aberrant eating patterns.

Comorbidity

Binge eating is strongly associated with both obesity and psychiatric disorder. It is well documented that obesity is linked to adverse medical and psychosocial outcomes. Preliminary findings also suggest that BED may be associated with poor health, independent of the effects of comorbid psychopathology or comorbid obesity.

Severity of binge eating is positively associated with degree of overweight. Additionally, there are important differences between overweight individuals with and without BED. BED patients report earlier onset of obesity, along with a history of more severe obesity, dieting, and weight fluctuations. When compared with equally overweight individuals without binge eating problems, BED patients report considerably less 'restraint' or control overeating, lower self-esteem, more fear of weight gain, more preoccupation with food, and higher body dissatisfaction.

Individuals with BED endorse high rates of psychiatric symptoms and disorders. For example, when compared to equally overweight individuals without binge eating problems, individuals with BED report significantly higher lifetime rates of major depressive disorder, substance abuse or dependence, and anxiety disorders. Some studies have shown that patients with BED report levels of eating disorder symptomatology, such as eating, shape, and weight concerns, that are comparable to those of normal weight patients with BN. Individuals with BED also have considerably higher rates of personality disorders than overweight individuals without an eating disorder. Thus, among individuals with BED, psychiatric symptomatology appears to be related to the binge eating rather than to the degree of obesity.

Treatment

Among those who seek treatment, BED tends to be a chronic and fluctuating disorder. The clinical picture in BED often involves onset in late adolescence or the early 20s, with numerous periods of relative control over eating, and weight loss during periods of successful calorie restriction, alternating with periods characterized by binge eating and weight gain. Individuals with BED often seek obesity treatment rather than treatment of disordered eating per se.

A variety of psychosocial and pharmacological interventions, as well as behavioral weight loss programs, can help individuals gain control over binge eating. **Figure 1** provides an overview of non-pharmacologic treatments and their postulated mechanisms of action; it should be noted that this list of treatments is not exhaustive. Furthermore, although the postulated treatment mechanisms reflect respective theoretical models of binge eating, the effects of psychosocial treatment usually lack specificity and the treatments often share common elements (e.g., self-monitoring is a central component of cognitive behavior therapy (CBT), dialectical behavior therapy (DBT), and behavioral weight control). Also, effects of psychosocial treatments often extend to areas that are not a focus of treatment (e.g., behavioral weight management programs that target changing eating and exercise also have been shown to improve mood). Thus, some of the treatments do overlap. Finally, it is important to note that a substantial number of patients are not abstinent from binge eating after treatment, suggesting

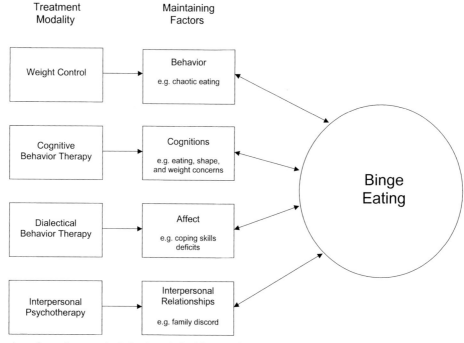

Figure 1 Overview of nonpharmacologic treatments for binge eating.

the need for clinical trials of novel therapeutic approaches as well as combinations and sequencing of treatments.

Psychosocial Treatments

Treatments for binge eating have been adapted from those that have been shown to be effective in reducing binge eating among individuals with BN. The majority of the research on psychosocial treatments has supported two structured, focused, short-term psychotherapies—CBT and interpersonal psychotherapy (IPT)—both of which have been shown to be more effective than no treatment in decreasing the frequency of binge eating and improving the psychopathology associated with binge eating. In addition, the use of DBT shows promise as an alternative treatment for BED.

Cognitive behavioral therapy CBT has been the most extensively studied treatment for individuals with binge eating. CBT for BED is based on the assumption that binge eating is maintained in the context of ongoing dietary restraint, weight concerns, negative emotions, and low self-esteem. Treatment focuses first on normalizing eating and then on the identification and restructuring of maladaptive thoughts and beliefs, particularly those related to eating, shape, and weight.

CBT for BED has been adapted to reflect important differences between individuals with BN and BED. Specifically, cognitions relating to having a large body size are directly targeted in treatment. Overweight individuals with BED may be helped to accept a larger than average body size and to change unrealistic expectations for weight loss. That is, for the majority of BED patients a 5- or 10-kg weight loss does not correspond with their desired weight loss, even though a modest weight loss may relate to improvements in binge eating and overall health. It is therefore important to help patients adopt realistic goals for the body weight and shape they are likely to achieve.

Another adaptation of CBT for BED relates to differences in the role of dieting between individuals with BED and those with BN. Although the treatment of BN stresses the role of dietary restraint in precipitating binge episodes, and treatment focuses on decreasing dietary restraint, patients with BED do not necessarily binge eat in response to restraint or hunger. Indeed, the preponderance of evidence suggests that increasing dietary restraint may help to ameliorate binge eating in obese individuals. Thus, CBT for BED does not stress decreased dietary restraint; rather, treatment encourages the development of a moderate, structured, healthy eating pattern.

Interpersonal psychotherapy Klerman and Weissman's IPT has also received empirical support in the treatment of individuals with BED. IPT for binge eating is based on the idea that dysfunctional eating behavior is maintained in the context of interpersonal difficulties. Treatment focuses on identifying and addressing specific, problematic interpersonal patterns in an effort to ameliorate binge eating. Treatment can focus on role disputes, such as marital or family discord; role transitions, such as the adjustment to motherhood or a new job; grief, such as the loss of a spouse or loved one; and interpersonal deficits, such as loneliness and social isolation.

IPT for BED does not directly target eating behaviors or attitudes about eating, shape, and weight. Although the ways in which CBT and IPT conceptualize and treat binge eating differ, both appear to be equally effective in reducing the frequency of binge eating.

Dialectical behavior therapy Developed by Linehan for the treatment of individuals with borderline personality disorder, DBT has shown promise in the treatment of BED. DBT is a comprehensive treatment program based on cognitive and behavioral principles and complemented by the use of mindfulness strategies derived primarily from Zen Buddhism. In addition to weekly individual outpatient treatment, traditional DBT prescribes a weekly group meeting in which the goal is to increase participants' behavioral skills. A group-only version of DBT for individuals with BED has also been shown to decrease binge eating and maladaptive attitudes about eating, shape, and weight. Additional research is needed to determine the efficacy of DBT relative to CBT and IPT.

Behavioral Weight Control

Because the majority of individuals with BED are also overweight and want to lose weight, and because obesity is associated with significant medical and psychosocial consequences, weight loss is a potentially important outcome in the treatment of BED. Numerous studies have documented that calorie restriction does not exacerbate binge eating in BED patients. Indeed, participation in behavioral weight control programs that focus on calorie restriction, provide education about sound nutritional principles, and promote physical activity may decrease binge eating and improve mood in BED patients. Therefore, concerns about the potentially deleterious effects of dieting should not deter obese patients who binge eat from attempting behavioral weight management.

Weight lost through dieting is frequently regained, and sustained weight change involves a permanent modification of eating and exercise patterns. However, it is not necessary to achieve large weight losses to improve risk factors for heart disease, diabetes, and other obesity-related comorbidities. There is evidence that sustained weight losses of approximately 10% of initial body weight can lead to significant improvements in modifiable risk factors such as blood pressure, lipids, and blood sugar levels.

Pharmacotherapy

Pharmacologic approaches to the treatment of BED that have empirical support include antidepressant and weight loss medications. Additionally, one study has demonstrated the potential utility of the anticonvulsant agent, topiramate. However, studies to date have not shown that pharmacotherapy increases the effectiveness of psychotherapy for BED.

Antidepressant treatment Because of their efficacy in ameliorating binge eating and purge behaviors in BN, antidepressants have been used in the treatment of BED. Early research comparing tricyclic antidepressants, such as desipramine and imipramine, to placebo showed greater reductions in binge eating among obese binge eaters treated with the drug than with a placebo. Recently, several selective serotonin reuptake inhibitors (e.g., fluoxetine) have been shown to be associated with moderate reductions in binge eating in BED patients. Moreover, the effects of antidepressant treatment on binge eating are independent of any effects on mood.

Antidepressant treatment also may be useful in treating depression associated with BED and has been associated with weight loss among obese binge eaters. Antidepressant treatment also may enhance dietary restraint or improve compliance with a weight loss program. Thus, it seems possible that longer term antidepressant treatment may be useful in breaking the cycle of negative mood, binge eating, and weight gain that characterizes BED.

Anorectic agents The utility of anorectic agents in the treatment of BED has been investigated in a few studies. Early research found that obese binge eaters treated with the serotoneric agent, d-fenfluarmine, experienced a significantly greater short-term reduction in binge eating than did those given placebo. However, because of the association between the longer term use of d-fenfluramine and the combination of phentermine and fenfluramine with serious pulmonary and cardiac problems, these medications have since been withdrawn from the market. Currently, two anorectic agents, sibutramine and orlistat, have been approved for long-term use in the treatment of obesity. Sibutramine has been investigated in the treatment of BED, with initial findings suggesting decreases in binge eating and body weight among obese women with BED.

Selection of Treatment for Specific Patients

No single treatment approach is effective for all patients. Future research may provide data to guide the selection of treatment for individual patients as well as evaluate alternative treatments. Until such information becomes available, clinicians and patients must decide on a course of treatment based on a careful assessment and thorough consideration of the pros and cons of available options.

Eating disorder and obesity history A history of early onset of binge eating, binge eating in the absence of obesity, or obesity in combination with numerous bouts of weight loss and regain over time ('yo-yo' dieting) suggests a course of psychosocial treatment. Such patients can be reassured that significant improvements in the aberrant eating and eating disorders psychopathology associated with BED can be obtained without weight loss.

On the other hand, clinical experience suggests that patients who report adult onset of binge eating and obesity, and do not have a history of marked weight fluctuations, may be more likely to benefit from a behavioral weight control approach. Behavioral weight control may also be indicated for patients who remain overweight after a trial of eating disorders treatment. Although behavioral weight control appears to be beneficial on average, it is important for each individual to evaluate the likelihood that he or she will be able to sustain lifelong changes in eating and exercise.

Psychiatric status Given the high psychiatric comorbidity in BED, a thorough evaluation is important for all patients who seek treatment. Although mild to moderate depression or anxiety is likely to improve during treatment of binge eating, the presence of marked or severe current illness suggests primary treatment of the mood or anxiety disorder. In addition, the presence of personality disorders characterized by emotional, dramatic, or impulsive behavior appears to be related to severity of binge eating but does not appear to predict treatment outcome.

Available resources   Clinicians trained in the use of psychosocial treatments for eating disorders are likely to be found in most metropolitan areas but may not be available in smaller cities or rural areas. Insurance companies vary in coverage for treatment of eating disorders, and some insurance plans may pay for obesity treatment only if there is a clear medical indication (e.g., hypertension or other cardiovascular risk). Thus, treatment decisions may need to take into account pragmatic factors, such as clinician availability and training or patient insurance plan coverage. Self-help programs may be appropriate for carefully screened, motivated patients with mild to moderate binge eating. However, comorbid psychopathology and high-frequency binge eating may require more intensive clinical intervention.

Conclusion

BED is a chronic and fluctuating disorder that is common among obese individuals who seek treatment, and it is associated with elevated rates of psychopathology. A biopsychosocial model shows most promise in understanding the etiology of aberrant eating. Once established, binge eating is maintained by a complex interplay of eating behaviors, cognitions, affect, and interpersonal factors. Nevertheless, available research indicates that most who binge eat can be helped with either a behavioral weight control program or an eating disorders treatment. Pharmacotherapy may also reduce binge eating but generally does not add to the effectiveness of psychosocial treatment. A careful assessment, review of the benefits and disadvantages of the different therapies, and consideration of the availability of trained clinicians should guide the choice of treatment for an individual with BED. More research is necessary to fully understand this problematic eating pattern and to improve strategies for management and treatment.

See also: **Eating Disorders**: Anorexia Nervosa; Bulimia Nervosa. **Obesity**: Fat Distribution; Complications; Treatment. **Weight Management**: Weight Maintenance.

Further Reading

American Psychiatric Association (2000) *Diagnostic and Statistical Manual of Mental Disorders*, 4th ed.–text revision. Washington, DC: American Psychiatric Association.

Cooper P (1995) *Bulimia Nervosa & Binge-Eating: A Guide to Recovery*. New York: New York University Press.

De Zwaan M (2001) Binge eating disorder and obesity. *International Journal of Obesity* 25(supplement 1): S51–S55.

Fairburn C (1995). *Overcoming Binge Eating*. New York: Guilford Press.

Fairburn CG and Brownell KD (eds.) (2002) *Eating Disorders and Obesity: A Comprehensive Handbook*. New York: Guilford Press.

Fairburn CG, Doll HA, Welch SL *et al.* (1998) Risk factors for binge eating disorder. *Archives of General Psychiatry* 55: 425–432.

Fairburn GG and Wilson GT (eds.) (1993) *Binge Eating: Nature, Assessment and Treatment*. New York: Guilford Press.

Levine MD and Marcus MD (1998). The treatment of binge eating disorder. In: Hoek H, Treasure J, and Katzman M (eds.) *The Integration of Neurobiology in the Treatment of Eating Disorders*, pp. 363–381. London: John Wiley & Sons.

Marcus MD and Kalarchian MA (2003) Binge eating in children and adolescents. *Int J Eat Disord.* 34(suppl.): S47–S57.

Marcus MD and Levine MD (2004) Obese patients with binge eating disorder. In: Goldstein DJ (ed.) *The Management of Eating Disorders*. Clifton, NJ: Humana Press.

Marcus MD and Levine MD (2004) Dialectical behavior therapy in the treatment of eating disorders: Brewerton T (ed.) *Eating Disorders*. New York: Marcel Dekker.

Striegel-Moore RH and Smolak L (2001). *Eating Disorders: Innovative Directions in Research and Practice*. New York: Guilford Press.

Stunkard AJ (1959) Eating patterns and obesity. *Psychiatric Quarterly* 33: 284–295.

Wadden TA and Stunkard AJ (eds.) (1994) *Handbook of Obesity Treatment*. New York: Guilford Press.

Walsh BT (ed.) (2003) The current status of binge eating disorder. *International Journal of Eating Disorders* 34.

Walsh BT and Devlin MJ (1998) Eating disorders: Progress and problems. *Science* 280: 1387–1390.

EGGS

D J McNamara and H S Thesmar, Egg Nutrition Center, Washington, DC, USA

Introduction

Eggs have been a staple in the human diet for thousands of years. From hunter–gatherers collecting eggs from the nests of wild birds, to the domestication of fowl for more reliable access to a supply of eggs, to today's genetically selected birds and modern production facilities, eggs have long been recognized as a source of high-quality protein and other important nutrients. Over the years, eggs have become an essential ingredient in many cuisines, owing to their many functional properties, such as water holding, emulsifying, and foaming.

An egg is a self-contained and self-sufficient embryonic development chamber. At adequate temperature, the developing embryo uses the extensive range of essential nutrients in the egg for its growth and development. The necessary proteins, lipids, carbohydrates, vitamins, minerals, and functional nutrients are all present in sufficient quantities for the transition from fertilized cell to newborn chick, and the nutrient needs of an avian species are similar enough to human needs to make eggs an ideal source of nutrients for us. (The one essential human nutrient that eggs do not contain is ascorbic acid (vitamin C), because non-passerine birds have active gulonolactone oxidase and synthesize ascorbic acid as needed.) This article summarizes the varied nutrient contributions eggs make to the human diet.

Egg Types

While the majority of eggs consumed today are chicken eggs, a variety of eggs from different species of bird are commercially available in different parts of the world, from the petite quail egg to the very large ostrich egg. The data presented in **Table 1** compare the caloric, protein, lipid, and cholesterol contents per 100 g for eggs from various species. Eggs from commercial chickens differ from those from wild breeds in that they have lower cholesterol and lipid contents. This difference could be the result of many years of genetic selection of breeds with increased feed-to-egg conversion ratios and faster rates of lay.

The commercial hen used in today's egg production has been selected for optimal feed conversion and egg production along with overall health, disease resistance, livability, and temperament. The majority of egg production is carried out using a battery cage system, which offers a high degree of control over environment, feed, water, hygiene, biosecurity, and egg collection. This system also facilitates mechanization. Other production systems include barn and free-range, which offer more freedom to the birds but often lead to higher disease and mortality rates and potentially to increased susceptibility to bacterial contamination of the eggs.

Shifting dietary patterns in the population have resulted in compensatory changes in the egg industry. A major change has been the increased use of eggs in egg products for the pre-prepared packaged-food industry. In the USA over 30% of the total egg production is used to make egg products, and

Table 1 Macronutrient composition of various raw eggs (per 100 g)

Nutrient	Species (average egg weight)				
	Quail (9 g)	Chicken (50 g)	Duck (70 g)	Turkey (79 g)	Goose (144 g)
Water (g)	74.35	75.84	70.83	72.50	70.43
Energy					
kJ	663	617	776	716	775
kcal	158	147	185	171	185
Protein (g)	13.05	12.58	12.81	13.68	13.87
Lipid (g)	11.09	9.94	13.77	11.88	13.27
SFA (g)	3.56	3.10	3.68	3.63	3.60
MUFA (g)	4.32	3.81	6.53	4.57	5.75
PUFA (g)	1.32	1.36	1.22	1.66	1.67
Cholesterol (mg)	844	423	884	933	852

USDA National Nutrient Database for Standard Reference, Release 16 (July 2003). Nutrient Data Laboratory Home Page, http://www.nal.usda.gov/fnic/foodcomp
SFA, saturated fatty acids; MUFA, monounsaturated fatty acids; PUFA, polyunsaturated fatty acids.

egg-product usage has been the most rapidly growing part of the industry, accounting for the majority of the increased per capita egg consumption over the past decade. Another area of growth has been the speciality egg market. As consumers become more health conscious, there has been an emphasis on functional components of foods that contribute to health and well-being. Eggs with enhanced nutrient benefits, especially with increased content of omega-3 fatty acids, are available worldwide.

Egg Macronutrient and Micronutrient Content and Distribution

The levels of many nutrients in an egg are influenced by the age and breed or strain of hen as well as the season of the year and the composition of the feed provided to the hen. While most variations in nutrients are relatively minor, the fatty acid composition of egg lipids can be significantly altered by changes in the hen's diet. The exact quantities of many vitamins and minerals in an egg are determined, in part, by the nutrients provided in the hen's diet.

Hen eggs contain 75.8% water, 12.6% protein, 9.9% lipid, and 1.7% vitamins, minerals, and a small amount of carbohydrates (Table 2). Eggs are classified in the protein food group, and egg protein is one of the highest quality proteins available. Virtually all lipids found in eggs are contained in the yolk, along with most of the vitamins and minerals. Of the small amount of carbohydrate (less than 1% by weight), half is found in the form of glycoprotein and the remainder as free glucose.

Egg Protein

Egg proteins, which are distributed in both yolk and white (albumen), are nutritionally complete proteins containing all the essential amino-acids (EAA). Egg protein has a chemical score (EAA level in a protein food divided by the level found in an 'ideal' protein food) of 100, a biological value (a measure of how efficiently dietary protein is turned into body tissue) of 94, and the highest protein efficiency ratio (ratio of weight gain to protein ingested in young rats) of any dietary protein.

The major proteins found in egg yolk include low density lipoprotein (LDL), which constitutes 65%, high density lipoprotein (HDL), phosvitin, and livetin. These proteins exist in a homogeneously emulsified fluid. Egg white is made up of some 40 different kinds of proteins. Ovalbumin is the major protein (54%) along with ovotransferrin (12%) and ovomucoid (11%). Other proteins of interest include flavoprotein, which binds riboflavin, avidin, which can bind and inactivate biotin, and lysozyme, which has lytic action against bacteria.

As shown in Table 3, egg protein contains substantial amounts of EAAs and nonessential amino-acids. The first column shows the amount of each amino-acid in one large egg. The second column indicates the amount of each amino-acid per 100 g of whole egg. The third column shows the dietary reference intake (DRI) for all of the EAAs per 50 g of total dietary protein, and the last column indicates the percentage of the DRI for each EAA provided by one large egg. While a large egg provides only 3% of the energy in a 2000 kcal (8394 kJ) diet, it provides 11% of the

Table 2 Macronutrient distribution in raw chicken egg (per 50 g large egg)

	Whole egg	Egg albumin	Egg yolk
Weight (%)	100	66	34
Water (g)	37.9	28.9	8.9
Energy			
kJ	308.5	71.3	228.8
kcal	73.5	17.2	54.7
Protein (g)	6.29	3.60	2.70
Lipid (g)	4.97	0.06	4.51
Sugars (g)	0.39	0.24	0.10

USDA National Nutrient Database for Standard Reference, Release 16 (July 2003). Nutrient Data Laboratory Home Page, http://www.nal.usda.gov/fnic/foodcomp

Table 3 Amino-acid content of a large egg

Amino-acid	Grams per large egg	Grams per 100 g whole egg	DRI (g) EAA per 50 g protein day^{-1}	Percentage EAA DRI per large egg
Alanine	0.38	0.69		
Arginine	0.42	0.77		
Aspartic acid	0.65	1.18		
Cystine[a]	0.15	0.28	1.25	12
Glutamic acid	0.85	1.54		
Glycine	0.22	0.40		
Histidine[a]	0.16	0.29	0.9	18
Isoleucine[a]	0.36	0.66	1.25	29
Leucine[a]	0.57	1.04	2.75	21
Lysine[a]	0.45	0.82	2.55	18
Methionine[a]	0.21	0.39	1.25	17
Phenylalanine[a]	0.35	0.64	2.35	15
Proline	0.26	0.48		
Serine	0.50	0.91		
Threonine[a]	0.32	0.59	1.35	24
Tryptophan[a]	0.11	0.19	0.35	31
Tyrosine[a]	0.28	0.51	2.35	12
Valine[a]	0.43	0.79	1.6	27

[a]Essential amino-acids (EAA) are not synthesized by the body and must be consumed in foods; therefore, only EAA have a dietary reference intake (DRI) value.
USDA National Nutrient Database for Standard Reference, Release 16 (July 2003). Nutrient Data Laboratory Home Page, http://www.nal.usda.gov/fnic/foodcomp

protein needs. The EAAs in an egg contribute between 12% and 31% of the DRI for the various EAAs.

Egg Lipids

A large egg yolk contains 4.5 g of lipid, consisting of triacylglycerides (65%), phospholipids (31%), and cholesterol (4%). Of the total phospholipids, phosphatidylcholine (lecithin) is the largest fraction and accounts for 26%. Phosphatidylethanolamine contributes another 4%. The fatty-acid composition of egg-yolk lipids depends on the fatty-acid profile of the diet. The reported fatty-acid profile of commercial eggs indicates that a large egg contains 1.55 g of saturated fatty acids, 1.91 g of monounsaturated fat, and 0.68 g of polyunsaturated fatty acids. (Total fatty acids (4.14 g) does not equal total lipid (4.5 g) because of the glycerol moiety of triacylglycerides and phospholipids and the phosphorylated moieties of the phospholipids). It has been reported that eggs contain less than 0.05 g of trans-fatty acids. Egg yolks also contain cholesterol (211 mg per large egg) and the xanthophylls lutein and zeaxanthin. The lipid profile of a large egg is presented in **Table 4**.

Egg Vitamins

Eggs contain all the essential vitamins except vitamin C, because the developing chick does not have a dietary requirement for this vitamin. As shown in **Table 5**, the yolk contains the majority of the water-soluble vitamins and 100% of the fat-soluble vitamins. Riboflavin and niacin are concentrated in

Table 4 Egg yolk lipid profile per large egg

Lipids	Amount
Fatty acids, total saturated (g)	1.55
8:0–14:0	0.02
16:0	1.16
18:0	0.41
20:0–24:0	0.01
Fatty acids, total monounsaturated (g)	1.99
16:1	0.16
18:1	1.82
20:1	0.02
Fatty acids, total polyunsaturated (g)	0.72
18:2	0.60
18:3	0.02
20:4	0.07
20:5–22:6 n-3	0.02
Cholesterol (mg)	211
Carotene, β (μg)	15
Carotene, α (μg)	6.5
Cryptoxanthin, β (μg)	5.6
Lutein + zeaxanthin (μg)	186

USDA National Nutrient Database for Standard Reference, Release 16 (July 2003). Nutrient Data Laboratory Home Page, http://www.nal.usda.gov/fnic/foodcomp

Table 5 Egg vitamin content per large egg

Vitamin	Whole	Albumen	Yolk
Thiamin (mg)	0.04	<0.01	0.03
Riboflavin (mg)	0.24	0.15	0.09
Niacin (mg)	0.04	0.04	<0.01
Pantothenic acid (mg)	0.72	0.06	0.51
Vitamin B_6 (mg)	0.07	<0.01	0.06
Folate, total (μg)	23.5	0	24.8
Vitamin B_{12} (μg)	0.65	0.03	0.33
Vitamin A (IU)	243.5	0	245.1
Choline (mg)	125.5	0	125.5
Retinol (μg)	70	0	63.1
Vitamin E (mg)	0.49	0	0.44
Vitamin D (IU)	17.3	0	18.3
Vitamin K (μg)	0.15	0	0.12

USDA National Nutrient Database for Standard Reference, Release 16 (July 2003). Nutrient Data Laboratory Home Page, http://www.nal.usda.gov/fnic/foodcomp

the albumen. The riboflavin in the egg albumin is bound to flavoprotein in a 1:1 molar ratio. Eggs are one of the few natural sources of vitamins D and B_{12}. Egg vitamin E levels can be increased up to tenfold through dietary changes. While no single vitamin is found in very high quantity relative to its DRI value, it is the wide spectrum of vitamins present that makes eggs nutritionally rich.

Egg Minerals

Eggs contain small amounts of all the minerals essential for life. Of particular importance is the iron found in egg yolks. Research evaluating the plasma iron and transferrin saturation in 6–12-month-old children indicated that infants who ate egg yolks had a better iron status than infants who did not. The study indicated that egg yolks can be a source of iron in a weaning diet for breast-fed and formula-fed infants without increasing blood antibodies to egg-yolk proteins. Dietary iron absorption from a specific food is determined by iron status, heme- and nonheme-iron contents, and amounts of various dietary factors that influence iron absorption present in the whole meal. Limited information is available about the net effect of these factors as related to egg iron bioavailability.

In addition to iron, eggs contain calcium, phosphorus, sodium, potassium, magnesium, zinc, copper, and manganese (**Table 6**). Egg yolks also contain iodine (25 μg per large egg), and this can be increased twofold to threefold by the inclusion of an iodine source in the feed. Egg selenium content can also be increased up to ninefold by dietary manipulations.

Egg Choline

Choline was established as an essential nutrient in 1999 with recommended daily intakes (RDIs) of 550 mg for

Table 6 Egg mineral content per large egg

Mineral	Whole	Albumen	Yolk
Calcium (mg)	26.5	2.3	21.9
Iron (mg)	0.92	0.03	0.46
Magnesium (mg)	6.0	3.63	0.85
Phosphorus (mg)	95.5	4.95	66.3
Potassium (mg)	67.0	53.79	18.53
Sodium (mg)	70.0	54.78	8.16
Zinc (mg)	0.56	0.01	0.39
Copper (mg)	0.05	0.01	0.01
Manganese (mg)	0.02	<0.01	0.01
Selenium (µg)	15.85	6.60	9.52

USDA National Nutrient Database for Standard Reference, Release 16 (July 2003). Nutrient Data Laboratory Home Page, http://www.nal.usda.gov/fnic/foodcomp

men and 450 mg for women. The RDI for choline increases during pregnancy and lactation owing to the high rate of choline transfer from the mother to the fetus and into breast milk. Animal studies indicate that choline plays an essential role in brain development, especially in the development of the memory centers of the fetus and newborn. Egg-yolk lecithin (phosphatidylcholine) is an excellent source of dietary choline, providing 125 mg of choline per large egg.

Egg Carotenes

Egg yolk contains two xanthophylls (carotenes that contain an alcohol group) that have important health benefits – lutein and zeaxanthin. It is estimated that a large egg contains 0.33 mg of lutein and zeaxanthin; however, the content of these xanthophylls is totally dependent on the type of feed provided to the hens. Egg-yolk lutein levels can be increased up to tenfold through modification of the feed with marigold extract or purified lutein. An indicator of the lutein + zeaxanthin content is the color of the yolk; the darker yellow-orange the yolk, the higher the xanthophyll content. Studies have shown that egg-yolk xanthophylls have a higher bioavailablity than those from plant sources, probably because the lipid matrix of the egg yolk facilitates greater absorption. This increased bioavailability results in significant increases in plasma levels of lutein and zeaxanthin as well as increased macular pigment densities with egg feeding.

Egg Cholesterol

Eggs are one of the richest sources of dietary cholesterol, providing 215 mg per large egg. In the 1960s and 1970s the simplistic view that dietary cholesterol equals blood cholesterol resulted in the belief that eggs were a major contributor to hypercholesterolemia and the associated risk of cardiovascular disease. While there remains some controversy regarding the role of dietary cholesterol in determining blood cholesterol levels, the majority of studies have shown that saturated fat, not dietary cholesterol, is the major dietary determinant of plasma cholesterol levels (and eggs contain 1.5 g of saturated fat) and that neither dietary cholesterol nor egg consumption are significantly related to the incidence of cardiovascular disease. Across cultures, those countries with the highest egg consumption actually have the lowest rates of mortality from cardiovascular disease, and within-population studies have not shown a correlation between egg intake and either plasma cholesterol levels or the incidence of heart disease. A 1999 study of over 117 000 men and women followed for 8–14 years showed that the risk of coronary heart disease was the same whether the study subjects consumed less than one egg a week or more than one egg a day.

Clinical studies show that dietary cholesterol does have a small influence on plasma cholesterol levels. Adding one egg per day to the diet would, on average, increase plasma total cholesterol levels by approximately $5\,mg\,dl^{-1}(0.13\,mmol/L)$. It is important to note, however, that the increase occurs in both the atherogenic LDL cholesterol fraction $(4\,mg\,dl^{-1}(0.10\,mmol/L))$ and the anti-atherogenic HDL cholesterol fraction $(1\,mg\,dl^{-1}(0.03\,mmol/L))$, resulting in virtually no change in the LDL:HDL ratio, a major determinant of cardiovascular disease risk. The plasma lipoprotein cholesterol response to egg feeding, especially any changes in the LDL:HDL ratio, vary according to the individual and the baseline plasma lipoprotein cholesterol profile. As shown in **Table 7**, adding one egg a day to the diets of three hypothetical patients with different plasma lipid profiles results in very different effects on the LDL:HDL ratio. For the individual at low risk there is a greater effect than for the person at high risk, yet in all cases the effect is quantitatively minor and would have little impact on their heart-disease risk profile. Overall, results from clinical studies indicate that egg

Table 7 Changes in plasma lipoprotein cholesterol levels with addition of one large egg per day to the diet

	Cholesterol ($mg\,dl^{-1}$)		LDL:HDL ratio
	LDL	HDL	(% change)
Baseline	125	50	2.50
+1 egg day^{-1}	129	51	2.53 (+1.2%)
Baseline	150	50	3.00
+1 egg day^{-1}	154	51	3.02 (+0.6%)
Baseline	175	50	3.50
+1 egg day^{-1}	179	51	3.51 (+0.3%)

feeding has little if any effect on cardiovascular disease risk. This is consistent with the results from a number of epidemiological studies.

A common consumer misperception is that eggs from some breeds of bird have low or no cholesterol. For example, eggs from Araucana chickens, a South American breed that lays a blue-green egg, have been promoted as low-cholesterol eggs when, in fact, the cholesterol content of these eggs is 25% higher than that of commercial eggs. The amount of cholesterol in an egg is set by the developmental needs of the embryo and has proven very difficult to change substantially without resorting to hypocholesterolemic drug usage.

Undue concerns regarding egg cholesterol content resulted in a steady decline in egg consumption during the 1970s, 1980s, and early 1990s, and restriction of this important and affordable source of high-quality protein and other nutrients could have had negative effects on the well-being of many nutritionally 'at risk' populations. Per capita egg consumption has been increasing over the past decade in North America, Central America, and Asia, has remained relatively steady in South America and Africa, and has been falling in Europe and Oceania. Overall, world per capita egg consumption has been slowly increasing over the past decade, in part owing to the change in attitude regarding dietary cholesterol health concerns.

Allergenic Aspects of Egg Proteins

Eggs are one of the most common causes of food allergies in infants and young children. Although the majority of egg allergies are caused by egg-white protein, proteins in both the egg white and the yolk are associated with allergies. The egg white contains 50% ovalbumin, which is the major allergen. Other egg-white allergenic proteins are ovomucoid, ovotransferrin, and lysozyme. Most egg allergies in young children are outgrown by the age of 5 years following an elimination diet.

Owing to the allergenicity of egg proteins, it is advised not to feed egg yolks to infants younger than 6 months of age and to wait until children are 12 months old to feed them egg whites. When feeding egg yolks to children between the ages of 6 months and 12 months, the eggs should be prepared in such a way that the egg white can be completely removed, as in hardboiled eggs.

Speciality Eggs

There is an increasing interest worldwide in the production and marketing of speciality eggs with enhanced nutrient benefits. The nutrient composition of an egg can be significantly modified by altering the composition of the feed. Commercially available nutrient-enhanced eggs contain increased amounts of omega-3 fatty acids, vitamin E, selenium, and lutein. Other enhancements include increased contents of vitamin D and the B vitamins as well as incorporation of conjugated linoleic acid.

Omega-3 Fatty Acids

The fatty-acid content of eggs is easily and significantly affected by the fatty-acid profile of the hen's feed. The omega-3 fatty-acid content of eggs can be increased by feeding hens a source of omega-3 fatty acids. In some countries, fish meal is used as a source of omega-3 fatty acids, but this can result in eggs with a fishy odour and taste. Marine algae are another source of omega-3 fatty acid and result in higher concentrations of eicosapentanoic acid and docosahexanoic acid (DHA) in egg yolks. Flaxseed oil is also used as a source of omega-3 fatty acids and results in increased levels of α-linolenic acid in egg yolks. The relative proportion of DHA to α-linolenic acid can be controlled by feeding a mixture of flaxseed oil and marine algae. It is possible to attain levels as high as 200 mg of omega-3 fatty acids per large egg.

Although omega-3 fatty-acid levels in eggs are well below levels found in fishes such as salmon and tuna, eggs can still be an important source of omega-3 fatty acids in the diet. For people who cannot eat fish, eggs with higher levels of omega-3 fatty acids can be an important way of including these beneficial fatty acids in the diet.

Other Nutrients in Speciality Eggs

By altering the content in the feed, other nutrients in eggs can be enhanced, for example lutein, vitamin E, and selenium. Vitamin E is usually added to the feed to serve as an antioxidant when the polyunsaturated fatty acids are increased. Vitamin E levels in eggs have been increased as much as 25-fold. The vitamin E in these eggs can provide an additional natural source of this important fat-soluble vitamin. Lutein (a xanthophyll) content can also be increased in eggs by increasing the amount in feed, usually in the form of marigold extract. Lutein is deposited in the egg yolk at levels as high as 2 mg per large egg, and the human body readily absorbs lutein from the egg phospholipid matrix. Nutritional needs for selenium vary widely owing to differences in the selenium content of regional soils. Egg selenium levels can be increased between 5-fold and 8-fold by the addition of an organo-selenium source to the feed.

Egg Food Safety

Eggs pose a unique food-safety problem because they can be contaminated internally with the pathogenic bacteria *Salmonella enterica* Serovar Enteritidis (SE). If SE infects the reproductive tracts of laying hens, it can be deposited in the eggs during formation. In addition to internal egg contamination by SE, eggshells can be contaminated with a number of microorganisms. Caution is required when selecting eggs for consumption. Only clean eggs should be consumed. Vaccinating hens against salmonella, together with temperature control, proper handling, and cooking are important control measures to reduce the incidence of SE illness.

When SE internally contaminates an egg, it is thought to be deposited at the yolk membrane in the egg white. The integrity of the vitelline membrane is very important in preventing SE from entering the yolk, where it could grow very rapidly in the nutrient-rich environment. The egg white has natural antimicrobial compounds, such as lysozyme, that help prevent SE from growing.

In naturally contaminated eggs, scientists have documented that between 10 and 100 cells of SE may be deposited in an egg. The bacterial cell count will remain low unless the egg is exposed to temperatures that would allow rapid growth of SE or the vitelline membrane breaks down. Even when flocks are infected with SE, only a small percentage of the eggs produced will contain SE. Properly cooking eggs to a temperature of $63\,°C$ for $3\,min$, $65\,°C$ for $1\,min$, or $70\,°C$ for $1\,s$ will destroy SE if it is present in an egg.

The Role of Eggs in the Diet

The nutritional contribution of eggs to a diet is determined by the per capita consumption profile of a given country. In countries such as Japan, with the highest per capita egg consumption, eggs play an important role as a source of nutrients, while in countries such as India, with very low per capita consumption, their role is minor. Worldwide there are many misperceptions and myths regarding eggs, which influence consumption patterns (**Table 8**).

Eggs are a nutrient-dense source of many EAA, vitamins, and minerals, and, as shown in **Figure 1**, eggs contribute a number of nutrients to the American diet in amounts proportionally greater than their caloric contributions. While providing only 1.3% of the calories, they provide nine different nutrients in amounts ranging from 2% to 6% of the DRI. Such nutrient-dense foods can play an

Table 8 Common myths and misperceptions about eggs

Myth	Fact
Brown eggs are healthier than white eggs; fertile eggs have less or no cholesterol; free-range eggs have more nutritional value than commercial eggs	There are no substantive nutritional differences between white eggs, brown eggs, fertile eggs, and free-range eggs; nutritional content is determined by the hen's diet
Eggs contain the hormones they give the hen to force her to lay eggs when there isn't a rooster around	Hens are not given hormones to produce eggs in the absence of a rooster; hens lay eggs with or without a rooster; there are no harmful hormones in eggs
Eggs contain the antibiotics they give hens to increase the number of eggs they'll lay	Antibiotics have no effect on egg production and there is no value in using them unless needed for therapeutic reasons
Eggs in the store are a mixture of fertile and non-fertile eggs; that stringy stuff is the embryo	Commercial eggs are not fertile (can be included in a lactoovo- or ovo-vegetarian diet); that stringy stuff (chalaza) is an egg protein that anchors the yolk in the centre of the egg
Eating eggs can cause liver problems	No study has ever shown that eggs cause liver problems
Eggs with blood or meat spots are fertilized or are bad	The tiny meat or blood spot is caused by the rupture of a blood vessel during egg formation; it has no adverse effect on the egg and can be either removed or eaten
If an egg floats in water, it is bad	As an egg ages the air sac expands and an egg will stand on end in water; this is not a sign that the egg is bad

Additional information and facts can be obtained from the American Egg Board *Eggcyclopedia*. (http://www.aeb.org/).

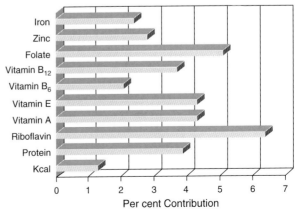

Figure 1 Nutrient contributions of eggs to the American diet.

important role in the diets of seniors who have decreased caloric intakes as well as in weight-reduction and weight-maintenance diets. Studies have shown that egg intake has a significant effect on satiety beyond what would be predicted from its protein and fat contents. Egg intake slows the rate of gastric emptying, resulting in a flatter blood glucose response and a lower insulin response. The effects on gastric emptying appear to be related to the effects of egg yolk (not white) intake on the secretion of cholecystokinin and gastric inhibitory peptide.

Summary

For nutritionally vulnerable populations, including the poor, the very young, the very old, pregnant women, and those suffering from chronic diseases, eggs are an affordable nutrient-dense source of high-quality protein important for maintaining health and facilitating recovery. Pregnancy is an especially important time to optimize the intake of high-quality protein and other essential nutrients to reduce the risk of low birth weight and the associated development of chronic diseases and other health problems during the infant's adult life. Eggs also serve as an important dietary source of choline during pregnancy and lactation, providing the fetus and newborn with choline for brain development. In addition, eggs provide a satiety effect, which, in view of the global problem of obesity, can be a valuable addition to weight-loss and weight-maintenance programs. For various populations, from infants to the aged, there are a multitude of health reasons to include nutrient-dense eggs as part of the diet, and for many of these groups it is economically feasible.

The high-quality protein, many nutritional components, low caloric content, affordability, blandness, ease of digestibility, and satiety response all make eggs ideal for inclusion in the diet at all ages, from very young to very old, and in times of both health and convalescence.

See also: **Antioxidants**: Diet and Antioxidant Defense. **Cholesterol**: Sources, Absorption, Function and Metabolism; Factors Determining Blood Levels. **Choline and Phosphatidylcholine**. **Coronary Heart Disease**: Lipid Theory. **Fatty Acids**: Omega-3 Polyunsaturated. **Food Allergies**: Etiology. **Food Safety**: Bacterial Contamination. **Phytochemicals**: Classification and Occurrence; Epidemiological Factors. **Pregnancy**: Nutrient Requirements. **Protein**: Requirements and Role in Diet; Digestion and Bioavailability; Quality and Sources.

Further Reading

American Egg Board. *Eggcyclopedia*, Chicago: American Egg Board. http://www.aeb.org/eggcyclopedia/main_frame_page.html

Egg Nutrition Center, Washington, DC. http://www.enc-online.org

Handelman GJ, Nightingale ZD, Lichtenstein AH, Schaefer EJ, and Blumberg JB (1999) Lutein and zeaxanthin concentrations in plasma after dietary supplementation with egg yolk. *American Journal of Clinical Nutrition* **70**: 247–251.

Herron KL and Fernandez ML (2004) Are the current dietary guidelines regarding egg consumption appropriate? *Journal of Nutrition* **134**: 187–190.

Hu FB, Stampfer MJ, Rimm EB *et al.* (1999) A prospective study of egg consumption and risk of cardiovascular disease in men and women. *JAMA* **281**: 1387–1394.

Humphrey TJ (1994) Contamination of egg shell and contents with *Salmonella enteritidis*: a review. *International Journal of Food Microbiology* **21**: 31–40.

McNamara DJ (2000) Dietary cholesterol and atherosclerosis. *Biochimica et Biophysica Acta* **1529**: 310–320.

McNamara DJ (ed.) (2000) Where would we be without the egg? A conference about nature's original functional food *Journal of the American College of Nutrition* **19**: 495S–562S.

Stadelman WJ and Cotterill OJ (1995) *Egg Science and Technology*, 4th edn. New York: Food Products Press.

Watson RR (ed.) (2002) *Eggs and Health Promotion*. Ames: Iowa State Press.

Yamamoto T, Juneja LR, Hatta H, and Kim M (1997) In *Hen Eggs: Their Basic and Applied Science*. Boca Raton: CRC Press.

Eicosanoids *see* **Prostaglandins and Leukotrienes**

ELECTROLYTES

Contents
Acid-Base Balance
Water–Electrolyte Balance

Acid-Base Balance

A G Jardine and P B Mark, University of Glasgow, Glasgow, UK

Introduction

Maintenance of cellular and extracellular pH (hydrogen ion concentration) is essential to life, in view of the exquisite pH dependence of processes such as enzyme function. Hydrogen ions (H^+) are generated by cellular metabolism and, to a lesser extent by the ingestion of acids in the diet. Acid-base homeostasis regulates pH between 7.36 and 7.44 (corresponding to a [H+] of 36–$44 \, nmol \, l^{-1}$) in extracellular fluids, such as blood, whereas intracellular pH is more acidic (pH 6.3–7.4) depending on individual organs and circumstances. The pH of subcellular organelles may be more acidic, reflecting their physiological function (e.g., lysosomes). Blood and extracellular fluid pH are tightly regulated by the presence of buffer systems, which attenuate changes as a consequence of acid load. These buffer systems, both extracellular and intracellular, include hemoglobin, other proteins, phosphate, and bicarbonate – the latter being of greatest importance. However, the acid load must ultimately be eliminated by the subsequent excretion of volatile acid by the lungs and fixed acids by the kidney.

Definitions, Acids, Bases, and Buffers

pH

The term pH is an expression of hydrogen ion (H^+) concentration (such that pH and H^+ are inversely related):

$$pH = -\log_{10}[H^+] \qquad [1]$$

Acids and Bases

Acids are substances that dissociate to donate H^+ (eqn [2]); the stronger the acid, the more readily it dissociates. The dissociation constant (pKa) is the pH at which 50% of the acid is dissociated. At pH values greater than pKa more H^+ will dissociate; the lower the pKa, the stronger the acid. A base is a substance that accepts hydrogen ions. In the following text the term 'fixed acid' is used to describe formed acid, and 'volatile acid' is used to describe the potential acid load imposed by carbon dioxide (CO_2). Where 'A' represents an acid, the following applies:

$$AH \leftrightarrow A^- + H^+ \qquad [2]$$

The importance of this relationship in physiological terms is that since the pKa of most organic acids is much lower than the pH of extracellular fluids, most organic acids exist in a dissociated state (as acid anion salts) the free H^+ being buffered. In urine, where the minimum achievable pH is around 5, most strong acids (with a pKa below this value) will be in a dissociated state, necessitating the excretion of H^+ together with urinary buffers.

Acidosis is the term used to describe conditions where pH is low and those where pH would be low were it not appropriately buffered; similarly, alkalosis is the term used for a high pH and for a potentially elevated pH that has been appropriately buffered. Acidemia and alkalemia reflect low or elevated blood pH. It is common to describe acidosis/alkalosis as respiratory or metabolic depending on their causation.

Buffers

Buffering is the ability of weak acids, present in excess, to accept H^+ donated from strong acids, thus limiting the changes in free H^+ concentrations and pH changes (equation [3]):

$$AH + Buffer \leftrightarrow Buffer\text{-}H^+ + A^- \qquad [3]$$

The principal buffer system in blood (and other extracellular fluids) is based on bicarbonate (HCO_3^-), accounting for approximately 70% of the buffering capacity of the blood. In blood, CO_2 (the major product of oxidative metabolism) reacts with water in the presence of the enzyme carbonic anhydrase (CA) to form carbonic acid (H_2CO_3). This compound is relatively unstable and tends to dissociate (eqn [4]). The rate of formation of carbonic acid is dependent on the concentration of carbon dioxide and the rate constant of reaction [i]; the dissociation of carbonic acid to generate H^+ and HCO_3^- is governed by the rate constant of reaction [ii]. In practice, these two reactions can be combined, and the relationship between pH ($[H^+]$), carbon dioxide, and bicarbonate is described by a single equation – the Henderson-Hasselbalch equation [5]:

$$\overset{[i]}{} \quad \overset{[ii]}{}$$
$$CO_2 + H_2O \leftrightarrow H_2CO_3 \leftrightarrow H^+ + HCO_3^- \qquad [4]$$

$$pH = 6.1 + \log_{10}([HCO_3^-]/K.S.PCO_2) \qquad [5]$$

pH reflects $-\log [H^+]$; 6.1 is the value of $-\log (1/K)$, K being the equilibrium constant describing the overall equation [4]; P_{CO_2} is the partial pressure of carbon dioxide; S is the solubility constant for carbon dioxide. $K.S.$ is constant and equal to 0.225 when P_{CO_2} is measured in kPa, 0.03 when P_{CO_2} is measured in mmHg). **Table 1** shows the normal range for these parameters in humans.

From eqn [5] the principles of acid-base balance can be appreciated. Acidification may occur in two ways: either by the production of CO_2 or by the consumption of bicarbonate (as part of the buffering of fixed acid). The excretion of CO_2 (see below) is controlled by the lungs, and the excretion of fixed acid takes place in the kidney.

The Henderson-Hasselbalch equation allows basic understanding of acid-base physiology, in health and disease, but has limitations. In the presence of either metabolic or respiratory derangement of acid-base homeostasis it does not allow assessment of the severity of the metabolic derangement, analogous to the respiratory component. It also does not assess the influence of other acids other than carbonic acid. For this reason some authors propose analysis of acid-base physiology using a more complex method based on the principles of physical chemistry. This method proposes that all changes pH in plasma can be explained in terms of relative concentrations of CO_2, relative electrolyte, and weak acid. This concept allows more rigorous interrogation of acid-base disorders and may permit greater insight into their pathophysiology and management.

Table 1 Normal ranges

Variable	Normal range
pH	7.36–7.44
Hydrogen ion (H^+)	37–44 nmol l^{-1}
Partial pressure CO_2 (P_{CO_2})	34–46 mmHg; 4.5–6.1 kPa
Bicarbonate (HCO_3^-)	24–30 mmol l^{-1}

Maintenance of the pH of the Blood and Extracellular Fluids

Acid and Alkali Load

The sources of acids (and alkalis) are from the diet and metabolism. The major potential source of acid is CO_2 ('volatile acid'; eqn [4]) generated by oxidative metabolism; a total of 12–20 mol of CO_2 are produced daily. Other metabolic products include lactic acid, other organic acids, and urea, the synthesis of which produces H^+. Because of its role in the metabolism of lactic acid and in the synthesis of urea, the liver plays a major role in acid-base homeostasis that is often not appreciated.

Volatile acid (CO_2) is excreted by the lungs, whereas the breakdown of sulfur and phosphorus-containing compounds are 'fixed' acids, requiring excretion by the kidney. For example, cysteine or methionine metabolism leads to the production of sulfuric and phosphoric acid (H_2SO_4, H_3PO_4), while the metabolism of other amino acids (lysine, arginine, and histidine) leads to the production of hydrochloric acid (HCl). In contrast, organic acids (e.g., lactate, fatty acids) may be completely metabolized to CO_2 and H_2O and thus excreted by the lungs. In addition, the absorption of dietary phosphate and the fecal loss of bicarbonate represent an additional acid load. In total, the net acid load of fixed acid is approximately 1 mmol kg^{-1} day^{-1} and may be increased by a high protein intake or reduced by a strict vegetarian diet.

There is surprisingly little information on the direct contributions of individual foods to the acid burden. However, this source of dietary acid is of increasing importance in view of current popular weight reduction diets (e.g., the Atkins diet). The major acids contained in food are citric acid (in fruit, fruit juices), acetic acid (as a preservative, pickles, vinegar), lactic acid (yogurt, fermented foods), malic acid (fruit), oxalic acid (vegetables that contain smaller amounts of citric and malic acids), and tartaric acid (wine). Oxalic acid precipitates in the gut to form calcium salts, which are excreted in the stool and little is absorbed. The other acids are absorbed but quickly metabolized and present an acid burden in the form of CO_2. The largest source of fixed acid comes from the metabolism of amino acids (particularly those from animal proteins – see above). The significance of this source of acid is readily demonstrated in patients consuming a high-protein diet (particularly one rich in animal protein) who have increased urinary acid excretion. Based on studies on the relationship between diet, renal excretion of acid, and urine pH it is theoretically feasible to quantify urinary acid excretion for individual foods. However, because of daily variation in diet (and therefore absence of a metabolic steady state) and inherent variation in the composition of foodstuffs, it has not been possible to date to estimate accurately the effects of diet on renal acid-base metabolism in circumstances reflective of normal dietary intake.

Alkalis are often prescribed to compensate for metabolic acidosis (see below) and in the past were often used to neutralize gastric acidity. Milk and milk products are also alkaline but seldom cause any disturbance, unless consumed in great excess. Excessive consumption of milk or alkali is now rarely seen.

Regulation

Blood and extracellular fluid pH is regulated at three levels: (1) buffering within the blood and tissues; (2) excretion of volatile acids by the lungs; and (3) excretion of fixed acids by the kidney. Whilst buffering is immediate, respiratory compensation occurs over minutes to hours and renal excretion takes many hours to days (**Table 2**).

Blood/Extracellular Fluid

Immediate buffering of an acid load, for example by the release of lactic acid and CO_2 by anaerobic and aerobic metabolism in exercising muscle, occurs in the blood and other extracellular fluids, which together contain approximately 350 mmol of bicarbonate buffer. Sixty to seventy per cent of the buffering capacity of blood is accounted for by the bicarbonate buffer system; 20–30% is dependent on direct binding to hemoglobin and to other proteins, including plasma proteins. Blood is in equilibrium with extracellular fluid H^+. H^+ ions move across cell membranes depending on concentration and charge; thus, H^+ ions may move into cells in exchange for K^+ (and to a lesser extent Na^+ ions) when extracellular H^+ is increased. Hence, acidosis is often accompanied by increased serum K^+, and alkalosis by low K^+. Large amounts of H^+ may be 'buffered' by direct binding to proteins within cells

and tissues, particularly bone where H^+ ions are also buffered by calcium salts, such as apatite.

Lungs

The lungs excrete volatile acid (CO_2) by changes in the rate and volume of respiration. This is regulated by respiratory centers in the brainstem that respond to changes in the pH of the cerebrospinal fluid (which is in equilibrium with extracellular fluids elsewhere in the body), and signals from chemoreceptors in the carotid and aortic bodies that are responsive to changes in pH and P_{CO_2} of the arterial blood (increased P_{CO_2} or reduced pH cause an increase in respiration). Thus, acidosis leads to an increase in respiratory rate and ventilatory volume (the pattern in severe acidosis being described as Kussmaul breathing) and alkalosis leads to the opposite effect.

Kidneys

The kidneys have two major roles in acid-base homeostasis: the recovery of filtered bicarbonate and generation of new bicarbonate; and the excretion of fixed acid (**Figures 1** and **2**; eqn [5]). Blood is filtered in the glomeruli and the glomerular filtrate is subsequently modified in the renal tubules so that the final urine volume is less than 1% of the glomerular filtrate volume. Plasma bicarbonate concentration is approximately $25 \, \text{mmol} \, l^{-1}$ and glomerular filtration rate (GFR) is $100 \, \text{ml} \, \text{min}^{-1}$, thus $3600 \, \text{mmol}$ of bicarbonate must be reabsorbed daily.

Table 2 Buffering and acid-base regulation

Mechanism	Site	Role (time)
Protein (e.g., Hb)	Cell	Rapid binding of H^+ (seconds)
Bicarbonate buffer	ECF	Buffering of H^+ (seconds)
Ventilation	Lungs	Excretion of CO_2, respiratory compensation (hours)
Fixed acid excretion	Kidney	Excretion of H^+, reabsorption and regeneration of bicarbonate, renal compensation (hours to days)

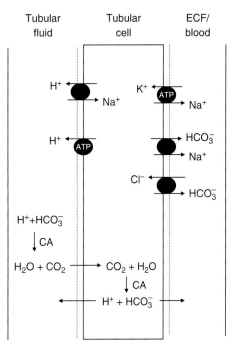

Figure 1 Recovery of filtered bicarbonate in the proximal convoluted tubule. CA, carbonic anhydrase.

Tubular   Tubular   ECF/
fluid   cell   blood

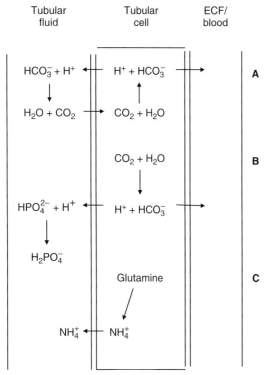

Figure 2 Excretion of acid in the collecting duct.

Bicarbonate reabsorption mainly occurs in the proximal convoluted tubule (PCT, **Figure 1**). Eighty-five per cent of filtered bicarbonate is reabsorbed at this site: 10% in the thick ascending limb of the loop of henle, the remainder being titrated to regulate total acid excretion in the collecting duct (**Figure 2**). As shown in the Figure, different mechanisms are involved at each tubular site. The enzyme carbonic anhydrase, on the luminal brush border of tubular cells, catalyzes the combination of filtered bicarbonate with H^+, secreted by the apical H^+-ATPase and Na^+/H^+ exchangers on tubular cells, to generate CO_2. CO_2 then diffuses into the tubular cells down its concentration gradient. Within the cell, carbonic anhydrase catalyzes the reverse reaction generating the production of H^+ and HCO_3^-. Hydrogen ions are then recycled to the tubular lumen and bicarbonate is secreted into the extracellular fluid (by basolateral anion exchangers or Na^+–HCO_3^- cotransporters) passing into the extracellular fluid and blood. The tubule cells are also exposed to CO_2 in the extracellular fluid and will continue to generate H^+ even in the absence of filtered bicarbonate. This H^+ is then buffered by other buffers in the glomerular filtrate including HPO_4^{2-} and, to a lesser extent, creatinine. Strong acids (e.g., H_2SO_4) with low pKa values will dissociate in the urine (pH range 5–8) and are buffered, whereas weaker acids may be excreted intact. In the presence of alkalosis,

the function of cellular transporters may be reversed so that H^+ secretion occurs on the basolateral membrane and HCO_3^- secretion on the brush border of tubular cells resulting in alkaline urine.

Classically, the final mechanism by which the kidney can excrete H^+ is by the generation of ammonium (NH_4^+) from the metabolism of glutamine by glutaminase (**Figure 2**), a process that is stimulated by low pH and increased P_{CO_2}. The excretion of H^+ as part of ammonium accounts for around 70 mmol day^{-1}, increasing several-fold (albeit over a period of days) in the face of an acid load. Whether this is truly a urinary buffer is the subject of some debate as ammonium (NH_4^+) is generated directly from glutamine rather than accepting additional protons. There are alternative mechanisms for the role of NH_4^+ in overall acid-base homeostasis that involve the liver. After being pumped into the glomerular filtrate, NH_4^+ may be reabsorbed by the tubule and used by the liver to synthesize urea, generating free H^+ ions. Thus, there is no net loss of H^+ and the overall role of NH_4^+ in acid-base balance is dependent on the balance between tubular reabsorption of NH_4^+ and the hepatic synthesis of urea. The latter function may also be directly influenced by extracellular pH.

Liver and Bone

The liver plays additional roles in acid-base balance that may be underestimated. For example, the liver metabolizes lactate and keto acids; the rate of metabolism is dependent on pH (e.g., ketogenesis is suppressed at low pH) and may be exceeded at higher concentrations of lactate or in liver disease. The synthesis of urea from ammonium and carbon dioxide (above) results in the genesis of two protons, and is reduced in the presence of acidosis. Some buffering also occurs in bone due to the slow exchange of bone calcium carbonate for extracellular phosphate.

Measurement of Urinary Acid Excretion

Urinary pH can be measured by commercially available 'dipstix' or by using a pH meter on a fresh sample of urine. The loss of CO_2 or the production of NH_4^+ from urea-splitting organisms in infected urine will alter the pH with time. The excretion of fixed acid can be determined by the chemical titration of urine to pH 7.4, and is commonly termed 'titratable' acidity. The amount of NH_4^+ is usually estimated from the difference between the most abundant cation (Na^+, K^+) and anion (Cl^-) concentrations in the urine.

Effects of Acid-Base Disturbance

In addition to the adaptive changes occurring in acidosis, a range of metabolic and pathophysiological changes occur; alkalosis tends to produce opposite but milder effects. The metabolism of carbohydrate is altered: both glycolysis and gluconeogenesis are inhibited in the liver. Delivery of oxygen to the tissues is increased by the reduced ability of hemoglobin to retain oxygen in an acid environment (the Bohr effect). Consciousness is impaired, leading to coma in severe cases. However, the most important effects from a clinical perspective are cardiovascular: vasodilatation occurs in peripheral tissues, cardiac contractility is impaired resulting in reduced blood pressure, and, when severe, in reduced tissue perfusion. It is these effects that contribute to the adverse effects of acidosis in, for example, septic shock and contribute to the high mortality in these conditions.

Abnormalities in Acid-Base Balance

Disturbances in acid-base balance are classified as either 'acidosis,' indicating an excess of H^+ ions in the blood (reduced pH) or alkalosis, indicating the opposite. In practice, acidosis is the more common, varied, and serious problem. Disturbances in acid-base balance are usually labeled according to their origin. For example, respiratory acidosis reflects a primary problem in gas exchange with impaired excretion of CO_2, whereas metabolic acidosis reflects the over-production of fixed acid or loss of bicarbonate. Compensation refers to the body's ability to offset the primary problem. Thus, the response to a primary metabolic acidosis is to increase the excretion of CO_2 – respiratory compensation. If the pH returns to normal the problem is said to be 'fully compensated' whereas most disturbances tend to be only partially compensated (Table 3).

Table 3 Changes in blood and ECF during acid-base disturbance, the mechanism and degree of compensation

Problem	$[H^+]$	$[HCO_3^-]$	P_{CO_2}	Compensation
Metabolic				
Acidosis	↑	1°↓	2°↓	Partial respiratory
Alkalosis	↓	1°↑	2°↑	Partial respiratory
Respiratory				
Acidosis	↑	2°↑	1°↑	Complete renal
Alkalosis	↓	2°↓	1°↓	Complete renal

↑, Increase; ↓, decrease; 1°, primary; 2°, secondary.

Metabolic Acidosis

The main causes of metabolic acidosis are excessive acid production, inappropriate urinary loss of bicarbonate, or failure of the kidney to excrete fixed acid. Although the Henderson-Hasselbalch equation provides mathematical information concerning the equilibrium of bicarbonate species, in practice it provides little information regarding the nature of the underlying cause of the acid-base disorder and the concept of 'anion gap' is useful in assessing the cause of metabolic acidosis. This is derived from the principle of electroneutrality and is calculated thus:

$$([NA^+] + [K^+]) - ([Cl^-] + [HCO_3^-]) \qquad [6]$$

The anion gap represents an artificial disparity between the concentrations of these cations and anions routinely measured in clinical practice, therefore signifying the concentration of unmeasured anions such as proteins (the most important in healthy subjects), sulfate, phosphate, and others. The normal anion gap is $10–18\ mmol\,l^{-1}$ although recent calculations using more sensitive measurements estimate this to be $6–12\ mmol\,l^{-1}$. This concept has limitations but is useful for dividing metabolic acidoses into those characterized by an increased anion gap as a marker of excess generation of organic acids and those with a normal anion gap due to decreased excretion of acid or external losses of bicarbonate. There are exceptions to this rule, e.g., the acidosis of chronic renal failure, but, nonetheless, it remains a useful concept in clinical practice. Classification of the causes of metabolic acidoses according to the presence of an increased or normal anion gap is shown in **Table 4**.

Diabetic Ketoacidosis

The absence of pancreatic insulin secretion in insulin-dependent diabetes results in increased plasma glucose and reduced tissue uptake and utilization of glucose. In the place of glucose, there is increased utilization of nonesterified fatty acid (NEFA) as an alternative source of energy that is metabolized to acetyl coenzyme A (acetyl-CoA). Under normal circumstances this substance is further metabolized in the liver via the tricarboxylic acid (TCA) cycle to CO_2 and water. In diabetic crises this cycle cannot accommodate the excess acetyl-CoA that is, instead, converted to acetoacetic acid, which can be further reduced to β-hydroxybutyric acid or decarboxylated to acetone. These three metabolites are known as 'ketone bodies' and their accumulation results in metabolic acidosis. In diabetic ketoacidosis, the homeostatic compensation is to increase ventilation

Table 4 Causes of metabolic acidoses according to the presence of an increased or normal anion gap

Increased anion gap	Normal anion gap
Ketoacidosis	Decreased renal acid
Diabetic	excretion
Starvation	Distal renal tubular acidosis
Alcoholic	
Inborn enzyme defects of	
metabolism	
Lactic acidosis	Loss of alkali
	Diarrhea
	Ureterosigmoidostomy
	(urinary conduit)
Renal failure	Increased renal bicarbonate
	loss
	Proximal renal tubular acidosis
	Azetazolamide
	Renal tubular damage
Intoxication	Increased HCl production
Salicylates	Ammonium chloride ingestion
Methanol	Increased catabolism of
Ethylene glycol	lysine, arginine
Paraldehyde	

and CO_2 excretion, leading to the characteristic pattern of ventilation known as Kussmaul respiration.

Lactic Acidosis

Reduced tissue perfusion, or perfusion that is inadequate to meet the metabolic demands of the tissues (such as exercising muscle), results in an inadequate supply of oxygen and a change from oxidative metabolism (the end products of which are CO_2 and H_2O) to anaerobic metabolism. The end product of anaerobic glycolysis is lactic acid, which is normally metabolized (to CO_2 and H_2O) by the liver or used in the synthesis of glucose (gluconeogenesis). The normal plasma [lactate] is less than $1\,mmol\,l^{-1}$ but may increase 10-fold in extreme exercise. When the ability to metabolize lactate is exceeded, either by increased production, or reduced delivery to the liver (in, for example, circulatory shock) or in the presence of impaired liver function, accumulation results in metabolic acidosis. Thus, lactic acidosis may occur in a variety of conditions, including circulatory shock, severe diabetic ketoacidosis, as a consequence of drugs (for example, the oral hypoglycemic agent metformin that inhibits gluconeogenesis and lactate transport), chronic liver disease, and poisoning (including ethanol and methanol).

Excess Bicarbonate Loss

The secretion of acid into the stomach is neutralized by alkaline secretions in the intestine. It follows that excessive loss of pure intestinal secretions (for example, in the presence of an enteric fistula) may lead to acidosis. A more common circumstance is the presence of an ileal conduit where the ureters are implanted into an isolated loop of intestine, which is then externalized (a 'urinary conduit'). The delivery of urine rich in chloride to the isolated intestine leads to exchange of Cl^- for HCO_3^-, and thence to excessive loss of HCO_3^- in the conduit, resulting in metabolic acidosis.

There are also a group of conditions known as renal tubular acidosis (RTA). These are mostly inherited but may be acquired, for example, as a consequence of recurrent infection. There are two major forms – proximal and distal – reflecting the site of the tubular defect in the nephron. In distal tubular RTA (type I) H^+ secretion is impaired resulting in impaired H^+ excretion, whereas in proximal RTA (type I) HCO_3^- reabsorption is impaired (usually as part of multiple tubular abnormalities) leading to net loss of bicarbonate. Both cause acidosis, the features of which are low pH and hypokalemia as a result of increased distal tubular H^+/K^+ exchange. The precise causes of these conditions is not known but is likely to reflect genetic defects on individual transporter subtypes, for example, those of the Na^+/H^+ exchanger (**Figure 2**).

Renal Failure

In progressive renal failure, renal clearance of all substances is impaired, reflecting the progressive loss of individual nephron function. Reduced excretion of fixed acid leads to bicarbonate consumption in the extracellular fluids and to acidosis. Tubular recovery of HCO_3^- may also be impaired (see RTA), as may the production of tubular NH_4^+, and may be associated with overproduction of urea in the liver.

Drugs and Other Causes

Many drugs can cause metabolic acidosis, generally in overdose. A classic example is aspirin (acetylacetic acid). Lactic acidosis is also associated with oral hypoglycemic agents (specifically metformin, used in the treatment of noninsulin-dependent diabetes), paracetamol, alcohol, and ethylene glycol (antifreeze) poisoning.

Compensation

The body's response to metabolic acidosis is a compensatory increase in ventilation to excrete excessive CO_2, restoring the equilibrium in the Henderson-Hasselbalch equation (eqn [5]). This respiratory compensation is usually incomplete, resulting in pH values or H^+ concentrations at, or marginally outside, the limits of 'normal' (**Table 3**). Complete compensation depends on renal excretion of excess H^+, or resolution of the underlying condition.

Treatment

Treatment of metabolic acidosis is essentially that of the underlying condition: correction of tissue hypoxia in lactic acidosis; correction of fluid depletion and insulin therapy in diabetic ketoacidosis; and dialysis in renal failure. Rapid correction of pH can be achieved by the administration of intravenous sodium bicarbonate if necessary; treatment of chronic metabolic acidosis (e.g., in chronic renal failure or RTA) may be achieved by the administration of oral sodium bicarbonate. In uremia the prescription of a low-protein diet will also reduce acid load.

Metabolic Alkalosis

Metabolic alkalosis may be caused either by the excessive loss of acid or intake of alkali. The latter may be iatrogenic or factitious, with the excessive intake of prescribed antacids (such as sodium bicarbonate for heartburn or peptic ulcer disease) – the 'milk-alkali' syndrome. The loss of acid-rich gastric secretions in severe vomiting, for example, in cases of gastric outlet obstruction (due to pyloric stenosis, or a consequence of peptic ulcer disease), also leads to alkalosis. Compensation is by reducing ventilation to promote retention of CO_2 and thus balance the Henderson-Hasselbalch equation. Treatment is of the underlying condition rather than by administration of acid.

Respiratory Acidosis

Impaired ventilation reduces CO_2 excretion, increases Pa_{CO_2}, and thus lowers pH. This may occur acutely or chronically. Causes of respiratory acidosis include factors that interfere with the neurological 'drive' for respiration (e.g., head injury, cardiac arrest, opiate and anesthetic drugs), diseases of the respiratory muscles (e.g., poliomyelitis, Guillain-Barré syndrome), or primary lung diseases (acute pulmonary edema or pneumonia, chronic bronchitis or emphysema). In acute conditions, pH may fall dramatically, whereas in chronic conditions, such as chronic lung disease, the pH is generally nearer normal. In chronic conditions complete compensation occurs in the kidney where elevated $PaCO_2$ levels are offset by the increased generation of bicarbonate and excretion of fixed acid by the kidney, to balance the Henderson-Hasselbalch equation.

Respiratory Alkalosis

Respiratory alkalosis occurs as a result of inappropriately increased ventilation and increased excretion of CO_2. This may occur as a transient response to pain or hysteria. Such stimuli tend to be short lived and can be offset by analgesia, sedation, or short-term re-breathing of expired air. Additional causes include the early phases of aspirin poisoning (where the respiratory centers are activated), hypoxia, stroke, and other conditions affecting the brainstem respiratory control centers. Most causes of respiratory alkalosis are short term and, although adaptive responses would be expected to require excretion of bicarbonate to balance the Henderson-Hasselbalch equation, resolution usually occurs by resolution of the underlying condition.

Transporter Mechanisms: Physiology and Pathophysiology

Developments in molecular biology have led to major improvements in our understanding of the physiology and pathophysiology of renal tubular function. It is now possible to subdivide the various types of renal tubular acidosis, for example, by the precise biochemical defect rather than simply the tubular location. Thus, distal (or type 1) RTA may be a consequence of impaired distal tubular H^+ excretion, either due to increased permeability to H^+ or to impaired secretion, the latter, in turn, being a consequence of a variety of defects that include carbonic anhydrase type 2 deficiency, mutations in anion transport protein AE1, or deficiency of collecting duct proton transport ATPase. Whilst specific knowledge of the molecular defect is not necessary to either diagnose or manage these disorders, it is likely that future classification of acid-base disorders will change to recognize the underlying defect.

See also: **Brain and Nervous System. Electrolytes:** Water–Electrolyte Balance.

Further Reading

Adrogue HJ and Madias NE (1998) Management of life-threatening acid-base disorders. Second of two parts. *New England Journal of Medicine* **338**(2): 107–111.

Adrogue HJ and Madias NE (1998) Management of life-threatening acid-base disorders. First of two parts. *New England Journal of Medicine* **338**(1): 26–34.

Corey HE (2003) Stewart and beyond: New models of acid-base balance. *Kidney International* **64**: 777–787.

Galla JH (2000) Metabolic alkalosis. *Journal of the American Society of Nephrology* **11**: 369–375.

Gluck SL (1998) Acid-base. *The Lancet* **352**: 474–479.

Gunnerson KJ and Kellum JA (2003) Acid-base and electrolyte analysis in critically ill patients: are we ready for the new millennium? *Current Opinion in Critical Care* **9**: 468–473.

Halperin ML and Goldstein MB (1999) *Fluid, Electrolyte and Acid-Base Physiology: A Problem-Based Approach*, 3rd edn. London: W.B. Saunders.

Kellum JA (2000) Determinants of blood pH in health and disease. *Critical Care* **4**(1): 6–14.

Palmer BF, Narins RG, and Yee J (2005) Clinical acid–base disorders. In: Davison AM, Cameron JS, Grünfeld J-P, Ponticelli C, Ritz E, Winearls CG, and van Ypersele C (eds.) *Oxford Textbook of Clinical Nephrology*, 3rd edn, vol. 1, Ch 2.6, pp. 321–346. Oxford: Oxford University Press.

Remer T (2000) Influence of diet on acid-base balance. *Seminars in Dialysis* **13**(4): 221–226.

Sirker AA, Rhodes A, Grounds RM, and Bennett ED (2002) Acid-base physiology: the 'traditional' and the 'modern' approaches. *Anaesthesia* **57**: 348–356.

Stewart PA (1983) Modern quatitative acid-base chemistry. *Canadian Journal of Physiology and Pharmacology* **61**: 1444–1461.

Williams AJ (1998) ABC of oxygen: Assessing and interpreting arterial blood gases and acid-base balance. *British Medical Journal* **317**: 1213–1216.

Water–Electrolyte Balance

S M Shirreffs and R J Maughan, Loughborough University, Loughborough, UK

Body Water and Electrolytes

Man is dependent on ready access to water for survival. Water is the largest component of the human body and the total body water content varies from approximately 45 to 70% of the total body mass; this therefore corresponds to about 33–53 l for a 75 kg man. The water content of the various tissues is maintained relatively constant; as adipose tissue has a low water content (**Table 1**)

Table 1 Water content of various body tissues for an average 75 kg man

Tissue	% water	% of body mass	Water per 75 kg (l)	% of total body water
Skin	72	18	9.7	22
Organs	76	7	4.0	9
Skeleton	22	15	2.5	5
Blood	83	5	3.1	7
Adipose	10	12	0.9	2
Muscle	76	43	24.5	55

From Sawka (1990).

Table 2 Body water distribution between the body fluid compartments in an adult male

	% of body mass	% of lean body mass	% of body water
Total body water	60	72	100
Extracellular water	20	24	33
Plasma	5	6	8
Interstitium	15	18	25
Intracellular water	40	48	67

From Sawka (1990).

the fraction of water in the body is determined largely by the fat content. The body's water can be divided into two components—the intracellular fluid and the extracellular fluid. The intracellular fluid is the major component and comprises approximately two-thirds of total body water. The extracellular fluid can be further divided into the interstitial fluid (that between the cells) and the plasma; the plasma volume represents approximately one-quarter of the extracellular fluid volume (**Table 2**).

Numerous electrolytes and solutes are dissolved within the body water compartments: an electrolyte can be defined as a compound which dissociates into ions when in solution. The major cations (positively charged electrolytes) in the body water are sodium and potassium, with smaller amounts of calcium and magnesium; the major anion (negatively charged electrolytes) is chloride, with smaller amounts of bicarbonate and protein. Sodium is the major electrolyte present in the extracellular fluid, while potassium is present in a much lower concentration (**Table 3**). Within the intracellular fluid the situation is reversed, and the major electrolyte present is potassium, while sodium is found in much lower concentrations. Maintenance of the transmembrane electrical and chemical gradients is of

Table 3 Ionic concentrations ($mmol\,l^{-1}$) of body water compartments[a].

Ion	Plasma	Intracellular fluid	Sweat
Sodium	140 (135–145)	12	20–80
Potassium	4.0 (3.5–4.6)	150	4–8
Calcium	2.4 (2.1–2.7)	4.0	0–1
Magnesium	0.8 (0.6–1.0)	34	<0.2
Chloride	104 (98–107)	4	20–60
Bicarbonate	29 (21–38)	12	0–35
Inorganic phosphate	1.0 (0.7–1.6)	40	0.1–0.2

[a]The normal ranges of the plasma electrolyte concentrations are shown.

paramount importance for maintaining the integrity of the body's cells and allowing electrical communication throughout the body.

Daily Regulation of Body Water

The body's total body water content is normally maintained within a small window of fluctuation on a daily basis by intake of food and drink to balance the excretion of urine and other losses. Hyperhydration is corrected by an increase in urine production and hypohydration by an increase in water intake via food or drink consumption initiated by thirst. Most of our water intake is related to habit rather than thirst, but the thirst mechanism is effective at driving intake after periods of deprivation. There are also water losses via the respiratory tract, the gastrointestinal tract, and the skin. The extent of these losses will vary from individual to individual and will be strongly influenced by environmental conditions and physical activity levels, but for a sedentary individual in a cool environment these generally represent only a small proportion of the total body water loss.

All the major textbooks of nutrition and physiology include data on the various components of water intake and output, although it is difficult to find the original data on which the various mean values and ranges are based. The Geigy Scientific Tables suggest that the minimum daily water intake for adults is on the order of 1.5 l, but others indicate that the minimum intake should be 2 l per day. Body size has a major influence on water turnover, but the total body water content will also be markedly affected by the body composition. Water turnover should therefore be more closely related to lean body mass than to body mass itself. It is expected, therefore, that there will be differences between men and women and between adults and children.

Environmental conditions will affect the basal water requirement by altering the losses that occur by the various routes (i.e., respiration, sweat, and urine). Water requirements for sedentary individuals living in the heat may be two or threefold higher than the requirement when living in a temperate climate, even when not accompanied by pronounced sweating. Transcutaneous and respiratory losses will be markedly influenced by the humidity of the ambient air, and this may be a more important factor than the ambient temperature. Respiratory water losses are incurred because of the humidification of the inspired air with fluid from the lungs. These losses are relatively small in the resting individual in a warm, moist environment

(amounting to about 200 ml per day) but will be increased approximately 2-fold in regions of low humidity, and may be as high as 1500 ml per day during periods of hard work in the cold, dry air at altitude. To these losses must be added insensible water loss through the skin (about 600 ml per day) and urine loss, which will not usually be less than about 800 ml per day.

Variations in the amount and type of food eaten have some effect on water requirements because of the resulting demand for excretion of excess electrolytes and the nonvolatile products of metabolism. An intake of electrolytes in excess of the amounts lost (primarily in sweat and feces) must be corrected by excretion in the urine, with a corresponding increase in the volume and osmolality of urine formed. The daily intake of electrolytes is subject to wide variation among individuals, with strong trends for differences among different geographical regions. Daily dietary sodium chloride intakes for 95% of the young male UK population fall between 3.8 and 14.3 g, with a mean of 8.4 g; the corresponding values for young women are 2.8–9.4 g, with a mean value of 6.0 g. For the same population, mean urinary sodium losses were reported to account for about 175 mmol per day, which is equivalent to about 10.2 g of sodium chloride.

There are also large differences among countries in the recommended intake of salt. The British health authorities advise a maximum of 6 g per day, but in Germany a maximum of 10 g per day is recommended. In contrast, Sweden recommends a maximum of 2 g per day, and Poland recommends a minimum of 1.4 g per day. The differences among countries reflect in part different interpretations with regard to the evidence linking salt intake and health, but also reflect regional consumption patterns dictated by food choices.

A high-protein diet requires a greater urine output to allow for excretion of water-soluble nitrogenous waste; this effect is relatively small compared with other routes of water loss but becomes meaningful when water availability is limited. The water content of the food ingested will also be influenced greatly by the nature of the diet, and water associated with food may make a major contribution to the total fluid intake in some individuals. Some water is also obtained from the oxidation of nutrients, and the total amount of water produced will depend on the total metabolic rate and is also influenced by the substrate being oxidized. An energy expenditure of 3000 kcal (12.6 MJ) per day, based upon a diet composed of 50% carbohydrate, 35% fat, and 15% protein, will yield about 400 ml of water per day. Reducing the daily energy expenditure to 2000 kcal (8.4 MJ), but keeping the same diet composition, will yield about 275 ml of water. The contribution of this water-of-oxidation to total water requirements is thus appreciable when water turnover is low but becomes rather insignificant when water losses are high.

Thirst and the Control of Intake

In man, daily fluid intake in the form of food and drink (plus that formed from substrate oxidation) is usually in excess of the obligatory water loss (transcutaneous, pulmonary, and renal output), with renal excretion being the main mechanism regulating body water content. However, conservation of water or electrolytes by the kidneys can only reduce the rate of loss; it cannot restore a deficit. The sensation of thirst, which underpins drinking behavior, indicates the need to drink and hence is critical in the control of fluid intake and water balance. While thirst appears to be a poor indicator of acute hydration status in man, the overall stability of the total water volume of an individual indicates that the desire to drink is a powerful regulatory factor over the long term.

The act of drinking may not be a direct consequence of a physiological need for water intake but can be initiated by habit, ritual, taste, or desire for nutrients, stimulants, or a warm or cooling effect. A number of the sensations associated with thirst are learned, with signals such as dryness of the mouth or throat inducing drinking, while distention of the stomach can stop ingestion before a fluid deficit has been restored. However, the underlying regulation of thirst is controlled separately by the osmotic pressure and volume of the body fluids and as such is governed by the same mechanisms that affect water and solute reabsorption in the kidneys and control central blood pressure.

Regulatory Mechanisms

Areas of the hypothalamus and forebrain, that are collectively termed the thirst control centers, appear to be central to the regulation of both thirst and diuresis. Receptors in the thirst control centers respond directly to changes in osmolality, volume, and blood pressure, while others are stimulated by the fluid-balance hormones that also regulate renal excretion. These regions of the brain also receive afferent input from systemic receptors monitoring osmolality, circulating sodium concentration, and alterations in blood volume and pressure. Changes in the balance of neural activity in the thirst control centers regulated by the different monitoring inputs

determine the relative sensations of thirst and satiety, and influence the degree of diuresis. Input from the higher centers of the brain, however, can override the basic biological need for water to some extent and cause inappropriate drinking responses. Cases of water intoxication (hyponatremia) during endurance sports events lasting more than about 6–8 h have been reported in which the major cause of the illness is due to overhydration as a result of overdrinking.

A rise of between 2 and 3% in circulating osmolality (i.e., about 6–8 mosm kg^{-1} H$_2$O) is sufficient to evoke a profound sensation of thirst coupled with an increase in the circulating concentration of antidiuretic hormone, also known as vasopressin. The mechanisms that respond to changes in intravascular volume and pressure appear to be less sensitive than those that monitor plasma osmolality, with hypovolemic thirst being evident only following a 10% decrease in blood volume. As fairly large variations in blood volume and pressure occur during normal daily activity, primarily in response to postural changes, this lack of sensitivity presumably prevents overactivity of the volume-control mechanisms. Prolonged exercise, especially in the heat, is associated with a decrease in plasma volume and a tendency for an increase in osmolality, but fluid intake during and immediately following exercise is often less than that required to restore normal hydration status. This appears to be due to a premature termination of the drinking response rather than to a lack of initiation of that response. Also, the composition of the beverage consumed has an effect on the volume of fluid ingested, with water prematurely abolishing the osmotic drive to drink, while sodium-containing drinks help maintain the osmotic drive to drink and increase voluntary intake.

When a water deficit is present and free access to fluid is allowed, the drinking response in man usually consists of a period of rapid ingestion, during which more than 50% of the total intake is consumed, followed by intermittent consumption of relatively small volumes of drink over a longer period. The initial alleviation of thirst occurs before significant amounts of the beverage have been absorbed and entered the body water. Therefore, although decreasing osmolality and increasing extracellular volume promote a reduction in the perception of thirst, other preabsorptive factors also affect the volume of fluid ingested. Receptors in the mouth, oesophagus, and stomach are thought to meter the volume of fluid ingested, while distension of the stomach tends to reduce the perception of thirst. These preabsorptive signals appear to be behavioural, learned responses and may be subject to disruption in situations which are novel to the individual. This may partly explain the inappropriate voluntary fluid intake in individuals exposed to an acute increase in environmental temperature or to exercise-induced dehydration.

Renal Function

As well as acting to regulate body water levels by an increase or decrease in the amount of urine produced, the kidneys are also responsible for the elimination of waste products from the body. This, therefore, also affects the daily urine volume. For example, a healthy individual eating a normal diet excretes approximately 600–800 mosmol of solute per square metre of body surface area per day, amounting to a total of about 1000–1500 mosmol day^{-1}. The kidneys can dilute urine to at least as low as 100 mosmol kg^{-1} and can concentrate it to 1200 mosmol kg^{-1}. Therefore, the daily solute load to be excreted can be accommodated in a volume ranging between approximately 500 ml and more than 13 l. To allow for waste product excretion, an obligatory minimum amount of urine must always be excreted, and this is generally in the region of 20–50 ml per hour. However, in the majority of healthy individuals in most situations, the volume of urine produced and excreted is in excess of these basal levels.

Hormonal Control of Urine Production

The volume of urine produced in a healthy individual is largely determined by circulating hormone levels, and in particular by levels of vasopressin. Vasopressin is a cyclic, nine-amino acid peptide. It is released from the posterior pituitary after having been transported there along the axons of neurons whose cell bodies are located in the paraventricular and supraoptic nuclei of the hypothalamus, the site of vasopressin synthesis. An increase in the rate of secretion of vasopressin results in a reduced urine production. Vasopressin acts on the renal distal tubules and collecting ducts to cause an increased permeability to water and hence an increased reabsorption of water from the filtrate. Therefore, a hyperosmotic urine can be formed and the solute load to be excreted can be accommodated in a small volume of water. A decrease in vasopressin secretion results in an increase in the volume of urine produced by causing a reduction in the permeability of the renal distal tubule and collecting ducts to water. Vasopressin secretion is largely influenced by changes in plasma osmolality. An increase in plasma osmolality results in a increased vasopressin secretion and vice versa. The vasopressin is released rapidly in response to the stimuli and begins to act within minutes. When the secretion is inhibited, the half-life of clearance from the circulation is approximately 10 minutes. Therefore, changes in body fluid tonicity are rapidly translated into changes in water excretion by this tightly regulated feedback system.

In addition to the influence of plasma osmolality on vasopressin secretion, other (nonosmotic) factors with an influence are baroregulation, nausea, and pharyngeal stimuli. A fall in blood pressure or blood volume will stimulate vasopressin release; vasopressin secretion is, however, less sensitive to these changes than to changes in osmolality. Nausea is an extremely potent stimulus to vasopressin secretion in man; vasopressin levels can increase 100- to 1000-fold in response to nausea induced by various chemical agents. After a period of water deprivation followed by access to drink, vasopressin levels fall before there is any change in plasma tonicity, suggesting activation of neuronal pathways from the oropharynx.

Aldosterone, a steroid hormone, is released into the circulation after synthesis by the zona glomerulosa cells of the adrenal cortex. Its primary role, in terms of renal function, is to increase renal tubular reabsorption of sodium and in doing so will bring about an increased excretion of potassium and, in association with vasopressin, increase water reabsorption in the distal segments of the nephron. Aldosterone causes this response by increasing the activity of the peritubular sodium/potassium pump and by increasing the permeability of the luminal membrane to both sodium and potassium. The increased luminal permeability allows potassium to move down its concentration gradient from the inside of the membrane cells into the tubule lumen. The majority of the sodium present is reabsorbed into the cell down the concentration gradient. The sodium absorption and potassium excretion are closely correlated with a 3 sodium:2 potassium ratio. Chloride follows the sodium to maintain the electrical neutrality of the urine.

The release of aldosterone is determined by a number of factors including the renin–angiotensin system: A fall in blood or extracellular fluid volume increases renin production and, via angiotensin II, results in an increase in aldosterone secretion.

The presence in the renal filtrate of ions such as bicarbonate and sulphate, which are not reabsorbed, promotes secretion of potassium into the distal tubule of the nephron and will also result in an increased urinary loss of potassium.

Sweat

Exercise, particularly in a warm environment, and diarrheal illness are two situations which will increase the requirement for salt to substantially greater levels. Sweating, therefore, is an important consideration in the area of water and electrolyte balance as this is the one route where there can be extensive losses of water and electrolytes from the body in a healthy individual. If these losses are not replaced, serious consequences can ensue.

Eccrine sweat is a clear, watery, odourless substance whose primary function is to promote heat loss by evaporation from the skin surface. When sweat is produced, the daily water losses increase and the intake must be increased or urine production decreased accordingly if euhydration is to be maintained.

Sweat Evaporation

There is a daily loss on the order of approximately 500 ml of water through the skin. However, when the body is exposed to a heat stress and behavioral and vasomotor mechanisms are insufficient to prevent a rise in temperature, the physiological responses generally include an increase in sweat production in an attempt to prevent hyperthermia; the high latent heat of vaporization of water makes the evaporation of sweat an effective heat loss mechanism (evaporation of 1 l of water from the skin surface will remove 2.4 MJ (580 kcal) of heat from the body). The heat stress may be of external origin (i.e., from the environmental conditions), of internal origin due to muscular work or fever, or from a combination of these factors.

In many individuals sweat rates can be in excess of 2 l per hour, especially in situations of exercise undertaken in a warm, humid environment, and these high sweat rates can be maintained for a number of hours. For example, body mass losses in marathon runners have been reported to range from about 1–6% (0.7–4.2 kg) at low (10 °C) ambient temperatures to more than 8% (5.6 kg) in warmer conditions. However, when sweat rates are high, a significant fraction of the sweat secreted onto the skin may drip from the body and is therefore ineffective at removing heat.

Mechanism of Sweat Secretion

The human body has approximately 2 million sweat glands. The eccrine sweat gland consists of a single tubule, opening onto the epidermis at one end and closed at the other. The proximal half of the tubule is the secretory coil and the distal half the reabsorptive duct. The sweat secreted onto the skin is the original tubular secretion minus the substances which are, further up the tubule, reabsorbed; from the isoosmotic fluid secreted by the coil most of the major electrolytes (Na^+, Cl^-, HCO_3^+, and lactate) are transported out of the duct back into the extracellular fluid in excess of water. The final sweat secreted onto the skin is therefore hypotonic with respect to body fluids.

Sweat Composition

The composition of human sweat is highly variable, both between individuals and within an individual over time. However, sodium and chloride are the major electrolytes lost in sweat, with other ions being present in smaller amounts relative to the whole body status. The sweat electrolyte composition of an individual seems to be related primarily to sweat rate but can be influenced by training status, extent of heat acclimation, and diet. However, the range of values for sweat electrolyte composition reported in the literature probably reflects not only the interindividual differences but also differences in the methodology used for collection of the sweat. This last factor may be the result of errors caused by contamination or incomplete collection of the sample, or it may reflect a real difference induced by the collection procedure.

Due to the secretion and reabsorption process involved in sweat production within the sweat gland and duct, sweat composition is influenced by sweat rate, at least within single ducts, such that a reduction in rate allows for greater reabsorption of certain electrolytes (Na^+, Cl^-, but not K^+) from the duct resulting in a lower concentration in the final sweat produced. There also appear to be regional variations in sweat composition, as evidenced by the different values obtained when the composition of sweat obtained from different parts of the body is compared, and the values obtained by regional collection also differ from those obtained by the whole body washdown technique. Reported values for sweat electrolyte composition are summarized in Table 3.

Restitution of Water and Electrolyte Balance

When substantial sweat losses have been incurred, restitution of water balance requires both volume repletion and replacement of electrolyte losses. This can be achieved by ingestion of electrolyte-containing drinks or by ingestion of water and consumption of electrolyte-containing foods. Problems may occur when large sweat losses are replaced with electrolyte-free drinks. Hyponatremia and blood volume expansion ensue and will promote a diuresis that will prevent effective recovery.

Conclusions

In healthy individuals, water is the largest single component of the body. Although water balance is regulated around a range of volumes rather than a finite set point, its homeostasis is critical for virtually all physiological functions. To further ensure proper regulation of physiological and metabolic functions, the composition of the individual body water compartments must also be regulated.

Humans continually lose water through the renal system, gastrointestinal system, skin, and respiratory tract, and this water must be replaced. Thirst is implicated in our water intake, but behavioral habits also have an important influence on drinking.

When exercise is undertaken or when an individual is exposed to a warm environment, the additional heat load is lost largely due to sweating and this can increase greatly the individual's daily water loss and therefore the amount that must be consumed. Sweat rates on the order of 2 to 3 l per hour can be reached and maintained by some individuals for a number of hours and it is not impossible for total losses to be as much as 10 l in a day. These losses must of course be replaced and when they are so extreme, the majority must be met from fluid consumption rather than food ingestion. A variety of drink types and flavors are likely to be favored by individuals who have extreme losses to replace. Sports drinks have an importance role in this recovery when no food is ingested by their contribution to sweat electrolyte loss replacement which is crucial for retention of the ingested water.

See also: **Calcium**. **Exercise**: Beneficial Effects. **Magnesium**. **Potassium**. **Sodium**: Physiology.

Further Reading

Briggs JP, Sawaya BE, and Schnermann J (1990) Disorders of salt balance. In: Kokko JP and Tannen RL (eds.) *Fluids and Electrolytes*, 2nd edn., pp. 70–138. Philadelphia: WB Saunders.

Costill DL, Coté R, and Fink W (1976) Muscle water and electrolytes following varied levels of dehydration in man. *Journal of Applied Physiology* 40: 6–11.

Engell DB, Maller O, Sawka MN *et al.* (1987) Thirst and fluid intake following graded hypohydration levels in humans. *Physiology and Behaviour* 40: 229–236.

Grandjean AC, Reimers KJ, Bannick KE, and Haven MC (2000) The effect of caffeinated, non-caffeinated, caloric and non-caloric beverages on hydration. *Journal of the American College of Nutrition* 19: 591–600.

Kirby CR and Convertino VA (1986) Plasma aldosterone and sweat sodium concentrations after exercise and heat acclimation. *Journal of Applied Physiology* 61: 967–970.

Lentner C (ed.) (1981) *Geigy Scientific Tables*, 8th edn. Basel: Ciba-Geigy Limited.

Maughan RJ (2001) Water, hydration status and human wellbeing. In: Berk Z *et al.* (ed.) *Water Science for Food, Health, Agriculture and Environment*, ISOPOW 8, pp. 43–57. Lancaster: Technomic.

Maughan RJ and Murray R (eds.) (2000) *Sports Drinks: Basic Science and Practical Aspects*. Boca Raton, FL: CRC Press.

Rose BD (1984) *Clinical Physiology of Acid–Base and Electrolyte Disorders*, 2nd edn. New York: McGraw-Hill.

Sawka MN (1990) Body fluid responses and hypohydration during exercise-heat stress. In: Pandolf KB, Sawka MN, and Gonzalez RR (eds.) *Human Performance Physiology and Environmental Medicine at Terrestrial Extremes*, pp. 227–266. Carmel: Cooper.

Shirreffs SM and Maughan RJ (1997) Whole body sweat collection in man: An improved method with some preliminary data on electrolyte composition. *Journal of Applied Physiology* 82: 336–341.

Sterns RH and Spital A (1990) Disorders of water balance. In: Kokko JP and Tannen RL (eds.) *Fluids and Electrolytes*, 2nd edn., pp. 139–194. Philadelphia: WB Saunders.

Taylor NAS (1986) Eccrine sweat glands. Adaptations to physical training and heat acclimation. *Sports Medicine* 3: 387–397.

Valtin H (2002) "Drink at least eight glasses of water a day." Really? Is there scientific evidence for "8 × 8"? *American Journal of Physiology* 283: R993–R1004.

ENERGY

Contents
Metabolism
Balance
Requirements
Adaptation

Metabolism

S Cox, London School of Hygiene and Tropical Medicine, London, UK

The energy required for the growth and maintenance of living organisms is acquired through the cellular respiration of organic compounds. In man and other nonphotosynthetic organisms, these metabolic fuels are obtained from food and consist of carbohydrates, fats, and proteins.

Metabolism

Metabolism is defined as the sum of anabolic or synthetic chemical reactions that require energy and the catabolic chemical reactions that break down large organic molecules into smaller molecules, thereby releasing energy for anabolic reactions.

Cellular Respiration and Adenosine Triphosphate

Cellular respiration can be defined generally as the process by which chemical energy is released during the oxidation of organic molecules. If it requires oxygen, it is called aerobic respiration, whereas if it takes place in the absence of oxygen it is anaerobic respiration.

Organic molecules, usually carbohydrate or fat, are broken down by a series of enzyme-catalyzed reactions. Many of these reactions release a small amount of energy that is channeled into molecules of a chemical nucleotide called adenosine triphosphate (ATP) (**Figure 1**).

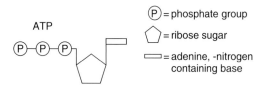

Figure 1   Structure of adenosine triphosphate (ATP).

ATP is the standard unit in which the energy released during respiration is stored. ATP is an instant source of energy within the cell. It is mobile and transports energy to wherever energy-consuming processes are occurring within the cell. The energy is released by the dephosphorylation of ATP to ADP, which can then be rephosphorylated to ATP by being coupled to the processes of respiration. ATP is found in all living cells and can be thought of as a universal energy transducer.

The principal metabolic fuel is glucose, and there are three stages in its oxidation to carbon dioxide, water, and energy, captured as ATP. This process can be summarized very simply by the following equation:

$$C_6H_{12}O_6 + 6O_2 \rightarrow 6CO_2 + 6H_2O + \text{energy (ATP)}$$

In the first stages, glucose and other metabolic fuels are oxidized, linked to the chemical reduction of coenzymes (nicotinamide adenine dinucelotide (NAD^+), flavin adenine dinucleotide (FAD), and flavin mononucleotide (FMN)). In the final stage, ATP is synthesized from ADP and phosphate via a common pathway using energy released from the oxidation and recycling of the reduced coenzymes (**Table 1**). Thus, the oxidation of metabolic fuels is tightly coupled to energy consumption and the production of ADP from ATP in energy-consuming processes (**Figure 2**).

Glycolysis

The main substrate for glycolysis is glucose. Glycolysis does not require oxygen and is important for the direct production of ATP when oxygen is limiting (i.e., in rapidly contracting muscle). Glycolysis results in the splitting of glucose, a six-carbon (6C) compound, into two molecules of pyruvic acid (3C), which in the cytoplasmic solution becomes pyruvate (**Figure 3**). Pyruvate can enter the mitochondrion and be metabolized by oxidative decarboxylation to CO_2, or if oxygen is unavailable it can be further metabolized to lactic acid resulting in the

Table 1 The three principal stages in the production of ATP from one molecule of glucose

Metabolic pathway	Location	O_2 required?	Net ATP or reduced coenzymes/glucose	Products
Glycolysis	Cytoplasm	Anaerobic	Net gain 2 ATP 2 NADH + H$^+$	Glucose → 2 pyruvate
Pyruvate → acetyl-CoA	Mitochondrial matrix	Aerobic	2 NADH + H$^+$	
TCA cycle	Mitochondrial matrix	Aerobic	2 GTP → 2 ATP 8 NADH + H$^+$ 2 FADH$_2$	2 Pyruvate → 6CO$_2$
Electron transfer chain (oxidative phosphorylation)	Mitochondrial crista and primary particles	Aerobic	12 NAD$^+$ + 2 FAD → 38 ATP^a	12H$_2$ + 6O$_2$ → 6H$_2$O

^{a}The exact net gain in the number of ATP produced from the oxidation of the reduced coenzymes NADH + H$^+$ and FADH$_2$ varies depending on the mechanism used to transport them across the crista membrane in the mitochondria, the site of oxidative phosphorylation.

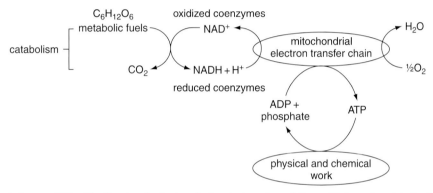

Figure 2 Linkage between ATP utilization in physical and chemical work and the oxidation of metabolic fuels. (Adapted with permission from Bender DA (2002) *Introduction to Nutrition and Metabolism*, 3rd edn. London: Taylor & Francis.)

regeneration of NAD$^+$ from NADH + H$^+$, thus allowing glycolysis to continue in the absence of oxygen. Red blood cells lack mitochondria and therefore glycolysis is the only source of energy metabolism. Thus, red cells can only metabolize glucose or other simple sugars and not fats or proteins. Red cells produce lactate that is excreted into the blood. Lactate is primarily metabolized back to pyruvate in the liver, where it is mostly used for the synthesis of glucose (gluconeogenesis), which is essentially the reverse of glycolysis except for the irreversible reaction of phosphoenolpyruvate (PEP) to pyruvate. Hence, in the liver pyruvate is converted back to PEP via oxaloacetate (**Figure 3**). This cycling of lactate and pyruvate is known as the Cori cycle.

Other sugars, such as fructose and galactose, can be fed into glycolysis at different points and then metabolized in the same way as glucose to pyruvic acid.

The pentose–phosphate shunt (sometimes also known as the hexose–monophosphate pathway) occurs when glucose-6-phosphate is metabolized via an alternative route to glycolysis to generate

pentose phosphates to be used as components in DNA and RNA nucleotides. Alternatively, pentose phosphates can be returned into the glycolytic pathway by conversion back to fructose-6-phosphate or glyceraldehyde-3-phosphate. Another purpose of this shunt is the production of NADPH + H$^+$ from NADP$^+$, which is the required coenzyme for fat synthesis (lipogenesis). Reduced NADP$^+$ is also required for the reduction and recycling of oxidized glutathione, an important intermediate in antioxidant defence and in the generation of the respiratory burst, used to kill parasites ingested by macrophages, a type of white blood cell.

Tricarboxylic Acid Cycle

The tricarboxylic acid (TCA) cycle (also known as the citric acid cycle) is located in the mitochondrial matrix and is a common metabolic pathway for all fuels. It is responsible for the production of the majority of the reduced coenzymes used for the generation of ATP in the electron transfer chain. It also plays a central role in the interconversion of

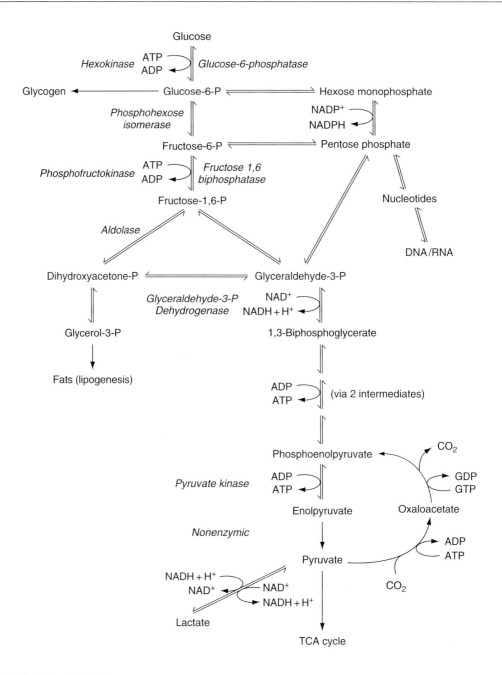

Figure 3 Glycolysis and its interactions with other metabolic pathways.

fuels and metabolites. The TCA cycle participates in gluconeogenesis from amino acids and lactate during fasting between meals and longer term in starvation. TCA cycle intermediates are the source of most of the nonessential amino acids, such as aspartate and glutamate. It is also involved in the conversion of carbohydrates to fat for storage after a carbohydrate-rich meal.

Pyruvate (3C) from glycolysis is oxidatively decarboxylated to acetyl-CoA (2C) in the mitochondria,

catalyzed by the multienzyme complex pyruvate dehydrogenase and the coenzyme A (Co-ASH):

$$\text{Pyruvate} + \text{Co-ASH} + \text{NAD}^+$$
$$\rightarrow \text{acetyl-CoA} + \text{Co}_2 + \text{NADH} + \text{H}^+$$

Pyruvate dehydrogenase requires several coenzymes derived from vitamins, including vitamin B_1 or thiamine, niacin (NAD), riboflavin (FAD), and pantothenic acid (a component of CoA). Deficiencies in any of these vitamins can affect energy metabolism, as

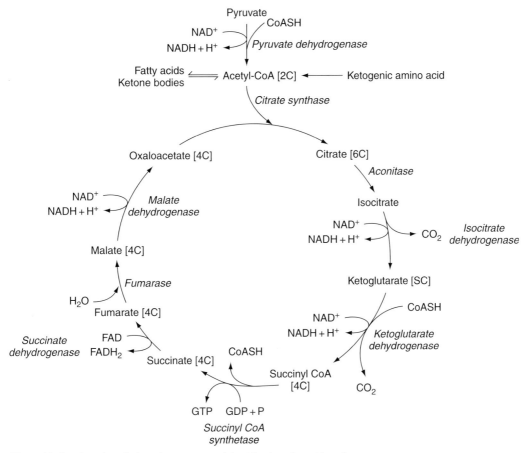

Figure 4 The oxidative decarboxylation of pyruvate and the tricarboxylic acid cycle.

evidenced by the increased cellular pyruvate and cardiac and skeletal muscle weakness in beriberi caused by thiamine deficiency. Pyruvate dehydrogenase catalyzes a central reaction in carbohydrate metabolism, and therefore its activity is regulated by both allosteric and covalent mechanisms.

Acetyl-CoA can be produced from pyruvate but also from fatty acids released from fat stores and from amino acids released from proteolysis of protein tissue, which can be converted to acetyl-CoA or cycle intermediates. In the first of the eight enzymatic reactions, acetyl-CoA (2C) combines with oxaloacetate (4C), forming citrate (6C) and releasing the CoA for further reactions with pyruvate to acetyl-CoA. A cycle of reactions follows in which two molecules of CO_2 are released and three molecules of $NADH + H^+$ and one of $FADH_2$ are produced along with one molecule of GTP (equivalent to ATP). At the end of the cycle, oxaloacetate is regenerated and able to react again with another molecule of acetyl-CoA, and so the cycle continues (**Figure 4**).

In the electron transfer chain, each $NADH + H^+$ yields approximately 3 ATP and $FADH_2$ yields 2

ATP. Thus, each rotation of the TCA cycle produces approximately 12 ATP (3 $NADH + H^+ \approx 9$ ATP + 1 $FADH_2 \approx 2$ ATP + 1 GTP). Because two molecules of acetyl-CoA are formed from one glucose molecule, the TCA cycle rotates twice for each molecule of glucose respired, producing a net of 24 ATP (**Table 1**).

Electron Transfer Chain (Oxidative Phosphorylation)

Oxidative phosphorylation occurs in the crista of mitochondria, formed by invaginations of the inner mitochondrial membrane (**Figure 5**). The hydrogen accepted by NAD^+ and FAD during glycolysis and the TCA cycle is oxidized to water by molecular oxygen with accompanying phosphorylation of $ADP \rightarrow ATP$. This is achieved by phosphorylation of ADP coupled with a series of redox reactions whereby the hydrogen ions (H^+) and their electrons (e^-) are passed along a chain of intermediate carriers in the crista membrane of the mitochondria

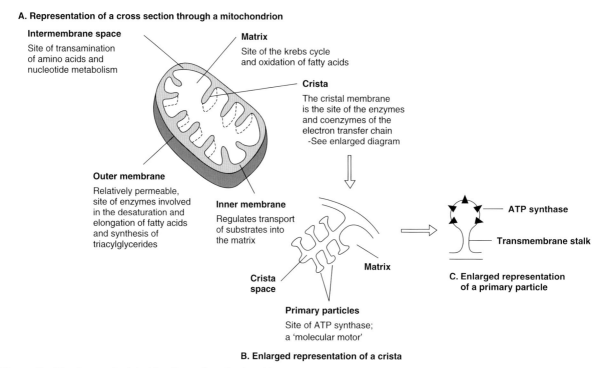

Figure 5   Structure and related functions of a mitochondrion.

(**Figure 6**), with each intermediate being reduced by the proceeding one and in turn reducing the next one and hence itself being oxidized. The chain consists of a flavoprotein and ubiquinone (coenzyme Q), both hydrogen carriers, followed by a series of cytochromes that are carriers of electrons only. Finally, at the end of the chain is cytochrome oxidase, which catalyzes the formation of water from hydrogen ions, electrons, and molecular oxygen. Unlike the other cytochromes, cytochrome oxidase contains copper (Cu^{2+}) in a prosthetic group instead of Fe^{3+} (in the form of a heme molecule), and this final stage can be inhibited by the irreversible binding of cyanide to Cu^{2+} preventing it from accepting electrons and therefore terminating the entire hydrogen electron transfer chain and hence all aerobic respiration. This is the basis of the toxicity of cyanide and also several other substances.

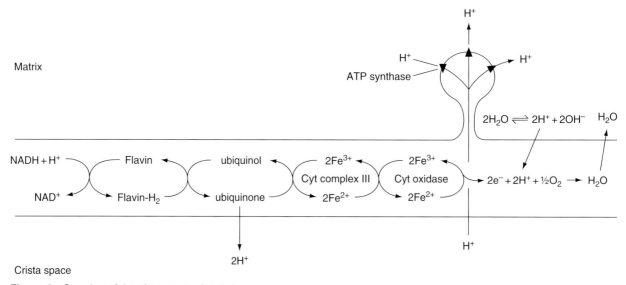

Figure 6   Overview of the electron transfer chain.

When the hydrogen from $NADH + H^+$ or $FADH_2$ is passed from ubiquinone to the first cytochrome, the hydrogen dissociates into a hydrogen ion (proton) and an electron. The proton is excreted into the crista space, whereas the electron carries on down the chain of cytochromes. This creates a proton gradient across the crista membrane. In the last step, the reduction of molecular oxygen to water, the hydrogen protons are obtained not from the hydrogen excreted into the crista space but from the mitochondrial matrix from the dissociation of water ($H_2O \leftrightarrow H^+ + OH^-$), thus maintaining a proton gradient across the crista membrane. The resulting movement of protons from the crista space to the matrix through the transmembrane stalk of the primary particle drives the multienzyme complex of ATP synthase. It is the energy of the flow of the protons that provides the energy required for the synthesis of ATP in a manner analogous to a water mill, where the flow of water can be used to turn a motor, grind wheat, or generate electricity.

The oxidation of $FADH_2$ and $NADH + H^+$ is normally tightly coupled to the phosphorylation of $ADP \rightarrow ATP$ because the phosphorylation of ADP cannot occur unless there is a proton gradient across the crista membrane of the mitochondria, resulting from the processes in the hydrogen electron transfer chain. Metabolic fuels can only be oxidized if there is NAD^+ and FAD available to be reduced. If there is no ADP because it has all been phosphorylated to ATP, protons cannot move down the concentration gradient across the crista membrane and through the 'water mill' of ATP synthase because it will not turn if there is no ADP to bind to it. Once a critical concentration of protons is reached in the crista space, it is no longer possible to extrude any more protons from the oxidation of FADH or $NAD + H^+$ during the transfer of hydrogen from ubiquinone to the first cytochrome. Hence, the whole chain stops and no more oxidized NAD^+/FAD is available for glycolysis or the TCA cycle.

The uncoupling of the electron transfer chain from the production of ATP can only occur if protons move down the concentration gradient across the crista membrane and through routes independent of ATP synthase. In some circumstances tissues, uncoupling proteins can be expressed in the crista membrane, which allow protons to flow down the concentration gradient into the mitochondrial matrix without passing through the ATP synthase and therefore not generating ATP but resulting in the generation of a large amount of heat energy. This is the basis of nonshivering thermogenesis, which is thought to occur mostly in brown adipose tissue in infants by the uncoupling protein thermogenin. In adults, the importance of brown adipose tissue compared with other uncoupling proteins in muscle and other tissues is unclear. In addition to maintenance of body temperature, uncoupling proteins may also be important in overall energy balance and body weight. Leptin, a hormone secreted from white adipose tissue, increases the expression of uncoupling proteins in muscle and adipose tissue, thus increasing energy expenditure and utilisation of adipose tissue fat reserves.

Energy Metabolism of Other Nutrients

The TCA cycle and pyruvate are central in the metabolism of carbohydrate, fat, and protein in the fed and fasting state. Pyruvate can have three main fates depending on the metabolic circumstances. It can be a substrate for gluconeogenesis, or it can undergo oxidative decarboxylation to acetyl-CoA and either enter the TCA cycle or be used for fatty acid synthesis.

Acetyl-CoA can be made from carbohydrates via pyruvate, from fatty acids via β-oxidation in the mitochondrial matrix, or from the proteolysis of proteins to amino acids, some of which are converted to acetyl-CoA.

There are three main stores of metabolic fuels: triacylglycerols in adipose tissue, glycogen as a carbohydrate reserve in liver and muscle, and protein as a source of amino acids that can be oxidized via the TCA cycle or used as a substrate for gluconeogenesis.

Overview of Fat Metabolism

β-Oxidation of Fatty Acids and Ketogenesis

Fats (triacylglycerides) are stored mainly in adipose tissue. Lipolysis breaks down fats into the constituent fatty acids and glycerol. Fatty acids can be oxidized via the β-oxidation pathway in the mitochondrial matrix. In this process, a cyclical series of reactions removes the last two carbon atoms from the carboxyl end of the fatty acyl-CoA, with the addition of another CoA to form a new fatty acyl-CoA that is two carbon atoms shorter plus acetyl-CoA. In muscle, the acetyl-CoA is metabolized via the TCA cycle to produce reduced coenzymes for the production of ATP. In the liver, it is shunted largely to the synthesis of ketone bodies (ketogenesis), which, like glucose, are exported for use in other tissues.

On the outer face of the mitochondrial membrane, fatty acids are esterified to CoA to form fatty acyl-CoA, which cannot enter the matrix of the mitochondria, the site of the enzymes for β-oxidation. This function is performed by the carnitine shuttle. On the outer mitochondria membrane, fatty acyl is transferred onto carnitine to form fatty acyl-carnitine that is transported across the inner and outer mitochondrial membranes on a countercurrent transporter system, in exchange for transporting free carnitine into the intermembrane space. Once in the matrix, the fatty acyl is esterified to CoA, thus releasing free carnitine. There is no dietary requirement for carnitine because it is readily synthesized from the amino acids lysine and methionine.

Most tissues have a limited capacity for β-oxidation. However, the liver can produce large amounts of acetyl-CoA by β-oxidation and can then convert some of this into four-carbon ketone bodies that can be easily transported to other tissues for use as a metabolic fuel. Acetoacetate is formed by the combination of 2 acetyl-CoA and the removal of the CoA molecules. This is unstable and undergoes a nonenzymic reaction to acetone, which is poorly metabolized, most of it being excreted in urine and exhaled air. Hence, most of the acetoacetate is reduced to β-hydroxybutyrate before being released from the liver. β-Hydroxybutyrate is metabolized by extrahepatic tissues by adding a CoA via succinate-CoA to form succinate and acetoacetyl-CoA that is then broken down into 2 acetyl-CoA by β-ketothiolase and CoA (**Figure 7**).

Synthesis of Fatty Acids and Triacylglycerides

The majority of fatty acids are supplied by the diet, but many tissues are capable of *de novo* synthesis, including the liver, brain, kidney, mammary glands, and adipose tissue. The *de novo* synthesis of fatty acids occurs in conditions of excess energy intake.

Fatty acid synthesis occurs in the cytosol but is essentially the reverse of β-oxidation of fatty acids (although it employs a separate set of enzymes), whereby fatty acids are synthesized from the successive additions of 2C acetyl-CoA followed by reduction.

Acetyl-CoA is formed in the mitochondrial matrix, but it cannot pass across the mitochondrial inner membrane. Hence, the source of acetyl-CoA for fatty acid synthesis is citrate, which can pass out of the mitochondria, where, with CoA, it is cleaved to produce acetyl-CoA and oxaloacetate. The oxaloacetate is returned indirectly to the mitochondrial matrix via its oxidation to pyruvate, which is linked to the generation of reduced NADP, required for fatty acid synthesis. Once in the mitochondrial matrix, the pyruvate is converted back to oxaloacetate and thus returned into the TCA cycle.

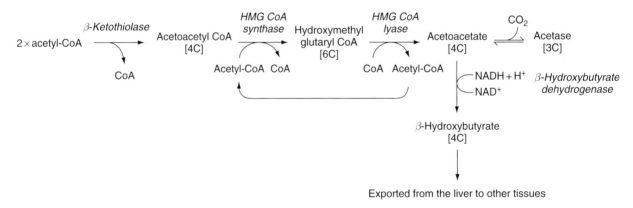

(A) Ketogenesis in the liver from acetyl-CoA

(B) Extrahepatic metabolism of β-hydroxybutyrate (Ketone bodies) to acetyl-CoA

Figure 7 The production (A) and metabolism (B) of ketones produced from acetyl-CoA.

The first step in fatty acid synthesis is the carboxylation of acetyl-CoA to malonyl-CoA, followed by the addition of a series of malonyl-CoA units by a complex series of reactions via the multienzyme complex fatty acid synthase. The carboxylation of acetyl-CoA to malonyl-CoA is regulated by the hormones insulin and glucagon, which affect the activity of the enzyme catalyzing this reaction. Hence, in the fed state insulin increases the activity of the enzyme, whereas in the fasting state glucagon decreases its activity. Also, malonyl-CoA inhibits the uptake of fatty acids into the mitochondria via acetyl carnitine-CoA so that when fatty acid synthesis is occurring, β-oxidation is inhibited by limiting the supply of substrate into the mitochondria.

Storage of fatty acids in adipose tissue can only occur when glycolysis is activated in the fed state because the source of glycerol in adipose tissue is blood glucose entering glycolysis and DHA-P removed to be converted to glycerol-3-P.

During fatty acid synthesis, desaturase enzymes can introduce double bonds to make mono- and polyunsaturated fatty acids. However, these enzymes cannot introduce double bonds after C10; this is why there is a requirement for the essential fatty acids linoleic acid (n-6) and linolenic acid (n-3), which can then be converted to the long-chain polyunsaturated fatty acids, arachidonic acid and eicosapentaenoic acid, which are important metabolic precursors.

Protein Metabolism

After a meal there is an increase in the synthesis of tissue protein from absorbed amino acids and the increased availability of metabolic fuel to provide ATP for protein synthesis. During fasting some of the relatively labile protein laid down in response to a meal can be mobilized and the amino acids used both as a metabolic fuel and as a source of TCA cycle intermediates for gluconeogenesis.

After removal of the nitrogen-containing amino group of amino acids, their carbon skeletons can undergo gluconeogenesis (gluconeogenic amino acids only), be converted into ketone bodies via acetyl-CoA (ketogenic amino acids), be fully oxidized to CO_2 and H_2O, be converted into fat or glycogen for storage, or be used as a precursor for a wide range of important biomolecules (**Figure 8**).

Gluconeogenesis

The brain can normally only metabolize glucose as an energy source. Therefore, it is very important to maintain relatively constant levels of circulating glucose. In normal circumstances, glycogen serves as a source of blood glucose as free fatty acids from adipose tissue and ketone bodies from the liver are used preferentially as metabolic fuels by muscle and some other tissues. However, this still leads to the exhaustion of glycogen reserves within 12–18 h.

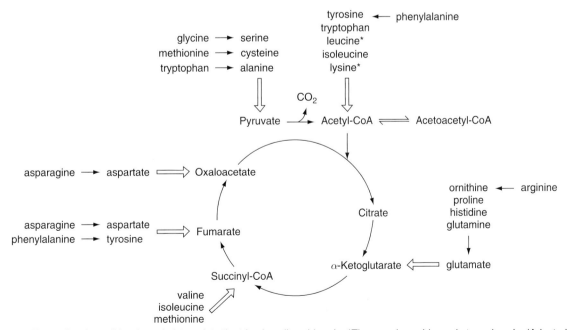

Figure 8   Entry of amino acid carbon skeletons into the tricarboxylic acid cycle. *These amino acids are ketogenic only. (Adapted with permission from Bender DA (2002) *Introduction to Nutrition and Metabolism*, 3rd edn. London: Taylor & Francis.)

Hence, the formation of glucose from noncarbohydrate sources (gluconeogenesis) is important.

Glucose can be formed from the gluconeogenic amino acids and from glycerol released from the lipolysis of TAGs in adipose tissue. Amino acids can enter the TCA cycle as intermediates and be converted to oxaloacetate, the excess of which can then be removed and metabolized to phophoenolpyruvate and then, by a process that is the reverse of glycolysis, be converted to glucose. Glycerol can be converted to an intermediate on the glycolytic pathway and therefore undergo gluconeogenesis if required.

Amino acids that can only be metabolized to acetyl-CoA cannot undergo gluconeogenesis because acetyl-CoA cannot be converted back to pyruvate and the inclusion of more acetyl-CoA will not generate a net increase in oxaloacetate, which can be removed from the cycle. Hence, fatty acids and ketones that are broken down into acetyl-CoA also cannot be used for gluconeogenesis.

There are three enzymes in gluconeogenesis that are different from those in glycolysis, and the relative activity of these compared to the equivalent glycolytic enzymes is tightly controlled by hormones, hence controlling whether glycolysis or gluconeogenesis is the dominant pathway.

Glycogen Metabolism

The red blood cells and the brain have an absolute requirement for glucose for energy metabolism. Glucose is absorbed from the intestines only for 2 or 3 h after a meal; therefore, there must be another source of glucose to maintain a constant blood glucose level. When blood glucose levels increase after a meal, the liver can uptake large amounts of glucose, where it is converted to glucose-6-phosphate that can be used to synthesize glycogen (glycogenesis). When glycogen stores are full, glucose-6-phosphate can enter glycolysis or be used to synthesize glycerol for the formation of fat. When blood glucose levels decrease, during fasting between meals, glycogen is broken down in the liver and glucose is released (glycogenolysis). In the fasting state, glycogen is broken down by the removal of glucose units as glucose-1-phosphate from the many ends of the molecule. This is then isomerised to glucose-6-phosphate. Only the liver can release free glucose because muscle tissue lacks glucose-6-phosphatase. The free glucose released by the liver is used by the brain and red blood cells.

Glucose-6-phosphate released in the muscle tissue from glycogen can enter directly into glycolysis for energy production by the muscle. Alternatively, it can be metabolized to pyruvate and then transaminated to alanine that is exported from the muscle to the liver, where it can be used as a substrate for gluconeogenesis. **Table 2** shows the relative importance of energy metabolic pathways in different tissues of the body.

See also: **Amino Acids**: Metabolism. **Energy**: Balance. **Fatty Acids**: Metabolism. **Glucose**: Metabolism and Maintenance of Blood Glucose Level. **Protein**: Requirements and Role in Diet. **Sports Nutrition**.

Further Reading

Bender DA (2002) *Introduction to Nutrition and Metabolism*, 3rd edn. London: Taylor & Francis.

Brody T (1999) Regulation of energy metabolism. In: *Nutritional Biochemistry*, 2nd edn, pp. 157–262. London: Academic Press.

Stillway W (1999) Bioenergetics and oxidative metabolism. In: Baynes J and Dominiczak M (eds.) *Medical Biochemistry*, pp. 83–94. St. Louis: Mosby.

Stillway W (1999) The tricarboxylic acid cycle. In: Baynes J and Dominiczak M (eds.) *Medical Biochemistry*, pp. 157–167. St. Louis: Mosby.

Wildman REC and Medeiros DM (2000) Energy metabolism. *Advanced Human Nutrition*, pp. 283–316 Boca Raton, FL: CRC Press.

Table 2 Summary of relative importance of different metabolic pathways in intermediary metabolism in different tissues

Tissue	Principal catabolic and anabolic pathways
Brain	25% basal O_2 consumption
	Metabolizes glucose only, except after prolonged starvation when it can adapt to uptake and metabolize ketones
Blood	Mature red blood cells have no mitochondria ∴ energy from anaerobic glycolysis: glucose → lactate
Muscle	Preferentially metabolize fatty acids and ketones produced from the liver
	Anaerobic glycolysis of glucose from glycogen stores
	Aerobic respiration of glucose from glycogen or fatty acids/ketones
Liver	Mostly amino acid oxidation for generation of ATP
	Most important tissue for maintaining blood glucose by gluconeogenesis from amino acids and lactate (via Cori cycle) and glycerol and also from breakdown of glycogen stores
	Fatty acid synthesis and synthesis of lipoproteins for transport
	Production of ketones into circulation
	Site of the pentose–phosphate pathway for generation of $NADPH + H^+$
Adipose tissue	Designed for the storage of fat
	Can synthesize fat from glucose
Kidneys	Gluconeogenesis
	Amino acid oxidation for ATP generation

Balance

Y Schutz, University of Lausanne, Lausanne, Switzerland

Introduction

To maintain physiologic functions, the human body continuously expends energy by oxidative metabolism. This energy is used to maintain chemical and electrochemical gradients across cellular membranes for the biosynthesis of macromolecules such as proteins, glycogen, and triglycerides, and for muscular contraction. Another part of the energy is lost as heat because of the inefficiency of metabolic transformations. Ultimately all the energy produced by the organism is dissipated as heat.

The energy expended by an individual can be assessed by two different techniques: indirect and direct calorimetry. The term indirect calorimetry stems from the fact that the heat released by chemical processes within the body can be indirectly calculated from the rate of oxygen consumption ($\dot{V}O_2$). The main reason for the close relation between energy metabolism and $\dot{V}O_2$ is that the oxidative phosphorylation at the respiratory chain level allows a continuous synthesis of adenosine triphosphate (ATP). The energy expended within the body to maintain electrochemical gradients, support biosynthetic processes, and generate muscular contraction

cannot be directly provided from nutrient oxidation. Almost all chemical processes requiring energy depend on ATP hydrolysis. It is the rate of ATP utilization that determines the overall rate of substrate oxidation and therefore $\dot{V}O_2$. With the exception of anaerobic glycolysis, ATP synthesis is coupled with substrate oxidation. The biochemical theory of oxidative phosphorylation considers that 3 mol of ATP are generated per gram-atom of oxygen consumed (i.e., a P:O ratio of 3:1). The energy expenditure per mole of ATP formed should be calculated from the heat of combustion of 1 mol of substrate, divided by the total number of moles of ATP generated in its oxidation. It is interesting to note that each mole of ATP generated is accompanied by the release of about the same amount of heat ($\sim$75 kJ/mol ATP) during the oxidation of carbohydrates, fats, or proteins. Because there is a proportionality between $\dot{V}O_2$ and ATP synthesis, and because each mole of ATP synthetized is accompanied by the production of a given amount of heat, one understands the rationale of using $\dot{V}O_2$ measurement to calculate heat production within the body.

Since indirect calorimetry measures the heat released by the oxidative processes and direct calorimetry assesses the heat dissipated by the body, a relationship exists between the two: for a subject in resting conditions, the difference between metabolic heat production and heat dissipation represents the body heat balance (**Figure 1**). The heat production from oxidative processes is equal to the sum of

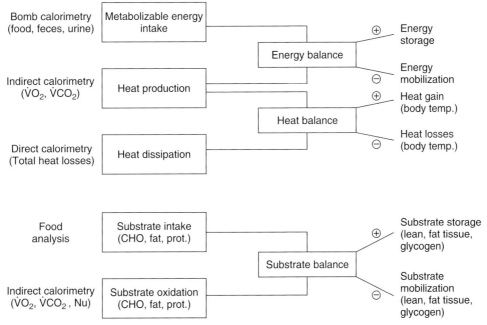

Figure 1 Heat balance, energy balance, and substrate balance: three different concepts.

the nonevaporative components (radiant heat exchange + convective + conductive heat transfer) plus the evaporative heat transfer. In order to assure the equality of the equation an additional term representing the rate of storage of body heat must be included:

$$\text{Heat production} = \text{Heat losses} \pm \text{Heat storage}$$

Heat storage can be positive when excess heat is gained, resulting in a rise in internal body temperature. Heat storage can be negative when excess heat is lost, resulting in a cooling of the body. The rate of heat storage can be estimated from the body weight, the specific heat capacity of the body (which depends upon body composition), and the rate of change in internal body temperature. In practice, this calculation remains somewhat uncertain since the changes in temperature within the body are not uniformly distributed within each tissue.

Under most environmental conditions, heat is lost by all channels (i.e., radiative + convective + conductive + evaporative). However, except during immersion in water, the rate of heat gain or loss by conduction constitutes a small proportion of the total heat loss (typically 3%). Heat can be lost by convection (air currents) but it can also be gained in very hot conditions such as in a desert characterized by high movement of hot air.

Energy Balance: Definition

Overall energy balance is given by the following equation:

$$\text{energy intake} = \text{energy expenditure} + \Delta \text{ energy stores}$$

Thus, if the total energy contained in the body (as fat, protein, and glycogen) is not altered (i.e., Δ energy stores $= 0$), then energy expenditure must be equal to energy intake. In this case, the individual is said to be in a state of energy balance.

If the intake and expenditure of energy are not equal, then a change in body energy content will occur, with negative energy balance resulting in the utilization of the body's energy stores (glycogen, fat, and protein) or positive energy balance resulting in an increase in body energy stores, primarily as fat.

The difference between the concepts of energy balance and heat balance is presented in **Figure 1**.

Model of Energy Balance: A Dynamic State

There are multiple reciprocal direct and indirect influences of energy intake on energy expenditure and vice versa: for example, energy intake influences

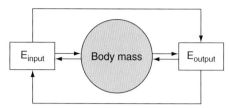

Figure 2 Simple model of energy (E) balance. Long-term constancy of body weight through the regulation of energy balance is achieved through a highly complex network of regulatory systems operating through changes in food intake, in energy expenditure, and body energy content (i.e., change in body composition).

resting energy expenditure by increasing postprandial and dietary-induced thermogenesis, whereas changes in energy expenditure via a modification of physical activity is susceptible to influence energy intake to maintain energy balance. In order to assure an accurate regulation of body stores, a double control is essential (see below). Body weight and body composition are not invariant with time but small corrections of both input and output from day-to-day or week-to-week, assure energy homeostasis (**Figure 2**). When attempting to explain the actual responses in energy balance and weight regulation in real life, we need to recognize that several factors may be operating at once on both sides of the energy balance equation. Compensatory adjustments occur in both intake and output, so unravelling the importance of one or other adjustment is not easy in man.

Gross and Metabolizable Energy

The traditional way of measuring the energy content of foostuffs is to use a 'bomb calorimeter' in which the heat produced when a sample of food is combusted (under high pressure of oxygen) is measured. When the food is combusted, it is completely oxidized to water, carbon dioxide, and other incompletely burned elements. The total heat liberated (expressed in kilocalories or kilojoules) represents the gross energy value or heat of combustion of the food. The heat of combustion differs between carbohydrates, proteins, and fats. There are also important differences within each category of macronutrient. The gross energy yield of sucrose, for example, is $16.5 \, \text{kJ g}^{-1}$, whereas starch yields $17.5 \, \text{kJ g}^{-1}$. The energy yield of butterfat is $38.5 \, \text{kJ g}^{-1}$ and of lard $39.6 \, \text{kJ g}^{-1}$. These values have been rounded off to give $17.3 \, \text{kJ g}^{-1}$ for carbohydrates rich in starch and poor in sugar, $39.3 \, \text{kJ g}^{-1}$ for average fat, and $23.6 \, \text{kJ g}^{-1}$ for mixtures of animal and vegetable proteins.

The gross energy value of foodstuffs (**Table 1**), however, does not represent the energy actually

Table 1 Metabolizable energy (ME) and Atwater's factors

Nutrient	Gross energy in $kJ\,g^{-1}(kcal\,g^{-1})$	% Absorbed (Atwater's values)	Digestible energy in $kJ\,g^{-1}(kcal\,g^{-1})$	Urinary loss in $kJ\,g^{-1}(kcal\,g^{-1})$	Metabolizable energy in $kJ\,g^{-1}(kcal\,g^{-1})$	Atwater's factor[1] $(kcal\,g^{-1})$
Starch	17.5 (4.2)	99	17.3 (4.15)	–	17.3 (4.15)	4
Glucose	15.6 (3.75)	99	15.4 (3.7)	–	15.4 (3.7)	4
Fat	39.1 (9.35)	95	37.1 (8.88)	–	37.1 (8.88)	9
Protein	22.9 (5.47)	92	21.1 (5.04)	5.2 (1.25)	15.9 (3.8)	4
Alcohol	29.8 (7.1)	100	29.8 (7.1)	Trace	29.8	7

[1]Values are rounded off.

available to the body, since no potentially oxidizable substrate can be considered available until it is presented to the cell for oxidation. None of the foodstuffs are completely absorbed; therefore, some energy never enters the body and is excreted in feces. Digestibility of the major foodstuffs, however, is high; on the average, 97% of ingested carbohydrates, 95% of fats, and 92% of proteins are absorbed from the intestinal lumen.

In the body, the tissues are able to oxidize carbohydrate and fat completely to carbon dioxide and water, but the oxidation of protein is incomplete, and results in the formation of urea and other nitrogenous compounds, which are excreted in the urine. Determination of both the heat of combustion and the nitrogen content of urine indicates that approximately $33.0\,kJ\,g^{-1}$ of urine nitrogen is equivalent to $5.2\,kJ\,g^{-1}$ of protein since 1 g urinary nitrogen arises from $\sim6.25\,g$ protein. This energy represents metabolic loss and must be subtracted from the 'digestible' energy of protein to obtain metabolizable energy.

With a mixed diet, rich in carbohydrates and fibers, the metabolizable energy of food is approximately 90% of the gross energy (heat of combustion) (**Figure 3**). The remaining 10% is mainly due to unabsorbed energy (fecal energy losses) and urinary excretion of metabolites.

The collection of representative samples of all food eaten combined with the collection of urine and feces for a week (i.e., complete nutritional balance) is technically difficult and cumbersome in practice. The pioneer investigator Atwater developed in the early 20th century a practical approach for calculating, rather than measuring, the metabolizable energy (ME) of a diet based on its composition of carbohydrates, fat, and proteins. A specific calorimetric factor was developed according to the digestibility and absorption of each macronutrient and the loss of energy in urine (measured by nutrition balance technique). These are the so-called 'Atwater factors.' The ME values for the three substrates and their derivation are shown in **Table 1**.

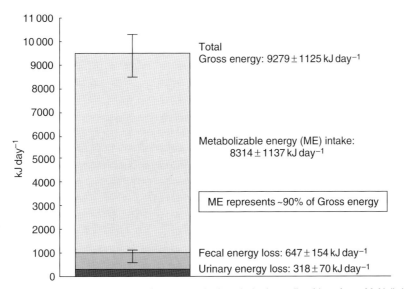

Figure 3 Gross and metabolizable energy intakes of a mixed, high-carbohydrate diet (data from McNeil (2000)). Calculation of metabolizable energy for 10 women on a high-carbohydrate, high-nonstarch polysaccharide (NSP) diet for a period of 7 days.

Assessment of Energy Expenditure

The study of energy metabolism in humans has recently raised a great interest in the regulation of these processes thanks to advances in the construction of open-circuit ventilated hood indirect calorimeters and comfortable respiration chambers.

With the only measurement of $\dot{V}O_2$ (in liters of O_2 STPD (standard temperature ($0\,°C$), pressure ($760\,mm\,Hg$), and dry) per min), metabolic rate (M), which corresponds to energy expenditure, can be calculated (in kilojoules per min) as follows:

$$\dot{M} = 20.3 \times \dot{V}O_2 \qquad [1]$$

The number 20.3 is a mean value (in $kJ\,l^{-1}$) of the energy equivalent for the consumption of $1\,l$ (STPD) of oxygen. The value of the energy equivalent of oxygen depends on the composition of the fuel mixture oxidized. However, the error in using equation 1 instead of an equation that takes into account the type of fuels oxidized (equations 2 and 3, see below) is no greater than ± 1 to 2%.

To take into account the heat released by the oxidation of the three macronutrients (carbohydrates, fats, and proteins), three measurements must be carried out: oxygen consumption ($\dot{V}O_2$), carbon dioxide production ($\dot{V}CO_2$), and urinary nitrogen excretion (N).

Simple equations for computing metabolic rate (or energy expenditure) from these three determinations are written under the following form:

$$\dot{M} = a\dot{V}O_2 + b\dot{V}CO_2 - cN \qquad [2]$$

The factors a, b, and c depend on the respective constants for the amount of O_2 used and the amount of CO_2 produced during oxidation of the three classes of nutrients. An example of such a formula is given below:

$$\dot{M} = 16.18\dot{V}O_2 + 5.02\dot{V}CO_2 - 5.99N \qquad [3]$$

where $\dot{M}$ is in kilojoules per unit of time, $\dot{V}O_2$ and $\dot{V}CO_2$ are in liters STPD per unit of time, and N is in grams per unit of time. As an example, if $\dot{V}O_2 = 600\,l\,day^{-1}$, $\dot{V}CO_2 = 500\,l\,day^{-1}$ (respiratory quotient, or RQ = 0.83), and $N = 25\,g\,day^{-1}$, then $\dot{M} = 12\,068\,kJ\,day^{-1}$. With the simpler equation (1) the results give a value of $12\,180\,kJ$ per day.

Slightly different factors for the amounts of O_2 used and of CO_2 produced during oxidation of the nutrients are used by other authors, and the values for the factors a, b, and c are modified accordingly. The difference in energy expenditure calculated by the various formulae is not greater than 3%.

Total Energy Expenditure and its Components

It is customary to consider energy expenditure as being made up of three components: the energy spent for basal metabolism (or basal metabolic rate), the energy spent on physical activity, and the increase in resting energy expenditure in response to a variety of stimuli (in particular food, cold, stress, and drugs). These three components are depicted in **Figure 4**.

Basal Metabolic Rate (BMR) or Resting Metabolic Rate (RMR)

This is the largest component of energy expenditure accounting for between half to three-quarters of daily energy expenditure. It is measured under standardized conditions, i.e., in an awake subject lying in the supine position, in a state of physical and mental rest in a comfortable warm environment, and in the morning in the postabsorptive state, usually 10–12 h after the last meal. There is an arbitrary distinction between RMR and BMR in the literature. RMR may be considered equivalent to BMR if the measurements are made in postabsorptive conditions. It seems difficult to partition RMR into various subcomponents since the metabolic rates of individual organs and tissues are hard to assess in humans under noninvasive experimental conditions. BMR can vary up to $\pm 10\%$ between individuals of the same age, gender, body weight, and fat-free mass (FFM), suggesting that genetic factors are also important. Day-to-day intraindividual variability in BMR is low in men (coefficient of variation of 1–3%) but is greater in women because the menstrual cycle affects BMR. In both women and men, sleeping metabolic rate is lower than BMR by

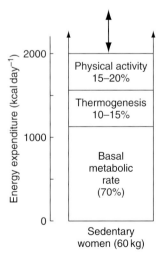

Figure 4 The three classical components of total energy expenditure. (Inactive person).

5–10%, the difference being explained by the effect of arousal. BMR is known to be depressed during starvation.

The major part of the whole-body RMR stems from organs with high metabolic activity such as the liver, kidneys, brain, and heart, although these account for a small proportion of the total body weight (5%). Per unit body weight, the kidneys and heart have a metabolic rate more than twice as high as the liver and the brain. In contrast, the metabolic rate of muscle per unit body weight is nearly 35 times lower than that of the heart and kidneys. Since the proportion of muscle to nonmuscle changes with age from birth to adulthood, the RMR per unit body weight is not constant with age. The tissue with the lowest metabolic activity per unit body weight is adipose tissue, which accounts for only 4% of the whole-body RMR in nonobese subjects. Calculations show that this value can increase up to 10% or more in obese subjects with a large excess in body fat. Skin and intestines (which have a relatively large protein mass and protein turnover), as well as bones and lungs, also contribute significantly to RMR.

Numerous studies have demonstrated that major factor explaining the variation in RMR between individuals is FFM. FFM is a heterogeneous component that can be partitioned into muscle mass and nonmuscle mass. Unfortunately, there is no simple and accurate way to assess these two subcomponents. Owing to the larger variation between individuals in fat mass, as compared to FFM, and because in grossly obese women fat mass can represent a nonnegligible component of total RMR, the prediction models for RMR that include both FFM and fat mass explain significantly more variance in RMR than FFM alone. In addition, age, sex, and family membership are additional factors that should be taken into account.

The effects of gender on resting metabolic rate are explained by differences in body composition. Caution should be used when comparing resting metabolic rate expressed per kilogram FFM in men and women, because the composition of FFM is influenced by gender. The muscle mass of men is greater than that is greater of women and this tends to give a lower value of RMR per kilogram FFM in men when compared to that of women. This is explained by a greater component of tissue with a low metabolic rate (resting muscle) in men than in women.

In clinical work, where body composition is difficult to assess, body weight, gender, and age can be used to estimate BMR and RMR (**Table 2**), bearing in mind that many important determinant of RMR, in addition to body size, have been tracked (**Table 3**).

Table 2 Simple formulae for the prediction of resting metabolic rate in men and women of different ages (equations for predicting basal metabolic rate from body weight alone)

Age range (years)	kcal per day	MJ per day
Males		
0–3	$60.9\,W - 54$	$0.255\,W - 0.226$
3–10	$22.7\,W + 495$	$0.0949\,W + 2.07$
10–18	$17.5\,W + 651$	$0.0732\,W + 2.72$
18–30	$15.3\,W + 679$	$0.0640\,W + 2.84$
30–60	$11.6\,W + 879$	$0.0485\,W + 3.67$
>60	$13.5\,W + 487$	$0.0565\,W + 2.04$
Females		
0–3	$61.0\,W - 51$	$0.255\,W - 0.214$
3–10	$22.5\,W + 499$	$0.0941\,W + 2.09$
10–18	$12.2\,W + 746$	$0.0510\,W + 3.12$
18–30	$14.7\,W + 496$	$0.0615\,W + 2.08$
30–60	$8.7\,W + 829$	$0.0364\,W + 3.47$
>60	$10.5\,W + 596$	$0.0439\,W + 2.49$

W, body weight expressed in kilograms; MJ, megajoules.
(Data from WHO (1986) *Energy and Protein Requirements*. Report of a Joint FAO/WHO/UNU Expert Consultation. Technical Report Series 724. Geneva: World Health Organization.)

Thermic Effect of Food or Postprandial Thermogenesis

The energy expenditure increases significantly after a meal. The thermic effect of food is mainly due to the energy cost of nutrient absorption and storage. The total thermic effect of food over 24 h represents −10% of the total energy expenditure in sedentary subjects. The thermic effect of nutrients mainly depends on the energy costs of processing and/or storing the nutrient. Expressed in per cent of the energy content of the nutrient, values of 8%, 2%, 20–30%, and 22% have been reported for glucose, fat, protein, and ethanol, respectively.

Glucose-induced thermogenesis mainly results from the cost of glycogen synthesis and substrate cycling. Glucose storage as glycogen requires 2 mol ATP/mol. In comparison with the 38 mol ATP produced on complete oxidation of glucose, the energy cost of glucose storage as glycogen corresponds to

Table 3 Determinants of resting (basal) metabolic rate

- Body size
- Body composition (lean vs. obese)
- Gender
- Age
- Physiological status (growth, pregnancy, and lactation)
- Genetic make-up
- Hormonal status (e.g., Follicular ve luteal phase)
  - Temperature (body internal and environment)
  - Pharmacological agents (e.g., nicotine and caffeine)
  - Disease (fever, tumors, burns, etc.)

5% (or 2/38) of the energy content of glucose stored. Cycling of glucose to glucose-6-phosphate and back to glucose, to fructose-1,6-diphosphate and back to glucose-6-phosphate, or to lactate and back to glucose, is occurring at variable rates and is an energy-requiring process that may increase the thermic effect of carbohydrates.

The thermic effect of dietary fat is very small; an increase of 2% of its energy content has been described during infusion of an emulsion of triglyceride. This slight increase in energy expenditure is explained by the ATP consumption in the process of free fatty acid reesterification to triglyceride. As a consequence, the dietary energy of fat is used very efficiently.

The thermic effect of proteins is the highest of all nutrients (20–30% of the energy content of proteins). Ingested proteins are degraded in the gut into amino acids. After absorption, amino acids are deaminated, their amino group transferred to urea, and their carbon skeleton converted to glucose. These biochemical processes require the consumption of energy amounting to ~25% of the energy content of amino acids. The second pathway of amino acid metabolism is protein synthesis. The energy expended for the synthesis of the peptide bonds also represents ~25% of the energy content of amino acids. Therefore, irrespective of their metabolic pathway, the thermogenesis induced after absorption of amino acids represents ~25% of their energy content.

Energy Expenditure Due to Physical Activity

The energy spent on physical activity depends on the type and intensity of the physical activity and on the time spent in different activities. Physical activity is often considered to be synonymous with 'muscular work', which has a strict definition in physics (force × distance) when external work is performed in the environment. During muscular work (muscle contraction), the muscle produces 3–4 times more heat than mechanical energy, so that useful work costs more than muscle work. There is a wide variation in the energy cost of any activity both within and between individuals. The latter variation is due to differences in body size and in the speed and dexterity with which an activity is performed. In order to adjust for differences in body size, the energy cost of physical activities are expressed as multiples of BMR. These generally range from 1 to 5 for most activities, but can reach values between 10 and 14 during intense exercise. In terms of daily energy expenditure, physical activity accounts for 15–40% of total energy expenditure but it can represent up to 70% of daily energy expenditure in an individual involved in heavy manual work or

Table 4 Exogenous and endogenous factors influencing the three components of energy expenditure

Components	Endogenous	Exogenous
• Basal metabolic rate	• Fat-free mass • Thyroid hormones • Protein turnover	
• Thermogenesis	• Nutritional status • Sympathetic nervous system activity • Insulin resistance (obesity)	• Macronutrient intake (+alcohol) • Cold exposure • Stress • Thermogenic stimuli (coffee, tobacco) • Thermogenic drugs
• Physical activity	• 'Fidgeting' • Muscular mass • Work efficiency • Fitness level ($\dot{V}O_2$max)	• Duration intensity, and frequency of physical activity

competition athletics. For most people in industrialized societies, however, the contribution of physical activity to daily energy expenditure is relatively small. The numerous factors influencing the 3 components of energy expenditure are outlined in **Table 4**.

The effect of body weight in average women (~60 kg) on energy expenditure is illustrated in **Figure 5**. The relationship is slightly curvilinear because of differences in body composition in terms of leanness and fatness. Resting metabolic rate is shown as a baseline value.

Just as described above for a specific activity, it has been customary to express total energy expenditure

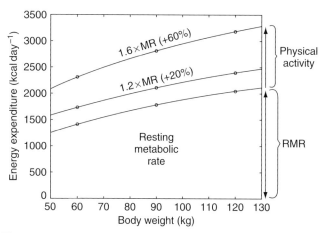

Figure 5 Effect of body weight on total energy expenditure at two levels of physical activity in young women. A physical activity level (PAL) of 1.2 represents minimal physical activity compatible with health, whereas a value of 1.6 represents a 'medium' level of physical activity.

(TEE) relative to RMR (TEE/RMR or TEE/BMR) to offset the large variation in RMR among subjects of difference body weight & body composition. This quotient is called physical activity level (PAL) and reflects multiples of RMR. A PAL of 1.5 indicates that TEE is 50% greater than RMR over 24 h.

Macronutrient Balance, Energy Balance, and Storage

Since macronutrients (carbohydrate, fat, protein, and alcohol) are the sources of energy, it is logical to consider energy balance and macronutrient balance together as the opposite side of the same coin.

There is a direct relationship between energy balance and macronutrient balance, and the sum of individual substrate balance (expressed as energy) must be equivalent to the overall energy balance. Thus:

carbohydrate balance = exogenous carbohydrate − carbohydrate oxidation

protein balance = exogenous protein − protein oxidation

lipid balance = exogenous lipid − lipid oxidation

It follows that Δ substrate balance $\equiv \Delta E$ balance. Fat balance is closely related to energy balance (**Figure 6**).

Indirect calorimetry also allows computation of the nutrient oxidation rates in the whole body. An index of protein oxidation is obtained from the total amount of nitrogen excreted in the urine during the test period. One approach to calculate the nutrient oxidation rate is based on the oxygen consumption and CO_2 production due to the oxidation rates of the three nutrients carbohydrate, fat, and protein (**Figure 6** respectively. In a subject oxidizing c grams per min of carbohydrate (as glucose), f grams per min of fat, and excreting n grams per min of urinary nitrogen, the following equations, can be used:

$$\dot{V}O_2 = 0.746c + 2.02f + 6.31n \qquad [4]$$

and

$$\dot{V}CO_2 = 0.746c + 1.43f + 5.27n \qquad [5]$$

We can solve equations 4 and 5 for the unknown c and f this way:

$$c = 4.59\dot{V}CO_2 - 3.25\dot{V}O_2 - 3.68n \qquad [6]$$

$$f = 1.69\dot{V}O_2 - 1.69\dot{V}CO_2 - 1.72n \qquad [7]$$

Because 1 g urinary nitrogen arises from approximately 6.25 g protein, the protein oxidation rate (p in grams per min) is given by the equation

$$p = 6.25n \qquad [8]$$

Energy stores (constituted mainly of fat stores) are big as a proportion of the food intake (2000 kcal day^{-1}, mixed diet in a 60-kg nonobese woman with 25% body fat). The total energy stored is about 90 times total daily energy intake: typically fat stores are 175 times daily fat intake, protein 133 times daily protein intake, and carbohydrate only 1.3 times daily carbohydrate intake (**Figure 7**).

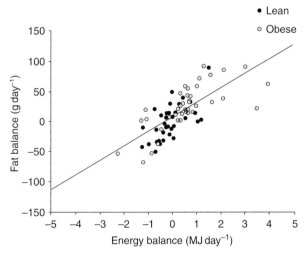

Figure 6 Relationship between energy balance and fat balance in lean and obese individuals. Note that at zero energy balance fat balance is zero. At an excess or deficit of 4.2 MJ day^{-1} (1000 kcal) the fat imbalance (about 100 g day^{-1} = 900 kcal day^{-1}) accounts for more than 90% of the magnitude of energy balance. (Reproduced from Schrauwen P, Lichtenbelt WD, Saris WH, Westerterp KR (1998) Fat balance in obese subjects: role of glycogen stores. *AM J Physiol.* **274**: E1027–33.)

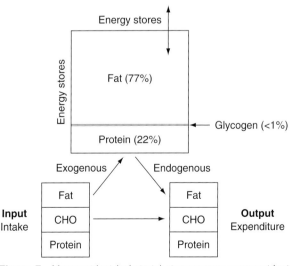

Figure 7 Macronutrient (substrate) stores versus macronutrient intake.

Energy Imbalance and Body Weight

Positive energy balance leads to body weight gain and negative energy leads to body weight loss. There is no fixed relationship between these two variables so that relatively small energy retention can be accompanied by large body weight gain and vice versa. The confounding factor is the associated water storage.

Long-term fluctuations in fat stores will be reflected in body weight. There is a difference in the energy value of fat mass and fat-free mass, the latter including the glycogen–water pool and the protein–water pool (**Table 5**).

Energy density of the tissue stored (or the substrate pool stored) represents an indicator of the composition of tissue stored or mobilized. It is defined as the total calorie per gram of substance. It is about $8 \, kcal \, g^{-1}$ for adipose tissue compared to the fat value (triglyceride) of $9 \, kcal \, g^{-1}$. This lower former value is due to the fact that fat is diluted out by the small amount of water (5–10%) and proteins the adipose tissue contains. As explained previously, the energy density of the glycogen–water pool is low, about $1 \, kcal \, g^{-1}$, since glycogen ($4.2 \, kcal \, g^{-1}$) is associated with approximately 3 times its weight of water.

Let us take an energy imbalance of say 1000 kcal. The body weight change will be approximately 8 times lower (i.e., $\approx 125 \, g$) if fat is stored in adipose tissue, as compared to glycogen stored (under the form of glycogen-water pool) in liver and muscles ($\approx 1000 \, g$). In other words, rapid weight gain (or weight loss) means little fat storage despite what the layman thinks. Day-to-day energy imbalance is generally accommodated by water retention due to changes in carbohydrate storage and sodium intake.

In real life, it is more reasonable to consider that the reserve is composed of a mixture in different proportions of fat and glycogen. If about half of the energy imbalance is accounted for by fat and half by glycogen storage, the energy density will be $4–5 \, kcal \, g^{-1}$. With the imbalance value described above, it will generate a body weight change of 400–500 g.

The energy balance varies from day to day. The changes in daily energy intake and expenditure are not necessarily synchronized. Positive energy balance on one day may not be spontaneously compensated by negative energy balance on the subsequent day, so that it is important to consider the overall energy balance regulation over a prolonged period of time. Short-term day-to-day energy imbalance is mostly accommodated by rapid changes in carbohydrate balance, whereas over a prolonged period of time, positive energy balance is mostly expressed as fat storage since carbohydrate stores are small (**Figure 6**).

To what extent do alterations in energy output contribute to the regulation of energy balance and stability of body weight? To understand the regulation of a system, it must be subjected to perturbation. Excess food intake during overfeeding or deficit in food intake during underfeeding disrupts the balance system.

Overfeeding Studies (Figure 8)

In a perfectly regulated system, any increase in energy intake should be offset by a change in energy expenditure of the same magnitude and direction. However, a 100% efficient adaptive process would obviously be counter productive, since this would signify that an increase in energy storage (required during nutritional rehabilitation) or an increase in energy mobilization (required for decreasing body weight) would be very limited. Adaptation to energy imbalance only occurs at the cost of increasing (or decreasing) body weight. In fact, excess energy intakes result in an increased metabolic turnover and energy flux through the mechanism of adaptive thermogenesis. The efficiency of energy storage is not constant and depends upon several factors including the magnitude of energy imbalance and the composition of the surfeit energy fed, as well as endogenous factors. As shown in **Figure 8**, the energy expenditure increases during acute overfeeding, an evidence of the 'flexibility' of the metabolism.

Table 5 Body stores of energy as different macronutrients

Substrate	Form of storage	Pool size	Tissues	% Water in tissues	Daily imbalance	Energy density (kcal/g^{-1})	Postprandial thermogenesis
Carbohydrate	Glycogen	Small (limited)	Liver + muscles	70–80	Large	$\simeq 4$	Average
Fat	Triglycerides	Moderate–large (unlimited)	Adipose tissue	5–10	Small	$\simeq 8$	Low
Protein	Protein	Moderate (limited)	Lean tissue (muscle)	70–75	Small	$\simeq 4$	High

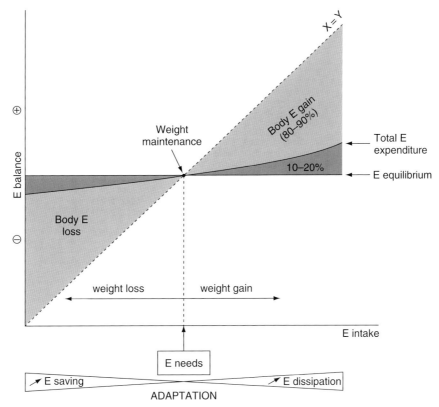

Figure 8 Energy balance in underfeeding (below maintenance) and overfeeding (above maintenance) conditions. E, energy.

Underfeeding Studies (Figure 8)

Analysis of underfeeding experiments shows that the decrease in energy expenditure has three components. First, if energy intake is decreased the thermic effect of feeding (about 10% of energy intake) is similarly decreased. Second, there is an adaptive decrease in metabolic rate during the first week, related in part to a decrease in sympathetic activity. The magnitude of this decrease is significantly related to the initial metabolic rate, and is usually about 5–8%. Third, there is a decrease in metabolic rate related to the weight lost: most investigators find a decrease of 10–12 kcal per day per kg weight loss. The effect of all three processes is that a person who lost weight from, say, 100 kg to 70 kg (a 30% reduction in weight) would experience about a 15% reduction in energy requirements for weight maintenance. Thus, a decrease in energy intake causes a reduction in body weight but, provided the decrease is not too great, a new equilibrium will be reached at which the reduced requirement will be satisfied by the reduced intake, and body weight will stabilize. Taken together we can conclude that the efficiency of energy utilization is lower in overfeeding than in underfeeding conditions because, substrate storage in tissues is energetically costly (ATP needs), whereas the process of energy mobilization requires

little energy. In the former situation excess energy must be dissipated.

Adaptive changes in thermogenesis do attenuate the impact on energy balance of excessive or insufficient food consumption (as compared to requirement). The magnitude of adaptive thermogeneis varies as a function of the nature of excess substrates fed (protein is higher than carbohydrate and fat).

Energy Expenditure is Less Effective than Food Intake as a Control Mechanism of Energy Balance

It should be stressed that the relationship between the change in energy intake below and above energy equilibrium and energy storage is not quite linear, indicating an increased net efficiency of energy utilization below energy maintenance and a decreased net efficiency of energy utilization above energy equilibrium (**Figure 8**).

Dynamics of Energy Balance with Overfeeding and Underfeeding (Figure 9)

To understand the dynamic aspect of energy balance while overfeeding is of the utmost important, since as mentioned previously the system is not invariant.

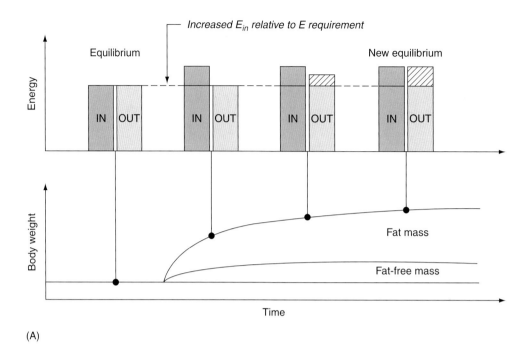

(A)

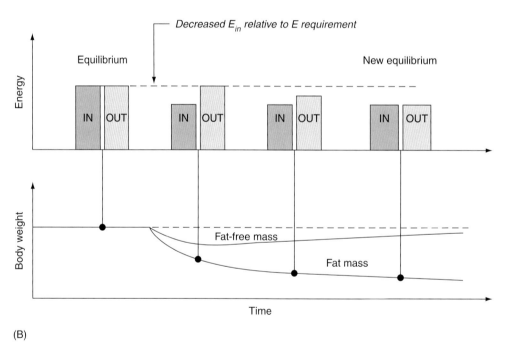

(B)

Figure 9 Dynamic change in energy balance following a step steady increase (A) overfeeding (or decrease) (B) underfeeding in energy intake. The time required to reach a new equilibrium in energy balance is very long (years) and depends upon the initial energy imbalance, the magnitude of adaptation of energy expenditure in response to change in energy intake, and on the factors related to the subject (obesity versus leanness). The figure shows that the static energy balance as such tells us nothing about the absolute level of energy intake and expenditure (see initial and final balance).

Continuous increase in energy intake above energy requirement will lead to a gradual gain in body weight. The size of the energy imbalance will progressively diminish with time as weight is gained. The reason for this is that the expansion of fat-free mass and fat mass (adipose tissue) will be accompanied by a rise in energy metabolism. A new equilibrium in weight is eventually reached after adaptation of each component of total energy expenditure, i.e., resting metabolic rate, diet-induced thermogenesis, and the increasing energy cost of supporting a heavier body weight. Note that each kg of excess body weight increases total energy expenditure by about 20–25 kcal day^{-1}, and 10–12 kg day^{-1} when RMR is considered (**Figure 5**).

Let us take the following practical example: small increase in daily intake, e.g., of 100–200 kcal, will induce small increases in body weight with its associated rise in energy expenditure as the mass of lean tissue increases. If these changes occur on a daily basis, month by month, and if after 3–5 years the adult is still eating 200 kcal day^{-1} more than at baseline, they will now be heavier, and have a higher energy expenditure, and will come into energy balance; therefore, they cease to gain more weight.

Summary

- Energy balance is the difference between metabolizable energy intake and total energy expenditure. It is strongly related to macronutrient balances, and the sum of the individual substrate balances, expressed as energy, must be equivalent to the overall energy balance.
- Energy in foods is furnished by carbohydrate, proteins, fats, and alcohol; only 5–10% is lost through the feces and urine.
- The energy available to the body, called 'metabolizable energy', is on average 17 kJ g^{-1} of carbohydrate, 17 kJ g^{-1} of protein, 37 kJ g^{-1} of fat, and 29 kJ g^{-1} of alcohol. These figures vary slightly according to the type of carbohydrate, protein, or fat in the diet.
- The energy used in the body, or energy expenditure, is classically assessed by indirect calorimetry. It involves measuring the oxygen consumption and carbon dioxide production by an individual.
- Short-term regulation of energy balance is poor, but (in most people) long-term regulation is accurate. The mechanism is unknown, but must include conscious alterations in lifestyle to correct unwanted changes in body weight.
- During long periods of energy imbalance the weight gained (or lost) is initially glycogen plus water with an energy density of ∼1.0 kcal g^{-1}. If the imbalance continues, after a week the tissue gained (or lost) is a mixture of mostly fat, water, and protein with an energy density of ∼7 kcal g^{-1}.
- Undernutrition leads to a decrease in energy expenditure. Part of the decrease in metabolic rate is related to weight loss.
- In overfeeding, although some of the excess energy intake will be stored in adipose tissue, there are compensatory increases in energy expenditure.
- The changes in modern affluent society can be considered in terms of energy balance. The increasing prevalence of overweight in industrialized society can be attributed to a profound change in the pattern of physical activity due to increased mechanization, robotics, and computerization, which have substantially reduced the need for even modest physical activity. Today, the demand for heavy labor is rare. In developed countries increased car ownership and heavy road traffic result in fewer opportunities to travel on foot. Television-watching now fills a large proportion of leisure time and numerous gadgets minimize housework.

See also: **Amino Acids**: Metabolism. **Energy**: Metabolism; Requirements; Adaptation. **Energy Expenditure**: Indirect Calorimetry; Doubly Labeled Water. **Fats and Oils**.

Further Reading

Blaxter K (1989) *Energy metabolism in animals and man.* Cambridge: Cambridge University Press.

Ravussin E and Bogardus C (2000) Energy balance and weight regulation: genetics versus environment. *Br J Nutr* **83**(Suppl 1): S17–20.

Ravussin E and Bogardus C (1989) Relationship of genetics, age, and physical fitness to daily energy expenditure and fuel utilization. *Am J Clin Nutr* **49**(Suppl): 968–75.

Schutz Y (1995) Macronutrients and energy balance in obesity. *Metabolism* **44**(Suppl 3): 7–11.

Requirements

W P T James, International Association for the Study of Obesity/International Obesity Task Force Offices, London, UK

The metabolic rate of the body is the overall rate of tissue oxidation of fuels by all the body's organs. The dietary fuels are the carbohydrate, fat, protein, alcohol, and minor dietary components that are oxidized in the tissues, with oxygen being taken up by the lungs and the combusted end products (carbon dioxide, water, and urea) being excreted by the lungs, urine, and skin. The total rate of body metabolism is assessed by monitoring the rate of oxygen uptake by the lungs. The sources of fuel can then be estimated from the proportion of carbon dioxide produced and the rate of urea production.

The energy equivalence of oxygen varies depending on the precise nature of the fuels being oxidized, but a value of 20 kJ per liter of oxygen is taken as an appropriate average.

Factors Affecting Metabolic Rate

The process of oxidation involves a series of enzymatically controlled biochemical reactions leading eventually to the combination of oxygen with the carbon and hydrogen components of the body's fuels to yield the carbon dioxide and metabolically derived water. The incompletely oxidized nitrogen is excreted as urea, which is synthesized by the liver and excreted by the kidneys. The intermediate steps in the metabolism of the body's fuels are linked biochemically to drive the generation of phosphate-containing organic molecules, such as adenosine triphosphate (ATP), which in turn serve as the direct energy sources for all the body's cell activities, including the synthesis of complex molecules, the maintenance of tightly controlled ionic gradients in the cell, and the excretion of ions and molecules outside the cell. Thus, the oxygen being taken up by the lungs reflects the tissue metabolism of the fuels needed to regenerate the ATP used up in either biochemical 'internal' work or mechanical external work undertaken by the body's muscles. The rate at which the body burns its own stored fuels in the fasted, resting, and relaxed state (i.e., in the basal state in a warm room) is called the basal metabolic rate (BMR). This varies with the age of the individual, mainly because of the varying sizes of metabolically very different organs at different ages. Thus, a child has a relatively large brain, liver, and intestine, with a higher metabolic rate per kilogram of body weight than a more muscular adult. Body fat cells are metabolically active but contain a substantial amount of inert fat so that the larger fat mass of a woman means she has a lower BMR per unit body weight than a man. However, if the oxygen uptake is calculated in terms of the metabolically active fat-free mass, then her metabolic rate is the same. As men and women age, they tend to lose lean tissue and store extra fat, so the BMR on a weight basis decreases with age.

Equations can be used to estimate a group's BMR from their sex, age, and body weight (**Table 1**), but there is a range of BMR amounting to $\pm 20\%$ of the mean value at each weight. Thus, in a 25-year-old woman who weighs 55 kg, the anticipated mean BMR is 5460 kJ (1305 kcal) per day but may vary under normal conditions from 4448 to 6473 kJ per-day. The kilojoule is the standard measure, and 4.184 kJ corresponds to 1 kcal, which was originally defined in energy terms as that required to increase the temperature of 1 g of pure water by 1 °C from 14.5 to 15.5 °C. The variation in BMR at a constant weight in part reflects differences in the fat content of individuals of the same weight. Thus, the BMR per unit fat-free mass varies by 12–15% rather than by $\pm 20\%$ as for weight. Approximately 40% of the BMR variation

Table 1 Equations for estimating basal metabolic rate (BMR) from body weight (kg)[a]

Age (years)	Males (MJ/day)	Females (MJ/day)
<3	BMR = 0.255 kg − 0.226	BMR = 0.244 kg − 0.130
3–9.9	BMR = 0.0949 kg + 2.07	BMR = 0.085 kg + 2.033
10–17.9	BMR = 0.74 kg + 2.754	BMR = 0.056 kg + 2.898
18–29.9	BMR = 0.063 kg + 2.896	BMR = 0.062 kg + 2.036
30–59.9	BMR = 0.048 kg + 3.653	BMR = 0.034 kg + 3.538
60–74	BMR = 0.0499 kg + 2.930	BMR = 0.0386 kg + 2.875
75+	BMR = 0.035 kg + 3.434	BMR = 0.0410 kg + 2.610

[a]The BMR values for infants and children are no longer used to calculate energy requirements but provide an indication of the likely values. The adult data are those from the original Schofield *et al.* analyses, with the data for 60-year-old and older adults derived from both the Schofield data and information provided to the UK Department of Health (1991).

may be explained by differences in the size of the body's organs (e.g., liver, intestine, and muscle), but there is a residual difference between individuals that seems to be explicable only in terms of differences in the rate at which every organ of the body metabolizes its fuel. This in turn is controlled principally by the circulating concentration of thyroid hormones. Adults with a normal but above average level of thyroid hormones in their blood tend to have a BMR in the upper normal range. Smokers also have a BMR that is approximately 5% above normal, but whether this relates to changes in thyroid hormones is unknown. Young women who have normal menstrual cycles show a change in BMR that is at its lowest in the late follicular phase, just before ovulation. On ovulation, the basal body temperature rises rapidly by approximately 0.5 °C. The BMR is also increased but rises further to a peak in the later luteal phase, immediately before menstruation. This metabolic cycle with changes of $\pm 5\%$ of the mean is independent of changes in food intake, but the recognized 5–10% decrease in intake during the follicular phase with a similar increase in the luteal phase may accentuate the hormonally dependent change in metabolism. The effects of contraceptives that inhibit ovulation and the subsequent increase in basal temperature are unknown. The previous day's food intake does not affect the BMR unless there has been substantial overeating. However, the mixture of fuels combusted during fasting is influenced by the proportion of the previous 3 or 4 days' intake, which is derived from carbohydrate, with much of the glucose from glycogen being metabolized in the fasting state if carbohydrate intake was previously high. When the carbohydrate store of glycogen in the liver is nearing exhaustion, the body's output of carbon dioxide declines as the body switches to using body stores of fat. The oxygen uptake for combusting the fatty acids continues since the demand for regenerating ATP is unaffected by the change in fuel supply, but a carbohydrate-rich diet tends to induce a slightly higher fasting metabolic rate than an energy-equivalent, fat-enriched diet, probably because of a slight induction of thyroid metabolism by dietary carbohydrates.

The BMR decreases 2–5% when individuals move to a tropical, warm environment, and in uninsulated houses seasonal changes in the BMR have been readily seen, with a 5–10% increase from summer to winter observed in the Japanese before World War II. The BMR formulas shown in **Table 1** ignore any temperature effects. The BMR of some people living in the tropics may be as much as 10% below the values shown, but these studies have been conducted on children and adults who are, or were, undernourished. Poor nutrition may have both an immediate and a long-term effect in lowering the BMR. Semistarvation leads to a decrease in BMR beginning on approximately day 4, and within 2 weeks the BMR can decrease by 15% as thyroid metabolism changes and the body's organs become more efficient. More prolonged or severe semistarvation leads to a progressive loss of the body lean tissues as well as fat, and the BMR therefore continues to decline in proportion to the loss of lean tissues. Body weight can eventually stabilize at a new low level, and if physical activity is also reduced, semistarved volunteers can return to energy balance on 50% of their initial intake. However, this requires a 40% loss of weight and marked lethargy if energy balance is to be preserved on such a low intake.

Components of Metabolic Rate

Traditionally, the metabolic rate is divided into three components: BMR, postprandial thermogenesis, and physical activity. The BMR usually comprises 50–60% of an individual's total energy expenditure and postprandial thermogenesis comprises 10%, which is used for the metabolic cost of processing (i.e., eating, absorbing, transporting, and storing food). The remaining energy is used for physical activity.

Postprandial Thermogenesis

The surge in oxygen uptake after a meal, known as postprandial thermogenesis, has been variously described as the specific dynamic action of food, dietary-induced thermogenesis, or the thermic effect of feeding. The last term is particularly favored by animal nutritionists. It is difficult to measure it accurately because after ingesting food with minimum physical effort, an individual has to lie at complete rest while oxygen uptake and carbon dioxide production are monitored for many hours until the metabolic rate has returned to the basal rate. This may take more than 10 h, which explains why BMR is measured after a 14-h fast. Separate feeding of different fuels shows that the maximum effect on oxygen uptake occurs after protein intake. This response is equivalent to approximately 30% of the protein's energy: Glucose induces a 5–10% effect; fat only a 2–5% effect, consistent with its slow absorption by the lymphatic tissue; and alcohol a 0–8% effect. Certain dietary components also increase metabolic rate; for example, a caffeine equivalent to two cups of tea increases metabolic rate by 1–3%, and spices, such as those found in an Indian curry, may increase it by 25% compared with a nonspiced meal. Moderate exercise amplifies the metabolic response to a standard meal so that the combined effect of exercise and food is greater than the sum of the response to each stimulus given separately. The effect, however, is small, amounting to 2% of the total energy expenditure.

Differences in postprandial energy expenditure have been sought as an explanation for the propensity of some individuals and animals to obesity. Results are often conflicting because in any person, the response tends to vary from day to day and is readily influenced by changes in gastric emptying. A proportion of obese subjects have a reduced metabolic response to a meal; this effect may depend on the degree of abdominal insulation since the response is reduced if volunteers are swathed in insulation to reduce abdominal heat loss, thereby increasing the temperature of the blood entering and leaving the liver. This seems to reduce the stimulus to body metabolism. Lactating mothers (and pregnant women) have a lower postprandial thermogenesis that returns to normal after they have stopped breast-feeding. Smoking and postprandial thermogenesis interact synergistically so the thermic output after a meal is enhanced. The small postprandial response during lactation is consistent with that observed in many species of animals in which brown adipose tissue is used as the organ for modulating heat production as a mechanism to maintain body temperature. However, this organ is not very active in humans.

Prolonged underfeeding and overfeeding lead to changes not only in postprandial thermogenesis but also in BMR. The effects of semistarvation when expressed per unit of tissue mass are modest, but overfeeding can produce a much greater response, provided that the intensity of overfeeding (especially with carbohydrate) is high. Thus, progressive over-consumption of 6.3 MJ (1500 cal) per day leads to a 33% increase in daily energy expenditure. This composite response to more prolonged overfeeding is usually classified as dietary-induced thermogenesis. Nevertheless, this apparent mechanism for dissipating excess energy is limited because, at most, 27% of the excess intake is metabolised, and the remaining 73% is stored—two-thirds as fat and approximately one-third as lean tissue. The majority of the excess response in metabolism is accounted for by the theoretical cost of fat synthesis from carbohydrate, although the human capacity to transform carbohydrate into fat is limited, with preference being given to the selective storage of the fat component of the ingested energy.

Physical Activity

The energy cost of physical activity is predictable, but in order to obtain a reasonable estimate of energy expenditure on a daily basis, an analysis of activity patterns on a minute-by-minute basis is required. Children can be very active, making a detailed analysis difficult because the type of activity needs to be specified if an energy cost is to be assigned to each type of activity. Weight-bearing movement and antigravitational moves (e.g., walking up a hill with a load) are particularly expensive. The simplest way to estimate individual costs is to use the extensive tables on the energy cost of different movements in children and adults. For simplicity, these can be expressed as a ratio of the BMR since, in this way, differences between the sexes and individuals of varying size are removed. **Table 2** illustrates how this is achieved for adults with a moderately active lifestyle. The physical activity ratios (PARs) (i.e., energy costs in relation to BMR) can be assigned on the basis of extensive measures of similar activities. Those involved in sports medicine also call this unit cost a metabolic equivalent (MET), where 1 MET is equal to the resting metabolic rate of approximately 4.2 kJ (1 kcal) per minute. If the average energy requirement of the individual is to be estimated, account must be taken of the different types of work involved throughout the year. Each day is compartmentalized on a minute-by-minute basis, with a division often being made for convenience between occupational and other work. Maintenance of the individual's household varies depending on the day of the week and the season. Integrating all these activities, the ratio of the total daily energy expenditure to the BMR is designated the physical activity level (PAL). Physical activity is of general health benefit, so it is desirable that the overall PAL of individuals should be 1.75 or higher, which requires at least 60 minutes of moderately vigorous activity daily. In sedentary societies, however, 30 minutes of moderately vigorous exercise three times a week benefits muscular tone and physical fitness. This improves cardiovascular health and insulin sensitivity and therefore is likely to limit the development of type 2 diabetes in susceptible individuals. **Table 3** provides a listing of PAL values for adults of all ages according to their activity patterns. Thus, by knowing the sex, age, and body weight of individuals, it is possible to estimate their BMR (see **Table 1**). Given this BMR figure in millijoules per day, multiply by the PAL value shown in **Table 3**, and the energy needs can be estimated. Note that individuals vary in their energy needs by 10% at equivalent weights and activity levels, so an individual's needs cannot be predicted very accurately

Table 2 Calculating the appropriate energy requirements as physical activity levels (PALs) for adults with an active or moderately active lifestyle[a]

Main daily activities	Time allocation (h)	Energy cost (physical activity ratio)	Time (h) × Energy cost	Mean PAL (multiple of 24-h BMR)
Sleeping	8	1	8.0	
Personal care (dressing, showering)	1	2.3	2.3	
Eating	1	1.5	1.5	
Standing, carrying light loads[b] (waiting on tables, arranging merchandise)	8	2.2	17.6	
Commuting to/from work on the bus	1	1.2	1.2	
Walking at varying paces without a load	1	3.2	3.2	
Low-intensity aerobic exercise	1	4.2	4.2	
Light leisure activities (watching TV, chatting)	3	1.4	4.2	
Total	**24**		**42.2**	**42.2/24 = 1.76**

[a]If this PAL was from a female population, 20–25 years old, with mean weight of 57 kg and mean BMR of 5.60 MJ/day (1338 kcal/day), TEE = 1.76 × 5.60 = 9.86 MJ (2355 kcal), or 173 kJ (41 kcal)/kg/day.
[b]Composite of the energy cost of standing, walking slowly, and serving meals or carrying a light load.

Table 3 Classification of lifestyles in relation to the intensity of habitual physical activity or physical activity level (PAL)

Category	PAL value[a]
Sedentary or light activity lifestyle	1.40–1.69
Active or moderately active lifestyle	1.70–1.99
Vigorous or vigorously active lifestyle	2.00–2.40

[a]PAL ranges apply to both men and women.
Reproduced with permission from FAO Human Energy Requirements. Food and Nutrition Technical Report Series No. 1. (2004) FAO, Rome.

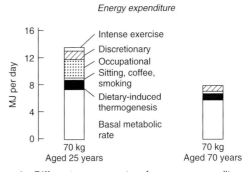

Energy expenditure

Figure 1 Different components of energy expenditure in a young man and the impact of ageing. Note that the energy expenditure decreases mainly because of a decline in physical activity. There is also a decrease in the basal metabolic rate, but this predominantly reflects a reduction in the lean tissues (i.e., fat-free mass) in the elderly.

unless his or her BMR is measured and account taken of his or her personal lifestyle (i.e., activity pattern). Nevertheless, the total energy expenditure of an individual child or adult is remarkably consistent from day to day, varying by only 1 or 2% provided that food intake and physical activity are meticulously standardized and account is taken in women of the stage of the menstrual cycle. The factors modulating BMR or the metabolic response to food are many, but their effect is small, so it is not surprising that energy expenditure is very predictable; the human body is thus a finely tuned and well-regulated machine. Abnormalities of regulation (e.g., in obesity) only arise because of a consistent discrepancy between the physiological controlled intake and expenditure, which, if discrepant by 1 or 2%, produces a 2- to 5-kg weight change in a year.

New measures of total energy expenditure estimated over 2 or 3 weeks can be obtained by using the double-labeled water technique, which relies on the difference in labeling of urine or saliva with the two heavy isotopes of water, deuterium and ^{18}O. The differential dilution of ^2H and ^{18}O in urinary water is monitored over a 2- or 3-week period following a single oral dose of $^2H_2^{18}O$. The ^{18}O content is diluted more rapidly than the ^2H because the oxygen in water exchanges rapidly with the body's bicarbonate pool, which turns over rapidly as carbon dioxide is produced by tissue metabolism. Thus, the difference in dilution rates of ^{18}O and deuterium provides a measure of the rate of carbon dioxide production. The technique is expensive and difficult to perform analytically but very convenient for the subject being studied since only single daily or occasional urine or saliva specimens are needed during the period of observation.

This method is increasingly used, and together in children with a heart rate monitoring system, has been used to revise the estimates of population energy requirements. These are accurate for groups of people but not for individuals, who vary not only

in their physical activity patterns but also in their metabolic rate at rest. PAL estimates are less useful in infants because their energy requirement includes not only their total energy expenditure but also their cost of growth; BMRs are also difficult to measure at this age, so the $^2H_2^{18}O$ method together with estimates of growth costs have been used to compile new lower estimates of energy needs than were originally estimated by the old factorial method.

Age-related changes in energy needs are important not only in children but also in adults for different reasons. **Figure 1** gives an indication of the decline in energy needs during adult life. This results from the atrophy of the lean tissues, which may be related to a decline in physical activity. Lack of exercise is therefore a handicap because it directly reduces energy expenditure, and it may also lead to a slow shrinkage of tissues, such as muscle, thereby producing a long-term decline in metabolism at rest. There may also be up to an additional 5% decrease in the rate of tissue metabolism. Thus, unless people adapt their intake extraordinarily well to this progressive decline in energy output, energy storage, weight gain, and obesity are inevitable.

Extra Energy Costs

The cost of growth amounts to 10–25 kJ/g of new tissue deposited; the value is higher if fat with little lean tissue is laid down. A newborn has a high energy requirement of approximately 460 kJ/kg, with a cost of weight gain amounting to 26 kJ/g; however, by 1 year of age the total daily requirement decreases to approximately 335 kJ/kg as growth slows, with growth now costing 10 kJ/g. Breast-fed infants have an energy requirement approximately 10% lower than that of bottle-fed infants (**Table 4**).

Table 4 Average energy requirements of infants (breast and bottle fed) and of children up to age 18 years

Infants (months)	Energy requirement (kJ/kg/day)			Children (years)	Weight (kg)	PAL	Energy requirement (kJ/kg/day)	Weight (kg)	PAL	Energy requirement (kJ/kg/day)
	Boys	Girls	Mean		Boys			Girls		
1	475	445	460	1.1–2	11.5	1.43	345	10.8	1.42	335
2	435	420	430	2.1–3	13.5	1.45	350	13.0	1.42	337
3	395	395	395	3.1–4	15.7	1.44	334	15.1	1.44	320
4	345	350	345	4.1–5	17.7	1.49	322	16.8	1.49	309
5	340	345	345	5.1–6	19.7	1.53	312	18.6	1.53	299
6	335	340	340	6.1–7	21.7	1.57	303	20.6	1.56	290
7	330	330	330	7.1–8	24.0	1.60	295	23.3	1.60	279
8	330	330	330	8.1–9	26.7	1.63	287	26.6	1.63	267
9	330	330	330	9.1–10	29.7	1.66	279	30.5	1.66	254
10	335	330	335	10.1–11	33.3	1.71	270	34.7	1.71	242
11	335	330	335	11.1–12	37.5	1.75	261	39.2	1.74	229
12	335	330	335	12.1–13	42.3	1.79	252	43.8	1.76	217
				13.1–14	47.8	1.82	242	48.3	1.76	206
				14.1–15	53.8	1.84	233	52.1	1.75	197
				15.1–16	59.5	1.84	224	55.0	1.73	189
				16.1–17	64.4	1.84	216	56.4	1.73	186
				17.1–18	67.8	1.83	210	56.7	1.72	185

The energy requirements of infants were derived from double-labeled water measurements of total energy expenditure to which was added the age-specific energy deposited during growth, taking into account the different proportions of lean and fat tissue laid down during infancy. The children's requirements were estimated from quadratic equations relating body weight to total energy expenditure of girls and boys measured separately or from estimates of total energy expenditure based on calibrated heart rate recordings. Again, the energy deposited as growth was added to give a requirement expressed on a weight basis to allow adjustments for children of different weights at each age.PAL, physical activity level.

Without sufficient energy, a child will fail to grow, but the causes of growth failure usually relate to a deficiency of other nutrients or to infection rather than to a lack of dietary energy. Adolescents, particularly boys, who are physically very active may have a high demand for energy. However, the actual cost of even rapid growth rates at this age is modest.

Traditionally, pregnancy is considered, incorrectly, a time of great demand for food. Good nutrition is extremely important, and a weight gain in pregnancy of approximately 12 kg is desirable for reducing the risk of maternal and fetal complications and preterm and low-birth-weight infants and increasing the probability of delivering a 3.3-kg infant. With a weight gain of 12 kg, increases in maternal BMR are 5, 10, and 25% in the first, second, and third trimester of pregnancy, respectively. In practice, the intensity of physical activity often declines, particularly in late pregnancy, and some enhanced metabolic efficiency seems to occur. Thus, the increase in total energy expenditure amounts to only 1, 6, and 17% in the three trimesters, respectively. Therefore, the need for additional energy is small, amounting to 85, 350, and 1300 kJ/day (20, 85, and 310 kcal/day) for sequential trimesters, and in practice this means that a pregnant women needs to increase her food intake by 1.5 MJ/day (360 kcal/day) in the second trimester and 2.0 MJ/day (475 kcal/day) in the third trimester.

Lactation imposes a greater demand on mothers since their milk contains 1.9 MJ/day after birth, increasing to approximately 2.3 MJ/day on exclusive breast-feeding at 3 months. Extra energy is involved in making this milk, and the total extra energy demand is 2.6 MJ/day. Part of this additional energy derives from the extra fat stored by the mother during pregnancy, with the average, well-nourished women losing 0.8 kg/month, so the mother needs to eat approximately 1.9 MJ/day (450 kcal/day). This explains why mothers are more hungry when nursing their child than when pregnant. During lactation, there are no significant changes in BMR, efficiency of work performance, or total energy expenditure, and in most societies women resume their usual level of physical activity in the first month postpartum or soon thereafter.

Convalescent patients who need to gain weight require extra food, but the cost of this weight gain is 20–40 MJ/kg. If 1 kg is gained per month, the extra food needed amounts to approximately 1 MJ/day.

See also: **Adolescents**: Nutritional Requirements. **Breast Feeding**. **Children**: Nutritional Requirements. **Energy**: Balance. **Energy Expenditure**: Indirect Calorimetry. **Exercise**: Diet and Exercise. **Infants**: Nutritional Requirements. **Lactation**: Dietary Requirements. **Obesity**: Definition, Etiology and Assessment; Childhood Obesity; Complications. **Pregnancy**: Nutrient Requirements; Energy Requirements and Metabolic Adaptations. **Protein**: Requirements and Role in Diet.

Further Reading

Department of Health (1991) *Dietary Reference Values for Food Energy and Nutrients for the United Kingdom*, No. 41. London: HMSO.

FAO Human Energy Requirements (2004) Food and Nutrition Technical Report Series No. 1. FAO, Rome.

James WPT and Schofield EC (1990) *Human Energy Requirements*. Oxford: Oxford Medical.

Schofield WN, Schofield C, and James WPT (1985) Basal metabolic rate: Review and prediction. *Human Nutrition: Clinical Nutrition* 39C: 1–96.

World Health Organization (1985) *Energy and Protein Requirements. Report of a Joint FAO/WHO/UNU Expert Consultation*, WHO Technical Report Series 724. Geneva: World Health Organization.

Adaptation

A G Dulloo, University of Fribourg, Fribourg, Switzerland
J Jacquet, University of Geneva, Geneva, Switzerland

Throughout much of evolutionary history, the mammalian species have been faced with periodic food shortages, specific nutrient deficiencies, and, sometimes, food abundance. Within such a lifestyle of famine and feast, it is conceivable that adaptive mechanisms—operating through adjustments in energy expenditure and in management of the body's main energy-containing compartments (fat and protein)—have evolved to the extent that they constitute key control systems in the regulation of body weight and body composition. These control systems and how they operate to enable the human body to adapt to nutritional stresses and to achieve body weight homeostasis are the focus of this article.

Beyond Adaptation through Mass Action

There is in fact a built-in stabilizing mechanism in the overall homeostatic system for body weight. Any imbalance between energy intake and energy requirements will result in a change in body weight that, in turn, will alter the maintenance energy requirements in a direction that will tend to counter the original imbalance and hence be stabilizing. The system thus exhibits 'dynamic equilibrium.' For example, an increase in body weight will be predicted to increase metabolic rate (on the basis of the extra energy cost for synthesis and subsequent maintenance of extra lean and fat tissues), which will tend to produce a negative energy balance and hence a subsequent decline in body weight toward its set or preferred value. Similarly, a reduction in body weight will result in a reduction in metabolic rate due to the loss in lean and fat tissues, which will tend to produce a positive balance and hence a subsequent return toward the 'set' or 'preferred' weight. In reality, however, the homeostatic system is much more complex than this simple effect of mass action since the efficiency of metabolism (or metabolic efficiency) may also alter in response to the alterations in body weight. Indeed, subjects forced to maintain body weight at a level 10% above their initial body weight showed an increase in daily energy expenditure even after adjusting for changes in body weight and body composition. Conversely, in subjects maintaining weight at a level 10% below the initial body weight, daily energy expenditure was also lower after adjusting for losses in weight and lean tissues. These compensatory changes in energy expenditure ($\sim$15% above or below predicted values) reflect changes in metabolic efficiency that oppose the maintenance of a body weight that is above or below the set or preferred body weight.

Interindividual Variability in Metabolic Adaptation

The experiments on forced changes in body weight have also revealed that there is a large interindividual variability in the ability to readjust energy expenditure, with some individuals showing little or no evidence for altered metabolic efficiency and others a marked capacity to decrease or increase energy expenditure through alterations in metabolic efficiency. Indeed, the most striking feature of virtually all experiments of human overfeeding (lasting from a few weeks to a few months) is the wide range of individual variability in the amount of weight gain per unit of excess energy consumed. Some of these differences in the efficiency of weight gain could be attributed to interindividual variability in the gain of lean tissue relative to fat tissue (i.e., variability in the composition of weight gain), but most are in the ability to convert excess calories to heat—that is, in the large interindividual capacity for diet-induced thermogenesis (DIT). A detailed reanalysis of data from approximately 150 humans participating in the various overeating experiments conducted between 1965 and 1999 suggested that at least 40% of these overfed subjects must have exhibited an increase in DIT, albeit to varying degrees. Part of this variation in DIT could be explained by differences in the dietary protein content of the diet, with DIT being more pronounced in unbalanced diets that are low or high in percentage protein. As shown in **Figure 1**, in a subgroup of volunteers who were overfed on two occasions—once on a normal protein diet and once on a low-protein diet—

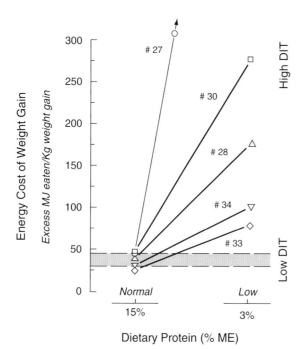

Figure 1 Interindividual variability in thermogenesis by low-protein overfeeding in humans. The data represent the energy cost of weight gain (excess MJ consumed per kilogram weight gained) during 3 or 4 weeks of overfeeding in the five human volunteers who participated in both the normal protein and low-protein overfeeding in the gluttony experiments of Miller and Mumford (1967). The horizontal broken lines (enclosing the shaded area) correspond to predicted energy cost of weight gain on the assumption that weight gain is either 100% fat (45 MJ/kg) or 60% fat (30 MJ/kg), the latter value including the cost of fat-free mass gain. The greater the deviation from the predicted values, the greater the likelihood that the excess calories were dissipated via enhanced diet-induced thermogenesis (DIT). Adapted from Dulloo AG and Jacquet J (1999) Low-protein overfeeding: A tool to unmask susceptibility to obesity in humans. *International Journal of Obesity* **23**: 1118–1121.

relatively small individual differences in DIT on balanced normal protein diet were amplified on the protein-deficient diet. That genes play an important role in variability in metabolism that underlies such susceptibility to weight gain and obesity has in fact been established from overfeeding experiments in identical twins. Conversely, a role for genotype in human variability in both the composition of weight loss (i.e., ratio of lean to fat tissue) and the enhanced metabolic efficiency (i.e., adaptive reduction in thermogenesis) during weight loss has been suggested from studies in which identical twins underwent slimming therapy on a very low-calorie diet. Taken together, it is evident that in addition to the control of food intake, changes in the composition of weight changes (via partitioning between lean and fat tissues) and in metabolic efficiency (via adaptive thermogenesis) also play an important role in the regulation of body weight and body composition, and the magnitude of these adaptive changes is strongly influenced by the genetic makeup of the individual.

What Constitutes Adaptive Thermogenesis?

The quantitative assessment of adaptive thermogenesis in the regulation of body weight and body composition is hampered by difficulties in determining which component(s) of energy expenditure may be contributing importantly to the changes in metabolic efficiency. As depicted in **Figure 2**, energy expenditure in the resting state is measured as basal metabolic rate (BMR) or as thermic effect of food (classically known as the specific dynamic action). Changes in the thermic effect of food (as percentage of calories ingested) or resting energy expenditure (after adjusting for changes in fat-free mass and fat mass) can be quantified, and they reflect changes in metabolic efficiency and hence in adaptive changes in thermogenesis. In contrast, any change in heat production from what is generally labeled nonresting energy expenditure is more difficult to quantify. The efficiency of muscular contraction during exercise is low (~25%), but that of spontaneous physical activity (SPA)—including fidgeting, muscle tone and posture maintenance, and other low-level physical activities of everyday life—is even lower since these essentially involuntary activities comprise a larger proportion of isometric work that is simply thermogenic. Since actual work done on the environment during SPA is very small compared to the total energy spent on such activities, the energy cost associated with SPA

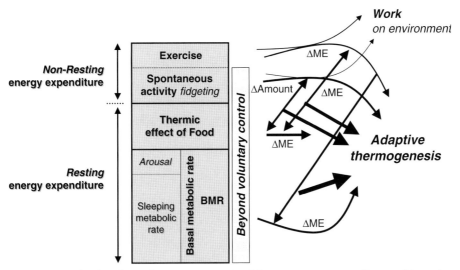

Figure 2 Schematic diagram showing the various compartments of human energy expenditure and how changes in metabolic efficiency (ΔME) both within and across these compartments can lead to adaptive changes in thermogenesis. The diagonal arrows depict possible *interactions* – between compartments of energy expenditure – that also constitute adaptive changes in thermogenesis; see text for details.

has been referred to as movement-associated thermogenesis or SPA-associated thermogenesis. It has also been argued that since SPA is essentially subconscious and hence beyond voluntary control, a change in the level or amount of SPA in a direction that defends body weight also constitutes autoregulatory changes in energy expenditure. In this context, an increase in the amount of SPA in response to overfeeding or a decrease during starvation also constitute adaptive changes in thermogenesis.

Spontaneous Physical Activity

The most direct evidence that changes in SPA contribute to autoregulatory changes in energy expenditure in humans derives from data obtained from the eight men and women who participated in the Biosphere 2 experiment. Biosphere 2 was a self-contained ecologic 'miniworld' and prototype planetary habitat built in Arizona. As a result of an unexpected shortage of food, their loss in body weight (8–25%) over a 2-year period was accompanied by a major reduction in SPA, which, like their reduced energy expenditure, persisted several months after the onset of weight recovery and disproportionate recovery of fat mass. Whether interindividual variability in the amount of SPA during overfeeding contributes to variability in resistance or susceptibility to obesity has also been the focus of a few human studies of energy expenditure. The importance of SPA-associated thermogenesis in human weight regulation was in fact underscored by the finding that even under conditions in which

subjects were confined to a metabolic chamber, the 24-h energy expenditure attributed to SPA (as assessed by radar systems) was found to vary between 100 and 700 kcal/day and to be a predictor of subsequent weight gain. In fact, a main conclusion of early overfeeding experiments conducted in the late 1960s was that most of the extra heat dissipation in some individuals resisting obesity by increased DIT could not be accounted for by an increase in resting metabolic rate but could be due to an increased energy expenditure associated with simple (low-level) activities of everyday life. This notion has recently gained support from the findings that more than 60% of the increase in total daily energy expenditure in response to an 8-week overfeeding period could be attributed to SPA, and that interindividual variability in energy expenditure associated with SPA, referred to as nonexercise activity thermogenesis (NEAT), was the most significant predictor of resistance or susceptibility to obesity.

Efficiency of Muscle Work

In addition to changes in SPA, there is also evidence that changes in the efficiency of muscle work also contribute to adaptive changes in energy expenditure. Indeed in experiments of forced changes in weight in which subjects maintained body weight at 10% above or 10% below their habitual body weight, changes in muscle work efficiency could account for a-third of the change in daily energy expended in physical activity. These findings are consistent with other reports of an increase in skeletal muscle work efficiency (i.e., decreased thermogenesis) after experimentally-induced weight reduction or in chronically undernourished subjects. Instead, changes in muscle work efficiency could account for one-third of the change in daily energy expended performing physical activity. These findings are consistent with other reports of an increase in skeletal muscle work efficiency (i.e., decreased thermogenesis) after experimentally induced weight reduction or in chronically undernourished subjects.

Interactions between Resting and Nonresting Energy Expenditure

It must be emphasized that the separation of adaptive thermogenesis between resting and nonresting is artificial, given the possibilities of their interactions illustrated in **Figure 2**. For example, energy expenditure during sleep, which is generally nested under resting energy expenditure, also comprises a nonresting component due to spontaneous movement (or SPA) occurring during sleep, the frequency of which seems to be highly variable between individuals. Furthermore, nonresting energy expenditure or NEAT may also include heat production resulting from the impact of physical activity (exercise or SPA) on postabsorptive metabolic rate or postprandial thermogenesis. There is evidence that relatively low-intensity exercise can lead to potentiation of the thermic effect of food, and that the effect of physical activity on energy expenditure can persist well after the period of physical activity (postexercise or post-SPA stimulation of thermogenesis). Reduction in postexercise stimulation of metabolic rate has also been proposed as a mechanism for energy conservation in individuals who are considered to be chronically energy deficient since childhood. Thus, any changes in metabolic efficiency in the resting or nonresting state that would tend to attenuate energy imbalance or to restore body weight and body composition toward its set or preferred value constitute adaptive changes in thermogenesis

Autoregulation of Body Weight and Body Composition

From a system physiology standpoint, the available evidence, based on classic longitudinal studies of starvation, refeeding, and overfeeding, suggests the adaptive mechanisms for optimal survival in an environment of famine and feast are embodied in three distinct autoregulatory control systems: the control of partitioning between protein and fat (the two main energy-containing compartments in

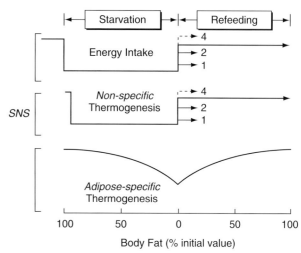

Figure 3 Schematic representation of the concept of two distinct control systems underlying adaptive thermogenesis during prolonged starvation and subsequent refeeding, showing (i) the *non-specific* control of thermogenesis, which is mediated primarily by the sympathetic nervous system (SNS) and which is a direct function of food energy supply, and (ii) the *adipose-specific* control of thermogenesis which is independent of the functional state of the SNS and which is a direct function of the state of depletion/repletion of the fat stores. Note that the different caloric loads during refeeding correspond to levels 1–4 of energy reavailability, with energy intake at level 1–2 below and level 4 above that prior to starvation, respectively. Adapted from Dulloo AG and Jacquet J (2001) An adipose-specific control of thermogenesis in body weight regulation. *International Journal of Obesity* **25**: (Supplement 5) S22–29.

the body) and two distinct control systems underlying adaptive changes in thermogenesis, as depicted in **Figure 3**. One control system is a direct function of changes in the food energy supply and responds relatively rapidly to the energy deficit. Its effector mechanisms are suppressed early during the course of starvation, and upon refeeding they are restored relatively rapidly as a function of energy reavailability and are activated further if hyperphagia occurs during refeeding, which may account for increased DIT. Because the efferent limb of this control system, which is primarily under the control of the sympathetic nervous system (SNS), is dictated not only by the dietary energy supply but also by a variety of other environmental factors, such as diet composition, specific nutrient deficiencies, ambient temperature, and psychological stress, it is referred to as the nonspecific control of thermogenesis. In contrast, the other control system has a much slower time constant by virtue of its response only to signals arising from the state of depletion/repletion of body fat stores; it is therefore referred to as the control system operating through an adipose-specific control of thermogenesis. The definitions of these two control systems underlying adaptive thermogenesis are thus made on the basis of their differential commands—either deriving solely from the state of adipose tissue fat stores or not.

A Compartmental Model

An overall integration of these autoregulatory control systems in the regulation of body weight and body composition during a cycle of weight loss and weight recovery is discussed with the help of a schematic diagram presented in **Figure 4**. This diagram embodies the finding that the control of body energy partitioning between protein and fat is an individual characteristic—that is, individuals vary in their partitioning characteristic (Pc) during weight loss and weight recovery—and takes into account the two distinct control systems for adaptive thermogenesis that can operate independently of each other.

During starvation, the control of partitioning determines the relative proportion of protein and fat to be mobilized from the body as fuel—the individual's Pc being dictated primarily by the initial body composition. The functional role of the control of partitioning is to meet the fuel needs of the individual in such a way that the energy reserve component in both the fat and the protein compartments (i.e., the part that can be lost without death or irreversible damage) would reach complete depletion simultaneously—a strategy that ensures the

maximum duration of survival for a given individual during long-term food scarcity. Furthermore, the energy conserved resulting from suppressed thermogenesis is directed at reducing the energy imbalance, with the net result that there is a slowing down in the rate of protein and fat mobilization in the same proportion as defined by the Pc of the individual. Indeed, the fact that the fraction of fuel energy derived from protein (i.e., the *P* ratio) remains relatively constant during the course of prolonged starvation, albeit in normal-weight humans, implies that neither control system underlying suppressed thermogenesis is directed at sparing specifically protein nor specifically fat but, rather, at sparing both protein and fat compartments simultaneously. Therefore, during starvation the functional role of both control systems underlying suppressed thermogenesis is to reduce the overall rate of fuel utilization (i.e., for energy conservation directed at sparing both lean and fat tissues).

During refeeding, the control of partitioning operates in such a way that protein and fat are deposited in the same relative proportion as determined by the Pc of the individual during starvation, and this serves to reestablish the individual's prestarvation capacity for survival during long-term food scarcity. Furthermore, the increased availability of food leads to the rapid removal of suppression upon the nonspecific (SNS-mediated) control of thermogenesis. In contrast, the suppression of thermogenesis under

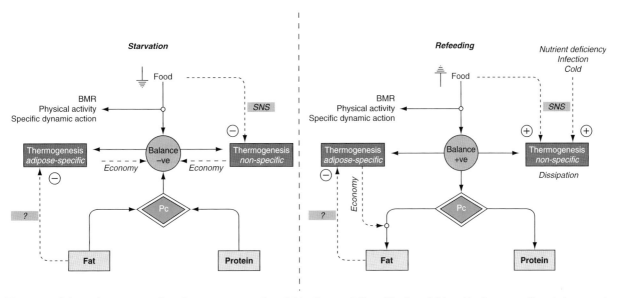

Figure 4 Schematic representation of a compartmental model for the regulation of body weight and body composition during a cycle of weight loss (prolonged starvation) and weight recovery (refeeding). In this model, the two distinct control systems underlying adaptive thermogenesis—the nonspecific control and the adipose-specific control—are integrated with the more 'basal' control of partitioning between the body fat and protein compartments as determined by the partitioning characteristic (Pc) of the individual. Adapted from Dulloo AG and Jacquet J (2001) An adipose-specific control of thermogenesis in body weight regulation. *International Journal of Obesity* **25**(supplement 5): S22–S29.

adipose-specific control is only slowly relieved as a function of fat recovery, such that the energy that continues to be spared is directed specifically at the replenishment of the fat stores. The net effect is that fat is deposited in excess of that determined by the Pc of the individual, thereby contributing to the disproportionate rate of fat relative to lean tissue recovery. This phenomenon of catch-up of fat (rather than catch-up of lean tissue) is often observed, both in adults after severe weight loss due to food unavailability and disease and in infants and children recovering from protein energy malnutrition and growth arrest.

Biological Significance

Such an adaptive phenomenon that accelerates the restitution of fat stores rather than diverting the energy saved toward compensatory increases in body protein synthesis (an energetically costly process) would have survival value in ancestral famine-and-feast lifestyle. This is because by virtue of the fact that body fat has a greater energy density and a lower energy cost of synthesis/maintenance than protein, it would provide the organism with a greater capacity to rapidly rebuild an efficient energy reserve and hence to cope with recurrent food shortage. Thus, the functional role of the adipose-specific control of thermogenesis during weight recovery is to accelerate specifically the replenishment of the fat stores whenever food availability is increased after a long period of food deficit and severe depletion of body fat stores. It provides an alternative mechanism to recover survival capacity in the absence of hyperphagia. However, equally important for the survival of mammals during weight loss and weight recovery is the need to retain the capacity to increase heat production (i.e., to activate thermogenesis) in response to a number of other environmental stresses, namely (i) for increased thermoregulatory needs in cold environments, (ii) for the generation of fever during exposure to infections, or (iii) for increased heat production as an adaptation to nutrient-deficient diets. The necessity to increase DIT in the face of nutrient-deficient diets probably had evolutionary survival advantage of 'homeostatic waste' because it enables individuals to overeat relatively large quantities of poor-quality food in order to obtain essential nutrients without the deposition of excess, nonessential energy as fat. Excessive weight gain would be a hindrance to optimal locomotion, hunting capabilities, and the ability to fight or flee. It has been proposed that DIT may have evolved as a means of regulating the metabolic supply of essential

nutrients (protein, minerals, and vitamins) with only a secondary role in regulating energy balance and body weight. Whatever the exact functional significance of DIT, however, it is clear that in the context of weight recovery an elevated efficiency for catch-up fat can be shown to persist even under conditions of hypermetabolism (a net increase in thermogenesis) induced by hyperphagia or nutrient-deficient diets. To explain this apparent paradox, the model presented in **Figure 4** provides a structural framework that illustrates how suppressed adipose-specific thermogenesis that results in enhanced fat deposition during refeeding, and that is postulated to occur in the skeletal muscle, persists under conditions when the nonspecific control of thermogenesis is activated in organs/tissues recruited by the SNS (liver, kidneys, heart, and brown adipose tissue). Such differentially regulated control systems for thermogenesis may thus have arisen during the course of mammalian evolution as dual-adaptive processes that can satisfy the need for energy conservation during weight loss or for catch-up fat during weight recovery, even under environmental stresses when SNS-mediated activation of heat production has equally important survival values.

Energy Adaptation during a Longitudinal Human Study of Weight Fluctuations

The existence and operation of this dual-control system for adaptive thermogenesis are consistent with the temporal changes of BMR and body composition during the unique longitudinal study of semistarvation, refeeding, and subsequent overfeeding in men participating in a Minnesota experiment. The pattern of changes in food intake and body weight, together with kinetics of altered thermogenesis (assessed as changes in BMR adjusted for fat-free mass (FFM) and fat mass and expressed as a percentage of baseline BMR value) are presented in **Figure 5**.

During the phase of weight loss, the operation of the two control systems for adaptive thermogenesis is suggested by the fact that reduction in thermogenesis is biphasic in nature, with an initial rapid reduction in adjusted BMR at week 4, corresponding to 10% of baseline BMR, followed by a slower reduction in adjusted BMR, corresponding to 20 and 25% of baseline BMR at weeks 20 and 24, respectively. At the latter time points during starvation (at S20 and S24), the magnitude of reduced adjusted BMR was found to be associated with the reduction in fat mass (i.e., the greater the degree of depletion of the fat stores, the greater the suppression of thermogenesis).

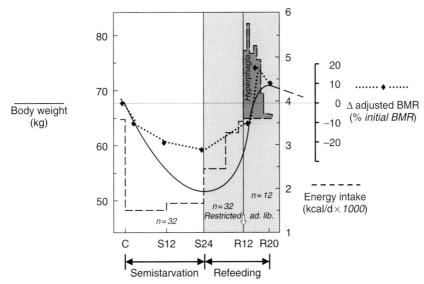

Figure 5 Pattern of changes in body weight, food intake, and adaptive thermogenesis during the various phases of the longitudinal 'Minnesota experiment' of human semistarvation and refeeding. The changes in adaptive thermogenesis at the various time points are assessed as changes in basal metabolic rate (BMR) after adjusting for changes in fat-free mass and fat mass and are expressed as a percentage of the baseline (control) BMR level. C, end of control (baseline) period; S12 and S24, week 12 and week 24 of semistarvation, respectively; R12 and R20, week 12 and week 20 after onset of refeeding, respectively. Data from Keys A, Brozek J, Henschel A, Mickelson O and Taylor HL (1950) *The Biology of Human Starvation*. Minneapolis: University of Minnesota Press; and Dulloo AG and Jacquet J (1998) Adaptive reduction in basal metabolic rate in response to food deprivation in humans: A role for feedback signals from fat stores. *American Journal of Clinical Nutrition* **68**: 599–606.

During the phase of weight recovery, the operation of the two control systems for thermogenesis is also suggested by the following:

1. The relation between the degree of depletion of fat stores and suppressed (adipose-specific) thermogenesis persists at week 12 of restricted refeeding, at which time point (R12) the mean adjusted BMR is still approximately 10% below baseline BMR level, the body fat is 80% recovered, and body weight and FFM recoveries are less than 50%.

2. After withdrawal of the dietary restriction during the subsequent period of ad libitum refeeding, the development of hyperphagia is accompanied by a prompt (perhaps SNS-mediated nonspecific) increase in thermogenesis, as judged by increases in adjusted BMR corresponding to approximately 20% of baseline BMR at week 14 of refeeding.

It is also noticeable that by week 20 after the onset of refeeding (R20), when FFM has been almost 100% recovered and body fat has overshot baseline (prestarvation) level by >70%—a phenomenon referred to as 'poststarvation obesity'—the adjusted BMR remains significantly higher (by approximately 10%) above baseline BMR despite the fact that hyperphagia is no longer present. This post-overfeeding sustained elevation of thermogenesis is consistent with a feedback mechanism existing between thermogenesis and body fat (i.e., the result of an activated adipose-specific control of thermogenesis), which may well have contributed to the subsequent slow return of body weight toward the baseline level after the phase of fat overshooting. Body fat was still higher than pre-starvation values when examined 33 weeks after the end of starvation, but was no longer significantly higher than pre-starvation values when examined 58 weeks after the end of starvation.

It should be noted that this study only enabled analysis of adaptive changes in thermogenesis in the BMR compartment since no measurements were performed pertaining to the thermic effect of food or to the energy cost of physical activity. The authors nonetheless observed that there was a profound decrease in SPA of the subjects, particularly during weeks S12 and S24 of semistarvation, thereby suggesting that adjustments in energy expenditure occurred in both resting and nonresting energy expenditure.

Energy Adaptation and Susceptibility to Leanness and Fatness

In addressing the issue of energy adaptation in human susceptibility to leanness and fatness, it must be noted that even in individuals who maintain a relatively stable lean body weight over decades, there is no 'absolute' constancy of body weight over days, weeks, and years. Instead, body weight tends to fluctuate or oscillate around a mean constant value, with deviations from a set or preferred value being triggered by events that are cultural (e.g., weekend parties and holiday seasons), psychological (e.g., stress, anxiety, or emotions), and pathophysiological (ranging from minor health perturbations to more serious disease states). Very short-term day-to-day changes in body weight have a standard deviation of approximately 0.5% of body weight, whereas longitudinal observations over periods of between 10 and 30 years indicate that individuals experience slow trends and reversal of body weight amounting to between 7 and 20% of mean weight. In such a dynamic state within which weight homeostasis occurs, it is likely that long-term constancy of body weight is achieved through a network of regulatory systems and subsystems through which autoregulatory changes in food intake, body composition, and energy expenditure are interlinked.

The autoregulatory control systems—operating through adjustments in energy partitioning and through the two distinct control systems underlying thermogenesis—can play a crucial role in attenuating and correcting deviations of body weight from its set or preferred value. The extent to which these adjustments are brought about is dependent on the environment (e.g., diet composition) and is highly variable from one individual to another, largely because of the previous nutritional status of the individual and because of genetic variations. They probably conferred varying capacities to defend the body's protein and fat stores in an ancestral hunter–gatherer lifestyle of famine and feast, but they now underlie varying metabolic susceptibilities to fatness in societies in which palatable foods are abundant year-round. The resultant subtle variations between individuals in energy partitioning and in adaptive thermogenesis can, over the long term, be important in determining constancy of body weight in some and in provoking drift toward obesity in others.

Furthermore, the adaptive responses to starvation, so far discussed in the context of experimentation in normal weight (lean) individuals, also persist in individuals in whom obesity has developed spontaneously and contribute the defense of the obese state once acquired. In fact, longitudinal studies in obese humans losing weight in response to therapeutic slimming also indicate that they show a reduction in BMR (even after adjustments for losses of lean and fat tissues) as well as in SPA during both the dynamic phase of weight loss and subsequent weight maintenance. These findings support the notion that suppressed thermogenesis in response to food deprivation is a factor that reduces the efficacy of therapeutic regimens and contributes to obesity relapse. Furthermore, since the initial body composition (percentage of fat) is the most important determinant of energy partitioning between lean and fat tissue (i.e., Pc of the individual) during weight loss and weight recovery, the higher percentage body fat (i.e., the more obese the individual), the lower the fraction of energy mobilized as protein and hence the greater the propensity to mobilize fat during weight loss and to subsequently deposit fat during recovery. The low partitioning characteristic of the obese, coupled with sustained (adipose-specific) suppression of thermogenesis in response to their relative state of body fat depletion, will contribute to the relapse of obesity.

Acknowledgments

This work was supported by Grant 3200B0-102156 from the Swiss National Science Foundation.

See also: **Body Composition**. **Energy**: Metabolism; Balance. **Obesity**: Treatment. **Starvation and Fasting**. **Weight Management**: Weight Cycling.

Further Reading

Dulloo AG (2002) A sympathetic defense against obesity. *Science* **297**: 780–781.

Dulloo AG and Jacquet J (1999) The control of partitioning between protein and fat during human starvation: Its internal determinants and biological significance. *British Journal of Nutrition* **82**: 339–356.

Dulloo AG, Jacquet J, and Montani J-P (2002) Pathways from weight fluctuations to metabolic diseases: Focus on maladaptive thermogenesis during catch-up fat. *International Journal of Obesity* **26**(supplement 2): S46–S57.

Elia M, Stubbs RJ, and Henry CJK (1999) Differences in fat, carbohydrate, and protein metabolism between lean and obese subjects undergoing total starvation. *Obesity Research* **7**: 597–604.

Henry CJK, Rivers J, and Payne RR (1998) Protein and energy metabolism in starvation reconsidered. *European Journal of Clinical Nutrition* **42**: 543–549.

Hirsch J, Hudgins LC, Leibel RL, and Rosenbaum M (1998) Diet composition and energy balance in humans. *American Journal of Clinical Nutrition* **67**(supplement): 551S–555S.

Levine JA, Eberhardt NL, and Jensen MD (1999) Role of nonexercise activity thermogenesis in resistance to fat gain in humans. *Science* **283**: 212–214.

Luke A and Schoeller D (1992) Basal metabolic rate, fat-free mass, and body cell mass during energy restriction. *Metabolism* **41**: 450–456.

Miller DS and Mumford P (1967) Gluttony 1. An experimental study of overeating low- or high-protein diets. *American Journal of Clinical Nutrition* **20**: 1212–1222.

Shetty PS (1999) Adaptation to low energy intakes: The responses and limits to low intakes in infant, children and adults. *European Journal of Clinical Nutrition* **53**(supplement 1): S14–S23.

Stock MJ (1999) Gluttony and thermogenesis revisited. *International Journal of Obesity* **23**: 1105–1117.

Weyer C, Walford RL, Harper IT *et al.* (2000) Energy metabolism after 2 y of energy restriction: The Biosphere 2 experiment. *American Journal of Clinical Nutrition* **72**: 946–953.

ENERGY EXPENDITURE

Contents
Indirect Calorimetry
Doubly Labeled Water

Indirect Calorimetry

A Raman and D A Schoeller, University
of Wisconsin–Madison, Madison, WI, USA

All living organisms require a source of energy for survival. Among animals, this energy is provided in the form of chemical energy in the nutrients they consume, which are converted to other forms of energy through respiration. This conversion is subject to the same laws of thermodynamics that govern all energy systems. The first law of thermodynamics states that energy can neither be created nor destroyed; it can only be exchanged from one system to another. Hence, the chemical energy consumed in the form of food is converted into mechanical energy for work performed by the body, thermic energy for maintenance of body temperature, or stored as chemical energy in tissues as fat, protein, or a small fraction as carbohydrates. This conservation of energy can be stated mathematically as

$$\text{Energy}_{in} = \text{Energy}_{work} + \text{Energy}_{heat} \pm \text{Energy}_{stored}$$

The sum of energy converted to work and heat is defined as metabolism. Although metabolism constitutes thousands of chemical reactions occurring at the same time throughout the body that cannot be individually measured, their sum can be measured as either the sum of work and heat energy or, in the absence of any measurable work, the rate of heat production by the body. This is based on the assumption that all the cellular events ultimately result in heat.

The process of measuring heat produced by the body during combustion of substances or nutrients in animals or humans is called calorimetry. The term 'direct calorimetry' is used when the rate of heat production is directly measured by placing a person in a thermally isolated chamber. The term 'indirect calorimetry' is used when heat production is not measured directly but is instead calculated from the measurement of the rates of oxygen consumption (V_{O_2}) and carbon dioxide production (V_{CO_2}). In both measurements, the rate of metabolism is commonly referred to as the rate of energy expenditure, which in the absence of work output is the rate at which chemical energy in food is converted to heat. The nutrients in food that provide this chemical energy are the macronutrients: carbohydrates, fat, protein, and alcohol. The chemical process that releases the chemical energy is respiration, in which each of these macronutrients is combined with oxygen to produce carbon dioxide and water. These chemical reactions are chemically equivalent to those that would be observed if the nutrient were combusted in a flame, except the reaction in the body is an enzymatic process that does not produce a flame.

For example, one molecule of sugar (glucose) breaks down as follows:

$$C_6H_{10}O_6 + 6O_2 \rightarrow 6CO_2 + 6H_2O$$

It should be noted that during this reaction, six molecules of CO_2 are produced and six molecules of O_2 are consumed. Thus, the ratio of CO_2 to O_2 has a value of 1.0. This ratio is commonly called the respiratory quotient (RQ), although many investigators prefer the term respiratory exchange ratio (RER) when it is applied to a whole body measurement. Similarly, when one molecule of fat (tripalmitin) is broken down completely, the chemical reaction is

$$C_{57}H_{104}O_6 + 80O_2 \rightarrow 57CO_2 + 52H_2O$$

In the instance of fat oxidation, 57 molecules of CO_2 are produced while 80 molecules of O_2 are consumed when 1 molecule of fat is oxidized. This yields an RER of 0.71. When only carbohydrate and fat are being used to support energy expenditure, this difference in RER makes it possible to calculate what percentage of energy expenditure is being supported by each of the two energy substrates.

There is, however, a third macronutrient that is oxidized to produce energy. The third macronutrient, protein, is more difficult to describe on a chemical basis because a protein is made from a mixture of amino acids, and for each dietary protein the number and composition of amino acids differ.

The breakdown of the average dietary protein, however, can be described by the chemical reaction

$$C_{100}H_{159}N_{26}O_{32}S_{0.7} + 105.3O_2$$
$$\rightarrow 13CON_2H_4 + 87CO_2 + 52.8H_2SO_4$$

In the instance of protein oxidation, 87 molecules of CO_2 are produced while 105.3 molecules of O_2 are consumed when 1 molecule of protein is oxidized. This yields an RER of 0.83. Although this RER value is intermediate between carbohydrate and fat, protein is unique among the three energy substrates because it is the only one to contain nitrogen. As such, urinary nitrogen can be assayed to obtain an estimate of protein oxidized by an individual. Combining this with the knowledge that the average protein is 16% nitrogen by weight, it is possible to use the previous chemical relationship to calculate the O_2 consumption and CO_2 production that result from the oxidation of the protein represented by the urinary nitrogen. Subtracting these from the total respiratory gas exchange yields a nonprotein O_2 consumption, CO_2 production, and nonprotein RER. This is used to calculate the nonprotein metabolic rate and eventually the carbohydrate and fat oxidation rates. Because urinary nitrogen is often not measured, results from indirect calorimetry often use the Weir equation to calculate the energy expenditure. This equation was derived assuming that protein oxidation supports 12% of total energy expenditure (**Table 1**).

Over the years, different instrumental methods of indirect calorimetry have been developed to accurately measure V_{O_2} and V_{CO_2} rates. Despite being a precise and accurate method of measurement of macronutrient oxidation and hence energy expenditure, constraints such as expense, portability, gas collection issues, samplers, and applicability of measurements to habitual expenditure prevented it from being available to different types of research. Hence,

the quest to develop new instrumental techniques is driven by the desire to make it a more generally applicable and easier to use technique.

Laboratory Methods

Whole Body Indirect Calorimetry

The advent of indirect calorimetry was a significant event in the history of animal and human nutrition. In whole body indirect calorimetry, the subject is kept in a sealed room or chamber, which is ventilated with a constant, measured supply of air. 'It is a setting similar to his habitual living and hence a more applicable measurement of energy expenditure.' The respiratory gas exchange of the subject is measured by the change in composition of the air going into the chamber and that of the air expelled from the chamber. Well-mixed samples of the chamber air are drawn to be analyzed for chamber air composition. The difference in O_2 and CO_2 composition of the incoming and outgoing chamber air is used to calculate the energy expenditure and macronutrient oxidation of the subject. Two main types of indirect calorimetry systems exist.

Closed-circuit indirect calorimetry involves the recirculation of the same air through the chamber. This can be performed by placing the subject in a sealed chamber. The recirculated air is kept breathable by removing the CO_2 produced by the subject and replacing the O_2 consumed by the subject. The replacement of O_2 is controlled by continuously monitoring the change in the volume of the gas in the closed breathing circuit. As the subject consumes O_2, a sensor detects the decrease in volume and a signal is sent to an external source to release constant calibrated pulses of O_2 back into the system to restore the original values. The rate of O_2 consumption is measured by recording the amount of O_2 that is added to the air during recirculation. The CO_2 produced by the subject is removed from the recirculated air by an absorber attached to the system and the CO_2 production is measured from the increased weight of the absorber (**Figure 1**).

Open-circuit indirect calorimetry involves a system in which both ends of the breathing system are open to the atmosphere. The inspired and expired air are kept separate by means of a three-way respiratory valve or non-rebreathing mask. The expired gases are collected into an air-tight bag or are frequently sampled or continuously analyzed for O_2 and CO_2 content.

These two terms are also used to describe some of the many other forms of smaller indirect calorimeters that have been developed over the years.

Table 1 Formulas for calculation of energy expenditure

Variable	Formula
Oxygen consumption (ml/min)	= (Volume of inspired air per minute × fraction of inspired O_2) − (volume of expired air per minute × fraction of expired O_2)
Carbon dioxide production (ml/min)	= (Volume of expired air per minute × fraction of expired CO_2) − (volume of inspired air per minute × fraction of inspired CO_2)
Respiratory exchange ratio (RER or RQ)	= V_{CO_2}/V_{O_2}
Weir Equation (TEE, kcal/min)	= (0.0039 × V_{O_2}) + (0.0011 × V_{CO_2}) − (2.2 × urinary nitrogen, g/min)

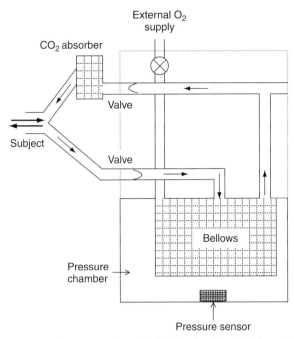

Figure 1 Closed-circuit metabolic chamber in which the subject's oxygen consumption is measured to calculate the corresponding energy expenditure. The change in volume of air in the system is constantly monitored by the sensors and a measured quantity of oxygen is added back to the system. Carbon dioxide is taken out of the recirculated air by a CO_2 absorber.

These can be categorized as laboratory or field techniques based on their portability. The instrumentation used for each varies in complexity and the degree to which they restrict the subject's movement.

Metabolic Carts

Metabolic cart is a common name for a semiportable respiratory gas analyzer that has been made small enough to be placed on a cart with wheels so that it can be rolled to different locations within a building. Two designs are generally available: the ventilated hood and the mouthpiece system.

The ventilatory hood system is an open-circuit indirect calorimeter that usually consists of a pliable plastic or rigid Perspex hood placed over the subject's head with a latex or thin plastic apron providing a rough seal around the neck or chest. These allow air to be drawn across a subject's face while in a reclining or lying position. For longer term measurements, ventilated plastic tents are available that cover all or part of the patient's bed. Since these hoods operate on a suction principle, a tight seal of the hood is not required. For field measurements, whole body transparent plastic ventilated boxes have been used successfully in infants. Many of the

ventilatory hoods are constructed by researchers from the components according to the requirements of their study. The components include a pump, a flow meter, and a means of regulating the airflow. Samples of the air drawn from the hood can be directed to gas analyzers, which are usually connected in series to the hood. Respiratory gas exchange is calculated from the difference in O_2 and CO_2 concentration between the air entering and exiting the hood and the controlled rate of airflow (**Figure 2**).

Instruments have been developed to operate in adult and pediatric applications and differ with respect to flow rates and internal volume because of the smaller metabolic rate of children. The expired air enters a mixing chamber within the instrument to eliminate concentration variation resulting from inspiration and expiration before the sample enters O_2 and CO_2 sensor analyzers, which measure the concentration differences between the expired and inspired air. For state-of-the-art instruments, the data are input into a microprocessor providing minute-by-minute calculation of the O_2 consumption, CO_2 production, RER, and energy

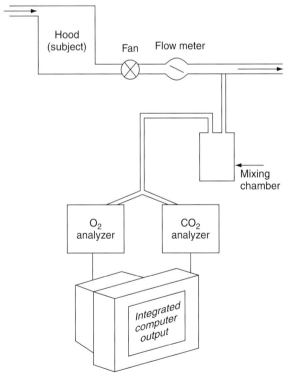

Figure 2 Ventilatory hood system showing a hood that is placed on the subject's head, a mixing chamber, and O_2 and CO_2 analyzers. A fan maintains a slight negative pressure in the hood to pull air into the chamber and also to prevent the escape of the expired air from the system. The air is mixed in the mixing chamber and is analyzed for oxygen and carbon dioxide by the respective analyzers. Results are calculated by the computer.

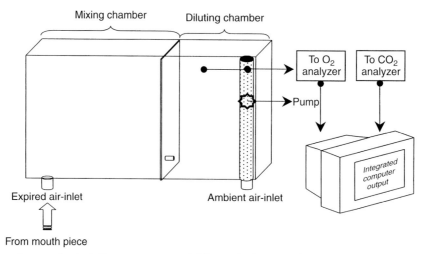

Figure 3 Metabolic unit measuring both O_2 consumption and CO_2 production rates during rest and exercise. In this type of system, expired air is diluted using ambient air before being analyzed by the respective analyzers.

expenditure. These instruments are generally used for measurements of subjects at rest as part of nutritional studies of energy expenditure and macronutrient utilization. These units can also be connected to mechanical ventilators for use in hospitalized patients.

Mouthpiece systems are similar to ventilated hood systems in principle, but instead of placing a hood over the subject's head, the subject wears a mouthpiece connected to the analyzer and nose clips to prevent breathing through the nose. The mouthpiece is connected to a valve system that allows the subject to breath in atmospheric air while directing the exhaled air to the gas analysis system. The expired breath is again subjected to analysis of O_2 and CO_2 concentration, but rather than passing the breath through a mixing chamber to smooth out the changes in concentration gradient of these gases from the start to end of an exhalation, the concentration profile is measured in real time along with the rate of gas flow from the exhalation. Again, the data are fed into a microprocessor for calculation of O_2 consumption and CO_2 production, but in this case the calculation is performed on a breath-by-breath basis. Results are averaged over time, usually provided as minute-by-minute averages of O_2 consumption, CO_2 output, and the rate of energy expenditure. The mouthpiece systems are generally used for studies of gas exchange and energy metabolism during exercise and provide a shorter measurement response time than the ventilated hood systems. The mouthpiece and nose clip used with some of the instruments make long time measurements highly cumbersome. Also, breathing through the mouthpiece often causes untrained subjects to involuntarily hyperventilate leading to inappropriate O_2 and CO_2 rates. It is also often difficult with mask systems to obtain an airtight seal without excessive pressure at the site of contact with the mask and face.

Different types of metabolic carts or monitors are available that are designed for various applications ranging from nutrition to exercise science. Most have built-in gas analyzers and data processing computers, making them highly user-friendly, handy tools for measurement of energy metabolism. They generally provide accurate and reliable data but do require periodic calibration. Ventilated hood systems often use a combination of gases with known concentrations and weighed ethanol or methanol burns for such calibration, whereas breath-by-breath systems use a combination of large volumetric syringes and gases of known O_2 and CO_2 concentration (**Figure 3**).

Field Methods

As for whole body indirect calorimetry, ambulatory and portable systems measure the respiratory gas exchange with the V_{O_2} and V_{CO_2} measurements. Ambulatory methods and less refined laboratory methods often dispense with the measurement of CO_2 to avoid the need for two gas analyzers. The error incurred by assuming a CO_2 production rate is several percentage points, which researchers are prepared to compromise on. When only O_2 consumption is measured, however, it is not possible to compute macronutrient-specific oxidation rates. The accuracy of ambulatory and portable methods is generally between $+4$ and -2%. Field methods involve the collection of expired air over a fixed period of time as in the Douglas bag or small online analysis systems that sample inspired and expired air through a mouthpiece.

Douglas Bag/Tissot Tank

The Douglas bag method is a classical example of collection of expired air to measure energy expenditure in the field during both rest and physical activity. It consists of a gas-impermeable bag with a capacity of ~100 l or a Tissot tank suspended over water, which is used to store the subject's expired air over a fixed, short time interval. A classic Douglas bag is made up of either a rubber sheeting cemented by two layers of canvas or plastic material lined by PVC or aluminum with welded seams. The rubber bags have leakage of CO_2 by diffusion, which is unavoidable, but PVC and metalized bags hold better. If the bags are filled to capacity and analyzed with 20 min of collection, the effects of diffusion can be minimized. The subject wears a nose clip and mouthpiece or a face mask. Outside air or its equivalent is inhaled through the mouthpiece or mask containing a one-way valve and exhaled into a Douglas bag or Tissot tank for a precise period of time. It is important that the mouthpiece and connecting tubing provide minimal resistance to airflow, or the cost of breathing will increase the energy expenditure. Ambient temperature, barometric pressure, and relative humidity are recorded for converting values under conditions of standard temperature and pressure. The volume of air collected in the bag or tank is measured and a sample of exhaled air is obtained to measure the O_2 and CO_2 concentrations using gas analyzers. The volume of oxygen consumed and carbon dioxide exhaled are calculated by analyzing the gas from the Douglas bag for the precise time period during which it was collected. This method is relatively simple and inexpensive yet gives reliable results. It is suitable only for short durations of field measurement, and wearing the mask and nose clip for the whole duration of the study may be cumbersome, interfere with daily activities, and is socially undesirable to the subject.

Spirometers were used in the past for measurement of the volume of the respired air. With the advent of continuous flow electronic analyzers and superior gas flowmeters, spirometers are now rarely used. Ambulatory methods also consist of a mouthpiece incorporating light action-sensitive but robust one-way gas valves, corrugated tubes, and three-way taps. The volume of air respired and the relative concentrations of O_2 and CO_2 in the expired air are measured using O_2 and CO_2 gas analyzers. These small analyzers have replaced the Haldane system or micro-Scholander chemical gas analyzers, which used reagents to absorb the CO_2 and O_2, with the weight of absorbents measured before and after the gases were absorbed.

Max Plank/Kofranyi–Michaels Respirometer

A Max Plank respiration gas meter is a small, compact, and lightweight backpack-mounted respirometer. It combines a gas volume meter and a sampling device for continuous sampling of each breath of expired air. The Max Plank respirometer consists of a dry, bellow-type gas meter for measuring the total volume of expired air during activity. The subject breathes through a low-resistance valve and the expired volume is monitored. A measured quantity of expired air is removed continuously (0.3 or 0.6%) by an aliquoting device to be sent to a small butyl rubber bag. This rubber sampling bag can be connected directly to the oxygen analyzer, eliminating the need for transfer of samples to gastight syringes for analysis. The respirometer is suitable for flow rates between 15 and 50 l/min or for periods of 110 min on a slow flow rate and 55 min on a faster rate. It is smaller, more compact, and lighter than the Douglas bag apparatus and can be used in studies involving light to moderate physical activity. Although the system has a low resistance, at higher ventilation rates the resistance increases substantially and hence cannot be used in higher flow rate scenarios. Also, this can be used in studies of shorter duration only. Due to the use of mouthpiece and nose clip, prolonged usage may cause discomfort to the subjects.

Telemetry Systems

The K2 system was the first of a series of portable systems that consists of a soft face mask with a turbine flowmeter attached to it. A transmitter and battery are attached to a chest harness, which transmits signals to a receiver unit. The flowmeter measures the rate of airflow, calculates the volume of expired air per minute, and counts the number of expirations per minute. A small capillary tube passes through to the transmitter unit, which contains an electrochemical gas analyzer used to measure the concentration of oxygen in expired air. The signals from this analyzer are transmitted to the receiver unit by the portable transmitter unit. The receiver unit processes the data and prints it in a desired format. The electrochemical gas analyzer is a polarographic electrode. It has a membrane through which oxygen permeates into an electrolyte solution generating an electrical impulse proportional to the rate of oxygen permeation through the membrane.

Since these systems are portable and easy to use, they have many potential uses in exercise science studies and rehabilitation medicine. They allow a breath-by-breath pulmonary gas exchange

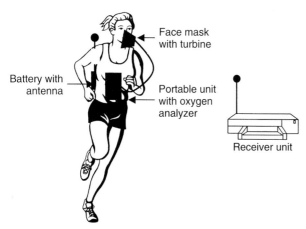

Figure 4 Telemetry system with a face mask attached to a turbine flowmeter, a transmitter, and a receiver unit. The flowmeter measures the rate and volume of airflow and the expiratory cycles per minute. The expired air is analyzed for oxygen concentration by an oxygen analyzer in the transmitter unit. The transmitter then transmits the signals to the receiver unit, which integrates the data and prints the results.

measurement while still being very light and portable, enabling a direct field assessment of human performance and cardiopulmonary limitations. The low-resistance flowmeter allows a wide range of oxygen flow rates to be measured, through these systems face the issue of air leakage from the face masks when subjects are made to exercise at high intensities. The measurement durations usually are limited to 1–5 h. The polarographic electrode membrane is known to have a short life span and hence monitoring of the usage of the instrument is essential. If CO_2 concentrations are essential for a study, this is not a good instrument to use (**Figure 4**).

Tracer Methods of Indirect Calorimetry

These are a third category of techniques that have gained popularity among investigators during the past two decades. These techniques provide a measure of CO_2 production through the use of dilution techniques using isotopic tracers.

Labeled Bicarbonate

A constant infusion-labeled bicarbonate method is useful in estimating the net CO_2 production and hence energy expenditure in animals and humans. This method is based on an isotopic dilution technique whereby the administered label is diluted by the CO_2 produced endogenously by the body. The extent of this isotope dilution is used to measure the rate of CO_2 production and is used to estimate the energy expenditure of the individual. A micro-infusion of ^{13}C- or ^{14}C-labeled bicarbonate is given

to an individual and the specific activity or enrichment of his or her physiological fluids, especially breath or urine, are measured to estimate the rate of label elimination and hence the rate of endogenous CO_2. Thus, variation in the endogenous CO_2 production rate will be reflected in the dilution of the body pool and consequently in the breath samples.

These measurements are accurate when energy expenditures are measured over a longer duration of time (>1 day) but are subject to effects of label sequestration over shorter periods. Sequestration refers to trapping, or fixation, of the label in tissues that utilize bicarbonate/CO_2 for their metabolic functions. Shorter duration of collection of breath samples requires a correction for the fraction of label that is sequestered. This is based on the assumption that similar amounts of label are sequestered in various individuals. When breath samples are collected over longer durations, the sequestration is often assumed to be negligible.

Some investigators have used a bolus bicarbonate administration rather than the continuous infusion. These investigators measured the rate at which the label concentration decreases with time as a measure of CO_2 turnover and the initial concentration as a measure of the body's bicarbonate pool size. Taken together, these provided a measure of energy expenditure during a short period of constant physical activity.

Doubly Labeled Water

This is an isotope dilution technique wherein deuterium and heavy oxygen-labeled water (doubly labeled water, DLW) are given to individuals and timed urine samples are collected to measure the elimination rates of ^2H and ^{18}O in the urine. ^2H label from DLW mixes with the body water and is eliminated as water in the urine. Similarly, ^{18}O label from DLW is eliminated as water, but it is also utilized in bicarbonate synthesis and hence is also eliminated in the breath as CO_2. The difference in turnover rates of isotopic ^2H-H and ^{18}O-labeled water is proportional to CO_2 production. Energy expenditure, oxygen consumption, water intake, and metabolic water production can be calculated using standard indirect calorimetry equations with an estimated RER (**Figure 5**).

In practice, a measured dose of DLW is given to the subject whose energy expenditure is to be measured. Body water samples, such as blood, urine, saliva, or breath water, are collected before dosing and after equilibrium is attained. The isotopic disappearance rates of ^{18}O and ^2H as CO_2 in breath or

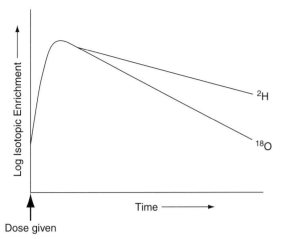

Figure 5 Time course on log scale for the enrichments of the stable isotopes 18-oxygen and deuterium when administered to the subject. Both the tracer enrichments increase rapidly in the body water pool until they reach distribution equilibrium (2–4 h). The enrichments then start to decline as the body water turns over during metabolism. 18-Oxygen is eliminated at a faster rate because it is excreted as water and CO_2 in breath, whereas deuterium is eliminated as water only. The difference in elimination rates of these two tracers is proportional to the rate of CO_2 production by the subject.

H_2O in urine, saliva, or breath water, respectively, are determined from the change in isotopic enrichments of the before dosing and after equilibrium samples.

The doubly labeled water method is both simple and noninvasive. It has been validated in various animals and humans, with the CO_2 production rate showing a mean measurement error of less than 5%. Unlike the majority of the other methods, the doubly labeled water method provides a measure of average energy expended over a period of 3–21 days without restricting the subject's movement and thus provides a better estimate of habitual energy expenditure than the other methods. The doubly labeled water method, however, does not provide any information on the pattern or intensity of any one activity during that time but the overall average energy expenditure. This method is also expensive due to the cost of the ^{18}O and it does require sophisticated mass spectrometric analyses.

Summary

Indirect calorimetry is a noninvasive, reliable, and valuable tool in assessing energy expenditure, evaluating fuel utilization by the body. It has been used extensively for both scientific investigation and medical evaluation and care. Scientists from various fields have used it effectively to measure energy expenditure, establish nutrient requirements, measure physical fitness, and evaluate macronutrient utilization during exercise and rest. Clinicians have used indirect calorimetry to optimize the nutritional support in metabolic disorders as in parenterally fed patients and to quantify the energy expenditure in mechanically ventilated patients. Indirect calorimetry is a reliable, convenient, and accurate diagnostic and prognostic tool in experimental and clinical settings. Indirect calorimetry has such universal appeal because animals and humans derive their energy for sustenance by transforming the chemical energy from the nutrients they consume to heat through respiration, and their existence depends on their ability to balance energy intake and expenditure.

See also: **Energy**: Metabolism; Balance; Requirements.

Further Reading

Elia M, Fuller NJ, and Murgatroyd PR (1992) Measurement of bicarbonate turnover in humans: Applicability to estimation of energy expenditure. *American Journal of Physiology* **263**: E676–E687.

Headley JM (2003) Indirect calorimetry. *AACN Clinical Issues* **14**(2): 155–167.

Jequier E, Acheson K, and Schutz Y (1987) Assessment of energy expenditure and fuel utilization in man. *Annual Review of Nutrition* **7**: 187–208.

Macfarlane DJ (2001) Automated metabolic gas analysis systems. *Sports Medicine* **31**(12): 841–861.

Molnar JA, Cunnigham JJ, Miyatani S *et al.* (1986) Closed-circuit metabolic system with multiple applications. *Journal of Applied Physiology* **61**(4): 1582–1585.

Murgatroyd PR, Shetty PS, and Prentice AM (1993) Techniques for the measurement of human energy expenditure: A practical guide. *International Journal of Obesity* **17**: 549–568.

Peel C and Utsey C (1993) Oxygen consumption using the K2 telemetry system and a metabolic cart. *Medicine and Science in Sports and Exercise* **25**(3): 296–400.

Schoeller DA and Webb P (1984) Five-day comparison of the doubly labeled water method with respiratory gas exchange. *American Journal of Clinical Nutrition* **40**(1): 153–158.

Simonson DC and DeFronzo RA (1990) Indirect calorimetry: Methodological and interpretive problems. *American Journal of Physiology* **258**: E399–E412.

Doubly Labeled Water

W A Coward, MRC Human Nutrition Research, Cambridge, UK

Like methods for the measurement of energy expenditure by respiratory gas analysis, the doubly labeled water (DLW) method is indirect. The disappearance of stable isotope tracers, given orally, is used to model water and water plus carbon dioxide turnover. Carbon dioxide production rate is then estimated by difference and energy expenditure calculated from it. In practice, this means that subjects merely drink labeled water, samples of body water (e.g., urine, saliva, or blood) are collected over a few days, and these are then passed to the laboratory for tracer analysis and calculation. The method is thus uniquely objective; it is noninvasive and nonrestrictive in that its application does not interfere with normal lifestyles and comparable results can in principle be obtained in any circumstances without subject or observer influence. Complex measurement techniques do not need to be exported to the site where the subjects are located. However, underlying the apparent simplicity are concepts and techniques that are not commonly tools of trade for many potential users of the methodology. In a complete review, these, as well as method practice and results, need to be explained.

Method Fundamentals

Stable Isotopes as Tracers

Although radioactive tracers are familiar tools, the use of tracer elements and compounds to measure metabolic processes was developed first with stable isotopes in the late 1930s by Schoenheimer and Rittenberg soon after ^2H and ^{15}N (both stable isotopes) became available. Unlike radioactive isotopes, which are largely man-made, unstable, and decay to other elements, stable isotopes do not decay and are ubiquitous. Virtually all elements exist in nature in at least two stable isotopic forms with the same numbers of electrons and protons but with differing numbers of neutrons in the nucleus. The level of a specific isotopic form in nature is called its natural abundance. For tracer experiments, an element or a simple compound containing it, enriched with one of the isotopes, is prepared by mass-dependent separation on an industrial scale. This is then incorporated into the substrate of interest for biological experiments. In the current context, ^2H_2O (deuterium oxide, heavy water) is readily available from the electrolysis of water. Water enriched with ^{18}O is prepared directly by fractional distillation or from nitric oxide after its cryogenic distillation.

No radioactivity is involved in the use of stable isotopes in human experiments; thus, the only effects that have to be considered in relation to risk to the subject are related to the physical properties of the isotopic labeled compound. There is inevitably some degree of isotopic discrimination in physical and enzymatic processes, but because stable isotopes are normally present in all biological material at natural abundance levels, the relevant consideration is only by how much and for how long amounts are changed in experimental procedures. Because highly precise measurement techniques are used, it is necessary only to increase isotopic enrichments in body water from natural abundance by very small amounts. In a typical experiment, ^2H enrichment might be increased from 150 to 300 parts per million (ppm) and ^{18}O from 2000 to 2400 ppm, and a return to natural abundance levels will occur with a biological half-life of 5–7 days. There is no evidence that amounts many times larger than these have any harmful effects.

Measuring Isotopic Enrichment

Mass spectrometry is a generic name for a family of methodologies in which compounds are ionised and separated on the basis of mass:charge ratio. The method of choice for the measurement of isotopic enrichment with sufficient precision for DLW experiments is isotope ratio mass spectrometry. This technique is applicable only to relatively simple molecules. It separates ions such as $[^2H-^1H]^+$ and $[^1H-^1H]^+$ (mass 3 and 2) or $[^{12}C^{16}O^{18}O]^+$ and $[^{12}C^{16}O^{16}O]^+$ (mass 46 and 44) and measures isotopic ratios (R) relative to an international standard, such as Vienna Standard Mean Ocean Water (V-SMOW; Table 1). For the DLW method, therefore, the isotopic enrichment in water from biological samples has to be measured as hydrogen or carbon dioxide. For hydrogen isotope analysis, a variety of methods have been used for the conversion including reduction by reaction with hot uranium or zinc, but these methods are difficult to automate. Currently favoured methods are the exchange of hydrogen in the water sample with gaseous hydrogen by equilibration in the presence of a platinum catalyst or reduction with hot chromium. Both of these techniques are automated in commercially available equipment. For oxygen isotopes, samples are usually equilibrated

Table 1 Typical isotopic ratios and equivalent enrichments measured in DLW experiments[a]

Sample	^2H isotope ratio (ppm)	^2H enrichment (‰)	^{18}O isotope ratio (ppm)	^{18}O enrichment (‰)
V-SMOW	155.76	0	2005.2	0
Background	152.28	−22.34	1995.74	−4.72
Postdose	342.67	1200	2305.98	150

[a]Enrichment $= 10^3 \left(\frac{R_{sample}}{R_{V-SMOW}} - 1 \right)$.

V-SMOW, Vienna Standard Mean Ocean Water.

Single Pool Kinetics

Considering only hydrogen, **Figure 1** represents a subject, in water balance, with a total body water of N mol with water (tracee) input and output rates of F mol/day containing ^2H at a naturally abundant molar concentration, C_b. A fractional output or rate constant is defined as $K = F/N$.

If a small quantity (D mol) of water labeled with ^2H tracer is added to the pool, it will be removed from it according to the monoexponential relationship

$$q_t - q_b = De^{-Kt}$$

where D is the amount of tracer given, q_t is the total amount (mol) in the body pool at time t (days), and q_b is the amount always present due to inflow at natural abundance. K is a fractional rate constant, sometimes defined in terms of the biological half-life $T_{1/2}$. This can be calculated as $T_{1/2} = \ln2/K = 0.693/K$.

Since input and output rates are the same and the amount of tracer added is small relative to the pool size, we can write

$$\frac{q_t - q_b}{N} = \left(\frac{D}{N}\right)e^{-Kt} \text{ or } C_t - C_b = (C_0 - C_b)e^{-Kt}$$

where $C_0 - C_b$ is the increment in isotopic concentration resulting from the administration of the dose, and N can be calculated as $N = D/(C_0 - C_b)$.

The foregoing equations have been written in terms of isotopic concentration (e.g., $C = {}^2H/({}^2H + {}^1H)$), but mass spectrometry measurements are in terms of ratio (e.g., $R = {}^2H/{}^1H$) and in practice, for DLW calculations R or enrichment relative to a standard is invariably substituted for C with no effect on results at the low levels of enrichment applied in this methodology.

Principles of the Method

When Lifson first began his physiological experiments with newly available ^{18}O in the mid-1950s, it was already well-known that oral dosing with ^2H_2O and its dilution in body water was a way of measuring body water mass and turnover. Lifson showed that the oxygen in carbon dioxide, the waste product of energy metabolism, was in equilibrium in the body with body water:

$$H_2O + CO_2 \Longleftrightarrow H_2CO_3$$

He realized, therefore, that the greater apparent turnover of body water measured with $H_2{}^{18}O$ in comparison to turnover measured with ^2H_2O (**Figure 2**) was a consequence of carbon dioxide production, as shown in **Figure 3**. Thus, there was potential for a method that would permit the measurement of total CO_2 output and hence energy expenditure over long periods merely by isotopic analysis of samples of body fluids. Initially, the method was applied only to small animals because

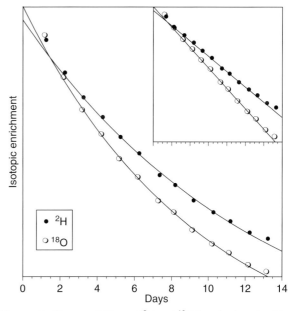

Figure 2 Exponential loss of ^2H and ^{18}O from body water. The insert shows the data on a log scale.

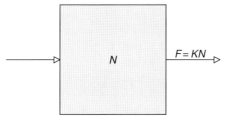

Figure 1 A simple one-compartment model of water turnover.

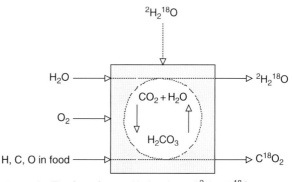

Figure 3 The fate of an oral bolus dose of ^2H and ^{18}O given as water (DLW).

the ^{18}O isotope was (and still is) expensive and instrumental limitations meant that relatively large doses had to be given to achieve adequate measurement precision. However, in the 1980s human studies, which are the focus of this article, became possible and in 1998 a basic unified methodological approach was established as a result of a meeting of the experts in the field (International Dietary Energy Consultancy Group). The publication derived from this meeting remains a valuable tool.

The following are the underlying assumptions of the method:

1. Body water is a single compartment that the isotopes label and from which they are lost.
2. ^{2}H is lost only as water.
3. ^{18}O is lost as water and carbon dioxide.
4. Total body water and output rates of water and carbon dioxide are constant.
5. Water and carbon dioxide loss occurs with the same enrichment as that coexisting in body water.
6. Background isotope intakes are constant.

Taking these in turn, assumption 1 is not correct. Evidence from many studies shows that the single compartments labelled by the isotopes are not the same size; ^{2}H space is approximately 3% larger than ^{18}O space. However, there is no evidence that isotope sequestration is a significant factor in human studies (assumptions 2 and 3). Water and carbon dioxide production rates are unlikely to be constant during a measurement period (assumption 4), but provided variations are random and not unidirectional during the measurement period, justifying the use of mean values for a period in any case, the method will not produce biased results.

Allowing assumptions 1–4, simple equations can be formulated (values of F and N are in mol and K in days^{-1}). F_{H_2O} is measured as

$$F_{H_2O} = K_D N_D$$

and the water plus carbon dioxide output (expressed in mol water equivalents) is

$$F_{H_2O+CO_2} = K_O N_O$$

Carbon dioxide production is then

$$F_{CO_2} = \frac{K_O N_O - K_D N_D}{2}$$

The factor of 2 arises because 2 mol of water is equivalent to 1 mol of carbon dioxide.

These simple relationships are in practice modified to correct for isotopic fractionation that, contrary to assumption 5, does occur. Where evaporative water losses occur, relatively less ^{2}H and ^{18}O leave the body in water vapour compared with liquid water. Fractionation factors are defined as

$$f_1 = \frac{\left(^{2}H/^{1}H\right)_{vapour}}{\left(^{2}H/^{1}H\right)_{liqiud}} = 0.941,$$

$$f_2 = \frac{\left(^{18}O/^{16}O\right)_{vapour}}{\left(^{18}O/^{16}O\right)_{liqiud}} = 0.991,$$

$$f_3 = \frac{\left(^{18}O/^{16}O\right)_{CO_2}}{\left(^{18}O/^{16}O\right)_{H_2O}} = 1.037$$

Thus, water vapour is isotopically depleted in ^{2}H and ^{18}O and carbon dioxide is relatively more enriched in ^{18}O compared to liquid water.

If it is assumed that a constant proportion (x) of water losses is fractionated, carbon dioxide production rate becomes

$$F_{CO_2} = \frac{K_O N_O}{2f_3} - \frac{K_D N_D(xf_2 + 1 - x)}{2f_3(xf_1 + 1 - x)}$$

This procedure is most frequently used for infants and young children, in whom values of x are assumed to be 0.15–0.20.

For adults, fractionated water losses (F_f) are often defined in terms of F_{CO_2} ($F_f = 2.1 F_{CO_2}$), in which case

$$F_{CO_2} = \frac{K_O N_O - K_D N_D}{2f_3 + 2.1(f_2 - f_1)}$$

Assumption 6 relates to the requirement that a predose sample should represent the effect of normal natural abundance isotope input. In most cases, background isotopic enrichment is likely to vary only randomly during a measurement period and so the issues are about the relationship between the background sample measured, the mean background and its random variation during the experimental period, the extent to which background variations in ^{2}H and ^{18}O are covariant, and the size of isotope doses and postdose enrichments in relation to these variations. In most experimental situations investigated with affordable isotopic doses, background variation contributes to the internal errors of the method and limits the extent to which better analytical precision improves results. In some circumstances (e.g., subjects moving from one place to another and use of large amounts of rehydration fluids in hospitalised patients), it is possible that a predose sample taken to represent isotopic background is not at all meaningful and the best advice may be to avoid these circumstances rather than try to correct for them.

Finally, F_{CO_2} values have to be converted into values for energy expenditure based on a fixed relationship between these quantities that depends on metabolic fuels used, expressed as a respiratory quotient (RQ). We can write

$$Energy\ expenditure\ (kJ) = F_{CO_2}\left(\frac{346.7}{RQ} + 124.3\right)$$

where F_{CO_2} is mol. RQ is calculated from dietary information or assumed to have a particular population value, such as 0.85.

Insertion of typical Western adult values ($N_O = 2000$, $N_D = 2066$, $K_O = 0.12$, and $K_D = 0.10$) into the relevant equations and 'what if' experimentation will allow the reader to test the effect of making changes to the assumptions and values. **Table 2** provides examples that show that serious errors or bias, for groups or individuals, are unlikely unless the applied population means for assumed values are grossly incorrect or the coefficient of variation (CV) is large.

Experimentation with the data, however, will also show that the magnitude of the difference between $K_O N_O$ and $K_D N_D$ is crucial. The method depends on precisely determining a relatively small difference between these two experimentally measured, larger values. This difference is approximately 20% in the example but can be much less when water turnover is high relative to carbon dioxide production (e.g., very young infants or subjects living in the tropics).

For the slopes (K_O and K_D) a minimum of two time points are required sufficiently far apart in time (two or three biological half-lives) to allow good precision on the slope determination with doses of sufficient magnitude to avoid detrimental effects of natural abundance variations and the limitations of analytical precision, especially at the end of the measurement period. In some protocols, more than two samples are measured, and this permits error calculations based on the goodness of fit of the data. Isotope distribution

spaces are calculated from samples taken soon after dose administration (the 'plateau method') or by extrapolation of the disappearance curves to $t = 0$. Distribution spaces may be normalized to population-based estimates (N'_D and N'_O) of their relation to total body water (TBW):

$$TBW = \frac{\dfrac{N_O}{1.007} + \dfrac{N_D}{1.041}}{2}$$

$$N'_O = 1.007(TBW)\ \ N'_D = 1.041(TBW)$$

Figure 4 illustrates some aspects of total imprecision and the origins of the variance for a typical subject defined in **Table 3** when different dosing regimes are applied, with ^{18}O enrichment being varied at a constant initial ^2H:^{18}O ratio of 8.

The following are general considerations:

1. Naturally occurring covariance in ^2H and ^{18}O enrichment in baseline samples can be used to mitigate errors resulting from physiological variation in these values if dose sizes are suitably tailored to the slope of the variation. Optimum doses in this respect are predicted by

$$\left(\frac{^2H}{^{18}O}\right)_{optimal} = S\frac{2^n - 1}{2^{pn} - 1}$$

where $(^2H/^{18}O)_{optimal}$ is the ratio of immediate post-dose - background enrichments (rel V-SMOW) for

Table 2 'What if' calculations for a typical subject ($N_O = 2000$, $N_D = 2066$, $K_O = 0.12$, $K_D = 0.10$)

Fractionated water losses defined in terms of F_{CO_2} ($F_f = 2.1\ F_{CO_2}$) for mean and assumed CV = 10%	CO_2 production relative to value for mean
−2 SD = 1.68 F_{CO_2}	1.010
Mean = 2.1 F_{CO_2}	1
+2 SD = 2.58 F_{CO_2}	0.981
Assumed RQ (typical mean ±2 SD)	Energy expenditure relative to value for mean
−2 SD = 0.825	1.024
Mean = 0.85	1
+2 SD = 0.875	0.978

CV, coefficient of variation; RQ, respiratory quotient.

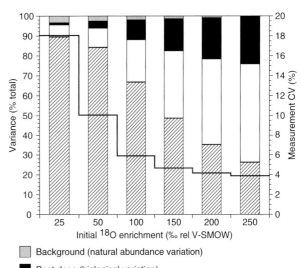

Figure 4 Origin of errors and their size in DLW experiments. The line and right axis show the total CV at different isotope doses in a typical subject defined in **Table 3**. The bars and left axis indicate the proportion of the total variance derived from each source of error.

Table 3 Typical estimates and measurement precision in a DLW experiment lasting 14 d

Parameter	Value
N_O	2000 mol
N_D	2066 mol
K_O	0.12 day^{-1}
K_D	0.10 day^{-1}
Proportional error in postdose ^{2}H samples originating from variations in water turnover (SD)	0.01
Variance in postdose ^{18}O accounted for by variance in ^{2}H (excluding analytical errors)	90%
^{18}O analytical error at baseline (SD)	0.15‰
^{2}H analytical error at baseline (SD)	1.5‰
^{18}O analytical error for enriched samples (SD)	0.5% of value + 0.15‰
^{2}H analytical error for enriched samples (SD)	0.5% of value + 1.5‰
^{18}O background variation (SD)	0.15‰
^{2}H background variation (SD)	1.2‰
Variance in background ^{2}H accounted for by variance in ^{18}O (excluding analytical errors)	100%
Slope of background ^{2}H enrichment on background ^{18}O enrichment	8

^{2}H and ^{18}O, S is the slope of background ^{2}H enrichment on background ^{18}O enrichment, n is the experiment duration in terms of the number of biological half-lives for the ^{2}H isotope, and p is K_O/K_D.

2. Much of the deviation of the ^{2}H and ^{18}O data from the model for the postdose samples is covariant because it relates to inconstancy of water turnover. Errors thus tend to cancel, and this considerably reduces the potential impact of variance from this source.

3. Although the analytical errors applied in this case are not the lowest reported, they are probably typical and it can be seen that they always account for much of the variance.

4. Errors consequent on background uncertainty become very important when amounts of dose are reduced, but in practice, cost always limits the amount of ^{18}O that can be given. For this example, adequate precision in the total energy expenditure(TEE) measurement is predicted for ^{18}O doses producing initial enrichment in the range of 100–150‰ rel V-SMOW.

Protocols

There are, of course, variations depending on the type of subjects to be investigated, and either exclusively urine or saliva samples can be collected. Typically, for adult subjects, after the collection of a predose sample of urine or saliva, they are asked to drink an accurately weighed mixture of the isotopes to give the required enrichment in body water. A small sample of the dose should be retained for isotope analysis. The dose bottle is then rinsed with a further amount of water (≈ 50 ml) and this is also drunk. Most investigators fast their subjects for at least 6 h and may restrict food and water intake during the time when the isotopes are equilibrating in body water. If a plateau method is used for the determination of dilution spaces, the requirement is to collect a sample after equilibration is complete but before turnover begins to reduce enrichment. This will usually require a series of three samples collected at successive hourly intervals between 4 and 8 h. If urine samples are used, the first one should be discarded. A further two samples are collected two or three biological half-lives apart. In most adult cases, experiments will last 14 days; however, for both the timing of the plateau samples and the length of time of the study, it is advisable to establish specific times for the population under investigation. If dilution spaces are to be calculated from the intercept of isotope disappearance curves, postdose samples should begin to be collected on day 1 postdose and on subsequent days during the measurement period. Minimally, samples should be collected at the beginning and end of the measurement period (e.g., days 1, 2, 13, and 14). If a plateau method is used, samples are best collected in the presence of the investigation team, but when the intercept method is used subjects can be instructed to collect, label, and store their own samples. A few ml of urine, or saliva are sufficient for analyses, and should be collected and capped immediately to avoid evaporation and possible contamination. For long-term storage, samples should be stored frozen but may be refrigerated in the short term and need not be frozen for shipping.

Experience suggests that often it is the dose administration and sample collection that cause method failures. A good technique and high precision are needed for enrichment measurements but samples can always be reanalysed. Failures consequent on poor technique in subject-related procedures cannot be rectified and can be costly, especially if they are repeated through a whole investigation. New users of the methodology are advised to test all procedures in pilot work before full-scale application in a study.

Enrichment of samples is best calculated in terms of fraction of the dose given; that is,

$$\left(\frac{18.02d}{TD}\right)\left(\frac{E_S - E_P}{E_D - E_T}\right)$$

where E is isotopic enrichment, d is a weight (g) of dose diluted in T (g) tap water, and D is the weight (g) of dose given. Subscripts S, P, D, and T refer to postdose sample, predose sample, diluted dose, and tap water, respectively. The reciprocal of plateau values is the isotope dilution space (N_D or N_O). The reciprocal of the value at the time zero intercept of a plot of its log value vs time provides alternative dilution space estimates. The slope is the rate constant (K_D or K_O).

Validations and Reproducibility

Comparisons between DLW and calorimetry suggest a precision of 4 or 5%, but it should be remembered that studies of this type are highly controlled and may not properly reflect the real-life situation to which the method is intended to apply. The closest useful estimates are therefore perhaps those provided by an analysis of test/retest situations in which the same subjects were measured in more or less the same physiological conditions. **Figure 5** shows a compilation of such data. Apart from the labourers studied in the tropics, where the precision of the estimates may have been limited by known

high water turnover rates, the data are quite consistent, with a mean of 8%. Subtraction of a likely contribution of 4% from total measurement error suggests a within-subject variation of 7%.

Applications of DLW in Nutrition

DLW and Energy Intake

Examination of the history of DLW in man suggests that there was an expectation that much would be learned in relation to the development of obesity as an outcome of identified long-term positive energy balance. Certainly in the initial phases of its use in human studies in the late 1980s, experimental protocols were most often designed to measure as accurately as possible the differences between energy intake and energy expenditure, but the findings from these experiments invariably exposed the limitations of energy intake measurements. Probably because the DLW concepts were then somewhat alien to conventional nutrition, the notion that intake measurements were more often than not inaccurate and underestimates was not at first easily accepted, but the most recent of several reviews records a very convincing body of evidence (**Figure 6**). However, although exposing a problem, most of these observations by themselves do nothing

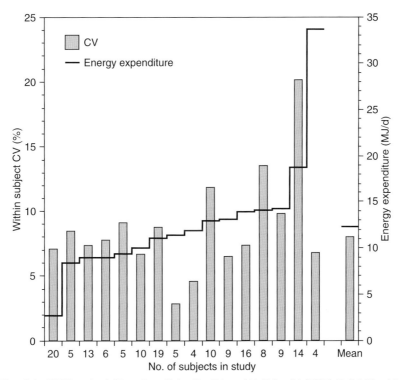

Figure 5   Reproducibility of the DLW method. (Data from Schoeller DA and Hnilicka JM (1996) Reliability of the doubly labeled water method for the measurement of total daily energy expenditure in free-living subjects. *Journal of Nutrition* **126**: 348S–354S.)

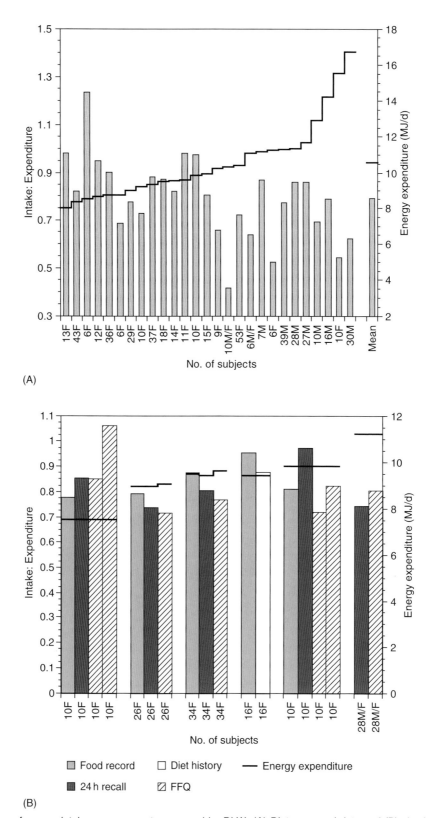

(A)

(B)

□ Food record   □ Diet history   — Energy expenditure

■ 24 h recall   ▨ FFQ

Figure 6 Accuracy of energy intake measurements assessed by DLW. (A) Dietary record data and (B) simultaneous use of more than one instrument. (Data from Trabulsi J and Schoeller DA (2001) Evaluation of dietary assessment instruments against doubly labeled water, a biomarker of habitual energy intake. *American Journal of Physiology (Endocrinology and Metabolism)* **281**: E891–E899.)

to solve it, not least because the studies are too small and indications of the nature and degree of correlation between DLW energy expenditure measurements and intake have not always been reported. The issue of detecting and correcting for bias in food and specific nutrient intake measurements remains a problem to which DLW is being applied as a biomarker of energy intake in large-scale studies.

DLW and Other Noninvasive Energy Expenditure Measurements

Although DLW can be regarded as the reference noninvasive total energy expenditure measurement, isotope cost and the need for mass spectrometric analyses will always limit it to specialist rather than widescale application. There is thus a need to validate or at least understand the limitations of preexisting methodologies and alternatives under development. A significant consideration is that although DLW measurements in an individual include basal metabolic rate as a component of the total expenditure, in alternatives the focus is most often on activities and their energy cost, and basal metabolic rate is measured separately or derived from prediction equations. This means that comparisons of total energy expenditure derived from DLW and the alternatives include a component representing approximately 70% of the total that is not dependent on the activity measurement method. In these circumstances, it is not surprising that activity-based TEE measurements often show good correlation between DLW and on average tend to be similar, but they should be treated with caution with respect to the validity of the activity measurements. Calculation of the energy cost of activity (TEE - resting metabolic rate) for comparison between methods is a much more useful comparison but is not always available.

DLW and Energy Requirements

The energy requirement of an individual is the intake from food that will balance expenditure when an individual has a body size and composition, and level of physical activity, consistent with long-term good health and that will allow for the maintenance of an economically necessary and socially desirable level of physical activity. In principle, these measurements could be obtained from the measurement of food intake or by factorial methods summing estimates of resting metabolic rate with the energy costs of activity. In practice, neither of these approaches is satisfactory; food intake is generally underestimated and no single instrument for the measurement of activity is sufficiently well validated to justify its general use. However, both in the United States (Standing Committee on the Scientific Evaluation of Dietary Reference Intakes) and internationally (FAO/WHO/UNU) the decision has been made to use DLW estimates of energy expenditure to provide the basis for the estimation of requirements. Given the relatively small number of laboratories involved in this work and its relatively short history, it is quite remarkable that sufficient data are available for this exercise. The normative US databases consist of adults ($n = 407$) and children ($n = 525$), obese adults ($n = 360$) and children ($n = 309$), and subsets for pregnant and lactating women. Regression equations derived from the data sets are used to predict requirements.

Conclusions

This article provided insight into how the DLW method works, showed how it should be used, and highlighted three areas in which it is clear that DLW has made, or at least has begun to make, a significant impact on nutrition research. The method is relatively expensive and uses scarce resources in terms of expertise, instruments, and materials. However, where the research requirement matches method capabilities, in terms of accuracy and precision, it is a uniquely effective tool.

See also: **Energy**: Metabolism; Balance; Requirements. **Energy Expenditure**: Indirect Calorimetry.

Further Reading

Ainslie P, Reilly T, and Westerterp K (2003) Estimating human energy expenditure: A review of techniques with particular reference to doubly labelled water. *Sports Medicine* 33: 683–698.

Black AE (2000) The sensitivity and specificity of the Goldberg cut-off for EI:BMR for identifying diet reports of poor validity. *European Journal of Clinical Nutrition* 54: 395–404.

Coward WA and Cole TJ (1991) The doubly labeled water method for the measurement of energy expenditure in humans: Risks and benefits. In: Whitehead RG and Prentice A (eds.) *New Techniques in Nutritional Research*, pp. 139–176. San Diego: Academic Press.

Food and Nutrition Board (2002) Energy. In *Dietary Reference Intakes for Energy, Carbohydrate, Fiber, Fat, Fatty Acids, Cholesterol, Protein, and Amino Acids (Macronutrients)*, pp. 93–206. Washington, DC: National Academies Press.

Jones PJ and Leatherdale ST (1991) Stable isotopes in clinical research: Safety reaffirmed. *Clinical Science (London)* 80: 277–280.

Koletzko B, Sauerwald T, and Demmelmair H (1997) Safety of stable isotope use. *European Journal of Pediatrics* 156(supplement 1): S12–S17.

Lifson N, Gordon GB, and McClintock R (1955) Measurement of total carbon dioxide production by means of $D_2{}^{18}O$. *Journal of Applied Physiology* 7: 704–710.

Prentice AM (ed.) (1990) *The Doubly-Labelled Water Method for Measuring Energy Expenditure*. Vienna: International Atomic Energy Agency.

Schoenheimer R and Rittenberg D (1939) Studies in protein metabolism. I. General considerations in the application of isotopes to the study of protein metabolism. The normal abundance of nitrogen isotopes in amino acids. *Journal of Biological Chemistry* 127: 285–290.

Speakman J (1997) *Doubly Labelled Water: Theory and Practice*. Dordrecht, The Netherlands: Kluwer Academic.

Schoeller DA (2002) Validation of habitual energy intake. *Public Health Nutrition* 5: 883–888.

Schoeller DA and DeLany P (1998) Human energy balance: What have we learned from the doubly labeled water method. *American Journal of Clinical Nutrition* 68: 930S–979S.

Wong WW (2003) Energy utilization with doubly labelled water. In: Abrams SA and Wong WW (eds.) *Stable Isotopes in Human Nutrition*, pp. 85–106. Cambridge, MA: CABI.

EXERCISE

Contents
Beneficial Effects
Diet and Exercise

Beneficial Effects

C Boreham and M H Murphy, University of Ulster at Jordanstown, Jordanstown, UK

This article examines the roles that physical activity, exercise, and fitness may play in the regulation of energy balance and in the etiology of major diseases such as coronary heart disease, cancer, and osteoporosis. Before proceeding, it is necessary to define the key terms of reference. 'Physical activity' can be defined as "any bodily movement produced by skeletal muscles that results in energy expenditure." 'Exercise' (often used interchangeably with 'physical activity') is defined as "physical activity which is regular, planned, and structured with the aim of improving or maintaining one or more aspects of physical fitness." 'Physical fitness' is "a set of outcomes or traits relating to the ability to perform physical activity."

Exercise and Energy Balance

Energy balance occurs when the total energy expenditure of an individual equals his or her total energy intake from the diet. If intake exceeds expenditure the result is an increase in the storage of energy primarily as body fat. If intake is below expenditure, body energy content or body fat decreases.

In humans, energy is expended in three ways: maintaining the physiological functions of the body at rest, often termed resting metabolic rate (RMR); ingesting food and digesting and assimilating nutrients, or the thermic effect of food (TEF); and skeletal muscular contractions involved in spontaneous physical activity or planned exercise. Of these components, the energy expenditure associated with physical activity and exercise is the factor that accounts for the greatest variability between individuals (**Table 1**). In addition, energy expenditure through physical activity is the only component that may be reasonably

Table 1 Estimated daily energy expenditure (approximate) for individuals of different age, weight, gender, and level of activity[a]

Status	Estimated daily energy expenditure (kcal)
Infant, male, age 3 months, body weight 6 kg	760 (3200 kJ)
Child, male, age 4 years, body weight 17 kg	1520 (6400 kJ)
Teenager, male, age 13 years, body weight 46 kg	2200 (9200 kJ)
Sedentary female[b]	1950 (8100 kJ)
Sedentary male[c]	2500 (10 200 kJ)
Female, moderately active[b]	2200 (9200 kJ)
Male, moderately active[c]	3000 (12 500 kJ)
Female, very active[b]	2500 (10 400 kJ)
Male, very active[c]	3200 (13 300 kJ)

[a]Values are based on estimated average requirements from a report by the Committee on Medical Aspects of Food Policy (1991). Dietary reference values are for food energy and nutrients for the *United Kingdom*.
[b]Based on female age 25 years, body weight 60 kg.
[c]Based on male age 25 years, body weight 70 kg.

controlled by an individual, and therefore it may represent an appropriate method for altering energy balance. Physical activity is estimated to make up 5–40% of daily energy expenditure depending on the activity habits of the individual, with RMR and TEF accounting for 60–75 and 10–15%, respectively.

Aside from its direct independent effect on daily energy expenditure, evidence suggests that exercise may also alter RMR, TEF, and the energy expenditure caused by spontaneous physical activity.

Energy Expenditure during Exercise

The magnitude of energy expenditure during exercise is dependent on several factors, including the mode, intensity, and duration of exercise, as well as the body mass of the individual.

When determining the metabolic cost of weight-bearing physical activity, energy expenditure needs to be expressed in relation to body size since a small person will expend less energy performing a given activity (e.g., walking up a flight of stairs) than a larger person performing the same activity. Therefore, to calculate the energy cost of a given activity it is necessary to know the energy cost in kcal (kJ) per kilogram of body weight. The term MET (metabolic equivalent) may also be used to indicate the ratio of the rate of energy expenditure during a given activity to resting metabolic rate (RMR). An example illustrates how METs are used to quantify energy expenditure during exercise. If an individual with a body mass of 70 kg expends 70 kcal (≈300 kJ) per hour at rest (RMR), and walking at a speed of 5.6 km per hour requires 280 kcal (≈1200 kJ) per hour, the energy cost of the activity is 4 METs or four times the RMR of the individual. Since body size is a determinant of both RMR and the energy expenditure during exercise, a heavier individual will have a higher RMR but will still require four times this level of expenditure (or 4 METs) to walk at the same speed. Table 2

Table 2   Energy costs of popular physical activities

Activity	Intensity	METs
Walking	6.4 km h^{-1}	4
Running	10.8 km h^{-1}	11
Cycling	20.9 km h^{-1}	8
Swimming	Front crawl, moderate	8
Tennis	Singles	8
Aerobics	Moderate	6

Adapted from Ainsworth BE, Haskell WL, Leon As *et al.* (1993). Compendium of physical activities: Classification of energy costs of human physical activities. *Medicine and Science in Sports and Exercise* **25**(1): 71–80.

indicates the energy cost in METS of many popular exercise modes.

Energy Expenditure after Exercise

In addition to the additional energy consumed during an exercise bout, several researchers have found that energy expenditure remains elevated for a period following exercise. However, conclusions regarding the magnitude and duration of this postexercise elevation in energy expenditure have been equivocal. Studies have found an increase in energy expenditure in the postexercise period varying in magnitude from 5 kcal (21 kJ) to 130 kcal (546 kJ), with some suggesting that this additional energy expenditure lasts a few minutes and others suggesting that the elevated metabolic rate persists for up to 24 h. The divergence in the findings may be accounted for by the various modes, durations, and intensities of exercise employed in the studies as well as the methods used for measuring alterations in energy expenditure and the confounding effects of food ingestion during the recovery period. In addition, alterations in postexercise energy consumption may exhibit intraindividual variations according to the fitness level of subjects. Several mechanisms underlying this increased energy expenditure during the postexercise period have been postulated, including the energy cost of replenishing fuel stores, the cost of dissipating by-products of adenosine triphosphate (ATP) resynthesis, restoration of cellular homeostasis, and the futile cycling of energy substrates. The magnitude of this increase may be related to the intensity and duration of exercise, with longer or more strenuous activity creating a greater perturbation to homeostasis and therefore causing greater energy expenditure in restoring the body to its preexercise condition.

Effects of Exercise Training on Resting Metabolic Rate

Aside from the transient increase in energy expenditure in the period immediately following exercise, several researchers have examined the chronic effect of exercise on RMR. Although findings are far from consistent, some investigators have found that regular exercise causes a persistent augmentation in RMR. The mechanism for effect has yet to be confirmed, but it has been hypothesized that this increase may be due to the high energy turnover associated with the elevated levels of energy intake and expenditure typical of trained individuals. One beneficial effect of exercise training on resting metabolic rate is the maintenance or increase in lean body mass. As a result of regular resistance exercise, muscle size increases (hypertrophy) or the age-related decline in muscle mass (atrophy) is reduced, contributing to an increase or maintenance of RMR.

Effects of Exercise on the Thermic Effect of Food

The TEF is largely dictated by the composition and energy content of the meal as well as an individual's body composition. However, some studies have indicated that pre- or postprandial exercise may enhance the TEF.

In addition to this acute effect of exercise, regular training may alter the TEF. In males, the thermic effect of a meal is lower in highly trained compared to untrained individuals. In one study, moderate levels of fitness were associated with a greater increase in the TEF than either high or low fitness. The authors suggest that very high or very low levels of fitness may decrease the thermic effect possibly by adaptive mechanisms, such as a lower insulin or lower noradrenaline response to feeding. Interestingly, no equivalent effect has been found in women. Studies on monozygotic twins also suggest a strong genetic factor controlling whether exercise has such an effect.

Effect of Exercise on Energy Expenditure in Spontaneous Physical Activity

In addition to the energy expenditure during planned exercise, other skeletal muscle contraction associated with spontaneous physical activity (including fidgeting) incurs an energy cost. Research indicates that the quantity of energy expended in spontaneous physical activity is highly variable between individuals. Studies show that in addition to its effect on RMR, participation in a planned exercise program increases the energy expenditure of an individual during nonexercising time.

Physiological Adaptations to Exercise Training

Aside from alterations in energy balance, regular exercise brings about many physiological adaptations. The human body is remarkably plastic in response to the increased metabolic demands of exercise training (overload), with many adaptations occurring that enable the body to function more efficiently. The nature and magnitude of these changes are dependent on the volume (duration and frequency), intensity, and type of exercise performed. For this reason, the physiological adaptation to training will be classified according to the nature of the exercise undertaken.

It is important to remember two principles when considering the physiological adaptations to exercise training. First, there is a degree of intraindividual variation in response to exercise training that may be attributed in part to hereditary factors. Second, whereas exercise training will cause adaptation, the removal of this stimulus will result in a reversal of adaptation, or 'detraining.'

Adaptations to Submaximal/Endurance Exercise Training

Submaximal exercise generally refers to an intensity of exercise that requires less than an individual's maximal oxygen uptake. Submaximal exercise challenges the body to deliver and utilise an increased amount of oxygen in the resynthesis of ATP. With training, changes occur that increase the body's ability to utilize oxygen. For simplicity, the adaptations to submaximal exercise training have been grouped according to the site at which they occur.

Central adaptations   Central adaptations to regular submaximal exercise include alterations in the morphology and function of the heart and circulatory systems that allow greater delivery of oxygen to the working muscle.

The pulmonary system in healthy individuals does not provide a significant limitation to exercise, and therefore little alteration in the lung volumes, respiratory rate, or pulmonary ventilation and diffusion occurs as a result of training.

Modest cardiac hypertrophy characterized by an increase in left ventricular volume occurs in response to training. This adaptation allows an increase in stroke volume, leading to a reduction in heart rate at rest and during submaximal workloads and an increased cardiac output during maximal workloads.

Finally, an increase in total plasma volume and an increase in the total amount of hemoglobin have been observed in response to submaximal endurance training.

Peripheral Adaptations

Peripheral adaptations refer principally to changes in the structure and function of skeletal muscle that enhance its ability to use oxygen to produce energy aerobically.

As a result of endurance training, there is an increase in blood supply to the working muscle. This is achieved by an increased capillarization in trained muscles, greater vasodilation in existing muscle capillaries, and a more effective redistribution of cardiac output to the working muscle.

An increase in the activity of aerobic enzymes and an increased mitochondrial volume density (approximately 4–8%) within trained muscle have been noted. These are coupled with increased glycogen storage within the muscle and increased fat mobilization allowing a higher rate of aerobic ATP resynthesis from free fatty acids and glucose.

High-Intensity Exercise and Strength Training

High-intensity exercise requires energy utilization rates that exceed the oxidative capabilities of the muscle. Activities such as sprinting require the anaerobic resynthesis of ATP to produce and maintain high levels of muscular force and are therefore limited in duration. Strength training also relies heavily on anaerobic energy sources and requires high force production by specific muscle groups.

Adaptations to High-Intensity Exercise and Strength Training

The main alterations that occur in response to regular high-intensity exercise or strength training are improvements in the structure and function of the neuromuscular system that allow more efficient production of the forces required for these activities and an enhanced ability to produce the energy required through anaerobic processes.

Neuromuscular The initial improvements in performance that occur with high-intensity exercise training are largely a result of improved coordination of the nervous system. Increased nervous system activation, more efficient neuromuscular recruitment patterns, and a decrease in inhibitory reflexes allow the individual to produce greater levels of force.

The maximum force a muscle can exert is largely determined by its cross-sectional area. In addition to the neural adaptations, strength training stimulates an increase in muscle size. This hypertrophy occurs preferentially in fast twitch muscle fibers and is brought about by increased protein synthesis in response to resistance training. The degree to which muscle hypertrophy occurs is dependent on many factors, including gender and body type. Although some researchers have suggested that strength training may increase the number of muscle cells (hyperplasia), the results of these studies are far from conclusive.

Since both high-intensity and strength training rely largely on anaerobic processes for energy production, adaptive alterations in oxygen delivery and utilization, such as increased capillarization or mitochondrial mass of muscle cells, are relatively minor.

Metabolic In addition to the neuromuscular alterations that occur with high-intensity and strength training, several metabolic adaptations improve the ability of the muscle to resynthesize ATP from anaerobic sources. Intramuscular stores of the anaerobic energy intermediates, such as creatine phosphate (CP) and glycogen, increase after a period of supramaximal training. The activity of enzymes involved in anaerobic production of energy, such as creatine kinase and myokinase, is also increased.

Studies on the Role of Exercise/Fitness in the Etiology of Coronary Heart Disease

Coronary heart disease (CHD) has a multifactorial etiology, and major 'biological' risk factors include elevated concentrations of blood total and low-density lipoprotein (LDL) cholesterol, reduced concentration of high-density lipoprotein (HDL) cholesterol, high blood pressure, diabetes mellitus, and obesity. In addition, 'behavioral' risk factors for CHD include cigarette smoking, a poor diet, and low levels of physical activity and physical fitness associated with the modern, predominantly sedentary way of living. Among these risk factors, a sedentary lifestyle is by far the most prevalent according to data from both the United States and England (**Figure 1**).

Scientific verification of a link between an indolent lifestyle and CHD has been forthcoming during the past 40 years, with the publication of more than 100 large-scale epidemiological studies investigating the relationships between physical activity and cardiovascular health. These studies, some of which are summarized in **Figure 2**, have produced consistently compelling evidence that regular physical activity can protect against CHD.

Pooled data and meta-analyses of the 'better' studies indicate that the risk of death from CHD increases about twofold in individuals who are physically inactive compared with their more active counterparts. Relationships between aerobic fitness and CHD appear to be at least as strong. For example, in a cohort of middle-aged men followed up for an average of 6.2 years, the risk of dying was approximately double in those whose exercise capacity at baseline was <5 METS compared with those whose capacity was >8 METS. For both physical activity and fitness, adjustment for a wide range of other risk factors only slightly weakens these associations, suggesting independent relationships.

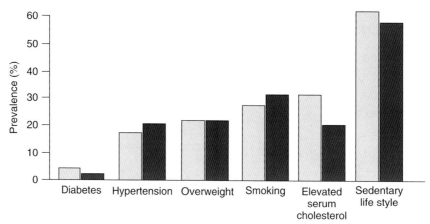

Figure 1   Estimates of the prevalence (%) of the U.S. population with selected risk factors for coronary heart disease and the population from England. In both studies, a sedentary lifestyle was taken as 'no physical activity' or irregular physical activity (i.e., fewer than three times per week and/or less than 20 minutes per session). (From Killoran AJ, Fentem P, and Caspersen C (eds.) (1994) *Moving On. International Perspectives on Promoting Physical Activity.* London: Health Education Authority, with permission.)

A common weakness of such studies is that they often rely on a single measurement of fitness or activity at baseline, with subsequent follow-up for mortality within the cohort. With such a design, it is difficult to discount the possibility that genetic or other confounding factors are influential in the observed relationship between physical activity/ fitness and mortality. A further weakness in single baseline studies is that subsequent changes in activity/ fitness during the follow-up are not monitored, even

though they may affect the observed relationships due to the phenomenon of 'regression to the mean.'

Some prospective studies have overcome these deficiencies by examining the effects of *changes* in physical activity and fitness on mortality. One study reported on the relationship of changes in physical activity and other lifestyle characteristics to CHD mortality in 10 269 alumni of Harvard University. Changes in lifestyle over an 11- to 15-year period were evaluated on the basis of questionnaire

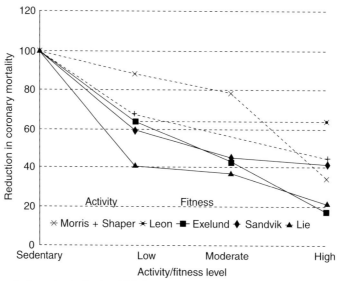

Figure 2   Summary of the results from six studies in which fitness level was determined (three studies) or activity level assessed by questionnaire (three studies) in individual populations. Follow-up was generally between 7 and 9 years except in Sandvik's study, which had a 16-year follow-up. The 'low level' group for each study represented in this figure was the activity/fitness level next to the least active/fit group. The 'high level' represents the group that was the most active/fit for the particular study. If the study participants were grouped by quintile, the 'moderate' group is the average of the third and fourth quintiles. (From Killoran AJ, Fentem P, and Caspersen C (eds.) (1994) *Moving On. International Perspectives on Promoting Physical Activity.* London: Health Education Authority, with permission.)

information, and subsequent mortality was assessed over an 8-year period. In men who were initially sedentary but started participating in moderately vigorous sports (intensity of 4.5 METS or greater), there was a 41% reduced risk of CHD compared to those who remained sedentary. This reduction was comparable to that experienced by men who stopped smoking. The second study examined changes in physical fitness and their effects on mortality. In this study of 9777 men, two clinical examinations (including treadmill tests of aerobic fitness) were administered approximately 5 years apart, with a mean follow-up of 5.1 years after the second examination to assess mortality. Results showed that men who improved their fitness (by moving out of the least fit quintile) reduced their aged-adjusted CHD mortality by 52% compared with their peers who remained unfit. Furthermore, such changes in fitness proved to be the most effective in reducing all-cause mortality when compared with changes in other health risk factors (**Figure 3**).

Mechanisms of Effect

Exercise appears to reduce the risk of CHD through both direct and indirect mechanisms. Regularly performed physical activity may reduce the vulnerability of the myocardium to fatal ventricular arrhythmia and reduce myocardial oxygen requirements. Aerobic training also increases coronary vascular transport capacity via structural adaptations and altered control of vascular resistance. Risk of thrombus formation

may also be reduced with regular exercise through its effects on blood clotting and fibrinolytic mechanisms. Regular endurance exercise may also improve the serum lipid profile (particularly in favor of an enhanced HDL: total cholesterol ratio) and have beneficial effects on adipose tissue lipolysis and distribution. Regular exercise may also reduce postprandial lipemia, increase glucose transport into muscle cells, and improve the elasticity of arteries.

Exercise Prescription

For protection against CHD and other diseases associated with inactivty, exercise needs to be habitual, predominantly aerobic in nature, and current. Evidence from work carried out on British civil servants suggests that to be cardioprotective, exercise should be moderately vigorous ($\geq 7.5\,\text{kcal min}^{-1}$ ($\geq 31.4\,\text{kJ min}^{-1}$) or 6 METS, equivalent to walking at approximately 3 miles per hour up a gradient of 1 in 20) and performed at least twice weekly. However, other studies have indicated that lower intensity activity is also effective as long as the total accumulated exercise energy expenditure is greater than approximately $2000\,\text{kcal week}^{-1}$ ($\geq 8368\,\text{kJ week}^{-1}$).

Thus, recommendations from the U.S. Surgeon General suggest that everyone older than the age of 2 years should accumulate 30 minutes or more of at least moderate-intensity physical activity on most—preferably all—days of the week. Such activity may embrace everyday tasks such as stair climbing and walking, recreational physical activities, and more

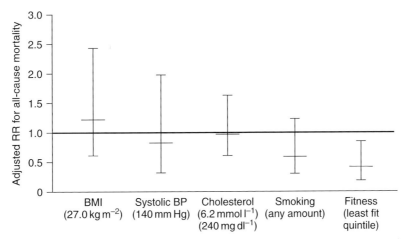

Figure 3 Relative risks (adjusted for age, family history of coronary heart disease, health status, baseline values, and changes for all variables in the figure, and interval in years between examinations) of all-cause mortality by favorable changes in risk factors between first and subsequent examinations. The analyses were for men at risk on each particular variable at the first examination. Cutoff points designating high risk are given parenthetically at the bottom of the figure. The number of men at high risk (and the number of deaths) for each characteristic were as follows: body mass index (BMI), 2691 (66); systolic blood pressure (BP), 1013 (55); cholesterol, 2212 (79); cigarette smoking, 1609 (45); and physical fitness, 1015 (56). (From Blair SN, Kohl HW, Barlow CE, Paffenbarger RS, Gibbons LW, and Macera CA, (1995) Changes in physical fitness and all-cause mortality. A prospective study of healthy and unhealthy men *JAMA*, **273**: 1093–1098, with permission.)

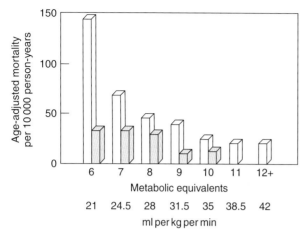

Figure 4 Age-adjusted, all-cause mortality rates per 10 000 person-years of follow-up by physical fitness categories in 3120 women and 10 224 men. Physical fitness categories are expressed as maximal metabolic equivalents (work metabolic rate/resting metabolic rate) achieved during the maximal treadmill exercise test. One metabolic equivalent equals $3.5 \, ml \, kg^{-1} \, min^{-1}$. The estimated maximal oxygen uptake for each category is shown also. (From Blair SN *et al.* (1989) Physical fitness and all-cause mortality. A prospective study of healthy men and women. *Journal of the American Medical Association* **262**: 2395–2401, with permission.)

formal aerobic exercise programs and sports. Intermittent or shorter bouts of activity (of at least 10 minutes duration) may be accumulated throughout the day to confer similar benefits to single, continuous 30-minute bouts of exercise. A consistent finding is that previous exercise that has been abandoned confers no benefit.

Desirable aerobic fitness levels have also been described for women (maximal aerobic power of approximately 9 METs [$32.5 \, ml \, kg^{-1} \, min^{-1}$]) and men (10 METs [$35 \, ml \, kg^{-1} \, min^{-1}$]) (**Figure 4**).

Studies on the Role of Exercise/Fitness in the Etiology of Other Diseases

Obesity

Obesity is defined as an excess of adipose tissue. This condition plays a central role in the development of diabetes mellitus and confers an increased risk for CHD, high blood pressure, osteoarthritis, dyslipoproteinemia, various cancers, and all-cause mortality. The prevalence of obesity has risen dramatically in recent years, despite a decline in daily energy expenditure during the past two decades in the United Kingdom of approximately $800 \, kcal \, day^{-1}$ ($3347 \, kJ \, day^{-1}$).

Based on the principles of energy balance, such circumstantial evidence indicates that physical inactivity may play a central role in the development of obesity in humans. However, confirmatory data are scarce, particularly from well-designed prospective studies. One large-scale national study in the United States evaluated the relationship of physical activity to weight gain over a 10-year follow-up of 3515 men and 5810 women. Individuals who were sedentary at both baseline and follow-up were much more likely (relative risk, 2.3 (95% confidence interval (CI), 0.9–5.8) in men and 7.1 (95% CI, 2.2–23.3) in women) to experience considerable weight gain ($>13 \, kg$) than subjects who were active at both examinations. Evidence suggests that women who gain weight ($\geq 6 \, kg$) over a 1-year period expend on average $212 \, kcal/day$ less in light to moderate activities than those who maintain their normal body weight.

Difficulties are also encountered in interpreting results from intervention studies investigating the effects of exercise and/or diet on body weight, body composition, and resting metabolic rate (the latter being the single greatest component of total energy expenditure). Both energy intake and physical activity are notoriously difficult to quantify accurately, as is body fat status and distribution. Methodological differences between studies, a lack of control for possible confounding factors, and the fact that weight loss leads to an enhanced metabolic economy (due to reductions in RMR, energy cost of physical activity, and the TEF) further complicate matters. Nevertheless, exercise, particularly of the moderate-intensity type such as walking or cycling, probably helps to protect fat-free mass while promoting the loss of fat mass, but it does not appear to prevent the decline in RMR during weight loss. Similarly, long-term physical activity has minimal effects on RMR beyond its effect on lean body mass. Although studies have shown that exercise alone can reduce body weight, due to the lower total energy deficit, the rate and amount of weight loss are less than can be achieved through dieting alone.

Although the combination of exercise and dieting might be expected to improve weight loss, most data show only a modest increase (2 or 3 kg). When the total daily deficit is kept constant, diet, exercise, and diet plus exercise result in similar weight loss, but the inclusion of exercise generally results in greater fat loss and an increased lean tissue mass. There is evidence that the long-term maintenance of weight loss may require more regular activity (approximately double the current guidelines of 30 min/day) than that required to prevent weight gain in the first place. The ideal dietary and exercise prescriptions to control body weight in the long-term remain elusive.

Osteoporosis

Osteoporosis-related fractures represent a major public health concern. Once established, osteoporosis may be irreversible, emphasizing the need for primary prevention strategies based on minimizing bone loss and maximizing peak bone mass. Nearly half the variation in bone mineral density (BMD) may be attributable to nonhereditary factors. Behavioural factors of importance include diet (particularly calcium and vitamin D intakes), smoking, and the amount and type of habitual physical activity. These factors may be particularly influential during adolescence when (depending on the site) up to 90% of adult bone mineral content may be deposited, prior to the attainment of peak bone mass in the third decade of life.

Several studies on the relation of physical activity to BMD have been conducted, allowing a few general conclusions to be drawn. Clearly, bone responds positively to the mechanical stresses of exercise. Regular physical activity is likely to boost peak bone mass in young women, probably slows the decline in BMD in middle-aged and older women, and may increase BMD in patients with established osteoporosis. More research is required to clarify the type and amount of exercise that is most effective for enchancing peak bone mass. Evidence favors relatively high-impact, weight-bearing exercises (such as dancing, jumping, and volleyball), particularly during the peripubertal and adolescent years. It is unclear how physical activity and other intervention strategies, such as calcium supplementation and oestrogen replacement therapy, might interact to promote bone health.

In addition to its osteogenic effects, regular exercise may also promote better coordination, balance, and ambulatory muscle strength, thus minimising the risk of falling. The reported reduced risk of fracture (relative risk, 0.41 in men and 0.76 in women) in active individuals compared to sedentary ones is likely due to these combined direct and indirect effects of physical activity.

Cancer

In general, data relating to associations between physical activity and breast, endometrial, ovarian, prostate, and testicular cancers are inconclusive, although the suggestion that activity in adolescence and young adulthood may provide subsequent protection against breast cancer is worthy of further study. To date, the only clear evidence in this field comes from epidemiological studies relating a reduced risk of cancer of the colon to both occupational and leisure time physical activity. One such study investigated 17 148 Harvard alumni, who were assessed for physical activity at two time points, 10–15 years apart. Those who were highly active (exercise energy expenditure ≥ 2500 kcal $(10\,460$ kJ$) \cdot$ week^{-1}) at both assessments displayed half the risk of developing colon cancer than those who were relatively inactive (≤ 1000 kcal $(4184$ kJ$) \cdot$ week^{-1}). Interestingly, higher levels of physical activity at one (but not both) assessment were not associated with lower cancer risk, suggesting that consistently higher levels of activity may be necessary to provide a measure of protection. Possible biological mechanisms for this association include exercise-induced alteration of local prostaglandin synthesis (particularly prostaglandin F_2-alpha) and a decreased gastrointestinal transit time—the latter possibly decreasing the duration of contact between the colon mucosa and potential carcinogens.

See also: **Bone. Cancer**: Epidemiology and Associations Between Diet and Cancer. **Coronary Heart Disease**: Prevention. **Energy**: Metabolism; Balance. **Energy Expenditure**: Indirect Calorimetry. **Exercise**: Diet and Exercise. **Obesity**: Definition, Etiology and Assessment; Treatment. **Osteoporosis**.

Further Reading

Ainsworth BE, Haskell WL, Leon AS *et al.* (1993) Compendium of physical activities: Classification of energy costs of human physical activities. *Medicine and Science in Sports and Exercise* **25**(1): 71–80.

Booth FW, Gordon SE, Carlson CJ *et al.* (2000) Waging war on modern chronic disease: Primary prevention through exercise biology. *Journal of Applied Physiology* **88**: 774–787.

Bouchard C, Shephard RJ, and Stephens T (eds.) (1994) *Physical Activity, Fitness and Health. International Proceedings and Consensus Statement.* Champaign, Ill, USA, Human Kinetics.

Goya Wannamethee S and Shaper AG (2001) Physical activity in the prevention of cardiovascular disease. An epidemiologocial perspective. *Sports Medicine* **31**(2): 101–114.

McKenna J and Riddoch C (eds.) (2003) *Perspectives on Health and Exercise.* Basingstoke, UK: Palgrave Macmillan.

Melanson EL, Sharp TA, Seagle HM *et al.* (2002) Effect of exercise intensity on 24-h energy expenditure and nutrient oxidation. *Journal of Applied Physiology* **92**: 1045–1052.

Poehlman ET (1989) A review: Exercise and its influence on resting energy metabolism in man. *Medicine and Science in Sports and Exercise* **21**(s): 510–525.

Poehlman ET, Denino WK, Beckett T *et al.* (2002) Effects of endurance and resistance training on total daily energy expenditure in young women: A controlled randomized trial. *Journal of Clinical Endocrinology and Metabolism* **87**: 1004–1009.

Poehlman ET, Melby CL, and Goran MI (1991) The impact of exercise and diet restriction on daily energy expenditure. *Sports Medicine* **11**(2): 78–101.

U.S. Department of Health and Human Services (1996) *Physical Activity and Health: A Report of the Surgeon General.* Atlanta, GA: U.S. Department of Health and Human Services, Centers for Disease Control and Prevention, National Center for Chronic Disease Prevention and Health Promotion.

Diet and Exercise

R J Maughan, Loughborough University, Loughborough, UK

Introduction

At an International Consensus Conference held at the offices of the International Olympic Committee in 1991, a small group of experts agreed a consensus statement that began by saying that "Diet significantly influences exercise performance." That is a bold and unambiguous statement, leaving little room for doubt. However, the statement went on to add various qualifications to this opening statement. These largely reflect the uncertainties in our current knowledge, but also reflect the many different issues that arise in considering the interactions between diet and exercise. Exercise may take many forms and may be undertaken for many different reasons: as the emphasis on physically demanding occupations has decreased in most parts of the world, so participation in recreational exercise and sport have increased. Even though physical activity programs have been heavily promoted in most developed countries, however, they rarely involve more than about 30% of the population, leaving a major part of the population who seldom or never engage in any form of strenuous activity.

In considering the interactions between diet and exercise, two main issues must be considered, each of which gives rise to many subordinate questions. The first question is how altered levels of physical activity influence the body's requirement for energy and nutrients: this then has implications for body composition (including the body content of fat, muscle, and bone), for the hormonal environment and the regulation of substrate metabolism, and for various disease states that are affected by body fatness, nutrient intake, and other related factors. The second question is how nutritional status influences the responses to and the performance of exercise. This has implications for those engaged in physically demanding occupations, and also for those who take part in sport on a recreational or competitive basis.

Influence of Physical Activity on Energy Balance

In the simple locomotor activities that involve walking, running, or cycling, the energy cost of activity is readily determined and can be shown to be a function of speed: where body mass is supported, as in running, or where it must be moved against gravity, as in cycling uphill, then body mass is also an important factor in determining the energy cost. For walking, running, and cycling at low speeds, there is a linear relationship between velocity and energy cost, if the energy cost is expressed relative to body mass. Across a range of speeds, the cost of locomotion is approximately $1 \, kcal \, kg^{-1} km^{-1}$. Therefore, energy expenditure depends on the distance covered and the body mass and is not influenced by walking speed. In purposeful walking, where the aim is to get from one place to another, the distance is set, but where walking is part of a physical activity program, activity is more often measured by time rather than distance, so walking speed becomes an important factor in determining the energy cost. At higher speeds, the relationship between energy expenditure and speed becomes curvilinear and the energy cost increases disproportionately.

It is often recommended that 20–30 min of moderate intensity exercise three times per week is sufficient exercise to confer some protection against cardiovascular disease: if this exercise is in the form of jogging, aerobics, or similar activities, the energy expenditure will be about 4 MJ (1000 kcal) per week for the average 70-kg individual, or an average of only about $150 \, kcal \, day^{-1}$ (**Table 1**). However, even a small daily contribution from exercise to total daily energy expenditure will have a cumulative effect on a long-term basis. For obese individuals, whose exercise capacity is low, the role of physical activity in raising energy expenditure is necessarily limited, but this effect is offset to some degree by the increased energy cost of weight-bearing activity.

Very high levels of daily energy expenditure are now rarely encountered in occupational tasks. The average daily metabolic rate of lumberjacks has

Table 1 Estimated average energy cost of physical activity, expressed as METS (multiples of BMR) and in kJ per kg body mass per h

Activity	MET	$kJ \, kg^{-1} h^{-1}$
Bicycling, leisure	4.0	17
Bicycling, racing $30 \, km \, h^{-1}$, no drafting	16.0	67
Dancing, ballroom	3.0–5.5	13–23
Forestry, fast chopping with axe	17	71
Soccer, casual	7.0	29
Walking, slow	3.5	15
Walking, brisk uphill	5.0–7.0	21–29
Writing, desk work	1.8	7.5

been reported to be about four times the basal metabolic rate, and similar values have been reported for other very demanding occupations, suggesting that this may be close to the upper limit of physical exercise that can be sustained on a long-term basis. In the short term, sporting activities can involve much higher levels of energy output: the world record for distance run in 24 h is 286 km, which requires an energy expenditure of about 80 MJ (20 000 kcal). Such an effort, however, results in considerable depletion of the body's energy reserves, and must be followed by a period of recovery.

For athletes, very high levels of daily energy expenditure are more often a feature of training than of competition, with very high levels of energy intake reported in many sports. Measurements on runners in steady state with regard to training load and body mass show good relationships between energy intake and distance run. There are some competitive events that require high levels of activity to be sustained for many consecutive days, the most obvious examples being the multi-stage cycle tours, of which the most famous is the Tour de France. Measurements on some of the competitors have shown that they manage to maintain body weight in spite of a mean daily energy expenditure of 32 MJ (8000 kcal) sustained over a 3-week period. It was suggested that those cyclists who were unable to meet the daily energy requirement were unable to complete the race.

Measurements of oxygen uptake, heart rate, and other variables made after exercise show that the metabolic rate may remain elevated for at least 12 h and possibly up to 24 h if the exercise is prolonged and close to the maximum intensity that can be sustained. After more moderate exercise, the metabolic rate quickly returns to baseline level. Therefore, it seems likely that the athlete training at near to the maximum sustainable level, who already has a very high energy demand, will find this increased further by the elevation of postexercise metabolic rate: this will increase the difficulties that many of these athletes have in meeting their energy demand. The recreational exerciser, for whom the primary stimulus to exercise is often to control body mass or to reduce body fat content, will not benefit to any appreciable extent from this effect.

The control of food intake in relation to energy expenditure is not well understood, but it is clear that both short-term and long-term regulatory mechanisms exist. These allow the adult body weight to be maintained within fairly narrow limits in spite of wide variations in energy expenditure. It is also clear from the growing prevalence of obesity, that these control mechanisms are not perfect. The acute

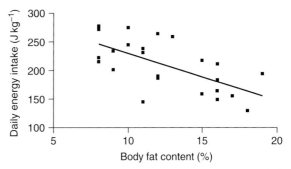

Figure 1 Association between daily energy intake and body fat content. (For further details see Maughan RJ and Piehl Aulin K (1997) Energy needs for physical activity. In: Simopoulos AP and Pavlou KN (eds.) *World Review of Nutrition*, vol. 82, pp. 18–32. Basel: Karger.)

effects of exercise on appetite and energy intake are also unclear. A period of activity may result in a stimulation of the appetite, leading to an increase in the energy intake: the magnitude of the increased intake may exceed the total energy expenditure of the activity itself. There are, however, reports that exercise may lead to a suppression of appetite, and this is likely to be true especially of high-intensity exercise. A modest training program involving energy expenditure of 200 kcal three times per week has been reported to have no effect on energy intake. In the study of distance runners referred to above, there was a negative association between the training load (expressed as distance run per week) and body fat and a positive association between training load and energy intake: this led to a somewhat paradoxical negative association between energy intake and body fat content (**Figure 1**).

Macronutrients and Physical Activity

Protein

The idea that protein requirements are increased by physical activity is intuitively attractive, and high-protein diets are a common feature of the diets of sportsmen and women. The available evidence does show an increased rate of oxidation of the carbon skeletons of amino acids during exercise, especially when carbohydrate availability is low. Protein contributes only about 5% of total energy demand in endurance exercise, but the absolute rate of protein breakdown is higher than at rest (where protein contributes about the same fraction as the protein content of the diet, i.e., typically about 12–16%) because of the higher energy turnover. Most recommendations suggest that individuals engaged in endurance activities on a daily basis should aim to achieve a protein intake of about

$1.2-1.4\,\mathrm{g\,kg^{-1}\,day^{-1}}$, whereas athletes engaged in strength and power training may need as much as $1.6-1.7\,\mathrm{g\,kg^{-1}\,day^{-1}}$. In strength and power sports such as weightlifting, sprinting, and bodybuilding, the use of high-protein diets and protein supplements is especially prevalent, and daily intakes in excess of $4\,\mathrm{g\,kg^{-1}}$ are not unusual. Scientific support for such high intakes is generally lacking, but those involved in these sports are adamant that such high levels of intake are necessary, not only to increase muscle mass, but also to maintain muscle mass. This apparent inconsistency may be explained by Millward's adaptive metabolic demand model, which proposes that the body adapts to either high or low levels of intake, and that this adjustment to changes in intake occurs only very slowly.

Protein synthesis and degradation are both enhanced for some hours after exercise, and the net effect on muscle mass will depend on the relative magnitude and duration of these effects. Several recent studies have shown that ingestion of small amounts of protein (typically about 35–40 g) or essential amino acids (about 6 g) either before or immediately after exercise will result in net protein synthesis in the hours after exercise, whereas net negative protein balance is observed if no source of amino acids is consumed. These observations have led to recommendations that protein should be consumed immediately after exercise, but the control condition in most of these studies has involved a relatively prolonged (6–12 h) period of fasting, and this does not reflect normal behavior. Individuals who consume foods containing carbohydrate and proteins in the hour or two before exercise may not further increase protein synthesis if additional amino acids or proteins are ingested immediately before, during, or after exercise.

Various low-(40%) carbohydrate, high-(30%) fat, high-(30%) protein diets have been promoted for weight loss and athletic performance. Proposed mechanisms include reduced circulating insulin levels, increased fat catabolism, and altered prostaglandin metabolism. These diets can be effective in promoting short-term weight loss, primarily by restricting energy intake (to $1000-2000\,\mathrm{kcal\,day^{-1}}$) and by restricting dietary choice. There is no evidence to support improvements in exercise performance, and what evidence there is does not support the concept.

Carbohydrate

Carbohydrate is stored in the body in the form of glycogen, primarily in the liver (about 70–100 g in the fed state) and in the skeletal muscles (about 300–500 g, depending on muscle mass and preceding diet). These stores are small relative to the rate of carbohydrate use during exercise. Fat and carbohydrate are the main fuels used for energy supply in exercise. In low-intensity exercise, most of the energy demand can be met by fat oxidation, but the contribution of carbohydrate, and especially of the muscle glycogen, increases as the energy demand increases. In high-intensity exercise, essentially all of the energy demand is met by carbohydrate metabolism, and carbohydrate oxidation rates of $3-4\,\mathrm{g\,min^{-1}}$ may be sustained for several hours by athletes in training or competition. When the glycogen content of the exercising muscles reaches very low levels, the work rate must be reduced to a level that can be accommodated by fat oxidation. Repeated short sprints will also place high demands on the muscle glycogen store, most of which can be converted to lactate within a few minutes.

Carbohydrate supplies about 45% of the energy in the typical Western diet: this amounts to about $200-300\,\mathrm{g\,day^{-1}}$ for the average sedentary individual, and is the amount that is necessary to get through normal daily activities. In an hour of hard exercise, up to 200 g of carbohydrate can be used, and sufficient carbohydrate must be supplied by the diet to replace the amount used. Replacement of the glycogen stores is an essential part of the recovery process after exercise; if the muscle glycogen content is not replaced, the quality of training must be reduced, and the risks of illness and injury are increased. Low muscle glycogen levels are associated with an increased secretion of cortisol during exercise, with consequent negative implications for immune function.

Replacement of carbohydrate should begin as soon as possible after exercise with carbohydrate foods that are convenient and appealing, and at least 50–100 g of carbohydrate should be consumed within the first 2 h of recovery. Thereafter, the diet should supply about 5–10 g of carbohydrate per kg body mass, including a mixture of different carbohydrate-rich foods. For athletes preparing for competition, a reduction in the training load and the consumption of a high carboydrate diet in the last few days are recommended: this will maximize the body's carbohydrate stores, and should ensure optimum performance, not only in endurance activities, but also in events involving short-duration high-intensity exercise and in field games involving multiple sprints.

The high-carbohydrate diet recommended for the physically active individual coincides with the recommendations of various expert committees that a healthy diet is one that is high in carbohydrate (at least 55% of energy) and low in fat (less than

30% of energy). However, where energy intake is either very high or very low, it may be inappropriate to express the carbohydrate requirement as a fraction of energy intake. With low total energy intakes, the fraction of carbohydrate in the diet must be high, but the endurance athlete with a very high energy intake may be able to tolerate a higher fat intake.

Fat

Fat is an important metabolic fuel in prolonged exercise, especially when the availability of carbohydrate is low. One of the primary adaptations to endurance training is an enhanced capacity to oxidize fat, thus sparing the body's limited carbohydrate stores. Studies where subjects have trained on high-fat diets, however, have shown that a high-carbohydrate diet during a period of training brings about greater improvements in performance, even when a high-carbohydrate diet is fed for a few days to allow normalization of the muscle glycogen stores before exercise performance is measured. It must be recognized, though, that these short-term training studies usually involve relatively untrained individuals and may not reflect the situation of the highly trained elite endurance athlete where the capacity of the muscle for oxidation of fatty acids will be much higher. For the athlete with very high levels of energy expenditure in training, the exercise intensity will inevitably be reduced to a level where fatty acid oxidation will make a significant contribution to energy supply and fat will provide an important energy source in the diet. Once the requirements for protein and carbohydrate are met, the balance of energy intake can be in the form of fat.

Micronutrients and Physical Activity

Many micronutrients play key roles in energy metabolism, and during strenuous physical activity the rate of energy turnover in skeletal muscle may be increased up to 20–100 times the resting rate. Although an adequate vitamin and mineral status is essential for normal health, marginal deficiency states may only be apparent when the metabolic rate is high. Prolonged strenuous exercise performed on a regular basis may also result in increased losses from the body or in an increased rate of turnover, resulting in the need for an increased dietary intake. An increased food intake to meet energy requirements will increase dietary micronutrient intake, but individuals who are very active may need to pay particular attention to their intake of iron and calcium.

Iron deficiency anemia affects some athletes engaged in intensive training and competition, but it seems that the prevalence is the same in athletic and sedentary populations, suggesting that exercise *per se* does not increase the risk. The implications of even mild anemia for exercise performance are, however, significant. A fall in the circulating hemoglobin concentration is associated with a reduction in oxygen-carrying capacity and a decreased exercise performance. Low serum ferritin levels are not associated with impaired performance, however, and iron supplementation in the absence of frank anemia does not influence indices of fitness.

Osteoporosis is now widely recognized as a problem for both men and, more especially, women, and an increased bone mineral content is one of the benefits of participation in an exercise program. Regular exercise results in increased mineralization of those bones subjected to stress and an increased peak bone mass may delay the onset of osteoporotic fractures; exercise may also delay the rate of bone loss. Estrogen plays an important role in the maintenance of bone mass in women, and prolonged strenuous activity may result in low estrogen levels, causing bone loss. Many very active women also have a low body fat content and may also have low energy (and calcium) intakes in spite of their high activity levels. All of these factors are a threat to bone health. The loss of bone in these women may result in an increased predisposition to stress fractures and other skeletal injury and must also raise concerns about bone health in later life. It should be emphasized, however, that this condition appears to affect only relatively few athletes, and that physical activity is generally beneficial for the skeleton.

Water and Electrolyte Balance

Few situations represent such a challenge to the body's homeostatic mechanisms as that posed by prolonged strenuous exercise in a warm environment. Only about 20–25% of the energy available from substrate catabolism is used to perform external work, with the remainder appearing as heat. At rest, the metabolic rate is low: oxygen consumption is about $250 \, ml \, min^{-1}$, corresponding to a rate of heat production of about 60 W. Heat production increases in proportion to metabolic demand, and reaches about 1 kW in strenuous activities such as marathon running (for a 70-kg runner at a speed that takes about $2\frac{1}{2}$ h to complete the race). To prevent a catastrophic rise in core temperature, heat loss must be increased correspondingly and this is achieved primarily by an increased rate of evaporation of sweat from the skin surface. In hard exercise in hot conditions, sweat rates can reach $3 \, l \, h^{-1}$, and trained athletes can sustain sweat rates in excess of $21h^{-1}$ for many hours. This represents a much higher fractional turnover rate of water than that of most other body components. In the sedentary individual living in a temperate climate, about 5–10% of total body water may be lost and replaced on a daily basis. When prolonged exercise is performed in a hot environment, 20–40% of total body water can be turned over in a single day. In spite of this, the body water content is tightly regulated, and regulation by the kidneys is closely related to osmotic balance.

Along with water, a variety of minerals and organic components are lost in variable amounts in sweat. Sweat is often described as an ultrafiltrate of plasma, but it is invariably hypotonic. The main electrolytes lost are sodium and chloride, at concentrations of about $20-70 \, \text{mmol} \, l^{-1}$, but a range of other minerals, including potassium and magnesium, are also lost, as well as trace elements in small amounts. When sweat losses are high, there can be a substantial electrolyte loss, and intake must increase accordingly.

Failure to maintain hydration status has serious consequences for the active individual. A body water deficit of as little as 1% of total body mass can result in a significant reduction in exercise capacity. Endurance exercise is affected to a greater extent than high-intensity exercise, and muscle strength is not adversely affected until water losses reach 5% or more of body mass. Hypohydration greatly increases the risk of heat illness, and also abolishes the protection conferred by prior heat acclimation.

Many studies have shown that the ingestion of fluid during exercise can significantly improve performance. Adding an energy source in the form of carbohydrate confers an additional benefit by providing an energy source for the working muscles. Addition of small amounts (perhaps about 2–8%) of carbohydrate, in the form of glucose, sucrose, or maltodextrin, will promote water absorption in the small intestine as well as providing exogenous substrate that can spare stored carbohydrate. The addition of too much carbohydrate will slow gastric emptying and, if the solution is strongly hypertonic, may promote secretion of water into the intestinal lumen, thus delaying fluid availability. Voluntary fluid intake is seldom sufficient to match sweat losses, and a conscious effort to drink is normally required if dehydration is to be avoided. Palatability of fluids is therefore an important consideration. If exercise is prolonged and sweat losses high, the addition of sodium to drinks may be necessary to prevent the development of hyponatremia. Ingestion of large volumes of plain water is also likely to limit intake because of a fall in plasma osmolality leading to suppression of thirst.

Replacement of water and electrolyte losses incurred during exercise is an important part of the recovery process in the postexercise period. This requires ingestion of fluid in excess of the volume of sweat lost to allow for ongoing water losses from the body. If food containing electrolytes is not consumed at this time, electrolytes, especially sodium, must be added to drinks to prevent diuresis and loss of the ingested fluid.

Dietary Supplementation for Active Individuals

The use of nutritional supplements in athletes and in the health-conscious recreationally active population is widespread, as it is in the general population. A very large number of surveys have been published. A meta-analysis of 51 published surveys involving 10 274 male and female athletes of varying levels of ability showed an overall prevalence of supplement use of 46%, but the prevalence varies widely in different sports, at different levels of age, performance etc., and in different cultural backgrounds.

A wide variety of supplements are used with the aim of improving or maintaining general health and exercise performance. In particular, supplement use is often aimed at promoting tissue growth and repair, promoting fat loss, enhancing resistance to fatigue, and simulating immune function. Most of these supplements have not been well researched, and anyone seeking to improve health or performance would be better advised to ensure that they consume a sound diet that meets energy needs and contains a variety of foods.

See also: **Anemia**: Iron-Deficiency Anemia. **Appetite**: Physiological and Neurobiological Aspects. **Bone**. **Carbohydrates**: Chemistry and Classification; Regulation of Metabolism; Requirements and Dietary Importance. **Electrolytes**: Water–Electrolyte Balance. **Energy**: Balance. **Exercise**: Beneficial Effects. **Fats and Oils**. **Osteoporosis**. **Protein**: Synthesis and Turnover; Requirements and Role in Diet. **Sports Nutrition**. **Supplementation**: Dietary Supplements; Role of Micronutrient Supplementation; Developing Countries; Developed Countries.

Further Reading

American College of Sports Medicine, American Dietetic Association, and Dietitians of Canada (2000) Joint Position Statement: Nutrition and athletic performance. *Medicine and Science in Sports and Exercise* 32: 2130–2145.

Devlin JT and Williams C (1992) *Foods, Nutrition and Sports Performance*. London: E and FN Spon.

Henriksson J and Hickner RC (1998) Adaptations in skeletal muscle in response to endurance training. In: Harries M, Williams C, Stanish WD, and Micheli LJ (eds.) *Oxford Textbook of Sports Medicine*, 2nd edn, pp. 45–69. Oxford: Oxford University Press.

Ivy J (2000) Optimization of glycogen stores. In: Maughan RJ (ed.) *Nutrition in Sport*, pp. 97–111. Oxford: Blackwell.

Kiens B and Helge JW (1998) Effect of high-fat diets on exercise performance. *Proceedings of the Nutrition Society* 57: 73–75.

Maughan RJ (1999) Nutritional ergogenic aids and exercise performance. *Nutritional Research Review* 12: 255–280.

Maughan RJ and Murray R (eds.) (2000) *Sports Drinks: Basic Science and Practical Aspects.* Boca Raton: CRC Press.

Maughan RJ and Piehl Aulin K (1997) Energy needs for physical activity. In: Simopoulos AP and Pavlou KN (eds.) *World Review of Nutrition,* vol. 82, pp. 18–32. Basel: Karger.

Millward DJ (2001) Protein and amino acid requirements of adults: current controversies. *Canadian Journal of Applied Physiology* 26: S130–S140.

Nieman DC and Pedersen BK (1999) Exercise and immune function. *Sports Medicine* 27: 73–80.

Noakes TD and Martin D (2002) IMMDA-AIMS advisory statement on guidelines for fluid replacement during marathon running. *New Studies in Athletics* 17: 15–24.

Shirreffs SM and Maughan RJ (2000) Rehydration and recovery after exercise. *Exercise and Sports Science Reviews* 28: 27–32.

Williams C (1998) Diet and sports performance. In: Harries M, Williams C, Stanish WD, and Micheli LJ (eds.) *Oxford Textbook of Sports Medicine*, 2nd edn, pp. 77–97. Oxford: Oxford University Press.

Wolfe RR (2001) Effects of amino acid intake on anabolic processes. *Canadian Journal of Applied Physiology* 26: S220–S227.

FAMINE

K P West Jr, Johns Hopkins University,
Baltimore, MD, USA

There are so many hungry people, that God can not
appear to them except in the form of bread.
Mahatma Gandhi

Famines in History

Famine has afflicted humankind, shaping its demo-
graphy and history from antiquity. Records of famine in ancient Egypt during the third millennium BC
are depicted in bas-relief on the Causeway of the
Pyramid of Unas in Saqqura. Biblical accounts of a
famine resulting from drought in Egypt during the
second millennium BC (Middle Kingdom) that
stretched to Mesopotamia describe the devastation
wrought on the land and society and the means by
which Joseph predicted and managed its consequences. The fall of the Roman Empire followed
repeated food shortages and famines from 500 BC
to 500 AD. China experienced some 1828 famines,
nearly one per year, from 108 BC to 1911 AD. The
ranks of the Crusades in the eleventh and twelfth
centuries swelled in response to promise of food.
The storming of the Bastille and French Revolution
followed decades of periodic rises in flour and bread
prices that had caused widespread hunger and hardship, and hundreds of 'food riots.'

Recurrent famine motivated the settling of the
New World. The Great Irish Famine in the late
1840s caused one and a half million deaths and an
equal number of migrations, mostly to America.
Decades of Russian famines following crop failures
in the late nineteenth century resulted in waves of
immigration to the US. Repeated famines led to the
overthrow of Czarist Russia that ushered in the
Bolshevik Revolution in the early twentieth century.
Using food deprivation to wage class warfare and
crush the Cossack revolution in the 1930s, Stalinist
policies led to the starvation and death of 3.5 million
Ukrainians. In China, multiple famines throughout the
nineteenth century reportedly led to over 50 million
deaths, and these continued throughout the first
half of the twentieth century. Maoist communism
rose to power in the 1940s understandably amidst
promises of land reform and freedom from chronic
hunger and periodic famine. However, collectivization of private farms and irrational rural industrialization schemes coupled with monopolistic control
of food grain movement, purchase and access, abu-
sive taxation, and repressive policies against the
peasantry left China mostly food insecure throughout the 1950s and primed for what has turned out
to be the worst single famine in human history
(1959–60). During this period an estimated 30 million people perished, in absence of worldview and
reaction, following the secretive, cultist policy failures of Mao's 'Great Leap Forward.' Famine was
notorious on the Indian subcontinent throughout
the mid-twentieth century, with the two final famines both occurring in Bengal in 1943, towards the
end of British rule and again in Bangladesh (formerly East Bengal) in 1974–75. An India free from
overt famine over the past half-century, despite
continuing chronic undernutrition, has been attributed, in part, to the country's economic rise, relative peace, and democratic and popular processes
that have included political accountability and a
flourishing free press; lessons that still remain to
be learnt by some modern states. In North Korea,
for example, the effects of repeated floods in the
late 1990s that ruined crops, combined with isolation, a collapsed centralized economy, and politicization and diversion of already insufficient
international food aid from those most in need led
to famine of devastating proportion.

In the late twentieth century famines have
inflicted heavy loss of life in Africa, especially in
the Greater Horn (i.e., Ethiopia, the Sudan, and
Somalia). At least one modern regime's demise,
that of Emperor Haile Selassie in 1974, followed
famine. Famines of seemingly increased complexity

in Africa have resulted from deteriorating crop production associated with steady rainfall decline, failures in development and commerce, repressive and corrupt governance, and armed conflict leading, at times, to outright anarchy. Tragically, famines over the past 30 years have occurred at a time in human history when general understanding of causes and consequences of famine, and a global ability to monitor antecedents and intervene to avert mass starvation, disease, and death have never been greater. Yet, with conflict, especially internal civil war, rising as the decisive and yet unpredictable trigger of modern famine, stable governance with democratic processes (e.g., free press, people's participation, fair trade, etc.) is increasingly recognized to be one of the most important means for its prevention. History has increased awareness and understanding of the need for a stable, peaceful, and equitable political economy to guide the developing world away from famine in the twenty-first century.

Definition of Famine

Definitions of famine vary but all contain the necessary elements of widespread inaccessibility to food leading to mass numbers of starved individuals. Importantly, lack of access is not equivalent to non-availability of food within a region, as most famines occur amidst food stocks sufficient to feed the afflicted population. More comprehensive definitions of famine may include elements of time dependency (e.g., steady, continuous erosion of or sudden collapse in food available for consumption), partial causation (e.g., due to natural calamity, armed conflict, or convergence of other complex causal events), class (e.g., affecting certain ethnic, geographic, economic or occupational groups more than others), and health consequence on a population scale (e.g., accompanied by epidemics of disease and high mortality) or other population responses (e.g., mass migration). While poverty-stricken communities tend to view famine as a continuum of increasing loss and oppression that typically begins long before mass casualty, formal 'external' definitions tend to invoke thresholds or shocks involving sudden inflections in trends for events that afflict large numbers of people. These may include spikes in prices of staple grains, levels of violence, destitution, mortality from starvation and infectious disease, and migratory movement. Threshold events tend to distinguish famine, which upon declaration demands a massive relief response, from endemic, chronic food deprivation, which results from extreme poverty, political corruption, developmental

neglect and food insecurity and which leads to chronic, high rates of malnutrition, disease, and mortality. Yet, these factors are ones that, often when acting together, predispose underserved populations of the developing world to risk of famine. Such conditioning factors are antecedent causal elements that require more continuous, sensitive, and specific indicators to detect as well as a set of longer term economic, political, and developmental solutions to prevent. Whether continuous and evolving or more sudden, unleashed famine – where thresholds have been transgressed by masses of people – is catastrophic, distinct, and a human tragedy of unparaleled proportion.

Causes of Famine

> Starvation is a matter of some people not having enough food to eat, and not a matter of there being not enough food to eat.
>
> Amartya Sen

Large numbers of people starve during famine, which is usually followed by epidemics of lethal infectious diseases. Typically, a plethora of forces or conditions act within society to deprive people of food to survive. General food decline in a population may be an important factor, but it is neither necessary nor sufficient as a cause, as amply revealed by critical treatises of numerous famines over the past two centuries. This has led analysts to recognize that famines are complex, often with many ('component') causes that vary in their attribution, depending on the classes of society affected, and their timing, severity, duration, and degree of interaction. The constellation of causes and potential solutions of famine can be examined from ecological, economic, social, and public health perspectives, each offering different insights into the ecology of famine. While each view is valid and informative, none are complete or mutually exclusive, making it necessary to integrate these diverse perspectives to understand the complexity of famine and approaches to its prevention. In offering an epidemiologic overview, there appear to be at least three dominant causes of famine that have emerged during the nineteenth and twentieth centuries that appear particularly relevant to understanding modern famine causation (**Figure 1**): (1) market failure; (2) armed conflict; and (3) failure in central planning. Importantly, none are sole-acting causes and, therefore, for each one there are other antecedent factors, sometimes operative for years before, as well as concurrent and late-acting components that together lead to famine.

Market failure

Great Bengal
Famine of 1943

Bangladesh Famine
of 1974

Ethiopia and Sudan
Famines of 1984–85

War or armed conflict

Dutch Hunger
Winter of 1944

Somalian Famine
of 1991–92

Central plan failure

Ukraine Famine of
1933–34

Great Leap Famine
of 1959–60

North Korea
Famine of 1997–98

Figure 1 Complex causal networks of selected modern famines, stratified by a dominant cause. Each pie illustrates a complete cause; each wedge illustrates an assumed, essential component cause, without any one of which famine would not occur. Inclusion of causes based on literature reviews; sizes of pie slices are subjective based on descriptions in the literature (causal concepts adapted from Rothman and Greenland, 1998). A: market failure – loss of direct or trade entitlement through a combination of: (1) increased food prices due to food shortage from decreased agricultural production or importation, hoarding and speculation, or other market forces leading to unfavorable terms of exchange; plus (2) loss of means to command food through cash, labor, credit, and other assets (endowment) by vulnerable groups of society. B: war or armed conflict – declared or internal; through siege, blockade, or other expression of force, during a time course leading up to and concurrent with famine. C: central plan failure – occurring within centrally planned states lacking democratic processes, notably in twentieth century communist states; directives that disrupt infrastructure, productivity, and economic well-being, and access to food through heavy taxation, extraction of food grains, livestock and other productive assets and terror, or restrict movement of food stocks outside free-market dynamics, leading to starvation of the masses. D: natural disaster – climatological and environmental catastrophes including floods, or single, repeated or chronic droughts. E: food availability decline – food shortage resulting from poor crop production, lack of trade, poor food transport, storage and marketing sytems. F: weak infrastructure – inadequate systems of finance, credit, roads, communications, agricultural production including irrigation or flood protection systems. G: poor/unstable governance – weak and ineffective forms of governance, including anarchy. H: inadequate aid response/administrative mismanagement – inadequate national or international counter-famine measures, including employment or food procurement policies as well as withheld, slow, ineffectual, or insufficient relief. I: other causes – a catch-all 'causal complement' to those listed above, of interacting prefamine and intrafamine sociological, governmental, environmental, and market forces that render each famine unique.

Market Failure

Market failure famines occur when free, competitive market forces, driven by agriculture, transportation, communication and trade, and enabled by an abiding government fail to assure minimal entitlement to food, either directly (through subsistence) or via trade for a large sector of society. Following Amartya Sen, entitlement failure is an economic phenomenon, broadly defined, in which individuals and households are

unable to obtain sufficient amounts of food through all available legal means (cash, labor, skills, credit, and other assets that comprise 'endowment') at the market's existing terms of exchange (costs of securing sufficient amounts of food). Combinations of loss of endowment and adverse shifts in the conditions of exchange (e.g., spikes in grain prices) can lead to certain classes of society being severely deprived of food. Component causes that lead to market failure-driven famine are complex, interacting over an extended time

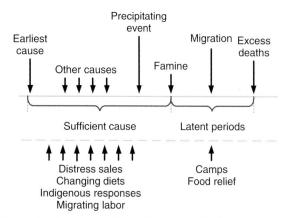

Figure 2 A model depicting actions of individual, or component, causes that can lead to a sufficient cause of famine, and societal, indigenous responses to famine predominantly caused by market failure. Famine may be latent or delayed from external view until migrations or excess deaths occur. Government relief is typically a late response to famine.

(**Figure 2**). Causes acting at various times in the pathway to market failure can be numerous, including long- and short-term adversity in climate leading to drought and excessive floods, pestilence and other causes of lost crop yield, reduced food imports or inefficient transport and marketing infrastructures. These all can lead to a national or, more often, regional declines in food availability, inflationary grain market responses to speculation and hoarding, other aspects of infrastructural neglect, ineffectual trade policies, political instability and corrupt governance, market depressions with year-round or seasonal job losses, and depletion of assets of the poor (endowment). Prior or present conflict can destabilize markets and contribute to such types of famine. Famines that can be classified as those primarily of market failure include the Great Irish Famine from 1844 to 1848, the Great Bengal Famine of 1943, the Bangladesh famine of 1974, and the Sudan famine of 1984–85. The Great Irish Famine was triggered by a potato blight that stripped the country of the only staple that Irish peasantry could afford to grow on their small parcels of land. Peasants who grew other staple grains had to sell them to pay rent to landlords. However, during these same years, there were substantial exports of wheat, barley, oats, and animal products by landowners to English markets. Food did not enter the local Irish markets because the peasants lacked effective demand.

Market or entitlement failures marked the last two great Bengal famines of the twentieth century: The Great Bengal Famine of 1943 and the Bangladesh Famine of 1974–75 (**Figure 1**). The 1943 famine, during which some 3 million people are estimated to have died, was originally judged by a Famine Inquiry Commission to be due to a shortage in rice

supply. However, a seminal in-depth analysis years later by Sen showed that the famine occurred in a year during which rice production in Bengal was only 5% lower than the average of the previous 5 years. It was also a year when most economic indicators of Bengal were showing a 'boom' in growth due to World War II. Rural food stocks were being procured by the government to support military needs, subsidize rations for civil servants, and stabilize general prices of rice in Calcutta, which drove up the price of rice in rural areas. This practice, coupled with 'boat blockade' and 'rice denial' policies imposed in regions along the Bay of Bengal for reasons of defense, left certain low wage-earning rural classes (agricultural workers, day laborers, artisans, and fishermen) disentitled, and unable to acquire enough food for their own survival.

In Bangladesh, at least 100 000 people died between 1974 and 1975 in a famine that followed an unusually severe flood. During the several years leading up to the famine there were events that brought the country to a highly vulnerable state, including a devastating cyclone and tidal wave, a civil war that led to the country's independence, and a series of partial crop failures, all superimposed on preexisting high burdens of malnutrition, disease, underdevelopment, and ensuing political chaos. The flood in the middle of 1974 was expected to destroy much of the major 'aman' rice to be harvested a few months later. In anticipation of impending rice shortage, rural traders began to hoard grains in early September of that year causing rice prices to spike across the country's rural markets in a contagious pattern (**Figure 3**). Rice prices remained at about twice their normal level for months thereafter, even after it became evident that the speculated poor rice harvest was, in fact, a normal one. Thus, total and per capita aggregate grain supplies in Bangladesh remained at about average levels throughout the famine. Local area food deficits and hoarding of grains by traders led to the observed points of inflection in the price of rice throughout the country that caused the entitlements of rural wage earners to collapse, initiating a famine that resulted in extremely high mortality and massive migrations to urban centers in search of relief.

The Horn of Africa has been wracked by famine or famine-like conditions, leading to what have become classically defined as 'complex emergencies' for much of the past three decades. Aggregate food shortage has appeared to play a more variable and, at times, prominent role in recent famines in the eastern Horn. In Ethiopia, Sudan, Eritrea, and Somalia large tracts of land are drought-prone, average annual rainfall has been declining since the

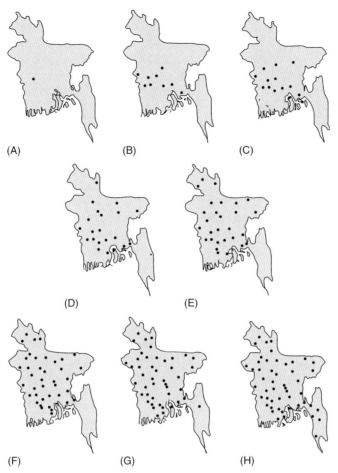

Figure 3 Consecutive weekly maps of a contagious spread of spikes in the price of rice in local markets throughout rural Bangladesh from (A) late August 1974 through to (H) the end of October 1974 during a flood-associated period of a famine that reportedly killed from 100 000 to 1 million persons. (Adapted from Seaman J and Holt J (1980) Markets and famines in the third world. *Disasters* **4**(3): 283–297.)

1930s, and robust, indigenous farming and animal husbandry practices have been weakened as agricultural land has increasingly been used for growing export crops. In the Ethiopian famine of 1972–75, in which over 100 000 people died, national crop production dropped to only ~7% below normal levels, a decline that, like in Bengal in 1943 and 1974, would not have been expected to trigger a famine. However, crop production had been severely below normal in Wollo Province, where the famine began. Although the famine subsequently spread to other areas of the country, a reluctance by the government to formally recognize the famine and excessive delays in mobilizing and targeting food aid within country (whether from national or international stocks) were deemed responsible for unleashing a famine that, based on national stocks, should have been averted. Famines during 1982–85 in Ethiopia and the Sudan appeared to be more closely tied to gradual declines in national food security during the preceding decade. These trends were exacerbated by repressive governments enacting targeted, famine-promotive rather than preventive policies, resulting in civil wars and severely deteriorating economic conditions that were compounded by weak international food aid responses.

Armed Conflict

A second major class of famine comprises those precipitated or triggered by declared war or armed insurgency, leading to a siege or food blockade by a foreign power (e.g., Allied blockade of Germany in 1915–18; Nazi blockade of Holland precipitating the Dutch Winter Famine of 1944–45, and the Nazi siege of Lenningrad in 1942–44) or, as occurring more in recent years, severe civil war that disrupts normal markets as well as emergency food delivery systems (e.g., the Somalian civil war and famine of 1991–92). Armed conflict can incapacitate or destroy a country's ability to govern, develop, produce and feed itself domestically or through food aid, as scores of people become displaced, destitute, starve and die from severe malnutrition and epidemic illness. The famine in Somalia in the early 1990s exemplifies the rapid emergence of military conflict as a precipitating cause of famine. With significant transfers of weaponry to rogue vigilante groups and increased deployments of land mines in other poor, warring countries in recent years, civil violence and lawlessness also pose a major hindrance to the effective provision of short-term relief during the acute phase of famine and to subsequent economic recovery.

Failure in Central Planning

A third class of modern famine, distinct from the other two, has resulted from failure by intent, indifference, ignorance, or incompetence of a centrally planned state to adequately provide food to all sectors of society, often as a result of totalitarian action to advance political goals outside of the rules of free trade or popular processes. Examples of this third type of famine in the twentieth century include those induced by the notorious policies of Stalin in Soviet Russia in the 1920s and 1930s. In an effort to achieve rapid industrial growth, Stalin waged class warfare among rural peasantry, abolished economic incentives, collectivized farms into massive (inefficient) production units and merged villages into socialist agro-towns, seized and exported grain for foreign exchange to fuel industrialization, restricted population movements across municipalities, and brutally suppressed all opposition. Agricultural production plummeted across regions of Russia leading to disastrous shortages (e.g., by 40% in some areas), further intensifying state seizures of food grain, especially in the grain-belt region of the Ukraine where Stalin sought to crush a nationalist revolt by forcibly extracting available food grains from the population. The actions induced the worst famine in Russian history. Between 1930 and 1937 it was estimated that nearly 15 million peasants died, of whom 7–8 million died in the Ukraine in 1933–34.

Under communist rule imposed by Mao Zedong, in 1959–60 China experienced the worst recorded famine in human history that left an estimated 30 million people dead. The Great Leap Famine was provoked through a causal chain of centrally planned policy steps during the preceding decade, modeled after Stalin and motivated by ill-conceived goals to 'Leap forward' MAO's aims were to achieve agricultural sufficiency and superiority through massive agricultural collectivization and the formation of huge peasant communes, and rapid rural industrialization through crash programs to increase steel production. The plight of tens of millions of rural peasants was tightly controlled by the state through brutal force, terror, propaganda, and state control of grain production, procurement and taxation motivated by a blind faith among civil servants in the vision and leadership of Mao. As a result of fabricated inflation of grain production figures, driven by a zeal to demonstrate success, China became a net exporter of more than a million metric tons of grain during the peak of famine mortality in the countryside in 1960, mimicking Stalinist Russia. Thus, in addition to events immediately leading to famine, some component causes contributing to the centrally planned Great Leap Famine can be traced back through the previous one to three decades and to influences beyond the borders of China.

Communist North Korea's inability to avert famine in 1997–98 amounts to the most recent example of a central planning failure, conditioned by chronic food insecurity over the previous decade and precipitated by poorly timed, torrential rains and floods in 1995–96 and drought in 1997. However, some causal elements related to how slowly and secretively the isolationist government responded, actions of governance that date back to the Korean War and Cold War politics, and politicization of food aid.

Coping Strategies

Most is known about household and community coping mechanisms in response to famines due to market failure. In cultures where food shortage or inaccessibility to large sectors of society is chronic, and threat of famine periodic, there exist indigenous responses that enable the local populace to cope, protect their entitlement, and minimize as best it can the risk of starvation as terms of exchange for food deteriorate (illustrated as a concept in **Figure 4**).

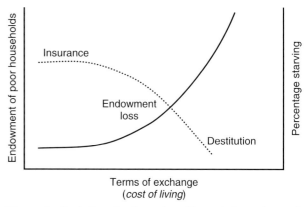

Figure 4 Illustration of collapse in entitlement. As endowment of the poor decreases toward a state of destitution with increasingly severe (costly) terms of exchange for food, the risk of starvation and famine increases.

A first line of responses may be viewed as 'insurance' against uncertainty; these are activities that can stem loss of endowment, such as restructuring the mix of crops grown or pastoral practices in ways that insulate against drought- or flood-induced shortages. Examples include planting more robust crops, dispersing crops across a wider area, staggering plantings, or increasing livestock diversity and mobility. Food preservation practices and dietary changes to include less commonly eaten foods can initially increase the size and diversity of the food base. As terms of exchange become worse, coping mechanisms aimed at survival increasingly cost households their endowment. These responses include working longer and at different jobs for lower wages, migrating far from home to find marginal work, reducing meal frequency, consuming the next planting's seeds, and expanding intake to include 'famine foods' poor in, or lacking, nutritional quality. At first these may include unusual tubers, leaves, flowers, and other plants. Household assets such as pots, utensils, watches, and small animals are increasingly sold as, eventually, are larger assets such as bullock carts, bicycles, and draft animals. Land mortgage or sales transactions become more numerous. With indebtedness and destitution, petty crime and child abandonment increase; famine foods may include tree bark, ground bone, and rodents; suicide and cannablism may occur. An indicator of severe entitlement loss in a community is the livestock-to-grain price ratio in local markets. Normally this ratio is of a figure that reflects the greater asset value of livestock compared to grain. However, it may invert as the cost of grain and feeding animals and the level of animal wasting all continue to rise, such that, at a peak of famine vulnerability, large numbers of animals may be sold at very low prices relative to the costs of grain.

Viewed over time, famine is a continuum. As household and community entitlements erode for increasing numbers due both to deteriorating conditions of exchange and endowment loss, destitution and starvation become more likely. **Figure 5** depicts a hypothetical shift in distribution of starving individuals in a poor population exposed to increasing risk of famine, where under usual conditions a small proportion of individuals routinely face the threat of starvation and wasting malnutrition (top panel). During periods of high or repeated stress, such as those of prolonged drought and internal conflict, while the population faces less food security coping mechanisms continue to protect most vulnerable groups from abject starvation, even as they near such a 'threshold' amidst inevitable losses of human and economic asset (middle

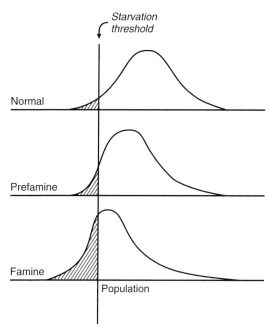

Figure 5 Shifting of a high-risk, undernourished population toward increased starvation during prefamine and famine conditions, particularly those most vulnerable. Truncated left tail area reflects hypothetical effects of coping strategies that prevent starvation. Right skew reflects polarizing of wealth, with some sectors profiting from famine.

panel). During severe distress of famine, entitlement has collapsed for the most vulnerable classes of society, pushing large numbers of persons into a state of starvation, leaving them destitute and migrating or dying (bottom panel). However, not all individuals starve. Some segments of society lose little or no economic ground, or benefit considerably from the plight of others by acquiring property and other assets at low prices, obtain labor at reduced wages or lend money at high interest rates. Still other segments, particularly those trading in famine relief goods and services, stand to gain large profits throughout the famine and recovery periods (depicted by the right skew). Postfamine, the economic landscape is nearly always one of greater polarization of wealth and an increase in size and vulnerability of society's poor and destitute. Peri-urban slums typically remain swollen following famine as a result of permanent migration.

Government and International Responses

Famine through the ages has invoked from law abiding governments preventive action, where believed indicated, and relief responses in the face of imminent catastrophe. In Genesis, Pharoah's grain taxes during years of plenty were aimed at relieving dwindling food stores in famine. During China's

Eastern Chou and Ch'in dynasties of the third century BC, as well as in India over 2000 years ago, steps formulated to prevent or relieve famine included disaster reporting procedures, cropping alterations, grain distribution, feeding kitchens, tax remissions, vulnerable group relocation, and public works construction to facilitate irrigation, food shipment or flood control. In sixteenth century England, to counter inflationary effects of speculative grain hoarding, the Tudor First Book of Orders called for enforced extraction and marketing of private grain stocks as a way to control staple prices and thwart famine. Policy response can also amount to inaction. The Great Irish Famine from 1844 to 1848 evoked a different response from the British Government: a flawed 'laissez-faire' policy intending to allow market forces to equilibrate on their own to meet local food needs, a course that never materialized as entitlement collapsed among Irish peasantry. However, learning from a century of repeated famine, Famine Codes emerged in British India in 1880 that called for massive public works coupled with food distribution and feeding centers for vulnerable groups, which served as the core famine relief policy on the subcontinent for more than a half century and have continued to guide famine relief efforts to the present day.

Today, modern preventive response by international agencies and governments can be informed and guided by surveillance systems with regional, national, and local data collection mechanisms. Examples are the Famine Early Warning System (FEWS), which functions across Sub-Saharan Africa and has been supported by the US Agency for International Development over the past two decades and the Global Information Early Warning System (GIEWS) managed by the Food and Agricultural Organization of the United Nations (FAO). The primary aim of surveillance is to detect worsening conditions in high-risk populations in sufficient time to permit effective preventive or pre-emptive action. The task is a 'tall order' given widespread, often complex, component causes that must converge in certain ways to cause famine, against a usual plethora of endemic risk factors. With early, adequate, and effective response serving as the criterion of success, modern surveillance has so far failed to prevent famine. In part, this may reveal a basic epidemiologic dilemma: Against a background of profound, widespread economic and nutritional need throughout the developing world, including numerous prefamine but intact situations arising under surveillance, famine is a rare event. Even with presumed high sensitivity and specificity, low predictive value stemming from infrequent occurrence makes action to prevent a particular famine unlikely given the enormous political and financial resources required to mount preventive responses.

Thus, the most effective preventive action relates to setting and enacting a development agenda that recognizes high risk areas and seeks to strengthen the productivity and well-being of famine-vulnerable population groups in those areas of a country. These can include boosting infrastructural, commercial, education, agricultural, and other inputs into priority areas that improve long-term economic conditions.

Preemptive government policies are directed toward relieving a prefamine condition once it becomes apparent. Setting up famine early warning systems that monitor climatic, agricultural, population mobility, economic, and nutritional indicators is considered preemptive in that such information is intended to identify high-risk trends so that corrective action could be taken long before famine becomes imminent. Normally, early warning surveillance is only possible in high-risk countries with significant international assistance. Another example is a government making large purchases of food on the international market and releasing the commodities through ration shops, food-for-work and other programs that do not disrupt the local food economy but stabilize local grain market prices instead as a means to prevent speculation throughout the period of high risk.

Lagged or relief-oriented responses comprise emergency responses to acute and enormous need that typically are enacted after famine begins and its harsh consequences are already evident in a population. These actions, usually in coordination with major international relief and donor agencies, are typically intended to relieve acute suffering and death and promote the rehabilitation of those masses who have survived to migrate, and reach encampments. By definition, lagged responses represent policy failure for governments intending to minimize the destruction, malnutrition, and mortality of famine.

See also: **Hunger**. **Malnutrition**: Primary, Causes Epidemiology and Prevention; Secondary, Diagnosis and Management. **Nutrition Policies In Developing and Developed Countries**. **Starvation and Fasting**.

Further Reading

Ahmed R, Haggblade S, and Chowdhury TE (2000) *Out of the Shadow of Famine: Evolving Food Markets and Food Policy in Bangladesh* Baltimore: Johns Hopkins University Press.
Aykroyd WR (1974) *The Conquest of Famine*. London: Chatto & Windus.
The Bible. Book of Genesis **47**: 4–26.

Cuny FC (1999) *Famine, Conflict and Response: A Basic Guide* West Harford: Kumarian Press.

Dreze J and Sen A (eds.) (1990) *The Political Economy of Hunger: Famine Prevention*, vol. 2: *WIDER Studies in Developmental Economics*, pp. 1–400. Oxford: Clarendon Press.

Edkins J (1996) Legality with a vengeance: Famines and humanitarian relief in "complex emergencies." *Millenium: Journal of International Studies* 25: 547–575.

Newman LF (ed.) (1992) *Hunger in History: Food Shortage, Poverty and Deprivation*. Oxford: Blackwell.

Ravallion M (1997) Famines and economics. *Journal of Economic Literature* 35: 1205–1242.

Rothman K and Greenland S (1998) *Modern Epidemiology*, pp. 7–28. Philadelphia: Lippincott-Raven.

Scrimshaw NS (1987) The phenomenon of famine. Annual Review of Nutrition 7: 1–21.

Seaman J and Holt J (1980) Markets and famines in the third world. *Disasters* 4(3): 283–297.

Sen A (1977) Starvation and exchange entitlements: a general approach and its application to the great Bengal famine. *Cambridge Journal of Economics* 1: 33–59.

Sevoy RE (1986) *Famine in Peasant Societies*. New York: Greenwood Press.

Yang DL (1996) *Calamity and Reform in China: State, Rural Society and Institutional Change since the Great Leap Forward*. Stanford: Stanford University Press.

Yip R (1997) Famine. In: Noji EK (ed.) *Public Health Consequences of Disasters*, pp. 305–335 New York: Oxford University Press.

Fat-Soluble Vitamins *see* **Vitamin A**: Biochemistry and Physiological Role. **Vitamin D**: Physiology, Dietary Sources and Requirements; Rickets and Osteomalacia. **Vitamin E**: Metabolism and Requirements. **Vitamin K**

Fat Stores *see* **Adipose tissue**

Fats *see* **Fatty Acids**: Metabolism; Monounsaturated; Omega-3 Polyunsaturated; Omega-6 Polyunsaturated; Saturated; *Trans* Fatty Acids. **Lipids**: Chemistry and Classification; Composition and Role of Phospholipids

---

FATS AND OILS

A H Lichtenstein, Tufts University, Boston MA, USA

Dietary fat is a macronutrient that has historically engendered considerable controversy and continues to do so. Contentious areas include optimal type and amount in the diet, role in body weight regulation, and importance in the etiology of chronic disease(s).

Dietary Fats and Oils: The Good, Bad, and Ugly

Dietary fats and oils are unique in modern times in that they have good, bad, and ugly connotations. The aspects of dietary fat that are classified as good include serving as a carrier of preformed fat-soluble vitamins, enhancing the bioavailability of fat-soluble micronutrients, providing essential substrate for the synthesis of metabolically active compounds, constituting critical structural components of cells membranes and lipoprotein particles, preventing carbohydrate-induced hypertriglyceridemia, and providing a concentrated form of metabolic fuel in times of scarcity. The aspects of dietary fat that can be classified as bad include serving as a reservoir for fat-soluble toxic compounds and contributing dietary saturated and *trans* fatty acids, and cholesterol. Aspects of dietary fat that can be classified as ugly include providing a concentrated form of metabolic fuel in times of excess and comprising the major component of atherosclerotic plaque, the underlying cause of heart disease, stroke, and phlebitis.

Lipids in Food and in the Body

Fatty Acids

Fatty acids are hydrocarbon chains with a methyl and carboxyl end. The majority of dietary fatty acids have an even number of carbons. The range in chain length of common dietary fatty acids is broad. Fatty acids with 16 and 18 carbons make up the majority of fatty acids present in plants and animals. However, they are by no means the most metabolically active. Long-chain unsaturated fatty acids, such as arachidonic acid (C20:4), are common precursors of regulatory compounds.

Essential nutrients are those that the body cannot synthesize or cannot synthesize in amounts adequate to meet needs. Linoleic acid (18:2) and/or fatty acids that can be derived from linoleic acid are essential fatty acids. These specific fatty acids are essential because humans cannot introduce a double bond above the ninth carbon from the carboxyl end of the acyl chain. To maintain optimal health, they must be supplied by the diet of humans. The metabolism of linoleic acid is represented in **Figure 1**.

A wide range of fatty acids occur in nature. There are a number of features of fatty acids that distinguish one from another. In addition to chain length, they also vary with regard to degree of saturation and location of the double bond(s). Fatty acids with a single double bond are referred to as monounsaturated fatty acids, and those with two or more double bonds are referred to as polyunsaturated fatty acids (**Figure 2**). The double bonds within unsaturated fatty acids can either be in the *cis* (hydrogen atoms on the same side of the acyl chain) or *trans* (hydrogen atoms on opposite sides of the acyl chain) conformation (**Figure 3**). The *cis* conformation is most commonly found in nature. Double bonds can also vary with regard to location within the acyl chain. The presence of double bonds, per se, and their number, position, and conformation, dictates the physical properties of the fatty acids.

Unsaturated fatty acids of the same length with an identical number of double bonds can occur in multiple forms due to variation in the conformation of one or more of the double bonds (*cis* versus *trans*). They are referred to as geometric isomers (**Figure 3**). A common example is oleic acid (18:1c-9) and elaidic acid (18:1t-9). The presence of a *cis* relative to a *trans* double bond results in a greater bend or kink in the hydrocarbon chain. This kink impedes the fatty acids from aligning or packing together, thereby lowering the melting point of the fat. In a cell membrane this will be reflected in increased fluidity. In food this will be reflected in an oil that is liquid or fat that is soft at room temperature.

Unsaturated fatty acids of the same length with an identical number of double bonds and conformation can also occur in multiple forms due to the location of the double bonds within the acyl chain. They are referred to as positional isomers. A common example is alpha-linolenic acid (18:3n-3) and gamma-linolenic acid (18:3n-6). The difference in location of double bonds results in small alterations to the melting point yet large differences in the metabolic properties of the fatty acids. The most common distinction made among positional isomers of fatty acids is the location of the first double bond from the methyl end of the acyl chain. A fatty acid in which the first double bond occurs three carbons from the methyl end is termed an omega-3 fatty acid, frequently denoted n-3 fatty acid. This class of fatty acids is distinguished from the major class of fatty acids in which the first double bond occurs six carbons from the methyl end, termed an omega-6 or n-6 fatty acid. Enzymes that metabolize fatty acids distinguish among both positional and geometric isomers. The metabolic products of the different positional isomers of fatty acids have different and, occasionally, opposite physiological effects.

Most double bonds within fatty acids occur in a nonconjugated sequence, both in the human body and in food. That is, a carbon atom with single carbon–carbon bonds separates the carbons making up the double bonds. Some double bonds occur in

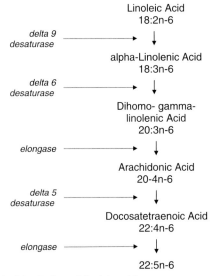

Figure 1 Metabolism of linoleic acid.

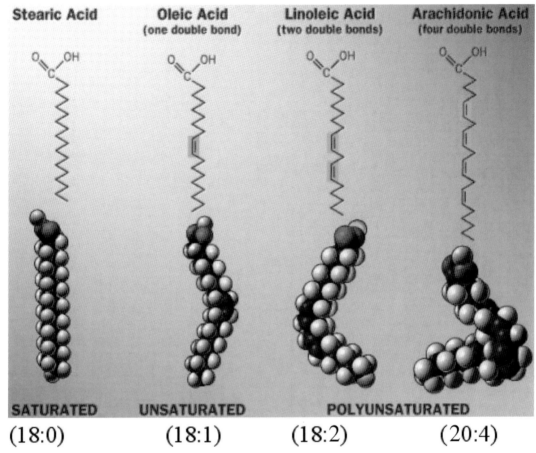

Figure 2 Saturated, monounsaturated, and polyunsaturated (n-3 and n-6) acids.

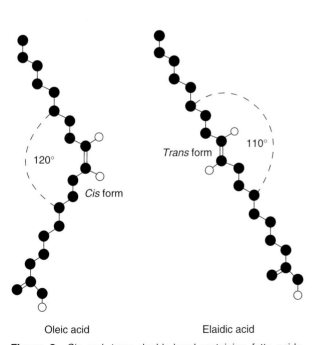

Figure 3 *Cis* and *trans* double-bond-containing fatty acids. (Copyright © The McGraw-Hill Companies, Inc.)

the conjugated form, without an intervening carbon atom separating the double bonds. Conjugated double bonds tend to be more reactive chemically (i.e., more likely to become oxidized). Although there is considerable speculation about the role of conjugated double bond-containing fatty acids and human health, the current state of knowledge is insufficient to draw any firm conclusions.

Triacylglycerol

Triacylglycerol is the major form of dietary lipid in fats and oils, whether derived from plants or animals. Triacylglycerol is composed of three fatty acids esterified to a glycerol molecule (**Figure 4**). The physical properties of the triacylglycerol are determined by the specific fatty acids esterified to the glycerol moiety and the actual position the fatty acid occupies. Each of the three carbons comprising the glycerol molecule allows for a stereochemically distinct fatty acid bond position: sn-1, sn-2, and sn-3. A triacylglycerol with three identical fatty acids is termed a simple triacylglycerol. These are exceedingly rare in nature. A triacylglycerol with two or three different fatty acids is termed a mixed

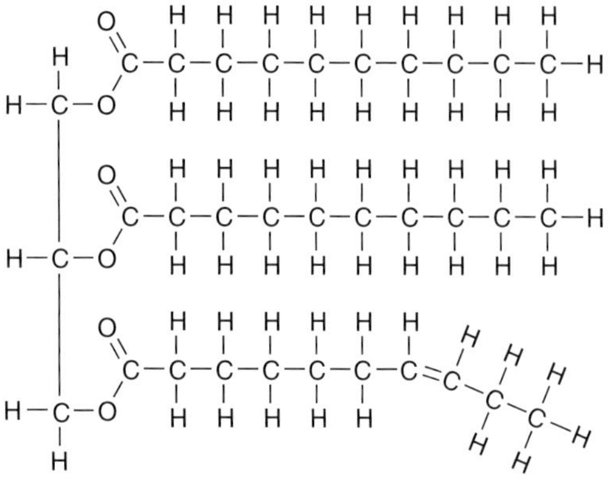

Figure 4 Triacylglycerol.

triacylglycerol, and these make up the bulk of the fat both in the human diet and in the body. The melting point of a triacylglycerol is determined by the position of the fatty acids esterified to glycerol and physical characteristics—their chain length and number, position, and conformation of the double bonds, and the stereochemical position.

Approximately 90% of the molecular weight of triacylglycerol is accounted for by the fatty acids. The fatty acid profile of the diet is reflected, in part, in the fatty acid profile of the adipose tissue triacylglycerol. Such data have been used to approximate long-term food intake patterns of humans. Manipulating the dietary fat provided to domesticated animals is being considered as one approach to modifying the fatty acid profile of meat.

Mono- and diacylglycerols have one and two fatty acids, respectively, esterified to glycerol. They rarely occur in large quantities in nature. Mono- and diacylglycerols are primarily intermediate products of triacylglycerol digestion and absorption, clearance from the bloodstream, or intracellular metabolism. They are frequently added to processed foods because of their ability to act as emulsifiers. Their presence in food products is noted on ingredient labels.

Once consumed, triacylglycerol are hydrolyzed to free fatty acids and monoglycerides in the small intestine prior to absorption. These compounds enter the intestinal cell and are used to resynthesize triacylglycerol. This lipid is then incorporated into a nascent triacylglycerol-rich lipoprotein particle, termed chylomicron, for subsequent release into peripheral circulation. Chylomicrons are secreted directly into the lymph prior to entering the bloodstream. Once in circulation, triacylglycerol are hydrolyzed before crossing the plasma membrane of peripheral cells for subsequent metabolism. The primary enzyme that hydrolyzes triacylglycerol in plasma is lipoprotein lipase. Lipoprotein lipase hydrolyzes triacylglycerol into two free fatty acids and 2-monoacylglycerol. The enzyme is attached to the luminal surface of capillary endothelial cells via a highly charged membrane-bound chain of heparin sulfate–proteoglycans. The ability of lipoprotein lipase to bind both the chylomicron particle and the cell surface ensures the cellular uptake of free fatty acids that are generated from the hydrolysis. Once inside the cell, free fatty acids can be oxidized to provide energy, metabolized to biologically active compounds, incorporated into phospholipid and cholesteryl ester, or resynthesized into triacylglycerol for storage as a potential reservoir of fatty acids for subsequent use.

Phospholipid

There are only trace amounts of phospholipid in dietary fats and oils. However, because the fatty acids in fats and oils provide substrate for the synthesis of phospholipid in the body, it is important to discuss this subtype of fat. Phospholipid is a critical structural component of all cells, both plant and animal. It is composed of two fatty acids on the sn-1 and sn-2 positions and a moiety frequently referred to as a polar head group on the sn-3 position of glycerol, the latter via a phosphate bond (**Figure 5**). Phospholipid molecules are amphipathic—that is, there are both hydrophobic and hydrophilic domains in the molecule. The two fatty acids confer hydrophobic properties and the polar head group hydrophilic properties. The specific fatty acids esterified to the glycerol backbone tend to be unsaturated fatty acids. The different polar head groups, most commonly phosphorylcholine, phosphorylserine, phosphorylinositol, or phosphorylethanolamine, result in phospholipids that vary in size and charge. Due to their amphipathic nature, phospholipids serve as the major structural component of cellular membranes by forming bilayers and in so doing also serve as a reservoir for metabolically active unsaturated fatty acids. Due to their amphipathic properties, in the

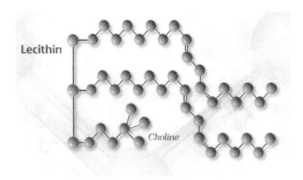

Figure 5 Phospholipid.

small intestine they play an important role in the emulsification and absorption of dietary fat and fat-soluble vitamins. On the surface of lipoprotein particles, they provide a critical component in the packaging and transport of lipid in circulation.

Cholesterol

Dietary sources of cholesterol are limited to foods of animal origin. Cholesterol is an amphipathic molecule that is composed of a steroid nucleus and a branched hydrocarbon tail (**Figure 6**). Cholesterol occurs naturally in two forms, either as free (nonesterified) cholesterol or esterified to a fatty acid (cholesteryl ester). If esterified, the fatty acid is linked to cholesterol at the number 3 carbon of the sterol ring.

Cholesterol serves a number of important functions in the body. Free cholesterol is a component of cell membranes and along with the fatty acid profile of the phospholipid bilayer determines membrane fluidity. The intercalation of free cholesterol into the phospholipid bilayer restricts motility of the fatty acyl chains and hence decreases fluidity. Free cholesterol is critical for normal nerve transmission. It makes up approximately 10% (dry weight) of total brain lipids. Cholesterol is a precursor of steroid hormones (i.e., estrogen and testosterone), vitamin D, adrenal steroids (i.e., hydrocortisone and aldosterone), and bile acids. This latter property is exploited in certain approaches to decrease plasma cholesterol levels by preventing the resorption of bile acids (recycling) and hence forcing the liver to use additional cholesterol for bile acid synthesis and in so doing creating an alternate mechanism for cholesterol excretion.

The receptor-mediated cellular uptake of cholesterol from lipoprotein particles is critical to maintaining intracellular and whole body cholesterol homeostasis. Once internalized, lipoprotein-associated cholesterol that is released from lysosomes has three major effects in the cell. The free cholesterol inhibits the activity of 3-hydroxy 3-methylglutaryl CoA reductase, the rate-limiting enzyme in endogenous cholesterol biosynthesis. This property serves to decrease cholesterol biosynthesis commensurate with the uptake of cholesterol from circulating lipoprotein particles and

hence protects the cell from accumulating excess intracellular cholesterol. Free cholesterol inhibits the synthesis of receptors that mediate the uptake of lipoproteins from the bloodstream, thereby limiting the amount of additional cholesterol taken up by the cell. Free cholesterol increases the activity of acyl CoA cholesterol acyltransferase (ACAT), the intracellular enzyme that converts free cholesterol to cholesteryl ester. A high level of intracellular free cholesterol is cytotoxic, whereas cholesteryl ester is a highly nonpolar molecule and coalesces into a lipid droplet within the cell, preventing interaction with intracellular components. Increased ACAT activity is an important mechanism in preventing the accumulation of intracellular free cholesterol.

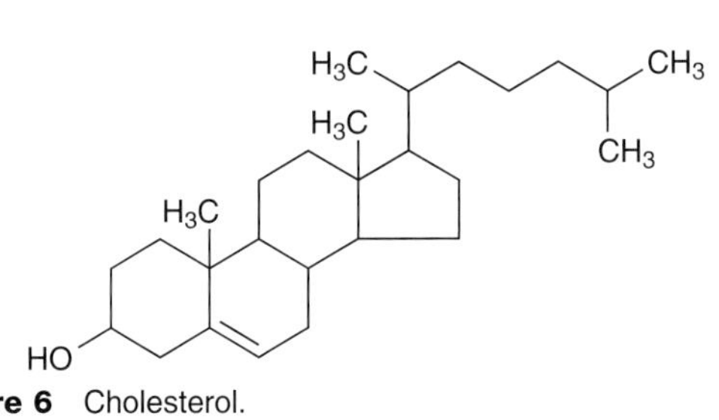

Cholesterol can be esterified intracellularly, as previously indicated, by ACAT. ACAT uses primarily oleoyl CoA as substrate and the resulting product is primarily cholesteryl oleate. Cholesterol can also be esterified in plasma by lecithin cholesterol acyltransferase (LCAT). LCAT uses phosphotidylcholine as substrate; the resulting products are primarily cholesteryl linoleate and lysolecithin. Cholesteryl ester is less polar than free cholesterol and this difference dictates how the two forms of cholesterol are handled—intracellularly and within lipoprotein particles.

Approximately one-third of cholesterol in plasma circulates as free cholesterol and approximately two-thirds as cholesteryl ester. Cholesterol in circulation is carried on all the lipoprotein particles (both intestinally derived chylomicrons and hepatically derived very low-density lipoprotein) or those generated during the metabolic cascade (intermediate-density lipoprotein, low-density lipoprotein (LDL), and high-density lipoprotein (HDL)). Free cholesterol is sequestered on the surface of lipoprotein particles within the phospholipid monolayer, whereas cholesteryl ester resides in the core of the lipoprotein particle. The majority of the cholesterol in circulation is carried on LDL particles. Cholesteryl ester is the major component of atherosclerotic plaque. In the arterial wall, cholesteryl ester is derived from the infiltration of lipoprotein-associated cholesteryl ester resulting from LCAT activity or is synthesized in situ as a result of ACAT activity. The fatty acid profile of the cholesteryl ester in arterial plaque can provide some indication of its source.

Other Sterols

Fats and oils derived from plants contain a wide range of phytosterols, compounds structurally similar to cholesterol. The difference between

Figure 6   Cholesterol.

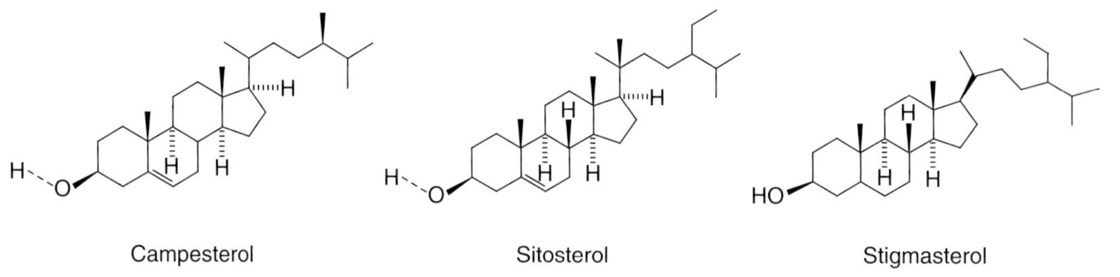

Figure 7 Plant sterols.

Campesterol   Sitosterol   Stigmasterol

phytosterols and cholesterol is related to their side chain configuration and/or steroid ring bond patterns. The most common dietary phytosterols are beta-sitosterol, campesterol, and stigmasterol (**Figure 7**). In contrast to cholesterol, phytosterols are only absorbed in trace amounts. For this reason, plant sterols have been used therapeutically to reduce plasma cholesterol levels. They compete with cholesterol for absorption; hence, they effectively reduce cholesterol absorption efficiency.

The absorption efficiency of cholesterol in humans ranges from approximately 40 to 60%. Because the relative absorption of plant sterols, however low, is correlated with the percentage of cholesterol absorbed in an individual, there is considerable interest in using circulating plant sterol concentrations as a surrogate marker for cholesterol absorption efficiency. Limited data suggest efficiency of cholesterol absorption may have a significant effect on lipoprotein profiles and cardiovascular disease risk. Whether circulating phytosterols have an independent effect on cardiovascular disease risk is under investigation.

Dietary Fats and Oils and Cholesterol

Dietary fat serves critical functions in the human body. It provides a concentrated source of energy, slightly more than twice per gram than protein or carbohydrate. For this reason, the causes of energy imbalances are often attributed to this component of the diet. However, definitive data in this area are lacking.

In addition to providing a source of metabolic energy, dietary fat provides a source of essential fatty acids, linoleic acid (18:2), and/or other fatty acids that are derived from linoleic acid. Dietary fat is the major carrier of preformed fat-soluble vitamins (vitamins A, D, E, and K). The bioavailability of these fat-soluble vitamins is dependent on fat absorption. Dietary fatty acids are incorporated into compounds that serve as structural components of biological membranes and lipoproteins, and as such they serve as a reservoir for fatty acids having subsequent metabolic fates.

Fatty Acid Profile of Common Dietary Fats

Dietary fats and oils derive from both animal and plant sources, primarily in the form of triacylglycerol. The fatty acid profile of dietary fats commonly consumed by humans varies considerably (**Figure 8**). In general, fats of animal origin tend to be relatively high in saturated fatty acids, contain cholesterol, and are solid at room temperature. A strong positive association has been demonstrated in epidemiological, intervention, and animal data between cardiovascular disease risk and intakes of saturated fatty acids. The exception is stearic acid (18:0), a saturated fatty acid of which a large proportion is metabolized to oleic acid (18:1), a monounsaturated fatty acid. Fats and oils of plant origin tend to be relatively high in unsaturated fatty acids (both monounsaturated and polyunsaturated) and are liquid at room temperature. Notable exceptions include plant oils termed tropical oils (palm, palm kernel, and coconut oils) and hydrogenated fat. Tropical oils are high in saturated fatty acids but remain liquid at room temperature because they contain a high proportion of short-chain fatty acids. Hydrogenated plant oils can be relatively high in saturated and/or *trans* fatty acids due to chemical changes induced during processing, including conversion of unsaturated to saturated bonds and *cis* to *trans* double bonds.

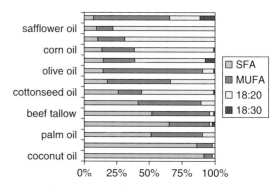

Figure 8 Relative composition of common dietary fats.

Major Contributors of Dietary Saturated, Monounsaturated, and Polyunsaturated Fatty Acids and Cholesterol

The major types of dietary fats and oils are generally broken down on the basis of animal and plant sources. The relative balance of animal and plant foods is an important determinant of the fatty acid profile of the diet. However, with the increasing prominence of processed, reformulated, and genetically modified foods, it is becoming more difficult to predict the fatty acid profile of the diet on the basis of the animal verses plant distinction.

According to the National Health and Nutrition Examination Survey (NHANES) recall data from 1999–2000, the 10 major dietary sources of saturated fatty acids in US diets are regular cheese (6.0% of the total grams of saturated fatty acids consumed), whole milk (4.6%), regular ice cream (3.0%), 2% low-fat milk (2.6%), pizza with meat (2.5%), French fries (2.5%), Mexican dishes with meat (2.3%), regular processed meat (2.2%), chocolate candy (2.1%), and mixed dishes with beef (2.1%). Hence, the majority of saturated fatty acids are contributed by regular dairy products (16%), and the top 10 sources contribute 30% of the total saturated fatty acids consumed. The increased prevalence of fat-free and low-fat dairy products provides a viable option with which to encourage a populationwide decrease in saturated fat intake. To put the value of decreasing populationwide intakes of saturated fat into perspective, it has been estimated that the isocaloric replacement of 5% of energy from saturated fatty acids with complex carbohydrate, on average, would reduce total cholesterol levels by 10 mg/dl (0.26 mmol/l) and LDL cholesterol by 7 mg/dl (0.18 mmol/l). For a person at moderately high risk of developing cardiovascular disease with a total cholesterol level of 220 mg/dl (5.69 mmol/l) and LDL cholesterol level of 140 mg/dl (3.62 mmol/l), such a dietary modification would decrease total and LDL cholesterol levels by 4.5 and 5%, respectively. Each 1% decrease in total cholesterol levels has been associated with a 2% reduction in the incidence of coronary heart disease. Using this example, that would theoretically translate into a 9% decrease in cardiovascular disease risk. However, it is important to note that decreasing the saturated fatty acid content of the diet should not necessarily be done by displacing fat with carbohydrate. As discussed in the next section, the quantity of dietary fat, relative to carbohydrate and protein, also impacts on blood lipid levels and lipoprotein profiles.

The 10 major dietary sources of monounsaturated fatty acids in US diets are French fries (3.3% of the total grams of monounsaturated fatty acids consumed), regular processed meat (2.5%), regular cookies (2.5%), regular miscellaneous snacks (2.4%), pizza with meat (2.4%), regular salad dressing (2.4%), regular cheese (2.3%), Mexican dishes with meat (2.3%), sausage (2.1%), and mixed dishes with beef (2.1%). There is little change in total or LDL cholesterol levels from the isocaloric replacement of monounsaturated fatty acids by complex carbohydrate. However, it is important to note that approximately one-half of the monounsaturated fatty acids consumed in the United States come from animal fats. Therefore, a decrease in saturated fatty acid intake would be predicted to decrease monounsaturated fatty acid intake unless vegetable oils high in monounsaturated fatty acids, such as canola or olive oil, replaced the animal fat.

The 10 major dietary sources of n-6 polyunsaturated fatty acids in US diets are regular salad dressing (8.8% of the total grams of polyunsaturated fatty acids consumed), regular white bread (4.2%), regular mayonnaise (3.0%), French fries (2.6%), regular cake (2.5%), regular cookies (2.1%), mixed dishes with chicken and turkey (2.1%), regular miscellaneous snacks (2.0%), regular potato chips (2.0%), and fried fish (2.0%). The distribution of polyunsaturated fatty acids among commonly consumed foods is wide. It has been estimated that the isocaloric replacement of complex carbohydrate with polyunsaturated fatty acids for 5% of energy, on average, will reduce total cholesterol levels by 5 mg/dl (0.13 mmol/l) and LDL cholesterol by 4 mg/dl (0.11 mmol/l). For a person at moderately high risk of cardiovascular disease with a total cholesterol level of 220 mg/dl (5.69 mmol/l) and LDL cholesterol level of 140 mg/dl (3.62 mmol/l), such a dietary modification would decrease total and LDL cholesterol levels by 2.1 and 3.6%, respectively, and potentially result in a 4% decrease in cardiovascular disease risk.

The 10 major dietary sources of cholesterol in US diets are fried eggs (16.6% of the total milligrams of cholesterol consumed), regular eggs including scrambled eggs (8.4%), mixed dishes with eggs (4.5%), mixed dishes with beef (2.9%), whole milk (2.6%), regular cheese (2.5%), fried fish (2.3%), mixed dishes with chicken and turkey (2.3%), lean cut meat (2.1%), and regular processed meat (2.1%). Eggs or foods high in eggs contribute approximately 30% of the total dietary cholesterol intake. It has estimated that reducing cholesterol intakes by 200 mg/day, on average, will reduce total cholesterol levels by 5 mg/dl (0.13 mmol/l) and LDL cholesterol by 2.6 mg/dl (0.10 mmol/l). Such a change would be predicted to have a similar risk effect as displacing 5% of energy as carbohydrate with polyunsaturated fatty acids—that is, reducing cardiovascular disease risk by approximately 4%.

Dietary Fat and Cardiovascular Prevention

Amount in Diet

When considering the percentage of energy contributed by dietary fats and oils (amount of fat) and cardiovascular disease prevention and management, there are two major factors—the impact on plasma lipoprotein profiles and body weight. The potential relationship with body weight is important because overweight and obesity are strongly associated with elevated lipid and lipoprotein levels, blood pressure, dyslipidemia, and type 2 diabetes—all potential risk factors for cardiovascular disease. With respect to plasma lipoprotein profiles, the focus is usually on triglyceride and HDL cholesterol levels or total cholesterol:HDL cholesterol ratios.

When body weight is maintained at a constant level, decreasing the total fat content of the diet, expressed as a percentage of total energy, and replacing it with carbohydrate frequently results in an increase in triglyceride levels, decrease in HDL cholesterol levels, and a less favorable (higher) total cholesterol:HDL cholesterol ratio. Low levels of HDL cholesterol are an independent risk factor for cardiovascular disease (<50 mg/dl in females [<1.3 mmol/l] and <40 mg/dl in males, [<1.0 mmol/l]). Very low-fat diets are of particular concern in diabetic and overweight individuals who tend to have low HDL cholesterol and high triglyceride levels or those individuals classified as having metabolic syndrome (having three or more of the following: abdominal obesity, elevated triacylglycerol levels, low HDL levels, hypertension, or elevated fasting glucose levels). Because of these findings, the Adult Treatment Panel of the National Cholesterol Education Program (NCEP) revised its guidelines in 2001 from recommending a diet with less than 30% of energy as fat to a diet with 25–35% of energy as fat. Similarly, the American Heart Association and the USDA/HHS 2000 Dietary Guidelines for Americans changed their recommendations to shift the emphasis from a general recommendation to limit intakes of total and saturated fat to limit saturated and *trans* fat.

With respect to the amount of dietary fats and oils and body weight, two reviews of the long-term data have been published. Both concluded that even a relatively large downward shift in dietary fat intake, approximately 10% of energy, results in only modest weight loss of 1.0 kg during a 12-month period in normal weight subjects and 3 kg in overweight or obese subjects. However, it is important to note that in contrast to what would have been predicted, during the course of the studies included in the reviews, in no case was weight gain reported.

Fatty Acid Profile

Early evidence demonstrated that diets relatively high in saturated fatty acids increased plasma total cholesterol levels. Subsequent work demonstrated that this elevation in total cholesterol levels is contributed to by increases in both LDL and HDL cholesterol levels. It also became clear that not all saturated fatty acids had identical effects on plasma lipoprotein levels. Very short-chain fatty acids (6:0 to 10:0) and stearic acid (18:0) produce little or no change in blood cholesterol levels, whereas saturated fatty acids with short- and intermediate-chain lengths—lauric (12:0), myristic (14:0), and palmitic (16:0) acids—appear to be the most potent in increasing blood cholesterol levels. Because a large proportion of stearic acid (18:0) is rapidly converted to oleic acid (18:1), it appears to have a relatively neutral effect. The underlying mechanism by which saturated fatty acids with 10 or fewer carbon atoms have different effects from those with 12–16 carbons is yet to be determined. The current dietary recommendation as defined in the NCEP Therapeutic Lifestyle Change diet to prevent and treat cardiovascular disease is to limit intakes of saturated fat to less than 7% of total energy. The major contributors of saturated fatty acids were discussed previously.

Compared to saturated fatty acids, unsaturated fatty acids, both monounsaturated and polyunsaturated fatty acids, lower both LDL and HDL cholesterol levels. The absolute magnitude of the change is greater for LDL cholesterol than HDL cholesterol. Most data suggest that monounsaturated fatty acids have a slightly smaller effect than polyunsaturated fatty acids in lowering both LDL and HDL cholesterol levels so that the total cholesterol:HDL cholesterol ratio is similar for both categories of fat.

Quantitatively, the major n-3 polyunsaturated fatty acid in the diet is alpha-linolenic acid (18:3n-3). Major dietary sources include soybean and canola oils (**Figure** 8). Two other n-3 polyunsaturated fatty acids, eicosapentaenoic acid (EPA, 20:5n-3) and docosahexaenoic acid (DHA, 22:6n-3), referred to as very long-chain n-3 fatty acids, are found predominantly in fish, specifically dark flesh fish such as salmon, tuna, and swordfish. Dietary intakes of very long-chain n-3 fatty acids are associated with decreased risk of heart disease and stroke. Intervention studies have substantiated these findings.

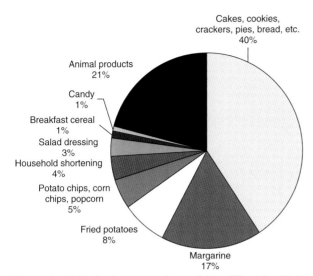

Figure 9 Major food sources of *trans* fat for US adults. (Data from www.cfsan.fda.gov/~dms/qatrans2.)

The beneficial effects of EPA and DHA are attributed to decreased ventricular fibrillation resulting in decreased sudden death, and also decreased triglyceride levels, platelet aggregation, and blood pressure. Evidence suggests that very long-chain n-3 fatty acids may decrease atherosclerotic plaque progression.

Dietary *trans* fatty acids occur naturally in meat and dairy products as a result of anaerobic bacterial fermentation in ruminant animals. *Trans* fatty acids are also introduced into the diet as a result of the consumption of hydrogenated vegetable or fish oils. Hydrogenation results in a number of changes in the fatty acyl chain: conversion of *cis* to *trans* double bonds; saturation of double bonds; and migration of double bonds along the acyl chain, resulting in multiple positional isomers. Oils are primarily hydrogenated to increase viscosity (change a liquid oil into a semiliquid or solid) and extend shelf life (decrease susceptibility to oxidation). Major contributors of *trans* fatty acids are commercially baked products (40%), animal products (21%), margarine (17%), and fried potatoes and chips (13%) (**Figure 9**). In intervention and observational studies, *trans* fatty acid intake has been associated with less favorable total cholesterol:HDL cholesterol ratios and increased risk of cardiovascular disease, respectively.

Composition of Dietary Fats

Types of fat relatively high in saturated fatty acids include butterfat (62%), beef tallow (50%), tropic oils (coconut, 87%; palm kernel, 81%; and palm oil, 49%), and lard (39%) (**Figure 8**). The content of cholesterol in these fats is 33, 14, 0, and 12 mg/tablespoon, respectively. Types of fat relatively high in monounsaturated fatty acids include canola oil (56%), olive oil (73%), and peanut oil (46%). Types of fat relatively high in polyunsaturated fatty acids include soybean oil (51%), corn oil (58%), safflower oil (74%), and sunflower oil (66%). None of the vegetable oils high in monounsaturated or polyunsaturated fatty acids contain cholesterol. The fatty acid profile of diets varies widely among individuals and depends on such factors as availability, cultural and religious dietary patterns, price, and personal preferences.

Summary

Dietary fats and oils have both positive and negative attributes with respect to health outcomes. This makes determining optimal dietary recommendations difficult. Fats and oils are primarily composed of triacylglycerol. The fatty acid composition of the triacylglycerol dictates the physical properties of the fat. During fatty acid biosynthesis, humans are unable to insert a double bond above the ninth carbon of the acyl chain. For this reason, linoleic acid and fatty acids derived from linoleic acid are essential and hence must be consumed preformed. Animal fats are the major contributors of saturated fatty acids to the diet. Vegetable oils such as canola and olive, and also animal fats, are the major contributors of monounsaturated fatty acids to the diet. Vegetable oils such as safflower, sunflower, and corn oils are the major contributors of polyunsaturated fatty acids to the diet. Dietary patterns high in saturated fatty acids have been associated with increased risk of developing cardiovascular disease, whereas dietary patterns high in unsaturated fatty acids (monounsaturated and polyunsaturated) have been associated with decreased risk. Two other subtypes of fatty acids derived from the diet potentially impact on human health: very long-chain n-3 fatty acids and *trans* fatty acids. Very long-chain n-3 fatty acids are derived primarily from fish, and intakes have been associated with decreased risk of developing cardiovascular disease. The majority of *trans* fatty acids are derived from foods made with hydrogenated fat and, to a lesser extent, from animal fats. Higher amounts in the diet have been associated with elevated LDL cholesterol levels and higher total cholesterol to HDL cholesterol ratios. Dietary fatty acid intakes are determined by the sum of individual food choices. Current general dietary recommendations from a number of sources suggest that one should consume a diet high in fruits and vegetables, whole grain products, low-fat and nonfat diary products, legumes, and lean meats. Such a dietary pattern, while accommodating personal preferences, is consistent with a diet low in saturated and *trans* fatty acids and is predicted to reduce the risk of developing cardiovascular and other chronic diseases.

See also: **Cholesterol**: Sources, Absorption, Function and Metabolism; Factors Determining Blood Levels. **Fatty Acids**: Metabolism; Monounsaturated; Omega-3 Polyunsaturated; Omega-6 Polyunsaturated; Saturated; *Trans* Fatty Acids. **Lipids**: Chemistry and Classification; Composition and Role of Phospholipids. **Lipoproteins**.

Further Reading

Clarke R, Frost C, Collins R *et al.* (1997) Dietary lipids and blood cholesterol: Quantitative meta-analysis of metabolic ward studies. *British Medical Journal* **314**: 112–117.

Expert Panel on Detection, Evaluation, and Treatment of High Blood Cholesterol in Adults (2001) Executive summary of the third report of the National Cholesterol Education Program (NCEP) Expert Panel on Detection, Evaluation, and Treatment of High Blood Cholesterol in Adults (Adult Treatment Panel III). *Journal of the American Medical Association* **285**: 2486–2497.

Hooper L, Summerbell CD, Higgins JP *et al.* (2001) Dietary fat intake and prevention of cardiovascular disease: Systematic review. *British Medical Journal* **322**: 757–763.

Krauss RM, Eckel RH, Howard B *et al.* (2000) AHA Dietary Guidelines: Revision 2000: A statement for healthcare professionals from the Nutrition Committee of the American Heart Association. *Circulation* **102**: 2284–2299.

Law M (2000) Plant sterol and stanol margarines and health. *British Medical Journal* **320**: 861–864.

Law MR, Wald NJ, and Thompson SG (1994) By how much and how quickly does reduction in serum cholesterol concentration lower risk of ischaemic heart disease? *British Medical Journal* **308**: 367–372.

Lichtenstein AH (2003) Dietary fat and cardiovascular disease risk: Quantity or quality? *Journal of Women's Health* **12**: 109–114.

Sacks FM and Katan M (2002) Randomized clinical trials on the effects of dietary fat and carbohydrate on plasma lipoproteins and cardiovascular disease. *American Journal of Medicine* **113**: 13S–24S.

Schaefer EJ (2002) Lipoproteins, nutrition, and heart disease. *American Journal of Clinical Nutrition* **75**: 191–212.

Tang JL, Armitage JM, Lancaster T *et al.* (1998) Systematic review of dietary intervention trials to lower blood total cholesterol in free-living subjects. *British Medical Journal* **316**: 1213–1220.

Watts GF and Burke V (1996) Lipid-lowering trials in the primary and secondary prevention of coronary heart disease: New evidence, implications and outstanding issues. *Current Opinion in Lipidology* **7**: 341–355.

Willett WC (1998) Is dietary fat a major determinant of body fat? (Comment; erratum appears in Am J Clin Nutr 1999 Aug;70(2):304). *American Journal of Clinical Nutrition* **67**: 556S–562S.

Yao M and Roberts SB (2001) Dietary energy density and weight regulation. *Nutrition Reviews* **59**: 247–258.

FATTY ACIDS

Contents
Metabolism
Monounsaturated
Omega-3 Polyunsaturated
Omega-6 Polyunsaturated
Saturated
Trans **Fatty Acids**

Metabolism

P A Watkins, Kennedy Krieger Institute and Johns Hopkins University School of Medicine, Baltimore, MD, USA

Introduction

Fatty acids and glucose are the primary metabolic fuels used by higher organisms, including man. As such, fatty acids occupy a central position in human nutrition. Fat, carbohydrate, and protein comprise the macronutrients. When nutritionists speak of fat, they are referring mainly to triacylglycerol (triglyceride), which consists of three fatty-acid molecules covalently linked to a backbone of glycerol. Several properties of fatty acids and triacylglycerol make them highly suited to the storage and provision of energy. When a gram of fatty acid is burned as fuel, about 9 kcal of energy is recovered – more than twice that yielded when a gram of carbohydrate or protein is utilized. Unlike carbohydrates, fat can be stored in an anhydrous compact state, allowing the organism to amass large quantities of fuel reserves in times of plenty. This property can have unfortunate consequences in prosperous societies, as evidenced by the increasing incidence of obesity. Fatty acids are also fundamental building blocks for the synthesis of most biologically important lipids, including phospholipids, sphingolipids, and cholesterol esters. They are the precursors of bioactive molecules such as prostaglandins and other eicosanoids. In addition, fatty acids and their coenzyme A derivatives have many metabolic regulatory roles.

Fatty-Acid Nomenclature Conventions

In this article, fatty acids will be identified by their chain length, the number of double bonds present, and the position of the first double bond from the methyl end of the molecule. Thus 14:0 denotes a saturated fatty acid with 14 carbon atoms, 16:1n-9 denotes a monounsaturated fatty acid with 16 carbon atoms in which one double bond occurs nine carbon atoms from the methyl end, and 20:4n-6 denotes a polyunsaturated fatty acid with 20 carbon atoms in which the first of four double bonds is found six carbon atoms from the methyl end. Unless otherwise noted, all double bonds are in the *cis* configuration and double bonds in polyunsaturated fatty acids are separated by a single methylene (–CH_2–) group. The carboxyl carbon atom of any fatty acid is carbon-1. The adjacent carbon atom is referred to as either carbon-2 or the α-carbon; the next is carbon-3 or the β-carbon, and so on. Some examples are shown in **Figure 1**.

Physical Properties of Fatty Acids

Fatty acids are aliphatic organic acids with the fundamental structure $CH_3(CH_2)_nCOOH$, where n can range from zero to more than 26. Thus, fatty acids range from the shortest, acetic acid (2:0), to the very long-chain fatty acids containing 26 or more carbon atoms (e.g., 26:0). Although fatty acids with an odd number of carbon atoms exist in nature, most common fatty acids have an even number. The most abundant fatty acids in human lipids and in dietary lipids are the long-chain fatty acids 16:0 (palmitic acid) and 18:1n-9 (oleic acid) (**Figure 1**). The hydrophobic nature of the hydrocarbon chain of fatty acids containing more than eight carbon atoms renders them quite insoluble in aqueous media. It has been estimated that for every two

additional carbon atoms in the fatty-acid chain its solubility decreases 10-fold.

Owing to the poor solubility of the most abundant fatty acids, free (non-esterified) fatty acids are often found associated with binding and/or transport proteins. Serum albumin has at least six binding sites for fatty acids and is the primary transporter of these molecules through the bloodstream. Several low-molecular-weight fatty-acid binding proteins have been identified and implicated in the intracellular transport of free fatty acids. While free fatty acids can associate with lipophilic cellular and organellar membranes, concentrations of these non-esterified compounds in membranes are typically very low.

Fatty-Acid Activation

Biochemically, fatty acids are rather nonreactive molecules unless they are first activated by thioesterification to coenzyme A (CoA). This reaction is catalyzed by acyl-CoA synthetases (also known as acid : CoA ligases, E.C. 6.2.1.x). The overall acyl-CoA synthetase reaction is

$$RCOOH + ATP + CoA\text{-}SH$$
$$\rightarrow RCO\text{-}S\text{-}CoA + AMP + PPi$$

where PPi is inorganic pyrophosphate, ATP is adenosine triphosphate, and AMP is adenosine monophosphate. Owing to the wide diversity of fatty-acid chain lengths, many enzymes with varied substrate specificities have been identified.

It is estimated that humans have more than 25 enzymes capable of activating fatty acids and/or fatty-acid-like compounds. Acyl-CoA synthetases that activate fatty acids of similar chain lengths often have different tissue-expression patterns and/or different subcellular locations. Thus, each enzyme may direct its fatty-acid substrates into a particular metabolic pathway.

Mitochondrial Fatty-Acid β-Oxidation

To recover their stored energy, fatty acids must be oxidized. Quantitatively, the most important energy-yielding degradation pathway is mitochondrial β-oxidation (**Figure 2**). Fatty acids must first enter cells or tissues. Serum triacylglycerol, usually associated with lipoproteins, is hydrolyzed by lipoprotein lipase located on the capillary endothelium, releasing fatty acids for cellular uptake. In addition, albumin-bound circulating free fatty acids (e.g., produced by the mobilization of adipocyte fat stores) reach the cell surface. Although

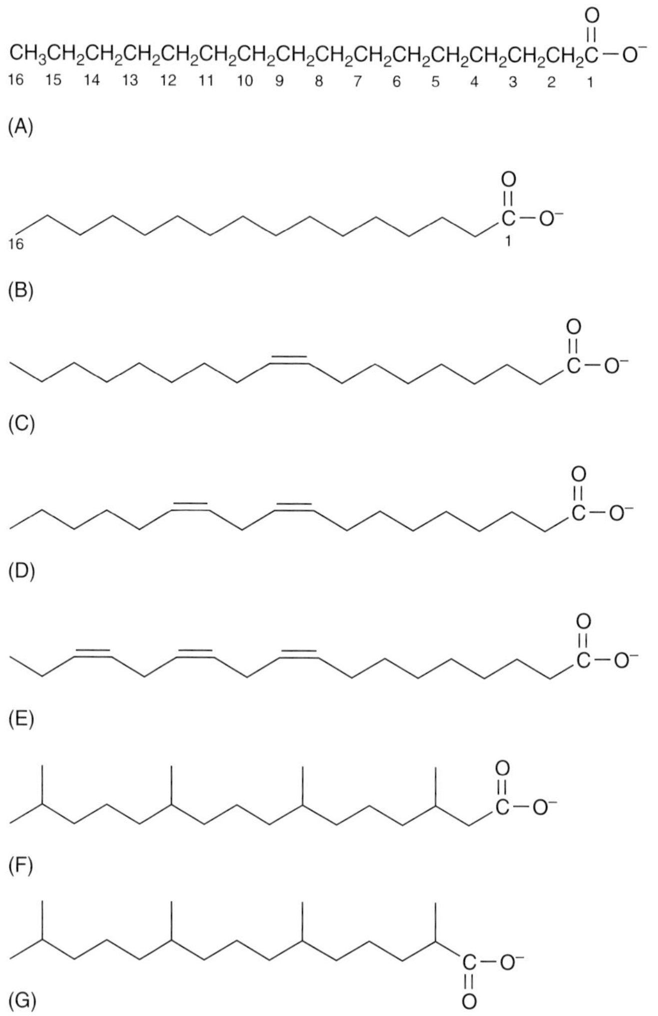

Figure 1 Fatty-acid structure and nomenclature. (A) Chemical formula and carbon atom numbering system for a 16-carbon saturated fatty acid (16:0). (B) Schematic representation of 16:0. (C) A monounsaturated fatty acid, 18:1n-9, showing the double bond nine carbon atoms from the methyl end (carbon 18). (D) The essential n-6 fatty acid 18:2n-6, where the first double bond is found six carbon atoms from the methyl end. The two double bonds are separated by a methylene (–CH$_2$–) group. (E) The essential n-3 fatty acid 18:3n-3, where the first double bond is found three carbon atoms from the methyl end. (F) Phytanic acid, a dietary β-methyl-branched-chain fatty acid (3,7,11,15-tetramethyl 16:0). The methyl group on carbon 3 prevents this fatty acid from degradation by β-oxidation. (G) Pristanic acid (2,6,10,14-tetramethyl 15:0) is the product of phytanic acid α-oxidation, in which a single carbon (carbon 1) is lost. The methyl group on carbon 2 does not preclude subsequent degradation by β-oxidation.

hydrophobic fatty acids can traverse the plasma membrane by simple diffusion, a role for membrane transport proteins in this process remains controversial. Once inside the cell, fatty acids are thought to be moved to the mitochondria (or other intracellular sites) by intracellular fatty-acid binding proteins.

Acyl-CoA synthetase activity towards long-chain fatty-acid substrates is present in the outer mitochondrial membrane. However, fatty acyl-CoAs do not readily traverse biological membranes such as the inner mitochondrial membrane. A highly sophisticated transport system has evolved to allow tight regulation of fatty-acid entry into the mitochondrion

(**Figure 2**). Carnitine palmitoyl transferase 1 (CPT1), located on the inner aspect of the outer mitochondrial membrane, catalyzes a transesterification reaction:

$$\text{fatty acyl-CoA} + \text{carnitine}$$
$$\rightarrow \text{fatty acyl-carnitine} + \text{CoA-SH}$$

Carnitine–acylcarnitine translocase (CACT), located in the inner mitochondrial membrane, carries the fatty acyl-carnitine inside the mitochondrion in exchange for a free carnitine molecule. CPT2, located inside the mitochondrion, then catalyzes the reversal of the CPT1 reaction. Thus, the concerted actions of CPT1, CACT, and CPT2

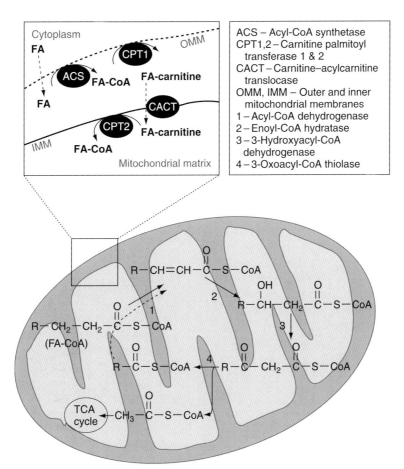

Figure 2 Mitochondrial fatty-acid (FA) β-oxidation pathway. Long-chain fatty acids are activated, converted to carnitine esters, transported across the inner mitochondrial membrane, and re-converted to their CoA thioester once in the mitochondrial matrix. Four sequential mitochondrial enzyme reactions shorten the fatty acyl-CoA (FA-CoA) by two carbon atoms, which are released as acetyl-CoA. The shortened fatty acyl-CoA can undergo additional cycles of degradation until the entire carbon chain has been converted to acetyl-CoA units. $FADH_2$ and NADH, produced in reactions 1 and 3, respectively, can enter the electron transport chain for ATP production. Acetyl-CoA enters the tricarboxylic acid (TCA) cycle, yielding additional NADH and $FADH_2$ for ATP production. Mitochondrial β-oxidation is the primary pathway for recovering the energy stored as triacylglycerol or 'fat'.

effectively translocate fatty acyl-CoA across the inner mitochondrial membrane.

Entry of fatty acids into the mitochondrion is regulated by several mechanisms. Although long-chain fatty acids can readily diffuse across the lipophilic inner mitochondrial membrane, the mitochondrial matrix lacks long-chain acyl-CoA synthetase activity. Thus, long-chain fatty acids cannot be activated intramitochondrially to enter the β-oxidation pathway. Control is also exerted extramitochondrially via malonyl-CoA, a cytoplasmic intermediate in fatty-acid biosynthesis and an indicator of high cellular energy status. Malonyl-CoA is a potent inhibitor of CPT1, prohibiting fatty acids from entering the mitochondria to be degraded.

As depicted in **Figure 2**, the four primary enzymes of mitochondrial β-oxidation act on

intramitochondrial fatty acyl-CoA by sequential dehydrogenation, hydration, dehydrogenation, and thiolytic cleavage reactions. The products are (1) fatty acyl-CoA that has been shortened by two carbon atoms, (2) acetyl-CoA, (3) reduced flavin adenine dinucleotide ($FADH_2$), and (4) reduced nicotinamide adenine dinucleotide (NADH). $FADH_2$ and NADH can directly enter the electron transport chain at complex 2 and complex 1, respectively, yielding about five ATP molecules. Acetyl-CoA can be further degraded to carbon dioxide and water by the tricarboxylic acid cycle, yielding additional reducing equivalents that can enter the electron transport chain and produce ATP. Importantly, the entire β-oxidation process can be repeated using the shortened fatty acyl-CoA as a substrate. This process can be repeated until the entire carbon skeleton of the fatty acid has been degraded to two-carbon acetyl-CoA units. Theoretically, complete oxidation of one molecule of 16:0 (β-oxidation and tricarboxylic acid cycle) will yield more than 160 ATP molecules.

Essentially all cells and tissues can use carbohydrate (glucose) for fuel, and a few (e.g., nerves and erythrocytes) are dependent on this fuel source. An important nutritional consideration is that carbon derived from fatty acids via β-oxidation cannot be converted to glucose in net quantities. In the postprandial state, however, most cell types other than nerves and erythrocytes derive the majority of their energy from fatty-acid oxidation under normal physiologic conditions. Some tissues, e.g., skeletal muscle, completely oxidize fatty acids to carbon dioxide and water. Others, e.g., liver, only partially oxidize fatty acids, using the acetyl-CoA product for biosynthethic needs. In particular, liver uses intramitochondrial acetyl-CoA for the synthesis of ketone bodies, acetoacetate and β-hydroxybutyrate (**Figure 3**). Ketone bodies can be oxidized by all tissues except the liver and provide an alternative fuel source during starvation. In particular, nervous tissue can oxidize ketone bodies. During prolonged starvation, increased ketone-body use spares the brain's requirement for glucose.

Peroxisomal Fatty-Acid β-Oxidation

Like mitochondria, peroxisomes contain pathways for the β-oxidation of fatty acids. The mechanism by which fatty acids enter peroxisomes is unclear but does not appear to involve the CPT1–CACT–CPT2 pathway. Long-chain and very-long-chain acyl-CoA synthetase activities are associated with peroxisomes, but it has not been established whether fatty acids or fatty acyl-CoAs traverse the peroxisomal membrane. The basic reactions of peroxisomal β-oxidation resemble those found in mitochondria, but the peroxisomal and mitochondrial enzymes are distinct proteins (**Figure 4**). In fact, peroxisomes contain two sets of β-oxidation enzymes, which appear to function with distinct substrates.

Unlike mitochondria, peroxisomes do not contain an electron transport chain or tricarboxylic acid cycle, and, thus, peroxisomal fatty-acid degradation is not directly coupled to energy production. Rather, peroxisomes have a more specialized fatty-acid oxidation role, degrading fatty-acid substrates that cannot be catabolized in mitochondria. Peroxisomes are indispensable for the degradation of very-long-chain fatty acids (containing more than 22 carbon atoms),

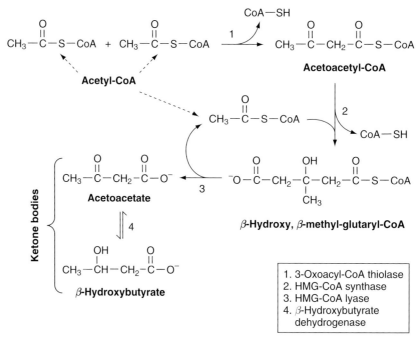

1. 3-Oxoacyl-CoA thiolase
2. HMG-CoA synthase
3. HMG-CoA lyase
4. β-Hydroxybutyrate dehydrogenase

Figure 3 Synthesis of ketone bodies. In the mitochondria of hepatocytes, acetyl-CoA derived from β-oxidation is converted to ketone bodies, primarily acetoacetate and β-hydroxybutyrate, rather than entering the tricarboxylic acid cycle. Two molecules of acetyl-CoA condense in a reversal of the last β-oxidation reaction (3-oxoacyl-CoA thiolase). The product, acetoacetyl-CoA, condenses with another molecule of acetyl-CoA, yielding β-hydroxy, β-methyl-glutaryl-CoA (HMG-CoA), a reaction catalysed by HMG-CoA synthase. Cleavage of HMG-CoA by HMG-CoA lyase yields acetoacetate, regenerating one molecule of acetyl-CoA. Acetoacetate is reversibly reduced to β-hydroxybutyrate via the NAD-dependent enzyme β-hydroxybutyrate dehydrogenase. These ketone bodies can traverse the inner mitochondrial membrane, eventually reaching the bloodstream for ultimate use by the brain and other tissues.

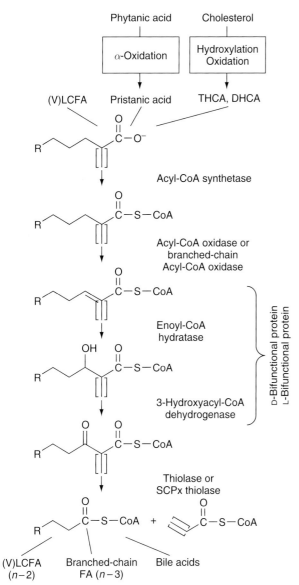

Figure 4 Peroxisomal fatty-acid (FA) β-oxidation pathways. While saturated long-chain fatty acids (LCFA) are preferentially degrade in mitochondria, saturated very-long-chain fatty acids (VLCFA) and some LCFA are shortened by peroxisomal β-oxidation. Degradation of pristanic acid, the product of phytanic acid α-oxidation, and the conversion of the cholesterol-derived 27-carbon bile-acid precursors dihydroxycholestanoic acid (DHCA) and trihydroxycholestanoic acid (THCA) to 24-carbon bile acids also require this pathway. The mechanism by which these substrates enter peroxisomes is unknown. Four enzymatic reactions serve to shorten the substrates by either two (LCFA, VLCFA) or three (pristanic acid, DHCA, THCA) carbon atoms. The 2-methyl group of the latter substrates is shown in brackets. SCPx thiolase refers to the thiolase activity of sterol carrier protein x.

which are neurotoxic if allowed to accumulate. These fatty acids undergo several cycles of peroxisomal β-oxidation until they are between eight and 10 carbon atoms long, after which they go to the

mitochondria for further catabolism. Degradation of xenobiotic fatty acyl-like compounds (e.g., sulphur-substituted fatty acids and many nonsteroidal anti-inflammatory drugs) takes place in peroxisomes. Oxidation of dicarboxylic acids (from the diet or from ω-oxidation) and 2-methyl-branched-chain fatty acids (from the diet or from α-oxidation) also occurs in peroxisomes.

The peroxisomal β-oxidation pathway also fulfils an important biosynthetic role. In the hepatic synthesis of bile acids from cholesterol, the aliphatic side chain, which resembles an α-methyl-branched-chain fatty acid, must be shortened. A single cycle of peroxisomal β-oxidation will remove a three-carbon portion of the side chain, converting the 27-carbon bile acid precursors dihydroxycholestanoic and trihydroxycholestanoic acids into the 24-carbon primary bile acids chenodeoxycholate and cholate, respectively.

Fatty-Acid α-Oxidation and ω-Oxidation

Other important fatty-acid catabolic pathways include α-oxidation and ω-oxidation. α-Oxidation is required for degradation of the dietary fatty acid phytanic acid (3,7,11,15-tetramethyl-16:0). This fatty acid cannot be degraded by β-oxidation owing to the methyl group on carbon-3. In the human diet, phytanic acid is obtained from the consumption of ruminant meats, fats, and dairy products. Rumen bacteria hydrolyze chlorophyll, releasing the phytol side chain; phytol is oxidized to phytanic acid and incorporated into triacylglycerol and phospholipids by the animal. Humans typically ingest 50–100 mg of phytanic acid per day. The current view of the α-oxidation pathway, which is found in peroxisomes, is shown in **Figure 5**. After activation to its CoA derivative, phytanoyl-CoA is hydroxylated on the 2-carbon. The next reaction catalyzes the removal of a one-carbon CoA derivative as formyl-CoA. The other product of this reaction is an aldehyde, pristanal, that can be oxidized to form pristanic acid (2,6,10,14-tetramethyl-15:0). This chain-shortening reaction effectively shifts the position of the first methyl group from carbon-3 (in phytanic acid) to carbon-2 (in pristanic acid). The 2-methyl-branched chain fatty acids can then be degraded further via peroxisomal β-oxidation.

Another mechanism for degradation of fatty acids that cannot undergo β-oxidation is known as ω-oxidation. In this process, the terminal methyl group (referred to as the ω-end) of a fatty-acid chain is oxidized to a carboxylic acid via cytochrome P450 isozymes, particularly the CYP52A family, in the endoplasmic reticulum. The resulting

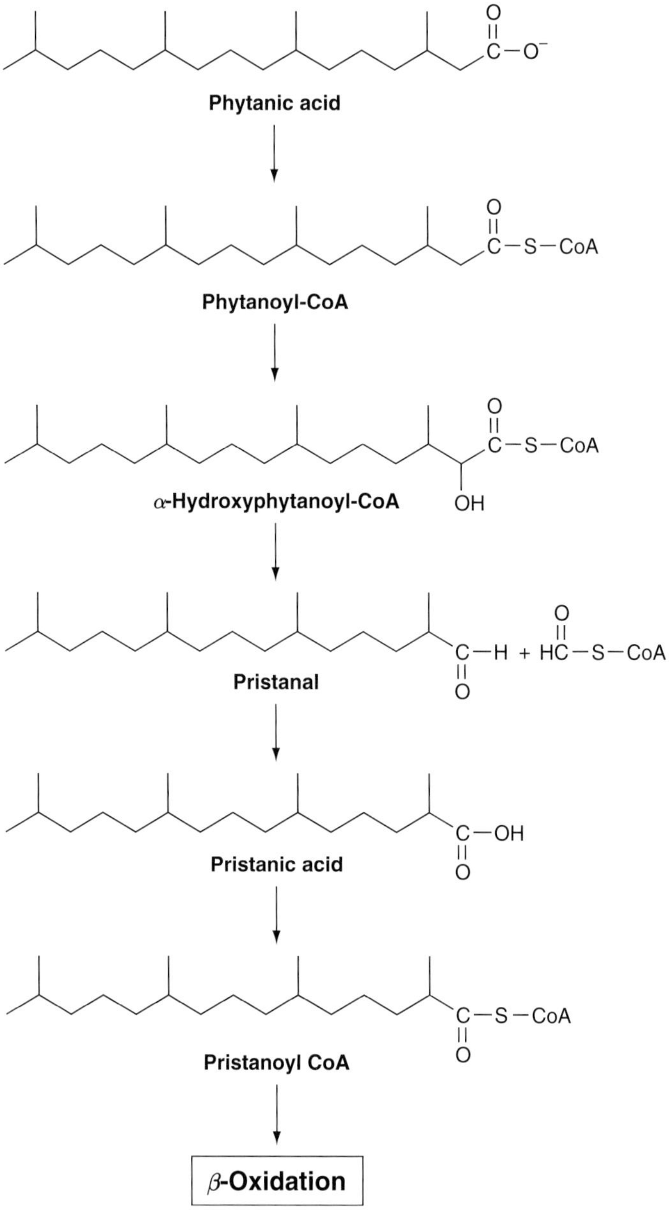

Figure 5 Peroxisomal phytanic acid α-oxidation pathway. The dietary 3-methyl-branched fatty acid phytanic acid is toxic if allowed to accumulate in the tissues. Its 3-methyl group prevents degradation by β-oxidation; therefore, this fatty acid is first shortened by one carbon atom. Like the substrates for peroxisomal β-oxidation, phytanic acid enters peroxisomes by an unknown mechanism. Activated phytanic acid is hydroxylated on carbon 2. Cleavage between carbons 1 and 2 yields a one-carbon CoA compound, formyl-CoA, and an aldehyde, pristanal. After oxidation and reactivation to the CoA derivative, pristanoyl-CoA can be degraded by β-oxidation.

dicarboxylic acids can then be at least partially degraded by β-oxidation from the ω-end, primarily in peroxisomes.

Fatty-Acid *de novo* Synthesis

Much of our need for fatty acids as constituents of phospholipids and other complex lipids is met by the diet. In addition, certain lipogenic tissues are capable of the *de novo* synthesis of fatty acids (**Figure 6**). These tissues include liver (hepatocytes),

adipose tissue, and lactating mammary gland. Much of the fatty acids synthesized by all three tissues is incorporated into triacylglycerol. Hepatic synthesis is primarily for export to other tissues (in very low-density lipoproteins), while synthesis in adipocytes and mammary gland is for local storage.

The carbon used for fatty-acid synthesis typically derives from the products of glycolysis. The end product of glycolysis, pyruvate, enters the mitochondria and becomes the substrate for two separate

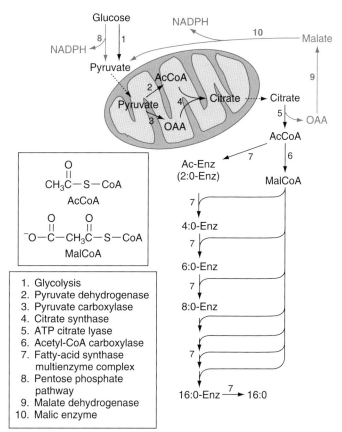

Figure 6 Fatty-acid biosynthesis. Cytoplasmic acetyl-CoA (AcCoA) is the primary substrate for *de novo* fatty-acid synthesis. This two-carbon compound most commonly derives from the glycolytic degradation of glucose, and its formation is dependent upon several reactions in the mitochondria. The mitochondrial enzyme pyruvate carboxylase is found primarily in tissues that can synthesize fatty acids. AcCoA is converted to malonyl-CoA (MalCoA) by acetyl-CoA carboxylase. Using AcCoA as a primer, the fatty-acid synthase multienzyme complex carries out a series of reactions that elongate the growing fatty acid by two carbon atoms. In this process MalCoA condenses with AcCoA, yielding an enzyme-bound four-carbon β-ketoacid that is reduced, dehydrated, and reduced again. The product is enzyme-bound 4:0. This process is repeated six more times, after which 16:0 is released from the complex. The reductive steps require NADPH, which is derived from enzyme reactions and pathways shown in grey. Enz refers to the fatty acid synthase multienzyme complex.

reactions. In one, pyruvate is decarboxylated via the pyruvate dehydrogenase complex, yielding acetyl-CoA. Lipogenic tissues also contain another mitochondrial enzyme, pyruvate carboxylase, which converts pyruvate to the four-carbon acid oxaloacetate (OAA). Acetyl-CoA and oxaloacetate condense to form the six-carbon acid citrate. As citrate accumulates within the mitochondrion, it is exported to the cytoplasm, where it is converted back to oxaloacetate and acetyl-CoA. Cytoplasmic acetyl-CoA is the fundamental building block for *de novo* synthesis of fatty acids.

The first enzyme unique to fatty-acid synthesis is acetyl-CoA carboxylase, which converts the two-carbon substrate acetyl-CoA into the three-carbon product malonyl-CoA. Citrate, in addition to being the precursor of cytoplasmic acetyl-CoA, has a regulatory role. Citrate is an allosteric activator of acetyl-CoA carboxylase and serves as a

signal that there is an ample carbon supply for fatty-acid synthesis. As noted above, malonyl-CoA is a potent inhibitor of CPT1. Cytoplasmic malonyl-CoA levels will be high only when there is significant flux through glycolysis, indicative of a high cellular energy state. Under these conditions, entry of fatty acids into the mitochondria (and subsequent β-oxidation) is prevented. Interestingly, there are two isoforms of acetyl-CoA carboxylase. One is found in the above-named lipogenic tissues. The other is found in many tissues that are not capable of synthesizing fatty acids, e.g., the heart. It is thought that the primary role of the second isozyme is to regulate mitochondrial fatty-acid β-oxidation by synthesizing malonyl-CoA when cellular energy needs are being met by carbohydrate metabolism.

The subsequent reactions of fatty-acid synthesis in humans are catalyzed by a multienzyme

Table 1 Distinctions between fatty-acid β-oxidation and fatty-acid synthesis

	Fatty-acid β-oxidation	Fatty-acid synthesis
Tissues with active pathway	Nearly all tissues except brain, nerve, and erythrocytes	Liver, adipose, and lactating mammary gland
Subcellular location	Mitochondria	Cytoplasm
Redox cofactors	NAD, FAD	NADPH
Acyl-group carrier	CoA	Enzyme-bound acyl carrier protein
Stereochemistry of 3-hydroxy intermediate	L-	D-

complex, fatty-acid synthase. After binding of one molecule each of acetyl-CoA and malonyl-CoA to unique binding sites within the complex, a condensation reaction occurs in which carbon dioxide is released and an enzyme-bound 4-carbon 3-ketoacid is formed. Subsequent reactions include a reduction step, a dehydration step, and a second reduction step. The intermediates produced in these reactions are similar to those seen in β-oxidation (**Figure 2**), in reverse order. The product (enzyme bound) is the saturated fatty acid 4:0, which can then condense with another molecule of malonyl-CoA to start the process anew. After seven such cycles, the ultimate product is 16:0, which is released from the complex.

The reductive steps in fatty-acid synthesis require reduced nicotinamide adenine dinucleotide phosphate (NADPH). Some NADPH is produced during recycling of the oxaloacetate formed during the cytoplasmic hydrolysis of citrate, described above. Oxaloacetate is first converted to malate (via cytoplasmic malate dehydrogenase). Malate is then decarboxylated to pyruvate in an $NADP^+$-dependent reaction catalyzed by malic enzyme; NADPH is produced in this reaction. NADPH for fatty-acid biosynthesis also comes from reactions in the pentose phosphate pathway (hexose monophosphate shunt).

In several respects, the enzymatic reactions of fatty-acid synthesis are the converse of those in fatty-acid oxidation. However, there are key differences, which are summarized in **Table 1**.

Fatty-Acid Elongation

The primary product synthesized by the *de novo* pathway is 16:0. While 16:0 is an important fatty acid, there is a need to synthesize longer-chain acids. Enzymes for elongation of fatty-acids have been found in membranes of the endoplasmic reticulum and mitochondria. However, these pathways are less well-characterized than that of fatty-acid synthesis. In the endoplasmic reticulum, the reactions involved in fatty-acid elongation are very similar to those of cytoplasmic fatty-acid synthesis. The donor of the added carbon atoms is also malonyl-CoA, indicating that an active acetyl-CoA carboxylase is required for elongation. Whereas the primary reactions of fatty-acid synthesis are found within the fatty-acid synthase multienzyme complex, individual proteins catalyze the four elongation reactions (condensation, reduction, dehydration, and reduction). Like synthesis, elongation in the endoplasmic reticulum requires reducing equivalents in the form of NADPH.

Fatty-acid elongation in mitochondrial membranes is thought to be slightly different from the process in the endoplasmic reticulum. The primary difference is that the donor of elongation units is thought to be acetyl-CoA, not malonyl-CoA. The four elongation reactions are similar, but may require NADH rather than NADPH as source of reducing equivalents. Little is known about how fatty-acid elongation in either the mitochondria or the endoplasmic reticulum is regulated.

Fatty-Acid Unsaturation and the Essential Fatty Acids

Monounsaturated and polyunsaturated fatty acids are extraordinarily important in human health and nutrition. Thus, the insertion of double bonds into the carbon skeleton of a fatty acid is a vital metabolic function. However, humans are in general not capable of inserting double bonds closer than nine carbon atoms from the methyl end of a fatty acid. Thus, we are incapable of the *de novo* synthesis of two important classes of fatty acids, the *n*-3 fatty acids such as docosahexaenoic acid (22:6*n*-3) and the *n*-6 fatty acids such as arachidonic acid (20:4*n*-6). The *n*-3 fatty acids have proven to be beneficial in the prevention of coronary artery disease. The fatty acid 22:6*n*-3 has been shown to be important for the normal development of the brain and retina, leading some manufacturers to include this fatty acid in their infant formula preparations. The *n*-6 fatty acids are important constituents of membrane lipids. The fatty acid 20:4 is also the well-known precursor of prostaglandins and other bioactive eicosanoids. Since we cannot synthesize these fatty acids *de novo*, we are dependent on the presence of at least some *n*-3 and some *n*-6 fatty acids in the diet. Linoleic acid (18:2*n*-6) and α-linolenic acid (18:3*n*-3) are the precursors of most biologically important *n*-3 and *n*-6 fatty acids; thus, they are referred to as essential fatty acids.

As noted earlier, the most abundant fatty acids in humans include a saturated fatty acid (16:0) and a monounsaturated fatty acid (18:1*n*-9). Humans can readily insert a *cis*-double bond nine carbons from the carboxyl carbon atom of a fatty acid (Δ9) in a reaction catalyzed by stearoyl-CoA desaturase (SCD1; so-named because the preferred substrate is the CoA derivative of 18:0, stearic acid). Because SCD1 is involved in the synthesis of such an abundant fatty acid, 18:1, the importance of this enzyme in metabolism was initially overlooked. However, 18:1 produced by SCD1 appears to be directed specifically towards triacylglycerol synthesis. Mice in which the SCD1 gene is disrupted have decreased adiposity. Furthermore, genetically obese leptin-deficient (ob–/ob–) mice in which the SCD1 gene is also disrupted have significantly reduced body weight compared with ob–/ob– mice, leading to the hypothesis that leptin regulates the synthesis of SCD1. Interestingly, dietary 18:1 seems to be more readily incorporated into lipids other than triacylglycerols, implying that the dietary and the SCD1-produced pools of this fatty acid are metabolically distinct. As with the *n*-3 fatty acids, dietary ingestion of monounsaturated fatty acids such as 18:1 has been associated with benefits to cardiovascular health.

Humans are also capable of inserting *cis*-double bonds either five or six carbon atoms from the carboxyl carbon atom of a fatty acid (Δ5 desaturase and Δ6 desaturase activity, respectively). These activities, when combined with the elongation pathways described above, form a powerful mechanism for synthesis of highly polyunsaturated fatty acids such as 20:4*n*-6 and 22:6*n*-3 from the dietary essential fatty acids. Previously, it was thought that humans also had the ability to insert a double bond four carbon atoms from the carboxyl carbon (Δ4 desaturase activity), as this activity was thought to be necessary for the conversion of 18:3*n*-3 to 22:6*n*-3. However, attempts to measure Δ4 desaturase activity experimentally were not successful. It is now thought that, through a series of elongation and desaturation reactions, 18:3*n*-3 is converted to the penultimate intermediate, 22:5*n*-3. Rather than using a Δ4 desaturase to complete the synthesis, 22:5*n*-3 is elongated to 24:5*n*-3, converted to 24:6*n*-3 by Δ6 desaturase, and finally chain-shortened to 22:6*n*-3 by one cycle of peroxisomal β-oxidation.

Fatty Acids as Components of Complex Lipids

Fatty acids are important building blocks for various cellular complex lipids (**Figure 7**). For simplicity, the pathways for incorporation of fatty acids into these lipids are outlined only briefly. More details can be found in any good biochemistry text. In most cases, fatty acyl-CoA and not free fatty acid participates in these biosynthetic reactions. Nearly all cells synthesize phospholipids, which are essential membrane constituents. Phospholipid synthesis takes place in the endoplasmic reticulum. It begins by fatty acylating the two free hydroxyl groups in α-glycerophosphate, a triose derived from glycolytic intermediates, yielding phosphatidic acid. Various head groups (e.g., choline, ethanolamine, inositol, or serine) can then be linked to the phosphate group. For synthesis of triacylglycerol, this phosphate moiety is removed, yielding diacylglycerol, and a third fatty acyl group is esterified to the free hydroxyl group.

Another type of lipid, the ether-linked phospholipids (e.g., plasmalogens), comprises about 20% of membrane phospholipids (**Figure 7**). Plasmalogen synthesis requires enzymes present in both peroxisomes and the endoplasmic reticulum. These lipids are thought to be part of the cellular defense mechanism against oxidative injury.

Fatty acids are also found esterified to the 3-hydroxyl group of cholesterol (cholesterol esters; ChE). ChE, which are more hydrophobic than free cholesterol, are a transport and storage form of cholesterol. ChE are found in high concentrations in low-density lipoproteins. Intracellular lipid droplets containing ChE are found in steroidogenic tissues and are thought to be a reservoir of cholesterol for steroid-hormone synthesis. The fatty acid most commonly found in ChE is 18:1. It must be activated to its CoA derivative before transfer to cholesterol in a reaction catalyzed by acyl-CoA cholesterol acyltransferase. ChE are also formed within lipoproteins by the transfer of one fatty acyl chain from phosphatidyl choline to cholesterol, a reaction catalyzed by circulating lecithin: cholesterol acyltransferase.

Synthesis of sphingolipids, which include sphingomyelin, ceramides, cerebrosides, and gangliosides, begins by the condensation of palmitoyl-CoA (16:0-CoA) with serine. The amino group of serine is then acylated by a second fatty acyl-CoA to form ceramide; the chain length of the second fatty acid can be variable. Transfer of phosphorylcholine (from the phospholipid phosphatidyl choline) to the hydroxyl group of ceramide yields

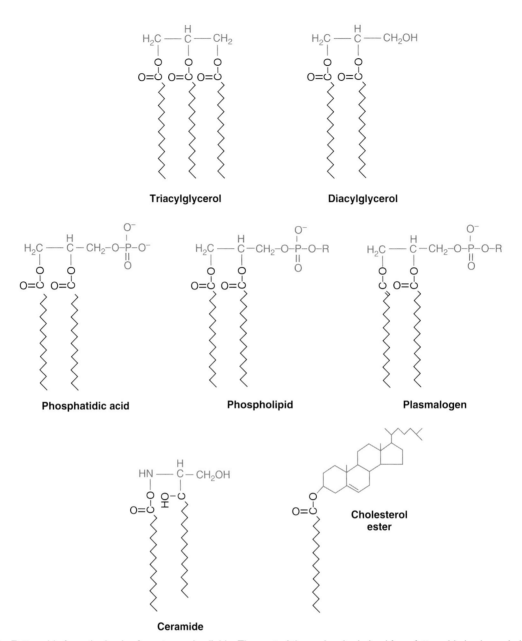

Figure 7 Fatty acids form the basis of most complex lipids. The part of the molecule derived from fatty acids is shown in black, and the part derived from other sources is shown in grey. For phospholipids and plasmalogens, R = choline, ethanolamine, inositol, serine, or a similar head group.

sphingomyelin. Alternatively, sugars (from sugar nucleotide donors) are added to produce the cerebrosides, gangliosides, and related lipids.

Eicosanoid Synthesis

The fatty acid 20:4n-6 (arachidonic acid) is the precursor of most eicosanoids, which include the prostaglandins, leukotrienes, and thromboxanes. Because it is an n-6 fatty acid, 20:4 must be derived from dietary lipids or synthesized by elongation and

unsaturation of the essential fatty acid 18:2n-6. As with other fatty acids, cellular concentrations of unesterified 20:4 are low. Conversion of 20:4 to eicosanoids begins with an agonist-induced release of the fatty acid from the sn-2 position of membrane phospholipids via the action of phospholipase A2. Unlike most reactions of fatty acids, eicosanoid synthesis appears to use free 20:4 rather than its CoA derivative as the substrate. Cyclooxygenases (COX1 and COX2) catalyze a complex molecular oxygen-requiring reaction that converts 20:4 to prostaglandin G2. This reaction involves carbon atoms in the middle of the acyl chain, rather than the methyl carbon (such as occurs in ω-oxidation) or the carboxyl carbon (such as occurs in nearly all other reactions of fatty acids). Prostaglandin G2 can subsequently be converted to other prostaglandins or to thromboxanes. As these compounds have potent biological effects, including mediation of inflammation, COX inhibitors are an important class of anti-inflammatory drugs. Free 20:4 is also the primary substrate for the enzyme 5-lipoxygenase, which is the first step in the synthesis of leukotrienes.

Fatty Acylation of Proteins

Covalent modification of proteins is a more recently discovered role of fatty acids. Fatty acylation of proteins frequently serves as a means of targeting or anchoring a protein to a membrane. Myristoylation, the addition of 14:0 to a protein, occurs at N-terminal glycine residues after removal of the initiator methionine. This process is generally co-translational and irreversible. N-myristoyl proteins include many signal-transduction-associated proteins, e.g., *src* and ADP-ribosylation factors. The enzyme N-myristoyltransferase catalyzes the reaction and uses 14:0-CoA as substrate.

Palmitoylation, the addition of 16:0 to a protein, is also commonly observed. This modification to the sulfydryl side chain of cysteine residues occurs post-translationally and is reversible. Both membrane-associated proteins and integral membrane proteins can be palmitoylated; examples are ion channels, neurotransmitter receptors, and sonic hedgehog. Protein palmitoyl transferases also use the CoA derivative of the fatty acid as a substrate. Several proteins are modified with both an N-terminal 14:0 and an S-linked 16:0 elsewhere in the protein chain. α-subunits of heterotrimeric G-proteins and endothelial nitric oxide synthase are examples of dually acylated proteins.

There are instances of acylation by fatty acids with chain lengths other than 14 or 16 carbon atoms. One nutritionally important example is the recently identified orexigenic peptide ghrelin. The active form of this 28-amino-acid peptide hormone has the medium-chain fatty acid 8:0 covalently esterified to the hydroxyl group of serine-3. Octanoylated ghrelin is believed to act at the level of the hypothalamus to stimulate appetite, perhaps via neuropeptide Y.

Vitamins and Fatty-Acid Metabolism

Several of the B vitamins are essential for normal fatty-acid metabolism (**Table 2**). Pantothenic acid is a constituent of CoA and is thus required for numerous reactions of fatty acids. Niacin and riboflavin are necessary for the synthesis of oxidized and reduced NAD(P) and FAD, respectively. These compounds play essential roles in fatty-acid oxidation, synthesis, and elongation. Biotin is a constituent of acetyl-CoA carboxylase and pyruvate carboxylase, both of which are involved in the synthesis of fatty acids from glucose. Thiamine is required for activity of the pyruvate dehydrogenase complex, which also participates in fatty-acid synthesis from glucose.

Regulation of Fatty-Acid Metabolism

A few specific aspects of the regulation of fatty-acid metabolism have been described above. More global regulatory mechanisms that deserve mention include those mediated by insulin and glucagon, sterol regulatory element-binding protein (SREBP) 1c, and peroxisome proliferator-activated receptor (PPAR) α. In the fed and fasted states, control of fuel metabolism is mediated to a large extent by insulin and glucagon, respectively. Effects of glucagon are mediated via cyclic adenosine monophosphate (cAMP)-dependent kinases and serve to decrease flux through glycolysis,

Table 2 Vitamins associated with fatty-acid metabolism

Vitamin	Active form	Enzymes	Pathways
Pantothenic acid	CoA	Many enzymes	Most reactions involving fatty acids
Niacin	NAD, NADH, NADP, NADPH	Dehydrogenases; reductases	Many pathways, particularly β-oxidation and fatty-acid synthesis and elongation
Riboflavin	FAD, FADH$_2$	Oxidases	β-Oxidation
Thiamine	Thiamine pyrophosphate	Pyruvate dehydrogenase complex; β-hydroxyphytanoyl-CoA lyase	Fatty-acid synthesis from glucose; phytanic acid β-oxidation
Biotin	Biocytin	Acetyl-CoA carboxylase; pyruvate carboxylase	Fatty-acid synthesis from glucose

thus decreasing the rate of *de novo* fatty-acid biosynthesis and increasing rates of mitochondrial β-oxidation and ketogenesis. Insulin effects are mediated through activation of its receptor tyrosine kinase and are in general opposite to those of glucagon, stimulating glycolysis and fatty-acid synthesis while inhibiting fatty-acid degradation. Insulin and glucagon have both acute and long-term effects on fatty-acid metabolism. The transcription factor SREBP1c is thought to mediate the action of insulin in upregulating genes involved in fatty-acid synthesis. Activation of PPARα on the other hand increases rates of fatty-acid oxidation and ketogenesis. Endogenous ligands for this nuclear receptor are thought to include polyunsaturated fatty acids and branched-chain fatty acids. The PPARs heterodimerize with the retinoid X receptor, and both receptors must be ligand-bound for transcriptional activation. Several mitochondrial, microsomal, and peroxisomal genes associated with fatty-acid catabolism are upregulated via PPARα stimulation.

See also: **Cholesterol**: Sources, Absorption, Function and Metabolism; Factors Determining Blood Levels. **Fatty Acids**: Monounsaturated; Omega-3 Polyunsaturated; Omega-6 Polyunsaturated; Saturated; *Trans* Fatty Acids. **Lipids**: Chemistry and Classification; Composition and Role of Phospholipids. **Obesity**: Definition, Etiology and Assessment.

Further Reading

Frohnert BI and Bernlohr DA (2000) Regulation of fatty acid transporters in mammalian cells. *Progress in Lipid Research* **39**: 83–107.

Gibbons GF (2003) Regulation of fatty acid and cholesterol synthesis: co-operation or competition? *Progress in Lipid Research* **42**: 479–497.

Gunstone FD, Harwood JL, and Padley FB (eds.) (1994) *The Lipid Handbook*, 2nd edn. London: Chapman & Hall.

Kunau WH, Dommes V, and Schulz H (1995) Beta-oxidation of fatty acids in mitochondria, peroxisomes, and bacteria: a century of continued progress. *Progress in Lipid Research* **34**: 267–342.

McGarry JD and Foster DW (1980) Regulation of hepatic fatty acid oxidation and ketone body production. *Annual Review of Biochemistry* **49**: 395–420.

Numa S (ed.) (1984) *Fatty Acid Metabolism and its Regulation*. New York: Elsevier.

Vance DE and Vance JE (eds.) (2002) *Biochemistry of Lipids, Lipoproteins and Membranes*, 4th edn. New Comprehensive Biochemistry 36. New York: Elsevier.

Wanders RJ, Vreken P, Ferdinandusse S *et al.* (2001) Peroxisomal fatty acid alpha- and beta-oxidation in humans: enzymology, peroxisomal metabolite transporters and peroxisomal diseases. *Biochemical Society Transactions* **29**: 250–267.

Watkins PA (1997) Fatty acid activation. *Progress in Lipid Research* **36**: 55–83.

Monounsaturated

P Kirk, University of Ulster, Coleraine, UK

This article is reproduced from the previous edition, pp. 744–751, © 1999, Elsevier Ltd.

Introduction

Fatty acids are described according to two characteristics: chain length and degree of saturation with hydrogen. Monounsaturated fatty acids (MUFA) have, as the name suggests, only one unsaturated bond attached to the carbon chain. This double bond is fixed in nature and is positioned on the ninth carbon atom counting from the methyl (omega) end of the fatty-acid chain. Four of these MUFA are found in significant quantities in food, the most common being oleic acid ($C_{18:1}$) (**Figure 1**). This n-9 fatty acid is capable of being synthesized by animals, including humans, but is predominantly incorporated via the diet. While butter and animal fats contain only small amounts of oleic acid, olive oil is a rich source. Olive oil, which comprises up to 70% of the fat intake in Mediterranean diets, is postulated to be effective in decreasing the risk of certain chronic diseases. These include such diseases as coronary heart disease, cancers, and inflammatory disorders, particularly rheumatoid arthritis.

Cholesterol Metabolism

Cholesterol metabolism is of fundamental biological importance. All vertebrates require cholesterol as a precursor for bile acids and hormones, including corticosteroids, sex steroids, and vitamin D. The amount of cholesterol found in tissues greatly exceeds the requirement for production of these hormones and bile acids, and the bulk of this excess is associated with the cell-membrane structure, where it is believed to modulate the physical state of phospholipid bilayers.

Cholesterol circulates in plasma as a component of lipoproteins. There are several distinct classes of plasma lipoprotein, which differ in several respects, including type of apolipoprotein and relative content of triacylglycerol and cholesterol.

Cholesterol transport

Chylomicron remnants deliver dietary cholesterol to the liver. It is then incorporated into very low-density lipoproteins (VLDL), which are secreted in

Figure 1 Structure of oleic acid, $C_{18:1}$.

plasma. The VLDL acquire cholesteryl esters and apolipoprotein E (apo E) from high-density lipoproteins (HDL) to produce intermediate-density lipoproteins (IDL), which are rapidly taken up by the liver or are further catabolized into low-density lipoproteins (LDL). These cholesterol-rich LDL particles are catabolized only slowly in human plasma and are therefore present at relatively high concentrations. Elimination of cholesterol from these extrahepatic cells is achieved by the delivery of cholesterol from cell membranes to plasma HDL in the first step of a pathway known as reverse cholesterol transport. This process allows for esterification of cholesterol and its delivery back to the liver.

LDL, HDL, and atherosclerosis

Membrane function is compromised if it contains either too much or too little cholesterol. Epidemiological studies have classified raised plasma cholesterol levels as a risk factor for atherosclerosis, and it is one of the more important predictors of coronary heart disease (CHD). Elevated plasma cholesterol concentration (hypercholesterolemia) is associated with an increased concentration of LDL, owing to either an increased rate of LDL formation or a decrease in the rate at which they are cleared from plasma, and usually a decreased concentration of HDL. Numerous dietary-intervention studies have aimed both to prevent CHD and to reduce total mortality, but almost all have been ineffective.

MUFA and CHD

Many of the trials conducted concentrated on the substitution of polyunsaturated vegetable oils for saturated fat from animal sources and on decreasing the amount of dietary cholesterol. These studies followed the reasoning that fats rich in saturated fatty acids (SFA) raised plasma cholesterol mainly by increasing plasma LDL cholesterol levels, and oils rich in polyunsaturated fatty acids (PUFA) lowered plasma cholesterol mainly by decreasing LDL cholesterol. The MUFA were first considered neutral in regard to their influence on plasma cholesterol, but more recent findings suggest a decrease in total LDL cholesterol concentration following substitution of SFA by MUFA. Moreover, clinical trials have also shown that a MUFA-rich diet does not decrease concentrations & HDL, the lipoprotein inversely correlated with CHD.

Although important links exist between cholesterol metabolism and aspects of cell function, other complicating factors must be considered. Cholesterol metabolism is sensitive to the inflammatory response that accompanies most pathological events.

Tumor necrosis factor (TNF) reduces LDL and HDL cholesterol levels and inhibits lipoprotein lipase, resulting in a fall in cholesterol and an increase in triacylglycerol levels. These changes may be perpetuated beyond the acute phase if an inflammatory process is present. Cholesterol metabolism is also sensitive to genetic and environmental factors, which may have independent effects on noncardiovascular disease. As a consequence, the relationship between cholesterol levels and the presence or absence of a disease state must be interpreted with caution.

Atherogenesis and Endothelial Dysfunction

Atherosclerosis can be considered as a chronic inflammatory disease, which slowly progresses over a period of decades before clinical symptoms become manifest. The atherogenic process comprises interactions between multiple cell types, which initiate a cascade of events involving alterations in vascular production of autocoids, cytokines, and growth factors. The endothelium, because of its location between blood and the vascular wall, has been implicated in the atherogenic process from the initial stages.

Function of endothelial cells

Owing to the strategic location of the endothelium, it is able to perform many different functions. In addition to acting as a protective barrier, endothelial cells have been shown to play important roles in control of homeostasis, capillary transport, and, more importantly, regulation of the tone of underlying vascular smooth muscle. The endothelium evokes relaxation of these muscle cells, allowing vasodilation via the chemical factor endothelium-derived relaxing factor (EDRF), which has been identified as nitric oxide (NO). The EDRF or NO is vital for maintaining the vasodilatory capacity of vascular muscle and also controls levels of platelet function and monocyte adhesion. Any endothelial injury or dysfunction could therefore be an important factor in atherosclerosis.

Endothelial dysfunction

Decrease in the production, release, or action of NO may lead to enhanced expression of adhesion molecules and chemotactic factors at the endothelial surface. The exact nature of endothelial dysfunction is unknown, although possibilities include a decreased expression of NO synthase, imbalance between the production of endothelium-derived constricting and relaxing factors, production of an endogenous NO synthase inhibitor, and overproduction of oxygen-derived free radicals including O_2^-. The release of the free radical O_2^- from smooth muscle cells is believed to be responsible for the oxidation of LDL cholesterol. Raised cholesterol levels and – more importantly – increased levels of oxidatively modified LDL cholesterol (OxLDL) are considered to be among the most powerful inhibitors of normal endothelial function and hence contribute to the process of atherogenesis.

Lipid peroxidation and atherosclerosis

Lipid peroxidation apparently plays a major role in the pathology of atherosclerosis. Atherosclerosis, which is usually a precondition for CHD, is a degenerative process leading to the accumulation of a variable mixture of substances including lipid in the endothelium of the arteries. This disease is characterized by the formation of a fatty streak and the accumulation of cells loaded with lipid: the foam cells. These cells are believed to arise from white blood cell-derived macrophages or arterial smooth muscle cells. Most of the lipid in the foam cells is in the form of LDL particles. Although research has determined that LDL receptors are responsible for the uptake of LDL by cells, the arterial uptake of LDL, which leads to development of foam cells, occurs by a different pathway. It is only when the LDL particles have undergone oxidative modification that they are available for uptake by macrophages via the scavenger receptor. During the course of oxidative modification, LDL cholesterol acquires various biological properties not present in native LDL that make it a potentially important mediator, promoting atherogenesis. The LDL, once oxidized, becomes cytotoxic and causes local cellular damage to the endothelium. This process, which enhances LDL uptake to generate foam cells, is considered one of the earliest events in atherogenesis (**Figure 2**).

MUFA and atherogenesis

Studies have looked at the oxidizability *in vitro* of LDL using nonphysiological oxidizing conditions to evaluate the susceptibility of LDL to oxidation and hence its atherogenic potential. It is well known that modification of LDL is inhibited by various antioxidants commonly present within plasma LDL particles. More recent studies, however, indicate that raising the ratio of $C_{18:1}$ to $C_{18:2}$ (linoleic acid) may also reduce the susceptibility of LDL to oxidation. The LDL is particularly vulnerable to peroxidation once PUFA form part of the lipoprotein fraction of cell membranes, as these fatty acids

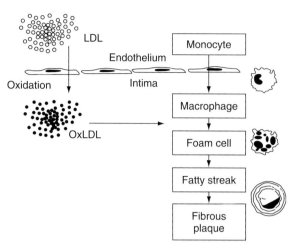

Figure 2 The role of oxidized LDL (OxLDL) in formation of foam cells. Reproduced with permission from Ashwell M (1993) *Diet and Heart Disease – A Round Table of Factors.* London: British Nutrition Foundation.

have reactive double bonds in their structures. The MUFA are much less easily oxidized as they have only one double bond. This property may confer a protective effect against CHD by generating LDL particles more resistant to oxidation. Further protection may be afforded from MUFA as they do not lower HDL. It is postulated that oxidized HDL, in contrast to oxidized LDL, is not avidly taken up by macrophages but instead inhibits the modification of LDL, thereby substantially decreasing oxidized LDL cellular uptake.

Oxidation of LDL cholesterol is, therefore, clearly linked to damage to the endothelium and hence to the process of atherogenesis. It has, however, more far-reaching effects, as it has also been linked to activation and aggregation of platelets. This process is involved in the production of occlusive thrombosis, which contributes significantly to the fibrous atherosclerotic plaque.

Thrombosis and Fibrinolysis

The importance of thrombosis in causing heart disease is receiving increasing attention. Thrombosis, in contrast to atherosclerosis, is an acute event resulting in the formation of a thrombus or blood clot, which is an aggregate of fibrin, platelets, and red cells. Blood clotting or coagulation is an important process as it is responsible for repairing tissues after injury. Under normal physiological conditions, a blood clot forms at the site of injury. Platelets are attracted to the damaged tissue and adhere to the surface. They are then activated to release substances that attract more platelets, allowing platelet aggregation and triggering coagulation mechanisms.

The coagulation cascade

The process of blood coagulation involves two pathways: the extrinsic and intrinsic pathways (**Figure 3**). The cascade is dependent on a series of separate clotting factors, each of which acts as a catalyst for the next step in the system. The process results in the formation of insoluble fibrin from the soluble protein fibrinogen. This then interacts with a number of blood components, including red blood cells, to form the thrombus. Any damage to the endothelium, therefore, causes platelet aggregation and adherence to the lining of the blood-vessel walls, thereby triggering the coagulation cascade. An imbalance of this process, by increasing the rate of thrombus formation, could increase the risk of CHD, and data have shown that levels of factor VII and fibrinogen are particularly important in balancing the coagulation cascade.

Factor VII and fibrinogen

There is accumulating evidence the factor VII is involved in arterial thrombosis and atherogenesis. The physiology of the factor VII system is intricate, not least since it can potentially exist in several forms. Activation of factor VIIc is generally achieved by tissue factor and initiates blood coagulation by subsequent activation of factors IX and X. It has been further suggested that tissue factor associated with the lipoproteins LDL and VLDL, but not HDL, may possibly generate factor VIIc activity, and a direct relationship is believed to exist between the level of factor VII complex in plasma and the dietary influence on plasma triacylglycerol concentration.

Several mechanisms have been suggested whereby an increase in plasma fibrinogen concentration may be linked to CHD. These include the involvement of fibrinogen and fibrin in the evolution of the atheromatous plaque through fibrin deposition and in

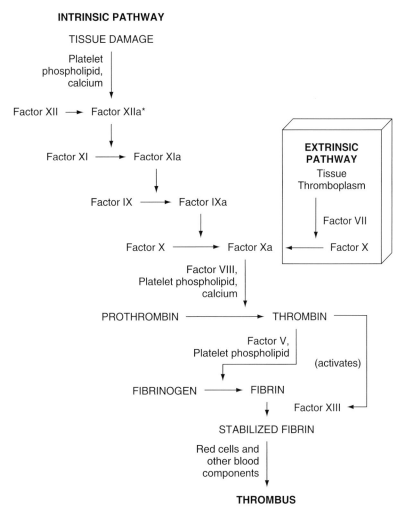

Figure 3 The coagulation cascade; a, active. Reproduced with permission from Buttriss JL and Gray J (1992) *Coronary Heart Disease II, Fact File 8*. London: National Dairy Council. Copyright National Dairy Council.

platelet aggregation through its impact on blood viscosity, which in turn is related to the risk of thrombosis. A mechanism exists to dissolve the thrombus by the breakdown or lysis of the fibrin meshwork (fibrinolysis). Plasminogen, which is generated by plasmin, is the zymosan that ultimately effects fibrinolysis. Failure of the mechanism to activate will cause obstruction of blood vessels and prevent normal blood supply.

Fibrinolysis

Investigators have shown that a decrease in the release of tissue plasminogen activator (tPA) and an elevation of plasminogen activator inhibitor 1 (PAI-1) will reduce fibrinolytic function. It has emerged that triacylglycerol-rich lipoproteins stimulate PAI-1 secretion from endothelial cells, and furthermore it has been shown that OxLDL induces secretion, whereas native LDL has no detectable effect. Lipoprotein (a) (Lp(a)) has also been linked with a decrease in fibrinolysis. Lp(a) is an LDL-like particle consisting of the protein apo(a). It is believed that apo(a) competes with plasminogen and plasmin for binding to fibrin, thus interfering with fibrinolysis; LDL and Lp(a) may represent, therefore, an important link between thrombotic and lipid mechanisms in atherogenesis.

MUFA and thrombosis

Results from animal studies have shown an elevation in platelet activation and hence greater risk of thrombosis as a result of feeding saturated fat. Platelet aggregation thresholds, however, decrease when total fat intake is decreased or when dairy and animal fats are partially replaced with vegetable oils rich in PUFA. These studies failed, however, to keep the intakes of SFA and total fat constant. More recent work has shown that, in fact, diets high in PUFA significantly increase platelet aggregation in animals, compared with MUFA-rich diets. The changes in fatty-acid composition may affect blood clotting because the increase in PUFA allows for oxidation of LDL. As previously mentioned, OxLDL is cyto-toxic, and this can cause endothelial damage leading to the activation of platelets, generation of factor VII, and hence thrombus formation. Increased dietary intakes of MUFA may also increase the rate of fibrinolysis by lowering levels of LDL cholesterol and reducing the susceptibility of LDL to oxidation, thereby affecting both PAI-1 secretion and apo(a) activity.

It must be noted that both atherosclerosis and thrombosis are triggered by inflammation, and evidence suggests that several hemostatic factors other than the glycoprotein fibrinogen not only have an important role in thrombotic events but are also recognized as potentially important CHD risk factors.

Inflammation and Oxidative Damage

Many diseases that have an inflammatory basis such as cancer, sepsis, and chronic inflammatory diseases such as rheumatoid arthritis (RA) have symptoms mediated by pro-inflammatory mediators named cytokines. These mediators, which include interleukins (IL) 1–8, tumor necrosis factors (TNF), and interferons, are essential for protection from invading bodies. They act by producing a situation in which immune cells are attracted to the inflammatory site and are activated. An inflammatory stimulus, such as tissue damage incurred by trauma or invasion of tissue by bacteria or viruses, induces production of IL-1, IL-6, and TNF from a range of immune cells, including phagocytic leucocytes and T and B lymphocytes. Once induced, IL-6, IL-1, and TNF further induce each other's production, leading to a cascade of cytokines, which are capable of producing metabolic and immune effects. Inflammatory stimuli also bring about the activation of neutrophils to release free radicals, which enhance the production of TNF and other cytokines. Overproduction of these pro-inflammatory mediators may, therefore, allow excessive release of reactive oxygen species (ROS) into extracellular fluid to damage its macromolecular components.

Oxidative damage

Free radicals are any species capable of an independent existence that contain one or more unpaired electrons. ROS is a collective term, referring not only to oxygen-centered radicals such as superoxide ($O_2^{\cdot}$) and the hydroxy radical ($^{\cdot}OH$), but also to hydrogen peroxide (H_2O_2), ozone (O_3), and singlet oxygen ($^1O_2$). These are produced as the by-products of normal metabolism and, as such, are highly reactive in chemical terms. In order to become more stable chemically, the free radical reacts with other molecules by either donating or taking an electron, in either case leaving behind another unstable molecule, and hence this becomes a chain reaction. So, although oxygen is essential for life, in certain circumstances it may also be toxic. Damage caused by ROS to cellular target sites includes oxidative damage to proteins, membranes (lipid and proteins), and DNA. PUFA are particularly vulnerable to ROS attack because they have unstable double bonds in their structure. This process is termed 'lipid peroxidation'; because PUFA are an essential part of the phospholipid fraction of cell membranes, uncontrolled lipid peroxidation can lead to considerable cellular damage. The balance of MUFA in cell membranes is also critical to cell function, but, as already noted, MUFA are far less vulnerable to lipid peroxidation.

MUFA and inflammation

Oxidative damage by ROS to DNA and lipids contributes significantly to the etiology of cancer and atherosclerosis. A decrease in production of proinflammatory mediators would, therefore, be beneficial by decreasing the release of ROS. Diminishing the production of cytokines is also believed to improve the symptoms of RA. It has been suggested that olive oil may have anti-inflammatory properties as it can reduce the production of these proinflammatory mediators. Although few studies have been carried out on the benefits of olive oil on symptoms of inflammation, it is possible that olive oil produces a similar effect to fish oil. Fish oils and butter have both been shown to reverse the proinflammatory effects of one cytokine, TNF. Further research, where $C_{18:1}$ was added to a diet containing coconut oil, resulted in responses to TNF that were similar to those seen in animals fed butter. It was assumed that, as the anti-inflammatory effects of butter appeared to be due to its oleic acid content, olive oil should be more anti-inflammatory. This was put to the test, and, while both butter and olive oil reduced the extent of a number of symptoms of inflammation, olive oil showed a greater potency than butter. From this, it can be concluded that dietary factors such as olive oil may play a significant protective role in the development severity of RA.

Carcinogenesis

Cancer is second only to CHD as a cause of death in Western countries. Cancer in humans is a multistep disease process in which a single cell can develop from an otherwise normal tissue into a malignancy that can eventually destroy the organism. Carcinogenesis is believed to proceed through three distinct stages. Initiation is brought about when carcinogens mutate a single cell. This mutation provides a growth advantage, and cells rapidly proliferate during the second stage, promotion. Tumor promotion produces relatively benign growths, which can be converted into cancer in the third stage, malignant conversion. While the causes of cancer are not known with certainty, both initiation and conversion require some form of genetic alteration, and ROS and other free radicals have long been known to be mutagenic (**Figure 4**).

Oxidation and cancer

Although PUFA are the most reactive of substrates for ROS attack leading to lipid peroxidation, interest is centering on the detection of oxidized nucleic acids as an indicator of pro-oxidant conditions. It

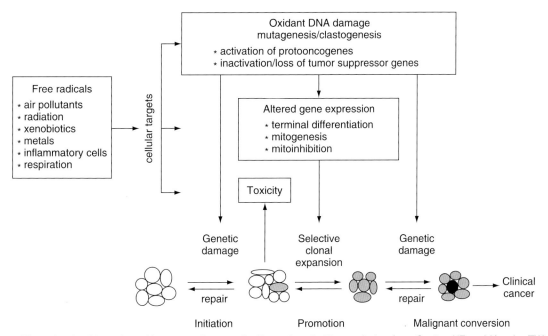

Figure 4 The role of oxidants in multistage carcinogenesis. Reproduced with permission from Guyton KZ and Kensler TW (1993) Oxidative mechanisms in carcinogenesis. *British Medical Bulletin* **49**: 523–544.

has been indicated that significant oxidative damage occurs *in vitro* and contributes to the etiology of cancer. It has become apparent that many genotoxic agents act through the common mechanism of oxidative damage to DNA. Oxidative processes may be responsible for initiating carcinogenic changes via DNA oxidative damage and may also act as tumor promoters, modulating the expression of genes that regulate cell differentiation and growth and act synergistically with the initiators. Animal studies have indicated diets containing high levels of $C_{18:2}$ as strong promoters of tumors, and this may be as a result of increased oxidative stress. The fact that MUFA are much less readily oxidized may therefore confer a protective effect against carcinogenesis.

Immune function and cancer

The diet is believed to play an important role in the onset of carcinogenesis, and there are a number of carcinogens present in food, including mycotoxins, polycyclic hydrocarbons, and pesticides. Associations have been made between dietary fat intake and morbidity and mortality from breast and colon cancer. Another possible mechanism for the proposed protective effects against cancer of olive oil compared with sunflower oil involves diet-induced alterations in host immune responses. Both the type and concentration of dietary fats have been reported to influence immune status in several animal models. The PUFA $C_{18:2}$ is necessary for T-cell-mediated immunity, but high intakes will suppress immune function and may therefore increase the risk of cancer. Furthermore, comparisons between the effects of diets rich in $C_{18:2}$ and those rich in $C_{18:1}$ on varying indicators of immune function in mice have shown that, while dietary $C_{18:2}$ predisposed animals to suppression of certain T-cell-mediated reactions, diets rich in $C_{18:1}$ did not. MUFA may therefore have a significant effect in humans against cancer, by lowering the risk of suppression of T-cell activity.

Other Physiological Effects

Because many, sometimes competing, mechanisms appear to mediate the relation between intake of MUFA and CHD incidence, no single surrogate biochemical or physiological response can predict with confidence the effect of a particular dietary pattern. For this reason examinations of the relation between specific dietary factors and CHD incidence itself are particularly valuable because such studies integrate the effects of all known and unknown mechanisms.

The extremely low rate of CHD in countries with high consumption of olive oil, for instance, suggests the benefits of substituting this fat for other fats. This kind of analysis has been expanded further by noting that MUFA intake is inversely associated with total mortality as well as with CHD. Some effects may well be because of the amount of antioxidant vitamins olive oil contains. Vegetable oils are the most important source of α-tocopherol in most diets, and olive oil contains about 12 mg per 100 g. Evidence indicates that α-tocopherol functions as a free-radical scavenger to protect cellular membranes from oxidative destruction. Oxidative stress has been linked to an increased risk of many chronic diseases, including atherosclerosis, cancer, and inflammatory disorders. Other injuries such as cataract and reperfusion injury are also associated with an increase in oxidative stress and a decrease in antioxidant activity.

A large body of evidence suggests a beneficial effect of MUFA in the diet. Although much remains to be learned about the mechanisms by which $C_{18:1}$ acts, it is believed to lower risks of CHD, several common cancers, cataracts, and other inflammatory disorders. It is suggested, therefore, that consuming MUFA, for instance in the form of olive oil as used widely in the Mediterranean diet, is likely to enhance long-term health.

See also: **Antioxidants**: Diet and Antioxidant Defense. **Arthritis**. **Cancer**: Epidemiology and Associations Between Diet and Cancer; Effects on Nutritional Status. **Cholesterol**: Sources, Absorption, Function and Metabolism; Factors Determining Blood Levels. **Coronary Heart Disease**: Hemostatic Factors; Lipid Theory; Prevention. **Cytokines**. **Dairy Products**. **Fats and Oils**. **Fatty Acids**: Metabolism; Monounsaturated; Omega-3 Polyunsaturated; Omega-6 Polyunsaturated; Saturated; *Trans* Fatty Acids. **Immunity**: Physiological Aspects. **Lipids**: Chemistry and Classification. **Lipoproteins**.

Further Reading

Ashwell M (1993) *Diet and Heart Disease – A Round Table of Factors*. London: British Nutrition Foundation.

Barter P (1994) Cholesterol and cardiovascular disease: basic science. *Australia and New Zealand Journal of Medicine* 24: 83–88.

Besler HT and Grimble RF (1993) Modulation of the response of rats to endotoxin by butter and olive and corn oil. *Proceedings of the Nutrition Society* 52: 68A.

Cerutti PA (1985) Prooxidant states and tumor promotion. *Science* 227: 375–381.

Daae LW, Kierulf P, Landass S, and Urdal P (1993) Cardiovascular risk factors: interactive effects of lipid, coagulation, and fibrinolysis. *Scandinavian Journal of Clinical Laboratory Investigation* 532: 19–27.

Dunnigan MG (1993) The problem with cholesterol. No light at the end of the tunnel. *British Medical Journal* **306**: 1355–1356.

Ernst E (1993) The role of fibrinogen as a cardiovascular risk factor. *Atherosclerosis* **100**: 1–12.

Guyton KZ and Kensler TW (1993) Oxidative mechanisms in carcinogenesis. *British Medical Bulletin* **49**: 523–544.

Halliwell B (1989) Tell me about free radicals, doctor: a review. *Journal of the Royal Society of Medicine* **82**: 747–752.

Hannigan BM (1994) Diet and immune function. *British Journal of Biomedical Science* **51**: 252–259.

Hoff HF and O'Neil J (1991) Lesion-derived low density lipoprotein and oxidized low density lipoprotein share a lability for aggregation, leading to enhanced macrophage degradation. *Arteriosclerosis and Thrombosis* **11**: 1209–1222.

Linos A, Kaklamanis E, and Kontomerkos A (1991) The effect of olive oil and fish consumption on rheumatoid arthritis – a case control study. *Scandinavian Journal of Rheumatology* **20**: 419–426.

Mensink RP and Katan MB (1989) An epidemiological and an experimental study on the effect of olive oil on total serum and HDL cholesterol in healthy volunteers. *European Journal of Clinical Nutrition* **43**(supplement 2): 43–48.

Morel DW, Dicorleto PE, and Chisolm GM (1984) Endothelial and smooth muscle cells alter low density lipoprotein *in vitro* by free radical oxidation. *Arteriosclerosis* **4**: 357–364.

National Dairy Council (1992) *Coronary Heart Disease*. Fact File No. 8. London: NDC.

Visioli F and Galli C (1995) Natural antioxidants and prevention of coronary heart disease: the potential role of olive oil and its minor constituents. *Nutrition Metabolism and Cardiovascular Disease* **5**: 306–314.

Omega-3 Polyunsaturated

A P Simopoulos, The Center for Genetics, Nutrition and Health, Washington, DC, USA

Introduction

Over the past 20 years many studies and clinical investigations have been carried out on the metabolism of polyunsaturated fatty acids (PUFAs) in general and on n-3 fatty acids in particular. Today we know that n-3 fatty acids are essential for normal growth and development. Research has been carried out in animal models, tissue cultures, and human beings. The original observational studies have given way to controlled clinical intervention trials. Great progress has taken place in our knowledge of the physiologic and molecular mechanisms of the n-3 fatty acids in health and disease. Specifically, their beneficial effects have been shown in the prevention and management of coronary heart disease, hypertension, type 2 diabetes, renal disease, rheumatoid arthritis, ulcerative colitis, Crohn's disease, and

chronic obstructive pulmonary disease. This chapter focuses on the sources, desaturation and elongation of n-6 and n-3 fatty acids; evolutionary aspects of diet relative to n-3 fatty acids and the n-6:n-3 balance; eicosanoid metabolism and biological effects of n-6 and n-3 fatty acids; nutrigenetics – interaction between the n-6:n-3 fatty acids and the genome; effects of dietary α-linolenic acid compared with long-chain n-3 fatty acid derivatives on physiologic indexes; human studies in growth and development; coronary heart disease; inflammation – a common base for the development of coronary heart disease, diabetes, arthritis, mental health and cancer; the need to return the n-3 fatty acids into the food supply for normal homeostasis; and future considerations.

n-6 and n-3 Fatty Acids: Sources, Desaturation and Elongation

Unsaturated fatty acids consist of monounsaturates and polyunsaturates. There are two classes of PUFA: n-6 and n-3. The distinction between n-6 and n-3 fatty acids is based on the location of the first double bond, counting from the methyl end of the fatty acid molecule. In the n-6 fatty acids, the first double bond is between the 6th and 7th carbon atoms and in the n-3 fatty acids the first double bond is between the 3rd and 4th carbon atoms. Monounsaturates are represented by oleic acid an n-9 fatty acid, which can be synthesized by all mammals including humans. Its double bond is between the 9th and 10th carbon atoms (**Figure 1**).

n-6 and n-3 fatty acids are also known as essential fatty acids (EFAs) because humans, like all mammals, cannot make them and must obtain them in their diet. n-6 fatty acids are represented by linoleic acid (LA; 18:2n-6) and n-3 fatty acids by α-linolenic acid (ALA; 18:3n-3). LA is plentiful in nature and is found in the seeds of most plants except for coconut, cocoa, and palm. ALA, on the other hand, is found in the chloroplasts of green leafy vegetables and in the seeds of flax, rape, chia, perilla, and in walnuts (**Tables 1, 2**, and **3**). Both EFAs are metabolized to longer chain fatty acids of 20 and 22 carbon atoms. LA is metabolized to arachidonic acid (AA; 20:4n-6) and LNA to eicosapentaenoic acid (EPA; 20:5n-3) and docosahexaenoic acid (DHA; 22:6n-3), increasing the chain length and degree of unsaturation by adding extra double bonds to the carboxyl end of the fatty acid molecule (**Figure 2**).

Humans and other mammals, except for carnivores such as lions, can convert LA to AA

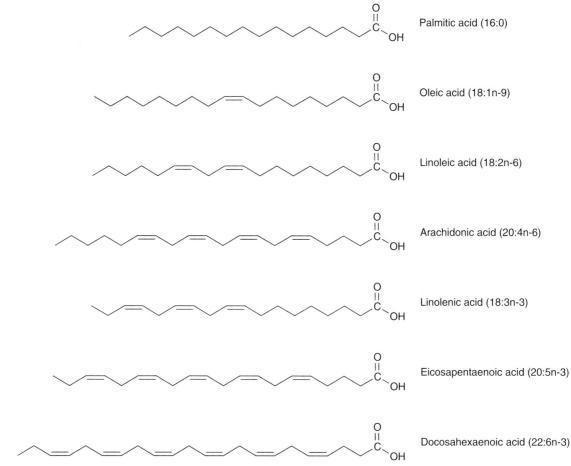

Figure 1 Structural formulas for selected fatty acids.

and ALA to EPA and DHA. This conversion was shown by using deuterated ALA. There is competition between n-6 and n-3 fatty acids for the desaturation enzymes. However, both Δ-4 and Δ-6 desaturases prefer n-3 to n-6 fatty acids. But a high LA intake interferes with the desaturation and elongation of ALA. *Trans*-fatty acids interfere with the desaturation and elongation of both LA and ALA.

Table 1 Polyunsaturated oils high in n-6 and n-3 fatty acids

n-6 oils	n-3 oils
Corn oil	Fish oil
Safflower oil	Chia oil
Sunflower seed oil	Perilla oil
Cottonseed oil	Flaxseed oil
Soybean oil	Canola oil
Peanut oil	Walnut oil
Sesame oil	Soybean oil[a]
Grapeseed oil	
Borage oil	
Primrose oil	

[a]note: soybean oil is higher in n-6 fatty acids than most n-3 oils, so it belongs in both categories.

Δ-6 desaturase is the limiting enzyme and there is some evidence that it decreases with age. Premature infants, hypertensive individuals, and some diabetics are limited in their ability to make EPA and DHA from ALA. These findings are important and need to be considered when making dietary recommendations. EPA and DHA are found in the oils of fish, particularly fatty fish (**Table 4**). AA is found predominantly in the phospholipids of grain-fed animals and eggs.

LA, ALA, and their long-chain derivatives are important components of animal and plant cell membranes. In mammals and birds, the n-3 fatty acids are distributed selectively among lipid classes. ALA is found in triglycerides, in cholesteryl esters, and in very small amounts in phospholipids. EPA is found in cholesteryl esters, triglycerides, and phospholipids. DHA is found mostly in phospholipids. In mammals, including humans, the cerebral cortex, retina, and testis and sperm are particularly rich in DHA. DHA is one of the most abundant components of the brain's structural lipids. DHA, like EPA, can be

Table 2 Comparison of dietary fats (fatty acid content normalized to 100%)

Dietary fat	Saturated fat	Polyunsaturated fat			Monounsaturated fat	Cholesterol
		LA	ALA	LA:ALA		
Flaxseed oil	10	16	53	(0.3)	20	0
Canola (rapeseed) oil	6	22	10	(2.2)	62	0
Walnut oil	12	58	12	(4.8)	18	0
Safflower oil	10	77	Trace	(77)	13	0
Sunflower oil	11	69	–	(69)	20	0
Corn oil	13	61	1	(61)	25	0
Olive oil	14	8	1	(8.0)	77	0
Soybean oil	15	54	7	(7.7)	24	0
Margarine	17	32	2	(16)	49	0
Peanut oil	18	33	–	(33)	49	0
Palm oil[a]	51	9	0.3	(30)	39	0
Coconut oil[a]	92	2	0	(2.0)	7	0
Chicken fat	31	21	1	(21)	47	11
Lard	41	11	1	(11)	47	12
Beef fat	52	3	1	(3.0)	44	14
Butter fat	66	2	2	(1.0)	30	33

[a]palm oil has arachidic of 0.2 and coconut oil has arachidic of 0.1.
Data on canola oil from data on file, Procter & Gamble. All other data from Reeves JB and Weihrauch JL (1979) *Composition of Foods, Agriculture Handbook No. 8-4*. Washington, DC: US Department of Agriculture.

derived only from direct ingestion or by synthesis from dietary EPA or ALA.

Evolutionary Aspects of Diet Relative to n-3 Fatty Acids and the n-6:n-3 Balance

On the basis of estimates from studies in Paleolithic nutrition and modern-day hunter-gatherer populations, it appears that human beings evolved consuming a diet that was much lower in saturated fatty acids than today's diet. Furthermore, the diet contained small and roughly equal amounts of n-6 and n-3 PUFAs (ratio of 1–2:1) and much lower amounts of *trans*-fatty acids than today's diet (**Figure 3**). The current Western diet is very high in n-6 fatty acids (the ratio of n-6 to n-3 fatty acids ranges between 10:1 and 30:1) because of the recommendation to substitute vegetable oils high in n-6 fatty acids for saturated fats to lower serum cholesterol concentrations. Furthermore, intake of n-3 fatty acids is much lower today because of the decrease in fish consumption and the industrial production of animal feeds rich in grains containing n-6 fatty acids, leading to production of meat rich in n-6 and poor in n-3 fatty acids. The same is true for cultured fish and eggs. Even cultivated vegetables contain fewer n-3 fatty acids than do plants in the wild. In summary, modern agriculture, with its emphasis on production, has decreased the n-3 fatty acid content in many foods: green leafy vegetables, animal meats, eggs, and even fish, while it has

increased the amount of n-6 fatty acids in foods, leading to high n-6 intake for the first time in the history of human beings in many countries around the world (**Table 5**). The traditional diet of Crete (Greece) is consistent with the Paleolithic diet relative to the n-6:n-3 ratio. The Lyon Heart Study, which was based on a modified diet of Crete, had an n-6:n-3 ratio of 4:1 resulting in a 70% decrease in risk for cardiac death. As shown in **Table 6**, the higher the ratio of n-6 to n-3 fatty acids in platelet phospholipids, the higher the death rate from cardiovascular disease. As the ratio of n-6 PUFAs to n-3 PUFAs increases, the prevalence of type 2 diabetes also increases (**Figure 4**). As will be discussed below, a balance between the n-6 and n-3 fatty acids is a more physiologic state in terms of gene expression, eicosanoid metabolism, and cytokine production.

Further support for the need to balance the n-6:n-3 PUFAs comes from studies that clearly show the ability of both normal rat cardiomyocytes and human breast cancer cells in culture to form all the n-3 fatty acids from n-6 fatty acids when fed the cDNA encoding n-3 fatty acid desaturase obtained from the roundworm *Caenorhabditis elegans*. The n-3 desaturase efficiently and quickly converted the n-6 fatty acids that were fed to the cardiomyocytes in culture to the corresponding n-3 fatty acids. Thus, n-6 LA was converted to n-3 ALA and AA was converted to EPA, so that at equilibrium, the ratio of n-6 to n-3 PUFAs was close to 1:1. Further studies

Table 3 Terrestrial sources of n-3 (18:3n-3) fatty acids (grams per 100 g edible portion, raw)

Nuts and seeds

Butternuts, dried	8.7
Walnuts, English/Persian	6.8
Chia seeds, dried	3.9
Walnuts, black	3.3
Beechnuts, dried	1.7
Soya bean kernels, roasted and toasted	1.5
Hickory nuts, dried	1.0

Oils

Linseed oil	53.3
Rapeseed oil (canola)	11.1
Walnut oil	10.4
Wheat germ oil	6.9
Soya bean oil	6.8
Tomato seed oil	2.3
Rice bran oil	1.6

Vegetables

Soya beans, green, raw	3.2
Soya beans, mature seeds, sprouted, cooked	2.1
Seaweed, Spirulina, dried	0.8
Radish seeds, sprouted, raw	0.7
Beans, navy, sprouted, cooked	0.3
Beans, pinto, sprouted, cooked	0.3
Kale, raw	0.2
Leeks, freeze-dried	0.2
Broccoli, raw	0.1
Cauliflower, raw	0.1
Lettuce, butterhead	0.1
Spinach, raw	0.1

Fruits

Avocados, raw, California	0.1
Raspberries, raw	0.1
Strawberries	0.1

Legumes

Soya beans, dry	1.6
Beans, common, dry	0.6
Cowpeas, dry	0.3
Lima beans, dry	0.2
Peas, garden, dry	0.2
Chickpeas, dry	0.1
Lentils, dry	0.1

Grains

Oats, germ	1.4
Wheat, germ	0.7
Barley, bran	0.3
Corn, germ	0.3
Rice, bran	0.2
Wheat, bran	0.2
Wheat, hard red winter	0.1

Data from United States Department of Agriculture. Provisional table on the content of n-3 fatty acids and other fat components in selected foods from Simopoulos AP, Kifer RR, and Martin RE (eds.) (1986) *Health Effects of Polyunsaturated Fatty Acids in Seafoods*. Orlando, FL: Academic Press.

demonstrated that the cancer cells expressing the n-3 desaturase underwent apoptotic death whereas the control cancer cells with a high n-6:n-3 ratio continued to proliferate.

Eicosanoid Metabolism and Biological Effects of n-6 and n-3 Fatty Acids

When humans ingest fish or fish oil, the ingested EPA and DHA partially replace the n-6 fatty acids (especially AA) in cell membranes, particularly those of platelets, erythrocytes, neutrophils, monocytes, and liver cells.

Because of the increased amounts of n-6 fatty acids in the Western diet, the eicosanoid metabolic products from AA, specifically prostaglandins, thromboxanes, leukotrienes, hydroxy fatty acids, and lipoxins, are formed in larger quantities than those formed from n-3 fatty acids, specifically EPA. As a result (**Figure 5**), ingestion of EPA and DHA from fish or fish oil leads to: (1) decreased production of prostaglandin E2 metabolites; (2) decreased concentrations of thromboxane A2, a potent platelet aggregator and vasoconstrictor; (3) decreased formation of leukotriene B4, an inducer of inflammation and a powerful inducer of leukocyte chemotaxis and adherence; (4) increased concentrations of thromboxane A3, a weak platelet aggregator and vasoconstrictor; (5) increased concentrations of prostacyclin prostaglandin I3 (PGI3), leading to an overall increase in total prostacyclin by increasing PGI3 without decreasing PGI2 (both PGI2 and PGI3 are active vasodilators and inhibitors of platelet aggregation); and (6) increased concentrations of leukotriene B5, a weak inducer of inflammation and a chemotactic agent. The eicosanoids from AA are biologically active in small quantities and if they are formed in large amounts, they contribute to the formation of thrombi and atheromas; the development of allergic and inflammatory disorders, particularly in susceptible people; and cell proliferation. Thus, a diet rich in n-6 fatty acids shifts the physiologic state to one that is prothrombotic and proaggregatory, with increases in blood viscosity, vasospasm, and vasoconstriction and decreases in bleeding time. Bleeding time is shorter in groups of patients with hypercholesterolemia, hyperlipoproteinemia, myocardial infarction, other forms of atherosclerotic disease, type 2 diabetes, obesity, and hypertriglyceridemia. Atherosclerosis is a major complication in type 2 diabetes patients. Bleeding time is longer in women than in men and in younger than in older persons. There are ethnic differences in bleeding time that appear to be related to diet. The hypolipidemic, antithrombotic, anti-inflammatory, and anti-arrhythmic effects of n-3 fatty acids have been studied extensively in animal models, tissue cultures, and cells (**Table 7**).

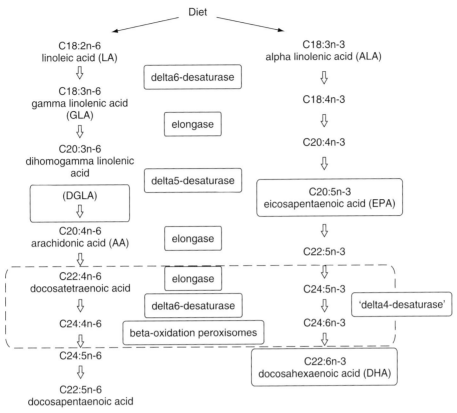

Figure 2 Essential fatty acid metabolism: desaturation and elongation of n-6 and n-3.

Nutrigenetics: Interaction between the n-6:n-3 Fatty Acids and the Genome

As expected, earlier studies focused on mechanisms that involve eicosanoid metabolites. More recently, however, the effects of fatty acids on gene expression have been investigated and this focus of interest has led to studies at the molecular level (Tables 8, 9). Previous studies have shown that fatty acids, whether released from membrane phospholipids by cellular phospholipases or made available to the cell from the diet or other aspects of the extracellular environment, are important cell signaling molecules. They can act as second messengers or substitute for the classic second messengers of the inositide phospholipid and cyclic AMP signal transduction pathways. They can also act as modulator molecules mediating responses of the cell to extracellular signals. It has been shown that fatty acids rapidly and directly alter the transcription of specific genes.

5-Lipoxygenase and Atherosclerosis: An Example of Nutrigenetics/Nutrigenomics

Leukotrienes are eicosanoids derived through the action of 5-lipoxygenase (5-LO). It has been recently shown that genetic variants of the 5-LO promoter, already known to be associated with variable sensitivity to anti-asthmatic medications, also influence atherosclerosis. Variant genotypes of the 5-LO gene were found in 6% of a cohort of 470 healthy middle-aged men and women. Carotid intima-media thickness (IMT), taken as a marker of the atherosclerotic burden, was significantly increased, by 80% in the variant group compared to carriers of the common allele, suggesting increased 5-LO promoter activity associated with the mutant (variant) allele. Furthermore, dietary AA intake significantly enhanced the proatherogenic effect of 5-LO gene variants, while intake of EPA and DHA decreased (blunted) the effect of 5-LO and was associated with less IMT. EPA and DHA decrease the formation of leukotrienes of the 4-series by competing with AA (Figure 5) as substrates for 5-LO and generate weaker leukotrienes of the 5-series. The results of this study suggest that person with genetic variants are at higher risk for atherosclerosis at higher AA intake. It also suggests that the effects of EPA and DHA may be stronger in individuals with genetic variants associated with increased 5-LO activity. Therefore, clinical trials in the future should be controlled for genetic variation.

Table 4   Content of n-3 fatty acids and other fat components in selected fish (grams per 100 g edible portion, raw)

Fish	Total fat	Fatty acids (g/100 g)			18:3	20:5	22:6	Cholesterol (mg/100 g)
		Total saturated	Total monounsaturated	Total polyunsaturated				
Anchovy, European	4.8	1.3	1.2	1.6	–	0.5	0.9	–
Bass, striped	2.3	0.5	0.7	0.8	Tr	0.2	0.6	80
Bluefish	6.5	1.4	2.9	1.6	–	0.4	0.8	59
Carp	5.6	1.1	2.3	1.4	0.3	0.2	0.1	67
Catfish, brown Bullhead	2.7	0.6	1.0	0.8	0.1	0.2	0.2	75
Catfish, channel	4.3	1.0	1.6	1.0	Tr	0.1	0.2	58
Cod, Atlantic	0.7	0.1	0.1	0.3	Tr	0.1	0.2	43
Croaker, Atlantic	3.2	1.1	1.2	0.5	Tr	0.1	0.1	61
Flounder, unspecified	1.0	0.2	0.3	0.3	Tr	0.1	0.1	46
Grouper, red	0.8	0.2	0.1	0.2	–	Tr	0.2	–
Haddock	0.7	0.1	0.1	0.2	Tr	0.1	0.1	63
Halibut, Greenland	13.8	2.4	8.4	1.4	Tr	0.5	0.4	46
Halibut, Pacific	2.3	0.3	0.8	0.7	0.1	0.1	0.3	32
Herring, Pacific	13.9	3.3	6.9	2.4	0.1	1.0	0.7	77
Herring, round	4.4	1.3	0.8	1.5	0.1	0.4	0.8	28
Mackerel, king	13.0	2.5	5.9	3.2	–	1.0	1.2	53
Mullet, striped	3.7	1.2	1.1	1.1	0.1	0.3	0.2	49
Ocean perch	1.6	0.3	0.6	0.5	Tr	0.1	0.1	42
Plaice, European	1.5	0.3	0.5	0.4	Tr	0.1	0.1	70
Pollock	1.0	0.1	0.1	0.5	–	0.1	0.4	71
Pompano, Florida	9.5	3.5	2.6	1.1	–	0.2	0.4	50
Salmon, Chinook	10.4	2.5	4.5	2.1	0.1	0.8	0.6	–
Salmon, pink	3.4	0.6	0.9	1.4	Tr	0.4	0.6	–
Snapper, red	1.2	0.2	0.2	0.4	Tr	Tr	0.2	–
Sole, European	1.2	0.3	0.4	0.2	Tr	Tr	0.1	50
Swordfish	2.1	0.6	0.8	0.2	–	0.1	0.1	39
Trout, rainbow	3.4	0.6	1.0	1.2	0.1	0.1	0.4	57
Tuna, albacore	4.9	1.2	1.2	1.8	0.2	0.3	1.0	54
Tuna, unspecified	2.5	0.9	0.6	0.5	–	0.1	0.4	–

Dashes denote lack of reliable data for nutrient known to be present; Tr, trace (<0.05 g/100 g food). Adapted from the United States Department of Agriculture Provisional Table on the Content of Omega-3 Fatty Acids and Other Fat Components in Seafoods as presented by Simopoulos AP, Kifer RR, and Martin RE (eds.) (1986) *Health Effects of Polyunsaturated Fatty Acids in Seafoods.* Orlando, FL: Academic Press.

Effects of Dietary ALA Compared with Long-Chain n-3 Fatty Acid Derivatives on Physiologic Indexes

Several clinical and epidemiologic studies have been conducted to determine the effects of long-chain n-3 PUFAs on various physiologic indexes. Whereas the earlier studies were conducted with large doses of fish or fish oil concentrates, more recent studies have used lower doses. ALA, the precursor of n-3 fatty acids, can be converted to long-chain n-3 PUFAs and can therefore be substituted for fish oils. The minimum intake of long-chain n-3 PUFAs needed for beneficial effects depends on the intake of other fatty acids. Dietary amounts of LA as well as the ratio of LA to ALA appear to be important for the metabolism of ALA to long-chain n-3 PUFAs. While keeping the amount of dietary LA constant (3.7 g) ALA appears to have biological effects similar to those of 0.3 g long-chain n-3 PUFAs with conversion of 11 g ALA to 1 g long-chain n-3 PUFAs. Thus, a ratio of 4 (15 g LA:3.7 g ALA) is appropriate for conversion. In human studies, the conversion of deuterated ALA to longer chain metabolites was reduced by ≅50% when dietary intake of LA was increased from 4.7% to 9.3% of energy as a result of the known competition between n-6 and n-3 fatty acids for desaturation. After ALA supplementation there is an increase in long-chain n-3 PUFAs in plasma and platelet phospholipids and a decrease in platelet aggregation. ALA supplementation does not alter triacylglycerol concentrations. Only long-chain n-3 PUFA have triacylglycerol-lowering effects. Supplementation with ALA to lower the n-6:n-3 ratio from 13:1 to 1:1 led to a 50% reduction in C-reactive protein (CRP), a risk factor for coronary heart disease.

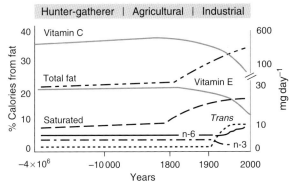

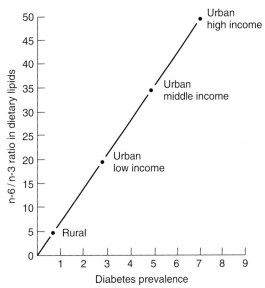

Figure 3 Hypothetical scheme of fat, fatty acid (n-6, n-3, *trans* and total) intake (as per cent of calories from fat) and intake of vitamins E and C (mg day⁻¹). Data were extrapolated from cross-sectional analyses of contemporary hunter-gatherer populations and from longitudinal observations and their putative changes during the preceding 100 years. *Trans*-fatty acids, the result of the hydrogenation process, have increased dramatically in the food supply during this century. (Reproduced with permission from Simopoulos AP (1999) Genetic variation and evolutionary aspects of diet. In: Papas A (ed.) *Antioxidants in Nutrition and Health*, pp. 65–88. Boca Raton: CRC Press.)

Figure 4 Relation between the ratio of n-6 to n-3 fatty acids in dietary lipids in the Indian diet and the prevalence of type 2 diabetes. (Reproduced with permission from Raheja BS, Sadikot SM, Phatak RB, and Rao MB (1993) Significance of the n-6/n-3 ratio for insulin action in diabetes. *Annals of the New York Academy of Science* **683**: 258–271.)

Table 5 n-6:n-3 ratios in various populations

Population	n-6:n-3
Paleolithic	0.79
Greece prior to 1960	1.00–2.00
Current Japan	4.00
Current India, rural	5–6.1
Current UK and northern Europe	15.00
Current US	16.74
Current India, urban	38–50

Reproduced with permission from Simopoulos AP (2003) Importance of the ratio of omega-6/omega-3 essential fatty acids: Evolutionary aspects. *World Review of Nutrition and Diet* **92**: 1–22.

Table 6 Ethnic differences in fatty acid concentrations in thrombocyte phospholipids and percentage of all deaths from cardiovascular disease

	Europe and US	Japan	Greenland Eskimos
Arachidonic acid (20:4n-6)	26%	21%	8.3%
Eicosapentaenoic acid (20:5n-3)	0.5%	1.6%	8.0%
Ratio of n-6:n-3	50%	12%	1%
Mortality from cardiovascular disease	45%	12%	7%

Modified from Weber PC (1989) Are we what we eat? Fatty acids in nutrition and in cell membranes: cell functions and disorders induced by dietary conditions. In: *Fish, Fats and your Health*, Report no. 4, pp. 9–18. Norway: Svanoybukt Foundation.

In Australian studies, ventricular fibrillation in rats was reduced with canola oil as much or even more efficiently than with fish oil, an effect attributable to ALA. Further studies should be able to show whether this result is a direct effect of ALA per se or whether it occurs as a result of its desaturation and elongation to EPA and possibly DHA.

The diets of Western countries have contained increasingly larger amounts of LA, which has been promoted for its cholesterol-lowering effect. It is now recognized that dietary LA favors oxidative modification of low-density lipoprotein (LDL) cholesterol, increases platelet response to aggregation, and suppresses the immune system. In contrast, ALA intake is associated with inhibitory effects on the clotting activity of platelets, on their response to thrombin, and on the regulation of AA metabolism. In clinical studies, ALA contributed to lowering of blood pressure. In a prospective study, ALA was inversely related to the risk of coronary heart disease in men.

ALA is not equivalent in its biological effects to the long-chain n-3 fatty acids found in fish oils. EPA and DHA are more rapidly incorporated into plasma and membrane lipids and produce more rapid effects than does ALA. Relatively large reserves of LA in body fat, as are found in vegans or in the diet of omnivores in Western societies, would tend to slow down the formation of long-chain n-3 fatty acids from ALA. Therefore, the role of ALA in human nutrition becomes important in terms of long-term

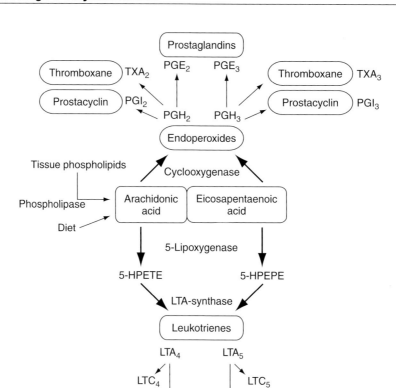

Figure 5 Oxidative metabolism of arachidonic acid and eicosapentaenoic acid by the cyclooxygenase and 5-lipoxygenase pathways. 5-HPETE denotes 5-hydroperoxyeicosatetranoic acid and 5-HPEPE denotes 5-hydroxyeicosapentaenoic acid.

dietary intake. One advantage of the consumption of ALA over n-3 fatty acids from fish is that the problem of insufficient vitamin E intake does not exist with a high intake of ALA from plant sources.

Human Studies in Growth and Development

Pregnancy and Fetal Growth

Since World War II, the role of maternal nutrition in fetal growth and development has been extensively studied in the context of protein-calorie malnutrition. The role of n-3 fatty acids has only recently come into focus, despite the evidence of its importance having been demonstrated in a series of studies between 1928 and 1930 involving rats and primates. Lipid nutrition during pregnancy and lactation is of special relevance to human development, because brain development in the human takes place during fetal life and in the first 2 years after birth. DHA is found in larger amounts in the gray matter of the brain and in the retinal membranes, where it accounts for 30% or more of the fatty acids in the ethanolamine and serine phospholipid. DHA accumulates in the neurons of the brain between weeks 26 and 40 of gestation in humans.

During the third trimester of human development, rapid synthesis of brain tissue occurs in association with increasing neuromotor activity. The increase in cell size, number, and type requires de novo synthesis of structural lipids, leading to accumulation of DHA in the brain of the human infant during the last trimester. The levels of ALA and LA are low in the brain, whereas marked accretion of long-chain desaturation products, specifically DHA and AA, occurs. More recent data indicate that the main developmental changes in the brain seem to be an increase in DHA at the end of gestation and a decrease in oleic acid (18:1n-9) and AA in phosphatidlyethanolamine (PE). Similar changes occur in the liver. Therefore, a premature infant (prior to 37 weeks' gestation) has much lower amounts of DHA in the brain and liver and is at risk of becoming deficient in DHA unless it is supplied in the diet. In the full-term newborn, about half of the DHA accumulates in the brain before birth and the other half after birth.

There is epidemiologic evidence that the birth weights of newborns in the Faroe Islands (where fish intake is high) are higher than those in Denmark, as is the length of gestation: 40.3 ± 1.7 weeks for the Faroese versus 39.7 ± 1.8 weeks for the Danish pregnant women. The average birth weight of primiparas is 194 g higher for the Faroe Islands. The higher dietary n-3 fatty acid intake quite possibly influences endogenous prostaglandin metabolism. It is

Table 7 Effects of n-3 fatty acids on factors involved in the pathophysiology of atherosclerosis and inflammation

Factor	Function	Effect of n-3 fatty acid
Arachidonic acid	Eicosanoid precursor; aggregates platelets; stimulates white blood cells	↓
Thromboxane A_2	Platelet aggregation; vasoconstriction; increase of intracellular Ca^{++}	↓
Prostacyclin ($PGI_{2/3}$)	Prevent platelet aggregation; vasodilation; increase cAMP	↑
Leukotriene (LTB_4)	Neutrophil chemoattractant; increase of intracellular Ca^{++}	↓
Fibrinogen	A member of the acute phase response; and a blood clotting factor	↓
Tissue plasminogen activator	Increase endogenous fibrinolysis	↑
Platelet activating factor (PAF)	Activates platelets and white blood cells	↓
Platelet-derived growth factor (PDGF)	Chemoattractant and mitogen for smooth muscles and macrophages	↓
Oxygen free radicals	Cellular damage; enhance LDL uptake via scavenger pathway; stimulate arachidonic acid metabolism	↓
Lipid hydroperoxides	Stimulate eicosanoid formation	↓
Interleukin 1 and tumor necrosis factor	Stimulate neutrophil O_2 free radical formation; stimulate lymphocyte proliferation; stimulate PAF; express intercellular adhesion molecule-1 on endothelial cells; inhibit plasminogen activator, thus, procoagulants	↓
Interleukin-6	Stimulates the synthesis of all phase proteins involved in the inflammatory response: C-reactive protein; serum amyloid A; fibrinogen; α_1-chymotrypsin; and haptoglobin	↓
C-reactive protein (CRP)	An acute phase reactant and an independent risk factor for cardiovascular disease	↓
Endothelial-derived relaxation factor	Reduces arterial vasoconstrictor response	↑
Insulin sensitivity		↑
VLDL		↓
HDL	Decreases the risk for coronary heart disease	↑
Lp(a)	Lipoprotein(a) is a genetically determined protein that has atherogenic and thrombogenic properties	↓
Triglycerides and chylomicrons	Contribute to postprandial lipemia	↓

Source: Updated and modified from Weber PC, Leaf A. Cardiovascular effects of omega-3 fatty acids. Atherosclerosis risk factor modification by omega-3 fatty acids. World Rev Nutr Diet 1991, **66**: 218–32. With permission.

hypothesized that the dietary n-3 fatty acids inhibit the production of the dienoic prostaglandins, especially PGF_{2a} and PGE_2, because they are involved in the mediation of uterine contractions and the ripening of the cervix that lead to labor and delivery. These important observations need to be further investigated, as the prevention of prematurity is one of the most critical issues to be overcome in perinatal medicine.

Human Milk and Infant Feeding

A number of studies from around the world indicate that human milk contains both LNA and LA and their long-chain n-6 and n-3 fatty acids, whereas cow's milk does not. The long-chain fatty acid composition of red blood cell membrane phospholipids may reflect the composition of phospholipids in the brain. Therefore, determination of red blood cell membrane phospholipids has been carried out by many investigators to determine the long-chain PUFA content in breast-fed and bottle-fed infants. As expected, the fatty acids 22:5n-3 and 22:6n-3 were higher in the erythrocytes from breast-fed

infants than those from bottle-fed babies and the 20:3n-9 was lower in the erythrocytes of the breast-fed infants.

Following birth, the amount of red blood cell DHA in premature infants decreases; therefore the amount of DHA available to the premature infant assumes critical importance. Preterm infants have a limited ability to convert LNA to DHA (**Figure 2**); therefore, a number of studies have been carried out on the DHA status of the premature infant. Premature babies have decreased amounts of DHA, but human milk contains enough DHA to support normal growth of the premature baby. The amount of n-3 fatty acids in human milk varies with the mother's diet; in particular, DHA is lower in vegetarians than in omnivores. One can increase the amount of DHA in human milk by giving fish oil rich in DHA to the mother.

The need to supplement infant formula with n-3 fatty acids and, particularly, DHA for the premature is now recognized and many countries have licensed infant formula enriched with n-3 fatty acids. DHA is essential for normal visual function and visual

Table 8 Effects of polyunsaturated fatty acids on several genes encoding enzyme proteins involved in lipogenesis, glycolysis, and glucose transport

Function and gene	Linoleic acid	α-Linolenic acid	Arachidonic acid	Eicosapentaenoic acid	Docosahexaenoic acid
Hepatic cells					
Lipogenesis					
FAS	↓	↓	↓	↓	↓
S14	↓	↓	↓	↓	↓
SCD1	↓	↓	↓	↓	↓
SCD2	↓	↓	↓	↓	↓
ACC	↓	↓	↓	↓	↓
ME	↓	↓	↓	↓	↓
Glycolysis					
G6PD	↓				
GK	↓	↓	↓	↓	↓
PK	—	↓	↓	↓	↓
Mature adiposites					
Glucose transport					
GLUT4	—	—	↓	↓	—
GLUT1	—	—	↑	↑	—

↓ = Suppress or decrease; ↑ = induce or increase
Source: Modified from Simopoulos AP. The role of fatty acids in gene expression: Health implications. Ann Nutr Metab 1996, **40**: 303–311. With permission.

maturation, particularly of the premature infant. Studies are currently in progress comparing the growth and development of both the premature and full-term infant who are fed mother's milk with those who are receiving formula supplemented with n-3 fatty acids and those whose formula is not supplemented, to define precisely the effects of DHA on intelligence quotient (IQ) and overall neuromotor development. **Tables 10** and **11** show the EFA dietary recommendations for adults,

pregnant women, and infants made by a scientific group at a workshop held at the National Institutes of Health in Bethesda, Maryland in 1999.

Aging

ALA deficiency has been found in patients on long-term gastric tube-feeding that included large amounts of skim milk without ALA supplementation. These patients, who were in nursing homes,

Table 9 Effects of polyunsaturated fatty acids on several genes encoding enzyme proteins involved in cell growth, early gene expression, adhesion molecules, inflammation, β-oxidation, and growth factors[a]

Function and gene	Linoleic acid	α-Linolenic acid	Arachidonic acid	Eicosapentaenoic acid	Docosahexaenoic acid
Cell growth and early gene expression					
c-fos	—	—	↑	↓	↓
Egr-1	—	—	↑	↓	↓
Adhesion molecules					
VCAM-1 mRNA[b]	—	—	↓	c	↓
Inflammation					
IL-1β	—	—	↑	↓	↓
β-oxidation					
Acyl-CoA oxidase[d]	↑	↑	↑	↑	↑↑
Growth factors					
PDGF	—	—	↑	↓	↓

[a]VCAM, vascular cell adhesion molecule; IL, interleukin: PDGF, platelet-derived growth factor. ↓ suppresses or decreases, ↑ induces or increases.
[b]Monounsaturated fatty acids (MONOs) also suppress VCAM1 mRNA, but to a lesser degree than does DHA. AA also suppresses to a lesser extent than DHA.
[c]Eicosapentachoic acid has no effect by itself but enhances the effect of docosahexachoic acid (DHA)
[d]MONOs also induce acyl-CoA oxidase mRNA
Source: Modified from Simopoulos AP. The role of fatty acids in gene expression: Health implications. Ann Nutr Metab 1996, **40**: 303–311. With permission.

Table 10 Adequate intake (AI) for adults

Fatty acid	Grams/day (2000 kcal diet)	% Energy
LA	4.44	2.0
(upper limit)[a]	6.67	3.0
ALA	2.22	1.0
DHA + EPA	0.65	0.3
DHA to be at least[b]	0.22	0.1
EPA to be at least	0.22	0.1
TRANS-FA		
(upper limit)[c]	2.00	1.0
SAT		
(upper limit)[d]	–	<8.0
MONOs[e]	–	–

[a]Although the recommendation is for AI, the Working Group felt that there is enough scientific evidence to also state an upper limit (UL) for LA of 6.67 g day^{-1} based on a 2000 kcal diet or of 3.0% of energy.
[b]For pregnant and lactating women, ensure 300 mg day^{-1} of DHA.
[c]Except for dairy products, other foods under natural conditions do not contain trans-FA. Therefore, the Working Group does not recommend trans-FA to be in the food supply as a result of hydrogenation of unsaturated fatty acids or high-temperature cooking (reused frying oils).
[d]Saturated fats should not comprise more than 8% of energy.
[e]The Working Group recommended that the majority of fatty acids are obtained from monounsaturates. The total amount of fat in the diet is determined by the culture and dietary habits of people around the world (total fat ranges from 15% to 40% of energy) but with special attention to the importance of weight control and reduction of obesity.
If sufficient scientific evidence is not available to calculate an estimated average requirement, a reference intake called an adequate intake is used instead of a recommended dietary allowance. The AI is a value based on experimentally derived intake levels or approximations of observed mean nutrient intakes by a group (or groups) of healthy people. The AI for children and adults is expected to meet or exceed the amount needed to maintain a defined nutritional state or criterion of adequacy in essentially all members of a specific healthy population.
LA, linoleic acid; ALA, α-linolenic acid; DHA, docosahexaenoic acid; EPA, eicosapentaenoic acid; TRANS-FA, trans-fatty acids; SAT, saturated fatty acids; MONOs, monounsaturated fatty acids.
Reproduced with permission from Simopoulos AP, Leaf A, and Salem N Jr (1999) Essentiality of and recommended dietary intakes for omega-6 and omega-3 fatty acids. *Annals of Nutrition and Metabolism* **43**: 127–130.

Table 11 Adequate intake (AI) for infant formula/diet

Fatty acid	Per cent of fatty acids
LA[a]	10.00
ALA	1.50
AA[b]	0.50
DHA	0.35
EPA[c]	
(upper limit)	<0.10

[a]The Working Group recognizes that in countries like Japan the breast milk content of LA is 6–10% of fatty acids and the DHA is higher, about 0.6%. The formula/diet composition described here is patterned on infant formula studies in Western countries.
[b]The Working Group endorsed the addition of the principal long-chain polyunsaturates, AA and DHA, to all infant formulas.
[c]EPA is a natural constituent of breast milk, but in amounts more than 0.1% in infant formula may antagonize AA and interfere with infant growth.
If sufficient scientific evidence is not available to calculate an estimated average requirement, a reference intake called an adequate intake is used instead of a recommended dietary allowance. The AI is a value based on experimentally derived intake levels or approximations of observed mean nutrient intakes by a group (or groups) of healthy people. The AI for children and adults is expected to meet or exceed the amount needed to maintain a defined nutritional state or criterion of adequacy in essentially all members of a specific healthy population.
LA, linoleic acid; ALA, α-linolenic acid; AA, arachidonic acid; DHA, docosahexaenoic acid; EPA, eicosapentaenoic acid; TRANS-FA, trans-fatty acids; SAT, saturated fatty acids; MONOs, monounsaturated fatty acids.
Reproduced with permission from Simopoulos AP, Leaf A, and Salem N Jr (1999) Essentiality of and recommended dietary intakes for omega-6 and omega-3 fatty acids. *Annals of Nutrition and Metabolism* **43**: 127–130.

symptoms, along with the biochemical determinations, provides additional support for the diagnosis. To verify the diagnosis, it is essential that the clinical symptoms disappear upon supplementation of the deficient diet with n-3 fatty acids.

With the increase in the number of elderly persons in the population, and the proliferation of nursing homes, particular attention must be given to the nutritional requirements of the elderly, especially those who are fed enterally or parenterally.

Coronary Heart Disease

Most epidemiologic studies and clinical trials using n-3 fatty acids in the form of fish or fish oil have been carried out in patients with coronary heart disease. However, studies have also been carried out on the effects of ALA in normal subjects and in patients with myocardial infarction.

The hypolipidemic effects of n-3 fatty acids are similar to those of n-6 fatty acids, provided that they replace saturated fats in the diet. n-3 fatty acids have the added benefit of not lowering high-density

developed skin lesions diagnosed as scaly dermatitis, which disappeared with ALA supplementation. A number of other patients were reported to have n-3 fatty acid deficiency, again patients on long-term gastric tube-feeding or prolonged total parenteral nutrition because of chronic illnesses. If a deficiency of total n-3 fatty acid intake is suspected, its concentration in plasma should be measured. A decrease in the concentration of 20:5n-3, 22:5n-3, and particularly 22:6n-3 in plasma or erythrocyte phospholipids indicates that the dietary intake of n-3 fatty acids has been low. The presence of clinical lipoprotein (HDL) and consistently lowering serum triacylglycerol concentrations, whereas the n-6 fatty acids do not and may even increase triglyceride levels.

Another important consideration is the finding that during chronic fish oil feeding postprandial triacylglycerol concentrations decrease. Furthermore, consumption of high amounts of fish oil blunted the expected rise in plasma cholesterol concentrations in humans. These findings are consistent with the low rate of coronary heart disease found in fish-eating populations. Studies in humans have shown that fish oils reduce the rate of hepatic secretion of very low-density lipoprotein (VLDL) triacylglycerol. In normolipidemic subjects, n-3 fatty acids prevent and rapidly reverse carbohydrate-induced hypertriglyceridemia. There is also evidence from kinetic studies that fish oil increases the fractional catabolic rate of VLDL (**Table 7**).

The effects of different doses of fish oil on thrombosis and bleeding time have been investigated. A dose of $1.8\,g\,EPA\,day^{-1}$ did not result in any prolongation in bleeding time, but $4\,g\,day^{-1}$ increased bleeding time and decreased platelet count with no adverse effects. In human studies, there has never been a case of clinical bleeding, even in patients undergoing angioplasty, while the patients were taking fish oil supplements. Clinical investigations indicate that n-3 fatty acids prevent sudden death. A series of intervention trials have clearly shown that the addition of n-3 fatty acids in the form of fish oil (EPA and DHA) decrease the death rate in the secondary prevention of coronary heart disease by preventing ventricular arrhythmias that lead to sudden death.

Antiarrhythmic Effects of n-3 Fatty Acids (ALA, EPA, and DHA)

Studies have shown that n-3 fatty acids, more so than n-6 PUFA, can prevent ischemia-induced fatal ventricular arrhythmias in experimental animals. n-3 fatty acids make the heart cells less excitable by modulating the conductance of the sodium and other ion channels. Clinical studies further support the role of n-3 fatty acids in the prevention of sudden death due to ventricular arrhythmias which, in the US, account for 50–60% of the mortality from acute myocardial infarction and cause 250 000 deaths a year. In the intervention trials, there was no change in lipid concentration, suggesting that the beneficial effects of n-3 fatty acids were due to their antithrombotic and antiarrhythmic effects.

The antiarrhythmic effects of n-3 fatty acids are supported by clinical intervention trials (Diet and Reinfarction Trial (DART), Lyon Heart Study, Gruppo Italiano per lo Studio della Sopravvivenza nell'Infarto miocardico (GISSI)-Prevenzione Trial,

Indo-Mediterranean Diet Heart Study). Their results strongly support the role of fish or fish oil in decreasing total mortality and sudden death in patients with one episode of myocardial infarction. Therefore, the addition of 1 g/d of n-3 fatty acids is highly recommended for the primary and secondary prevention of coronary heart disease.

Inflammation: a Common Base for the Development of Coronary Heart Disease, Diabetes, Arthritis, Mental Health, Neurodegenerative Diseases and Cancer

Anti-inflammatory Aspects of n-3 Fatty Acids

Many experimental studies have provided evidence that incorporation of alternative fatty acids into tissues may modify inflammatory and immune reactions and that n-3 fatty acids in particular are potent therapeutic agents for inflammatory diseases. Supplementing the diet with n-3 fatty acids (3.2 g EPA and 2.2 g DHA) in normal subjects increased the EPA content in neutrophils and monocytes more than sevenfold without changing the quantities of AA and DHA. The anti-inflammatory effects of fish oils are partly mediated by inhibiting the 5-lipoxygenase pathway in neutrophils and monocytes and inhibiting the leukotriene B_4 (LTB_4)-mediated function of LTB_5 (**Figure 5**). Studies show that n-3 fatty acids influence interleukin metabolism by decreasing IL-1β and IL-6. Inflammation plays an important role in both the initiation of atherosclerosis and the development of atherothrombotic events. An early step in the atherosclerotic process is the adhesion of monocytes to endothelial cells. Adhesion is mediated by leukocyte and vascular cell adhesion molecules (CAMs) such as selectins, integrins, vascular cell adhesion molecule 1 (VCAM-1), and intercellular adhesion molecule 1 (ICAM-1). The expression of E-selectin, ICAM-1, and VCAM-1, which is relatively low in normal vascular cells, is upregulated in the presence of various stimuli, including cytokines and oxidants. This increased expression promotes the adhesion of monocytes to the vessel wall. The monocytes subsequently migrate across the endothelium into the vascular intima, where they accumulate to form the initial lesions of atherosclerosis. Atherosclerosis plaques have been shown to have increased CAM expression in animal models and human studies.

Diabetes is a major risk factor for coronary heart disease. EPA and DHA increase sensitivity to insulin and decrease the risk of coronary heart disease. Rheumatoid arthritis has a strong inflammatory component characterized by an increase in interleukin (IL)-1β. n-3 fatty acids decrease IL-1β as well as the number of swollen and painful joints. Supplementation with EPA and DHA, changing the ratio of n-6:n-3 of the background diet by increasing the n-3 and decreasing the n-6 intake, is now standard treatment for patients with rheumatoid arthritis along with medication in a number of centers around the world. Similarly, changing the background diet in patients with asthma has led to decreases in the dose of nonsteroidal anti-inflammatory drugs.

These studies suggest the potential for complementarity between drug therapy and dietary choices and that increased intake of n-3 fatty acids and decreased intake of n-6 fatty acids may lead to drug sparing effects. Therefore, future studies need to address the fatty acid composition and the ratio of n-6:n-3 of the background diet, and the issue of concurrent drug use. A diet rich in n-3 fatty acids and low in n-6 fatty acids provides the appropriate background biochemical environment in which drugs function.

Psychologic stress in humans induces the production of proinflammatory cytokines such as interferon gamma (IFNγ), TNFα, IL-6, and IL-10. An imbalance of n-6 and n-3 PUFA in the peripheral blood causes an overproduction of proinflammatory cytokines. There is evidence that changes in fatty acid composition are involved in the pathophysiology of major depression. Changes in serotonin (5-HT) receptor number and function caused by changes in PUFAs provide the theoretical rationale connecting fatty acids with the current receptor and neurotransmitter theories of depression. The increased 20:4n-6/20:5n-3 ratio and the imbalance in the n-6:n-3 PUFA ratio in major depression may be related to the increased production of proinflammatory cytokines and eicosanoids in that illness. Studies have shown that EPA and DHA prolong remission, that is, reduce the risk of relapse in patients with bipolar disorder. There are a number of studies evaluating the therapeutic effect of EPA and DHA in major depression.

Earlier studies in rodents showed that ALA intake improved learning, memory and cognition. In Zellweger's syndrome (a genetic neurodegenerative disease) high amounts of DHA early in life decreased somewhat the rate of progression of the disease. A number of studies have suggested that people who eat a diet rich in fish are less likely to develop Alzheimer's disease. Learning and memory depend on dendritic spine action assembly and DHA. High DHA consumption is associated with reduced risk for Alzheimer's disease, yet mechanisms and therapeutic potential remain elusive. In an Alzheimer's disease mouse model, reduction of dietaty n-3 fatty acid resulted in 80%-90% losses of the p85 alpha subunit of phosphoinositol 3-kinase and the postsynaptic action-regulating protein drebrin as in the brain of patients with Alzheimer's disease. The loss of postsynaptic proteins was associated with increased oxidation without concomitant neuron or presynaptic protein loss. Treatment of the n-3 fatty acid restricted mice with DHA protected against these effects and behavioral deficits. Since n-3 fatty acids are essential for p85-mediated central nervous system insulin signaling and selective protection of postsynaptic proteins, these findings have implications for neurodegenerative diseases, where synaptic loss is critical, especially in Alzheimer's disease. A few case control studies suggest that higher EPA and DHA intake is associated with lower risk of Alzheimer's disease and severity of the disease. Inflammation is a risk factor for Alzheimer's disease. It remains to be determined whether low n-3 fatty acids, especially low DHA status, in patients with Alzheimer's disease is a causal factor in the pathogenesis and progression of Alzheimer's disease and other neurodegenerative diseases.

Cancer is characterized by inflammation, cell proliferation, and elevated IL-6 levels. Since EPA and DHA suppress IL-6, fish oil supplementation suppresses rectal epithelial cell proliferation and PGE$_2$ biosynthesis. This was achieved with a dietary n-6:n-3 ratio of 2.5:1, but not with the same absolute level of fish oil intake and an n-6:n-3 ratio of 4:1. Case control studies in women with breast cancer support the hypothesis that the balance between n-6 and n-3 in breast adipose tissue plays an important role in breast cancer and in breast cancer metastasis.

Future Work, Conclusions, and Recommendations

n-3 fatty acids should be added to foods rather than be used solely as dietary supplements, which is a quasi-pharmaceutical approach. Furthermore, the development of a variety of n-3-rich foodstuffs would allow increased n-3 dietary intakes with little change of dietary habits. n-3 fatty acids maintain their preventative and therapeutic properties when packaged in foods other than fish. Efficient use of dietary n-3 fatty acids will require the simultaneous reduction in the food content of n-6 fatty acids and their substitution with monounsaturated oils. Dietary n-3 fats give rise to higher tissue levels of EPA when the 'background' diet is low in n-6 fats. Compared to n-6 fatty acids, olive oil increases the incorporation of n-3 fatty acids into tissues.

In the past, industry focused on improvements in food production and processing to increase shelf life of the products, whereas now and in the future the focus will be on nutritional quality in product development. This will necessitate the development of research for the nutritional evaluation of the various food products and educational programs for professionals and the public. The definition of food safety will have to expand in order to include nutrient structural changes and food composition. The dawn of the twenty-first century will enhance the scientific base for product development and expand collaboration among agricultural, nutritional, and medical scientists in government, academia, and industry. This should bring about a greater involvement of nutritionists and dieticians in industrial research and development to respond to an ever-increasing consumer interest in the health attributes of foods.

Today, more is known about the mechanisms and functions of n-3 fatty acids than other fatty acids. It is evident that Western diets are relatively deficient in n-3 fatty acids and that they contain much higher amounts of n-6 fatty acids than ever before in the evolution of human beings. Research has shown that DHA is essential for the development of the premature infant relative to visual acuity, visual function, and maturation. In the full-term infant, DHA may influence visual acuity and neural pathways associated with the developmental progression of language acquisition. These findings have led to the inclusion of DHA and AA in infant formulas in most countries around the world.

Most of the research on the role of n-3 fatty acids in chronic diseases has been carried out in patients with coronary heart disease. Intervention trials have clearly shown that n-3 fatty acids decrease sudden death and all cause mortality in the secondary prevention of coronary heart disease and in one study also in the primary prevention of coronary heart disease. The decrease in sudden death is most likely due to the anti-arrhythmic effects of n-3 fatty acids.

Most recent research suggests that the response to n-3 fatty acids may be genotype dependent, since certain individuals respond more than others. The time has come to take genetic variation into consideration when setting up clinical intervention trials. We need to move away from the long-term prospective studies and proceed with genotype-specific clinical intervention trials.

Inflammation and cell proliferation are at the base of many chronic diseases and conditions, especially atherosclerosis and cancer, but also diabetes, hypertension, arthritis, mental health, and various autoimmune diseases. Individuals carrying genetic variants for these conditions are much more prone to develop them because the high n-6:n-3 ratio leads to proinflammatory and prothrombotic states.

The time has come to return to high n-3 fatty acid levels in the diet and to decrease the n-6 intake.

There is good scientific evidence from studies on the Paleolithic diet, the diet of Crete, other traditional diets (Okinawa), intervention studies, and finally studies at the molecular level using transgenic rodents that the physiologic n-6:n-3 ratio should be 1:1 or 2:1. Japan has already recommended a ratio of 2:1. Industry has moved in the direction of including n-3 fatty acids in various products starting with n-3 enriched eggs, which are based on the *Ampelistra* (Greek) egg as a model obtained under completely natural conditions and which has a ratio of n-6:n-3 of 1:1.

It is essential that Nutrition Science drives Food Science and the production of foods rather than Food Technology. This is of the utmost importance in the development of novel foods. The scientific evidence is strong for decreasing the n-6 and increasing the n-3 fatty acid intake to improve health throughout the life cycle. The scientific basis for the development of a public policy to develop dietary recommendations for EFA, including a balanced n-6:n-3 ratio, is robust. What is needed is a scientific consensus, education of professionals and the public, the establishment of an agency on nutrition and food policy at the national level, and willingness of governments to institute changes. Education of the public is essential to demand changes in the food supply.

Abbreviations

ALA	α-linolenic acid
CAM	cell adhesion molecule
CRP	C-reactive protein
DHA	docosahexaenoic acid
EFA	essential fatty acid
EPA	eicosapentaenoic acid
FAS	fatty acid synthase
GK	glucokinase
GLUT	glucose transporter
ICAM	intercellular adhesion molecule
IFN	interferon
IL	interleukin
IMT	intima-media thickness
LA	linoleic acid
LO	lipoxygenase
ME	malic enzyme
PDGF	platelet-derived growth factor
PE	phosphatidylethanolamine
PG	prostaglandin
PK	pyruvate kinase
PUFA	polyunsaturated fatty acid
TNF	tumor necrosis factor
VCAM	vascular cell adhesion molecule

See also: **Aging**. **Arthritis**. **Breast Feeding**. **Cancer:** Effects on Nutritional Status. **Coronary Heart Disease:**

Hemostatic Factors; Lipid Theory; Prevention. **Diabetes Mellitus**: Dietary Management. **Fatty Acids**: Omega-6 Polyunsaturated. **Lactation**: Dietary Requirements. **Pregnancy**: Nutrient Requirements; Safe Diet for Pregnancy.

Further Reading

Burr ML, Fehily AM, Gilbert JF, Rogers S, Holliday RM, Sweetnam PM, Elwood PC, and Deadman NM (1989) Effect of changes in fat fish and fibre intakes on death and myocardial reinfarction: diet and reinfarction trial (DART). *Lancet* **2**: 757–761.

Calon F, Lim GP, Yang F, Morihara T, Teter B, Ubeda O, Rostaing P, Triller A, Salem N Jr, Ashe KH, Frautschy SA, and Cole GM (2004) Docosahexaenoic acid protects from dendritic pathology in an Alzheimer's disease mouse model. *Neuron* **43**: 633–645.

de Lorgeril M, Renaud S, Mamelle N, Salen P, Martin JL, Monjaud I, Guidollet J, Touboul P, and Delaye J (1994) Mediterranean alpha-linolenic acid rich-diet in the secondary prevention of coronary heart disease. *Lancet* **343**: 1454–1459.

Dwyer JH, Allayee H, Dwyer KM, Fan J, Wu H, Mar R, Lusis AJ, and Mehrabian M (2004) Arachidonate 5-lipoxygenase promoter genotype, dietary arachidonic acid, and atherosclerosis. *New England Journal of Medicine* **350**: 29–37.

GISSI-Prevenzione Investigators (1999) Dietary supplementation with n-3 polyunsaturated fatty acids and vitamin E after myocardial infarction: results of the GISSI-Prevenzione trial. *Lancet* **354**: 447–455.

Kang JX, Wang J, Wu L, and Kang ZB (2004) *Fat-1 mice convert n-6 to n-3 fatty acids*. *Nature* **427**: 504.

Maes M, Smith R, Christophe A, Cosyns P, Desynder R, and Meltzer H (1996) Fatty acid composition in major depression: decreased omega 3 fractions in cholesteryl esters and increased C20:4 omega 6/C20:5 omega 3 ratio in cholesteryl esters and phospholipids. *Journal of Affective Disorders* **38**(1): 35–46.

Mechanisms of Action of LCPUFA (2003) Effects on infant growth and neurodevelopment. Proceedings of a conference held in Arlington, Virginia, May 14–15, 2002. *Journal of Pediatrics* **143**(supplement 4): S1–S109.

Simopoulos AP (2001) N-3 fatty acids and human health: defining strategies for public policy. *Lipids* **36**: S83–S89.

Simopoulos AP (2002) Omega-3 fatty acids in inflammation and autoimmune diseases. *Journal of American College of Nutrition* **21**: 494–505.

Simopoulos AP and Cleland LG (eds.) (2003) *Omega-6/Omega-3 Essential Fatty Acid Ratio: The Scientific Evidence*. World Review of Nutrition and Dietetics, vol. 92 Basel: Karger.

Simopoulos AP, Leaf A, and Salem N Jr (1999) Essentiality of and recommended dietary intakes for omega-6 and omega-3 fatty acids. Annals of Nutrition and Metabolism **43**: 127–130.

Simopoulos AP and Nestel PJ (eds.) (1997) *Genetic Variation and Dietary Response. World Review of Nutrition and Dietetics*, vol. 80, Basel: Karger.

Simopoulos AP and Robinson J (1999) In *The Omega Diet. The Lifesaving Nutritional Program Based on the Diet of the Island of Crete*. New York: Harper Collins.

Simopoulos AP and Visioli F (eds.) (2000) *Mediterranean Diets. World Review of Nutrition and Dietetics*, vol. 87. Basel: Karger.

Singh RB, Dubnov G, Niaz MA, Ghosh S, Singh R, Rastogi SS, Manor O, Pella D, and Berry EM (2002) Effect of an Indo-Mediterranean diet on progression of coronary artery disease in high risk patients (Indo-Mediterranean Diet Heart Study): a randomised single-blind trial. *Lancet* **360**(9344): 1455–1461.

Yehuda S (2003) Omega-6/omega-3 ratio and brain-related functions. *World Review of Nutrition and Dietetics* **92**: 37–56.

Omega-6 Polyunsaturated

J M Hodgson and T A Mori, University of Western Australia, Perth, WA, Australia
M L Wahlqvist, Monash University, Victoria, VIC, Australia

Structure, Function, and Nutritional Requirements

Omega-6 (n-6) fatty acids are a class of polyunsaturated fatty acids (PUFA). They have two or more *cis* double bonds, with the position of the first double bond six carbon atoms from the methyl end of the molecule. The general formula of n-6 fatty acids is $CH_3(CH_2)_4(CH{=}CHCH_2)_x(CH_2)_yCOOH$ [where $x = 2$–5]. Linoleic acid (*cis*-9, *cis*-12-octadecadienoic acid, 18:2n-6, LA) and α-linolenic acid (*cis*-9, *cis*-12, *cis*-15-octadecatrienoic acid, 18:3n-3, ALA) are the precursor fatty acids of the n-6 and omega-3 (n-3) fatty acids, respectively. These two fatty acids cannot be made by mammals and are therefore termed essential fatty acids (EFA). In addition, mammals are unable to interconvert LA and ALA, or any of the n-6 and n-3 fatty acids, because mammalian tissues do not contain the necessary desaturase enzyme. Plant tissues and plant oils tend to be rich sources of LA. ALA is also present in plant sources such as green vegetables, flaxseed, canola, and some nuts. Once consumed in the diet, LA can be converted via chain elongation and desaturation to γ-linolenic acid (GLA, 18:3n-6), dihomo-γ-linolenic acid (DGLA, 20:3n-6), and arachidonic acid (AA, 20:4n-6) (**Figure 1**). The same enzymes involved in elongation and desaturation of the n-6 fatty acids are common to the n-3 series of fatty acids (**Figure 1**). Thus, ALA can be converted to eicosapentaenoic acid (EPA, 20:5n-3) and docosahexaenoic acid (DHA, 22:6n-3). EPA and DHA are found in relatively high proportions in marine oils.

The n-6 and n-3 fatty acids are metabolically and functionally distinct and often have important opposing physiological functions. Indeed, the balance of EFA is important for good health and normal development. Historically, human beings evolved on a diet in which the ratio of n-6 to n-3 fatty acids was about 1:1. In contrast, Western diets have a ratio of

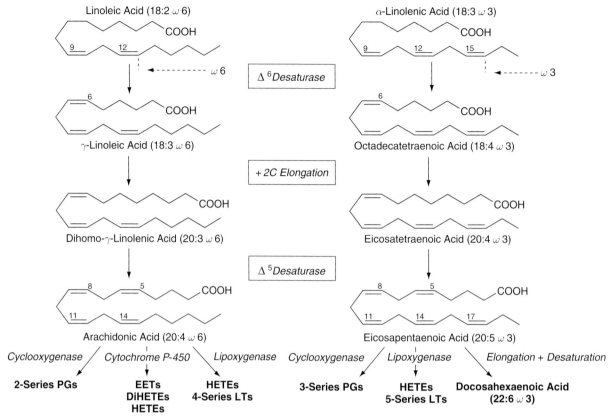

Figure 1   Essential fatty acid metabolism.

approximately 15:1. Evidence for this change in diet through history comes from studies on the evolutionary aspects of diet, modern-day hunter–gatherers, and traditional diets. Modern agriculture has led to a substantial increase in n-6 fatty acids at the expense of n-3 fatty acids, which has resulted in excessive consumption of n-6 fatty acids by humans.

The n-6 EFAs have two main functions. First, they act as structural components of membranes forming the basis of the phospholipid component of the lipid bilayer of plasma membranes in every cell in the body, thus providing a membrane impermeable to most water-soluble molecules. The length and degree of saturation of the fatty acids determine how the phospholipid molecules pack together and consequently affect membrane fluidity, signal transduction, and the expression of cellular receptors. The second role of n-6 fatty acids is as precursors to the eicosanoids (**Figure 1**). The eicosanoids are a family of 'hormone-like' compounds including prostaglandins (PGs), leukotrienes (LTs), and hydroxy- (HETEs), dihydroxy- (DiHETEs), and epoxy- (EETs) fatty acids. Eicosanoids, however, are distinct from most hormones in that they act locally, near their sites of synthesis, and they are catabolized extremely rapidly. Thus, they are

considered to be locally acting hormones. The eicosanoids modulate renal and pulmonary function, vascular tone, and inflammatory responses. The enzymes involved in AA metabolism include the cyclooxygenases and lipoxygenases, which yield the 2-series PGs and 4-series LTs, respectively. Lipoxygenase also utilizes AA for the formation of the HETEs. A third pathway for the utilization of AA involves the cytochrome P-450 enzymes found in the liver, kidney, lung, intestines, heart, small blood vessels, and white blood cells. AA metabolized via cytochrome P-450 yields EETs, DiHETEs, as well as HETEs. The cytochrome P-450 metabolites play an important role as paracrine factors and second messengers in the regulation of pulmonary, cardiac, renal, and vascular function and modulate inflammatory and growth responses.

Endothelial Function, Atherosclerosis, and Cardiovascular Disease

Differences in n-6 fatty acid intake have the potential to influence several chronic diseases and disorders. This article will focus on the effects of n-6 fatty acids on cardiovascular disease and atherosclerosis.

The vascular endothelium is the most important organ controlling vascular function and consists of a single layer of epithelial cells lining blood vessels. Its primary function is to regulate vascular tone, but it plays a critical role in modulating coagulation and fibrinolysis, inflammation, smooth muscle cell proliferation, and macrophage function. Many of these functions are regulated through the release of various mediators including eicosanoids. There is multiple and close interaction of the endothelial cells with circulating cells, smooth muscle cells, and macrophages. There is also evidence that endothelial dysfunction precedes clinically apparent atherosclerosis.

Atherosclerosis is an inflammatory disease involving multiple cellular and molecular responses that lead to an alteration in vascular function and structure, and the development and progression of cardiovascular disease. Atherosclerosis is characterized by degenerative changes, deposition of cholesterol, proliferation of smooth muscle cells, involvement of a range of circulating proinflammatory cell types, and fibrosis. Resulting atheromatous plaques cause narrowing of arteries and increase the likelihood of thrombosis and occlusion. When this process occurs in the coronary arteries, the outcome is myocardial infarction and with possible death.

Eicosanoids: Relevance to Endothelial Function, Thrombosis, Inflammation, and Atherosclerosis

In general, the eicosanoids derived from AA have potent prothrombotic and proinflammatory activity. In contrast, the eicosanoids derived from EPA have reduced biological activity and are less prothrombotic and proinflammatory. Eicosanoid production is generally tightly controlled through homeostatic mechanisms. However, eicosanoid production can be significantly altered in situations in which endothelial dysfunction, atherosclerosis and plaque rupture, or various thrombotic or inflammatory conditions are present.

Prostaglandins and Leukotrienes

Prostaglandins have a central role in the regulation of platelet aggregation and vascular tone. In this regard, two of the major prostaglandins derived from AA are thromboxane A_2, produced in platelets, and prostacyclin I_2, produced in endothelial cells. Thromboxane A_2 promotes platelet aggregation and blood vessel constriction, while prostacyclin I_2 has the opposite effects. An increase in availability of EPA can decrease platelet thromboxane A_2 and increase thromboxane A_3, the latter having

considerably less physiological activity. EPA supplementation also stimulates formation of prostacyclin I_3, while prostacyclin I_2 is unaffected. Prostacyclin I_3 and prostacyclin I_2 are equipotent in their biological activity. The net result following intake of n-3 fatty acids is a shift in the thromboxane/prostacyclin balance toward a reduced prothrombotic state.

Leukotriene B_4 is a potent inflammatory mediator produced by neutrophils from 20:4n-6 at the site of injury. Leukotriene B_4 is also a powerful chemotactic factor responsible for attracting neutrophils to the site of injury. Leukotriene B_5, which is produced from EPA, has significantly lower biological activity. Therefore an increased availability of EPA has the potential to reduce inflammation.

Fatty Acid Intake and Eicosanoids

The proportional concentration of the eicosanoid precursor fatty acids both circulating and in tissues depends on dietary intake. DGLA and AA can be obtained from animal meat and fat, and by desaturation and chain elongation of LA. The major dietary source of EPA is fish. EPA can also be obtained indirectly from ALA, although desaturation and chain elongation of ALA appears to be a less important pathway in humans.

Only the free form of the fatty acid precursors of eicosanoids can be utilized by the enzymes for conversion to the biologically active metabolites. However, the amount of precursor free fatty acid in the cytoplasm and circulating is usually low and so too is basal eicosanoid formation. Furthermore, basal eicosanoid formation may depend on dietary and adipose tissue fatty acid composition. The amount of eicosanoid precursor free fatty acids is controlled to a large extent by incorporation and release from cellular phospholipids. Which eicosanoids are produced during stimulated synthesis may depend on membrane fatty acid composition as well as the cell type involved. Dietary fatty acid composition, therefore, has the potential to effect basal and stimulated synthesis of eicosanoids and influence endothelial function and thrombotic and inflammatory responses.

n-6 Fatty Acids and Risk of Cardiovascular Disease

Evidence that differences in n-6 fatty acid intake can influence cardiovascular disease risk derives from several sources. Population studies may provide useful data for establishing optimal intakes of n-6 fatty acids. However, valuable information on the potential mechanisms and effects of these fatty acids is derived from studies focusing on their impact on thrombosis, inflammation, endothelial function, and other cardiovascular risk factors.

Cardiovascular Disease: Population Studies

The incidence of cardiovascular disease within populations with either very high or very low intakes of n-6 fatty acids may provide some indication for optimal intakes of n-6 fatty acids. Within populations with low n-6 fatty acid intakes ($\leq$3%) there would appear to be a benefit of having a higher n-6 fatty acid intake on cardiovascular disease risk reduction. These observations suggest that very low n-6 fatty acid intakes increase the risk for cardiovascular disease. The presence of EFA deficiency in a significant proportion of such populations may explain the increased risk. Several populations, including the Israelis, Taiwanese, and !Kung bushmen in the African Kalahari desert, have high to very high intakes of n-6 fatty acids. The contribution of n-6 fatty acids to total energy intake is about 10% in the Israelis and Taiwanese and about 30% in the !Kung bushmen. Rates of cardiovascular disease are low in the Taiwanese, where dietary n-6 fatty acids are obtained mainly from soybean oil, and estimated to be very low in the !Kung bushmen, where dietary n-6 fatty acids were obtained mainly from the monongo fruit and nut. In the Taiwanese, the soybean oil is refined but is accompanied by a diet rich in antioxidant polyphenols, notably from tea, fruits, and vegetables. In the !Kung bushmen the oil is unrefined and is therefore likely to contain a range of phytochemicals. There is, however, a high prevalence of cardiovascular disease in the Israeli population, where n-6 PUFAs are obtained largely from refined sources. These observations suggest that a high n-6 fatty acid intake can be compatible with low risk of cardiovascular disease, but the dietary context may be very important. Given that n-6 fatty acids are susceptible to lipid peroxidation, high n-6 fatty acid intake may increase risk for cardiovascular disease when consumed against a background diet low in antioxidants. The potential impact on eicosanoid metabolism remains uncertain.

Several factors may need to be considered in the interpretation of the results of population studies. First, the effect of LA on atherosclerosis and cardiovascular disease may depend on the background intake in the population being studied. Second, any relationships observed may be confounded by intake of other foods from which LA derives. Third, LA may have differential effects on aspects of the aetiology of cardiovascular disease, including endothelial function, thrombosis, arrhythmia, and atherosclerosis.

Thrombosis

Dietary fatty acids influence thrombosis by altering the activity and function of endothelial cells, platelets, and other circulating cells—effects that can be mediated, in part, by alterations in eicosanoid metabolism. Replacement of dietary saturated fatty acids with unsaturated fatty acids, including n-6 fatty acids, generally lowers the risk of thrombosis and cardiovascular disease. Furthermore, studies have shown that an increase in n-3 fatty acid intake can increase vasodilation, attenuate platelet aggregation, and alter circulating concentrations of factors involved in coagulation and fibrinolysis. The net effect of increasing n-3 fatty acid intake is a tendency toward reduced risk for thrombosis. These findings are supported by population studies demonstrating that n-3 fatty acids may reduce the risk of thrombosis. It remains uncertain whether the major factor influencing these functions is the absolute increase in n-3 fatty acids or the relative proportions of n-6 and n-3 fatty acids in the diet and cell membranes. There is evidence, however, that increased n-3 fatty acid intake may be more beneficial in populations consuming relatively small quantities of fish, which includes many Western populations.

Much of the evidence for a potential impact of n-6 fatty acids on thrombosis derives from research on platelet function. The role of platelets in thrombosis is established and the influence of fatty acid intake on platelet function has been assessed in many studies. Platelets play a part in thrombosis by adhering to, and aggregating at, the site of injury. Platelet reactivity and increased platelet activation may increase the risk of thrombosis. *In vitro* and *in vivo* studies assessing effects of n-6 fatty acids on platelet aggregation are inconsistent. To date there is little evidence that a high n-6 fatty acid diet in humans decreases platelet aggregation and some studies are suggestive of increased aggregation with high n-6 fatty acid diets, primarily in the form of LA. The effects of AA on platelet aggregation are also not clear. One of the main difficulties in interpreting these studies is the unresolved issue as to how the *in vitro* aggregation test reflects platelet function *in vivo*.

Inflammation

Conditions of increased inflammation, such as inflammatory arthritis, dermatological conditions such as psoriasis and atopic dermatitis, chronic inflammatory bowel disease, autoimmune diseases, and bronchial asthma, appear to be beneficially influenced by n-3 fatty acids but not by n-6 fatty acids.

Whether or not increased intake of n-6 fatty acids can exacerbate inflammation *via* increased production of proinflammatory eicosanoids remains uncertain. Results of *in vitro* studies and intervention studies in humans are generally consistent with this theoretical potential of n-6 fatty acids to enhance inflammation, at least in comparison to n-3 fatty acids and probably n-9 monounsaturated fatty acids. The importance of absolute and relative intakes of n-6 fatty acids to inflammatory processes also remains unclear. The effects of changes in n-6 fatty acid intake on inflammatory processes may depend on the background dietary fatty acid intake, as well as proportional and absolute intake of n-3 fatty acids.

Cholesterol and Lipoproteins

The major classes of circulating lipoproteins in human plasma are chylomicrons, very low-density lipoproteins (VLDL), low-density lipoproteins (LDL), and high-density lipoproteins (HDL). High fasting plasma concentrations of LDL cholesterol and triglycerides—predominantly circulating as part of VLDL—and low plasma concentrations of HDL cholesterol are associated with increased risk of cardiovascular disease. Dietary fatty acids can influence lipoprotein metabolism and therefore have the potential to influence atherosclerosis and cardiovascular disease risk. Most studies examining the effects of n-6 PUFAs on cholesterol metabolism have focused on LA, the major dietary n-6 fatty acid.

It is now established that LDL cholesterol lowering reduces the risk of cardiovascular disease. In the fasting state LDL is the major cholesterol carrying lipoprotein in human plasma. The mechanisms through which raised plasma LDL cholesterol concentrations increase cardiovascular disease risk are not entirely understood but oxidative modification of LDL is thought to be involved. An increase in LA intake results in a lowering of plasma LDL cholesterol concentrations and therefore has the potential to reduce cardiovascular disease risk. These effects may not be linear over the entire range of LA intake and most of the benefits appear to be gained by moving from lower (<2% of energy) to moderate (~4–5% of energy) intakes. In addition, it is worthy of note that the effects of dietary n-6 PUFAs are less than half that of lowering dietary saturated fatty acids. Therefore, if total fat intake is maintained,

the LDL cholesterol lowering effects of increasing n-6 PUFA intake are greatly enhanced if saturated fatty acid intake is decreased.

HDL cholesterol is inversely associated with cardiovascular disease risk. The mechanism by which HDL reduces cardiovascular disease risk may involve reverse cholesterol transport and reductions in cholesterol accumulation in the arterial wall. Intakes of LA within the normal ranges of intakes in most populations do not appear to alter HDL cholesterol concentrations. However, very high intakes—above 12% of energy—can lower HDL cholesterol concentrations.

Oxidative Stress

Several lines of evidence suggest that oxidatively modified LDL plays an important role in the development of atherosclerosis. Oxidative modification of LDL involves peroxidation of PUFAs. LDL particles enriched in PUFAs have been shown to be more susceptive to oxidative modification compared to LDL particles rich in monounsaturated fatty acids. Others have also suggested that a diet high in PUFAs may overwhelm the antioxidant defenses of cells. In particular, studies have shown that LA-enriched LDL is more prone to *in vitro* oxidation than oleic acid-enriched LDL. Concern also remains with respect to the potential for increased lipid peroxidation following n-3 fatty acids. To date, however, the data *in vivo* are inconclusive, with observations of increased, unchanged, and decreased lipid peroxidation. The most plausible explanation relates to differences in the methodologies employed to assess lipid peroxidation. Much of the literature relating to PUFAs and lipid peroxidation is based on indirect and nonspecific assays, including measurement of LDL oxidative susceptibility, which relies on the isolation of LDL from plasma. In this regard, the recent discovery of F_2-isoprostanes, which are nonenzymatic prostaglandin-like products of free radical peroxidation of arachidonic acid, has allowed for the direct assessment of *in vivo* lipid peroxidation. There is now good evidence that quantitation of F_2-isoprostanes provides a reliable measure of *in vivo* oxidative stress. Using measurement of F_2-isoprostanes, recent data have demonstrated that n-3 fatty acids decrease oxidative stress. It has also been suggested that the concentration of PUFAs may be a more important factor affecting lipid peroxidation than the degree of unsaturation. Further research using better markers of lipid peroxidation is required before definitive statements can be made relating to the effect of n-6 fatty acids, and indeed PUFAs in general, on oxidative stress.

Blood Pressure

The possible effects of dietary fatty acids on blood pressure have been explored in population studies and dietary intervention trials. With the exception of studies comparing vegetarian and nonvegetarian populations, from which there is a suggestion of a blood pressure lowering effect of diets high in PUFAs, including LA, and lower in saturated fatty acids, the results of most within- and between-population studies have generally not found significant associations. The results of intervention studies suggest that n-6 fatty acids, LA in particular, may be responsible for a small blood pressure lowering effect. However, these studies are also inconsistent, with several failing to find a significant blood pressure lowering effect.

Conclusions

Diets low in n-6 fatty acids, principally LA, appear to be associated with an increased risk of cardiovascular disease. The results of studies examining the effects of LA on risk factors for atherosclerosis and cardiovascular disease are consistent with this observation. An increase in n-6 PUFA intake from a low to a moderate intake level, in conjunction with decreases in total and saturated fat intake, may beneficially influence lipoprotein metabolism, lower blood pressure, and reduce cardiovascular disease risk. Observations in populations with high n-6 PUFA intake indicate that high intakes of n-6 fatty acids (>10%) can occur together with low rates of cardiovascular disease and possibly also cancer. However, where antioxidant composition of the diet is low, there is the potential for increased risk of cardiovascular disease. An increased susceptibility of PUFAs to oxidative damage, particularly in the presence of low concentrations of protective antioxidants, may be an important factor involved. The source of n-6 PUFAs in the diet, refined versus unrefined, and the composition of the background diet may therefore be important determinants of whether high n-6 fatty acid intake increases or decreases risk of cardiovascular disease. In addition, the proportion of n-6 to n-3 fatty acids in the diet may also play an important role in determining cardiovascular risk.

The available evidence suggests that n-6 fatty acid-derived eicosanoids are generally proinflammatory and prothrombotic. In contrast, eicosanoids derived from n-3 fatty acids have attenuated biological activity on cardiovascular risk factors. The effects of altering n-6 PUFA intake, in conjunction with changes in other polyunsaturated fatty acids, as well as other classes of fatty acids, on endothelial function, thrombosis, and inflammation are not understood. The relative proportion of all the classes of fatty acids in the diet may well be more important and relevant to cardiovascular risk reduction than any single class of fatty acids. Clearly such research warrants further investigation.

See also: **Cholesterol**: Sources, Absorption, Function and Metabolism; Factors Determining Blood Levels. **Coronary Heart Disease**: Lipid Theory. **Fatty Acids**: Metabolism; Monounsaturated; Omega-3 Polyunsaturated; Saturated; *Trans* Fatty Acids. **Fish**. **Lipoproteins**. **Prostaglandins and Leukotrienes**.

Further Reading

Grundy SM (1996) Dietary fat. In: Ziegler EE and Filer LJ Jr. (eds.) *Present knowledge in Nutrition*, 7th edn., pp. 44–57. Washington, DC: ILSI Press.

Hodgson JM, Wahlqvist ML, Boxall JA, and Balazs NDH (1993) Can linoleic acid contribute to coronary artery disease? *American Journal of Clinical Nutrition* 58: 228–234.

Hodgson JM, Wahlqvist ML, and Hsu-Hage B (1995) Diet, hyperlipidaemia and cardiovascular disease. *Asia Pacific Journal of Clinical Nutrition* 4: 304–313.

Hornsrtra G, Barth CA, Galli C *et al.* (1998) Functional food science and the cardiovascular system. *British Journal of Nutrition* 80(supplement 1): S113–S146.

Horrobin DF (ed.) (1990) *Omega-6 Essential Fatty Acids: Pathophysiology and Roles in Clinical Medicine*. New York: Wiley-Liss.

Jones GP (1997) Fats. In: Wahlqvist ML (ed.) *Food and Nutrition, Australia, Asia and the Pacific*, pp. 205–214. Sydney: Allen & Unwin.

Jones PJH and Kubow S (1999) Lipids, sterols and their metabolism. In: Shils ME, Olson JA, Shike M, and Ross AC (eds.) *Modern Nutrition in Health and Disease*, 9th edn., pp. 67–94. Baltimore: Williams & Wilkins.

Knapp HR (1997) Dietary fatty acids in human thrombosis and hemostasis. *American Journal of Clinical Nutrition* 65(supplement 5): 1687S–1698S.

Lyu LC, Shieh MJ, Posner BM *et al.* (1994) Relationship between dietary intake, lipoproteins and apolipoproteins in Taipei and Framingham. *American Journal of Clinical Nutrition* 60: 765–774.

Mensink R and Connor W (eds.) (1996) *Nutrition. Current Opinion in Lipidology* 7: 1–53.

National Health and Medical Research Council (1992) *The role of polyunsaturated fats in the Australian diet: Report of the NHMRC working party*. Canberra: Australian Government Publishing Service.

Salem N, Simopoulos AP, Galli, Lagarde M, and Knapp HR (eds.) (1996) Fatty acids and lipids from cell biology to human disease: Proceedings of the 2nd International Congress of the International Society for the Study of Fatty Acids and Lipids. *Lipids* 31 (supplement).

Truswell AS (1977) Diet and nutrition of hunter gatherers. *Ciba Foundation Symposium*, 213–221.

Yam D, Eliraz A, and Berry EM (1996) Diet and disease—The Israeli paradox: Possible dangers of a high omega-6 polyunsaturated fatty acid diet. *Israeli Journal of Medical Sciences* 32: 1134–1143.

Saturated

R P Mensink, Maastricht University, Maastricht, The Netherlands
E H M Temme, University of Leuven, Leuven, Belgium

Fats and oils always consist of a mixture of fatty acids, although one or two fatty acids are usually predominant. **Table 1** shows the fatty acid composition of some edible fats rich in saturated fatty acids. In the Western diet, palmitic acid ($C_{16:0}$) is the major saturated fatty acid. A smaller proportion comes from stearic acid ($C_{18:0}$), followed by myristic acid ($C_{14:0}$), lauric acid ($C_{12:0}$), and short-chain and medium-chain fatty acids (MCFA) ($C_{10:0}$ or less).

When discussing the health effects of the total saturated fat content of diets, this class of fatty acids has to be compared with some other component of the diet that provides a similar amount of energy (isoenergetic). Otherwise, two variables are being introduced: changes in total dietary energy intake and, as a consequence, changes in body weight. Normally, an isoenergetic amount from carbohydrates is used for comparisons.

Cholesterol Metabolism

Lipoproteins and their associated apoproteins are strong predictors of the risk of coronary heart disease (CHD). Concentrations of total cholesterol, low-density lipoproteins (LDL), and apoprotein B are positively correlated with CHD risk; high-density lipoprotein (HDL) and apoprotein Al concentrations are negatively correlated. Controlled dietary trials have now demonstrated that the total saturated fat content and the type of saturated fatty acid in the diet affect serum lipid and lipoprotein levels.

Total Saturated Fat Content of Diets

Using statistical techniques, results from independent experiments have been combined to develop equations that estimate the mean change in serum lipoprotein levels for a group of subjects when carbohydrates are replaced by an isoenergetic amount of a mixture of saturated fatty acids. The predicted changes for total LDL and HDL cholesterol and triacylglycerols are shown in **Figure 1**. Each bar represents the predicted change in the concentration of that particular lipid or lipoprotein when a particular fatty acid class replaces 10% of the daily energy intake from carbohydrates. For a group of adults with an energy intake of 10 MJ daily, 10% of energy is provided by about 60 g of carbohydrates or 27 g of fatty acids.

A mixture of saturated fatty acids strongly elevates serum total cholesterol levels. It was predicted that when 10% of dietary energy provided by carbohydrates was exchanged for a mixture of saturated fatty acids, serum total cholesterol concentrations would increase by 0.36 mmol l^{-1}. This increase in total cholesterol will result from a rise in both LDL and HDL cholesterol concentrations. Saturated fatty acids will also lower fasting triacylglycerol concentrations compared with carbohydrates. Besides affecting LDL and HDL cholesterol concentrations, a mixture of saturated fatty acids also changes the concentrations of their associated apoproteins. In general, strong associations are observed between changes in LDL cholesterol and changes in apo-B and between changes in HDL cholesterol and apo-Al.

Figure 1 also shows that total and LDL cholesterol concentrations decrease when saturated fatty acids are replaced by unsaturated fatty acids. In addition, slight decreases of HDL cholesterol concentrations are then predicted.

Effects of Specific Saturated Fatty Acids

Cocoa butter raises total cholesterol concentrations to a lesser extent than palm oil. This difference in

Table 1 Composition of fats rich in satured fatty acids

	Weight per 100 g of total fatty acids (g)								
	$\leq C_{10:0}$	$C_{12:0}$	$C_{14:0}$	$C_{16:0}$	$C_{18:0}$	$C_{18:1}$	$C_{18:2}$	$C_{18:3}$	Other
Butterfat	9	3	17	25	13	27	3	1	2
Palm kernel fat	8	50	16	8	2	14	2		
Coconut fat	15	48	17	8	3	7	2		
Palm oil			1	45	5	39	9		1
Beef fat			3	26	22	38	2	1	8
Pork fat (lard)			2	25	12	44	10	1	6
Cocoa butter				26	35	35	3		1

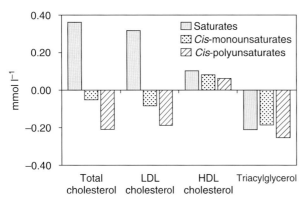

Figure 1 Predicted changes in serum lipids and lipoproteins when 10% of energy from dietary carbohydrates is replaced by an isoenergetic amount of saturated fatty acids. From Mensink *et al.* (2003) *American Journal of Clinical Nutrition* **77**: 1146–1155. Reproduced with permission by the *American Journal of Clinical Nutrition*. © Am J Clin Nutr. American Society for Clinical Nutrition.

the serum cholesterol-raising potency of two fats high in saturated fatty acids (see **Table 1**) showed that not all saturated fatty acids have equal effects on cholesterol concentrations. **Figure 2** illustrates the effects of lauric, myristic, palmitic, and stearic acids on LDL and HDL cholesterol concentrations. Compared with other saturated fatty acids, lauric and myristic acids have the strongest potency to increase serum total and LDL cholesterol concentrations and also HDL cholesterol concentrations. Effects of lauric acid on HDL are stronger than those of myristic acid.

Scientists are not unanimous about the cholesterol-raising properties of palmitic acid, the major dietary saturated fatty acid. Many studies have

indicated that, compared with carbohydrates, palmitic acid raises serum total and LDL cholesterol levels but has less effect on HDL cholesterol (**Figure 2**). However, a few studies indicated that palmitic acid might not raise total and LDL cholesterol concentrations compared with carbohydrates. It has been proposed that this negative finding is only present when the linoleic acid content of the diet is adequate (6–7% of energy). It is hypothesized that the increased hepatic apo-B100 production caused by palmitic acid, and the consequent elevation of concentrations of serum very low density lipoproteins (VLDL) and LDL particles, is counteracted by an increased uptake of LDL particles by the LDL receptor which is upregulated by linoleic acid. To explain the discrepancy with other studies, it has been suggested that in some situations, such as hypercholesterolaemia or obesity, linoleic acid is unable to increase LDL receptor activity sufficiently to neutralize the cholesterol-raising effects of palmitic acid. This theory, however, awaits confirmation, and for now it seems justified to classify palmitic acid as a cholesterol-raising saturated fatty acid.

Stearic acid, a major fatty acid in cocoa butter, does not raise total, LDL, and HDL cholesterol levels compared with carbohydrates. Also, MCFA have been reported not to raise LDL and HDL cholesterol concentrations compared with carbohydrates, but data are limited. Like carbohydrates, diets containing large amounts of MCFA increase fasting triacylglycerol concentrations compared with the other saturated fatty acids. However, such diets are the sole energy source only in parenteral or enteral nutrition or in sports drinks. Other saturated fatty acids have not been reported to raise

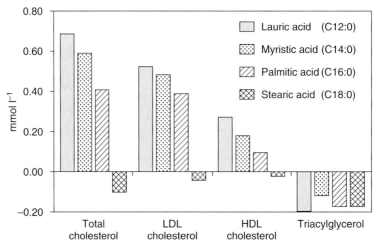

Figure 2 Overview of the effects of particular fatty acids on serum total, LDL, and HDL cholesterol concentration when 10% of energy from dietary carbohydrates is replaced by an isoenergetic amount of a particular saturated fatty acid. From Mensink *et al.* (2003) *American Journal of Clinical Nutrition* **77**: 1146–1155. Reproduced with permission by the *American Journal of Clinical Nutrition*. © Am J Clin Nutr. American Society for Clinical Nutrition.

triacylglycerol concentrations compared with each other, but lower triacylglycerol concentrations compared with carbohydrates.

Platelet Aggregation

Increased platelet aggregation may be an important risk marker for the occurrence of cardiovascular disease, and different types of fatty acids can modify platelet aggregation *in vitro*. However, reports of research on this topic are confusing. All measurements have their limitations, and it is not known whether measurement *in vitro* of platelet aggregation reflects the reality of platelet reactivity *in vivo*.

Many methods are available to measure platelet aggregation *in vitro*. First, the blood sample is treated with an anticoagulant to avoid clotting of the blood in the test tube or in the aggregometer; many different anticoagulants are used, which all differ in their mechanism of action. Second, platelet aggregation can be measured in whole blood, in platelet-rich plasma, or (to remove the influence of the plasma constituents) in a washed platelet sample. Finally, the platelet aggregation reaction in the aggregometer can be initiated with many different compounds, such as collagen, ADP, arachidonic acid, and thrombin. Platelet aggregation can also be studied by measuring the stable metabolites of the proaggregatory thromboxane A_2 (TxA_2), thromboxane B_2 (TxB_2), the stable metabolite of the antiaggregatory prostaglandin (prostacyclin: PGI_2), or 6-keto-PGF1α.

Total Saturated Fat Content of Diets

Platelet aggregation and clotting activity of plasma were studied in British and French farmers, who were classified according to their intake of saturated fatty acids. A positive correlation was observed between thrombin-induced aggregation of platelet-rich plasma and the intake of saturated fatty acids. Aggregation induced by ADP or collagen, however, did not correlate with dietary saturated fat intake. In a follow-up study, a group of farmers consuming high-fat diets were asked to replace dairy fat in their diets with a special margarine rich in polyunsaturated fatty acids. Besides lowering the intake of saturated fatty acids, this intervention also resulted in a lower intake of total fat. A control group of farmers did not change their diets. After this intervention the thrombin-induced aggregation of platelet-rich plasma decreased when saturated fat intake decreased. Aggregation induced by ADP, however, increased in the intervention group. From these

studies, it is not clear whether the fatty acid composition of the diets or the total fatty acid content is responsible for the changes in platelet aggregation. Furthermore, it is not clear if one should favor increased or decreased platelet aggregation after decreasing the saturated fat content of diets as effects did depend on the agonist used to induce platelet aggregation. Saturated fatty acids from milk fat have also been compared with unsaturated fatty acids from sunflower and rapeseed oils. Aggregation induced by ADP or collagen in platelet-rich plasma was lower with the milk fat diet than with either oil.

One of the mechanisms affecting platelet aggregation is alteration of the proportion of arachidonic acid in the platelet phospholipids. Arachidonic acid is a substrate for the production of the proaggregatory TxA_2 and the antiaggregatory PGI_2, and the balance between these two eicosanoids affects the degree of platelet activation. The proportion of arachidonic acid in membranes can be modified through changes in dietary fatty acid composition. Diets rich in saturated fatty acids increase the arachidonic acid content of the platelet phospholipids, but this is also dependent on the particular saturated fatty acid consumed (see below).

Diets rich in saturated fatty acids have also been associated with a lower ratio of cholesterol to phospholipids in platelet membranes, which may affect receptor activity and platelet aggregation. However, these mechanisms have been described from studies *in vitro* and on animals and have not adequately been confirmed in human studies.

Effects of Specific Saturated Fatty Acids

Diets rich in coconut fat have been reported to raise TxB_2 and lower 6-keto-PGF$_{1\alpha}$ concentrations in collagen-activated plasma compared with diets rich in palm or olive oils, indicating a less favourable eicosanoid profile. The main saturated fatty acids of coconut fat — lauric and myristic acids — did not, however, change collagen-induced aggregation in whole-blood samples compared with a diet rich in oleic acid. Also, diets rich in MCFA or palmitic acid did not change collagen-induced aggregation in whole-blood samples. Compared with a diet rich in a mixture of saturated fatty acids, a stearic acid diet increased collagen-induced aggregation in platelet-rich plasma. In addition, a decreased proportion of arachidonic acid in platelet phospholipids was demonstrated after a cocoa butter diet compared with a diet rich in butterfat. Changes in eicosanoid metabolite concentrations in urine, however, were not observed after either diet. These results are conflicting and it is debatable whether measurement *in vitro* of platelet aggregation truly reflects the situation *in vivo*.

Coagulation and Fibrinolysis

Processes involved in thrombus formation include not only those required for the formation of a stable thrombus (platelet aggregation and blood clotting) but also a mechanism to dissolve the thrombus (fibrinolysis). Long-term prospective epidemiological studies have reported that in healthy men factor VII coagulant activity (factor VIIc) and fibrinogen concentrations were higher in subjects who developed cardiovascular diseases at a later stage of the study. Factor VIIc in particular was associated with an increased risk of dying from cardiovascular disease. A high concentration of plasminogen activator inhibitor type 1 (PAI-1) indicates impaired fibrinolytic capacity of the plasma and is associated with increased risk of occurrence of coronary events.

Saturated fatty acids can affect the plasma activity of some of these coagulation and fibrinolytic factors and thus the prethrombotic state of the blood. However, the effects of saturated fatty acids on coagulation and fibrinolytic factors in humans, unlike effects on cholesterol concentrations, have received little attention, and few well-controlled human studies have been reported. Also, regression equations derived from a meta-analysis, which predict the effects on coagulation and fibrinolytic factors of different fatty acid classes compared with those of carbohydrates, do not exist. Therefore, the reference fatty acid is dependent on the experiment discussed. In the epidemiological studies that have found associations between CHD risk and factors involved in thrombogenesis or atherogenesis, subjects were mostly fasted. Also, the effects of saturated fatty acids on cholesterol metabolism, platelet aggregation, and coagulation and fibrinolysis have been studied mainly in fasted subjects. It should be noted, however, that concentrations of some coagulation factors (e.g., factor VIIc) and fibrinolytic factors change after a meal.

Total Saturated Fat Content of Diets

Coagulation Results of studies on the effects of low-fat diets compared with high-fat diets provide some insight into the effects of decreasing the saturated fat content of diets. However, in these studies multiple changes are introduced which makes interpretation of results difficult.

Figure 3 demonstrates that decreased factor VIIc levels were observed in subjects on low-fat diets

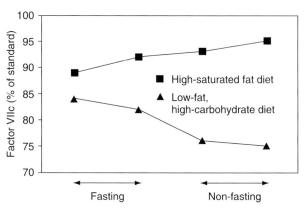

Figure 3 Effects of a high-saturated fat diet on fasting and postprandial factor VIIc activity From Miller (1998) *American Journal of Clinical Nutrition* **67**(supplement): 542S–545S. Reproduced with permission by the *American Journal of Clinical Nutrition*. © Am J Clin Nutr. American Society for Clinical Nutrition.

compared with those on high-saturated fat diets. In many of these studies, the low-fat diet provided smaller quantities of both saturated and unsaturated fatty acids and more fiber than the high-saturated fat diets. The combined results, however, suggest that, apart from a possible effect of dietary fiber, saturates increase factor VII levels compared with carbohydrates. Effects on other clotting factors are less clear. Measurements of markers of *in vivo* coagulation (e.g., prothrombin fragment $1+2$) might have provided more information on the effect of saturates on blood coagulation but were unfortunately not measured in most experiments.

Fibrinolysis Effects of low-fat and high-fat diets on the fibrinolytic capacity of the blood have also been studied. A similar problem, as stated before, is that multiple changes were introduced within a single experiment. Results of longer term and shorter term studies with dietary changes of total fat (decrease of saturated and unsaturated fatty acids contents) and increased fiber content indicate beneficially increased euglobulin fibrinolytic capacity of the blood. However, when the saturated fatty acid and fiber content of two diets were almost identical and only the unsaturated fatty acid content was changed, no significant differences in fibrinolytic capacity were observed.

Little is known about the relative effects on fibrinolytic capacity of saturated fatty acids compared with unsaturated fatty acids. It has been reported, however, that diets rich in butterfat decreased PAI-1 activity compared with a diet rich in partially hydrogenated soybean oil, but whether this is because of changes in the saturated acid or the *trans* fatty acid content is not clear from this study.

As for coagulation factors, the findings on the fibrinolytic effects of saturates are still inconclusive and need to be examined by more specific assays, measuring the activities of the separate fibrinolytic factors such as tPA and PAI-1.

Effects of Specific Saturated Fatty Acids

Coagulation   The interest in the effects of particular fatty acids on coagulation and fibrinolytic factors has increased since the observation that different saturated fatty acids raise serum lipids and lipoproteins in different ways (see section on cholesterol metabolism). Although results are conflicting, some studies indicate that the most potent cholesterol-raising saturated fatty acids also increase factor VII activity.

Diets rich in lauric plus myristic acids compared with a diet rich in stearic acid also increase concentrations of other vitamin K-dependent coagulation proteins. In addition, this mixture of saturated fatty acids raised F1 + 2 concentrations, indicating increased *in vivo* turnover of prothrombin to thrombin. This agreed with a study in rabbits where increased F1 + 2 concentrations were associated with increased hepatic synthesis of vitamin K-dependent clotting factors.

Diets rich in certain saturated fatty acids (lauric acid and palmitic acid) and also diets rich in butterfat have been reported to raise fibrinogen concentrations, but increases were small.

Postprandially, increased factor VIIc concentrations have been demonstrated after consumption of diets rich in fat compared with fat-free meals (**Figure 3**). The response is stronger when more fat is consumed, but this occurs regardless of whether the fat is high in saturated or unsaturated fatty acids. Only meals with unrealistically high amounts of MCFA have been reported not to change factor VIIc levels in comparison with a meal providing a similar amount of olive oil.

Fibrinolysis   Increased PAI-1 activity of a palmitic acid-rich diet has been observed compared with diets enriched with oleic acid, indicating impaired fibrinolytic capacity of the plasma. However, this was not confirmed by other experiments on the effects of particular saturated fatty acids (including palmitic acid), which did not indicate changes in fibrinolytic capacity of the blood, measured as tPA, PAI-1 activity, or antigen concentrations of tPA and PAI-1.

Conclusion

Saturated fatty acids as a group affect factors involved in cholesterol metabolism. Relative to the carbohydrate content of the diet, a decrease in saturated fat content induces a favorable decrease in serum total and LDL cholesterol concentrations but unfavorably reduces HDL cholesterol concentrations. Both increasing and decreasing effects of saturates on platelet aggregation have been observed, as well as the absence of effect, so results are inconsistent and difficult to interpret. Whether the beneficial effect of a diet low in saturated fat on the prethrombotic state of blood depends on the dietary fiber content is still unclear.

Of the saturated fatty acids, lauric and myristic acids have the strongest potency to raise total and LDL cholesterol concentrations. In addition, both of these saturated fatty acids raise HDL cholesterol levels. Palmitic acid raises total and LDL cholesterol levels compared with carbohydrates but is less potent than lauric and myristic acids. Stearic acid does not raise LDL and HDL cholesterol concentrations compared with carbohydrates. Lauric, myristic, and palmitic acids increase factor VII activity in a similar way, whereas the effects of MCFA and stearic acid seem limited.

See also: **Cholesterol**: Sources, Absorption, Function and Metabolism; Factors Determining Blood Levels. **Coronary Heart Disease**: Hemostatic Factors; Lipid Theory; Prevention. **Fats and Oils**. **Fatty Acids**: Metabolism. **Lipids**: Chemistry and Classification. **Lipoproteins**.

Further Reading

Hornstra G and Kester ADM (1997) Effect of the dietary fat type on arterial thrombosis tendency: Systematic studies with a rat model. *Atherosclerosis* **131**: 25–33.

Khosla P and Sundram K (1996) Effects of dietary fatty acid composition on plasma cholesterol. *Progress in Lipid Research* **35**: 93–132.

Kris-Etherton PM, Kris-Etherton PM, Binkoski AE *et al.* (2002) Dietary fat: Assessing the evidence in support of a moderate-fat diet; The benchmark based on lipoprotein metabolism. *Proceedings of the Nutrition Society* **61**: 287–298.

Masson LF, McNeill G, and Avenell A (2003) Genetic variation and the lipid response to dietary intervention: A systematic review. *American Journal of Clinical Nutrition* **77**: 1098–1111.

Mensink RP, Zock PL, Kester AD, and Katan MB (2003) Effects of dietary fatty acids and carbohydrates on the ratio of serum total to HDL cholesterol and on serum lipids and apolipoproteins: A meta-analysis of 60 controlled trials. *American Journal of Clinical Nutrition* **77**: 1146–1155.

Miller GJ (1998) Effects of diet composition on coagulation pathways. *American Journal of Clinical Nutrition* **67**(supplement): 542S–545S.

Mutanen M and Freese R (1996) Polyunsaturated fatty acids and platelet aggregation. *Current Opinion in Lipidology* **7**: 14–19.

Mutanen M and Freese R (2001) Fats, lipids and blood coagulation. *Current Opinion in Lipidology* **12**: 25–29.

Sacks FM and Katan M (2002) Randomized clinical trials on the effects of dietary fat and carbohydrate on plasma lipoproteins and cardiovascular disease. *American Journal of Medicine* **113**(Supplement 9B): 13S–24S.

Temme EHM, Mensink RP, and Hornstra G (1998) Saturated fatty acids and effects on whole blood aggregation in vitro. *European Journal of Clinical Nutrition* **52**: 697–702.

Temme EHM, Mensink RP, and Hornstra G (1999) Effects of diets enriched in lauric, palmitic or oleic acids on blood coagulation and fibrinolysis. *Thrombosis and Haemostasis* **81**: 259–263.

Tholstrup T, Miller GJ, Bysted A, and Sandström B (2003) Effect of individual dietary fatty acids on postprandial activation of blood coagulation factor VII and fibrinolysis in healthy young men. *American Journal of Clinical Nutrition* **77**: 1125–1132.

Trans Fatty Acids

M J Sadler, MJSR Associates, Ashford, UK

Chemistry

The *trans* fatty acids are unsaturated fatty acids that contain one or more ethylenic double bonds in the *trans* geometrical configuration, i.e., on opposite sides of the carbon chain (**Figure 1**). The *trans* bond is more thermodynamically stable than the *cis* bond and is therefore less chemically reactive.

Trans bonds have minimal effect on the conformation of the carbon chain such that their physical properties more closely resemble those of saturated fatty acids than of *cis* unsaturated fatty acids. The conformation remains linear, compared with *cis* fatty acids, which are kinked (**Figure 2**). Hence, *trans* isomers can pack together more closely than their *cis* counterparts.

Trans fatty acids have higher melting points than their *cis* counterparts, while saturated fatty acids have higher melting points than both *trans* and *cis* fatty acids. For example, the melting points of C_{18}

$$CH_3-(CH_2)_x-\overset{\overset{\displaystyle H}{|}}{C}=\overset{\overset{\displaystyle H}{|}}{C}-(CH_2)_y-COOH$$

cis configuration

$$CH_3-(CH_2)_x-\overset{\overset{\displaystyle H}{|}}{C}=\underset{\underset{\displaystyle H}{|}}{C}-(CH_2)_y-COOH$$

trans configuration

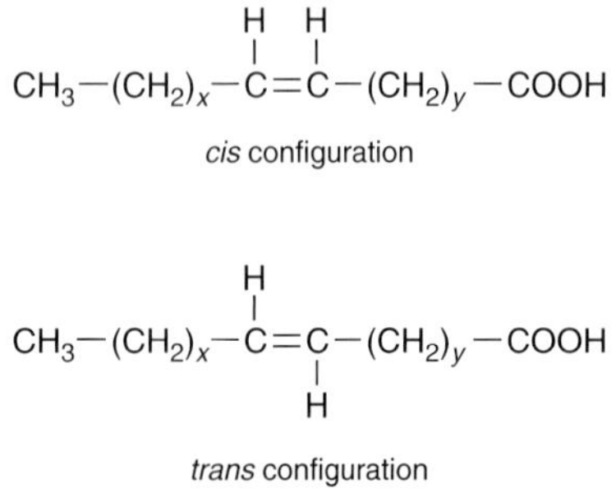

Figure 1 The *trans* and *cis* configurations of unsaturated bonds. Reproduced with kind permission of the British Nutrition Foundation.

$$CH_3-(CH_2)_x-CH$$
$$HOOC-(CH_2)_y-CH$$

cis conformation

$$CH_3-(CH_2)_x-CH$$
$$HC-(CH_2)_y-COOH$$

trans conformation

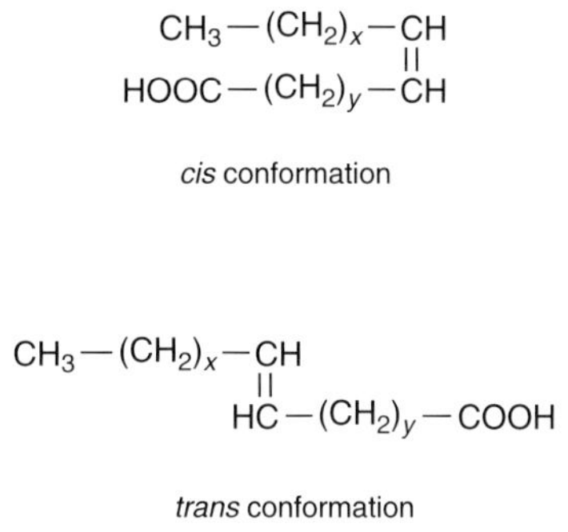

Figure 2 Conformation of the carbon chain with *trans* and *cis* bonds. Reproduced with kind permission of the British Nutrition Foundation.

fatty acids are 69.6 °C for stearic acid (18:0), 44.8 °C for elaidic acid (*trans*-18:1), and 13.2 °C for oleic acid (*cis*-18:1). The relative proportion of these different types of fatty acids influences the physical properties of cooking fats and their suitability for different uses in the food processing industry.

In addition to geometrical isomerism (*cis* and *trans*), unsaturated fatty acids also exhibit positional isomerism, where the double bonds can occur in different positions along the chain in fatty acids which have identical chemical formulae. As with *cis* fatty acids, *trans* fatty acids also occur as mixtures of positional isomers.

Occurrence

Trans fatty acids present in the diet arise from two origins. The first is from bacterial biohydrogenation in the forestomach of ruminants, which is the source of *trans* fatty acids present in mutton and beef fats. These are present at a concentration of 2–9% of bovine fat. *Trans*-11-octadecenoic acid is the main isomer produced although *trans*-9- and *trans*-10-octadecenoic acid are also produced. Thus, *trans* fatty acids occur in nature and cannot be considered to be foreign substances.

The second origin is from the industrial catalytic hydrogenation of liquid oils (mainly of vegetable origin, but also of fish oils). This produces solid fats and partially hydrogenated oils and is undertaken to increase the thermal stability of liquid oils and to alter their physical properties. The margarines, spreads, shortenings, and frying oils produced are thus more useful in the food processing industry than liquid oils. Chemically, a range of *trans* isomers is produced that, for vegetable oils containing predominantly C_{18} unsaturated fatty acids, is qualitatively similar to those produced by biohydrogenation, although the relative proportions of the isomers may differ. Use of fish oils containing a high proportion of very long-chain (C_{20} and C_{22}) fatty acids with up to six double bonds produces more complex mixtures of *trans*, *cis*, and positional isomers. However, the use of hydrogenated fish oils in food processing is declining, owing to a general fall in edible oil prices and to consumer preference for products based on vegetable oils.

Analysis

Methods available for the estimation of total *trans* unsaturation and to determine individual *trans* fatty acids are outlined in **Table 1**. At present there is no one simple and accurate method suitable for both research applications and for use in the food industry. In dietary studies data for *trans* fatty acid intake are generally expressed as the sum of the fatty acids containing *trans* double bonds, and there is generally no differentiation between the different isomers.

A report from the British Nutrition Foundation (BNF) in 1995 highlighted concerns over the variations in estimations of *trans* fatty acid concentrations in some food products provided by different analytical techniques. A thorough review of the available analytical techniques was called for.

Sources and Intakes

The main sources of *trans* fatty acids in the UK diet are cereal-based products (providing 27% of total *trans* fatty acid intake), margarines, spreads, and frying oils (22%), meat and meat products (18%), and milk, butter, and cheese (16%). In the USA, the main sources of intake are baked goods (28%), fried foods (25%), margarine, spreads, and shortenings (25%), savory snacks (10%), and milk and butter (9%).

Typical ranges of *trans* fatty acids in foods are shown in **Table 2**. *Trans* isomers of $C_{18:1}$ (elaidic acid) are the most common *trans* fatty acids, accounting for 65% of the total *trans* fatty acids in the UK diet.

Intakes of *trans* fatty acids are difficult to assess because of:

- analytical inaccuracies;
- difficulties of obtaining reliable information about food intake.

A number of countries have attempted to assess intakes of *trans* fatty acids (**Table 3**). Reliable intake data are available for the UK, based on a 7-day weighed intake of foods eaten both inside and outside the home, for 2000 adults aged 16–64 years (**Table 3**). Data from the UK National Food Survey,

Table 1 Analytical methods for *trans* fatty acids

General method	Determines	Advantages	Disadvantages
Infrared (IR) absorption spectrometry	Total *trans* unsaturation	Inexpensive; reliable results provided concentrations of *trans* isomers exceed 5%; can analyze intact lipids	Unreliable results if concentrations of *trans* isomers less than 5%; interpretive difficulties—need to apply correction factors
Fourier transform IR spectroscopy	Total *trans* unsaturation	Reliable results if concentrations of *trans* isomers less than 2%	Does not distinguish between two esters each with one *trans* bond or between one ester with two *trans* bonds and one with none
Gas–liquid chromatography (GLC)	Individual *trans* fatty acids		Presence of unidentified compounds can give false estimates of *trans* fatty content
Argentation—GLC	Individual *trans* fatty acids	Saturated, monounsaturated, and diunsaturated fatty acids can be resolved	Method is time-consuming
Capillary column GLC	Individual *trans* fatty acids which can be summated to give total *trans* unsaturation	Accurate resolution of fatty acid esters including *cis* and *trans* isomers	Great skill required for preparing columns and interpretation of chromatograms
High-performance liquid chromatography	Individual *trans* fatty acids	*cis,cis-* and *trans,trans*-dienoic fatty acids can be separated	
Nuclear magnetic resonance (NMR)	Individual *trans* fatty acids	Intact lipids can be analyzed; can identify *trans*-diene isomers by use of proton (^{1}H) NMR	Equipment is costly; more use as a research tool than for general analysis

Table 2 Typical content of *trans* fatty acids in a range of foods

Food	Content of trans fatty acids per 100 g product (g)
Butter	3.6
Soft margarine, not high in PUFA	9.1
Soft margarine, high in PUFA	5.2
Hard margarine	12.4
Low-fat spread, not high in PUFA	4.5
Low-fat spread, high in PUFA	2.5
Blended vegetable oil	1.1
Vegetable oil (sunflower, safflower, soya, sesame)	0
Commercial blended oil	6.7
Potato crisps	0.2
Whole wheat crisps	0.2
Low-fat crisps	0.3
Beefburger, 100% beef frozen, fried, or grilled	0.8
Sausage, pork, fried	0.1
Sausage roll, flaky pastry	6.3
Hamburger in bun with cheese, take-away	0.5
Biscuits, cheese-flavored	0.2
Biscuits, chocolate, full coated	3.4
Chocolate cake and butter icing	7.1
Chips, old potatoes, fresh, fried in commercial blended oil	0.7
Chips, frozen, fine cut, fried in commercial blended oil	0.7

PUFA, polyunsaturated fatty acids. *Trans* fatty acid methyl esters were determined by capillary gas chromatography.
Reproduced with kind permission of the British Nutrition Foundation.

which does not include food eaten outside the home, show a steady decline in intake of *trans* fatty acids from 5.6 g per person per day in 1980 to 4.8 g in 1992. In the UK *trans* fatty acids account for approximately 6% of dietary fat, and in the USA

Table 3 Estimated intakes of *trans* fatty acids in various countries

Country	Estimated daily intake of total trans fatty acids (g)	Year published and basis for estimation
UK	5.6 (men) 4.0 (women)	1990: 7-day weighed intake undertaken in 1986–87 including food eaten outside the home
USA	8.1	1991: availability data
	3.8	1994: food frequency questionnaire
Denmark	5.0	1995: availability data
Finland	1.9	1992: duplicate diets
Spain	2.0–3.0	1993: calculated from food consumption data
Norway	8.0	1993: food frequency questionnaire

for approximately 7–8% of dietary fat. Estimates of *trans* fatty acid intake are likely to show a downward trend because of:

- improved analytical techniques which give lower but more accurate values for the *trans* fatty acid content of foods;
- the availability of values for *trans* fatty acids in a wider range of foods which allows more accurate estimation of intakes;
- the reformulation of some products which has led to a reduction in the concentration of *trans* fatty acids in recent years.

Advances in food technology that are enabling a gradual reduction in the *trans* fatty acid content include:

1. refinements in hydrogenation processing conditions which will enable the reduction and in the future, the elimination of *trans* fatty acids;
2. the interesterification (rearrangement of fatty acids within and between triacylglycerols) of liquid oils with solid fats;
3. the future genetic modification of oils.

Physiology of *trans* Fatty Acids

Extensive reviews of the health effects of *trans* fatty acids conducted in the 1980s found no evidence for any adverse effects of *trans* fatty acids on growth, longevity, reproduction, or the occurrence of disease, including cancer, from studies conducted in experimental animals.

Digestion, Absorption, and Metabolism

Trans fatty acids are present in the diet in esterified form, mainly in triacylglycerols but those from ruminant sources may also be present in phospholipids. Before absorption into the body, triacylglycerols must be digested by pancreatic lipase in the upper small intestine. There is no evidence of differences in the hydrolysis and absorption of *trans* fatty acids, in comparison with that of *cis* fatty acids. *Trans* fatty acids are transported from the intestine mainly in chylomicrons, but some are also incorporated into cholesteryl esters and phospholipids.

Trans fatty acids are incorporated into the lipids of most tissues of the body and are present in all the major classes of complex lipids. The positional distribution of *trans* fatty acids tends to show more similarity to that of saturated fatty acids than to that of the corresponding *cis* fatty acids. Some selectivity between tissues results in an uneven distribution of *trans* fatty acids throughout the body.

Trans fatty acids occur mainly in positions 1 and 3 of triacylglycerols, the predominant lipids in adipose tissue. The concentration of *trans* fatty acids in adipose tissue is approximately proportional to long-term dietary intake, and determination of the concentrations in storage fat is one method used to estimate *trans* fatty acid intake. However, this is not entirely straightforward as variation has been reported in the composition of adipose tissue obtained from different sites and depths, and factors that influence adipose tissue turnover rates such as dieting and exercise are also complicating factors. *Trans*-18:1 isomers account for approximately 70% of the *trans* fatty acids found in adipose tissue, and *trans*-18:2 isomers (*trans,trans, trans,cis,* and *cis,trans*) account for about 20%.

In heart, liver, and brain, *trans* fatty acids occur mainly in membrane phospholipids. The position of the double bond as well as the conformation of the carbon chain may determine the pattern of *trans* fatty acid esterification in phospholipids, but there is evidence that *trans*-18:1 fatty acids are preferentially incorporated into position 1 of the phosphoacylgly-cerols, as are saturated fatty acids; in contrast, oleic acid is randomly distributed.

The turnover of *trans* fatty acids parallels that of other types of fatty acids in the body, and *trans* fatty acids are readily removed from the tissues for oxidation. Studies in which human subjects were fed labelled carbon-13 isotope have demonstrated that the whole-body oxidation rate for *trans*-18:1 is similar to that for *cis*-18:1. *Trans* fatty acids are a minor component of tissue lipids, and their concentrations in tissues are much lower than their concentrations in the diet. However, research has focused on C_{18} *trans* fatty acids, and more studies are needed to investigate the effects of very long-chain *trans* fatty acids derived from the hydrogenation of fish oils.

Interactions with Metabolism of Essential Fatty Acids

From experiments mainly with laboratory animals, it has been demonstrated that relatively high intakes of *trans* fatty acids in the diet in conjunction with marginal intakes of essential fatty acids (less than 2% dietary energy from linoleic acid) can lead to the presence of Mead acid (*cis*-5,8,11–20:3) in tissue lipids and an increase in the ratio of 20:3 n-9 to 20:4 n-6. This has been interpreted to suggest early signs of essential fatty acid deficiency, with potentially increased requirements for essential fatty acids. Mead acid can accumulate in the presence of linoleic acid, if large amounts of nonessential fatty acids are

also present. Two mechanisms have been suggested to explain these observations in relation to intake of *trans* fatty acids:

- that *trans* fatty acids may compete with linoleic acid in metabolic pathways;
- that *trans* fatty acids may inhibit enzymes involved in elongation and further desaturation of linoleic acid.

The consensus is that the significance of Mead acid production in humans has not been established, and further research is needed in this area. It is unlikely that a competitive effect between polyunsaturated fatty acids (PUFA) and *trans* fatty acids would arise, because of the relatively high intakes of linoleic acid in people freely selecting their own diets. Also, as there is a large body pool of linoleic acid available for conversion to long-chain PUFA, it is unlikely that the *trans* fatty acids in the body would interfere even at relatively low ratios of dietary linoleic acid to *trans* fatty acids. The appearance of Mead acid is not specifically induced by *trans* fatty acids, and experiments in animals have not demonstrated any adverse health effects of its production.

Effect of *trans* Fatty Acids on Plasma Lipoproteins

Raised plasma concentrations of low-density lipoprotein (LDL) are considered to be a risk factor for coronary heart disease (CHD); in contrast, reduced concentrations of high-density lipoprotein (HDL) are considered to increase risk. It therefore follows that to help protect against CHD, diets should ideally help to maintain plasma concentrations of HDL cholesterol and to lower those of LDL cholesterol. Dietary factors that raise LDL and lower HDL concentrations would be considered to be undesirable in this context.

Several trials have evaluated the effects of C_{18} *trans* monounsaturated fatty acids on plasma lipoproteins (**Figure 3**). The results have been relatively consistent, and the following general conclusions have been drawn from these studies:

- C_{18} monounsaturated *trans* fatty acids raise LDL cholesterol concentration; the cholesterol-raising effect is similar in magnitude to that of the cholesterol-raising saturated fatty acids, i.e., myristic (14:0) and palmitic (16:0) acids.
- C_{18} monounsaturated *trans* fatty acids decrease HDL cholesterol concentration; this is in contrast to saturated fatty acids which produce a small rise in HDL levels.
- In comparison with the effects of oleic and linoleic fatty acids, C_{18} monounsaturated *trans* fatty acids raise LDL cholesterol and lower HDL cholesterol levels.

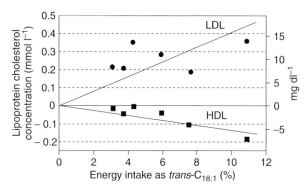

Figure 3 Effects of monounsaturated C_{18} *trans* fatty acids on lipoprotein cholesterol concentrations relative to oleic acid (*cis*-$C_{18:1}$). Data are derived from six dietary comparisons between *trans* and *cis* monounsaturated fatty acids; differences between diets in fatty acids other than *trans* and *cis* monounsaturated fatty acids were adjusted for by using regression coefficients from a meta-analysis of 27 controlled trials. The regression lines were forced through the origin because a zero change in intake will produce a zero change in lipoprotein concentrations. From Zock *et al.* (1995), reproduced with kind permission of the *American Journal of Clinical Nutrition*.

It has been calculated that 'theoretically', each 1% increase in energy from *trans* fatty acids (18:1) in place of oleic acid (*cis*-18:1) would raise plasma LDL concentration by 0.040 mmol l^{-1} (an approximately 1% increase based on average UK plasma cholesterol concentration); HDL would be decreased by 0.013 mmol l^{-1} (a 1% decrease).

The 1995 BNF Task Force calculated that, in the UK, replacing 2% energy from *trans* fatty acids with 2% energy from oleic acid would reduce mean plasma LDL cholesterol concentration by 0.08 mmol l^{-1}; plasma HDL concentration would rise by 0.026 mmol l^{-1}, and the HDL ratio would fall from 3.92 to 3.77. From estimates of the effect of changes in LDL and HDL concentrations on CHD risk, this was predicted to reduce the risk of CHD by 5–15%. In comparison, replacing *trans* fatty acids with either saturated fatty acids or carbohydrate would decrease risk by up to 8%.

The influence of *trans* fatty acids on plasma lipoproteins in relation to CHD risk would thus appear to be more unfavorable than that of saturated fatty acids, as determined by the effect on the ratio of LDL to HDL cholesterol. However, the overall magnitude of the effect would be dependent on the relative intakes of *trans* fatty acids and saturated fatty acids. In the UK *trans* fatty acids contribute about 2% of dietary energy, in contrast to saturated fatty acids which contribute about 15% dietary energy, and this needs to be considered when formulating dietary advice. The Task Force also estimated, on the same basis, that a reduction of 6% in

energy from saturated fatty acids would decrease risk by 37%.

However, these conclusions of the adverse effect of *trans* fatty acid on plasma lipoprotein concentrations are not universally accepted. It has been commented that some trials used an inappropriate basis for comparison of the different diets and did not always control for other fatty acids that are known to influence blood cholesterol levels.

Several studies have suggested that *trans* fatty acids raise the plasma concentration of lipoprotein(a), particularly in individuals with already raised levels. Lipoprotein(a) has been suggested to be an independent risk marker for CHD, although this is not universally accepted.

Atherosclerosis and Hemostasis

Despite the reported effects of *trans* fatty acids on blood lipoproteins, experiments with laboratory animals have not provided evidence that dietary *trans* fatty acids are associated with the development of experimental atherosclerosis, provided that the diet contains adequate levels of linoleic acid. Similarly, there is no evidence that *trans* fatty acids raise blood pressure or affect the blood coagulation system. However, there has been no thorough evaluation of the effect of *trans* fatty acids on the coagulation system, and this is an area worthy of investigation.

The Role of *trans* Fatty Acids in Coronary Heart Disease

A number of epidemiological studies have suggested an association between *trans* fatty acids and CHD.

Case–Control Studies

A study by Ascherio in 1994 demonstrated that in subjects who had suffered acute myocardial infarction (AMI), past intake of *trans* fatty acids, assessed from a food frequency questionnaire, was associated with increased risk. *Trans* fatty acid intake per day in the top quintile was 6.5 g compared with 1.7 g in the lowest quintile. After adjusting for age, energy intake, and sex, relative risk of a first AMI for the highest compared with the lowest quintile was 2.44 (95% confidence interval, 1.42–4.10). However, there was not a clear dose–response relationship.

A case–control study of sudden cardiac death found that higher concentrations of *trans* isomers of linoleic acid in adipose tissue, compared with lower concentrations, were associated with increased risk of sudden death. After controlling for smoking and making an allowance for social class, this relationship became insignificant.

A multicenter study in eight European countries plus Israel found that the risk of AMI was not significantly different across quartiles of the concentration of *trans*-18:1 fatty acids in adipose tissue, the multivariate odds ratio being 0.97 (95% confidence interval, 0.56–1.67) for the highest compared with the lowest quartiles. However, there were significant differences within countries. In Norway and Finland, relative risk was significantly increased in the highest compared with the lowest quartiles, but in Russia and Spain relative risk was significantly decreased in these groups. Exclusion from the multicenter analysis of the Spanish centers, which had particularly low intakes of *trans* fatty acids, resulted in a tendency to increased risk of AMI in the highest quartiles of *trans*-18:1 concentration. However, the trend was not statistically significant, and adjustment for confounding factors had no effect on the results.

A Prospective Study

The relationship between *trans* fatty acid intake and subsequent CHD events was investigated in approximately 85 000 US nurses (the Nurses Health Study). *Trans* fatty acid intake was calculated from food frequency questionnaires for women who had been diagnosed free from CHD, stroke, diabetes, and hypercholesterolemia. The subjects were followed up for 8 years and CHD events were recorded. The relative risk of CHD in the highest compared with the lowest quintile was 1.5 (95% confidence interval, 1.12–2.0), after adjustment for age, energy intake, social class, and smoking. However, there was no clear dose–response relationship between the highest and the lowest intake groups. The intake of *trans* fatty acids in the top quintile was 3.2% dietary energy compared with 1.3% in the lowest quintile.

It has been commented on that the benefit predicted by the authors, that individuals in the top quintile of intake could halve their risk of myocardial infarction by reducing their intake of *trans* fatty acids to that of the lowest quintile, seems a large effect in view of the small difference in intakes between these groups (3.3 g). The changes in plasma lipoprotein cholesterol concentrations that would be predicted to occur as a result of lowering *trans* fatty acid intake would not explain all of the observed increase in risk. Also, the study was carried out in a selected population of women and it is unclear that the findings are applicable to the whole population or to other population groups.

Cancer

Although there is much evidence concerning the effect of different intakes of different types of fats on experimental carcinogenesis, data for *trans* fatty acids are limited and are hampered by confounding due to the lack of a suitable control diet.

Studies using different tumor models in mice and rats have shown no effect of *trans* fatty acids on tumor development. Increasing the intake of *trans* fatty acids, in place of *cis* fatty acids, has not demonstrated an adverse outcome with regard to cancer risk. In humans, there is little to suggest that *trans* fatty acids are adversely related to cancer risk at any of the major cancer sites. Early studies did not generally find that *trans* fatty acids were an important risk factor for malignant or benign breast disease. One study did report an association between the incidence of cancer of the colon, breast, and prostate and the use of industrially hydrogenated vegetable fats in the USA; however, other known risk factors were not allowed for.

Cancer of the Breast

Some epidemiological evidence suggests that total fat intake may be related to increased risk of cancer of the breast, although this is by no means conclusive. There is no strong evidence that intake of *trans* fatty acids *per se* is related to increased risk of breast cancer and many studies have not reported examining this relationship. A study in which adipose tissue concentrations of *trans*-18:1 fatty acids were assessed in 380 women with breast cancer at various stages and in controls revealed no consistent pattern of association. A similar, smaller study suggested an increased risk with higher body stores of *trans* fatty acids, but it was concluded that any such association may be modified by adipose tissue concentrations of polyunsaturated fatty acids.

Cancer of the colon

Epidemiological data from the Nurses Health Study suggested a link between intake of meat and meat products and colon cancer. The data indicated that high intakes of total, animal, saturated, and monounsaturated fat were associated with increased risk. Consuming beef, pork, or lamb as a main dish was positively associated with risk; though beef and lamb contain *trans* fatty acids, there was no evidence that high intakes of *trans* fatty acids increased risk. The Health Professionals Follow-up Study (a prospective study in male health professionals of parallel design to the Nurses Health Study) found similar dietary associations for colon cancer risk, with no suggestion of any link with intake of *trans* fatty acids.

Prostate Cancer

Dietary associations with risk of prostate cancer were also assessed from the Health Professionals Follow-up Study. High intakes of total, saturated, and monounsaturated fatty acids and of α-linolenic acid were associated with increased risk, whereas high intakes of saturated fatty acids and linoleic acid were found to be protective. Intake of *trans* fatty acids was not found to be associated with risk of prostate cancer.

Dietary Guidelines

The details of population dietary guidelines for the quality and quantity of fat intake differ between countries. However, in consideration of prevention of CHD, dietary guidelines generally reflect advice to reduce average total fat intakes to 30–35% dietary energy and to lower saturated fat intakes to approximately 10% of dietary energy. Though the effect of *trans* fatty acids on the plasma LDL/HDL ratio is less favorable than that of saturated fatty acids, dietary advice needs to reflect the relative intakes of these two types of fatty acids. Since the contribution of saturated fat intake to dietary energy is approximately 5–7 times higher than that of *trans* fatty acids, advice on *trans* fatty acids should not assume more importance than advice to lower saturated fatty acids. However, because of the unfavorable effect of *trans* fatty acids on plasma lipoprotein concentrations, the 1995 BNF Task Force report concluded that the average intake of *trans* fatty acids in the UK diet (2% of energy) should not rise, and that dietary advice should continue to focus on reducing intake of saturated fatty acids as a priority.

Extreme consumers of *trans* fatty acids may be at greater risk, and individuals with high intakes may benefit from advice to lower their intake. It has been calculated that lowering total fat and increasing carbohydrate intake (which reduces plasma HDL cholesterol) will have minimal effect on risk of CHD. Substituting *cis* unsaturated fatty acids for saturated and *trans* fatty acids would be predicted to have a greater impact. For individuals at risk of CHD, high intakes of *trans* fatty acids would appear to be undesirable. Most dietary guidelines call for a reduction in *trans* fatty acids "as much as possible" recognizing that small amounts of *trans* fats are naturally present in the food chain. The food industry in general has reduced or eliminated *trans* in many products by improving manufacturing techniques and reducing *trans* fats generated during the hydrogenation process. Additionally, several countries now have regulations requiring that *trans* fatty acid be listed on products' labels. In some cases, like in the US, *trans* must be added to the saturated fat content reported on the Nutrition Facts label, based on their similar adverse effects on health. Although listing both fats together may not be correct in chemical terms, it is a practical way to allow consumers to quickly assess the content of unhealthy fat in a product.

Conclusions

Several lines of evidence indicate that *trans* fats have an adverse effect on the lipoprotein profile and likely on risk of cardiovascular disease. Although reducing intake of *trans* fats is a desirable goal, public health policy should keep as a central recommendation the reduction of saturated fats, which constitute four to six times more percent calories in the diet than *trans* fats. Since the largest proportion of *trans* fats is generated during food processing, industry bears the main responsibility for reducing the *trans* content of its products, thus helping the general public to lower their intake of this type of fat.

See also: **Cancer**: Epidemiology and Associations Between Diet and Cancer. **Cholesterol**: Factors Determining Blood Levels. **Coronary Heart Disease**: Lipid Theory. **Dairy Products. Dietary Guidelines, International Perspectives. Dietary Intake Measurement**: Methodology; Validation. **Dietary Surveys. Food Composition Data. Hyperlipidemia**: Nutritional Management. **Lipids**: Chemistry and Classification; Composition and Role of Phospholipids. **Lipoproteins. Meat, Poultry and Meat Products. Socio-economic Status**.

Further Reading

AIN/ASCN (1996) Position paper on *trans* fatty acids. *American Journal of Clinical Nutrition* 63: 663–670.

Aro AV, Kardinal AFM, Salminen I *et al.* (1995) Adipose tissue isomeric *trans* fatty acids and the risk of myocardial infarction in different countries: the EURAMIC study. *Lancet* 345: 273–278.

Ascherio A, Hennekens CH, Buring JE *et al.* (1994) *Trans* fatty acids intake and risk of myocardial infarction. *Circulation* 89: 94–101.

Berger KG (1996) In *Lipids and Nutrition: Current Hot Topics*. Bridgwater: PJ Barnes.

British Nutrition Foundation (1995) *Trans* Fatty Acids. Report of the British Nutrition Foundation Task Force. London: BNF.

Giovannucci E, Rimm E, Colditz GA *et al.* (1993) A prospective study of dietary fat and risk of prostate cancer. *Journal of the National Cancer Institute* **85**: 1571–1579.

Giovannucci E, Rimm EB, Stampfer MJ *et al.* (1994) Intake of fat, meat and fiber in relation to risk of colon cancer in men. *Cancer Research* **54**: 2390–2397.

Gurr MI (1996) Dietary fatty acids with *trans* unsaturation. *Nutrition Research Reviews* **9**: 259–279.

International Life Sciences Institute (1995) *Trans* fatty acids and coronary heart disease risk. Report of the expert panel on *trans* fatty acids and coronary heart disease. *American Journal of Clinical Nutrition* **62**: 655S–707S.

Ip C and Marshall JR (1996) *Trans* fatty acids and cancer. *Nutrition Reviews* **54**: 138–145.

Mensink RP and Katan MB (1990) Effect of dietary fatty acids on high density and low density lipoprotein levels in healthy subjects. *New England Journal of Medicine* **323**: 439–444.

Willett WC, Stampfer MJ, Manson JE *et al.* (1993) Intake of *trans* fatty acids and risk of coronary heart disease among women. *Lancet* **341**: 581–585.

Zock PL, Katan MB, and Mensink RP (1995) Dietary *trans* fatty acids and lipoprotein cholesterol. *American Journal of Clinical Nutrition* **61**: 617.

FERTILITY

R E Frisch, Harvard Center for Population and Development Studies, Cambridge, MA, USA

Linking Body Fat and Reproduction

It is well documented that women who are underweight, or too lean, because of injudicious dieting, excessive athletic activity, or both, experience disruption of their reproductive ability. It is also well documented that moderate weight loss, approximately 10–15% of normal weight for height, unassociated with anorexia nervosa (where weight loss is approximately 30% below ideal weight), results in amenorrhea due to hypothalamic dysfunction. Weight loss in this moderate range is equivalent to a loss of one-third of body fat. If the excessive leanness occurs before menarche, menarche may be delayed until as late as the age of 19 or 20 years.

In addition to the disruptive effects of weight loss and athletic activity on the menstrual cycle, women who exercise moderately or who are regaining weight into the normal range may have a menstrual cycle that appears to be normal but that actually has a shortened luteal phase or is anovulatory. All of these partial or total disruptions of reproductive ability are usually reversible, after varying periods of time, following weight gain, decreased athletic training, or both.

Excessive fatness is also associated with infertility in women; fertility is restored by loss of weight. Too little or too much fat are thus both associated with infertility. It is hypothesized that these associations are causal, and that the high percentage of body fat—26–28% in women after completion of growth—is necessary for and may directly influence reproduction.

The basic question is how does the hypothalamus, the part of the brain controlling reproduction, 'know' how much fat is stored in the body? The discovery of leptin, a protein hormone made by body fat cells of women and men, provides the biochemical link between body fat and reproductive ability. Friedman and colleagues cloned a gene that encoded leptin. Leptin controls food intake, energy metabolism, and reproduction. Receptors for leptin are located in the hypothalamus, the part of the brain that controls all three of these functions in addition to temperature control and stress.

Even before the leptin discovery, the 'critical fatness' hypothesis of Frisch and McArthur led to the prediction of minimum or threshold weights for height for the onset and maintenance of regular ovulatory menstrual cycles. These weights have been found to be useful clinically as target weights for the restoration of ovulatory cycles in cases of amenorrhea due to weight loss. Both the absolute and the relative amounts of fat are important since the lean mass and the fat must be in a particular absolute range as well as a relative range (i.e., the woman must be large enough to reproduce successfully).

Why Fat? The Energy Cost of Reproduction

A human pregnancy and lactation each have a high energy cost: A pregnancy requires approximately 336 MJ (74 000 kcal) in addition to normal metabolic requirements. Lactation requires approximately 2.5 MJ (600 kcal) per day. In premodern times, lactation was an essential part of reproduction.

While the reproductive system is slowly maturing during growth, the body changes in composition as well as in size and proportions. Direct measurements of body water of girls from birth to completion of growth at ages 16–18 years show a continuous

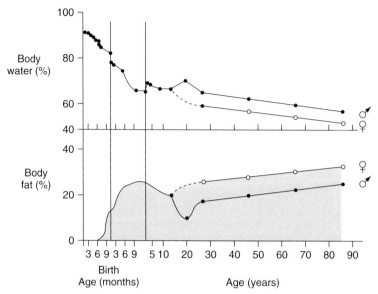

Figure 1 Changes in body water as percentage of body weight throughout the life span, and corresponding changes in the percentage of body fat. (Adapted from Friis-Hansen B (1965) Hydrometry of growth and aging. In: Brozek J (ed.) *Human Body Composition*, vol. 7, Symposia of the Society for the Study of Human Biology, pp. 191–209. Oxford: Pergamon Press.)

decline in the proportion of body water because girls have a large relative increase in body fat (**Figure 1**). This decrease is particularly rapid during the adolescent growth spurt in height and weight, which precedes menarche.

At the completion of growth, between ages 16 and 18 years, the body of a well-nourished woman contains approximately 26–28% fat and approximately 52% water, whereas the body of a man at completion of growth contains approximately 12% fat and 61% water. A young girl and boy of the same height and weight (**Table 1**) differ markedly in the percentages of body water and fat. The main function of the 16 kg of stored female fat, which is equivalent to more than 600 MJ (144 000 kcal), may be to provide energy for a pregnancy and for approximately 3 months of lactation. In prehistoric times when the food supply was

scarce or fluctuated seasonally, stored fat would have been necessary for successful reproduction. Fat is the most labile component of body weight. Body fat therefore would reflect environmental changes in food supplies more rapidly than other tissues.

Body Weight and Infant Survival

Infant survival is correlated with birth weight, and birth weight is correlated with the prepregnancy weight of the mother and, independently, her weight gain during pregnancy. From a teleologic and evolutionary view, it is economical to hypothesize that the physical ability to deliver a viable infant and the hypothalamic control of reproduction are synchronized. Adipose tissue may be the synchronizer.

Other Inputs of Adipose Tissue on Female Reproductive Ability

In addition to the message of leptin to the hypothalamus on the amount of body fat, adipose tissue makes other hormones that may directly affect ovulation and the menstrual cycle and, hence, fertility:

1. Adipose tissue is a significant extragonadal source of estrogen. Conversion of androgen to estrogen takes place in the adipose tissue of the breast and abdomen, the omentum, and the fatty marrow of the long bones. This conversion accounts for approximately one-third of the circulating estrogen of premenopausal women and is the main source of

Table 1 Total body water as percentage of body weight: an index of fatness[a]

Variable	Girl	Boy
Height (cm)	165.0	165.0
Weight (kg)	57.0	57.0
Total body water (l)	29.5	36.0
Lean body weigt (kg)	41.0	50.0
Fat (kg)	16.0	7.0
Fat/body weight (%)	28.0	12.0
Total body water/body weight (%)	51.8	63.0

[a]Comparison of an 18-year-old girl and a 15-year-old boy of the same height and weight.
Lean body weight = total body water/0.72.
Fatness/body weight % = 100 − [(total body water/body wt %)/0.72].

estrogen in postmenopausal women. Men also convert androgen into estrogen in body fat.

2. Body weight, and hence fatness, influences the direction of estrogen metabolism to more potent or less potent forms. Very thin women have an increase in the 2-hydroxylated form of estrogen, which is relatively inactive and has little affinity for the estrogen receptor. Lean female athletes also have an increase in the 2-hydroxylated form of estrogen. In contrast, obese women metabolize less of the 2-hydroxylated form and have a relative increase in the 16-hydroxylated form, which has potent estrogenic activity.

3. Obese women and young girls who are relatively fatter have a diminished capacity for estrogen to bind to serum sex hormone-binding globulin (SHBG); this results in an elevated percentage of free serum estradiol. Since SHBG regulates the availability of estradiol to the brain and other target tissues, the changes in the proportion of body fat to lean mass may influence reproductive performance through the intermediate effects of SHBG.

4. The adipose tissue of obese women stores steroid hormones.

Changes in relative fatness may also affect reproductive ability indirectly through disturbance of the regulation of body temperature and energy balance by the hypothalamus. Very lean women, both anorexic and nonanorexic, display abnormalities of temperature regulation in addition to delayed response, or lack of response, to exogenous luteinizing hormone-releasing hormone.

Hypothalamic Dysfunction, Gonadotropin Secretion, and Weight Loss

It is now recognized that the amenorrhea of underweight and excessively lean women is due to hypothalamic dysfunction. Hypothalamic dysfunction has also been implicated in the amenorrhea of athletes. Consistent with the view that this type of amenorrhea is adaptive, the pituitary–ovarian axis is apparently intact and functions when exogenous gonadotropin-releasing hormone (GnRH) is given in pulsatile form or in a bolus.

Women with this type of hypothalamic amenorrhea have both quantitative and qualitative changes in the secretion of the gonadotropins, luteinizing hormone (LH) and follicle-stimulating hormone (FSH), and of estrogen:

1. Levels of LH, FSH, and estradiol levels are low.
2. The secretion of LH and the response to GnRH are reduced in direct correlation with the amount of weight loss.

3. Underweight patients respond to exogenous GnRH with a pattern of secretion similar to that of prepubertal children; the FSH response is greater than the LH response. The return of LH responsiveness is correlated with weight gain.
4. The maturity of the 24-h LH secretory pattern and body weight are related. Weight loss results in an age-inappropriate secretory pattern resembling that of prepubertal or early pubertal children. Weight gain restores the postmenarcheal secretory pattern.
5. A reduced response or absence of response to clomiphene, a pituitary hormone which stimulates ovulation, is correlated with the degree of the loss of body weight and hence of fat. A normal response occurs after weight gain to the normal range.

Supportive of the view that this type of hypothalamic amenorrhea is adaptive is the finding of one study that women in whom ovulation had been induced had a higher risk of having babies who were small for their age, and this risk was greatest (54%) in those who were underweight. The authors of this study concluded that the most suitable treatment for infertility secondary to weight-related amenorrhea is dietary rather than induction of ovulation.

Physiological Basis of Reproductive Ability

Weight at Menarche

The idea that relative fatness is important for female reproductive ability followed findings that the events of the adolescent growth spurt, particularly menarche in girls, were closely related to an average critical body weight. This result was unexpected for human beings, although it was well-known for rats and monkeys that puberty (defined by vaginal opening or, more precisely, by first estrus) was more closely related to body weight than to chronological age.

In the United States, the mean weight at menarche for girls was 47.8 ± 0.5 kg at a mean height of 158.5 ± 0.5 cm and mean age of 12.9 ± 0.1 years. This mean age included girls from Denver, who had a slightly later age of menarche than that of sea-level populations due to the slowing effect of altitude on prenatal and postnatal weight growth.

Secular Trend Toward an Earlier Age of Menarche

Even before the meaning of the critical weight for an individual girl was analyzed, the idea that menarche is associated with a critical weight for a population explained simply many observations associated with early or late menarche. Observations of earlier menarche are associated with attaining the critical weight more quickly. The most important example is the secular (long-term) trend to an earlier menarche of approximately 3 or 4 months per decade in Europe in the past 100 years (**Figure 2**). The explanation is that children become larger sooner; therefore, girls on average reach 46 or 47 kg, the mean weight at menarche of US and many European populations, more quickly. Theoretically, the secular trend should end when the weight of children of successive cohorts remains the same because of the attainment of maximum nutrition and child care; this has happened in the United States.

Conversely, a late menarche is associated with body weight growth that is slower prenatally, postnatally, or both so that the average critical weight is reached at a later age: Malnutrition delays menarche, twins have later menarche than do singletons of the same population, and high altitude delays menarche.

Components of Weight at Menarche

Individual girls have menarche at varied weights and heights. To make the notion of a critical weight meaningful for an individual girl, the components

of body weight at menarche were analyzed. We investigated body composition at menarche because total body water (TW) and lean body weight (LBW; TW/0.72) are more closely correlated with metabolic rate than is body weight since they represent the metabolic mass as a first approximation. Metabolic rate was considered to be an important clue since Kennedy hypothesized a food intake–lipostat–metabolic signal to explain his elegant findings on weight and puberty in the rat.

The greatest change in estimated body composition of both early and late-maturing girls during the adolescent growth spurt was a large increase in body fat from approximately 5 to 11 kg (a 120% increase) compared to a 44% increase in lean body weight. There was thus a change in the ratio of lean body weight to fat from 5:1 at initiation of the spurt to 3:1 at menarche. The shortest, lightest girls at menarche had a smaller absolute amount of fat (8.9 ± 0.4 kg) compared to the tallest, heaviest girls (12.3 ± 0.6 kg) (the mean of all subjects was 11.5 ± 0.3 kg). However, both extreme groups had approximately 22% of their body weight as fat at menarche, as did all subjects, and the ratio of lean body weight to fat of both groups was in the range of 3:1, as it was for all subjects.

Since adipose tissue can convert androgens to estrogens, the relative degree of fatness can be

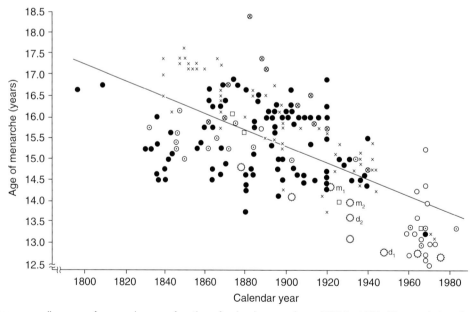

Figure 2 Mean or median age of menarche as a function of calendar year from 1790 to 1980. The symbols refer to England ⊙; France ●; Germany ⊗; Holland □; Scandinavia (Denmark, Finland, Norway, and Sweden) X; Belgium, Czechoslovakia, Hungary, Italy, Poland (rural), Romania (urban and rural), Russia (15.2 years at an altitude of 2500 m and 14.4 years at 700 m), Spain, and Switzerland, all labeled ○; and the United States ○ (data not included in the regression line). Twenty-seven points were identical and do not appear on the graph. The regression line cannot be extended indefinitely. The age of menarche has already leveled off in some European countries, as it has in the United States. (From Wyshak and Frisch (1982) Evidence for a secular trend in age of menarche. *New England Journal of Medicine* **306**: 1033–1035, with permission from the *New England Journal of Medicine*.)

directly related to the quantity of circulating estrogen. The biological effectiveness of the estrogen is also related to body weight. Rate of fat gain, therefore, is a neat mechanism for relating rate of growth, nutrition, and physical work to the energy requirements for reproduction.

Fatness as a Determinant of Minimal Weights for Menstrual Cycles

As shown in **Table 1** and **Figure 1**, total body water as a percentage of body weight is an index of fatness. In a study in the United States, this index in each of the 181 girls followed from menarche to the completion of growth at ages 16–18 years provided a method of determining a minimal weight for height necessary for menarche in primary amenorrhea and for the resumption of normal ovulatory cycles in cases of secondary amenorrhea, when the amenorrhea was due to undernutrition or intensive exercise. These weights have been found useful in the evaluation and treatment of patients with primary or secondary amenorrhea due to weight loss.

Percentiles of total body water/body weight, which are percentiles of fatness, were made at menarche and for the 181 girls at age 18 years, the age at which body composition stabilized. Patients with amenorrhea due to weight loss, other possible causes having been excluded, were studied in relation to the weights indicated by the diagonal percentile lines of total water/body weight percent (**Figure 3**). It was found that 56.1% of total water/body weight, the 10th percentile at age 18 years (equivalent to approximately 22% fat of body weight), indicated a minimal weight for height necessary for the restoration and maintenance of menstrual cycles. For example, a 20-year-old woman whose height is 165 cm (65 in.) should weigh at least 49 kg (108 lb) before menstrual cycles would be expected to resume (**Figure 3**).

The weights at which menstrual cycles ceased or resumed in postmenarcheal patients age 16 years and older were approximately 10% greater than the minimal weights for the same height observed at menarche (**Figure 4**). The explanation was that both early and late-maturing girls gain an average of 4.5 kg of fat from menarche to age 18 years. Almost all of this gain is achieved by age 16 years, when mean fat is 15.7 ± 0.3 kg, 27% of body weight. At age 18 years, mean fat is 16.0 ± 0.3 kg, 28% of the mean body weight of 57.1 ± 0.6 kg. Reflecting this increase in fatness, the total water/body weight percent decreases from $55.1 \pm 0.2\%$ at menarche (12.9 ± 0.1 years in this sample) to $52.1 \pm 0.2\%$ (standard deviation 3.0) at age 18 years.

Because girls are less fat at menarche than when they achieve stable reproductive ability, the minimal weight for onset of menstrual cycles in cases of primary amenorrhea due to undernutrition or exercise is indicated by the 10th percentile of fractional body water at menarche, 59.8%, which is equivalent to approximately 17% of body weight as fat. For example, a 15-year-old girl whose completed height is 165 cm (65 in.) should weigh at least 43.6 kg (96 lb) before menstrual cycles can be expected to begin (**Figure 4**).

The minimum weights indicated in **Figure 4** would be used also for girls who become amenorrheic as a result of weight loss soon after menarche, as often occurs in cases of anorexia nervosa in adolescent girls.

The absolute and relative increase in fatness from menarche to ages 16–18 years coincides with the period of adolescent subfecundity. During this time, there is still rapid growth of the uterus, ovaries, and oviducts.

Other factors such as emotional stress affect the maintenance or onset of menstrual cycles. Therefore, menstrual cycles may cease without weight loss and may not resume in some subjects even though the minimum weight for height has been achieved. Also, these standards apply only to Caucasian US females and European females since different races have different critical weights at menarche and it is not known whether the different critical weights represent the same critical body composition of fatness.

Since the prediction of the minimum weights for height is based on total water/body weight percent (not fat to body weight percent), successful prediction may be related to the ratio of lean mass to fat, which is normally approximately 3:1 at menarche and 2.5:1 at the completion of growth at age 18 years. No prediction can be made above the threshold weight for a particular height.

Physical Exercise, Delayed Menarche, and Amenorrhea

Does intense exercise cause delayed menarche and amenorrhea of athletes, or do late maturers choose to be athletes and dancers? We found that the mean age of menarche of 38 college swimmers and runners was 13.9 ± 0.3 years, significantly later ($p < 0.001$) than that of the general population (12.8 ± 0.05 years), in accord with other reports. However, the mean menarcheal age of the 18 athletes whose training began before menarche was 15.1 ± 0.5 years, whereas the mean menarcheal age

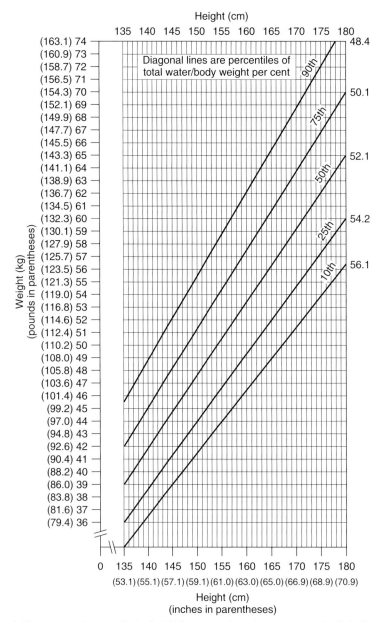

Figure 3 The minimal weight necessary for a particular height for restoration of menstrual cycles is indicated on the weight scale by the 10th percentile diagonal line of total water/body weight percent, 56.1%, as it crosses the vertical height line. For example, a 20-year-old woman whose height is 165 cm (65 in.) should weigh at least 49 kg (108 lb) before menstrual cycles would be expected to resume. (Adapted from Frisch and McArthur (1974) Menstrual cycles: Fatness as a determinant of minimum weight for height necessary for their maintenance or onset. *Science* **185**: 949–951, with permission from *Science*.)

of the 20 athletes whose training began after menarche was 12.8 ± 0.2 years ($p < 0.001$). The latter mean age was similar to that of the college controls (12.7 ± 0.4 years) and the general population. Therefore, training, not preselection, is the delaying factor. Each year of premenarcheal training delayed menarche by 5 months (0.4 years). This suggests that one constructive way to reduce the incidence of teenage pregnancy would be to have girls join teams at age 8 or 9 years and maintain regular moderate

exercise. Such a program might reduce the risk of serious diseases of women in later life, as discussed later.

Training also directly affected the regularity of the menstrual cycles during the training year. Of the premenarche trained athletes, only 17% had regular cycles; 61% were irregular and 22% were amenorrheic. In contrast, 60% of the postmenarche trained athletes were regular, 40% were irregular, and none were amenorrheic. However, during intense

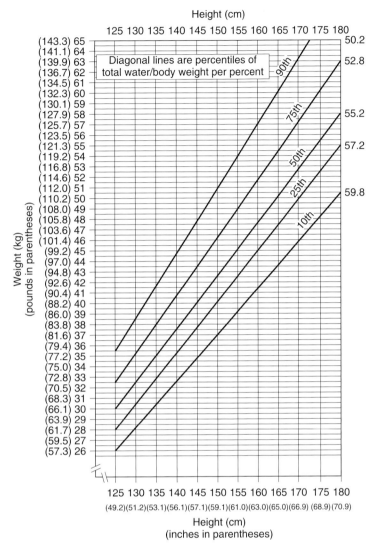

Figure 4 The minimal weight necessary for a particular height for onset of menstrual cycles is indicated on the weight scale by the 10th percentile diagonal line of total water/body weight percent, 59.8%, as it crosses the vertical height lines. The height growth of girls must be completed or approaching completion. For example, a 15-year-old girl whose completed height is 165 cm (65 in.) should weigh at least 43.6 kg (96 lb) before menstrual cycles can be expected to start. (Adapted from Frisch and McArthur (1974) Menstrual cycles: Fatness as a determinant of minimum weight for height necessary for their maintenance or onset. *Science* **185**: 949–951, with permission from *Science*.)

training, the incidence of oligomenorrhea and amenorrhea increased in both groups.

As other workers have found, plasma gonadotropins and estrogen levels were in the low-normal range in this study for the athletes with irregular cycles or amenorrhea. Progesterone was at the follicular phase level. Thyroid hormones, however, were in the normal range. These athletes had increased muscularity and decreased adiposity compared to nonathletes. The explanation for their menstrual disturbances may therefore be the same as that for dieting, nonathletic women—too little fat in relation to lean mass. Some of the swimmers and track and field athletes were above average weight for height.

A raised lean mass:fat ratio may nevertheless have caused their menstrual problems because their body weight represented a greater amount of muscle and less adipose tissue than the same weight of nonathletic women.

Psychologic Stress and Changes in Weight

The psychologic stress of competition, which may increase the secretion of adrenal corticosteroids and catecholamines, thus affecting the hypothalamic control of gonadotropins, may be involved, but stress does not seem to be the main factor in many individuals.

Nutrition and Male Reproduction

Undernutrition delays the onset of sexual maturation in boys in a similar way to the delaying effect of undernutrition on menarche. Undernutrition and weight loss in men also affect their reproductive ability. The sequence of effects, however, is different from that in females. In men, loss of libido is the first effect of a decrease in energy intake and subsequent weight loss. Continued energy reduction and weight loss result in a loss of prostate fluid and then decreases in sperm motility and sperm longevity. Sperm production ceases when weight loss is approximately 25% of normal body weight. Refeeding results in a restoration of function in the reverse order of loss.

Effects of Exercise on Men

Men marathon runners have been shown to have decreased hypothalamic GnRH secretion. Also reported are changes in serum testosterone levels with weight loss in wrestlers, a reduction in serum testosterone and prolactin levels in male distance runners, and changes in reproductive function and development in relation to physical activity.

Body Mass Index

Recognition of the importance of relative fatness levels for general health and successful reproductive outcome has led to the use of the body mass index (BMI) to estimate relative fatness levels.

BMI is calculated as weight (kg)/height $(m)^2$.

A BMI of $20-25 \, kg/m^2$ is recommended for good health and is associated with normal fertility.

A weight for height equivalent to a BMI of $18 \, kg/m^2$ and lower is considered too low for successful reproductive ability. Research indicates that the hormonal environment for a successful pregnancy outcome will be improved with a BMI higher than $19 \, kg/m^2$.

A BMI of $25-27 \, kg/m^2$ is associated with a slight reduction in fertility, and that higher than $27 \, kg/m^2$ is associated with a significantly reduced fertility.

BMI standards may not apply to athletes who train regularly because of their increased muscle mass.

Magnetic Resonance Imaging of Body Fat of Athletes and Controls

Using magnetic resonance imaging for direct quantification of body fat showed that athletes who did not differ in body weight from nonathletes had 30–40% less fat than the nonathletes. Muscles are heavy (80% water), so the body weight of an athlete does not necessarily indicate body composition.

Athletes had a more sensitive insulin response to a glucose tolerance test compared to controls. The insulin area under the curve of athletes and controls was significantly related to their total fat as a percentage of total volume, determined by magnetic resonance imaging.

Athletes with menstrual disorders had significantly decreased subcutaneous and internal fat, overall and at all regional sites, compared to controls. The extent of estradiol 2-hydroxylation to 2-hydroxyoestrone, determined by radiometric analysis, was significantly ($p = 0.005$) inversely related to total fat as a percentage of total volume and to subcutaneous fat as a percentage of total volume ($p = 0.004$) overall and at each of the regional fat depots. This inverse relationship may be a determinant of the anovulatory cycles and amenorrhea of excessively lean women by a feedback to the hypothalamus since 2-hydroxyoestrone is antiestrogenic.

Long-Term Regular Exercise Lowers the Risk of Sex Hormone-Sensitive Cancers

The amenorrhea and delayed menarche of athletes raised the question: Are there differences in the long-term reproductive health of athletes with moderate training compared to nonathletes?

A study of 5398 college graduates ages 20–80 years, of whom 2622 were former athletes and 2776 were nonathletes, showed that the former athletes had a significantly lower lifetime occurrence of breast cancer and cancers of the reproductive system compared to the nonathletes. More than 82.4% of the former college athletes began their training in high school or earlier, compared to 24.9% of the nonathletes. The analysis controlled for potential confounding factors, including age, age of menarche, age of first birth, smoking, and cancer family history. The relative risk (RR) for nonathletes compared to athletes for cancers of the reproductive system was 2.53 (95% confidence limit (CL), 1.17–5.47) (**Figure 5**). The RR for breast cancer was 1.86 (95% CL, 1.00–3.47). The former college athletes were leaner in every age group compared to the nonathletes.

Although one can only speculate as to the reasons for the lower risk, the most likely explanation is that long term, the former athletes had lower levels of estrogen because they were leaner, and more estrogen was metabolized to the nonpotent catechol estrogens. Also, the former athletes may have consumed diets lower in fat and saturated fat. Such diets shift the pattern of estrogen metabolism toward the less active catechol estrogens.

Compared to the nonathletes, the former college athletes also had a lower lifetime occurrence

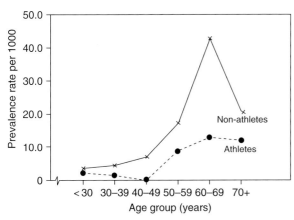

Figure 5 Prevalence rate of cancers of the reproductive system for athletes (circles) and nonathletes (crosses) by age group. (From Frisch RE, Wyshak G, Albright NL *et al.* (1985) Lower prevalence of breast cancer and cancers of the reproductive system among former college athletes compared to non-athletes. *British Journal of Cancer* **52**: 885–891, with permission from the *British Journal of Cancer.*)

(prevalence) of benign tumors of the breast and reproductive system; a lower prevalence of diabetes, particularly after age 40 years; and no greater risk of bone fractures, including risk of wrist and hip fractures, in the menopausal period.

These data indicate that long-term exercise, which was not at Olympic or marathon level but moderate

and regular, reduces the risk of sex hormone-sensitive cancers and the risk of diabetes for women in later life. Data showing that moderate exercise also reduces the risk of nonreproductive system cancers suggest that other factors, such as changes in immunosurveillance, may also be involved.

Nutrition, Physical Work, and Natural Fertility

The effects of hard physical work and nutrition on reproductive ability suggest that differences in the fertility of populations, historically and today, may be explained by a direct pathway from food intake to fertility (**Figure 6**), in addition to the classic Malthusian pathway through mortality. Charles Darwin described this commonsense direct relationship between food supplies and fertility, observing the following:

1. Domestic animals that have regular, plentiful food without working to get it are more fertile than the corresponding wild animals.
2. "Hard living retards the period at which animals conceive."
3. The amount of food affects the fertility of the same individual.
4. It is difficult to fatten a cow that is lactating.

All of Darwin's dicta apply to human beings.

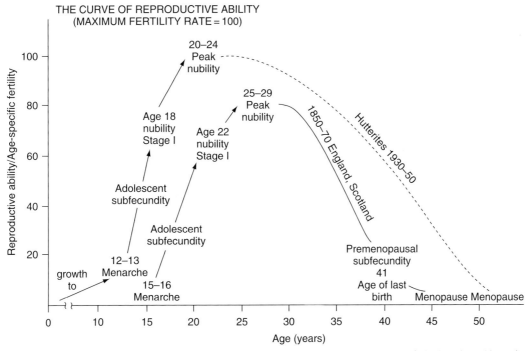

Figure 6 The mid-nineteenth century curve of female reproductive ability (variation of the rate of childbearing with age) compared with that of the well-nourished, modern Hutterites who do not use contraception. The Hutterite fertility curve (broken line) results in an average of 10–12 children; the 1850–1870 fertility curve (solid line) in approximately 6–8 children. (From Frisch (1978) Population, food intake and fertility. *Science* **199**: 22–30, with permission from *Science.*)

The Paradox of Rapid Population Growth in Undernourished Populations

In many historical populations with slow population growth, poor couples living together to the end of their reproductive lives had only 6 or 7 living births. Most poor couples in many developing countries today also have 6 or 7 living births during their reproductive life span. This total fertility rate is far below the human maximum of 11 or 12 children observed among well-nourished couples not using contraception, such as the Hutterites. However, 6 children per couple today in developing countries results in a very rapid rate of population growth because of decreased mortality rates due to the introduction of modern public health procedures. The difference between the birth rate per 1000 and the death rate per 1000, which gives the percentage growth rate, is currently as high as 2–4%. Populations growing at 2, 3, and 4% double in 35, 23, and 18 years, respectively.

British data from the mid-nineteenth century on growth rates, food intake, age-specific fertility, sterility, and ages of menarche and menopause show that females who grew relatively slowly to maturity, completing height growth at ages 20 or 21 years (instead of 16–18 years, as in well-nourished contemporary populations), also differed from well-nourished females in each event of the reproductive span: Menarche was later, for example, 15.0–16.0 years compared with 12.8 years; adolescent sterility was longer, and the age of peak nubility was later; the levels of specific fertility were lower; pregnancy wastage was higher; the duration of lactational amenorrhea was longer; the birth interval was longer; and the age of menopause was earlier, preceded by a more rapid period of perimenopausal decline (**Figure 6**). Thus, the slower, submaximal growth of women to maturity is subsequently associated with a shortened and less efficient reproductive span. The differences in the rate of physical growth of women and men result not only in a displacement of the age-specific fertility curve in time but also in a difference in the ultimate level: The faster the growth of females and males, the earlier and more efficient the reproductive ability.

Endocrinological data show that undernourished women have a longer lactational amenorrhea than do well-nourished women. The amount of suckling is not the only factor, as has been suggested in explaining reduced natural fertility. In addition, age of menarche and the other events of the reproductive span, which are known to be affected by the nutritional state, are pertinent to overall fertility.

See also: **Exercise**: Beneficial Effects; Diet and Exercise. **Growth and Development, Physiological Aspects**. **Low Birthweight and Preterm Infants**: Causes, Prevalence and Prevention. **Obesity**: Definition, Etiology and Assessment; Complications. **Pregnancy**: Role of Placenta in Nutrient Transfer; Nutrient Requirements; Energy Requirements and Metabolic Adaptations; Weight Gain; Safe Diet for Pregnancy; Prevention of Neural Tube Defects; Pre-eclampsia and Diet. **Weight Management**: Weight Maintenance.

Further Reading

Chehab FF, Mounzih K, Ronghva L et al. (1997) Early onset of reproductive function in normal female mice treated with leptin. *Science* 275: 88–90.

Clement K, Vaisse C, Lahlou N et al. (1998) A mutation in the human leptin receptor gene causes obesity and pituitary dysfunction. *Nature* 392: 398–401.

Friis-Hansen B (1965) Hydrometry of growth and aging. In: Brozek J (ed.) *Human Body Composition*, vol. 7, Symposia of the Society for the Study of Human Biology, pp. 191–209. Oxford: Pergamon Press.

Frisch RE (1978) Population, food intake and fertility. *Science* 199: 22–30.

Frisch RE (1981) What's below the surface? *New England Journal of Medicine* 305: 1019–1020.

Frisch RE (ed.) (1990) *Adipose Tissue and Reproduction*. Basel: Karger.

Frisch RE (2002) *Female Fertility and the Body Fat Connection* Chicago: University of Chicago Press.

Frisch RE and McArthur JW (1974) Menstrual cycles: Fatness as a determinant of minimum weight for height necessary for their maintenance or onset. *Science* 185: 949–951.

Frisch RE, Snow RC, Johnson L et al. (1993) Magnetic resonance imaging of overall and regional body fat, estrogen metabolism and ovulation of athletes compared to controls. *Journal of Clinical Endocrinology and Metabolism* 77: 441–477.

Frisch RE, Wyshak G, Albright NL et al. (1985) Lower prevalence of breast cancer and cancers of the reproductive system among former college athletes compared to non-athletes. *British Journal of Cancer* 52: 885–891.

Frisch RE, Wyshak G, and Vincent L (1980) Delayed menarche and amenorrhea of ballet dancers. *New England Journal of Medicine* 303: 17–19.

Halaas JL, Gajiwala KS, Maffei M et al. (1995) Weight-reducing effects of the plasma protein encoded by the obese gene. *Science* 269: 543–546.

Hileman SM, Pierroz DD, and Flier JS (2002) Leptin, nutrition and reproduction: Timing is everything. *Journal of Clinical Endocrinology and Metabolism* 85: 804–807.

Strobel A, Issad T, Camoin L et al. (1998) A Leptin missense mutation associated with hypogonadism and morbid obesity. *Nature Genetics* 18: 213–215.

Vigersky RA, Andersen AE, Thompson RH et al. (1977) Hypothalamic dysfunction in secondary amenorrhea associated with simple weight loss. *New England Journal of Medicine* 297: 1141–1145.

Wyshak G and Frisch RE (1982) Evidence for a secular trend in age of menarche. *New England Journal of Medicine* 306: 1033–1035.

Fetal Origins of Disease *see* Early Origins of Disease: Fetal; Non-Fetal

Fiber *see* Dietary Fiber: Physiological Effects and Effects on Absorption; Potential Role in Etiology of Disease; Role in Nutritional Management of Disease

FISH

A Ariño, J A Beltrán, A Herrera and P Roncalés, University of Zaragoza, Zaragoza, Spain

Introduction

In discussing the food uses of fishes, the term 'fish' refers to edible species of finfish, molluscs, and crustacea coming from the marine or freshwater bodies of the world, either by capture fisheries or by aquaculture. Accordingly, "fishery products" means any human food product in which fish is a characterizing ingredient, such as dried, salted, and smoked fish, marinated fish, canned seafood, minced fish flesh such as surimi, and miscellaneous products.

Fish is a source of high-quality animal protein, supplying approximately 6% of the world's protein requirements and 16.4% of the total animal protein. According to Food and Agriculture Organization figures, the contribution of fish to the total animal-protein intake is 26.2% in Asia, 17.4% in Africa, 9.2% in Europe, 9% in the former USSR, 8.8% in Oceania, 7.4% in North and Central America, 7.2% in South America, and 21.8% in the low-income food-deficit countries (including China). There are wide differences among countries in fish consumption measured as the average yearly intake per person, ranging from countries with less than 1.0 kg per person to countries with over 100 kg per person.

Edible fish muscle contains 18–20% protein and 1–2% ash; the percentage of lipids varies from less than 1% to more than 20% (in high-fat finfish), and fish has the added advantage of being low in saturated fat. In general, lean fish is not an important source of calories, which are mostly obtained from the staple carbohydrates in the diet. Fatty fish, however, is a significant energy source in many fish-consuming communities in both the developed and the developing worlds. Today it is recognized that fish is probably more important as a source of micronutrients, minerals, and particularly essential fatty acids than for its energy or protein value. The essential micronutrients and minerals in fish include vitamins A and D, calcium, phosphorus, magnesium, iron, zinc, selenium, fluorine, and iodine (in marine fishes).

The protective effect of a small amount of fish against mortality from coronary heart disease (CHD) has been established by numerous epidemiological studies. A diet including two or three servings of fish per week has been recommended on this basis, and researchers have reported a 50% reduction in CHD mortality after 20 years with intakes of as little as 400 g of fish per week.

It has been suggested that the long-chain omega-3 (*n*-3) polyunsaturated fatty acids (PUFAs) (eicosapentanoic acid (EPA; C20:5) and docosahexanoic acid (DHA; C22:6)) in fish offer this protection against CHD. Several recent studies have shown that a large intake of omega-3 fatty acids is beneficial in lowering blood pressure, reducing triacylglycerols, decreasing the risk of arrhythmia, and lowering the tendency of blood platelets to aggregate.

As fish become more popular, the reports of food-borne diseases attributed to fish have increased. Food-borne diseases linked with exposure to fish can result from the fish itself (i.e., toxic species, allergies) or from bacterial (i.e., *Clostridium botulinum*, *Listeria monocytogenes*, *Salmonella*, *Vibrio*, and *Staphylococcus*), viral (i.e., hepatitis, Norwalk gastroenteritis), or parasitic (i.e., *Anisakis* and related worms) contamination. Also, naturally occurring seafood toxins (i.e., scombrotoxin, ciguatoxins, shellfish poisoning from toxic algae) or the presence of additives and chemical residues due to environmental contamination can cause food-borne illnesses. In recent years, reports of contamination of some fish with methylmercury have raised concerns about the healthfulness of certain fish for some populations.

General Characteristics of Finfish

A very large number of species of finfish are used for food by the world's population. The dressing percentage of finfish (60–70%) is similar to that of beef, pork, or poultry. The percentage of edible tissue in the dressed carcasses of finfish (without head, skin, and viscera) is higher than that of other food animals, because fishes contain less bone, adipose tissue, and connective tissue. There are three main categories of finfish that are widely used as foods. The bony fishes (teleosts) provide two compositional categories: white fishes (or lean fishes) and fatty fish. The third category is the cartilaginous elasmobranch fishes.

White fishes

The flesh of these fishes is very low in fat and consists primarily of muscle and thin layers of connective tissue. The concentrations of most of the B vitamins are similar to those in mammalian lean meats, although fish may contain higher amounts of vitamins B_6 and B_{12}. The mineral levels are also similar, although the very fine bones that are eaten with the fish flesh can raise the calcium content; fish is also a significant source of iodine. These fishes accumulate oils only in their livers, which are a rich source of vitamin A (retinol), vitamin D, and long-chain PUFAs in their triacylglycerols (TAGs).

Fatty Fishes

These fishes have fat in their flesh, which is usually much darker than that of white fishes, with similar blocks of muscle and connective tissue. The amount of fat is related to the breeding cycle of the fish, so that the fat content falls considerably after breeding. The flesh of fatty fishes is generally richer in the B vitamins than that of white fishes, and significant amounts of vitamins A and D are present. The mineral concentrations are not very different, but fatty fish is a better source of iron. The oil of these fishes is particularly rich in very-long-chain PUFA, especially those of the omega-3 (*n*-3) series such as EPA and DHA. These fishes accumulate oils in their muscles, belly flap, and skin (subdermal fat).

Cartilaginous Fishes

The cartilaginous fishes include the sharks and rays, whose flesh is rich in connective tissue and relatively low in fat, although they do accumulate oils in their livers. The concentrations of vitamins and minerals are very similar to those in white fish. These fishes contain urea in relatively large amounts, and so protein values based on total nitrogen are overestimated. The ammonia smell of cooked sharks and rays is not an indication that the fish is spoiled but rather is the result of enzymatic degradation of urea.

General Characteristics of Shellfish

The term 'shellfish' includes any aquatic invertebrate, such as molluscs or crustaceans, that has a shell or shell-like exoskeleton. The cephalopods have an internal shell (as in squids) or no shell (as in octopods). Owing to the presence of the tough exoskeleton, the edible portion in shellfish (around 40%) is less than that in finfish, with the exception of cephalopods, whose dressing percentage is 70–75%. The lipid content of the edible parts of most shellfish is low, as bivalves store their energy surplus as glycogen and not as depot fat, while crustaceans and cephalopods store their fat in their digestive glands (hepatopancreas). In many fish-eating communities, these foods are very highly valued gastronomically.

Molluscs

A wide range of molluscs are eaten by man, including bivalves (such as mussels, oysters, and scallops), gastropods (such as winkles and whelks), and cephalopods (such as squids and octopuses). The flesh is muscular with low levels of fat, although the fat is more saturated and richer in cholesterol than that of finfish. The mineral levels in shellfish are usually somewhat higher than those in finfish, and the vitamin concentrations are low. Bivalves and gastropods are often eaten whole after boiling or sometimes raw; usually, only the muscular mantles of cephalopods are eaten. In some cultures, only selected parts are eaten; for example, only the white adductor muscle of the scallop is eaten in North America.

Crustaceans

Crustaceans include a range of species, both freshwater (such as crayfish) and marine (such as crabs, shrimps, prawns, and lobsters). These animals have a segmented body, a chitinous exoskeleton, and paired jointed limbs. The portions eaten are the muscular parts of the abdomen and the muscles of the claws of crabs and lobsters. The flesh is characteristically low in fat and high in minerals, with vitamin levels similar to those found in finfish.

Nutritional Value of Fish and Shellfish: Introductory Remarks

Fish and shellfish are excellent sources of protein. A 100 g cooked serving of most types of fish and shellfish provides about 18–20 g of protein, or about a third of the average daily recommended protein intake. The fish protein is of high quality, containing an abundance of essential amino-acids, and is very digestible by people of all ages. Seafood is also loaded with minerals such as iron, zinc, and calcium.

The caloric value of fish is related to the fat content and varies with species, size, diet, and season. Seafood is generally lower in fat and calories than beef, poultry, or pork. Most lean or low-fat species of fish, such as cod, hake, flounder, and sole, contain less than 100 kcal (418 kJ) per 100 g portion, and even fatty fish, such as mackerel, herring, and salmon, contain approximately 250 kcal (1045 kJ) or less in a 100 g serving. Most crustaceans contain less than 1% fat in the tail muscle because depot fat is stored in the hepatopancreas, which is in the head region.

Interest in the health benefits of fish and shellfish began decades ago when researchers noted that certain groups of people – including the Inuit and the Japanese, who rely on fish as a dietary staple – have a low rate of ischemic diseases (i.e., heart attack or stroke). Fish, particularly fatty fish, is a good source of the omega-3 fatty acids EPA and DHA. These fats help to lower serum triacylglycerols and cholesterol, help prevent the blood clots that form in heart attacks, and lower the chance of having an irregular heartbeat. In fact, one study found that women who ate fish at least once a week were 30% less likely to die of heart disease than women who ate fish less than once a month. Similar benefits have been found for men. Fish consumption is also related to slower growth of atherosclerotic plaque and lower blood pressure. Especially good sources of omega-3 fats are salmon, tuna, herring, mackerel, and canned tuna and sardines.

When included in the diet of pregnant and breast-feeding women, DHA is thought to be beneficial to infant brain (learning ability) and eye (visual acuity) development. Scientists have found that women who ate fatty fish while pregnant gave birth to children with better visual development. Babies of mothers who had significant levels of DHA in their diet while breastfeeding experienced faster-than-normal eyesight development. Preliminary research also suggests that a diet rich in omega-3 fatty acids – and in DHA in particular – may help to decrease the chance of preterm birth, thus allowing the baby more time for growth and development.

Recent research found that eating just one serving a week of fish decreased the risk of developing dementia by 30%. Eating fatty fish several times a week may also lower the risk of developing prostate cancer by as much as half. A Swedish study of 3500 postmenopausal women eating two servings of fatty fish a week found that they were 40% less likely to develop endometrial cancer than those eating less than one-fourth of a serving a week.

Eating a variety of fish and seafood, rather than concentrating on one species, is highly recommended for both safety and nutrition. It is recommended that pregnant women should avoid certain species of fish and limit their consumption of other fish to an average of 400 g of cooked fish per week. The reason for this recommendation is that, whereas nearly all fish contain trace amounts of methylmercury (an environmental contaminant), large predatory fish, such as swordfish, shark, tilefish, and king mackerel, contain the most. Excess exposure to methylmercury from these species of fish can harm an unborn child's developing nervous system. It is also suggested that nursing mothers and young children should not eat these particular species of fish.

Fish Lipids

In fish, depot fat is liquid at room temperature (oil) and is seldom visible to the consumer; an exception is the belly flaps of salmon steaks. Many species of finfish and almost all shellfish contain less than 2.5% total fat, and less than 20% of the total calories come from fat. Almost all fish has less than 10% total fat, and even the fattiest fish, such as herring, mackerel, and salmon, contains no more than 20% fat (**Table 1**). In order to obtain a good general idea of the fat contents of most finfish species, flesh color might be considered. The leanest species, such as cod and flounder, have a white or lighter color, while fattier fishes, such as salmon, herring, and mackerel, have a much darker color.

The triacylglycerol depot fat in edible fish muscle is subject to seasonal variation in all marine and freshwater fishes from all over the world. Fat levels tend to be higher during times of the year when fishes are feeding heavily (usually during the warmer months) and in older and healthier individual fishes. Fat levels tend to be lower during spawning or reproduction. When comparing fat contents between farmed and wild-caught food fish, it should be remembered that farmed species have a tendency to show a higher proportion of muscle fat than their wild counterparts. Also, the fatty-acid composition of farmed fish depends on the type of dietary fat

Table 1 Fat levels in marine and freshwater fish and shellfish commonly found in the marketplace

Low (<2.5% fat) less than 20% of total calories from fat	Medium (2.5–5% fat) between 20% and 35% of total calories from fat	High (>5% fat) between 35% and 50% of total calories from fat
Saltwater fish		
Cod	Anchovy	Dogfish
Grouper	Bluefish	Herring[a]
Haddock	Sea bass	Mackerel[a]
Hake	Swordfish	Salmon[a]
Most flatfishes (flounder, sole, plaice)	Tuna (yellowfin)	Sardine
Pollock		Tuna (bluefin)
Shark		
Skate		
Snapper		
Whiting		
Most crustaceans		
Most molluscs		
Freshwater fish		
Pike	Bream	Catfish (farmed)
Perch, bass	Carp	Eel[a]
Tilapia	Trout (various)	Whitefish

[a]More than 10% fat.

Reproduced with permission from Ariño A, Beltran JA, and Roncalés P (2003) Dietary importance of fish and shellfish. In: Caballero B, Trugo L, and Finglas P (eds.) *Encyclopedia of Food Sciences and Nutrition*, 2nd edn. Oxford: Elsevier Science Ltd. pp. 2471–2478.

used in raising the fish. Cholesterol is independent of fat content and is similar in wild and cultivated fishes.

Most protein-rich foods, including red meat and poultry as well as fish, contain cholesterol. However, almost all types of fish and shellfish contain well under 100 mg of cholesterol per 100 g, and many of the leaner types of fish typically have 40–60 mg of cholesterol in each 100 g of edible muscle. It is known that most shellfish also contain less than 100 mg of cholesterol per 100 g. Shrimp contain somewhat higher amounts of cholesterol, over 150 mg per 100 g, and squid is the only fish product with a significantly elevated cholesterol content, which averages 300 mg per 100 g portion. Fish roe, caviar, internal organs of fishes (such as livers), the tomalley of lobsters, and the hepatopancreas of crabs can contain high amounts of cholesterol.

Omega-3 PUFA in Fish and Shellfish

The PUFA of many fish lipids are dominated by two members of the omega-3 (*n*-3) family, C20:5 *n*-3 (EPA) and C22:6 *n*-3 (DHA). They are so named because the first of several double bonds occurs

three carbon atoms away from the terminal end of the carbon chain.

All fish and shellfish contain some omega-3, but the amount can vary, as their relative concentrations are species specific (**Table 2**). Generally, the fattier fishes contain more omega-3 fatty acids than the leaner fishes. The amount of omega-3 fatty acids in farm-raised products can also vary greatly, depending on the diet of the fishes or shellfish. Many companies now recognize this fact and provide a source of omega-3 fatty acids in their fish diets. Omega-3 fatty acids can be destroyed by heat, air, and light, so the less processing, heat, air exposure, and storage time the better for preserving omega-3 in fish. Freezing and normal cooking cause minimal omega-3 losses, whereas deep frying and conditions leading to oxidation (rancidity) can destroy some omega-3 fatty acids.

The beneficial effects of eating fish for human health have been well documented. Research has shown that EPA and DHA are beneficial in protecting against cardiovascular and other diseases (**Table 3**). Studies examining the effects of fish consumption on serum lipids indicate a reduction in triacylglycerol and VLDL-cholesterol levels, a factor that may be protective for some individuals. Research also indicates that EPA in particular reduces platelet aggregation, which may help vessels injured by plaque formation. Fish oils also appear to help stabilize the heart rhythm, a factor that may be important in people recovering from heart attacks.

Table 2 Selected fish and shellfish grouped by their omega-3 fatty-acid content

Low-level group (<0.5 g per 100 g)	Medium-level group (0.5–1 g per 100 g)	High-level group (>1 g per 100 g)
Finfish		
Carp	Bass	Anchovy
Catfish	Bluefish	Herring
Cod, Haddock, Pollock	Halibut	Mackerel
Grouper	Pike	Sablefish
Most flatfishes	Red Snapper	Salmon (most species)
Perch	Swordfish	Tuna (bluefin)
Snapper	Trout	Whitefish
Tilapia	Whiting	
Shellfish		
Most crustaceans	Clams	
Most molluscs	Oysters	

Reproduced with permission from Ariño A, Beltran JA, and Roncalés P (2003) Dietary importance of fish and shellfish. In: Caballero B, Trugo L, and Finglas P (eds.) *Encyclopedia of Food Sciences and Nutrition*, 2nd edn. Oxford: Elsevier Science Ltd. pp. 2471–2478.

Table 3 Summary of the beneficial effects of eating fish for cardiovascular and other diseases

Cardiovascular disease	Other diseases
Protects against heart disease	Protects against age-related macular degeneration
Prolongs the lives of people after a heart attack	Alleviates autoimmune diseases such as rheumatoid arthritis
Protects against sudden cardiac arrest caused by arrhythmia	Protects against certain types of cancer
Protects against stroke (thrombosis)	Mitigates inflammation reactions and asthma
Lowers blood lipids such as triacylglycerols and VLDL-cholesterol	
Lowers blood pressure	

VLDL, very low-density lipoprotein.
Reproduced with permission from Ariño A, Beltran JA, and Roncalés P (2003) Dietary importance of fish and shellfish. In: Caballero B, Trugo L, and Finglas P (eds.) *Encyclopedia of Food Sciences and Nutrition*, 2nd edn. Oxford: Elsevier Science Ltd. pp. 2471–2478.

The major PUFA in the adult mammalian brain is DHA. It is among the materials required for development of the fetal brain and central nervous system and for retinal growth in late pregnancy. Brain growth uses 70% of the fetal energy, and 80–90% of cognitive function is determined before birth. However, the placenta depletes the mother of DHA, a situation that is exacerbated by multiple pregnancies. Dietary enhancement or fortification with marine products before and during pregnancy, rather than after the child is born, would be of great benefit to the child and mother. Furthermore, the food sources that are rich in DHA are also rich in zinc, iodine, and vitamin A, so it may be possible to provide several dietary supplements at one time. Deficiencies of the latter micronutrients are established causes of mental retardation and blindness.

The typical Western diet has a ratio of omega-6 to omega-3 essential fatty acids of between 15:1 and 20:1. Several sources of information suggest that a very high omega-6 to omega-3 ratio may promote many diseases, including cardiovascular disease, cancer, and inflammatory and autoimmune diseases. Fish provides an adequate intake of these omega-3 fats, thus improving the omega-6 to omega-3 fatty-acid ratio. Most experts do not advise the routine use of fish-oil supplements: they favor eating fish and shellfish regularly in the context of a healthy diet and a regular pattern of physical activity. Whereas some research shows benefits of fish-oil supplements, research has also shown that people with weakened immune systems should avoid large doses of fish oil. The final conclusion as to whether it is possible to substitute fish consumption with fish oils or omega-3 fatty-acid supplements, and gain the same reduction in mortality from CHD, awaits more studies. However, the protective role of fish consumption is unquestioned.

Fish Proteins

Both finfish and shellfish are highly valuable sources of proteins in human nutrition. The protein content of fish flesh, in contrast to the fat content, is highly constant, independent of seasonal variations caused by the feeding and reproductive cycles, and shows only small differences among species. **Table 4** summarizes the approximate protein contents of the various finfish and shellfish groups. Fatty finfish and crustaceans have slightly higher than average protein concentrations. Bivalves have the lowest values if the whole body mass is considered (most of them are usually eaten whole), whereas values are roughly average if specific muscular parts alone are consumed; this is the case with the scallop, in which only the adductor muscle is usually eaten.

The essential amino-acid compositions of fish and shellfish are given in **Table 5**. Fish proteins, with only slight differences among groups, possess a high nutritive value, similar to that of meat proteins and slightly lower than that of egg. It is worth pointing out the elevated supply, relative to meat, of essential amino-acids such as lysine, methionine, and threonine. In addition, owing in part to the low collagen content, fish proteins are easily digestible, giving rise to a digestibility coefficient of nearly 100.

The recommended dietary allowances (RDA) or dietary reference intakes (DRI) of protein for human male and female adults are in the range of 45–65 g per day. In accordance with this, an intake of 100 g of fish would contribute 15–25% of the

Table 4 Protein content of the different groups of fish and shellfish

Fish group	g per 100 g
White finfish	16–19
Fatty finfish	18–21
Crustaceans	18–22
Bivalves	10–12
Cephalopods	16–18

Reproduced with permission from Ariño A, Beltran JA, and Roncalés P (2003) Dietary importance of fish and shellfish. In: Caballero B, Trugo L, and Finglas P (eds.) *Encyclopedia of Food Sciences and Nutrition*, 2nd edn. Oxford: Elsevier Science Ltd. pp. 2471–2478.

Table 5 Content of essential amino-acids in fish and shellfish (g per 100 g of protein)

Fish group	Isoleucine	Leucine	Lysine	Methionine	Phenylalanine	Threonine	Tryptophan	Valine
Finfish	5.3	8.5	9.8	2.9	4.2	4.8	1.1	5.8
Crustaceans	4.6	8.6	7.8	2.9	4.0	4.6	1.1	4.8
Molluscs	4.8	7.7	8.0	2.7	4.2	4.6	1.3	6.2

Reproduced with permission from Ariño A, Beltran JA, and Roncalés P (2003) Dietary importance of fish and shellfish. In: Caballero B, Trugo L, and Finglas P (eds.) *Encyclopedia of Food Sciences and Nutrition*, 2nd edn. Oxford: Elsevier Science Ltd. pp. 2471–2478.

total daily protein requirement of healthy adults and 70% of that of children. A look at the dietary importance of the Mediterranean diet is convenient: one of its characteristics is the high consumption of all kinds of fish, chiefly fatty fish. In many Mediterranean countries, fish intake averages over 50 g per day (edible flesh); thus, fish protein contributes over 10% of the total daily protein requirements steadily over the whole year in those countries.

Less well known is the fact that the consumption of fish protein, independently of the effect exerted by fish fat, has been related to a decrease in the risk of atherogenic vascular diseases. In fact, it has been demonstrated that diets in which fish is the only source of protein increase the blood levels of high-density lipoprotein relative to those resulting from diets based on milk or soy proteins.

Nonprotein Nitrogen Compounds in Fish

Nonprotein nitrogen (NPN) compounds are found mostly in the fiber sarcoplasm and include free amino-acids, peptides, amines, amine oxides, guanidine compounds, quaternary ammonium molecules, nucleotides, and urea (**Table 6**). NPN compounds account for a relatively high percentage of the total nitrogen in the muscles of some aquatic animals, 10–20% in teleosts, about 20% in crustaceans and molluscs, and 30–40% (and in special cases up to 50%) in elasmobranchs. In contrast, NPN compounds in land animals usually represent no more than 10% of total nitrogen.

Most marine fishes contain trimethylamine oxide (TMAO); this colorless, odorless, and flavorless compound is degraded to trimethylamine, which gives a 'fishy' odor and causes consumer rejection. This compound is not present in land animals and freshwater species (except for Nile perch and tilapia from Lake Victoria). TMAO reductase catalyzes the reaction and is found in several fish species (in the red muscle of scombroid fishes and in the white and red muscle of gadoids) and in certain microorganisms (*Enterobacteriaceae, Shewanella putrefaciens*).

Creatine is quantitatively the main component of the NPN fraction. This molecule plays an important role in fish muscle metabolism in its phosphorylated form; it is absent in crustaceans and molluscs.

Table 6 Nonprotein nitrogen compounds in several commercially important fish species and mammalian muscle (mg per 100 g wet weight)

Compounds	Cod	Herring	Shark species	Lobster	Mammal
Total NPN	1200	1200	3000	5500	3500
Total free amino-acids:	75	300	100	3000	350
Arginine	<10	<10	<10	750	<10
Glycine	20	20	20	100–1000	<10
Glutamic acid	<10	<10	<10	270	36
Histidine	<1.0	86	<1.0	—	<10
Proline	<1.0	<1.0	<1.0	750	<1.0
Creatine	400	400	300	0	550
Betaine	0	0	150	100	—
Trimethylamine oxide	350	250	500–1000	100	0
Anserine	150	0	0	0	150
Carnosine	0	0	0	0	200
Urea	0	0	2000	—	35

NPN, nonprotein nitrogen.
Reproduced with permission from Ariño A, Beltran JA, and Roncalés P (2003) Dietary importance of fish and shellfish. In: Caballero B, Trugo L, and Finglas P (eds.) *Encyclopedia of Food Sciences and Nutrition*, 2nd edn. Oxford: Elsevier Science Ltd. pp. 2471–2478.

Endogenous and microbial proteases yield some free amino-acids; taurine, alanine, glycine, and imidazole-containing amino-acids seem to be the most frequent. Glycine and taurine contribute to the sweet flavor of some crustaceans. Migratory marine species such as tuna, characterized by a high proportion of red muscle, have a high content (about 1%) of free histidine. A noticeable amount of this amino-acid has been reported in freshwater carp. The presence of free histidine is relevant in several fish species because it can be microbiologically decarboxylated to histamine. Cooking the fish may kill the bacteria and destroy the enzymes, but histamine is not affected by heat, thus becoming a hazard to consumers. The symptoms of the resulting illness (scombroid poisoning) are itching, redness, allergic symptoms, headache, diarrhea, and peppery taste. Scombroid poisoning is most common after ingesting mahi-mahi, tuna, bluefish, mackerel, and skipjack.

Nucleotides and related compounds generally play an important role as coenzymes. They participate actively in muscle metabolism and supply energy to physiological processes. They have a noticeable participation in flavor; moreover, some of them may be used as freshness indices. Adenosine triphosphate (ATP) is degraded to adenosine diphosphate (ADP), adenosine monophosphate (AMP), inosine monophosphate (IMP), inosine, and hypoxanthine. This pattern of degradation takes place in finfish, whereas AMP is degraded to adenosine and thereafter to inosine in shellfish. The degradation chain to IMP and AMP in finfish and shellfish, respectively, is very fast. IMP degradation to inosine is generally slow, except in scombroids and flat fishes. Inosine degradation to hypoxanthine is slower. IMP is a flavor potentiator, whereas hypoxanthine imparts a sour taste and it is toxic at high levels. ATP, ADP, and AMP decompose quickly leading to a build-up of inosine and hypoxanthine. As this corresponds well to a decline in freshness, the ratio of the quantity of inosine and hypoxanthine to the total quantity of ATP and related substances is called the K-value and used as a freshness index of fish meat.

Guanosine is an insoluble compound that gives fish eyes and skin their characteristic brightness. It is degraded to guanine, which does not have this property; therefore, brightness decreases until it completely disappears.

The NPN fraction contains other interesting compounds, such as small peptides. Most of them contribute to flavor; besides this, they have a powerful antioxidant activity. Betaines are a special group of compounds that contribute to the specific flavors of different aquatic organisms: homarine in lobster and glycine-betaine, butirobetaine, and arsenic-betaine in crustaceans. Arsenic-betaine has the property of fixing arsenic into the structure, giving a useful method for studying water contamination.

Fish Vitamins

The vitamin content of fish and shellfish is rich and varied in composition, although somewhat variable in concentration. In fact, significant differences are neatly evident among groups, especially regarding fat-soluble vitamins. Furthermore, vitamin content shows large differences among species as a function of feeding regimes.

The approximate vitamin concentration ranges of the various finfish and shellfish groups are summarized in **Table 7**. The RDA for adults is also given, together with the percentage supplied by 100 g of fish. Of the fat-soluble vitamins, vitamin E (tocopherol) is distributed most equally, showing relatively high concentrations in all fish groups, higher than those of meat. However, only a part of the vitamin E content is available as active tocopherol on consumption of fish, since it is oxidized in protecting fatty acids from oxidation. The presence of vitamins A (retinol) and D is closely related to the fat content, and so they are almost absent in most low-fat groups. Appreciable but low concentrations of vitamin A are found in fatty finfish and bivalve molluscs, whereas vitamin D is very abundant in fatty fish. In fact, 100 g of most fatty species supply over 100% of the RDA of this vitamin.

Water-soluble vitamins are well represented in all kinds of fish, with the sole exception of vitamin C (ascorbic acid), which is almost absent in all of them. The concentrations of the rest are highly variable; however, with few exceptions, they constitute a medium-to-good source of such vitamins, comparable with, or even better than, meat. The contents of vitamins B_2 (riboflavin), B_6 (pyridoxine), niacin, biotin, and B_{12} (cobalamin) are relatively high. Indeed, 100 g of fish can contribute up to 38%, 60%, 50%, 33%, and 100%, respectively, of the total daily requirements of those vitamins. Fatty fish also provides a higher supply of many of the water-soluble vitamins (namely pyridoxine, niacin, pantothenic acid, and cobalamin) than does white fish or shellfish. Crustaceans also possess a relatively higher content of pantothenic acid, whereas bivalve molluscs have much higher concentrations of folate and cobalamin.

Table 7 Vitamin content of the different groups of fish and shellfish (mg or μg per 100 g)

	A (μg)	D (μg)	E (mg)	B₁ (mg)	B₂ (mg)	B₆ (mg)	Niacin (mg)	Biotin (μg)	Pantothenic acid (mg)	Folate (μg)	B₁₂ (μg)	C (mg)
White finfish	Tr	Tr	0.3–1.0	0.02–0.2	0.05–0.5	0.15–0.5	1.0–5.0	1.0–10	0.1–0.5	5.0–15	1.0–5.0	Tr
Fatty finfish	20–60	5–20	0.2–3.0	0.01–0.1	0.1–0.5	0.2–0.8	3.0–8.0	1.0–10	0.4–1.0	5.0–15	5.0–20	Tr
Crustaceans	Tr	Tr	0.5–2.0	0.01–0.1	0.02–0.3	0.1–0.3	0.5–3.0	1.0–10	0.5–1.0	1.0–10	1.0–10	Tr
Molluscs	10–100	Tr	0.5–1.0	0.03–0.1	0.05–0.3	0.05–0.2	0.2–2.0	1.0–10	0.1–0.5	20–50	2.0–30	Tr
Cephalopods	Tr	Tr	0.2–1.0	0.02–0.1	0.05–0.5	0.3–0.1	1.0–5.0	1.0–10	0.5–1.0	10–20	1.0–5.0	Tr
RDA	900	5	15	1.2	1.3	1.3	16	30	5.0	400	2.4	90
% RDA/100 g	0–11	0–100	2–20	1–20	2–38	5–60	1–50	3–33	2–20	0.3–12	40–100	0
% RDA/Md	2	50	7	5	15	25	18	5	8	2	100	0

Tr, trace; RDA, recommended dietary allowance; Md, Mediterranean diet.
Reproduced with permission from Ariño A, Beltran JA, and Roncalés P (2003) Dietary importance of fish and shellfish. In: Caballero B, Trugo L, and Finglas P (eds.) *Encyclopedia of Food Sciences and Nutrition*, 2nd edn. Oxford: Elsevier Science Ltd. pp. 2471–2478.

Table 8 Selected mineral content of the different groups of fish and shellfish (mg per 100 g)

	Na	K	Ca	Mg	P	Fe	Zn	Mn	Cu	Se	Cr	Mo	I
White finfish	50–150	200–500	10–50	15–30	100–300	0.2–0.6	0.2–1.0	0.01–0.05	0.01–0.05	0.02–0.1	0.005–0.02	0.005–0.02	0.01–0.5
Fatty finfish	50–200	200–500	10–200	20–50	200–500	1.0–5.0	0.2–1.0	0.01–0.05	0.01–0.05	0.02–0.1	0.005–0.02	0.005–0.02	0.01–0.5
Crustaceans	100–500	100–500	20–200	20–200	100–700	0.2–2.0	1.0–5.0	0.02–0.2	0.1–2.0	0.05–0.1	0.005–0.02	0.01–0.05	0.01–0.2
Molluscs	50–300	100–500	50–200	20–200	100–300	0.5–10	2.0–10	0.02–0.2	0.02–10	0.05–0.1	0.005–0.02	0.01–0.2	0.05–0.5
Cephalopods	100–200	200–300	10–100	20–100	100–300	0.2–1.0	1.0–5.0	0.01–0.1	0.02–0.1	0.02–0.1	0.005–0.02	0.01–0.2	0.01–0.1
RDA			1000	420	700	8	11	2.3	0.9	0.055	0.035	0.045	0.15
% RDA/100 g			1–20	4–50	15–100	2–50	1–90	0–10	1–100	25–100	15–60	10–100	8–100
% RDA/Md			6	5	30	18	2		2	100		100	100

RDA, recommended dietary allowance; Md, Mediterranean diet.
Reproduced with permission from Ariño A, Beltran JA, and Roncalés P (2003) Dietary importance of fish and shellfish. In: Caballero B, Trugo L, and Finglas P (eds.) *Encyclopedia of Food Sciences and Nutrition*, 2nd edn. Oxford: Elsevier Science Ltd. pp. 2471–2478.

A Mediterranean diet rich in fish – and especially in fatty finfish – contributes steadily over the year to an overall balanced vitamin supply. The last row of **Table 7** illustrates this; the supply of vitamins D, B_2, B_6, B_{12}, and niacin from this particular diet is more than 15% of the daily requirements; all other vitamins, except ascorbic acid, are supplied to a lesser, but significant, extent.

Fish Minerals

The approximate amounts of selected minerals contained in fish are given in **Table 8**. The first point to note is that all kinds of finfish and shellfish present a well-balanced content of most minerals, either macroelements or oligoelements, with only a few exceptions. Sodium content is low, as in other muscle and animal origin foods. However, it must be remembered that sodium is usually added to fish in most cooking practices in the form of common salt; also, surimi-based and other manufactured foods contain high amounts of added sodium. Potassium and calcium levels are also relatively low, though the latter are higher in fish than in meat; in addition, small fish bones are frequently eaten with fish flesh, thus increasing the calcium intake. Fish is a good source of magnesium and phosphorus, at least as good as meat. These elements are particularly abundant in crustaceans; fatty finfish show elevated levels of phosphorus, and bivalve molluscs have high amounts of magnesium.

Fish is a highly valuable source of most oligoelements. Fatty fish provides a notable contribution to iron supply, similar to that of meat, whereas shellfish have higher concentrations of most dietary minerals. In particular, crustaceans and bivalve molluscs supply zinc, manganese, and copper concentrations well above those of finfish. Worth mentioning is the extraordinary dietary supply of iodine in all kinds of finfish and shellfish; however, this depends on the concentration present in feed, particularly in planktonic organisms.

In summary, 100 g of fish affords low levels of sodium and medium-to-high levels of all the remaining dietary minerals. In fact, it can contribute 50–100% of the total daily requirements of magnesium, phosphorus, iron, copper, selenium, and iodine. A Mediterranean diet, rich in fatty fish and all kinds of shellfish, can lead to an overall balanced mineral supply, which may well reach over 20% of daily requirements of phosphorus, iron, selenium, and iodine.

See also: **Cancer**: Epidemiology and Associations Between Diet and Cancer. **Coronary Heart Disease**: Prevention. **Dietary Guidelines, International Perspectives**. **Fatty Acids**: Omega-3 Polyunsaturated. **Food Composition Data**. **Food Safety**: Bacterial Contamination; Other Contaminants; Heavy Metals. **Hyperlipidemia**: Nutritional Management. **Iodine**: Physiology, Dietary Sources and Requirements. **Protein**: Quality and Sources. **Stroke, Nutritional Management**. **Supplementation**: Dietary Supplements.

Further Reading

Ackman RG (1995) Composition and nutritive value of fish and shellfish lipids. In: Ruiter A (ed.) *Fish and Fishery Products: Composition, Nutritive Properties and Stability*, pp. 117–156. Wallingford: CAB International.

Ariño A, Beltran JA, and Roncalés P (2003) Dietary importance of fish and shellfish. In: Caballero B, Trugo L, and Finglas P (eds.) *Encyclopedia of Food Sciences and Nutrition*, 2nd edn., pp. 2471–2478. Oxford: Elsevier Science Ltd.

Exler J (1987, updated 1992) *Composition of Foods: Finfish and Shellfish Products, Human Nutrition Information Service Agriculture Handbook 8-15* Washington DC: US Department of Agriculture.

Food and Agriculture Organization of the United Nations (1989) *Yield and Nutritional Value of the Commercially More Important Species. FAO Fisheries Technical Paper 309*. Rome: Food and Agriculture Organization.

Food and Drug Administration (1989) *The Fish List, FDA Guide to Acceptable Market Names for Food Fish Sold in Interstate Commerce 1988*. Washington DC: US Government Printing Office.

Haard NF (1995) Composition and nutritive value of fish proteins and other nitrogen compounds. In: Ruiter A (ed.) *Fish and Fishery Products: Composition, Nutritive Properties and Stability*, pp. 77–115. Wallingford: CAB International.

Holland B, Brown J, and Buss DH (1993) Fish and fish products. In: *Supplement to the 5th Edition of McCance and Widdowson's The Composition of Foods*. London: The Royal Society of Chemistry and Ministry of Agriculture, Fisheries and Food.

Huss HH (1995) *Quality and Quality Changes in Fresh Fish*, FAO Fisheries Technical Paper 348. Rome: Food and Agriculture Organization.

Lands WEM (1988) *Fish and Human Health* Orlando, FL: Academic Press.

Lovell RT (1989) *Nutrition and Feeding of Fish* New York: Van Nostrand Reinhold.

National Fisheries Institute. http://www.nfi.org.

Nettleton JA (1993) *Omega-3 Fatty Acids and Health* New York: Chapman & Hall.

Southgate DAT (2000) Meat, fish, eggs and novel protein. In: Garrow JS, James WPT, and Ralph A (eds.) *Human Nutrition and Dietetics*, 10th edn. Edinburgh: Churchill Livingstone.

United States Department of Agriculture. Composition of foods. http://www.nal.usda.gov/fnic/foodcomp.

Valdimarsson G and James D (2001) World fisheries – utilisation of catches. *Ocean and Coastal Management* 44: 619–633.

Flavonoids *see* **Phytochemicals**: Classification and Occurrence; Epidemiological Factors

Folate *see* **Folic Acid**

FOLIC ACID

J McPartlin, Trinity College, Dublin, Ireland

Introduction

Folic acid was initially distinguished from vitamin B_{12} as a dietary anti-anemia factor by Wills in the 1930s. The subsequent chemical isolation of folic acid and the identification of its role as a cofactor in one-carbon metabolism led to the elucidation of deficiency diseases at the molecular level. The term 'folate' encompasses the entire group of folate vitamin forms, comprising the naturally occurring folylpolyglutamates found in food and folic acid (pteroylglutamic acid), the synthetic form of the vitamin added as a dietary supplement to foodstuffs. 'Folate' is thus the general term used for any form of the vitamin irrespective of the state of reduction, type of substitution, or degree of polyglutamylation.

Folate functions metabolically as an enzyme cofactor in the synthesis of nucleic acids and amino-acids. Deficiency of the vitamin leads to impaired cell replication and other metabolic alterations, particularly related to methionine synthesis. The similar clinical manifestations of cobalamin deficiency and folate deficiency underline the metabolic interrelationship between the two vitamins. Folate deficiency, manifested clinically as megaloblastic anemia, is the most common vitamin deficiency in developed countries. Much attention has focused recently on a number of diseases for which the risks are inversely related to folate status even within the range of blood indicators previously considered 'normal.' Food-fortification programs introduced to prevent neural-tube defects (NTD) have proved effective in increasing folate intakes in populations and may be shown potentially to reduce the risk of cardiovascular disease.

Physiology and Biochemistry

Chemistry and Biochemical Functions

Folic acid (**Figure 1**) consists of a pterin moiety linked via a methylene group to a para-aminobenzoylglutamate moiety. Folic acid is the synthetic form of the vitamin; its metabolic activity requires reduction to the tetrahydrofolic acid (THF) derivative, addition of a chain of glutamate residues in γ-peptide linkage, and acquisition of one-carbon units.

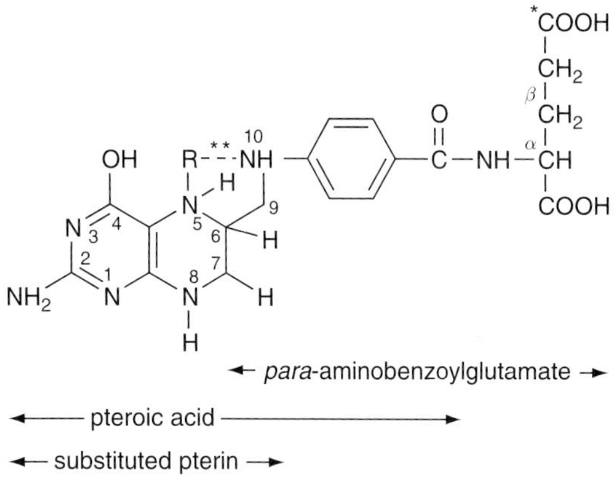

Figure 1 Structural formula of tetrahydrofolate (THF) compounds. In tetrahydrofolic acid R = H; other substituents are listed in **Table 1**. The asterisk indicates the site of attachment of extra glutamate residues; the hatched line and double asterisk indicates the N5 and/or N10 site of attachment of one-carbon units.

Table 1 Structure and nomenclature of folate compounds (see **Figure 1**)

Compound	R	Oxidation state
5-formylTHF	—CHO	Formate
10-formylTHF	—CHO	Formate
5-formiminoTHF	—CH=NH	Formate
5,10-methenylTHF	—CH=	Formate
5,10-methyleneTHF	—CH$_2$—	Formaldehyde
5-methylTHF	—CH$_3$	Methanol

One-carbon units at various levels of oxidation are generated metabolically and are reactive only as moieties attached to the N5 and/or N10 positions of the folate molecule (**Table 1**).

The range of oxidation states for folate one-carbon units extends from methanol to formate as methyl, methylene, methenyl, formyl, or formimino moieties. When one-carbon units are incorporated into folate derivatives, they may be converted from one oxidation state to another by the gain or loss of electrons.

The source of one-carbon units for folate One-carbon units at the oxidation level of formate can enter directly into the folate pool as formic acid in a reaction catalyzed by 10-formylTHF synthase (**Figure 2**). Entry at the formate level of oxidation can also take place via a catabolic product of histidine, formaminoglutamic acid. The third mode of entry at the formate level of oxidation involves the formation of 5-formylTHF from 5,10-methenylTHF by the enzyme serine hydroxymethyl transferase (SHMT). The 5-formylTHF may be rapidly converted to other forms of folate.

The enzyme SHMT is involved in the entry of one-carbon units at the formaldehyde level of oxidation by catalyzing the transfer of the β-carbon of serine to form glycine and 5,10-methyleneTHF. Other sources of one-carbon entry at this level of oxidation include the glycine cleavage system and the choline-dependent pathway; both enzyme systems generate 5,10-methylene in the mitochondria of the cell.

The removal and use of one-carbon units from folate Single-carbon units are removed from folate by a number of reactions. The enzyme 10-formylTHF dehydrogenase provides a mechanism for disposing of excess one-carbon units as carbon dioxide. (Folate administration to animals enhances the conversion of ingested methanol and formate to carbon dioxide, diminishing methanol toxicity.) Additionally, single-carbon units from 10-formylTHF are used for the biosynthesis of purines (**Figure 2**).

The one-carbon unit of 5,10-methyleneTHF is transferred in two ways. Reversal of the SHMT reaction produces serine from glycine, but since serine is also produced from glycolysis via phosphoglycerate this reaction is unlikely to be important. However, one-carbon transfer from 5,10-methyleneTHF to deoxyuridylate to form thymidylic acid, a precursor of DNA, is of crucial importance to the cell. While the source of the one-carbon unit, namely 5,10-methyleneTHF, is at the formaldehyde level of oxidation, the one-carbon unit transferred to form thymidylic acid appears at the methanol level of oxidation. Electrons for this reduction come from THF itself to generate dihydrofolate as a product. The dihydrofolate must in turn be reduced back to THF in order to accept further one-carbon units.

A solitary transfer of one-carbon units takes place at the methanol level of oxidation. It involves the transfer of the methyl group from 5-methylTHF to homocysteine to form methionine and THF. This reaction is catalyzed by the enzyme methionine synthase and requires vitamin B$_{12}$ as a cofactor. The substance 5-methylTHF is the dominant folate in the body, and it remains metabolically inactive until it is demethylated to THF, whereupon polyglutamylation takes place to allow subsequent folate-dependent reactions to proceed efficiently.

Clinical implications of methionine synthase inhibition The inhibition of methionine synthase due to vitamin B$_{12}$ deficiency induces megaloblastic anemia that is clinically indistinguishable from that caused by folate deficiency. The hematological effect in both cases results in levels of 5,10-methyleneTHF that are inadequate to sustain thymidylate biosynthesis. Clinically, it is essential to ascertain whether the anemia is the result of folate deficiency or vitamin B$_{12}$ deficiency by differential diagnostic techniques. Vitamin B$_{12}$ is essential for the synthesis of myelin in nerve tissue, a function probably related to methionine production from the methionine synthase reaction and the subsequent formation of S-adenosyl-methionine. Hence, vitamin B$_{12}$ deficiency probably leads to nervous disorders in addition to the hematological effects. While the latter respond to treatment with folic acid, the neurological effects do not. Thus, inappropriate administration of folic acid in patients with vitamin B$_{12}$ deficiency may treat the anemia but mask the progression of the neurological defects. Where possible, vitamin B$_{12}$ and folate statuses should be checked before giving folate supplements to treat megaloblastic anemia. The main objection to fortifying food with folate is the potential to mask

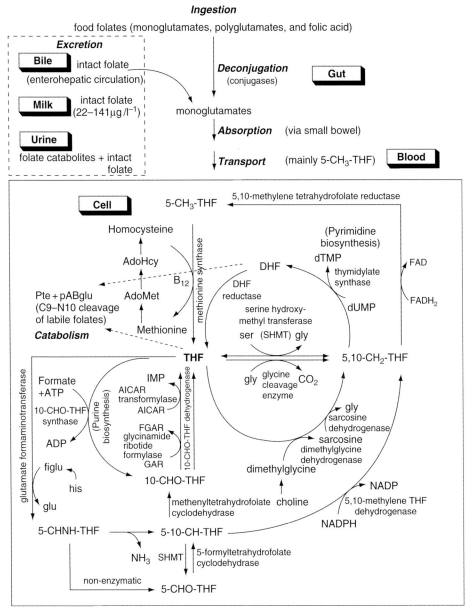

Figure 2 Physiology and metabolism of folate. GAR, glycinamide ribonucleotide; FGAR, formylglycinamide ribonucleotide; AICAR: aminoimidazolecarboxamide ribonucleotide; figlu, formiminoglutamic acid; IMP, inosine monophosphate.

vitamin B_{12} deficiency in the elderly, who are most prone to it.

In summary, the biochemical function of folate coenzymes is to transfer and use these one-carbon units in a variety of essential reactions (**Figure 2**), including *de novo* purine biosynthesis (formylation of glycinamide ribonucleotide and 5-amino-4-imidazole carboxamide ribonucleotide), pyrimidine nucleotide biosynthesis (methylation of deoxyuridylic acid to thymidylic acid), amino-acid interconversions (the interconversion of serine to glycine, catabolism of histidine to glutamic acid, and conversion of homocysteine to

methionine (which also requires vitamin B_{12})), and the generation and use of formate.

Many of the enzymes involved in these reactions are multifunctional and are capable of channelling substrates and one-carbon units from reaction to reaction within a protein matrix. Another feature of intracellular folate metabolism is the compartmentation of folate coenzymes between the cytosol and the mitochondria. For instance, 5-methylTHF is associated with the cytosolic fraction of the cell, whereas most of 10-formylTHF is located in the mitochondria. Similarly, some folate-dependent enzymes are associated with one or other compartment, though some are found in both. Metabolic products of folate-dependent reactions, such as serine and glycine, are readily transported between the two locations, but the folate coenzymes are not.

Folate Deficiency and Hyperhomocysteinemia An important consequence of folate deficiency is the inability to remethylate homocysteine (**Figure 2**). Indeed, there is an inverse correlation between the levels of folate and those of homocysteine in the blood of humans. Many clinical studies, beginning with the observations of children with homocysteinuria presenting with vascular abnormalities and thromboembolism, have demonstrated an association between hyperhomocysteinemia and an increased risk of premature atherosclerosis in the coronary, carotid, and peripheral vasculatures. Even mild hyperhomocysteinemia is recognized to be an independent risk factor for cardiovascular disease. The risk of heart disease was found to increase proportionately in most, but not all, studies, throughout the full of range of blood homocysteine concentrations. An increase in plasma homocysteine of $5\,\mu mol\,l^{-1}$ is associated with a combined odds ratio of 1.3 for cardiovascular disease. Plasma homocysteine is usually shown to be a greater risk factor for cardiovascular disease in prospective studies than in retrospective studies, probably because the populations in the former studies are older. Metabolically, homocysteine may be disposed of by the methionine synthase reaction (dependent on folate and vitamin B_{12}), the transsulfuration pathway (dependent on vitamin B_6), and the choline degradation pathway. Marginal deficiencies of these three vitamins are associated with hyperhomocysteinemia. Of the three vitamins, however, folic acid has been shown to be the most effective in lowering levels of homocysteine in the blood. Convincing evidence of the potential role of folate intake in the prevention of vascular disease has come from a significant inverse relationship between serum folate levels and fatal coronary heart disease. While most studies have focused on the homocysteine-lowering effects of folate, other benefits have also been reported. Potential mechanisms include antioxidant actions and interactions with the enzyme endothelial nitric oxide synthase.

Absorption of Folates

Food folates mainly consist of reduced polyglutamates, which are hydrolyzed to monoglutamates in the gut prior to absorption across the intestinal mucosa. The conjugase enzyme that hydrolyzes dietary folates has been found on the luminal brush border membrane in the human jejunum and has equal affinity for polyglutamates of various chain lengths. Transport is facilitated by a saturable carrier-mediated uptake system, although changes in luminal pH and the presence of conjugase inhibitors, folate binders, or other food components can adversely affect the rate of hydrolysis and intestinal absorption. Such factors account for the wide variation in the bioavailability of the vitamin from foods of plant and animal origins. Some metabolism of the resultant monoglutamate, mainly to 5-methylTHF, appears to occur during the absorption process, though this may not be necessary for transport across the basolateral membrane of the intestinal mucosa into the portal circulation. The degree of metabolic conversion of dietary folic acid depends on the dose; pharmacological amounts are transported unaltered into the circulation.

Transport in the Circulation, Cellular Uptake, and Turnover

Folate circulates in the blood predominantly as 5-methylTHF. A variable proportion circulates freely or bound either to low-affinity protein binders such as albumin, which accounts for about 50% of bound folate, or to a high-affinity folate binder in serum, which carries less than 5% of circulating folate. The physiological importance of serum binders is unclear, but they may control folate distribution and excretion during deficiency.

Though most folate is initially taken up by the liver following absorption, it is delivered to a wide variety of tissues in which many types of folate transporters have been described. Because these transporters have affinities for folate in the micromolar range, they would not be saturated by normal ambient concentrations of folate. Therefore, folate uptake into tissues should be responsive to any increases in serum folate levels arising from folate supplementation. An important determinant of folate uptake into cells is their mitotic activity, as would be expected given the dependence of DNA biosynthesis on folate coenzyme function. Folate accumulation is more rapid in actively dividing cells than in quiescent cells, a factor that is probably related to the induction and activity of folylpoly-γ-glutamate synthase. This enzyme catalyzes the addition of glutamate by γ-peptide linkage to the initial glutamate moiety of the folate molecule. Although polyglutamate derivatization may be considered a storage strategem, this elongation is the most efficient coenzyme form for normal one-carbon metabolism. The activity of folylpoly-γ-glutamate synthase is highest in the liver, the folate stores of which account for half of the estimated 5–10 mg adult complement. Retention within the cell is facilitated by the high proportion of folate associated with proteins, and this is likely to be increased in folate deficiency.

The mobilization of liver and other stores in the body is not well understood, particularly in deficiency states, though some accounts describe poor turnover rates in folate-depleted rats. Transport across cell membranes during redistribution requires deconjugation of the large negatively charged polyglutamates. Mammalian γ-glutamylhydrolases that hydrolyze glutamate moieties residue by residue and transpeptidases that can hydrolyze folylpolyglutamates directly to mono- or di-glutamate forms of the vitamin have been described for a number of tissues. Thus, mammalian cells possess two types of enzyme that can play a key role in folate homeostasis and regulation of one-carbon metabolism: the folylpolyglutamate synthetase that catalyzes the synthesis of retentive and active folate, and a number of deconjugating enzymes that promote the release of folate from the cell. Polyglutamate forms released into the circulation either through cell death or by a possible exocytotic mechanism would be hydrolyzed rapidly by plasma γ-glutamyl-hydrolase to the monoglutamate form.

Catabolism and Excretion

Folate is concentrated in bile, and enterohepatic recirculation from the intestine accounts for considerable re-absorption and reuse of folate (about $100\,\mu g\,day^{-1}$). Fecal folates mostly arise through biosynthesis of the vitamin by the gut microflora, with only a small contribution from unabsorbed dietary folate. Urinary excretion of intact folates accounts for only a small fraction of ingested folate under normal physiological conditions. The greater amount of excretion in urine is accounted for by products that arise from cleavage of the folate molecule at the C9–N10 bond, consisting of one or more pteridines and p-acetamidobenzoylglutamate. The rate of scission of the folate molecule increases during rapid-mitotic conditions such as pregnancy and rapid growth. Scission of folate is perhaps the major mechanism of folate turnover in the body.

Human Folate Requirements

The folate requirement is the minimum amount necessary to prevent deficiency. Dietary recommendations for populations, however, must allow a margin of safety to cover the needs of the vast majority of the population. As is the case with most nutrients, the margin of safety for folate requirement corresponds to two standard deviations above the mean requirement for a population and should therefore meet the needs of 97.5% of the population. Thus, international dietary recommendations contain allowances for individual variability, the bioavailability of folate from different foodstuffs, and periods of low intake and increased use. Current international folate recommendations for FAO/WHO, USA/Canada, and the European Union are listed in **Table 2**.

Table 2 Recommended dietary folate allowances for various population groups ($\mu g\,day^{-1}$)

Category	Age	FAO/WHO (1998)	USA/Canada RDA (1998)	EU (1993)
Infants	Up to 6 months	80	65	100
	6 months–1 year	80	80	100
	1–3 years	160	150	100
Children	4–6 years	200	200	130
	7–10 years	300 (age 9–13 years)	300	150
Males	11–14 years	400	300	180
	15–18 years	400	400	200
	19–24 years	400	400	200
	25–50 years	400	400	200
	Over 50 years	400	400	200
Females	11–14 years	400	300	180
	15–18 years	400	400	200
	19–24 years	400	400	200
	25–50 years	400	400	200
	Over 50 years	400	400	200
Pregnant women		600	600	400
Lactating women		500	500	350

The 1998 recommendations for folate are expressed using a term called the dietary folate equivalent (DFE). The DFE was developed to help account for the difference in bioavailability between naturally occurring dietary folate and synthetic folic acid. The Food and Nutrition Board of the US National Academy of Sciences reasoned that, since folic acid in supplements or in fortified food is 85% bioavailable, but food folate is only about 50% bioavailable, folic acid taken as supplements or in fortified food is 85/50 (i.e., 1.7) times more available. Thus, the calculation of the DFE for a mixture of synthetic folic acid and food is μg of DFE = μg food folate + (1.7 × μg synthetic folate).

International recommendation tables are constantly subject to review, particularly in view of the relationship between folate status and the risk of NTD and specific chronic diseases including coronary artery disease and colorectal cancer.

Pregnancy

The crucial role of folate in the biosynthesis of precursors for DNA suggests that folate requirements may vary with age, though folate use is most obviously increased during pregnancy and lactation. Maintaining adequate folate status in women in their child-bearing years is particularly important since a large proportion of pregnancies are unplanned and many women are likely to be unaware of their pregnancy during the first crucial weeks of fetal development. Pregnancy requires an increase in folate supply that is large enough to fulfil considerable mitotic requirements related to fetal growth, uterine expansion, placental maturation, and expanded blood volume. The highest prevalence of poor folate status in pregnant women occurs among the lowest socioeconomic groups and is often exacerbated by the higher parity rate of these women. Indeed, the megaloblastic anemia commonly found amongst the malnourished poor during pregnancy probably reflects the depletion of maternal stores to the advantage of the fetal–placental unit, as indicated by the several-fold higher serum folate levels in the newborn compared with the mother. Considerable evidence indicates that maternal folate deficiency leads to fetal growth retardation and low birth weight. The higher incidence of low-birth-weight infants among teenage mothers compared with their adult counterparts is probably related to the additional burden that adolescent growth places on folate resources.

The lack of hard evidence about the extent of supplementation required in pregnancy prompted the development of a laboratory-based assessment of metabolic turnover, which involved the assay of total daily folate catabolites (along with intact folate) in the urine of pregnant women. The rationale of the procedure was that this catabolic product represents an ineluctable daily loss of folate, the replacement of which should constitute the daily requirement. Correcting for individual variation in catabolite excretion and the bioavailability of dietary folate, the recommended allowances based on this mode of assessment are in close agreement with the latest recommendations of the USA/Canada and FAO/WHO. The data produced by the catabolite-excretion method may provide a useful adjunct to current methods based on intakes, clinical examination, and blood folate measurements to provide a more accurate assessment of requirement.

Folate and Neural-Tube Defects

Much attention has focused over the past 15 years on a number of diseases for which the risks are inversely related to folate status even within the range of serum folate levels previously considered 'normal.' Foremost among these is NTD, a malformation in the developing embryo that is related to a failure of the neural tube to close properly during the fourth week of embryonic life. Incomplete closure of the spinal cord results in spina bifida, while incomplete closure of the cranium results in anencephaly. The risk of NTD was found to be 10-fold higher (6 affected pregnancies per 1000) in people with poor folate status (i.e., less than 150 μg red cell folate per litre) than in those with good folate status ($400 \, \mu g \, l^{-1}$). International agencies have published folic acid recommendations for the prevention of NTD. To prevent recurrence, 5 mg of folic acid daily in tablet form is recommended, while 400 μg daily is recommended for the prevention of occurrence, to be commenced prior to conception and continued until the 12th week of pregnancy. Given the high proportion of unplanned pregnancies, the latter recommendations are applicable to all fertile women. This amount, however, could not be introduced through fortification because high intakes of folic acid by people consuming fortified flour products would risk preventing the diagnosis of pernicious anemia in the general population and of vitamin B_{12} deficiency in the elderly.

The introduction of 140 μg of folic acid per 100 g of flour in the USA, calculated to increase individual consumption of folic acid by $100 \, \mu g \, day^{-1}$, has reduced the incidence of abnormally low plasma folate from 21% to less than 2%, the incidence of mild hyperhomocysteinemia from 21% to 10%, and, most importantly, the incidence of NTD by about 20% over the first years of universal fortification. Because 30% of the population takes vitamin supplements and presumably would not be expected to derive significant benefit from fortification, the actual effect may be closer to a 30% decrease due to fortification. Recent calculations suggest that, for a variety of reasons, the overall fortification amount was about twice the mandatory amount.

On balance, the introduction of food fortification with folate is regarded as beneficial not only in preventing NTD but also in reducing the incidences of hyperhomocysteinemia (mentioned earlier), colorectal cancer, and a number of neurological and neuropsychiatric diseases in which folate is postulated to play a protective role.

Lactation

Unlike during pregnancy, in which the bulk of folate expenditure arises through catabolism, during lactation the increased requirement is chiefly due to milk secretion. Several observations indicate that mammary tissue takes precedence over other maternal tissues for folate resources. For instance, maternal folate status deteriorates in both early and late lactation, but milk folate concentration is maintained or increased. Moreover, supplemental folate appears to be taken up by mammary epithelial cells preferentially over hematopoietic cells in lactating women with folate deficiency, indicating that maternal reserves are depleted to maintain milk folate content in lactating women. Recommendations are based on the maintenance requirement of nonpregnant non-lactating women and the estimated folate intake required to replace the quantity lost in milk. This increment of between 60 μg and 100 μg daily is based on a milk secretion rate of 40–60 μg l^{-1} and an absorption rate from dietary sources of between 50% and 70%. The official recommendations might be underestimated, however. On the one hand, a less efficient absorption rate of 50% from a mixed diet is more likely, and, on the other hand, the most recent estimations of milk folate secretion are as high as 100 μg daily. Therefore, an additional 200 μg of folate daily or a total of 500 μg daily seems a more realistic recommended amount for lactating women.

Infants and Children

The high concentration of circulating folate in newborn infants coincides with the rapid rate of cell division in the first few months of life and is reflected in the higher folate requirement for infants on a weight basis than for adults. Though the recommendation standards (see **Table 2**) may underestimate the quantities consumed by many breast-fed infants, intake is generally sufficiently above the recommendations that folate deficiency is unlikely.

Data on requirements for older children are sparse, so recommendations for up to adolescence are based on interpolations between the values for very young children and those for adults. Daily recommended levels are above 3.6 μg per kg of body weight, an amount associated with no overt folate deficiency in children and shown to maintain plasma folate concentrations at a low but acceptable level.

Adolescents and Adults

Folate recommendations for adolescents are set at a similar level to that for adults, the smaller weights of adolescents being compensated for by higher rates of growth.

The Elderly

Although folate deficiency occurs more frequently in the elderly than in young adults, recommendations are set at the same level for both groups. Reference recommendations apply to healthy subjects. However, a significant proportion of the elderly are likely to suffer from clinical conditions and to be exposed to a range of factors such as chronic smoking, alcohol, and prescription drugs that may have a detrimental effect on folate status.

Food Sources of Folate

Folate is synthesized by microorganisms and higher plants but not by mammals, for which it is an essential vitamin. The most concentrated food folate sources include liver, yeast extract, green leafy vegetables, legumes, certain fruits, and fortified breakfast cereals. Folate content is likely to depend on the maturity and variety of particular sources. Foods that contain a high concentration of folate are not necessarily those that contribute most to the overall intakes of the vitamin in a population. For example, liver is a particularly concentrated source, providing 320 μg of folate per 100 g, but it is not eaten by a sufficient proportion of the population to make any major contribution to total dietary folate intakes. The potato, on the other hand, although not particularly rich in folate, is considered a major contributor to folate in the UK diet, accounting for 14% of total folate intake because of its high consumption. Prolonged exposure to heat, air, or ultraviolet light is known to inactivate the vitamin; thus, food

Table 3 Contributions of the main food groups to the average daily intake of folate in British and US adults (%)

Food group	USA (1994)	UK (1998)
Dairy products	8.1	9.8
Meat, poultry, fish	8.5	6.5
Grain products	21.2[a]	31.8
Fruit, fruit juices	10.2	6.9
Vegetables	26.4	31.8
Legumes, nuts, soy	18.5	—
Eggs	5.1	2.4
Tea	—	4.1
Other food	2.1	5.7

[a]Prior to mandatory fortification of flour-based products.

preparation and cooking can make a difference to the amount of folate ingested; boiling in particular results in substantial food losses. The major source of folate loss from vegetables during boiling may be leaching as opposed to folate degradation. Broccoli and spinach are particularly susceptible to loss through leaching during boiling compared with potatoes because of their larger surface areas. The retention of folate during cooking depends on the food in question as well as the method of cooking. Folates of animal origin are stable during cooking by frying or grilling. In addition to highlighting good food sources, public-health measures promoting higher folate intake should include practical advice on cooking. For example, steaming in preference to boiling is likely to double the amount of folate consumed from green vegetables.

While cultural differences and local eating habits determine the contribution of different foodstuffs to folate intake (**Table 3**), as with other nutrients, globalization and the integration of the international food industry may lead to more predictable 'Westernized' diets in the developed and developing world. Internationally, much of the dietary folate in the 'Western' diet currently comes from fortified breakfast cereals, though this foodstuff is likely to be joined shortly in this regard by fortified flour products in the light of the experience of the US food fortification program. In the main, though, adherence to dietary recommendations to increase the consumption of folate-rich foods is likely to enhance the intake not only of folate but also of other nutrients essential to health.

See also: **Adolescents**: Nutritional Requirements. **Amino Acids**: Chemistry and Classification; Metabolism; Specific Functions. **Anemia**: Megaloblastic Anemia. **Breast Feeding. Cobalamins. Food Fortification**: Developed Countries; Developing Countries. **Fruits and Vegetables. Infants**: Nutritional Requirements. **Lactation**: Physiology; Dietary Requirements. **Pregnancy**: Safe Diet for Pregnancy; Prevention of Neural Tube Defects.

Further Reading

Bailey LB (ed.) (1995) *Folate in Health and Disease*. New York: Marcel Dekker.

Blakley R (1969) The biochemistry of folic acid and related pteridines. In: Newbergen H and Taton EL (eds.) *North Holland Research Monographs Frontiers of Biology*, vol. 13, Amsterdam: North Holland Publishing Company.

Boushey CJ, Beresford SA, Omenn GS, and Motulsky AG (1995) A quantitative assessment of plasma homocysteine as a risk factor for vascular disease. *JAMA* **274**: 1049–1057.

Chanarin I (1979) *The Megaloblastic Anaemias*, 2nd edn. Oxford: Blackwell Scientific Publications.

Duthie SJ (1999) Folic acid deficiency and cancer: mechanisms of DNA instability. *British Medical Bulletin* **55**: 578–592.

Homocysteine Lowering Trialists' Collaboration (1998) Lowering blood homocysteine with folic acid based supplements: meta-analysis of randomised trials. *BMJ* **316**: 894–898.

National Academy of Sciences (1998) *Dietary Reference Intakes: Folate, other B Vitamins and Choline*. Wasington, DC: National Academy Press.

Refsum H, Ueland PM, Bygard MD, and Vollset SE (1998) Homocysteine and cardiovascular disease. *Annual Review of Medicine* **49**: 31–62.

Reynolds EH (2002) Folic acid, ageing, depression, and dementia. *BMJ* **324**: 1512–1515.

Scott JM and Weir DG (1994) Folate/vitamin B_{12} interrelationships. *Essays in Biochemistry* **28**: 63–72.

UK Department of Health (2000) *Folic Acid and the Prevention of Disease. Report of the Committee on Medical Aspects of Food and Nutritional Policy*. Norwich: Her Majesty's Stationary Office.

FOOD ALLERGIES

Contents
Etiology
Diagnosis and Management

Etiology

T J David, University of Manchester, Manchester, UK

The concept that certain foods can produce adverse reactions in susceptible individuals has a long history. Hippocrates (460–370 BC) reported that cow's milk could cause gastric upset and urticaria. Later, Galen (131–210 BC) described a case of intolerance to goat's milk. It was Lucretius (96–55 BC) who said, "What is food to one man may be fierce poison to others." In the 1920s and 1930s, a fashion developed of blaming food intolerance for a large number of hitherto unexplained disorders. The uncritical and overenthusiastic nature of the claims, in addition to the anecdotal evidence on which they were based, generally discredited the whole subject. Indeed, the field of food intolerance has been described as "a model of obstruction to the advancement of learning." The whole area has provoked much controversy. The introduction of double-blind provocation tests has placed studies on a more scientific footing, but they are impractical in routine management. The lack of objective and reproducible diagnostic laboratory tests that could eliminate bias has ensured that controversy about food intolerance continues.

Definitions

The word 'allergy' is frequently misused and applied indiscriminately to any adverse reaction, regardless of the mechanism. An allergic response is a reproducible adverse reaction to a substance mediated by an immunological response. The substance provoking the reaction may have been ingested, injected, inhaled, or merely have come into contact with the skin or mucous membranes. Food allergy is a form of adverse reaction to food in which the cause is an immunological response to a food. The much broader term of 'food intolerance' does not imply any specific type of mechanism and is simply defined as a reproducible adverse reaction to a specific food or food ingredient. Outside the United Kingdom, the terminology used sometimes differs. It has been suggested that the term 'food hypersensitivity' should be used to cover all adverse reactions to food, which are then subdivided into food allergy (i.e., immunologically mediated) and food intolerance, which implies a nonimmunologically mediated event.

The term 'food aversion' comprises food avoidance, where the subject avoids a food for psychological reasons such as distaste or a desire to lose weight, and psychological intolerance. The latter is an unpleasant bodily reaction caused by emotions associated with the food rather than the food itself. Psychological intolerance will normally be observable under open conditions but will not occur when the food is given in an unrecognizable form. Psychological intolerance may be reproduced by suggesting (falsely) that the food has been administered.

The term 'anaphylaxis' or 'anaphylactic shock' is taken to mean a severe and potentially life-threatening reaction of rapid onset with circulatory collapse. The term anaphylaxis has also been used to describe any allergic reaction, however mild, that results from specific IgE antibodies, but such usage fails to distinguish between a trivial reaction (e.g., a sneeze) and a dangerous event.

An antigen is a substance that is capable of provoking an immune response. An antibody is an immunoglobulin that is capable of combining specifically with certain antigens. An allergen is a substance that provokes a harmful (allergic) immune response.

Immunological tolerance is a process that results in the immunological system becoming specifically unreactive to an antigen that is capable in other circumstances of provoking antibody production or cell-mediated immunity. The immunological system nevertheless reacts to unrelated antigens given simultaneously and via the same route.

Atopy is the ability to produce a weal-and-flare response to skin prick testing with a common antigen, such as house dust mite or grass pollen. The atopic diseases are asthma (all childhood cases but not all adult cases), atopic eczema, allergic rhinitis, allergic conjunctivitis, and some cases of urticaria.

Mechanisms of Food Allergy

Understanding of the mechanisms of food allergy is poor, and in many cases the precise mechanism is obscure.

Sensitization

The following are possible factors that contribute to immunological sensitization leading to food intolerance:

1. Genetic predisposition: food allergy is commonly familial, suggesting the importance of genetic factors.
2. Immaturity of the immune system or the gastrointestinal mucosal barrier in newborn infants may predispose to sensitisation. The numerous studies that have been performed to determine if food allergy or atopic disease can be prevented by interventions during pregnancy or lactation are based on the idea that there is a critical period during which sensitization can occur.
3. Dosage of antigen: It may be that high dosage leads to the development of tolerance, and low dosage leads to sensitization. This might help to explain the well-documented phenomenon of infants who become allergic to traces of foods that reach them through their mother's breast milk.
4. Certain food antigens are especially likely to lead to sensitization, such as egg, cow's milk, and peanut. The reason why certain foods are more likely to provoke an allergic reaction than others is poorly understood.
5. A triggering event, such as a viral infection: The evidence is anecdotal, but there is a suggestion that food allergy may develop in a previously nonallergic subject after a viral infection such as infectious mononucleosis (glandular fever).
6. Alteration in the permeability of the gastrointestinal tract, permitting abnormal antigen access: The best example of this is the suggestion that acute viral gastroenteritis may damage the small intestinal mucosa, allowing abnormal absorption of food proteins, leading to sensitization. Thus, some data suggest that in a few cases the onset of cow's milk protein allergy follows soon after an episode of gastroenteritis.

Immunological and Molecular Mechanisms

Despite the gastrointestinal barrier, small amounts of immunologically intact proteins enter the circulation and are distributed throughout the body. In normal individuals, the gut-associated lymphoid tissue (GALT), although capable of mounting a rapid and potent response against foreign substances, develop tolerance to ingested food antigens. The means by which tolerance develops is poorly understood, but it is believed that failure to develop tolerance leads to food allergy. The relatively low salivary secretory IgA concentrations, together with the large amount of ingested protein, contributes to the large amount of food antigens confronting the immature GALT. In genetically predisposed infants, these food antigens may stimulate the excessive production of IgE antibodies or other abnormal immune responses.

Heat Treatment

Heat treatment clearly affects certain (but not all) foods, most commonly rendering them less likely to provoke an allergic reaction in a subject who is allergic. Occasionally, the reverse occurs, as in the celebrated case of Professor Heinz Küstner, who was allergic to cooked and not raw fish.

In cow's milk, whey proteins are easily denatured by heat but casein is highly resistant. This observation led to the suggestion that the heat treatment of whey proteins may be a simple and logical strategy for producing a hypoallergenic infant milk formula. However, double-blind, placebo-controlled oral challenges gave rise to immediate hypersensitivity reactions to heat-treated whey protein in four of five children with cow's milk protein intolerance. The reason for these reactions is not known, but one possibility is a reaction to residual casein, which is often present in trace amounts in commercial whey preparations. The small proportion of patients with cow's milk protein intolerance likely to tolerate heat-treated cow's milk, such as evaporated milk, means that heat-treated milk is unlikely to be suitable as a substitute for a cow's milk infant formula.

Cooking reduces the allergenicity of eggs by 70%. However, one of the major allergens in eggs, ovomucoid, a heat-resistant glycoprotein that contributes to the gel-like structure of thick white, is resistant to heating. Heat appears to render a large number of fruits and vegetables less likely to provoke adverse reactions in subjects who are intolerant. Thus, for example, it is not uncommon to see children who are allergic to raw potatoes or fresh pineapple, but almost all such children can tolerate cooked potatoes or tinned pineapples. In some situations, it appears that heat can accelerate a process of denaturation that can in time occur on its own. For example, there have been studies of patients who reacted to fresh melon, pear, peach, pineapple, grape, and banana.

In each case, stewed or tinned fruit caused no reaction. Studies of fresh extracts of these fruits showed that when stored in a refrigerator, the extracts lost their ability to provoke a positive skin test after approximately 3 days.

Heating can increase the allergenicity of certain proteins through the induction of covalent modifications that lead to new antigens or increased stability. In peanuts, for example, the roasting process produces end products with greater resistance to digestion and heightened allergenicity compared with those produced by frying or boiling. This finding may partly account for the low prevalence of peanut allergy in China, where peanut is widely consumed but not roasted.

Prevalence

Unreliability of Self-Reported Food Allergy

Reports of food allergy from individuals or parents of children are notoriously unreliable. Such reports have to be treated with scepticism. It is common for parents to believe that foods are responsible for a variety of childhood symptoms. Double-blind provocation tests in children with histories of reactions to food only confirm the story in one-third of all cases. In the case of purely behavioral symptoms, the proportion that could be reproduced under blind conditions was zero. The same is true of adults' beliefs about their own symptoms. If unnecessary dietary restrictions are to be avoided, one has to be sceptical, and it may be necessary in some cases to seek objective confirmation of food intolerance. The gross overreporting of food allergy has to be borne in mind when examining data on prevalence that are based on unconfirmed subjective reports.

Population Studies

In the European Community Respiratory Health Survey administered to 17 280 adults in 15 countries covering the period 1991–1994, 12% of respondents reported a food allergy or intolerance, ranging from 4.6% in Spain to 19.1% in Australia. The foods most commonly reported to cause shortness of breath were peanut in the United States; fruit in Iceland, Belgium, Ireland, and Italy; and hazelnut in Norway, Sweden, and Germany. The reason for the variation in the reported food triggers is unknown.

A population-based study of 33 110 people in France defined food allergy on the basis of self-reported typical allergic symptoms only and found a rate of 3.5%. In adults, the main foods reported to trigger allergic reactions were seafood, fruit, and vegetables, whereas in children the main foods were egg and milk.

In a questionnaire offered to approximately 30 000 people in 11 388 households in the High Wycombe area of Britain, 3188 of the 18 582 responders (17%) thought that they had some sort of reaction to foods or food additives. A check on the nonresponders showed that they had almost no food-provoked symptoms. Particular attention was then paid to food additives, and it was found that 1372 of the 18 582 responders (7.4%) believed they had adverse reactions to food additives. Of the 1372, 649 attended for a detailed interview, and 132 gave a history of reproducible clinical symptoms after ingestion of food additives. Eighty-one of these completed a trial of double-blind, placebo-controlled challenges with 11 food additives, but a consistent adverse reaction was found in only 2 subjects. One was a 50-year-old atopic man who reported headaches after ingesting coloring agents and who reacted to challenge with annatto, which reproduced his headache at both low (1 mg) and high (10 mg) dose after 4 and 5 h, respectively. He also reacted to placebo on one occasion. The second was a 31-year-old nonatopic woman who reported abdominal pain after ingestion of foods. She had related this to ingestion of preservatives and antioxidants. Her symptoms were reproduced on challenge with annatto at low and high dose.

The parents of 866 children from Finland were asked to provide a detailed history of food allergy, and for certain foods the diagnosis was further investigated by elimination and open challenge at home. Food allergy was reported in 19% by the age of 1 year, 22% by 2 years, 27% by 3 years, and 8% by 6 years. In a prospective study of 480 children in the United States of America up to their third birthday, 16% were reported to have had reactions to fruit or fruit juice and 28% to other food. However, open challenge confirmed reactions in only 12% of the former and 8% of the latter.

Estimates of the prevalence of cow's milk protein allergy are reported to range from 0.3 to 7.5% of subjects.

Natural History

The natural history of food allergy has been little studied. It is well-known that a high proportion of children with food intolerance in the first year of life lose their intolerance in time. The proportion of children to which this happens varies with the food and probably with type of symptoms that are produced. Thus, it is common for allergy to cow's milk or egg to spontaneously disappear with time, whereas peanut allergy is usually lifelong. In the North American study referred to previously, it was found that the offending food or fruit was back in the diet after only 9 months in half the cases, and virtually all the offending foods were back in the diet by the third birthday. A further study of nine children with very severe adverse reactions to food showed that despite the severity, three were later able to tolerate normal amounts of the offending food and four became able to tolerate small amounts.

Although it is clear that the majority of children with food intolerance spontaneously improve, it remains to be established to what extent this depends on the age of onset, the nature of the symptoms, the food itself, and other factors such as associated atopic disease.

In adults with food allergy, the problem is far more likely to be lifelong. Nevertheless, some adults do become tolerant to foods to which they were allergic. In one adult follow-up study, approximately one-third of adults were found to lose their allergy after maintaining an elimination diet for 1 year.

Cross-Reactions

This term refers to cross-reaction between different species and between different foodstuffs that may or may not belong to the same botanical family.

Animal Milk

There is a marked antigenic similarity between the proteins that cause food allergy in the milk of cows, goats, and sheep. It is often not appreciated that almost all subjects who are allergic to cow's milk protein are allergic to the milks of these other animals. This is one of the many reasons why goat's milk is not an appropriate milk substitute for an infant with cow's milk allergy.

Eggs

The eggs from turkeys, duck, goose, and seagull all contain ovalbumen, ovomucoid, and ovotransferrin, the major allergens in hens' eggs. The eggs of hens and turkeys have a similar relative potency of allergenicity. The immunochemical identity of proteins in the egg white of ducks and geese differs somewhat from that of hens, and they may have less potency as allergens. Of all the bird's eggs listed previously, the eggs of the seagull are the least allergenic and bear the least immunochemical similarity with hen's eggs.

Legumes

It is not always obvious which plants belong to the same family. The Leguminosae include beans, peas, soya, lentils, peanuts, liquorice, carob, and gum arabic. Clinical cross-reactivity is uncommon, and the degree of genetic relationship may be of little relevance. Thus, for example, patients with soya allergy are not uncommonly allergic also to peanuts, although the two legumes are not closely related.

Seafood

The taxonomic diversity (fish, molluscs, and crustaceans) suggests that complete cross-reactivity for all seafood is unlikely to be common. In one study, of 20 children with a history of allergy to cod, there was a history of allergy to sole in 11 (55%), to tuna in 7 (35%), and to mackerel, anchovy, sardine, red mullet, and salmon each in 1 (5%). Most studies of cross-reactivity are based on skin prick and IgE antibody test results, which are of little relevance to clinical sensitivity.

Food and Pollen

Cross-reactions can occur between inhaled pollen and ingested food allergens. There is a well-documented association between allergy to birch tree pollen and allergy to apple, carrot, celery, potato, orange, and tomato. This and other similar types of associations are explained by the conservation of protein across species, and a number of so-called panallergens have been described:

1. Profilins in birch pollen, hazelnut, and apple
2. Class 1 chitinases in avocado, banana, and latex
3. Lipid transfer proteins in apple and peach
4. Tropomyosin in insects and shellfish

Cross-reacting IgE antibodies reactive with related foods can often be detected in people who are allergic to a member of these food groups, but clinical reactions are uncommon.

Special Requirements for the Occurrence of Allergic Reaction to Food

In some individuals, there is a clear one-to-one relationship between the ingestion of a food and a reaction. An example is an individual with allergy to cod. Every time the subject eats cod, there is an immediate allergic reaction. In other individuals, the relationship between the food and an allergic reaction is less precise. There are a number of possible reasons for this.

Timing of Reaction and Delayed Reactions

Most allergic reactions to foods occur within minutes of ingestion of the food. However, sometimes a reaction may be delayed. This is best documented in cow's milk protein allergy, in which three types of reaction are recognized: early skin reaction, early gut reaction, and late reaction. An affected individual usually exhibits only one of these types of reaction. In the early skin reaction group, symptoms begin to develop within 45 min of cow's milk challenge. Almost all patients in this group have a positive skin prick test to cow's milk. In the early gut reaction group, symptoms begin to develop between 45 min and 20 h after cow's milk challenge. Approximately one-third of patients in this group have a positive skin prick test to cow's milk. In the late reaction group, symptoms begin to develop approximately 20 h after cow's milk protein challenge. Only approximately 20% of this late reaction group have a positive skin prick test to cow's milk, and these are mostly children with atopic eczema. Almost all children in the late reaction group present over the age of 6 months, and as a group their age at presentation is significantly higher than that of the two other groups.

Quantity of Food

The quantity of cow's milk, for example, required to produce an allergic reaction varies from patient to patient. Some patients are highly sensitive and develop anaphylaxis after ingestion of less than 1 μg of casein, β-lactoglobulin, or α-lactalbumin. In contrast, there are children and adults who do not react to 100 ml of milk but who do react to 200 ml or more. There is a relationship between the quantity of milk required and the time of onset of symptoms. In one study, the median reaction onset time in those who reacted to 100-ml milk challenges was 2 h, but the median reaction onset time in those who required larger amounts of milk to elicit reactions was 24 h.

Food-Dependent Exercise-Induced Anaphylaxis

In this unusual condition, attacks only occur when the exercise follows within a couple of hours of the ingestion of specific foods, such as celery, shellfish, squid, peaches, or wheat. The mechanisms that result in food-dependent exercise-induced anaphylaxis are obscure. This disorder, although rare, is important in the interpretation of dietary challenge studies of food intolerance because in these patients a simple double-blind food challenge without exercise will fail to validate a history of food intolerance.

Drug-Dependent Food Allergy

There are individuals who only react to specific foods while taking a drug. The best recognised examples of this are individuals who only react to foods while taking salicylate (aspirin).

Effect of Disease Activity

It is a common but poorly understood observation that children with eczema and food allergy can often tolerate some or all food triggers when the skin disease clears (usually when the child is vacationing in a sunny location).

Other Possibilities

It is not known whether food allergy can be confined to occasions when the pollen count is high or when the individual consumes certain other foods. There are no objective studies that address the complex issue of the possible additive effect of orally ingested and possibly inhaled antigens. There are subjects with allergy to foods in whom the severity of adverse reactions clearly varies from time to time, but the reasons for this variability are not known.

See also: **Dairy Products**. **Eggs**. **Food Allergies**: Diagnosis and Management. **Food Intolerance**. **Fruits and Vegetables**. **Immunity**: Physiological Aspects. **Nuts and Seeds**.

Further Reading

Bentley SJ, Pearson DJ, and Rix KJB (1983) Food hypersensitivity in irritable bowel syndrome. *Lancet* **2**: 295–297.

Bernhisel-Broadbent J and Sampson HA (1989) Cross-allergenicity in the legume botanical family in children with food hypersensitivity. *Journal of Allergy and Clinical Immunology* **83**: 435–440.

Bock SA (1987) Prospective appraisal of complaints of adverse reactions to foods in children during the first three years of life. *Pediatrics* **79**: 683–688.

Bush RK, Taylor SL, Nordlee JA, and Busse WW (1985) Soybean oil is not allergenic to soybean-sensitive individuals. *Journal of Allergy and Clinical Immunology* **76**: 242–245.

David TJ (1987) Reactions to dietary tartrazine. *Archives of Disease in Childhood* **62**: 119–122.

David TJ (1993) *Food and Food Additive Intolerance in Childhood*. Oxford: Blackwell Scientific.

De Martino M, Novembre E, Galli L *et al.* (1990) Allergy to different fish species in cod-allergic children: *In vivo* and *in vitro* studies. *Journal of Allergy and Clinical Immunology* **86**: 909–914.

Dreborg S (1988) Food allergy in pollen-sensitive patients. *Annals of Allergy* **61**: 41–46.

Herian AM, Taylor SL, and Bush RK (1990) Identification of soybean allergens by immunoblotting with sera from soy-allergic adults. *International Archives of Allergy and Immunology* **92**: 193–198.

Johansson SGO, Bieber T, Dahl R *et al.* (2004) Revised nomenclature for allergy for global use: Report of the Nomenclature

Review Committee of the World Allergy Organisation, October 2003. *Journal of Allergy and Clinical Immunology* **113**: 832–836.

Pastorello EA, Stocchi L, Pravettoni V *et al.* (1989) Role of the elimination diet in adults with food allergy. *Journal of Allergy and Clinical Immunology* **84**: 475–483.

Pauli G, Bessot JC, Dietemann-Molard A, Braun PA, and Thierry R (1985) Celery sensitivity: Clinical and immunological correlations with pollen allergy. *Clinical Allergy* **15**: 273–279.

Sampson HA (2004) Update on food allergy. *Journal of Allergy and Clinical Immunology* **113**: 805–819.

Sicherer SH (2002) Food allergy. *Lancet* **360**: 701–710.

Young E, Patel S, Stoneham M, Rona R, and Wilkinson JD (1987) The prevalence of reaction to food additives in a survey population. *Journal of the Royal College of Physicians of London* **21**: 241–247.

Diagnosis and Management

T J David, University of Manchester, Manchester, UK

Documenting Possible Food Allergies

The diagnosis of food allergy is made from the history, supported by investigations and by responses to avoidance of specific food triggers. Since the value of investigations is limited, it is especially important to obtain a clear history. There are a number of practical points to be made:

- **Speed of onset.** In general, the quicker the onset of the allergic reaction, the more reliable is the history. If a child develops a violent allergic reaction within a minute or two after ingesting a food, it is much easier to link the reaction to a specific food than if a reaction only occurs hours or days after eating a food.
- **Coincidences need to be excluded.** If a child becomes unwell (e.g., starts wheezing) an hour after eating a specific food, the wheezing could be caused by the food, or it could just be a coincidence. The more times that such a sequence has been observed, the more likely it is that there is a cause and effect relationship.
- **Observations need to be tested for internal consistency.** Someone may believe that he or she is allergic to a food if a symptom (e.g., urticaria) occurs on (say) three occasions after eating a specific food. It is important to find out:
  1. Whether the subject has had the same symptoms on other occasions when the suspect food trigger was not taken.

  2. Whether the subject has taken the suspect food on one or more other occasions without any adverse effects.

Failure to seek inconsistencies such as these is one factor that is responsible for the overdiagnosis of food allergy.

Documenting a Diagnosis of Food Allergy

If it is reported that someone is allergic to an item, it is important to probe further and find out on what basis the person has been deemed allergic. It is common to find children and adults who are believed to be allergic to a food solely on the basis of tests such as skin tests or blood tests, which are in fact almost wholly unreliable (see below). It is also common for people to believe that they are allergic to something because a health professional said so one day, which on further enquiry turns out to be on flimsy or nonexistent grounds.

Another common problem is the misinterpretation of a sequence of events. For example, a child with an ear infection is given an antibiotic, and 3 days later gets diarrhea, so the parents come to believe the child is allergic to the antibiotic. In fact the cause of the diarrhea is far more likely to be either an underlying viral infection, or a disturbance of the gut flora. Another example is the report of a child who is believed to be allergic to sesame seeds because of reactions occurring after eating buns coated with sesame seeds; many such children are in fact not allergic to sesame seeds but are reacting to the egg glaze that has been used as an adhesive for the seed coating. Another common example is the child with asthma who coughs and wheezes after drinking a diluted orange squash drink, with the result that it is believed that the child is reacting to the yellow-orange coloring agent tartrazine. If fact such reactions are more likely to be due to sulfite preservatives in the squash; sulfites trigger symptoms in 60% or more of children with asthma.

Practical Diagnostic Difficulties

Multiple Mechanisms

Reactions to foods are a heterogeneous group of disorders caused by a variety of different immunological and pharmacological mechanisms. In any individual case, the precise mechanism is often not known. No single type of laboratory test could possibly cover all the different types of possible mechanisms of reactions to foods. Even if one focuses on food allergy, there are a number of different possible immunological mechanisms, including IgE-antibody mediated, cell mediated, and circulating immune complexes.

Inability to Predict Outcome

In many situations (e.g., atopic disease), the subject wants to know whether there will be any benefit from food avoidance (e.g., not drinking cows' milk or not eating apples). Even if there were valid tests for the diagnosis of food intolerance, the outcome of avoidance measures depends on a number of other variables. Allergen avoidance may succeed for the following reasons:

1. the patient was intolerant to the item;
2. coincidental improvement; and
3. placebo response.

The reasons why a trial of food avoidance may fail to help can be summarized as:

1. The subject is not allergic to the food.
2. The period of elimination was too short. For example, where a child has an enteropathy (damage to the small intestine) due to food allergy, it may take a week or more for improvement in symptoms to occur.
3. The food has been incompletely avoided. This may happen in a subject supposedly on a cows' milk protein-free diet who still continues to receive food that contains cows' milk proteins such as casein or whey.
4. The subject is allergic to other items, which have not been avoided. For example, a child with an allergy to cows' milk protein who fails to improve when given a soy-based milk to which they also have an allergy.
5. Coexisting or intercurrent disease, for example, gastroenteritis in a child with loose stools who is trying a cows' milk-free diet.
6. The patient's symptoms are trivial and have been exaggerated or do not exist at all and have either been imagined or made up by the parents.

It is unrealistic to expect there to be a simple test that can overcome all these problems.

Diagnostic Tests

Skin Prick Tests

The principle of skin prick tests is that the skin weal and flare reaction to an allergen demonstrates the presence of mast-cell-fixed antibody, which is mainly IgE antibody. IgE antibody is produced in plasma cells, and is distributed in the circulation to all parts of the body, so that sensitization is generalized and therefore can be demonstrated by skin testing. In the presence of specific IgE antibody, mast cells in the skin release histamine, which in turn causes a visible weal and flare reaction in the skin.

The procedure involves a drop of allergen solution being placed on the skin, which is then pricked with a hypodermic needle. Two control solutions should also be used: the diluent, in order to detect false-positive reactions; and a positive control (e.g., a histamine solution), to enable comparison with a positive result of an allergen solution. The skin prick test induces a response that reaches a peak in 8–9 min for histamine and 12–15 min for allergens. The size of the weal reaction (and not the larger red flare) is measured.

There are numerous problems with skin prick tests, including:

1. There is no agreed definition about what constitutes a positive reaction.
2. The size of the weal depends to some extent on the potency of the extract.
3. Antihistamines and tricyclic antidepressants suppress the histamine-induced weal and flare response of a skin test. The suppressive effect of antihistamines may last from a week up to several months for some of the more recently introduced nonsedating antihistamines.
4. False-positive tests: skin prick test reactivity may be present in subjects with no clinical evidence of allergy or intolerance. This is sometimes described as 'asymptomatic hypersensitivity' or 'subclinical sensitization.' Whilst many with positive skin prick tests will never develop the allergy, some subjects with positive skin prick tests do develop symptoms later. However, since the test cannot identify those who are going to develop symptoms, the skin test information is of no practical value.
5. False-positive results: skin prick test reactivity may persist after clinical evidence of intolerance has subsided. For example, in a study of children with egg allergy, it was noted that 5 out of 11 who grew out of egg allergy had persistently positive skin prick tests after the allergy had disappeared.
6. False-negative tests: skin prick tests are negative in some subjects with genuine food allergies.
7. Skin prick tests mainly detect IgE antibody. However, many adverse reactions to food are not IgE mediated, in which case skin prick tests can be expected to be negative. Taking cows'

milk protein intolerance as an example, patients with quick reactions often have positive skin prick tests to cows' milk protein, but those with delayed reactions usually have negative skin prick tests.

8. False-negative results are a problem in infants and toddlers, when the weal size is much smaller than later in life.

9. There is a poor correlation between the results of provocation tests (e.g., double-blind food challenges) and skin prick tests. For example, in one study of 31 children with a strongly positive (weal >3 mm in diameter) skin prick test to peanut, only 16 (56%) had symptoms when peanuts were administered.

10. Commercial food extracts (sometimes heat treated) and fresh or frozen raw extracts may give different results (more positives with raw foods), reflecting the fact that some patients are allergic to certain foods only when taken in a raw state. In others the reverse is the case.

Skin prick tests are mainly used in research studies. The results of skin tests cannot be taken alone, and standard textbooks on allergy acknowledge that "the proper interpretation of results requires a thorough knowledge of the history and physical findings." The problems in clinical practice are, for example, whether or not a subject with atopic disease (eczema, asthma, or hay fever) or symptoms suggestive of food intolerance will benefit from attempts to avoid certain foods or food additives. However, skin prick test results are unreliable predictors of response to such measures.

Skin test results are known to be misleading in cases of inhalant allergy (e.g., allergy to dust mites or grass pollen) but skin prick tests for food allergy are especially unreliable because of the large number of false-positive and false-negative reactions.

Intradermal Testing

Intradermal testing comprises the intradermal injection of 0.01–0.05 ml of an allergen extract. It can cause fatal generalized allergic reaction (anaphylaxis), and is only performed if a preliminary skin prick test is negative. Intradermal tests are more sensitive than skin prick testing, and hence also produce even more false-positive reactions, making the interpretation of the results of intradermal testing even more difficult than that for skin prick testing. The difficulty in interpretation of the results, the pain of intradermal injections, and the risk of anaphylaxis mean that intradermal testing has no place in the routine investigation of food allergy.

Skin Application of Food Prior to Food Challenges

There is one situation where direct application of food to the skin may be of practical value, and that is prior to a food challenge in a child in whom one fears an anaphylactic reaction. An example might be a 6-month-old infant with a history of a severe allergic reaction to egg. If the parents wish to see if the child has outgrown the allergy without directly administering egg and risking a violent reaction, a simple approach is to rub some raw egg white into the skin and observe the skin for a few minutes. If the skin application of egg in this way causes an urticarial reaction, then a gradual diminution and disappearance of this response during the succeeding months and years can probably be taken to indicate the development of tolerance, and a continuing brisk response to skin contact would constitute a deterrent to an oral challenge. However, this is only an approximate guide, and there are a number of possible reasons why such testing may give false-positive (e.g., using a raw food when the food is usually eaten cooked, such as egg or potato) or false-negative (e.g., the child is receiving antihistamine drug) results.

Tests for Circulating IgE Antibodies: the Radioallergosorbent (RAST) Test

The radioallergosorbent (RAST) test is the best known of a number of laboratory procedures for the detection and measurement of circulating IgE antibody. Unfortunately, the clinical interpretation of RAST test results is subject to most of the same pitfalls as that for skin prick testing. Additional problems with RAST tests are the cost, and the fact that a very high level of total circulating IgE (e.g., in children with severe atopic eczema) may cause a false-positive result. Depending upon the criteria used for positivity, there is a fair degree of correlation between the RAST test and skin prick test results.

Provocation Tests

A provocation test may be useful to confirm a history of allergy. An example might be a child who developed wheezing and urticaria minutes after eating a rusk that contained, as its main ingredients, wheat and cows' milk protein. To determine which component, if any, caused the reaction, oral challenges with individual components can be conducted.

However, the results of provocation tests cannot prove that improvement in a disease has been caused by food avoidance. For example, a child with atopic eczema is put on a diet avoiding many foods, and the eczema improves. This improvement could be a coincidence, a placebo effect, or due to the diet. Just because the child is shown to react to a single food does not prove that avoidance of that food was the cause of the improvement.

Open and blind challenges   Where the subject and the observer knows the identity of the administered material at the time of the challenge, the procedure is said to be an 'open' challenge. In a 'single-blind challenge' the observer but not the patient or family know the identity of the test material. To avoid bias on the part of the observer, a double-blind challenge is required. A 'double blind' challenge involves exposing the subject to a challenge substance, which is either the item under investigation or an indistinguishable inactive (placebo) substance. Neither the subject nor the observer knows the identity of the administered material at the time of the challenge or during the subsequent period of observation.

The purpose of provocation tests   The aim of a food challenge is to study the consequences of food or food additive ingestion. Provocation tests are helpful:

1. to confirm a history (parents' observations of alleged food allergy are notoriously unreliable, as are adults' beliefs about their own allergies);
2. to confirm the diagnosis, for example, of cows' milk protein allergy in infancy, where the diagnostic criteria include improvement on elimination diet and relapse on reintroduction;
3. to see if a subject has grown out of a food intolerance; and
4. as a research procedure.

The food challenge should replicate normal food consumption in terms of dose, route, and state of food. It should also be performed in such a way that the history can be verified. Thus, for example, there is no point solely looking for an immediate reaction if the parents report a delayed reaction.

Open food challenges are the simplest approach, but open food challenges run the risk of bias influencing the parents' (or doctors') observations. Often this is unimportant. But in some cases belief in food intolerance may be disproportionate, and where this is suspected there is no substitute for a double-blind placebo-controlled challenge. An open challenge may be an open invitation to the overdiagnosis of food intolerance. For example, in the UK parents widely believe that there is an association between food additives and bad behavior, but in one series, double-blind challenges with tartrazine and benzoic

acid were negative in all cases in a study of 24 children with a clear parental description of adverse reaction.

The double-blind placebo-controlled challenge is regarded as the state-of-the-art technique to confirm or refute histories of adverse reactions to foods. The ability to unravel food-related problems is said to be limited only by the imagination of the physician and a clever dietitian. In fact, the technique is subject to a number of potential limitations, not all of which can be overcome.

Effect of dose   In some cases of food intolerance, minute quantities of food (e.g., traces of cows' milk protein) are sufficient to provoke florid and immediate symptoms. In other cases, much larger quantities of food are required to provoke a response. Hill *et al.* demonstrated that whereas 8–10 g of cows' milk powder (corresponding to 60–70 ml of milk) was adequate to provoke an adverse reaction in some patients with cows' milk protein allergy, others (with late onset symptoms and particularly atopic eczema) required up to 10 times this volume of milk daily for more than 48 h before symptoms developed.

Concealing large doses is difficult   Standard capsules that contain up to 500 mg of food are suitable for validation of immediate reactions to tiny quantities of food, but concealing much larger quantities of certain foods (especially those with a strong smell, flavor, or color) can be very difficult.

Route of administration   Reactions to food occurring within the mouth are likely to be missed if the challenge by-passes the oral route, e.g., administration of foods in a capsule or via a nasogastric tube. In practice, patients whose symptoms are exclusively confined to the mouth are unusual, and where there is a history of purely oral reactions an alternative challenge procedure can be employed. In subjects who are intolerant to sulfites, it is well recognized that the administration of sulfites in capsules or directly into the stomach via a nasogastric tube usually fails to provoke an adverse reaction, whereas the oral administration of solution will succeed in doing so.

Problems with capsules   Capsules are unsuitable for use in children who cannot swallow large capsules, and this is a major limitation as most cases of suspected food allergy are in infants and toddlers. Furthermore, it is unsatisfactory to allow patients or parents to break open capsules and mix the contents with food or drink, as the color (e.g., tartrazine) or smell (e.g., fish) will be difficult or impossible to conceal and the challenge will no longer be blind.

Anaphylactic shock danger There is a danger of producing anaphylactic shock, even if it had not occurred on previous exposure to the food. For example, in Goldman's classic study of cows' milk protein intolerance, anaphylactic shock had been noted prior to cows' milk challenge in 5 out of 89 children, but another 3 developed anaphylactic shock as a new symptom after cows' milk challenge. In a study of 80 children with atopic eczema treated with elimination diets, anaphylactic shock occurred in 4 out of 1862 food challenges. The risk appears to be greatest for those who have received elemental diets.

Effect of disease activity A food challenge performed during a quiescent phase of the disease (e.g., urticaria, eczema, or asthma) may fail to provoke an adverse reaction.

Additive effect of triggers Although some patients react repeatedly to challenges with single foods, it is possible (but unproven) that some patients only react adversely when multiple allergens are given together. There certainly are some subjects who only react in the presence of a nonfood trigger, such as exercise or taking aspirin.

Special types of provocation testing Other than giving a suspect food by mouth, and asking the subject to swallow it, there are some alternative approaches, which are outlined below.

Oral mucosal challenge A small portion of food is applied to the mucosa inside the mouth, and one looks for reactions such as swelling of the lips, and tingling or irritation of the mouth or tongue, possibly followed by other more generalized symptoms such as urticaria, asthma, vomiting, abdominal pain, or anaphylactic shock. Patients with food intolerance commonly make use of these oral symptoms, spitting out and avoiding further consumption of a food that provokes the symptom.

Gastric mucosal challenge In this procedure, an allergen is applied directly to the gastric mucosa via an endoscope, and the mucosa is then observed for signs of a reaction. In addition, it is possible to take biopsies of the gastric mucosa to study the histological changes and measure the tissue concentration of mediators of inflammation such as histamine.

Rectal challenges The standard test to confirm a diagnosis of celiac disease is the jejunal biopsy, in which a small portion of jejunal mucosa is obtained with the aid of a special capsule that is swallowed, and which passes into the small intestine. When in the correct location, the capsule is triggered and withdrawn; it contains a portion of intestinal mucosa, which can then be examined under the microscope. Alternatively, gluten can be instilled into the rectum, in order to look for a reaction that would signify celiac disease. This procedure requires multiple biopsies from the rectum, and it is uncertain whether the results are reliable.

Management

Dietary Elimination

The management of food allergy consists largely of elimination from the diet of the trigger food or foods. Elimination diets are used either for the diagnosis or the treatment of food intolerance, or for both. A diet may be associated with an improvement in symptoms because of intolerance to the food, a placebo effect, or the improvement may have been a coincidence. The degree of avoidance that is necessary to prevent symptoms is highly variable. Some patients are intolerant to minute traces of food, but others may be able to tolerate varying amounts. Strict avoidance and prevention of symptoms are the aims in certain instances, but in many cases it is unknown whether allowing small amounts of a food trigger could lead to either enhanced sensitivity or to the reverse, increasing tolerance. The duration required for dietary avoidance varies. For example, intolerance to food additives may last only a few years, whereas intolerance to peanuts is usually lifelong. Although food allergy is common in children, most have grown out of the problem by the age of 5 years; an important exception is those with nut allergy.

Malnutrition

Malnutrition is a major risk of unsupervised diets.

Calcium Cows' milk is an important source of calcium, and avoidance of cows' milk and its products carries the risk of an inadequate intake of calcium. Unfortunately, it is far from clear what constitutes an adequate intake for various different age groups.

Protein, energy Milk, eggs, fish, meat, wheat, and their respective manufactured food products are important sources of protein and energy. Avoidance of these without the provision of alternative sources of protein and energy runs the risk of an inadequate intake, and growth failure, serious malnutrition, and weight loss are well documented sequelae of unsupervised and inappropriate dietary elimination.

Iodine Cows' milk and dairy products are important sources of dietary iodine. Exclusion of cows' milk products and a number of other items from the diet, coupled with the consumption of large amounts of soy milk, which has been reported to cause hypothyroidism by increasing fecal loss of thyroxine, have resulted in hypothyroidism and growth failure due to dietary iodine deficiency.

High-risk factors The risk of malnutrition from an elimination diet is particularly high in the following situations:

1. The diet is not supervised by a dietitian.
2. There is chronic disease prior to diagnosis, or concurrent chronic disease such as severe atopic eczema. The subject's nutrient requirements may be increased.
3. Malabsorption or enteropathy increases the risk of malabsorption of nutrients.
4. The subject is avoiding sunlight. The risk of vitamin D deficiency may compound the effects of a low calcium intake.
5. The subject is already on a diet that excludes multiple foods, e.g., vegan or macrobiotic diet.

The Role of the Dietitian

The dietitian has three roles in the management of elimination diets. One is to ensure that the resulting diet is nutritionally adequate, and to prevent potential deficiency states by recommending (in an infant) appropriate amounts of infant milk formula, and (in older children or adults) supplements of calcium, vitamins, and so on. Another role is to advise how to avoid specific foods, particularly those contained in manufactured foods. Third, the dietitian makes suggestions as to how to make the diet practical and palatable, and suggests recipes for use with a limited range of foods (e.g., how to make biscuits with potato flour).

Cows' Milk Protein Avoidance

Any form of cows' milk, whether fresh, skimmed, condensed, or evaporated, needs to be avoided. Also forbidden are milk products that contain casein, whey, and nonfat milk solids. Where milk substitutes are required, the choice lies between formulas based on soy protein, casein hydrolysate, or whey hydrolysate. Soya formulas are cheaper, but unsuitable for those who are also intolerant to soya.

Butter, margarine, cream, cheese, ice cream, and yogurt all need to be avoided. Fats that can be used instead include margarines made from pure vegetable fat (e.g., Tomor) and lard. Caution is required with baby foods, as a large number of manufactured products, e.g., rusks, contain milk protein. A common trap is so-called 'vegetarian' cheese, often wrongly believed to be safe for subjects with cows' milk allergy. In fact, it differs from ordinary cheese only in the use of nonanimal rennet and is unsuitable for people with cows' milk allergy. Meat, game, and poultry are all allowed, but sausages and pies should be avoided unless it is known that they are milk free. Intolerance to cows' milk protein is not a reason to avoid beef. Eggs are allowed, but not custard or scrambled egg which may contain milk. Fish is permitted, unless it is cooked in batter (which unless otherwise stated should be assumed to contain milk) or milk. Lemon curd, chocolate spread, chocolate (unless stated to be milk-free), toffee, fudge, caramels, and butterscotch are all unsuitable. All ordinary cereals (e.g., oats) are allowed, but caution is required with manufactured breakfast cereals, some of which contain milk powder.

It is essential to check the list of ingredients on the label of any manufactured foods. There is a special problem with unwrapped foods, because there is no label of ingredients. Examples include bread, sausages, or confectionery.

Egg Avoidance

Eggs (both the white and the yolk) and all products that contain egg or albumen must be avoided. As well as hen's eggs, eggs of other birds such as geese, turkeys, and quails must be avoided. Eggs are widely used to make cakes and are sometimes used in the manufacture of bread. Egg wash or glaze is commonly brushed on to the surface of rolls, buns, or baps, and also bread, cakes, and pastry used in puddings (e.g., apple pie). Sweets can be a hazard because they are usually sold without information about ingredients, and egg is included in several products.

Mayonnaise normally contains egg; custard usually does not, with the exception of egg custard and egg custard tarts. Eggs are an essential ingredient of souffles and certain sauces, such as Bearnaise or Hollandaise sauce.

Egg allergy is not a reason to avoid eating chicken.

Soy Avoidance

The major difficulty is mass-produced bread, because in the UK soy is often included as an ingredient in flour. Soy is also found in manufactured products that contain hydrolyzed or textured vegetable protein, and minced beef, which unless described as 'pure beef' has been known to include quantities of soy protein.

Wheat-Free and Gluten-Free

These terms cause confusion; they are not interchangeable. Subjects who are allergic to wheat cannot tolerate foods that contain any type of wheat. Subjects with celiac disease can tolerate all wheat proteins other than the gluten fraction.

Peanut Avoidance

Peanut is also known as groundnut or arachis, so these three names need to be sought on labels of manufactured foods as well as some pharmaceutical products. The difficulty comes with 'vegetable oil,' which may include peanut oil; only by writing to the manufacturer of individual products can the composition of the vegetable oil be determined. It is not known to what extent subjects with peanut allergy should avoid peanut oil. Most peanut oil used in food manufacture is highly refined, and contains only very minute quantities of peanut protein. In a number of small-scale studies, subjects with peanut allergy were found not to react when given highly refined peanut oil. However, it remains possible that such oil contains traces of protein sufficient to result in enhanced reactivity, such that when the subject does ingest peanut accidentally the reaction is worse than previously. On this basis, subjects with peanut allergy should really be advised to avoid peanut oil.

Drug Treatment in the Management of Food Allergy

At present, drug treatment has little part to play in the management of food allergies. There are two exceptions. First, there are a very small number of cases in which the reaction to a food is exclusively gastrointestinal, and in whom the reaction can be blocked by taking the drug sodium cromoglycate by mouth 20 min before the trigger food is swallowed. Second, there are a small number of individuals who develop the life-threatening reaction, of anaphylactic shock when exposed to a trigger food. There are three ways in which anaphylactic shock may prove fatal. First, rapid swelling of the soft tissues in the pharynx may completely obstruct the airway; the treatment is to bypass the obstruction, either by passing an endotracheal tube, or by performing a tracheostomy. Another mechanism is severe shock, with a profound drop in blood pressure; the life-

saving treatment is to restore the circulating volume with intravenous fluids and to give oxygen. The third mechanism is severe bronchoconstriction (asthma); here, the life-saving treatment is with bronchodilator drugs and artificial ventilation. If patients with life-threatening anaphylactic shock are to be saved, they must be given urgent (within minutes) medical attention. For individuals who have already experienced a life-threatening allergic reaction to a food, it is common practice to provide them with a syringe preloaded with adrenaline (epinephrine), with the aim that this should be administered while waiting for medical help. Unfortunately, self-administered adrenaline is not without its hazards (e.g., inadvertent intravenous administration causing fatal cardiac arrest), and there is no proof that it is life saving; indeed, there are many cases in which the subject died despite the use of epinephrine. Nevertheless, it is the best one can do when faced with someone who is experiencing a life-threatening allergic reaction to a food. The need for urgent medical help cannot be overemphasized.

There is little evidence that antihistamine drugs are of any value. It would be reasonable to take a nonsedating fast-acting antihistamine such as terfenadine if experiencing an allergic reaction to a food, but it is questionable whether it will have much effect.

A number of new approaches to the treatment of IgE-mediated food allergy are being examined. In a double-blind placebo-controlled study of monthly injections of a preparation of anti-IgE antibodies, treated patients with peanut allergy required significantly greater amounts of peanut protein to elicit allergic symptoms compared with control subjects. Another anti-IgE preparation has been used in the treatment of asthma but has not been evaluated in peanut allergy. Theoretically, anti-IgE antibody treatment should be protective against multiple food allergens, although it would have to be administered indefinitely. Other experimental approaches include a concoction of traditional Chinese herbs, injection of heat-killed *Escherichia coli* containing mutated recombinant peanut proteins Ara h 1 to Ara h 3, the use of immunostimulatory sequences, and the use of chimeric protein that could form complexes with allergen-specific IgE bound to mast cells and basophils.

Desensitization

In theory it ought to be possible to desensitize subjects with food allergy by giving injections of gradually increasing quantities of an appropriate extract of the food trigger. In practice, such treatment is not available. One at present insurmountable difficulty is that desensitization (also known as hyposensitization) treatment carries a small risk of death from the treatment itself. A subject has a series of injections without any major problem, but then without warning drops dead from anaphylaxis after the next injection. There is some data to show that desensitization performed in this way can work, but such subjects would probably require maintenance injections on a permanent basis, and the very subjects most at risk of fatal anaphylaxis from accidental injection are quite probably also the ones most at risk from fatal anaphylaxis resulting from desensitization treatment.

See also: **Celiac Disease**. **Eggs**. **Food Allergies**: Etiology. **Food Intolerance**. **Lactose Intolerance**. **Malnutrition**: Secondary, Diagnosis and Management.

Further Reading

Acciai MC, Brusi C, Francalanci S, Gola M, and Sertoli A (1991) Skin tests with fresh foods. *Contact Dermatitis* 24: 67–68.

Ancona GR and Schumacher IC (1950) The use of raw foods as skin testing material in allergic disorders. *California Medicine* 73: 473–475.

Bernstein IL (1988) Proceedings of the task force guidelines for standardizing old and new techniques used for the diagnosis and treatment of allergic diseases. *Journal of Allergy and Clinical Immunology* 82: 487–526.

Bock SA, Buckley J, Holst A, and May CD (1977) Proper use of skin tests with food extracts in diagnosis of hypersensitivity to food in children. *Clinical Allergy* 7: 375–383.

Bock SA, Sampson HA, Atkins FM *et al.* (1988) Double-blind, placebo-controlled food challenge as an office procedure: a manual. *Journal of Allergy and Clinical Immunology* 82: 986–997.

Buttriss J (ed.) (2002) *Adverse Reactions to Food.* The Report of a British Nutrition Foundation Task Force. Oxford: Blackwell.

Curran WS and Goldman G (1961) The incidence of immediately reacting allergy skin tests in a "normal" adult population. *Annals of Internal Medicine* 55: 777–783.

David TJ (1984) Anaphylactic shock during elimination diets for severe atopic eczema. *Archives of Disease in Childhood* 59: 983–986.

David TJ (1987) Reactions to dietary tartrazine. *Archives of Disease in Childhood* 62: 119–122.

David TJ (1989) Hazards of challenge tests in atopic dermatitis. *Allergy* 44(suppl. 9): 101–107.

David TJ (1993) In *Food and Food Additive Intolerance in Childhood.* Oxford: Blackwell Scientific Publications.

Demoly P, Piette V, and Bousquet J (1998) In vivo methods for study of allergy. Skin tests, techniques, and interpretation. In Adkinson NF, Yunginger JW, Bisse WW *et al.* (eds.) *Middleton's Allergy Principles & Practice*, 6th edn, pp. 631–643. St. Louis Mosby.

Fontana VJ, Wittig H, and Holt LM (1963) Observations on the specificity of the skin test. The incidence of positive skin tests in allergic and nonallergic children. *Journal of Allergy* 34: 348–353.

Ford RPK and Taylor B (1982) Natural history of egg hypersensitivity. *Archives of Disease in Childhood* 57: 649–652.

Fries JH and Glazer I (1950) Studies on the antigenicity of banana, raw and dehydrated. *Journal of Allergy* 21: 169–175.

Goldman AS, Anderson DW, Sellers WA *et al.* (1963) 1. Oral challenge with milk and isolated milk proteins in allergic children. *Pediatrics* 32: 425–443.

Hill DJ, Duke AM, Hosking CS, and Hudson IL (1988) Clinical manifestations of cows' milk allergy in childhood. II. The diagnostic value of skin tests and RAST. *Clinical Allergy* 18: 481–490.

Josephson BM and Glaser J (1963) A comparison of skin-testing with natural foods and commercial extracts. *Annals of Allergy* 21: 33–40.

Lessof MH, Buisseret PD, Merrett J, Merrett TG, and Wraith DG (1980) Assessing the value of skin tests. *Clinical Allergy* 10: 115–120.

Meglio P, Farinella F, Trogolo E, and Giampietro PG (1988) Immediate reactions following challenge-tests in children with atopic dermatitis. *Allergie Immunologie* 20: 57–62.

Metcalfe DD, Sampson HA, and Simon RA (eds.) (1997) *Food Allergy: Adverse Reactions to Foods and Food Additives*, 2nd edn. Oxford: Blackwell.

Nater JP and Zwartz JA (1967) Atopic allergic reactions due to raw potato. *Journal of Allergy* 40: 202–206.

Patel L, Radivan FS, and David TJ (1994) Management of anaphylactic reactions to food. *Archives of Disease in Childhood* 71: 370–375.

Patterson R, Grammer LC, and Greenberger PA (eds.) (1997) *Allergic Diseases. Diagnosis and Management*, 5th edn. Philadelphia: Lippincott-Raven.

Simons FER (2004) First-aid treatment of anaphylaxis to food: focus on epinephrine. *Journal of Allergy and Clinical Immunology* 113: 837–844.

Voorhorst R (1980) Perfection of skin testing technique. *Allergy* 35: 247–261.

FOOD CHOICE, INFLUENCING FACTORS

A K Draper, University of Westminster, London, UK

Food choice is about why we eat the foods we do. This would appear to be a simple and relatively straightforward matter, but human food choice is a complex phenomenon, difficult to predict, and its analysis is not a simple affair. Many factors influence our food choice, and these encompass biological, psychological, economic, social, and cultural influences. These all operate on different aspects of food choice and vary in terms of their relative strength and influence from person to person and context to context. That said, it is a topic of public health importance for two broad reasons. First, it is important to understand the etiology of those nutritional disorders that can be attributed to dysfunctional patterns of dietary intake. This applies to both deficiency disorders, such as vitamin A deficiency, that are due to inadequate nutrient intakes and diet-related chronic diseases, such as coronary heart disease, that are partly attributable to overconsumption or an imbalanced intake of certain foods and/or nutrients. Second, it is important to reduce morbidity and mortality from these disorders via interventions, such as health education, that are designed to either increase or decrease consumption of specific foods and nutrients. The successful achievement of these objectives relies on an understanding and manipulation of the factors that influence food choice, and there is currently much emphasis on the need for health promotion to be more 'evidence-based.' Food choice, like other so-called health behaviors, is thus an important determinant of health and nutritional status and has been the focus of much research.

One of the significant features of this research is that many different theoretical frameworks drawn from both the natural and the social sciences have been used to study the phenomenon of food choice. These derive from many academic disciplines that include biology and physiology, psychology, social psychology, geography, economics, history, sociology, anthropology, political science, and even philosophy. These all approach the study of food choice in very different ways and identify different factors that influence it. This in part derives from the differing ways in which the phenomenon of food choice and the act of eating have been conceptualized. As noted previously, the question of why we eat what we do is deceptively straightforward, but eating, like sex, presents an ontological or analytical problem: Is eating a purely biological act founded on natural need and determined by physiological mechanisms and whose primary function is the meeting of nutritional requirements or is it a form of intentional social behaviour driven by social, psychological, or economic factors and that may serve nonnutritional ends, such as maintaining social relationships or expressing identity? The particular way in which the nature of food and eating are conceptualized inevitably leads to the identification of different types of factors that are seen to influence it. These methodological differences are compounded in that food choice can also be seen as the outcome of a number of different processes or phases ranging from food production and processing to shopping and finally the act of eating or consumption. Again, different academic disciplines have tended to address different steps within this chain and the way in which they impact on the choice of individuals, households, or wider social groups. Finally, the word 'choice' is somewhat problematic; it is rarely explicitly defined, but it is variously used to refer to acts of food selection that range from unconscious behavioral responses to physiological cues and conscious acts of decision making.

This lack of commensurability in research methods, definition of terms, and the actual object of study thus makes it difficult to review and summarize research findings from across different disciplines regarding the different types of factors that influence food choice. However, the main categories of influence on human food choice can be crudely divided into biological and behavioral factors, psychological factors, economic factors, and social and cultural factors. Within each of these categories, particular factors may be either positive or negative influences in that they may act to encourage or discourage choice of particular food items. These categories of influence are discussed in relation to the theoretical frameworks with which they have been studied and with a brief examination of their explanatory value is given.

Biological and Behavioral Influences

There has been an enormous amount of experimental research conducted on both humans and animals that has sought to identify biological and behavioral mechanisms that regulate food intake. This work is grouped together here with the influences on food choice identified by it because most of this work is based on the assumption that food selection or food choice can be explained by internal physiological processes, and that the principal function served by food and eating is to satisfy nutritional requirements. The notion of choice implicit in such models is therefore not one of conscious decision making but, rather, of choice as the outcome of a physiological or behavioral response to a cue or stimulus that may be either internal or external. The notion of choice thus tends to be elided with that which is eaten, and the unit of analysis is generally that of the individual organism or species.

Many different biological models of food selection have been developed and most of these are based on homeostatic models (i.e., systems that work to maintain a balance between the intake of energy and/or specific nutrients and requirements for them) and are seen to operate via stimulus–response mechanisms of various kinds. Food choice is thus seen as driven either via some kind of internal biofeedback loop that responds to internal physiological states or stimuli, such as states of physiological need, feelings of hunger or satiety, and the energy and nutrient composition of meals, or via detection and response to external cues or influences, such as taste, smell, or the palatability of foods. Various mechanisms have been identified that act to regulate intake of energy as well as individual nutrients, although the evidence to support innate biological mechanisms governing food choice is probably strongest for overall energy intake. Some mechanisms also only appear to act in fairly extreme physiological circumstances, such as the craving for carbohydrates that follows administration of large doses of insulin. With perhaps the exception of salt and water, the evidence linking physiological needs states or cravings with the choice of specific foods is also equivocal.

The regulation of energy balance and appetite in particular has been the subject of a large amount of research. Much of this work has been carried out in relation to obesity and whether this can be linked to a faulty mechanism or genetic defect of some kind. This work is reviewed in detail elsewhere in this encyclopedia, but a number of different mechanisms have been proposed whereby energy intake and balance might be regulated. These include the adaptive thermogenesis theory (now largely discounted, this proposed that energy expenditure was flexible in some individuals and increased to expend excessive energy intakes); nutrient-based models of feeding in which the energy and/or nutrient composition of the diet is considered to lead to appetite suppression via complex gut-fill cues (e.g., the effect of carbohydrates on neurotransmitters and the central nervous system); and the glucostat, lipostat, and leptin theories, which are considered to operate via satiety effects. However, although experimental studies have shown that complex physiological changes are indeed associated with eating, that these vary with what is eaten, and that humans can respond to the covert manipulation of the energy and nutrient composition of our diets, these studies cannot explain the wide variation and flexibility in human food selection or the development of dysfunctional food habits. Humans appear to be more efficient at regulating up (i.e., eating more) when the energy content of the diet is reduced than regulating down. It has been hypothesized that this is the result of evolutionary adaptation to environments in which food supplies were scarce and/or unreliable and in which the ability to deposit energy stores would carry significant advantages. Thus, although there is evidence to support the idea that humans have some kind of appetite control knob (or even knobs) to regulate energy intake, this knob (or knobs) can be overridden, as evidenced by the increasing rates of obesity in many areas of the world.

In relation to external or behavioral cues influencing food choice, there has also been much work investigating relationships between the organoleptic or sensory properties of food, such as taste and palatability, and food preferences and choice. The palatability of food is a complex construct that combines both the sensory qualities of food (taste, smell, and texture) and our hedonic or pleasure response to that food. There has been much work on what makes certain foods more or less palatable. A high fat content, for instance, enhances the palatability of foods, and a liking for high-fat foods appears to be a universal biological disposition. A liking for sweetness and a dislike of bitter flavors also appear to be universal. Again, it has been argued that these carry evolutionary advantages because sweetness is often linked with good dietary energy sources and bitter tastes with foods containing alkaloids and other poisons. Beyond this, however, most likes and dislikes for specific tastes, flavors, textures, and food appear to be learned, often at an early age. Many food aversions, for instance, are very culturally specific.

In summary, although various stimuli, both internal and external, have been shown to influence certain aspects of human food choice, innate biological or behavioral mechanisms alone cannot explain the enormous diversity in human food choice that we see over time and place. As Rozin, a key researcher in the field of food choice, has pointed out, we need to remember that as a species humans are not specialized feeders; we can and do eat an enormous range of foods and diets that satisfy our nutritional requirements. Thus, although there is undoubtedly a physiological base to human nutrition, biology alone cannot explain the complexity of human food choice.

Psychological influences

Much research has been conducted by psychologists and social psychologists on eating behavior, and they have developed a number of different theoretical models within which food choice is conceptualised as a function of specific psychological characteristics or factors. Psychological factors that have been shown to influence food choice include our knowledge, attitudes, emotions, beliefs, intentions, social norms, feelings of self-control or efficacy, cues to act, our early and ongoing experiences, and our relationships with others, including our mothers and other caretakers. These cannot all be reviewed here, but two models that have been particularly influential in relation to the study and attempted manipulation of food choice are discussed. Note that only psychological influences on normative food choice are discussed here and not the etiology of complex psychological disorders, such as anorexia nervosa.

The knowledge–attitudes–practice model (also known as knowledge–attitudes–behavior) is perhaps one of the most enduring models of food choice. This is a knowledge-based theory in which it is assumed that a particular practice or behavior is derived from certain attitudes, which in turn flow from our knowledge base. Although attractive in its simplicity, any causal link between nutritional knowledge alone and subsequent food choice is far from proven, and increasing an individual's level of knowledge does not necessarily lead the individual to alter his or her diet. This model has been largely discounted as providing a valid account of human behavior, but it still remains the model of food choice implicit in health education activities that seek to change our behavior via the provision of information and enhancement of knowledge about nutrition.

A number of more complex and sophisticated models of health behavior have been developed that draw on social psychology and social learning theory. These are called social cognition models because in addition to our attitudes, they incorporate the beliefs and norms that we hold about our social environment. A social cognition model that has been widely applied to the study of food choice is the theory of planned behavior developed by Fishbein and Azjen (originally called the theory of reasoned action). The theory of planned behavior has been very influential and, in brief, it posits that the principal determinant of behavior, including food choice, is our intention to perform it (i.e., our behavioral intention), which in turn is determined by our attitude toward that behavior, our social and subjective norms (these are our beliefs about what we think other people want us to do and our motivation to comply or not with their wishes), and our perceived behavioral control ('Do I think that I can do it?'—a construct similar to that of self-efficacy). Studies using this model have shown correlations between the various components of the model and consumption differences; for instance, women tend to consume less high-fat foods and also tend to have more negative attitudes toward them. They thus illustrate that in terms of psychological influences on our food choice, we tend to eat what we like to eat and intend to eat, although our likes and intentions are modified to some extent by what we think we should eat and feel we can eat.

Economic Influences

Economics has also been called the 'science of choice,' and there has been much important work by economists on the analysis of economic influences on food choice. Within economic approaches, food choice is conceptualized as an act of consumption broadly equivalent to the consumption of other goods, whether they be clothes, tractors, or dishwashers. Food choice is thus largely conflated with purchase by economists and, as with other commodities, a range of economic factors have been identified that act to both constrain and encourage our purchase of particular foods, mostly centering on the interplay between price, demand, and income.

The simplest economic model of food choice is the demand curve, which describes an individual's choice of foods as a function of his or her income and the price of the food. Thus, as the price of a particular food commodity decreases, we tend to buy more of it. As income increases, we also tend to buy more of the food as well as spend more money on food overall (although it constitutes a smaller proportion of overall expenditure, a phenomenon known as Engel's law). As consumers, however, we do not just buy for cheapness or price, and various more sophisticated economic explanations have developed, such as utility theory and indifference theory. These incorporate the notion of demand or satisfaction in addition to price or income. Utility theory states that when making choices to purchase a particular good or product from a bundle of goods, as consumers we seek to achieve maximum utility. The term 'utility' refers to the satisfaction of needs, wants, tastes, and aspirations, and choice is conceptualized in terms of maximizing these. Thus, the purchase of a food with high prestige value, such as caviar, makes 'sense' in terms of utility theory if not in terms of nutrition. Indifference theory takes the concept of satisfaction further to explain how we make choices between different combinations of goods or foods for maximum satisfaction; as we eat less of one food, such as vegetables, and more of another, such as fruit, the less willing we become to give up some vegetables to get even more fruit. Economic explanations thus move from accounts of choice on the basis of cheapness to combinations of cost-consciousness with maximizing satisfaction or utility within the budgetary constraints of income.

A number of elegant economic laws have been developed to explain and predict food consumption and patterns of expenditure, such as the wonderfully named law of starchy staples. This predicts that as income increases, traditional staple foods are replaced with more refined staples (e.g., the replacement of sorghum or millet with white rice or wheat), and this is a pattern of change that is being seen today in countries in transition. Such 'laws' and economic analyses demonstrate how factors such as price and income influence food choice and set constraints to it.

Social and Cultural Influences

As Douglas, a famous anthropologist, stated, food is not feed, and food and eating serve many nonnutritional social functions, such as the expression of identity whether individual or national, the maintenance or rupture of social relationships, and religious and symbolic functions. These subtly influence not only what we eat but also how and where we eat and with whom we eat. Food and drink are not taken at random, but within the context of social exchanges between people and within social contexts, such as the family. Therefore, argue the social scientists, to understand the food choices of individuals we must understand the social contexts within which they occur and also the social rules that influence many aspects of our food choice. These can be seen to work at a number of different levels or in a number of ways on the food choice of individuals.

At the most basic level, it is arguably cultural rules of food use that specify the edible versus the inedible. Although the definition of 'food' might appear to be self-evident, there is huge variation cross-culturally in what is classified as edible. This is perhaps illustrated best by examining differences in what are considered edible animal species in different societies (guinea pigs—a tasty snack or domestic pet?). Beyond this basic definition of the edible versus inedible, in all cultures foods are further classified into complex subgroupings, such as hot and cold foods, foods appropriate for meals, snacks, and special events, foods to be eaten/avoided during pregnancy, and so forth. Cultural rules may also specify the food needs of different categories of people (e.g., the young or the pregnant), meal formats and their patterning over time, the way in which food is eaten and prepared, and the allocation of food within an household.

Taken as a whole, sociological studies of food can be read as a form of lay epidemiology that illustrates that not only are the attributes and values that we give to food largely culturally derived but also beliefs about food are culturally constructed and not the product of ignorance or irrational prejudices. Social science approaches to food choice thus study how choices about food are constructed and negotiated in the context of everyday life and how social rules and contexts influence this, and they can offer insights into what otherwise might appear to be irrational or dysfunctional food choices.

Table 1 A hierarchical model of food choice

Edible substances (as defined by culture and physiology)	
Excluded by	**Subsets of**
Culture and rules of allocation	Permissible foods
Availability and cost	Available and affordable foods
Palatability preferences, attitudes, experience	Preferred and chosen foods

A Hierarchy of Constraints?

There is thus a large range of factors that influence human food choice. These are a complex blend of both positive and negative influences that either encourage or constrain our choice of particular foods as well as a combination of biological, psychological, economic, and social factors. These all operate in very different ways and on different aspects of this phenomenon called food choice. How can these be sorted into any kind of scheme or hierarchy to assess their relative importance in any particular context? Various composite models of food choice have been developed, but these often become so global as to be almost meaningless. Following Wheeler, one solution is to turn the issue on its head and start with an analysis of the factors that constrain or limit choice and so identify the range of choice open to an individual in any particular context and what determines this (**Table 1**).

The relative importance of particular influences or constraints will vary from one context to another and also with how they interact, but such a hierarchical framework allows identification of what the relevant factors may be in any given situation and their relative importance for any given individual and thus what degree of choice is actually available to them.

See also: **Appetite**: Physiological and Neurobiological Aspects; Psychobiological and Behavioral Aspects. **Eating Disorders**: Anorexia Nervosa; Bulimia Nervosa; Binge Eating. **Energy**: Balance; Adaptation. **Hunger**. **Obesity**: Definition, Etiology and Assessment. **Religious Customs, Influence on Diet**. **Socio-economic Status**.

Further Reading

Beardsworth A and Keil T (1997) *Sociology on the Menu: An Invitation to the Study of Food and Society.* London: Routledge.

Conner M and Norman P (eds.) (1995) *Predicting Health Behaviour.* Buckingham, UK: Open University Press.

Fine B, Heasman M, and Wright J (1996) *Consumption in the Age of Affluence: The World of Food.* London: Routledge.

French SJ (1999) The effects of specific nutrients on the regulation of feeding behaviour in human subjects. *Proceedings of the Nutrition Society* 58: 533–540.

Germov J and Williams L (eds.) (1999) *A Sociology of Food and Nutrition: The Social Appetite*. Oxford: Oxford University Press.

Messer E (1984) Anthropological perspectives on diet. *Annual Review of Anthropology* **13**: 205–249.

Murcott A (1998) Food choice, the social sciences and the 'Nation's Diet' research programme. In: Murcott A (ed.) *The Nation's Diet: The Social Science of Food Choice*. New York: Longman.

Rozin P (1996) Towards a psychology of food and eating: From motivation to model to meaning, morality and metaphor. *Current Directions in Psychological Science* **5**: 1–7.

Rozin P and Schulkin J (1990) Food selection. In: Stricker EM (ed.) *Handbook of Behavioral Neurobiology*, vol. 10, pp. 297–328. New York: Plenum.

Wheeler EF (1992) What determines food choice and what does food choice determine? *BNF Bulletin* **17**: 65–73.

FOOD COMPOSITION DATA

S P Murphy, University of Hawaii, Honolulu, HI, USA

Overview: Why Compile Food Composition Tables?

Food composition data are an integral component of evaluating and planning nutrient intakes. Without information on the nutrient content of foods, it is not possible to convert dietary intake data, based on foods consumed, into nutrient intake data. The science of developing accurate food composition data has advanced substantially with the advent of sophisticated laboratory equipment and methods for food analyses as well as increasingly powerful computers that are used to compile and store the results. The International Network of Food Data Systems (INFOODS) at the Food and Agriculture Organization has provided guidelines and training to help countries improve their food composition tables. However, comprehensive analyses of the many nutrients and other bioactive components of foods remain both challenging and expensive, and given the enormous variety of foods consumed throughout the world, food composition tables are often incomplete. Often, the intake calculations that are based on these tables must be regarded as estimates of true nutrient intakes. Nonetheless, for many purposes related to promoting health, nutrient intake estimates are essential and can lead to actions that improve the health of both individuals and populations.

Procedures for Compiling Food Composition Data

Nutrients to Include

As the number of recognized biologically active components of foods increases, compilers of food composition tables are faced with an ever-expanding list of possible nutrients and other components to include. Some of these are given in **Table 1**. The current version of the US Department of Agriculture's Standard Reference Database (release 16-1) contains up to 125 components for each of more than 6600 foods. Because a wide variety of analytic methods is available for determining and reporting nutrient levels in foods, it is useful to have a common convention for naming the nutrients. Many compilers are using standard nutrient names, called tag names, that have been proposed by INFOODS.

Nutrient values in a food composition table normally reflect the level in 100 g of the food item. Thus, the intake of a nutrient from a specific food can be calculated if the amount consumed is recorded in gram weights (e.g., if 100 g of whole milk has 119 mg of calcium, and a person drank a cup of milk weighing 244 g, then the intake of calcium from the cup of milk would be 291 mg). Many food composition tables also contain the weight of typical portions of each food item, and thus the nutrient profile for these portions can readily be calculated.

A related issue is whether to show nutrient profiles per 100 g of the food as consumed or 100 g of the food as purchased. Because some parts of a food may be discarded as inedible, the nutrients per 100 g as purchased will be lower for these foods. For example, a banana skin is approximately one-third of the weight of a banana. If 100 g of a banana without peel has an energy content of approximately 90 kcal, then the energy content of 100 g of banana with peel is only 60 kcal. Composition tables may simply carry a variable for the average percentage of the food that is edible, but it is obviously important to match the method used to measure the food intake (with or without inedible portions) with the way the composition of the food is given in the table.

Foods to Include

There is also a constantly expanding number of foods available in most regions of the world due to changing

Table 1 Nutrients and other food components that are often included in food composition tables

Macronutrients	Typical units (usually per 100 g)	Related components that may be present in a table
Energy	kcal and/or kJ	
Protein	g	Individual amino acids; nitrogen
Fat	g	
Carbohydrate	g	May be calculated by difference (100 minus grams of the other macronutrients)
Alcohol	g	
Water	g	
Ash	g	
Carbohydrates and fiber		
Sugars	g	Individual monosaccharides and disaccharides
Starch	g	
Dietary fiber	g	May be divided into soluble and insoluble fiber
Nonstarch polysaccharides	g	
Lignans	μg	
Glycemic load	g	Glycemic index
Fats		
Saturated fatty acids	g	Individual fatty acids
Monounsaturated fatty acids	g	Individual fatty acids
Polyunsaturated fatty acids	g	Individual fatty acids
Omega-3 fatty acids	g	
Omega-6 fatty acids	g	
Trans fatty acids	g	
Conjugated linoleic acid	mg	
Cholesterol	mg	
Minerals		
Calcium	mg	
Phosphorus	mg	
Magnesium	mg	
Iron	mg	Heme iron, non-heme iron
Zinc	mg	
Sodium	mg	
Potassium	mg	
Selenium	μg	
Copper	μg	
Chromium	μg	
Molybdenum	μg	
Manganese	mg	
Fluoride	mg	
Iodine	μg	
Vitamins		
Vitamin A	IU, μg RE, μg RAE	
Carotenoids	mg	Individual carotenoids
Retinol	μg	
Vitamin E	mg α-tocopherol	mg α-tocopherol equivalents, synthetic α-tocopherol
Tocopherols	mg	Individual tocopherols
Vitamin C	mg	
Vitamin D	μg	
Thiamin	mg	
Riboflavin	mg	
Niacin	mg	Niacin equivalents
Folate	μg, μg dietary folate equivalents	Synthetic folic acid
Vitamin B_6	mg, μg	
Vitamin B_{12}	μg	
Pantothenic acid	mg	
Biotin	μg	
Vitamin K	μg	
Other food components		
Isoflavonoids	mg	Individual isoflavonoids
Flavonoids	mg	Individual flavonoids

agricultural practices, increases in imported foods, and new commercial product formulations. Including all these foods in a single composition database has not been attempted, and instead, regions and countries have focused on compiling food composition tables that are specific for their populations. Several types of foods are usually found in such composition tables.

Basic agricultural commodities are considered essential in most tables. These include both plant and animal foods that are typically consumed by the population of interest. Frequently, composite values are given in composition tables and reflect an average of multiple samples collected from different regions of the country. For example, nutrient profiles of oranges in the United States are an average of different species of oranges grown primarily in California and Florida; the average is weighted to reflect the production of different types of oranges. Composition tables may contain both cooked and raw values for a food item, which can be helpful if a food is consumed both ways (e.g., tomatoes). Because nutrients may be lost during cooking, and also because the water and fat contents may change, it is important to have nutrient values that correspond to the form of the food that is actually consumed. In addition to cooked and uncooked forms, basic foods may also be available in processed forms, such as canned, frozen, or dried. Many of these processing procedures can alter the nutrients in foods, and thus it is sometimes desirable to have composition data for the differently processed forms of the food.

In addition to basic foods and ingredients, food composition tables usually also contain values for mixed dishes. Some of these mixtures may reflect common recipes that are used in the home, and others may represent commercially available foods, either in food stores or in restaurants. Because recipes may vary greatly, it is particularly useful if the software that accesses the composition table allows the user to alter the recipe ingredients.

Food Descriptors to Use

It is a challenging task to clearly and completely describe the foods that are in the food composition table. Food names for most tables are devised by the compilers using common names plus appropriate descriptors (e.g., cooked, raw, and canned). Ideally, the food descriptors should fully define the food item so there is no ambiguity about the scientific name, the part of the plant or animal that is consumed, and any cooking or processing that has been applied. Several schemes for describing foods have been proposed, including guidelines from INFOODS and the LanguaL system that is used by several European countries.

Sources of Composition Data

Food composition data come from a variety of sources (**Table 2**). Those that are based on laboratory analyses of foods are considered the gold standard for composition tables. Appropriate methods are often specified by the Association of Official Analytical Chemists. Accurate analytic procedures also should incorporate quality control methods, including the proper use of internal standards, and the analysis of duplicate samples to determine intersample variability.

The scheme that is used to obtain and prepare the food samples for analysis is also important. Ideally, the sample collection scheme would match the foods that are reported by the population of interest. For example, if the purpose of the analysis is to determine the nutrient content of a specific person's diet, then the analyses should be performed for a composite of the foods actually consumed or, in the case of feeding studies, for a composite of the foods to be fed. Because such analyses are usually not feasible, more general composition data are often used. Most food composition tables are intended for use across a broad population, and thus the sampling scheme should reflect the types of foods typically consumed. Often, this is an

Table 2 Sources of data for food composition tables

Source	Comments on accuracy
Analytic values	
By the table compilers	Generally the most accurate type of data if sampling and analyses are appropriate.
From published literature	May not be correct if the food items differ on important characteristics.
From the food industry	Values from food labels may be underestimates for nutrients added to foods.
From another composition table	May not be correct if the food items differ on important characteristics.
Imputed values	
Based on a similar food	The accuracy of this process depends on how closely the foods can be matched.
Assumed zero	Can be very accurate for some nutrients (fiber in animal products; vitamin B_{12} in plant products)
Calculated values	
From another form of the same food	Usually requires assumptions about changes such as losses due to cooking.
From a recipe	Typical recipe ingredients and proportions may be difficult to collect.
From a product formulation	Useful method for obtaining nutrient values that are not on the product label.

expensive and challenging task, particularly for national and regional tables. Once the sampling plan is devised, it is also necessary to decide on the protocol for storing and preparing the samples for analysis. Considerable nutrient losses can occur if samples are handled improperly because many nutrients are labile to heat, light, and exposure to oxygen. Methods of indicating the quality of analytic data for foods have been proposed, including attaching a confidence code to each data point so that users can decide if the composition data are appropriate for their purposes.

Analytic data are published in various forms. Many countries or regions publish tables, either printed or in electronic form. For example, large tables are compiled by the US Department of Agriculture and also by the Royal Society of Chemistry and the Department for Environment, Food and Rural Affairs in the United Kingdom. Other sources of analytic data include journal articles and books. A particularly useful journal for food composition values is the *Journal of Food Composition and Analysis*, edited by the INFOODS secretariat.

However, analytic data may not be available for all foods and nutrients of interest, and time and cost constraints may prohibit chemical analyses of these foods. In some cases, these values are left blank, and such missing values are assumed to be the same as zero values by most programs that calculate nutrient intakes. Because an appropriately estimated value for a nutrient is usually superior to a value of zero, several methods are used to derive such estimations. A frequent approach is to obtain data from the food composition table of another region or country. If the foods are of the same genus and species, then the nutrient profiles should be similar. Although variations can occur due to different cultivars within a species, as well as different conditions during growing, storage, and processing, such borrowed composition values are considered preferable to a missing value. Another approach to estimating nutrient profiles is to impute a value from a similar food that does have analytic data. If the known nutrients are similar for two foods (e.g., the macronutrient profiles), and the type of food is similar (e.g., dark green vegetables), then the missing value may be replaced with an imputed value from the similar food. Sometimes, calculations are performed to adjust for differences between the foods. Values for a cooked food can be imputed from a raw food by applying factors for nutrient losses during cooking and adjusting for differences in moisture (and sometimes also fat) content.

Another common method of obtaining composition data is to calculate the values from the ingredients in a mixture. For home-prepared foods, such calculations involve determining the proportions of each ingredient (a recipe) and any changes in moisture content during preparation (the yield). There are many challenges in determining recipes that are appropriate for a large group of individuals, but it is equally challenging to try to collect appropriate samples of these mixtures for chemical analysis. For some mixtures, multiple recipes, and thus multiple entries on the food composition table, may be needed (e.g., home-prepared beef stew, commercially canned beef stew, and beef stew from a restaurant).

Composition data may also be obtained from the nutritional labels on commercial food products, if they are available. Most countries require a list of ingredients on the label, and if the proportions of each can be estimated, then a recipe can be devised. It is more useful, however, if the label gives information on the nutrient profile, for at least some of the main nutrients. These values can be incorporated directly into the composition table and also are useful in estimating the proportions of each ingredient (e.g., the amount of wheat flour may be estimated from the carbohydrate content). Because even the most comprehensive nutrition labels seldom give values for all nutrients of interest for the users of food composition tables, recipes will be needed to estimate values for nutrients not shown on the label. Caution should be used with label values for nutrient-fortified products. Good manufacturing practice dictates that the label underestimate the levels of any nutrient, particularly vitamins, that may degrade with time. This ensures that nutrient levels are at least as high as those stated on the label, even after a substantial time on the shelf. Thus, it is always preferable to obtain average nutrient values directly from the product manufacturer if possible.

Compilations of Composition Data for Dietary Supplements

As the use of dietary supplements increases worldwide, there is an increasing need to quantify intakes of nutrients and botanical products from these sources. Compiling nutrient profiles of such products into tables can be very time-consuming because the number of products continues to grow and formulations of existing products often change over time. Furthermore, average analytic data are seldom available from the supplement manufacturers, and thus database compilers must rely on whatever information is available from the product label. In many countries, a label showing the amount of each nutrient in the product is required.

Uses of Food Composition Data

Evaluate or Plan Nutrient Intakes

Uses of food composition data are varied, and the method of compiling the data may need to be tailored to the application of interest. Perhaps the most common use of composition data is to estimate intakes of individuals. Dietitians and other health professionals may wish to evaluate the quality of a person's current diet or to plan for changes in a diet to meet specific nutrient goals. For example, a person with elevated serum cholesterol may be counseled to reduce saturated fat and cholesterol intakes and given specific menus of diets low in these nutrients. In order to compile these menus, a nutritionist would require access to composition data for saturated fat and cholesterol in a variety of commonly consumed foods. Although the composition data are often averages across many samples of a food, this level of precision is usually acceptable for counseling applications, where long-term compliance with dietary recommendations is being examined.

Similarly, researchers often evaluate or plan diets for individuals as part of nutrition studies. However, for these applications, the required level of precision of the data may be higher. In a feeding study, it may be crucial that the composition of the menus be tightly controlled, and thus average values across many samples are not appropriate. Indeed, it may be necessary to conduct laboratory analyses of the diets that are used in feeding studies rather than rely on more general composition data.

Food composition data are also used to plan and evaluate intakes of population groups, as in dietary surveys, or in choosing menus for institutions such as schools and hospitals. When intakes are to be evaluated and averaged across a large number of people, the use of aggregated food composition data is appropriate and would lead to less error in the estimates than relying on only a small number of samples.

Some users of food composition data may wish to evaluate the nutrient content of foods as purchased at stores or markets. For example, food consumption data may be evaluated for households rather than for individuals, and these data are usually recorded as foods that are purchased for the household. In this case, the composition data must also be given per quantity of food as purchased, before any inedible portions are removed, and before cooking. Likewise, nutrition education for families may focus on making shopping lists of nutritious foods for the household, and composition data for foods as purchased will be helpful.

Food composition data may be used at an even more aggregated level in estimating food use for a region or country. For example, the US Department of Agriculture estimates the nutrient content of the US food supply annually in order to track trends. These data, often called disappearance data, assign nutrient composition values to the major commodities that are produced (minus any exports) or imported for use as food (e.g., flour, sugar, and butter). The amount of each commodity that is available for consumption is multiplied by the corresponding nutrient composition to give an estimate of nutrient consumption per capita.

Estimate Nutrient Profiles for Product Labels

The food industry also uses food composition data to justify health claims for their products (e.g., to indicate that a food product is low in fat) and, in many countries, to obtain information for printing nutrient information on the product labels. Nutrition labels are often required and are considered an important consumer guide to selecting healthy diets. Large manufacturers of processed foods usually obtain laboratory analyses of the nutrients in their products, but smaller companies may rely on calculating nutrient profiles from the product's ingredients. Restaurant chains are also increasingly likely to provide nutrient composition data for the items on their menus.

Evaluate or Plan Food Intakes

Another use of food composition data is to examine intakes from food groups—at the level of the individual, the population group, or the country. Such analyses are facilitated if each of the food items in a food composition table is assigned to a food group using a predetermined food grouping scheme. Once foods are categorized into groups, it is possible to examine intakes from each group (as grams per day) as well as nutrient intakes from each group (e.g., dietary fiber from grains). A further refinement of the food group assignments includes an indication of the number of servings that each food contains (usually per 100 g of the food). Thus, 100 g of orange juice contains approximately one-half of a serving of fruit (assuming $\frac{3}{4}$ cup, or 188 g, of juice is considered a serving). Using such a scheme, it is possible to calculate the number of servings consumed from each food group in a day and compare these intakes to dietary guidance for a country. The Food Guide Pyramid is used for such guidance in the United States, and the US Department of Agriculture has developed a Pyramid Servings Database that may be used to calculate intakes of 30 food groups (**Table 3**).

Limitations of Food Composition Data

Poor Analytic Procedures

Accurate chemical analysis of the nutrient content of foods is a challenging process and may yield

Table 3 Food groups in the USDA Pyramid Servings Database

Grain group	Total grain
	Whole grain
	Nonwhole grain
Vegetable group	Total vegetables
	Dark-green leafy vegetables
	Deep-yellow vegetables
	White potatoes
	Other starchy vegetables
	Tomatoes
	Other vegetables
Fruit group	Total fruits
	Citrus fruits, melons and berries
	Other fruits
Dairy group	Total dairy
	Milk
	Yogurt
	Cheese
Meat group	Meat, poultry, fish
	Meat (beef, pork, veal, lamb, game)
	Organ meats
	Frankfurters, sausage, luncheon meats
	Poultry (chicken, turkey, other)
	Fish (fish, shellfish, other)
	Eggs
	Soybean products (tofu, meat analogs)
	Nuts and seeds
	Cooked dry beans and peas
Pyramid tip	Discretionary fat
	Added sugars
	Alcohol

inaccurate results for a variety of reasons. For some nutrients (and other food components of interest), accurate procedures may not be available. For example, the usual procedures for analyzing the folate content of foods are known to underestimate the actual levels, and thus estimates of folate intakes are likely to be low. Both the extraction procedures and the enzyme digestion treatments may be less than optimal for food folate, and although recent procedures solve some of these problems, folate values on most food composition tables are probably underestimated. Dietary fiber in foods provides another example of possibly incorrect methods. Many older food composition tables contain a variable named fiber, but the values are for crude fiber. Crude fiber is measured using procedures that destroy some of the physiologically important fibers, and thus it is an underestimate of the true dietary fiber content. Recent methods measure either total dietary fiber (defined as all fibers that are not digested in the human gut, including lignans) or nonstarch polysaccharides (excluding lignans).

Inaccurate analyses may also occur when access to the best laboratory equipment is not available, either because the costs are too high or because the technical expertise to use the equipment is not available. For many of the antioxidant compounds, such as carotenoids and tocopherols, quantification by mass spectrometry (MS) yields the most sensitive detection limits, although analysis using high-performance liquid chromatography (HPLC) is adequate in most cases. However, because the equipment, maintenance, and reagents are often too expensive, laboratories (particularly in developing countries) may use older methods, such as spectrophotometry combined with open-column chromatography. Nutrient values derived using such methods are less accurate than those resulting from HPLC and MS methods.

Users of food composition tables should ask when and how analytic values were obtained. Likewise, compilers of these tables should clearly document the analytic procedures used to obtain all values and ensure that such information is readily available to users.

Inappropriate Sampling Procedures

The way foods are sampled and collected can also impact the quality of the composition data. Many nutrient values vary substantially across multiple samples of the same food. Nutrient composition can be affected not only by the species and cultivar of a plant but also by the growing conditions, time of harvest, and length of storage. Because it is seldom feasible to match all these factors with the diets to be analyzed, composite values, based on the average of multiple samples, are usually given in food composition tables.

Inappropriate Nutrient Forms and Expressions

An important limitation for some food composition tables is the method of expressing the activity of the nutrient. The estimation of nutrient activity is a large and expanding field of research and includes studies of both the absorption of the nutrient and its bioavailability for metabolic processes. For example, iron bioavailability has been debated extensively, and many algorithms for calculations have been proposed. Virtually all these require separating iron that is found as heme-iron in animal products from nonheme sources of iron. If these two variables are not carried on the composition table, it will not be possible to calculate iron bioavailability for specific intakes.

Vitamin A also illustrates the complexity of properly expressing the physiologically meaningful form of a nutrient. Until 1967, the vitamin A value of foods was expressed in international units (IUs), which was equivalent to 0.3 μg of retinol and 0.6 μg of β-carotene. This form of expression is still used in many composition tables and also on nutrition labels for both foods and dietary supplements. A more relevant unit of activity, micrograms of retinol equivalents (REs), was adopted in 1967 and has been used to set recommended nutrient intake levels. A lower relative pro-vitamin A activity of carotenoids was assumed, and thus it is not possible to directly convert IUs into REs, unless both the retinol and the carotenoid levels of a food are given. Recently, the estimated pro-vitamin activity of carotenoids has been further reduced and a newer unit proposed: micrograms of retinol activity equivalents (RAEs). Again, it is not possible to convert between REs and RAEs (or between IUs and RAEs), unless the retinol and carotenoid components of a food are available. Increasingly, food composition tables are carrying separate variables for the specific forms of nutrients such as vitamin A and iron, but this is not the case for many of the older tables. Such disaggregation is an obvious advantage because it allows for recalculation of nutrient activity when there is a scientific consensus that new availability factors are needed. Tables that cannot be easily updated to reflect new information will lag behind the current knowledge and thus will have more limited usefulness.

Lack of Internal Consistency and Integrity

Compiling food composition tables involves recording nutrient profiles for many foods and many nutrients, and errors can easily occur during this process. Quality control is important in this field, just as it is in the development of any product. Developers of the most accurate composition tables always include procedures to ensure that the numbers are correct. In addition to having several people review any new data before they are added to a table, several automated types of integrity checks are possible. For example, the energy value of a food item should approximate the value calculated from the main components (4 kcal/g times the grams of protein and carbohydrate, plus 9 kcal/g times the grams of fat, plus 7 kcal/g times the grams of alcohol), and any deviations should be investigated. Likewise, the sum of all the macronutrients (water, protein, fat, carbohydrate, alcohol, and ash) should be approximately 100 g if the nutrient profiles are given per 100 g of the food. Quality control procedures such as these should be an integral part of the compilation of food composition data.

Conferences on Food Composition Issues

Most of the issues discussed in this article have been addressed at conferences specifically convened to present advances in food composition data. In the United States, the National Nutrient Databank Conference has been held annually for the past 28 years. In addition, the International Food Data Conference has been held biannually for the past 10 years. The proceedings from several recent conferences have been published in the *Journal of Food Composition and Analysis*.

See also: **Dietary Intake Measurement**: Methodology; Validation. **Iron. Supplementation**: Dietary Supplements; Role of Micronutrient Supplementation; Developing Countries; Developed Countries. **Vitamin A**: Biochemistry and Physiological Role.

Further Reading

AOAC International (2002) *Official Methods of Analysis of AOAC International, 17th edn* Gaithersburg, MD: Association of Official Analytical Chemists.

Braithwaite E and Selley B (2004) *International Nutrient Databank Directory.* Available at www.medicine.uiowa.edu/gcrc/nndc/survey.html.

Burlingame B (2004) Fostering quality data in food composition databases: Visions for the future. *Journal of Food Composition and Analysis* 17: 251–258.

Food Standards Agency (2002) *McCance and Widdowson's The Composition of Foods, 6th edn* Cambridge: Royal Society of Chemistry.

Greenfield H and Southgate DAT (2003) *Food Composition Data. Production, Management and Use.* Rome: Food and Agriculture Organization.

Harrison GG (2004) Fostering data quality in food composition databases: Applications and implications for public health. *Journal of Food Composition and Analysis* 17: 259–265.

INFOODS (2004) *Directory of International Food Composition Tables,* Available at www.fao.org/infoods/directory.

Klensin JC, Feskanich D, Lin V, Truswell AS, and Southgate DAT (1989) *Identification of Food Components for Data Interchange* Tokyo: United Nations University.

Møller A and Ireland J (2000) *LanguaL 2000—The LanguaL Thesaurus.* Report by the COST Action 99–EUROFOODS Working Group on Food Description, Terminology and Nomenclature, Report No. EUR 19540, European Commission.

Rand WM, Pennington JAT, Murphy SP, and Klensin JC (1991) *Compiling Data for Food Composition Data Bases* Tokyo: United Nations University Press.

Truswell AS, Bateson DJ, Madifiglio KC *et al.* (1991) INFOODS guidelines: A systematic approach to describing foods to facilitate international exchange of food composition data. *Journal of Food Composition and Analysis* 4: 18–38.

US Department of Agriculture (2004) *Pyramid Servings Database.* Available at www.barc.usda.gov/bhnrc/cnrg.

US Department of Agriculture (2004) *Nutrient Database for Standard Reference*, Release 16-1. Available at www.nal.usda.gov/fnic/foodcomp.

US Department of Agriculture (2004) *Food and Nutrient Database for Dietary Studies*, Release 1.0. Available at www.barc.usda.gov/bhnrc/foodsurvey.

FOOD FOLKLORE

J Dwyer and J Freitas, Tufts University, Boston, MA, USA

Introduction

Food folklore consists of traditional beliefs, legends, and customs about food that have been transferred from one generation to the next by word of mouth. For thousands of years, folklore espousing food's nutritional and medicinal benefits has influenced dietary practices. In this chapter, the history and evolution of food folklore is reviewed, and a guide is provided for determining the scientific validity of food folk beliefs.

History of Food Folklore

In addition to sustaining life, food has come to play a symbolic role in both religious ceremonies and cultural traditions. For example, rice has been associated with fertility in many cultures for millennia and continues to be thrown on newly married couples today. Similarly, bread has been regarded as a symbol of divinity and has played an important role in religious services and observances.

Curative properties have also been ascribed to many foods for thousands of years. In ancient Rome, cabbage was considered the perfect medicinal plant and was prescribed frequently for a wide range of ailments including warts, deafness, and drunkenness. Apples, herbs, garlic, honey, milk, peppers, and many other foods were also highly regarded in ancient cultures for their therapeutic qualities. The prescription of foods as medicines was not necessarily based on scientific fact but instead was often based on early medical theories or magic. The ancient Greeks believed that the body was composed of four humors: blood (hot and moist), phlegm (cold and moist), yellow bile (hot and dry), and black bile (cold and dry). Health was thought to result from a balance of the humors, and illness resulted from an imbalance. To counteract imbalances and restore health, physicians often prescribed specific foods, based on their perceived degree of 'heat' and 'moisture'. For example, fever, a 'hot' 'dry' condition, was attributed to an excess of yellow bile, and 'cool' 'moist' foods, such as cucumbers, were prescribed to treat it. In contrast, oedema, a 'cool' 'moist' condition, was treated with foods that were viewed as 'warm' and 'dry'. The hot, cold, moist, and dry properties of food were also regarded as important in other ancient societies, including China, where achieving a balance between the opposing forces of yin (cold/moist) and yang (hot/dry) has guided traditional medical practice for centuries and continues to be popular today.

The Doctrine of Signatures, based on the notion that 'like cures like', was also popular in the nineteenth century. Therapies were chosen on the basis of similarities of color, aroma, shape, and other characteristics. For example, beet juice, which is deep red, was thought to be an effective cure for blood diseases, while yellow plants were believed to alleviate jaundice and other liver ailments. The pungent odours of onions and garlic were thought to ward off disease, stimulate strength and bravery, arouse libido, and banish evil spirits. Walnuts resemble the brain and so were eaten to improve intellect. The ginseng root, with its resemblance to the human torso, was used by the Chinese as a panacea (**Figure 1**).

The common names of many foods reflect folklore about their curative properties, as shown in **Table 1**. For example, the word ginseng is derived from the root words *gin*, meaning man, and *sing*, meaning essence.

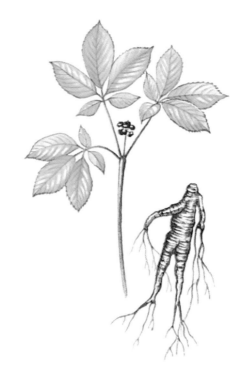

Figure 1 The universal healing properties of ginseng were attributed to the resemblance of its root to the human body. Reproduced with permission from The American Heritage Dictionary of the English Language, Boston, 4th edn, 2000.

Table 1 Food names related to food folklore

Herb (botanical name)	Folklore
Blackeye root (*Tamus communis*)	Heals bruises, removes discoloration
Bloodroot (*Sanguinaria candensis*)	Cures blood disorders and heart disease
Birthwort (*Aristolochia longa*)	Alleviates complications associated with childbirth
Eyebright (*Euphrasia officinalis*)	Cures disorders of the eyes
Ginseng (*Panax quinquefolium*)	General human panacea
Heartsease (*Viola tricolor*)	Relieves heart ailments
Liverwort (*Anemone hepatica*)	Relieves liver disorders
Lungwort (*Sticta pulmonaria*)	Cures pulmonary diseases
Maidenhair fern (*Asplenium trichomanes*)	Prevents balding, promotes hair growth
Snakeroot (*Aristolochia serpentaria*)	Antidote for snake bites
Spleenwort (*Asplenium*)	Remedy for disorders of the spleen

Food Folklore Today

While some food folk beliefs continue to be passed down from generation to generation, others have been discarded over the years, and new ones have been introduced. Today, food folklore is spread not only by word of mouth from person to person, but also to large numbers of people simultaneously via the mass media and the Internet. The growing popularity of alternative therapies, organic products, and functional foods has led to the development of new food folklore and increased the popularity of some traditional notions. Several examples of commonly held food folk beliefs of both the past and present are provided in **Table 2**.

Food and nutrition-science concepts that have developed over the past two centuries are newcomers to human thinking about the relationships between food and health. Although some food beliefs, such as the association of carrots with eyesight, have some scientific basis, many others remain unsupported by, or in opposition to, recent scientific findings. Pseudoscience, rather than sound evidence, provides the basis for much of today's food folklore. It is important for food and nutrition professionals to be knowledgeable about current food folk beliefs, because these ideas influence popular views about diet–health relationships. In order to identify beliefs that are of major health significance, it is useful to consider the strength of the belief in folklore and the strength of the scientific evidence surrounding it, as shown in **Table 3**.

When folkloric belief and scientific evidence are both strong and in agreement with each other, the folklore is unlikely to pose a major health threat. Similarly, when food folklore and the scientific evidence surrounding it are both weak, few practical problems exist. However, when scientific findings refute, or fail to support, popular food folk beliefs, public health may be threatened. For example, despite folklore that ephedra promotes rapid weight loss, a recent evidence-based review suggests that it does not and that it may even be harmful. Often, though, it is not that the scientific evidence regarding food folklore is weak but that it is unproven or undetermined, indicating that more research needs to be done.

Folklore and Evidence: Fact or Fiction?

Totality of the Evidence

Food folklore cannot be taken as fact without evidence. Single studies are usually inadequate for demonstrating cause–effect relationships, and no single study alone is enough to prove that something is fact or folklore. It is important to consider the totality of evidence and the type and quality of the available research. When many different types of evidence are all supportive of a relationship, the weaknesses of individual studies are mitigated and causal inference is strengthened.

Ideally, the best way to conduct a scientific evaluation of a question is to perform an evidence-based expert review of many randomized double-blind placebo-controlled clinical trials, meta-analyses, and other studies. An evidence-based review often entails the use of statistical techniques to reanalyze the results of many small studies, as well as expert judgment. If all systematic evidence-based reviews produce comparable conclusions, the scientific evidence is good that the folklore belief is justified.

Comprehensive reviews are especially important for far-reaching questions that have implications for large populations. They are also necessary for questions regarding important issues, including life and death, and those that involve very large costs or imply large reimbursements. However, because such reviews are significantly time consuming and require much expertise and money, they can be done only for a few very important questions. For example, the National Institutes of Health (NIH) has sponsored such reviews of obesity treatment, the American Institutes of Cancer Research has done reviews to substantiate their population-based recommendations, and the health

Table 2 Food folkore: current and historic beliefs

Food	Folklore
Fruits	
Apple	'An apple a day keeps the doctor away'; prevents cavities and tooth decay
Blueberries	Cure for kidney and urinary-tract ailments; improves vision and memory
Cherries	Cherry gum dissolved in wine relieves a cough; ensure continued fertility
Citrus fruits	Prevent scurvy; Cause low blood pressure; cure the common cold
Cranberries	Prevent scurvy; prevent cure or urinary-tract infections
Currant	Relieves sore throat
Fig	Relieves toothache; mild laxative
Grapefruit	Should be avoided completely when taking medication; burns calories, dissolves fat, aids in weight loss; is 'good for you'
Raspberry	Raspberry leaf tea promotes contractions and aids in labor
Vegetables	
Beets	An effective cure for anemia; help build iron-rich blood
Carrots	Important for good eyesight
Celery	Promotes weight loss
Garlic	Stimulates digestion; inhibits germs; cleanses the blood and intestines; lowers cholesterol and blood pressure
Lettuce	Induces sterility
Onions	Cooked onions cure the common cold; good for the heart
Peppers	Cure for a cold
Potatoes	A historic cure for impotence; prevent scurvy; soothe and soften the skin; are fattening
Spinach	Builds strong muscles
Grains	
Bread	Is the body of the supernatural; cures disease and protects against evil; is a fattening; food brown bread has more fiber than white bread
Flaxseed	Effective cure for constipation; prevents cancer; lowers cholesterol
Oats	Oatmeal and oat bran can prevent heart disease
Dairy	
Milk	Prevents scurvy; helps to heal ulcers; causes constipation; unpasteurized milk has more nutrients than pasteurized; a glass of milk before bed causes drowsiness; mothers who drink a lot of milk have colicky babies; milk and other dairy products are fattening and should be avoided on a low-fat diet; the calcium in milk and other foods causes kidney stones
Yoghurt	Prevents vaginal yeast infections; cures vaginitis, constipation, and diarrhea; yoghurt applied topically heals a sunburn
Meat	
Beef	Eating beef and other red foods causes high blood pressure; extra protein from beef makes muscles stronger
Chicken soup	Cure for the common cold
Eggs	Drinking raw eggs helps build muscle; brown eggs are healthier than white eggs; people with high cholesterol should not eat eggs
Legumes	Beans are a natural laxative
Seafood	Fish is a brain food; fish is good for the heart and prevents heart attacks; pregnant women should avoid eating fish; oysters increase sexual potency
Fat, sweets, and alcohol	
Olive oil	Protects against breast cancer
Cod liver oil	Relieves rheumatism, aching muscles, and stiff joints; prevents rickets
Sugar	Causes tooth decay; causes hyperactivity; eating too much causes diabetes and heart disease
Honey	Is natural and will not raise blood-sugar levels; a mix of honey and water is a good cure for colic
Chocolate	Causes acne; eating chocolate helps to prevent heart disease
Salt	A no-salt diet protects against high blood pressure; sea salt is healthier than table salt; salt tablets prevent muscle cramps
Alcohol	Helps to warm the body in cold weather; acts as a sleep aid if consumed before bedtime; red wine is good for the heart; a nip of brandy cures a cold; drinking alcohol with raw oysters ensures they are safe

effects of ephedrine were recently summarized in an evidence-based review by the Office of Dietary Supplements. Unfortunately, for much food folklore, such studies have never been done.

Type of Evidence

In determining the validity of food folklore, not only the totality of evidence but also the type and quality of available evidence are important. As shown in

Table 3 Folklore: separating fact from fiction

	Scientific evidence	
	Strong	Weak
Folklore Strong	Fact[a]	Fiction/ undetermined[b]
Folklore Weak	Emerging science[a]	Fiction[a]

[a]Unlikely to be a major threat
[b]Potential threat to public health

Table 4, the strength of the association between eating a food (cause) and a health outcome (effect) can be ranked according to the type of evidence presented. The best evidence comes from studies that have the most control over the claim or treatment being evaluated and eliminate other factors that may suggest an effect was present, when really it was not. Although randomized double-blind placebo-controlled clinical trials are considered the 'gold standard' for determining diet–health relationships, such studies are rarely available. Lesser levels of evidence must usually be used.

Randomized double-blind placebo-controlled trials When randomized double-blind placebo-controlled trials show a relationship between a specific food and a health effect, the evidence is considered to be very good. These studies exert rigorous control over the claim or treatment being evaluated and over the people who are subjected to

Table 4 Ranking the quality of the evidence

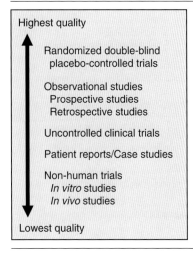

it (by randomization) and the assumptions of both the experimenters and the participants (by placebos and blinding). Multiple studies of this type, with an expert review of all other types of data, are considered to be the 'gold standard' for establishing cause–effect relationships. Other types of evidence and studies are lower in the hierarchy, because they are not as definitive in identifying true cause and effect.

Although single randomized trials and non-randomized clinical studies are somewhat less definitive, they are still valuable, because they also permit control over the treatment being evaluated. Often, however, these studies are not large enough, or the study sample is not representative, so the results cannot be generalized to the problem at hand. Other factors that may weaken these studies are not counting of dropouts, lacking or unconvincing placebos, and inappropriate points or biomarkers serving as surrogate end points.

Observational studies Human studies that involve observation rather than direct intervention provide evidence that is satisfactory but less conclusive. These studies are designed to test a relationship between an exposure of interest (folk belief) and a health outcome. Observational studies include both cohort studies (prospective) and case–control studies (retrospective). In a prospective study, a group exposed to the treatment of interest and an unexposed group are followed forward in time. The health outcomes in both groups are observed and evaluated after controlling for confounding factors with the use of statistics. In contrast, retrospective studies compare individuals who have already developed an outcome of interest (case) against those who have not (control). Factors contributing to the development of the outcome are then determined by looking backward in time. Because observational studies cannot be precisely controlled, it is more difficult to establish cause and effect. However, when confounding factors can be adequately controlled for, these studies provide suitable evidence to support diet–health relationships.

Uncontrolled clinical trials Clinical studies in which everyone is treated, in which only those who ask for the treatment are treated, or in which some are treated based on unsubstantiated clinical convictions are suspect. In such studies, no randomization occurs and neither the researcher nor the participant is blinded to the treatment. Therefore, it cannot be determined whether the treatment is actually the cause of the observed results or whether biased convictions of both experimenters and study participants are falsely contributing to the results. Better evidence is needed before it can be stated with assurance that the folklore based on such observations is true.

Patient reports, case studies, and folklore Even weaker human evidence of cause and effect comes from single medical case reports and anecdotal evidence. These types of evidence are also biased since those who experience success from the treatment are much more likely to report their stories than those who do not.

Animal studies and laboratory experiments Non-human studies involving living animals (*in vivo* studies) or tissue cultures (*in vitro* studies) are useful in providing information on the possible biological plausibility, dose response, and action of a treatment. However, their ability to predict outcomes in humans is poor. Therefore, these studies are unconvincing and should be used only to support other types of evidence.

Guide for Separating Food Folklore Facts from Fiction in Clinical Situations, and A Practical Example

For summarizing and evaluating food folklore involving diet–health relationships, health professionals need to not only evaluate the evidence but also use their clinical judgment and communications skills to relate this to clients or patients. How can food folklore be evaluated in discussions with laypeople and in counselling situations? The strategies are similar to those employed in research and in more formal evidence-based reviews, but contextual realities require tailoring of the approach. One method of evaluation is provided, as shown in **Table 5**, and an actual clinical example follows.

The problem One example of currently popular food folklore is the notion that people on medication should not drink grapefruit juice. Although there is scientific evidence that grapefruit juice interacts with certain medications, making them

Table 5 Steps to evaluating food folklore in clinical situations

1. Report
2. Review
3. Recall
4. Relate
5. Recommend
6. Revise

incompatible, the facts do not suggest either that grapefruit must be eliminated from the diet of those taking medications or that all drugs exhibit these interactions. The process of reviewing this food folklore with the patient to arrive at this conclusion is outlined in detail below.

In the late 1980s, in a study examining the interaction between alcohol and felodopine (a calcium antagonist used to lower blood pressure), it was accidentally discovered that grapefruit juice, which was being used as a placebo, dramatically altered the drug's metabolism. The drug was a common one, the juice dose – about 6 ounces (180 ml) – was within the range many people drink, and the effects were large (similar to a doubling of the drug dose). Therefore, it was of potential clinical importance. Since then, more than 200 scientific papers have been published in peer-reviewed journals on the issue of drug interactions with grapefruit, confirming the original observations. By the mid-1990s, the finding had received a great deal of media coverage and the notion that grapefruit juice was dangerous for those on prescription drugs had become a subject of food folklore. This particular bit of folklore is an example of a strongly held belief for which there is some scientific evidence. Under the circumstances, how should clinicians advise patients?

Report In counselling, it is important for the clinician to relate to the patient and establish two-way communication to learn about the folk belief. It may be useful to determine the strength of the individual's conviction about this folklore as well as the source of the belief and whether there is a potential conflict of interest. When the health professional actively listens, it is more likely that the patient will listen, understand, accept, and follow recommendations.

Review In clinical situations, it is also important for health professionals to review all the evidence surrounding the patient's professed food folk belief. A vital piece of information to consider is safety. Although many prescription drugs have side-effects, they are taken under the supervision of a physician, who can monitor adverse effects and take steps to control them. Because folk remedies are often self-administered, such safeguards are lacking. If there is evidence that the implementation of food folklore is likely to be hazardous to health, it must be discouraged. Folk remedies that are effective for one purpose but have negative side-effects must also be cautioned against.

For example, when the patient's prescription drug is one that is metabolized by cytochrome 3A (CYP 3A), a dramatic effect can occur if grapefruit juice or other forms of the fruit are consumed. Grapefruit juice enhances the effects of these drugs over time by decreasing their oral clearance. However, the effects of the interaction depend on the nature of the drug (for some drugs there is little or no effect) and the size of the interaction. Interaction occurs only if the drug is metabolized by CYP 3A, if it normally undergoes pre-systemic extraction with CYP 3A, and if it is given orally. The interactions vary. For example, with the statins – drugs commonly used to lower serum cholesterol – they are strong for simvastatin and lovastatin, moderate for atorvastatin and cervastatin, and low for fuvastatin and pravastatin. Similarly, sedatives, hypnotics, and other drugs vary as to whether they induce interactions or not.

Recall The CYP P450 superfamily consists of many enzymes. They are labelled as follows: CYP (family 1, 2, 3, etc.) (subfamily A, B, C, etc.) (isoform 1, 2, 3, 4, etc.). There is individual variability in the expression of these enzymes, which is probably in part genetic.

CYP 3A is an enzyme that is involved in the metabolism of many drugs. It is present in the liver and gut mucosa and is induced or inhibited by drugs and other chemicals. Under certain conditions, components of foods can also affect it. The CYP 3A enzyme in the gut mucosa (enteric CYP 3A) is affected by grapefruit juice, but CYP 3A in the liver is not. The phytochemicals that are thought to have these effects are furanocoumarin derivatives in the juice, which reversibly and irreversibly inhibit the CYP 3A in the gut mucosa. When grapefruit juice and certain drugs are taken together orally, this leads to effects on their pre-systemic extraction (first-pass metabolism). In consequence, pre-systemic extraction of the drug is reduced, and, because of this, more of the drug reaches the circulation over time. With this increased systemic exposure to the drug, there is an increased drug effect. The duration of the juice's effect depends on the dose and on the time it takes for the enzyme to regenerate. The liver CYP 3A is not affected by grapefruit juice (although it may be affected by some drugs that also affect gut CYP 3A). Thus, the grapefruit–drug interaction does not happen with drugs administered intravenously, since they bypass the gut.

About one-fifth of American households consume grapefruit juice, and it is considered a 'good food' since it has the American Heart Association heart check and the American Cancer Society endorsement. Many older people take their medications and juice together at breakfast. Many people who are elderly take medications, and some of these drugs may pose problems. Therefore, this folklore is highly relevant from the clinical standpoint.

For the grapefruit interaction to take place, the patient must be taking a drug that affects the gut CYP 3A and he or she must express a significant amount of CYP 3A. People differ in these respects, and there may be racial as well as other genetic differences.

Relate The clinician or nutrition scientist must build on his or her own knowledge and that available from expert reviews or sources and place it in the clinical context. Common sense is needed to fit the information to the patient's realities. The facts, which are that most drugs do not interact with grapefruit, must be related to the folklore and the patient's actual condition. Many grapefruit–drug interactions are modest and not clinically important. Fortunately, for every therapeutic class of drugs there is an option that is not affected by the grapefruit interaction.

Recommend In responding and making recommendations, considerations include their importance, feasibility, and effectiveness for the patient. The information is then particularized to fit the patient or questioner's problem and needs.

This is the time to particularize for the patient and lead him or her to the next level of understanding. With many drugs there is no interaction, and the patient can be told to drink the juice if he or she wishes but to alert the physician if adverse reactions occur. It may be possible to change the medication if a major interaction exists, or, for modest interactions, it may be enough to avoid taking drugs and grapefruit juice at the same time and to avoid consuming large quantities (four or more glasses) of juice.

The patient should be praised for asking about possible food–drug interactions and told that these reactions sometimes occur, but do not usually exist. Is the information relevant – that is, if the patient is on a statin, is it the type that is involved in interactions? Does the patient *want* to drink grapefruit juice? If not, the issue is moot. What are patient reactions, and is reassurance needed?

Revise Fortunately, in counselling, although a relatively rapid response is usually required, there is an ongoing relationship with the individual that permits follow-up. The clinician can follow up and revisit the issue later if necessary when more information becomes available or when additional questions arise.

For example, a patient might ask whether, since the drug effect is enhanced with the consumption of grapefruit juice, he or she could save money by taking more grapefruit juice and continuing with lovastatin. The response to this legitimate question is no, not because it is theoretically impossible but because it is difficult to titre the drug, individual differences exist, and reactions are unpredictable, so such a strategy is not recommended.

Conclusions

Food folklore is alive and well and is likely to continue. For summarizing and evaluating food folklore involving diet–health relationships, health professionals need to not only evaluate the evidence but also use their clinical judgment and communications skills to relate this to patients. The six Rs (report, review, recall, relate, respond, recommend, and revise if necessary) provide a guide for evaluating food folklore in clinical situations.

See also: **Dietetics. Drug–Nutrient Interactions. Food Choice, Influencing Factors. Fruits and Vegetables. Functional Foods**: Regulatory Aspects.

Further Reading

Duyff RL American Dietetic Association (1999) *Food Folklore: Tales and Truth About What We Eat.* Minneapolis: Chronimed Publishing.

Anderson H, Blundell J, and Chiva M (eds.) (2002) *Food Selection: From Genes to Culture.* Brussels Belgium: Chauvehid, Stavelot, Juillet.

Andrews T (2000) In *Nectar and Ambrosia: An Encyclopedia of Food in World Mythology.* Santa Barbara: ABC-CLIO.

August DA (2000) Clinical guidelines: an evidence based tool to lead nutrition practice into the new millennium. *Nutrition in Clinical Practice* 15: 211–212.

Cavendish R (1983) *Man Myth and Magic: The Illustrated Encyclopedia of Mythology, Religion and the Unknown.* New York: Marshall Cavendish Corporation.

Green TA (ed.) (1997) *Folklore: An Encyclopedia of Beliefs, Customs, Tales, Music and Art.* Santa Barbara: ABC-CLIO.

Kennett F (1976) *Folk Medicine: Fact and Fiction.* New York: Crescent Books.

Kiple KF and Orneals KC (2000) *The Cambridge World History of Food.* Cambridge: Cambridge University Press.

Koretz RL (2000) Doing the right thing: the utilization of evidence based medicine. *Nutrition in Clinical Practice* 15: 213–217.

Leach M and Fried J (eds.) (1949) *Funk & Wagnall's Standard Dictionary of Folklore, Mythology, and Legend.* New York: Funk & Wagnall Company.

Lehner E and Lehner J (1962) In *Folklore and Odysseys of Food and Medicinal Plants.* New York: Tudor Publishing Company.

Rinzler CA (1979) *The Dictionary of Medical Folklore.* New York: Thomas Y Crowell Publishers.

Visser M (1991) *The Rituals of Dinner: The Origins, Evolution, Eccentricities, and Meaning of Table Manners.* New York: Penguin Books.

Walker ARP (1998) Food folklore overview. In: Sadler MJ, Strain JJ, and Caballero J (eds.) *Encyclopedia of Human Nutrition,* vol. 2, pp. 875–880. San Diego: Academic Press.

Wilson DS and Gillespie AK (eds.) (1999) *Rooted in America: Foodlore of Popular Fruits and Vegetables.* Knoxville: The University of Tennessee Press.

FOOD FORTIFICATION

Contents
Developed Countries
Developing Countries

Developed Countries

R Nalubola, Center for Food Safety and Applied Nutrition, US Food and Drug Administration, MD, USA

Published by Elsevier Ltd.

Introduction

Food fortification is increasingly recognized as an effective public health intervention to alleviate nutritional deficiencies. Nutrients may be added to foods to either restore nutrients lost during processing (restoration or enrichment), introduce nutrients not naturally found in the food, or increase the levels of nutrients to above those naturally present in the food (fortification). The terms 'enrichment' and 'fortification' are often used interchangeably to simply refer to the addition of nutrients to food; however in some countries these terms have specific regulatory definitions. In this article, food fortification refers to all such nutrient additions.

History and Current Market Place

Food fortification has been practiced for several decades in developed countries. Historically, certain staple foods have been fortified to alleviate deficiency diseases in the general population, such as the iodization of salt to alleviate goiter, addition of vitamin D to milk to prevent rickets, and enrichment of cereal products with thiamin and niacin to alleviate beriberi and pellagra. For example, in the US, fortification began with the iodization of salt in the State of Michigan in 1924. The practice of salt iodization had spread rapidly throughout the rest of the country by 1928. With the revolution of nutritional science and the elucidation of chemical structures of several nutrients in the 1930s, the production of synthetic preparations of nutrients became possible. By 1934, vitamin D was routinely being added to milk. Although an effort to enrich cereal flours and products with B vitamins and iron started in the 1930s, the enrichment program began in earnest only in 1941 with about 40% of the flour in the country being fortified by 1942. Furthermore, in 1951, the Committee of Food and Nutrition of the National Research Council recommended the addition of vitamin A to table fats (margarine). Several other developed countries experienced similar initiation and implementation of food fortification as a strategy to alleviate nutrient deficiencies in the general population. More recently, cereals fortified with folic acid have been introduced in several countries to increase the folic acid intake of women of childbearing age and reduce the rates of neural tube defects, and the results are already measurable. Foods commonly fortified in developed countries are listed in **Table 1**.

Although the original intent of food fortification was to correct or prevent widespread nutrient deficiencies, the focus now has shifted in developed countries to optimal intakes of nutrients for the prevention of chronic diseases and for overall health and well-being. Classic nutrient deficiency diseases such as goiter and pellagra are no longer common in developed countries at least, in part, due to food fortification programs. However, suboptimal intakes of nutrients such as calcium and vitamin D may occur. In addition, there is heightened consumer awareness and demand for more healthful foods. Consequently, food industries perceived a market for foods with improved nutritional profiles, resulting in a proliferation of fortified foods in the current market place. Ready-to-eat breakfast cereals are a prime example of industry-initiated food fortification. Published reports indicate that in 1969, only about 16% of the breakfast cereals in the US market place were fortified; that number rose to about 92% in 1979 following certain legislative actions providing more flexibility to industry for the addition of nutrients to foods. A market survey in Germany highlights the heterogeneity of current fortification practices: a total of 288 fortified foods in six different food categories (beverages, sweets, cereals, milk products, powdered instant beverages, and ready-to-eat meals) were found to be fortified with a wide range of nutrients.

Characteristics of a Fortification Program

Food fortification can be mandatory (required by government regulations) or voluntary (permitted by government regulations and policies). Some characteristics of both types of fortification programs are presented in **Table 2**. As with any intervention, each of these has certain advantages and limitations that have to be considered to determine the regulatory course that is most appropriate for the country and for the public health concern at hand. For example, it is reported that voluntary fortification of foods with folic acid in Australia and New Zealand, while demonstrating benefits, has not reached the target population to the extent intended. Therefore, policymakers are considering mandatory fortification as an option to ensure sufficient folate intake among all women in Australia and New Zealand.

At the international level, the Codex Alimentarius Commission has adopted a set of criteria which allow for the rational addition of nutrients to improve the nutritional quality of the overall food supply and prevent indiscriminate fortification of foods, while acknowledging that the need for, and appropriateness of, addition of nutrients to foods will depend on the nutritional problems of a country, the characteristics of the target populations, and

Table 1 Foods commonly fortified in developed countries

Foods	Nutrients
Cereal grain flours and products	Thiamin, riboflavin, niacin iron, and folic acid
Milk and milk products	Vitamins A and D
Fats and spreads	Vitamins A and D
Salt	Iodine
Ready-to-eat breakfast cereals	Many vitamins and minerals
Juices and other beverages	Vitamin D and calcium
Infant foods	Many vitamins and minerals

Table 2 Characteristics of mandatory and voluntary food fortification

Mandatory fortification	Voluntary fortification
• Initiated by government[a]	• May be initiated by government or by industry
• Regulations require addition of nutrients	• Regulations provide for optional addition of nutrients
• Food vehicle(s) are staple foods consumed in significant and relatively stable amounts	• Both staple and nonstaple foods are used as food vehicles
• Driven primarily by a documented need for a public health intervention	• Driven primarily by consumer demand and market forces
• Resource-intensive, coordinated multi-sector effort	• Relatively fewer resources are needed, particularly from the public sector
• Targeted to reach populations at risk of deficiency	• Can be introduced quickly
• Excessive intakes of fortified nutrients are minimized	• In the case of breakfast cereals, proven to make substantial contributions to nutrient intakes
• Adverse effects on other nutrient intakes or health conditions due to fortification are curtailed	• Random fortification and overfortification of the food supply is a potential concern although this can be minimized by appropriate regulatory restrictions
• Fortification levels and food vehicles are tightly controlled	
• A cost-effective nutrition intervention for governments	
• Proven to be an effective strategy to eliminate micronutrient deficiencies in the general population	

[a]While government-initiated fortification is usually mandatory, it can be 'voluntary' in that food companies have the option of selling unfortified versions of the food provided they are appropriately labeled. For example, in Canada, 'flour' or 'enriched flour' is required to contain specified amounts of thiamin, riboflavin, niacin, folic acid, and iron (B.13.001, Food and Drug Regulations) and 'milk' is required to be fortified with vitamin D (B.08.003, Food and Drug Regulations). In the US, however, 'enriched flour' is required to contain these nutrients, but 'flour' is not (Title 21 of the Code of Federal Regulations, sections 137.105 and 137.165) and 'milk, vitamins A and D added' is required to contain specified amounts of these vitamins, but 'milk' is not (21 CFR 131.110).

their food consumption patterns. The Codex general principles for the addition of essential nutrients to foods (CAC/GL 09-1987) state the following:

• The nutrient should be present at a level that will not result in an excessive or an insignificant intake of the added nutrient considering the amounts from other sources in the diet.
• The nutrient should not result in an adverse effect on the metabolism of any other nutrient.
• The nutrient should be sufficiently stable in the food during packaging, storage, distribution, and use.
• The nutrient should be biologically available from the food.
• The nutrient should not impart undesirable characteristics to the food, or unduly shorten shelf-life.
• The additional cost should be reasonable for the intended consumers, and the addition of nutrients should not be used to mislead the consumer concerning the nutritional quality of the food.
• Adequate technology and processing facilities should be available, as well as methods of measuring and/or enforcing the levels of added nutrients.

The Codex principles mirror the criteria proposed in the US (in 1974) as conditions to be met to support food fortification, including the following:

• There should be a demonstrated need for increasing the intake of an essential nutrient in one or more population groups.

• The food selected as a vehicle should be consumed by the population at risk and intake of this food should be stable and uniform.
• The amount of nutrient added should be sufficient to correct or prevent the deficiency when the food is consumed in normal amounts by the population at risk.
• The addition of the nutrient should not result in excessive intakes.

Many developed countries have adopted various regulations to either require or permit manufacturers to fortify their food products in a safe and appropriate manner, and to market such products in a manner that is truthful and not misleading to consumers. In some countries, such as Norway, Finland, and Denmark, voluntary fortification has been considered unnecessary and potentially harmful and, therefore, is generally restricted. However, in many other countries, such as the US, UK, Canada, Switzerland, and Belgium, regulations are less restrictive allowing foods to be fortified voluntarily as long as fortification is safe and harmful levels of nutrients are avoided.

Contribution of Food Fortification to Nutrient Intakes

Individual nutrient intakes in developed countries are strongly influenced by food fortification. The amounts of thiamin, riboflavin, niacin, and iron in

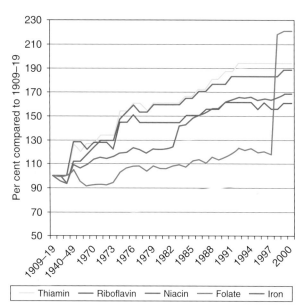

Figure 1 Trends in the amounts of thiamin, riboflavin, niacin, folic acid, and iron in the US food supply between 1909 and 2000. Fortification of cereal grain products with thiamin, riboflavin, niacin, and iron was initiated in 1941 and fortification levels were adjusted in 1973. The levels of iron were reversed in 1978 and then increased in 1981. Folate fortification began in 1998. Source of data: Gerrior S, Bente L, and Hiza H (2004) *Nutrient Content of the United States Food Supply, 1909–2000*. Home Economics Research Report No. 56. United States Department of Agriculture, Center for Nutrition Policy and Promotion, Alexandria, VA, USA.

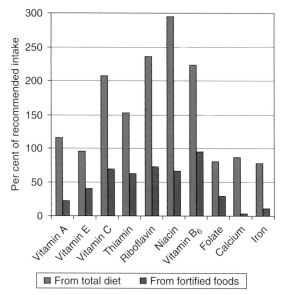

Figure 2 Nutrient intakes from the total diet and fortified foods among 2–13-year-old German children in 1996. Source of data: Sichert-Hellert W, Kersting M, Alexy U, and Manz F (2000) Ten-year trends in vitamin and mineral intake from fortified food in German children and adolescents. *European Journal of Clinical Nutrition* **54**(1): 81–86.

the US food supply markedly improved following fortification of cereal grain products in the 1940s (**Figure 1**). Cereal grain products provided about 31% of the thiamin in the food supply in 1909–19 compared to about 59% in 2000; 14% of riboflavin in 1909–19 to 39% in 2000; 30% of niacin in 1909–19 to 45% in 2000; and 33% of iron in 1909–19 to 52% in 2000. Similarly, fortification sharply increased the amounts of folate in the food supply since its inception in 1998. Cereal grain products accounted for 23% of folate in the food supply in 1909–19, which rose to 35% in 1997 and, following fortification, jumped to 70% in 1998 and remained there in the most recent data of 2000.

An analysis of food consumption patterns between 1985 and 2000 among German children and adolescents showed that food fortification increased the intakes of several vitamins and minerals by 20–50%. In the case of vitamins A, C, thiamin, riboflavin, niacin, and B₆, fortification raised already adequate intakes from nonfortified foods. In the case of vitamin E and folate, inadequate intakes from nonfortified foods were increased to 100% and 80%, respectively, of reference intake levels (**Figure 2**). Fortified foods accounted for less than 5% of total calcium intake, 10–20% of iron, vitamin

A, and folate intakes, 40–50% of vitamin C, E, thiamin, riboflavin, and niacin intakes, and up to 80% of vitamin B₆ intake among this population group.

Calcium fortification of flour is estimated to have supplied up to 30% of the total calcium intake in Danish adults and 13% of total calcium intake in adolescents in Britain. A Swedish multicenter study, 1980–81, on food habits and nutrient intake in children aged 1–15 years revealed that enriched low-fat milk and margarine are important food sources of vitamin A in this population group. Vitamin D-fortified margarine is estimated to provide up to 48% of the total vitamin D intake among Australian men and women.

While government-initiated fortification of foods can greatly change the nutritional profile of the food supply, the contribution of foods voluntarily fortified by industry should also be considered. In the US, such fortified foods are reported to increase intakes of several nutrients, some of which are already adequately provided by nonfortified foods and standardized enriched foods (**Table 3**). Among voluntarily fortified foods, ready-to-eat breakfast cereals are the most significant food category, accounting for the top food source of many vitamins and minerals in several countries, including the US, UK, France, and Spain. Fortified juices and beverages appear to be another substantial contributor, primarily for intakes of vitamins C and D. Fortified breakfast cereals are associated with higher intakes

Table 3 Contribution of voluntary food fortification to nutrient intakes in the US population $\geq$ 1 year of age[a]

Nutrient	Median intake (% RDA)		Contribution of voluntarily fortified food[b] sources to median intake (% RDA)
	Excluding voluntarily fortified food[b] sources	Including voluntarily fortified food[b] sources	
Vitamin A	70	85	15
Vitamin C	98	122	24
Thiamin	101	113	14
Riboflavin	107	119	12
Niacin	104	117	13
Folate	99	122	23
Calcium	76	76	0
Iron	84	96	12
Zinc	66	70	4

[a]Source of data: Berner LA, Clydesdale FM, and Douglass JS (2001) Fortification contributed greatly to vitamin and mineral intakes in the United States, 1989–91. *Journal of Nutrition* **131**: 2177–2183.
[b]In this analysis, researchers determined the contribution of voluntarily fortified foods, namely the food categories ready-to-eat cereals and fortified cooked cereals, vitamin-and mineral-fortified drinks, meal replacements and supplements, and calcium-fortified milk beverages and juices. Standardized, enriched foods (i.e., foods governed by federal food standards of identity), including enriched flour, enriched bread, enriched rice, enriched pasta, and vitamin-fortified milk, were excluded in this analysis.

of vitamin A among children in Spain and Northern Ireland. In the UK, which has a long tradition of fortification, fortified foods contribute positively to nutrient intakes. For example, in the UK, in 1950, red meat and vegetables were the primary sources of iron and vitamin C, respectively, among 4-year-olds. However, by 1992, most dietary iron came from fortified breakfast cereals and most vitamin C was provided by fortified beverages. Similarly, fortified breakfast cereals were found to be the principal source of folic acid and the second most important food source of vitamins B_6 and D among children in Spain.

Effectiveness of Food Fortification as a Public Health Intervention

The benefits, at a national level, of historical fortification efforts are generally not well documented; however, epidemiological evaluations of pilot-scale programs are considered to have played an important role in the widespread implementation of these programs. Iodization of salt was found to decrease the incidence of goiter by 74–90% in different counties in the State of Michigan in the US in the first 10 years of the program (1924–35). Salt iodization is credited with the elimination of endemic cretinism and endemic goiter in Switzerland. Since its inception in 1922, periodic evaluations of the program triggered increases in fortification of levels of iodine, most recently in 1998. In 2001, an evaluation of a national sample of Swiss school children and pregnant women showed adequate iodine status,

underscoring the importance of iodized salt in that nation's food supply and the value for periodic monitoring in the success of a fortification program.

A successful intervention with vitamin A-fortified margarine initiated in Newfoundland in 1944–45 led to a marked improvement in vitamin A status, as indicated by serum retinol levels in a sample of the population. Similarly, observations on the curative effects of milk fat, but not of margarine, eventually led to the enrichment of margarine with vitamin A in Denmark.

An evaluation of the possible health impact of niacin fortification of cereal grains in the US showed that fortification played a significant role in the decline of pellagra-attributed mortality in the 1930s and 1940s and, finally, in the elimination of pellagra in the country. Fortification was particularly significant during a period when food availability and variety were considerably less than are evident today.

Effectiveness of iron fortification is less clear owing primarily to the complex etiology of anemia. Several cereal grain products and other foods, especially breakfast foods, are commonly fortified with iron in developed countries and iron fortification is generally assumed to be responsible, at least in part, for the marked reduction in the prevalence of iron deficiency anemia in these countries. However, many other factors, such as improved socioeconomic conditions, increased meat intake, and iron supplementation may have played important roles. Furthermore, the most common iron source used in cereal fortification in Western countries is reduced iron, which has been found to be poorly bioavailable. Nevertheless, the effectiveness of iron fortification is apparent in some cases. For example, in Sweden, fortification of flour with iron was withdrawn in January, 1995, because the benefits of such fortification were considered uncertain. However, recent investigations suggest that, after accounting for possible confounding factors, iron intake decreased by 39% and iron deficiency anemia increased by 28% among adolescent girls in the 6 years following withdrawal of iron fortification. The effectiveness of iron fortification is also clear in the case of targeted fortification of infant foods. The use of iron-fortified infant formulas and cereals is credited with the virtual elimination of iron deficiency among American infants.

The effectiveness of food fortification as a public health strategy is evident in the case of recent folate fortification efforts. Since its inception in November, 1998, folic acid fortification (150 μg per 100 g of food) in Canada has produced measurable benefits. In Newfoundland, the average rates of neural tube defects, which remained unchanged between 1991 and 1997, fell by 78% with concurrent increases in blood folate levels of women after the implementation of folic acid fortification. This survey did not find evidence of improved folate status masking hematological manifestations of vitamin B_{12} deficiency, which was a concern carefully considered in setting the fortification levels of folic acid. Studies in other Canadian provinces also report significant reductions in neural tube defects: up to 32% in Quebec, 48% in Ontario, and 54% in Nova Scotia. Folate fortification is also reported to be associated with a 60% reduction in neuroblastoma, an embryonic tumor, among Canadian children.

In the US, enriched cereal grain products have been required to be fortified with 140 μg of folic acid per 100 g of food since January, 1998. Since then, folate levels of baked products, cereal grains, and pasta have doubled or tripled and breakfast cereals are one of the most highly fortified food sources of folate. Consequently, typical folic acid consumption in the country is estimated to have increased by more than $200\,\mu g\,day^{-1}$ due to fortification, along with a substantial improvement in folate status of different population groups. According to the Centers for Disease Control and Prevention, the rates of neural tube defects fell by about 26% from 1995–96 to 1999–2000 in the US although there is debate that this figure may be an underestimate. Careful monitoring and surveillance of the long-term effects of these fortification programs is needed to ensure desired benefits without unintended consequences.

Several factors are considered essential for the success of fortification as a public health intervention. Key among them are:

- a documented need for food fortification, i.e., assessing the gap between current and desired intakes;
- choosing an appropriate food vehicle(s) that is consumed by most of the population in relatively constant amounts;
- setting a fortification level that is not only efficacious in the target population but also safe for the general population;
- resolving any concerns of adverse nutrient interactions;
- establishing clear fortification regulations and policies;
- a public education campaign to increase consumer awareness; and
- periodic assessments of the impact of the intervention to determine any necessary adjustments to the fortification policy to ensure that the desired benefits are achieved and that excessive intakes are minimized.

Relevant government bodies, food industry, professional health organizations, consumer associations, and trade organizations play important roles in formulating a coordinated and concerted effort in the successful implementation of the fortification program.

Emerging Issues

As noted above, both mandatory and voluntary fortifications have played important roles in the overall nutritional adequacy of food supply in developed countries. While classic nutrient deficiency diseases have been alleviated, there is increasing awareness that suboptimal intakes of nutrients may occur in some population subgroups. For example, calcium and vitamin D intakes may be inadequate, particularly among women and the elderly. In the US, median calcium intakes among adolescent girls and adult women are below the recommended Adequate Intake levels. Similarly, the lowest dietary intakes of vitamin D in the US are reported by female teenagers and female adults, with only about 30% of adolescent girls and 20–25% of women cosuming sufficient dietary vitamin D to meet the Adequate Intake levels. Dietary patterns are changing among teenagers with a preference for soft drinks over milk and other dairy beverages. Up to 90% of older adults in the US are reported to consume inadequate amounts of vitamin D. In Australia and New Zealand, women and the elderly are also considered high-risk groups for marginal vitamin D status. In Europe, a substantial percentage of the elderly are reported to have low vitamin D status, ranging from about 10% in the Nordic countries to about 40% in France. Current scenarios of food fortification do not appear to be reaching the population groups most at risk of these deficiencies.

In contrast, overfortification and random fortification of the food supply is also a growing concern. Where the regulatory system in the country permits, a wide variety of foods are being fortified with a broad spectrum of nutrients. The need for such a vast number of fortified foods for generally nutritionally adequate populations, particularly given the wide consumption of vitamin and mineral supplements, is questioned. Recently, advances in scientific knowledge have enabled estimations of upper (safe) levels of intake and various government agencies have established tolerable upper intake levels for different micronutrients. These upper levels of nutrient intake are being carefully considered as countries continue to monitor their existing fortification programs and policies to appropriately balance risks of deficiency and toxicity in well-nourished populations.

Another emerging issue relates to the so-called 'functional foods' as consumers look for foods associated with health benefits beyond basic nutrition. Nutrition research in the recent past has shifted from evaluating the benefits of the whole food itself to the benefits of bioactive components isolated from such foods. Substances such as lycopene, lutein, and probiotics are being added to foods with claimed health benefits, although the efficacy of such fortification is largely unknown.

Conclusion

Fortification of foods commonly consumed by populations at risk of micronutrient deficiencies has been demonstrated to be an effective public health intervention. Iodization of salt, fortification of milk with vitamin D, and the addition of thiamin, riboflavin, niacin, and iron to cereal grain products have a long history in several developed countries, some starting as early as the 1920s. More recently, several countries have either required or permitted the fortification of cereal grain products with folic acid. In addition, where the regulatory environment permits, the food industry has voluntarily fortified a variety of foods with a wide array of nutrients. The importance of food fortification in the diets of developed countries is clear. Surveys indicate that fortified foods make significant contributions to the intakes of nutrients among different population groups,

resulting in improved nutrient status and/or related health conditions. The success of food fortification in developed countries can be attributed to several factors, notably cooperation among different sectors to raise consumer awareness and demand for more healthful foods. However, as the popularity of fortified foods grows and trends toward random fortification and overfortification of the food supply continue, careful monitoring of existing fortification programs and policies become more critical to ensure not only the adequacy but, perhaps more importantly, the safety of food fortification in generally well-nourished populations.

See also: **Ascorbic Acid**: Deficiency States. **Calcium**. **Cobalamins**. **Folic Acid**. **Food Fortification**: Developing Countries. **Functional Foods**: Regulatory Aspects. **Iodine**: Deficiency Disorders. **Niacin**. **Riboflavin**. **Thiamin**: Beriberi. **Vitamin A**: Deficiency and Interventions. **Vitamin D**: Rickets and Osteomalacia. **Vitamin B$_6$**.

Further Reading

Allen L, de Benoist B, Dary O, and Hurrell R (2005) *Guidelines on Food Fortification with Micronutrients*. World Health Organization, Geneva.

Backstrand JR (2002) The history and future of food fortification in the United States: a public health perspective. *Nutrition Reviews* 60(1): 15–26.

Bauerfeind JC and Lachance PA (eds.) (1991) *Nutrient Additions to Foods*. Trumbull, CT: Food and Nutrition Press.

Food and Agriculture Organization (1996) *Food Fortification: Technology and Quality Control*. Report of an FAO technical meeting held in Rome, 20–23 November, 1995. FAO Food and Nutrition Paper 60. Food and Agriculture Organization of the United Nations, Rome.

Gerrior S, Bente L, and Hiza H (2004) *Nutrient Content of the United States Food Supply, 1909–2000*. Home Economics Research Report No. 56. United States Department of Agriculture, Center for Nutrition Policy and Promotion Alexandria, UA, USA.

Liu S, West R, Randerll E *et al.* (2004) A comprehensive evaluation of food fortification with folic acid for the primary prevention of neural tube defects. *BMC Pregnancy and Childbirth* 4: 20.

Meltzer HM, Aro A, Andersen NL, Bente K, and Alexander J (2003) Risk analysis applied to food fortification. *Public Health Nutrition* 6(3): 281–290.

Prynne CJ, Paul AA, Price GM *et al.* (1999) Food and nutrient intake of a national sample of 4-year-old children in 1950: comparison with the 1990s. *Public Health Nutrition* 2(4): 537–547.

Sichert-Hellert W, Kersting M, Alexy U, and Manz F (2000) Ten-year trends in vitamin and mineral intake from fortified food in German children and adolescents. *European Journal of Clinical Nutrition* 54(1): 81–86.

Yetley EA and Rader JI (2004) Modeling the level of fortification and post-fortification assessments: U.S. experience. *Nutrition Reviews* 62(6): S50–S59.

Developing Countries

O Dary and J O Mora, The MOST Project, Arlington, VA, USA

Introduction

Micronutrient deficiencies are a consequence of diets with low variety, which are common in developing countries where the diet is based on starchy foods. Fortification of commonly consumed edible products is a potential solution to increase the intake of micronutrients. However, feasibility and effectiveness of fortification depends on production in the industrial setting, reliable food control mechanisms, and frequent and sufficient consumption of the fortified products. These criteria are not common in developing countries, and this limits the potential of this intervention to improve the health of their inhabitants. Nevertheless, some examples already exist that show that food fortification is feasible and useful in developing countries. Increasing, urbanization in these countries makes fortification an essential food technology for their immediate future.

The Need to Improve Micronutrient Intakes in Developing Countries

Micronutrient deficiency is a consequence of a lack of variety in the diet. This condition is aggravated in developing countries, where the diets consist primarily of low-cost starchy foods. **Table 1** shows the micronutrient density of wheat, wheat flour, maize-meal, corn-masa flour, and rice. In all cases, the cereal-based derivatives are good sources of energy, but are very poor in most micronutrients, in particular zinc, iron, calcium, and vitamins associated with foods of animal origin, such as vitamins A, B_2, and B_{12}. These products are also poor in folate and vitamin C. Extraction of flour from cereal grains increases the energy density by two times in the case of corn, and by three times in the case of wheat (**Table 1**), but reduces the original micronutrient content of the grain by 30–85%. **Table 1** illustrates that white wheat flour (extraction rate lower than 80%) is not a good source of any micronutrient, whereas rice and, especially, corn derivatives maintain satisfactory quantities of vitamin B_6 and niacin. Corn sub products also retain some zinc, and adequate amounts of vitamin B_1. Iron content is also higher, but the presence of strong iron-absorption inhibitors, especially in corn-masa flour, makes corn derivatives poor sources of this nutrient. Processing of the corn grains with lime (calcium oxide) to produce masa-flour increases the content of zinc, calcium, and niacin. Nevertheless, considering that 50% or more of energy is satisfied through the consumption of these foods in poor populations of developing countries, it is easy to explain why they are at very high risk of suffering the consequences of vitamin and mineral deficiencies.

Table 2 illustrates that, in general, diets in developing countries are not only poor in energy (less than 77% adequacy) but also in zinc, iron, calcium, vitamin B_{12}, folate, vitamin A, and vitamin B_2. Adequacies of these micronutrients are from 35% to 70% of the estimated average requirement (EAR). Vitamin B_1, niacin, and vitamin C have better adequacies, although these are still unsatisfactory, being in the order of 70–100% of the EAR. Iodine deficiency, as in most human societies in the world, is

Table 1 Micronutrient density of main energy sources in developing countries (per 100 g of product)

Nutrient	EAR[a]	Wheat	White wheat flour	Maize-meal		Corn-masa flour	Rice
Energy (kcal)		112	364	361	(% EAR)	365	360
Zinc	11.7 mg	26	6	15		21	10
Iron	21.6 mg[b]	17	8	16		8	4
Calcium	833 mg	4	2	2		17	1
B_{12}	2.0 µg	0	0	0		0	0
Folate	320 µg	14	6	8		0	3
Vitamin A	429 µg	0	0	0		0	0
B_1	1.0 mg	40	6	25		31	7
B_2	1.1 mg	16	5	11		5	5
B_6	1.1 mg	9	4	34		31	14
Niacin	12 mg	50	8	14		20	13
Vitamin C	37 mg	0	0	0		0	0

[a]EAR, estimated average requirement is the average (median) daily nutrient intake level estimated to meet the needs of half the healthy individuals in a particular age and gender group.
[b]EAR for white wheat flour (low extraction flour) = 10.8 mg; and for corn-masa flour = 43.2 mg.

Table 2 Nutrient adequacy in some developing countries (approximate % EAR in diet)[a]

Nutrient	EAR	S. Africa (1999)	Bangladesh (1995–96)	Nicaragua (1993)	Mexico (2000)	Philippines (1998)[b]
Energy (kcal)		77	75	75	67	70
Zinc	11.7 mg	56	–	77	51	–
Iron	21.6 mg	65	53	48	38	61
Calcium	833 mg	61	41	82	77	58
B_{12}	2.0 µg	280	–	90	–	–
Folate	320 µg	89	–	35	66	–
Vitamin A[c]	429 µg	106	66	50	60	49
B_1	1.0 mg	140	118	70	–	76
B_2	1.1 mg	157	45	82	–	73
B_6	1.1 mg	118	–	128	–	–
Niacin	12 mg	127	155	71	–	89
Vitamin C	37 mg	193	87	140	83	119

[a]Almost all individuals in the population should have an intake equal or greater than the corresponding EAR. In this table, adequacy rates smaller than 100% means that half or more of the population is not fulfilling the nutritional requirement.
[b]Data for children 4–8 years old.
[c]Conversion factor for vitamin A from plant sources was changed from 1:6 to 1:12 (retinol:β-carotene).

also widespread due to the absence of foods containing this nutrient. It seems that only vitamin B_6 may be the exception for micronutrient deficiencies in developing countries. Improvement in micronutrient adequacy cannot be expected with a simple increase of the consumption of food (in order to satisfy the daily energy requirements) without changes in the quality of the diet, because inadequacies originate from the low-micronutrient content of the usual foods consumed.

In South Africa, nutrient adequacy for vitamin B_{12}, vitamin A, and vitamin B_2 was better than in the other countries included in **Table 2**; this may be a consequence of the greater consumption of eggs and milk in this country. Similarly, Nicaragua and Mexico presented lower deficiency for calcium, which is obviously associated with the consumption of corn-masa flour.

It is generally recognized that developing countries require not only an increase in intake of iodine, vitamin A, and iron, but also most vitamins and minerals.

Conditions Limiting the Implementation of Effective Food Fortification Programs in Developing Countries

Many of the micronutrient deficiencies in developing countries might be solved by raising the consumption of foods of animal origin (eggs, milk, fish, poultry, and meat). However, this strategy is difficult to implement in the short term because of its high cost, as well as cultural and religious beliefs. Thus, food fortification seems an attractive

alternative. However, fortification is not a simple task in developing countries, as explained below.

Small Proportion of Centrally Produced Foods

Food fortification is a technology, and hence it necessitates the existence of processing centers (industrial plants or fortification facilities), which must have a minimum technological development that is compatible with the advantages of large market economies and quality control procedures. If this requirement is not satisfied, it would be wasteful, worthless, and risky to try to implement a food fortification program, because of prohibitive cost and unsafe practices. The salt iodization program is occasionally mentioned as an example against this statement, but this cannot be used as a model of other food fortification programs, as explained later. Factories for processed foods (breakfast cereals, pastas, vegetable fats, beverages, and the like) exist in most developing countries but, unlike the situation in developed countries, their products are generally out of the reach of the populations at risk. Food staples such as corn, rice and, in some situations wheat, are produced and processed locally in very small facilities, and hence they are very difficult or impossible to fortify. Fortification of rice still faces cost and technological constraints, especially in regions where rice is the main staple.

The difficulty of finding suitable vehicles to be fortified in the developing world has led to investigation of the fortification of oil, sugar, salt, fish and soy sauces, curry powder, and, in the past, other condiments such as monosodium glutamate. The main limitation of these food vehicles is that they allow the addition of only one or very few micronutrients.

Low Consumption of Potential Food Vehicles

The effectiveness of food fortification in developing countries is hampered by the fact that those edible products that are amenable to fortification, are not consumed frequently enough or in sufficient amounts by the most at risk individuals. In the past, it was assumed that increasing the level of micronutrients in the food vehicle may overcome this constraint. It is now realized that the content of micronutrients in widely consumed products depends on keeping their consumption safe for everyone (especially for individuals with very large consumption), on maintaining the technological compatibility with the properties and uses of the food vehicle, and on maintaining the price of the product within an acceptable range. As a consequence, the fortification formulations are more or less fixed by maximum possible values, which in turn determine that a minimum daily consumption of the fortified vehicles is necessary in order to provide useful amounts of micronutrients. This condition reduces the potential benefits of food fortification for very poor families, as well as for small children, because they usually consume low amounts of industrially manufactured products.

Table 3 illustrates the minimum consumption amounts of industrially produced foods to supply from 20% to 70% of the EAR of iodine, iron, and vitamin A through fortification. This range was selected under the assumption that a source of a nutrient is one that provides at least 20% of the EAR of that nutrient, and if a food supplies 70% EAR it means that that food might be sufficient to supply all of the amount needed to complement the diet with that nutrient. Daily consumption amounts should be in the following ranges: oil, 5–20 ml for vitamin A; sugar, 10–35 g for vitamin A; low-extraction wheat flour, 40–140 g for iron, and 50–150 g for vitamin A; salt, 4–15 g for iron, and slightly less for vitamin A and iodine; and fish/soy sauce, 6–20 ml for iron. Ideally, consumption patterns should be equal to or higher than the uppermost figure of the range, but never below the lowest value to have public health significance. If consumption is within the range, then probably more than one product should be fortified and consumed.

Weak Enforcement and Monitoring Capabilities

Many developing countries have regulations and laws making food fortification mandatory. However, those legal instruments often remain without compliance because of the impossibility of enforcing them. There are also many examples of false, misleading, and exaggerated claims regarding the presence of micronutrients in the foods. These claims are used as simple advertizing tools but without checking that the products really contain the vitamins and minerals in the amounts that are declared on the labels. The lack of reliable food control mechanisms is a barrier to the effectiveness of fortification in developing countries.

Low Bioavailability of Iron and Other Minerals

Iron is a relatively abundant mineral in plant sources, but its bioavailability is very low. Iron in cereal-based diets – without fermentation or elimination of the bran – might be $\leq 5\%$ absorbed.

Table 3 Consumption range of fortified foods to supply 20–70% EAR[a] (range of consumption/(minimum fortification level in ppm[b]))

Nutrient	Oil	Sugar	Wheat flour	Salt	Fish/soy sauce
Iodine	–	–	–	$\dfrac{1.5\text{–}5.0\,\text{g}^{c}}{(25\,\text{ppm})}$	–
Iron[d]	–	–	$\dfrac{45\text{–}165}{(45\,\text{ppm})}$	$\dfrac{4.0\text{–}15.0\,\text{g}}{(500\,\text{ppm})}$	$\dfrac{6\text{–}20\,\text{ml}}{(350\,\text{ppm})}$
Vitamin A	$\dfrac{5\text{–}20\,\text{ml}}{(20\,\text{ppm})}$	$\dfrac{10\text{–}35\,\text{g}}{(10\,\text{ppm})}$	$\dfrac{50\text{–}175\,\text{g}}{(2.0\,\text{ppm})}$	$\dfrac{3.0\text{–}10.0\,\text{g}}{(35\,\text{ppm})}$	–

[a]Approximately equivalent to 15–50% Recommended Nutrient Intake (RNI). It is assumed that a food should supply at least 20% EAR of a nutrient to be considered as a source of that nutrient; and that a supply of 70% would mean that that food would be sufficient to complement the whole recommendations of that nutrient.
[b]Higher levels cannot be used because risk of excessive intakes for individuals who consume large amounts of these foods; high cost; or technological incompatibility. Supply of EAR was estimated considering losses during storage, transportation and distribution, and after food preparation.
[c]In the case of iodine, because iodized salt is almost its only source, the nutritional goal should be to supply 100%EAR, which means that the usual salt consumption should be 7 grams/day.
[d]In all cases, assuming a diet with iron bioavailability of 10%.

Many developing countries assume that their diets have 10% bioavailability for iron, but in fact this is not the case. This fact has caused iron deficiency to be underestimated, and the estimation of the potential impact of iron fortification overestimated. Perhaps a similar situation may be happening with zinc and calcium.

In a diet with abundant iron-absorption inhibitors (rice, high extraction wheat and corn flours, and corn-masa flour), even the most absorbable iron compounds, such as NaFeEDTA and ferrous bisglycinate, have absorption rates not higher than 10%. Water-soluble or acid-soluble iron salts, such as ferrous sulfate and ferrous fumarate, respectively, are absorbed at rates of from 5% to 10%, depending on the content of iron absorption inhibitors in the diet. Electrolytic iron and other difficult to dissolve iron compounds are absorbed in even lower proportions. This condition combined with the fact that the most absorbable iron compounds change the sensory characteristics of foods (color, flavor, and odor) makes the improvement of iron status in cereal-based diets through food fortification a very difficult challenge.

Use of electrolytic iron deserves a special mention because, once in the fortified food, it cannot be distinguished from other types of elemental iron, such as reduced iron and atomized iron, whose bioavailability rates are even lower. The impossibility of enforcement makes the use of electrolytic iron an unattractive option under the conditions in developing countries.

Price of Fortified versus Nonfortified Product

When fortification is being considered as a public health strategy, feasibility analyses regarding cost implications and trade practices are usually neglected in favor of biological efficacy trials. This approach has produced reports and publications showing biological impact but it has not supported the creation of true and effective programs. This was

the case when monosodium glutamate was fortified with vitamin A in the Philippines and Indonesia in the 1980s. The nutrient was bioavailable and metabolically efficacious, but the fortified product had a very short life span in the market. This was principally due to the 17% reduction in weight of the sachets in order to keep the price similar to the unfortified product. The consumers noticed the difference and preferred to choose the unfortified alternative. The fortified product also had problems with color and micronutrient segregation, but the uncompetitive price was the main reason for the failure of the program.

Table 4 shows the annual cost per person of providing 70% of the EAR through food fortification. In the case of iodine, the annual cost is only US$0.003 per person. Iodine is the only micronutrient to combine several properties that permit us to recommend a 'universal' measure to provide iodine in most countries of the world. These characteristics are: its mineral nature (resistant to environmental factors, mainly in the form of potassium iodate even when combined with raw salt); very low cost; very small interactions with the food matrix; very low nutritional requirements (microgram range); and absence of foods that are good sources of this nutrient. These properties make it possible to use only one carrier, i.e., salt, without the need to consider other ways to complement the amounts of iodine supplied by this means. No other nutrient has all these attributes. Therefore, iodization of salt is the exception and not the model for food fortification.

Table 4 also shows that independently of the food vehicles that can be used to increase the dietary iron, the annual investment would depend on the price of the type of iron that must be used to be compatible with the food matrix. Thus, to supply 70% EAR throughout the year using ferrous fumarate would cost US$0.045 per person' using encapsulated ferrous sulfate US$0.257, and using NaFeEDTA US$0.405. These iron compounds are compatible with white wheat flour, salt and fish/soy sauce, respectively.

Table 4 Annual cost per person of providing 70% EAR through food fortification[a] (US$)

Nutrient	Oil	Sugar	Wheat flour	Salt	Fish/soy sauce
Iodine	–	–	–	0.003	–
Iron	–	–	0.045[b]	0.257[c]	0.405[d]
Vitamin A[e]	0.023	0.150	0.130	0.175	–
Total	0.023	0.150	0.175	0.435	0.405

[a]At the levels of fortification and consumption indicated in **Table 3**.
[b]Ferrous fumarate.
[c]Encapsulated ferrous sulfate.
[d]NaFeEDTA.
[e]All cases, except oil, use microencapsulated vitamin A. Oil uses fat-soluble vitamin A.

The nature of the two latter vehicles does not allow use of other iron alternatives at this time.

Similarly, the cost of fortification with vitamin A would change if the nutrient is added to an oily matrix (US$0.023/year per person), or to a dry or water-soluble matrix (US$0.130 to US$0.150/year per person) such as wheat flour, sugar, or salt.

In principle, the less costly alternatives should be used preferentially, but if these food matrixes are not consumed regularly nor in sufficient amounts, then the more expensive options are necessary. **Table 4** illustrates that the total annual costs, even in the most costly cases of food fortification, are inexpensive enough compared with the large public health benefits that are expected from the prevention of the consequences of these micronutrient deficiencies.

However, the viability of the fortification program depends not only on the total annual cost, but also on the relative price increase of the food vehicle, because the difference in price compared to the unfortified choice will determine the feasibility of production, trade, and enforcement. Thus, using the case of salt as an example (**Table 5**), adding iodine increases the price by 0.6%, iron by 16.7%, and vitamin A by 11.7%. Then, it is logical to conclude that considering salt as a vehicle of iron and vitamin A, although it might be technologically compatible and biologically efficacious, would face a lot of opposition from the producers with high risk of noncompliance in the absence of strong enforcement capabilities. In theory, this type of fortification is possible and has potential biological impact, but in practice the substantial challenges might impede their implementation.

Table 5 also includes the production cost and the price increase for other fortification examples. It is easy to see that double or triple fortification of salt, or iron fortification of fish/soy sauce, would need very strict and reliable enforcement systems and permanent financial mechanisms, in order to be sustainable and efficient interventions.

Table 5 and **Table 6** show that flours are suitable for the addition of several micronutrients simultaneously, and that the price increase is relatively low. Therefore, flours should be used to their maximum potential wherever and whenever it is possible.

Examples of Food Fortification Programs in Developing Countries

Despite the multiple limitations that affect food fortification in the developing world, there are several examples that confirm its feasibility and benefits.

Vegetable Fats and Oil Fortified with Vitamin A and D

Addition of vitamin A to margarine and other vegetable fats started in 1918 in Denmark, when cases of xerophthalmia were associated with the replacement of butter by margarine. Then, the practice of nutritional equivalence, that is emulating the nutritional composition of butter, was adopted by the industry. Thus, vitamin A and D started to be added to margarine and other vegetable fats. Despite the fact that the bioavailability and utilization of vitamin A has been confirmed experimentally in the Philippines and other countries, the compliance and effectiveness of this practice at the national level has not been documented. Similarly, the addition of vitamin A in oil has been proven to be efficacious in

Table 5 Production cost of food fortification[a]

Food (price)	Oil (US$0.50/kg)	Sugar (US$0.40/kg)	Wheat flour (US$0.40/kg)	Salt (US$0.30/kg)	Fish/soy sauce (US$0.50/kg)
Nutrient			(US$ per Metric Ton/(% price)		
Iodine	–	–	–	1.75 (0.6%)	–
Iron	–	–	0.90[b] (0.2%)	50.00[c] (16.7%)	55.00[d] (11.0%)
Vitamin A[e]	3.50 (0.7%)	12.00 (2.7%)	2.02 (0.5%)	35.00 (11.7%)	–

[a]At the levels of fortification indicated in **Table 3**.
[b]Ferrous fumarate.
[c]Encapsulated ferrous sulfate.
[d]NaFeEDTA.
[e]All cases, except oil, microencapsulated vitamin A.

Table 6 Characteristics of a suggested fortification formulation for white wheat flour[a]

Nutrient	Level (mg kg^{-1})	Cost (US$ per Metric Ton)	% Price[b]	% EAR in 100 g consumption[c]
Zinc	30.0	0.16	0.04	52
Iron	45.0	0.90	0.22	48
B$_{12}$	0.01	0.59	0.15	45
Folic acid	2.0	0.32	0.08	97[d]
Vitamin A	2.0	2.02	0.51	39
B$_1$	6.0	0.30	0.08	45
B$_2$	4.0	0.24	0.06	39
B$_6$	5.0	0.25	0.06	47
Niacin	45.0	0.54	0.14	38
Total	–	5.32	1.34%	–

[a]Formulation adequate for daily consumption of 50–200 g day^{-1}. If consumption is greater, micronutrient levels should be reduced. Countries might reduce the levels of some micronutrients based on their particular nutritional profile and presence of other fortification programs with large public health coverage.
[b]Assuming US$0.40/kg.
[c]Considering losses during food preparation.
[d]Dietary folate $= 1.7 \times$ folic acid.

Brazil, but national effectiveness studies are still pending. Oil is currently fortified with vitamin A in Coted'Ivoire, Mali, Morocco, Nigeria, Oman, Philippines, Uganda, and Yemen. These programs have been designed to provide at least 100 µg vitamin A (23% EAR), which may have some biological consequence in a portion of the population. The main restriction of this practice is the destruction of vitamin A when oil is exposed to light inside transparent bottles.

Sugar Fortified with Vitamin A

In the 1970s, the Central American countries suffered from vitamin A deficiency. The only food that was identified as a good vehicle for fortification (centrally produced, affordable fortification cost, and widely consumed) was sugar. The technology of the addition of vitamin A was developed and, together with the introduction of the intervention, its biological effectiveness was evaluated. Vitamin A level increased in serum and breast milk of individuals in poor communities. Sugar is now the most important source of this nutrient in El Salvador, Guatemala, Honduras, and Nicaragua. It supplies 200–1000 µg of vitamin A (50–200% EAR), depending on the daily consumption pattern (30–150 g day^{-1}). Nowadays, vitamin A deficiency is practically nonexistent in those countries. Zambia started this program in 1998 but, differentiate from, Central America, the impact has been modest due to the lower sugar consumption (20 g day^{-1}) and sugar use (50% of population compared with nearly 100% in Central America). Nevertheless, sugar is the main source of vitamin A for those who consume it in Zambia. Nigeria has already started to implement this program for all sugar refined in the country. The vitamin A added to sugar is microencapsulated, and hence the type of packaging has little influence on its stability.

Wheat Fortified with Multiple Micronutrients

The practice of adding micronutrients to restore the nutritional quality of wheat grain with iron, vitamins B$_1$ and B$_2$, niacin, and sometimes calcium has been followed by many wheat flour mills in developing countries since the 1950s, especially in those industries with links to companies in the US and Canada. Nevertheless, attention to fortification of wheat flour was raised in the 1990s as a measure advocated by international organizations to reduce iron deficiency. Generally, the iron source is elemental iron, either electrolytic or reduced iron; exceptions are Central America where ferrous fumarate is used, and Peru, Cuba, and Chile, which use ferrous sulfate. A study in Sri Lanka, where an additional 12 mg day^{-1} of reduced (28% EAR) or electrolytic (56% EAR) iron was provided, did not find any improvement in hemoglobin levels after 2 years of treatment. Similarly, a study in Bangladesh, which supplied 3.3 mg day^{-1} of reduced iron (35% EAR) to 6–15-year-old children failed to modify any parameter associated with iron status. Only Chile has indirect evidence that iron from fortified wheat flour contributes to maintain good nutritional status of this nutrient. Wheat flour consumption in that country (250 g day^{-1}) provides 7.5 mg day^{-1} iron from ferrous sulfate (69% EAR). Other studies are on-going with the purpose of assessing if it is legitimate to use electrolytic iron for the fortification of wheat flour.

Most recently, attention has been given to folic acid, after evidence that neural tube defects in the US and Canada were reduced by the intake of an additional $200\,\mu g\,day^{-1}$ of folic acid (106% EAR), by means of the consumption of cereals fortified with this nutrient. These results have been confirmed in Chile, where bioavailability and biological utilization of folic acid was also clearly demonstrated.

Experimental efficacy trials of wheat flour fortified with vitamin A in the Philippines and Bangladesh have established that biological impact can be found with intake levels of $100–200\,\mu g\,day^{-1}$ (25–50% EAR). Despite this finding, vitamin A has not been widely considered as a micronutrient to be added to wheat flour, although South Africa, Nigeria, and the Philippines have regulations including this micronutrient as part of the formulation. In comparison with sugar, addition of vitamin A to wheat flour has a lower cost and slightly better stability.

In addition to iron and folic acid, many countries also include vitamins B_1, B_2, and niacin in the fortification formulations. This is the practice followed by most Latin American countries. Now, Latin America is also considering the incorporation of vitamin B_{12} and zinc. Biological effects of the presence of other nutrients apart from iron and vitamin A have not been systematically evaluated in developing countries. However, when wheat flour fortification started in the US, it was documented that cases of beriberi, ariboflavinosis, and pellagra, associated with vitamins B_1, B_2, and niacin deficiencies, respectively, decreased drastically.

Wheat flour fortification has now extended to Bahrain, Jordan, Morocco, Saudi Arabia, Pakistan, Iran, Indonesia, and some regions of China, Central Asian countries and a few African countries.

Corn Products Fortified with Multiple Micronutrients

In Venezuela, precooked and degermed corn flour is fortified with iron (reduced iron and ferrous fumarate, in a mixture 2:3), vitamins B_1, B_2, niacin, and vitamin A. The usual consumption of this food provides $2.4\,mg$ of iron from ferrous fumarate (22% EAR), and $1.6\,mg$ from reduced iron (3.7% EAR). It also supplies $200\,\mu g$ of vitamin A (47% EAR). A formal evaluation of this program has not been carried out, although it has been associated with maintenance of the iron status of the population despite the economical deterioration of the country. This argument is controversial because the additional supply of iron is not high, and the prevalence of anemia was low only in the year when fortification was introduced, whereas anemia rates after fortification were similar to those existent before fortification. Without a study under controlled conditions it is difficult to assign the

mentioned effect to this program. Fortified precooked corn flour is theoretically more important as a source of vitamin A than iron, but no experimental evidence has been obtained in this regard. Nevertheless, it is interesting to note that a national nutritional survey, carried out in 2002, did not find vitamin A deficiency in Venezuelan preschoolers.

In Africa, maize-meal is currently being used as a vehicle for iron, zinc, vitamin A, and B complex vitamins, including in some cases vitamin B_{12}. Biological impact has not been evaluated.

Masa-corn flour is fortified with iron (reduced, or ferrous fumarate, or ferrous bisglycinate), and vitamins B_1, B_2, and niacin, in some Central American countries, and in Mexico also with zinc. Efficacy trials have shown the better bioavailability of NaFeEDTA over reduced iron in this matrix, although NaFeEDTA has not been used as yet in an industrial setting.

Salt Fortified with Iodine and Fluoride

Most developing countries have joined the initiative for universal salt iodization; evidence obtained worldwide confirms that this provides sufficient iodine to human populations. However, some countries have started to reduce the content of iodine, because of concerns of unnecessary or excessive supply. A few countries, such as Colombia, Costa Rica, Jamaica, Mexico and Uruguay, have also utilized salt as a vehicle for delivering fluoride with the purpose of reducing tooth decay. In Costa Rica, tooth decay was reduced 65% after 12 years of initiating the program. As in the case of iodine, fluoride content has recently been lowered after epidemiological monitoring determined that excessive fluoride was being supplied.

Soy/Fish Sauces and Curry Powder Fortified with Iron

Efficacy trials carried out with soy sauce in China and fish sauce in Vietnam that were fortified with NaFeEDTA have shown an impact on reduction of anemia and improvement in the iron status indicators. The amount of iron supplied was $10\,mg\,day^{-1}$, which is about 93% of the EAR assuming a diet with 10% iron bioavailability. The plan is now to make these experiences national programs. A similar study with curry powder in South Africa provided similar conclusions. In these cases, effectiveness and technical feasibility have been proven, and the existence of the program depends now on assuring industrial acceptance, permanent financing, and continuous enforcement.

Implications and Conclusion

The examples described in the previous section demonstrate that food fortification is possible and that it can be effective in developing countries. However, it is important to point out that the biological impact depends on the chemical properties and amounts of the micronutrients that are supplied and not on the fortified food itself. It is not a surprise that biological impact has been found in efficacy trials using many edible products as the fortification vehicles, such as biscuits, milk, sugar-based beverages, and "sprinkles." If these products contain the proper form and amount of micronutrients, it is highly probable that they will produce the expected biological outcomes.

Although food fortification has limitations in developing countries, mainly due to low accessibility and affordability of industrially produced foods by poor sectors of the population, the increasing trend of urbanization makes this strategy very important. Quality of the diets will be improved, and hence the health and well being of millions of persons. The aim is to supply sufficient micronutrients to populations having poor-quality diets, and fortification is one of the most efficient mechanisms to achieve this goal.

See also: **Ascorbic Acid**: Physiology, Dietary Sources and Requirements; Deficiency States. **Calcium**. **Folic Acid**. **Food Fortification**: Developed Countries. **Iodine**: Physiology, Dietary Sources and Requirements; Deficiency Disorders. **Iron**. **Niacin**. **Nutrition Policies In Developing and Developed Countries**. **Riboflavin**.

Sodium: Salt Intake and Health. **Supplementation**: Developing Countries. **Vitamin A**: Biochemistry and Physiological Role; Deficiency and Interventions. **Vitamin B$_6$**.

Further Reading

Allen L, de Benoist B, Dary O, and Hurrell R (2004) *Guidelines on Food Fortification with Micronutrients*. Geneva: World Health Organization.

Bauerfeind JC and Lachance PA (eds.) (1991) *Nutrient Additions to Foods*. Trumbull, CT: Food and Nutrition Press.

Hetzel BS, Dunn JT, and Stanbury JB (eds.) (1987) *The Prevention and Control of Iodine Deficiency Disorders*. Amsterdam: Elsevier Press.

Hurrell R (2002) How to ensure adequate iron absorption from iron-fortified food. *Nutrition Reviews* 60(II): S7–S15.

Hurrell R, Bothwell T, Cook JD, Dary O, Davidsson L, Fairweather-Tait S, Hallberg L, Lynch S, Rosado J, Walter T, and Whittaker P (2002) The usefulness of elemental iron for cereal flour fortification: A SUSTAIN Task Force Report. *Nutrition Review* 60: 391–406.

Micronutrient Initiative (ed.) (1998) *Food Fortification to End Micronutrient Malnutrition*. Arlington, UA: State of the Art.

Mora JO, Dary O, Chinchilla D, and Arroyave G (2000) *Vitamin A Sugar Fortification in Central America. Experience and Lessons Learned* Arlington, VA: MOST/USAID Micronutrient Program.

Nestel P (1993) *Food Fortification in Developing Countries*. Arlington, UA: VITAL, USAID, Micronutrient Initiative.

Pan American Health Organization (2002) Iron compounds for food fortification: Guidelines for Latin America and the Caribbean 2002. *Nutrition Reviews* 60(II): S50–S61.

Roche (2003) Vitamins. Nutriview (special issue 12). http://www.nutrivit.org/vic/staple/N2003_spec.pdf.

Food Intake *see* **Dietary Intake Measurement**: Methodology; Validation. **Dietary Surveys**. **Meal Size and Frequency**

FOOD INTOLERANCE

T J David, University of Manchester, Manchester, UK

Definition of Food Intolerance

Food intolerance can be defined as a reproducible adverse reaction to a specific food or food ingredient, and it is not psychologically based. Although this appears straightforward, there are a number of difficulties with this definition, and these are discussed below.

Lack of Definition of 'Adverse Reaction'

One problem with our definition of food intolerance is the lack of definition of what constitutes an adverse reaction. All eating causes reactions, which include satiety, feeling warm, the urge to defecate (due to the gastrocolic reflex), and weight gain.

Variation in Tolerance

People vary in their tolerance of events. For some, flatus is an unacceptable and embarrassing problem, whereas for others it is the normal effect of eating baked beans.

Any Food taken in Excess may be Harmful

The definition above does not take into account dosage. Large quantities of certain foods may result in disease in certain individuals, although such disorders are not usually included in the category of food intolerance. Any food, however harmless, can be harmful if taken in excess. Notable examples of this are:

1. Apples, pears, and honey are rich sources of fructose, a sugar which in early childhood is not well absorbed if taken in large quantities. Thus, if a child takes a quantity of fructose in excess of that which can be absorbed in the gastrointestinal tract, the result will be loose stools (diarrhea) due to the osmotic effect of unabsorbed fructose. It should be noted that whereas this applies to normal children, there is in addition a small number of children who are especially poor at handling ingested fructose, and in these children even small quantities of fructose-containing foods will cause florid diarrhea.
2. Chicken liver is a rich source of vitamin A. There are reported cases of infants who were fed large quantities of chicken liver, and who developed raised intracranial pressure as a consequence of vitamin A toxicity.
3. In those who are genetically predisposed, ingestion of an excess of purine-rich foods contributes to hyperuricemia, leading to gout, a disorder which is not usually regarded as a form of food intolerance.

Principal Mechanisms and Pathophysiology of Food Intolerance

The principal mechanisms resulting in food intolerance and the pathophysiology (where this is understood) are discussed below.

Food Allergy

The term 'allergy' implies a definite immunological mechanism. This could be antibody mediated, cell mediated, or due to circulating immune complexes. The clinical features of an allergic reaction include urticaria (nettle rash), angioedema, rhinitis (sneezing, nasal discharge, blocked nose), worsening of pre-existing atopic eczema, asthma (wheezing, coughing, tightness of the chest, shortness of breath), vomiting, abdominal pain, diarrhea, and anaphylactic shock.

Enzyme Defects

Inborn errors of metabolism may affect the digestion and absorption of carbohydrate, fat, or protein. In some subjects the enzyme defect is primarily gastrointestinal, causing defects in digestion or absorption. An example is lactase deficiency (see below). In other subjects, the enzyme defect is systemic. An example is the rare disorders of hereditary fructose intolerance, described below.

Lactase deficiency An example of an enzyme defect causing food intolerance is lactase deficiency. In this condition, which is primarily a disorder that affects infants and young children, there is a reduced or absent concentration of the enzyme lactase in the small intestinal mucosa. Affected individuals are unable to break down ingested lactose, the main sugar found in milk, and which if unabsorbed passes into the large intestine, where there are two consequences. One is an osmotic diarrhea. The other is that some of the unabsorbed lactose is broken down by intestinal bacteria, accompanied by the production of gas (hydrogen) leading to abdominal distension and flatus and the production of organic acids that cause perianal soreness or excoriation. The production of hydrogen, its absorption into the bloodstream, and its excretion in the breath lead to a very simple and elegant test for sugar intolerance: the breath hydrogen test. In this test, the subject swallows a portion of the sugar which one suspects the subject cannot absorb. Breath is collected every half an hour and the hydrogen content is measured. In the normal individual, the sugar is absorbed and hydrogen is not produced. In the intolerant individual, the sugar is not absorbed, hydrogen is produced, and a steep rise in hydrogen concentration is found in the exhaled air.

The management of lactose intolerance is to avoid foods that contain lactose (mainly cows' milk and its products). For infants it is worth noting that the soya-based infant formulas are lactose free. In theory, an alternative is to add microbial β-galactosidase to cows' milk, which can produce a lactose-free milk, with the inconvenience that it has a sweeter flavor and requires a 24-h incubation period at 4 °C.

In infants and young children, lactase deficiency is usually a transient problem occurring after an episode of gastroenteritis, but it is commonly a feature of any disease that causes damage to the intestinal mucosa (e.g., celiac disease). Levels of lactase tend to fall during mid to later childhood, and in a number of populations (e.g., African, Mexican, Greenland Eskimo) a high proportion of adults have very little lactase activity. This adult deficiency is believed to have a genetic basis. Man is the only animal apart from the domestic cat that drinks milk after weaning, and deficiency of lactase in adults could in certain populations be considered the normal state.

Hereditary fructose intolerance In this condition, which has autosomal recessive inheritance, there is deficiency of the liver enzyme fructose 1,6-bisphosphate aldolase. As a result, fructose-1-phosphate accumulates in liver cells, and acts as a competitive inhibitor for phosphorylase. The resulting transient inhibition of the conversion of glycogen to glucose leads to severe hypoglycemia (low blood glucose concentration). Affected infants are symptom free as long as their diet is limited to human milk. If they receive milk formulas or any food that contains fructose they develop attacks of hypoglycemia, shock, coma and convulsions. There may be jaundice, an enlarged liver, and sometimes progressive liver disease. The treatment requires the complete elimination of fructose from the diet, which may be difficult as fructose is a widely used food additive and sweetener. A trivial but interesting feature of the condition in survivors is a notable reduction in dental caries, a beneficial result from the need to avoid many types of confectionery.

Pharmacological Mechanisms

Caffeine A good example of a pharmacological agent found in food with the ability to cause adverse reactions is caffeine. The stimulant effect, which may be welcome at times but unwelcome at others, of 60 mg caffeine in a cup of tea or 100 mg caffeine in a cup of coffee are well recognized. What is less well recognized is that heavy coffee or tea drinkers can suffer a number of other side effects of caffeine, which stimulates gastric secretion and can cause heartburn, nausea, vomiting, diarrhea, and intestinal colic. Also common are irregular heartbeats, episodes of rapid pulse, sweating, tremor, anxiety, and sleeplessness. Caffeine also has a diuretic effect.

Sodium nitrite Another pharmacological effect occurs when unusually large quantities of sodium nitrite are ingested. Sodium nitrite is an antioxidant used as an antibacterial agent, and in quantities of 20 mg or more it can cause dilatation of blood vessels causing flushing and headache, and urticaria.

Tyramine, histamine, and other vasoactive amines A further example of a pharmacological mechanism is the adverse effect of various vasoactive amines such as tyramine, serotonin, tryptamine, phenylethylamine, and histamine, which are found in a range of foods such as tuna, pickled herring, sardines, anchovy fillets, bananas, cheese, yeast extracts (such as Marmite), chocolate, wine, spinach, tomato, and sausages. There appear to be three main mechanisms in operation:

1. An abnormally high intake of vasoactive amines, such as histamine or tyramine, either because of a high content in food or because of synthesis of these chemicals in the gut by bacteria.
2. An abnormal effect whereby drugs or chemicals in food interfere with the enzymes that break down vasoactive amines.
3. An abnormal release from mast cells of histamine and other mediators of inflammation, triggered by eating certain foods such as strawberries, shellfish, and alcohol.

Vasoactive amines are the normal constituents of many foods. They arise mainly from the decarboxylation of amino acids, but they may also develop during normal food cooking and during the storage of food. **Table 1** shows the histamine level of various sausages. The term 'semi-dry' when applied to sausages (**Table 1**) means sausages that are fermented for varying periods. During this sausage ripening process, the histamine concentration increases, depending upon the length of the ripening process. It is estimated that 70–1000 mg of histamine ingested in a single meal is necessary for the

Table 1 Histamine levels in sausages

Type of sausage	Histamine level (mg/100g)	
	Mean	Range
Cooked sausages[a]		
Bologna	0.55	0.19–0.84
Cooked salami	0.83	0.47–5.86
Kosher salami	0.50	0.33–0.97
Semidry sausages[a]		
Thuringer cervelat	2.35	1.03–3.63
Thuringer	1.19	0.31–2.56
Dry sausages[a]		
Italian dry salami	2.14–24.5[b]	0.42–36.4[b]
Pepperoni	1.03–38.1[b]	0.72–55.0[b]
Chorizo	2.29	0.60–8.08

[a]The sausages were obtained from retail markets in the San Francisco Bay area.
[b]Depending upon the brand tested.
Source: Taylor SL, Leatherwood M, Lieber ER (1978) A survey of histamine levels in sausages. *Journal of Food Protection* **41**: 634–637.

onset of toxicity, depending on individual sensitivity. Thus, 130 g of the pepperoni sample that contained 55.0 mg histamine per 100 g (see **Table 1**) would be necessary to cause symptoms in the most sensitive individuals.

The largest amounts of histamine and tyramine are found in fermented foods such as cheese, alcoholic drinks, sausage, sauerkraut, and tinned fish. Badly stored food (see below) such as mackerel and tuna can also contain large amounts of histamine.

The effects of large doses of tyramine, histamine, and other vasoactive amines are extremely variable. Histamine causes flushing (by dilatation of blood vessels), constriction of smooth muscle in the intestine and the bronchi, increased heart rate, headache, fall in blood pressure, and asthma. Tyramine causes constriction of blood vessels, and it stimulates the release of noradrenaline from nerve endings. It can also cause the release of histamine and prostaglandins from mast cells. Dietary tyramine is known to induce hypertension and headache in patients who are taking monoamine oxidase inhibitor drugs. This effect has been shown to be due to inhibition, by these drugs, of intestinal and hepatic metabolism of tyramine, so that the amine accumulates.

The variable effect of histamine taken by mouth is in part due to the varying degree of inactivation in the gastrointestinal tract. Histamine is inactivated by mucoproteins that are produced in the gastrointestinal tract mucosa, but this inactivation can be blocked by other amines such as cadaverine and putresceine, which also bind strongly to mucoproteins. Thus, when food is taken that contains cadaverine and putresceine, more histamine can be absorbed. In fact, most of the histamine that is absorbed is degraded as it is transported across the mucosa by the intestinal enzyme diamine oxidase. Cadaverine and putresceine also have a high affinity for diamine oxidase, and can also interfere with the inactivation of histamine by this enzyme. Another barrier to the absorption of histamine is provided by the liver enzyme methyl transferase.

Thus, the effect of histamine and other vasoactive amines on an individual will depend on a number of factors, which include:

1. The amount of vasoactive amine that is present in food.
2. The amount of histamine released (as a result of an allergic process).
3. The permeability of the gastrointestinal tract, including inactivation by mucus and by mechanisms in the gut mucosa.
4. Interference with the synthesis or release of enzymes involved in amine breakdown (e.g., liver damage causing reduced activity of methyl transferase).

Tyramine and migraine   There has been interest in a possible relationship between dietary tyramine and migraine. One hypothesis is that some patients with migraine have defective metabolism of ingested tyramine in the intestinal wall, which leads to increased absorption, apparently explaining why foods that contain tyramine can provoke attacks in susceptible individuals. However, there is no evidence that the activity of monoamine oxidase, the main tyramine metabolizing enzyme, is lower in patients with food-induced migraine than in other individuals prone to migraine, although levels of monoamine oxidase in platelets are generally lower in patients with migraine.

Set against these theoretical arguments, in fact most attempts to induce migraine by tyramine challenge in children and adults have been unsuccessful. Furthermore, a controlled study of exclusion of dietary vasoactive amines in children with migraine failed to demonstrate benefit. In the latter study, patients were randomly allocated to either a high-fiber diet low in dietary amines or a high-fiber diet alone. Although there was no significant difference in the results for the two groups, both groups showed a highly significant decrease in the number of headaches, emphasizing the need for a control diet in studies designed to show that dietary manipulation improves disease.

Of the foods reported to be common triggers of attacks of migraine, only cheese is rich in tyramine. Chocolate is low in this and other vasoactive amines, and red wine usually contains no more tyramine than white wine. Alcoholic drinks, particularly red wine, are commonly reported to provoke attacks of migraine. Whether these attacks are due to the alcohol itself or some other compound is a matter of debate. The major chemical difference between red and white wine is the former's high concentration of phenolic flavonoids such as anthocyanins and catechins, which as well as having direct effects on blood vessels may also inhibit the enzyme phenolsulfotransferase. Patients with food-induced migraine were shown to have significantly lower levels of platelet phenolsulfotransferase activity, and it has been hypothesized (but not proven) that low activity of this enzyme could lead to an accumulation of phenolic or monoamine substrates, which in turn might directly or indirectly provoke attacks of migraine.

Regardless of the possible mechanism, there are a number of subjects with migraine who are made worse by specific dietary triggers such as cheese or wine, for whatever reason, and avoidance of specific food triggers in susceptible subjects may prove helpful in reducing the frequency of attacks.

11β-hydroxysteroid dehydrogenase and liquorice
Liquorice contains an enzyme that inhibits 11 β-hydroxysteroid dehydrogenase, resulting in sodium and water retention, hypertension, hypokalemia, and suppression of the renin–aldosterone system.

Irritant Mechanisms

Certain foods have a direct irritant effect on the mucous membranes of the mouth or gut, such as the irritant effect of coffee or curry. In certain individuals, food intolerance only occurs in the presence of a coexisting medical disorder. For example, the ingestion of spicy food, coffee, or orange juice provoke esophageal pain in some patients with reflux esophagitis. This effect is unconnected to the temperature or acidity of the food, or to any effect on the lower esophageal sphincter. The treatment in susceptible individuals is to avoid the trigger food item.

Specific Drug–Food Combinations

One example of drug-induced food intolerance is potentiation of the pressor effects of tyramine-containing foods (e.g., cheese, yeast extracts, and fermented soya bean products) by monoamine oxidase inhibitor drugs. Another is the effect of taking alcohol in patients with alcohol dependence during treatment with disulfiram (Antabuse). The reaction, which can occur within 10 min of alcohol and may last for several hours, consists of flushing and nausea.

Toxic Mechanisms

Nature has endowed plants with the capacity to synthesize substances that are toxic, and thus serve to protect them from predators whether they be fungi, insects, animals, or humans. Thus, many plant foods contain naturally occurring toxins. On a worldwide scale, reactions to naturally occurring toxins may outnumber allergic reactions, although it is currently fashionable to pay more attention to the latter.

Protease inhibitors Soya beans were originally introduced into the US as a source of oil, the extracted meal being used as a by-product that could provide animals with a source of protein. However, it was recognized that it was necessary to subject soya beans to heat treatment if they were to support the growth of animals. It was later found that the substance responsible for growth inhibition in raw soya beans was a protease (trypsin) inhibitor and it is now known that protease inhibitors are widely distributed throughout the plant kingdom, particularly in legumes, and to a lesser extent in cereal grains and tubers. In addition to inhibition of growth, one of the most characteristic responses of most animals to trypsin inhibitor is enlargement of the pancreas. The depression of growth is believed to result from endogenous loss of protein (i.e., loss into the gastrointestinal tract) due to hypersecretion by the pancreas. Soya beans products that have been adequately heat treated to inactivate trypsin inhibitor are safe for consumption.

Lectins There is a protein present in most legumes and cereals that has the property of being able to agglutinate the red blood cells of various species of animals: the so-called phytohemagglutinins or lectins. Some of these lectins, such as ricin from the castor bean, are extremely toxic. Others, such as those in the soya bean, are nontoxic. Lectins appear to be responsible for the fact that many other legumes, unless properly cooked, not only fail to support the growth of animals but can lead to death. Lectins are found in many food items commonly consumed in the human diet including tomatoes, bean sprouts, raw vegetables, fruits, spices, dry cereals, and nuts, and it is not known whether these are harmful in any way. However, it is well recognized that inadequate cooking of red kidney beans can cause severe gastrointestinal upset, with vomiting and diarrhea. It is for this reason that it is recommended that raw red kidney beans should be cooked by initially boiling hard for 10 min.

Lathyrogens Lathyrism is a paralytic disease that is associated with the consumption of chickling pea or vetch, *Lathyrus sativus*. The causative factor is believed to be an amino acid derivative, β-N-oxalyl-, -diaminopropionic acid; this is a metabolic antagonist of glutamic acid, a substance that is involved in the transmission of nerve impulses in the brain.

Mimosine Mimosine is an amino acid that comprises 1–4% of the dry weight of the legume *Leucaena leucocephala*, and consumption of its leaves, pods, and seeds leads to hair loss in animals. Mimosine is also a goitrogen (see below).

Djenkolic acid In parts of Sumatra the djenkol bean is a popular food item. The bean is a seed of the leguminous tree, *Pithecolobium lobatum*, and resembles the horse chestnut in size and color. Consumption of this seed leads to kidney failure that is accompanied by blood and needle-like clusters in the urine, which have been identified as containing the amino acid djenkolic acid.

Goitrogens Substances capable of producing goiter are present in plants belonging to the cabbage family, including cabbage, turnip, broccoli, cauliflower, brussel sprouts, kale, rape seed, and mustard seed. Cows' milk is a vector for the transmission of goitrogens from animals fed kale and turnips, and may have been responsible for endemic goiter in countries such as Australia and Finland.

Cyanogens A number of plants are potentially toxic because they contain glycosides from which hydrogen cyanide may be released by enzymatic hydrolysis. The most common plants eaten by humans, in order of their potential cyanide content, are: lima beans (*Phaseolus lunatus*), sorghum, cassava, linseed meal, black-eyed pea (*Vigna sinensis*), garden pea (*Pisum sativum*), kidney bean (*Phaseolus vulgaris*), Bengal gram (*Cicer arietinum*), and red gram (*Cajanus cajans*).

Vicine and convicine These are β-glucosides that are present in broad beans (*Vicia faba*). When consumed by individuals with deficiency of the enzyme glucose-6-phosphate dehydrogenase, these substances precipitate the condition of favism, which is characterized by anemia caused by hemolysis of red blood cells. The enzyme deficiency is a genetic disorder that is confined largely to inhabitants of countries surrounding the Mediterranean basin (Italy, Sicily, Lebanon, Israel, and north Africa) although individuals of the same ethnic background residing in other countries may also suffer from favism.

Cycasin Cycad seeds or nuts are obtained from *Cycad circinalis*, a palm-like tree that grows throughout the tropics and subtropics. The seeds, unless thoroughly washed, are extremely toxic, causing poisoning in humans and tumors in experimental animals. The toxic ingredient methyl-azoxy-methanol, the aglycone of cycasin, is released on hydrolysis of cycasin by intestinal bacteria.

Pyrrolizidine derivatives Pyrrolizidine alkaloids are found in a wide variety of plant species. The toxic ingredient belongs to a class of compounds that are derivatives of pyrrolizidine. Large numbers of people have been poisoned through consumption of cereal and grain crops contaminated with pyrrolizidine-containing plants. It is also possible that milk from cows grazing on pastures that contain such plants could act as a vector for the transmission of pyrrolizidine to humans. In one part of western USA one such plant, the tansy ragwort (*Senecio jacobea*) is readily consumed by cows and goats, and the milk from such animals has been shown to contain significant amounts of a pyrrolizidine derivative, jacoline.

Lupin alkaloid Milk from animals that have eaten plants from the lupin family, notably *Lupinus latifolius*, may contain quinolizidine alkaloids such as anagyrine. There is strong evidence that these alkaloids are teratogenic in animals, causing severe bony deformities, and there is some evidence that similar defects may occur in the offspring of human mothers who drink alkaloid-containing milk in pregnancy.

Other examples There are numerous other examples of toxic substances present in foodstuffs. These include solanidine in potatoes, cyanide in tapioca, mycotoxins in mushrooms and cereal grains, and phototoxic furocoumarins in angelica, parsley, dill and celeriac, which in sufficient quantities can give rise to a wide variety of toxic reactions (**Table 2** and **Table 3**).

Table 2 Examples of toxic constituents of plant foodstuffs and their role in plant physiology

Toxic constituent	Type of food containing toxic constituent	Physiological role of toxic constituent	Role in plant defense: mechanism of toxic constituent
Protease inhibitors	Legumes, cereals, potatoes, pineapple	?Prevents degradation of storage protein during seed maturation	Part of defense against invading microbes following mechanical damage to leaves
Hemagglutinins	Legumes, cereals, potatoes	(a) Attach glycoprotein enzymes (b) Role in embryonic development/ differentiation (c) Role in sugar transport or store (d) ?Involved in root nodule nitrogen-fixing bacteria symbiosis	(a) Counteract soil bacteria (b) Antifungal (c) Protect against seed predators
Glucosinolates	Radish, horseradish, turnip, cabbage, rape seed	?Disease & insect resistance role	
Cyanogens	Almonds, cassava, corn, peas, butter beans, bamboo shoots		
Saponins	Alfalfa, French beans, soya beans		

Adapted from: Leiner IE (ed.) (1980) *Toxic Constituents of Plant Foodstuffs*, 2nd edn. New York: Academic Press.

Table 3 Examples of foodborne toxins or toxin-producing organisms, excluding plant foodstuffs

Pathogen or toxin	Principal symptoms	Common food source
Bacillus cereus	(a) diarrhea	Proteinaceous food, vegetables, sauces, puddings
	(b) Vomiting	Fried rice
Bacillus subtilis	Vomiting, diarrhea	Meat and pastry
	Flushing, sweating	Meat/seafood with rice
Bacillus licheniformis	Diarrhea	Cooked meat and vegetables
Clostridium botulinum	Neuroparalytic disease (botulism)	Meat, fish, vegetables, hazelnut conserve
Clostridium perfringens	Diarrhea, abdominal pain	Meat, poultry
Salmonella enteridis	Diarrhea, abdominal pain, fever, vomiting	Poultry, eggs
Staphylococcus aureus	Vomiting, abdominal pain, diarrhea	Numerous but specially cooked high-protein foods
Verotoxin-producing Escherichia coli	Hemorrhagic colitis	Ground beef
Listeria monocytogenes	Listeriosis	Unpasteurized cheese, undercooked meat
Dioxins and dibenzofurans	Adverse effects uncertain when consumed in quantities found in food	Fish
Cantharidin	Sensitivity to urethra and genitalia; priapism	Frogs that have Meloidae (blister beetles)
Methyl mercury	Brain damage	Fish, bread
Toxic alkaloid (saxitoxin) in dinoflagellates and plankton	Diverse neurological disorders (paralytic shellfish poisoning)	Clams, oysters, scallops, and mussels
Brevetoxins	Paraesthesia, abdominal pain, diarrhea, transient blindness, paralysis, death (neurotoxic shellfish poisoning)	Clams, oysters, scallops, and mussels
Ciguatera toxin	Diverse gastrointestinal and neurological disorders	Fish (especially reef predators)
Tetrodotoxin	Diverse gastrointestinal and neurological disorders	Puffer fish, certain newts
Domoic acid	Vomiting, diarrhea, hyperexcitation, seizures, memory loss (amnesic shellfish poisoning)	Mussels
Okadaic acid, dinophysis toxins, yessotoxin, pectenotoxins	Diarrhea, vomiting, abdominal pain (diarrhetic shellfish poisoning)	Mussels, scallops
Scombrotoxin (usually histamine)	Headache, palpitations, gastrointestinal disturbance	Mackerel, tuna, and related species
Tetramine (red whelk poisoning)	Diplopia, dizziness, leg pains	Whelks
Grayanotoxins (in honey from areas of Turkey where Rhododendrons are grown)	Hypotension, bradycardia, vomiting, sweating	Honey
Unknown (? in algae) (turtle flesh poisoning)	Cardiorespiratory failure, death	Turtles

Food Storage

Chemical changes in food during storage can produce substances that cause food intolerance. An example is intolerance to ripe or stored tomatoes in subjects who can safely eat green tomatoes, where ripening of the fruit produces a new active glycoprotein. Some adverse reactions resulting from food storage come into the category of toxic reactions, such as the rise in levels of histamine and tyramine in certain foods during storage as a result of bacterial decarboxylation. An example of this is the production of histamine in badly stored mackerel and other fish: scombroid fish poisoning. Contamination of food by antigens such as storage mites or microbial spores may give rise to adverse effects, particularly asthma and eczema. Contamination of food by microorganisms may result in adverse effects. For example,

celery, parsnip, and parsley may become infected with the fungus *Sclerotinia scleriotiorum* ('pink rot'), resulting in the production of the photosensitizing chemicals psoralen, 5-methoxypsoralen, and 8-methoxypsoralen.

Practical Applications

Food arouses not only the appetite but also the emotions. The passion for food that is natural (i.e., free from extraneous ingredients) is not new; in 1857, a survey of adulterants in food showed that childrens' sweets were commonly colored by red lead (lead oxide), lead chromate, mercuric sulfide, and copper arsenite. By the late 1850s, 'pure and unadulterated' had become the stock advertising slogan of those anxious to cash in on the then newly awakened fears of the public. The current scale of the use of additives in food comes as a surprise to most people, and it is understandable that many should find these substances vaguely menacing. Nonetheless, the current phobia of food additives and food processing, and the obsession for so-called natural or health food arises largely out of misinformation and ignorance. Obsession with so-called natural or health food ignores the wide range of naturally occurring toxins in foods. The concept of health food is wholly misleading. For example, a survey of 'crunchy' peanut butter showed that 11 out of 59 samples from health food producers contained over $100 \, \mu g \, kg^{-1}$ of aflatoxins, over 10 times the proposed maximum permitted level for total aflatoxins. Only one of the 26 samples from other producers contained aflatoxins in excess of $10 \, \mu g \, kg^{-1}$, and none contained more than $50 \, \mu g \, kg^{-1}$.

See also: **Caffeine**. **Food Allergies**: Etiology; Diagnosis and Management. **Food Safety**: Mycotoxins. **Fructose**. **Lactose Intolerance**. **Vitamin A**: Biochemistry and Physiological Role; Deficiency and Interventions.

Further Reading

Ashwood-Smith MJ, Ceska O, and Chaudhary SK (1985) Mechanism of photosensitivity reactions to diseased celery. *British Medical Journal*, vol. **290**: 1249.

Bjarnason I, Levi S, Smethurst P, Menzies IS, and Levi AJ (1988) Vindaloo and you. *British Medical Journal* **297**: 1629–1631.

Bleumink E, Berrens L, and Young E (1967) Studies on the atopic allergen in ripe tomato fruits. *International Archives of Allergy* **31**: 25–37.

Ciegler A (1975) Mycotoxins: occurrence, chemistry, biological activity. *Lloydia* **38**: 21–35.

Conning DM and Lansdown ABG (eds.) (1983) *Toxic Hazards in Food*. London: Croom Helm.

Edwards CRW (1991) Lessons from licorice. *New England Journal of Medicine* **325**: 1242–1243.

Farese RV, Bigieri EG, Shackleton CHL, Irony I, and Gomez-Fontes R (1991) Licorice induced hypermineralocorticoidism. *New England Journal of Medicine* **325**: 1223–1227.

Forsythe WI and Redmond A (1974) Two controlled trials of tyramine in children with migraine. *Developmental Medicine and Child Neurology* **16**: 794–799.

Gibson GG and Walker R (eds.) (1985) *Food Toxicology – Real or Imaginary Problems?* London: Taylor & Francis.

Gumbmann MR, Spangler WL, Dugan GM, and Rackis JJ (1986) Safety of trypsin inhibitors in the diet: effects on the rat pancreas of long-term feeding of soy flour and soy protein isolate. In: Friedman M (ed.) *Nutritional and Toxicological Significance of Enzyme Inhibitors in Foods*, pp. 33–79. New York: Plenum Press.

Hall MJ (1987) The dangers of cassava (tapioca) consumption. *Bristol Medico-Chirurgical Journal* **102**: 37–39.

Harris JB (ed.) (1986) *Natural Toxins. Animal, Plant, and Microbial*. Oxford: Clarendon Press.

Horwitz D, Lovenberg W, Engelman K, and Sjoerdsma A (1964) Monoamine oxidase inhibitors, tyramine, and cheese. *Journal of the American Medical Association* **188**: 90–92.

Kaufman HS (1986) The red wine headache: A pilot study of a specific syndrome. Immunology and Allergy Practice **8**: 279–284.

Knudson EA and Kroon S (1988) In vitro and in vivo phototoxicity of furocoumarin-containing plants. *Clinical Experimental Dermatology* **13**: 92–96.

Leiner IE (ed.) (1980) *Toxic Constituents of Plant Foodstuffs*, 2nd edn. New York: Academic Press.

Lessof MH (1992) *Food Intolerance* London: Chapman & Hall.

Littlewood JT, Glover V, Davies PTG, Gibb C, Sandler M, and Rose FC (1988) Red wine as a cause of migraine. *Lancet* **1**: 558–559.

Mahoney CP, Margolis MT, Knauss TA, and Labbe RF (1980) Chronic vitamin A intoxication in infants fed chicken liver. Pediatrics 1980; **65**: 893–896.

Masyczek R and Ough CS (1983) The "Red Wine Reaction" syndrome. *American Journal of Enology and Viticulture* **34**: 260–264.

Moffett A, Swash M, and Scott DF (1972) Effect of tyramine in migraine: a double-blind study. *Journal of Neurology, Neurosurgery and Psychiatry* **35**: 496–499.

Moffett AM, Swash M, and Scott DF (1974) Effect of chocolate in migraine: a double-blind study. *Journal of Neurology, Neurosurgery and Psychiatry* **37**: 445–448.

Morgan RGH, Crass RA, and Oates PS (1986) Dose effects of raw soyabean flour on pancreatic growth. In: Friedman M (ed.) *Nutritional and Toxicological Significance of Enzyme Inhibitors in Foods*, pp. 81–89. New York: Plenum Press.

Noah ND, Bender AE, Reaidi GB, and Gilbert RJ (1980) Food poisoning from raw red kidney beans. *British Medical Journal* **281**: 236–237.

Price SF, Smithson KW, and Castell D (1978) Food sensitivity in reflux esophagitis. *Gastroenterology* **75**: 240–243.

Rackis JJ, Wolf WJ, and Baker EC (1986) Protease inhibitors in plant foods: content and inactivation. In: Friedman M (ed.) *Nutritional and Toxicological Significance of Enzyme Inhibitors in Foods*, pp. 299–347. New York: Plenum Press.

Salfield SAW, Wardley BL, Houlsby WT, Turner SL, Spalton AP, Beckles-Wilson NR, and Herber SM (1987) Controlled study of exclusion of dietary vasoactive amines in migraine. *Archives of Disease in Childhood* **62**: 458–460.

Sandler M, Youdim MBH, and Hanington E (1974) A phenylethylamine oxidising defect in migraine. *Nature* **250**: 335–337.

Taylor SL (1986) Histamine food poisoning: toxicology and clinical aspects. *CRC Critical Reviews in Toxicology* **17**: 90–128.

Wuthrich B and Ortolani C (eds.) (1996) *Highlights in Food Allergy*. Basel: Karger.

FOOD SAFETY

Contents
Mycotoxins
Pesticides
Bacterial Contamination
Other Contaminants
Heavy Metals

Mycotoxins

J D Groopman and T W Kensler, Johns Hopkins University, Baltimore, MD, USA

Mycotoxins are toxic fungal metabolites of enormous chemical diversity that naturally contaminate the human food supply. These compounds induce an array of toxicologic effects when consumed in sufficient quantities. The three major genera of mycotoxin-producing fungi are *Aspergillus*, *Fusarium*, and *Penicillium*. This field has been comprehensively reviewed by the Council for Agricultural Science and Technology (CAST) and concisely by Etzel. The potential production of mycotoxins is insidious since fungal growth can occur both prior to and after grain harvest. Ecological conditions such as drought or damage to seeds by insects or mechanical harvesting can enhance mycotoxin production during both growth and storage. Mycotoxin production also occurs over a wide range of moisture content, relative humidity, and temperature. The major crops affected throughout the world are corn, peanuts, cotton, wheat, rice, and the processed food derived from these commodities.

Following the discovery of the carcinogenic aflatoxins 40 years ago, the search for mycotoxins has led to the identification of more than 100 toxigenic fungi and more than 300 mycotoxins worldwide. Most of these mycotoxins have not been linked to any toxic syndromes in animals or people, but some, such as aflatoxins, certain trichothecenes, fumonisins, and ochratoxins, have been implicated in highly lethal episodic outbreaks of mold poisoning in exposed animals and/or human populations. Mycotoxins with carcinogenic potency in experimental animal models include aflatoxins, sterigmatocystin, ochratoxin, fumonisin, patulin, and penicillic acid. Of these agents, aflatoxin B_1 has been classified as a category I human carcinogen by the International Agency for Research on Cancer

(IARC). This article briefly describes the occurrence, biological effects, mechanistic studies, and where available, epidemiological associations of dietary exposure to major mycotoxins with human disease outcomes.

Aflatoxins

Chemistry and Occurrence

The aflatoxins (AFs) were discovered as the causative agent of turkey X disease, which resulted in the death of thousands of turkey poults, ducklings, and chicks fed a contaminated peanut meal. Chemically, the AFs are a highly substituted coumarin moiety containing a fused dihydrofurofuran moiety. Four major AFs designated B_1, B_2, G_1, and G_2 are produced by *A. flavus* and *A. parasiticus*. AFB_1 and AFB_2 were named because of their strong blue fluorescence under ultraviolet light, whereas AFG_1 and AFG_2 fluoresced greenish-yellow.

Commodities most often shown to contain AFs are peanuts, various other nuts, cotton seed, corn, and rice. Human exposure can occur from consumption of AFs from these sources and the products derived from them, as well as from tissues, eggs, and milk (AFM_1) from animals that have consumed contaminated feeds. When contamination occurs, AFB_1 generally predominates. Although contamination by the molds may be universal within a given geographical area, the levels or final concentrations of AFs in the grain product can vary from less than 1 ppb to greater than 12,000 ppb. It is important to note that obvious contamination of a commodity with *A. flavus* or *A. parasiticus* does not necessarily indicate the presence of AFs, and the appearance of a sound, uninfected sample of commodity does not preclude the existence of significant quantities of AFs.

Widespread concern regarding the toxic effects of AFs in humans and animals and possible transfer of residues from animal tissues and milk to humans has led to regulatory actions governing the interstate as well as global transport and consumption of AF-contaminated food and feed commodities. The US Food and Drug Administration has set the action levels of AF in commodities. For feeding mature nonlactating animals, the action level is 100 ppb; for commodities destined for human consumption and interstate commerce, it is 20 ppb; and for milk it is 0.5 ppb.

Toxic Effects

AFs are potent liver toxins, and their effects in animals vary with dose, length of exposure, species, breed, and diet or nutritional status. These toxins may be lethal when consumed in large doses; sublethal doses produce a chronic toxicity, and low levels of chronic exposure can result in cancer, primarily liver cancer, in many animal species. AFB_1, the most potent and most commonly occurring AF, is acutely toxic to all species of animals, birds, and fishes tested. Sheep and mice are the most resistant, whereas cats, dogs, and rabbits are the most sensitive species. Chronic aflatoxicosis is characterized by bile duct proliferation, periportal fibrosis, icterus, and cirrhosis of liver. Prolonged exposure to low levels of AFB_1 leads to hepatoma, cholangiocarcinoma, or hepatocellular carcinoma and other tumors. The molecular basis for the toxicology of aflatoxin has been reviewed by Wild and Turner.

Some cases of acute aflatoxicosis in humans have been reported in the literature, especially in the subpopulations of developing countries. Clinical manifestations were characterized by vomiting, abdominal pain, pulmonary edema, and fatty infiltration and necrosis of the liver. There was a putative aflatoxin poisoning in western India when there was consumption of heavily molded corn. There were at least 97 fatalities, and these deaths occurred only in households where the contaminated corn was consumed. Histopathology of liver specimens revealed extensive bile duct proliferation, a lesion often noted in experimental animals after acute AF exposure. An incident of acute aflatoxicosis in Kenya was also associated with consumption of maize highly contaminated with AF. There were 20 hospital admissions with a 20% mortality. Also, the consumption of AF-contaminated noodles resulted in acute hepatic encephalopathy in children in Malaysia. Up to 3 mg of AF was suspected to be present in a single serving of contaminated noodles.

Carcinogenicity in Animals

AFB_1 is a potent liver carcinogen in many species of animals, including rodents, nonhuman primates, and fish. In appropriate circumstances, dependent on such variables as animal species and strain, dose, route of administration, and dietary factors, significant incidences of tumors have been induced at sites other than the liver, such as kidney and colon. AFB_1 has been demonstrated to induce liver tumors in two species of lower primates: the tree shrew (*Tupaia glis*) and the marmoset (*Saguinus oedipomidas*). All liver tumors of the tree shrew were classified as hepatocellular carcinoma (HCC) and developed in a manner similar to those of the rat. Unlike the case with rats, in the marmoset histologic observation revealed the association of cirrhotic changes with liver tumor development. Rhesus monkeys have also proven to be susceptible to AFB_1 carcinogenicity. Data from 47 monkeys, representing three species (rhesus, cynomolgus, and African green), that had received AFB_1 have been published. Primary liver tumor incidence was 19% (5/26) in animals surviving for longer than 6 months, and total tumor incidence in these animals was 50% (13/26).

Metabolism

Metabolism plays a critical role in the biological activity and disposition of AF. To produce a DNA damage product, AFB_1 undergoes an initial two-electron oxidation by the cytochrome P450 family members CYP1A2 and CYP3A4, yielding aflatoxin B1-8,9-oxide. This epoxide reacts with the N7 atom of guanine to form a pro-mutagenic DNA adduct (aflatoxin–N7–guanine). The aflatoxin–DNA adduct is unstable and undergoes depurination, leading to its urinary excretion. Aflatoxin B1-8,9-oxide is also a substrate for several isoforms of human glutathione S-transferases (GSTs), which yield a stable, nontoxic, polar product that is excreted in the bile. The aflatoxin–glutathione product also undergoes sequential metabolism in the liver and kidneys to be excreted as a mercapturic acid (aflatoxin–N-acetylcysteine) in the urine. Aflatoxin B1 also undergoes extensive oxidation, which is catalyzed by cytochrome P450s. In addition to formation of the 8,9-oxide, oxidation by CYP1A2 yields a stable urinary metabolite, aflatoxin M1, that is excreted in milk. Aflatoxin M1 is less carcinogenic or mutagenic than aflatoxin B1, but it is equally toxic. The oxidation products of aflatoxin can be excreted without further biotransformation or can be conjugated by UDP-glucuronosyl transferases. Collectively, these end products of aflatoxin biotransformation are biomarkers of exposure to aflatoxin and risk of hepatocellular carcinoma.

Aflatoxin and Human Cancer

HCC is the fifth leading cause of cancer mortality throughout the world, and in areas of Asia and Africa it accounts for nearly 70% of all cancer deaths. Furthermore, due to the lack of symptoms in the early stages and rapid growth rates of tumors, most HCCs are discovered in very advanced stages. The 5-year mortality rate for individuals diagnosed with HCC is greater than 95%. In the People's Republic of China, HCC is the third leading cause of cancer mortality and accounts for at least 250,000 deaths per year, with an incidence in some counties approaching 100 cases per 100,000 per year. Moreover, in high-risk regions of the world the median age of onset of HCC is decades earlier than in the United States.

In the early 1990s, nested case–control studies conducted in Shanghai utilized these biomarkers to establish a significant association between aflatoxin exposure and HCC. They showed that the risk of HCC increased dramatically (60-fold) in individuals who had been exposed to aflatoxin and had chronic hepatitis infection compared to those with neither the chemical nor viral exposures. Additional studies in Qidong and Taiwan have confirmed this striking chemical–viral interaction. The underlying mechanism for this interaction remains poorly understood.

The relationship between aflatoxin exposure and development of human HCC is further highlighted by molecular biological studies on the *p53* tumor suppressor gene, the most common mutated gene detected in many human cancers. The initial results came from three independent studies of *p53* mutations in HCCs occurring in populations exposed to high levels of dietary AF and found high frequencies of G $\rightarrow$ T transversions, with clustering at codon 249. On the other hand, studies of *p53* mutations in HCCs from Japan and other areas where there is little exposure to AF revealed no mutations at codon 249.

A positive correlation has been observed between population estimates of aflatoxin exposure and the proportion of HCC cases with a *p53* 249[ser] mutation detected in plasma. Kirk and colleagues analyzed restriction length fragment polymorphisms to detect this mutation in the plasma of liver cancer patients in The Gambia, West Africa. Jackson *et al.* subsequently used mass spectrometry to detect the same mutation in matched plasma and tumor samples from cancer patients in Qidong. Continuing validation of this biomarker in a prospective cohort has shown that it can be detected 1 or more years in advance of HCC diagnosis. Collectively, these genetic serum markers reveal a new paradigm for early identification of at-risk individuals and HCC diagnosis.

Fumonisins

Occurrence

The fumonisins are a class of mycotoxins produced by *Fusarium moniliforme*, a fungus that is a ubiquitous contaminant of corn, and are also found at high levels in milk and cereal products. Six fumonisins have been isolated and characterized from *F. moniliforme*. They are designated as fumonisin B_1 (FB_1), B_2, B_3, B_4, A_1, and A_2. Only FB_1 and FB_2 appear to be toxicologically significant and have been studied to any extent. FB_1 and FB_2 were first isolated in 1988 and invariably occur together, with FB_2 at levels of 15–35% of FB_1. Levels of FB_1 have annual variation but are consistently in the 0.5 to 2 ppm range in US cornmeal and have been reported as high as 150 ppm in corn destined for human consumption in South Africa. Regulatory limits for fumonisins in commodities are currently being promolugated worldwide.

Toxicity

Fusarium moniliforme contaminated corn has been associated with several human and animal diseases, including luekoencephalomalacia (LEM) in horses, pulmonary edema in swine, and hepatoxicity in horses, swine, and rats. Both culture material from *F. moniliforme*-inoculated corn and pure FB_1 are capable of producing similar effects in animals. Neurotoxic signs and symptoms, including loss of feed consumption, lameness, ataxia, oral and facial paralysis, and recumbency, begin within days after initial consumption of moldy corn or by direct administration of FB_1 and may be rapidly followed by seizures and morbidity. Focal malacia and liquefaction of cerebral white matter with peripheral hemorrhage is the pathognomonic finding.

Studies have provided possible insights into the mechanisms of toxicity. The fumonisins bear considerable structural similarity to the long-chain (sphingoid) base backbones of sphingolipids. It was demonstrated that incubation of rat hepatocytes with fumonisins inhibited sphingosine biosynthesis. FB_1 increased the amount of the biosynthetic intermediate sphinganine, which suggests that fumonisins inhibit the conversion of sphinganine to N-acyl-sphinganines. It was subsequently shown, using mouse cerebellar neurons in culture, that FB_1 inhibited ceramide synthase in mouse brain microsomes with a competitive-like kinetic behavior with respect to both sphinganine and stearoyl-CoA. Thus, disruption of the *de novo* pathway of sphingolipid biosynthesis may be a critical event in the diseases that have been associated with consumption of fumonisins.

Carcinogenicity in Animals

Rats fed a diet supplemented with maize contaminated with the *F. moniliforme* that had caused an outbreak of LEM in horses all developed hepatic nodules, cholantiofibrosis, or cholangiocarcinomas within 6 months. Lifetime studies in rats fed diets containing maize inoculated with *F. moniliforme* yielded a high incidence of liver tumors. The carcinogenicity of FB_1 has been directly assessed in a study in which a semipurified diet containing 50 mg/kg of pure (>90%) FB_1 was fed to rats. Ten out of 15 FB_1-treated rats (66%) developed primary HCC.

Human Health Effects

In an initial study in high-risk and low-risk regions of Transkei (South Africa) for esophageal cancer, cancer rates were correlated with the proportion of maize samples infected by *F. moniliforme*. In a follow-up study, the mean proportions of maize kernel infected with *F. moniliforme* in both healthy and moldy maize samples from households in the high-incidence esophageal cancer area were significantly higher than those in the low incidence area. FB_1 and FB_2 levels in healthy maize samples from the low-risk area were approximately 20 times lower than those in healthy samples from high-risk areas. One study estimated that naturally poisoned horses consumed levels of fuminisins equivalent to those shown to be toxic experimentally, and that humans in high esophageal cancer risk areas can potentially consume levels higher than those shown to be carcinogenic in rats.

A number of surveys have been conducted in Henan Province in northern China. Fungal strains from samples of wheat, corn, dried sweet potato, rice, and soya beans were cultured and isolated in five counties with a high incidence of esophageal cancer and three with a low incidence. The frequency of contamination by *F. moniliforme* was significantly higher in food samples from high-risk areas, although the frequency of contamination by all other fungi analyzed was also significantly higher in samples from the high-risk counties. Although these studies, as well as those conducted in South Africa, demonstrate correlations between high esophageal cancer rates and contamination of foods, primarily corn, with *F. moniliforme*, the specific role of the fumonisins or other related toxins in the etiology of this cancer remains to be firmly established.

Ochratoxins

Occurrence

Ochratoxins are a group of structurally related metabolites that are produced by *A. ochraceus* and related species, as well as *P. viridicatum* and certain other *Penecillium* species. The major mycotoxin in this group is ochratoxin A (OA), which appears to be the only one of major toxicological significance. Chemically, OA contains an isocoumarin moiety linked by a peptide bond to phenylalanine. OA has been detected in many food commodities throughout the world but is found primarily in grains grown in northern temperate areas resulting in contamination of breads and cereal products. In addition to cereals, animal products such as sausage can be significant human dietary sources of OA. Although OA has been found in many foodstuffs in many countries, the highest frequency of OA contamination in foods (~10%) was encountered in Croatia, where Balkan endemic nephropathy (BEN) is highly prevalent. Moreover, average concentrations are higher in foods from nephropathic regions. Many countries have set regulatory limits for OA ranging from 1 to 50 ppb for food and from 100 to 1000 ppb for animal feeds.

Toxicity

The toxicity of OA varies considerably with dose and between species. Dogs and pigs are the most sensitive species (0.2 and 1 mg/kg body weight, respectively). Synergistic effects of OA with other mycotoxins, such as citrinin and penicillic acid, on the LD_{50} were seen in mice following intraperitoneal injection. OA is nephrotoxic to a number of animal species, and the presence of OA in feed is believed to be the most important cause of spontaneous mycotoxic porcine and poultry nephropathy. OA also produces hepatic toxicity at high doses. OA is teratogenic in mice, rats, and hamster, and the major target in the fetus is the developing central nervous system. OA is also immunosuppressive at low doses, affecting immune function at both the level of antibody synthesis and natural killer cell activity. The toxic mechanism of OA has been shown to be inhibition of protein synthesis by competition with phenylalanine in the phenylalanyl-tRNA synthetase-catalyzed reaction. OA also inhibits other enzymes that use phenylalanine as a substrate, such as phenylalanine hydroxylase. The effect of OA on protein synthesis is followed by an inhibition of RNA synthesis, which may affect proteins with a high turnover. OA has also been found to enhance lipid peroxidation *in vivo*.

Carcinogenicity

OA has been tested for carcinogenicity by oral administration in mice and rats. The kidney, and in particular the tubular epithelial cells, was the major target organ for OA-induced lesions. In male ddY and DDD mice, atypical hyperplasia, cystadenomas, and carcinomas of the renal tubular cells were induced, as were neoplastic nodules and hepatocyte tumors of the liver. In B6C3F1 mice, tubular-cell adenomas and carcinomas of the kidneys were induced in male mice, and the incidences of hepatocellular adenomas and carcinomas were increased in male and female mice. In male and female F344 rats, OA induced neoplastic effects in the kidneys.

Human Health Effects

It has been suggested for several decades that excessive exposure to OA plays a substantive role in the development of BEN. BEN is a bilateral, noninflammatory, chronic nephropathy in which the kidneys are extremely reduced in size and weight and show diffuse cortical fibrosis. Functional impairments are characterized by progressive hypercreatininemia, hyperuremia, and hypochromic anemia. In an endemic area of Croatia, an extremely high incidence of urinary tract tumors in the endemic areas for BEN, particularly urothelial tumors of the pelvis and ureter, has been reported. In Bulgaria, 16 cases of urinary tract tumors were reported among 33 autopsied patients with BEN. A causal relationship between exposure to OA and these human diseases is suggested by (i) similarities in the morphological and functional renal impairments induced by OA in animals and those observed in BEN and (ii) the finding that foods from the endemic areas are more heavily contaminated with OA than foods from disease-free areas. Analyses of serum samples in European countries from nearly a dozen studies revealed that blood from healthy humans was contaminated with OA at concentrations of 0.1–40 ng/ml. The frequency of contamination of human sera, which ranged from 4 to 57%, seems to indicate continuous, widespread exposure of humans to OA.

An association between BEN and/or urinary tract tumors and OA content in blood samples has been reported. Among 61 patients with BEN and/or urinary tract tumors, 14.8% had levels of 1 or 2 ng/ml and 11.5% had more than 2 ng/ml OA in their blood. This proportion was significantly higher than that in a control group of 63 individuals from unaffected families in the endemic villages (7.9 and 3.2%, respectively). A case–control study provided molecular evidence for the possible role of ochratoxin in the development of urinary tract tumors in Bulgaria.

Trichothecenes

The trichothecenes are a family of more than 150 structurally related compounds produced by several fungal genera (*Fusarium*, *Cephalosporium*, *Myrothecium*, *Stachybotrys*, and *Trichoderma*). Chemically, they are sesquiterpenes characterized by a double bond at position C-9, an epoxide ring at C-12, and various patterns of hydroxy and acetoxy substitutions at positions C-3, C-4, C-15, C-7, and C-8. There are four naturally occurring trichothecene mycotoxins (deoxynivalenol, nivalenol, T-2 toxin, and diacetoxyscirpenol) produced in food and feed by *Fusarium* species.

Deoxynivalenol

Deoxynivalenol (DON) is probably the most widely distributed *Fusarium* mycotoxin. Its occurrence in foods in North America, Japan, and Europe is common, but the concentration is relatively low; however, its contamination in cereals in some developing countries, particularly in southern China and areas of South America and Africa, is usually high during some years. In 1980 and 1981 in Canada and 1982 in the United States, DON was found in wheat as the result of severe infestations with the wheat scab fungus, *F. graminearum*. In both countries, the soft winter wheats were the most severely affected. In Canada, dried corn was found to contain higher levels of DON. Several countries have set guidelines or official tolerance levels for DON in food and feed. The range varies from 0.005 to 4 mg/kg. Acute mycotoxicoses affecting fairly large numbers of people and caused by ingestion of DON-contaminated food have been reported in China, India, and other countries.

T-2 Toxin

T-2 toxin is produced primarily by *F. sporotrichioides* and has been reported in many areas of the world. It is formed in large quantities in the unusual circumstance of prolonged wet weather at harvest. Natural contamination of foods and feeds by T-2 toxin in the United States has been reported in only one incident involving heavily molded corn. An official tolerance level of 0.1 mg/kg was established for T-2 toxin in grains in Russia.

T-2 toxin, as the representative trichothecene, has been well studied for its toxic effects on various animal models and has been reviewed in detail.

General signs of toxicity in animals include weight loss, decreased feed conversion, feed refusal, vomiting, bloody diarrhea, severe dermatitis, hemorrhage, decreased egg production, abortion, and death. Histologic lesions consist of necrosis and hemorrhage in proliferating tissues of the intestinal mucosa, bone marrow, spleen, testis, and ovary. T-2 toxin can alter hemostasis and affect cellular immune response in animals, and it is a strong inhibitor of protein and DNA synthesis. T-2 toxin is also teratogenic in mice and rats. As the major trichothecene mycotoxin, T-2 toxin has been implicated in a variety of animal and human toxicosis, such as alimentary toxic aleukia, Msleni joint disease, scabby grain toxicosis, and Kashin–Beck disease.

Other Mycotoxins

Zearalenone

Zearalenone (ZEN) is produced primarily by *F. graminearum* and is among the most widely distributed *Fusarium* mycotoxins. It is associated mainly with maize but occurs in modest concentrations in wheat, barley, sorghum, and other commodities. An official tolerance level of 1 mg/kg ZEN in grains, fats, and oils was established in Russia. Proposed levels in other countries are 0.2 mg/kg ZEN in maize in Brazil and 0.03 mg/kg in all food in Romania. ZEN has estrogenic effects in domestic pigs and experimental animals. F-2 toxicosis and hyperestrogenism are two diseases in pigs caused by ZEN. ZEN is teratogenic to mice and rats and induces chromosomal anomalies in cultured rodent cells. Its carcinogenicity was tested by administration in the diet of mice in one experiment and in that of rats in two experiments. An increased incidence of hepatocellular adenomas was observed in female mice, and an increased incidence of pituitary adenomas was observed in mice of both sexes. No increase in the incidence of tumors was observed in rats.

Sterigmatocystin

Sterigmatocystin is produced by several species of *Aspergillus*, *Penicillium luteum*, and a *Bipolaris* species. Chemically, sterigmatocystin resembles the AFT and is a precursor in the biosynthesis of AFT. It has been detected at low concentrations in green coffee, moldy wheat, and in the rind of hard Dutch cheese. Sterigmatocystin is a hepatotoxin and is less potent than the AFT. It was mutagenic in the Ames test, the *Rec* assay, and the *Bacillus subtilis* assay. It can covalently bind to DNA and form DNA adducts. It has been proven that sterigmatocystin is carcinogenic to rats and mice, mainly inducing liver tumors.

Patulin

Patulin is produced primarily by *P. expansum*. Other *Penicillium* and *Aspergillus* species can also be patulin producers. Commodities found contaminated with patulin are mainly fruits and fruit juices in Europe and North America. Patulin is appreciably stable in apple and grape juices, and it may constitute a potential threat to humans. Currently, 11 countries have set regulatory limits for patulin in fruit juice ranging from 30 to 50 ppb. The toxicity of patulin has been studied in many experimental models, including chicken, quail, cat, cattle, rabbit, mice, and rats. The toxic effects on these animals were found to be edema and hemorrhage in brain and lungs; capillary damage in the liver, spleen, and kidney; paralysis of motor nerves; and convulsions. Patulin is also an immunosuppressive agent that inhibits multiple aspects of macrophage function.

See also: **Cancer**: Effects on Nutritional Status. **Liver Disorders. Nuts and Seeds.**

Further Reading

Chen J-G *et al.* (1998) Population-based cancer survival in Qidong, People's Republic of China. *IARC Scientific Publications* 145: 27–35.

Council for Agricultural Science and Technology (CAST) (2003) *Mycotoxins: Risks in Plants, Animals and Human Systems.* Washington, DC: CAST.

Etzel RA (2002) Mycotoxins. *Journal of the American Medical Association* 287: 425–427.

Harris CC (1996) *p53* tumor suppressor gene: from the basic research laboratory to the clinic—an abridged historical perspective. *Carcinogenesis* 17: 1187–1198.

IARC Working Group on the Evaluation of Carcinogenic Risks to Humans (1993) *Some Naturally Occurring Substances: Food Items and Constituents, Heterocyclic Aromatic Amines and Mycotoxins*, vol. 56. Lyon, France: IARC.

Jackson PE, Qian G-S, Friesen MD *et al.* (2001) Specific *p53* mutation detected in plasma and tumors of hepatocellular carcinoma patients by electrospray ionization mass spectrometry. *Cancer Research* 61: 33–35.

Kirk GD, Camus-Randon AM, Mendy M *et al.* (2000) Ser-249 *p53* mutations in plasma DNA of patients with hepatocellular carcinoma from The Gambia. *Journal of the National Cancer Institute* 92: 148–153.

Li L and Rao K (eds.) (2001) *Cancer Incidence and Mortality in Cities and Counties of P. R. China 1988–1992.* China Medical Science and Technology Press.

Lye MS, Ghazali AA, Mohan J, Alwin N, and Nair RC (1995) An outbreak of acute hepatic encephalopathy due to several aflatoxicosis in Malaysia. *American Journal of Tropical Medicine and Hygene* 53: 68–72.

Park D and Troxell T (2002) US perspective on mycotoxin regulatory issues. *Advances in Experimental Medicine and Biology* 504: 277–285.

Parkin DM, Pisani P, and Ferlay J (1999) Estimates of the worldwide incidence of 25 major cancers in 1990. *International Journal of Cancer* 80: 827–841.

Sun Z-T *et al.* (1999) Increased risk of hepatocellular carcinoma in male hepatitis B surface antigen carriers with chronic hepatitis who have detectable urinary aflatoxin metabolite M1. *Hepatology* 30: 379–383.

Wang L-Y, Hatch M, Chen CJ *et al.* (1996) Aflatoxin exposure and the risk of hepatocellular carcinoma in Taiwan. *International Journal of Cancer* 67: 620–625.

Wild CP and Turner PC (2002) The toxicology of aflatoxins as a basis for public health decisions. *Mutagenesis* 17: 471–481.

Yu MW, Lien JP, Chiu YH *et al.* (1997) Effect of aflatoxin metabolism and DNA adduct formation on hepatocellular carcinoma among chronic hepatitis B carriers in Taiwan. *Journal of Hepatology* 27: 320–330.

Pesticides

M Saltmarsh, Alton, UK

This article is reproduced from the previous edition, pp. 869–874, © 1999, Elsevier Ltd.

What are Pesticides?

Pesticide is a generic term that covers a wide range of natural and synthetic chemicals (over 700 in total) that are used to protect crops from attack from pests, both before and after harvest. There are many different sorts of pests. The term includes insects, slugs and snails, nematode worms, mites, rodents, weeds, molds, bacteria and viruses. The chemicals can be applied before and during growth of the plant or on to the stored crop as, for example, fumigants, which are used to kill pests that have infested stored cocoa or grain. Chemicals used to treat pests on animals are not included; they are considered as veterinary medicines.

The pesticide formulation used by the farmer will include the pesticide chemical itself and a number of other chemicals that enable it to be applied and to work as effectively as possible. These will include solvents, adhesives, and surface-active agents such as emulsifiers. In some cases other chemicals, known as 'safeners,' are applied to minimize the damage done to the crop while maintaining the effectiveness of the spray on the target.

It is estimated that worldwide usage of pesticides is around 2.5 million tons with a cost in 1997 of US$21 billion.

Why Do We Need Pesticides?

Food crops are subject to attack by a multitude of pests and diseases and pesticides are applied to minimize the damage to the crop. It has been estimated that without protection world cereal crop yields would fall by between 46 and 83%. History is littered with records of crop failures and famine caused primarily by rodent, insect or fungus. Some of these events have had a wide-ranging and long-lasting effect, like the 1845–1846 Irish potato famine and the 1917–1918 German 'turnip winter,' the latter so called because the potatoes rotted and turnips were the only stored root crop that was available to feed the population through the winter. Both these events, in which 1.5 million and 700 000 people died, respectively, were caused by potato blight, infection by the fungus *Phytophthora infestans*. Famine caused by massive swarms of locust is still all too common in Northern Africa and Arabia. Less spectacular but as disastrous is the loss of an estimated 30% of harvested crops in India to rodents.

In addition to the loss of the crop, pesticides are used to control agents which make the crop toxic rather than healthy. Two examples are the toxins caused by fungi. When an insect bores into a peanut it allows spores of the fungus *Aspergillus flavus* to enter and grow, producing the aflatoxins, a series of carcinogens. When rye (*Secale cereale*) grows in damp conditions a fungus, *Claviceps purpurea*, can grow on the seed. If this seed is subsequently ground into flour and made into bread it can cause consumers to suffer hallucinations, gangrene, and death. Outbreaks amounting to epidemics were common in the Middle Ages in Europe and one occurred as recently as 1951 in France.

A second reason relates not so much to quantity as to quality. Supermarkets in the developed nations offer a wide range of fresh produce at competitive prices. Consumers do not like holes made by slugs and snails in their fresh lettuce. They do not expect scab marks on their apples, or holes made by small maggots in their carrots. Flour millers do not expect to have to clean the grain from weed seeds before milling. Even small defects can dramatically reduce the value of the crop, or indeed make it unsaleable, and the need for a competitive price requires minimal labor input so that application of pesticide is essential.

Types of Pesticides

There are currently around 600 pesticides, both natural and synthetic. Natural pesticides include both chemicals derived from plant sources and biological agents such as parasitic wasps, mites, bacteria, and chemicals contained within or exuded by plants or bacteria. While there is no inherent reason why natural products should be any safer than synthetic ones (after all, insect venoms and toxins and poisonous plants are natural), it appears that the risks do lie in their potential impact on the environment rather than on their effect in food. There are also increasing numbers of cases where plants have been given a gene which expresses a natural pesticide (see *Bacillus thuringiensis*, below).

At the time of writing, naturally derived pesticides make up less than 5% of the world pesticide market, but a great deal of work is being devoted to the screening of natural sources and this proportion will certainly increase. The most successful natural product development so far has been that of the pyrethrin insecticides, of which 33 are currently available.

The largest classes of pesticides are pyrethrins, organochlorines, organophosphates, and carbamates, although there are many smaller classes with only one or two members. The chemical structures of the key members of the major groups are given in **Table 1**.

Important Pesticide Groups

This list covers the important pesticide groups and some individual pesticides but does not attempt to be comprehensive.

Pyrethrins

Pyrethrins are chemically related to pyrethrin, which is a secondary metabolite found in the flowers of the pyrethrum plant (*Chrysanthemum cinerariaefolium*). Dried pyrethrum flowers were used as an insecticide in ancient China and in the middle ages in Persia. The dried flowers are still used. Current production is around 20 000 tons per annum centered in Kenya and Tanzania. The pyrethrins are effective insecticides, having very low dose rates and rapid knockdown of insects but being harmless to mammals under all normal conditions. Natural pyrethrins break down rapidly under the influence of oxygen and UV light. This limits their use in agriculture, but recently synthetic analogs have been developed to overcome these problems. Starting from the structure of the natural product a large number of synthetic compounds have been made. It is worth noting how they differ in effectiveness: deltamethrin is a broad range insecticide; allethrin is particularly toxic to house flies (*Musca domestica*) but much less effective with other insects; flumethrin is active against cattle ticks; while others are acaricides or miticides with little or no insecticidal activity.

Bacillus thuringiensis

Bacillus thuringiensis is a widely distributed bacterium that during sporulation produces a crystal inclusion which is insecticidal when ingested by the larvae of a number of insect orders. Susceptible orders include Lepidoptera, Diptera, and Colcoptera. The action of *B. thuringiensis* was first observed in 1901 as the cause of a disease of silkworms. Several strains of the bacterium have been identified with activity against a range of insects including cabbage looper, tobacco budworm, mosquito, black fly, and more recently nematodes, ants and fruit flies. While the bacterium appears an ideal insecticide (having a toxicity 300 times greater than synthetic pyrethroids), it requires careful use. It is most effective against neonates and early larval instars so that spraying must be timed for egg hatch. It also has no contact activity and must be ingested so the plant must be well covered to ensure the insect receives a lethal dose. Furthermore it has a half-life in the field as short as 4 h, so careful timing is essential for it to be effective. Despite these limitations, it has been shown to be an important component of crop management programes.

One way of overcoming the problems of application of *B. thuringiensis* is to incorporate the gene responsible for expression of the protein into the crop plant. This has been achieved with maize (*Zea mays*) to protect against the European corn borer, with cotton (*Gossypium hirsutum*) to protect against a range of budworms and bollworms, and with potato (*Solanum tuberosum*) against Colorado beetle. (Cotton may seem irrelevant in a text on food but cottonseed oil is used extensively in cooking oils, margarines, and industrial fats.) This genetic modification has great benefits but care has to be taken that the food product has not changed in some unpredicted way. All genetically modified foods have to be extensively tested and cleared by regulatory agencies before release.

Neem oil

This is an oil obtained from the neem tree, *Azadirachta indica* A. Juss. It has been used as an insecticide in India and Africa but is increasingly being developed as a significant commercial product. It contains a number of compounds, one of the most active being azardirachtin, which is an insect antifeedant but also shows growth inhibitory and endocrine disrupting effects. This product and its individual components is at the beginning of its commercial development, which is likely to result in a series of products as significant as those from pyrethrum.

Table 1　Chemical structure and acceptable daily intake (ADI) of some pesticides

Compound	Class	Structure	ADI (mg per kg body weight)
Deltamethrin	Pyrethrin		0.01
DDT	Organochlorine		0.02
Lindane (HCH)	Organochlorine		0.008
Chlorfenvinphos	Organophosphate (mixture of two isomers)		0.002
Malathion	Organophosphate	$(CH_3O)_2PSCHCH_2CO_2CH_2CH_3$ (S double bond on P); $CO_2CH_2CH_3$	0.02
Propoxur	Carbamate	$OCONHCH_3$; $OCH(CH_3)_2$	0.02
Simazine	Triazine		0.005
Glufosinate		$CH_3PCH_2CH_2CHCO_2H$ with $=O$, OH, NH_2	0.02
Glyphosate		$HO_2CCH_2NHCH_2P(OH)_2$ with $=O$	0.3

Microbial phytotoxins

These are herbicides and include the highly commercially successful glufosinate, a synthetic form of phosphinothricin, first isolated from *Streptomyces hygroscopicus*, a soil-borne microbe. This compound is a potent, irreversible inhibitor of glutamine synthetase which is used in plants for photorespiration. Many attempts have been made to make synthetic variants of phosphinothricin without success. Other members of this group include anisomycin and herboxidiene, derived from other *Streptomyces* strains. The veterinary insecticide, avermectin is derived from *Streptomyces avermitilis*.

Organochlorines

The organochlorines were the first group of synthetic insecticides and without them the dramatic decrease in malaria observed in the 1950s would have been impossible. The best known of this class is DDT (dichlorodiphenyltrichloroethane) but others include 2,4 DD, hexachlorbenzene, and lindane. Of these only lindane (γ-hexachlorocyclohexane, see **Table 1**) is still in use in the developed world.

These compounds are very slow to break down in the environment and one result of this persistance was the decline in bird numbers graphically described by Rachel Carson in the book *Silent Spring*. The problem was that DDT was concentrated through the food chain and predator birds in particular were failing to raise chicks. Since the organochlorine pesticides and other sources of organochlorines in the environment have been largely phased out, numbers of many species of birds are rising again. It is recognized that pesticides are still having an adverse influence on numbers of some birds that inhabit farmland. However, this is not a straightforward effect. In the case of the grey partridge, for example, it is because herbicides have reduced the number of weeds, which in turn has reduced the number of insects that feed on the weeds, resulting in fewer insects for the chicks to eat.

The mechanism of action of the organochlorines is not known in detail although they appear to act on the central nervous system. In humans the organochlorine compounds tend to accumulate in the body fat and in mothers' milk. While there is no direct evidence that they cause mutations or cancers, there is concern that lindane may be a carcinogen and its role in breast cancer is still under review. However, in contrast, DDT and γ-HCH have both been shown to inhibit tumors in mice initiated by aflatoxin B_1.

Although organochlorine pesticides have largely been phased out in Europe, analysis for them continues and low levels of lindane are still being detected in milk in the UK (typically at $0.005 \, \text{mg} \, \text{kg}^{-1}$ compared with the maximum residue limit (see below) of $0.008 \, \text{mg} \, \text{kg}^{-1}$ and an acceptable daily intake (see below) of $0.05 \, \text{mg}$ per kg body weight).

Organophosphorus compounds

Organophosphorus compounds generally contain both sulfur and phosphorus linked to carbon atoms. Their discovery was a by-product of the development of nerve gases. The group includes parathion, malathion, dimethoate, diazinon, and chlorfenvinphos. They are used as herbicides, insecticides, and fungicides. They break down quickly in the environment and do not concentrate in body fats, although they may be stored for some time. However, their mode of action – inhibition of acetylcholine esterase – means that they affect both insects and mammals and their use depends on the effective dose in the target species being below the sensitivity of other species.

Acute effects of sublethal doses of organophosphates in man include sweating, salivation, abdominal cramps, vomiting, muscular weakness, and breathing difficulties. Concern has also been expressed about long-term effects following acute exposure. Research suggests that some victims may show reductions in some neurobehavioral tests when tested some months after exposure. There are also concerns that people who do not appear to have suffered acute poisoning have subsequently developed debilitating illnesses. Symptoms include extreme exhaustion, mood changes, memory loss, depression, and severe muscle weakness.

Carbamates

Carbamates are derived from carbamic acid and are used against both insects and weeds. They are also acetylcholine esterase inhibitors. They are very reactive and are used up rapidly after application.

Methyl bromide

Methyl bromide was for many years the fumigant of choice for destroying insects in stored crops, but it is now being withdrawn as part of the general restriction on volatile organohalogen compounds because of their damaging effect on the ozone layer. It is being replaced by a number of less environmentally damaging compounds, including phosphine, although none currently available is as effective or as cheap as methyl bromide.

Phosphine

Phosphine has been used as a fumigant for many years. It is highly reactive and leaves no residues but great care has to be taken in its application because it is very toxic to humans.

Control of Pesticides

Control over pesticides is exercised in two ways: stringent testing on new pesticides before they are permitted and measurement of the residue in the crop.

Testing pesticides

There are a number of national and international bodies that approve new pesticides within their areas of responsibility. These include Codex Alimentarius, the European Union, and the US Food and Drug Administration (USFDA). Currently, within the European Union, registration of pesticides is being harmonized under Directive 91/414 EEC. Annexe 1 of this directive will identify all active ingredients permitted in pesticides. As yet this annexe is incomplete and member states are still acting under their national laws.

Within the UK pesticide registration is carried out under the Control of Pesticide Regulations 1986 and is the responsibility of the Ministry of Agriculture, Fisheries, and Food who are advised by the Advisory Committee on Pesticides.

In the USA a new Food Quality Protection Act of 1996 replaced both the Food, Drug, and Cosmetic Act and the Insecticide, Fungicide, and Rodenticide Act to provide a comprehensive regulatory scheme for pesticides.

In order to gain approval for use, pesticides are subjected to an extensive testing program including toxicity tests on mammals, plants, insects, fungi, birds, bees, fish, earthworms, and other soil organisms. The toxicity studies include effects of pesticides on fetuses and infant animals. There are also environmental tests which include laboratory tests on the breakdown and movement of the chemical in plants, soil, water, air, mammals, birds, and fish. These latter tests determine the rate of decay in the various species. Laboratory tests are followed by prolonged field trials to determine the fate of the chemical and its breakdown products in the environment and to estimate how the pesticide is concentrated up the food chain. On average it takes about 10 years to develop a new pesticide at a cost of about £50 million. The complete dossier of results has to be submitted to the approval body who determine whether the tests have been sufficiently rigorous to allow an acceptable daily intake (ADI) of the pesticide to be set. The ADI is defined as the amount of a pesticide that can be taken in each day throughout a person's life with the practical certainty, on the basis of all known facts, that no harm will result. This is determined on the basis of the highest level at which the pesticide has no observable effect in animal tests. This is then reduced by a factor of 10 in case humans are more sensitive than the animals used in the tests, and by a further factor of 10 to allow for cases where some humans may be more sensitive than others. In some cases, where the data show unusual effects, the safety factor can be increased from 100 to 500 or 1000. In practice the amount of pesticides to which the population is exposed is far below this level.

Table 1 includes the ADI for a number of the more common pesticides. There is no evidence that there are any cases where the combined effects of two pesticides are greater than the sum of their individual effects, in other words there is no evidence of synergy in toxicology between the different pesticides. Once maximum residue limits (MRL see below) for foodstuffs have been set on the basis of good agricultural practice, a total dietary intake is determined by considering all commodities in which the pesticide is likely to be used, and assuming the upper range of consumption, all foodstuffs at the MRL and no losses during transport, storage or food preparation. This figure is then compared with the ADI. For all permitted pesticides in the UK the figure is below the ADI.

Maximum residue limits

Maximum residue limits (MRLs) are statutory limits set on individual active ingredient and foodstuff combinations. They are based on residue levels which result when the pesticide is used according to the instructions on the label and in accordance with good agricultural practice (GAP). MRLs may be used to ensure that the pesticides are only being used in accordance with GAP. Many countries have codes of good operating practice with training for farmers and operators to ensure that pesticides are used at optimal levels. Some countries rely on the Codex Alimentarius Committee on Pesticide Residues to establish MRLs, while others set their own. (Codex Alimentarius is an international body which has over 120 countries as members and their standards are increasingly being accepted as the basis of world trade in foodstuffs.)

In the USA the FDA used to set tolerances for pesticide/foodstuff combinations but under the 1996 Act it sets a level for each pesticide in all foods based on the principle of a reasonable certainty of no harm. This is defined as a lifetime cancer risk of less than 1 in a million. There is also a requirement that residue tolerances must be specifically determined as being safe for children.

Within the EU, individual member states have historically set their own MRLs which differ from state to state. Directive 76/895 established a common MRL setting regime and a series of subsequent directives has fixed the levels for a series of pesticides in fruit, vegetables, cereal products, and products of animal origin. There is an ongoing program to harmonize the levels throughout the Union.

Most industrialized countries have pesticide surveillance programs which cover both home-produced and imported commodities and these report annually. The EU has an annual specific coordinated program to check compliance in nominated combinations of pesticide and foodstuff. MRLs require sophisticated equipment for their determination because the levels are so low and the minimum detectable limit depends on the foodstuff. For example the tolerance for aldrin and dieldrin (two organochlorines) in the USA is between 0.05 and $0.1 \, mg \, kg^{-1}$ (parts per million), depending on the foodstuff. There are over 600 different active ingredients available commercially. Because there are so many, laboratories around the world have developed sophisticated rapid analytical techniques to allow them to screen pesticides by class so that retailers, food manufacturers, and governments can carry out analyses as a matter of routine.

The MAFF 7th Report of the UK Working Party on Pesticide Residues in 1996 showed 68% of samples had no detectable residue, 31% had residues below the MRL, and <1% were over the MRL. Similar results were obtained by the FDA who report results with relation to the tolerance to the pesticide/commodity combination. In 1995, of over 9000 samples analyzed, 64% had no detectable residues, 34% had residues below the tolerance, <1% had residues over the tolerance and <1% had residues for which there is no tolerance in that particular pesticide/commodity combination.

In all cases where MRLs or tolerances are exceeded follow-up action is taken. For home-produced materials, this involves investigation of the grower and prosecution if necessary. For imports, exceeding the level causes the consignment to be refused entry.

Maximum levels of pesticides are also set for drinking water. Pesticides get into water from spraying, runoff, percolation or from treatment of fish in aquaculture. Good practice is increasingly being developed to minimize the levels in raw water and treatment works are developing systems to reduce incoming levels to levels acceptable for drinking water.

Endocrine Disruption

The possibility that a number of chemicals discharged into the environment as a result of human activity may disrupt the endocrine system of a wide range of mammals has recently been given considerable prominence. Among the chemicals cited are the organochlorine pesticides, most of which have now been withdrawn for other reasons. While there is no doubt that there are a significant number of cases of endocrine disruption, the evidence to point to any particular chemical as a cause is lacking. It is also worth noting that deliberate endocrine disruption is a mechanism of a number of natural insecticides which act so as to inhibit development of juvenile larvae to adults. Fortunately these pesticides are reactive and usually have a short life in the field.

It is also true that there are very many naturally occurring endocrine disruptors, including the phytoestrogens present in vegetables, notably soya beans, peas, beans, cabbage, and hops. However, since this issue is very serious a considerable amount of work has now been initiated and its results will have implications for future testing of pesticides.

Future Prospects

In many parts of the world it is recognized that there has been too great a reliance on pesticide use and not enough on improving agricultural practices. There is increasing pressure to move towards minimizing pesticide usage in order to both improve the environment and to reduce cost. This is being done by using newer, more specific pesticides and by adopting improved agricultural practices and integrated pest management (a combination of biological and chemical control).

Biological control is not new. In the 1930s *Macrocentrus homonae* was introduced into Sri Lanka from Indonesia to control the tea small leaf roller (*Adoxophyes*) with such success that no chemical control measures are needed for this pest even today. More recently there have been some impressive results from using predator insects, for example in the control of cassava green mite (*Mononchellus tanajoa*) in West Africa and white fly in European greenhouses.

In terms of agricultural practice, improved crop hygiene, crop rotation, better understanding of optimal timing of application, and varying sowing dates, together with the development of more powerful and more discriminating pesticides has brought about a decrease in pesticide inputs. This is seen dramatically in the case of oil seed rape (canola). Less than 1% of the weight of herbicide applied to this crop in 1983 was applied in 1993.

Unfortunately pests develop resistance to individual pesticides over time and research is continually needed to develop both new pesticides and resistant varieties of crops to keep the pests in check. There has been some success with new pesticides having new modes of action such as the antifeedants and antimolting agents, but this will be a continuing battle for the foreseeable future.

See also: **Phytochemicals**: Classification and Occurrence; Epidemiological Factors.

Bacterial Contamination

N Noah, London School of Hygiene and Tropical Medicine, London, UK

The burden of gastroenteritis (GE) in the world, in terms of both morbidity and mortality, is enormous. In the developing world (e.g., Southeast Asia), diarrhea vies with acute respiratory tract infection as the leading cause of death in childhood. Even in the more developed world, infectious GE is a significant cause of illness and time lost from work, and death does occur. Infectious intestinal disease in England is estimated to cost the country £743 million p.a. (in 1994–95 prices). GE caused by bacteria was far more costly than that caused by viruses. The more sophisticated surveillance systems become, the more GE they uncover.

Not all GE is caused by food. Probably most GE is caused by poor hygiene leading to direct or indirect transmission of infection without the assistance of food. Nevertheless, a major cause of infectious GE throughout the world is contaminated food. The definition of food poisoning (FP) is not straightforward. In essence, FP is an acute gastroenteritis caused by food. Hepatitis A, typhoid, and brucellosis, however, are not usually considered as FP, whereas botulism is, even though it causes paralysis and not GE, as is listeria, which causes septicemia and meningitis.

Bacteria are the most common known cause of FP and, with the possible exception of the Norwalk-like viruses, of GE also. As one would expect, bacterial FP is more common in summer than winter.

Bacteria produce their effects on the intestinal tract either by direct invasion of the mucosa or by the production of toxin. Some of the toxins are produced outside the intestinal tract—in the food; others are formed in the intestine. Some invasive bacteria also produce a toxin in the intestine. This article provides an overview of the bacterial causes of FP.

Bacterial Toxins

There are three main forms of bacterial enteric toxin:

Enterotoxin producing excess fluid secretion into the gut (cholera and some types of *Escherichia coli*)
Cytotoxin causing inflammation and mucosal damage (shigella and enterohemorrhagic *E. coli*)
Neurotoxin affecting the nervous system (botulism and staphylococcal toxin)

Some *E. coli* strains produce toxin; these are dealt with under Invasive Bacteria. Red kidney bean, scombrotoxin and other fish toxins, and heavy metal poisoning are dealt with elsewhere in this book.

Staphylococcal Food Poisoning

Background Staphylococcal food poisoning (SFP) is one of the few causes of bacterial FP that can commonly be attributed to a food handler. Humans frequently carry staphylococci either in an infected site or asymptomatically. Infected sites include wounds and abscesses, which may be the source of large numbers of staphylococci. Asymptomatic sites include throat, nostrils, fingernails, or hair. In general, only coagulase-positive staphylococci (*Staphylococcus aureus*), and only certain types, produce enterotoxin. Rarely, some coagulase-negative strains may occasionally produce toxin. Because the organism is also carried by many animals, outbreaks attributable to inadequate processing of a precontaminated food can occur also.

Growth and survival Staphylococci are killed by normal cooking temperatures. Any staphylococci that survive because of inadequate heat penetration or, more frequently, by postcooking contamination from a food handler will, if it is an enterotoxigenic strain and given the right conditions of warmth, moisture, pH, and time, produce toxin. Growth of staphylococci and production of toxin are optimum at approximately 20–37 °C, but growth can occur between 8 and 48 °C. This toxin is fairly heat stable; boiling for approximately 30 min is required to destroy it. Canning is usually, but not always, sufficient. The toxin is also resistant to radiation.

Many foods can cause SFP. Because the organism can grow in foods with high salt or sugar content (possibly because there is less competition from other organisms), ham is a common cause of SFP, as are desserts, especially those containing cream. Other foods implicated include meats and other high-protein foods, salads with mayonnaise, canned mushrooms, cream, cheese, salami, and eggs (and probably any moist food). Cows with mastitis may occasionally infect milk.

Characteristic sequence of events A whole leg of ham is prepared for consumption and cooked. It is then sliced warm by a chef who has no skin lesions. The slices are overlapped on a tray. The tray is covered and left to cool for several hours before being refrigerated. Staphylococci from the nose of the chef are conveyed to the warm ham slices. Because of the large surface area, and the large bulk of covered overlapping slices of meat taking time to cool, staphylococci grow and toxin is formed. Refrigerating or reheating the meat will not destroy toxin. Similarly, ice cream may be contaminated during the preparation process by a food handler. If it is then left at room temperature, it will allow the staphylococci to grow and form toxin. Freezing the dish afterwards does not destroy toxin, and consumers are likely to contract SFP regardless of how long the ice cream is kept frozen.

Clinical features The toxin is an enterotoxin and a receptor in the gut appears to be necessary. There may also be a neurotoxic effect that acts on the vomiting center in the brain. With SFP, onset of symptoms is often dramatic. Vomiting is the most prominent symptom. It occurs between 2 and 4 h but may range from 30 min to 8 h after eating. Nausea, abdominal colic, and diarrhea are also common. Generally, as with most toxins, the higher the concentration (or the greater the amount ingested), the shorter the incubation period and the more severe the symptoms. Individual susceptibility is also a determining factor in severity. The illness is usually over in a day or two, but deaths have occurred, sometimes as a result of acute hypotension (another well-known but rare effect of the toxin).

Diagnosis Because many people carry staphylococci, it is important to ensure that the type causing an outbreak of FP is the same in the carrier and those affected; merely showing that a food handler carries staphylococci is insufficient. The organism can be grown from, or enterotoxin can be detected in, implicated foods, which usually contain $>10^6$ organisms/g. The organism can also be isolated from vomit or stool of patients and from the hands, nose, abscess, or infected wound of the food handler. Phage typing of strains, with detection and typing of enterotoxin, can also be performed.

Enterotoxins A–I are recognized, although type A used to be the most common. With the advent of polymerase chain reaction, other types are being seen more frequently. As with all FP, the absence of laboratory-supporting evidence does not necessarily mean that the diagnosis is wrong or the implicated food innocent.

Bacillus cereus

Background *Bacillus cereus* is widely distributed in the environment and is not a contaminant of food. It is found in rice and other natural foods, such as herbs and spices, cream, and dry foods.

Growth and survival Unlike the staphylococci, *B. cereus* is a spore-forming organism that survives prolonged boiling. It causes two fairly distinct types of food poisoning, emetic and diarrheic. The diarrheal toxin is heat labile and, like *Clostridium perfringens*, formed in the gut. The foods commonly associated with it are 'proteinaceous' and, like *C. perfringens*, associated with meats, stews, desserts, and sauces. The emetic type is 'farinaceous,' associated mainly with cooked rice, and produces an illness similar to SFP. Different serotypes of *B. cereus* cause these two different forms of FP, and the toxins are different also. Other members of *Bacillus* sp. are discussed later. Some strains will grow at refrigeration temperatures in milk and other foods.

Clinical features and characteristic sequence of events The emetic type of *B. cereus* FP is caused by preformed toxin (cereulide) in food, usually rice that has cooled slowly. This usually happens when a large bulk of rice, as in Chinese restaurants, is allowed to cool at room temperature for many hours, often overnight. The center of the mass will stay warm for a long enough period for the spores of the bacillus to germinate and form toxin. The toxin is heat stable and will survive the quick frying given to it in a Chinese restaurant. The incubation period is usually short (1–6 h), and the symptoms, predominantly vomiting, tend to be milder than those for SFP, which it otherwise resembles.

The diarrheal form of *B. cereus* FP is similar to that caused by *C. perfringens*. The toxin, unlike the emetic type, is an enterotoxin formed in the intestine and is heat labile. The predominant symptoms are diarrhea and abdominal colic. The incubation period, as expected for an organism that multiplies in the intestine and then produces its toxin, is also longer (8–16 h). This type of *B. cereus* FP can be caused by a wide variety of foods, including meat, vegetables, and dairy products.

Diagnosis   The mere presence of *B. cereus* in a food is insufficient because it is a normal contaminant of many natural foods. The diagnosis is confirmed by the finding of the organism in high concentrations [10^6–10^8/g, minimum 10^5] in cooked rice, or other food for the diarrheic type, and obtaining it from the stool or vomit of cases. Alternatively, the same serotype should be present in food and patient specimen. Detection of the toxin in the food may also be sufficient.

Clostridium botulinum

Background   *Clostridium botulinum* is an anaerobic spore-forming bacterium widely distributed in soil and mud. The toxin is the most lethal substance known to man, with a LD_{50} of 0.00003 μg/kg body weight. In one incident, an adult was paralysed for more than 6 months after eating less than two teaspoonfuls of a rice salad. Tetanus toxin from *Clostridium tetani* and ricin from the castor bean (the next most toxic substances) have LD_{50} values of 0.0001 and 0.02 μg/kg, respectively. The seven toxin types, A–G, affect the nervous systems of vertebrates, animals, and birds more commonly than man. Birds in aquatic environments seem especially susceptible to mass die-offs caused by botulism. Invertebrates are not susceptible but can harbor the bacteria and toxins in their bodies. Types A, B, and E are the only toxins that affect man. Type E is acquired from fish. Type C is the main bird toxin, although types D and E are also important.

Growth and survival   Because the organism grows anaerobically, special conditions have to be present for it to cause FP. Fortunately, although the organism is ubiquitous, FP caused by it is rare. First, the spores have to be present, which is not uncommon because they are widely, although patchily, distributed in soil and aquatic environments. Second, the spores have to survive cooking, which again is not difficult because they can survive heating at 100 °C for 2 h. Third, they have to be allowed to germinate and grow in anaerobic conditions. This accounts for the rarity of botulism, although accidents have occurred, and occasionally still occur, with home canning (once popular in the United States), and it occasionally occurs in preserved meat in Europe (the term botulism is derived from *botulus*, the Latin term for sausage) and in preserved rotting or fermenting food in the Arctic and areas of the Far East. Large bulks of certain types of food (e.g., canned hazelnut puree) may also be susceptible to growth and toxin formation. Commercial canning, except for the occasional accident, destroys spores by the heating processes

used. The vegetative forms of *C. botulinum* are as susceptible as most other vegetative bacteria to heat, and the toxin is also destroyed by boiling—the human types A, B, and E in 2 min at 70 °C and all toxins for 5 min at 80 °C. The pH is also important: The lower the pH, the less resistant are the spores to heat, and a low pH (<4.5) affects the ability of the spores to form toxin. Hence, bottled pickled vegetables in vinegar tend to be safe. High concentrations of salt also affect the viability and toxin-forming properties of *C. botulinum*.

Clinical features   The incubation period is 12–36 h (range, 6 h–10 days).The toxin destroys the cholinergic nerves in the motor end plates (MEPs). These are the junctions of the nerves with muscle, preventing the release of acetylcholine from the cholinergic nerves in the MEP and paralysing the muscle. Once this has happened, no amount of antitoxin or antibiotic is going to help. The combination of nausea, vomiting, or diarrhea followed by symmetrical descending paralysis of cranial and autonomic nerves is almost diagnostic. Thus, the characteristic neurological symptoms are blurred vision, dry mouth, difficulty swallowing, dysarthria, diplopia, and descending paralysis. Recovery has to wait until new MEPs form. There is a high fatality rate, but with modern technology patients can often be kept alive artificially until new nerve terminals have formed new MEPs, which may take several months.

Baby botulism

Some babies, usually younger than 6 months of age, acquire a form of botulism that is usually mild. It is thought to be caused by ingested spores multiplying in and colonizing the baby's intestine, forming toxin. The initial symptom is often constipation, leading to poor feeding, irritability, neck paralysis, and generalized weakness. Honey is thought to be one cause of baby botulism.

Diagnosis   The diagnosis is made by the demonstration of botulinus toxin in food, stool, or serum. Growing the organism from food is suggestive but not diagnostic, whereas fecal isolates are rare except in affected individuals.

Clostridium perfringens

Background   Food poisoning caused by *C. perfringens* is also toxin mediated. It differs, however, from those described previously in that toxin is formed in the intestine after ingestion of the bacteria. Like other clostridia, it is anaerobic, gram positive, and spore forming. There are five types, classified A–E according to the enterotoxin formed; type A is the one that causes FP. Some strains, but not generally those that cause FP, can cause gas gangrene. *Clostridium perfringens* is primarily found in soil and is transmitted to animals and man by ingestion of vegetables and other plants. It is thus commonly found in the intestine of man and animals. When animals are eviscerated, the organism contaminates the inside of the carcass. Flies can transmit the organism to food.

Clostridium perfringens FP is common. Fortunately, it is rarely fatal except in those who are debilitated or immunocompromised.

Growth and survival *Clostridium perfringens* does not tend to multiply on the surface of raw meat. It grows optimally at warm temperatures of approximately 43–47 °C (range, 20–50 °C) and low oxygen levels found in the interior of a cooked dish. The cooking process will have driven off oxygen and thus facilitated sporulation and subsequent growth of the organism. Vegetative cells are not resistant to heat, but spores of the FP strains of *C. perfringens* can survive boiling for several hours. If cooling is slow, vegetative cells reform and grow rapidly. After ingestion, toxin is formed from multiplying cells in the intestine, although both toxin and vegetative cells appear to be necessary to produce symptoms.

Clinical features and characteristic sequence of events A casserole is prepared containing, among other ingredients, cubed meat. It is heated to boiling and allowed to cook for 1 or 2 h until ready. However, it is not needed immediately, and because of its bulk and lack of refrigeration facilities it is left overnight in a warm kitchen. It is warmed the next day before serving. Symptoms of diarrhea with abdominal pain begin 8–24 h later. The illness may last only a few hours, and there are no sequelae, except in those who are already debilitated.

Diagnosis The organism can be cultured from the stools of affected people and should be compared with that isolated from food for toxin production. Enterotoxin detection in stools is important confirmatory evidence. The organism has to be detected in high numbers in food to be significant. Molecular typing methods are available to compare isolates from food and feces.

Vibrio cholerae

Background Cholera appears to have originated in India. It first spread to Asia in 1817–1823, the first pandemic. The second pandemic reached Europe in 1826–1837, and subsequent to this there were five additional pandemics. The most recent began inexplicably in 1961 with a mild strain, the el Tor biotype, which had been endemic in Indonesia since 1937. More recently, it has become endemic in areas of South America. *Vibrio cholerae* 0139 is a new strain that emerged in the Indian subcontinent in 1992.

It is mainly to cholera that we owe the introduction of sanitation and the development of 'public health.' Although not a common cause of FP or GE in developed countries, the vibrios, especially *V. cholerae*, still cause large, mainly waterborne outbreaks in the developing world. It is the only gastrointestinal infection that is internationally notifiable. Because large numbers of organisms are required for infection, case-to-case transmission is uncommon.

Growth and survival The bacteria are aquatic and prefer briny waters. They can be found in many warm plankton-rich coastal waters, including the Mediterranean, Gulf of Mexico, and those of Southeast Asia and South America. Bivalved molluscs concentrate them, as they do many other bacteria. Other fish and shellfish can be contaminated, and inadequate cooking and storage will allow growth sufficient to cause FP. They prefer moist, slightly salty foods. Unfortunately, the el Tor strain is more likely to produce asymptomatic infections, persist longer in the environment, multiply more rapidly in food, and produce less immunity than the classical type. The organism produces an enterotoxin in the intestine.

Clinical features Cholera, in its most dramatic form, is characterized by an acute outpouring of watery diarrhea (rice water stools) and vomiting causing death within 24 h by acute loss of fluid and electrolytes. However, the clinical syndrome ranges from the symptomless to the mild and less dramatic forms. The organism is not invasive, and if the loss of fluid and salts can be counterbalanced by infusion of equal amounts of fluid supplemented by electrolytes, the patient will survive. Patients with an absence of acid in the stomach, and those with blood group O, are especially prone to severe disease. The incubation period is 1–3 days (range, 12 h–5 days).

Characteristic sequence of events Sewage-contaminated seafood or water is by far the most common source of infection. The vibrio can grow successfully in cooked rice and other grains contaminated by food handlers, and salad vegetables can be contaminated by water. However, the organism often seems to find an 'environmental niche' and may persist in some communities for years.

Diagnosis The organism is usually isolated from the stool using special media. It can also be distinguished by light microscopy, and specific antisera will halt motility of the organisms. Agglutination tests with serum will distinguish 01 from 0139 and other strains. The organism can also be isolated from the environment using enriched media. Toxin production or the presence of the toxin gene can, and should, also be demonstrated. A 4-fold or greater rise in antibody is also helpful in diagnosis.

Invasive Bacteria

Salmonella Infections

Background Salmonellae are the most common known cause of bacterial FP in developed (and possibly less well-developed) countries of the world. Other bacteria such as campylobacter commonly cause GE but not necessarily FP.

There are a large number of serotypes of salmonella. They are typed according to their somatic [O] or flagellar [H phases 1 and 2] antigens according to the Kauffman–White scheme and are generally named after a geographical location. Further typing, usually by phages, can be done to distinguish the more common serotypes. Some serotypes are pathogenic for man, some for animals, others for birds including poultry, and some for humans as well as animals and birds. They are gram-negative bacilli that do not form spores but can survive for remarkably long periods on dried foods.

Salmonellae are widely distributed in and excreted by living creatures so that environmental contamination is inevitable. Protein foods processed in bulk for animals and poultry can cause widespread infection in them and subsequently in humans. In the United Kingdom, for example, fishmeal imported from Peru and fed to poultry caused a large outbreak of *Salmonella agona* infection in humans that lasted for several years through the late 1960s and early 1970s. Since then, there have been outbreaks of *S. hadar* infection in turkeys, and more recently various phage types of *S. enteritidis* infection in poultry and hens' eggs have caused outbreaks in many countries. In eggs, transmission is mainly 'vertical' (i.e., through oviducts). Before this, salmonellae gained entry to the insides of eggs mainly through the shell. If eggs were shelled in bulk, contamination of just one or two shells would be enough to contaminate the whole bulk of eggs and

then grow given the right conditions. However, mayonnaise, paradoxically, is best kept at room rather than refrigerator temperatures if contaminated with salmonella. This is because acid, in the form of lemon juice or vinegar, kills salmonella more efficiently at warm than cool temperatures.

Other potent sources of contamination are sewage, polluted water, or direct fecal contamination of foodstuffs. Thus, many foods are bought already contaminated. Recent examples include mung beans, black pepper, dried herbs and spices, chocolate, spent yeast (used as a flavoring vehicle in packet potato crisps), infant dried milk, salamis, and sausages. Indeed, it is important to note that almost any food can be contaminated given the right circumstances. A multistate outbreak of salmonellosis in the United States was traced to tomatoes that had been washed in a contaminated water bath. An extensive outbreak in the United Kingdom was shown to be caused by lettuce. These episodes are particularly worrying because they show that any vegetable eaten raw may cause a salmonella infection. Cross-contamination from raw meat to relishes and dressings in a kitchen may also occur. Direct contamination of a food by a food handler, at any rate enough to cause an outbreak, is rarely documented. Indeed, infected food handlers are nearly always victims of the food they have prepared, not the source of contamination. Cases of human carriers with prolonged carriage occur.

Growth and survival Although salmonellae do not form spores, and are fairly easily destroyed by heat, they survive for a remarkably long period in the environment. An outbreak of *S. virchow* and *S. saint-paul* infection was caused in several countries in Europe by green lentils (mung beans) imported from Queensland. They were used to make bean sprouts, which required overnight growth in a warm waterbath. Slow drying of salmonellae makes them more resistant to dry heat. Moisture is important when using heat to kill bacteria.

Salmonellae grow best at 37 °C, and the danger temperatures are 30–45 °C. Growth stops below approximately 7 °C and above approximately 63 °C. Antibiotic-resistant strains are becoming more common.

The infective dose of salmonellae in humans is quite large—approximately 10^7 organisms. However, in certain circumstances, much lower doses may cause symptoms. Fatty foods such as chocolate, cheese, salami, and mayonnaise seem to require much smaller doses, and patients with immunosuppression, low acid levels in their stomach (achlorhydria), as well as the elderly and debilitated may also be especially vulnerable. Thus, salmonellae may be transmitted nosocomially, especially in geriatric or psychogeriatric wards, and in such outbreaks it may be a waste of time to pursue a food source. Growing antibiotic resistance in salmonellae is proving to be a problem.

Characteristic sequence of events Various scenarios are described here:

A chicken dish is undercooked and then left in a warm environment for some hours before consumption. Alternatively, the chicken may be thoroughly cooked but is then replaced in an unwashed container or plate, or cut with a knife that was used for raw chicken, and allowed to stand. The contaminated utensil may be used on another dish, thus contaminating it.

A dried herb or spice, such as black pepper, is added to a dish after cooking but while still warm, and the dish is then left to stand.

Raw egg is added to a product without cooking, as with mayonnaise or mousse, or only lightly cooked. When the light cooking involves several hundred eggs, 1 contaminated egg and time in the warmth are enough to create many infective doses. In one outbreak, 800 eggs were used and left for a considerable period before being lightly cooked to make a hollandaise sauce. More than 100 guests at the wedding were affected. Subsequent examination of leftover unused eggs from the same batch suggested that the rate of contamination of eggs was very low, perhaps less than 1 per 1000. Low rates of contamination of a common food that is generally eaten after light cooking or raw can cause a large number of salmonella infections.

Clinical features The incubation period of salmonella infection is 12–36 h but can range from 6 to 72 h. Clinical features of salmonella infection range from asymptomatic to mild and enteric fever. Enteric fever (typhoid) is usually caused by *S. typhi* or *S. paratyphi* A. More commonly, salmonellae cause severe diarrhea with fever and abdominal pain. Vomiting is uncommon. Some salmonellae, such as *S. cholerae-suis*, may cause multiple abscesses, and people with sickle cell disease may have bone abscesses with any salmonella. Septicaemia (blood poisoning), meningitis, and other localised infections are also occasional complications of salmonellosis. Patients with AIDS and other immunosuppressive conditions are particularly vulnerable to severe complications.

Salmonellae and hens eggs In the late 1980s, *S. enteritidis* rapidly became the most common cause of salmonella infections in the United Kingdom. Previously, *S. typhimurium* had been by far the most frequently reported salmonella species. Between 1984 and 1987, the number of human *S. enteritidis* infections increased by approximately 50% per year. In 1988, the number more than doubled and by 1993 it was virtually 10 times that diagnosed in 1984. By 1993, *S. enteritidis* accounted for approximately five times the number of *S. typhimurium* infections. Most of this was due to eggs, although some of it was also attributable to chicken. Many European countries and countries elsewhere experienced similar trends.

Diagnosis The diagnosis of a salmonella infection is usually made by isolation of the organism from stool or food. Some salmonellae, such as *S. typhimurium* and *S. enteritidis*, are so common that further differentiation is necessary for epidemiological purposes. Further characterization of the organism can be undertaken by phage typing and antibiotic resistance profiles. Plasmid analysis may also be useful in differentiating strains of the same phage type.

Campylobacter Infections

Background The importance of campylobacter as a cause of GE was only recognized in the mid-1970s. They are now the most common known bacterial cause of GE in most developed countries. (In less developed countries, asymptomatic infection is more common.) *Campylobacter jejuni* is the most common species, but *C. coli* is common in some areas.

Campylobacter spp. are found in the intestines of many animals and birds, including cattle and horses, household pets, and chickens. Rates of contamination of chicken carcasses vary from >75% in the United Kingdom and The Netherlands to <30% in Sweden and Norway. Some of these differences may be due to the method of isolation used.

The reported incidence of human infection in Western Europe is high. In a survey of 15 countries, the annual incidence varied from 2.9 to 166.8 per 10^5 population, with a mean of 71 (1999 data). Because these are laboratory-confirmed infections, the true incidence will be considerably higher. The wide range of incidences almost certainly reflects rates of laboratory diagnosis and reporting rather than variation in incidence.

Growth and survival The reason for the late recognition of campylobacters is their fastidiousness: They grow best in an O_2 concentration of 5%, in a special medium, and at a temperature of 42 °C. They are also sensitive to heat, being destroyed readily by cooking, and do not survive for long (probably a few hours only) on the surfaces of foods. They nevertheless are highly successful in causing infection, probably because of their ubiquity in the environment, domestic animals, and birds and the small dose required for infection (possibly no more than 200 organisms may be enough).

Characteristic sequence of events and clinical features Although campylobacters undoubtedly cause FP, the source of infection in most instances, especially sporadic cases, is unknown. It is highly probable that many cases, perhaps even most cases, are caused by direct contact with animals, birds, the environment (both domestic and outside), meat carcasses, and possibly other people. Food-borne outbreaks in the past have been traced to untreated water and milk and also milk from bottles whose tops have been pecked by birds. Undercooked poultry is undoubtedly a risk factor, and meat prepared at barbecues, which includes pork, veal, and beef as well as chicken, has also been implicated. In one study, consuming organic products, both meat and vegetables, and eating in a restaurant were risk factors. In another, eating grapes was found to be a risk factor, and salads have also been implicated, but it is possible that some of these foods were contaminated from another source or directly by a food handler.

Other risk factors include travel to foreign countries; handling and cooking of food, especially raw meat; contact with animals and pets (especially those with diarrhea) and visiting an animal farm; swimming; and sailing.

The incubation period of 3–5 days is long compared to that of most other FP bacteria. As with most gastrointestinal (GI) infections with a long incubation period, symptoms are mostly associated with the lower GI tract. Thus, vomiting is uncommon, and abdominal pain and diarrhea are the main symptoms. An accompanying fever is usual, and the diarrhea is often bloody. The illness may last a few days, and the antibiotic ciprofloxacin is now the treatment of choice for severe or prolonged illnesses.

Septicemia or other localized infections are rare complications. One of the well-known complications of campylobacter infection is Guillain–Barre syndrome, in which a symmetrical paralysis affects the body some weeks after the infection. Recovery is usually spontaneous but may take several months. In the acute phases of the illness, respiratory support may be needed.

Diagnosis The organism can be grown from stools, rectal swabs, and food. Special media and O_2 concentrations of 5–10% are needed for campylobacter. Two typing systems are available—Penner and Lior.

Escherichia coli

Background *Escherichia coli* are a remarkable group of organisms with a wide range of infections, including meningitis, septicaemia, and urinary infections. They are often also nonpathogenic. Those that cause GE also have a wide range of pathogenic mechanisms and are divided into various fairly distinct groups: enteropathogenic (EPEC), enterohemorrhagic (EHEC), enteroinvasive (EIEC), and enterotoxigenic (ETEC) are the main ones, although some groups—diffusely adherent (DAEC) and enteroaggregative (EAEC)—have recently been described. Some EHEC strains produce a shiga (or verocyto-) toxin, STEC, which includes *E. coli* O157:H7 as well as other strains. However, because the O157 strains are much more common, STEC strains are classified as O157 and non-O157. Shiga toxin is produced by other bacteria also, including *S. dysenteriae* type 1. Only these verocytotoxin-producing strains are considered in detail here because they are commonly foodborne and can cause serious illness and death.

Escherichia coli GE is not a notifiable infection, so there are few if any data on its impact on communities. Moreover, ETEC is not identified routinely by the stool culture methods commonly used. Infections with ETEC strains are common worldwide at all ages. These strains are the most common known cause of travellers' diarrhea but can also be spread by food. This toxigenic group includes strains that produce heat-labile and heat-stable enterotoxins. Heat-labile enterotoxin is closely related to cholera toxin and causes profuse watery diarrhea. EPEC strains are common infections in neonates and infants, tend to spread from person to person, and are not commonly known to be associated with food. EIEC and the two newer strains are rare. EIEC outbreaks related to food have been occasionally described, including one caused by French cheese exported to the United States.

In the United States, *E. coli* O157:H7 is estimated to cause 20 000 cases and 250 deaths annually, 67% of outbreaks are foodborne, 8% waterborne, and 22% transmitted case to case. Swimming in contaminated water can also transmit the infection. *Escherichia coli* O157:H7 was recognized as a cause of FP only in 1982. Some strains with the verocytotoxin (VT) gene produce a toxin that causes the hemolytic–uraemic syndrome (HUS). Other *E. coli* strains also produce VT.

Escherichia coli, including *E. coli* O157:H7, is a normal inhabitant of the intestines of many mammals, including cattle, sheep, and goats. Contamination can occur directly from the intestines to carcass to meat or via the faeces of these animals to raw vegetables and other foods.

Growth and survival The organism can survive for a considerable length of time on contaminated meat and vegetables. In two outbreaks caused by apple juice, the organism was present on the surface of apples that had fallen to the ground. The orchard was frequented by deer that were subsequently found to be carrying the organism. Manure was also used. The apples were not processed adequately to kill most organisms, and waxing may have sealed the organisms onto the surface of the fruit. The cider was not pasteurized. The organism is more resistant than salmonella to acid: *E. coli* O157:H7 has been shown to survive for 21 days in cider at a pH of 3.7–3.9 at 4 °C, with only approximately a 5% kill-off. It can grow very successfully over several weeks in manure slurries. The infectious dose is thought to be small, so case-to-case infection may occur. Like most vegetative organisms, it is destroyed by heat.

Characteristic sequence of events In a town in North Cumbria, England, 61 patients had diarrhea, many with blood, over three weeks. A total of 114 people were found to be infected, ranging in age from 3 months to 85 years. Investigations implicated a farm supplying pasteurized milk. Nine days before the first case, a problem had occurred in the heat-exchanger plates of the pasteurization unit. No tests were undertaken after new plates were fitted, and temperature monitoring was inadequate. The unit was one that a few months before had been the subject of a food hazard warning. *Escherichia coli* O157 was isolated from 66 environmental and animal feces samples on the farm but not from the milk or the pasteurization plant.

In an outbreak in the United States, 501 patients became ill after eating inadequately processed hamburgers from a restaurant chain. HUS developed in 45 cases, and 3 died.

Undercooked hamburgers and ground beef are a common cause of *E. coli* O157:H7 infection. The process of grinding beef can spread the organism from the surface of the meat to the inside. Other vehicles of infection include raw milk, unchlorinated water, apple juice, unwashed fruits and vegetables including alfalfa sprouts and radish tops, or swimming in unchlorinated pools.

Clinical features The infectious dose for *E. coli* O157:H7 is thought to be fewer than 700 organisms. The incubation period of 3–5 days is long compared with that of most other FP bacteria. As with most GI infections with a long incubation, symptoms are mostly associated with the lower GI tract. Vomiting is uncommon, and abdominal pain and diarrhea, often bloody, are the main symptoms. Fever is usual. The illness may last a few days, and the antibiotic ciprofloxacin is now the treatment of choice for severe or prolonged illnesses. HUS is characterized by hemolytic anemia, thrombocytopenic purpura, renal failure, and a death rate of 3–5%.

Diagnosis The usual method of diagnosis is to isolate the organism from stools or food, which is straightforward. However, because most of the *E. coli* in the intestine is part of the normal flora and nonpathogenic, it is necessary to demonstrate virulence by further tests or assigning it to a serotype, which normally requires more sophisticated techniques in specialist laboratories. Serotyping is performed on the somatic cell wall antigens (O antigen) and the flagellar antigen (H). On the basis of the serotyping of the O antigens, the organisms can be classified as EPEC, ETEC, etc. DNA tests are increasingly being used. Thus, *E. coli* O111 is an EPEC strain, O115 with an H antigen is an ETEC strain, O115 without an H antigen is an EIEC strain, and O157:H7 is an EHEC strain. Toxins are now tested for using enzyme-linked immunosorbent assay or DNA probes. For EIEC strains, the conjunctival sac of a guinea pig is used. Serology tests are also used, but they are not reliable indicators of recent infection.

Other Organisms

Shigella

Shigella requires a very low dose to cause infection and does not grow very well in food. Thus, it is more commonly spread case to case, especially among kindergarten and primary school children. Affected patients may excrete the organisms for weeks. Nevertheless, some large and important outbreaks have been caused by food contaminated by sewage-polluted water or food handlers. In 1995, an extensive *S. sonnei* outbreak caused by lettuce imported from Spain affected people in many countries in northern Europe. In another outbreak caused by shrimp, infection was transmitted by a food handler who mixed the shrimp by hand with mayonnaise and tomato sauce. The incubation period is 24–48 h, and although bloody or mucoid diarrhea is the usual symptom, it is characteristically accompanied by tenesmus—a feeling of wanting to defecate without being able to do so.

Listeria

Listeriosis, caused by the bacterium *Listeria monocytogenes*, is an unpleasant and rare infection that affects the more vulnerable, such as fetuses, infants, pregnant women, the elderly, and the immunocompromised. It causes septicaemia and meningitis, which is unusual for a FP organism. Fatality rates for invasive disease are high, as many as one in three. GI symptoms may be absent or mild. Also unusual, it can grow (albeit slowly) at normal refrigeration temperatures (0–4 °C). It is also very resistant in the environment, both to cold and to heat, so that it can survive for long periods. Normal pasteurization processes will inactivate it, but some organisms can survive the high-temperature/short-time process. The incubation period for invasive disease tends to be long (up to 3 weeks), but for GI symptoms very short periods of 1 day have been recorded. Dairy products, including soft cheese and butter, and pate are the most common sources of listerial FP, and a large and sustained outbreak in England and Wales between 1987 and 1989 was thought to be due to Belgian pate. The list of foods also includes hot dogs and other ready-to-eat delicatessen meats.

Yersinia enterocolitica

Like Listeria, *Y. enterocolitica* can reproduce at refrigeration temperatures. It is often missed in the laboratory because it requires special media and grows best at 25 °C. Many strains are nonpathogenic, but it is difficult to predict which strains are pathogenic and which not using current laboratory methods, although serotypes 3, 8, and 9 are most commonly associated with illness. The organism is found in many pets and other animals, and it may survive pasteurization, especially high-temperature/short-time milk treatment. Outbreaks have been associated with raw milk and dairy products. Undercooked pork and tofu have also caused outbreaks, and in one incident a caregiver who handled pork sausages passed the infection on to some infants. These infections appear to be more common in Scandinavia than elsewhere. The incubation period is 24–48 h to 5 days. Infants and young children are most often affected. Clinical features are characteristically fever and profuse watery diarrhea, but it may mimic acute appendicitis, risking an unnecessary operation. Occasionally, in vulnerable patients, septicaemia may occur.

Vibrio parahaemolyticus

Like *V. cholerae* (and several other aquatic organisms described later), *V. parahaemolyticus* is an aquatic organism that thrives in shallow coastal waters. Deep-sea fish do not tend to harbor the organism and usually become contaminated in fish markets. Precooked frozen shrimp may be contaminated and cause FP if served without further cooking, as in a seafood cocktail. *Vibrio parahaemolyticus* FP is associated with raw, undercooked, or contaminated seafood and is especially common in Japan and probably other countries in which seafood is a staple of the diet. Contamination from raw to cooked seafood is a common cause. The incidence of *V. parahaemolyticus* FP has increased in many Asian countries and the United States since 1996, and this is thought to be caused by a pandemic clone. Diarrhea, abdominal pain, and nausea are the predominant symptoms. The diarrhea can be severe, with blood or mucus in the stool. Vomiting is a less common feature, but fever can occur. The incubation period ranges from 4 h to 4 days, but most cases occur between 12 and 24 h. Death is uncommon.

The diagnosis is made by culture of the organism from feces or food. *Vibrio parahaemolyticus* can be easily isolated from most aquatic environments, but such strains are predominantly Kanagawa negative. Only the Kanagawa-positive strains (i.e., those producing a thermostable hemolysin that can be confirmed in a laboratory) cause GE, and it is thought that they multiply selectively in the human intestine. The infectious dose can be fairly small, 2×10^5 to 3×10^7.

Vibrio vulnificus

Like the other vibrios, infection with this organism is acquired from seafood. The epidemiology is similar but the organism appears to be the most common vibrio causing FP in the United States. It also causes septicaemia by ingress through a skin lesion in the food handler and in people with chronic liver disease through consumption of raw seafood. Gastroenteritis can also occur.

Aeromonas and *Plesiomonas shigelloides*

Aeromonas is another aquatic organism that prefers brackish and fresh water. It is generally accepted as a cause of FP, after initial doubts, in both adults and children. A profuse watery diarrhea is typical, although a dysentery-like syndrome is sometimes associated with it. The incubation period is 18–24 h. Sporadic infections are more common than full-blown outbreaks. Consumption of raw shellfish should be avoided (not only for aeromonas). *Plesiomonas shigelloides* is also an aquatic organism, and FP from it is rare. Its role in FP has not been fully elucidated. Diarrhea is the usual symptom, and the incubation period is approximately 24 h.

Bacillus subtilis and Bacillus licheniformis

Bacillus subtilis is a member of the Bacillus genus and is similar to B. cereus, except that its natural habitat is slightly different, and so the foods causing illness also differ. It has been recognized increasingly as a cause of GE, characterized mainly by vomiting. The incubation period is short, 2 or 3 h, although many cases occur within 1 h. Foods implicated include meat and vegetable products such as meat pies, sausage rolls, curries with accompanying rice dishes, and even bread, crumpets, and pizza. The organism is present at high levels in implicated food (10^5–10^9 cfu/g) and can be isolated easily from both food and feces. Another member of this genus, Bacillus licheniformis, tends to cause diarrhea. Cooked meats and vegetables have been implicated. The median incubation period is approximately 8 h. Other members of this genus can also cause FP.

Bacillus anthracis

Rare in developed countries, anthrax FP is caused by the consumption of severely infected meat that has been insufficiently cooked. Bloody diarrhea is characteristic, accompanied by nausea, vomiting, and acute abdominal pain. The incubation period is from 2 days to many weeks.

Brucellosis

Although not usually considered as FP, brucellosis deserves mention because it is commonly caused by food. Brucella melitensis in particular is nearly always foodborne, and cheese, milk, and other dairy products made from unpasteurized milk are common vehicles. Occasionally, contaminated meats may be responsible. Brucella abortus is associated with cows and cow products, B. melitensis with goats, and B. suis with pigs. Brucellosis is a serious and prolonged systemic illness, with fever, night sweats, headache, aches and pains, and, sometimes, profound depression. Many developed countries have eradicated brucella from livestock.

Streptococcal Pharyngitis

Notwithstanding the definition of FP as causing GE, streptococcal sore throat with fever has been well documented to spread in this way. Usually, a food handler has a streptococcus group A in his or her throat, which may or may not be causing symptoms, and transfers this to a food that is then left in a warm environment for some time before consumption. Foods implicated include cheese, milk, eggs, and meat. The incubation period is 24–48 h. To confirm a source, typing of strains is important, as is sound epidemiological evidence, because many people carry these streptococci in their throats.

Prevention of Bacterial Food Poisoning

With the increasing trend toward the manufacturing of foods in large quantities for distribution not only nationally but also internationally, the potential for vast outbreaks of foodborne disease is considerable. Outbreaks of salmonellosis and E. coli FP caused by cheese, salami, chocolate, beef jerky, infant dried milk, minced beef, hamburgers, and even potato crisps have all been documented. In one outbreak of E. coli O157:H7 infection, 34 lots of 281 000 lb of beef patties were manufactured in one plant, and 7 of 21 lots tested were found to be contaminated. The introduction of HACCP (hazard analysis and critical control point) in food manufacturing processes has been a significant advance in the production of safer food and the prevention of FP. Microbiological guidelines now exist for ready-to-eat foods. The establishment of Enternet in countries in Europe and elsewhere is an important step in the early detection of such outbreaks and the curtailment of their effects. This is a voluntary surveillance system that shares information on organisms causing FP. For example, an outbreak of FP affecting several tourists from different countries after staying at a hotel on the Mediterranean coast will be detected more quickly and enable an early warning to be instituted. If a contaminated food is distributed through several countries, the country that first detected a problem can issue an early warning.

Fortunately, most outbreaks of FP are more localized, although large numbers of people may still be affected. The most common problems in the preparation of food are inadequate cooking, leaving prepared food too long at too high a temperature, and allowing cross-contamination from raw to cooked food.

All foods entering the kitchen should be considered to be potentially hazardous. In any investigation, it is important not to assume that a food cannot be the cause just because it is unlikely or not known to have caused FP in the past. Salads and other vegetables or fruit eaten raw may be contaminated, and outbreaks have been caused by lettuce (S. sonnei and E. coli VTEC 0157), raspberries and strawberries (Cyclospora cayetanensis and hepatitis A), alfalfa sprouts (S. enteritidis), and radish sprouts grown hydroponically (E. coli VTEC

0157). Some of these foods were contaminated at the source by water or sewage, others during processing by infected food handlers (NLV and hepatitis A), and others by food handlers during preparation. It is difficult to avoid or prevent such infections in the kitchen short of cooking everything, and more stringent codes for hygiene at the growing farms and processing plants are required.

In the kitchen, it is important to keep raw and ready-to-eat foods entirely separate. Salad and fruit fall into the ready-to-eat category. Raw meats especially should have their own utensils, surfaces, and cutting boards. For cooked food entirely different utensils, surfaces, and cutting boards should be used, unless washed thoroughly in very hot water and detergent or a dishwasher and then left to dry. Otherwise, FP organisms will transfer from raw to cooked food and grow.

Cooking food, especially meat, thoroughly will destroy vegetative organisms, including salmonellas, although spores will survive. If the cooling down period is too long—normally approximately 1 h is considered the limit before refrigeration is necessary—C. perfringens or B. cereus that have survived as spores will grow. So will salmonellas and many other FP bacteria if the food was inadequately cooked. Cooking will not normally destroy preformed toxins of S. aureus. Infected food handlers may occasionally cause outbreaks of FP, but with the exception of staphylococci, bacterial FP from this source is rarer than is generally thought. Salmonellae almost always originate in a food, and B. cereus and C. perfringens always arise from the food. Food handlers whose hands have been contaminated usually transmit shigella, hepatitis A, or norovirus.

Thus, moist food needs to be kept either hot (above approximately 60 °C) or cold (below 8 °C, preferably 4 °C). Cooling food, even freezing it, will not destroy organisms (except for some helminths). Undercooked chicken that has been refrigerated will still need thorough cooking before it is fit to eat. A large bulk of frozen meat or poultry will need to be thawed before cooking. Large frozen turkeys may need several days in a refrigerator to thaw fully. The inside of the meat is the last to thaw and the last to cook.

Grinding meat will disperse organisms through it. Thus, hamburgers and sausages need thorough cooking.

Drinking raw milk is hazardous: A large number of organisms, from tuberculosis to *Streptococcus zooepidemicus*, can be spread in this way. Hens' eggs caused many cases of salmonella FP (mainly *S. enteritidis*) in the 1980s and 1990s throughout much of Europe and the United States. The rate of contamination was low, probably not more than 2 or 3 per 1000 eggs, but the number of cases was large because of the popularity of eggs as a food and because it is normal to eat them less than fully cooked, not only on their own but also in other dishes such as sauces and mousse. Fortunately, screening and vaccination of flocks in recent years have made this a less hazardous source of salmonellosis. Irradiation of food is effective but is not popular with the public.

Education of food handlers may be straightforward, but, especially in countries in which food handlers have low status and pay, compliance is more difficult. Nevertheless, education of the general public has been slow but has progressed: Most people now realize the importance of thawing poultry and meat thoroughly before cooking, and the large outbreaks of salmonella FP that used to occur at Christmas time in England and Wales caused by inadequately defrosted and cooked turkeys are now very rare.

See also: **Dairy Products. Eggs. Fish. Food Safety:** Mycotoxins. **Meat, Poultry and Meat Products.**

Further Reading

Campylobacter Sentinel Surveillance Scheme Collaborators (2003) Point source outbreaks of campylobacter jejuni infection—Are they more common than we think and what might cause them? *Epidemiology and Infection* 130: 367–375.

Centers for Disease Control and Prevention. Staphylococcal food poisoning. Available at www.cdc.gov/mmwrrhtml/00050415.htm

Eley AR (1996) *Microbial Food Poisoning*, 2nd edn. London: Chapman & Hall.

Evans MR, Salmon RL, Nehaul L *et al.* (1999) An outbreak of *Salmonella typhimurium* DT170 associated with kebab meat and yoghurt relish. *Epidemiology and Infection* 122: 377–383.

Gilbert RJ and Humphrey TJ (1998) Foodborne bacterial gastroenteritis. In: Collier L, Balows A, and Sussman M (eds.) *Topley and Wilson's Microbiology and Microbial Infections.* London: Edward Arnold.

Hedberg CW, Angulo FJ, White KE *et al.* (1999) Outbreaks of salmonellosis associated with eating uncooked tomatoes: Implications for public health. *Epidemiology and Infection* 122: 385–393.

Horby PW, O'Brien SJ, Adak GK *et al.* (2003) A national outbreak of multiresistant Salmonella enterica serovar typhimuriom DT 104 associated with consumption of lettuce. *Epidemiology and Infection* 130: 169–178.

Mintz ED, Tauxe RV, and Levine MM (1998) The global resurgence of cholera. In: Noah ND and O'Mahony M (eds.) *Communicable Disease: Epidemiology and Control.* Chichester, UK: John Wiley.

Neimann J, Engberg J, Molbak K, and Wegener HC (2003) A case–control study of risk factors for sporadic campylobacter infections in Denmark. *Epidemiology and Infection* 130: 353–366.

Noah ND (1992) Food poisoning. In: Truswell AS (ed.) *ABC of Nutrition.* London: British Medical Journal.

Osterholm MT and Norgan AP (2004) The role of irradiation in food safety. *New England Journal of Medicine* **350**: 1898–1901.

Perales I and Garcia MI (1990) The influence of pH and temperature on the behaviour of S. enteritidis phage type 4 in homemade mayonnaise. *Letters in Applied Microbiology* **10**: 19–22.

Roberts JA, Cumberland P, Sockett PN *et al.* (2002) The study of infectious intestinal disease in England: Socioeconomic impact. *Epidemiology and Infection* **129**: 1–11.

Takkinen J, Ammon A, Robstad O, Breuer T, and the Campylobacter Working Group (2003) European Survey of Campylobacter surveillance and diagnosis 2001. *Eurosurveillance* **8**: 207–213.

Tuttle J, Gomez T, Doyle MP *et al.* (1999) Lessons for a large outbreak of *E. coli* O157:H7 infections: Insights into the infectious dose and method of widespread contamination of hamburger patties. *Epidemiology and Infection* **122**: 185–192.

Zaidi AKM, Awasthi S, and deSilva HJ (2004) Burden of infectious diseases in South Asia. *British Medical Journal* **328**: 811–815.

Other Contaminants

C K Winter, University of California at Davis, Davis, CA, USA

Food may be contaminated with many chemicals that pose the potential for toxicological consequences in humans consuming the contaminated food items. In addition to the presence of contaminants such as mycotoxins, pesticide residues, and heavy metals, food may contain numerous organic contaminants that enter the food supply from environmental sources or as a result of chemical reactions that occur during food processing. This article focuses on three types of food contaminants: dioxins (including dibenzofurans and polychlorinated biphenyls), acrylamide, and perchlorate. Each of these classes has been subject to considerable regulatory scrutiny, scientific study, and popular media coverage. It is likely that concerns regarding the presence of these contaminants in the food supply will continue throughout the next decade or longer, and that significant efforts will be made to reduce human exposure to these substances from food. This article discusses how these types of food contaminants enter the food supply, the types of food items in which they are most likely to occur, and the potential toxicological consequences resulting from exposure to these contaminants.

Dioxins

Dioxins are organic chemicals that comprise a family of ubiquitous environmental contaminants. Technically speaking, the dioxins of potential toxicological concern are polychlorinated dibenzo-*p*-dioxins (PCDDs). They are related, both structurally and toxicologically, to polychlorinated dibenzofurans (PCDFs) and polychlorinated biphenyls (PCBs). Structures of generic PCDDs, PCDFs, and PCBs are shown in **Figure 1**. Due to their structural and toxicological similarity and to avoid confusion, all three related groups of chemicals are considered to represent "dioxins" for the purposes of this article. Specific chemicals belonging to this family are referred to as congeners. Collectively, there are more than 200 dioxin-related congeners, and each possesses unique toxicological and chemical properties.

Occurrence in the Environment and in Food

PCDDs and PCDFs are primarily introduced into the environment as by-products of combustion processes. These by-products have been identified in the exhaust gases from sources such as cigarette smoke; industrial and municipal waste incinerators; power plants burning coal, oil, or wood; and automobiles. In addition to these human sources, PCDDs and PCDFs are also produced naturally by combustion in forest fires and from volcanic eruptions.

Historically, PCDDs and PCDFs have also been produced as impurities during organic chemical synthesis. The most notable and most toxic dioxin congener, 2,3,7,8-tetrachlorodibenzo-*p*-dioxin (TCDD), has been shown to be produced in the synthesis of the herbicide 2,4,5-T, one of the herbicide components of Agent Orange, notoriously used in the Vietnam War. Although 2,4,5-T is now banned for use in the United States because of TCDD and other dioxin impurities, health concerns over the exposure of military veterans to Agent Orange and to TCDD continue to be raised. PCDDs and PCDFs can also be produced through the use of chlorine

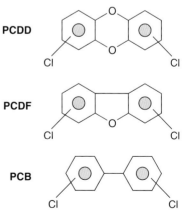

Figure 1 Chemical structures of generic PCDDs, PCDFs, and PCBs.

to bleach wood pulp, although most bleaching processes now use nonchlorine agents such as hydrogen peroxide.

PCBs have been produced synthetically since the 1930s and have been widely used for industrial applications, such as dielectric fluids in transformers (due to their inflammability) and capacitors in electrical machinery. Like their PCDD and PCDF counterparts, PCBs are extremely persistent in the environment and are of toxicological concern. As a result, the synthesis and industrial use of PCBs were significantly curtailed in the 1970s, although environmental residues of PCBs are still commonly detected today.

Although dioxin release into the environment has been known to occur for several decades, data are still limited with respect to the degree to which dioxins contaminate the food supply. Dioxin analysis in the laboratory is extremely expensive because methods must identify hundreds of different congeners, detection limits are required in the sub-part per trillion range, and significant precautions must be taken to minimize exposure of laboratory personnel to the analytical standards used for dioxin congeners.

Dioxins are highly fat soluble and have been shown to accumulate in the fat of birds, fish, and food animals. The US Environmental Protection Agency (EPA) has estimated that more than 95% of human exposure to dioxins results from dietary intake of animal fats. The major food sources for dioxin exposure include fish, poultry, meats, milk, and milk products. Dioxins are excreted in human breast milk and result in exposures to nursing infants.

Historically, it has been shown that human dioxin exposures, as determined by analyzing human tissues and environmental samples, have decreased significantly since 1987 due to engineering controls to limit dioxin emissions during combustion processes and to increased regulatory control over other sources of dioxin exposure. Dietary dioxin exposures to UK consumers were reduced by nearly two-thirds from 1982 to 1992, and subsequent studies showed even lower exposures in 1997. Nevertheless, dioxins are still ubiquitous in the environment and human exposure still occurs.

Toxicological Considerations

Dioxin exposure at significant dose levels has been linked to a large number of adverse health effects. Large acute exposures, resulting from chemical accidents and/or occupational exposure to dioxins, have caused a severe skin condition known as chloracne.

A variety of other skin effects, such as rashes and discoloration, have also been attributed to acute dioxin exposures, as has liver damage.

Concerns from chronic exposure to dioxins include cancer, reproductive effects, and developmental effects. The most toxic dioxin congener, TCDD, was classified by the International Agency for Research on Cancer as a human carcinogen.

From a biochemical standpoint, PCDDs, PCDFs, and PCBs appear to cause their toxic effects through chemical binding to a specific cellular receptor known as the Ah receptor. Specific dioxin congeners vary dramatically with respect to their abilities to bind with the Ah receptor; TCDD binds extremely effectively, whereas other congeners are more limited in their binding capabilities. The degree to which various dioxin congeners bind with the Ah receptor seems to be directly related to the number and location of chlorine atoms on the congeners.

Assessing the potential human health risks from exposure to dioxins presents significant challenges. Dioxin levels in specific food items can be quite variable, and, as discussed previously, data concerning dioxin levels on foods are frequently not available.

Another difficulty encountered in assessing dioxin risks is to appropriately account for exposures to the various congeners and to account for the toxicological differences among congeners. This is most appropriately achieved through a toxic equivalency factor (TEF) approach that assigns a potency factor to each of the congeners relative to that of the most toxic dioxin TCDD. For example, the TEF for TCDD is 1 and the TEF for 1,2,3,4,7,8-hexachlorodibenzo-p-dioxin (with chlorines added to the 1 and 2 positions and otherwise similar to TCDD) is 0.1 based on findings that 1,2,3,4,7,8-hexachlorodibenzo-p-dioxin is 10 times less capable of binding to the Ah receptor than is TCDD. To calculate a total dioxin exposure, the dietary contributions of each of the dioxin congeners are multiplied by their corresponding TEFs and summed to determine a TCDD equivalent exposure.

According to the World Health Organization (WHO), a tolerable daily intake (TDI) for TCDD was established at 10 pg TCDD per kilogram bodyweight per day in 1990, although revisions by WHO reduced the TDI range to 1–4 pg/kg/day in 1999. A 1997 UK survey of dioxin consumer exposure provided an upper bound of 1.8 pg TCDD equivalent/kg/day. Surveys from other countries, using slightly different TEF approaches, yielded exposures of 0.7 pg/kg/day in Italy, 1.4 pg/kg/day in Norway, 2.4–3.5 pg/kg/day in Spain, and 0.2 pg/kg/day in New Zealand.

The US Food and Drug Administration (FDA) has been monitoring finfish, shellfish, and dairy products for dioxins since 1995 and initiated dioxin analysis of foods analyzed in its Total Diet Study in 1999. Specific findings from the FDA's annual Total Diet Study can be obtained from the FDA, although human exposure estimates, in terms of the amount of TCDD equivalent exposure per kilogram of body weight per day, have not been published by the FDA.

The EPA recommends that consumers follow the existing Federal Dietary Guidelines to reduce fat consumption and, subsequently, dioxin exposure. Such guidelines suggest that consumers choose fish, lean meat, poultry, and low- or fat-free dairy products while increasing consumption of fruits, vegetables, and grains. Dioxin exposure can be further minimized by trimming visible fat from meats, removing the skin of fish and poultry, reducing the amount of butter or lard used in cooking, and replacing cooking methods such as frying with methods such as boiling or oven broiling.

Acrylamide

Acrylamide is a widely used and versatile industrial chemical. Its most common use is as a coagulant in water treatment and purification. It is also used as a soil conditioner, in the sizing of paper and textiles, in ore processing, and as a construction aid for the building of tunnels and dam foundations.

Acrylamide is considered by the International Agency for Research on Cancer to be "probably carcinogenic to humans" based on the results of several animal carcinogenicity studies. As a result, there has been widespread concern about the potential risks from exposure to acrylamide among industrial, manufacturing, and laboratory workers. Consumer exposure to acrylamide in treated drinking water has posed a much lower concern since drinking water is subject to special treatment techniques that control the amount of acrylamide in drinking water.

Swedish researchers developed laboratory techniques that allowed for the detection of biological reaction products (hemoglobin adducts) of acrylamide in human blood samples; results from their studies allowed correlations to be made between occupational activities and acrylamide exposures. The findings that acrylamide occurred in tobacco smoke and that smokers had increased levels of hemoglobin adducts relative to nonsmokers provided a suggestion that acrylamide may be formed during incomplete combustion of organic matter or during heating. Interestingly, the researchers found

significant levels of hemoglobin adducts in blood samples of nonsmoking humans not exposed occupationally to acrylamide. This led to speculation that the human diet could contain significant quantities of acrylamide. In April 2002, Swedish researchers published results of research that demonstrated the presence of acrylamide in several common foodstuffs, with the highest levels found in fried and baked foods. These findings stimulated worldwide interest in identifying the potential mechanisms for acrylamide formation in foods, in assaying a wide variety of foods for acrylamide levels, and in developing risk assessment and risk mitigation procedures.

Occurrence in Food

The findings from the initial Swedish study indicated that the highest levels (150–4000 μg/kg) of acrylamide were detected in carbohydrate-rich foods such as potatoes and in heated commercial potato products (potato chips) and crispbread. Moderate levels (5–50 μg/kg) were measured in protein-rich foods that were heated, whereas unheated or boiled foods showed no detectable acrylamide (<5 μg/kg).

The governments of several countries throughout the world performed similar analyses of acrylamide in foods and findings were fairly consistent with those reported in the Swedish study. The FDA analyzed dozens of foods for acrylamide levels and concluded that the highest levels were observed in french fries (29 samples; range, 117–1030 μg/kg) and in potato chips (40 samples; range, 117–2762 μg/kg). Multiple samples from different lots of the same commercial food products showed significant variability, with the highest levels often several times greater than the lowest levels. Commercial potato products that could be prepared by baking or by other methods showed much higher levels of acrylamide in the baked products. Acrylamide levels in baby food ranged from below the detection level (<10 μg/kg) to 130 μg/kg. All infant formula samples had levels below 10 μg/kg, and acrylamide levels in dairy products were also low.

The widespread findings of acrylamide in foodstuffs throughout the world provided the basis for numerous studies designed to elucidate the mechanisms for acrylamide formation in foods. It has been demonstrated that acrylamide can be formed from classical Maillard reactions as well as from reaction of the fatty acid oxidation product acrolein with ammonia and subsequent oxidation steps. The most plausible explanation for the relatively high acrylamide levels in fried potato products derives from a mechanism involving the reaction of the amino group of the amino acid asparagine with the

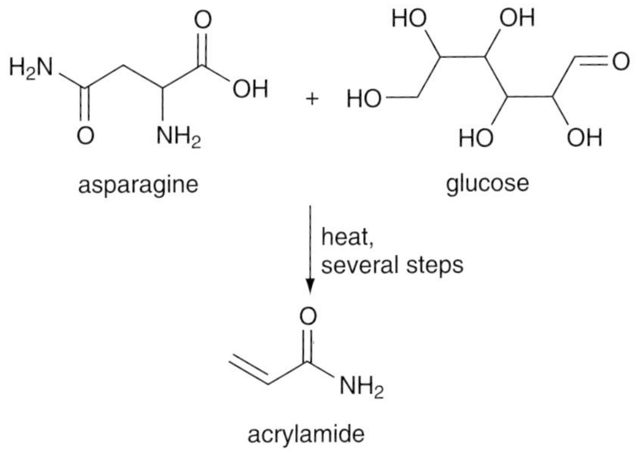

Figure 2 Proposed mechanism for acrylamide formation in foods.

carbonyl group of a reducing sugar such as glucose during baking and frying. This mechanism is shown in **Figure 2**. Potatoes are high in asparagine and in reducing sugars, and they are commonly prepared for consumption by frying or baking; all of these factors help explain the relatively high levels of acrylamide in heated potato products.

Toxicological Considerations

Laboratory toxicology studies have indicated that acrylamide is carcinogenic and also has been associated with the development of reproductive toxicity, genotoxicity, and neurotoxicity. Epidemiological and analytical studies of people exposed to acrylamide in the workplace have indicated that acrylamide does indeed enter the bloodstream of workers and can be detected and quantified as hemoglobin adducts, thus indicating both exposure and absorption of acrylamide. Such studies have not, however, indicated increases in cancer rates among those exposed occupationally to acrylamide. To date, the only documented toxicological effect observed in epidemiological studies of workers exposed to acrylamide is neurotoxicity. This effect is primarily an acute effect caused by large exposures to acrylamide for relatively short periods of time, leading to nervous system damage, weakness, and incoordination of limbs.

From a biochemical standpoint, it is likely that the health effects caused by high levels of exposure in humans and in laboratory animals may result from a Michael-type nucleophilic addition reaction of amino acids (both amino and sulfhydryl groups), peptides, and proteins to acrylamide because of the presence of the α,β-unsaturated conjugated structure in acrylamide. This is a common toxicological pathway for many reactive compounds. It is likely that high doses of acrylamide may overwhelm the defensive mechanisms of the body such as glutathione

conjugation and may cause reaction with biologically significant nucleophiles, leading to mutations and possible carcinogenicity.

Although it is clear that humans have been consuming significant amounts of acrylamide in their diets for a long time, the relatively new discovery of acrylamide as a food contaminant has raised several questions. Significant efforts are currently being made to better understand the levels of acrylamide throughout the food chain and to estimate dietary exposure to acrylamide. In addition, there is much emphasis on developing food processing approaches that can reduce acrylamide formation.

Regulatory limits for acrylamide in food have yet to be established since dietary acrylamide risk assessments are still being developed. In the meantime, the FDA recommends that consumers eat a balanced diet that includes a wide variety of foods low in trans fat and saturated fat and rich in high-fiber grains, fruits, and vegetables.

Perchlorate

Perchlorate exists as an anion (ClO_4^-) with a central chlorine atom surrounded by four oxygen atoms arranged in a tetrahedron. Perchlorate is manufactured in the United States and is used as the primary ingredient of solid rocket propellant. Perchlorate wastes from the manufacture and/or improper disposal of perchlorate-containing chemicals are frequently detected in the soil and water. Levels of perchlorate have been detected in 58 California public water systems and in water samples from 18 states.

The widespread water contamination by perchlorate and its potential to cause health effects in those consuming contaminated drinking water have led four US agencies—the EPA, Department of Defense, Department of Energy, and National Aeronautics and Space Administration—to request that the US National Academy of Sciences convene a study on "Toxicological Assessment of Perchlorate Ingestion."

Occurrence in Food

Although the primary concerns from perchlorate contamination result from drinking water consumption, recent evidence has indicated that perchlorate may contaminate food items as well. A small survey of 22 lettuce samples purchased in northern California showed perchlorate contamination in 4 samples. A subsequent study of California lettuce showed detectable perchlorate levels in all 18 samples tested. The toxicological significance of such findings has not been established, but the studies clearly indicate that perchlorate can enter lettuce, presumably from growing conditions in which perchlorate has contaminated water or soil.

Milk has also been shown to be subject to perchlorate contamination. A small survey of seven milk samples purchased in Lubbock, Texas, indicated that perchlorate was present in all of the samples at levels ranging from 1.12 to 6.30 μg/l. To put such findings in perspective, the State of California has adopted an action level of 4 μg/l for perchlorate in drinking water, whereas the EPA has yet to establish a specific drinking water limit.

Toxicological Considerations

Perchlorate is thought to exert its toxic effects at high doses by interfering with iodide uptake into the thyroid gland. This inhibition of iodide uptake can lead to reductions in the secretion of thyroid hormones that are responsible for the control of growth, development, and metabolism. Disruption of the pituitary–hypothalamic–thyroid axis by perchlorate may lead to serious effects, such as carcinogenicity, neurodevelopmental and developmental changes, reproductive toxicity, and immunotoxicity. Specific concerns relate to the exposures of infants, children, and pregnant women because the thyroid plays a major role in fetal and child development.

The ability of perchlorate to interfere with iodide uptake is due to its structural similarity with iodide. In recognition of this property, perchlorate has been used as a drug in the treatment of hyperthyroidism and for the diagnosis of thyroid or iodine metabolism disorders.

Ammonium perchlorate was found to be nongenotoxic in a number of tests, which is consistent with the fact that perchlorate is relatively inert under physiological conditions and is not metabolized to active metabolites in humans or in test animals.

Workers exposed to airborne levels of perchlorate absorbed between 0.004 and 167 mg perchlorate per day. These workers showed no evidence of thyroid abnormality, and a No Observed Adverse Effect Level was established at 34 mg absorbed perchlorate/day. Perchlorate does not accumulate in the human body, and 85–90% of perchlorate given to humans is excreted in the urine within 24 h.

See also: **Cancer**: Epidemiology and Associations Between Diet and Cancer. **Fish**. **Food Intolerance**. **Food Safety**: Mycotoxins; Pesticides; Bacterial Contamination; Heavy Metals.

Further Reading

Becher G (1998) Dietary exposure and human body burden of dioxins and dioxin-like PCBs in Norway. *Organohalogen Compounds* **38**: 79–82.

Buckland SJ (1998) Concentrations of PCDDs, PCDFs and PCBs in New Zealand retain foods and assessment of dietary exposure. *Organohalogen Compounds* **38**: 71–74.

Environmental Protection Agency (2001) *Dioxin: Scientific Highlights from Draft Reassessment*. Washington, DC: US Environmental Protection Agency, Office of Research and Development.

Food and Drug Administration (2002) *Exploratory Data on Acrylamide in Foods*. Washington, DC: US Food and Drug Administration, Center for Food Safety and Applied Nutrition.

Friedman M (2003) Chemistry, biochemistry, and safety of acrylamide. A review. *Journal of Agricultural and Food Chemistry* **51**: 4504–4526.

Jimenez B (1996) Estimated intake of PCDDs, PCDFs and co-planar PCBs in individuals from Madrid (Spain) eating an average diet. *Chemosphere* **33**: 1465–1474.

Kirk AB, Smith EE, Tian K, Anderson TA, and Dasgupta PK (2003) Perchlorate in milk. *Environmental Science and Technology* **37**: 4979–4981.

Sharp R and Walker B (2003) *Rocket Science: Perchlorate and the Toxic Legacy of the Cold War* Washington, DC: Environmental Working Group.

Tareke E, Rydberg P, Karlsson P, Eriksson S, and Tornqvist M (2002) Analysis of acrylamide, a carcinogen formed in heated foodstuffs. *Journal of Agricultural and Food Chemistry* **50**: 4998–5006.

Urbansky ET (2002) Perchlorate as an environmental contaminant. *Environmental Science and Pollution Research* **9**: 187–192.

Zanotto E (1999) PCDD/Fs in Venetian foods and a quantitative assessment of dietary intake. *Organohalogen Compounds* **44**: 13–17.

Heavy Metals

G L Klein, University of Texas Medical Branch at Galveston, Galveston TX, USA

Food that we are culturally habituated to consume is usually thought to be safe. However, some foods are naturally contaminated with substances, the effects of which are unknown. Crops are sprayed with pesticides while they are being cultivated; some animals are injected with hormones while being raised. Meanwhile, other foods are mechanically processed in ways that could risk contamination. This article discusses food contamination with heavy metals, the heavy metals involved, their toxicities, and their sources in the environment. A brief consideration of medical management is also included. Five metals are considered in this category: lead, mercury, cadmium, nickel, and bismuth.

Lead

How Does Lead Contaminate Food?

Although lead is primarily known as an environmental contaminant that is ingested in paint chips by young children in urban slums or from contaminated soil or inhaled in the form of house dust or automobile exhaust, it may also enter the food and water supply. Ways in which this can occur include fuel exhaust emissions from automobiles that may contaminate crops and be retained by them, especially green leafy vegetables. Animals used for food may graze on contaminated crops and thus may also be a potential source of lead. Moreover, lead from soldered water pipes may contaminate tap water used for drink or for food production.

Permissible Intakes

In the United States, the maximum quantity of lead in the water supply that is permitted by the Environmental Protection Agency is $15 \mu g$ ($0.07 \mu mol\, l^{-1}$). The Food and Drug Administration (FDA) Advisory Panel recommends that no more than $100 \mu g$ ($50 \mu mol$) of lead per day should be ingested from food products.

Dietary Lead: Absorption and Consequences

People with certain macronutrient and micronutrient deficiencies are prone to experience increased absorption of lead in the diet. Thus, depletion of iron, calcium, and zinc may promote lead absorption through the gastrointestinal tract. Whereas adults may normally absorb approximately 15% of their lead intake, pregnant women and children may absorb up to 3.5 times that amount, and the explanation for this difference is not clear.

The effects of the entry of lead into the circulation depend on its concentration. Thus, the inhibition of an enzyme active in hemoglobin synthesis, δ-amino levulinic acid dehydratase (ALAD), occurs at blood lead concentrations of $5–10 \mu g\, dl^{-1}$ ($0.25–0.5 \mu mol\, l^{-1}$). Another enzyme active in heme biosynthesis, erythrocyte ferrochelatase, is inhibited at a blood lead level of $15 \mu g\, dl^{-1}$ ($0.75 \mu mol\, l^{-1}$). Reduction of the renal enzyme 25-hydroxyvitamin D-1-α hydroxylase, which converts circulating 25-hydroxyvitamin D to its biologically active steroid hormone, $1\alpha,25$-dihydroxyvitamin D ($1,25(OH)_2D$) or calcitriol, is observed at a blood lead concentration of $25 \mu g\, dl^{-1}$ ($1.25 \mu mol\, l^{-1}$). Behavioral changes and learning problems may begin to occur at blood levels previously thought to be normal, $10–15 \mu g\, dl^{-1}$ ($0.5–0.75 \mu mol\, l^{-1}$).

Manifestations of Lead Toxicity

Perhaps due to their increased absorption of lead from the diet, children appear to be more susceptible to the toxic effects of lead. These involve the nervous system, including cognitive dysfunction; the liver; the composition of circulating blood; kidney function; the vitamin D endocrine system and bone (**Table 1**); and gene function, possibly with resultant teratogenic effects. Chronic exposure results in high blood pressure, stroke, and end-stage kidney disease in adults.

Neurologic Full-blown lead encephalopathy, including delirium, truncal ataxia, hyperirritability, altered vision, lethargy, vomiting, and coma, is not common. Although peripheral nerve damage and paralysis may still be reported in adults, the most common toxicity observed is learning disability and an associated high-frequency hearing loss occurring in children with blood lead levels previously assumed to be safe. At low blood levels of lead (less than $10 \mu g\, dl^{-1}$), children may lose IQ points, possibly due to the interference of lead in normal calcium signaling in neurons and possibly by blocking the recently reported learning-induced activation of calcium/phospholipid-dependent protein kinase C in the hippocampus.

The physicochemical basis of these changes derives largely from small animal data. Rats exposed to lead from birth develop mitochondrial dysfunction, neuronal swelling, and necrosis in both the cerebrum and the cerebellum. Exposure on day 10 of life elicited only the cerebellar pathology, and lead exposure after $3\frac{1}{2}$ weeks of life failed to produce any of these changes. In combination with manganese, lead has also produced peroxidative damage to rat brains and has been shown to inhibit nitric oxide synthase in the brains of mice. Additionally, an increase in blood arachidonic acid and in the ratio of arachidonic to linoleic acid following lead exposure in several species, including humans, may provide evidence in support of a peroxidative mechanism of damage to neural tissue following lead exposure.

Lead has also produced necrosis of retinal photoreceptor cells and swelling of the endothelial lining of retinal blood vessels in rats. Lead may also damage the auditory nerves in rats, and it may be partially responsible for the high-frequency hearing loss observed in humans. Finally, organic lead compounds may also disturb brain microtubular assembly.

Liver Although there are no outwardly recognizable manifestations of lead toxicity to the liver, studies in

Table 1 Heavy metal toxicities by tissues

Tissue	Heavy metal	Dietary source(s)	Toxicity
Neurologic	Lead	Green, leafy vegetables, canned food with lead solder, water	Learning disability, ataxia, encephalopathy, irritability
	Mercury	Seafood, agricultural crop contamination	Psychomotor retardation, paralysis, microcephaly, convulsions, choreoathetotic movements
	Bismuth	Medications	Paraesthesias, tremors, ataxia, reduced short-term memory
Bone	Lead	See above	Reduced conversion of vitamin D to active form, ?reduced osteoclast function
	Mercury	See above	?Reduced bone formation and bone density
	Cadmium	Seafood, plant roots in contaminated soil	?High bone turnover, secondary hyperparathyroidism
Bone marrow	Lead	See above	Decreased hemoglobin synthesis, decreased erythrocyte survival
	Mercury	See above	Increased hemolysis, alteration of T helper and T suppressor lymphocytes
	Cadmium	See above	?Reduced erythrocyte count
	Nickel	Vegetables, especially legumes, spinach and nuts	Decreased helper T cells and increased suppressor T cells
Gastrointestinal	Lead	See above	Decreased binding of L-tryptophan to hepatocellular nuclei
	Mercury	See above	Anorexia, fetal hepatic cell damage
	Cadmium	See above	Abdominal pain, vomiting, diarrhea
Renal	Lead	See above	Proximal tubular dysfunction: glycosuria, aminoaciduria, hyperphosphaturia, decreased renal conversion of 25-hydroxyvitamin D to 1,25-dihydroxyvitamin D, the biologically active form
	Mercury	See above	Renal tubular dysfunction, proteinuria, autoimmune damage
	Cadmium	See above	Proteinuria, glycosuria

rats indicate that amino acid binding to hepatocyte nuclei may be altered by lead. Thus, liver function may be subtly or subclinically affected and further studies are needed to elucidate this possibility.

Blood composition The major consequences of lead toxicity to the blood are microcytic anemia and decreased erythrocyte survival. The anemia is largely due to the inhibition of ALAD and erythrocyte ferrochelatase, which are critical to heme biosynthesis. Although the pathogenesis of the decreased red blood cell survival is not clear in humans, animal data indicate that the pentose phosphate shunt and glucose-6-phosphate dehydrogenase (G6PD) are inhibited by lead, suggesting that increased hemolysis may also contribute to the reduction in erythrocyte survival.

Kidney function Studies from the US National Institute of Occupational Safety and Health have reported that lead exposure reduced glutathione S-transferase expression in the kidneys of rabbits, indicating increased susceptibility to peroxidative damage. Renal proximal tubular dysfunction is described with lead intoxication and can result in glycosuria, aminoaciduria, and hyperphosphaturia as well as a reduced natriuretic response to volume

expansion. This latter effect of lead exposure may possibly offer an explanation of how lead accumulation may contribute to hypertension.

Vitamin D endocrine system and bone As previously mentioned, lead can contribute to the reduced conversion of 25-hydroxyvitamin D to $1,25(OH)_2D$. The extent to which this action may contribute to vitamin D deficiency is not known, but there is at least the potential for lower circulating levels of $1,25(OH)_2D$ to play a role in reduced intestinal calcium absorption. This in turn may result in further lead absorption. Additionally, lead accumulating in bone has been reported to cause osteoclasts to develop pyknotic nuclei and manifest inclusion bodies, possibly lead, in the nucleus and cytoplasm. Although it has yet to be proven, these findings suggest a reduction in the resorptive function of osteoclasts. This may be a protective mechanism by the body to prevent the liberation of lead stored in bone, but at the same time lead may prevent the uptake by bone of additional calcium.

Genetic/teratogenic effects Lead has been reported to alter gene transcription by the reduction of DNA binding to zinc finger proteins. This interruption of transcription has the potential to produce congenital anomalies in animals or humans. Studies have reported that lead crossing the placenta has produced urogenital, vertebral, and rectal malformations in the fetuses of rats, hamsters, and chick.

Management

Chelation therapy with dimercaprol succinic acid is recommended for anyone with a blood lead level higher than $25 \mu g l^{-1}$ ($1.2 \mu mol l^{-1}$), as shown in Table 2.

Mercury

How Does Mercury Contaminate Food?

The primary portal of mercury contamination of food is via its industrial release into water, either fresh or salt water, and its conversion to methyl mercury by methanogenic bacteria. As the marine life takes up the methyl mercury, it works its way into the food chain and is ultimately consumed by humans. This is the scenario that occurred following the release of inorganic mercury from an acetaldehyde plant into Minimata Bay in Japan in 1956 and 1965 and is responsible for the so-called 'Minimata disease.' Furthermore, acid rain has increased the amount of mercury available to be taken up by the tissues of edible sea life and can enhance the toxicity of certain fish. An unfortunate consequence of seafood contamination with methyl mercury is the contamination of fish meal used to feed poultry, resulting in mercury accumulation in the poultry as well as in the eggs. Additionally, mercury-containing pesticides can contaminate agricultural products. In Iraq in 1971 and 1972, wheat used in the baking of bread was contaminated with a fungicide that contained mercury.

Permissible Intakes

Limits of mercury intake set by the UN Food and Agriculture Organization (FAO) and the World Health Organization (WHO) are 0.3 mg per person per week, of which no more than 0.2 mg should be methyl mercury. Furthermore, FAO and WHO have set limits of mercury contamination of foods as not to exceed 50 parts per billion wet weight ($50 \mu g l^{-1}$). Hair mercury content is used as a marker of methyl mercury burden.

Dietary Mercury: Absorption and Consequences

Although the precise mechanism of mercury absorption and transport has not been clarified, one possibility is its use of molecular mimicry. Studies of methyl mercury show that it binds to reduced sulfhydryl groups, including those in the amino acid cysteine and glutathione. Methyl mercury-1-cysteine is similar in conformation to the amino acid methionine and may be taken up by the methionine transport system in the intestine. Also, inasmuch as it has been shown that deep-frying of fish, with or without breading, will increase the mercury content, it has been postulated that mercury may be absorbed with the oil from the frying process.

A Swedish study reported a direct correlation between the amount of seafood consumed by pregnant mothers and the concentration of methyl mercury in their umbilical cord blood. Although fetal tissue mercury concentration is generally lower than the maternal concentration, the exception to this is liver. According to a Japanese study, mercury is stored in the fetal liver, bound to metallothionein. With development, the amount of metallothionein decreases and the mercury in liver is redistributed primarily to brain and kidney. In studies of offspring of animals exposed to mercury vapors, behavioral changes have been detected.

With regard to toxicity, mercury affects the skin, kidneys, nervous system, and marrow, with

Table 2 Recommended management of toxic symptoms caused by heavy metal contaminants in food

Element	Agent	Comments
Lead	Dimercaptosuccinic acid	Blood lead levels greater than 25 μg (1.2 μmol) l⁻¹; treatment of children with blood levels exceeding 10 μg (0.5 μmol) l⁻¹ advocated due to learning problems
Mercury	Dimercaptosuccinic acid	Dimercaprol and D-penicillamine have also been used, but dimercaprol complicated by increased amount of mercury in brain
Cadmium	Diethyldithiocarbamate	Also used: dimercaprol, D-penicillamine, and dicalcium disodium EDTA
Nickel	Insufficient studies for recommended agent	Parenteral administration of diethyldithiocarbamide for acute toxicity may be helpful but unproven
Bismuth	Insufficient studies for recommended agent	Dimercaprol has been used anecdotally and reversed the symptoms of myoclonic encephalopathy; many choose to stop bismuth-containing drugs with a gradual resolution of symptoms

consequent effects on the blood cells, immune system, and bone formation.

Manifestations of Mercury Toxicity

Skin Mercury produces a symptom complex called acrodynia. Its main features are redness of the lips and pharynx, a strawberry tongue, tooth loss, skin desquamation, and pink or red fingertips, palms, and soles. The eyes are also affected, and photophobia and conjunctivitis are seen. In addition, there is enlargement of the cervical lymph nodes, loss of appetite, joint pain, and, occasionally, vascular thromboses, possibly by the induction of platelet aggregation, which has been shown in *in vitro* experiments. There is also a neurological component to this symptom complex: irritability, weakness of the proximal muscles, hypotonia, depressed reflexes, apathy, and withdrawal.

Kidneys Mercury has been hypothesized to stimulate T lymphocytes to produce a glomerular anti-basement membrane antibody, which produces sufficient damage to lead to the proteinuria observed with mercury toxicity (**Table 1**). The basis for this theory derives from studies in rats in which mercuric chloride injection produced these antibodies, both as IgG and IgM. There was also an observed increase in CD8$^+$ (suppressor) T cells in the glomeruli. In addition, the rats developed proximal tubular necrosis. However, it is not clear that this theory is correct because methyl mercury can induce apoptosis, or programmed cell death, of the T lymphocytes, possibly by damaging mitochondria and inducing oxidative stress.

Nervous system In the large epidemics of methyl mercury ingestion reported in both Japan and Iraq, infants were reported to have psychomotor retardation, flaccid paralysis, microcephaly, ataxia, choreoathetotic motions of the hands, tonic seizures, and narrowing of the visual fields (**Table 1**). Studies of neonatal rats injected with methyl mercuric chloride reported postural and movement changes during the fourth week of life. These were associated with degeneration of cortical interneurons, which produce γ-aminobutyric acid (GABA) as a neurotransmitter. In the caudate nucleus and putamen, these GABAergic and somatostatin immunoreactive interneurons manifested the abnormalities. Pregnant rats given methyl mercury by intraperitoneal injection demonstrated rapid (within 2 h) effects on their fetuses, including mitochondrial degeneration of cerebral capillary endothelial cells, which led to

hemorrhage. In turn, the bleeding disrupted normal neuronal migration.

In addition, methyl mercury may disrupt neuronal microtubular assembly and, perhaps by molecular mimicry (as described previously), may bind to the sulfhydryl groups of glutathione, causing peroxidative injury to the neurons. Following intracerebral injection in the rat, methyl mercuric chloride distributes in the Purkinje and Golgi cells of the cerebellum as well as in three different layers of cerebral cortical cells—III, IV, and VI.

Mercury exposure in humans can result in deficits in attention and concentration, especially under pressure of time deadlines. One report suggests that this may be due to mercury damage to the posterior cingulate cortex, where these functions are regulated.

Finally, *in vitro* studies of rat cerebellar granular cells suggested that incubation with methyl mercury caused an increased, although delayed, phosphorylation of certain proteins. The 12- to 24-h time course from mercury exposure to phosphorylation was believed to be consistent with the alteration of gene expression by mercury. Thus, the effects of mercury on the nervous system are multiple.

Bone marrow: Immune cells, blood cells, and bone formation A toxic effect of mercury on bone marrow would explain the abnormalities in red cell production, immune cell production, and bone formation (**Table 1**); all of the cells involved arise from stem cells found in the marrow and are presumably affected by mercury.

With regard to the immune cells, mercury induces an autoimmune response manifested by an increase in CD4$^+$ (helper) and CD8$^+$ (suppressor) T lymphocytes and in B lymphocytes in peripheral lymphoid tissue. This may explain in part the autoimmune nephropathy as well as the enlarged lymph nodes of acrodynia, previously described. Additionally, mercury may impair integrin signaling pathways in neutrophils, which may give rise to neutrophil dysfunction.

Hemolysis of red blood cells resulting from mercury exposure may be at least in part due to peroxidative damage inasmuch as studies on workers chronically exposed to mercury vapors demonstrate a reduction in erythrocyte enzyme activity of glutathione peroxidase and superoxide dismutase, as well as in G6PD.

Finally, although the effects of mercury exposure on bone have not been studied in humans, experiments in mice indicate that the administration of an anti-metallothionein antibody and mercury results in decreased biochemical markers of bone formation and decreased bone mineral density. The mechanism for this is unknown, but mercury interference with differentiation of osteogenic precursor cells is postulated.

Genetic/teratogenic effects   The uptake and redistribution of mercury by fetal hepatic tissue have been previously discussed. Abnormalities described with in utero exposure to mercury during the epidemics in Japan and Iraq have included low birth weight, malformation of the brain (both cerebrum and cerebellum), an abnormal migratory pattern of neurons, mental retardation, and failure to achieve developmental milestones. This remains a problem today for pregnant women who consume seafood. The FDA recommends that intake of large predator fish, such as swordfish and shark, be limited since they contain large amounts of mercury. Even tuna is considered to contain more mercury than most other seafood.

Management

Chelation with dimercaptosuccinic acid is recommended (**Table 2**).

Cadmium

How Does Cadmium Contaminate Food?

Cadmium enters the food chain in much the same way that lead and mercury do—by means of industrial contamination. Cadmium is often used as a covering of other metals or in the manufacture of batteries and semiconductors; it readily transforms into a gas as the metal ores are smelted. The cadmium then condenses to form cadmium oxide, which deposits in soil and water near the source. Cadmium accumulates in lower marine life, such as plankton, mollusks, and shellfish, and continues through the food chain as these organisms are consumed. However, contamination of the human food supply is limited by this route since cadmium is toxic to fish and fish embryos. In contrast to seafood, vegetables are affected differently because cadmium is taken up by the leaves and roots of plants, so those near industrial sources may be very high in cadmium.

Permissible Intakes

A 1991 study of adults consuming rice contaminated with cadmium in the Kakehashi River Basin of Ishikara, Japan, correlated cadmium intake with renal tubular dysfunction and established a maximum allowable intake of 110 µg per day.

Canadian studies have estimated daily intake in study populations to be approximately half that, and the French have estimated cadmium exposure in the diet as being only 3 or 4 µg per day. The Provisional Tolerable Weekly Intake (PTWI) established by FAO/WHO is 7 µg kg^{-1} body weight per week, a slightly more conservative estimate than the Japanese study but still in general agreement with it.

Dietary Cadmium: Absorption and Consequences

Fortunately, only 2–8% of dietary cadmium is absorbed and significant cadmium ingestion is accompanied by vomiting. Therefore, the gastrointestinal route is not as significant as inhalation of dust particles as a source of significant exposure.

Manifestations of Toxicity

Toxic manifestations of cadmium ingestion include renal dysfunction, osteoporosis and bone pain, abdominal pain, vomiting and diarrhea, anemia, and bone marrow involvement (**Table 1**).

Gastrointestinal toxicity   The mechanisms for cadmium's effects on the gastrointestinal tract are not certain. Whether these toxicities stem from an irritative effect of the metal or whether there is cellular damage has not been resolved in animal or *in vitro* studies. One possibility is that *in vitro* studies of neural tissue suggest that cadmium blocks adrenergic and cholinergic synapses. Therefore, it is possible that cadmium interferes with autonomic nervous system influence on gastrointestinal motility.

Renal toxicity   Renal tubular dysfunction is manifest in patients with itai itai disease as glycosuria and proteinuria, including excessive excretion of α- and β-microglobulin. Approximately 50–75% of cadmium accumulation in the body occurs in the liver and kidneys. Urinary cadmium excretion of 200 µg (1.78 µmol) g^{-1} of renal cortical tissue has been associated with tubular dysfunction. In the kidney, cadmium is bound to metallothionein. When the amount of intracellular cadmium accumulation exceeds metallothionein binding capacity, this is the point at which renal toxicity is hypothesized to occur.

Bone marrow and bone   In short-term accumulation of cadmium in the marrow, there is a proliferation of cells in the myeloid/monocyte category. However, with longer term burden, marrow hypoplasia is reported, including decreased production of erythropoietin. Although a reduction in marrow cells may indicate that the osteogenic precursors in the marrow may also be reduced (**Table 1**), this is not borne out by studies both in humans and in rats. In these cases, biochemical markers of bone formation (osteocalcin) and resorption (deoxypyridinoline) are both increased, indicating a high turnover state. In rats, circulating parathyroid hormone levels are also elevated, suggesting that the high turnover is due to secondary hyperparathyroidism and subsequent inability of the bone matrix to mature and bind calcium and phosphate. Parenteral administration of 1,25-dihydroxyvitamin D has been reported to decrease circulating parathyroid hormone in the rat and to reduce bone turnover. Moreover, other animal studies report that cadmium interferes with hydroxyapatite nucleation and growth, thus making it difficult for bone matrix to bind to calcium.

Management

Chelation therapy is recommended using calcium, disodium ethylene diaminetetraacetic acid, dimercaprol, D-penicillamine, or diethyldithiocarbamate (**Table 2**).

Nickel and Bismuth

Dietary Contamination

Nickel and bismuth are not considered to be common dietary contaminants. Nickel is mainly inhaled as a dust by workers, whereas bismuth is mainly ingested in bismuth-containing medications such as Pepto-Bismol. Vegetables contain more nickel than other foods, and high levels of nickel can be found in legumes, spinach, lettuce, and nuts. Baking powder and cocoa powder may also contain excess nickel, possibly by leaching during the manufacturing process. Soft drinking water and acid-containing beverages can dissolve nickel from pipes and containers. Daily nickel ingestion can be as high as 1 mg (0.017 mmol) but averages between 200 and 300 μg (3.4 and 5.1 μmol).

Permissible Intakes

The maximum permissible intake of nickel is not known. Bismuth intake is related to whole blood bismuth levels. If these levels exceed $100\,\mu g\,l^{-1}$, bismuth-containing medication should be discontinued.

Toxicity

Nickel ingestion by women resulted in an increase in interleukin-5 levels 4 h after ingestion and a decrease in $CD4^+$ and an increase in $CD8^+$ lymphocytes 24 h

following the nickel intake. Thus, alterations in the immune response may be associated with excessive nickel ingestion, consistent with reports of tumor production in animals and humans by inhalation of nickel-containing dust or powders. The mechanism for nickel-associated toxicity is purported to be oxidative. For bismuth, neurotoxicity, including irritability, numbness and tingling of the extremities, insomnia, poor concentration, impairment of short-term memory, tremors, dementia masquerading as Alzheimer's disease, and abnormal electroencephalograms, has been reported. Discontinuation of the bismuth may result in restoration of normal neurological function. Production of these symptoms in animals was associated with a brain bismuth concentration of $8\,\mu g\,g^{-1}$ brain tissue; a brain bismuth concentration of $4\,\mu g\,g^{-1}$ brain tissue was not associated with these neurotoxic manifestations. However, hydrocephalus was reported. At $1\,\mu g$ bismuth g^{-1} brain tissue, no neurotoxic features were observed in animals. Nephropathy, osteoarthropathy, and thrombocytopenia have also been reported with bismuth toxicity.

Management

Insufficient controlled clinical trials have been performed to make clear-cut recommendations for pharmacotherapy for toxicity from either nickel or bismuth. Diethyl dithiocarbamide chelation therapy when promptly administered intravenously has been reported to be effective in acute nickel carbonyl poisoning. In addition, there have been anecdotal case reports of the reversal of myoclonic encephalopathy caused by bismuth with use of dimercaprol. However, no recommendations can be given at the present time.

See also: **Ascorbic Acid**: Physiology, Dietary Sources and Requirements; Deficiency States. **Food Safety**: Other Contaminants. **Vitamin D**: Physiology, Dietary Sources and Requirements.

Further Reading

Bierer DW (1990) Bismuth subsalicylate: History, chemistry and safety. *Reviews of Infectious Disease* **12**(supplement 1): S3–S8.

Bjomberg KA, Vahter M, Peterson-Grawe K *et al.* (2003) Methyl mercury and inorganic mercury in Swedish pregnant women and in cord blood: Influence of fish consumption. *Environmental Health Perspectives* **111**: 637–641.

Blumenthal NC, Cosma V, Skyler D *et al.* (1995) The effect of cadmium on the formation and properties of hydroxyapatite in vitro and its relation to cadmium toxicity in the skeletal system. *Calcified Tissue International* **56**: 316–322.

Burger J, Dixon C, Boring CS et al. (2003) Effect of deep frying fish on risk from mercury. Journal of Toxicology and Environmental Health 66: 817–828.

Jin GB, Inoue S, Urano T et al. (2002) Induction of anti-metallothionein antibody and mercury treatment decreases bone mineral density in mice. Toxicology and Applied Pharmacology 115: 98–110.

Knowles S, Donaldson WE, and Andrews JK (1998) Changes in fatty acid composition of lipids in birds, rodents, and pre-school children exposed to lead. Biological Trace Element Research 61: 113–125.

Kollmeier H, Seeman JW, Rothe G et al. (1990) Age, sex and region adjusted concentrations of chromium and nickel in lung tissue. British Journal of Industrial Medicine 47: 682–687.

Kurata Y, Katsuta O, Hiratsuka H et al. (2001) Intravenous 1-α,25 (OH)$_2$ vitamin D$_3$ (calcitriol) pulse therapy for bone lesions in a murine model of chronic cadmium toxicosis. International Journal of Experimental Pathology 82: 43–53.

Murata K, Weche P, Renzoni A et al. (1999) Delayed evoked potential in children exposed to methylmercury from seafood. Neurotoxicology and Teratology 21: 343–348.

Needleman HL, Schell A, Bellinger D et al. (1990) The long-term effects of exposure to low doses of lead in childhood. An 11-year follow-up report. New England Journal of Medicine 322: 83–88.

Report of the International Committee on Nickel Carcinogenesis in Man (1990) Scandinavian Journal of Work and Environmental Health 49: 1–648.

Royce SC and Needleman HL (1990) Agency for Toxic Substances and Disease Registry Case Studies in Environmental Medicine, pp. 1–20. Atlanta: US Department of Health and Human Services, Public Health Service.

Simon JA and Hudes ES (1999) Relationship of ascorbic acid to blood lead levels. Journal of the American Medical Association 281: 2289–2293.

Watanabe C, Yoshida K, Kasanume Y et al. (1999) In utero methylmercury exposure differentially affects the activities of selenoenzymes in the fetal mouse brain. Environmental Research 80: 208–214.

Worth RG, Esper RM, Warra NS et al. (2001) Mercury inhibition of neutrophil activity: Evidence of aberrant cell signaling and incoherent cellular metabolism. Scandinavian Journal of Immunology 53: 49–55.

Fortification *see* **Food Fortification**: Developed Countries; Developing Countries

FRUCTOSE

N L Keim, US Department of Agriculture, Davis, CA, USA
P J Havel, University of California at Davis, Davis, CA, USA

Published by Elsevier Ltd.

Fructose, a monosaccharide, is naturally present in fruits and is used in many food products as a sweetener. This article reviews the properties and sources of fructose in the food supply, the estimated intake of fructose in Western diets, the intestinal absorption of fructose, and the metabolism of fructose and its effect on lipid and glucose metabolism. The health implications of increased consumption of fructose are discussed, and inborn errors of fructose metabolism are described.

Properties and Sources of Fructose

Fructose has a fruity taste that is rated sweeter than sucrose. Sweetness ratings of fructose are between 130% and 180% (in part dependent on the serving temperature) compared to the standard, sucrose, rated at 100%. Both sucrose and fructose are used extensively in foods to provide sweetness, texture, and palatability. These sugars also contribute to the appearance, preservation, and energy content of the food product.

Natural sources of dietary fructose are fruits, fruit juices, and some vegetables. In these foods, fructose is found as the monosaccharide and also as a component of the disaccharide, sucrose (**Table 1**). However, the primary source of fructose in Western diets is in sugars added to baked goods, candies, soft drinks, and other beverages sweetened with sucrose and high-fructose corn syrup (HFCS). HFCS is produced by hydrolyzing the starch in corn to glucose using α-amylase and glucoamylase. This is followed by treatment with glucose isomerase to yield a mixture of glucose and fructose. The process typically produces a HFCS composed of 42% fructose, 50% glucose, and 8% other sugars (HFCS-42). By fractionation, a concentrated fructose syrup containing 90% fructose can be isolated (HFCS-90). HFCS-42 and HFCS-90 are blended to produce HFCS-55, which is 55% fructose, 41% glucose, and 4% other sugars. HFCS-55 is the preferred sweetener used by the soft drink industry, although HFCS-42 is also commonly used as a sweetener in many processed food products. Concentrated

Table 1 Sucrose, glucose, and fructose contents of fruits, vegetables, and sweeteners

Food item	Serving size	Sucrose (g)	Glucose (g)	Fructose (g)
Apple	1 medium	2.86	3.35	8.14
Apple juice	1 cup	4.22	6.20	13.89
Banana	1 medium	2.82	5.88	5.72
Blueberries	1 cup	0.16	7.08	7.21
Cantaloupe	1/8 melon	3.00	1.06	1.29
Cherries	1 cup	0.18	7.71	6.28
Grapes	1 cup	0.24	11.52	13.01
Oranges	1 medium	5.99	2.76	3.15
Peaches	1 medium	4.66	1.91	1.50
Pears	1 medium	1.29	4.58	10.34
Plums	1 medium	1.04	3.35	2.03
Pineapple	1 cup diced	8.48	2.70	3.18
Raspberries	1 cup	0.25	2.29	2.89
Strawberries	1 cup	0.20	3.39	4.15
Watermelon	1/16 melon	3.46	4.52	9.61
Avocado	1 fruit	0.10	0.14	0.14
Broccoli	1 cup	0.09	0.43	0.60
Carrots, baby	10 small	2.70	1.00	1.00
Corn, sweet	1 ear	1.85	0.45	0.43
Cucumber	1 cup	0.00	0.75	0.89
Onions	1 slice	0.44	0.74	0.44
Peas, green	1 cup	7.24	0.17	0.57
Potatoes	1 medium	0.36	0.70	0.58
Spinach	1 cup	0.02	0.03	0.04
Sweet potato	1 medium	3.28	1.25	0.91
Tomatoes	1 medium	0.00	1.54	1.69
Honey	1 Tbsp	0.19	7.51	8.60
Maple syrup	1 Tbsp	11.26	0.47	0.18
Molasses	1 Tbsp	5.88	2.38	2.56

Values obtained from US Department of Agriculture nutrient database accessed at www.nal.usda.gov/fnic/foodcomp.

fruit juices, such as apple juice and white grape juice, are also used to sweeten beverages. The amount of fructose in fruit juices varies, as does its proportion with glucose, but clearly the use of concentrated apple juice provides more fructose relative to glucose (**Table 1**), compared to either sucrose or HFCS-55. Nevertheless, considering the variety of sweeteners commonly available, it is likely that fructose constitutes approximately 50% of energy from added sweeteners.

As a result of the addition of sweeteners and sugars to so many food products, the consumption of fructose has increased from the mid-1970s to the mid-1990s. Sugars added to the diet are difficult to quantify accurately, but based on food intake survey data, total fructose consumption provides approximately 12% of adult energy intake or ~60 g/day based on a 2000-kcal diet. Individuals who are avid consumers of soft drinks, such as adolescent males, typically consume more than two times the average intake or more than 100 g/day of fructose from added sweeteners. Considering the US population as a whole, and based on both food disappearance data and food survey data, total fructose consumption has increased approximately 25% during the past three decades.

Absorption of Fructose

Dietary fructose is ingested as the simple monosaccharide and also as part of the disaccharide sucrose. Sucrose is hydrolyzed by sucrase at the intestinal brush border to yield one molecule of glucose and one of fructose. Glucose is rapidly absorbed via a sodium-coupled cotransporter and arrives at the liver via the portal circulation. Fructose absorption is accomplished primarily by a fructose-specific hexose transporter, GLUT-5. This transporter is found in the jejunum on both the brush border and the basolateral membranes. Expression of GLUT-5 increases within hours of exposure to a fructose-enriched diet, indicating that the transporter is regulated by luminal signals. However, consumption of a large amount of pure fructose can exceed the capacity of intestinal fructose absorption, resulting in diarrhea. Several studies have shown that when a single dose of 50 g of fructose is consumed by healthy adults, more than half experience malabsorption, and in some studies malabsorption is also observed with a 25-g dose. Fructose malabsorption results in abdominal bloating, flatulence, and diarrhea. However, the intestinal absorptive capacity for fructose increases when glucose is consumed along with fructose. Thus, coingesting glucose to roughly balance fructose, as occurs when most fruits or sucrose is consumed, largely alleviates problems of fructose malabsorption. In addition, fructose absorption increases during sustained fructose consumption, suggesting adaptation to increased fructose intake.

Fructose Metabolism

The predominant site of fructose metabolism is the liver, where fructose enters the intermediary pathways of carbohydrate metabolism. Fructose is readily extracted by the liver because of the presence of an active hepatic enzyme system for metabolizing fructose, and the majority of ingested fructose is cleared in a single pass through the liver. Thus, the concentration of fructose circulating in blood is low after consumption of moderate amounts of fructose. Other tissues that take up small quantities of fructose include the kidney, skeletal muscle, and adipose tissue. The GLUT-5 transporter is expressed in these tissues but at relatively low levels.

In the liver, fructose is phosphorylated and forms fructose-1-phosphate. This reaction requires ATP and is catalyzed by fructokinase (EC 2.7.1.4), an enzyme with high affinity and specificity for fructose. Fructose-1-phosphate is then cleaved by hepatic aldolase (aldolase B; EC 4.1.2.13) to form dihydroxyacetone

phosphate (DHAP) and glyceraldehyde. DHAP is an intermediate metabolite in both the gluconeogenic and glycolytic pathways. Thus, a portion of the original fructose carbon structure forms glucose, and, in fact, a small increase in circulating glucose occurs after ingestion of fructose. The glyceraldehyde intermediate is phosphorylated by triokinase (EC 2.7.1.28) to form glyceraldehyde-3-phosphate, another intermediate in the glycolytic pathway. The triose phosphate compounds provide substrate for glycolysis and oxidative metabolism, formation of glycogen, and synthesis of glucose and fatty acids. With the formation of the triose phosphates, the metabolism of fructose and glucose converges. However, prior to this step, there are important differences in fructose and glucose metabolism that impact both carbohydrate and lipid metabolism. The initial reaction that primes fructose for entry to the glycolytic pathway allows it to bypass the critical rate-limiting step of glycolysis. This critical step precedes the formation of triose phosphates; glucose carbons pass through an intermediate step in which fructose-6-phosphate is converted to fructose-1,6-bis-phosphate. This reaction is catalyzed by the allosterically regulated enzyme phosphofructokinase (PFK; EC 2.7.1.11) and is the most important control point in the glycolytic sequence. Among the multiple effectors of PFK are ATP and citrate; these products of glucose oxidation exert an inhibitory effect on the enzyme (**Figure 1**). The

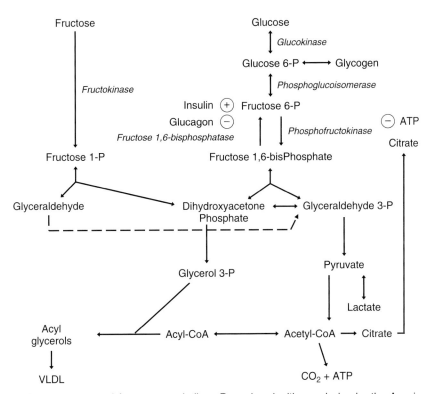

Figure 1 The intermediary pathways and fructose metabolism. Reproduced with permission by the American Journal of Clinical Nutrition. Copyright *Am J Clin Nutr.* American Society for Clinical Nutrition.

allosteric inhibition of PFK effectively reduces the rate of glycolysis and decreases hepatic glucose uptake overall. In contrast, the entry of fructose carbons through the pathway proceeds without this limitation.

Fructose and Lipid Metabolism

When large amounts of fructose are ingested, the glycolytic pathway becomes saturated with intermediates. In these circumstances, the intermediates become substrates for triacylglycerol synthesis: DHAP can be converted to glycerol, and acetyl-CoA can enter the lipogenic pathway to form fatty acids that are then esterified to the glycerol molecule to form triacylglycerols. During the initial step of lipogenesis, malonyl-CoA is formed. This intermediate serves to inhibit the transport of fatty acids into the mitochondria, where they are oxidized. By this regulatory mechanism, esterification of the newly synthesized fatty acids is reinforced. Studies have shown that the ingestion of fructose results in increased synthesis of fatty acids compared to ingestion of a comparable amount of glucose. The increased availability of fatty acids and subsequent triacylglycerol synthesis results in the production and secretion of triacylglycerols from the liver in the form of very low-density lipoproteins. Studies in animals have demonstrated that when large quantities of fructose or sucrose are consumed, an increase in blood triacylglycerol concentration occurs. Similar findings have been observed in humans, although some humans appear to be more susceptible to fructose consumption than others. For example, the lipogenic sequence may be accentuated in humans with preexisting hypertriacylglycerolemia or in those who are insulin resistant. Since high circulating triacylglycerol levels have been identified as a risk factor for coronary heart disease, long-term exposure to high levels of dietary fructose may contribute to a chronic, unfavorable lipid profile and increase risk of coronary heart disease.

Fructose and Glucose Metabolism

With fructose ingestion, there is an increased flux through the glycolytic pathway, with formation of pyruvate and lactate. As fructose-1-phosphate is formed, at the initial priming stage of glycolysis, it feeds forward and enhances the activation of pyruvate kinase (EC 2.7.1.40), thereby facilitating the passage of fructose carbon to pyruvate and lactate. With fructose ingestion, it is common to observe increases in blood lactate concentrations.

In the postprandial state, fructose serves to promote the formation of glycogen, but only when it is consumed along with glucose. This occurs through the activation of glycogen synthase (EC 2.4.1.11) and the inhibition of glycogen phosphorylase (EC 2.4.1.1).

In the starved state, fructose actively serves as a substrate for gluconeogenesis and glucose production. The gluconeogenic pathway and the glycolytic pathway share many common intermediates and enzymes, but the direction of the carbon flux through these pathways is controlled by several allosteric enzymes unique to each pathway. Since fructose enters the glycolytic pathway beyond the major gluconeogenic–glycolytic pivotal point (the interconversion between fructose-6-phosphate and fructose-1,6-bisphosphate), it does not exert an inhibitory effect on the gluconeogenic rate-limiting enzyme, fructose-1,6-bisphosphatase (EC 3.1.3.11). Consequently, there is no inhibition of gluconeogenesis by fructose as fructose carbons proceed through the glycolytic pathway. When a large quantity of fructose is infused intravenously, hepatic glucose production and output increase.

Consumption of large amounts of fructose is also associated with an impairment of glucose disposal. Prolonged feeding of fructose or sucrose to animals impairs insulin signaling and induces insulin resistance. Less is known about the effect of fructose ingestion on glucose tolerance and insulin resistance in humans because the scientific literature contains conflicting results. However, the lipogenic effects of fructose may contribute to insulin resistance indirectly since increased blood levels of triacylglycerols and fatty acids and deposition of lipid in liver and skeletal muscle have been implicated in the etiology of insulin resistance.

Fructose and Diabetes

Historically, in the nutritional management of diabetes mellitus, the ingestion of fructose was recommended as a sweetener for diabetics because it causes smaller increases in blood glucose following ingestion compared to similar amounts of glucose, sucrose, or starches. In fact, fructose, in small quantities, increases the hepatic uptake of glucose and promotes glycogen storage, probably by stimulating the activity of hepatic glucokinase (EC 2.7.1.2). Also, in individuals with type 2 diabetes mellitus, the addition of a small amount of fructose to an oral glucose tolerance test improves the glycemic response, indicating improved glycemic control. It must be emphasized, however, that the consumption of large quantities of fructose is not recommended, particularly for diabetics who, as a group, are at increased risk for cardiovascular disease, because of potentially adverse effects of fructose on lipid metabolism, body weight regulation, and oxidative stress that may contribute to diabetic complications.

Fructose Consumption, Body Weight, and Obesity

With the increase in fructose intake, primarily as sugar-sweetened beverages, occurring coincidently with the increase in prevalence of overweight and obesity during the past two decades, it is important to examine the evidence that links fructose consumption and body weight gain. In epidemiological studies, consumption of larger amounts of soft drinks and sweetened beverages is associated with greater weight gain in women and increased energy intake and higher body mass index in children. In experimental studies, when fructose- or sucrose-sweetened beverages are added to the diet, subjects do not compensate for the additional energy provided by these beverages by reducing energy intake from other sources, and total energy intake increases. Possibly, this lack of compensation may be explained by the lack of a significant effect of fructose ingestion on the secretion of hormones involved in the long-term regulation of food intake.

Data comparing the effects of ingesting fructose- and glucose-sweetened beverages with meals indicate that fructose ingestion results in smaller increases in blood glucose and insulin concentrations following the meals. In addition, circulating leptin concentrations are lower, and the normal suppressive effect of meal consumption on ghrelin concentrations is attenuated with fructose beverages. Glucose, insulin, leptin, and ghrelin are all involved in the long-term control of food intake and body weight regulation through the central nervous system. Since these key signals are absent or weakened with fructose consumption, chronic consumption of a diet high in fructose could contribute, along with dietary fat and inactivity, to increased energy intake, weight gain, and obesity.

Inborn Errors of Fructose Metabolism

Several genetically based abnormalities in fructose metabolism have been described in humans. Fructokinase deficiency leads to high levels of fructose in the blood and urine. In the absence of fructokinase, fructose can be metabolized to fructose-6-phosphate by hexokinase (EC 2.7.1.1), although at a low rate. Consequently, no serious health problems are associated with this abnormality.

The aldolase A, B, and C enzymes catalyze the reversible conversion of fructose-1-diphosphate into glyceraldehyde-3-phosphate and dihydroxyacetone phosphate, and deficiencies in the A and B enzymes have been identified. Aldolase A is expressed in embryonic tissues and adult muscle. Possibly owing to the importance of this enzyme in fetal glycolysis, its deficiency results in mental retardation, short stature, hemolytic anemia, and abnormal facial appearance. There is no known treatment for aldolase A deficiency. Aldolase B is expressed in liver, kidney, and intestine, and a deficiency of this enzyme is more common and can be exhibited at first exposure to fructose during infancy or can have its onset in adulthood. Upon ingestion of fructose-containing foods, vomiting and failure to thrive are apparent. Hypoglycemia (in some cases severe), increased blood uric acid, and liver dysfunction also occur. Fortunately, this disorder can be treated effectively by completely eliminating fructose from the diet.

Deficiency of fructose-1,6-bisphosphatase is also considered a genetic disorder of fructose metabolism. This enzyme has a critical role in the enzyme complex regulating glycolysis and gluconeogenesis. Deficient individuals exhibit hypoglycemia, acidosis, ketonuria, hyperventilation, and often hypotonia and hepatomegaly. The urinary excretion of many organic acids is altered; notably, urinary glycerol is elevated and is useful in the diagnosis of this disease. The treatment includes avoidance of dietary fructose, sorbitol, and prolonged fasting.

D-Glyceric aciduria is caused by D-glycerate kinase (EC 2.7.1.31) deficiency. Only 10 cases have been documented, with symptoms ranging from none to metabolic acidosis, failure to thrive, psychomotor retardation, spastic tetraparesis, and seizures. The absence of significant symptoms in some suggests that this enzyme deficiency is essentially benign, and other associated enzyme deficiencies may underlie the more severe symptoms.

See also: **Diabetes Mellitus**: Etiology and Epidemiology; Classification and Chemical Pathology; Dietary Management. **Glucose**: Chemistry and Dietary Sources; Metabolism and Maintenance of Blood Glucose Level. **Inborn Errors of Metabolism**: Classification and Biochemical Aspects. **Obesity**: Definition, Etiology and Assessment.

Further Reading

Bray GA, Nielsen SJ, and Popkin BM (2004) Consumption of high-fructose corn syrup in beverages may play a role in the epidemic of obesity. *American Journal of Clinical Nutrition* 79: 537–743.

Elliott SS, Keim NL, Stern JS, Teff K, and Havel PJ (2002) Fructose, weight gain, and the insulin resistance syndrome. *American Journal of Clinical Nutrition* 76: 911–922.

Forbes AL and Bowman BA (eds.) (1993) Health effects of dietary fructose. *American Journal of Clinical Nutrition* 58(supplement 5): 1S–823S.

Fried SK and Rao SP (2003) Sugars, hypertriacylglycerolmia, and cardiovascular disease. *American Journal of Clinical Nutrition* 78: 873S–880S.

Havel PJ (2001) Peripheral signals conveying metabolic information to the brain: Short-term and long-term regulation of food intake and energy homeostasis. *Experimental Biology and Medicine* 26: 963–977.

Havel PJ (2003) Regulation of energy homeostasis and insulin action by gastrointestinal and adipocyte hormones. In: Strasburger CJ (ed.) *Pituitary and Periphery: Communication in and out*, pp. 89–114. Bristol, UK: BioScientifica.

Havel PJ (2004) Update on adipocyte hormones: Regulation of energy balance and carbohydrate/lipid metabolism. *Diabetes* 53(supplement 1): S143–S151.

Havel PJ (2005) Dietary fructose: Implication for dysregulation of energy homeostasis and lipid/carbohydrate metabolism. Nutrition reviews. (In press).

Joost HG and Thorens B (2001) The extended GLUT-family of sugar/polyol transport facilitators: Nomenclature, sequence characteristics, and potential function of its novel members (Review). *Molecular Membrane Biology* 18: 247–256.

Keim NL, Levin RJ, and Havel PJ (2005) Carbohydrates. In: Shils ME, Ross AC, Shike M, Caballero B, Weinseir RL, and Cousins RJ (eds.) *Modern Nutrition in Health and Disease*, 10th editon. Baltimore: Lippincott, Williams & Wilkins, Inc. In press.

Kelley DE (2003) Sugars and starch in the nutritional management of diabetes mellitus. *American Journal of Clinical Nutrition* 78: 858S–864S.

McGuinness OP and Cherrington AD (2003) Effects of fructose on hepatic glucose metabolism. *Current Opinion in Clinical Nutrition and Metabolic Care* 6: 441–448.

Skoog SM and Bharucha AE (2004) Dietary fructose and gastrointestinal symptoms: A review. *American Journal of Gastroenterology* 99: 2046–2050.

Teff KL, Elliott SS, Tschoep M, Kieffer TJ, Rader D, Heiman M, Townsend RR, Keim NL, D'Allesio D, and Havel PJ (2004) Dietary fructose reduces circulating insulin and leptin, attenuates postprandial suppression of ghrelin, and increases triglycerides in women. *Journal of Clinical Endocrinology & Metabolism* 89: 2963–2972.

Wright EM, Martin MG, and Turk E (2003) Intestinal absorption in health and disease—Sugars. *Best Practice & Research Clinical Gastroenterology* 17: 943–956.

FRUITS AND VEGETABLES

A E Bender, Leatherhead, UK

This article is a revision of the previous edition, article by A E Bender, pp. 902–906, © 1999, Elsevier Ltd.

Fruits and vegetables have considerable potential as a source of nutrients but the amounts eaten vary enormously both within and between countries. Some 3000 species are known to be edible and there are said to be more than 1500 species of wild tropical plants. In the foreword to *Traditional Plant Foods*, published by the Food and Agriculture Organization of the United Nations, it is stated that "rural Africa is rich in nutritious plant foods but in recent decades social and economic changes have militated against their propagation and use." This is because the promotion of major cereals has led to the eclipse of traditional plants. Furthermore, in developing regions many plant foods are regarded as being 'merely' children's food or poor man's food. Indeed, more fruits and vegetables are eaten in industrialized countries where there is an abundance of foods of all kinds than in developing countries, where any addition to the food supply is valuable.

For example, the average daily intake of fruit and vegetables in some underdeveloped regions is only 10–12 g per day compared with the recommendation in Western countries of five (and even up to nine) helpings (at least 375 g per day).

Definition

Plant foods are usually divided into seeds (including cereals), nuts, and a third combined group of fruits and vegetables.

Fruits are the fleshy seed-bearing parts of plants, while stems, roots, shoots, leaves, some seeds (including peas, beans, and lentils), tubers (underground storage organs such as potato, Jerusalem artichoke, sweet potato, yam), underground stems (taro, onion), and flower buds and flowers (cauliflower, broccoli) are all classed as vegetables.

However, through popular usage some fruits such as tomato and cucumber are classed as vegetables, and rhubarb, a stem, as fruit. So the group includes a large number of very diverse foods which differ considerably in nutritional value.

Macronutrients

Fruits and vegetables contain a very high proportion of water (e.g., up to 96% in cucumber) and so, with some exceptions, supply only small amounts of macronutrients. The exceptions are those few eaten in sufficiently large amounts as to constitute a staple food, such as potato, plantain, cassava, and taro (colocasia, also known as eddo, dasheen, and old cocoyam). These are also lower in water content than many other members of the group and make a significant contribution to the carbohydrate and so the energy intake, and a small contribution of protein. For example, a 1000 kcal (4200 kJ) portion of plantain (*Musa* spp.) supplies 10 g protein. Cassava (manioc, *Manihot utilissima*) is extremely hardy and prolific and is a valuable staple in some communities, although a poor source of protein (1%).

Even in Western countries the potato (*Solanum tuberosum*) makes a contribution to the carbohydrate and protein of the diet, as well as supplying significant amounts of thiamin and ascorbic acid, because several hundred grams are often eaten per day.

One fruit, avocado (*Persea americana*), is a source of fat—17–27%—two-thirds of which is monounsaturated. Olives (*Olea europea*) contain 10–12% fat, two-thirds of which is monounsaturated, and of course are a commercial source of oil. Leafy vegetables are very watery (80–90%) and make an insignificant contribution to the intake of macronutrients. However, such proteins that are supplied are relatively rich in the amino acid lysine and to some extent, depending of course on the amount eaten, complement the relative deficiency of lysine in cereals (see Leaf Protein below).

The legumes—peas, beans, and lentils—play a special role in the diet since, as eaten, they contain more dry matter than most fruits and vegetables, around 30%. Unlike fresh fruits and vegetables they are usually stored for long periods in the dry state. After rehydration and cooking most of them including 'baked beans' (mature haricot beans, *Phaseolus vulgaris*) supply 5–8 g protein, 10–15 g carbohydrate, 300–400 kJ (80–100 kcal), and 4–5 g dietary fiber per 100 g. Legumes are sometimes described as rich sources of protein, but this is based on the dried product, not as eaten. When rehydrated and cooked their protein content is less than that of cereal products.

Garden peas (*Pisum sativum*) are commonly cooked from the fresh or frozen state, i.e., wet, but the macronutrient content is similar to that quoted above.

Green beans/French beans (pods and seeds of *Phaseolus vulgaris*) contain only 10% dry matter and 2 g protein, 100 kJ (25 kcal), and 2 g dietary fiber per 100 g.

Sprouted beans, commonly mung beans (*Vigna radiata*) but also alfalfa (lucerne, *Medicago sativa*) and adzuki beans (*Vigna angularis*), are also low in dry matter content and supply macronutrients in amounts similar to those in French beans.

Micronutrients

The major contribution of fruits and vegetables to the diet lies in their content of vitamins and minerals, but there are enormous variations between different types and between varieties of the same type.

Vitamins

The vitamin C content of different types of fruits ranges between some thousands of milligrams per 100 g in the instance of the West Indian cherry (acerola/Barbados cherry, *Malpighia punificolia*) to a few milligrams in apples (species of *Malus sylvestris*) and pears (varieties of *Pyrus communis*). The yellow–orange colored fruits (e.g., apricots, *Prunus armeniaca*, pawpaw, *Carica papaya*) supply carotene, as also do all green vegetables, while it is absent from white types. Leafy vegetables are rich sources of vitamin K and many fruits and vegetables are significant sources of folate.

Growing conditions including soil, fertilizer (type, amount, and time of application) and the state of maturity influence the vitamin content, particularly of vitamin C. In some foods, such as citrus fruits and tomato, the vitamin C is influenced by exposure to sunshine. One further cause of variation in vitamin content, again applying particularly to vitamin C and to a lesser extent to folate, is the loss after cropping, particularly from leaves that are bruised or wilted. Consequently it is not possible, apart from very broad generalizations, to state the vitamin content of a particular fruit or vegetable. Furthermore, new varieties have been and are being developed that are particularly rich in some vitamins.

Comparisons between food composition tables from various national authorities are unrealistic. Thus among six such tables (Australia, Germany, Great Britain, Spain, Italy, and the USA) the range of carotene in pumpkins is quoted from 0.24 to 19 mg per 100 g; for thiamin between 0.15 and 0.5 mg per 100 g; and for vitamin C between 10 and 50 mg per 100 g. For tomato the carotene ranges between 0.8 and 4 mg per 100 g. Even within one set of tables, in which the same sampling and analytical techniques are presumably used, there is a range of carotene in sweet potatoes (*Ipomea batatas*) from 0.3 to 4.6 mg per 100 g; and for lettuce (*Lactuca sativa*) from 0.16 to 1.6 mg per 100 g.

Mineral Salts

These are stable compared with some of the vitamins but the amounts can vary with different growing conditions, though to a lesser extent than described above for vitamins. Chemical analysis can be misleading since part of the mineral may be present in the food in a bound, unavailable form which is not liberated during digestion. In addition there may be other substances present in the same food or eaten at the same meal that interfere with absorption. Substances such as oxalates, phytates, tannins, and dietary fiber reduce the amount absorbed.

Generally, vegetables are good sources of potassium with a very high potassium/sodium ratio, but rather poor sources of iron of low availability, although the amount absorbed is a balance between enhancement by the vitamin C present and various factors that reduce absorption. Vegetables are also a minor source of iodine depending on the content in the soil water.

Both fruits and vegetables are often described as sources of calcium but they are minor sources, i.e., many supply around 50 mg per 100 g compared with milk at 120 mg (which is consumed in much larger quantities) and cheese at several hundred mg per 100 g. Some common fruits and vegetables do not contain any calcium and the richer sources such as parsley at 330 mg and watercress at 220 mg per 10 g are eaten in relatively small amounts. Spinach stands out with 600 mg calcium per 100 g, but this is partly unavailable.

Dietary Fiber

All fruits and vegetables are sources of dietary fiber—more precisely nonstarch polysaccharides—but in different amounts. Thus, taken from the same food composition tables, they vary in fruits from around 0.5 g per 100 g in grapes, lychees, melons, and cherries, through 1.5 g per 100 g in oranges, peaches, pineapple, plums, rhubarb, and apples, 2.5 g per 100 g in mangoes, olives, and pears, to nearly 4 g per 100 g guava, blackberries, and blackcurrants (Englyst method of analyis). Similarly vegetables vary from 1–1.5 g (potatoes, cauliflower, celery, lettuce) to 2 g (aubergine, French beans, cabbage), 4 g (baked beans, lentils, Brussels sprouts), and 6–7 g per 100 g (broad beans, kidney beans).

Leaf Protein

Leafy vegetables contain so little protein that excessive amounts would have to be consumed to make a significant contribution to the diet: Such amounts would include unacceptable intakes of dietary fiber (chiefly cellulose). This problem has been overcome by extracting the protein from leaves, including grass; the soluble proteins are separated from the fibrous parts and concentrated by heat coagulation. This product can be added on the domestic scale without further purification to foods such as stews or can be further refined to remove color and dried for storage, which adds to the cost and the technology required. Since grass and many leaves provide a continuing crop leaf protein offers considerable possibilities in developing countries but has been little exploited.

Developing Regions

As quoted in the introduction, there are numerous species of wild plants that could make useful contributions to the diet. The Food and Agriculture Organization has frequently drawn attention to the possibility of collecting wild plant foods, of growing them under protection, or of cultivating them. It has been calculated, for example, that adding 100 g of leafy vegetables to the diet of a 6-year-old child whose staple is cereal or cassava could supply three times the daily need for vitamins A and C, all the folate, calcium, and iron, 15% of the B vitamins, and 15% of the protein. Regular consumption of amaranth leaves and leaves of the drumstick tree (*Moringa olifera*) is recommended for children as a public health measure in many areas of the world, particularly to overcome the widespread problem of vitamin A deficiency.

Vegetarians

Although there is little evidence that the avoidance of animal products results in malnutrition, indeed, in some instances the reverse may be true, the intake of some nutrients may be at risk if all animal foods (including fish, eggs, and milk products) are shunned. Vitamin B_{12} is present only, with very few exceptions (e.g., some yeasts), in animal foods, so supplementation of the diet is virtually essential.

The average intake of carnitine by strict vegetarians is only one-tenth of that of people eating a mixed diet but plasma levels are within 'normal' limits. However, dietary carnitine may be required by premature infants and possibly by full-term infants and may be required by adults taking certain drugs.

There are very few plant sources of taurine and it is not known to what extent this may be a dietary essential. However, plasma levels in strict vegetarians are close to the 'normal' range.

Toxins and Contaminants

Fruits and vegetables contain large numbers of nonnutrients, some of which are toxic, but they are rarely harmful under ordinary conditions. Antinutritional substances in plant foods include antienzymes that interfere with digestion, antivitamins, and substances such as oxalates, phytates, tannins, and dietary fiber that can interfere with the absorption of some minerals. Glucosinolates, which are responsible for the characteristic flavor of vegetables of the families Cruciferae and Brassicaceae, are goitrogenic but appear to be an insignificant hazard to human health in the amounts usually eaten. In addition some legumes contain lectins in amounts sufficient to have been the cause of occasional cases of food poisoning when incompletely destroyed by cooking.

Most of these substances are destroyed by heat and have been found harmful to animals when included in feed in the raw state. Some are present in salad vegetables that are eaten raw, but in amounts too small to be harmful.

Cassava, especially the bitter variety, contains cyanide. This is usually removed in traditional food processing but not infrequently is a source of harm when the food is not properly treated.

Plantains eaten as a staple provide sufficient 5-hydroxytryptamine to affect central and peripheral nervous systems. Unripe ackee fruit (*Blighia sapida*) contains a toxin (hypoglycin) which causes vomiting sickness and hypoglycaemia. Rhubarb contains oxalate, and although the amounts in stems are harmless, poisoning has resulted from eating the leaves which contain a much higher concentration.

Potatoes contain small, usually harmless, amounts of solanine, but this is increased to toxic levels by exposure to light and subsequent 'greening.'

Some plant foods have been the cause of occasional outbreaks of poisoning in special circumstances. For example Jimson weed, *Datura stramonium*, contains alkaloids including scopolamine which produce hallucination; and the hemp plant, *Cannabis indica*, and the peyote, containing mescaline, have been consumed deliberately for their psychic effects.

Contamination

Some vegetables accumulate environmental toxins such as lead and radioactive fallout but the main cause for concern is from residues of agricultural chemicals, pesticides, and weedkillers. The danger of these chemicals is mainly to those handling them in production and manufacture, but there is concern over the small amounts remaining in the crops since these may be consumed over a long period, and the toxins may possibly be cumulative. Among these are the organochlorine insecticides including DDT and dieldrin. Both the substances and their degradation products persist in crops and so find their way into the human food chain. The fact that they are fat soluble and accumulate in the adipose tissue has given rise to concern but there is no evidence that these quantities merit alarm.

Nevertheless, they are restricted in use and are under continuous observation.

Role in Diet

There is considerable epidemiological evidence that a high intake of fruits and vegetables is protective against certain forms of cancer. Vitamins C, E, and β-carotene, when individually subjected to trials by dietary supplementation, have not been shown to be protective and it has been suggested either that there may be a synergistic effect between the various anti-oxidants found in plant foods or that some of the numerous other substances in the food may be the protective agent(s). These include lycopene, lutein, indoles, and phenols. Overall there are many hundreds of nonnutrients in plant foods whose functions in the diet, if any, have been little investigated.

Health Effects

Cardiovascular Disease

Observational studies during the past decade have shown consistent associations between consumption of fresh fruits and vegetables (FF&V) and reduction in cardiovascular disease (CVD) outcomes. An inverse correlation between fruits and vegetables intake and CVD mortality has also been shown in two studies. Similarly, a few, well-controlled randomized clinical trials have shown positive effects on CVD events or biomarkers of risk. The DASH trial (Dietary Approaches to Stop Hypertension), in which a high intake of fresh fruits and vegetables was a major component of the intervention, showed a significant decrease in systolic blood pressure after only 8 weeks. It is less clear whether these beneficial effects are primarily related to antioxidant effects of substances present in fresh fruits and vegetables or to the increased potassium intake associated with high consumption of fruits and vegetables.

Table 1 Sources of vitamin C in the average British diet

Food	% Average intake
Potatoes	16
Other vegetables	19
Fruit juices	18
Fruit	17
Salad vegetables	8
Milk products	5
Meat	4
Soft drinks	4
Enriched cereal products	3

From Gregory *et al.* (1990).

Diabetes

Cohort and cross-sectional studies indicate a protective effect of FF&V for type 2 diabetes. The European EPIC study reported an inverse association between FF&V intake and Hgb A1C levels. Other studies have shown a similar inverse correlation with fasting glucose and with glucose levels during an oral glucose tolerance test.

Cancer

The evidence of a protective effect of FF&V on several forms of cancer has been summarized by the International Agency for Research in Cancer (IARC), the World Health Organization, and the World Cancer Research Fund. The IARC report concluded that there is strong evidence of the protective effects of FF&V for cancers of the I gastrointestina tract (including colon) and lungs, but not for others. Some studies have suggested that the intake level necessary for cancer protection may be higher than the traditional recommendation five of servings per day.

See also: **Antioxidants**: Observational Studies; Intervention Studies. **Bioavailability**. **Dietary Fiber**: Physiological Effects and Effects on Absorption. **Food Safety**: Pesticides. **Legumes**. **Nutrition Policies In Developing and Developed Countries**. **Nutritional Surveillance**: Developing Countries. **Nuts and Seeds**. **Phytochemicals**: Epidemiological Factors. **Vegetarian Diets**.

Further Reading

Appel LJ *et al.* (1997) DASH: A clinical trial of the effects of dietary patterns on blood pressure. New England. *Journal of Medicine* **336**: 1117–1124.

FAO (1998) *Traditional food plants*. Food and Nutrition, Paper 42, Rome.

Ford ES and Mokhdad AH (2001) Fruit and vegetable consumption and diabetes mellitus incidence among US adults. *Preventive Medicine* **32**: 33–39.

Gregory J, Foster K, Tyler H, and Wiseman M (1990) *The Dietary and Nutritional Survey of British Adults*. London: HMSO.

Holland B, Welch AA, Unwin ID, Bass DH, Paul AA, and Southgate DAT (1991) *The Composition of Foods*, 5th edn. Cambridge: Royal Society of Chemistry.

Liener IE (1980) *Toxic Constituents of Plant Foodstuffs*, 2nd edn. New York: Academic Press.

Liu S, Manson JE, Lee IM *et al.* (2000) Fruit and vegetable intake and risk of cardiovascular disease: The Women's Health study. *American Journal of Clinical Nutrition* **72**: 922–928.

Oomen HAPC and Grubben GJH (1978) *Tropical leaf vegetables in human nutrition*. Communication 69 Amsterdam: Department of Agriculture Research.

Souci SW, Fachmann W, and Kraut H (1989) *Food Composition and Nutrition Tables*. Stuttgart: Wissen-schaftliche Verlagsgesellschaft mbH.

Watson DH (ed.) (1987) *Natural Toxicants in Food*. Chichester: Ellis Horwood.

World Cancer Research Fund and American Institute of Cancer Research (1997) *Nutrition and the Prevention of Cancer, a Global Perspective*. Washington, DC: AICR.

FUNCTIONAL FOODS

Contents
Health Effects and Clinical Applications
Regulatory Aspects

Health Effects and Clinical Applications

L Galland, Applied Nutrition Inc., New York, NY, USA

Introduction

Functional foods are foods with health benefits that exceed those attributable to the nutritional value of the food. The term is usually applied to foods that have been modified or combined in order to enhance the health benefits but may include any food that naturally possesses components with demonstrable pharmacologic activity. Functional foods are most often selected because they contain ingredients with immune-modulating, antioxidant, anti-inflammatory, antitoxic, or ergogenic effects. The most widely studied functional ingredients are plant-derived phenolic chemicals, probiotic bacteria, and fiber or other poorly digested carbohydrates, but colostrum, egg yolk, and other nonplant foods may also serve as functional food sources. Although pharmacologic activity of most of these substances is well established *in vitro* or in small mammals, establishing clinical effects in humans poses a challenge for functional food research.

Concept and Definition

The concept of functional foods derives from the observation that certain foods and beverages exert beneficial effects on human health that are not explained by their nutritional content (i.e., macronutrients, vitamins, and minerals). The definition of functional foods varies among countries for reasons that are historical, cultural, and regulatory. In its broadest use, functional foods are food-derived products that, in addition to their nutritional value, enhance normal physiological or cognitive functions or prevent the abnormal function that underlies disease. A hierarchy of restrictions narrows the definition. In most countries, a functional food must take the form of a food or beverage, not a medication, and should be consumed the way a conventional food or beverage is consumed. If the ingredients are incorporated into pills, sachets, or other dosage forms they are considered dietary supplements or nutraceuticals, not functional foods. In Japan and Australia, the functional food appellation has been applied only to food that is modified for the purpose of enhancing its health benefits; in China, Europe, and North America, any natural or preserved food that enhances physiological function or prevents disease might be considered a functional food. If food is modified, there is lack of international consensus as to whether a vitamin or mineral-enriched food (e.g., folate-fortified flour or calcium-fortified orange juice) should be considered a functional food, or whether functional foods are described by the presence of their nonnutritive components (e.g., fiber or polyphenols). Future development of functional foods is likely to be driven by scientific research rather than government regulation, so it is likely that the concept (if not the definition) of functional foods will remain fluid and flexible.

History

If the broadest, least restrictive definition is employed, the use of functional foods for promoting health and relieving symptoms is as old as the practice of medicine. Specific dietary recommendations for treating or preventing various types of illness have been documented in Hippocratic and Vedic texts and the canons of traditional Chinese medicine. Traditional Chinese remedies frequently contain recipes for combining specific foods with culinary and nonculinary herbs to produce healing mixtures. Folk medicine, East and West, has always depended upon functional foods. Peppermint (*Mentha piperita*) tea has a long history of use for digestive complaints. Peppermint oil contains spasmolytic components that block calcium channels in smooth muscle. Cranberry (*Vaccinium macrocarpon*) juice contains proanthocyanidins that inhibit the attachment of *E.coli* to the epithelium of the urinary bladder, explaining its efficacy in prevention of bacterial cystitis and its traditional use for treatment of urinary infection.

Herbs and spices are added to food to enhance flavor and initially were used to inhibit spoilage. Many of these have documented medicinal uses that render them functional foods, broadly defined. Thyme (*Lamiaceae* spp.) was used to treat worms in ancient Egypt. Thyme oils possess potent antimicrobial properties. Ginger (*Zingiber officinale* root), cinnamon (*Cinnamomum* spp. bark), and licorice (*Glycyrrhiza glabra* root) are common ingredients in Chinese herbal tonics and have been widely used in Western folk medicine for treating digestive disorders. Ginger contains over four hundred biologically active constituents. Some have antimicrobial, anti-inflammatory, or anti-platelet effects; others enhance intestinal motility, protect the intestinal mucosa against ulceration and dilate or constrict blood vessels. Cinnamon oil contains cinnamaldehyde and various phenols and terpenes with antifungal, antidiarrheal, vasoactive, and analgesic effects. Recent research has identified phenolic polymers in cinnamon with actions that increase the sensitivity of cells to insulin, leading to the recognition that regular consumption of cinnamon may help to prevent type 2 diabetes. The most studied component of licorice, glycyrrhizin, inhibits the enzyme 11 beta-hydroxysteroid dehydrogenase type 2, potentiating the biological activity of endogenous cortisol. Glycyrrhizin also inhibits the growth of *Helicobacter pylori*. Glycyrrhizin and its derivatives may account for the anti-inflammatory and anti-ulcerogenic effects of licorice.

Fermentation is a form of food modification initially developed for preservation. The health-enhancing effects of fermented foods have a place in folk medicine. Several fermented foods have health benefits that exceed those of their parent foods and can be considered functional foods, broadly defined. These include red wine, yogurt, and tempeh. Red wine is a whole fruit alcohol extract that concentrates polyphenols found primarily in the seed and skin of the grape. Its consumption is associated with protection against heart disease, perhaps because red wine polyphenols inhibit the production of free radicals and lipid peroxides that result from the simultaneous ingestion of cooked meat. Fresh yogurt contains live cultures of lactic acid-producing bacteria that can prevent the development of traveler's diarrhea, antibiotic-induced diarrhea, rotavirus infection, and vaginal yeast infection, decrease the incidence of postoperative wound infection following abdominal surgery and restore the integrity of the intestinal mucosa of patients who have received radiation therapy. Tempeh is made from dehulled, cooked soy beans fermented by the fungus *Rhizopus oligosporus*. Not only is its protein content higher than the parent soy bean, but it also has antibiotic activity *in vitro* and the ability to shorten childhood diarrhea *in vivo*.

Modification of a food to make it less harmful by removing potential toxins or allergens may create a functional food. Using this criterion, infant formula, protein hydrolysates, low-sodium salt substitutes, low-fat dairy products, and low-erucic-acid rapeseed oil (canola oil) might be considered functional foods.

If the most restrictive definition of functional foods is employed, the functional food movement began in Japan during the 1980s, when the Japanese government launched three major research initiatives designed to identify health-enhancing foods to control the rising cost of medical care. In 1991, a regulatory framework, Foods for Special Health Uses (FOSHU), was implemented, identifying those ingredients expected to have specific health benefits when added to common foods, or identifying foods from which allergens had been removed. FOSHU products were to be in the form of ordinary food (not pills or sachets) and consumed regularly as part of the diet. Initially, 11 categories of ingredients were identified for which sufficient scientific evidence indicated beneficial health effects. The Japanese Ministry of Health recognized foods containing these ingredients as functional foods. They were intended to improve intestinal function, reduce blood lipids and blood pressure, enhance calcium or iron absorption, or serve as noncariogenic sweeteners (see **Table 1**). In addition, low-phosphorus milk was approved for people with renal insufficiency and protein-modified rice for people with rice allergy.

Interest in the development of functional foods quickly spread to North America and Europe, where the concept was expanded to include any food or food component providing health benefits in addition to its nutritive value. In Europe, functional food proponents distinguished functional foods from dietetic foods, which are defined by law. European dietetic foods are intended to satisfy special nutritional requirements of specific groups rather than to enhance physiologic function or prevent disease through nonnutritive influences. They include infant formula, processed baby foods

Table 1 Some ingredients conferring FOSHU status on Japanese functional foods

Ingredient	Physiological function
Dietary fiber	Improve gastrointestinal function
Psyllium seed husk	
Wheat bran	
Hydrolyzed guar gum	
Oligosaccharides	Improve gastrointestinal function
Xylo-, fructo-, isomalto-	and mineral absorption
Soy-derived	
Polydextrose	
Bacterial cultures	Improve gastrointestinal function
Lactobacilli	
Bifidobacteria	
Soy protein isolates	Reduce cholesterol levels
Diacylglycerols	Reduce triglyceride levels
Sugar alcohols	Prevent dental caries
Maltitol	
Palatinose	
Erythritol	
Green tea polyphenols	Prevent dental caries
Absorbable calcium	Improve bone health
Calcium citrate malate	
Casein	
phosphopeptide	
Heme iron	Correct iron deficiency
Eucommiacea (tochu)	Reduce blood pressure
leaf glycosides	
Lactosucrose, lactulose,	Improve gastrointestinal function
indigestible dextrin	

(weaning foods), low-calorie foods for weight reduction, high-calorie foods for weight gain, ergogenic foods for athletes, and foods for special medical purposes like the treatment of diabetes or hypertension. In the US, functional food proponents have distinguished functional foods from medical foods, defined by law as special foods designed to be used under medical supervision to meet nutritional requirements in specific medical conditions. In both domains, functional foods have been viewed as whole foods or food components with the potential for preventing cancer, osteoporosis, or cardiovascular disease; improving immunity, detoxification, physical performance, weight loss, cognitive function, and the ability to cope with stress; inhibiting inflammation, free-radical pathology and the ravages of aging; and modulating the effects of hormones. Researchers have sought to validate biomarkers that demonstrate functional improvement in response to dietary intervention, identify the chemical components of functional foods responsible for those effects, and elucidate the mechanism of action of those components. The scientific substantiation of claims is a major objective.

In China, functional foods (referred to as health foods) have been viewed as part of an unbroken medical tradition that does not separate medicinal herbs from foods. Over 3000 varieties of health foods are available to Chinese consumers, most derived from compound herbal formulas for which the active ingredients and their mechanism of action are unknown, all claiming multiple effects on various body systems, with little experimental evidence for safety and efficacy but widespread acceptance due to their history of use.

Edible Plants and Phytochemicals

Because their consumption is known to enhance health, vegetables, fruits, cereal grains, nuts, and seeds are the most widely researched functional foods. The health benefits of a plant-based diet are usually attributed to the content of fiber and of a variety of plant-derived substances (phytonutrients and phytochemicals) with antioxidant, enzyme-inducing, and enzyme-inhibiting effects. Some phytochemicals may also exert their health effects by modifying gene expression. Carotenoids, for example, enhance expression of the gene responsible for production of Connexin 43, a protein that regulates intercellular communication. The protective effect of carotenoid consumption against the development of cancer is more strongly related to the ability of individual carotenoids to upregulate Connexin 43 expression than their antioxidant effects or conversion to retinol. Dietary supplementation with beta-

carotene reduces the blood levels of other carotenoids, some of which are more potent inducers of Connexin 43 than is beta-carotene. The unexpected and highly publicized increase in incidence of lung cancer among smokers taking beta-carotene supplements may be explained by this mechanism.

Phytochemicals associated with health promotion and disease prevention are described in **Table 2**. The most studied food sources of these phytonutrients are soy beans (*Glycine max*) and tea (*Camellia sinensis* leaves), but tomatoes (*Lycopersicon esculentum*), broccoli (*Brassica oleracea*), garlic (*Allium sativum*), turmeric (*Curcuma longa*), tart cherries (*Prunus cerasus*), and various types of berries are also receiving considerable attention as functional food candidates. An overview of the research on soy and tea illustrates some of the clinical issues encountered in the development of functional foods from edible plants.

Soy protein extracts have been found to lower cholesterol in humans, an effect that appears to be related to amino acid composition. Soy protein extracts frequently contain nonprotein isoflavones, which have received considerable attention because of their structural similarity to estrogen. Soy isoflavones are weak estrogen agonists and partial estrogen antagonists. Epidemiologic and experimental data indicate that isoflavone exposure during adolescence may diminish the incidence of adult breast

Table 2 Phytochemicals associated with health promotion and disease prevention

Group	Typical components	Biological activities	Food sources
Carotenoids	Alpha- and beta-carotene cryptoxanthin, lutein, lycopene, zeaxanthin	Quench singlet and triplet oxygen, increase cell–cell communication	Red, orange and yellow fruits and vegetables, egg yolk, butter fat, margarine
Glucosinolates, isothiocyanates	Indole-3-carbinol sulphoraphane	Increase xenobiotic metabolism, alter estrogen metabolism	Cruciferous vegetables, horseradish
Inositol phosphates	Inositol hexaphosphate (phytate)	Stimulate natural killer cell function, chelate divalent cations	Bran, soy foods
Isoflavones	Genistein, daidzein	Estrogen agonist and antagonist, induce apoptosis	Soy foods, kudzu
Lignans	Enterolactone, enterolactone	Estrogen agonists and antagonists, inhibit tyrosine kinase	Flax seed, rye
Phenolic acids	Gallic, ellagic, ferulic, chlorogenic, coumaric	Antioxidant, enhance xenobiotic metabolism	Diverse fruits, vegetables
Phytoallexins	Resveratrol	Antioxidant, platelet inhibition, induce apoptosis	Red wine, grape seed
Polyphenols	Flavonoids, chalcones, catechins, anthocyanins, proanthocyanidins	Antioxidant, enhance xenobiotic metabolism, inhibit numerous enzymes	Diverse fruits, vegetables, red wine, tea
Saponins	Glycyrrhizin, ginsenosides	Antimicrobial, immune boosting, cytotoxic to cancer cells	Legumes, nuts, herbs
Sterols	Beta-sistosterol, campestrol	Bind cholesterol, decrease colonic cell proliferation, stimulate T-helper-1 cells	Nuts, seeds, legumes, cereal grains
Sulfides	Diallyl sulfides	Antimicrobial, antioxidant	Garlic, onions

cancer. *In vitro* studies show conflicting effects. On the one hand, soy isoflavones induce apoptosis of many types of cancer cells; on the other hand, estrogen receptor-bearing human breast cancer cells proliferate in tissue culture when exposed to isoflavones. Although the widespread use of soy in Asia is cited in support of the safety of soy foods, the intake of isoflavones among Asian women consuming soy regularly is in the range of 15–40 mg day^{-1}, significantly less than the isoflavone content of a serving of soymilk as consumed in the US. In clinical trials, soy isoflavones have not been effective in relieving hot flashes of menopausal women but do diminish the increased bone resorption that causes postmenopausal bone loss. In premenopausal women, soy isoflavones may cause menstrual irregularities. The successful development of soy derivatives as functional foods will require that these complex and diverse effects of different soy components in different clinical settings be better understood.

Regular consumption of tea, green or black, is associated with a decreased risk of heart disease and several kinds of cancer. These benefits are attributed to tea's high content of catechin polymers, especially epigallocatechin gallate (ECGC), which has potent antioxidant and anti-inflammatory effects, that may lower cholesterol in hyperlipidemic individuals and alter the activity of several enzymes involved in carcinogenesis. Catechin content is highest in young leaves. Aging and the fermentation used to produce black tea oxidize tea catechins, which polymerize further to form the tannins, theaflavin and thearubigen. Although ECGC is a more potent antioxidant than theaflavin, theaflavin is far more potent an antioxidant than most of the commonly used antioxidants, like glutathione, vitamin E, vitamin C, and butylated hydroxytoluene (BHT). Both ECGC and theaflavin are partially absorbed after oral consumption, but a clear dose–response relationship has not been established. Tea-derived catechins and polymers are being intensively studied as components of functional foods, because the results of epidemiologic, *in vitro*, and animal research indicate little toxicity and great potential benefit in preventing cancer or treating inflammation-associated disorders. Clinical trials have shown a mild cholesterol-lowering effect and perhaps some benefit for enhancing weight loss.

Probiotics and Prebiotics

Probiotics are live microbes that exert health benefits when ingested in sufficient quantities. Species of lactobacilli and bifidobacteria, sometimes combined with *Streptococcus thermophilus*, are the main bacteria used as probiotics in fermented dairy products. Most probiotic research has been done with nutraceutical preparations, but yogurt has been shown to alleviate lactose intolerance, prevent vaginal candidosis in women with recurrent vaginitis, and reduce the incidence or severity of gastrointestinal infections.

Prebiotics are nondigestible food ingredients that stimulate the growth or modify the metabolic activity of intestinal bacterial species that have the potential to improve the health of their human host. Criteria associated with the notion that a food ingredient should be classified as a prebiotic are that it remains undigested and unabsorbed as it passes through the upper part of the gastrointestinal tract and is a selective substrate for the growth of specific strains of beneficial bacteria (usually lactobacilli or bifidobacteria), rather than for all colonic bacteria, inducing intestinal or systemic effects through bacterial fermentation products that are beneficial to host health. Prebiotic food ingredients include bran, psyllium husk, resistant (high amylose) starch, inulin (a polymer of fructofuranose), lactulose, and various natural or synthetic oligosaccharides, which consist of short-chain complexes of sucrose, fructose, galactose, glucose, maltose, or xylose. The best-known effect of prebiotics is to increase fecal water content, relieving constipation. Bacterial fermentation of prebiotics yields short-chain fatty acids (SCFAs) that nourish and encourage differentiation of colonic epithelial cells. Absorbed SCFAs decrease hepatic cholesterol synthesis. Fructooligosaccharides (FOSs) have been shown to alter fecal biomarkers (pH and the concentration of bacterial enzymes like nitroreductase and beta-glucuronidase) in a direction that may convey protection against the development of colon cancer.

Several prebiotics have documented effects that are probably independent of their effects on gastrointestinal flora. Whereas the high phytic acid content of bran inhibits the absorption of minerals, FOSs have been shown to increase absorption of calcium and magnesium. Short-chain FOSs are sweet enough to be used as sugar substitutes. Because they are not hydrolyzed in the mouth or upper gastrointestinal tract, they are noncariogenic and noninsulogenic. Bran contains immunostimulating polysaccharides, especially beta-glucans and inositol phosphates, which have been shown to stimulate macrophage and natural killer cell activity *in vitro* and in rodent experiments. The poor solubility and absorption of beta-glucans and inositol phosphates are significant barriers to clinical effects in humans.

Immune Modulators

Several substances produced by animals and fungi have been investigated for immune-modulating effects. Fish oils are the most studied. As a source of n-3 fatty acids, fish oil consumption by humans has been shown to influence the synthesis of inflammatory signaling molecules like prostaglandins, leukotrienes, and cytokines. In addition to direct effects on prostanoid synthesis, n-3 fats have also been shown to directly alter the intracellular availability of free calcium ions, the function of ion channels, and the activity of protein kinases. Generally administered as nutraceuticals rather than as functional foods, fish oil supplements have demonstrated anti-inflammatory and immune suppressive effects in human adults. A high intake of the n-3 fatty acids eicosapentaenoic (20:5n-3) and docosahexaenoic (22:6n-3) acid (DHA) from seafood or fish oil supplements has also been associated with prevention of several types of cancer, myocardial infarction, ventricular arrhythmias, migraine headaches, and premature births, and with improved control of type 2 diabetes mellitus, inflammatory bowel disease, rheumatoid arthritis, cystic fibrosis, multiple sclerosis, bipolar disorder, and schizophrenia. 20:5n-3 but not 22:6n-3 is effective for schizophrenia and depression; 22:6n-3 but not 20:5n-3 improves control of blood sugar in diabetics. The benefits of fish oil supplements have prompted efforts at increasing the n-3 fatty acid content of common foods by adding fish oil or flax oil extracts. Consumption of these has been associated with decreased levels of some inflammatory biomarkers, including thromboxane B2, prostaglandin E2, and interleukin 1-beta.

Feeding flax seed meal or fish meal to hens enriches the n-3 fatty acid content of the yolks of the eggs they lay. Consumption of these eggs increases the n-3 fatty acid content of plasma and cellular phospholipids and produces an improved blood lipid profile when compared with consumption of standard eggs. Egg yolk is not only a source of fatty acids, but also of carotenoids and immunoglobulins. The xanthophyll carotenoids zeaxanthin and its stereoisomer lutein are readily absorbed from egg yolk. Their consumption is associated with a decreased incidence of macular degeneration and cataract. Immunizing hens to specific pathogens and extracting the antibodies present in their egg yolks yields a functional food that has been shown to prevent enteric bacterial or viral infection in experimental animals.

Bovine colostrum, the milk produced by cows during the first few days postpartum, has a long history of use as a functional food. Compared to mature milk, colostrum contains higher amounts of immunoglobulins, growth factors, cytokines, and various antimicrobial and immune-regulating factors. Consumption of bovine colostrum has been shown to reduce the incidence of diarrheal disease in infants and the symptoms of respiratory infection in adults. Specific hyperimmune bovine colostrums, produced by immunizing cows to pathogenic organisms like *Cryptosporidium parvum*, *Helicobacter pylori*, rotavirus, and *Shigella* spp., may prevent or treat infection by these organisms.

Human studies have also shown that consumption of bovine colostrum can improve anaerobic athletic performance and prevent the enteropathy induced by use of nonsteroidal anti-inflammatory drugs.

Mushrooms play a major role in traditional Chinese medicine and as components of contemporary Chinese health foods. Many *Basidiomycetes* mushrooms contain biologically active polysaccharides in fruiting bodies, cultured mycelium, or culture broth. Most belong to the group of beta-glucans that have both beta-$(1\rightarrow3)$ and beta-$(1\rightarrow6)$ linkages. Although they stimulate macrophages and natural killer cells, the anticancer effect of mushroom polysaccharide extracts appears to be mediated by thymus-derived lymphocytes. In experimental animals, mushroom polysaccharides prevent oncogenesis, show direct antitumor activity against various cancers, and prevent tumor metastasis. Clinical trials in humans have shown improvement in clinical outcome when chemotherapy was combined with the use of commercial mushroom polysaccharides like lentinan (from *Lentinus edodes* or shiitake), krestin (from *Coriolus versicolor*), or schizophyllan (from *Schizophyllum commune*). Mushroom extracts may fulfill their potential more as medicines than as functional foods.

Designer Foods

An important direction in the development of functional foods is the combination of numerous ingredients to achieve a specific set of goals, rather than efforts to uncover the potential benefits of a single food source. Infant formula was probably the first area for designer foods of this type, because of the profound influence of nutrients on the developing brain and immune system. The addition of DHA to infant formula for enhancing brain and visual development, the alteration of allergenic components in food, and the possible use of probiotics and nucleotides to enhance immune response are important developments in this area.

Sports nutrition is another established arena for designer foods. Specific nutritional measures and dietary interventions have been devised to support athletic performance and recuperation. Oral rehydration products for athletes were one of the first categories of functional foods for which scientific evidence of benefit was obtained. Oral rehydration solutions must permit rapid gastric emptying and enteral absorption, improved fluid retention, and thermal regulation, to enhance physical performance and delay fatigue. Carbohydrates with relatively high glycemic index combined with whey protein concentrates or other sources of branched chain amino acids have been shown to enhance recovery of athletes. Caffeine, creatine, ribose, citrulline, L-carnitine, and branched chain amino acids have each been shown to improve exercise performance or diminish postexercise fatigue. Whether combinations of these ingredients, blended into foods or beverages, will perform better than the individual ingredients will help to determine the design of future sports foods.

Optimal cardiovascular health involves prevention of excessive levels of oxidant stress, circulating homocysteine, cholesterol, triglycerides and fibrinogen, and protection of the vascular endothelium. A mix of ingredients supplying all of these effects could consist of soy protein powder, oat beta-glucan, plant sterols and stanols, folic acid, L-arginine, 22:6n-3, magnesium, and red wine or green tea polyphenols. Evidence suggests that addressing multiple nutritional influences on cardiovascular health will be more beneficial than addressing only one influence, but more definitive studies are needed. Genetic factors may need to be incorporated for designer foods to achieve their full potential. Polyunsaturated fatty acids, for example, raise the serum concentration of HDL-cholesterol among individuals who carry the Apo A1-75A gene polymorphism, but reduce HDL-cholesterol levels of individuals who carry the more common Apo A1-75G polymorphism.

See also: **Alcohol**: Absorption, Metabolism and Physiological Effects. **Carotenoids**: Chemistry, Sources and Physiology; Epidemiology of Health Effects. **Dietary Fiber**: Physiological Effects and Effects on Absorption. **Fatty Acids**: Omega-3 Polyunsaturated. **Functional Foods**: Regulatory Aspects. **Microbiota of the Intestine**: Prebiotics; Probiotics. **Phytochemicals**: Classification and Occurrence; Epidemiological Factors. **Protein**: Quality and Sources. **Sports Nutrition**. **Tea**.

Further Reading

Ashwell M (2001) Functional foods: a simple scheme for establishing the scientific basis for all claims. *Public Health Nutrition* 4(3): 859–862.

Bellisle F, Diplock AT, Hornstra G *et al.* (eds.) (1998) Functional food science in Europe. *British Journal of Nutrition* 80(supplement 1): S1–S193.

Clydesdale FM and Chan SH (eds.) (1995) First International Conference on East–West Perspectives on Functional Foods. *Nutrition Reviews* 54(11, part II): S1–S202.

Constantinou AI and Singletary KW (eds.) (2002) Controversies in functional foods. *Pharmaceutical Biology* 40(supplement): 5–74.

Diplock AT, Aggett PJ, Ashwell M *et al.* (eds.) (1999) Scientific Concepts of Functional Foods in Europe: Consensus Document. *British Journal of Nutrition* 81(supplement): S1–S27.

Farnworth ER (2003) *Handbook of Fermented Functional Foods*. USA: CRC Press.

Goldberg I (ed.) (1994) *Functional Foods, Designer Food, Pharmafoods, Nutraceuticals*. New York: Chapman and Hall.

ILSI North America Technical Committee on Food Components for Health Promotion (1999). *Food Component Report*. Washington, DC: ILSI Press.

Knorr D (1999) Technology aspects related to microorganisms in functional food. *Trends in Food Science and Technology*. 9(8–9, Special Issue): 295–306.

Langseth L (1995) *Oxidants, Antioxidants and Disease Prevention: ILSI Europe Concise Monograph Series*. Washington, DC: ILSI Press.

Langseth L (1996) *Nutritional Epidemiology: Possibilities and Limitations: ILSI Europe Concise Monograph Series*. Washington, DC: ILSI Press.

Langseth L (1999) *Nutrition and Immunity in Man: ILSI Europe Concise Monograph Series*. Washington, DC: ILSI Press.

Meskin MS, Biidlack BI, Davies AJ, and Omaye ST (eds.) (2002) *Phytochemicals in Nutrition and Health*. USA: CRC Press.

Roberfroid MB (2000) Defining functional foods. In: Gibson G and Williams C (eds.) *Functional Foods*. Cambridge: Woodhead Publishing Ltd.

Truswell AS (1995) *Dietary Fat: Some Aspects of Nutrition and Health and Product Development: ILSI Europe Concise Monograph Series*. Washington, DC: ILSI Press.

Regulatory Aspects

H H Butchko, Exponent, Inc., Wood Dale, IL, USA
B J Petersen, Exponent, Inc., Washington DC, USA

Although there is no universally accepted definition of functional food, the International Life Sciences Institute of North America (ILSI NA) defines such foods as those that provide a health benefit beyond basic nutrition through the presence of physiologically active food components. Health Canada considers functional food as "similar in appearance to a conventional food, consumed as part of the usual diet, with demonstrated physiological benefits, and/

or to reduce the risk of chronic disease beyond basic nutritional functions." The Institute of Medicine of the US National Academy of Sciences has a more limited definition of functional foods as those in which the concentrations of one or more ingredients have been manipulated or modified to enhance their contribution to a healthful diet.

Under a broad definition, functional foods may include conventional foods; fortified, enriched, or enhanced foods; and dietary supplements because they provide essential nutrients often beyond quantities necessary for normal maintenance, growth, and development and/or other biologically active components that impart health benefits or desirable physiological effects. Thus, fruits and vegetables, such as broccoli, carrots, and tomatoes, are the simplest forms of functional foods because they provide physiologically active components such as sulforaphane, β-carotene, and lycopene, respectively.

Although functional foods can play a key role in promoting a healthier population, the government regulation of such foods is important to ensure protection of consumers from fraud and to ensure that any claims provide accurate information, are not misleading, and are scientifically valid. Governments have developed or are developing regulatory frameworks of nutrition and health claims to assist consumers in choosing foods for health promotion. The regulation of functional foods, the types and wording of claims communicated to consumers, and their place in national regulatory frameworks is evolving globally.

Regulation of Functional Foods in Japan

In the 1980s, the Japanese government funded large-scale research programs for systemic analysis of food functions and the physiological regulation of the function of food and the molecular design of functional foods. In 1991, the government established the Japanese Foods for Specified Health Use (FOSHU) to define foods with potential health benefits to help stem the rising cost of health care in Japan.

Under the FOSHU system, health claims are approved for specific products. Companies make an application for FOSHU approval to the Ministry of Health and Welfare (MHW). FOSHU are those foods that have a specific health benefit due to the presence of certain constituents or foods. Allergens cannot be present. Scientific substantiation, including the scientific evidence of safety and efficacy of the food and the medical or nutritional basis for the claim, must be provided to the MHW for

consideration. To be classified as FOSHU, it must be demonstrated that the final food product, not just individual components, is likely to have a beneficial health effect when consumed as part of the normal diet. FOSHU must be in the form of food and not pills or capsules.

The labeling of FOSHU foods must not be misleading and must include the approved health claim, the recommended daily intake, relevant nutrition information, guidance on healthful eating, and any necessary warnings regarding excessive intake. Domestic products have an 'approved' mark from the MHW, whereas imported products have a "permitted" mark.

Regulation of Functional Foods in the United States

Current US food regulations do not specifically address functional foods but, rather, include them in several categories within conventional foods, food additives, dietary supplements, medical foods, or foods for special dietary use. All of these fall under the amended Federal Food, Drug and Cosmetic Act (FDCA) of 1938 and are implemented under regulations from the Food and Drug Administration (FDA). Four types of claims can be used to communicate the usefulness of functional foods to consumers: health claims, qualified health claims, structure–function claims, and nutrient content claims.

Health Claims

The Nutrition Labeling and Education Act (NLEA) of 1990 authorizes the FDA to allow approved disease risk-reduction claims, known as health claims, to appear on food labeling. NLEA allows claims that "characterize the relationship of any substance to a disease or health-related condition." For example, "diets low in sodium may reduce the risk of high blood pressure." Health claims may not be false or misleading in any respect and must not suggest that a food will diagnose, treat, mitigate, cure, or prevent any disease, or they would be considered drug claims under the FDCA. If a manufacturer fails to comply with all of the requirements for an approved health claim, the FDA would consider that the food is either misbranded (mislabeled and therefore illegal) or an illegal drug because it would not comply with all applicable drug requirements.

The scientific standard for authorization of a health claim under NLEA mandates that there be significant scientific agreement among qualified experts about the validity of the relationship described in the proposed claim. The FDA has approved 12 health claims that meet the significant scientific agreement standard (**Table 1**).

The FDA Modernization Act of 1997 (FDAMA) provides an additional expedited process for manufacturers to use health claims. FDAMA allows health claims if they are based on current, published, authoritative statements from certain federal government official scientific bodies, such as the National Institutes of Health, the Centers for Disease Control and Prevention, and the National Academy of Sciences. Under FDAMA, manufacturers are required to notify and provide specific wording of the claim to the FDA 120 days in advance of use of the claim. During this time period, the FDA is expected to review the claim and may prohibit or modify the claim. If the FDA fails to act within the 120-day period, the claim is authorized by statue; the FDA is not required to issue a regulation. Since July 6, 1999, when the first health claim under the FDAMA was authorized, only one additional health claim has been allowed (**Table 2**).

Qualified Health Claims

Qualified health claims allow disease risk-reduction statements but, unlike health claims, must be qualified to indicate that the level of scientific support is not conclusive. Qualified health claims for dietary supplements were first authorized under a 1999 court decision in the case of *Pearson versus Shalala* regarding health claims for dietary supplements. In December 2002, the FDA announced the institution of a new labeling scheme for qualified health claims. The FDA indicated that it will depart from its standard of significant scientific agreement for health claims in evaluating qualified health claims. Qualified health claims may be based on the weight of the scientific evidence. In July 2003, the FDA announced a ranking system and proposed language for qualified health claims. Under the new scheme, claims are ranked by strength of scientific evidence. A claim designated as 'A' is actually an unqualified health claim with the standard of significant scientific agreement. Claims 'B,' 'C,' and 'D' would have progressively less supportive scientific evidence, and the FDA has suggested appropriate qualifying language for these claims (**Table 3**). To date, the FDA has allowed qualified health claims regarding certain foods, food components, and dietary supplements and the risk of cancer, cardiovascular disease, cognitive function and dementia, and neural tube defects (**Table 4**).

Structure–Function Claims

Structure–function claims for conventional foods focus on effects derived from nutritive value, whereas such claims for dietary supplements may focus on nutritive as well as nonnutritive effects. Structure–function claims describe the role of a nutrient or dietary ingredient that affects normal structure or function of the body (e.g., "calcium builds strong bones") without linking it to a specific disease. Structure–function claims may also characterize the mechanism by which a nutrient or dietary ingredient acts to maintain such structure or function (e.g., "fiber maintains bowel regularity"). They may also relate general well-being to consumption of a nutrient or dietary ingredient or describe a benefit related to a nutritional deficiency disease (e.g., deficiency of vitamin C and the occurrence of scurvy), which must be accompanied by a statement that describes the prevalence of such a disease in the United States. Structure–function claims on conventional foods are not preapproved by the FDA; it is the manufacturer's responsibility to ensure the accuracy and truthfulness of its claims and that such claims are not misleading.

The Dietary Supplement Health and Education Act of 1994 established special regulatory procedures for structure–function claims for dietary supplements. When such claims are used with a dietary supplement, the label must include a disclaimer that the FDA has not evaluated the claim and also that the product is not intended to "diagnose, treat, cure, or prevent any disease." Manufacturers of dietary supplements that make structure–function claims on labels or in labeling are required to submit a notification to the FDA no later than 30 days after marketing the dietary supplement. Although this notification must include the text of the structure–function claim, there is no requirement that the manufacturer include the scientific evidence supporting the claim with this notification.

Nutrient Content Claims

A nutrient content claim either expressly or implicitly characterizes the level of a nutrient in a product (e.g., "high in vitamin C" or "low in sodium"). In general, nutrient content claims cannot be used in food labeling unless the claim is made in accordance with existing FDA regulations or an authoritative statement by a scientific body. The FDA has allowed nutrient content claims for certain substances for which it has established Daily Reference Values or Reference Daily Intakes (RDIs). In general, the FDA allows nutrient content labeling for "high in," "rich in," or an "excellent source of" a vitamin or mineral

Table 1 FDA-approved health claims that meet the significant scientific agreement standard

Food or dietary component	Disease claim	Model claim
Calcium 21 CFR 101.72	Osteoporosis	"Regular exercise and a healthy diet with enough calcium helps teens and young adult white and Asian women maintain good bone health and may reduce their high risk of osteoporosis later in life."
Dietary fat 21 CFR 101.73	Cancer	"Development of cancer depends on many factors. A diet low in total fat may reduce the risk of some cancers."
Dietary saturated fat and cholesterol 21 CFR 101.75	Coronary heart disease	"While many factors affect heart disease, diets low in saturated fat and cholesterol may reduce the risk of this disease."
Dietary noncariogenic carbohydrate sweeteners 21 CFR 101.80	Dental caries	**Full claim**: "Frequent between-meal consumption of foods high in sugars and starches promotes tooth decay. The sugar alcohols in [name of food] do not promote tooth decay." **Shortened claim** (on small packages only): "Does not promote tooth decay."
Fiber-containing grain products, fruits, and vegetables 21 CFR 101.76	Cancer	"Low-fat diets rich in fiber-containing grain products, fruits, and vegetables may reduce the risk of some types of cancer, a disease associated with many factors."
Folate 21 CFR 101.79	Neural tube birth defects	"Healthful diets with adequate folate may reduce a woman's risk of having a child with a brain or spinal cord defect."
Fruits and vegetables 21 CFR 101.78	Cancer	"Low-fat diets rich in fruits and vegetables (foods that are low in fat and may contain dietary fiber, vitamin A, or vitamin C) may reduce the risk of some types of cancer, a disease associated with many factors. Broccoli is high in vitamin A and C, and it is a good source of dietary fiber."
Fruits, vegetables, and grain products that contain fiber, particularly soluble fiber 21 CFR 101.77	Coronary heart disease	"Diets low in saturated fat and cholesterol and rich in fruits, vegetables, and grain products that contain some types of dietary fiber, particularly soluble fiber, may reduce the risk of heart disease, a disease associated with many factors."
Sodium 21 CFR 101.74	Hypertension	"Diets low in sodium may reduce the risk of high blood pressure, a disease associated with many factors."
Soluble fiber from certain foods 21 CFR 101.81	Coronary heart disease	"Soluble fiber from foods such as [name of soluble fiber source, and if desired, name of food product], as part of a diet low in saturated fat and cholesterol, may reduce the risk of heart disease. A serving of [name of food product] supplies __ grams of the [necessary daily dietary intake for the benefit] soluble fiber from [name of soluble fiber source] necessary per day to have this effect."
Soy protein 21 CFR 101.82	Coronary heart disease	(1) "25 grams of soy protein a day, as part of a diet low in saturated fat and cholesterol, may reduce the risk of heart disease. A serving of [name of food] supplies __ grams of soy protein." (2) "Diets low in saturated fat and cholesterol that include 25 grams of soy protein a day may reduce the risk of heart disease. One serving of [name of food] provides __ grams of soy protein."
Stanols/sterols 21 CFR 101.83	Coronary heart disease	(1) "Foods containing at least 0.65 gram per serving of vegetable oil sterol esters, eaten twice a day with meals for a daily total intake of at least 1.3 grams, as part of a diet low in saturated fat and cholesterol, may reduce the risk of heart disease. A serving of [name of food] supplies __ grams of vegetable oil sterol esters." (2) "Diets low in saturated fat and cholesterol that include two servings of foods that provide a daily total of at least 3.4 grams of plant stanol esters in two meals may reduce the risk of heart disease. A serving of [name of food] supplies__ grams of plant stanol esters."

From *Label Claims, Health Claims That Meet Significant Scientific Agreement*. Available at www.cfsan.fda.gov/~dms/lab-ssa.html.

Table 2 Health claims allowed under the FDAMA

Food or dietary component	Disease	Basis
Potassium	High blood pressure and stroke	National Academy of Sciences report *Diet and Health: Implications for Reducing Chronic Disease Risk*
Whole grain foods	Heart disease and certain cancers	National Academy of Sciences report *Diet and Health: Implications for Reducing Chronic Disease Risk*

From *Label Claims, FDA Modernization Act of 1997 (FDAMA) Claims.* Available at www.cfsan.fda.gov/~dms/labfdama.html.

for which the agency has established an RDI if the food provides 20% or more of the RDI per reference amount customarily consumed. The FDA has also published regulations authorizing and establishing detailed requirements for "good source," "more," and "light" (or "lite") claims, and certain claims about calorie content, sodium content, and fat, fatty acid, and cholesterol content.

If a manufacturer wants to make a claim about a food as a good source of a nutrient for which no FDA nutrient content claim regulation exists, such a claim would not be allowed, even if the claim is truthful and not misleading, unless and until the FDA issues a regulation approving the use of the claim.

Table 3 Standardized language for qualified health claims by category

FDA category	Level of scientific evidence	Proposed qualifying language
B	Second level: Moderate/good level of comfort	"Although there is scientific evidence supporting this claim, the evidence is not conclusive."
C	Third level: Low level of comfort	"Some scientific evidence suggests ... however, FDA has determined that this evidence is limited and not conclusive."
D	Fourth level: Extremely low level of comfort	"Very limited and preliminary scientific research suggests ... FDA concludes that there is little scientific evidence supporting this claim."

From *Guidance for Industry and FDA. Interim Procedures for Qualified Health Claims in the Labeling of Conventional Human Food and Dietary Supplements.* Available at www.cfsan.fda.gov/~dms/hclmgui3.html.

European Regulations for Functional Foods

The concept of functional foods was first evaluated in Europe in the 1990s when the International Life Sciences Institute in Europe (ILSI Europe) developed a project on functional foods that became a European Commission (EC) concerted action, Functional Food Science in Europe. Approximately 100 experts in nutrition and medicine in Europe reviewed the scientific literature about foods and food components and their effects on body functions, and they developed a global framework that included a framework for the identification and development of functional foods and for the scientific substantiation of their health-related effects. From this evaluation, two types of claims for functional foods were suggested: enhanced function claims and reduction of disease risk claims. From this evaluation, the "Concepts of Functional Foods" was produced by ILSI followed by publication of "Scientific Concepts of Functional Foods in Europe: Consensus Document." According to this concept document, "a food can be regarded as functional if it is satisfactorily demonstrated to beneficially affect one or more target functions in the body, beyond adequate nutritional effects, in a way which is relevant to either an improved state of health and well-being, or reduction of risk of disease." As in the United States, this definition of a functional food specifically excludes the treatment of disease. However, unlike the case in the United States, where functional foods can include dietary supplements in pill or capsule form, in Europe functional foods must be foods that have a positive health benefit in amounts normally consumed in the diet.

There are currently no final regulations or legislation at the European Union (EU) level that define permissible nutrition and health claims on foods. However, various member states have adopted local legislation to regulate their use, which has resulted in numerous differences throughout the EU in the definition of terms and the circumstances when claims are warranted. In 2003, the EU Commission issued a "Proposal for a Regulation of the European Parliament and of the Council on Nutrition and Health Claims Made in Foods" for harmonization of claims throughout the EU. Under this proposed regulation, although functional food is not defined, both nutrition and health claims would be allowed. Nutrition and health claims must be based on, and substantiated by, generally accepted scientific data and not be false, ambiguous, or misleading or imply doubts about the safety or nutritional adequacy of other foods. This proposal is being evaluated by the member states.

Table 4 Qualified health claims permitted by FDA

Food or food component	Disease	Eligible food	Required claim statement
Selenium	Cancer	Dietary supplements containing selenium	(1) "Selenium may reduce the risk of certain cancers. Some scientific evidence suggests that consumption of selenium may reduce the risk of certain forms of cancer. However, FDA has determined that this evidence is limited and not conclusive." or, (2) "Selenium may produce anticarcinogenic effects in the body. Some scientific evidence suggests that consumption of selenium may produce anticarcinogenic effects in the body. However, FDA has determined that this evidence is limited and not conclusive."
Antioxidant vitamins	Cancer	Dietary supplements containing vitamin E and/or vitamin C	(1) "Some scientific evidence suggests that consumption of antioxidant vitamins may reduce the risk of certain forms of cancer. However, FDA has determined that this evidence is limited and not conclusive." or, (2) "Some scientific evidence suggests that consumption of antioxidant vitamins may reduce the risk of certain forms of cancer. However, FDA does not endorse this claim because this evidence is limited and not conclusive." or, (3) "FDA has determined that although some scientific evidence suggests that consumption of antioxidant vitamins may reduce the risk of certain forms of cancer, this evidence is limited and not conclusive."
Nuts	Heart disease	Whole or chopped nuts or foods containing nuts with at least 11 g per reference amount customarily consumed; types of nuts — almonds, hazelnuts, peanuts, pecans, some pine nuts, pistachio nuts, walnuts	"Scientific evidence suggests but does not prove that eating 1.5 ounces per day of most nuts [such as *name of specific nut*] as part of a diet low in saturated fat and cholesterol may reduce the risk of heart disease."
Walnuts	Heart disease	Whole or chopped walnuts	"Supportive but not conclusive research shows that eating 1.5 ounces per day of walnuts, as part of a low saturated fat and low cholesterol diet and not resulting in increased caloric intake, may reduce the risk of coronary heart disease. See nutrition information for fat [and calorie] content."
Omega-3 fatty acids	Coronary heart disease	Dietary supplements containing the omega-3 long-chain polyunsaturated fatty acids eicosapentanoic acid (EPA) and/or docosahexanoic acid (DHA)	"Consumption of omega-3 fatty acids may reduce the risk of coronary heart disease. FDA evaluated the data and determined that, although there is scientific evidence supporting the claim, the evidence is not conclusive."

Continued

Table 4 Continued

Food or food component	Disease	Eligible food	Required claim statement
B vitamins	Vascular disease	Dietary supplements containing vitamin B_6, B_{12}, and/or folic acid	"As part of a well-balanced diet that is low in saturated fat and cholesterol, Folic Acid, Vitamin B_6 and Vitamin B_{12} may reduce the risk of vascular disease. FDA evaluated the above claim and found that, while it is known that diets low in saturated fat and cholesterol reduce the risk of heart disease and other vascular diseases, the evidence in support of the above claim is inconclusive."
Phosphatidylserine	Cognitive function and dementia	Dietary supplements containing soyderived phosphatidylserine	(1) "Consumption of phosphatidylserine may reduce the risk of dementia in the elderly. Very limited and preliminary scientific research suggests that phosphatidylserine may reduce the risk of dementia in the elderly. FDA concludes that there is little scientific evidence supporting this claim." *or,* (2) "Consumption of phosphatidylserine may reduce the risk of cognitive dysfunction in the elderly. Very limited and preliminary scientific research suggests that phosphatidylserine may reduce the risk of cognitive dysfunction in the elderly. FDA concludes that there is little scientific evidence supporting this claim."
Folic acid (0.8 mg)[a]	Neural tube birth defects	Dietary supplements containing folic acid	"0.8 mg folic acid in a dietary supplement is more effective in reducing the risk of neural tube defects than a lower amount in foods in common form. FDA does not endorse this claim. Public health authorities recommend that women consume 0.4 mg folic acid daily from fortified foods or dietary supplements or both to reduce the risk of neural tube defects."

[a]FDA has approved a health claim for folic acid in food and does not endorse that the 0.8 mg is more effective than lower amounts found in food.
From *Summary of Qualified Health Claims Permitted*. Available at www.cfsan.fda.gov/~dms/qhc-sum.html.

Nutrition Claims

A nutrition claim is defined as "any claim which states, suggests, or implies that a food has particular nutrition properties due to" energy or nutrients or other substances (i.e., provides, provides at a reduced or increased rate, or does not provide). The proposed regulation calls for establishment of a list of permitted claims and their specific conditions of use, which would be regularly updated. In the current proposed regulation, the list of nutrients includes fat, saturated fat, unsaturated fat, monounsaturated fat, polyunsaturated fat, omega-3 fatty acids, sugar, sodium, fiber, protein, vitamins/minerals, or other substances.

Health Claims

A health claim is defined in the proposed regulation as "any claim that states, suggests, or implies that a relationship exists between a food category, a food, or one of its constituents and health." A reduction in disease risk claim is defined as "any health claim that states, suggests, or implies that the consumption of a food category, a food, or one of its constituents significantly reduces a risk factor in the development of a human disease." As in the United States, medicinal products in Europe are those that treat, prevent, or diagnose disease or restore, correct, or modify physiological functions. In the European Directive 2000/13/EC on labeling, presentation, and advertising of foods, there is a specific prohibition on attributing prevention, treatment, or cure of a human disease or any reference to such properties to a food. However, there is a distinction made between prevention and significant reduction of a major disease risk factor, and the directive acknowledges that diet and certain foods are important for supporting and maintaining health and can affect certain disease risk factors.

Under the proposed regulation, health claims will only be allowed if the following information is included on the label: (i) a statement describing the importance of a varied and balanced diet and healthy lifestyle; (ii) the quantity of the food and pattern of consumption required to obtain the claimed beneficial heath effect: (iii) a statement addressed to people who should avoid the food, if appropriate; and (iv) a warning for products that may result in a health risk if consumed in excess. A reduction of risk claim must also include a statement that diseases may have many risk factors and that altering only one of these factors may or may not have a beneficial effect. Claims regarding a "slimming, slimness-producing, or weight-reducing" effect, those that refer to reducing hunger or increasing satiety, and those that claim a reduction in available energy from the diet would not be permitted.

The European Food Safety Authority (EFSA) is designated as the body that will be responsible for evaluating and authorizing health claims. EFSA would be required to make a decision within 6 months of receipt of an application. Once EFSA makes a decision, it would be forwarded to the Commission, which would be required to draft a decision within 3 months, followed by publication in the *Official Journal of the European Communities*. It is also anticipated that the Commission would establish and maintain a "community register of nutrition and health claims on food."

Nutrition and Health Claims at Codex

Many countries use decisions of the Codex Alimentarius Commission (Codex) as a basis for national regulations. Codex decisions are also used by the World Trade Organization (WTO) as the basis for resolution of trade disputes between nations. In May 2004, the Codex Committee on Food Labeling adopted draft guidelines for the use of nutrition and health claims; the commission officially adopted these draft guidelines in June 2004. Nutrition and health claims would not be allowed for foods for infants and young children unless specifically provided for in relevant Codex standards or national legislation.

Nutrition Claims

According to Codex, a nutrition claim "states, suggests, or implies that a food has particular nutritional properties, including but not limited to the energy and to the content of protein, fat, and carbohydrates, as well as the content of vitamins and minerals." The only nutrition claims permitted are those relating to energy, protein, carbohydrate, and fat and components thereof, fiber, sodium, and vitamins and minerals for which Nutrient Reference Values (NRVs) have been laid down in the Codex Guidelines for Nutrition Labelling. Two types of nutrition claims were defined. A nutrient content claim is defined as a nutrition claim that describes the level of a nutrient contained in a food—for example, "source of calcium," "high in fiber," and "low in fat." A nutrient comparative claim is one that compares the nutrient levels and/or energy value of two or more foods—for example, "reduced," "less than," "fewer," "increased," and "more than" (**Table 5**).

Table 5 Nutrient content claims at Codex

Food component	Content claim	Requirements Not more than
Energy	Low	40 kcal (170 kJ) per 100 g (solids) or 20 kcal (80 kJ) per 100 ml (liquids)
	Free	4 kcal per 100 ml (liquids)
Fat	Low	3 g per 100 g (solids), 1.5 g per 100 ml (liquids)
	Free	0.5 g per 100 g (solids) or 100 ml (liquids)
Saturated fat	Low[a]	1.5 g per 100 g (solids), 0.75 g per 100 ml (liquids) and 10% of energy
	Free	0.5 g per 100 g (solid) or 100 ml (liquids)
Cholesterol	Low[a]	0.02 g per 100 g (solids), 0.01 g per 100 ml (liquids)
	Free[a]	0.005 g per 100 g (solids), 0.005 g per 100 ml (liquids) and, for both claims, less than 1.5 g saturated fat per 100 g (solids), 0.75 g saturated fat per 100 ml (liquids) and 10% of energy of saturated fat
Sugars	Free	0.5 g per 100 g (solids), 0.5 g per 100 ml (liquids)
Sodium	Low	0.12 g per 100 g
	Very low	0.04 g per 100 g
	Free	0.005 g per 100 g
Protein	Source	10% of NRV per 100 g (solids), 5% of NRV per 100 ml (liquids) or 5% of NRV per 100 kcal (12% of NRV per 1 MJ) or 10% of NRV per serving
	High	2 times the values for 'source'
Vitamins and minerals	Source	15% of NRV per 100 g (solids), 7.5% of NRV per 100 ml (liquids) or 5% of NRV per 100 kcal (12% of NRV per 1 MJ) or 15% of NRV per serving
	High	2 times the values for 'source'

[a]*Trans* fatty acids should be taken into account where applicable.
NRV, nutrient reference value.
From Codex Alimentarius Commission (2004) *Joint FAO/WHO Food Standards Programme. Twenty-Seventh Session Rome, 28 June–3 July 2004. ALINORM 04/27/22 Report of the Thirty-Second Session of the Codex Committee on Food Labeling. Montréal, Canada, 10–14 May 2004.* Available at www.codexalimentarius.net.

Any comparisons are to be based on a relative difference of at least 25% in the energy value or macronutrient nutrient content and a 10% difference in the NRV for micronutrients between the compared foods. The use of the word "light" follows the same criteria as for "reduced" and should include an indication of the characteristics that make the food "light."

Health Claims

Health claims are defined by Codex as "any representation that states, suggests, or implies that a relationship exists between a food or a constituent of that food and health." Health claims must be based on the current relevant scientific data and be sufficient to substantiate the claimed effect and the relationship to health; Codex also envisions a re-review of claims as additional data may become available. Health claims should include information on the physiological role of the nutrient or the diet–health relationship as well as information on the composition of the product relevant to the physiological role of the nutrient or the accepted diet–health relationship. Codex defined three types of health claims: nutrient function claims, other function claims, and reduction of disease risk claims.

A nutrient function claim describes the physiological role of a nutrient in growth, development, and normal functions of the body. For example, "Nutrient A (naming a physiological role of nutrient A in the body in the maintenance of health and promotion of normal growth and development). Food X is a source of/high in nutrient A."

Other function claims convey specific beneficial effects of the consumption of foods or their constituents in the context of the total diet on normal functions or biological activities of the body. Such claims relate to a positive contribution to health, to the improvement of a function, or to modifying or preserving health. For example, "Substance A (naming the effect of substance A on improving or modifying a physiological function or biological activity associated with health). Food Y contains x grams of substance A."

Reduction of disease risk claims convey that consumption of a food or food constituent, in the context of the total diet, is related to a reduced risk of developing a disease or health-related condition. Risk reduction is defined as "significantly altering a major risk factor(s) for a disease or health-related condition." Because diseases have multiple risk factors and altering one of these risk factors may or may not have a beneficial effect, the risk reduction claims must have appropriate language and reference to other risk factors to ensure that consumers do not interpret them as prevention claims. For example, reduction of risk claims may include statements such as "A healthful diet low in nutrient or substance A may reduce the risk of disease D. Food X is low in nutrient or substance A" or "A healthful diet rich in nutrient or substance A may reduce the risk of disease D. Food X is high in nutrient or substance A."

Claims Related to Dietary Guidelines or Healthy Diets

Claims describing a food as part of a healthy diet should be permitted only if they are related to the pattern of eating contained in dietary guidelines officially recognized by the appropriate national authority, contain a statement relating the food to the pattern of eating to that in the guidelines, and are consistent with such guidelines. Such claims should not describe the food itself as healthy or imply that the food in and of itself will impart health. Foods that are allowed such claims should meet certain minimum criteria for major nutrients in the dietary guidelines. Codex stated that there should be some flexibility in the wording of such claims as long as they "remain faithful to the pattern of eating outlined in the dietary guidelines."

Conclusion

With the growing recognition of the connection between diet and health along with soaring health care costs, both consumers and governments have had great interest in capitalizing on the benefits of functional foods for health promotion. Although there is no standard accepted definition of functional food, most regulations and guidelines incorporate the concept that such foods, food components, and supplements provide a benefit to health beyond basic nutrition. There has been considerable progress by governments and Codex to develop systems to allow such products and to communicate their benefits to consumers through labeling claims. Some national regulatory agencies have laid down scientific standards for demonstrating the safety and efficacy of functional foods for different types of nutrition and health claims. Regulatory agencies are especially concerned that claims on foods or supplements are truthful and not misleading and aid consumers in making informed choices for health promotion. In the future, it is expected that functional foods will gain in importance, and regulatory agencies will need to continue to ensure that any claims on such products meet consumer needs.

See also: **Bioavailability**. **Food Composition Data**. **Food Fortification**: Developed Countries; Developing Countries. **Fruits and Vegetables**. **Functional Foods**: Health Effects and Clinical Applications. **Supplementation**: Dietary Supplements; Role of Micronutrient Supplementation; Developing Countries; Developed Countries.

Further Reading

American Dietetic Association (2004) Position of the American Dietetic Association: Functional foods. *Journal of the American Dietetic Association*, **104**,: 814–826.

Ashwell M (2002) *Concepts of Functional Foods. ILSI Europe Concise Monograph Series.* Brussels: International Life Sciences Institute. Available at www.ilsi.org.

Codex Alimentarius Commission (2004) *Joint FAO/WHO Food Standards Programme. Twenty-Seventh Session Rome, 28 June–3 July 2004. ALINORM 04/27/22 Report of the Thirty-Second Session of the Codex Committee on Food Labelling. Montréal, Canada, 10–14 May 2004.* Available at www.codexalimentarius.net.

European Commission (2004) *Proposal for a Regulation of the European Parliament and of the Council on Nutrition and Health Claims Made in Foods*, 11028/04. Brussels: European Commission.

Food and Drug Administration, Center for Food Safety and Applied Nutrition (2004) *Label Claims.* Available at www.cfsan.fda.gov/~dms/lab-hlth.html.

Hasler CM (2002) Functional foods: Benefits, concerns and challenges—A position paper from the American Council on Science and Health. *Journal of Nutrition* **132**: 3772–3781.

Health Canada (2001) Product-specific authorization of health claims for foods. A proposed regulatory framework. Bureau of Nutritional Sciences. Food Directorate. Health Products and Food Branch. October, 2001.

ILSI North America Technical Committee on Food Components for Health Promotion (1999) Safety assessment and potential health benefits of food components based on selected scientific criteria. *Critical Reviews in Food Science and Nutrition* **39**(3): 203–316.

ILSI North America Technical Committee on Food Components for Health Promotion (2002) Scientific criteria for evaluating health effects of food components. *Critical Reviews in Food Science and Nutrition* **42**(supplement): 651–676.

Institute of Food Technologists (2004) *Expert Report on Functional Foods* (Draft). Chicago Institute of Food Technologists.

International Food Information Council (2002) *International Food Information Council: Functional Foods Attitudinal Research.* Available at www.ific.org/research/funcfoodres00.cfm.

Sloan AE (2004) The top ten functional food trends 2004. *Food Technology* **58**(4): 28–51.

GALACTOSE

A Abi-Hanna and J M Saavedra,
Johns Hopkins School of Medicine, Baltimore,
MD, USA

This article is reproduced from the previous edition,
pp. 915–922, © 1999, Elsevier Ltd.

Lactose, a disaccharide composed of glucose and galactose, is the principal sugar of mammalian milk and the principal carbohydrate energy source for infants and children; thus galactose plays a central metabolic role in human nutrition. Lactose is hydrolyzed in the intestine into glucose and galactose, which together with other sources of these monosaccharides are absorbed and metabolized and used as energy. Galactose additionally is an important constituent of complex polysaccharides, galactolipids, and other glycoconjugates of structural and functional importance. Both absorptive as well as metabolic defects affecting galactose have been described.

Dietary Sources of Galactose

Lactose is by far the most abundant source of galactose in the diet of most humans. However, lactose can also be found in a considerable number of sources. These include drugs and medications, which use lactose as an excipient, in part because of its excellent tablet-forming capacity. Additionally, small amounts of galactose can be present in many fruits and vegetables, and considerable amounts can also be found in legumes (beans and peas) and in other food plants. Galactose polysaccharides with various glycolytic linkages such as $\alpha(1-6)$, $\beta(1-3)$, and $\beta(1-4)$ are ubiquitous in animals and plants. The bioavailability of galactose in these linkages found in foods is not well known. Some galactosidasis in plants can liberate galactose, and foods fermented by microorganisms for preparation or preservation may also contain free galactose. The role of free and bound galactose in cereals, fruits, legumes, nuts, and other vegetables may contribute to sources of galactose that are not readily obvious. Bound galactose is also present in raffinose oligosaccharides and other sugars.

Galactose Absorption

Lactose is hydrolyzed in the intestine by the enzyme lactase-phlorizin hydrolase to glucose and galactose. In humans, D-glucose and D-galactose are the only nutritionally significant monosaccharides that are actively absorbed. Although glucose and galactose can cross the intestinal mucosa down a diffusion gradient, the slowness of this method is such that water would diffuse in the opposite direction leading to a lessening in the concentration gradient. Thus, a rapid transport mechanism exists for glucose and galactose, particularly in infants. The 'coupled carrier' hypothesis is generally accepted as the main mechanism. In the small intestine and proximal tubule of the kidney, D-glucose is absorbed by epithelial cells via a sodium-dependent cotransport system existing at the luminal membrane level and a sodium-independent transport system at the basolateral membrane level. It is suggested that the potential difference across the brush border membrane of the cell also plays an important role in the mechanism which concentrates sugar in the cell.

The genetic functional defects of this cotransport system are expressed in two main clinical entities; selective congenital glucose and galactose malabsorption by the intestine discussed below, and familial renal glycosuria. Once galactose is absorbed, it must be converted to glucose for utilization. This occurs primarily by the pathways explained below. Three distinct enzymatic defects are responsible for the conditions generally described as galactosemia.

Glucose–Galactose Malabsorption

Pathophysiology and Clinical Manifestation

Glucose and galactose malabsorption is a rare congenital disease resulting from a selective defect in the intestinal transport of glucose and galactose. It is characterized by the neonatal onset of severe, watery, acidic diarrhea. The diarrhea is profuse and contains sugar. In children given lactose, fecal sugar mainly consists of glucose and galactose with only small amounts of lactose, since lactase activity is usually adequate. Hyperosmotic dehydration and metabolic acidosis are the rule. Related gastrointestinal signs and symptoms include increase of abdominal gas, distension, and vomiting. Intermittent or permanent glycosuria after fasting or after a glucose load is frequent. Thus the combination of reducing sugar in the stool and slight glycosuria despite low blood glucose levels is highly suggestive of glucose–galactose malabsorption.

The major characteristic in glucose–galactose malabsorption is the lack of intracellular glucose or galactose accumulation against a concentration gradient. The transport of other molecules such as alanine or leucine via a sodium cotransporter is typically intact.

The abnormality of carbohydrate metabolism is confined to glucose transport in the small intestine and the proximal renal tube. The main defect appears to be the absence of a functional sodium-dependent glucose contransporter. Electrolytes can be secreted in the jejunal mucosa together with fluids, suggesting that the combined glucose–sodium water absorption process is effective. Sucrose can undergo normal hydrolysis and fructose can be absorbed typically without problems. Glucose entry into the erythrocytes is normal and so are fasting blood glucose levels. Oral glucose tolerance tests usually yield a flat glucose curve while breath hydrogen tests done separately for glucose and galactose are consistent with malabsorption.

The functionality of the cotransporter at the brush border membrane is either absent or reduced. Additionally, the participation of a mutarotase in sugar transport has recently been suggested in the absence of this enzyme and has been demonstrated in glucose–galactose malabsorption. However, full understanding of this condition requires additional information on the liquid composition of the membrane and on other characteristics and genetic control of this transport system.

Diagnosis

Children affected with glucose–galactose malabsorption are of diverse origin. There is high consanguinity rate and no clear-cut vertical transmission, suggesting an autosomal recessive mode of inheritance.

The diagnosis can be established by a clinical history of watery diarrhea with glucose–water solution or milk and rapid cessation of the problem when these are discontinued. Oral glucose or galactose tolerance tests and breath hydrogen analysis can aid in the diagnosis. The differential diagnosis includes congenital lactase deficiency, sucrose–isomaltose deficiency, and congenital chloride-secreting diarrhea. Most other monosaccharide malabsorption and intolerance is secondary to mucosal injury and responds to adequate nutritional management with complete resolution.

Management

Treatment consists of immediate rehydration, adequate maintenance of hydration, and initiation of a glucose- and galactose-free diet. Since fructose is tolerated, most of the carbohydrate initially can be given as fructose, using other dietary modular products of protein and fat as well as micronutrients.

Biochemistry and Physiology of Galactose

The main pathway of galactose metabolism in humans is the conversion of galactose to glucose, without disruption of the carbon skeleton. The name 'galactosemia' has been associated with a syndrome of toxicity associated with the administration of galactose to patients with an inherited disorder of galactose utilization, leading to multiple clinical manifestations, including malnutrition, mental retardation, liver disease, and cataracts. The clinical manifestations are linked to specific enzymatic defects. Thus the term 'galactosemia' should be qualified by the specific defect. Three enzymatic steps are required to metabolize galactose to UDP-glucose. Two alternate pathways, oxidation and reduction, are used in the absence of enzymes of the main route.

Step 1: Galactokinase

Galactose is phosphorylated by galactokinase with ATP to form galactose 1-phosphate. The equilibrium is far in the direction of sugar phosphorylation, but the reaction is reversible. Galactokinase has been studied in detail in human red cells, leucocytes, fibroblasts, placenta, liver, and various human fetal tissues. It is detectable in fetal liver from 10 weeks of gestation onwards and the activity of the enzyme in liver and red cells is higher in the second and third trimester. Its activity is higher in red blood cells from human infants than in cells from adults, and in reticulocytes than with aged red cells. Cultured human fibroblasts show enhanced galactokinase activity when grown in the presence of galactose, whereas in the liver the activity does not appear to be regulated by dietary galactose. The red cell enzyme, like that of the liver, undergoes substrate and product inhibition.

The assignment of the gene for galactokinase has been made to human chromosome 17, and its regional localization of the chromosome has been assigned to band q21–22.

Step 2: Transferase

Galactose 1-phosphate reacts with UDP-glucose to produce UDP-galactose and glucose 1-phosphate. This step is catalyzed by galactose-1-phosphate uridyltransferase, an enzyme present in bacteria and most mammalian tissues. Like galactokinase, galactose-1-phosphate uridyltransferase is detectable in fetal liver from 10 weeks of gestation, with the liver enzyme-specific activity being highest at 28 weeks of gestation. The rate of reaction may be regulated by substrate concentration and limited by UDP-glucose substrate inhibition of transferase. Glucose 1-phosphate is a potent inhibitor of the enzyme. Uridine nucleotides such as uridine di- and triphosphate are powerful competitive inhibitors of substrate UDP-glucose.

Galactose-1-phosphate uridyltransferase deficiency is the most commonly reported defect in galactosemic patients. In the young infant galactose is a major energy source and its metabolism to glucose 1-phosphate is essential, but this is not the case in the fetus in whom glucose is the main energy source. However, the metabolism of galactose in the fetus is important to prevent accumulation of toxic galactose metabolites. Thus in galactose-1-phosphate uridyl-transferase deficiency the fetus could be at a disadvantage as early as the 10th week of gestation. Dietary and hormonal influences on the liver enzyme have not been reported. In the rat a galactose-rich diet increases transferase activity.

Galactose-1-phosphate uridyltransferase is localized on chromosome 9p13. At least 32 variants in the nucleotide sequence of the galactose-1-phosphate uridyltransferase gene have been identified, with the most frequent being change in amino acid codon position 188 in which an arginine is substituted for a glutamine, the Q188R mutation. This Q188R mutation is associated with 'classical' galactosemia with virtually no galactose-1-phosphate uridyl-transferase activity detectable. However, there are other variant forms of the enzyme which have diminished but detectable activity, known as Duarte, Indiana, Rennes, Los Angeles, Münster, and Chicago. Heterozygotes for normal and Duarte alleles are presumed to have 75% of normal galactose-1-phosphate uridyltransferase activity. Homozygotes for the Duarte allele could have 50% activity, and compound heterozygotes for the Duarte allele and the classical galactosemia allele have 25% activity in peripheral erythrocytes.

Step 3: Epimerase

The UDP-galactose is converted to UDP-glucose by UDP-galactose 4'-epimerase. The UDP-glucose thus formed can then enter the reaction again in a cyclical fashion until all the free galactose coming into the pathway is converted to glucose 1-phosphate. This enzyme is responsible for the inversion of the hydroxyl group at the C-4 carbon of the hexose chain to form glucose from galactose; it is also important for the conversion of UDP-glucose to UDP-galactose when only glucose is available and galactose is required as a constituent of complex polysaccharides. The epimerase maintains a cellular equilibrium of UDP-glucose to UDP-galactose in a ratio of about 3:1.

The purified enzyme is a dimer of identical subunits that consists of a mixture of catalytically active subunits (epimerase-NAD$^+$) and inactive subunits (epimerase-NADH-uridine nucleotide). The NAD binds to the enzyme and induces a conformational change resulting in enzymatic activity. For liver enzyme activity, exogenous NAD is required and NADH is a potent inhibitor of the enzyme. Any process disturbing the NAD/NADH ratio, such as ethanol metabolism which generates NADH, will impair galactose utilization. Cellular levels of UDP-glucose and other uridine nucleotides may also exert rate-regulating effects. Cells not exposed to free galactose form the sugar from glucose in adequate amounts to satisfy normal growth and development. Epimerase activity of the intestinal mucosa increases with age, whereas human red cells have a higher activity in newborns than adults. The intestinal enzyme activity can be enhanced by feeding diets high in glucose or galactose content. Less information is available on fetal levels of UDP-galactose 4'-epimerase, but one fetus of 16 weeks' gestation had liver enzyme activity comparable with that of children and adults. In epimerase deficiency, when the amount of entering galactose is low, an elevated level of galactose 1-phosphate in red blood cells may be reduced to normal but the UDP-galactose level stays elevated. The gene for epimerase has been assigned to human chromosome 1.

Alternative Pathway: Reduction

The polyol pathway was first identified in placenta and seminal vesicles and is responsible for the fructose content of seminal fluid. Two enzymatic reactions involving aldose reductase and sorbitol dehydrogenase catalyze the conversion of glucose to fructose with sorbitol as the intermediate. In certain cells, such as renal collecting duct cells, retinal pigment epithelial cells, and renal glomerular endothelium, and under certain conditions, aldose reductase functions to produce sorbitol which acts as an intracellular osmolyte. The acyclic polyols such as sorbitol, galactitol, and mannitol are the end product of metabolism and have osmotic properties. The presence of galactitol in the urine and plasma of patients with transferase-, galactokinase-, and epimerase-deficiency galactosemia is suggestive of the importance of the reduction of galactose as an alternative pathway. However, the high K_m of this enzyme indicates that reduction will occur only when galactose levels in tissues are very high.

Patients with classical galactosemia have markedly elevated levels of galactitol in plasma and urine, which remain above age-matched control levels after treatment with galactose-free diet, whereas high urinary galactose levels return to normal in all patients. Aldose reductase has been localized to the Schwann cells of peripheral nerves and to renal paptillae cells. Kinetic studies suggest that neither glucose nor galactose are preferred substrates. Only when tissue levels of galactose are much elevated would reduction be important. Aldose reductase activity of lens and other tissue is stimulated by sulfate ions and ATP and is inhibited by various keto acids, fatty acids, and ADP. Increased production of galactitol is felt to play an important role in the pathogenesis of cataracts in the infant with galactose-1-phosphate uridyltransferase, galactokinase, and UDP-galactose epimerase deficiency. The toxicity of polyols in the ocular lens is probably related to their ability to act as osmotically active particles within the lens cells, which leads to accumulation of water and eventually cell dysfunction.

Cataracts are the primary manifestation of disease in untreated patients with galactokinase deficiency, who manifest accumulation of galactitol but not galactose 1-phosphate in tissues. Thus the galactose 1-phosphate and not galactitol toxicity is probably a necessary mediator in both transferase and epimerase deficiencies for expression of hepatic disease, renal tubular dysfunction, and increased red blood cell turnover.

Alternative Pathway: Oxidation

In the absence of galactose-1-phosphate uridyltransferase activity, galactose 1-phosphate and galactose accumulate behind the block. The second alternate pathway, besides reduction of galactose to sugar alcohol, galactitol, is the oxidation of galactose to sugar acid, galactonate. Galactonate, for example, appears in the urine of transferase-deficient individuals. Galactonate can be further metabolized to xylulose, a sugar capable of further metabolism. This pathway accounts for about 50% of oxidation of galactose by galactosaemic patients. Patients with transferase-deficient galactosemia excrete galactonate in urine after galactose is administered, and galactonate has been found in the liver of a transferase-deficient subject.

Disorders of Galactose Metabolism

Clinical Manifestations

Galactose is an important constituent of the complex polysaccharides which are part of cell glycoconjugates, key elements of immunologic determinants, hormones, cell membranes structures, endogenous animal lectins, and numerous other glycoproteins. In addition galactose is incorporated in galactolipids, important structure elements of the central nervous system. It is not difficult to assume that the abnormal galactose metabolism in galactosemic patients could have profound and widespread effects on glycoconjugate structures and their biological function.

Classically, the term 'galactosemia' was associated with an inherited disorder of galactose utilization characterized by malnutrition, liver disease, cataracts, and mental retardation, resulting from the specific deficiency of galactose-1-phosphate uridyltransferase. However, other enzymatic defects with variations of clinical presentation can also lead to galactosemia (**Table 1**). Thus it is preferably better to refer to these abnormalities of metabolism by the specific enzymatic deficiencies which are described below.

Transferase deficiency Failure to thrive is the most common initial clinical sign of galactose-1-phosphate uridyltransferase deficiency, and it is present in all cases. Vomiting or diarrhea is present in almost all patients, usually starting within a few days of milk ingestion. Jaundice, hepatomegaly, or both are present almost as frequently after the first week of life. The jaundice of intrinsic liver disease may be accentuated by severe hemolysis in some

Table 1 Disorders of galactose metabolism

Enzyme deficiency	Primary clinical manifestations
Galactose-1-phosphate uridyltransferase	Failure to thrive
	Emesis/diarrhea
	Jaundice, hepatomegaly
	Cataracts
	Galactosuria
	Gonadal dysfunction
	Developmental delay, neurologic symptoms
	Cataracts
Galactokinase	Similar manifestations as transferase deficiency, but with no liver, kidney, or gonadal dysfunction
UDP-galactose 4'-epimerase	Mostly asymptomatic
	Rarely same manifestations as transferase deficiency but with no gonadal dysfunction

patients. Abnormal liver function tests and ascites may develop. The reason for liver toxicity remains obscure. The liver of affected patients has a characteristic acinar formation, and liver biopsy on occasion has been helpful in establishing the diagnosis. There is high frequency of neonatal death due to *Escherichia coli* sepsis, possibly caused by the inhibition of leucocyte bactericidal activity.

Galactose 1-phosphate and galactitol have been detected in the kidneys of patients with galactosemia. Renal toxicity may manifest as renal tubular dysfunction and a defect in urine acidification mechanisms. Galactosuria, hyperchloremic acidosis, albuminuria, and aminoaciduria may also occur. Hyperchloremic acidosis could be also secondary to the gastrointestinal disturbance and poor food intake. Galactosuria may be intermittent, depending on oral intake, and can disappear within 3–4 days with the use of intravenous glucose. The finding of urinary reducing substances which do not react in a glucose oxidase test should raise the suspicion of galactosemia. This finding, however, does not establish the diagnosis, since galactosuria can also occur in intestinal lactase deficiency and in severe liver disease due to other causes.

Ovarian atrophy appears to be an important manifestation of galactose toxicity, with clinical and biochemical evidence of ovarian dysfunction present in nearly all affected females. The basis of the toxicity has not been defined. The consequences of the gonadal dysfunction range from failure of pubertal development, through primary amenorrhea to secondary amenorrhea or premature menopause (75–76% of affected females). Although gonadal function has been described as early as infancy based on elevations of follicle stimulating hormones

(FSH) and abnormal stimulation testing, no predisposing factor for gonadal dysfunction can be found. Previous recommendations that dietary lactose restriction from birth may be beneficial have in fact not prevented gonadal dysfunction. In the galactosemic male, a complete understanding of gonadal dysfunction has not yet been described. The majority—but not all—of male galactosemic patients had normal pubertal development, and a few individuals have been found to have normal semen.

Cataracts have been observed within a few days of birth. These may be found only on slit-lamp examination and can be missed with an ophthalmoscope, since they consist of punctate lesions in the fetal lens nucleus. Several hypotheses have been postulated to account for their formation and are mentioned above. It seems conclusive that the initiator of the process in rats is galactitol and not galactose 1-phosphate. Galactose 1-phosphate accumulates only late in the process and is absent in patients with galactokinase deficiency who present with cataracts.

Development of mental retardation may be apparent after the first months of life. Signs of increased intracranial pressure and cerebral oedema have been observed as a presenting feature.

Many of the toxicity symptoms can rapidly resolve with institution of dietary lactose restriction. However, a substantial percentage of children have subnormal IQs and speech and language deficits, but rarely devastating neurological sequelae. Most galactosemic patients with lactose restriction are deficient of cognitive functioning in one or more areas. The deficits are variable and do not appear to be related to the age, diagnosis, or the severity of illness at presentation. The pathophysiology of these impairments in galactosemia remains unknown. Several hypotheses are suggested, including toxic oedema due to increased brain galactitol concentrations, changes in the second messenger pathway, and changes of the energy status of the brain.

Galactokinase deficiency Galactokinase deficiency is characterized by the occurrence of cataracts without liver, kidney, or ovarian dysfunction and no increased risk of infections. A number of infants are reported to have pseudotumor cerebri, with very rare neurological involvement, suggesting that retardation is not a feature. The absence of liver and kidney damage in galactokinase deficiency and the presence of damage to these organs in transferase deficiency make it likely that toxicity in the later condition is in some way associated with galactose 1-phosphate formation.

Epimerase deficiency Elevated red cell levels of galactose 1-phosphate with absence of UDP-galactose 4′-epimerase have been described in a patient with normal growth, development, and normal ability to metabolize ingested galactose. Several cases of biochemical deficiency have been described but symptomatic cases are extremely rare. A few had cataracts, sepsis, liver, kidney, and brain abnormalities, including a few with neurosensory deafness. There appears to be no ovarian dysfunction. The absence of ovarian dysfunction suggests that elevated UDP-galactose levels may protect the ovary from damage observed in transferase deficiency. Screening programs have been established in Japan, where the incidence is reported to be 1 in 23 000. In epimerase deficiency, when dietary galactose is low, galactose 1-phosphate concentrations in red blood cells may be reduced to normal, but UDP-galactose concentrations remain elevated. Despite the many phenotypic similarities between transferase and epimerase deficiency, the latter is characterized by elevated red cell levels of UDP-galactose even with modest galactose intake.

Diagnosis

The presence of reducing substance in urine which does not react with glucose oxidase reagents is consistent with galactosuria; however, occasionally some infants (particularly premature babies) also develop galactosuria. It is important to note that the presence of lactose, fructose, and pentose in the urine may give the same results. The presence of cataracts in infants without other systemic symptoms suggests the possibility of galactokinase deficiency. The presence of cataracts in older patients with the absence of gastrointestinal dysfunction or failure to thrive in galactosemic patients helps to differentiate between galactokinase deficiency and transferase deficiency.

The diagnosis of transferase deficiency is suggested by abnormally high amounts of red cell galactose 1-phosphate and confirmed by direct assay of red cell transferase activity. The red cell UDP-glucose consumption test may help to differentiate homozygous patients with a complete absence of transferase in red cells from heterozygous patients who have intermediate levels. Normal red cell values are of 6 mmol UDP-glucose consumed per hour per millilitre of red blood cells. In galactokinase deficiency the diagnosis can be made by the presence of normal amounts of galactose-1-phosphate uridyltransferase and the absence of galactokinase in the red blood cells.

Galactose-1-phosphate uridyltransferase deficiency can be diagnosed prenatally, by assay of galactose-1-phosphate uridyltransferase activity in cultured amniotic fluid cells or chorionic villi, and by galactitol measurement in amniotic fluid supernatant. The perinatal diagnosis is undertaken rarely, because the transferase deficiency is seen as a treatable condition.

Methods for mass screening of newborns for galactosemia are available, although galactosemia is rare. The incidence in Norway is 1 in 96 000, in Sweden 1 in 81 000, in the USA 1 in 62 000, in Switzerland 1 in 58 000, in Germany 1 in 40 000, and the worldwide incidence is about 1 in 70 000. Newborn screening has not been introduced in Great Britain, the Netherlands, or in some states of the USA. Most newborn screening programs designed for the detection of anomalies of galactose metabolism use tests to measure either blood galactose or the activity of galactose-1-phosphate uridyltransferase. Beutler and Baluda developed a fluorescence test in which the activity of uridyltransferase in the dried blood spot is required for the reduction of NADP, yielding fluorescence under long-wave ultraviolet light; the intensity of the fluorescence corresponds to the activity of uridyltransferase. The main advantage of this test is that it can be completed in short time, although false positive results do occur. The disadvantage of this test is that patients with galactokinase deficiency are not detected by this method. Guthrie and Paigen described a more efficient test using the principle of metabolite inhibition; galactose inhibited the growth of an *E. coli* mutant strain lacking uridyltransferase. Later, Paigen used an *E. coli* mutant strain which lacks UDP-galactose 4′-cpimerase activity. Using the Paigen test it is possible to detect galactokinase and uridyltransferase deficiencies. Epimerase deficiency can also be detected by the Paigen test if alkaline phosphatase is added to hydrolyze galactose phosphatase. In many screening laboratories the Beutler test is combined with the microbiological Paigen test.

Management

A galactose-free diet is the current treatment for galactosemia. It is important to know that galactose is present not only in milk but in other sources of food. A strict galactose-free diet in galactosemic patients with transferase deficiency is not harmful. The quality of the galactose-free diet and patient compliance are usually monitored by measuring free galactose in plasma and galactose 1-phosphate in erythrocytes.

Growth retardation, cognitive impairment, speech impediment, tremor, ataxia, and ovarian failure are frequent complications in spite of a strict galactose-free diet. Elevated galactose phosphate levels may occur in erythrocytes of even well-treated galactosemic patients. This elevation is attributed to endogenous production of the metabolite. A galactose-free diet is recommended from birth. It is recommended to restrict galactose in the diet of pregnant mothers diagnosed perinatally with transferase deficiency; a galactose-free diet should be started as soon as the diagnosis is made in the infant regardless of any preexisting manifestation of toxicity. The strict galactose-free diet will cause regression of symptoms and findings. It is important for the families to be aware of the high incidence of verbal dyspraxia even on a very strict diet. The speech intervention program and language stimulation are recommended as early as the first year of life. Many patients with normal IQ values who were treated from birth have learning disabilities, speech and language deficit, and psychological problems. Neurological sequelae have been described also in patients on strict galactose-free diets. These sequelae include cerebellar ataxia, tremor, choreoathetosis, and encephalopathy. Gonadal dysfunction in female galactosemic patients is an almost universal finding, even with a strict galactose-free diet. There is no current therapy for ovarian dysfunction except palliative replacement of oestrogen and progesterone. This is suggested in galactosemic females to develop secondary sexual characters and establish regular menses. There is no universal recommendation for the management of newborns screened positive nor for galactosemic heterozygotic patients.

In patients with epimerase deficiency, UDP-glucose cannot be converted to UDP-galactose. Thus a complete absence of galactose from the diet and the lack of formation of UDP-galactose via transferase would have serious consequences. There would be an inability to form complex polysaccharides and an inability to provide an adequate galactose component for brain cerebrosides. The treatment of epimerase deficiency relies on providing a small amount of dietary galactose.

See also: **Early Origins of Disease**: Fetal. **Glucose**: Chemistry and Dietary Sources; Metabolism and Maintenance of Blood Glucose Level; Glucose Tolerance. **Glycemic Index**. **Inborn Errors of Metabolism**: Classification and Biochemical Aspects. **Liver Disorders**.

Further Reading

Acosta PB and Gross KC (1995) Hidden sources of galactose in the environment. *European Journal of Paediatrics* **154**(supplement 2): S87–92.

Berry GT (1995) The role of polyols in the pathophysiology of hypergalactosemia. *European Journal of Paediatrics* **154**(supplement 2): S53–64.

Beutler E and Baluda M (1996) Biochemical properties of the human red cell galactose-1-phosphate uridyl transferase (UDP Glucose: alpha-D Galactose-phosphate uridyl transferase) from normal and mutant subjects. *Laboratory and Clinical Medicine* **67**: 947.

Gitzelmann R and Boshard NU (1995) Partial deficiency of galactose-1-phosphate uridyltransferase. *European Journal of Paediatrics* **154**(supplement 2): S40–44.

Jakobs C, Vleijer W, Allen Y, and Holton JB (1995) Prenatal diagnosis of galactosemia. *European Journal of Paediatrics* **154**(supplement 2): S33–36.

Jakobs C, Schweitzer S, and Dorland B (1995) Galactitol in galactosemia. *European Journal of Paediatrics* **154**(supplement 2): S50–52.

Kaufman FR, McBride-Chang C, Morris F, Wolf J, and Nelson M (1995) Cognitive functioning, neurologic starters and the brain imaging in galactosemia. *European Journal of Paediatrics* **154**(supplement 2): 2–5.

Liu Y, Vanhooke JL, and Perry PA (1996) UDP-galactose 4-epimerase: NAD$^+$ content and a charge-transfer band associated with the substrate-induced conformational transition. *Biochemistry* **35**(23): 7615–7620.

Ng WG, Xu YK, Kauffman DR, and Donnell GN (1989) Deficit of uridine diphosphate galactose in galactosemia. *Journal of Inherited and Metabolic Disease* **12**: 257–266.

Sagal S (1995) Defective galactosylation in galactosemia; low cell UDP galactose an explanation? *European Journal of Paediatrics* **154**(supplement 2): S65–71.

Segal S (1989) Disorders of galactose metabolism. In: Scriver CR, Beaudet AL, Sly WS, and Vale D (eds.) *The Metabolic Basis of Inherited Disease*, 6th edn, pp. 453–480. New York: McGraw-Hill.

Segal S (1995) Galactosemia unsolved. *European Journal of Paediatrics* **154**(supplement 2): S97–102.

Schweitzer S (1995) Newborn mass screening of galactosemia. *European Journal of Paediatrics* **154**(supplement 2): S37–39.

GALL BLADDER DISORDERS

B Nejadnik and L Cheskin, Johns Hopkins
University, Baltimore, MD, USA

The incidence of gall bladder disease in the United States exceeds 20 million cases annually. The total cost of gall bladder disease in the United States is more than that of any other gastrointestinal illness, including colorectal cancer and peptic ulcer disease.

Gall bladder disease has an intimate relationship with diet and nutrition. On the one hand, there has been a great deal of interest in the role of dietary constituents and nutritional habits in the etiology of gall bladder disease. On the other hand, an individual's nutritional status has a direct impact on the risk of acquiring gall stones. For instance, obesity as well as rapid weight loss and total parenteral nutrition (TPN) predispose the patient to a higher risk of gall bladder disease. Of course, there are multiple other risk factors that play an important role in the formation and manifestations of gall bladder disease, including female gender, family history of first-degree relative with gall stone disease, pregnancy, and drug use. Approximately three-fourths of gall stones detected in the general population are cholesterol gall stones.

According to a large study of the Danish population published in 1991, the 5-year incidence of gall stones in men and women aged 30 years was 0.3% and 1.4%, respectively. At age 60, the incidence had increased to 3.3% and 3.7% for men and women, respectively. It seems that the difference in incidence between men and women disappears with age. This may be related to the difference in estrogenic hormones between the two genders, which follows the same pattern.

Normal Biliary Physiology

Bile, which is formed in the hepatic lobules, is secreted into the canaliculi, small bile ductules, and larger bile ducts that drain it into portal tracts. Interlobular bile ducts join to form larger septal bile ducts that coalesce to form the right and left hepatic ducts, which in turn join to form the common hepatic duct. The common hepatic duct is joined by the cystic duct of the gall bladder to form the common bile duct, which enters the duodenum (often after joining the main pancreatic duct) through the ampulla of Vater.

The largest bile components are water (82%), bile acids (12%), lecithin and other phospholipids (4%), and unesterified cholesterol (0.7%). The total daily basal secretion of hepatic bile is approximately 500–600 ml. The primary bile acids, cholic acid and chenodeoxycholic acid, are synthesized from cholesterol in the liver, conjugated with glycine or taurine, and excreted into the bile. Secondary bile acids, including deoxycholate and lithocholate, are formed in the colon as bacterial metabolites of the primary bile acids. The normal bile acid pool size is approximately 2–4 g. Bile salts play an important role not only in facilitating the biliary excretion of cholesterol but also in intestinal absorption of dietary fats. They are absorbed passively in the entire gut and actively absorbed by the terminal ileum. The bile acid pool circulates approximately 5–10 times daily.

Cholesterol is poorly soluble in water, and its solubility in bile depends on its lipid concentration and the quantity of bile acids and lecithin. Usually, cholesterol is solubilized and forms mixed micelles. Supersaturation of cholesterol provokes the precipitation of cholesterol crystals in bile.

Cholecystokinin (CCK) is the most powerful stimulator of gall bladder contraction. It is released from the duodenal mucosa in response to the ingestion of fats and amino acids. CCK plays its role through contraction of the gall bladder, reducing resistance of the sphincter of Oddi, increasing hepatic secretion of bile, and therefore enhancing flow of biliary contents into the duodenum.

Pathophysiology of Stone Formation

Morphology and Composition

There are three kinds of gall stone: cholesterol, black pigment, or brown pigment stones. Cholesterol stones constitute 75–90% of all gall stones. They are composed purely of cholesterol or have cholesterol as the major chemical constituent. Most cholesterol gall stones are of mixed composition. Pigmented stones get their color and their name from precipitated bilirubin. Increased production of unconjugated bilirubin causes black pigmentation. Formation of black pigment stones is typically associated with chronic hemolysis, cirrhosis, and pancreatitis. Brown pigment stones are usually associated with infection. Cytoskeletons of bacteria can be seen microscopically in brown pigment stones, and bacterial infection seems to be a prerequisite for brown stone formation.

Pathogenesis

Three factors have been recognized in gall stone formation: cholesterol supersaturation, accelerated nucleation, and gall bladder hypomotility. Among these, the degree of cholesterol saturation in gall bladder bile is the most important factor in crystal formation.

Cholesterol supersaturation Cholesterol is hydrophobic and not easily soluble in water. Its solubility is dependent on the presence of bile salts and lecithin. It is easy to imagine that as the ratio of cholesterol to bile salts and lecithin increases, cholesterol precipitation, crystal formation, and therefore stone formation ensue.

Nucleating and antinucleating factors Pronucleators include mucin glycoproteins, immunoglobulin G (IgG) and IgM, aminopeptidase N, haptoglobin, and α_1 acid glycoprotein; the most prominent of these is mucin glycoproteins. The hydrophobic centers of these proteins can bind to cholesterol, phospholipids, and bilirubin.

Gall bladder hypomotility The gall bladder concentrates and acidifies the bile. The most powerful stimulant of gall bladder contraction is CCK. CCK release is stimulated by (in order of decreasing potency) long-chain fatty acids, amino acids, and carbohydrates.

Risk Factors Associated with Cholesterol Gall Stone Formation

Major risk factors predisposing to gall stones are age, sex, genetic profile, nutritional status (including the route of nutrition), hormones, drugs, and some other diseases such as diseases of the terminal ileum. A summary of these elements is provided in **Table 1**.

Age, sex, and genetic profile As mentioned previously, women are affected more than men, and the incidence of gall stone increases with age. A positive family history of gall bladder disease increases risk to more than twice that of the general population. Native Americans and Scandinavians are more predisposed to this disease than other ethnic groups.

Obesity, weight loss, and total parenteral nutrition Obesity is a well-known risk factor for cholelithiasis. A large prospective study of obese women found a strong linear association between

Table 1 Risk factors associated with cholesterol gall stone formation

Age
Female gender
Genetics
    Prima Indians
    Chileans
    Family history of gall stone
Pregnancy
Small bowel diseases
    Crohn's disease
    Terminal ileum resection
Drugs
    Estrogens
    Ceftriaxone
    Lipid-lowering agents (Clofibrate)
    Octreotide
Nutritional status
    Obesity
    Rapid weight loss
    Total parenteral nutrition
    Diabetes
Other conditions
    Immobility
    Cirrhosis
    Spinal cord injury

body mass index and the reported incidence of cholelithiasis. In this study, those with the highest body mass index ($>45 \, \mathrm{kg/m^2}$) had a 7-fold increased risk of development of gall stones compared to non-obese controls. This relationship is somewhat weaker in men than in women. The association between obesity and gall stone formation may result from increased secretion of cholesterol into the bile as a result of higher 3-hydroxy-3-methylglutaryl-coenzyme A (HMG-CoA).

In studies of gall bladder motility in obese patients, no impairment in gall bladder contraction has been documented. Abnormal processing of the cholecystokinin receptor gene has been reported in one obese patient who had gall stones. Such an abnormality could lead to gall bladder stasis and ultimately to cholelithiasis.

Rapid weight loss is a recognized risk factor for cholesterol gall stone formation. As many as 30% of obese patients on restricted calorie intake may develop (usually asymptomatic) gall stones. This rate is higher, up to 50%, for obese patients who undergo gastric bypass surgery. It has been shown that hepatic cholesterol secretion increases in patients with low calorie intake. Other predisposing factors for the same patients are increased mucin secretion and decreased gall bladder motility. Gall stone formation may be prevented in this high-risk population possibly through prophylactic administration of a bile salt, ursodeoxycholic acid.

Low-fat diet by itself seems to be a predisposing factor. Cholecchia *et al.* studied 32 gall-stone-free obese patients and concluded that during a significant weight loss period, 54% of subjects following the low-fat diet, but none in the high-fat intake group, formed asymptomatic gall stones.

Total parenteral nutrition (TPN) is associated with the development of acalculous cholecystitis as well as cholelithiasis, cholecystitis, and gall bladder sludge. The latter can occur as early as 3 weeks after initiation of TPN. After 3 or 4 months of TPN, approximately 45% of patients will develop gall stones. Prolonged fasting resulting in gall bladder hypomotility seems to be the major cause of the bile stasis. Cholecystokinin–octapeptide 50 ng/kg intravenous infusion for 10 minutes once daily has been shown to prevent gall bladder sludge and gall stone formation in patients on TPN.

Hormones and drugs Hormones such as estrogen and progesterone have a significant effect on the risk of gall stone formation. One interesting illustration of these effects is seen in pregnant woman. Increased estrogen levels during pregnancy cause increased cholesterol secretion and supersaturation of bile, which results in more lithogenic bile. Progesterone, on the other hand, reduces gall bladder motility, resulting in stasis and sludge formation in 30% of cases.

Among lipid-lowering drugs, Clofibrate seems to have the greatest association with increased gall stone formation. The role of statins in gall bladder disease remains to be elucidated. Approximately one-third of patients treated with octreotide, a somatostatin analog, develop new gall stones. Ceftriaxone (Rocephin) has been shown to cause sludge formation in children. A large fraction of ceftriaxone is secreted in bile (40%) and forms complexes with calcium, resulting in an insoluble salt. The sludge disappears when ceftriaxone is discontinued.

Diet and lipid profile The ingestion of refined sugars has been shown to be associated with gall stone disease. However, no such association has been shown for alcohol or tobacco. It is not clear if high serum cholesterol predisposes to gall stone formation. In fact, the contrary has been shown in some studies. This is also the case for dietary cholesterol ingestion, which was shown to be a protective factor for gall stone formation in one study. Hypertriglyceridemia, on the other hand, is positively associated with an increased incidence of gall stones.

Dietary antioxidant deficiency, particularly of α-tocopherol, as well as low intakes of linoleic acid and essential amino acids may increase the incidence of gall stone disease. One study showed that there is an inverse correlation between the incidence of gall stone disease and the amount of certain foods, particularly fish and fruits, consumed per day. The gall stone subjects ate fewer meals per day but ate more cereals, oils, sugars, and meats. They also had more fluctuation in their weight. They consumed less fiber, folate, magnesium, vitamins, and minerals.

Other conditions predisposing to gall bladder disease Insulin-resistant diabetes predisposes to cholelithiasis. A Swedish study showed that the prevalence of gall stones in Crohn's disease was twice that seen in the general population. Cirrhosis is another major risk factor for gall stones. The incidence of gall stone formation in cirrhosis is 10 times that seen in the general population. The incidence increases with the severity of cirrhosis, being worse in Child's class B and C disease and in patients with higher body mass index. High estrogen level and reduced hepatic synthesis and transport of bile salts are reasons for the increased risk in cirrhosis. The Physicians' Health Study showed that 30 minutes of endurance-type exercise five times per week prevents approximately one-third of cases of symptomatic gall stones in men. The Nurses' Health Study confirmed the same trend in women.

Clinical Manifestations and Diagnosis of Gall Stone Disease

Approximately 80% of people with gall stones are asymptomatic. The presentation of gall bladder disease can be episodic pain when a brief cystic duct obstruction occurs or acute cholecystitis when the obstruction lasts longer and results in local and relatively extensive inflammation and edema. The complications include infection of the biliary system (cholangitis) and pancreatitis.

Symptoms and Signs

Pain related to the gall bladder is usually felt in the right upper quadrant or in the epigastrium. It may radiate to the back, going around the right flank. In some cases, it may radiate to the shoulder area or be felt in the chest. In acute cholecystitis, the pain is steady, as opposed to cramping or colicky. It typically occurs after a meal and may be accompanied by nausea and vomiting. Continuous obstruction of the cystic duct causes gall bladder distention and inflammation. Extension of the inflammation into the common bile duct area may cause edema and obstruction of the duct, resulting in jaundice. The physical signs of acute cholecystitis include right upper quadrant tenderness and Murphy's sign, which refers to severe right upper quadrant tenderness and inhibition of inspiration on deep palpation under the right subcostal margin.

Laboratory Findings

In acute cholecystitis, liver enzymes are normal or mildly elevated. Marked increase in liver enzymes should raise the possibility of bile duct obstruction concomitant with, or instead of, acute cholecystitis. In the case of bile duct obstruction, alanine aminotransferase and aspartate aminotransferase increase rapidly to levels 10 times normal and then decrease quickly toward normal, even if the obstruction persists. Alkaline phosphatase, on the other hand, will continue to increase unless the obstruction resolves. Mild to moderate leukocytosis is common in acute cholecystitis. Bile levels may increase if the obstruction lasts long enough.

Imaging

Ultrasonography, with a sensitivity of 96%, is a major diagnostic tool in gall bladder disease. The sonographic evidence of acute cholecystitis includes gall bladder size, its wall thickness, and pericholecystic fluid conformation. Among these signs, the latter is the most sensitive. Computed tomography is less sensitive and more expensive than ultrasonography. Its main role is to rule out other intra-abdominal processes. Magnetic resonance imaging has become an important means of detecting bile duct stones. Its sensitivity is approximately 85% for bile duct stones. Oral cholecystography has almost completely been replaced by ultrasonography. Endoscopic retrograde cholangiopancreatography (ERCP) is mostly used for its diagnostic and especially its therapeutic capability for removing bile duct stones. Hepatobiliary scintigraphy consists of the uptake by the gall bladder of an intravenously administered, ^{99m}Tc-labeled iminodiacetic acid derivative. The liver excretes the isotope into the bile ducts. A normal hepatobiliary scan using diisopropyliminodiacetic acid effectively rules out acute cholecystitis. If, on the other hand, the isotope does not appear in the bile ducts within 4 h, the likelihood of acute cholecystitis is very high.

Management

The decision about the treatment of gall stones will depend strongly on the presentation of the patient. Asymptomatic gall stones should not be treated surgically. This recommendation is based on multiple studies, including several prospective studies, that showed that patients with asymptomatic gall stones, observed over many years, develop symptoms or biliary complications only on rare occasions. In one study of 123 people with asymptomatic gall stones followed for 11–24 years, biliary pain developed in 2% during each of the first 5 years, followed by a decreasing incidence thereafter. Complications were seen in only 3 people and were preceded by warning signs of pain in all cases.

Prophylactic cholecystectomy has been performed in diabetic patients because of concern of higher rates of complications from acute cholecystitis and also in patients with sickle cell disease. In the latter group, the main reason for prophylactic cholecystectomy is that the pain of sickle crises is not easily distinguished from acute cholecystitis. Cholecystectomy should be undertaken in patients with 'porcelain' gall bladder and Native Americans with gall stones because these groups have a higher incidence of gall bladder carcinoma. However, the risk of gall bladder carcinoma is not high enough to justify cholecystectomy in other asymptomatic patients. Symptomatic gall stones should be treated surgically unless contraindicated. More than 60% of patients with symptomatic gall stones will have recurrent episodes within 1 or 2 years. Moreover, approximately 3% will develop biliary complications annually.

Nutritional Considerations

Prevention of gall stone formation   The importance of nutritional factors in the formation of gall stones was discussed previously. Thus, modification of those risk factors (obesity, rapid weight loss, TPN, etc.) or application of a remedy to correct the underlying offensive mechanism will perhaps reduce the chance of gall stone formation.

Some studies have shown beneficial effects of dietary fiber in the prevention of gall bladder disease during weight loss in obese patients. However, this effect seems to be limited. During rapid weight loss, patients are occasionally given a small amount of dietary fat in order to reduce the risk of gall stone formation. Some studies have confirmed this technique, especially when a lower amount of fat has been used (2 vs. 10 g fat/day); others have shown that this strategy is not effective when the comparison was made between higher amounts (16 vs. 30 g fat/day). However, some studies support the concept that factors other than gall bladder motility are involved in gall stone formation in patients undergoing rapid weight loss. The weight loss by itself will eventually be beneficial in the prevention of future gall stones.

In one study, fish oil (n-3-polyunsaturated fatty acids) was shown to prevent cholesterol gall stone formation in obese women during rapid weight loss.

A high-calcium diet has also been prescribed in order to change the output of deoxycholic acid. This diet has a modest beneficial effect on gall stone formation.

Multiple small meals as opposed to one or two larger meals per day will empty the gall bladder on a regular basis and prevent stasis. It also prevents long interruptions of the enterohepatic circulation of bile acids.

Cholecystokinin increases bile acid synthesis and, more important, promotes gall bladder contraction. Therefore, CCK is theoretically an effective agent in the prevention of gall stones in patients with TPN. In practice, though, this effect seems to be quite variable.

The Third National Health and Nutrition Examination Survey found that a history of clinical or asymptomatic gall stones was inversely correlated with serum ascorbic acid levels in women but not in men. Coffee consumption has been found to be associated with a reduced risk of symptomatic gall stones. Consumption of two or three cups of regular coffee per day reduces the risk of symptomatic gall stones by approximately 40% over 10 years. Table 2 summarizes the different preventive measures available to reduce the risk of gall stone formation.

Complementary and alternative medicine Factors reducing hyperinsulinemia, such as dietary unrefined carbohydrates and aerobic exercise, have been suggested to reduce the risk of cholelithiasis. Holistic health providers have been prescribing herbal medicines, such as turmeric, Oregon grape, bupleurum, and coin grass, with the belief that they may reduce gall bladder inflammation and relieve liver congestion.

Medical Treatment

Ursodeoxycholic acid is approved for gall stone dissolution in appropriate patients. This drug is a bile acid that forms soluble vesicles and prolongs the nucleation time of bile. Moreover, it inhibits HMG-CoA reductase and secondarily reduces cholesterol saturation. A year of treatment with ursodeoxycholic acid will result in complete dissolution of 50% of gall stones. This agent works on the surface of the stones; thus, the larger the stone, the less the efficacy of ursodeoxycholic acid. This drug is used in patients who refuse surgery or have a high risk for cholecystectomy. Shiffman *et al.* studied the efficacy of ursodeoxycholic acid in patients undergoing dietary-induced weight reduction and found it to be highly effective in preventing gall stone formation. The cost of this drug ($4 per day) is an important impediment for its long-term use.

Nonsteroidal antiinflammatory drugs may have some beneficial effect in the prevention of gall stone formation, but studies have not been conclusive. Extracorporeal shock wave lithotripsy has been used for fragmentation of gall stones by high-amplitude

Table 2 Prevention of gall stone formation

Dietary fiber	Limited efficacy
During rapid weight less	
Small amount of dietary fats	Depends on the amount of fat
Fish oil	Prevents cholesterol gall stone formation in obese women
Nonsteroidal antiinflammatory drugs	Studies have not been conclusive
Ursodeoxycholic acid	Effective in secondary prevention
Reduce insulin resistance	
Exercise	
Gradual weight loss	
During total parenteral nutrition	
Cholecystokinin	Increases bile acid synthesis and promotes gall bladder contraction; efficacy variable
Nutritional factors	
Ascorbic acid	Inverse correlation with gall stone formation in women but not in men
Reduce ingestion of refined sugars	Prevents insulin resistance and secondarily prevents gall bladder immobility
Dietary antioxidants, fiber, folate, magnesium, vitamins, minerals, linoleic acid, and essential amino acids	Unknown mechanism
Multiple small meals as opposed to few large meals	Prevents gall bladder stasis
High-calcium diet	Preventive
Coffee consumption	May reduce risk of symptomatic gall stone

shock waves generated by external piezoelectric devices. The waves are guided toward the stones by ultrasound imaging. This procedure was first used for kidney stones. Its efficacy in gall bladder stone treatment has been much less impressive. Its complications are the consequence of migration of stone fragments and include postprocedure biliary colic and pancreatitis. The availability of laparoscopic cholecystectomy has limited the need for lithotripsy.

Surgical Treatment

Patients admitted with suspected acute cholecystitis should initially be made NPO (nothing by mouth) and intravenously hydrated. Administration of broad-spectrum antibiotics early in the course is recommended because secondary infection often supervenes in what is initially a noninfectious process. If the diagnosis of acute cholecystitis is made within 24–48 h of onset of symptoms, early surgery leads to reduced morbidity and mortality rates.

Laparoscopic cholecystectomy   The first successful laparoscopic cholecystectomy in Europe in 1987 transformed gall bladder surgery very rapidly. The minimal injury to the abdominal wall tissues resulted in faster discharge and rapid return to normal activities. In approximately 1 in 10 patients, laparoscopic cholecystectomy must be converted to open surgery. The rates of complications in both procedures are approximately 5%.

Laparotomy (open cholecystectomy)   Today, open cholecystectomy is almost always a consequence of conversion of a laparoscopic procedure. On rare occasions, such as when there is suspicion of gall bladder cancer, a history of prior extensive abdominal surgery resulting in adhesions, or in patients with common bile duct stones that cannot be removed by ERCP, surgeons will perform open cholecystectomy at the outset of the operation.

Conclusions

Gall bladder disease is intimately tied to nutrition with respect to its etiology, treatment, and prevention. Attention to nutritional considerations can have a meaningful impact in particular on the prevalence and incidence of asymptomatic and symptomatic gall stones. Certain nutriments can change the likelihood of gall stone formation or change the course for preexisting stones. Nutritional status, including obesity and rapid weight loss, is an important predisposing factor. TPN increases the risk of gall stones considerably. Diagnosis of gall stone disease is based on history and physical examination as well as the laboratory and ultrasonographic evidence. Therapeutic decisions depend on the patient's presentation. Asymptomatic patients should not be treated surgically, except those with sickle cell disease or if there is a higher risk of gall bladder carcinoma (as in Native Americans and in patients with porcelain gall bladder). Laparoscopic surgery is the treatment of choice in symptomatic patients.

Nutritional interventions, such as fish oil, ascorbic acid, and coffee, seem to be protective against gall stone formation. Dietary fiber and the administration of small amounts of dietary fat have shown limited preventative efficacy for patients at higher risk of gall stone formation. CCK may be useful in patients receiving TPN. Ursodeoxycholic acid is effective in preventing gall stone formation in patients undergoing diet-induced weight reduction. Some authors have recommended the use of nonsteroidal antiinflammatory drugs in the prevention of gall stones, but studies have not been conclusive.

See also: **Cholesterol**: Sources, Absorption, Function and Metabolism; Factors Determining Blood Levels. **Diabetes Mellitus**: Etiology and Epidemiology. **Obesity**: Complications.

Further Reading

Andersen T (1992) Liver and gall bladder disease before and after very-low-calorie diets. *American Journal of Clinical Nutrition* **56**(1 supplement): 235S–239S.

Dam H (1969) Nutritional aspects of gall stone formation with particular reference to alimentary production of gall stones in laboratory animals. *World Review of Nutrition and Dietetics* **11**: 199–239.

Festi D, Colecchia A, Larocca A *et al.* (2000) Review: Low caloric intake and gall bladder motor function. *Alimentary Pharmacology and Therapeutics* **14**(supplement 2): 51–53.

Hayes KC, Livingston A, and Trautwein EA (1992) Dietary impact on biliary lipids and gall stones. *Annual Review of Nutrition* **12**: 299–326.

Hofmann AF (1988) Pathogenesis of cholesterol gall stones. *Journal of Clinical Gastroenterology* **10**(supplement 2): S1–S11.

Lee SP and Ko CW (2003) gall stones. In *Yamada Textbook of Gastroenterology*.

Rescorla FJ (1997) Cholelithiasis, cholecystitis, and common bile duct stones. *Current Opinion in Pediatrics* **9**(3): 276–282.

Rosen GH (1992) Somatostatin and its analogs in the short bowel syndrome. *Nutrition in Clinical Practice* **7**(2): 81–85.

Trotman BW (1991) Pigment gall stone disease. *Gastroenterology Clinics of North America* **20**(1): 111–126.

Geriatric Nutrition *see* **Older People**: Physiological Changes; Nutritional Requirements; Nutrition-Related Problems; Nutritional Management of Geriatric Patients

GLUCOSE

Contents
Chemistry and Dietary Sources
Metabolism and Maintenance of Blood Glucose Level
Glucose Tolerance

Chemistry and Dietary Sources

D J A Jenkins, R de Souza, L S A Augustin and C W C Kendall, University of Toronto, Toronto, ON, Canada

Glucose and its polymers are important energy sources for living organisms and structural components of plants. Because of the diversity of compounds in which glucose occurs, it may be helpful to first discuss nomenclature.

Nomenclature and Chemical Structure

Glucose

The compound D-glucose (Greek *gleucos*, 'sweet wine') or dextrose is 2,3,4,5,6-pentahydroxyhexaldehyde, more conventionally expressed as $C_6H_{12}O_6$, with a molecular weight of 180.16 kDa. Glucose is readily soluble in water in a powder form. Below 50 °C, α-D-glucose hydrate is the stable form; at 50 °C the anhydrous form is obtained; and at higher temperatures, α-D-glucose is obtained. Glucose is also present in the diet as part of the disaccharides sucrose (glucose and fructose), lactose (glucose and galactose), and maltose (glucose).

Glucose Oligosaccharides

Oligosaccharides (Greek *oligo*, 'few') are sugar polymers; the term usually refers to compounds containing 2–9 units but may include polymers containing up to 19 units. The dimer, trimer, and tetramer forms in which glucose molecules are joined by (1–4) linkages are referred to as maltose, maltotriose, and maltotetrose, respectively, since these substances are the products of starch digestion in the malting process. Sucrose, maltose, and lactose are common dietary disaccharides.

Starches

Starches are large-molecular-weight, α-linked polymers of glucose $(C_6H_{10}O_5)n$. Most starches show a mixture of $\alpha(1–4)$ and $\alpha(1–6)$ linkages. The $\alpha(1–4)$-linked polymer forms a linear structure that allows for hydrogen bonding between polymer chains and a more compact starch structure. Introduction of (1–6) linkages results in branch points and a more open structure that allows the (1–4)-linked backbone with the hemiacetal bond in the alpha configuration to coil like a spring into a helical form. Branched starches with the (1–6) linkage are more readily hydrated and digested compared to the (1–4)-linked linear starch. The (1–4)-linked starches are referred to as amylose starch, and (1–6)-linked starches are amylopectin starches.

Resistant Starch

Resistant starches are defined by their resistance to digestion in the human upper gastrointestinal tract. As with the term 'dietary fiber,' the definition is largely physiological. One proposed classification divides resistant starches into three classes: RS_1, RS_2, and RS_3. The first class, RS_1, is starch that escapes small intestinal digestion owing to the food form and incomplete enzymatic attack (e.g., large particle size or compact nature of food, or starch entrapment by dietary fiber). The second, RS_2, includes the more crystalline starches that resist digestion (e.g., high-amylose starches that resist gelatinization). The RS_3 starches are retrograded starches (e.g., high-amylose starches that upon cooling after cooking form a compact, hydrogen-bonded crystalline structure that excludes water).

Cellulose

Like starch, cellulose is a (1–4)-linked glucose polymer $(C_6H_{10}O_5)n$, but in this instance the glucose molecules are β-linked, allowing the development of a linear polymer with strong intrachain hydrogen bonding. Cellulose polymers may consist of as many as 10 000 glucose monomer units. Cellulose is both resistant to small intestinal digestion and insoluble in cold or hot water and most dilute acids and alkali. It is partially degraded by colonic bacteria; the proportion degraded is dependent on the source, with cellulose from vegetables broken down to a greater extent than cellulose from cereals such as wheat.

β-Glucans

In many ways, these predominantly (1–4)-linked glucose polymers are the cellulose equivalent of the starch amylopectin. Here, it is the (1–3) linkages interspersed throughout the polymer that prevent the compact structure achieved with the cellulose polymer where only the (1–4) linkages exist. As a result of the more open molecular structure of the β-glucan, unlike cellulose, it is readily hydrated and soluble in water, forming a solution of high viscosity. The viscosity, in turn, is dependent on the molecular weight and the presence of the (1–3) linkages. The greater the molecular weight, the greater the viscosity. Thus, reduction of molecular weight by acid or enzymatic hydrolysis, which may also occur during food processing, may greatly reduce viscosity. The common feature shared by cellulose and the β-glucans is that both are resistant to digestion by small intestinal enzymes. However, whereas cellulose is only partially fermented by the colonic bacteria, β-glucans are completely fermented.

Hemicellulose

The term 'hemicellulose' should not be taken to imply a class of (1–4)-linked glucose polymers. The similarity with cellulose lies not in the chemical structure but in the fact that hemicellulose is also insoluble in hot or cold water or hot dilute acid. It is, however, soluble in dilute alkali. The polymeric structure is heterosaccharitic with two or more sugars (e.g., arabinoxylans found in cereals), with a relatively small molecular size (50–200 saccharide units).

Occurrence

Glucose is the primary carbohydrate energy source of vertebrates. In healthy humans, fasting blood glucose levels are approximately 3.5–5.5 mmol/l (depending on the laboratory) and increase postprandially to values considerably less than 10 mmol/l (the renal threshold for complete reabsorption, above which glucose 'spills' over into the urine). Blood levels higher than 7.8 mmol/l 2 h after a 75-g glucose load are one of the diagnostic criteria for diabetes. Glucose is stored as glycogen, an α-linked polymer, predominantly in the liver and muscles ('animal starch'). On average, a 70-kg man may store 500 g of glycogen. Glucose can also be synthesized de novo by gluconeogenesis from the gluconeogenic amino acids lactate, glycerol, and pyruvate.

Erythrocytes, renal tissue, and nervous tissue require glucose as an energy source. In erythrocytes and renal tissue, the glucose is not oxidized but is returned to the liver as part of the Cori cycle for glucose synthesis. The brain oxidizes glucose and requires 140 g per day. From this figure the carbohydrate requirement was derived in the recent DRI assessment (**Table 1**). Despite this requirement, carbohydrate is still recommended to comprise between 45 and 65% of dietary calories.

Glucose is present in fruit and vegetables and, although less sweet on a per gram basis than fructose or sucrose, it is responsible together with fructose and sucrose for the sweet taste of vegetables and fruit. With the exception of fruit such as green banana, seeds (grain and dried legumes), and tubers, in which starch is the major carbohydrate form, foods containing glucose, fructose, and sucrose in various ratios comprise the major available (i.e., absorbable in the small intestine) carbohydrate sources. The relative proportions of the sugars have not been generally determined, and data are not available for many foods.

The main sources of dietary starch are cereal grains, dried legumes, and tubers. The major part of the available carbohydrate in these foods is

Table 1 Estimation of brain glucose requirements of adult humans

Glucose consumption (μmol/100 g brain/min)	Estimated brain weight (g)	Brain glucose consumption	
		mg/min	g/day
31–38	1450	81–99	117–142

Based on data from Sokoloff et al. (1977), Gottstein and Held (1979), Scheinberg and Stead (1949), and Reinmuth et al. (1965).

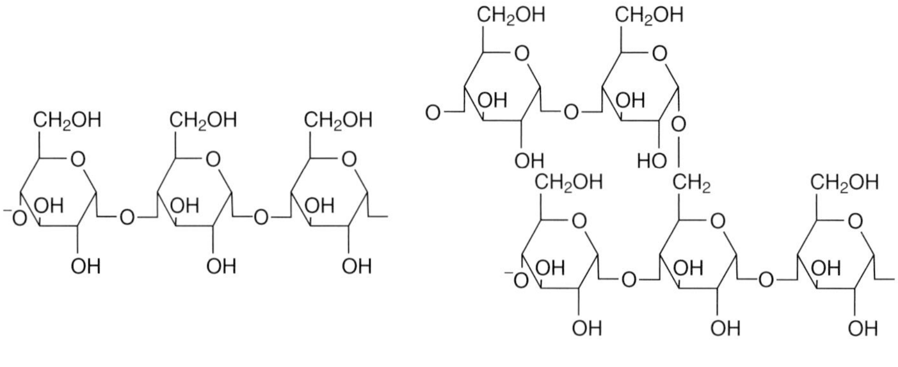

Figure 1 Partial structures of amylose (linear) and amylopectin (branched) starches.

starch. Starches contain both $\alpha(1–4)$ and $\alpha(1–6)$ linkages (i.e., amylose and amylopectin) (**Figure 1**). In most studies amylose predominates, with a ratio of amylose to amylopectin of 2–3:1. In general, legumes contain higher amylose levels than do cereals. Cultivars of corn have been bred with high amylose levels.

Resistant starches comprise a small proportion of most industrialized Western diets. Increased starch malabsorption may be induced by coarse milling or large particle size of cereal grains (e.g., whole-grain pumpernickel or bulgur wheat). Such foods may be said to contain resistant starch (RS_1). Resistant starches that are crystalline in nature and resist hydration (RS_2) are found in green banana, high-amylose corn, and relatively high-amylose legumes (peas, beans, and lentils). Starches, especially high-amylose starches that are cooked and then allowed to cool, undergo retrogradation with more crystalline realignment. These starches (RS_3) are produced in common foods such as potato, rice, and bread. Resistant starches in this category are produced commercially from high-amylose cornstarch by enzymatically debranching the remaining (1–6) linkages and allowing the resulting (1–4)-linked starch to 'retrograde' into a highly crystalline, digestion-resistant starch.

Cellulose is an important structural component of plant cell walls. In human nutrition, it forms an important part of the 'insoluble' dietary fiber component reported in food composition tables. However, values for the actual proportion of the total dietary fiber that is composed of cellulose are only available in special food composition tables for a relatively small number of foods.

From the standpoint of human nutrition, β-glucans are found predominantly in cereals, notably oats and barley, with trace amounts in wheat. In oats, the β-glucan is concentrated in the outer bran layer and may comprise 50% of the dietary fiber value and possibly 8 or 9% of the so-called oat bran derived from standard milling practices. In barley, the β-glucan is more dispersed through the endosperm, and thus a bran concentrate is less easy to achieve. In both cases, high β-glucan cultivars may greatly increase the yield of β-glucan. In addition, 'wet' processing techniques may yield a high-concentration β-glucan bran and purified β-glucan oat gum.

Analysis

Analysis of glucose may involve chemical, enzymatic, electrochemical, and high-performance liquid chromatography (HPLC) systems. Prior to the introduction of enzyme-based analyses, chemical techniques were based on the reducing ability of glucose, and techniques employing copper sulfate were popular. Such techniques were influenced by other reducing sugars and reducing substances, including uric acid and vitamin C. With the introduction of the more specific glucose oxidase-based tests, the chemical tests were abandoned, although there was debate over the potential carcinogenicity of the early chromogens, O-dianizadine and O-toluidine. Later, more specific, hexokinase-based enzyme assays were introduced. Current methods for rapid determination of blood glucose, which no longer require prior precipitation of plasma proteins, involve electrochemical detection. These methods rely on silver electrodes to detect electrons generated by the oxidation of glucose by glucose oxidase contained in membranes on the surface of the electrodes. For determination of glucose and α-limit dextrins resulting from starch digestion, HPLC techniques have proved useful.

Much attention has been given to the analysis of the glucose polymers—starches, resistant starches, cellulose, and β-glucans—in the context of dietary fiber. The ultimate assessment depends on the use of specific enzymes or enzyme systems to break the macromolecules down to their component glucose and other sugars when mixtures containing other polymers (dietary fibers) are being analyzed. These are then assessed by gas chromatography or HPLC and the ratios of the sugars determined. More routine assessment may involve a variety of chemical techniques combined with enzymatic digestion and, in the case of a popular Association of Official Analytical Chemists (AOAC)-approved technique for dietary fiber analysis, with a gravimetric determination. However, there is debate as to whether the resistant starch, which in the gravimetric AOAC technique is analyzed as dietary fiber, should be included as fiber or whether it is physiologically distinct. It is also debated whether a determination of β-glucan is sufficient without knowledge of its viscosity and molecular weight—factors that determine its physiological effect.

Physiology

The physiology of the gastrointestinal absorption of (and the energy retrieved from) the glucose molecule

along the length of the gastrointestinal tract in its various forms is discussed in the following sections, together with the influence of other dietary factors (**Figure 2**).

Absorption

In its simplest form, glucose ingested by mouth is rendered isotonic in the stomach by the gastric juices and expelled through the pylorus into the duodenum, where active transport takes place at the brush border by way of a sodium-linked glucose transporter. The absorbed glucose that is taken up by way of the portal vein suppresses hepatic glucose output but does not markedly alter the glucose balance across the liver. The major part of the absorbed glucose is taken up by muscle and also adipose tissue under the action of insulin. Similarly, sucrose, maltose, and lactose are both split and absorbed at the brush border by the brush border enzymes sucrase–isomaltase, maltase, and lactase. Although sucrose deficiency is exceedingly rare, hypolactasia is common in adult life in most of the world's populations, with the exception of those of northern European origin. Thus, unlike sucrose malabsorption, small-intestinal lactose malabsorption is common, with significant amounts of lactose entering

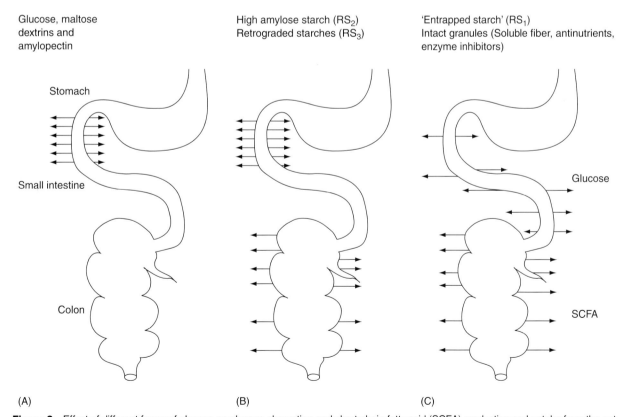

Figure 2 Effect of different forms of glucose on glucose absorption and short-chain fatty acid (SCFA) production and uptake from the gut.

the colon, resulting in gas production, short-chain fatty acid (SCFA) synthesis, and, in some instances, diarrhea.

On the other hand, purified, fully hydrated, cooked amylopectin starch commences digestion in the mouth under the action of salivary amylase. Enzyme activity ceases under the acidic conditions of the stomach and resumes in the duodenum under the action of pancreatic amylase. Amylolytic digestion in both mouth and stomach results predominantly in the production of free glucose, maltose, maltotriose, and the α-limit dextrins of greater polymeric length. The free glucose is taken up by the brush border glucose transporter, and the uptake of maltose and maltotriose is effected by brush border enzymes, notably the sucrase–isomaltase complex.

In both situations, absorption in the small intestine is considered to be complete.

However, foods as eaten do not usually comprise pure glucose and pure amylopectin starch as their carbohydrate components. Many factors influence small-intestinal absorption in terms of both rate and amount (**Table 2**). Some of these factors were previously discussed in connection with amylose and resistant starch.

Food Components

Insoluble fiber may form a coat around starchy foods, limiting the penetration of enzymes and thus reducing the rate and amount digested. Viscous soluble fibers may also reduce the rate of

Table 2 Factors influencing glycemia and gastrointestinal events

Factors influencing the availability of carbohydrate	Physiological effect					
	Glycemia	Stomach, gastric emptying	Small intestine, absorption rate	Motility	Colon	
					Baterial fermentation	Fecal bulk
Food components						
Fiber						
Soluble (viscous)	−	− − −	− −	−?	+++	+
Insoluble	0 ?	+	+	+	+	+++
Macronutrients						
Protein–starch interaction	−	−?	− −	?	+	?
Fat–starch interaction	−	−	− −	?	+	?
Starches						
Amylopectin	+	?	++	?	0	0
Amylose	−	−	− − −	?	++	+
Sugars and glucose polymers						
Glucose	++	−?	+	0	0	0
Maltose	++	−?	+	0	0	0
Maltodextrins	++	0	+	0	0	0
Antinutrients						
Phytates	−	?	−	?	+	?
Tanins	−	?	−	?	+	?
Saponins	?	?	−	?	+	?
Lectins	−	−	−	?	+	?
Amylase inhibitors	−	0	−	?	+	?
Alpha-glucosidase inhibitors	−	0	−	?	+	?
Food processing						
Cooking						
Starch gelatinisation	+	0	++	?	0	0
Starch regtrogradation	−	?	− −	?	+	+
Parboiling (e.g., rice)	−	?	−	?	?	0
Particle size						
Milling						
Crushing	+	+	+	?	0	0
Flaking	+	?	+	?	0	0
Extruding	+	?	+	?	0	0
	−	?	−	?	0	0

+, increase, promote; −, inhibit, reduce; 0, no effect; ?, uncertain.

absorption through prolonging gastric emptying and by acting as a barrier to diffusion in the small intestine. Starch–protein interactions (as seen with gluten in wheat products) and starch–fat interactions have been shown to reduce the rate of digestion, and fat is known to slow gastric emptying. A number of the so-called 'antinutrients' present in foods, notably lectins, phytates, and tannins, have been shown to reduce the digestibility of foods. For example, it is considered that phytate, by binding calcium ions that catalyse starch digestion by amylase, reduces the rate of small-intestinal starch digestion.

Food processing may influence the rate of digestion by removing or reducing the level and activity of inhibitory food components. It may also modify the structure of the food or its components to make the food more available to digestive enzyme attack. Examples are cooking, resulting in starch gelatinization, and reducing the particle size (and hence increasing the surface area available to digestive enzymes) by milling, crushing, or flaking. On the other hand, processing may also reduce digestibility by parboiling, cooking with retrogradation of the starch, and extrusion, as in the production of pasta, producing a more compact physical structure.

Increasing the frequency of meals and reducing their size spreads the nutrient load over time and hence prolongs the time spent in the absorptive state. It is perhaps the 'clearest' model of slowing the rate of absorption and is referred to again to explain the metabolic consequences of reducing the absorption rate.

Finally, enzyme inhibitors of carbohydrate absorption have been developed for pharmacological use in the treatment of diabetes, and these work by reducing the rate of carbohydrate uptake from the small intestine. One example of this class of substances is acarbose, an α-glycoside hydrolase inhibitor that has antiamylase and anti-sucrase–isomaltase activity and thus inhibits both intraluminal and brush border carbohydrate digestion and absorption of starch, sucrose, and maltose.

Possible Effects of Prolonging Absorption Time of Carbohydrate

The question remains as to what physiological effects are produced when carbohydrate is absorbed more slowly (**Table 3**). Studies have demonstrated the effectiveness of carbohydrate-absorption enzyme inhibitors in treating diabetes but also in preventing the development of diabetes in high-risk subjects treated with acarbose over a 3-year period. A further way to reduce the rate of absorption of

Table 3 Possible effects of prolonging absorption time of carbohydrates

Flatter postprandial glucose profile
Lower mean insulin levels postprandially and throughout the day
Reduced gastric inhibitory polypeptide response
Reduced 24-h urinary C peptide output
Prolonged suppression of plasma free fatty acids
Reduced urinary catecholamine output
Lower fasting and postprandial serum total and LDL cholesterol levels
Reduced hepatic cholesterol synthesis
Lower serum apolipoprotein B levels
Lower serum uric acid levels
Increased urinary uric acid excretion

carbohydrate without altering its composition is to change the rate of ingestion of carbohydrate substrates.

A number of effects appear to be beneficial when glucose is sipped slowly rather than drunk as a bolus or when starchy meals are eaten more frequently but in smaller amounts. Studies by Ellis in the 1930s first demonstrated a reduction in insulin requirements in patients with diabetes when glucose and insulin were administered in small, frequent doses. Since then, a range of metabolic benefits have been ascribed to increased meal frequency (the 'nibbling versus gorging' phenomenon). Early studies reported lower total cholesterol levels with increased meal frequency. Subsequent studies showed low-density lipoprotein (LDL) cholesterol reduction in subjects eating 3 meals a day compared to those eating from 6 to as many as 17 meals daily for periods of 2–8 weeks. An extreme model of slowing absorption, in which 17 meals daily were fed, demonstrated lower levels of apolipoprotein B in addition to total and LDL cholesterol. Population studies also indicated that total cholesterol levels were lower in those who ate more meals daily. Studies using stable isotopes showed that cholesterol synthesis was reduced at greater meal frequencies. Furthermore, mevalonic acid excretion (a water-soluble marker of cholesterol synthesis) suggested that the change in cholesterol levels was also related to the change in urinary mevalonic acid output. Since insulin is known to stimulate HMG-CoA reductase activity, a rate-limiting enzyme in cholesterol synthesis, the depressed cholesterol synthesis was attributed to the lower insulin levels observed. In addition, the reduction in serum cholesterol levels on 'nibbling' may have resulted from increased bile acid losses due to more frequent bile acid cycling through the gut following increased meal frequency.

Studies of non-insulin-dependent diabetes have shown depressed glucose and insulin levels during the day with increased meal frequency. In non-diabetic subjects, the major effect of reducing the absorption rate (by sipping glucose over 3 h instead of taking the same amount of glucose as a bolus within 5 minutes) was to reduce insulin secretion. In addition, insulin suppression of free fatty acids and branched-chain amino acid levels was prolonged, and following glucose challenge no counter-regulatory response was observed.

Finally, serum uric acid, an independent risk factor for coronary heart disease, was reduced and increased urinary uric acid excretion was seen with increased food frequency. As with the reduction in serum cholesterol levels, the effects of lower insulin levels were used to explain these differences. It was suggested that insulin promoted renal reabsorption of uric acid, as demonstrated in the context of sodium reabsorption and hypertension in hyperinsulinemic states.

Further effects of food frequency on diabetes have been assessed. It has been suggested that increased food frequency may limit obesity by reducing adipose tissue enzyme levels. Acute studies in humans failed to show an increased thermogenic response with increased meal frequency. Nevertheless, when satiety was assessed in acute studies, fluctuations in satiety were less over the whole day; long-term studies have yet to be undertaken. Concern still remains that 'snacking' may increase body weight in susceptible individuals. Despite these concerns, the demonstration that increased meal frequency can improve certain aspects of lipid and carbohydrate metabolism makes it a valuable model for other methods of 'spreading the nutrient load' (e.g., reducing the rate of glucose absorption).

Colonic Function

A portion of the starch, together with dietary fiber including cellulose and β-glucan, enters the colon and is fermented by the colonic microflora with the growth of the fecal biomass and the production of SCFA, hydrogen, and methane. The extent to which this occurs varies from individual to individual and is based on the nature of the resistant starch and the source of the cellulose (e.g., vegetable cellulose is more readily fermented than cereal cellulose). Although some individuals may have starch in their feces, the majority of subjects show little or no fecal starch. Furthermore, all the β-glucan is broken down by bacterial action in the colon. A large proportion of the cellulose escapes colonic bacterial fermentation

and contributes directly to fecal bulk. Thus, a significant proportion of glucose molecules are not absorbed in the small intestine but enter the colon and are salvaged after conversion to SCFAs. The SCFAs are rapidly absorbed and contribute to the host's energy metabolism. They are usually produced in the ratio of 60% acetate, 20% propionate, and 20% butyrate, but the relative ratios of these three fatty acids vary depending on the substrate and the rate of fermentation. Of the three SCFAs, only acetate appears in the peripheral circulation to any significant extent. Propionate is of interest since it is gluconeogenic and has been suggested to inhibit hepatic cholesterol synthesis. It is largely extracted by the liver at first pass. Butyrate, on the other hand, is taken up and used by colonocytes. The slower the fermentation, the higher the butyrate levels. Starches have been claimed to increase colonic butyrate and in some instances propionate production, and butyrate is said to have antineoplastic properties.

The Glycemic Index

The differing effects of different carbohydrate foods in raising the blood glucose concentration postprandially have long been recognized. The glycemic index classification was proposed to indicate the rates at which different starchy foods were digested. It was hoped that selection of foods with lower glycemic indices would contribute to prolonging the absorption of nutrients and thus improve the glycemic profile and reduce levels of fasting blood lipids.

However, a number of acute (up to 1 day) mixed meal studies during the mid- and late 1980s suggested that a glycemic index classification of foods had no clinical utility. Nevertheless, a number of subsequent reports have documented improved glycemic control in both type 1 and 2 diabetes as judged by serum fructosamine and glycosylated hemoglobin levels in studies lasting from 2 weeks to 2 months. Furthermore, some studies also noted reductions in serum lipids. Many high-fiber foods that lower LDL cholesterol levels also have low glycemic indices (barley, beans, etc.). Extensive glycemic index tables have been published that will help in food selection for therapeutic and study purposes.

Many of the traditional starchy foods from different cultures have a low glycemic index (**Table 4**). Finally, results of cohort studies suggest that consumption of foods with a low glycemic index, especially in the context of a high-fiber

during its passage from the gut to the periphery and converted into glycogen, triglycerides, and other metabolites.

Volunteers given a meal consisting of glucose (1 g per kilogram bodyweight) as a 45% solution on an empty stomach reduced their normal basal release of glucose from preformed glycogen in the liver from $9\,g\,h^{-1}$ to approximately $2.2\,g\,h^{-1}$ (i.e., approximately 75%). This persists for the period (3 or 4 h) during which glucose is absorbed from the gut. In other words, although there is a small net uptake of glucose by the liver following a carbohydrate-rich meal, the liberation of glucose from preformed glycogen does not cease completely. Glycogenolysis and gluconeogenesis take place simultaneously but at different rates, depending on whether glucose is being absorbed as well as on the amount and nature of the hormones released by the pancreas and intestine in response to the presence of food.

Fructose and Galactose

Before being absorbed, sucrose is cleaved into glucose and fructose, and lactose is cleaved into glucose and galactose. Galactose shares a transporter mechanism with glucose, whereas fructose uses a less efficient one of its own. Fructose and galactose, and a percentage of absorbed glucose, are removed on their first pass through the liver and converted into glycogen. This provides a store of carbohydrate that is released as glucose into the body pool when absorption from the gut is no longer occurring and gluconeogenesis has not yet become fully reestablished.

Starches and their partial hydrolytic products are converted enzymatically into glucose in the gut lumen and mucosal brush border at a rate that depends on their composition and physical form. Some starches are absorbed as rapidly as preformed glucose, whereas others are absorbed much more slowly. This is reflected in the rate and magnitude of the increase in blood glucose concentration that follows their ingestion and is referred to as the glycemic index.

The Postabsorptive Stage

The exact duration of the absorptive phase following ingestion of a meal depends on many factors, including the size of the meal, its composition, physical nature, and energy density as well as the rate of gastric emptying. Studies based on measurement of intestinal hormones that are released only in response to the absorption of food indicate that the average adult who eats three meals per day is rarely truly postabsorptive except during the night. During this comparatively brief fasting period, glucose lost from the glucose pool by its constant drain into the brain is replaced by glucose derived from the breakdown of liver glycogen. This can come either from reserves built up during the absorptive phase of a meal or by synthesis from glucose precursors, such as lactate, pyruvate, glycerol, and alanine, brought to it in the blood from peripheral tissues during fasting. Glucose synthesis, or gluconeogenesis, is increased by rising levels of glucagon and fatty acids in the blood, which are a consequence of decreasing plasma insulin levels.

The amount of glycogen in the liver varies with the nature of the diet and the size, composition, and timing of the last meal. The average amount of glycogen in the liver after an overnight fast is approximately 44 g (range, 15–80 g) and surprisingly does not increase very much after a meal. Nevertheless, after 36 h without food, liver glycogen stores may decline to as low as 4–8 g. Paradoxically, more prolonged fasting has little additional effect: Indeed, hepatic glycogen stores may actually be replenished as the brain shifts from using glucose to β-hydroxybutyrate as its main source of energy.

Glycogen probably never disappears from the liver completely, except *in extremis*, and there is evidence that it may be an intermediary in the production of glucose by the gluconeogenic pathway. Striatal muscles, which lack glucose-6-phosphatase, cannot convert the glycogen they contain into glucose and release it into the blood. Instead, they release its main breakdown products, lactate and pyruvate (and the latter's transamination partner, alanine), into the blood for conversion into glucose in the liver.

Gluconeogenesis

Gluconeogenesis is the process wherein the liver and, to a smaller but often significant extent, the kidneys make new glucose molecules from chemically simpler compounds. In humans, lactate is probably the most important glucose precursor, especially during exercise. Others, in order of importance, are alanine, pyruvate, glycerol, and some glucogenic amino acids, including glutamate. Glutamate is especially important in gluconeogenesis in the kidney. Fatty acids, apart from propionate formed in the colon by bacterial fermentation of nonabsorbable carbohydrates, do not serve as glucose precursors to any significant degree but do provide the conditions under which it can take place. So too do specific hormones, such as glucagon and cortisol.

The contribution by alanine to gluconeogenesis has probably been exaggerated. Although formed along with other amino acids by proteolysis of non-structural muscle proteins during periods of prolonged fasting and starvation, its main role under normal conditions is to transport, after transamination, three-carbon skeletons (e.g., pyruvate) derived from muscle glycogen to the liver, where it is converted into glucose during fasting.

Eating inhibits gluconeogenesis mainly through an increase in insulin and decrease in glucagon action. Fasting produces the opposite effect. Alcohol specifically inhibits gluconeogenesis from lactate but not other substrates, such as alanine. It does so by adversely changing the redox potential within the hepatocytes and reducing the availability of

nicotinamide adenine dinucleotide, which is an essential component in the formation of glucose from lactate. The inhibition of gluconeogenesis by quite modest amounts of alcohol can sometimes be so profound that people, especially children, with reduced liver glycogen stores may develop hypoglycemia of a severity that can be fatal.

Hormones and Glucose Homeostasis

Insulin is the only major hormone capable of lowering blood glucose levels (**Table 1**). It does so by inhibiting glycogen breakdown in the liver and inhibiting gluconeogenesis and by encouraging glucose uptake by peripheral tissues. It achieves this mainly by activating the glucose transporter protein, GLUT-4, an action that is enhanced by exercise and hyperglycemia. Consequently, insulin lowers

Table 1 Hormones that affect blood glucose concentrations

Hormones concerned with glucose homeostasis

Hormone	Source	Stimuli	Inhibitors	Main effect on glucose homeostasis
Insulin	B-cells of islets	Hyperglycemia, incretins (i.e., GIP & GLP-1), glucagon, some amino-acids e.g., arginine, leucine: parasympathetic nervous system i.e., vagus	Hypoglycemia, sympathetic nervous system and adrenaline, somatostatin	Reduced blood glucose concentration by Inhibition of hepatic glycogenolysis and gluconeogenesis, permitting peripheral glucose uptake
GIP	K-cells of duodenum, jejunum, ileum	Actively absorbed sugars e.g., glucose and galactose, actively absorbed fats, especially polyunsaturated	Glucagon; insulin	Incretin: stimulates insulin secretion only in presence of hyperglycemia
GLP-1	L-cells of the ileum and colon	Ingested food; whether absorbed or not	Glucagon; insulin	Incretin: stimulates insulin secretion only in presence of hyperglycemia: inhibits glucagon secretion. Inhibits gastric emptying: reduces appetite
Glucagon	A-cells of islets	Hypoglycemia, adrenaline, some amino-acids e.g., arginine	Insulin, hyperglycemia.	Increases glycogenolysis in liver (not peripheral tissues), enhances gluconeogenesis
Adrenaline	Adrenal medulla	Hypoglycemia, through sympathetic nervous stimulation, physical and mental stress.		Increases glycogenolysis in liver and peripheral tissues, inhibits insulin secretion, stimulates glucagon secretion, impairs peripheral glucose utilization and increases lipolysis (i.e., raises plasma NEFA levels)
Cortisol	Adrenal cortex	Hypoglycemia through hypothalamic release of ACTH		Decreases peripheral glucose uptake, induces insulin resistance, permits hepatic glycogenesis
Growth Hormone	Anterior pituitary	Hypoglycemia, through hypothalamus, ghrelin released from stomach following ingestion of food	Hyperglycemia, Somatostatin, alcohol	Decreases peripheral glucose uptake; increases adipocytes lipolysis
Vasopressin	Hypothalamus and posterior pituitary	Hypoglycemic stress; dehydration	Hypo-osmolality: alcohol	Stimulates hepatic glycogenolysis

blood glucose by two independent mechanisms. Which of the two actions predominates depends on the circumstances, including the actual concentration of insulin in the blood. Another is whether it is of exogenous or endogenous (pancreatic) origin. Exogenous insulin reaches peripheral tissues at a concentration in blood equal to or greater than that in blood perfusing the liver and is unaccompanied by C-peptide. Endogenous insulin, on the other hand, reaches the liver at a higher concentration than peripheral tissues and is accompanied by C-peptide, for which there is increasing evidence of synergism with insulin action.

Insulin released into the portal circulation is partially or, when its concentration in portal blood is low, almost completely removed by the liver. Not all tissues on which insulin acts are equally sensitive to its actions.

At the concentration at which insulin normally circulates in peripheral blood of fasting subjects ($<30 \, \text{pmol} \, l^{-1}$) it depresses, but does not completely suppress, the release of fatty acids from adipocytes and completely inhibits glucose uptake by striatal muscle. At insulin concentrations seen in peripheral blood in the absorptive phase of a meal ($\sim150–600 \, \text{pmol} \, l^{-1}$) it enhances peripheral glucose uptake and is responsible for the marked arteriovenous glucose difference observed at this time.

The release of insulin from the B cells of the pancreatic islets depends on the concentration of glucose in the blood perfusing them. At blood glucose levels less than approximately $3.5–4.0 \, \text{mmol} \, l^{-1}$, insulin secretion is minimal (constitutive). This means that as the arterial blood glucose declines toward its basal level in the postabsorptive state, plasma insulin levels also decline. However, they never decline low enough in the nondiabetic subject to permit uncontrolled liberation of glucose by the liver or fatty acids by adipocytes. This does, of course, happen when the B cells are destroyed, as in C-peptide negative type 1 diabetes, and is the cause of the hyperglycemia and ketosis that are the hallmark of this illness.

During prolonged starvation (20–50 days without food), small amounts of insulin still reach the liver. However, the amount reaching the adipocytes is sufficiently small to permit lipolysis by adipocytes, and their release of fatty acids into the circulation is sufficient to produce hyperketonemia ($10–20 \, \text{mmol} \, l^{-1}$) comparable to that seen in diabetic ketoacidosis. The situation differs, however, from that in diabetes, in that the restraining effect of insulin on hepatic gluconeogenesis and glycogenolysis remains. Consequently, blood glucose levels remain normal rather than grossly elevated and few ill effects develop except weight loss.

An important consequence of reduced insulin secretion as blood glucose levels decline after absorption of a meal is emancipation of the A cells, which are 'down stream' of B cells in the islet, from its suppressive effect on their own release of glucagon. Glucagon reaching its target organ, the liver, promotes both glycogenolysis and gluconeogenesis, thus reversing the effect exerted by insulin during the absorptive phase. In other words, each of the approximately 1 million pancreatic islets functions independently as a miniature glucostat.

Counterregulatory Hormones

Although it is possible to explain the control of blood glucose largely by means of the servoregulatory control of insulin and glucagon secretion described previously, the body has many other neural and hormonal mechanisms to correct or overcome a decline in blood glucose below the critical level (approximately $3.5 \, \text{mmol} \, l^{-1}$) necessary to maintain normal brain function. The sensors for this regulatory function are located in at least two anatomically distinct sites—within the brain and in the portal vein.

The following are the most important mechanisms involved:

Stimulation of the sympathetic and parasympathetic nervous systems, which in turn leads, respectively, to release of adrenaline from the adrenal medulla and noradrenaline from nerve terminals in the liver, and glucagon from the pancreas

Secretion of growth hormone, prolactin, and adrenocorticotrophic hormone by the anterior pituitary gland, cortisol by the adrenal cortex, and vasopressin by the posterior pituitary gland

None of these hormones, apart from cortisol, appears to be absolutely essential for the maintenance of normal glucose homeostasis, but all are brought into play under adverse conditions. They produce their hyperglycemic effects in a variety of ways that can be summarized as follows:

1. Increasing the liberation of glucose by the breakdown of preformed glycogen in the liver (e.g., glucagon, adrenaline, noradrenaline, and vasopressin)
2. Increasing gluconeogenesis in the liver (e.g., glucagon and cortisol)
3. Decreasing peripheral glucose utilization by peripheral tissues (e.g., growth hormone, cortisol, and prolactin)

Hyperglycemia and the Glycemic Index

In contrast to the numerous processes that protect against blood glucose falling too low, there is only one that protects the body from hyperglycemia—the release of insulin into the blood in response to the ingestion of food. Plasma insulin concentration, although neither its rate of increase nor its effectiveness (which depend on intrinsic physiology of the B cells and peripheral insulin sensitivity, respectively), is in large part determined by the increase in arterial blood glucose concentration that follows ingestion of a carbohydrate-containing meal. People who develop type 2 diabetes often have a delayed B cell response to intravenous glucose before showing overt evidence of impaired glucose tolerance in response to a meal. This is because their B cells, although relatively insensitive to hyperglycemia alone, remain sensitive to the hormones GIP and GLP-1, collectively known as incretins and that are released into the circulation from endocrine cells in the intestine in response to actively absorbed carbohydrates and fats. The incretins are able to stimulate insulin secretion only in the presence of hyperglycemia and do not do so when the meal contains little or no carbohydrate, thereby avoiding the risk of hypoglycemia following ingestion of a high-fat meal that does release GIP but virtually no insulin.

Other hormones released from the intestine in response to dietary constituents indirectly affect disposal of absorbed nutrients into the tissues and appetite as well as regulate gastrointestinal functions, such as the rate of gastric emptying and secretion of digestive enzymes.

There is a school of thought that maintains that the rate and magnitude of increase in blood glucose following ingestion of a carbohydrate-containing food compared to those of a comparable amount of glucose in solution or white bread eaten alone can usefully be expressed as its glycemic index. It further avers that low glycemic index foods are nutritionally preferable to high glycemic index foods, the ingestion of which various chronic illnesses are attributed. This has been disputed, and there is little evidence that the concept has much relevance to people with healthy pancreatic endocrine function eating combinations of diverse foods in their everyday life. There is indirect evidence that it may have value in determining dietary choices by people with diabetes whose pancreatic endocrine function is faulty or absent.

Glycosuria

Approximately 100 g of glucose is normally filtered from the blood at the glomeruli of the kidneys each day, more than 99% of which is reabsorbed by the kidney tubules. As a result, healthy people lose less than 150 mg of glucose in their urine each day, an amount too small to be detected by most simple screening procedures for glycosuria. When, for any reason—the most common cause of which is a blood glucose concentration of $10 \, \text{mmol} \, l^{-1}$ or higher—the amount of glucose filtered at a glomerulus is more than can be reabsorbed by its tubule, glucose appears at high concentration in the urine. The osmotic diuresis so produced is associated with an increased excretion of water, sodium, chloride, and potassium and is often the first clue to the existence of hyperglycemia, the characteristic hallmark of diabetes. Moreover, it is their loss and not that of glucose that leads to the fatal outcome of diabetic ketoacidosis in patients with untreated type 1 diabetes.

Because their concentration in blood is ordinarily extremely low, except in certain rare diseases, neither fructose nor galactose occur in the urine of healthy people.

See also: **Diabetes Mellitus**: Etiology and Epidemiology; Classification and Chemical Pathology; Dietary Management. **Fructose. Galactose. Glucose**: Chemistry and Dietary Sources; Metabolism and Maintenance of Blood Glucose Level; Glucose Tolerance.

Further Reading

Bolli GB and Fanelli CG (1999) Physiology of glucose counter-regulation to hypoglycemia. *Endocrinology and Metabolism Clinics of North America* **28**: 467–493.

Foster-Powell K, Holt SHA, and Brand-Miller JC (2002) International table of glycaemic index and glycaemic load values: 2002. *American Journal of Clinical Nutrition* **76**: 5–56.

Jackson RA, Blix PM, Mathews JA *et al.* (1983) Comparison of peripheral glucose uptake after oral glucose loading and a mixed meal. *Metabolism* **32**: 706–710.

Ludwig DS (2002) The glycaemic index: Physiological mechanisms relating to obesity, diabetes and cardiovascular disease. *Journal of the American Medical Association* **287**: 2414–2423.

Marks V (1989) Glycaemic responses to sugars and starches. In: J Dobbing (ed.) *Dietary Starches and Sugars: A Comparison*, pp. 150–167. London: Springer-Verlag.

Marks V, Samols E, and Stagner J (1992) Intra-islet interrelationship. In: Flatt PR (ed.) *Nutrient Regulation of Insulin Secretion*, pp. 41–57. London: Portland Press.

Olson AL and Pessin JE (1996) Structure, function, and regulation of the mammalian facilitative glucose transporter gene family. *Annual Review of Nutrition* **16**: 235–256.

Wahren J and Johansson B-L (1998) New aspects of C-peptide physiology. *Hormone & Metabolic Research* **30**: A2–A5.

Glucose Tolerance

B Ahrén, Lund University, Lund, Sweden

Definition and Impact of Glucose Tolerance

The prevalence of type 2 diabetes is steadily increasing and it has been estimated that the prevalence will increase during the next 25 years to reach epidemic levels. It is assumed that within 25 years, if the trend is not altered, more than 25% of the global adult population older than 65 years of age will be affected by diabetes. The prevalence also shows ethnic differences, with prevalence ranging by a factor of 10 between different populations. Also, the prevalence of diabetic complications is high, resulting in high and significant morbidity. Diabetes is also a major risk factor for cardiovascular diseases, and the majority of deaths in those with diabetes are due to cardiovascular or cerebrovascular disorders. Altogether, this makes diabetes a major burden for global health and health economy.

A most important factor underlying the morbidity in diabetes, its complications and concurrent cardiovascular diseases, is hyperglycemia. Importantly, even at such a low degree as not to reach the limit criteria for diabetes, hyperglycemia is related to morbidity. Lifestyle changes and pharmacological interventions to reduce or even normalize the hyperglycemia exist, and consistent adherence to such regimen will reduce the morbidity. However, hyperglycemia is initially without symptoms and therefore usually remains undetected for a long period of time. Therefore, it is important to have reliable methods for the detection of hyperglycemia in its initial stages for proper actions to be taken. Such detection relies on analysis of the circulating glucose in the fasting state or after a challenge. Thus, it is important to recognize that hyperglycemia is subdivided into two different entities. The first entity is fasting hyperglycemia. This is mainly due to inappropriately high release of glucose from the liver, which is in turn caused by excessive glucagon levels in combination with low insulin levels and/or deficient action of insulin to restrain glucose release from the liver. Standardization of the sample is usually defined as 8- or 12-h fast. The second entity of hyperglycemia is postchallenge hyperglycemia, which occurs after meal or glucose ingestion. This is called 'glucose intolerance' and is equivalent to an impairment to dispose glucose after a challenge. Several modes to diagnose glucose intolerance exist. However, the gold standard for its diagnosis is the oral glucose tolerance test (OGTT). This article describes this test, its advantages and limitations, and its potential role for early detection of patients with increased risk for developing type 2 diabetes and cardiovascular diseases. The article also summarizes the basic mechanisms determining glucose tolerance as well as epidemiological and clinical aspects of glucose intolerance, including the potential of treating the condition for prevention of diabetes and cardiovascular diseases.

Glucose Tolerance Tests

History and Definition of Oral Glucose Tolerance Tests

A major breakthrough in the understanding of glucose intolerance as a basis and risk factor for development of type 2 diabetes and cardiovascular diseases was the introduction of a worldwide standardization of the OGTT in the 1970s. By this introduction, glucose tolerance became a standardized entity, which enabled studies in metabolism, physiology, and clinical medicine with detection of risk factors as well as progressive follow-up studies using a standard recognized worldwide. At the same time, and also of significant importance for the generation of present-day knowledge within the field, was the introduction of the clinical entity impaired glucose tolerance (IGT), which replaced the term "borderline" diabetes. A problem with the term borderline diabetes was that its definition was not uniform, which was partly due to inconsistencies in the procedure of performing a glucose tolerance test, with the amount of glucose ingested varying from 50 to 100 g or given on a kilogram basis. IGT as an entity was thus introduced simultaneously with the suggestion that glucose tolerance in a clinical test should be determined following ingestion of 75 g glucose, with a blood sample for the measure of glucose to be taken 2 h later.

The evaluation of the standardized OGTT in the clinical setting relies on the 2-h glucose value. This value during the 75 g OGTT usually displays a normal distribution slightly skewed to the right. **Figure 1** shows the distribution pattern of 2-h glucose levels obtained from 802 Caucasian subjects in the Malmö Prevention Study, an epidemiological study from Sweden. From this distribution, normal values may be defined statistically from mean and variance values for statistical definition of the distribution. The mean value, as in most studies, is ≈ 7 mmol/l and standard deviation is ≈ 1 mmol/l. By defining reference values as 95% confidence intervals, the cutoff value for normality would be

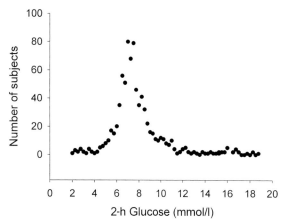

Figure 1 Distribution of the 2-h glucose value in an OGTT performed in 802 Caucasian subjects from the Malmö Prevention Study (unpublished data).

approximately 9 mmol/l and, hence, values higher than 9 mmol/l would indicate diabetes. By using such a definition of diabetes, a large number of subjects would have the disease, the clinical relevance of which is doubtful. Therefore, the definition of diabetes has instead been based on prospective studies evaluating the risk for microvascular disease and the cutoff-levels have been defined as levels increasing this risk. Therefore, a cutoff value of 11.1 mmol/l glucose has been used for the definition of type 2 diabetes.

OGTT was frequently used during the 1980s and 1990s for the clinical diagnosis of type 2 diabetes and in epidemiological studies, which markedly increased our knowledge of these conditions. By the end of the 1990s, however, definitions of IGT and clinical tests to be performed were again discussed. This resulted in revised cutoff levels and the introduction of a new entity called impaired fasting glycemia (IFG), which is defined as high fasting glucose. **Table 1** shows the new cutoff values

for the three diagnostic entities—IFG, IGT, and diabetes. It was also suggested that fasting glucose was sufficient for the diagnosis of glucose intolerance and type 2 diabetes.

The suggestion that a fasting sample is sufficient for the diagnosis of abnormal glycemia has been questioned, however, mainly because studies have shown that such a strategy will reduce the numbers at risk who are diagnosed and detected. This is because a large proportion of subjects with IGT have a normal fasting glucose but an elevated 2-h glucose value. In fact, there are populations with IFG alone, IGT alone, and IFG and IGT together, and these populations may represent different risks for diabetes and cardiovascular diseases. Consequently, those having a high 2-h glucose value but a normal fasting glucose, who also have increased risk for cardiovascular diseases, will be missed by the suggested strategy. A study by Larsson and collaborators from Sweden identified this dilemma since it was demonstrated that out of 414 subjects with abnormal fasting or 2-h glucose values during an OGTT, only 140 (34%) had elevation of both values. The largest group comprised subjects with high 2-h glucose values but normal fasting glucose values (i.e., IGT but not IFG), which were seen in 235 subjects (57%), whereas only 39 subjects (9%) had high fasting but normal 2-h glucose values (i.e., true IFG). The individual subgroups were shown to have similar risk factor patterns in terms of degree of obesity, blood pressure, and lipid levels. Therefore, it is now obvious that for a proper strategy to detect early cases at risk for diabetes and cardiovascular diseases, an OGTT needs to be performed since this test includes both fasting and postchallenge glucose determination.

Procedures and Evaluation of the Oral Glucose Tolerance Test

Glucose tolerance is defined as the ability to dispose a glucose load, and therefore glucose intolerance is defined as an impaired ability for glucose disposal. The gold standard technique is to challenge with an oral glucose load, with measurement of circulating glucose before and after the challenge—the OGTT. As routinely performed, this test determines the ability to dispose glucose after oral administration of 75 g glucose. The test is standardized such that it is performed in the morning after a 12-h overnight fast and blood samples are taken before the glucose load and after 2 h. Furthermore, the diet during the 3 days preceding the test should contain at least 250 g carbohydrates per day and the subjects should rest during the test in a semirecumbent position

Table 1 Cutoff values for fasting and 2-h glucose values (mmol/l) of impaired glucose tolerance (IGT), impaired fasting glucose (IFG), and type 2 diabetes (T2D) in an oral glucose tolerance test according to guidelines by the American Diabetes Association

	Plasma	Whole blood	
	Venous	Venous	Capillary
T2D			
Fasting glucose	≥7.0	≥6.1	≥6.1
2-h glucose	≥11.1	≥10.0	≥11.1
IGT			
2-h glucose	7.8–11.0	6.7–9.9	7.8–11.0
IFG			
Fasting glucose	6.1–6.9	5.6–6.0	5.6–6.0

without smoking. The glucose given should be dissolved in 250–300 ml fluid, and sometimes fruit-flavored water is used to improve the taste. There has been much debate about how to take the blood sample. The original diagnostic criteria used values obtained from plasma derived from blood taken venously in tubes containing additives for prevention of coagulation. However, valid results are also obtained when glucose is measured in whole blood and when capillary samples are taken, although cutoff levels need to be adjusted for the different glucose concentrations in these samples. Arterial samples are also theoretically possible but rarely, if ever, used. Sometimes, mainly for research purposes, more frequent samples are taken and the test may last 3 h; however, for clinical purposes, the routine OGTT lasts 2 h, with a sample taken at that time point.

As shown in **Figure 2**, in a normal person, circulating levels of glucose increase within the first 15 min after the oral ingestion of glucose to reach a peak after 30 min. Thereafter, a progressive decline occurs, with the 2-h value usually approximately 25% higher than the fasting value. Usually, it takes 3 h for a return to baseline glucose levels. In subjects with IGT, there is usually also a peak at 30 min, albeit at a higher level than in normal subjects, but the main difference versus normal subjects is that the glucose disposal is impaired, which results in a higher 2-h glucose value. In diabetics, there is usually not a peak at 30 min but a continuous rise throughout the 2-h study period. The currently used cutoff values are shown in **Table 1**. Note that the mode of measuring glucose is important with regard to the cutoff values used.

Limitations of the Oral Glucose Tolerance Test

An important limitation of the OGTT is the variability in results when the test is repeated. Actually, the coefficiency of variance (CV) is usually 15% and in some studies 20%, which is higher than that for most other clinical tests. It is not clear why OGTT has such a high CV. The variance is not, however, dependent on CV in the measurement of glucose, which is a procedure with very small error and CVs usually below 3%. Therefore, biological variation probably explains the high CV of OGTT. Factors explaining this variation may be preceding diet, exercise, emotions, stress, drugs taken for various diseases, and gender, which are all factors influencing gastric emptying, carbohydrate absorption, islet hormone secretion, hepatic glucose production, and peripheral glucose uptake (i.e., all processes contributing to the 2-h glucose value). Because of the high variability in the 2-h glucose value, a diagnosis of IGT or diabetes, particularly if intervention is planned, should not be based on a single OGTT. Instead, a clinical recommendation is to perform two OGTTs and use the mean of the two 2-h glucose values as the diagnostic value. The time interval between the two OGTTs should not exceed 3 months.

Metabolic Basis for Oral Glucose Tolerance

Oral ingestion of glucose initiates a series of metabolic perturbations, which comprise the 2-h glucose value. These metabolic perturbations are complex and involve glucose entering the bloodstream, changes in neural activity and islet hormone secretion, suppression of hepatic glucose production, and stimulation of peripheral glucose uptake. From a quantitative standpoint, of most importance with regard to the 2-h value are the changes in islet hormone secretion, which include stimulation of insulin secretion and inhibition of glucagon secretion, and the suppression of hepatic glucose production. In fact, there is an inverse linear relation between the inhibition of hepatic glucose production and the 2-h glucose value and, similarly, a linear inverse relation between stimulation of the early (first 30 min) insulin secretion and 2-h glucose. This section briefly summarizes these processes.

A first series of events in the OGTT is initiated during the anticipation of the oral glucose ingestion, through olfactory stimuli and through receptors located in the oral cavity. This response is called

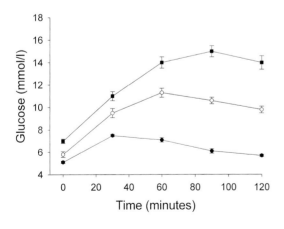

Figure 2 Venous plasma glucose levels during OGTT in subjects with normal impaired glucose tolerance, impaired glucose tolerance, and diabetes. From Ahrén B, unpublished data. Means ± SEM are shown.

the cephalic phase and activates sensory nerves, which give input to the central nervous system. This information is integrated in the hypothalamus for initiation and adjustment of a vagal nerve response to release insulin from the pancreatic islets. Therefore, when analyzed in detail, there is an increase in circulating insulin after glucose or meal ingestion already before glucose levels become elevated. After passage of glucose through the oral cavity, glucose passes to the stomach and through a regulated mechanism delivered into the gut. Since glucose is a monosugar, it is readily absorbed in the small intestine and reaches the splanchnic venous drainage. Glucose then passes to the portal vein and the liver. In the portal vein, glucose activates glucosensitive receptors, which through afferent sensory nerves send signals centrally to the brain for further integration with the previous signals in the hypothalamus for adjustment of efferent nerve activity. Furthermore, glucose in the liver inhibits hepatic glucose production, which is high after the overnight fast. Then, glucose passes to the general circulation to reach the pancreatic islets and the peripheral cells. The glucose load to the gut also stimulates the release of intestinal hormones, such as glucose-dependent insulinotropic polypeptide and glucagon-like peptide-1 (GLP-1). These hormones then pass through the circulation to reach the pancreas, where they stimulate insulin secretion and, as for GLP-1, inhibit glucagon secretion. In the pancreatic islets, vagal activation, intestinal hormones, and glucose stimulate insulin secretion, and glucose, GLP-1, and insulin inhibit glucagon secretion. These islet responses are of major importance for a normal glucose tolerance, and defects in these islet responses are major determinants of IGT and type 2 diabetes. Following passage of insulin into the venous drainage of the pancreas, the islet hormones reach the portal vein and the liver, and a main function of insulin is to potently suppress hepatic glucose production. This is a major process with regard to the degree of hyperglycemia during the test; in subjects with inappropriately high hepatic glucose production, the glucose level after oral glucose is high. This suppression of hepatic glucose production is augmented by the reduction in circulating levels of glucagon, which is initiated by the direct action of glucose and GLP-1 on the glucagon-producing cells and also by the action of insulin to inhibit glucagon secretion. After the liver, glucose and insulin reach the peripheral circulation and peripheral cells, where glucose is transported across the cell membranes and therefore leaves the circulation. In most cells, a major proportion of glucose uptake is sensitive to insulin; therefore, the amount of insulin, in relation to the insulin sensitivity of the cell, is of major importance for the delivery rate of glucose. However, insulin-independent mechanisms also exist, even in tissues, which are also insulin sensitive, and glucose uptake is thus also dependent on glucose. Of most importance for glucose disposal after oral glucose is the muscle cells, which have a high capacity for glucose uptake. From all these processes, the glucose level at 2 h can be determined.

It is important to realize that the metabolic processes underlying glucose tolerance are different from those underlying the fasting glucose value. Fasting glucose is mainly determined by hepatic glucose delivery during the night, which in turn is governed by the ability to maintain normal basal insulin and glucagon levels. Therefore, mechanisms underlying IFG include defective insulin secretion, defective suppression of glucagon secretion, defective sensitivity in the liver for the action of insulin, and defective peripheral glucose disposal at low glucose levels, which is a sign of insulin resistance. Although mechanisms underlying fasting and 2-h glucose values differ, there is a high correlation between fasting and 2-h glucose values in normal subjects, as shown in **Figure 3**. Nevertheless, there is a limited overlap between IGT and IFG in a population; in fact, most subjects with IGT have normal fasting glucose, and most subjects with IFG have a normal 2-h glucose value. This suggests that different pathophysiological processes underlie IGT and IFG, which in turn suggests that OGTT should be undertaken more frequently than performed today.

Differential Tests for Glucose Tolerance

Diagnoses of type 2 diabetes or stages preceding its occurrence can be undertaken by other means

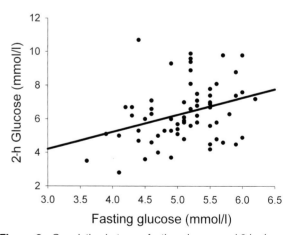

Figure 3 Correlation between fasting glucose and 2-h glucose during an OGTT in nondiabetic subjects. The regression is significant ($r = 0.32$, $p = 0.008$). From Ahrén B, unpublished data.

besides OGTT. As previously stated, the use of fasting glucose has been suggested as the gold standard for diagnosis during recent years. Although it has a lower CV than the 2-h glucose value after OGTT and is simpler and more convenient for both the subject and the staff, the problem with this method is that a large number of subjects with IGT, namely those with a normal fasting glucose, will be missed.

As an alternative to OGTT, glucose tolerance may also be determined by administering glucose intravenously. In the intravenous glucose tolerance test (IVGTT), glucose is injected intravenously, usually at a dose of 0.3, 0.5, or 1 g/kg, and circulating glucose is determined before and 8, 10, 15, 20, 30, 40, 50, 60, and 80 min after injection. Glucose tolerance is estimated from the elimination rate, where a glucose elimination constant (k_g) is calculated. The theory behind this is that the glucose elimination after intravenous glucose displays an exponential function (i.e., after logarithmic transformation of the data, the elimination is linear. k_g is thus calculated as the slope for the glucose curve following logarithmic transformation of the individual glucose values and is calculated from the formula $k_g = (0.693 \times 100)/t_{1/2}$, where $t_{1/2}$ is the half-time of glucose elimination (in minutes). The unit for k_g is percentage of glucose decay per minute. **Figure 4** shows this condition. Before OGTT was routinely used, IVGTT was undertaken more frequently. Unless very specific questions are asked, it is currently not used in clinical practice because it is more cumbersome to perform and it identifies only some of the metabolic processes underlying glucose tolerance, mainly insulin secretion, insulin sensitivity, and glucose uptake. Thus, other important aspects, such as glucagon secretion, release of incretin hormones, and hepatic glucose output, which are involved in the overall glucose tolerance and included in the 2-h glucose value after OGTT, contribute only marginally to the k_g after IVGTT.

It has been suggested that measurement of HbA_{1c} (i.e., the fraction of hemoglobin being glycosylated) may be used for the diagnosis of IGT and type 2 diabetes. The rationale is that hemoglobin is irreversibly glycosylated in proportion to the glucose level, and therefore the proportion of HbA_{1c} should reflect the mean of the glucose levels during the preceding 2 or 3 months. However, although this theoretical assumption is true, measurements of HbA_{1c} are not precise, have not been standardized at levels near the normal levels, and, consequently, slight elevations of HbA_{1c} will not distinguish normal from impaired glucose tolerance with fairly high precision. In addition, most subjects with IGT have HbA_{1c} levels within the normal distribution.

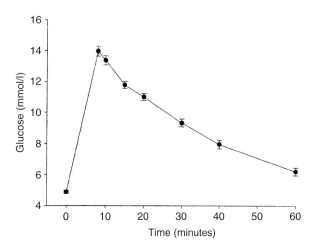

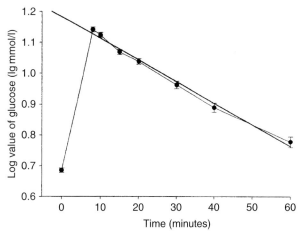

Figure 4 Glucose levels during an IVGTT in 41 healthy subjects with normal glucose tolerance. Glucose (0.3 g/kg) was injected intravenously at time 0. Linear regression curve for the logarithmic values from minutes 8 to 60. k_g value = $1.61 \pm 0.08\%$/min. From Ahrén B, unpublished data. Means $\pm$ SEM are shown.

Clinical Aspects of IGT

Epidemiology of IGT

During the 1980s, studies on the prevalence of IGT and type 2 diabetes were performed in several different populations. It became apparent that the prevalence of these conditions, although high in many populations, varied markedly between different populations. Thus, for some populations, mainly in Africa, data from only a few percent were published, whereas an exceedingly high prevalence (60%) was reported in some populations, such as Pima Indians. **Figure 5** shows a collaborative study from 1993 in which data from several populations throughout the world are summarized. Studies during the past 10 years have further increased our knowledge since they have included additional populations and demonstrated that the

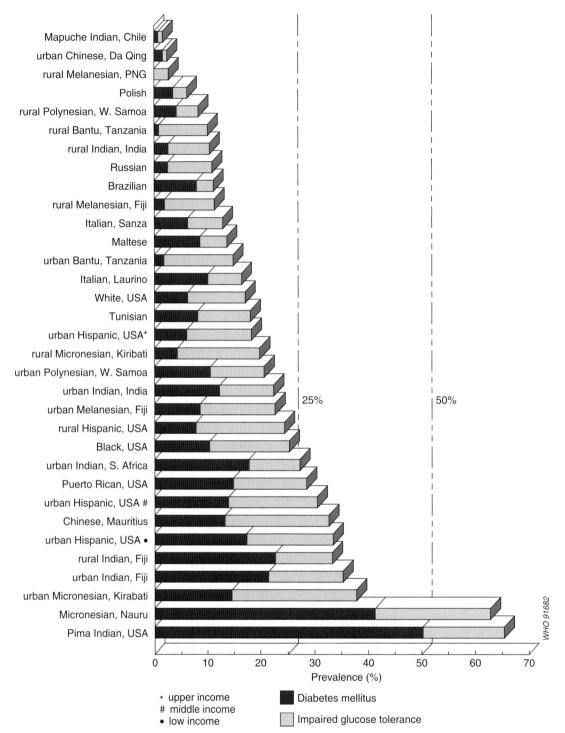

Figure 5 Prevalence (%) of diabetes and IGT in selected populations in the age range of 30–64 years; genders combined. Copyright © 1993 American Diabetes Association. From *Diabetes Care* volume 16, page 170. Reprinted with permission from the American Diabetes Association.

prevalence of IGT and type 2 diabetes is steadily increasing. Hence, the prevalence reported in 1993 is an underestimation of the prevalence today. It has to be emphasized, however, that the difference in reported prevalence rates between different populations may be partially explained by methodological differences. For example, the prevalence of IGT and type 2 diabetes is increased by age, and in many populations there is also a higher prevalence in women than in men, at least in younger age groups. Different studies have not controlled for these confounders. Furthermore, due to migration patterns in some populations, generalization of study results is questionable, and there may also be differences in the likelihood of subjects attending a study between different populations. Nevertheless, a true ethnic difference seems to exist, with extremely high values in some Pacific island and North American Indian populations and a low prevalence in South American Indian and Bantu populations. An interesting observation is that the increase in prevalence of IGT and type 2 diabetes seems to be higher in populations with low prevalence rates and vice versa, which probably will result in diminished differences in prevalence rates between different populations in the future.

Clinical Consequences of IGT

IGT is an important risk factor for development of type 2 diabetes. However, prospective and long-term studies report different predictive values for the development of type 2 diabetes in different populations. In general, the risk of transition of IGT into type 2 diabetes ranges from 1–2% to 5% and as high as 15–20% per year. The risk is higher for those older than 50 years of age. There is also evidence that hyperglycemia, even at levels not reaching the threshold for type 2 diabetes, is associated with a substantial risk for the development of cardiovascular diseases. One explanation for this is that glucose initiates metabolic perturbations of importance for developing angiopathy, such as tissue peroxidation, production of plasminogen activation inhibition-1, and impairment of endothelial function, such as nitric oxide production. Another explanation is that hyperglycemia is associated with a number of risk factors for cardiovascular diseases, such as high blood pressure, hyperinsulinemia, dyslipidemia, and microalbuminuria, which all are included in the metabolic syndrome. In fact, if hyperglycemia is present, the risk for developing cardiovascular diseases for each of the other risk factors is augmented. Attempts to define cutoff values of glucose for cardiovascular risks have been problematic, however, probably due to the fact that the risk is continuously increased across the glucose ranges. Hence, the use of defined cutoff values is more a convenient practical issue, which is important in a clinical setting, but offers limitations from a theoretical standpoint.

Since IGT is a risk factor for type 2 diabetes and cardiovascular diseases, it is also a risk factor for overall mortality. Alberti and coworkers attempted to quantify this by performing a meta-analysis on 13 prospective studies, and they identified a hazard ratio of 1.34 (95% confidence interval, 1.14–1.57) by comparing subjects with IGT to those with normal glucose tolerance. The hazard ratio is higher for subjects with IGT than for subjects with IFG, suggesting that the 2-h glucose value is more predictive of mortality than the fasting glucose value. This shows that an individual with IGT has an increased risk not only for type 2 diabetes but also for cardiovascular diseases and hence mortality. This indicates that attempts should be made to prevent IGT from progressing to cardiovascular diseases and type 2 diabetes.

Treatment of IGT

During recent years, the issue of whether IGT may be treated to prevent progression to type 2 diabetes or cardiovascular diseases has gained considerable interest. On the one hand, it has been argued that it is important to prevent progression of IGT. On the other hand, it has been argued that treating such a large population group as those with IGT would be risky. **Table 2** lists criteria that need to be fulfilled to justify prevention of a condition. In fact, most of these criteria are met for IGT; therefore, it may be argued that treating IGT is now justified. The optimal preventive intervention for IGT is not known, however. The intervention may include lifestyle changes, notably increased physical activity and dietary regulations. Such interventions have been shown to be efficient in highly motivated populations and study centers. However, whether generalization of these results to the general population is possible is not known. A clinical experience is that the outcome of advice on lifestyle changes is often disappointing in the long term. Another mode of

Table 2   Criteria for recommending population-based intervention for preventing a disease[a]

Criterion 1: The disease (IGT and type 2 diabetes) should pose a major health problem.

Criterion 2: Early development and natural history of the disease (IGT and type 2 diabetes) should be understood to identify parameters that measure its progression.

Criterion 3: Tests should exist for diagnosing the presumptive population (OGTT).

Criterion 4: Preventive methods should be safe, efficient, and reliable.

Criterion 5: Effort to find subjects and cost of intervention should not be burdensome and should be cost-effective.

[a]Based on recommendations from the American Diabetes Association (2004).

IGT, impaired glucose tolerance; OGTT, oral glucose tolerance test.

intervention is pharmacological treatment using compounds to stimulate insulin secretion, suppress hepatic glucose production, and/or enhance insulin sensitivity. These may be efficient, perhaps more efficient than advice on lifestyle changes, but may in turn pose other questions concerning long-term efficiency and potential adverse events. These two strategies are not mutually exclusive, however, and introducing pharmacological intervention without giving lifestyle advice is not appropriate in a clinical setting.

Recently, interesting data from large population studies on the prevention of progression of IGT have been obtained. Two studies, the Finnish diabetes prevention study and the Diabetes Prevention Program, have shown that lifestyle changes (i.e., individualized diet and exercise counseling) in subjects with IGT reduced the incidence of diabetes by more than 50%. In addition, in the Diabetes Prevention Program, it was shown that metformin (which reduces glucose output from the liver) reduces the risk by approximately 30%. This suggests that pharmacological treatment of IGT prevents development of type 2 diabetes. Several large studies are ongoing and results are expected within a few years.

Whether interventional programs on IGT are valid also for the prevention of cardiovascular diseases is not clearly established, mainly because long-term studies have not been performed. The STOP-NIDDM study, however, showed that acarbose, which reduces glucose absorption from the gut, reduced cardiovascular events by more than 30% during a 3-year study period. This suggests that cardiovascular diseases may be prevented by treating IGT. It should be noted, however, that for prevention of cardiovascular diseases and mortality, more studies and longer follow-up periods are required.

Conclusion

Because of the risk of developing type 2 diabetes and cardiovascular diseases in subjects with IGT, and also in those with IFG albeit at a lower level, it is important to diagnose and treat these conditions. This means that OGTT should be undertaken more frequently, at least in subjects found to have high fasting glucose. These subjects should be regarded similarly as other subjects with risk factors for cardiovascular diseases (i.e., those with hypertension and dyslipidemia). This implies that subjects with IGT should be given lifestyle advice and be checked regularly. Ongoing large and long-term prevention trials will also provide information on whether pharmacological treatment should be added.

See also: **Diabetes Mellitus**: Etiology and Epidemiology; Classification and Chemical Pathology; Dietary Management. **Glucose**: Metabolism and Maintenance of Blood Glucose Level.

Further Reading

American Diabetes Association (2004) Clinical practice and recommendations 2004. *Diabetes Care* **27**(supplement 1).

Chiasson JL, Josse RG, Gomis R *et al.* (2002) Acarbose for prevention of type 2 diabetes mellitus: The STOP-NIDDM randomised trial. *Lancet* **359**: 2072–2077.

DECODE Study Group (1999) Glucose tolerance and mortality: Comparison of WHO and American Diabetes Association diagnostic criteria. *Lancet* **354**: 617–621.

De Vegt F, Dekker JM, Ruhe HG *et al.* (1999) Hyperglycaemia is associated with all-cause and cardiovascular mortality in the Hoorn population: The Hoorn Study. *Diabetologia* **42**: 926–931.

Expert Committee on the Diagnosis and Classification of Diabetes Mellitus (1997) Report of the Expert Committee on the Diagnosis and Classification of Diabetes Mellitus. *Diabetes Care* **20**: 1183–1197.

Isomaa B (2003) A major health hazard. The metabolic syndrome. *Life Sciences* **73**: 2395–2411.

King H, Rewers M and WHO Ad Hoc Diabetes Reporting Group (1993) Global estimates for prevalence of diabetes mellitus and impaired glucose tolerance in adults. *Diabetes Care* **16**: 157–177.

Knowler WC, Barrett-Connor E, Fowler SE *et al.* (2002) Reduction in the incidence of type 2 diabetes with lifestyle intervention or metformin. *New England Journal of Medicine* **346**: 393–403.

Larsson H, Ahrén B, Lindgärde F, and Berglund G (1995) Fasting blood glucose in determining prevalence of diabetes in a large, homogenous population of Caucasian middle-aged women. *Journal of International Medicine* **237**: 537–541.

Larsson H, Berglund G, Lindgärde F, and Ahrén B (1998) Comparison of ADA and WHO criteria for diagnosis of diabetes and glucose intolerance. *Diabetologia* **41**: 1124–1125.

Larsson H, Lindgärde F, Berglund G, and Ahrén B (2000) Prediction of diabetes using ADA or WHO criteria in postmenopausal women: A 10-year follow-up study. *Diabetologia* **43**: 1224–1228.

Tuomilehto J, Lindström J, Eriksson JG *et al.* (2001) Prevention of type 2 diabetes mellitus by changes in lifestyle among subjects with impaired glucose tolerance. *New England Journal of Medicine* **344**: 1343–1350.

Unwin N, Shaw J, Zimmet P, and Alberti KGMM (2002) Impaired glucose tolerance and impaired fasting glycaemia: The current status on definition and intervention. *Diabetic Medicine* **19**: 708–723.

Weyer C, Bogardus C, and Pratley RE (1999) Metabolic characteristics of individuals with impaired fasting glucose and/or impaired glucose tolerance. *Diabetes* **48**: 2197–2203.

World Health Organization (1999) *Definition, diagnosis and classification of diabetes mellitus and its complications. Report of a WHO consultation. Part 1: Diagnosis and classification of diabetes mellitus.* Geneva: World Health Organization.

Zimmet P, Alberti KG, and Shaw J (2001) Global and societal implications of the diabetes epidemics. *Nature* **414**: 782–787.

Zimmet P, Shaw J, and Alberti KGMM (2003) Preventing type 2 diabetes and the dysmetabolic syndrome in the real world: A realistic view. *Diabetic Medicine* **20**: 693–702.

GLYCEMIC INDEX

G Frost and A Dornhorst, Imperial College at
Hammersmith Hospital, London, UK

In the past 10 years, a number of important epidemiological and experimental studies have linked glycemic index to postprandial glucose metabolism, insulin resistance, and cardiovascular risk factors. The World Health Organization (WHO) and the Food and Agriculture Organization (FAO) recommended that the physiological effects of dietary carbohydrates be classified according to their glycemic index. This review examines the historical and scientific background of the glycemic index.

Background and Definition

In 1939, Conn and Newburgh noted how different carbohydrate-containing foods could have the same macronutrient composition but different glycemic responses. Insulin responses elicited by different carbohydrates also vary. These observations led to the first classification of carbohydrate foods according to their glycemic response, which then allowed different dietary carbohydrates to be exchanged within a meal without altering postprandial glucose levels. The 'glycemic index' was introduced as a means of quantifying the glycaemic response of different dietary carbohydrates.

Glycemic indices of several foods are published in international nutritional tables, the most recent of which was published in 2002. Methodology on their derivation is available from previous reviews. Glycemic index of a food is a measure of postprandial glucose response after a 50-g load of available carbohydrate from the food (**Figure 1**) and provides a standardized comparison of a carbohydrate's 2-h postprandial glucose response with that of glucose (**Table 1**). Low glycemic index carbohydrates have lower 2-h incremental areas under the glucose curve than glucose, whereas high glycemic index foods have higher areas. Although the insulin response is not used to define glycemic index, the lower the glycemic index of a food, the more attenuated is the insulin response to a standard test meal. It has been argued that it is the insulin response to foods and not the glycemic response that is important in the pathogenesis of insulin resistance and related metabolic disturbances and disease risk. Although still an area of debate in general, glycemic index is

a surrogate marker of the insulin response to different carbohydrates, with the possible exception of diary products. Indeed, the insulin response in non-diabetic subjects to a wide range of foods (glycemic indices between 32 and 100) are highly correlated. The exception to this is possibly diary products which have an insulin response high than predicted but the glycemic index. This remains unexplained at present. Dietary carbohydrates stimulate insulin secretion both directly by stimulating the pancreatic β cell and indirectly through their secretion effect. The pattern of insulin secretion caused by different

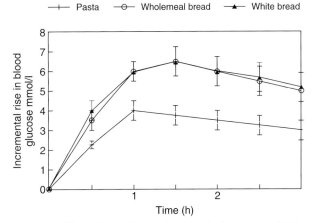

Figure 1 Mean blood glucose increment after equi-available carbohydrate meals. (Data from Jenkins DJ, Wolever TM and Jenkins AL (1988) Starchy foods and glycemic index. *Diabetes Care* 11: 149–159.)

Table 1 The glycemic index model

$$\frac{\text{Incremental area under blood glucose response curve for the test food containing 50 g of carbohydrate}}{\text{Corresponding area after equicarbohydrate portion of glucose}} \times 100$$

Calculation of the glycemic index of a mixed meal containing three separate carbohydrate-containing foods

Glycemic index/mixed meal $(GI_1)(PCF_1) + (GI_2)(PCF_2) + (GI_3)(PCF_3)$

Where
The three carbohydrate-containing foods are 1, 2, and 3
The glycemic index for each carbohydrate-containing food is GI_1, GI_2, and GI_3
The carbohydrate content is **C** 1, **C** 2, and **C** 3 g
The total meal carbohydrate (TMC) is [**C** 1 + **C** 2 + **C** 3] g
The proportion of carbohydrate from each food (PCF) is PCF1 **C** 1/TMCg, PCF2 **C** 2/TMCg, and PCF3 **C** 3/TMCg

carbohydrates reflects their different intestinal transit times.

Type of Dietary Carbohydrate and the Glycemic Index

The glycemic index of a carbohydrate is influenced by its rate of intestinal absorption, which in turn is influenced by its composition, tertiary structure, type of starch, and susceptibility to enzymic digestion.

Chain Length and Composition

Complex carbohydrates are polymeric chains of repeating monosaccharide units. Starches comprise repeating glucose units. The glycemic indexes of different starches are determined by their susceptibility to enzymic digestion, not chain length. White bread and pasta have similar chain lengths, but bread has a higher glycemic index due to its tertiary structure and solubility that ensures greater exposure to salivary and pancreatic amylases.

Short-chain carbohydrates are rapidly absorbed; however, when they contain nonglucose sugars, the glycemic index is lowered proportionally. The disaccharides sucrose and lactose consist of 50% glucose and 50% fructose or galactose, respectively, and both have a lower glycemic index than maltose, the disaccharide formed from two molecules of glucose.

Amylose and Amylopectin

The starches in cereal grains, rice, potatoes, and all green plants are composed of repeating glucose units arranged in straight (amylose) and branched-chained (amylopectin) polysaccharides. The absorption rate, and hence the glycemic index, of these starches is influenced by the ratio of amylose to amylopectin. The more compact structure of amylose than amylopectin results in a smaller surface area being available for amylase digestion. Amylose-enriched starches therefore have lower glycemic indexes than those enriched in amylopectin.

Relationship of Insoluble and Soluble Nonstarch Polysaccharides (Fiber) to Glycemic Index

Nondigestable complex carbohydrates are commonly known as dietary fiber; the more correct terminology is nonstarch polysaccharides (NSPs). NSPs are either soluble or insoluble. Clinical studies have shown that diets rich in soluble fiber/NSPs, such as guar gum, pectin, and sugar beet fibers, lower postprandial blood glucose and insulin levels. Guar gum, a β-glactomannan from the Indian locust bean, also reduces postprandial lipemia. Nonsoluble NSPs have no effect on dietary glycemic index.

Soluble NSPs, such as pulse vegetables, whole fruits, oats, and barley, form gelatinous gels within the stomach that delay gastric emptying and enzymic digestion, the latter by forming a physical barrier around the carbohydrate. Insoluble NSPs have little effect on gastric emptying and no effect on glucose absorption. High-fiber/high-NSP diets are therefore not necessarily synonymous with low glycemic foods. Cellulose is the most widely used NSP in household cereals, whole meal bread, and brown rice, and since it is insoluble, these foods have the same glycemic index whether replete or deplete of their dietary fiber/NSPs. For unknown reasons, Albran is an exception, and despite its high insoluble fiber content, it has a low glycemic index.

The solubility of dietary fiber/NSPs have benefits on postprandial glycemia and hyperinsulinemia. The reason for this are multifactorial including slowing of gastric emptying, a physical barrier to amylase, possible thickening of the unstirred lear and possative effects on gut incretin hormones such as GLP-1 and GIP. The lack of effect on increasing nonsoluble fiber NSPs on glucose and insulin should not detract from important effects on bowel function and bowel pathology.

Cell Structure, Food Preparation, and Processing

Cooking and food preparation can modify the glycemic index. Highly processed convenience foods tend to have high glycemic indexes. When cooking and processing disrupt the cell wall, the starch granules are broken open, optimizing amylase digestion and increasing the glycemic index. Cooked pulse vegetables have low glycemic indexes because their cell walls are resistant to cooking. The intact cereal grains of pumpernickel rye bread, granary bread, and bulgur wheat all have low glycemic indexes. However, when granary bread is processed to wholemeal bread, these grains are disrupted and the glycemic index rises. Cooling can paradoxically lower the glycemic index of certain starches, such as potatoes, due to the formation of retrograde starches that are resistant to amylase digestion.

Effects of the Upper Gastrointestinal Tract

For many foods, their glycemic index is determined by the process of chewing and swallowing. Chewing can reduce food particle size, which increases absorption rates. This explains why boiled and mashed potatoes have different glycemic indexes. Chewing can also change the constituency of the food such that with bread the particle size is reduced to such an extent that it behaves more as a fluid on swallowing and is therefore very rapidly absorbed. In contrast, pastes retain their structure on swallowing and are more slowly absorbed. The rate of gastric emptying also influences the glycemic index, with lower glycemic index foods being retained in the stomach for longer periods than high glycemic index foods.

Concerns Related to the Glycemic Index

Whereas the 1998 WHO/FAO dietary carbohydrate guidelines and the 1998 European dietetic guidelines advocate greater use of the glycemic index, the American Diabetes Association's evidence-based guidelines are more cautious, suggesting a "B"-level evidence grade. This is basically due to the lack of long-term studies, there is only one randomized control trial which had a study period of longer than 6 months. Also there remains concerns regarding the effects of mixed meals are difficult to predict. Against this is the observation in well conducted randomized control trials, blood glucose during the low glycemic index diet is lower than the high glycemic index diet. Studies of the long-term efficacy of low glycemic index diets in diabetes, obesity, and coronary risk groups using randomized control methodology are under way and will report during the next 5 years. The issue regarding the predictability of the glycemic index of mixed meals remains a matter of debate, but evidence suggests that the glycemic index of a mixed meal is reasonable when the fat content is low and deteriorates as the fat content of the meal rises. However, this academic debate should not detract from the fact the evidence from randomized control trial suggests positive benefits on glucose, insulin and lipids from low glycemic index diets.

Reproducibility

Within-subject variation The variability of the glycemic response for a given food for any individual is similar to that seen for the oral glucose tolerance test. In one study, a 25% coefficient of variation (CV) within individuals was seen when 11 healthy subjects had their glycemic response to different carbohydrates tested on eight separate occasions. In another study, the CV of the glycemic response in 22 healthy subjects given 50 g of white bread was 22%. This variability is reduced when the glycemic response is expressed in terms of the 'glycemic index.'

Between-individual variation The variability of the glycemic responses between individuals is larger than that within individual subjects. In a study that included 11 nondiabetic individuals, 10 non-insulin-treated type 2 diabetic subjects, 12 insulin-treated type 2 diabetic subjects, and 14 type 1 diabetic subjects, the CV between individuals within each group was 26, 34, 23, and 34%, respectively. From this it can be seen that comparing the absolute glycemic responses both within and between subjects is unreliable. However, this problem is considerably lessened when the glycemic response to any given food is expressed as a percentage of that individual's glycemic response to a standardized food substance, which in the case of the glycemic index is usually 50 g of glucose. By expressing the glycemic response of a test food against an equal amount of a standard carbohydrate in an individual, variations that occur with age, sex, body mass index, and ethnicity as well as medical conditions such as diabetes are minimized. By using the glycemic index, the between-individual CV of the glycemic response is reduced from approximately 40 to 10%.

Reproducibility of the Glycemic Index

The glycemic index measurement of certain foods can vary between individuals. For example, one study reported that the glycemic index of lentils ranged between 23 and 70 for different subjects. However, this large variability can be minimized to approximately 10% when both the food to be tested and the standard, usually white bread, are each measured in triplicate.

Problems arising from Different Methodologies Used to Calculate the Glycemic Index

Prior to the 1998 WHO nutritional report that standardized the methodology of assessing the glycemic index, different groups used different techniques to calculate the area under the glucose curve and to assess the postprandial glycemic response. The biggest change has been the standardization of the standard used from white bread to glucose. To allow comparison to historic data published glycemic index tables provide conversion factors or present tables using different methods.

Mixed Meals and Other Nutrients

Carbohydrate foods are frequently taken as part of a mixed meal, and the addition of fat and protein to a carbohydrate-containing meal tends to lower the glycemic response. Although the addition of protein or fat to carbohydrate foods reduces the glycemic response, the relative response of one carbohydrate to another remains, such that lentils will always have a lower response than white bread when part of a mixed meal.

The glycemic index of a mixed meal can be calculated from the different proportions of each of the carbohydrate-containing foods and their individual glycemic index values. For example, when bread and beans are mixed in equal portions, the resulting glycemic response is midway between that of bread alone and that of beans alone. A formula for calculating the glycemic index of mixed meals has been derived by Wolever and Jenkins (**Table 1**). For accuracy, this method requires all individual carbohydrate components of a mixed meal to be pretested. Other methods of calculating the glycemic responses of mixed meals relying on a single measurement of the area under the glycemic curve for the mixed meal or an estimation that does not account for all the carbohydrate-containing foods will be less accurate. To be fair, this remains an area of debate; a recent study suggested that the ability to predict the glycemic index of a mixed meal is poor, particularly those with a high fat content.

The Second Meal Effect

Dietary carbohydrates can influence the glycemic response of a second meal consumed during the postprandial period. The blood glucose response to a lunchtime meal is lower when taken after a low glycemic index breakfast than after a high glycemic index breakfast. Similarly, the glycemic response of a second meal taken during the postprandial period after lunch or dinner is influenced by the glycemic index of the preceding meal.

Wolever attributed the differences in the glycemic response to a second meal during the postprandial period to differences in intermediary metabolism and insulin action associated with rapidly and slowly absorbed carbohydrates. Rapidly absorbed carbohydrates produce large increases in blood insulin levels that result in blood glucose levels decreasing sufficiently quickly to stimulate several counterregulatory hormones that inhibit insulin action and glucose disposal. Both carbohydrate drinks and meals consumed rapidly rather than sipped or eaten slowly are associated with significantly higher serum concentrations of glucagon, catecholamines, growth hormone, and nonesterified fatty acid (NEFA) levels postprandially. The addition of guar to a meal, which slows glucose absorption and lowers the glycemic response, reduces postprandial NEFA and β-hydroxybutyrate levels and improves insulin action. In contrast, nibbling high glycemic index

foods between meals increases the glycemic response of a subsequent meal.

Clinical Significance of Postprandial and Fasting Hyperglycemia in Diabetic and Nondiabetic Populations

As with fasting blood glucose levels, postprandial hyperglycemia in nondiabetic populations is a predictor of insulin resistance and cardiovascular disease (CVD). The combined 20-year mortality data on men from the Whitehall, Paris prospective, and Helsinki policemen studies showed that the highest quintile compared with the lowest for the 2-h post-plasma glucose load was associated with a 2.7 increased risk of CVD mortality. The fasting glucose values were less predictive for CVD, with only the top 2.5% conferring a 1.8-fold increased mortality risk. During a 7-year period, elderly women with isolated postprandial hyperglycemia and a 2-h value more than 11.1 mmol/l and fasting value less than 7.0 mmol/l on a 75-g oral glucose tolerance test had an approximately threefold increased risk of heart disease compared with women whose 2-h values were less than 11.1 mmol/l.

In established diabetes, postprandial glycemia appears to have a stronger relationship with microvascular and macrovascular disease than fasting blood glucose. Similarly, in gestational diabetes adverse pregnancy outcome is more closely related to postprandial glycemia than fasting and premeal glycemic values.

Benefits of Low Glycemic Index Carbohydrates on Diabetic Control

This is the area in which there is most evidence of clinical efficacy. Two independent systematic reviews of the world evidence demonstrated the efficacy of low glycemic index diets on glycemic control in both type 1 and type 2 diabetes. Clinical studies have shown that after 3 months of a diet containing low glycemic index carbohydrates, glycemic control is improved in both type 1 and type 2 diabetes. With low glycemic diets, postprandial glucose and insulin concentrations decrease in type 2 diabetic subjects, whereas both postprandial glucose values and insulin requirements decrease in type 1 diabetic subjects. Good glycemic control and favorable lipid and fibrinolytic profiles have also been reported in individuals with either type 1 or 2 diabetes who habitually consume low glycemic index dietary carbohydrates. It remains to be shown whether these diets bestow long-term benefits on micro- or macrovascular complications.

Benefits of Low Glycemic Index Carbohydrates on Cardiovascular Disease Risk Factors

High glycemic index foods induce postprandial hyperinsulinemia, which is a powerful predictor for metabolic risk factors and CVD in epidemiological studies. Both cross-sectional and prospective population studies have shown favorable lipid profiles in association with high carbohydrate diets. Initially, these benefits were attributed to a high fiber content. However, when the glycemic index is controlled for, it is the low glycemic index diets rather than high fiber content that have the greatest influence on high-density lipoprotein (HDL) cholesterol, insulin sensitivity, and fibrinolytic parameters. In a cross-sectional study on more than 2000 middle-aged subjects, the glycemic index was a stronger determinant of HDL cholesterol than any other dietary factor, be it carbohydrate or fat. In this study, the HDL cholesterol of the women whose habitual diet was within the lowest quintile for glycemic index was 0.25 mmol/l higher than that for women whose dietary carbohydrate was within the highest quintile. Extrapolating from the Framingham data that showed a 3% decrease in female and a 2% decrease in male cardiovascular morbidity to be associated with a 0.026 mmol/l increase in HDL cholesterol, one would predict a 29% difference in CHD morbidity between women in the lowest and highest quintile for dietary glycemic index. A similar calculation for men with dietary carbohydrates in the lowest and highest quintile for glycemic index found a 7% decrease in CHD morbidity associated with the 0.09 mmol/l difference in HDL cholesterol concentrations. Low glycemic index diets have also been shown to lower serum cholesterol and triglyceride levels in hyperlipidemic subjects.

Glycemic Index and the Prevention of Type 2 Diabetes

Changes in diet and physical activity levels, both alone and in combination, reduce the progression of impaired glucose tolerance to diabetes. Two large US prospective population studies have demonstrated a doubling of the relative risk of developing type 2 diabetes for both men and women when the habitual diet is characterized by a high glycaemic index and high fat content. A similar protective effect against diabetes has been reported in populations consuming high-fiber foods and high quantities of fruit, and one would predict that these diets would also have a low glycemic index.

Obesity and Glycemic Index

Obesity contributes to the pathogenesis and morbidity of type 2 diabetes. Obesity is associated with changes in carbohydrate and fat metabolism that are central to the development of insulin resistance. Although low glycemic index diets enhance insulin sensitivity and improve metabolic cardiovascular risk factors, they will not reduce weight unless part of an energy-deficient diet. However, in obese subjects, when low glycemic carbohydrates are incorporated into a hypocaloric diet, there is a greater decrease in insulin resistance than can be accounted for by weight loss alone. Evidence from both animal and human studies demonstrates a change in body composition (decrease in fat but no change on overall weight) when exposed to a low glycemic index diet.

Pregnancy and Glycemic Index

Throughout pregnancy in well-nourished urbanized women consuming typical Western diets, glucose tolerance deteriorates. During pregnancy, African women living in traditional rural populations and consuming high-carbohydrate/low glycemic index diets do not invariably experience deterioration in their glucose tolerance. Clinical studies in the West show that women consuming similar high-carbohydrate/low glycemic index diets throughout pregnancy also have no deterioration of glucose tolerance despite the physiological increase in insulin resistance that occurs secondary to maternal and placental hormones. When the proportion of dietary carbohydrate increases above 50% in women with gestational diabetes, if no emphasis on low glycemic index carbohydrates is given, glucose tolerance will deteriorate.

Proposed Mechanism by which Dietary Carbohydrates/Glycemic Index Influence Insulin Resistance

Adipocyte metabolism is central to the pathogenesis of insulin resistance and dietary carbohydrates influence adipocyte function. The previous simplistic view that insulin resistance resulted from the downregulation of the insulin receptors in response to hyperinsulinemia is being replaced by the hypothesis that high circulating NEFA levels both impair insulin action and reduce pancreatic β cell secretion. It is plausible that low glycemic index carbohydrates reduce insulin resistance by their ability to reduce adipocyte NEFA release. There is evidence of a loss of suppression of hormone-sensitive lipase (HSL), an enzyme that breaks down triglyceride to free fatty acids and glycerol, to small physiological amounts of insulin and, to a lesser extent, insulin insensitivity of lipoprotein lipase. HSL is normally very sensitive to small increases in insulin levels and is totally suppressed at much lower concentrations than those required for glucose uptake. In insulin-resistant subjects, HSL is less sensitive to small changes in insulin levels and adipocyte NEFA release is increased. A relationship between increased adipocyte NEFA release and insulin resistance has been shown in subjects with coronary heart disease. The metabolic consequences of increased circulating NEFA are multiple and are beyond the scope of this review, but they include adverse lipoprotein and coagulation changes and have been reported to affect insulin secretion and have a lipotoxic effect on the β cell. Accumulation of triglyceride within the β cell also impairs insulin secretion.

Many of the metabolic benefits associated with low glycemic index carbohydrates can be attributed to their ability to reduce adipocyte NEFA release. Low glycemic index foods have been consistently shown to reduce insulin resistance, and animal studies have shown that improvements in fat and muscle insulin sensitivity are accompanied by decreases in fatty acid synthatase activity, adipocyte size, and lipid storage. Although human studies have shown that low glycemic index diets consumed for 3 weeks increase adipocyte insulin sensitivity, no direct effect on adipocyte metabolism has been identified.

Low glycemic index diets attenuate the insulin response for approximately 4 h postprandially. This slightly high postprandial insulin is insufficient to affect glucose transport but does suppress the insulin-sensitive enzyme, HSL, and thus ensures prolonged suppression of postprandial NEFA output. The ability of low glycemic carbohydrates to do this is in stark contrast with high glycemic diets that can cause an elevation of NEFA release postprandially by stimulating the counterregulatory hormones, as discussed previously. Low glycemic meals taken in the evening can effectively suppress circulating NEFA concentrations and hepatic glucose output throughout the night. These metabolic effects are predicted to promote insulin sensitivity.

Our own work has shown that insulin-resistant adults with a history or who are at risk of CHD improve their adipocyte insulin sensitivity after consuming a low glycemic index diet for 3 weeks and their circulating NEFA levels decline. These human studies complement animal work showing that low glycemic index diets improve insulin sensitivity by modulating adipocyte metabolism.

Conclusion

The glycemic index of a diet is an indicator of postprandial metabolism, which is important in contributing to cardiovascular risk. Dietary carbohydrates are absorbed and metabolized differently and therefore influence postprandial glucose, insulin, and NEFA concentrations differently. In Western society, the proportion of the day that we spend in the postprandial state is increasing as the tendency to snack throughout the day replaces sit-down meals. The known detrimental consequences of high glycemic foods and snacks on postprandial metabolism should encourage us to advocate low glycemic diets to counter the current epidemic of insulin resistance-related diseases, notably CVD and diabetes. The relevance of the glycemic index to these two major preventable diseases of the Western world argues strongly for its greater acceptance in current nutritional guidelines.

See also: **Carbohydrates**: Chemistry and Classification; Regulation of Metabolism; Requirements and Dietary Importance; Resistant Starch and Oligosaccharides. **Diabetes Mellitus**: Dietary Management. **Dietary Fiber**: Physiological Effects and Effects on Absorption. **Fructose. Galactose. Glucose**: Chemistry and Dietary Sources. **Obesity**: Complications. **Pregnancy**: Nutrient Requirements; Safe Diet for Pregnancy. **Sucrose**: Nutritional Role, Absorption and Metabolism. **World Health Organization**.

Further Reading

American Diabetic Association (2004) Nutrition principles and recommendations in diabetes. *Diabetes Care* **27**: S36.

Connor H, Annan F, Bunn E *et al.* Nutrition Subcommittee of the Diabetes Care Advisory Committee of Diabetes UK (2003) The implementation of nutritional advice for people with diabetes. *Diabetic Medicine* **20**(10): 786–807.

FAO/WHO (1998) *Carbohydrates in Human Nutrition. Report of a Joint FAO/WHO Committee, Rome 14–18 April, 1997,* Paper No. 66. Rome: FAO.

Foster-Powell K, Holt SH, and Brand-Miller JC (2002) International table of glycemic index and glycemic load values: 2002. *American Journal of Clinical Nutrition* **76**(1): 5–56.

Ha KK and Lean MEJ (1998) Recommendations for the nutritional management of patients with diabetes mellitus. *European Journal of Clinical Nutrition* **52**: 467–481.

Jenkins DJ, Wolever TM, and Jenkins AL (1988) Starchy foods and glycemic index. *Diabetes Care* **11**: 149–159.

Lean MEJ, Brenchley S, Connor H *et al.* (1992) Dietary recommendations for people with diabetes: An update for the 1990s. Nutrition Subcommittee of the British Diabetic Association's Professional Advisory Committee. *Diabetic Medicine* **9**(2): 189–202.

Goitre *see* **Iodine**: Deficiency Disorders

GOUT

L A Coleman, Marshfield Clinic Research Foundation, Marshfield, WI, USA
R Roubenoff, Millennium Pharmaceuticals, Inc., Cambridge, MA, USA and Tufts University, Boston, MA, USA

A diagnosis of gout refers to a group of metabolic conditions resulting from the deposition of monosodium urate crystals around and in the tissues of joints. The precise mechanism by which uric acid leads to gouty arthritis remains somewhat unclear; various contributing factors are discussed. Clinically, gout typically involves an episodic monoarthritis; if untreated, acute gout can segue into a deforming, chronic polyarthritis that may be difficult to distinguish from rheumatoid arthritis. Improved prevention and treatment of gout have occurred during the latter half of the twentieth century; however, recent research has focused on the link between serum urate, coronary artery disease, and insulin resistance syndrome. Dietary management of gout no longer seems to be focused on restriction of foods with a high purine content but, rather, on the treatment of metabolic disorders commonly associated with gout: obesity, insulin resistance syndrome, and dyslipidemia.

Definition and Etiology

Gout, from the Latin *gutta* or drop (of evil humor), is an ancient disease that was included in Hippocrates' Aphorisms. In the first edition of his textbook, *Principles and Practice of Medicine* (1892), Osler defined gout as "a nutritional disorder associated with an excess formation of uric acid." Today, we recognize that this definition is partly true, but that most cases of gout are not due to excess formation of uric acid but, rather, to insufficient clearance of the substance. Hyperuricemia occurs when there is too much uric acid in the blood, a condition that is generally agreed to exist when the serum or plasma uric acid exceeds

the saturation point at $37\,°C$, which is approximately $7.0\,mg\,dl^{-1}$. Hyperuricemia is a requirement for gout, but it is not always present when a patient presents with a first episode of gout, presumably because the acute deposition of uric acid in a joint reduces blood levels transiently. However, hyperuricemia is present at some point in virtually all gout patients. It is important to distinguish hyperuricemia, an asymptomatic condition, from gout, a painful disease that afflicts only a minority of people with elevated uric acid levels. Hyperuricemia can result from overproduction of uric acid in 10–15% of cases (generally because of enzyme deficiency or overactivity) or from underexcretion of uric acid, which accounts for 85–90% of cases of gout (due to decreased renal clearance of uric acid, even in the setting of a normal glomerular filtration rate).

Chemical Pathology

Uric acid is a by-product of purine metabolism in humans and certain apes who lack uricase, the enzyme that breaks down uric acid (**Figure 1**).

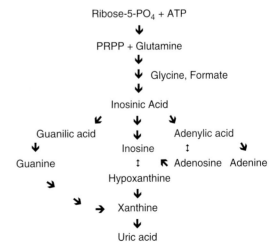

Figure 1 Simplified pathway of uric acid metabolism. PRPP, 5-phosphoribosyl-*l*-pyrophosphate. (Modified from Seegmiller JE, Rosenbloom FM and Kelly WN (1967) Enzyme defect associated with a sex-linked human neurological disorder and excessive purine synthesis. *Science* **155**: 1682–1684.)

When uric acid production is normal, and its clearance by the kidneys is normal, this metabolic quirk has no ill effects. However, this minor metabolic inconvenience becomes of pathological importance because uric acid is so poorly soluble in aqueous solutions that it can crystallize and cause the various conditions recognized as gout. Uric acid can be ingested directly in the diet (especially in organ meats such as liver, kidney, and sweetbreads), or it can be produced in the body by two pathways involved in purine metabolism (**Figure 1**). The de novo synthesis of uric acid proceeds directly from ribose-5-phosphate, whereas the salvage pathway consists of production of the uric acid precursors inosine from adenosine and xanthine from guanine. The medication allopurinol, which blocks the conversion of xanthine to uric acid by xanthine oxidase, is effective because xanthine is far more soluble in aqueous solutions than is uric acid.

The precise mechanism by which uric acid leads to gouty arthritis remains somewhat unclear. However, uric acid is known to be proinflammatory in that it can initiate an immune response with recruitment of white blood cells after uric acid crystals are phagocytosed by polymorphonuclear leukocytes or macrophages. These white blood cells also release tumor necrosis factor and interleukin-1, recruiting more white cells, which release lysosomal enzymes that lead to cartilage destruction and joint erosions with repeated attacks. In addition, ingestion of uric acid leads to death of the phagocytosing cells, leading to release of the uric acid and additional proteolytic enzymes, thus reinforcing the inflammatory condition. However, the crystals become progressively less phlogistic after several cycles of ingestion and release, and the inflammation relents over a period of 10–14 days. The natural history of untreated gout progresses through four stages from (i) asymptomatic hyperuricemia to (ii) acute gouty arthritis, (iii) intercritical gout, and (iv) chronic tophaceous gout. In addition, renal manifestations of gout develop in up to 50% of patients, depending on the amount of uric acid they excrete.

Prevalence and Risk Factors

Gout is the most common inflammatory arthritis in men; more than 2 million men and women in the United States are afflicted. The prevalence of gout in the United States tripled between 1969 and 1981 but recently seems to have stabilized. This increase is thought to be due to a combination of factors, including aging of the US population, increased prevalence of diuretic treatment of hypertension, better access to health care, and better diagnosis and reporting of gout. The incidence of gout (i.e., the development of new cases) is linked to serum uric acid levels, increasing from 0.9 cases per 1000 person-years for uric acid levels less than 7.0 mg dl^{-1} to 70 cases per 1000 person-years for levels higher than 10.0 mg dl^{-1}. However, even in the highest category, only 30% of men developed gout during the 5 years after their uric acid level was determined, confirming that only a minority of hyperuricemic men develop acute gout.

Risk factors for acute gout other than hyperuricemia have been identified. All risk factors act either by increasing serum uric acid levels or by reducing the solubility of uric acid in the joints. For example, male sex, alcohol ingestion, obesity, and weight gain are associated with increased uric acid production, whereas diuretics (thiazides and loop diuretics), low-dose salicylates, and renal insufficiency lead to reduced clearance of uric acid. Hypertension has been associated with increased risk of gout, but this effect probably operates through renal insufficiency, which occurs as a result of hypertension and diuretic therapy. Lead, on the other hand, has been shown to directly reduce the solubility of uric acid in synovial fluid, whereas lead nephropathy also leads to reduced clearance of uric acid; the gout associated with lead toxicity is known as saturnine gout. Joint trauma and cooling of distal joints also reduce solubility of uric acid and increase the risk of an acute attack. Gout was known in the eighteenth century as 'pheasant hunter's toe' when aristocratic gentlemen developed *podagra* (acute inflammation of the first metatarsophalangeal (MTP) joint) after a day of hunting in the cold marshes and a night of drinking alcohol, especially sherry shipped in lead-lined casks. In more recent times, saturnine gout has been associated with drinking illegal 'moonshine' whiskey distilled through lead-lined stills. An independent association has been shown between kidney stone disease and gout, strongly suggesting that they share a common underlying pathophysiological mechanism.

Insulin resistance has been increasingly implicated in the pathogenesis of gout. The lipoprotein abnormalities described in subjects with hyperuricemia are similar to those found in individuals with insulin resistance, and insulin has an impact on renal urate excretion. Although the precise frequency of insulin resistance syndrome in patients with gout is not known, it is estimated to be as high as 76% for insulin resistance syndrome and 95% for hyperinsulinemia. It has been suggested that elevated serum urate may even serve as a surrogate marker for insulin resistance syndrome.

Clinical Features

Gout is typically an episodic monoarthritis, although polyarticular gout (involving three or more joints) occurs in approximately 10% of cases. The description of the pain of acute gout by Thomas Sydenham in the seventeenth century remains among the best:

> The victim goes to bed and sleeps in good health. About two o'clock in the morning he is awakened by a severe pain in the great toe; more rarely in the heel, ankle, or instep. This pain is like that of a dislocation ... then follow chills and a little fever. The pain ... becomes more intense.... Now it is a violent stretching and tearing of the ligaments—now it is a gnawing pain and now a pressure and tightening. So exquisite and lively meanwhile is the feeling of the part affected, that it cannot bear the weight of the bed-clothes nor the jar of a person walking in the room. The night passes in torture.

More than half of patients present with podagra, and 75–90% of patients eventually develop podagra. This joint is thought to be most susceptible to gout because it is very prone to trauma and cooling, both of which reduce the solubility of uric acid. After the first MTP, acute gout most commonly involves the ankles, knees, instep, but it can also involve the wrists, elbows, and small joints of the hands and feet. Large axial joints, such as hips, shoulders, and vertebral joints, are rarely affected. Acute gout often involves a component of tenosynovitis (inflammation of tendon sheaths), and gouty cellulitis (sterile inflammation with urate crystals in the skin) and bursitis have also been described. As Sydenham stated, the onset is generally explosive, but many patients also describe a series of minor attacks leading up to the full-blown episode. Untreated gouty arthritis lasts from days to weeks, but minor bouts may resolve spontaneously in a few hours. At this stage, joint radiographs are normal except for soft tissue swelling. If untreated, acute gout can segue into a deforming, chronic polyarthritis that may be difficult to distinguish from rheumatoid arthritis.

Because a significant proportion of people, perhaps as many as one-third, who have a single acute gouty attack do not have another for 1 year or longer, no further therapy is indicated after the first attack has subsided. Once a patient has demonstrated recurrent attacks of acute gout, or if he or she has had a uric acid stone (or another type of stone in the setting of hyperuricosuria), treatment aimed at reducing serum uric acid below the point of solubility is indicated. In general, patients who develop a second attack and have a serum creatinine concentration less than $2.0\,\mathrm{mg\,dl^{-1}}$ should be evaluated further with a 24-h urine collection for creatinine clearance and uric acid output while consuming their regular diet. If the 24-h urinary uric acid totals more than 1000 mg, the patient is classified as an overproducer of uric acid and should be treated with allopurinol if he or she is not allergic. If the 24-h uric acid production is under 700 mg, then the patient is an underexcreter and may first be treated with a uricosuric agent, which is safer and less expensive than allopurinol. Renal insufficiency will reduce both creatinine clearance and urinary uric acid output, and allopurinol is the drug of choice in this situation, so the utility of a 24-h urine collection is reduced. Patients who produce between 700 and 1000 mg of uric acid are in a gray zone, and clinical judgment regarding optimal therapy is necessary, balancing issues of safety, cost, and convenience in the management of a chronic disease.

Chronic tophaceous gout occurs with an average of 10 years of untreated or inadequately treated gout. Over time, the acute attacks become less noticeable, and the patient develops a chronic, often deforming arthritis. This arthritis may mimic rheumatoid arthritis, although it should be less symmetric. At this time, the radiological hallmarks of gout, which include large, well-demarcated erosions in the absence of joint space narrowing ('rat-bite erosions'), are often visible. Tophi, which are subcutaneous deposits of uric acid, may be found in and around joints, bursae (especially the olecranon), tendons (Achilles and infrapatellar), and the extensor surfaces of the forearms. Less commonly, they may arise in the pinna of the ear, cardiac valves, cornea and sclera, and nasal cartilage. Needle aspiration or spontaneous rupture of tophi elicits a white, chalky material that is full of urate crystals under microscopy and is diagnostic of tophaceous gout. The presence of tophi is always an indication for allopurinol in nonallergic patients.

Dietary Management

There has been a substantial change in the predominant view regarding the relationship between diet and gout. It has even been said that "dietary considerations now play a minor role in the treatment of hyperuricemia, despite a fascinating history and abundant literature."

The relationship between gout and gluttony (overindulgence of food and alcohol) dates back to ancient times. In the fifth- century BC, Hippocrates attributed gout to dietary excesses of food and wine; he advised dietary restriction and reduction of alcohol consumption. Historically, the dietary management of gout has focused on two goals: (i) reducing the amount of uric acid that may be deposited as crystals in joints or soft tissues, leading to the clinical syndrome of gout, and (ii) managing the disorders that occur with increased frequency among patients with gout, including diabetes mellitus, obesity, hyperlipidemia, hypertension, and atherosclerosis.

Although some practitioners may still advocate the traditional low-purine, low-protein, alcohol-restricted diet, there is increasing support for the more 'contemporary' view that dietary management should focus on weight reduction with a restricted intake of calories and carbohydrates along with proportional increases in both protein and unsaturated fats and no restriction of purine content.

Traditional Low-Purine Diet

The primary dietary modification that has traditionally been recommended to reduce uric acid production is a low-purine diet (<75 mg/24 h; **Table 1**). Uric acid is the end product of purine metabolism in humans, formed by oxidation of its precursors, the oxypurines, hypoxanthine and xanthine. With the advent of more powerful and effective urate-lowering drugs, however, dietary restriction of purine-rich foods is of decreasing importance. Although patients may be advised to avoid large quantities of food and alcoholic beverages that they know may precipitate a gouty attack (i.e., large amounts of organ meats or beer), a rigid purine-restricted diet is no longer viewed as a mainstay of dietary management.

Many patients with gout are overweight, and a combination of caloric reduction and exercise can have a beneficial impact on any associated hypertension, hyperlipidemia, and insulin resistance syndrome via enhanced renal excretion of urate and reduced serum urate levels. However, although weight reduction, purine restriction, and reduced alcohol consumption may transiently reduce serum urate, there are no long-term studies demonstrating the efficacy of such an approach. Any benefit that does occur is likely to be small, and any limited reduction in serum urate levels is likely to be offset by the difficulty of maintaining such an improvement over the long term.

Contemporary Low-Calorie, Carbohydrate-Restricted Diet

In view of the well-recognized link between insulin resistance syndrome, hyperuricemia, and gout, a diet emphasizing reduced calorie intake with moderate restriction of carbohydrates and liberalization of protein and unsaturated fat consumption has been espoused for patients with gout. Low-purine foods are often high in both carbohydrate and saturated fats; these foods tend to further decrease insulin sensitivity, thereby contributing to even higher levels of insulin, glucose, triglycerides, and low-density lipoprotein cholesterol and lower high-density lipoprotein cholesterol levels, all of which result in increased risk of coronary heart disease among these patients. Conversely, a calorie-restricted, weight-reduction diet that is low in carbohydrates (40% of total calories) and relatively high in protein (approximately 120 g per day compared to 80–90 g in the typical Western diet) and unsaturated fat content, with no limitation of purine content, has been studied and found to result in weight loss and reductions in serum urate, lipids, and gouty attacks. These benefits seem to relate to the coexistence of hyperlipidemia and glucose intolerance in patients with gout.

In summary, both the traditional and the contemporary approaches to dietary modification need to be studied over the long term, but it appears that the most benefit can be gained by focusing efforts on reducing calorie intake and carbohydrate consumption rather than on limiting the purine content of the diet. It appears that restriction of alcoholic beverages is advisable in the management of gout.

Prognosis

Gout is unusual among the rheumatic diseases in that its etiology, treatment, and prevention are well understood. Thus, the long-term sequelae of gout should be completely avoidable with adequate treatment, making the overall prognosis excellent. Noncompliance with medication, lack of access to adequate medical care, and inability to tolerate one or more of the medications used to treat gout can lead to a worse outcome. A number of dietary and lifestyle factors may contribute to the increased uric acid production among patients with gout. If these factors can be identified and appropriate changes made, the serum uric acid concentration may decline substantially. However, many patients require medication to control the hyperuricemia. The

Table 1 Foods to avoid on a purine-restricted diet

Meats, organ meats (sweetbreads, liver, kidney), fish, eggs, sausages, meat extracts and gravies
Beans, peas, spinach, asparagus, cauliflower, mushrooms
Oatmeal
Legumes
Chocolate
Yeast and yeast extracts
Tea, coffee, cola beverages, alcoholic beverages

Touger-Decker R (1996) Nutritional Care in Rheumatic Diseases. In: Mahan LK and Escott-Stumps S (eds.) *Krause's Food, Nutrition, & Diet Therapy*, 9th edn. pp. 889–898. Philadelphia, PA: W.B. Saunders Company.

predominant dietary approach to gout is that dietary advice, other than the restriction of overly excessive alcohol intake, is likely to be limited to weight reduction.

See also: **Alcohol**: Disease Risk and Beneficial Effects. **Arthritis**. **Diabetes Mellitus**: Etiology and Epidemiology. **Hypertension**: Dietary Factors.

Further Reading

Brand FN, McGee DL, Kannel WB, Stokes J, and Castelli WP (1985) Hyperuricemia as a risk factor of coronary heart disease: The Framingham Study. *American Journal of Epidemiology* **121**: 11–18.

Dessein PH, Shipton EA, Stanwix AE, Joffe BI, and Ramokgadi J (2000) Beneficial effects of weight loss associated with moderate calorie/carbohydrate restriction, and increased proportional intake of protein and unsaturated fat on serum urate and lipoprotein levels in gout: A pilot study. *Annals of Rheumatic Disease* **59**: 539–543.

Emmerson BT (1996) The management of gout. *New England Journal of Medicine* **334**: 445–451.

Fam AG (2002) Gout, diet, and the insulin resistance syndrome. *Journal of Rheumatology* **29**: 1350–1355.

Lawrence RC, Helmick CG, Arnett FC *et al.* (1998) Estimates of the prevalence of arthritis and selected musculoskeletal disorders in the United States. *Arthritis & Rheumatism* **41**: 778–799.

Roubenoff R (1990) The epidemiology of gout and hyperuricemia. *Rheumatic Disease Clinics of North America* **16**: 539–550.

Roubenoff R (1996) Gout and other crystal diseases. In: Stobe JD, Ledenson PW, Traill TA, Petty BG, and Helliman DB (eds.) *Principles and Practice of Medicine*, 23rd edn., pp. 233–239. Hartford, CT: Appleton.

Roubenoff R, Klag MJ, Mead LA *et al.* (1991) Incidence and risk factors for gout in white men. *Journal of the American Medical Association* **266**: 3004–3007.

Snaith ML (2001) Gout: Diet and uric acid revisited. *Lancet* **358**: 525.

Sydenham T (1850) *The Works of Thomas Sydenham* (translated from Latin by RG Lathan), vol. 2, pp. 124. London: New Sydenham Society.

Terkeltaub RA (2001) Gout: Epidemiology, pathology, and pathogenesis. In: Klippel JH (ed.) *Primer on the Rheumatic Diseases*, 12th edn., pp. 307–312. Atlanta: Arthritis Foundation.

Touger-Decker R (1996) Nutritional Care in Rheumatic Diseases. In: Mahan LK and Escott-Stump S (eds) *Krause's Food, Nutrition, & Diet Therapy*, 9th edn. pp. 889–898. Philadelphia, PA: W.B. Saunders Company.

Wortmann RL (2002) Gout and hyperuricemia. *Current Opinions in Rheumatology* **14**: 281–286.

Grains *see* **Cereal Grains**

GROWTH AND DEVELOPMENT, PHYSIOLOGICAL ASPECTS

W W Hay Jr, University of Colorado Health Sciences Center, Aurora, CO, USA

Introduction

Growth and development refers to the growth of the individual in size as determined by anthropometric measurements of body weight, length, circumference, and weight/length ratio, as well as changes in body composition. This article will focus on growth and development of the fetus, as most of the relevant concepts about growth and development apply to the fetal period of development and this period encompasses the greatest changes in body proportion and composition during the life of the individual. Fetal growth occurs by increases in cell number and size. In the first third of gestation, during the embryonic period, growth occurs primarily by increased cell number (hyperplasia); in the middle third of gestation, cell size also increases (hypertrophy), while the rate of cell division becomes stable. In the last third of gestation, the rate of cell division declines, while cell size continues to increase.

Many terms are used to describe variations in growth. For example, human newborns are classified as having normal birth weight (greater than 2500 g), low birth weight (less than 2500 g), very low birth weight (less than 1500 g), or extremely low birth weight (less than 1000 g). Obviously, classification by weight alone says little about growth rate, as most infants with less than normal birth weights are the result of a shorter than normal gestation, i.e., they are preterm. Similarly, classifying newborns according to duration of gestation (e.g., preterm, term, or post-term) on the basis of birth weight also is erroneous, because infants with intrauterine growth restriction (IUGR) are smaller and macrosomic infants of diabetic mothers are larger than normal at any gestational age. Furthermore, it is inappropriate to label newborns as abnormally grown when their birth weight is less than some arbitrarily determined 'normal' birth weight, but their mother was quite small to begin with; such newborns are considered constitutionally small but not abnormal.

Growth of Fetal Size

What should be considered more important for growth assessment than birth weight (at any gestational age) is the genetic growth potential of the infant, which may or may not be limited by maternal size. Under usual conditions, the fetus grows at its genetic potential. Small fetuses of small parents or large fetuses of large parents do not reflect fetal growth restriction or fetal overgrowth, respectively; in fact, their rates of growth are normal for their genome. If the mother is unusually small, however, she might limit fetal growth by 'maternal constraint,' which represents a limited uterine size (primarily endometrial surface area) and thus the capacity to support placental growth and nutrient supply to the fetus. A clear example of maternal constraint is shown in **Figure 1**, showing the reduced rate of fetal growth of multiple fetuses in a species, i.e., human, that optimally supports only one fetus.

Fetal weight tends to increase exponentially in the middle part of gestation, producing the typical S-shaped curve of fetal weight versus gestational age that is derived from cross-sectional measurements of newborn weights at different known gestational ages (**Figure 2**). The length of gestation is more strongly related to the growth of neural tissue (range $0.015–0.033\,\mathrm{g}^{1/3}$/day – a 2.2-fold range) than to the growth of the fetal body (range 0.033 to $0.25\,\mathrm{g}^{1/3}$/day – a 7.6-fold range). The physiological significance of this relationship is not known, but intrauterine development of a large brain/body mass ratio in humans is favored in a single fetus and is made possible by a slow rate of somatic growth.

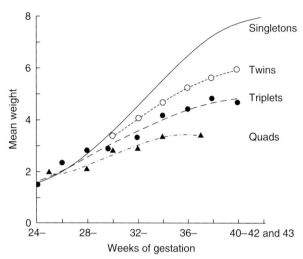

Figure 1 Mean birth weight of single and multiple fetuses related to duration of gestation. (Reproduced with permission from Ounsted M and Ounsted C (1973) *On Fetal Growth Rate.* Spastics International Medical Publications (Clinics in Developmental Medicine No. 46), p. 17. London: William Heinemann Medical Books Ltd.)

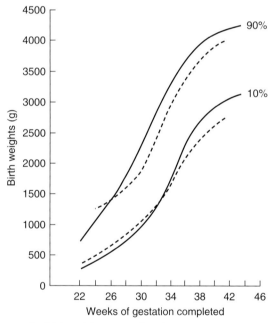

Figure 2 Birth-weight percentiles for gestational age. Solid lines represent California total singleton live births, 1970–1976: dotted lines represent Colorado General Hospital (Denver, Colorado) live births, 1948–1960. (Reproduced with permission from Creasy R and Resnik R (1989) Intrauterine growth retardation. In: Creasy R and Resnik R (eds.) *Maternal-Fetal Medicine*, 2nd edn, pp. 549–564. Philadelphia: W.B. Saunders.)

Developmental Change of Fetal Body Composition

Fetal growth during the last third of gestation requires large increases in nutrient supplies and appropriate utilization of these nutrients. Nutrient substrate supply is coupled with increased development of anabolic hormones and growth factors in fetal tissues and fetal plasma to produce increased nitrogen and carbon deposition in protein, carbohydrate deposition in glycogen, and fatty acid, glycerol and triglyceride deposition in adipose tissue. Growth of these tissues gradually replaces water in the fetal extracellular space.

Chemical composition studies of normal human infants are limited. Based on data from 15 studies that included 207 infants, nonfat dry weight and nitrogen content (predictors of protein content) show a linear relationship with fetal weight and an exponential relationship with gestational age (**Figure 3**). As gestation proceeds, larger fetuses grow faster than smaller fetuses, and protein accretion follows accordingly.

Water

Fetal water content increases directly with body weight, but not proportionally to body weight, as fetal body water, expressed as a fraction of body weight, decreases with advancing gestation. The relatively large growth of adipose tissue in the human fetus further dilutes the body concentration of water. Extracellular water, as a fraction of fetal body weight, also decreases more than intracellular water as gestation advances; this is mainly due to increasing cell number and increasing cell size, rather than the intracellular concentration of osmotic substances.

Nonfat dry weight

Comparative aspects of fetal chemical and physical growth in six species are summarized in **Table 1**. Despite growth rate variations up to 20-fold and weight-specific fat content variances at term up to 16-fold among these species, nonfat dry weight and protein weight-specific contents (as percentages of total weight at term) are constant. Protein

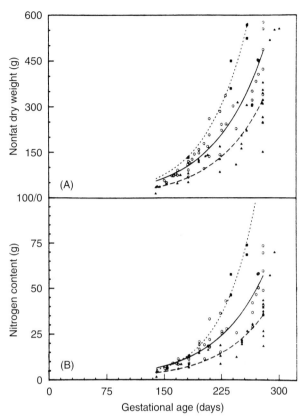

Figure 3 Nonfat dry weight (A) and nitrogen content (B) are plotted against gestational age for LGA (■, ····), AGA (O, —), and SGA (◆, – – –) infants. (Reproduced with permission from Sparks JW (1992) Intrauterine growth and nutrition. In: Polin RA and Fox WW (eds.) *Fetal and Neonatal Physiology*, p. 184. Philadelphia: W.B. Saunders.)

concentration is about 12% in all species at term and fetal protein content is linearly related to fetal weight; thus, protein accretion in the fetal rat occurs about 23 times as fast as it does in the human. These species-related differences in growth rate are remarkable and require marked differences in the placental capacity to supply nutrients to the fetus.

Table 1 Growth characteristics and chemical composition at term of selected mammals and a representative human fetus

	Human	Monkey	Sheep	Pig	Rabbit	Rat
Gestation (days)	280	163	47	67	30	21.5
Number of fetuses	1	1	1	3–5	4–6	10–12
Growth rate (g kg^{-1} day^{-1})	15	44	60	70	300	350
Fetal weight (g)	3500	500	4000	100	60	5
Dry weight (g/% body wt)	1050/30	125/25	760/19	25/25	9/15	0.2/4
Nonfat dry weight (g/% body wt)	490/14	–	640/16	14/14	–	–
Protein (g/% body wt)	420/12	–	480/12	12/12	7.2/12	0.6/12

From McCance RA and Widdowson EM (1985) In: Falkner F and Tanner JM (eds.) *Human Growth*, 2nd edn, vol. 1 p. 139. New York: Plenum Press.

Nitrogen Balance, Protein Turnover, and Protein Synthesis

According to animal data, only about 80% of the nitrogen content of the fetus is found in protein; the rest is found in urea, ammonia, and free amino acids. Additional nitrogen requirements for urea excretion and for other possible nitrogen excretion products are not known for human fetuses.

Radioactive and stable isotopic tracers of selected amino acids, especially essential amino acids such as leucine and lysine, have been used to measure fetal protein synthesis, breakdown, and accretion. Limited human data is consistent with data in the fetal sheep, the only species studied in significant detail. **Figure 4** shows results of experiments in fetal sheep over the second half of gestation, comparing fractional protein synthesis rates derived from tracer data and fractional body growth rates derived from body composition data. Whole body weight-specific protein turnover rate is higher in the early-gestation fetus primarily from increased rates of amino acid uptake from the placenta (exogenous entry of amino acids into the fetal circulation) and protein synthesis. These processes produce a 50% higher rate of net protein accretion in the mid-gestation fetus.

Mechanisms underlying the decrease in protein synthesis rate over gestation are not well understood, but they appear to be intrinsic to the fetus and not to a limitation of nutrient supply by the

Table 2 Fetal organ weight as per cent of body weight

	50% Gestation	67% Gestation	90% Gestation
Liver	6.5	5.1	3.1
Kidneys	1.6	1.2	0.7
Heart	0.9	0.8	0.8
Brain	3.4	2.9	1.7
Hindquarters	14.5	15.1	22.0

Reproduced with permission from Bell AW *et al.* (1987) Relation between metabolic rate and body size in the ovine fetus. *Journal of Nutrition* **117**: 1181–1186. Used with permission.

placenta. At least a partial explanation can be offered according to the changing proportion of body mass contributed by the major organs (**Table 2**). Based on the increased mass of skeletal muscle with advancing gestation, fetal whole body fractional synthesis rate should be lower, as skeletal muscle has a relatively lower fractional protein synthetic rate in late gestation than in earlier gestation. A direct relationship between anabolic growth-promoting substances acting as principal regulators of fetal protein synthesis rate, and thus fetal growth rate, cannot be made, however, as plasma concentrations or secretion rates of these substances increase in the fetus as gestation proceeds, while protein synthetic rates decline.

Glycogen

Many tissues in the fetus, including brain, liver, lung, heart, and skeletal muscle, produce glycogen over the second half of gestation. Liver glycogen content, which increases over the gestation period, is the most important store of carbohydrate for systemic glucose needs, because only the liver contains sufficient glucose-6-phosphatase for release of glucose into the circulation. Skeletal muscle glycogen content increases during late gestation and forms a ready source of glucose for glycolysis within the myocytes. Lung glycogen content decreases in late gestation with change in cell type, leading to loss of glycogen-containing alveolar epithelium, development of type II pneumocytes, and onset of surfactant production. Cardiac glycogen concentration decreases with gestation owing to cellular hypertrophy, but cardiac glycogen appears essential for postnatal cardiac energy metabolism and function. At term, fetal liver glycogen concentration in most species ($80–120\,mg\,g^{-1}$) is at least twice the adult concentration, but in the relatively slow-growing human fetus, glycogen synthesis rates are low (about $2\,mg\,day^{-1}\,g^{-1}$), representing less than 2% of estimated whole body glucose utilization rate.

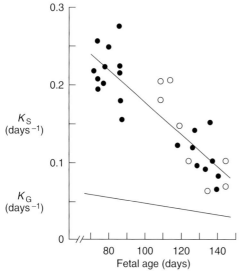

Figure 4 Fractional rate of protein synthesis (K_s) over gestation in fetal sheep studied with leucine (•) and lysine (O) radioactive tracers compared with the fractional rate of growth (K_G) (lower portion of the figure, —). (Reproduced with permission from Hay WW Jr (1992) Fetal requirements and placental transfer of nitrogenous compounds. In: Polin RA and Fox WW (eds.) *Fetal and Neonatal Physiology*, p. 439. Philadelphia: W.B. Saunders.)

The principal source of fetal glycogen is glucose derived from placental transport of glucose from the mother. Smaller fractions come from lactate and amino acids such as glutamine. Glycogen content of the fetus and selected fetal organs is directly related to the maternal and thus fetal plasma glucose concentrations. Thus, macrosomic fetuses of diabetic mothers have very high body and organ contents of glycogen, while IUGR fetuses that result from sustained maternal hypoglycemia or placental insufficiency and decreased placental glucose supply to the fetus have markedly decreased glycogen contents.

Cortisol and glucose provide developmental regulation, while adrenaline (epinephrine) and glucagon provide acute and more variable regulation. Experimentally, cortisol infusion decreases glycogen content of the liver while deficiencies in hypothalamic-pituitary regulation of the adrenal gland leads to cortisol deficiency and glycogen deficiency. Insulin acts synergistically with glucose to increase hepatic glycogen stores. Glucose also acts independently to activate glycogen phosphorylase and glycogenolysis to keep hepatic glycogen content constant at higher glucose concentrations.

Fat

Fetal fat content as a fraction of fetal weight varies several fold among species (**Figure 5**). The fat content of newborns at term of almost all land mammals is 1–3% and is considerably less than that of the human (15–20%). Differences in body fat content among species are due primarily to the capacity of the placenta to transfer fat to the fetus and to the capacity of the fetus to synthesize triglycerides and fat. Even in those species that take up fat from the placenta and deposit fat in fetal tissues, the rate of fetal fatty acid oxidation is presumed low, because plasma concentrations of fatty acids (and keto acid products such as β-hydroxybutyrate and acetoacetate) are low, and because the carnitine palmitoyl transferase enzyme system is not sufficiently developed to deliver long-chain fatty acids to the respiration pathway inside the mitochondria.

In the human fetus, calories produced by the complete oxidation of glucose and lactate can fully meet energy required for maintenance metabolism and for conversion of glucose and lactate to fatty acids. The portion of glucose converted into fat has been estimated to be $23 \, \mathrm{kcal \, kg^{-1} \, day^{-1}}$. This would permit accumulation of $2.4 \, \mathrm{g \, kg^{-1} \, day^{-1}}$ of fat. In the human fetus between 26 and 30 weeks' gestation, nonfat and fat components contribute equally to the carbon content of the fetal body. After that period, fat accumulation considerably exceeds that of the nonfat components. At 36 weeks' gestation, 1.9 g of fat accumulates for each gram of nonfat daily weight gain, and by term, the deposition of fat accounts for over 90% of the carbon accumulated by the fetus. The rate of fat accretion is approximately linear between 36 and 40 weeks' gestation, and by the end of gestation, fat accretion ranges from 1.6 to $3.4 \, \mathrm{g \, kg^{-1} \, day^{-1}}$. At 28 weeks' gestation, it is slightly less and ranges between 1.0 and $1.8 \, \mathrm{g \, kg^{-1} \, day^{-1}}$. By term, fat content of the human fetus is 15–20% of body weight, ranging from less than 10% in IUGR fetuses to 25% or more in macrosomic infants of diabetic mothers.

Energy Accretion in the Fetus

Fat has a high energy content ($9.5 \, \mathrm{kcal \, g^{-1}}$) and a very high carbon content (approximately 78%). Thus, differences in fetal fat concentration among species lead to large differences in calculated energy accretion rates and carbon requirements of the fetal tissues for growth. The energy concentration of nonfat dry weight is fairly consistent across species and also within species at different developmental stages, indicating that the ratio of protein to nonprotein substrates in the tissues is relatively constant. Thus, energy accretion rate of any fetus can be estimated from the growth curve of the fetus in question and the changing fat and water concentrations.

Data for energy accretion and distribution in the human fetus are shown in **Table 3**. Because growth of fat and nonfat (protein plus other) tissues are metabolically linked through energy supply that is used for protein synthesis and the production of

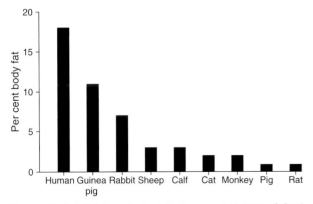

Figure 5 Fetal fat content at term as a per cent of fetal body weight among species. (Reproduced with permission from Hay WW Jr (1996) Nutrition and development of the fetus: carbohydrate and lipid metabolism. In: Walker WA and Watkins JB (eds.) *Nutrition in Pediatrics*, 2nd edn, p. 376. Hamilton: B. C. Decker.)

Table 3 Calculation of the energy distribution in the term human infant

	Wet weight	Fat	Nonfat wet weight	Nonfat dry weight
Weight (g)	3450	386	3064	511
Total calories (kcal)	5950	3650	2300	2300
Energy concentration (kcal g^{-1})	1.73	9.45	0.75	4.5

From Ziegler EE *et al.* (1979) Body composition of the reference fetus. *Growth* **40**: 329–341.

anabolic hormones that promote positive protein, fat, and carbohydrate growth, restriction of nutrient supply is likely to produce growth deficits of all tissues, not just fat (i.e., growth retardation involves limitation of muscle growth as well as fat and glycogen). Indeed, chronic experimental selective energy (glucose) restriction in the fetal sheep leads to increased protein breakdown as well as to lower rates of fetal growth and lipid content. In contrast, as shown by the growth curves in **Figure 6** from human infants born prematurely at different times

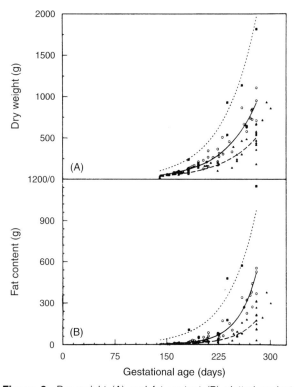

Figure 6 Dry weight (A) and fat content (B) plotted against gestational age in the same newborn human infants shown in **Figure 3** for LGA (■, ····), AGA (O, —), and SGA (◆, – – –) infants. (Reproduced with permission from Sparks JW (1992) Intrauterine growth and nutrition. In: Polin RA and Fox WW (eds.) *Fetal and Neonatal Physiology*, p. 184. Philadelphia: W. B. Saunders.)

over the last third of gestation, there is a bias towards thinner, SGA infants with less fat relative to nonfat weight and nitrogen content, raising the possibility that in a species that does lay down considerable fetal fat during late gestation, differences in intrauterine growth rate may reflect fat deposition more than the growth of nonfat, protein-containing tissues.

Mineral Accretion in the Fetus

Fetal calcium content is best correlated with fetal body length; this is true for both AGA and SGA infants. Using this index, fetal calcium content increases exponentially with a linear increase in length. Using this estimate, the human fetal rate of calcium accretion is about 85 mg kg^{-1} day^{-1}. Accretion of other minerals varies more directly with body weight, and according to the distribution of the minerals into extracellular (e.g., sodium) or intracellular (e.g., potassium) spaces.

Regulation of Fetal Growth

Fetal growth is the result of interaction among maternal, placental, and fetal factors, representing a mix of genetic mechanisms and environmental influences through which the genetic factors are expressed and modulated. The single most important environmental influence that affects fetal growth is the nutrition of the fetus. Nutrient supply to the fetus and the resulting increases in fetal tissue and plasma concentrations of anabolic hormones and growth factors are regulated by maternal health, maternal nutrition, uterine growth (including uterine blood flow and endometrial surface area), and placental growth and function.

Genetic Factors

Many genes contribute to fetal growth and birth weight of the normal term fetus. Maternal genotype is more important than fetal genotype in the overall regulation of fetal growth. **Table 4** presents estimates of the quantitative contribution of fetal and parental factors to fetal growth and birth weight at term. The more modest regulation by the paternal genotype, acting through the fetal genotype, is essential for trophoblast development. In fact, overexpression of the paternal genotype can produce trophoblast tumors. More specific gene targeting studies have shown the importance of genomic imprinting on fetal growth. For example, in mice normal fetal and placental growth require that the IGF$_2$ gene be paternal and the IGF$_2$ receptor gene be maternal, and paternal disomy producing IGF$_2$ gene overexpression results in fetal overgrowth while

Table 4 Factors determining variance in birth weight

	Per cent of total variance
Fetal	
Genotype	16
Sex	2
	18
Maternal	
Genotype	20
Maternal environment	24
Maternal age	1
Parity	7
	52
Unknown	30

From Penrose LS (1954) *Proceedings of the 9th International Congress on Genetics*, Part 1; and Milner RDG and Gluckman PD (1996) Regulation of intrauterine growth. In: Gluckman PD and Heymann MA (eds.) *Pediatrics and Perinatology*, 2nd edn, p. 285. London: Arnold.

maternal disomy producing IGF_2 underexpression results in fetal dwarfism. In humans, isopaternal inheritance of IGF_2 alleles is associated with the Beckwith-Wiedemann syndrome, which includes hyperinsulinism and fetal macrosomia.

Nongenetic Maternal Factors

There is a high correlation between birth weights of siblings that extends to cousins. The nongenetic, maternal nature of this effect is demonstrated by embryo transfer and cross-breeding experiments. For example, a small-breed embryo transplanted into a large-breed uterus will grow larger than a small-breed embryo remaining in a small-breed uterus. Furthermore, partial reduction in fetal number in a polytocous species such as the rat produces greater than normal birth weights in the remaining offspring. Conversely, embryo-transfer of a large-breed into a small-breed uterus will result in a newborn that is smaller than in its natural large-breed environment. Such evidence demonstrates that fetal growth is normally constrained, and that this constraint comes from the maternal environment. This is a physiological process and includes the maternal-specific capacity of uterine size, placental implantation surface area of the uterus, and uterine circulation, which together support the growth of the placenta and its function.

Maternal Nutrition

Normal variations in maternal nutrition have relatively little effect on fetal growth, because they do not markedly alter maternal plasma concentrations of nutrient substrates or the rate of uterine blood flow, the principal determinants of nutrient substrate delivery to and transport by the placenta. Human epidemiological data from conditions of prolonged starvation, as well as nutritional deprivation in experimental animals, indicate that even severe limitations in maternal nutrition only limit fetal growth by 10–20%. Restriction of caloric and protein intakes to less than 50% of normal for a considerable portion of gestation are needed before marked reductions in fetal growth are observed; such severe conditions often result in fetal loss before the impact on late gestation fetal growth rate and fetal size at birth are manifested. Similarly, fetal macrosomia is only common in pregnancies complicated by gestational diabetes mellitus in which maternal plasma hyperglycemia and hypertriglyceridemia, plus fetal hyperinsulinemia, combine to produce excessive fetal adiposity.

The Placenta

The placenta exerts strong control over fetal growth by providing nutrients directly or in metabolically altered form and amount. Naturally and experimentally, placental growth precedes fetal growth, and failure of placental growth is directly associated with decreased fetal growth. There is considerable variation in this control. For example, experiments in sheep that limited placental growth did not result in proportionately reduced fetal weight, indicating that either the capacity of the smaller placenta to transport nutrients to the fetus increased adaptively, or that the fetus developed increased capacity to extract nutrients from the placenta and direct those nutrients to growth. More characteristically, though, limitation in placental function to transfer nutrients to the fetus directly limits fetal growth. In fact, fetal growth retardation is seen as a natural and reproductively successful (though not perfect) adaptation to nutrient limitation. There is a direct relationship between fetal weight and placental weight in humans, indicating that placental size and fetal size are directly interrelated, although functional interrelationships between placenta and fetus also are important to fetal growth and development.

Maternal Endocrine Influences on Fetal Growth

Changes in maternal circulating growth hormone and growth hormone-like peptides such as placental lactogen, which increase during pregnancy, have combined effects that induce maternal insulin resistance and lead to higher circulating concentrations of glucose and lipids. These in turn are transported in increased amounts to the fetus where, combined with their stimulatory effects on fetal insulin and IGF_1 and IGF_2, promote fetal adiposity (or macrosomia, as in the infant of the diabetic mother) and limit fetal protein breakdown, both of which promote fetal growth.

Influence of Fetal Endocrine and Autocrine/Paracrine-Acting Growth Factors on Fetal Growth

Growth hormone, which classically acts as the major regulator of postnatal growth, has no demonstrable influence on fetal growth. Fetal insulin does regulate fetal growth, although the complete absence of insulin does not abolish fetal growth. In sheep, for example, fetal pancreatectomy in late gestation limits fetal growth rate only by 20–30%, and pancreatic agenesis in humans produces IUGR fetuses who are 30–50% less than normal weight near term. Insulin infusions into the fetus and excessive fetal insulin secretion enhance fetal glucose utilization and produce increased adiposity, but only a 10–15% increase in fetal nonfat growth. Such hyperinsulinemic conditions also limit protein breakdown, which leads to increased protein accretion, although by limiting protein breakdown, as well as by enhancing amino acid synthesis into proteins, insulin actually decreases plasma concentrations of amino acids, thereby limiting protein synthesis at the same time. Therefore, it is not clear how increased fetal insulin enhances, or its deficiency limits, protein accretion. The primary action of fetal insulin may be to promote glucose utilization and, in turn, enhance protein accretion by providing more energy substrate to fuel protein synthesis and to substitute glucose carbon for amino acids to fuel oxidative metabolism. For example, removal of insulin from the fetus increases fetal glucose concentration and the transfer of glucose from mother to fetus via the placenta, which reduces net fetal carbon accretion. Insulin also directly activates proteins in its signal transduction pathway, promoting the incorporation of amino acids into protein synthesis, and by activation of the MAP-kinase pathway; this occurs even when glucose utilization and oxidation rates are limited by reduction of glucose supply.

Interaction of amino acids with insulin also regulates amino acid synthesis into proteins. Recent studies in the fetal sheep have shown that amino acid infusion, independent of insulin, increases the skeletal muscle concentration of mTOR and elF4E, the key regulatory proteins for ribosomal synthesis of amino acids into protein. In contrast, increases in phosphorylated mTOR and 4EBP1 were only demonstrated when insulin concentrations were also elevated. These observations indicate that amino acids can independently upregulate particular signal transduction proteins during late gestation fetal growth, and emphasize, as does the data showing insulin activation of the MAP-kinase pathway, that nutrient–hormone interaction is central to regulation of growth.

Both IGF₁ and IGF₂ regulate fetal growth. Mice lacking the IGF₁ gene have markedly reduced rates of fetal growth in late gestation. IGF₂ knockouts also have delayed fetal growth that is more pronounced in early to mid-gestation. IGF₁ receptor knockout mice are more growth retarded than either IGF₁ or IGF₂ knockouts alone. These IGF₁ receptor knockouts are growth restricted to the same extent as mice in which both IGF₁ and IGF₂ genes are deleted, confirming that receptor activation is the principal growth-regulating step in IGF₁ and IGF₂ action. Infusions of IGF₁ into fetal sheep demonstrate limited insulin-like effects on fetal glucose metabolism, but they do limit fetal protein breakdown, particularly when sustained hypoglycemia is present in the presence of increased proteolysis. IGFs also regulate fetal growth by regulating placental growth. IGF₂ gene knockout mice have small placentas and, in turn, lower IGF₁ and IGF₂ binding proteins. IGF binding proteins modulate effects of IGF₁ and IGF₂ on fetal growth. Circulating IGF₂ receptors limit IGF₂ effects by binding most of it in the circulation. IGFBP-1 and -2 levels are relatively high in fetal plasma, perhaps limiting the effectiveness of IGF₁, while IGFBP-3 is low in the plasma of fetuses with IUGR, perhaps due to simultaneous insulin deficiency.

Interpretation of Growth Curves

Cross-sectional growth curves have been developed from anthropometric measurements in populations of infants born at different gestational ages. Such curves have been used to estimate whether growth of an individual fetus or preterm newborn is within or outside of the normal range of fetal growth, which is defined as between the 10th and 90th percentile, although what the curves actually show is simply how big a given fetus or newborn is relative to others at any given gestational age. Fetuses and newborn infants who are between the 10th and 90th percentiles for weight vs. gestational age are considered appropriate for gestational age (AGA), those who are less than the 10th percentile are considered small for gestational age (SGA), and those who are greater than the 90th percentile are considered large for gestational age (LGA). In general, SGA infants come from small parents (particularly the mother) and LGA infants come from large parents (again, particularly when the mother is big as well as the father).

Standard fetal and preterm neonatal growth curves represent the third trimester in humans. Each curve is based on local populations with variable composition of maternal age, parity, socioeconomic status, race, ethnic background, body size, degree of obesity or thinness, health, pregnancy-related problems, and nutrition, as well as the number of fetuses per mother, the number of infants included in the study, and how and how well measurements of body size and gestational age were made. Estimates of gestational age often are imprecise because of variable maternal postimplantation bleeding and irregular menses, onset and appearance of physical features of maturation in the infant, and interobserver assessments of an infant's developmental stage.

Mathematical analyses of various growth curves have been used to determine growth rates over relatively short gestational periods or at discrete gestational ages. The data used in the Lubchenco growth curves (**Figure 2**), for example, reflect a simple exponential function showing fetal weight increasing at about $15\,g\,kg^{-1}\,day^{-1}$ for average-sized infants; this rate will be lower for smaller infants and greater for the larger infants.

More recent growth curves have been developed from serial ultrasound measurements of fetal growth in normal pregnancies, providing continuous rather than cross-sectional growth patterns. The growth of a preterm infant is better correlated with serially determined fetal growth rates than with cross-sectional neonatal growth curves. Serial ultrasound measurements of fetal growth also more accurately determine how environmental factors can inhibit (for example, maternal undernutrition globally, or hypoglycemia specifically) or enhance (for example, maternal overnutrition globally or hyperglycemia specifically) growth.

Extremes of Growth and Development: Intrauterine Growth Restriction and Macrosomia

Newborn birth weights have been steadily increasing since the 1970s throughout much of the developed world, although in developed countries, this increase has been tempered by the increased number of preterm infants born as multiple births following *in vitro* fertilization procedures. However, the relative proportions of the two extremes of birth weight, very small infants with intrauterine growth restriction (IUGR) and those who are excessively large with macrosomia, remain constant, and within some populations are actually increasing.

Intrauterine Growth Restriction (IUGR)

In developed countries, 3–7% of newborns are classified as IUGR. These infants weigh less than two standard deviations below the mean of a population born at the same gestational age. Most of these infants experienced suboptimal nutrient supply, and consequently a restriction of fetal growth, as a result of some form of placental insufficiency. IUGR imposes increased risks of specific types of fetal and neonatal morbidity and mortality (**Table 5**).

Table 5 Risks of specific types of fetal and neonatal morbidity and mortality in IUGR infants

Problem	Pathogenesis/pathophysiology
Intrauterine death	Chronic hypoxia
	Placental insufficiency
	Growth failure
	Malformation
	Infection
	Infarction/abruption
	Pre-eclampsia
Asphyxia	Acute hypoxia/abruption
	Chronic hypoxia
	Placental insufficiency/pre-eclampsia
	Acidosis
	Glycogen depletion
Meconium aspiration	Hypoxia
Hypothermia	Cold stress
	Hypoxia
	Hypoglycemia
	Decreased fat stores
	Decreased subcutaneous insulation
	Increased surface area
	Catecholamine depletion
Persistent pulmonary hypertension	Chronic hypoxia
Hypoglycemia	Decreased hepatic/muscle glycogen
	Decreased alternative energy sources
	Heat loss
	Hypoxia
	Decreased gluconeogenesis
	Decreased counter-regulatory hormones
	Increased insulin sensitivity
Hyperglycemia	Low insulin secretion rate
	Excessive glucose delivery
	Increased catecholamine and glucagon effects
Polycythemia/ hyperviscosity	Chronic hypoxia
	Maternal–fetal transfusion
	Increased erythropoiesis
Gastrointestinal perforation	Focal ischemia
	Hypoperistalsis
Acute renal failure	Hypoxia/ischemia
Immunodeficiency	Malnutrition
	Congenital infection

From Anderson S, Hay WW, Jr. The small-for-gestational-age Infant. In: Avery GB, Fletcher MA, MacDonald MG (Eds), *Neonatology*: Pathophysiology and Management of the Newborn, 5th Edition. Lippincott-Raven, Philadelphia, pp. 411–444, 1999.

Possible adult disorders resulting from intrauterine growth restriction Interest in IUGR has been enhanced recently by retrospective epidemiological, clinical follow-up, and animal studies that indicate long-term consequences in adult life of IUGR offspring, including higher incidences of obesity, insulin resistance, impaired glucose tolerance, enhanced hepatic glucose production, pancreatic insulin secretion deficiency, type 2 diabetes mellitus, hypertriglyceridemia, and cardiovascular disease, particularly hypertension. These conditions, often called syndrome X or the metabolic syndrome, may represent an example of 'programing,' in which an insult, when applied at a critical or sensitive stage in development, produces lasting, even lifelong, effects on the structure or function of the organism. Mechanisms responsible for these later-life morbidities are not yet established. There is some evidence of diminished pancreatic growth and development, which might become manifest in later life as pancreatic insufficiency when the adult starts and then continues eating a diet rich in simple carbohydrates and lipids. Peripheral insulin resistance may develop in the same way, and hypertension in adulthood may be the result of restricted renal and adrenal development. A common theme among these observations is that excessive weight gain starting at any weight percentile is the strongest predictor of syndrome X or metabolic syndrome disorders.

Macrosomia

At the other end of the birth weight spectrum are macrosomic or large-for-gestational age (LGA) infants. These infants were exposed to excess nutrient supply *in utero*, principally carbohydrates and lipids. Macrosomic newborns have increased specific morbidities primarily associated with metabolic complications of maternal diabetes mellitus during pregnancy and associated birth complications and birth injuries as a result of excessive fetal size.

Macrosomia is defined in a newborn as a birth weight more than two standard deviations above the mean percentile for gestational age or a birth weight greater than 4000 g at term. Neonatal macrosomia has a strong ethnic predisposition affecting up to 50% of Latino and Native American pregnant women versus 19% of African-American pregnant women. Macrosomia is characteristic of infants of diabetic mothers (IDMs) who were hyperglycemic during pregnancy. The diabetes can be long standing, but the most common group producing macrosomic infants are women with gestational diabetes mellitus (GDM), which complicates 3–5% of all pregnancies. The risk of macrosomia is not consistent a cross all classes of diabetes; it primarily reflects the degree and duration of maternal hyperglycemia and hypertriglyceridemia and particularly high spikes of these conditions following meals that are more common in gestational diabetes. The hyperglycemia results in fetal hyperglycemia and hyperinsulinemia, while the hypertriglyceridemia contributes to the effect of the excess glucose and insulin to produce excess fat deposition.

Development of type 2 diabetes in later life in macrosomic offspring IDMs, particularly those with macrosomia, have increased risk of developing type 2 diabetes earlier in life. Mechanisms responsible for this sequence of events include insulin resistance and insufficient insulin secretion (β-cell dysfunction) in response to hyperglycemia. Typically, glucose intolerance from obesity and increased insulin resistance progresses to fasting hyperglycemia and the inability of β-cells to compensate by increasing insulin secretion. This form of β-cell failure appears to be reversible over short periods by improved glycemic control, but long-term exposure to hyperglycemia can lead to β-cell exhaustion and specific inhibition of insulin secretion, which are irreversible by glycemic normalization. The insulin resistance also extends to the liver where glucose production increases. This triad of insulin resistance, reduced β-cell insulin secretion, and increased hepatic glucose production results in type 2 diabetes.

See also: **Diabetes Mellitus**: Etiology and Epidemiology; Classification and Chemical Pathology. **Growth Monitoring. Infants**: Nutritional Requirements. **Low Birthweight and Preterm Infants**: Nutritional Management. **Pregnancy**: Role of Placenta in Nutrient Transfer; Nutrient Requirements; Energy Requirements and Metabolic Adaptations.

Further Reading

Barker DJ (1993) The fetal and infant origins of adult disease. *British Medical Journal* **301**: 1111.

Barker DJ (1995) Intrauterine programming of adult disease. *Molecular Medicine Today* **1**(9): 418–423.

Battaglia FC and Meschia G (1986) *An Introduction to Fetal Physiology.* Orlando: Academic Press.

Davis JA and Dobbing J (1974) *Scientific Foundations of Paediatrics.* Philadelphia: W.B. Saunders.

Hay WW Jr (1991) Glucose metabolism in the fetal-placental unit. In: Cowett RM (ed.) *Principles of Perinatal-Neonatal Metabolism*, pp. 337–367. New York: Springer-Verlag.

Hay WW Jr (1995) Current topic: Metabolic interrelationships of placenta and fetus. *Placenta* **16**: 19–30.

Hay WW Jr (2003) Nutrition and development of the fetus: carbohydrate and lipid metabolism. In: Walker WA, Watkins JB, and Duggan CP (eds.) *Nutrition in Pediatrics (Basic Science and*

Clinical Applications), 3rd edn, pp. 449–470. Hamilton, ON: BC Decker Inc Publisher.

Hay, WW Jr and Anderson MS. Fuel homeostasis in the fetus and neonate. In: DeGroot LJ and Jameson JL (eds.) *Endocrinology*, 5th edn. Philadelphia: W.B. Saunders (in press).

Hay WW Jr, Catz CS, Grave GD, and Yaffe SJ (1997) Workshop summary: fetal growth: its regulation and disorders. *Pediatrics* 99: 585–591.

Hay WW Jr and Regnault TRH (2003) Fetal requirements and placental transfer of nitrogenous compounds. In: Polin RA, Fox WW, and Abman SH (eds.) *Fetal and Neonatal Physiology*, 3rd edn, pp. 509–527. Philadelphia: W.B. Saunders.

Milner RDG and Gluckman PD (1993) Regulation of intrauterine growth. In: Gluckman PD and Heymann MA (eds.) *Pediatrics and Perinatology, The Scientific Basis*, 2nd edn. pp. 284–289. London: Arnold.

Molteni RA, Stys SJ, and Battaglia FC (1978) Relationship of fetal and placental weight in human beings: Fetal/placental weight ratios at various gestational ages and birth weight distributions. *Journal of Reproductive Medicine* 21: 327–334.

Nimrod CA (1992) The biology of normal and deviant fetal growth. In: Reece EA, Hobbin JC, Mahoney MJ, and Petrie RH (eds.) *Medicine of the Fetus & Mother*, pp. 285–290. Philadelphia: JB Lippincott Co.

Ounsted M and Ounsted C (1973) *On Fetal Growth Rate: Clinics in Developmental Medicine*, No. 46. Philadelphia: J. B. Lippincott.

Philipps AF (2003) Oxygen consumption and general carbohydrate metabolism in the fetus. In: Polin RA, Fox WW, and Abman SH (eds.) *Fetal and Neonatal Physiology*, 3rd edn, pp. 465–477. Philadelphia: W.B. Saunders.

Robinson JS, Owens JA, and Owens PC (1994) Fetal growth and fetal growth retardation. In: Thorburn GD and Harding R (eds.) *Textbook of Fetal Physiology*, pp. 83–94. Oxford: Oxford University Press.

Sharp F, Fraser RB, and Milner RDG (1989) *Fetal Growth*. London: Royal College of Obstetricians and Gynaecologists.

Smart J (1986) Undernutrition, learning and memory: review of experimental studies. In: Taylor TG and Jenkins NK (eds.) *Proceedings of XII International Congress of Nutrition*, p. 74. London: John Libbey.

Sparks JW (1984) Human intrauterine growth and nutrient accretion. *Seminars in Perinatology* 8(2): 74–93.

Sparks JW and Cetin I (1991) Intrauterine growth. In: Hay WW Jr (ed.) *Neonatal Nutrition and Metabolism*, pp. 3–41. St. Louis: Mosby Year Book.

Sparks JW, Girard JR, and Battaglia FC (1980) An estimate of the caloric requirements of the human fetus. *Biology of the Neonate* 38(3–4): 113–119.

GROWTH MONITORING

T J Cole, Institute of Child Health, London, UK

Growth is the single quality that most clearly distinguishes between children and adults—children grow, whereas adults do not. This in turn means that healthy children grow well and ill children often grow poorly. For this reason, the monitoring of growth is a logical and effective procedure for detecting child ill health—not just specific growth disorders but also more general conditions that affect growth indirectly.

A Cochrane Review on growth monitoring defined it as "the regular recording of a child's weight, coupled with some specified remedial actions if the weight is abnormal in some way." So the key elements are one or more measurements of weight, plus a protocol for recording, plotting, and interpreting the measurements, leading in suitable cases to some intervention.

The primary purpose of growth monitoring is to detect and treat illness in the individual child. The reasonable question asked by the Cochrane Review is "Does it work?" The Review found only two randomised clinical trials measuring the impact of growth monitoring, and they differed in their conclusions. One found that infants whose growth was monitored for 30 months were no healthier than age-matched controls, whereas the other showed that mothers trained to use a growth chart were more knowledgeable after 4 months. So there is little research on the subject, and even less evidence to justify its use, which is surprising given the enormous resources devoted each year to growth monitoring throughout the industrialized and developing worlds.

A possible reason for this lack of evidence is that growth monitoring is seen as intrinsically 'a good thing.' Parents are always interested to know how their children are growing, and the benefit to them of measuring the child regularly, although difficult to quantify, is assumed. So there is uncertainty as to exactly what growth monitoring is for and what outcome it might lead to.

Purpose and Outcome

The primary aim of growth monitoring is to improve child health by regular anthropometry (which literally means measurement of man and refers to body measures such as weight, height, and mid-upper arm circumference). However, the measurements are useful only if they are properly recorded and interpreted and a suitable intervention is introduced when the child's growth is suboptimal.

It is important to target the purpose, measurement, and intervention to the environment in which they are used. In practice, this makes growth monitoring a very different proposition in the developing and industrialized worlds due to differences in the burden of disease, resources, and training.

The disease burden is much greater in the developing world, with diarrhea, malaria, respiratory infection, tuberculosis, and HIV all common. Here, effective growth monitoring can in principle save lives. In contrast, in the industrialized world such conditions are less common and milder, so the focus is more on growth disorders such as growth hormone deficiency or Turner's syndrome, where mortality is not the issue.

This different focus also affects the target age range when children are monitored. Mortality risk in the developing world is greatest during infancy, and it is increased by low birth weight. So poor early growth is a potent risk factor for infant mortality, and infancy is the period when growth monitoring is likely to be of greatest value. In contrast, the main concerns in the industrialized world are growth disorders that usually show themselves after infancy, although infant failure to thrive is also a concern. So in the developing world growth monitoring targets the preschool years, whereas in the industrialized world it covers all childhood up to and including puberty.

Throughout the world mothers are encouraged to take their infants to the clinic for regular anthropometry and immunizations. But in the developing world, where infants are much more likely to grow poorly, it makes economic sense to educate mothers, who have the greatest influence over their infant's environment, about the principles of growth monitoring. This education component is not stressed in the same way in the industrialized world.

Maternal education is thus a secondary aim of growth monitoring in the developing world. If growth monitoring makes mothers more aware of their child's state of health, then it should also have an impact on the child's health.

In addition to detecting disease and raising parental awareness at the individual level, growth monitoring in the sense of information gathering has potential benefits at the population level. It provides information about average child growth that is useful for comparison, policy, and planning. For example, a knowledge of mean height for age and weight for age in children from different regions is useful for identifying areas where the prevalence of malnutrition is highest, which in turn allows resources of emergency aid and support staff to be effectively targeted.

Growth monitoring also supports scientific research on the prevention and treatment of disorders affecting growth. Evidence-based child health relies on well-designed studies to test the impact of interventions on child health outcomes. Growth is a proxy for child health and is a common choice of outcome. So growth monitoring fits naturally into the framework of a randomized clinical trial, in which it is used to measure the impact of the intervention. This is different from the situation considered by the Cochrane Review, in which growth monitoring was the intervention. Strictly, the use of repeated anthropometry as an outcome should not be called growth monitoring because it omits the important final stage in which some intervention depends on it.

The Process of Growth Monitoring

The process of growth monitoring involves three stages: anthropometry, interpretation, and referral.

Anthropometry

In infancy, the most common routine measurement is weight. It is simple to do, the required equipment is reasonably cheap, and it provides a convenient global summary of the infant's size. Birth weight in particular is a useful proxy for fetal growth. An advantage of weight is that it relates closely to the mother's own perception of her child's size.

Infant length is more difficult to measure for several reasons. The optimal equipment is a length board with a sliding footboard, which is expensive and needs regular calibration. Simpler equipment such as a tape measure increases the measurement error dramatically. Most important, proper length measurement requires two trained observers—one to hold the infant's head against the headboard and the other to position the footboard and take the measurement. For these reasons, infant length is often measured either poorly or not at all.

Arm circumference (or mid-upper arm circumference (MUAC)) is a popular alternative to weight in the developing world but less so in the industrialized world. This is because arm circumference measurement can detect malnutrition using a simple cutoff. The equipment (a specially marked inextensible tape) is cheaper and easier to use than weighing scales, and arm circumference is highly correlated with weight.

In the industrialized world, head circumference measured in infancy can detect some rare conditions such as hydrocephalus, which is indicated by a rapid increase in head circumference at approximately the time of birth.

Once past infancy, priorities change. Height becomes much more important, particularly in the industrialized world, where the emphasis is on detecting primary growth disorders such as growth hormone deficiency or Turner's syndrome. Children can be measured standing at approximately 2 years of age using a freestanding stadiometer with counterbalanced headboard. The child's head is positioned in the Frankfort plane (looking straight ahead with the line between the ear hole and eye horizontal), with the child's shoulders, buttocks, and heels touching the back plate, and the observer brings the headboard down gently and reads the height. Alternatively, a second observer can take the measurement while the first checks the child's position. Measurement technique is crucial for height, particularly when it is measured repeatedly. Height velocity is relatively low after infancy, so the height increment over a period of 6 months, for example, may be only 2 or 3 cm depending on age, which can result in excessive measurement error. A competent observer should be able to achieve a measurement error of less than 0.3 cm.

Weight and height are highly correlated, so their assessments are often similar: On average, a tall child is heavy and a short child is light. Once past infancy, weight can be more informative when expressed as an index of weight adjusted for height. There are many weight-for-height indices, but among the most common in the industrialized world is the body mass index, calculated as weight (measured in kilograms) divided by the square of height (in meters). It has been used in adults for decades (the index was originally proposed by Quetelet in the nineteenth century) but in children only relatively recently, and mainly in the area of child obesity. Note that it requires adjustment for age, in the same way as for weight and height. Other weight-for-height indices, used mainly in the developing world, adjust weight for height ignoring the child's age, which is an advantage when the age is not known. However, this leads to biases at certain ages, notably infancy and puberty, when a child's expected weight depends on their age as well as their height.

With the recent steep increase in the prevalence of child obesity, waist circumference has become useful as a measure of central body fatness. Body mass index is less useful because it does not distinguish between fat mass and muscle mass. A child may become fatter over time without becoming heavier simply by losing muscle mass (through inactivity)

Table 1 The suitability of anthropometry for growth monitoring at different ages[a]

Anthropometry	Infancy	Preschool	Childhood and adolescence
Weight	***	**	*
Length/height	*	***	***
Body mass index	*	***	***
Arm circumference	**	*	*
Head circumference	***	*	*
Waist circumference	*	***	***

[a]More asterisks indicate better suitability.

and gaining an equal mass of fat, as occurred in US adolescents during the 1980s. It is easier to measure waist circumference than skinfold thickness (e.g., triceps or subscapular skinfold), and the required equipment is also simpler—an inextensible tape as opposed to a skinfold caliper (the appearance of which often frightens parents and young children).

Table 1 summarizes the value of anthropometry at various stages of childhood, as described previously. The process of anthropometry requires attention to detail: suitable equipment that is regularly maintained and calibrated; observers who are trained in correct measurement technique; and regular quality control sessions in which observers are checked, against both themselves and each other, for measurement precision and accuracy. Only in this way can accuracy and precision be maintained.

Plotting and Chart Interpretation

The second stage of growth monitoring involves interpreting the anthropometry. The growing child increases in size over time, so the way to assess the child's growth is by comparison with a set of age-specific norms, usually in the form of a growth chart. This involves plotting the child's measurement on the chart and then interpreting it in the context of any previous measurements. First, growth charts and how they are constructed are discussed.

Growth Chart Construction

Charts to Measure Size

A growth chart summarizes the distribution of the measurement (e.g., weight) as it changes with age in some prespecified reference population (e.g., British children measured in 1990). At its simplest, the chart consists of the median curve, a smooth curve connecting median weight for the population at different ages. Usually, however, there are curves for other distribution centiles as well, extending typically from the 3rd to the 97th centile, to give an idea of the spread of measurements at each age. A centile corresponds to a given percentage (between 0 and 100) and is a measurement below which that percentage of children in the reference population will be found. For example, in the British 1990 boys weight reference, median (or 50th centile) weight at 1 year is 10.1 kg, whereas the 3rd and 97th centiles are respectively 8.3 and 12.3 kg. Therefore, 50% of British boys aged 1 year weigh less than 10.1 kg, whereas 3% weigh less than 8.3 kg and 97% weigh less (and 3% weigh more) than 12.3 kg.

The lowest centile curve on the chart is often used as a cutoff to detect poor growth. Children with measurements falling below this centile are viewed as 'at risk' and may be referred for more detailed examination. **Figure 1** shows the British weight reference for boys in infancy, which has nine centile curves ranging from the 0.4th at the bottom to the 99.6th centile at the top. The value of these more extreme centiles for screening is explained later.

Using a centile curve as the cutoff on the chart is just one approach to identifying at-risk children. In the developing world, where the concept of centiles can be difficult to explain, a simpler alternative is 'percent of the median.' Here, the cutoff is constructed as a curve that is, for example, 80% of the median weight curve, which is broadly similar in shape to the 3rd centile curve. A child whose weight falls below the cutoff is said to be below 80% weight for age.

Another approach to defining cutoffs involves standard deviation (SD) scores, also called z scores. These are linked to centiles through the underlying frequency distribution, in particular the SD of the measurement at each age. With a normal distribution, the median and mean coincide and the SD

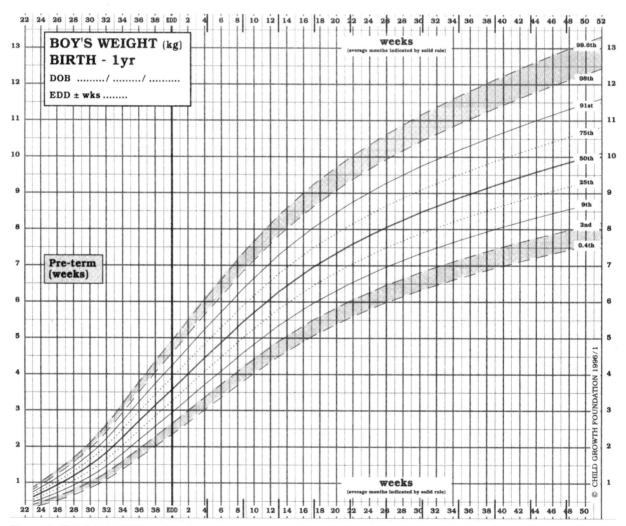

Figure 1 The British 1990 boys infant weight chart, covering 22 weeks of gestation to 12 months. The nine centiles range from the 0.4th to the 99.6th, and infants whose weights fall outside the extreme centiles are referred. (© Child Growth Foundation.)

score is 0. The 2nd centile is approximately 2 SDs below the median at all ages, whereas the 75th centile is 1.3 SDs above the median. Therefore, the 2nd centile corresponds to an SD score of −2 and the 75th centile to +1.3.

Height is normally distributed, but much anthropometry including weight is not—it has a skew distribution. The link between centiles and SD scores can be extended to measurements that are not normally distributed using a technique called the LMS method, which is the basis for many growth reference charts. The telltale sign of a skewness-adjusted chart is that the centile curves are asymmetrically spaced at each age; for example, the gap between the 25th and 50th centile curves is less than the 50th–75th centile gap.

The British growth reference centiles (**Figure 1**) are defined by their corresponding SD scores. The centiles are spaced two-thirds of an SD score apart, so the 0.4th centile corresponds to −2.67 SD scores. Similarly, the WHO chart spaces its centiles 1 SD score apart, from −3 to +3, which allows it to cover the wide range of anthropometry seen internationally.

Charts for use in the developing world tend to be simpler in design, often with only two or three centile curves. They highlight a region on the chart where children's individual growth curves should lie, and mothers are taught that children with curves within this region are healthy children. One common chart is the Road to Health chart (**Figure 2**). The advantage of the chart is that it can also include public health information about the timing of breast feeding, immunizations, etc.

The most difficult part of the measurement process is plotting the data accurately. For use in the developing world, the Direct Reading scale is a clever device that links the weighing scale to the chart so that as the child is weighed a pen records the scale deflection on the chart. This and the Road to Health chart can be obtained via Teaching Aids at Low Cost (TALC).

Another direct-reading chart is the Nabarro height-for-weight wall chart (also available through TALC). The child is first weighed, and then he or she stands against the chart at the point corresponding to his or her weight. The chart consists of

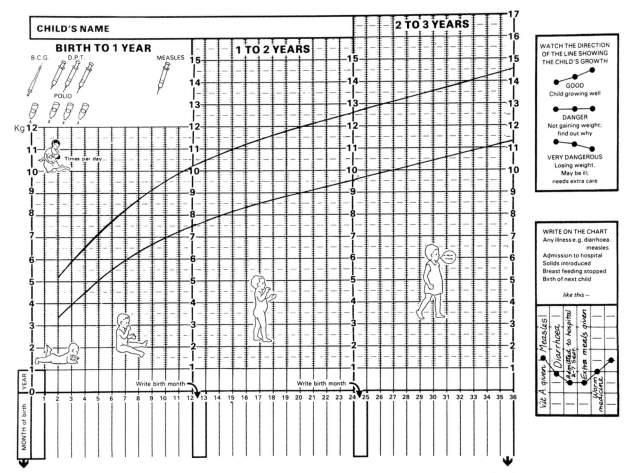

Figure 2 The TALC Road to Health chart. (Reproduced by kind permission of Teaching-Aids at Low Cost.)

vertical bars, and the height of the relevant bar is compared to the child's height. If the child is thin, he or she will be taller than other children of the same weight, and the upper section of the bar is color coded in red to flag excessive thinness, also known as wasting.

Familial Height Adjustment

Child height is strongly correlated with parental height, so many short children have short parents. Short children from tall families are easier to detect if their height is adjusted for midparent height. Tanner published a chart to do perform this adjustment in 1970, but it proved cumbersome to use, and currently the target height method is preferred. This method uses midparent height to estimate the child's likely height centile as an adult and compares it with the child's current centile.

However, the target height approach is also cumbersome and relies on the heights of both parents, one of which may not be available. A familial height chart has been described that compares the child's current height centile with that of his or her mother and/or father and/or sibling(s). The advantages of the chart are that it uses all the available familial height information (a sibling is as close genetically as a parent), it avoids all calculations (apart from reading the centiles off the height chart), and it adjusts for the secular trend in height by using an older height reference for the parents.

Ethnicity

A growth chart reflects the size and growth of its reference population. When the target population is materially different in size, as happens with ethnic minorities in the industrialized world (e.g., Hispanics in the United States or Asians in the United Kingdom), the chart's centiles can be misleading. More than 3% of such children may be found below the 3rd height centile, and the relevant cutoff for referral should take ethnicity into account. One simple way to do this is to estimate an offset, measured in SD score units, to apply to the chart for a given ethnic minority group. For example, Southeast Asian children in the United Kingdom are approximately 0.4 SDs shorter than ethnic Caucasians, corresponding to approximately half a channel width on the chart, the distance between adjacent centiles.

The differences in height between ethnic groups can be explained partly by genetics (i.e., differences in parental height) and partly by differences in the environment. However, the parental height differences reflect the environment of previous generations, so it is not feasible to ascribe the differences

purely to genes or the environment—the two are inextricably linked. If the child's height is appropriate for the heights of his or her parents, this should provide reassurance.

Charts to Measure Growth

Growth charts are usually constructed using cross-sectional data—each reference child contributes a single measurement to the data set. This allows children in each age group to be ranked by size to identify the required centiles, which can then be plotted against age. James Tanner coined the term "distance to indicate size attained," meaning the distance the child has travelled on the journey from conceptus to adult.

Growth is the rate of change of size, or velocity in Tanner's notation. To measure growth in an individual child requires at least two measurements separated in time. However, the growth chart is based on cross-sectional data, which provide no information about growth. This is an irony of the conventional growth chart: It is designed to measure size, not growth. It flags poor growth when the child's growth curve rises more slowly than the centile curve, but it does not distinguish between mild and severe faltering. The chart effectively has only three growth categories: normal (i.e., tracking along centiles as recommended by the Road to Health chart), above average growth (i.e., crossing centile curves upwards), and below average growth or crossing centiles downwards. Within the latter two categories, the chart does not grade the rate of centile crossing.

Tanner introduced notation to distinguish between distance or size charts, on the one hand, and velocity or growth charts, on the other hand. Velocity charts display centiles of growth velocity by age, and probably the most useful such chart is for height velocity measured over 1 year. In theory, velocity is better than distance for detecting short-term growth faltering, but in practice it is more difficult to measure because it involves two measurement errors, not one. It is also more complicated to monitor because the process of charting velocity involves taking the two measurements, calculating the velocity in units of cm/year or kg/year, and then plotting it at the mid-age point on the velocity chart.

Other forms of charts have been described that provide more information about growth velocity. Thrive lines are extra lines superimposed on the centile chart to quantify the rate of centile crossing of weight in infancy. Infants with monthly weight measurements who are growing on the 5th velocity centile track along the thrive lines. If they track in this way for 1 month it is a sign of moderate weight faltering, but if it continues then the faltering is progressively more severe. The thrive lines take into account the child's age and sex and adjust for regression to the mean. **Figure 3** illustrates the thrive lines superimposed on the weight chart of **Figure 1**. An infant measured twice 4 weeks apart whose weight curve tracks along the thrive lines (i.e., crosses centiles downwards) is growing on the 5th velocity centile, indicating moderate weight faltering.

Wright designed a weight monitoring chart in which the centile curves are spaced according to the infant's chance of crossing them in a given period of time. Large infants tend to cross centiles downwards more rapidly than small infants—this is a consequence of regression to the mean. Therefore, the centiles are relatively widely spaced at the top end and become progressively closer together at lower centiles. The chart is designed to simplify the assessment of infants recovering from failure to thrive.

Interpretation

The choice of charts for growth monitoring is bewildering—size charts, growth charts, and parental adjustment, each with many different cutoffs. In the industrialized world, the aim is to detect growth disorders as early as possible, and the key question is "Which form of growth monitoring is most effective at detecting disease?"

A common view is that growth monitoring requires measurements on two or more occasions, whereas growth screening involves a single measurement, and monitoring is therefore better than screening. Indeed, this is a fundamental tenet of growth monitoring as practiced in the developing world. Yet there is no direct evidence either way.

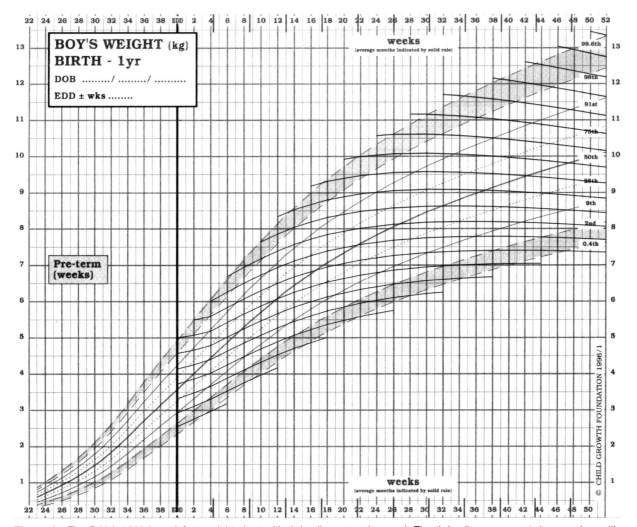

Figure 3 The British 1990 boys infant weight chart with thrive lines superimposed. The thrive lines represent downwards centile crossing corresponding to the 5th velocity centile, i.e., moderate weight faltering. (© Child Growth Foundation.)

A Dutch study by van Buuren and colleagues for the first time addressed this question, treating height monitoring as a diagnostic test with associated sensitivity and specificity. The study aimed to detect Turner's syndrome in girls using a regional growth survey as the corresponding normal population. Three measures of size and growth were used: height SD score, height SD score adjusted for parental height, and height velocity, each with a range of cutoffs. The study found that height alone was not very effective at identifying cases of Turner's syndrome, whereas height adjusted for parental height was very effective. Height velocity was useful for ruling out Turner's syndrome, but it was poor at ruling it in. Overall, the study emphasized the value of height adjusted for parental height and tended to discount the value of repeated measurements.

Similar studies need to be done for other outcomes, but until they are performed, the choice of charts and cutoffs needs to be based on simpler criteria. The British height reference uses the 0.4th centile to screen for short stature (**Figure 1**), which screens in 0.4% of the population and corresponds to a specificity of approximately 99.6%. It is very important for the false-positive rate to be as low as 0.4% to avoid overwhelming growth clinics with referred patients. In the United Kingdom, height velocity is viewed as too noisy, because of the two measurement errors involved, to justify its routine use.

Of course, these conclusions apply to growth monitoring in the industrialized world. They should not be extended uncritically to the developing world, where the purpose of growth monitoring is different—to reduce malnutrition. Here, underweight is judged by the Road to Health chart and is the universal indicator of malnutrition. Weight can fluctuate rapidly due to disease, and encouraging mothers to weigh their infants regularly is a logical way of encouraging the child to grow along the 'road to health.' This philosophy is just one component of UNICEF's GOBI program, which combines growth monitoring, oral rehydration, breast feeding, and immunization.

When height is also available, weight-for-age can be separated into height-for-age and weight-for-height, where low values are known as stunting and wasting. Stunting reflects long-term malnutrition and wasting short-term malnutrition. The implications of the two conditions are different, the latter indicating a need for medical intervention, possibly urgent, and the former is a proxy for more deeply seated socioeconomic problems that are less amenable to intervention. In practice, however, height is rarely measured in infancy and the main focus is on detecting underweight.

Nature of the Intervention

The intervention arising from growth monitoring may be quite specific (e.g., the identification and treatment of a particular growth disorder) or it may be more general (e.g., referral to a growth clinic, a dietician, or a feeding station). If the mother is involved, it may alter her view of her child's health and so modify her child care. At the population level, it may affect the allocation of resources (e.g., between regions for malnutrition relief).

If growth monitoring is evaluated in the spirit of the Cochrane Review, the outcome it leads to needs to be quantifiable and objective. Also, the Cochrane Review evidence, such as it is, suggests that growth monitoring in the developing world is ineffective. However, several potential outcomes are too diffuse to quantify (e.g., increased parental interest and education), and this needs to be recognized. The absence of an evidence base in favor of growth monitoring should not necessarily be interpreted as evidence that it lacks benefit. The benefits may simply be too subtle to detect using conventional trials.

See also: **Growth and Development, Physiological Aspects. Low Birthweight and Preterm Infants**: Causes, Prevalence and Prevention. **Malnutrition**: Primary, Causes Epidemiology and Prevention; Secondary, Diagnosis and Management. **Nutritional Assessment**: Anthropometry. **Nutritional Surveillance**: Developed Countries; Developing Countries. **Obesity**: Childhood Obesity.

Further Reading

British 1990 growth charts at http://www.healthforallchildren.co.uk.

Cole TJ (1993) The use and construction of anthropometric growth reference standards. *Nutrition Research Reviews* 6: 19–50.

Cole TJ (1997) 3-in-1 weight monitoring chart [Research letter]. *Lancet* 349: 102–103.

Cole TJ (2000) A simple chart to assess non-familial short stature. *Archives of Disease in Childhood* 82: 173–176.

Hall DMB (2000) Growth monitoring. *Archives of Disease in Childhood* 82: 10–15.

International Information Support Centre at http://www.asksource.info/

Jelliffe DB and Jelliffe EFP (1990) *Growth Monitoring and Promotion in Young Children.* Oxford: Oxford University Press.

Panpanich R and Garner P (2003) *Growth Monitoring in Children* [Cochrane review], The Cochrane Library, Issue 3. Oxford: Update Software.

Teaching-Aids at Low Cost at http://www.talcuk.org/

US CDC 2000 growth charts at http://www.cdc.gov/growthcharts/

van Buuren S, van Dommelen P, Zandwijken GRJ *et al.* (2004) Towards evidence based referral criteria for growth monitoring. *Archives of Disease in Childhood* **89**: 336–341.

WHO (1986) *The Growth Chart: A Tool for Use in Infant and Child Health Care.* Geneva: WHO.

WHO (1995) *Physical Status: The Use and Interpretation of Anthropometry.* Geneva: WHO.

Wright CM (2000) Identification and management of failure to thrive: A community perspective. *Archives of Disease in Childhood* **82**: 5–9.

Gut Flora *see* **Microbiota of the Intestine**: Probiotics; Prebiotics

HANDICAP

Contents
Down's Syndrome
Prader–Willi Syndrome
Cerebral Palsy

Down's Syndrome

M Collins and A Laverty, Muckamore Abbey
Hospital, Antrim, UK

Down's syndrome, named after John Langdon Down, is the most widely recognized chromosomal disorder found in humans and falls into a category of chromosomal disruptions known as trisomies; hence the other term for the condition, trisomy 21. People with Down's syndrome vary widely in their abilities, but the syndrome is the most common genetic cause of learning disability. The syndrome is characterized by abnormalities of both structure and function, some of which may be amenable to nutritional intervention.

More than 90% of Down's syndrome individuals have a total of 47 chromosomes in cells instead of the usual 46. The remaining cases are mainly either translocations, where there is a rearrangement of fragments of chromosomes, or mosaics, in whom there are both normal and trisomic cells (i.e., mosaic trisomy 21). There is a relationship between the frequency of Down's syndrome births and age, with both very young mothers and older mothers having a higher incidence of the syndrome. It has been suggested that nutrition may be implicated in the nondisjunction of the chromosomes. The additional chromosomal material in Down's syndrome usually comes from the mother, but it can come from the father, and one study reported that the maternal age relationship had been found associated with paternal origin of the additional chromosome. This observation may be indicative of hormonal changes in the older mother that reduce the likelihood of spontaneous abortion in an abnormal pregnancy.

The incidence of Down's syndrome is approximately 1 in 600–1000 live births. Prevalence is rising as life expectancy has improved in recent years with advancing medical knowledge and higher standards of care, but concurrently there is a declining incidence of live births in industrialized countries due to prenatal diagnostic screening and abortion.

Physical defects common in Down's syndrome include congenital anomalies of the gastrointestinal tract, which occur in approximately 12% of infants with Down's syndrome. Most of these anomalies require the neonate to be operated on immediately to allow nutrition. Congenital heart disease occurs in approximately 40% of infants with Down's syndrome. Children with congenital heart disease may present with failure to thrive, but after surgical repair of heart defects these children usually improve. Immune dysfunction, increased susceptibility to leukemia, and premature aging with Alzheimer-like changes in the brain are major features of the syndrome.

Thyroid dysfunction is more common in people with Down's syndrome, with the incidence increasing as they get older. Hypothyroidism is most frequently reported, but hyperthyroidism can also occur. Correction of thyroid function is essential to allow normal learning processes to take place and to aid weight control.

There are many biochemical anomalies associated with the syndrome, mainly quantitative rather than qualitative. It is presumed that the overexpression of genes on chromosome 21 contributes to both the structural and the functional pathology. Overdose effects of the genes already mapped to chromosome

Table 1 Nutritional complications of Down's syndrome

Physical	Problems with muscle tone, oral health and dentition, chewing, and swallowing
Metabolic	Anomalies in carbohydrate protein and lipid metabolism
	Increased demands on antioxidant defence system and methylation pathways
	Increased incidence of diabetes, coeliac disease, obesity, and thyroid disorders
Behavioral	Food consumption and exercise choices

21 are thought to alter pathways controlling the production of monocarbons, purines, pyrimidines, tubulins, and myelin.

The nutritional complications associated with Down's syndrome are summarized in **Table 1**.

Nutritional Status

It is debatable how relevant reference data from normal groups are for people with Down's syndrome.

Dietary Assessment

In children with Down's syndrome, conflicting reports have shown energy intake to be less than, similar to, or more than that of age-matched comparison groups, with a small percentage of children exceeding the recommended daily intake by more than 50%. However, because children with this syndrome tend to be shorter than age-matched children, energy intake comparisons need to be calculated per unit of body height.

Lower than recommended intakes of nonstarch polysaccharide coupled with higher than recommended consumption of protein and fats have also been reported. Some, but not all, researchers have reported low intakes of calcium, particularly in preschool and school-age children who refuse or limit milk consumption. Iron intakes have been reported to be low, particularly non-hem iron. Vitamins A and C intakes are limited in those who have a poor intake of fruit and vegetables. Intake of B vitamins has also been reported as low.

Laboratory Assessment

Carbohydrate Metabolism

Fasting blood glucose levels are usually in the normal range, but the glucose tolerance curve has been reported to be flatter and often with a double-humped curve, suggestive of delayed absorption.

There is an increased incidence of both type 1 (insulin dependent) and type 2 diabetes in Down's syndrome.

Protein Metabolism

Disturbances in protein metabolism are common in Down's syndrome. An increased level of immunoglobulin A and immunoglobulin G antibodies to food antigens has been reported, and several studies have reported an increased prevalence of coeliac disease. Abnormal levels of fasting plasma and urinary amino acids have been reported.

Lipid Metabolism

One study reported no significant differences between study and control groups, drawn from within the same families, in levels of total cholesterol, low-density lipoprotein, apolipoprotein B, and the apolipoprotein B-to-apolipoprotein A-I ratio. Triacylglycerol levels were significantly increased and serum high-density lipoprotein cholesterol-to-total cholesterol ratio was significantly decreased in Down's syndrome. This suggests increased risk for coronary heart disease. The results of this study and other studies reporting no difference between Down's syndrome and comparison groups with regard to atherosclerosis contrast with early reports that suggested a decreased incidence of coronary artery disease in Down's syndrome. It is not clear whether the differences reflect nutritional variables or population variable changes reflecting the increased survival rate in infancy.

There is evidence of increased lipid peroxidation in Down's syndrome.

Vitamins

Some, but not all, studies have reported biochemical evidence of deficiency of thiamin, nicotinic acid, pyridoxine, cobalamin, folate, ascorbic acid, retinol, β-carotene, and α-tocopherol. Vitamin D metabolites have been reported to be in the normal range in a Spanish study that demonstrated wide seasonal variation linked to intensity of solar radiation.

Minerals

Low iron, calcium, manganese, and zinc concentrations have been reported, and the iron-to-copper ratio has been reported to be decreased. Studies reported that intracellular zinc in blood mononuclear cells was approximately 47% lower than that of normal controls, and it is possible that this may play a role in thyroid dysfunction, immunodeficiency, retarded growth, and faulty DNA repair. Further research is required to determine if zinc supplements are beneficial and at what level. Supplementation with selenium aimed at increasing levels of the selenium-dependent enzyme glutathione peroxidase is reported to have led to a decrease in initially high blood mononuclear cell levels of copper, but it did not affect iron or zinc.

Vitamin and mineral levels have been held to reflect not just nutrient intake but also abnormal metabolism. Assessments of antioxidants and oxidation by-products are useful indicators of nutritional status in people with Down's syndrome. The overexpression of the superoxide dismutase system, the purine synthesis pathway, and cystathionine β-synthase are thought to create extra demands for antioxidants and for folate, but despite gene dosage effects the many biochemical anomalies that have been reported in people with Down's syndrome show a great deal of individual variation.

Anthropometric Assessment

Growth delay is one of the main characteristics of Down's syndrome, but impaired growth velocity is particularly evident at certain stages of development.

Fetal growth has usually been reported to be relatively normal and the length of the neonate is often within normal limits, allowing for gestation. Some studies have reported prenatal growth delay, and a major Italian study comparing neonatal length, weight, head circumference, and weight/length squared reported all percentiles of growth variables lower in Down's syndrome infants except for weight/length squared percentiles.

At approximately the age of 6 months, when growth starts to become regulated by growth hormone, growth velocity usually begins to show a marked reduction from normal levels. Although for the Down's syndrome child the period between birth and 2 years and the period between 6 years and 10 years of age are times of accelerated growth, the deviation from normal levels remains significant. Slow growth velocity is also a particular feature of adolescence, although there is a pubertal growth spurt. The deviation of adult stature from the means of reference groups is greater than the deviations in early infancy.

The short stature in Down's syndrome seems to be mainly the result of impaired growth of the long bones of the leg, because sitting height measurements show that the growth of the vertebral column is closer to normal.

Why there is growth delay in Down's syndrome is not entirely clear, and several hypotheses have been

advanced. Both human growth hormone therapy and zinc sulfate supplementation of the diet have been reported to accelerate growth.

Children with Down's syndrome tend to be not only shorter but also heavier than reference children. Charting the height and weight of a child with Down's syndrome using reference norms from the general population will show the abnormality of the growth pattern. However, it is more useful clinically to compare the height and weight of an individual against syndrome-specific norms because this will identify any deviation from the growth patterns of children with Down's syndrome.

Italian percentile charts have been drawn up for neonates with Down's syndrome based on a large sample of consecutively born infants. Specific growth charts for children with Down's syndrome have been constructed based on anthropometric assessments of US children, Sicilian children (thought to be representative of southern European children), and Dutch children (thought to be representative of northern European children). On average, the Dutch children were taller than the US children, and the US children were taller than the Sicilian children.

Nutritional Requirements

Children and adults with Down's syndrome need the same range of nutrients as the general population. Energy intake standards based on age groups are not appropriate for children with Down's syndrome. Energy intakes in both children and adults need to be tailored to height and weight and to physical activity.

Nutritional Therapy

In the 1970s and 1980s, hopes were raised that megadoses of vitamins and minerals would boost intelligence in children with Down's syndrome, but rigorous studies have shown these doses lead neither to higher intelligence nor to better health. In addition, there is anxiety about possible side effects, particularly from the fat-soluble vitamins.

As more has been learned about the genes on chromosome 21, interest has shifted to targeted nutritional intervention aimed at correcting the metabolic anomalies that are common in Down's syndrome due to genetic overexpression, with the emphasis on nutrients to maintain health and prevent disease. Targeted nutritional supplementation with vitamins, minerals, amino acids, digestive enzymes, and essential fatty acids is still controversial. Clinicians have reported differences between children treated and not treated in health, growth, and cognitive and speech functions, and extensive double-blind studies are planned.

Dietary Management

Dietary Guidelines

Dietary recommendations are as for the general population until research proves otherwise. There are no specific dietary guidelines for the woman pregnant with a Down's syndrome child or for the pregnant Down's syndrome woman. There are indications that antioxidant and essential fatty acid intake may be particularly important, and folic acid supplements beneficial, but dietary advice is currently the same as for other pregnant women.

The situation is similar for infant feeding. Brain lipids in the human infant are known to change with changing intakes of fatty acids. The needs of a newborn with Down's syndrome for the long-chain polyunsaturated fatty acids docosahexenoic acid and arachidonic acid have not been determined. Since breast milk contains the preformed dietary very long-chain fatty acids that seem to be essential for the development of the brain and the retina, it seems prudent to encourage breast-feeding.

The antioxidant defence system has a particularly important role in Down's syndrome, and parents and caregivers can be advised on providing a diet rich in antioxidants. Dietary intakes need to be considered for the sulfur amino acids (which are needed for glutathione synthesis); fat-soluble vitamins A, C, and E; water-soluble vitamins B_6, B_{12}, and folic acid; and the minerals selenium and zinc. In latitudes where no vitamin D is synthesized in the winter months, it is particularly important to ensure exposure to sunlight during summer months to maintain adequate stores of the vitamin throughout the year because studies indicate an increase in the incidence of osteoporosis in Down's syndrome.

Feeding Behavior

Feeding skills tend to be delayed in the young child with Down's syndrome, but the sequence of the emergence of the skills is the same as that for other children if appropriate learning opportunities are provided.

Infants with Down's syndrome have a smaller oral cavity, which makes it easier for liquids to spill from the sides of the mouth. If a child is hypotonic, the tongue is likely to flatten out when the child sucks instead of forming a groove around the nipple, so the child will have a weak suck, may gag, and milk will leak from the mouth. Feeding will be exhausting, and particularly when the child has a cardiac defect, the child may have difficulty taking in enough milk to meet energy requirements. Tube feeding may be necessary until the child develops better tongue control. As infants with Down's syndrome are often placid, sleepiness may be overlooked and feeding will be easier if the infant is wide awake. Extra support for the infant during feeding, and in particular supporting the infant's chin to help steady the jaw, can help encourage intake. Because of the benefits of breast feeding, it is essential that nursing mothers are given help and advice when their infants have initial difficulties. Breathing during feeding may be helped if the mouth and nose are cleared of mucus with a syringe before feeding.

As with other children, it is important to introduce textured food when the child is developmentally ready, and information should be provided to parents and caregivers regarding both appropriate expectations and helpful feeding techniques as well as dietary advice. In children with Down's syndrome, poor neuromotor control of the tongue may result in the continued use of pureed food. There may be slow initiation of the swallow response, possibly because of hypotonic pharyngeal muscles, and oral sensitivity problems may also make the transition to textured foods difficult. Persistent feeding problems merit multidisciplinary assessment and therapy. Impaired swallow can result in food being aspirated and contribute to respiratory problems. The presence of the tongue protrusion reflex past the age of 12–18 months can result in delayed progression to solid food and can contribute to malocclusion of teeth. Also, dental abnormalities can exacerbate difficulties with chewing and can contribute to poor nutrition because children who have problems chewing may be offered soft, often high-energy food and be given little opportunity to accept meats, fresh fruits, and vegetables, which are lower in energy.

Fresh fruit and vegetables also provide the non-starch polysaccharide that can help prevent the constipation common in Down's syndrome. Prunes, fruit juices, and water between meals also help with constipation. Because the hypotonia in Down's syndrome also contributes to sluggish bowel habits, this is another reason for children and adults to be encouraged to take part in physical activity. If constipation does not respond to dietary management, there should be a medical assessment to exclude gastrointestinal and thyroid problems.

Dental Problems

Dental anomalies in Down's syndrome include changes in tooth structure, reduced total number of teeth, and delayed or abnormal eruption. Together with the physical abnormalities of the facial appearance and oral cavity, these can all impact on feeding. Dental disease is common in Down's syndrome because teeth are more at risk of wear through bruxism and decay due to fragile enamel. In addition, gum disease (gingivitis) and oral infections due to mouth breathing can lead to teeth becoming loose and falling out. A healthy balanced diet, low in sugar-containing fluids and fizzy drinks (including 'diet' varieties), without frequent snacks and plenty of fruit and vegetables will help preserve teeth.

Obesity

Obesity is not inevitable in Down's syndrome, but it is common. Obesity in children with Down's syndrome has been reported from different cultures and different ethnic backgrounds. From Australian and North American studies, it has been reported that by 2 or 3 years of age more than 30% of children with trisomy 21 are overweight, and by 9 years of age the average child with Down's syndrome is obese; from the age of 10 years, the average weight of Dutch children with Down's syndrome is above the 90th percentile of weight-for-height curves of healthy children. Since the 1960s, obesity has been increasing rapidly in school-age children in Japan, and in 1994 a survey of children at special schools reported that more than 20% of school children with Down's syndrome were obese.

High rates of overweight and obesity have been reported in adults with Down's syndrome, both living in the community and at home, and more commonly in females than males. Overweight and obesity are particularly associated with living in the family home compared to supervised community units or hospitals, but they are not significantly associated with the degree of learning disability.

Because excessive weight gain in childhood often leads to adult obesity, it is important to encourage healthy choices in childhood. Why children with Down's syndrome have a tendency to become fat is not clear, but it is likely that several factors influence the weight gain. Retardation of growth

resulting in short stature may be of prime importance. Obesity in people with Down's syndrome has also been linked to poor eating behaviour, excessive energy intake, depressed resting metabolic rate, hypotonia, reduced exercise, and endocrine abnormalities such as hypothyroidism. Abnormal substrate fat oxidation may also be implicated (**Table 2**).

Prepubescent children with Down's syndrome have a decreased resting metabolic rate compared to control children matched for body mass index. Children of approximately the same body composition, whether or not they have Down's syndrome, expend similar levels of energy in physical activity. Since obesity is negatively correlated with motor performance, it is likely to lead to a reduction in sporting and physical recreation activities, and thus obesity has social as well as health implications, in children with Down's syndrome as in other children. However, children and adolescents with Down's syndrome have been shown to have difficulty with sustained physical exercise in both laboratory and recreational situations, and this has been attributed to physiological impairments, notably cardiovascular, as well as to lack of motivation.

Children, adolescents, and adults with Down's syndrome have a deficit in isokinetic strength, and by the age of 14 years adolescents with testosterone levels in the normal range fail to show the pubertal muscle strength increase. Progressive resistance exercise programs can help to build muscle strength, and regular aerobic exercise will improve exercise tolerance. Often, individuals can attain high standards in competitive gymnastics and swimming. The overexpression of collagen genes on chromosome 21 affects both muscle and connective tissue, and it has been claimed that targeted nutritional treatment leads to rapid improvement in both muscle strength and joint stability.

In a cross-sectional study of men and women with Down's syndrome, body mass index (weight in kilograms divided by height in meters squared)

Table 2 Factors predisposing to obesity in Down's syndrome

Factor	Increased	Decreased
Poor eating behavior	↑	
Calorie intake	↑	
Resting metabolic rate		↓
Muscle tone		↓
Exercise		↓
Thyroid function		↓
Substrate fat oxidation		? ↓

declined with increasing age. Further research is needed to clarify whether individuals lose weight as they age or whether there is a shorter life expectancy for individuals with higher body mass indices.

Aging

The rapid aging that characterizes Down's syndrome is in line with the accumulating evidence that many degenerative diseases are associated with deleterious activated oxygen species reactions. Activated oxygen species can damage genetic material and inactivate membrane-bound enzymes as well as cause lipid peroxidation in cell membranes. Of particular relevance to Down's syndrome is evidence relating to cancer, inflammatory joint disease, diabetes, degenerative vascular disorders, degenerative eye disease, and senile dementia—all reported to have increased prevalence in Down's syndrome.

The gene for copper/zinc superoxide dismutase is on chromosome 21, and copper/zinc superoxide dismutase levels are elevated by 50% in a range of cells of people with Down's syndrome, including erythrocytes, blood platelets, leucocytes, and fibroblasts. The increase has also been reported in fetal cerebral cortical cells. Although copper/zinc superoxide dismutase usually functions as an antioxidant, it seems likely that in Down's syndrome the raised levels lead to oxidative stress. When the increased production of hydrogen peroxide through catalysis of superoxide free radicals is not matched by a sufficient increase in glutathione peroxidase to metabolize the additional hydrogen peroxide to water and oxygen, there is thought to be an increase in highly reactive hydroxyl radicals leading to increased lipid peroxidation.

Fibroblasts derived from people with Down's syndrome show elevated lipid peroxidation, and levels of thiobarbituric reaction products, which indicate the extent of lipid peroxidation, have been reported to be raised in erythrocytes from Down's syndrome subjects compared to controls.

A reported increase in the activity of the hexose monophosphate pathway in Down's syndrome is thought to be a compensatory mechanism to deal with increased hydrogen peroxide, allowing greater production of the reduced form of nicotinamide-adenine-dinucleotide phosphate, thus improving the ability of cells to reduce oxidized glutathione. However, it has been suggested that this shift of glucose utilization from energy production to reducing power may compromise cellular cation pumps.

Among the genes identified on chromosome 21 is that for the β-amyloid precursor protein. Amyloidosis is evident in the brain tissue of both patients with Alzheimer's disease and those with Down's syndrome. Studies are investigating the implications of the anomalies in the expression of the β-amyloid precursor protein and also the effect on cobalamin/folate metabolism of the gene for the enzyme cystathionine β-synthase, also on chromosome 21. The overexpression of both these genes is believed to contribute substantially to the development of dementia of the Alzheimer type. Although all people with Down's syndrome have evidence of brain pathology similar to Alzheimer's disease by their early thirties, not all show Alzheimer-like behavior changes as they age.

It may be that an increase in dietary antioxidants could delay the onset of Alzheimer-type symptoms, but more research is required. However, standard dietary recommendations for healthier lifestyles (i.e., eating more fruit and vegetables and including more oily fish in the diet) may have the added potential benefits of increasing antioxidant intake. Unfortunately, these are often the foods least favored by individuals with Down's syndrome.

Low vitamin E levels have been found to be associated with dementia, not only in the elderly but also in those with Down's syndrome. Vitamin E may have a potential therapeutic role in Alzheimer-like neurological changes by protecting the integrity of the muscarinc receptors. Continuing research into the etiology of the Down's syndrome phenotype is expected to lead to advances in the treatment of both Down's syndrome and Alzheimer's disease.

Care in the Community

Most people with Down's syndrome live in the community; some live with parents or caregivers, but adults often live independently or semi-independently. Many people with Down's syndrome can learn about healthy eating and manage their own diets. A dietitian's role in a community learning disability support team is likely to encompass not only individual assessment but also teaching and educating people with Down's syndrome as well as parents, caregivers, and other professionals.

See also: **Aging**. **Antioxidants**: Diet and Antioxidant Defense; Observational Studies; Intervention Studies. **Dental Disease**. **Fatty Acids**: Metabolism. **Growth and**

Development, Physiological Aspects. Immunity: Physiological Aspects. **Infants**: Nutritional Requirements. **Obesity**: Definition, Etiology and Assessment; Fat Distribution; Childhood Obesity; Complications; Prevention; Treatment. **Weight Management**: Approaches; Weight Maintenance; Weight Cycling. **Zinc**: Physiology.

Further Reading

Ani C, Grantham-McGregor S, and Muller D (2000) Nutritional supplementation in Down's syndrome: Theoretical considerations and current status. *Developmental Medicine and Child Neurology* 42: 207–213.

Antila E, Westermarck T, Huovinen K, Lehto J, and Johansson E (1996) Indications for nutritional supplementation in Down's syndrome, 10th World Congress of the International Association for the Scientific Study of Intellectual Disabilities. *Trends in Biomedicine in Finland* 7(supplement): 50–53.

Bell EJ, Haidonis J, and Townsend GC (2002) Tooth wear in children with Down's syndrome. *Australian Dental Journal* 47(1): 30–35.

Chumlea WC and Cronk CE (1981) Overweight among children with trisomy 21. *Journal of Mental Deficiency Research* 25: 275–280.

Clementi M, Calzolari E, Turolla L, Volpato S, and Tenconi R (1990) Neonatal growth patterns in a population of consecutively born Down syndrome children. *American Journal of Medical Genetics* 7(supplement): 71–74.

Cremers MJG, van der Tweel I, Boersma B, Wit JM, and Zonderland M (1996) Growth curves of Dutch children with Down's syndrome. *Journal of Intellectual Disability Research* 40(5): 412–420.

Cronk CE (1978) Growth of children with Down's syndrome: Birth to age three years. *Pediatrics* 61: 564–568.

Cronk C, Crocker AC, Pueschel SM *et al.* (1988) Growth charts for children with Down's syndrome: 1 month to 18 years of age. *Pediatrics* 81(1): 102–110.

Hennequin M, Faulks D, Veyrune JL, and Bourdiol P (1999) Significance of oral health in persons with Down syndrome: A literature review. *Developmental Medicine and Child Neurology* 41: 275–283.

Hewitt P and Smith D (1983) Down's syndrome—Nutritional aspects. In: Macrea K, Robinson RK, and Sadler MJ (eds.) *Encyclopaedia of Food Science, Food Technology and Nutrition*, vol. 2, London: Academic Press.

Lejeune J (1990) Pathogenesis of mental deficiency in trisomy 21. *American Journal of Medical Genetics* 7(supplement): 20–30.

Pipes PL (1988) Feeding management of children with Down syndrome. In: Dmitriev V and Oelwein P (eds.) *Advances in Down's Syndrome*. Seattle: Special Child Publications.

Piro E, Pennino C, Cammarata M *et al.* (1990) Growth charts of Down syndrome in Sicily: Evaluation of 382 children 0–14 years of age. *American Journal of Medical Genetics* 7(supplement): 66–70.

Prasher VP (1995) Overweight and obesity amongst Down's syndrome adults. *Journal of Intellectual Disability Research* 39(5): 437–441.

Pruess JB, Fewell RR, and Bennett FC (1989) Vitamin therapy and children with Down syndrome: A review of research. *Exceptional Children* 55(4): 336–341.

Prader–Willi Syndrome

A O Scheimann, Johns Hopkins School of Medicine, Baltimore, MD, USA

Introduction

Prader–Willi syndrome (PWS) is a genetic disorder caused by deletion of the paternally derived genes in the proximal arm of chromosome 15. Patients with PWS manifest several common features, including hypotonia, decreased fetal movement, obesity, hyperphagia, short stature, growth hormone deficiency, hypogonadism, strabismus, and small hands and feet. Clinical features of PWS present ongoing medical and nutritional management issues.

Clinical History

Infants with PWS exhibit decreased fetal movement, weak cry, neonatal hypotonia, genital hypoplasia (cryptorchidism and clitoral hypoplasia), and failure to thrive (due to hypotonia and poor feeding). Toddlers with PWS acquire major motor milestones later than controls (walk at 24 months). Hyperphagia becomes evident between 18 months and 7 years of age. The majority of patients with PWS have growth hormone deficiency with short stature manifest during childhood and lack of a pubertal growth spurt. Individuals with PWS have an elevated pain threshold and vomiting threshold, with reports of delayed diagnoses of fractures, appendicitis, and gastroenteritis with significant morbidity. Obesity-related comorbidities, including sleep apnea, diabetes, and cor pulmonale, will shorten life expectancy without aggressive interventions. Behavioral problems, including obsessive–compulsive behavior (skin picking and rectal digging), stubbornness, and food foraging (including garbage and frozen food), are common; 5–10% of adults with PWS have features of psychosis.

Genetics of Prader–Willi Syndrome

Prader–Willi syndrome (PWS) is the first human disorder caused by altered imprinting. The incidence has been estimated between 1 in 8,000 to 1 in 25,000. During the process of imprinting, genes are differentially expressed based upon the parent of origin. Prader–Willi syndrome results from loss of imprinted genetic material localized to the paternal 15q11.2–13 region; loss of maternal genes in the same region results in Angelman's syndrome. The majority of cases are sporadic mutations. Nearly 70% of PWS patients have deletions of the paternal 15q11.2–13 region; 28% of patients have maternal uniparental disomy. Approximately 1% of patients have mutations within the imprinting center, which has a higher recurrence risk unlike patients with deletions and uniparental disomy.

Fulfillment of diagnostic criteria and genetic testing confirm in individuals suspected with PWS. In 1993, age-stratified diagnostic criteria were published by Holm *et al.* PWS is very likely in children <3 years of age with 5 points (3 from major criteria) or in those >3 years of age with 8 points (4 from major criteria). Major diagnostic criteria for PWS (1 point for each) include infantile central hypotonia, feeding difficulties in infancy, accelerated weight gain in early childhood, hypgonadism, developmental delay and typical facial features (narrow bifrontal diameter, almond palpebral fissures, narrow nasal bridge, down-turned mouth). Current minor diagnostic criteria for PWS (1/2 point each) include decreased fetal movement, sleep apnea, short stature, hypopigmentation, small hands/feet, narrow hands with straight ulnar border, esotropia/myopia, thick saliva, skin picking and speech problems. Other commonly reported features of individuals with PWS include high pain threshold, decreased vomiting, temperature instability, premature adrenarche and osteoporosis.

In those suspected of having Prader–Willi syndrome, genetic testing should be pursued. Genetic testing for PWS includes chromosomal analysis and assessment for methylation patterns in the PWS region on chromosome 15. Flourescent in situ hybridization (FISH) is diagnostic in patients with deletions of the 15 q11.2–13 regions. Analysis for underlying uniparental disomy requires samples from both parents and the index case for DNA methylation patterns.

Nutritional Assessment

Nutritional monitoring in Prader–Willi syndrome requires attention to growth, body composition, and intake. Infants and children should be weighed on calibrated scales in minimal garments with heights obtained via a stadiometer. PWS-specific charts are available through the Prader–Willi Syndrome Association (www.pwsausa.org) to monitor linear growth.

Nutritional Management

Long-term management of patients with PWS presents unique evolving nutritional challenges. During infancy, muscle hypotonia impairs oral feeding and causes inadequate caloric intake and failure to thrive. The combination of altered body composition (with diminished metabolically active lean mass), growth hormone deficiency, and excessive intake results in obesity unless intake is restricted. Without aggressive nutritional interventions, the life expectancy is shortened for individuals with PWS due to obesity comorbidities.

Prior studies have reported metabolic differences among individuals with PWS. Adults with PWS have a low basal metabolic rate (BMR) dependent on the technique of body composition analysis. Despite differences in body composition, energy expenditure during physical activity is similar to that of controls but their overall activity level is less than that of controls. The combination of diminished BMR and activity level necessitates lower caloric intake to avoid significant obesity.

Dietary Interventions

Nutritional support for patients with PWS requires ongoing adaptation to meet age-specific needs. During infancy, hypotonia of the muscles associated with sucking limits the volume of caloric intake during feedings. Through the use of adaptive bottles/nipples, thickening agents (Thick-It and cereal), formula concentration, and short-term nasogastric tubes, infants with PWS can meet caloric requirements without placement of a gastrostomy. The feeding therapy utilized is determined by the adequacy of swallowing skills and nutritional status under the supervision of an oromotor therapist and nutritionist.

During infancy and early childhood, caloric intake should conform to the current guidelines from the Nutrition Committee of the American Academy of Pediatrics. During the first 6 months of life, breast milk or infant formulas are primary nutritional sources, followed by introduction of solids at 5 or 6 months of age. Solid textures are gradually advanced based on oromotor skills (jaw strength and tongue mobility). Due to the high likelihood for development of hyperphagia and obesity, the majority of parents avoid exposure of the PWS child to high-calorie solids, desserts, and juices. Via close nutritional follow-up during the first 2 years, oral intake can be appropriately adjusted to maintain weight for height between the 25th and 80th percentiles. Caloric restriction under the guidance of an experienced nutritionist is employed only if weight gain becomes excessive.

Nutritional strategies beyond the toddler years focus on avoidance of obesity. A number of studies have evaluated the caloric requirements for individuals with PWS. Weight maintenance has been reported with intakes of 8–11 kcal/cm/day (non-PWS children require 11–14 kcal/cm/day); weight loss has been documented with intakes of 7 kcal/cm/day. Proper implementation of caloric restrictions requires attention to all potential sources of intake, including cafeterias, school buses, classroom activities ('life skills'), vending machines, neighbors, convenience stores, as well as home access (e.g., pantry, garbage cans, refrigerator, and tabletop).

Individuals with PWS and significant obesity-related comorbidities may require more aggressive weight loss interventions. To promote aggressive inpatient weight loss, a protein-sparing modified fast diet with micronutrient supplementation has been used over short time periods. Ongoing monitoring of food access is essential for long-term weight management.

Bariatric surgery causes weight loss through either a diminished capacity for intake or malabsorption. A long-term analysis of 10 non-PWS adolescents with a mean weight of 148 kg demonstrated a mean 5-year weight loss of >30 kg in 90% of patients; only 1 patient regained the weight. Bariatric surgery was initially attempted in PWS in the early 1970s. Gastroplasties were performed with the goal of decreasing PWS-related hyperphagic tendencies. More than half of PWS patients required subsequent revisions of the gastric pouch due to inadequate weight loss. The overall experiences with bariatric surgery in PWS are summarized in **Table 1**. The reported outcomes of bariatric

Table 1 Outcomes of bariatric surgery in Prader–Willi syndrome

Year	Author	Type of surgery	No. of patients	Media age (years)	Median weight (kg)	Success rate	Complications
1974	Soper	Gastroplasty	7	15	92.5	43%?	57% required revisions due to inadequate weight (wt) loss
1980	Anderson	91% gastric bypass; 9% gastroplasty	11	13	85		1 (9%) wound infection 54% required revision due to inadequate wt loss 1 dumping/diarrhea 1 death from uncontrolled wt gain
1981	Fonkalsrud	Vagotomy	1	17	120	?	29-kg initial wt loss followed by 20-kg gain
1983	Touquet	Jejunoileal bypass	1	24	181	62 kg (1 year)	Postoperative wound infection DVT/pulmonary embolus 4 or 5 stools/day
1991	Laurent-Jacard	Biliopancreatic diversion	3	27.6	84.5	Significant wt loss 1st year followed by wt gain ($2\frac{1}{2}$–6 years)	Diarrhea Vitamin D, vitamin B_{12}, folate, and iron deficiency
1992	Dousei	Vertical banded gastroplasty	1	21	57.4	Initial improved DM control	Short-term wt loss followed by break of staple line and wt gain
1997	Chelala	Laparoscopic adjustable gastric band	1	?	?		Death 45 days postoperatively from GI bleeding
2000	Grugni	Biliopancreatic diversion	1	24	80	Initial wt loss but wt gain without restriction	Diarrhea, severe osteopenia, anemia, hypoproteinemia
2001	Marinari	Biliopancreatic diversion	15	21	127	56–59% wt loss at 2–3 years; then regain 10–20% of wt lost	2 deaths from unrelated causes; no vitamin levels or bone density data provided

Adapted from Scheimann (2003) Management of nutrition issues in Prader–Willi syndrome. In *Management of Prader–Willi syndrome*, 3rd edn.

procedures have been less than satisfactory, with short-term weight loss followed by weight gain.

Micronutrients

Adequate vitamin and mineral supplementation is imperative for the patient with PWS. Hypocaloric diets required for patients with PWS preclude acquisition of adequate vitamin and minerals from traditional dietary sources. Commonly used meal plans for individuals with PWS are deficient in calcium, iron, vitamin D, vitamin E, biotin, pantothenic acid, magnesium, zinc, and copper.

See also: **Obesity**: Definition, Etiology and Assessment; Childhood Obesity; Treatment. **Weight Management**: Weight Maintenance.

Further Reading

Anderson AE, Soper RT, and Scott DH (1980) Gastric Bypass for Morbid Obesity in Children and Adolescents. *J Pediatr Surg* 15: 876–881.

Bistrian BR, Blackburn GL, and Stanbury JB (1977) Metabolic Aspects of a Protein-sparing Modified Fast in the Dietary Management of Prader-willi Obesity. *NEJM* 296: 774–9.

Chelala E, Cadiere GB, Favretti F, Himpens J, Vertruyen M, Bruyns J, Maroquin L, and Lise M (1977) Conversions and Complications in 185 Laparoscopic Adjustable Silicone Gastric Banding Cases. *Surg Endosc* 11: 268–71.

Collier SB and Walker WA (1991) Parenteral Protien-sparing Modified Fast in an Obese Adolescent with Prader-willi Syndrome. *Nutr Rev* 49: 235–8.

Dousei T, Miyata M, Izukura M, Harada T, Kitagawa T, and Matsuda H (1992) Long-term Follow-up to Gastroplasty in a Patient with Prader-willi Syndrome. *Obesity Surgery* 2: 189–93.

Fonkalsrud EW and Gray G (1981) Vagotomy for Treatment of Obesity in Childhood Due to Prader-willi Syndrome. *J Pediatr Surg* 16: 888–89.

Gavranich J and Selikowitz M (1989) A Survey of 22 Individuals with Prader-willi Syndrome in New South Wales. *Aust Paediatr J* 25: 43–46.

Greenswag LR and Alexander RC (1995) *Management of Prader-willi Syndrome Second Edition.* Springer-Verlag.

Grugni G, Guzzaloni G, and Morabito F (2000) Failure of Biliopancreatic Diversion in Prader-willi Syndrome. *Obesity Surgery* 10: 179–81.

Hill JO, Kaler M, Spetalnick B, Reed G, and Butler MC (1990) Reating Metabolic rate in Prader-willi Syndrome. *Dysmorphol Clin Genet* 4: 27–32.

Pipes PL and Holm VA (1973) Weight Control of Children with Prader-willi Syndrome. *J Am Diet Assoc* 62: 520–23.

Holm VA and Pipes PL (1976) Food and Children with Prader-willi Syndrome. *Am J Dis Child* 130: 1063–7.

Laurent-Jacard A, Hofstetter J-R, Saegesser F, and Chapuis G (1991) Long-trem Result of Treatment of Prader-willi Syndrome by Scopinaro's Bilio-pancreatic Diversion. Study of Three Cases and the Effect of Dextrofenfluramine on the Postoperative Evolution. *Obesity Surgery* 1: 83–87.

Marinari GM, Camerini G, Novelli GB, Papadia F, Murelli F, Marini P, Adami GF, and Scopinaro N (2001) Outcome of Biliopancreatic Diversion in Subject with Prader-willi Syndrome. *Obesity Surgery* 11: 491–95.

Nardella MT, Sulzbacher SI, and Worthington-Roberts BS (1983) Activity Levels of Persons with Prader-willi Syndrome. *Am Jour Mental Deficiency* 87: 498–505.

Schoeller DA, Levitsky LL, Bandini LG, Dietz WW, and Walczak A (1988) Energy Expenditure and Metabolism in Prader-willi Syndrome. *Metabolism* 37: 115–20.

Soper RT, Mason EE, Printen KJ, and Zellweger H (1975) Gastric Bypass for Morbid Obesity in Children and Adolescents. *J Pediatr Surg* 10: 51–58.

Stadler DD (1995) Nutritional Management in *Management of Prader–willi Syndrome: 2nd Edition.* Greenswag LR and Alexander RC (eds.) Springer.

Strauss RS, Bradley LJ, and Brolin RE (2001) Gastric Bypass Surgery in Adolescents with Morbid Obesity. *J Pediatr* 138: 499–504.

Touquet VLR, Ward MWN, and Clark CG (1983) Obesity Surgery in a Patient with the Prader-willi Syndrome. *Br J Surg* 70: 180–81.

Van Mil EA, Westerterp KR, Gerver WJ, Curfs LM, Schrander-Stumpel CT, Kester AD, and Saris WH (2000) Energy Expenditure at Rest and During Sleep in Children with Prader-willi Syndrome Is Explained by Body Composition. *Am J Clin Nutr* 71: 752–6.

Cerebral Palsy

J Krick and P Miller, Kennedy–Krieger Institute, Baltimore, MD, USA

This article focuses on cerebral palsy (CP) and its nutritional implications. The first section defines CP and describes its causes, prevalence, and classification types. Associated deficits related to CP are also explored. The topic of nutritional assessment of children with CP includes discussions on growth, body composition, and energy, protein, fluid, and nutrient needs. Feeding and swallowing problems and the influence of muscle tone on the ability to eat safely are discussed in-depth, as are alternative feeding routes. The interdisciplinary approach is emphasized throughout as the ideal model to provide services to people with CP in order to ensure quality of life in the community.

Definition and Etiology

Cerebral palsy is a term that refers to a number of nonprogressive disorders of movement and posture that result from an injury to the central nervous system during early brain development (**Table 1**).

Table 1 Causes of cerebral palsy

Cause	% of cases
Perinatal	44
First trimester	
– Teratogens	
– Genetic syndromes	
– Chromosomal abnormalities	
– Brain malformations	
Second and third trimesters	
– Intrauterine infections	
– Problems in fetal/placental functioning	
Labor and delivery	19
Preeclampsia	
Complications of labor and delivery	
Perinatal	8
Sepsis/central nervous system infection	
Asphyxia	
Prematurity	
Childhood	5
Meningitis	
Traumatic brain injury	
Toxins	
Not obvious	24

Adapted from Hagberg B and Hagberg G (1984) Prenatal and perinatal risk factors in a survey of 681 Swedish cases. In: Stanley F and Alberman E (eds.) *The Epidemiology of the Cerebral Palsied*, pp. 116–134. Philadelphia: JB Lippincott.

Classification

There are several different classifications of CP. The three most predominant types are pyramidal, extrapyramidal, and mixed-type. The type of CP and the degree of involvement play an important part in nutritional assessment and treatment.

Pyramidal (spastic) cerebral palsy Children with spastic CP have increased muscle tone with a clasped-knife quality. In spastic quadriplegia (30% of cases of pyramidal CP), all four extremities are involved. In spastic diplegia (25%), both lower extremities are spastic with minimal upper extremity involvement. Hemiplegia (45%) implies involvement on only one side of the body, with the upper extremity usually more affected than the lower extremity.

Extrapyramidal cerebral palsy Choreoathetosis involves the presence of abrupt, involuntary movements of the upper and lower extremities. This condition can greatly increase energy expenditure and is further discussed in the energy needs section.

Mixed-type cerebral palsy Mixed-type CP includes characteristics of both the pyramidal and the extrapyramidal types. For example, a child may have rigidity in the upper extremities and spasticity in the lower extremities.

Associated Disabilities/Deficits

Associated deficits of CP are important to note since they impact on nutritional status. Cognitive impairments are quite common. Mental retardation occurs in 60% of CP cases, with the remainder at high risk for some type of learning disability. Sensory deficits are prevalent, including those in the visual and auditory modalities. Seizures occur in 20–30% of cases, with the highest proportion in the spastic type. Feeding, behavioral, or emotional problems are also frequently noted.

Nutritional Assessment

The goal for nutritional assessment and intervention is to have healthy, alert, interactive individuals who are able to take advantage of all that the environment has to offer. Each person must be able to participate to his or her capacity in the learning and therapeutic habilitative processes and in social, community, and leisure activities.

Growth

The literature describes children with CP who are shorter and lighter than the reference standard. This may be the result of several factors. Individuals with CP have alterations in muscle tone affecting their limbs and torso, depending on the level of severity and topography. They often exhibit muscle contractures, depending on the type of CP; muscle spasticity may retard bone growth. Limited physical activity may impede growth. Immobilization may be required after orthopedic surgery. Immobilization inhibits bone formation and longitudinal growth and results in suppression of certain growth-stimulating hormones. It has been suggested that dysregulation of growth hormone secretion may be another factor affecting growth.

A growth reference for children with spastic quadriplegia has been developed to facilitate uniformity in clinical appraisal as well as to simplify comparative interpretation of growth data. These growth curves can be seen in **Figures 1–6**. It is important to view the velocity of rate of growth from one measurement to another to aid clinical management. The rate of growth in children with CP is slower so that as they get older, the difference from the standard becomes greater.

Both nutritional and nonnutritional factors influence growth in children with CP. Nonnutritional

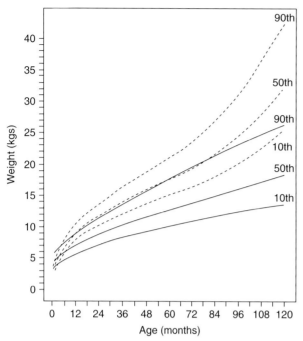

Figure 1 Weight for age for girls aged 0–120 months. The solid line represents girls with quadriplegic cerebral palsy, and the dotted line represents the National Center for Health Statistics standard curve for 10th, 50th, and 90th percentiles. (Reproduced with permission from Krick J, Murphy-Miller P, Zeger S, and Wright E (1996) Pattern of growth in children with cerebral palsy. *Journal of the American Dietetic Association* **96**: 680–685.)

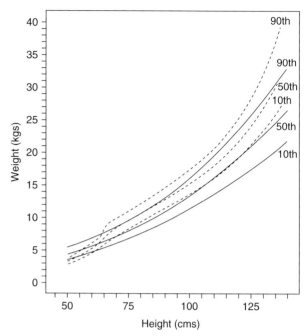

Figure 3 Weight for length for girls aged 0 to 120 months. The solid line represents girls with quadriplegic cerebral palsy and the dotted line represents the National Center for Health Statistics standard curve for 10th, 50th and 90th percentiles.

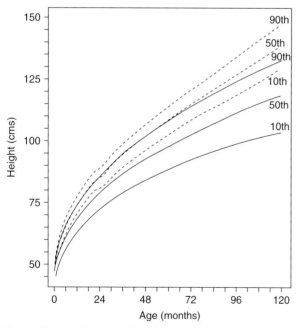

Figure 2 Length for age for girls aged 0 to 120 months. The solid line represents girls with quardriplegic cerebral palsy and the dotted line represents the National Center for Health Statistics standard curve for 10th, 50th and 90th percentiles.

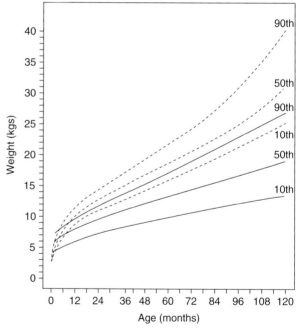

Figure 4 Weight for age for boys aged 0 to 120 months. The solid line represents boys with quadriplegic cerebral palsy and the dotted line represents the National Center for Health Statistics standard curve for 10th, 50th and 90th percentiles.

influences that have been suggested to impact growth include weight-bearing opportunities and,

by extension, interventions using aggressive physical therapy, growth hormones, and electrical stimulation of muscle. In 1995, Stevenson reviewed growth in hemiplegics and noted that there is diminished

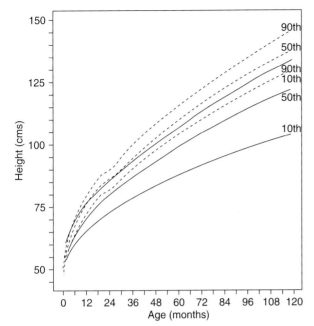

Figure 5 Length for age for boys aged 0 to 120 months. The solid line represents boys with quadriplegic cerebral palsy and the dotted line represents the National Center for Health Statistics standard curve for 10th, 50th and 90th percentiles.

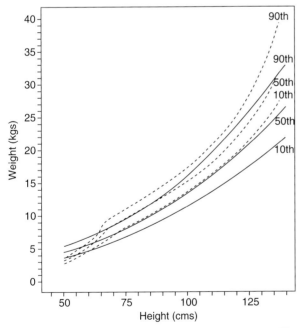

Figure 6 Weight for length for boys aged 0 to 120 months. The solid line represent boys with quadriplegic cerebral palsy and the dotted line represents the National Center for Health Statistics standard curve for 10th, 50th and 90th percentiles.

growth, decreased muscle mass, and decreased fat stores on the affected side, and that the magnitude of the differences increases with age and functional severity. Gender, age, cognitive impairment, and ambulatory status have also been noted to contribute to the slow growth seen in this population.

Measurement of length or height for individuals with CP may require techniques and standards using arm span, lower leg length, or segmental measurements because of the difficulties encountered with joint contractures and/or scoliosis. The use of height age, rather than chronological age, is a common technique and is defined as the age at which the child's height crosses the 50th percentile on the National Center for Health Statistics chart.

The use of z scores for length-for-age, weight-for-age, and weight-for-length promotes an accurate evaluation of discrete changes from one measurement date to another. Percentile tables describe ranges, and consequently detection of movement within the range is difficult to describe. The z score denotes standard deviation units from the median and allows the practicing clinician and investigator to pinpoint precisely any given measurement.

For screening purposes, conventional length/height and weight measures can be completed and compared to the Centers for Disease Control and Prevention growth charts. Reference standards for body mass index for children with CP do not exist; therefore, one must use body mass index data in conjunction with body composition data to determine adequacy of growth. Samson-Fang and Stevenson recommend using the TSF as a screening for identifying suboptimal fat stores in children with CP.

When trying to obtain growth measurements, joint contractures, muscle spasms, and poor cooperation will impact accuracy. Upper extremity (arm) length, tibial length, and knee height are often noted in the literature as valid proxies for length in children with CP up to the age of 18 years. (See **Table 2** for estimation of height using segmental measures.)

Researchers from the multicenter North American Growth in Cerebral Palsy Project suggest that a practical method to assess nutritional status in a child with CP is to measure body fat. This can be done in the form of either the triceps skin fold or

Table 2 Estimation of height from segmental measures

Age 0–12 years
$(4.35 \times UAL) + 21.8$
$(3.26 \times TL) + 30.8$
$(2.68 \times KH) + 24.2$

Age 6–18 years
White male $(2.22 \times KH) + 40.54$
Black male $(2.18 \times KH) + 39.60$
White female $(2.15 \times KH) + 43.21$
Black female $(2.02 \times KH) + 46.59$

UAL, upper arm length; TL, tibia length; KH, knee height.

both the TSF and subscapular skin folds. However, patient cooperation with the measuring techniques, required for accuracy and safety, may be difficult to obtain or maintain. For some individuals with CP, the process may be difficult, and training is needed to learn the technique for body fat measures and segmental measures mentioned previously.

Ideal Body Weight

The estimate of ideal body weight (IBW) is also in part determined by the severity of the CP. The IBW should be aimed at maintaining adequate fat and muscle stores to endure repeated surgeries or a common virus while facilitating daily physical care and management. Weight-for-length is an indicator of nutritional status, which obscures the issue of chronological age and addresses whether the individual is proportionate. IBW can be expressed as this ratio. Those with cerebral palsy should attain and maintain an IBW that takes into account their age, level of physical ability, and their independence. Measurement of arm anthropometry will provide a description of body composition and support clinical judgments related to IBW. For example, children with spastic quadriplegia are the most dependent and the 10th percentile weight-for-length would be designated as the IBW. However, this assignment is done in tandem with assessment and monitoring of body composition, and if either the arm fat or the arm muscle area were less than the 5th percentile, then the IBW would be adjusted upward.

Body Composition

Since the 1970s, researchers reviewing body composition have noted reduced lean body mass in children with CP. Recent work examining adults with CP and their age-matched controls found no difference in lean body mass or percentage of body fat.

Bone Mineral Density

Bone mineral density (BMD) is markedly reduced in nonambulatory children with CP, placing them at risk for nontraumatic fractures. Osteopenia defined as <2 standard deviations below the mean was found in the femur of most nonambulatory children by the age of 10 years. Decreased BMD results from a combination of factors, including immobilization, antiepileptic therapy, and nutritional deficiencies. Serum levels of calcium, phosphate, alkaline phosphatase, and osteocalcin were not found to be reliable indicators of low BMD when studied by Henderson. The same author noted that fracture rate is fourfold higher following spica casting and more than threefold higher following an initial fracture.

Many nonambulatory children require and are given less calories than recommended for their non-CP counterparts; therefore, the clinician is obliged to review the adequacy of the micronutrients, specifically calcium. Most likely, their diets will require supplementation to meet 100% of the DRI standards for age and gender.

Methods to increase BMD include weight-bearing activities, dietary adequacy, and the use of bisphosphonates. In several studies, bisphosphonate use has demonstrated increased bone density by 20–89% with no obvious adverse effects.

Energy Needs

Equations that are frequently used to predict energy requirements were developed using healthy children and adults in usual environmental and physical activity conditions and do not provide an accurate assessment of the needs of those with CP. From a nutrition perspective, wide-ranging studies demonstrate underreporting of energy needs on food records, which at best provide a qualitative measure of intake. Therefore, clinicians have turned to the use of more sophisticated technology, such as doubly labeled water and indirect calorimetry, to assess the energy needs of this population. Additionally, the energy cost of movement, whether it be wheelchair propulsion, crutch ambulation, or the involuntary movements of the individual with athetosis, must be considered. Those with CP may undergo repeated orthopedic surgery that insults nutritional status, resulting in increased nutrient and energy demands. It has also been hypothesized that whole body metabolic rate may be related to differences in skeletal muscle fiber proportions and/or differences in enzymatic activity. People with CP have abnormal variation in the size of muscle fibers and altered distribution of fiber types.

Altered energy needs are common among those with CP and differ widely from the norm. Clinicians use a variety of approaches to estimate energy needs, such as the Dietary Reference Intakes (DRIs) for chronological age, the RDAs for height age, and the World Health Organization equation. When estimating energy needs, information related to muscle tone, activity level, and needs for growth or catchup growth must be added to the estimate for resting energy expenditure (REE).

One equation designed specifically for this population is:

$$\text{REE} \times \text{muscle tone factor} \times \text{activity factor} + \text{growth factor(s)} = \text{kcal per day}$$

The REE can be determined using indirect calorimetry or can be derived from estimating body surface area standard metabolic rate 24 h. Body surface area (m²) is calculated from length and weight using the nomogram derived from the formula of DuBois and DuBois, and the standard metabolic rate (kcal/m²/h) is identified using height age and sex applying Fleisch data. The modifying factors are applied as follows:

- Muscle tone factors: Multiply by 10% for high tone (hypertonicity) and decrease by 10% for low tone (hypotonicity); no adjustment for normal tone.
- Activity factors: Multiply by 15% for bedridden state, 20% for wheelchair, and 30% for ambulation.
- Growth factors: Add 5 kcal (20.92 kJ) per gram of desired growth, expected growth, and catchup.

Energy needs must be viewed on an individual basis assimilating the concepts noted previously. The use of any approach is regarded as a guidepost and requires careful monitoring of body weight. Modifications to the diet should be based on clinical observation and measurement. There is a subset of individuals with CP who require significantly less kilocalories than anticipated (as few as perhaps 15 kcal/kg). Care should be exercised to provide adequate nutrients, protein/kg, and fluid despite the very low calorie needs.

Nutrient and Fluid Needs

Nutrient and protein needs are based on DRIs similar to those of the population without CP. Height age is often used in these determinations.

Fluid needs are based on body size rather than calorie intake. **Table 3** demonstrates how to calculate fluid needs. Constipation is a chronic problem for most children with CP and is related to muscle tone, loss of sensation, limited physical activity, medication side effects, and inadequate dietary fiber and/or fluid intake. Oral motor dysfunction results in diminished intake as well as in food and fluid loss. Modified food and fluid textures result in

less free water and fiber in the diet. Discomfort associated with constipation may decrease appetite and increase gastroesophageal reflux. Dietary intervention may therefore be limited and medical management may be necessary.

Assessment of Feeding Skills and Safety

Eating skills are acquired in a sequential pattern so that a developmental history will be helpful in evaluating current function and planning treatment options. Factors affecting feeding performance are shown in **Table 4**.

Oral Motor Evaluation

Feeding and swallowing problems are common in the child with CP, depending on the type of muscle tone, the presence of primitive reflexes, movement patterns, and the integrity of the sensory system. Clinical indicators of feeding and swallowing dysfunction are shown in **Table 5**. Problems often include poor intake, inefficient and lengthy mealtimes, abnormal oral motor patterns, inappropriate progression of feeding skills, and/or physiological compromise with feeding. Sensory, cognitive, and language deficits may also complicate the feeding process. An interdisciplinary team evaluation is

Table 4 General factors affecting feeding performance

Neuromotor performance	Constipation
Perceptual deficits	Amount of physical and verbal assistance required
Cognition and communication skills	Physiological support
Vision and hearing	Oral motor skills and swallowing status
Behavior/interaction	Medications
Growth	Dental and gum disease
Dietary adequacy	Multiple orthopedic procedures
GER and other gastrointestinal-related issues	Family/psychosocial stressors

Table 3 Fluid needs based on body weight[a]

Body weight (kg)	Fluid need (cm³ kg⁻¹)
≤10	100
11–20	+50
≥21	+25

$$\text{Fluid need } (cm^3\,kg^{-1})$$

[a]Suggest monitoring urine-specific gravities when available and quantity, color, and odor of urine, and adjust for periods of stress and temperature. Example: 28-kg child

  100 ml × 10 kg = 1000 ml
  50 ml × 10 kg = 500 ml
  25 ml × 8 kg = 200 ml
  Total need = 1700 ml

Table 5 Clinical indicators of feeding and swallowing dysfunction

Congestion	Difficulty managing secretions
Noisy 'wet' sounds	History of upper respiratory infections
Multiple swallows to clear bolus	Apnea during feeding
Unexplained fevers, unexplained irritability	Failure to thrive, failure to maintain weight
Coughing/choking/gagging before, during, or after swallow	
Food refusal	

essential for the assessment, development of appropriate goals, and facilitation of a treatment plan that respects the developmental progression. A clinical assessment of the feeding process should include observance of facial muscle tone, oral reflex activity, functional oral motor skills, structural abnormalities, sensory responses, behavior and interaction during feeding, respiratory and phonatory status, and posture and positioning.

Radiographic and ultrasound studies can provide more detailed information about the oral structures and the competency of the oral, pharyngeal, and esophageal phases, including the detection of aspiration. Cervical auscultation can also be helpful in evaluating the pharyngeal phase of swallowing. In addition, these techniques can assist in determining the suitable solid and liquid texture and appropriate head and neck positioning. Hypertonicity leads to abnormal movements of the tongue, lip, and jaw. These abnormal movements can be manifested as tongue retraction, tongue tip elevation, tongue thrust, tonic biting, jaw thrust, jaw instability, lip retraction, and lip/cheek instability. An abnormally strong gag reflex, tactile hypersensitivity in the oral area, and drooling can also complicate feeding. Individuals with CP are also at risk for dental problems due to poor oral hygiene, teeth grinding, hypersensitivity in the oral area, and hyperplasia of the gums from long-term use of phenytoin, a medicine commonly prescribed for seizure management.

Aspiration and Gastroesophageal Reflux

Clinical signs of aspiration may include coughing, choking, gagging, inability to handle oral secretions, wet upper airway sounds with poor vocal quality, apnea, food refusal, frequent upper respiratory infections, and aspiration pneumonia. Aspiration of food may occur without physical evidence if the protective cough or gag is not functioning, sensory deficits exist, and/or the swallowing mechanism is dysfunctional. This results in what is termed silent aspiration. Although aspiration from solid food can be detected, the possibility of aspiration from gastroesophageal reflux (GER) may also need to be considered. The regurgitation of gastric contents from the stomach into the esophagus can lead to irritability during or after feeding, arching, esophagitis, and ultimately food refusal. Other symptoms of GER include respiratory compromise, apnea, and drooling. Treatment for GER includes the use of antacids, H2 blockers, medications to increase gut motility, reduction in feeding rate, positioning, thickening of foods or liquids, or surgical

intervention. Small, frequent feedings help to decrease the volume in the stomach at one time.

Fatigue may occur in the child who is not able to sustain the work involved with feeding and may be expressed by an increase in respiratory rate, diaphoresis, or increased work of breathing. The causes may be muscular, respiratory, or cardiac, and they may increase the risk of aspiration or hypoxia. The work required to eat a meal is accomplished at a higher physiological cost to the child, thereby increasing caloric needs.

Muscle Tone and Positioning

It is important to understand the influences of muscle tone and proper positioning on the ability to eat safely and efficiently in this population. Increased or decreased muscle tone contributes to difficulty preserving a patent airway, compromised self-feeding skills, poor rib cage expansion and esophageal motility, and difficulty in maintaining a stable supported base for seating. Fluctuating muscle tone leads to involuntary movements and limited postural stability. Despite the type of muscle tone, optimal positioning is crucial for feeding and swallowing. The proper feeding position includes neutral alignment of head and neck, midline orientation, symmetrical trunk position, 90° pelvic/femoral alignment, and symmetrical arm position with neutral shoulders. An example of proper positioning can be seen in **Figure 7**. Consultations with orthopedists and/or rehabilitation physicians to address current and potential musculoskeletal problems, physical and occupational therapists for functional assessment, orthotists for deformity management, and durable medical equipment specialists to customize standard wheelchair components are valuable.

Underweight and Overweight

Overweight Most children with CP who are overweight or obese have low muscle tone. Their nutritional status impacts sleeping and breathing patterns, mobility, physical care, and peer relationships. It is difficult to attain an ideal body weight because energy needs are significantly reduced and the options for exercise are limited.

Underweight Typically, children with athetosis struggle to maintain weight given their excessive involuntary movements, which significantly increase energy needs. As these children age, the problem becomes more apparent, and many of these children will require enteral supplementation. One evaluation of this population noted that the basal energy requirement was 40% higher than expected.

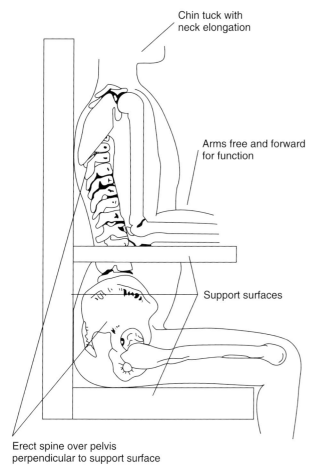

Chin tuck with neck elongation

Arms free and forward for function

Support surfaces

Erect spine over pelvis perpendicular to support surface

Figure 7 Proper seating position. (Reproduced with permission from: *The Handbook of Assistive Technology.* Singular Publishing Group, Inc.)

Superior Mesenteric Artery Syndrome

Superior mesenteric artery (SMA) syndrome is a condition in which the third portion of the duodenum is intermittently compressed by the overlying SMA, resulting in gastrointestinal obstruction. Symptoms include recurrent vomiting, abdominal distension, weight loss, and postprandial distress. People with CP are at high risk for several of the reported causes of SMA syndrome, including body cast compression, severe weight loss, prolonged supine positioning, and scoliosis surgery. Consequently, it is important to recognize the symptoms and know the appropriate treatments for this syndrome. Most people can be treated nonsurgically with gastric aspiration and nasojejunal or gastrojejunal feedings distal to the obstruction. One study also found that turning to the left from a supine position displaces the SMA from the right to the left side of the aorta in scoliosis cases. Thus, positioning can help alleviate symptoms and special

considerations may be indicated in light of the limitations imposed by the CP.

Behaviors at Mealtimes

Parent–child interactions can also influence feedings. Ineffective communication, lack of bonding, the absence of social interaction or poor interactive skills, family dysfunction, and decreased environmental stimuli can exacerbate feeding difficulties or lead to frustration and anxiety with subsequent food refusal or parental withdrawal. Aversion to oral feeds can also be an outcome of medical complications, such as esophagitis and GER, or lack of feeding experience at critical milestones secondary to prolonged tube feedings. Behavioral treatment should only be undertaken after thorough medical, nutritional, and neurodevelopmental assessments are completed.

Feeding Issues

The feeding plan should be safe, promote growth or weight maintenance without excessive energy expenditure in order to obtain the required calories, and meet the needs of the family. It should reflect their resources in time and skill, and it should address their concerns and expectations. The goals for treatment once feeding and swallowing problems are identified are to prevent aspiration and thereby respiratory compromise; provide adequate calories, protein, vitamins, minerals, and fluid; and educate caregivers regarding nutritional requirements.

Oral Motor Considerations

Management strategies for daily mealtime feeding include positioning, modification of the sensory properties of the food, oral motor facilitation techniques, and equipment adaptations. For individuals with increased energy needs, the nutrient density of their meals may need to be maximized. **Table 6** lists

Table 6 Calorie boosters

Instant breakfast	Margarine, butter, oils, gravy
Powdered, evaporated milk	Sugar, honey, syrup
Whole milk cheeses	Cream cheese
Peanut butter	Sour cream
Wheat germ	Concentrate juices
Yogurt, pudding, custards	Breading or cracker meal
Milkshakes, eggnog	Fruit canned in heavy syrup
Supplements such as Polycose, Promod, Microlipid, Pediasure, and Ensure	

commonly used calorie boosters. It is important to acknowledge the inability to change the underlying feeding problem while providing a method of circumventing the problem to allow adequate nutrition and growth. For example, facilitative techniques to minimize excessive jaw movement may entail the feeder providing physical jaw control/support; a change in the food consistency, texture, temperature, or taste to improve the ability to propel a bolus through the oropharynx; the careful selection of adaptive feeding equipment to assist with self-feeding and/or increased intake; and an appropriate seating system. Proper positioning also allows the feeder use of both hands.

Alternative Feeding Routes

Many children with CP are not able to meet some or all of their calorie needs by mouth due to one or more of the following conditions: oral motor dysfunction, excessive energy needs, recurrent infections, illnesses, and orthopedic surgical interventions. Consequently, if the gastrointestinal tract is functioning, supplemental or total tube feedings may be indicated. Early intervention with enteral nutrition may prevent protein–energy malnutrition and its complications. Studies have shown improvements in weight gain (fat mass as opposed to fat-free mass) with supplemental tube feedings, which better enables individuals to endure short-term medical insults.

Enteral nutrition may be delivered by nasogastric, nasojejunal, gastrostomy, gastrostomy–jejunal, and jejunostomy tubes. The degree of GER and risk of aspiration determine where the tube is placed, whereas the length of time needed for tube feedings determines whether a nasoenteral or surgically placed tube is required. The decision regarding continuous, intermittent, or combination tube feeds is dependent on the individual needs of the patient.

Tube feedings should be considered a tool to improve nutritional status rather than failure of the child's ability to eat. Based on the medical diagnosis and developmental stage of the child, the prognosis for return to oral feeding varies, and the length of time to achieve this goal is extremely variable. For some children, the goal of returning to full or partial oral feeding is not realistic. In a study evaluating the health of children with CP, Liptak describes those who were tube fed as having the lowest mental age, requiring the most health care resources, using the most medications, and having the most respiratory problems. These children were characterized as especially frail and required numerous health-related resources and treatments. Oral motor therapy

Table 7 Benefits of nonnutritive oral stimulation

Maintains oral sensation and tolerance
Facilitates saliva production, swallowing, and other oral motor patterns
Maintains or develops coordination of respiration and swallowing
Facilitates parent–child interactions

should focus on maintaining existing oral motor skills, encouraging pleasurable oral experiences, and tolerance of oral hygiene practices. Nonnutritive oral stimulation must be performed when tube feedings are employed as the route of nutrition. The benefits are listed in **Table 7**. Improvement in nutritional status can result in positive changes in oral feeding.

Parenteral nutrition should only be used when the gastrointestinal tract is dysfunctional. When initiating feedings in patients with major weight loss or failure to thrive, whether enteral or parenteral nutrition is used, it is important to be aware of the 'refeeding syndrome.' This syndrome refers to phosphorus depletion and alterations in potassium, magnesium, and glucose metabolism, resulting in severe metabolic and physiological complications. It is imperative to increase calorie delivery slowly with close laboratory monitoring.

Medications

Drug–nutrient interactions should be considered for all children receiving long-term medications for seizure disorders, alterations in muscle tone, attentional deficits, gastrointestinal disorders, and/or other chronic conditions. One drug or the combination of multiple drugs may affect nutrition in many ways, such as causing decreased appetite, interference with absorption of specific nutrients, nausea, and vomiting.

Medication treatment options offer challenges to nutrition. For instance, diazepam, often used to decrease spasticity, increases the potential for drooling. This raises concerns of fluid loss/balance as well as loss of the protective effect of saliva on esophageal mucosa. Additionally, attention must be paid to tone reduction in the trunk and oral structures that would compromise safety of feeding skills.

Tone-lowering drugs potentially reduce energy expenditure and, as a result, require increased vigilance to avert excessive weight gain. Anecdotally, as tone is significantly reduced in children for whom intrathecal Baclofen pumps are used, so is the energy requirement. Most of these children seen have been on tube feedings with a constant intake over time.

With the use of the Baclofen pump, weight gain is seen and adjustments in the kilocaloric level may be necessary.

Repeated Orthopedic Surgeries

These are common in children with CP, and each surgery must be preceded by an evaluation of nutritional status and assessment of the child's ability to physically heal and recover quickly from the trauma. Many children who are marginal oral feeders will decompensate, lose weight, and have a difficult time healing because of a cascade of events including pain, poor positioning for safe feeding, worsening constipation, minimal intake, lethargy, and increased medications for pain that may have a sedative effect. They may require supplemental feedings prior to surgery or during the postoperative period.

Coordinated Services

The provision of nutrition services and prevention of further disabling conditions can be done in a variety of health care, school, vocational, home, and community settings. It is the responsibility of the family in concert with the health care team to promote nutrition care planning in these settings. More than 90% of children with CP live to adulthood; however, their life expectancy is less than that of the general population. The chronicity of nutrition problems for individuals with CP is recognized and has in part created a need for care coordination and integrated service planning to provide meaningful and cost-effective services.

See also: **Energy Expenditure**: Indirect Calorimetry; Doubly Labeled Water. **Nutritional Support**: Adults, Enteral.

Further Reading

Capute A and Acardo PJ (eds.) (1996) *Developmental Disabilities in Infancy and Childhood*, 2nd edn., vol. 2. Baltimore: Paul H Brookes.

Case-Smith J (ed.) (1993) *Pediatric Occupational Therapy and Early Intervention*. Stoneham, UK: Butterworth-Heinemann.

Cherney L (1994) *Clinical Management of Dysphagia in Adults and Children*. Gaithersburg, MD: Aspen.

Eicher PS and Batshaw ML (1993) Cerebral palsy. *Pediatric Clinics of North America* 40: 537–551.

Ekvall SW (ed.) (1993) *Pediatric Nutrition in Chronic Diseases and Developmental Disorders: Prevention, Assessment and Treatment*. New York: Oxford University Press.

Henderson CR, Lark KR, Gurka JM et al. (2002) Bone density and metabolism in children and adolescents with moderate to severe cerebral palsy. *Pediatrics* 110(1).

Hogan SE (1999) Knee height as a predictor of recumbent length for individuals with mobility-impaired cerebral palsy. *Journal of the American College of Nutrition* 18(2): 201–205.

Klein M and Delaney T (1994) *Feeding and Nutrition for the Child with Special Needs*. Tucson, AZ: Therapy Skill Builders.

Krick J, Murphy-Miller P, Zeger S, and Wright E (1996) Pattern of growth in children with cerebral palsy. *Journal of the American Dietetic Association* 96: 680–685.

Liptak GS et al. (2001) Health status of children with moderate to severe CP. *Developmental Medicine and Child Neurology* 43: 364–370.

Samson-Fang LJ and Stevenson RD (1998) Linear growth velocity in children with cerebral palsy. *Developmental Medicine and Child Neurology* 40(10): 689–692.

Samson-Fang LJ and Stevenson RD (2000) Identification of malnutrition in children with cerebral palsy: Poor performance of weight-for-height centiles. *Developmental Medicine and Child Neurology* 42(3): 162–168.

Stallings VA, Charney EB, Davies JC, and Cronk CE (1993) Nutrition related growth failure in children with quadriplegic cerebral palsy. *Developmental Medicine and Child Neurology* 35: 126–138.

Stevenson RD (1995) Use of segmental measures to estimate stature in children with cerebral palsy. *Archives of Pediatrics & Adolescent Medicine* 149(6): 658–662.

Heart Disease *see* **Coronary Heart Disease**: Hemostatic Factors; Lipid Theory; Prevention

---

Height *see* **Nutritional Assessment**: Anthropometry

HOMOCYSTEINE

J W Miller, UC Davis Medical Center, Sacramento, CA, USA

Introduction

Homocysteine is a sulfur amino acid and an intermediate in the biochemical conversion of methionine to cysteine, a process called trans-sulfuration. Vincent Du Vigneaud and others elucidated the biochemistry of homocysteine over the period from the 1930s to the 1950s. In the early 1960s, the description and characterization of the inborn error of metabolism, homocystinuria, initiated a 40-year (and continuing) period of investigation that has revealed homocysteine as an independent risk factor for vascular disease. The association between elevated blood levels of homocysteine (hyperhomocysteinemia) and vascular disease may be similar in magnitude to the association between cholesterol and vascular disease, thus implicating hyperhomocysteinemia as a significant public health concern. Currently, large-scale intervention trials are being conducted to determine if supplements of the B vitamins folate, vitamin B_{12}, and vitamin B_6, each of which plays an integral role in homocysteine metabolism, reduce the incidence of vascular disease. If successful, B vitamin supplements may prove to be an inexpensive and safe prophylactic to reduce the risk of heart attacks and strokes.

Structure and Forms

The structure of homocysteine is shown in **Table 1** along with the related structures of cysteine and methionine. The most prominent features of homocysteine and cysteine are the free sulfhydryl groups located at the end of the side-chains of both amino acids. These sulfhydryl groups are highly susceptible to oxidation and the formation of disulfide linkages with other sulfhydryl compounds. The primary forms of homocysteine found in the blood (**Table 1**) consist of homocysteine in disulfide linkage with: (1) cysteine residues within the primary sequences of albumin and other plasma proteins (protein-bound); (2) free cysteines or cysteine-containing peptides (mixed disulfides); and (3) other homocysteine molecules (homocystine). Only about 1% of homocysteine in the blood is in the free-reduced form. Methionine, in contrast, does not have a free sulfhydryl group, and thus does not form disulfide compounds.

Biosynthesis and Metabolism

The biosynthesis and metabolism of homocysteine is presented in **Figure 1**. The ultimate source of homocysteine is dietary methionine. Methionine is first activated by addition of an adenosyl group (from ATP) to form S-adenosylmethionine (SAM). SAM is an important intermediate known as the universal methyl donor for its role as the methylating agent in a variety of essential reactions, including those involving DNA, RNA, proteins, membrane phospholipids,

Table 1 Structures and forms of homocysteine and related amino acids

Structures of homocysteine and related amino acids		Forms of homocysteine found in blood	
$H-\overset{\overset{\displaystyle NH_3^+}{\mid}}{\underset{\underset{\displaystyle COOH}{\mid}}{C}}-CH_2-CH_2-SH$	Homocysteine	HCY-S—S-CYS-albumin	Protein-bound
$H-\overset{\overset{\displaystyle NH_3^+}{\mid}}{\underset{\underset{\displaystyle COOH}{\mid}}{C}}-CH_2-SH$	Cysteine	HCY-S—S-CYS	Mixed disulfide
		HCY-S—S-HCY	Homocystine
$H-\overset{\overset{\displaystyle NH_3^+}{\mid}}{\underset{\underset{\displaystyle COOH}{\mid}}{C}}-CH_2-CH_2-S—CH_3$	Methionine	HCY-SH	Free reduced

HCY, homocysteine; CYS, cysteine.

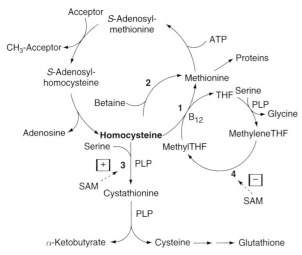

Figure 1 The biosynthesis and metabolism of homocysteine. Reactions that are regulated by S-adenosylmethionine (SAM) are indicated by positive and negative signs. Key enzymes: (1) methyltetrahydrofolate-homocysteine methyltransferase or methionine synthase; (2) betaine-homocysteine methyltransferase; (3) cystathionine β-synthase; (4) methylenetetrahydrofolate reductase. Abbreviations: THF, tetrahydrofolate; PLP, pyridoxal-5′-phosphate (vitamin B_6).

neurotransmitters, and the synthesis of creatine. A product of all SAM-dependent methylation reactions is S-adenosylhomocysteine (SAH), which in turn is metabolized to form adenosine and homocysteine. Homocysteine is then at a metabolic crossroad: it can be remethylated to form methionine or catabolized through cystathionine synthesis.

In remethylation, homocysteine reacquires a methyl group in a reaction catalyzed by methionine synthase (5-methyltetrahydrofolate-homocysteine methyltransferase) (EC 2.1.1.13) with methyltetrahydrofolate serving as the methyl donor and vitamin B_{12} serving as a cofactor. This reaction occurs in all mammalian cells. Alternatively, homocysteine can be remethylated in a folate- and vitamin B_{12}-independent reaction utilizing betaine as the methyl donor and catalyzed by betaine-homocysteine methyltransferase (EC 2.1.1.5). This reaction occurs primarily in the liver, and to a lesser extent in the kidney and possibly the brain.

Homocysteine catabolism occurs through cystathionine synthesis in a condensation reaction with serine. This reaction is catalyzed by cystathionine β-synthase (EC 4.2.1.22), which requires vitamin B_6 in the form of pyridoxal-5′-phosphate (PLP) as a cofactor. Cystathionine is then cleaved to form α-ketobutyrate and cysteine in a second PLP-dependent reaction catalyzed by cystathionase (EC 4.4.1.1). Further metabolism of cysteine leads to the formation of glutathione or inorganic sulfate.

Regulation of Metabolism

An important aspect of homocysteine metabolism is that it is subject to allosteric control. In addition to serving as the universal methyl donor, SAM also is an activator of cystathionine β-synthase and an inhibitor of methylenetetrahydrofolate reductase (MTHFR) (EC 1.7.99.5), the enzyme responsible for the synthesis of methyltetrahydrofolate (**Figure 1**). These allosteric functions serve to control whether homocysteine is recycled to form methionine or catabolized to form cystathionine. When dietary supply of methionine is high, i.e., after a protein meal, intracellular SAM levels increase. The high concentration of SAM activates cystathionine β-synthase and inhibits MTHFR, thus promoting homocysteine catabolism and limiting homocysteine remethylation. This serves to reduce the recycling of homocysteine when there is an adequate dietary supply of methionine. Conversely, under fasting conditions when there is no dietary influx of methionine, intracellular SAM levels go down. Cystathionine β-synthase is then not activated and the inhibition of MTHFR is relieved, thus promoting homocysteine remethylation over catabolism. Consequently, this maintains intracellular methionine levels during times of limited dietary supply.

An additional level of control of homocysteine metabolism is exerted by oxidative stress. Though the biochemical mechanism remains undefined, oxidative stress tends to divert homocysteine toward cystathionine synthesis away from methionine synthesis. This serves to increase synthesis of glutathione, a product of homocysteine metabolism through the trans-sulfuration pathway and an important intracellular antioxidant.

As discussed below, alterations in homocysteine metabolism also occur after menopause, in diabetes, and in hypothyroidism. These observations suggest that hormones, including estrogen, insulin, thyroxine, and thyroid-stimulating hormone, may directly or indirectly affect homocysteine metabolism. As for oxidative stress, the mechanisms by which these hormones affect homocysteine metabolism are poorly understood.

Hyperhomocysteinemia

Under conditions of maximal metabolic efficiency, plasma levels of homocysteine range from 4 to $10 \, \mu mol \, l^{-1}$. Metabolic blocks in homocysteine metabolism lead to accumulation of intracellular homocysteine with subsequent export into the blood. Depending on the magnitude of the metabolic impairment, plasma homocysteine levels can rise to varying degrees, as defined in **Table 2**.

Table 2 Degrees of hyperhomocysteinemia

Total plasma homocysteine	Designation
4–10 μmol l^{-1}	Normal
11–25 μmol l^{-1}	Mild to moderate
26–50 μmol l^{-1}	Intermediate
>50 μmol l^{-1}	Severe

Genetic Defects

Severe elevations in plasma homocysteine (concentrations as high as several hundred μmol l^{-1}) are observed in individuals with homozygous genetic defects affecting cystathionine β-synthase, MTHFR, or any of several enzymes responsible for the conversion of vitamin B$_{12}$ to its methionine synthase-associated cofactor form. These autosomal recessive genetic disorders, collectively termed homocystinuria because homocysteine accumulates in the urine as well as the blood, are associated with severe premature vascular disease, including thrombosis and atherosclerosis, mental retardation, dislocation of the eye lens (ectopia lentis), and skeletal malformations. Premature death (often in childhood) usually results from a major thrombotic or embolic event. Notably, one of the genetic defects that afflicts a significant proportion of homocystinuria patients reduces the affinity of cystathionine β-synthase for its vitamin B$_6$ cofactor, PLP. For these patients, the metabolic defect can be overcome to some extent with high-dose vitamin B$_6$ supplements, which significantly lower plasma homocysteine levels, reduce morbidity, and increase life expectancy. Interestingly, for other genetic defects involving cystathionine β-synthase that cause homocystinuria independent of the affinity of the enzyme for PLP, high-dose vitamin B$_6$ supplements nonetheless have a therapeutic effect despite having little or no influence on plasma homocysteine levels.

B Vitamin Deficiencies

Hyperhomocysteinemia is also caused by B vitamin deficiencies. Deficiencies of folate and vitamin B$_{12}$ lead to impaired remethylation of homocysteine causing mild, moderate, or severe elevations in plasma homocysteine, depending on the severity of the deficiency, as well as coexistence of genetic or other factors that interfere with homocysteine metabolism (see below). Because riboflavin is required for the synthesis of flavin adenine dinucleotide (FAD), and because FAD serves as a cofactor for MTHFR, riboflavin deficiency can also affect homocysteine remethylation, and thus contribute to elevations in plasma homocysteine. Vitamin B$_6$ deficiency leads to impairment of homocysteine catabolism and thus also causes hyperhomocysteinemia. However, the nature of hyperhomocysteinemia caused by vitamin B$_6$ deficiency differs from that caused by folate and vitamin B$_{12}$ deficiencies: In vitamin B$_6$ deficiency, fasting blood levels of homocysteine are usually not elevated or only slightly elevated. Only after a protein meal or after consumption of an oral methionine load (see below), does plasma homocysteine become abnormally elevated in vitamin B$_6$-deficient patients. In contrast, plasma homocysteine levels tend to be elevated regardless of prandial state in patients with folate or vitamin B$_{12}$ deficiency. The basis for these different manifestations is likely due to differential effects of the vitamin deficiencies on intracellular SAM levels and consequent disruption of the allosteric control of homocysteine metabolism.

Recently, there has been growing interest in the concept of nutritional genomics. This refers to genetic variability among individuals and its effect on nutritional requirements. A prime example of this concept is a common polymorphism in MTHFR (677C→T) in which an alanine is replaced by valine at codon 222 in the primary sequence of the enzyme. Individuals with the homozygous variant (677TT) of this gene (10–15% of the general population; lower in blacks, higher in Latinos and in some parts of Europe, e.g., Southern Italy) have an enzyme that is thermolabile, with reduced affinity for its substrate (methylenetetrahydrofolate) and its cofactor (FAD). Consequently, 677TT individuals require a higher intake of folate and riboflavin to maintain optimal enzyme activity than those with the wild-type isoform of the enzyme (677CC). This is reflected by the fact that blood homocysteine levels are higher in people with the 677TT isoform than in those with the 677CC isoform, but only when overall folate and/or riboflavin status is low. When overall folate and riboflavin status is high, no difference in homocysteine levels is observed between the isoforms.

The clinical and public health importance of the MTHFR polymorphism is that women with the 677TT isoform are at increased risk of having a child with a neural tube defect (e.g., spina bifida, *sp.* anencephaly). This risk can be reduced by folic acid supplements, an observation that underlies the decision by the US government to mandate folic acid fortification of grain products as of January, 1998. This program has been highly successful, having reduced the prevalence of folate deficiency from over 20% to about 1%, the prevalence of hyperhomocysteinemia by about 50%, and the incidence of neural tube defects by at least 20%. The success of the folic acid fortification program in the US spawned similar programs in several countries in the Americas, including Canada, Chile, and Costa Rica. Folic acid fortification has also been initiated in Hungary and Israel, but other European countries, most notably the UK, have been slow to adopt this intervention strategy. This is due to concerns about the feasibility of fortification, a hesitancy to impose manditory fortification on the population, lingering concerns over masking B_{12} deficiency, and the possibility of other unrecognized health consequences associated with excess folic acid intake.

Other polymorphisms in MTHFR and other enzymes involved in homocysteine metabolism (e.g., methionine synthase, methionine synthase reductase (EC 1.16.1.8), cystathionine β-synthase) have been identified and their overall influence on homocysteine metabolism, B vitamin requirements, and disease risk have been and continue to be evaluated.

Other Causes of Hyperhomocysteinemia

Other pathophysiological causes of hyperhomocysteinemia include renal dysfunction and hypothyroidism. The kidney is a major site of homocysteine metabolism and renal disease leads to a significant reduction in the body's overall capacity to metabolize this amino acid. The resulting moderate to severe hyperhomocysteinemia can be attenuated, in part, by high-dose B vitamin supplements, which putatively maximize the residual renal metabolism, as well as the metabolic capacities of the extrarenal organs. Mild elevations in homocysteine occur in patients with hypothyroidism, which resolve to normal with thyroid replacement therapy. This observation implies that thyroxine and/or thyroid-stimulating hormone influence homocysteine metabolism directly, perhaps through up- or downregulation of key homocysteine-metabolizing enzymes. Alternatively, homocysteine may become elevated in hypothyroid patients secondary to mild impairment of renal function that may accompany the disorder.

Patients with diabetes (both insulin dependent and insulin independent) tend to have mild hyperhomocysteinemia. However, this seems to be confined to those patients whose diabetic condition has progressed to involve renal insufficiency. Interestingly, in the absence of renal involvement, homocysteine levels in diabetic patients tend to be lower than normal. Insulin has been shown to inhibit homocysteine catabolism through cystathionine synthesis. Therefore, reduced insulin levels in diabetic patients may actually promote homocysteine catabolism, thus leading to lower plasma levels.

Premenopausal women tend to have lower plasma homocysteine than men of similar age, and

homocysteine levels tend to rise in women after the menopause. Hormone replacement therapy reduces homocysteine back to premenopausal levels. Moreover, homocysteine decreases in male to female transsexuals, and increases in female to male transsexuals, primarily related to the estrogen and androgen regimens that such individuals respectively follow. Taken together, these observations strongly suggest an influence of sex hormones on homocysteine metabolism, though the mechanisms are not well understood.

Drugs can also affect homocysteine metabolism and lead to elevations of homocysteine in the blood. Certain anticancer drugs, such as methotrexate, and antiepilepsy medications, such as valproate and carbamazepine, are inhibitors of folate metabolism. The resulting functional folate deficiency leads to hyperhomocysteinemia. The anti-Parkinsonian drug, levodopa or L-dopa, causes elevations in blood homocysteine levels by a different mechanism: a significant proportion of an oral dose of L-dopa is methylated by SAM, leading to increased intracellular synthesis of SAH and homocysteine. The excess synthesis of homocysteine can overwhelm the capacities of the homocysteine metabolic pathways, particularly when B vitamin status is suboptimal, leading to hyperhomocysteinemia.

Homocysteine and Vascular Disease

The current interest in homocysteine is primarily related to its recognized status as an independent risk factor for cardiovascular, cerebrovascular, and peripheral vascular disease. This homocysteine theory of vascular disease comes directly from a seminal observation made by Kilmer McCully. In the early to mid-1960s, it was recognized that a prominent characteristic of patients with homocystinuria caused by defects in cystathionine β-synthase were very high elevations of both homocysteine and methionine in the blood. Therefore, it was not clear whether the vascular complications of this disorder were the consequence of hyperhomocysteinemia or hypermethioninemia. McCully observed that a patient with homocystinuria caused by a defect in a B_{12}-metabolizing enzyme had hyperhomocysteinemia, but not hypermethioninemia. Nonetheless, this patient had similar (though not identical) vascular pathology to that observed in patients with homocystinuria caused by cystathionine β-synthase deficiency. From this McCully concluded that the vascular culprit was homocysteine, and not methionine.

McCully's hypothesis, however, was not immediately embraced. The prevailing theory of atherosclerosis at the time centered on cholesterol, and it proved difficult for McCully to convince his peers and national funding agencies of the potential importance of this new and competing hypothesis. Contributing to this was a lack of a reproducible animal model of homocysteine-induced vascular disease and a lack of a sensitive method to measure homocysteine in the blood. Consequently, McCully's hypothesis went into temporary obscurity.

In the mid-1970s, David and Bridget Wilcken reinvigorated McCully's hypothesis with their observation that a subset of patients with premature coronary artery disease had reduced ability to metabolize homocysteine. Notably, this association was observed in individuals who did not have any of the severe genetic defects that underly homocystinuria, suggesting that less severe or modest impairment of homocysteine metabolism may contribute to vascular disease risk. Subsequently, the advent of reliable, high-throughput assays for total plasma or serum homocysteine in the 1980s (see below) allowed for large-scale epidemiological assessment of associations between homocysteine and vascular diseases, both cross-sectionally and longitudinally. Through the 1990s, an explosion of population and case–control studies established that hyperhomocysteinemia is, indeed, a risk factor for heart attack, stroke, thrombosis, and peripheral atherosclerotic disease. Moreover, the risk associated with hyperhomocysteinemia is independent of other prominent risk factors, such as hypertension, hypercholesterolemia, hyperlipidemia, smoking, male gender, and others. Further indication of the importance of homocysteine with respect to vascular disease is the estimate that the relative risk of coronary artery disease associated with hyperhomocysteinemia is about equivalent to that associated with hypercholesterolemia. As the evidence mounted, McCully was vindicated and his contribution became widely recognized.

Homocysteine, Cognitive Function, and Dementia

As the relationship between homocysteine and vascular disease became increasingly apparent, researchers also addressed the hypothesis that hyperhomocysteinemia may affect cognitive function and the risk of dementia in older adults. This was based primarily on the recognized association between homocysteine and cerebrovascular disease, but also the observation that homocysteine and its metabolite, homocysteic acid, can induce excitotoxicity in neurons. Throughout the 1990s and into the new century, many cohort studies revealed significant inverse correlations between plasma homocysteine concentration and performance on a variety of cognitive function tests. Moreover, individuals with Alzheimer's disease were found to have higher plasma homocysteine than age- and gender-matched controls, while baseline homocysteine levels predicted the risk of incident dementia.

Homocysteine and Pregnancy Outcomes

Hyperhomocysteinemia has also been suspected as a risk factor for pregnancy complications and birth defects. Elevated plasma homocysteine levels have been associated with placental vasculopathy, pre-eclampsia, and placental infarction, as well as recurrent premature delivery, low birth weight, and spontaneous abortion. Birth defects associated with hyperhomocysteinemia in the mother include neural tube defects, orofacial clefts, clubfoot, and Down's syndrome. The protective effect of folic acid supplementation and fortification against neural tube defects, and perhaps the other abnormal birth outcomes cited, may be related to reduced homocysteine levels.

Mechanisms

In parallel with epidemiological studies, a significant amount of basic research has focused on the mechanism(s) by which homocysteine may induce atherosclerosis and thrombosis. A definitive answer has proven elusive. Potential mechanisms with significant experimental support include, but are not limited to, the following: (1) modification of the endothelial cell surface; (2) modification of plasma proteins by formation of disulfides; (3) activation of platelets; (4) modification of monocyte functions; (5) increased expression or activity of vascular adhesion molecules; and (6) oxidative damage induced by peroxides formed during disulfide bond formation.

A seventh potential mechanism relates to a known quirk of homocysteine synthesis and metabolism. The equilibrium of the interconversion between SAH and homocysteine (catalyzed by SAH hydrolase) actually favors SAH synthesis (**Figure 1**). *In vivo*, this reaction proceeds toward homocysteine synthesis because of product removal, i.e., the efficient metabolism of homocysteine back to methionine or through cystathionine synthesis. However, when there is a block in homocysteine metabolism, as occurs in the genetic defects, B vitamin deficiencies, and other causes delineated above, homocysteine accumulates intracellularly. Consequently, SAH also accumulates within cells. The significance of this phenomenon is that SAH is a feedback inhibitor of all SAM-dependent methylation reactions. Therefore, hyperhomocysteinemia may cause or contribute to vascular disease through SAH-mediated inhibition of methylation.

Another area that is receiving increasing attention is the relationship between homocysteine, nitric oxide, and endothelial function. One of the roles of nitric oxide is as a vasodilator. Homocysteine has been shown to be an inhibitor of nitric oxide synthesis, and thus can inhibit vasodilatation. This has led to the hypothesis that hyperhomocysteinemia, by inhibiting nitric oxide synthesis, impairs the ability of the vascular endothelium to maintain homeostasis of vascular tone. This in turn may directly or indirectly increase susceptibility to vascular insults, thus promoting atherosclerosis and thrombosis.

The search for the definitive pathogenetic mechanism implicating homocysteine as a cause of vascular disease continues, and it is recognized that several mechanisms may contribute synergistically. However, some have questioned whether homocysteine is a cause of vascular disease, or simply a consequence.

Cause or Effect?

Though there is considerable evidence, both epidemiological and experimental, that homocysteine is a causative factor in vascular disease, there are data that contradict this conclusion. First, though cross-sectional and case–control studies fairly consistently demonstrate that hyperhomocysteinemia is associated with vascular disease, some prospective studies have found no relationship between baseline homocysteine levels and risk of incident vascular events. Second, several studies have found no relationship between the MTHFR 667C→T polymorphism and venous thrombosis, despite the association of this polymorphism with elevated plasma homocysteine levels.

With these observations in mind, a plausible alternative hypothesis has been put forward to explain the association between hyperhomocysteinemia and vascular disease. One of the organs that can be significantly affected by vascular disease is the kidney. Reduced kidney function caused by atherosclerosis may lead to renal insufficiency and reduced capacity to metabolize homocysteine. In this way, hyperhomocysteinemia may actually result from vascular disease. This hypothesis remains to be tested. The possibility of a vicious cycle, i.e., one in which vascular disease causes homocysteine to become elevated in the blood, which in turn induces further vascular damage, must also be considered.

B Vitamin Supplementation

Currently, several large-scale intervention trials are underway to determine if B vitamin supplements (folic acid, B_{12}, B_6), which effectively lower blood homocysteine levels, reduce the incidence of vascular disease (**Table 3**). If proven effective, such supplements would be an inexpensive and relatively

Table 3 Intervention trials to determine the effect of B vitamin supplements on homocysteine and the risk of vascular disease

Study	Location	Start date
Cambridge Heart Antioxidant Study 2 (CHAOS-2)	UK	1998
Heart Outcomes Prevention Evaluation 2 (HOPE-2)	Canada	1999
Norwegian Multi-Center B-Vitamin Intervention Study (NORVIT)	Norway	1998
Prevention with a Combined Inhibitor and Folate in Coronary Heart Disease (PACIFIC)	Australia	2000
Study of Effectiveness of Additional Reductions in Cholesterol and Homocysteine (SEARCH)	UK	1999
Vitamins in Stroke Prevention (VISP)	USA	1998
Vitamins to Prevent Stroke (VITATOPS)	Australia	1999
Western Norway B-Vitamin Intervention Trial (WENBIT)	Norway	1999
Women's Antioxidant and Cardiovascular Disease Study (WACS)	USA	1998

innocuous means by which the risk of vascular disease may be reduced. However, it must be recognized that if these trials are successful, they will not serve as definitive proof that homocysteine is a vascular toxin. It may be the case that one or more of the B vitamins influences vascular disease risk through separate mechanisms. For example, several studies have shown that low B_6 status has an association with vascular disease independent of homocysteine. The uncertain relationship between hyperhomocysteinemia, B vitamins, and vascular disease is summarized in **Figure 2**. If homocysteine is not a vascular toxin, it may still serve as a marker of both vascular disease and as an indicator of the efficacy of B vitamin supplementation.

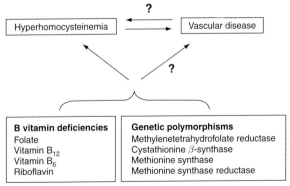

Figure 2 Hyperhomocysteinemia, B vitamins, genetic polymorphisms, and vascular disease. There is still some question whether elevated plasma homocysteine is a cause or consequence of vascular disease and whether there are influences of B vitamins and related polymorphisms on vascular disease risk that are independent of homocysteine.

Measurement of Blood Levels

A variety of assays have been developed to quantify blood homocysteine levels, with those employing high-pressure liquid chromatography perhaps being the most common. These assays have proven to be relatively accurate and precise (coefficients of variation less than 10%), and are relatively simple and quick to perform. The development of such assays in the 1980s was the technological breakthrough that spurred the exponential increase in homocysteine-related research over the last 15–20 years and the establishment of hyperhomocysteinemia as an independent risk factor for vascular disease.

As described above, homocysteine comes in several forms in the blood, including protein-bound, mixed disulfides, homocystine, and free-reduced. Assays for homocysteine usually measure the sum total of all these forms, i.e., total homocysteine. To accomplish this, the first procedure in homocysteine assays is a reduction step to break all disulfide bonds, thus converting all homocysteine to the free-reduced form. The free-reduced form is then quantified by one of various methods.

Blood sample collection and processing are critical factors in the determination of homocysteine concentrations. Typically, blood samples for homocysteine analysis are collected in tubes containing an anticoagulant (e.g., EDTA, heparin). Prompt separation of plasma from the blood cells after centrifugation is required to avoid excess release of intracellular homocysteine into the plasma or removal of homocysteine from the plasma by metabolically active leucocytes after blood draw. Keeping the blood sample cold until centrifugation and separation (ideally within 4 h of blood draw) minimizes this problem. Serum homocysteine concentrations typically exceed plasma concentrations by 20%. This is likely due to the fact that blood collected to isolate serum (i.e., without an anticoagulant) must clot at room temperature for 30–60 min before centrifugation and separation. Therefore, plasma is preferred for measurement of homocysteine. Once separated from the blood cells, the concentration of homocysteine in plasma or serum remains stable for years when stored frozen.

Another important issue in the measurement of homocysteine is the prandial state of the individual. For individuals with adequate B vitamin status, no genetic abnormalities, and no pathophysiological conditions that affect homocysteine metabolism, plasma homocysteine levels after an overnight fast are similar to levels after a meal (even high-protein meals containing methionine). However, for individuals with low vitamin B_6 status or heterozygous genetic defects in cystathionine β-synthase, post-prandial homocysteine levels can be significantly higher than fasting levels. Because of the nutritional or genetic block in the conversion of homocysteine to cystathionine, there is decreased capacity to metabolize the influx of homocysteine synthesized from dietary methionine. This, in fact, is the basis for the methionine load test for detection of impaired cystathionine β-synthase activity. In this test, baseline blood is drawn after an overnight fast, and then again 4 h after consumption of a large dose of methionine dissolved in orange juice (100 mg methionine per kilogram body weight). Plasma homocysteine increases to a greater extent in individuals with low vitamin B_6 status or heterozygous genetic defects in cystathionine β-synthase than in individuals without these problems. Importantly, individuals with elevated fasting homocysteine and those with normal fasting levels, but elevated post-methionine load levels, are both at increased risk of vascular disease.

See also: **Amino Acids**: Chemistry and Classification; Metabolism; Specific Functions. **Cobalamins**. **Folic Acid**. **Riboflavin**. **Vitamin B_6**.

Further Reading

Blom H, Fowler B, Jakobs C, and Koch H-G (eds.) (1998) Disorders of homocysteine metabolism. *European Journal of Pediatrics* 157(supplement 2): S39–S142.

Boushey CJ, Beresford SAA, Omenn GS, and Motulsky AG (1995) A quantitative assessment of plasma homocysteine as a risk factor for vascular disease: probable benefits of increasing folic acid intakes. *JAMA* 274: 1049–1057.

Brattström L and Wilcken DEL (2000) Homocysteine and cardiovascular disease: cause or effect? *American Journal of Clinical Nutrition* 72: 315–323.

Carmel R and Jacobsen DW (2001) *Homocysteine in Health and Disease*. Cambridge: Cambridge University Press.

Christen WG, Ajani UA, Glynn RJ, and Hennekens CH (2000) Blood levels of homocysteine and increased risks of cardiovascular disease: causal or casual? *Archives of Internal Medicine* 160: 422–434.

Clarke R, Smith AD, Jobst KA, Refsum H, Sutton L, and Ueland PM (1998) Folate, vitamin B_{12}, and serum total homocysteine levels in confirmed Alzheimer disease. *Archives of Neurology* 55: 1449–1455.

Finkelstein JD (1990) Methionine metabolism in mammals. *Journal of Nutritional Biochemistry* 1: 228–237.

Finkelstein JD (2000) Homocysteine: a history in progress. *Nutrition Reviews* 58: 193–204.

Graham I, Refsum H, Rosenberg IH, and Ueland PM (eds.) (1997) *Homocysteine Metabolism: From Basic Science to Clinical Medicine*. Boston, MA: Kluwar Academic Publishers.

Green R (1998) Homocysteine and occlusive vascular disease: culprit or bystander? *Preventive Cardiology* 1: 31–33.

Green R and Jacobsen DW (1995) Clinical implications of hyper-homocysteinemia. In: Bailey LB (ed.) *Folate in Health and Disease*, pp. 75–122. New York: Marcel Dekker.

Green R and Miller JW (1999) Folate deficiency beyond megaloblastic anemia: hyperhomocysteinemia and other manifestations of dysfunctional folate metabolism. *Seminars in Hematology* **36**: 47–64.

Homocysteine Lowering Trialists' Collaboration (1998) Lowering blood homocysteine with folic acid based supplements: meta-analysis of randomised trials. *British Medical Journal* **316**: 894–898.

Jacques PF, Selhub J, Bostom AG, Wilson PW, and Rosenberg IH (1999) The effect of folic acid fortification on plasma folate and total homocysteine concentrations. *New England Journal of Medicine* **340**: 1449–1454.

McCully KS (1996) Homocysteine and vascular disease. *Nature Medicine* **2**: 386–389.

Meleady R and Graham I (1999) Plasma homocysteine as a cardiovascular risk factor: causal, consequential, or of no consequence? *Nutrition Reviews* **57**: 299–305.

Miller JW (2000) Homocysteine, Alzheimer's disease, and age-related cognitive decline. *Nutrition* **16**: 675–677.

Miller JW, Selhub J, Nadeau M, Thomas CA, Feldman RG, and Wolf PA (2003) Effect of L-Dopa on plasma homocysteine in PD patients. *Neurology* **60**: 1125–1129.

Mudd SH, Levy HL, and Skovby F (1995) Disorders of transsulfuration. In: Scriver CR, Beaudet AL, Sly WS, and Valle D (eds.) *The Metabolic and Molecular Bases of Inherited Disorders*, 7th edn, pp. 1279–1327. New York: McGraw Hill.

Pfeiffer CM, Huff DL, Smith SJ, Miller DT, and Gunter EW (1999) Comparison of plasma total homocysteine

measurements in 14 laboratories: an international study. *Clinical Chemistry* **45**: 1261–1268.

Refsum H, Smith AD, Ueland PM *et al.* (2004) Facts and recommendations about total homocysteine determinations: an expert opinion. *Clinical Chemistry* **50**: 3–32.

Refsum H, Ueland PM, Nygard O, and Vollset SE (1998) Homocysteine and cardiovascular disease. *Annual Review of Medicine* **49**: 31–62.

Robinson K (ed.) (2000) *Homocysteine and Vascular Disease*. Norwell, Massachusetts: Kluwar Academic Publishers.

Selhub J, Jacques PF, Wilson PWF, Rush D, and Rosenberg IH (1993) Vitamin status and intake as primary determinants of homocysteinemia in an elderly population. *JAMA* **270**: 2693–2698.

Selhub J and Miller JW (1992) The pathogenesis of homocysteinemia: interruption of the coordinate regulation by S-adenosylmethionine of the remethylation and transsulfuration of homocysteine. *American Journal of Clinical Nutrition* **55**: 131–138.

Seshadri S, Beiser A, Selhub J *et al.* (2002) Plasma homocysteine as a risk factor for dementia and Alzheimer's disease. *New England Journal of Medicine* **346**: 476–483.

Stacey M (1997) The fall and rise of Kilmer McCully. *New York Times Magazine*, August **10**: 26–29.

Ueland PM, Refsum H, Beresford SAA, and Vollset SE (2000) The controversy over homocysteine and cardiovascular risk. *American Journal of Clinical Nutrition* **72**: 324–332.

Welch GN and Loscalzo J (1998) Homocysteine and atherothrombosis. *New England Journal of Medicine* **338**: 1042–1050.

Wilcken DEL and Wilcken B (1998) B vitamins and homocysteine in cardiovascular disease and aging. *Annals of the New York Academy of Sciences* **854**: 361–370.

HUNGER

J C G Halford, University of Liverpool, Liverpool, UK
A J Hill and J E Blundell, University of Leeds, Leeds, UK

This article is a revision of the previous edition article by A J Hill and J E Blundell, pp. 1015–1020, © 1999, Elsevier Ltd.

Hunger is a familiar but commonly misunderstood and mistrusted part of our eating behavior. This article will clarify the meaning of the term, describe the common procedures for measuring hunger, the ways in which hunger and satiety are interrelated, and the adaptability of hunger experience in a learning framework. The relationship between hunger and eating behavior will be examined at both a methodological and conceptual level, and putative disorders of hunger will be briefly examined.

Definition

The term hunger is used in more than one sense by both scientists and the lay public. World hunger is a widely used phrase to describe the shortage of food and state of malnutrition experienced by a substantial proportion of the world's population. Its use is emotive and largely descriptive. It is in the study of motivation that the term takes on a more precise and individual definition. In this context, hunger describes the drive or the motivational force that urges us to seek and consume food. It is the expression of a biological need to sustain growth and life. Hunger is therefore a purposeful experience that possesses a clear biological function.

There are two ways in which the term hunger is used within nutritional science. One is its use as a motivational construct in a scientific theory. Here, hunger is inferred from directly observable and measurable events. In this way, inferring increased or high levels of hunger from a long period of food deprivation or an increased willingness to expend effort in order to obtain food, hunger becomes a mediating concept or intervening variable. However, a more familiar use of the word is that collection of conscious feelings or sensations that are linked to a desire to obtain and eat food. This is the sense in which lay people understand the term hunger and is what researchers attempt to capture by means of rating scales and other measurement devices.

The first serious investigation of the everyday experience of hunger used a questionnaire in which people were asked to note the presence of physical sensations in a number of bodily areas, together with moods, urges to eat, and preoccupation with thoughts of food. It was found that the observation, 'I feel hungry,' is typically based on the perception of bodily feelings, which at times are very strong. Gastric sensations, a hollow feeling or stomach rumbling, are frequent indicators of hunger, although people also report sensations in the mouth, throat, and head. These accompany more diffuse feelings of restlessness and excitability as well as an urge to eat. The consumption of food changes both the pattern of physical sensations and the accompanying emotional feelings, with unpleasant and aversive sensations becoming replaced by more pleasant ones. So, for example, an aching stomach becomes relaxed and the feeling of excitement and irritability is replaced by one of contentment.

Subsequent research has confirmed these general patterns of characteristic premeal sensations and feelings, particularly with regard to the salience of gastric sensations. However, it has also noted a great deal of variability both within and between individuals. In other words, hunger demands neither the consistent presence of single sensations prior to every act of eating nor in every person sitting down to eat. Despite this variability people are able to, and frequently do, make judgments regarding their state of hunger, partly through reference to these sensations.

The Measurement of Hunger

The process of measuring hunger is not as straightforward as it might seem. One reason is the frequently raised mistrust of subjective reports. Critics point to the variability in response between individuals and the absence of any objective 'standard' by which internal experience can be calibrated. However, as argued later, this issue of 'validity' is more complex than this criticism suggests. A second reason is the failure to appreciate the distinction made previously between an individual's assessment of his or her disposition to eat and inferring hunger from the amount of food consumed or from some part of the act of eating (e.g., eating speed). While in many circumstances they will be

in accord, the subjective report and inferred construct can as easily diverge.

The two most common methods for quantifying hunger are fixed-point rating scales and visual analog scales (**Figure 1**). Fixed-point scales are quick and simple to use, and the data they provide are easy to analyze. Past examples of these scales show they vary greatly in complexity. In considering the appropriate number of points to be included in this type of scale, the freedom to make a range of possible responses must be balanced against the precision and reliability of the device. Research seems to indicate that scales with an insufficient number of fixed points can be insensitive to subtle changes in subjective experience. In addition, the fixed points are important determinants of the way people use the scales and distribute their ratings.

One way of overcoming some of these failings is to abolish the points completely. Thus, visual analog scales are horizontal lines (often 100 or 150 mm long), unbroken and unmarked except for word anchors at each end. The user of the scale is instructed to mark the line at the point that most accurately reflects the intensity of the subjective feeling at that time. The researcher measures the distance to that mark in millimeters from the negative end (no hunger), thus yielding a score of 0–100 (or 150). This is done either by hand or automatically if presented by computer screen. By doing away with all of the verbal labels except the end definitions, visual analog scales retain the advantages of fixed-point scales, while avoiding many of the problems with uneven response distributions.

An important aspect of these methods concerns the interpretation of differences between the fixed points or intervals on a visual analog scale. So, for example, it should not be assumed that the difference between 20 and 30 mm on a hunger scale is

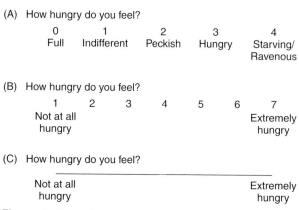

Figure 1 Examples of different types of scales used in the assessment of hunger: (A) fixed-point scale with points defined, (B) fixed-point scale, and (C) visual analog scale.

perceptually the same as the difference between 80 and 90 mm. Nor can a hunger rating of 80 mm be said to represent a feeling of hunger that is twice the intensity of that rated at 40 mm. Related to this is the problem of 'end effects.' This refers to the reluctance of a minority of subjects to make ratings away from the upper or lower end points of the scale, despite clear instructions. Despite these limitations, data from such scales are often analyzed using parametric statistical procedures, such as analysis of variance, and in general this appears to be a satisfactory approach.

Hunger and Satiety

If hunger is that feeling that reminds us to seek food, then eating relieves hunger, albeit until the next snack or meal. The capacity of a food to reduce the experience of hunger is called 'satiating power' or 'satiating efficiency.' This power is the product of the body's handling of the nutritional composition and structure of the food eaten. It follows that some foods will have a greater capacity to maintain suppression over hunger than other foods.

The distinction between hunger and satiety is both conceptual and technical. As hunger diminishes, satiety rises. But it is useful to further separate those events that occur across the course of a meal from those between meals. In this way the process of satiation can be clearly distinguished from the state of satiety. Satiation can be regarded as the process that develops during eating and that eventually brings a period of eating to an end. Accordingly, satiation can be defined in terms of the measured size of an eating episode (such as its energy, weight, or volume). Hunger declines as satiation develops and usually reaches its lowest point at the end of a meal. Satiety is defined as the state of inhibition over further eating that follows at the end of a meal and that arises from the consequences of food ingestion. The intensity of satiety can be measured by the duration of time until eating starts once more, or by the amount consumed at the next meal. The strength of satiety is also measured by the time that hunger is suppressed. And as satiety weakens, hunger is restored.

In examining the mechanisms responsible for suppressing hunger and maintaining its low state, it is clear that they range from those that occur when food is initially sensed to the effects of metabolites on body tissues following the digestion and absorption of food (across the wall of the intestine and into the bloodstream). By definition, satiety is not an instantaneous event but occurs over a considerable time period. The different phases of satiety and their associated mechanisms are shown in **Figure 2**.

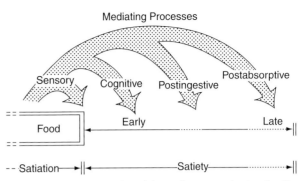

Figure 2 A representation of the satiety cascade showing the different phases of satiety and their associated mechanisms.

Sensory effects are generated through the smell, taste, temperature, and texture of food, and it is likely that these factors have effects on eating in the very short term. Cognitive influences represent the beliefs held about the properties of foods, and these factors may also help inhibit hunger in the short term.

The category identified as postingestive processes includes a number of possible actions, such as gastric distension and rate of emptying, the release of hormones such as cholecystokinin, and the stimulation of certain receptors along the gastrointestinal tract. The postabsorptive phase of satiety includes those mechanisms arising from the action of metabolites after absorption into the bloodstream. These include the action of glucose and amino acids, which act directly on the brain after crossing the blood–brain barrier, and which influence the brain indirectly via neural inputs following stimulation of peripheral chemoreceptors. The most important suppression and subsequent control of hunger is brought about by postingestive and postabsorptive mediating processes.

It follows from this framework that foods of varying nutrient composition will have different effects on the mediating processes and will therefore differ in their effects on hunger, satiation, and satiety. There is considerable interest, for example, in whether protein, fat, and carbohydrate differ in their satiating power.

The balance of evidence shows that per unit energy, protein (within normal dietary limits) has the greatest satiating efficiency of all the macronutrients. This is particularly true in short-term studies and is observed in lean and obese subjects alike. Longer term evidence of this effect is currently lacking. However, of great practical and theoretical interest is the comparative effect of carbohydrate and fat since they form the majority of our routine energy intake. Research shows that carbohydrates are efficient hunger relievers. A variety of carbohydrates, including glucose, fructose, sucrose, and maltodextrins, all suppress later test meal energy intake. This suppression is roughly equivalent to their energy value, although the time course of this effect varies according to the rate at which they are metabolized. In contrast, high-fat foods appear to stimulate energy intake (in contrast to low-fat, high-carbohydrate foods), or at least have a disproportionately weak action on satiety. The mechanisms responsible for this may include the effect of fat-promoting food palatability, the high-energy density of fat, and the absence of inhibitory feedback from body fat stores. Taken together, these findings show why diets high in fat can promote weight gain and lead to obesity.

Hunger: Physiological Determinants

Stomach distension and the detection of macronutrients such as fat or protein within the gut are all powerful satiety cues. They bring a meal to an end and for a time inhibit further consumption. Eventually, hunger again prevails and food intake follows. The flux between hunger and satiety is episodic and underpins the expression of our eating behavior throughout the day. However, it is not just the absence of episodic satiety cues (e.g., stomach distension and intestinal or absorbed nutrients) that influence the expression of hunger. Reduction in blood glucose levels or in levels of the circulating adipose tissue hormone leptin indicates a deficit in available energy and in energy reserves. Fluctuation of these factors indicates the metabolism and storage of the body's energy reserves. These are a tonic class of physiological signals that also influence the expression of appetite. Like episodic satiety signals, these tonic signals normally act on inhibitory mechanisms with the hypothalamus (anorexogenic circuits). Their absence elicits an active feeding response. Other tonic factors that indicate the body's energy status, such as adiponectin, cytokines, and gonadal hormones, also appear to act on energy regulator centres within the brain, particularly the hypothalamus, mainly to suppress hunger.

However, not all physiological signals, episodic or tonic, inhibit hunger. For instance, blood levels of the recently discovered gut hormone ghrelin have been shown to increase prior to a meal. Subsequent intake has been shown to suppress ghrelin release. Further studies have shown that ghrelin infusions increase food intake. Thus, this is a hormone that acts to promote food intake. Interestingly, ghrelin receptors are found in various hypothalamic locations that form part of the orexogenic circuits promoting food intake. These circuits contain many neuropeptides, such as neuropeptide Y, orexins, melanocortin concentrating hormone, and galanin, which all stimulate

food intake. The precise nature of the physiological and neurobiological regulation of appetite is discussed elsewhere in this encyclopedia. Finally, it should be noted that the biological mechanisms critical to the expression of hunger are not independent of psychological ones. Indeed, the sensory and cognitive cues that stimulate hunger produce physiological changes that anticipate the ingestion and metabolism of energy and subsequently aid these processes. This brings on the psychological factors critical in the expression of appetite.

Conditioned Hunger

One of the essentials for an omnivore faced with a variety of new and different foods is the capacity to learn. It is not possible for an inborn preference or aversion to guide the choice of every possible food. Therefore, we learn which foods are beneficial (and which are not) by eating them. This learning involves the association between the sensory and the postabsorptive characteristics of foods. In this way the sensory characteristics of foods act as cues and come to predict the impact that foods will later have. Consequently, these cues should suppress hunger according to their relationship with subsequent physiological events.

It is possible to demonstrate experimentally how human beings adapt their eating to a food's energy content. A distinctively flavored food which contains 'extra' hidden energy, presented on several occasions, will result in a change in eating and in preference. When deprived of food, subjects' preference for the taste increases with gained experience. If presented when satiated, preference for the taste decreases. This process is also observable in young children, who eat smaller meals following a taste previously associated with a high-energy snack, and larger meals following a taste previously associated with a low-energy snack.

The idea that we can have conditioned hunger for specific nutrients is far more contentious. The concept of conditioned hunger suggests that the organism, faced with a diet deficient in a single important nutrient, will seek an alternative food source that contains the missing nutrient. However, earlier evidence from animals has largely been reinterpreted from the standpoint of conditioned aversions. Indeed, conditioned aversions are far more potent examples of the impact of learning on eating behavior than any examples of conditioned hunger. A conditioned aversion that will be familiar to many readers is the profound dislike that occurs in response to a food or drink that was eaten prior to vomiting or illness. An example of a conditioned taste aversion was famously described by learning theorist Martin Seligman. Steak with sauce

Béarnaise was Seligman's last meal before a bout of gastric flu. Yet knowing that it was the flu rather than the food that made him sick did not prevent the subsequent aversion to sauce Béarnaise. In fact, surveys show that conditioned taste aversions are commonplace and reported by 40–60% of people.

Conditioned taste aversions are important in the present context not because they represent a special form of one-trial learning that we are biologically pre-prepared to acquire. Rather, they show that the strength of cue–consequence learning in the area of food intake depends on the stability and reliability of the relationship between tastes (sensory cues) and physiological effects (metabolic consequences) of food. When there is distortion, variation, or extreme complexity in the relationship between sensory characteristics and nutritional properties, then the conditioned control of hunger is weakened or lost. In many respects, the variety of foods available to us represents a cacophony of different sensory characteristics and has the added complication of ingredients that preserve the sensory qualities while altering their nutritive value. Learned hunger therefore is a relatively less important factor when the food supply contains many food items with identical tastes but differing metabolic properties.

Hunger and Eating Behavior

If hunger is biologically useful and a subjective experience that indicates a depleted nutritional state, then a close correspondence between hunger and eating would be expected. So hunger should be either a necessary or a sufficient condition for eating to occur. However, this is not invariably the case. Instances of people deliberately refraining from eating in spite of hunger (fasting for moral or political conviction) show hunger not to be a sufficient condition. And examples in research and daily experience, of eating a tempting food when otherwise satiated, show hunger not to be necessary for eating to take place. But while the relationship between hunger and eating is not based on biological inevitability, in many circumstances they are closely linked.

Unfortunately, the lack of a one-to-one correspondence between hunger and eating has been used as another way to question the validity of hunger ratings. But should a high correlation between hunger ratings and subsequent food intake be expected in all circumstances? The previous examples show that in certain circumstances the two can be disengaged. So, for example, eating can occur when hunger is low (such as when highly palatable food is offered unexpectedly) and not at other times when hunger is high (when food is unavailable or other activities have

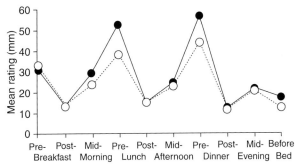

Figure 3 Ratings of hunger made across the day by a group of obese women taking an appetite suppressant drug (dotted lines) or placebo (solid lines).

priority). In addition, many experimental analyzes of the correlational relationship between hunger and food intake report the relationship only when subjects are hungry. In other words, the correlation is only examined for a small portion of the available scale. Very few studies have looked at the association between hunger and food intake when hunger has been represented in all its possible degrees.

It is clear that hunger ratings cannot be used simply as a proxy measure for food intake. Equally, there is good evidence that in most circumstances self-report ratings of hunger correlate statistically and meaningfully with eating. This association exists not simply across single meals, but across the entire day as shown in **Figure 3**. The rhythmic oscillation of hunger is tied closely to the overall pattern of food intake in this group of individuals. As such, it presents an elegant and experimentally useful way of examining diurnal variations in the experience of hunger.

In questioning the relationship between hunger and eating, we are also forced to place the action of hunger within a broader context of social and psychological variables that moderate food choice and eating behavior. Eating patterns are maintained by enduring habits, attitudes and opinions about the value and suitability of foods, and an overall liking for them. These factors, derived from the cultural ethos, largely determine the range of foods that will be consumed and sometimes the timing of consumption. The intensity of hunger experienced may also be determined, in part, by the culturally approved appropriateness of this feeling and by the host of preconceptions brought to the dining table. Hunger is therefore only one portion of the range of determinants of eating in any given situation.

Disorders of Hunger

The clinical eating disorders, anorexia nervosa and bulimia nervosa, are commonly believed to encompass major disturbances of hunger. Yet the role that hunger may play is not entirely clear. Contrary to the literal meaning of the term, 'anorexia' is not experienced as a loss of appetite. Rather, clinicians recognize that anorexics may endure intense periods of hunger during their self-restricted eating. For some, their strength in resisting intense episodes of hunger provides a feeling of self-mastery and control that is absent in other areas of their lives. Research suggests that restricting anorexics (compared with those who binge) have the greatest blunting of hunger response, and that this disturbance in hunger is not a product of other areas of perceptual confusion.

There is evidence that in conditions of total starvation hunger may become temporarily diminished. This circumstance is extremely rare and obviously relatively brief. Once eating is recommenced, hunger returns rapidly and with extreme intensity. The accounts of the male volunteers who submitted to a 6-month period of semistarvation during World War II (the 'Minnesota Experiment') are a testament to the extreme power of hunger. Referred to as semistarvation neurosis, these men's activities were shaped by their need for food. And their hunger experience was extreme. Nearly two-thirds reported feeling hungry all the time and a similar proportion experienced physical discomfort due to hunger. Participants described a marked increase in what was referred to as 'hunger pain.' For some this was mildly discomforting and vaguely localized in the abdomen. For others, it was extremely painful. This account is especially useful in reminding why energy-reduced diets aimed at achieving weight loss are often difficult to maintain and easy to abandon.

Like anorexia, bulimia finds its literal meaning in changed hunger — 'ox hunger.' Again, however, the term is imprecise. Close analysis of the precursors of binge episodes show hunger to be lower than it is prior to a normal meal. In addition, while the urge to eat may be strong during a binge, the large amount of food consumed implies some defect in satiation rather than in hunger. And binging is often a well-practised behavior that develops and changes with time. As with anorexics, it is likely that a stable eating pattern is necessary in order to normalize the experience of hunger, a process that may take a long time to establish.

The question of whether obesity reflects a disorder of hunger is now regarded as largely redundant. Obesity is strictly a disorder of weight, and as such reflects potentially long-term failure in the regulation of energy balance. There is hardly any evidence of heightened levels of hunger contributing to excessive energy input. However, an exception to this is the rare disorder Prader–Willi syndrome. Genetically determined and characterized mainly by intellectual disability, obesity is a well-recognised feature of the syndrome. Emerging research suggests that the excessive levels of food intake are associated with both a delayed reduction in hunger while eating and a more rapid return to premeal states when eating has finished. Clearly, a better understanding of the biological events that accompany such aberrant eating patterns will strengthen understanding of the psychobiological framework that supports hunger.

See also: **Appetite**: Physiological and Neurobiological Aspects; Psychobiological and Behavioral Aspects. **Carbohydrates**: Requirements and Dietary Importance. **Eating Disorders**: Anorexia Nervosa; Bulimia Nervosa. **Famine. Food Choice, Influencing Factors. Obesity**: Definition, Etiology and Assessment. **Starvation and Fasting. Weight Management**: Approaches.

Further Reading

Blundell JE (1980) Hunger, appetite and satiety—Constructs in search of identities. In: Turner M (ed.) *Nutrition and Lifestyles*, pp. 21–42. London: Applied Sciences Publishers.

Booth DA (1977) Satiety and appetite are conditioned reactions. *Psychosomatic Medicine* 39: 76–81.

Cornell CE, Rodin J, and Weingarten H (1989) Stimulus-induced eating when satiated. *Physiology and Behaviour* 45: 695–704.

Flint A, Raben A, Blundell LE, and Astrup A (2000) Reproducibility, power and validity of visual analogue scales in assessment of appetite sensations in single test meal studies. *International Journal of Obesity* 24: 38–48.

Friedman MI, Ulrich P, and Mattes RD (1999) A figurative measure of subjective hunger sensations. *Appetite* 32: 395–404.

Halmi KA and Sunday SR (1991) Temporal patterns of hunger and fullness ratings and related cognitions in anorexia and bulimia. *Appetite* 16: 219–237.

Hill AJ, Rogers PJ, and Blundell JE (1995) Techniques for the experimental measurement of human eating behaviour and food intake: A practical guide. International Journal of Obesity 19: 361–375.

Keys A, Brozek J, Henscher A *et al.* (1950) In *The Biology of Human Starvation*. Minneapolis: University of Minnesota Press.

Kirkmayer SV and Mattes RD (2000) Effects of food attributes on hunger and food intake. *International Journal of Obesity* 24: 1167–1175.

Kissileff HR (1984) Satiating efficiency and a strategy for conducting food loading experiments. *Neuroscience and Biobehavioural Reviews* 8: 129–135.

Monello LF and Mayer J (1967) Hunger and satiety sensations in men, women, boys and girls. *American Journal of Clinical Nutrition* 20: 253–261.

Ogden J (2002) The Psychology of Eating. *From Healthy to Disordered Behaviour*. Oxford: Blackwell.

Womble LG, Wadden TA, Chandler JM, and Martin AR (2003) Agreement between weekly vs. daily assessment of appetite. *Appetite* 40: 131–135.

HYPERACTIVITY

M Wolraich, Vanderbilt University, Nashville, TN, USA

This article is reproduced from the previous edition, pp. 1021–1025, © 1999, Elsevier Ltd.

To discuss the issues of hyperactivity and diet, it is first important to understand the issues related to the diagnosis of hyperactivity, or what is now called the 'attention deficit/hyperactivity disorder' (ADHD). Since most of the recommendations for dietary changes have been for children who have been diagnosed with ADHD, this article will first review the historic and current changes in the diagnosis of ADHD and then review the diets that have been recommended for treatment and the evidence as to their efficacy.

Diagnostic Issues

Hyperactivity, or ADHD, is a condition that has been recognized for many years and has been quite extensively researched, but the diagnostic criteria and treatment continue to be controversial. The symptoms of ADHD were first described by a German physician, Heinrich Hoffman, in a children's book written in 1848. The symptoms were represented by two children, Harry, who looks in the air (inattention), and Fidgety Phil (hyperactivity). In 1902, George Still presented a lecture in England about 20 children who were aggressive, defiant, excessively emotional and lacking inhibitory volition, and who were also noted to have impaired attention and overactivity. A more etiological conceptualization of the condition did not occur until after World War I.

Symptoms of hyperactivity and inattention were suspected to be caused by the influenza epidemic that occurred after World War I, when postencephalitic behavior manifestations in children included extreme examples of hyperactivity and inattention. This led to the suggestion that these symptoms were due to organic brain damage. The concept of inattention and hyperactivity being part of a spectrum with less intense manifestations secondary to subtle injuries became known as the syndrome of 'minimal brain damage' in the 1960s. However, the lack of clear evidence for brain damage eventually resulted in a shift to a more descriptive labeling of the disorder. This is reflected in the American Psychiatric Association classification system (DSM) defining the 'hyperkinetic reaction of childhood.' The same disorder was similarly described in the United Kingdom, as reflected in the World Health Organization (WHO) classification. However, the conditions described differed in that the British disorder included more severe symptomatology and required that the symptoms had to be present in all settings.

In 1980, the US characterization of inattention and hyperactivity was changed in several ways. It was conceptually defined by three symptom dimensions: inattention, impulsiveness, and hyperactivity, with inattention playing a more prominent role. In addition, to address the heterogeneity within the disorder, two subtypes ('attention deficit disorder with hyperactivity' and 'attention deficit disorder without hyperactivity') were defined. Again, different from the British criteria, the symptoms were only required to be present in one setting such as school. Retaining the concept that the major contributions to the symptoms were related to innate characteristics in the child rather than to environmental influences, the symptoms were required to have been present before the age of 7 years and to have lasted for at least 6 months. The British system continued to use the term 'hyperkinetic syndrome of childhood' and to include the pervasive nature of the symptoms.

The most recent changes in diagnostic criteria used by the American Psychiatric Association (DSM-IV) and the WHO have moved the definitions closer to agreement. Considering the most recent studies, there is evidence to support two dimensions. In DSM, the first dimension, inattention, is characterized by the 'often' occurrence of at least six of nine of the inattentive behaviors presented in **Table 1**. The second dimension consists of both hyperactivity and impulsiveness and is characterized by the 'often' occurrence of at least six of nine of the hyperactive and/or impulsive behaviors presented in **Table 1**. The WHO definitions are similar but do not attempt to quantify the specific behaviors and do not include impulsiveness in the hyperactivity dimension.

In DSM, the two dimensions define three subtypes: predominantly inattentive type (meeting criteria on the inattentive dimension), predominantly hyperactive/impulsive type (meeting criteria on the hyperactive/impulsive dimension), and combined type (meeting criteria on both dimensions). In addition, there are other general criteria including the onset of symptoms before 7 years of age, the presence of symptoms for at least 6 months, the presence of symptoms in two or more settings (e.g., home, school, or work), and evidence that

Table 1 DSM-IV behaviors for ADHD

Inattention
Careless mistakes
Difficulty sustaining attention
Seems not to listen
Fails to finish tasks
Difficulty organizing
Avoids tasks requiring sustained attention
Loses things
Easily distracted
Forgetful

Hyperactivity
Fidgeting
Unable to stay seated
Moving excessively (restless)
Difficulty engaging in leisure activities quietly
'On the go'
Talking excessively

Impulsiveness
Blurting answers before questions completed
Difficulty awaiting turn
Interrupting/intruding upon others

the symptoms cause significant clinical impairment in social, academic, or occupational functioning. The WHO condition has been renamed 'disturbances of activity and attention.'

Treatments Other Than Diet

In considering dietary interventions, it is important to note that there are two other forms of treatment with proven efficacy. These are stimulant medications and behavior modification. Considerations about dietary interventions have to be considered in the context of these other interventions. The nature of the main beneficial treatments, stimulant medication and behavioral interventions, makes the issue of diagnostic criteria for ADHD extremely important. Both of these treatments are not specific for the disorder so that the determination about which children are treated is very dependent on who is diagnosed.

The stimulant medications consist of methylphenidate (Ritalin), dextroamphetamine (Dexedrine), and pemoline (Cylert). They are particularly popular in the United States because they represent safe, effective, and low-cost treatment. A review of numerous studies has shown that stimulants improve the core behaviors of inattention, impulsiveness, and hyperactivity for the duration of action of the medication, as well as providing temporary improvement of associated features including aggression, social interaction, and academic productivity. The margin of safety is very high, and the side effects on appetite, sleep, and,

infrequently, tics or bizarre behavior are all reversible when the medication is stopped. The concern about growth has proved to be insignificant, and although abused by adults, the stimulants are rarely abused by the children who take them because they usually do not find taking the medication pleasurable. While there is no long-term evidence that the use of stimulant medication or behavioral interventions on their own have any long-term benefits, there is evidence of long-term benefits when they are used in combination.

Effective behavioral interventions have generally consisted of direct contingency management programs (e.g., point or token programs or a response cost program) and social skills training. Like stimulant medication, these interventions are not specific to ADHD and have no proven long-term benefit when used in isolation. Other approaches, such as traditional psychotherapy and play therapy, have not been found to be effective with this group of children. Likewise, cognitive behavioral techniques, where a therapist teaches a child to control his or her behavior, have usually not been effective for children with ADHD because of the difficulty these children experience in generalizing the techniques beyond the therapeutic sessions.

Dietary Interventions

The concept that specific dietary components may adversely affect behavior has rested on three hypotheses:

1. Oligoallergenic diet
2. Sugar restriction
3. Feingold diet.

The idea that food might have an adverse effect on behavior was first raised in 1922 by Shannon. This concept was further elaborated in 1947 by Randolph in his description of the 'tension fatigue syndrome,' a behavioral extension of the vomiting reaction to milk proteins, and was also promoted by Speer. Their theory suggested that some children have atypical allergic reactions to various foods, consisting of subtle and behavioral effects. Their treatment entailed placing a child on a restricted diet and then adding foods one at a time to determine which foods caused an adverse reaction. This has been referred to as the oligoallergenic diet by a recent clinical/research group.

A specific focus on sugar as a nutrient adversely affecting behavior first appeared in the 1970s, with a study reported by Langseth and Dowd. Among 271 hyperactive children, these authors found a large number of children who, during glucose tolerance tests, had patterns of blood glucose levels similar to the pattern seen in adults with functional reactive hypoglycemia. Similar results have also been found in aggressive criminal offenders. A subsequent study showed that the patterns that Langseth and Dowd found can be normal variations in childhood, but the Langseth and Dowd study was followed by two correlational studies that suggested an association between sugar intake and hyperactivity. The hyperactive children who consumed more sugar displayed more hyperactive and aggressive behavior.

The third dietary intervention suggested to improve behavior was proposed by Dr. Benjamin Feingold in 1975. He reported that at least 50% of hyperactive and learning-disabled children improved when placed on diets that were salicylate and additive free. Over time, the three dietary interventions have been combined so that proposed dietary restrictions now tend to incorporate all three in their recommendations. However, it is useful to examine the scientific evidence for each of these three dietary interventions.

Objective Standards

In discussing the evidence for the efficacy of dietary interventions in improving behavior in children, it is first important to review the concepts important to prove efficacy. The major point to emphasize is that it is impossible to prove the null hypothesis. It is virtually impossible to prove definitively that no relationship exists between dietary constituents and behavior or cognitive function. This is because it is impossible to test every possible variation or type of child. Therefore, a realistic approach needs to be similar to that taken by the US Food and Drug Administration (FDA) for the criteria it requires to license a new medication. Basically, pharmaceutical companies are required to demonstrate that a new medication is both efficacious and does not cause significant harm. It is not the role of the FDA to disprove the efficacy of a drug treatment. With dietary interventions, they should not be recommended as a primary intervention for behavioral problems until there is clear evidence of their efficacy.

The main criteria required to evaluate objectively the efficacy of psychotropic medications are presented in **Table 2**. It is useful to use these criteria to evaluate the scientific merit of any studies on interventions affecting behavior. It is also important to examine the pattern of results of multiple studies from different research groups. Ideally, where other efficacious therapies are available (e.g., stimulant medication and behavior modification for children

Table 2 Objective study criteria

Uniformity of subjects
Standard doses
Objective verifiable dependent measures
Control group
Placebo
Double-blind

with ADHD), the proposed therapy should be compared with existing therapies. This latter examination, by and large, has not been undertaken with any of the three dietary interventions.

Study Designs

There are two designs that can be employed to study the effects of nutrients on behavior. The most commonly employed design is the challenge study. This first places the children on the diet under study for a period of time and then challenges them with a food containing the offending agent (e.g., sucrose or tartrazine) or a food that does not contain the offending agent but looks and tastes identical to the offending agent, referred to as a placebo. This is the most commonly employed design because it is the easier and less expensive type to complete. The other design develops diets that appear similar, but the diets differ in what they contain (e.g., sugar or artificial sweeteners). In both designs the children, their families, and the researchers need to be blind about which diet or challenge food the children receive at any given time. In most studies, the children are used as their own controls (crossover studies). They are able to receive both diets or challenges in a sequence because the diets are not believed to result in permanent changes lasting once the diet is stopped.

The measures used to assess the effects (dependent measures) are then completed within the few hours after a challenge or repeatedly while the children are on diets. While parents, clinicians, and teachers are utilized as observers (completing behavior rating scales), ideally multiple measures are employed including some that are by independent observers or include objective assessments (e.g., performance on a continuous performance test and measuring activity level). Finally, it is important not to base results on one study. There need to be multiple studies performed by different groups of researchers, and a clear pattern of effects should emerge. When a number of studies have been completed, it is possible to combine them statistically with such techniques as meta-analysis to gain a more definitive picture.

Oligoallergenic Diet

While this is the oldest of the three dietary interventions, few controlled studies meeting the objective criteria outlined previously have been undertaken. Five investigations have studied the effects of placing children on restricted diets. These studies all included restricting the dietary intake of additives and simple sugars. The studies found beneficial effects from placing children on restricted diets compared with a placebo diet, or they found worsening behaviors in children on the restricted diets when they were challenged with offending foods compared with placebo challenges. In all but one of the studies, the only successfully completed dependent measure was behavior rating scales completed by the parents. While these are important measures and are collected in most studies, the raters are not independent of the children's behaviors. One study had multiple measures, but only those of the parents and physician found a significant difference between the offending agent and placebo challenges. More extensive research by additional research groups and additional independent measures are required to document the efficacy of this intervention before a decision can be made about its efficacy. Since the initial diet is extremely restrictive, care must be taken to make sure that the diet is adequately balanced and contains adequate nutrition.

Sugar Restriction

Sugar restriction usually refers to limiting the amount of sucrose in the diet. While most of the studies examined sucrose restriction, some also examined restriction of fructose or glucose. The artificial sweetener employed as a placebo was most frequently aspartame, but several studies used saccharin or both aspartame and saccharin as separate conditions. The type of sweetener used did not seem to affect the results.

Sugar restriction has been studied as a treatment for children since 1982. There have been a total of 23 appropriate objective studies contained within 16 reports employing a wide variety of types of children, including children with ADHD and aggression as well as normal children, and varying in age from preschool children to adolescents. All of the studies with two exceptions were challenge crossover studies in which children were challenged with drinks containing either sugar (sucrose in most studies) or an artificial sweetener (mostly aspartame). The other two studies consisted of giving the children diets that were high in sucrose content or low in sucrose and sweetened with aspartame or saccharin. A meta-analysis of the 23 studies did not find any significant behavioral or

cognitive effects from sugar. There were not enough studies to reach a definitive conclusion, and there was insufficient statistical power to detect small effects or to detect effects on a small subset of children. To date, there is not enough evidence to warrant the recommendation to restrict a child's sugar intake for the purpose of improving the child's behavior or cognitive functioning.

Feingold Diet

The Feingold diet restricts foods with dyes, preservatives, and salicylate compounds. Investigations of this diet, which were reviewed in 1986, generally involved children with ADHD. In most of the studies the children were kept on an additive-free diet and then challenged with a food containing an additive or an additive-free food as placebo. Two studies used additive-containing and additive-free diets. A problem in comparing studies was the variation in type and dose of additives used. There were a total of 13 controlled studies. The summation of the findings found little, if any, effect. At best, there was some suggestion that a small percentage of children (1%) were adversely affected by additives. However, a recent study found that 24 of 34 children referred for hyperactivity (no formal diagnosis was established) who responded in an open clinical trial to an additive-free diet responded adversely to challenges with varying doses of tartrazine compared with placebo, whereas all except 2 of 20 in a comparison group did not. The dependent measures were two behavior rating scales completed by the parents. There appeared to be a dose response that would be contrary to a usual allergic response. This is a much higher rate of response than found in any previous study including those using tartrazine. Further study is required to substantiate these results since they run contrary to most of the previous research. Overall, the evidence to date does not confirm the efficacy of the Feingold diet to warrant its promotion as a treatment for most children with behavioral problems. In addition, if the diet is strictly maintained including foods containing salicylate compounds, the diet may be deficient in vitamin C.

Potential Side Effects of Diets

With all the diets, maintaining compliance may be difficult. Children who have behavioral problems are generally less likely to be compliant, and it can require a major effort to maintain the diet, detracting from efforts to control other areas of behavior. Diets are also problematic because they require the children to eat foods different from their peers. In children who are already singled out as different, this can further reduce their self-esteem. Care has to be taken to weight the benefits of diets with as yet objectively unproved effects against the potential harm and difficulties in administering them.

Conclusions

ADHD is a mental disorder and its diagnosis is based on a child manifesting the symptoms of inattention, hyperactivity, and impulsiveness to the extent that the symptoms impair the child's ability to function. The main beneficial treatments are two nonspecific treatments, stimulant medication and behavioral interventions. While neither alone has any proven long-term benefits, there is evidence that the combination of both treatments does have some long-term benefits.

Dietary interventions have included (1) restriction of allergenic foods starting with a generally restricted diet and adding those foods that do not worsen the child's behavior, (2) restriction of food additives and preservatives referred to as the Feingold diet, and (3) restriction of sugar. These dietary interventions have not been proved to be efficacious and more study is required to determine their effects.

See also: **Food Allergies**: Diagnosis and Management. **Sucrose**: Nutritional Role, Absorption and Metabolism.

Further Reading

American Psychiatric Association (1994) *Diagnostic and Statistical Manual of Mental Disorders*, 4th edn. Washington, DC: American Psychiatric Association.

Baumgaertel A, Copeland L, and Wolraich ML (1996) Attention deficit hyperactivity disorder. In: Wolraich ML (ed.) *Disorders of Development and Learning*, 2nd edn. St Louis: Mosby-Yearbook.

Egger J, Stolla A, and McEwen LM (1992) Controlled trial of hyposensitisation in children with food induced hyperkinetic syndrome. *Lancet* **339**: 1150–1153.

Pelham WE and Sams SE (1992) Behavior modification. *Child and Adolescent Psychiatric Clinics of North American* **1**: 505–517.

Sprague RL and Werry JS (1971) Methodology of psychopharmacological studies with the retarded. *International Review of Research into Mental Retardation* **5**: 147–157.

Swanson JM, McBurnett K, Wigal T *et al.* (1993) Effects of stimulant medication on children with ADD: A review of reviews. *Exceptional Children* **60**: 154–162.

Wender EH (1986) The food additive-free diet in the treatment of behavior disorders: A review. *Journal of Developmental and Behavioral Pediatrics* **7**: 35–42.

Wolraich ML, Lindgren SD, Stumbo PJ *et al.* (1994) Effects of diets high in sucrose or aspartame on the behavioral and cognitive performance of children. *New England Journal of Medicine* **330**: 301–307.

Wolraich ML, Wilson DB, and White JW (1995) The effect of sugar on behavior or cognition in children: A meta-analysis. *Journal of the American Medical Association* **274**: 1617–1621.

World Health Organization (1992) *The ICD-10 Classification of Mental and Behavioural Disorders*. Geneva: World Health Organization.

HYPERLIPIDEMIA

Contents
Overview
Nutritional Management

Overview

T R Trinick and E B Duly, Ulster Hospital, Belfast, UK

Normal Lipid Metabolism

Lipids are a heterogeneous group of substances soluble in organic solvents but insoluble in water. They are largely intracellular but circulate in blood as lipoprotein particles. There are four general functions for lipids:

- Structural components of membranes
- Storage forms of metabolic fuel
- Transport forms of metabolic fuel
- Protective functions as an outer coating of the organism

Lipids consist of cholesterol and its derivatives, fatty acids, triacylglycerols, phospholipids, and apolipoproteins. The lipoprotein particle has a core of neutral lipids (cholesterol esters and triacylglycerol) and a surface coat of polar lipids (unesterified cholesterol and phospholipids) and apolipoproteins. They are classified in terms of density. The following are the main lipoproteins:

- Chylomicrons
- Very low-density lipoprotein (VLDL)
- Immediate-density lipoprotein (IDL)
- Low-density lipoprotein (LDL)
- High-density lipoprotein (HDL)

Synthesis of lipoproteins occurs in the intestine or liver. They are then modified by enzymes and taken up by cell surface receptors in processes largely regulated by the apolipoproteins. A series of receptors, transporters, and enzymes are important in lipoprotein metabolism and function as detailed later. The physicochemical characteristics of the main lipoprotein classes are shown in **Table 1**.

Interest in lipids lies in circulating lipid concentrations and their relationship to atherosclerosis, particularly coronary heart disease, stroke, and peripheral vascular disease.

Cholesterol

Cholesterol is a sterol with the structure shown in **Figure 1**. Daily cholesterol intake is 0.5–1.0 g, half of which is absorbed. On a low-cholesterol diet (<300 mg/day) the body synthesizes approximately 800 mg of cholesterol per day, mainly in the liver and, to a lesser extent, in the intestine.

The rate-limiting step in synthesis is highly sensitive to cellular levels of cholesterol, themselves sensitive to circulating levels of cholesterol. This feedback regulation occurs through changes in the amount and activity of an enzyme called 3-hydroxy-3-methylglutaryl CoA reductase (HMG-CoA reductase), which catalyzes the formation of mevalonate, the rate-limiting step in cholesterol biosynthesis. The rate of synthesis of HMG-CoA reductase mRNA is

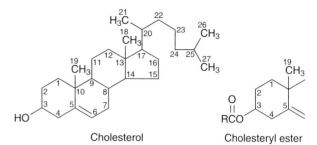

Figure 1 Structure of cholesterol and cholesteryl ester.

controlled by the sterol regulatory element binding protein (SREBP). SREBP in its inactive state is attached to the endoplasmic reticulum or nuclear membrane, but when cholesterol levels decline the amino-terminal domain is released from its association with the membrane by proteolytic cleavage; it migrates to the nucleus and binds to the sterol regulatory element (SRE) on the 5′ side of the reductase gene to enhance transcription. As cholesterol levels increase, the proteolytic release of SREBP is blocked, SREBP in the nucleus is rapidly degraded, and cholesterol synthesis is switched off.

Cholesterol is found in the body largely as free cholesterol in membranes, but in the plasma it is two-thirds esterified, mainly as cholesterol linoleate and cholesterol oleate. Free cholesterol in plasma exchanges freely with cholesterol in membranes. The major route of cholesterol excretion is through the bile, directly as cholesterol or after conversion to bile salts, some of which are reabsorbed from the terminal ileum in the enterohepatic circulation.

Triacylglycerol

Triacylglycerols are glycerol molecules esterified with three fatty acid molecules (**Figure 2**). Diacylglycerols and monoacylglycerols have two and one fatty acid molecules, respectively. Triacylglycerols constitute the main energy storage form in mammals and are the main storage form of fatty acids.

Table 1 Physicochemical characteristics of the major lipoprotein classes

Lipoprotein	Density (g/ml)	Molecular weight (Da × 10⁶)	Diameter (nm)	Triacylglycerol (% lipid)	Cholesterol (% lipid)	Phospholipid (% lipid)	Source
Chylomicrons	0.95	>400	75–1200	80–95	2–7	3–9	Intestine
VLDL	0.95–1.006	10–80	30–80	55–80	5–15	10–20	Liver
IDL	1.006–1.019	5–10	25–35	20–50	20–40	15–25	Catabolism of VLDL
LDL	1.019–1.063	2.3	18–25	5–15	40–50	20–25	Catabolism of IDL
HDL	1.063–1.21	1.7–3.6	5–12	5–10	15–25	20–30	Liver, intestine

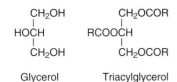

$$
\begin{array}{cc}
CH_2OH & CH_2OCOR \\
| & | \\
HOCH & RCOOCH \\
| & | \\
CH_2OH & CH_2OCOR \\
\\
\text{Glycerol} & \text{Triacylglycerol}
\end{array}
$$

Figure 2 Structure of glycerol and triacylglycerol. 'R' denotes the position of a fatty acid within the triacylglycerol.

Fatty Acids

Fatty acids can be present as triacylglycerol, as part of lipoprotein particles, and as free fatty acids (bound to albumin). Common fatty acids and their sources are listed in **Table 2**.

Fatty acids are straight-chain compounds of differing lengths connecting a hydrocarbon group to a hydroxyl group. With only single bonds in the straight chain, the fatty acid is saturated; with one or more additional double bonds, the fatty acid is unsaturated. Fatty acids with only one double bond are said to be monounsaturated (e.g., oleic acid, C18:1), whereas fatty acids with two or more double bonds are said to be polyunsaturated (e.g., arachidonic acid, C20:4). The presence of a double bond allows there to be two isomers, depending on whether the hydrogen atoms attached to the carbon atoms on either side of the double bond lie on the same side (*cis*) or opposing sides (*trans*). *Cis* isomers are the only naturally occurring isomers and form kinks in the fatty acid chain. *Trans* isomers occur as part of food processing and maintain the straight direction of fatty acid chains. The common saturated fatty acids are palmitic (C16:0) and stearic (C18:0) acids.

Diets rich in omega-3 polyunsaturated fatty acids (n-3 PUFAs), such as α-linoleic acid, eicosapentanaenoic acid, and decosahexaenoic acid, are associated with less coronary heart disease, and conjugated linoleic acids have beneficial effects against atherosclerosis. n-3 PUFAs function mainly by changing membrane lipid composition, cellular metabolism, signal transduction, and regulation of gene expression. It is postulated that receptors exist for fatty acids or their metabolites that are able to regulate gene expression and affect metabolic or signalling pathways associated with coronary heart disease. Three nuclear receptors are thought to be fatty acid receptors that respond to dietary and endogenous ligands: peroxisome proliferator activated receptors, retinoid X receptors, and liver X receptors.

Phospholipids

The common phospholipids in plasma are derived from glycerol and consist of triacylglycerol containing phosphate and a nitrogenous base (glycerophospholipids). The phosphate group is usually attached at position 3 of the glycerol molecule, and the nitrogenous base is usually an amino acid or an alcohol. The phosphatidyl cholines (lecithins) are the most common phospholipid and are found in plasma and in cell membranes. Lecithin–cholesterol acyl transferase (LCAT) catalyzes the transfer of a fatty acyl group at position 2 on glycerol to cholesterol to produce cholesteryl ester and leaves monoacyl glycerophosphate (lysolecithin). Another class of phospholipids, the cephalins, includes phosphatidyl ethanolamine, phosphatidyl serine, and phosphatidyl inositol.

Phospholipids are able to bridge nonpolar lipids and water and act to allow lipids to mix with water in an emulsion. The nonpolar hydrocarbon end of the phospholipid is attracted to lipid, whereas the polar phosphate group is attracted to water. In a lipid droplet, the inner oily centre is surrounded by phospholipid, which has its outer phosphate group attracted to the surrounding water environment, to form a micelle.

Table 2 Fatty acids and their sources

Fatty acid	Structure	Source	Melting point (°C)
Saturated			
Lauric	C12:0	Coconut oil, palm kernel oil	44
Palmitic	C16:0	Palm oil, milk, butter, cocoa, butter, beef, pork, lamb	63
Stearic	C18:0		69
Behanic	C22:0	Some seed oils, especially peanut	80
Lignoceric	C24:0		84
Unsaturated			
Oleic	C18:1	Olive oil, most commonly occurring fatty acid	11
Linoleic	C18:2	Corn oil, soya bean oil, sunflower oil and sunflower seed oil	−5
Linolenic	C18:3	Linseed oil	−11
Arachidonic	C20:4	Fish oils	−50
Eicosapentenoic	C20:5	Cod, salmon, pilchard, mussel, oyster	−54
Docosahexenoic	C22:6		

From Durrington PN (2004) *Hyperlipidaemia: Diagnosis and Management.* London: Hodder Arnold.

Apolipoproteins A, B, C, and E

The lipoprotein particle (VLDL, LDL, and HDL) is composed of lipid and protein molecules. Among the protein molecules are a group of proteins found at the surface of the lipoprotein particle called apolipoproteins. Their function is integral to the metabolism of lipoproteins. They interact with phospholipids to solubilize cholesterol esters and triacylglycerol, regulate the reaction of enzymes (LCAT, lipoprotein lipase, and hepatic lipase) with lipid, and bind with cell surface receptors to determine the metabolism of lipoproteins.

Apolipoprotein A

This is the main protein of HDL and has two forms, apoA-I and apoA-II. ApoA-I is the main protein component in HDL, and the production and catabolism of apoA-I determine the plasma concentration of HDL cholesterol. It acts as an activator of LCAT, which is responsible for esterification of free cholesterol in plasma, and allows the binding of HDL to many cell surfaces. ApoA-II is a structural component of HDL.

Apolipoprotein A-I Milano

ApoA-I Milano is a specific form of apoA-I seen in some Italian families, which appears to protect against the development of atherosclerosis.

Apolipoprotein B

ApoB-100 is the main protein component of LDL and is synthesized in the liver. It is also found in chylomicrons and VLDL. ApoB-48 is synthesized from the intestine and is the amino-terminal half of apoB-100 synthesized from the same gene. ApoB-100 is the receptor ligand for the LDL receptor.

Apolipoprotein C

ApoC is composed of three separate apolipoproteins. ApoC-I is mainly found in VLDL but also in chylomicrons and HDL. ApoC-II is present in a circulating reservoir of HDL, transferring to chylomicrons and VLDL, where it acts as an activator of lipoprotein lipase, allowing the lipolysis of triacylglycerols from circulating triacylglycerol-rich lipoproteins. ApoC-III is the most abundant form of apoC and may act as a modulator of lipoprotein lipase.

Apolipoprotein E

ApoE is a glycoprotein with several isoforms designated as apoE-2, -E-3, and -E-4. ApoE-3 is the most common isoform. It is present in VLDL, IDL, and HDL (mainly HDL$_2$). ApoE facilitates chylomicron remnant metabolism through the chylomicron remnant and VLDL receptors of the liver. ApoE-3 and -E-4 bind avidly with hepatic receptors, whereas apoE-2 is poorly bound. Patients with only apoE-2 isoform clear chylomicron remnants and IDL slowly, and apoE-2 is associated with dysbetalipoproteinemia (type III hyperlipoproteinemia). ApoE also facilitates metabolism through the LDL receptor (particularly the apoE-4 isoform). A large number of tissues express mRNA for apoE, including the brain, although the reason for this is unclear.

Apolipoprotein (a)

Apo(a) joined together with one LDL particle, which contains apoB, constitutes a lipoprotein called Lp(a). Interest in Lp(a) arose because apo(a) shows close sequence homology with plasminogen, suggesting that a high level of Lp(a) would impair thrombolysis. Lp(a) is an independent risk factor for developing vascular disease, with levels above a cutoff value of 300 mg/l placing individuals at risk, especially if combined with other risk factors.

Lipoproteins

The main function of the lipoproteins is to transport lipids from one organ to another. Their main characteristics are shown in **Table 1**.

Chylomicrons

These are the largest lipoproteins, consisting mainly of triacylglycerol with apoB-48 and apoA, -C, and -E. Triacylglycerol is hydrolyzed with endothelial-bound lipoprotein lipase, changing the chylomicron into a chylomicron remnant rich in cholesteryl ester. These remnants are removed from the circulation by interaction with the remnant receptors mainly present on hepatocytes. Peak chylomicronemia occurs 3–6 h after a meal, with a half-life of less than 1 h, and is cleared from the circulation after a 12-h fast.

Very low-density lipoproteins

These triacylglycerol-rich lipoproteins are secreted mainly by the liver, with apoB-100 and apoE on their surface, whereas some VLDLs are synthesized by the gut. They are transformed into mature VLDLs by accumulating cholesterol ester, apoC, and apoE from HDLs. They then either interact with lipoprotein lipase to convert into IDLs, which can be taken up by the liver, or convert to LDLs by interacting with hepatic triglyceride lipase.

VLDL particles vary in size. Small VLDL is converted into LDL, via IDL, to a greater extent than large VLDL, which is converted to a form of IDL that appears to be removed from the plasma before conversion to LDL.

Intermediate-density lipoproteins IDLs are intermediate particles formed from the conversion of VLDL to LDL. Also known as VLDL remnants, some are removed directly from plasma, whereas some convert into LDL.

Low-density lipoproteins LDL is the major cholesterol-carrying particle in the plasma. The core is cholesterol ester and has one apolipoprotein, apoB-100, per LDL particle. There are different sizes of LDL. Approximately one-third of the intravascular pool is catabolized per day and three-fourths of the circulating LDL is cleared through the liver, mainly through the LDL receptor. Small, dense LDL is more common in some dyslipidemias and may be more easily oxidized than larger LDL. Normal LDL does not cause foam cell formation, but lipid peroxidation of LDL makes the LDL a ligand for certain receptors (the scavenger receptor and perhaps a specific receptor for oxidized LDL) and results in the formation of cholesterol-laden foam cells. In addition, oxidized LDL in the cell wall stimulates the production of cytokines and growth factors, resulting in monocyte recruitment and the proliferation of smooth muscle cells. This mechanism underlies one model of atherogenesis.

High-density lipoproteins Nascent HDL is secreted by the liver and gut. It acquires unesterified cholesterol in the circulation, catalysed by LCAT to cholesteryl ester. HDL can pass cholesteryl ester to VLDL in exchange for triacylglycerol, facilitated by cholesterol ester transfer protein (CETP), or HDL can be taken up by the liver directly. The idea that HDL protects against coronary heart disease (CHD) comes from epidemiological studies. A 0.026 mmol/l increase in plasma HDL cholesterol decreases CHD risk by 2% in men and 3% in women.

Enzymes and Transfer Proteins

Acylcoenzyme A Cholesterol acyltransferase (ACAT; EC 2.3.1.26) ACAT-1 and ACAT-2 are membrane-bound proteins responsible for cholesterol ester formation, metabolizing excess cholesterol within cells to cholesterol ester, which is allosterically activated by cholesterol.

Adenosine-binding cassette transporter In peripheral tissues, adenosine-binding cassette transporter (ABCA-1) protein facilitates transfer of intracellular cholesterol out of cells to lipid-poor apoA-1 or pre-β HDL particles. When it is deficient or inactive, cholesterol accumulates in peripheral tissues as in Tangier disease or familial HDL deficiency.

Cholesterol Ester transfer protein CETP mediates the exchange of cholesteryl ester from HDL with triacylglycerol from VLDL or chylomicrons.

Fatty acid binding protein Fatty acid binding proteins (FABPs) play a role in the solubilization of long-chain fatty acids (LCFAs) and their CoA-esters to various intracellular organelles. FABPs serve as intracellular receptors of LCFAs and are involved in ligand-dependent transactivation of peroxisome proliferator-activated receptors (PPARs) in trafficking LCFAs to the nucleus.

Hepatic lipase (EC 3.1.1.3) Hepatic lipase (HL) is an endothelial-bound enzyme that removes triacylglycerol from lipoproteins in the metabolism of chylomicrons, VLDL, and HDL. HL hydrolyzes HDL triacylglycerol and phospholipids to form HDL_3 from HDL_2, contributing to the process of HDL regeneration in the reverse cholesterol transfer process.

Lecithin-cholesterol acyltransferase (EC 2.3.1.43) LCAT mediates the esterification of cholesterol by transferring a fatty acid from lecithin to cholesterol to form cholesteryl ester.

Lipoprotein lipase (EC 3.1.1.34) Lipoprotein lipase and hepatic lipase are endothelial-bound enzymes that remove triacylglycerol from lipoproteins. Lipoprotein lipase is activated by apoC-II and is involved in catabolism of chylomicrons and VLDL. Endothelial lipase, lipoprotein lipase, and hepatic lipase belong to the same gene family.

Microsomal triglyceride transfer protein Microsomal triglyceride transfer protein is present in enterocytes and hepatocytes, and it is responsible for adding neutral lipid to apoB to protect it from ubiquitinylation and degradation.

Phospholipid transfer protein Phospholipid transfer protein transfers phospholipids from other lipoproteins to HDL, contributing to the functionality of HDL.

Sterol regulatory element binding protein SREBP is a protein that binds with part of the LDL receptor promoter to increase cholesterol synthesis.

Receptors

A large number of lipoprotein receptors have been identified. Some of the more important receptors are discussed here. Lipoprotein uptake at the cell membrane may be non-receptor-mediated, perhaps by pinocytosis, where 'binding' is of low affinity but is not saturable.

LDL receptor The LDL receptor (LDLR) is a transmembrane glycoprotein present on most cell surfaces, encoded on chromosome 19. Free cholesterol, building up in the cell through the receptor, reduces both cell synthesis of cholesterol and cell uptake of more LDL cholesterol.

LDL receptor-related protein The LDL receptor-related protein (LRP) is a multifunctional receptor (binding VLDL/chylomicron remnants and other nonlipid ligands such as bacterial toxins) present in nearly all tissues. It has a high affinity for apoE and a low affinity for apoB-100.

VLDL receptor This receptor binds VLDL, β-VLDL, and IDL. It recognizes apoE and is located mainly in adipose tissue and muscle.

Scavenger receptors These receptors are found on macrophages and hepatic endothelium. They bind and degrade chemically modified LDL, such as oxidized or acetylated LDL. They are not downregulated by intracellular cholesterol accumulation. Hepatocellular uptake of HDL and/or its cholesteryl ester content is facilitated by a scavenger receptor and a HDL receptor.

Other remnant receptors The lipolysis-stimulated receptor found on fibroblasts recognizes surface apoE and takes up VLDL, chylomicrons, and LDL. Two membrane-binding proteins (MBP 200 and MBP 235) have been described on macrophages and appear to bind VLDL. Remnants from both chylomicrons and VLDL (after hydrolysis of more than 70% of their triacylglycerol content) appear to be removed by both the LDL and the LRP receptors.

Peroxisome proliferator-activated receptors PPARs are a family of intranuclear receptors, including PPARα and PPARδ, that regulate a variety of genes involved in lipid metabolism, thrombosis, and inflammation.

Exogenous (Dietary) Lipid Pathways

Ingestion of food containing fat (triacylglycerol) and cholesterol results in absorption into the enterocyte of fatty acids, monoacylglycerols, free cholesterol, and lysolecithin. In the enterocyte, reesterification of fatty acids into triacylglycerol and cholesterol into cholesteryl ester occurs to form chylomicrons, to which is added a surface layer of apoB-48, -A-I, -A-II, and -A-IV, phospholipid, and free cholesterol. This allows secretion of the chylomicron into the intestinal lymphatics. ApoB-48 is required for secretion of the chylomicron. ApoB-48 is a truncated form of apoB-100, synthesized in the liver but missing the LDL receptor-binding domain of apoB-100. The action of the apoB-editing enzyme in enterocytes changes a nucleotide base in apoB mRNA to a stop codon. There is one apoB-48 per intestinal triglyceride-rich particle.

Chylomicrons in the circulation take up apoC from HDL (releasing it back to HDL later) and acquire apoE. ApoC-II allows the chylomicron to activate lipoprotein lipase on capillary endothelial cells of muscle and fat. This allows hydrolysis of triacylglycerol, releasing glycerol and fatty acids to be taken up by local tissue. Surface phospholipids, free cholesterol, and apoC transfer to HDL as the particle shrinks. This small chylomicron is called a chylomicron remnant and is catabolized through the LDL receptor and other remnant receptors on the liver. This transport of dietary lipid from the intestinal to the peripheral tissues is shown in **Figure 3**.

Endogenous Lipid Pathways

The liver is the main source of endogenous lipid (**Figure 4**). In particular, the liver secretes the triacylglycerol-rich lipoprotein VLDL. Triacylglycerol, which is formed from fatty acids either newly synthesised or taken up from plasma, together with free cholesterol, synthesised from acetate or delivered to the liver in chylomicron remnants, join with apoB and phospholipids to form VLDL. ApoC and apoE are added in the circulation. Triacylglycerol is progressively removed from VLDL in the same way as occurs with chylomicrons. Free cholesterol transfers to HDL and is esterified with LCAT and transferred back to VLDL, using a protein called cholesteryl ester transfer protein (CETP), in exchange for triacylglycerol transfer from VLDL to HDL. In this way, VLDL becomes smaller and transforms to become IDL, although some small VLDLs may be removed directly. IDL is further changed through interaction with hepatic lipase to LDL. In this way, most VLDL is transformed to LDL.

Reverse Cholesterol Transport

Lipids are transported to the peripheries from the gut and the liver. They return to the liver via HDL in a process known as reverse cholesterol transport (**Figure 5**). HDL particles arise in the liver and gut from a coalescence of apoA-I and phospholipid to

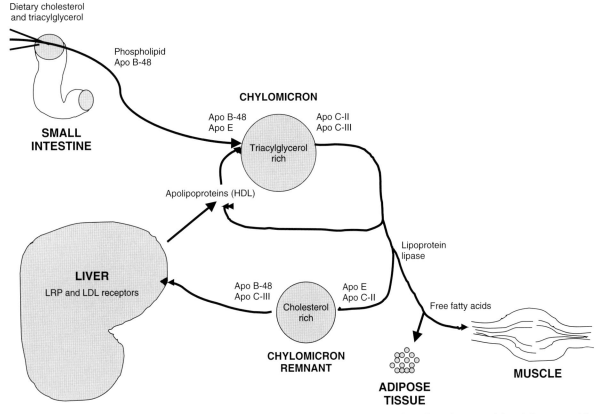

Figure 3 Exogenous (dietary) lipid pathway. This shows the transport of dietary lipid from intestine to peripheral tissues and liver. Movement of apolipoprotein between high-density lipoprotein (HDL) and chylomicrons is shown. LRP, low-density lipoprotein (LDL) receptor-related protein.

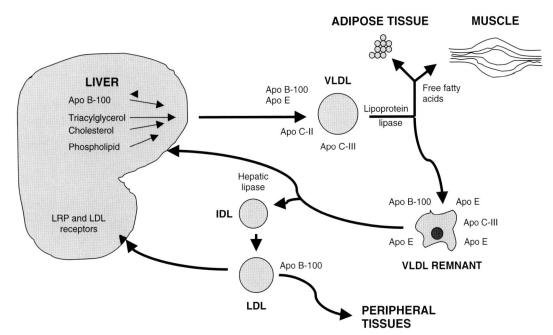

Figure 4 Endogenous lipid pathway. This shows the formation of very low-density lipoprotein (VLDL) lipid particles (VLDL$_1$ and VLDL$_2$) in the liver with the interconversion, through the action of lipoprotein lipase, to VLDL remnant and through immediate-density lipoprotein (IDL) to LDL. Lipids are taken up from LDL both peripherally and in the liver. LRP, low-density lipoprotein receptor-related protein.

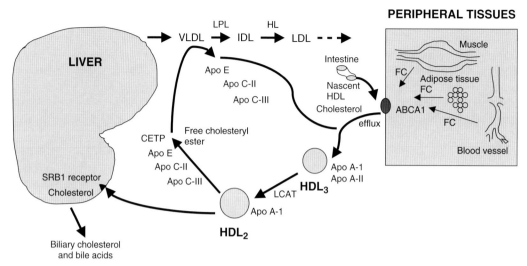

Figure 5   Reverse cholesterol transport. Nascent high-density lipoprotein (HDL$_3$) picks up free cholesterol from the peripheries to become HDL$_2$, by a lecithin–cholesterol acyl transferase (LCAT)-mediated conversion. Cholesterol is then transported to the liver with uptake by the SRBI receptor. A second method of transport to the liver involves CETP-mediated esterification of HDL and conversion into immediate-density lipoprotein (IDL) and low-density lipoprotein (LDL), which is then taken up by the LDL receptor. This transfer of lipid between HDL$_2$ and VLDL/IDL maintains a cycle within HDL, and IDL/LDL deliver cholesterol from the peripheries to the liver. HDL may also deliver cholesterol directly to the liver. FC, free cholesterol.

form cholesterol-deficient bilayered discs in the form of HDL$_3$. Circulating HDL particles, particularly a subset of HDL$_3$ called pre-β HDL or lipid-poor apoA-I, come into contact with cells, and ABCA-1 acts to move free cholesterol from the cell surface and out of the cells. This cholesterol is converted by LCAT to cholesteryl ester and moves into the core of the HDL, forming mature cholesterol-rich HDL. After accumulating cholesterol, the HDL starts to accept other apolipoproteins and becomes HDL$_2$. In turn, HDL$_2$ appears to pass cholesteryl ester to triglyceride-rich lipoproteins such as chylomicrons, chylomicron remnants, and VLDL under the influence of CETP. The cholesterol then finds its way back to the liver in the form of chylomicron remnants, IDL, and LDL. Some of the HDL$_2$ particles may lose cholesterol directly to the liver and some may be taken up directly by the liver.

Consequences of Hyperlipidemia

Clear evidence exists that as serum cholesterol rises, the risk of CHD rises, and as serum cholesterol falls, the risk of developing CHD falls. The epidemiological evidence comes from within-country studies, between-country studies, and migration studies. Support comes from animal studies and there is evidence of the beneficial effects of reducing serum cholesterol in both primary and secondary prevention of ischemic heart disease.

The within-country studies include the Multiple Risk Factor Trial Intervention (MRFIT) study, which followed 360 000 middle-aged men screened and followed up for CHD mortality. MRFIT showed a strong positive correlation between cholesterol levels at initial screening and later death from CHD. The Framingham Heart Study, started in 1949, is another prospective survey that followed a large cohort of Americans and examined lipid levels and risk of CHD, particularly the relationships between lipoprotein fractions and CHD. It showed a strong association between elevated LDL cholesterol and increased incidence of CHD and an inverse association between HDL cholesterol and CHD risk. Framingham has drawn attention to the value of the ratio of total cholesterol to HDL cholesterol, where a ratio of 3 or less suggests the disease is static and a ratio of 4 or higher suggests the disease is progressive. Framingham also drew attention to the incremental effect of additional risk factors in the development of CHD, such as hypertension, hyperglycemia, and smoking. Combinations of risk factors occur in the metabolic syndrome, in which insulin resistance appears to be the common denominator.

The best known between-country study is the Seven Countries Study by Ancel Keys linking diet, hypercholesterolemia, and CHD. He showed that a plot of each country's median total cholesterol against deaths from CHD was highly correlated. The variations in serum cholesterol were highly correlated with the ratio of saturated to unsaturated fats in the diet.

Studies of migration and CHD include the Ni-Hon-San Study, in which cholesterol levels and CHD rates were compared in Japanese living in Japan, Honolulu, and San Francisco. There was a rise in both cholesterol levels and CHD rates across these groups, suggesting that as Japanese adopted a Western lifestyle their cholesterol increased and their risk of CHD increased.

Evidence that treatment of hyperlipidemia influences CHD is substantial. The methods of treating hyperlipidemia have varied from diet to drugs, surgery, meditation, and multiple risk factor reduction. The conclusion is that treatment of hyperlipidemia improves CHD morbidity and mortality. The Lipid Research Clinics Coronary Primary Prevention Trial, started in the 1970s, examined 4000 men without evidence of CHD but with hypercholesterolemia, randomized to receive cholestyramine or placebo. After 7 years, despite a relatively minor difference in cholesterol levels, there was a 20% decrease in CHD in the drug-treated group.

In the Oslo study, high-risk Norwegian men were given antismoking and dietary advice, resulting in a significant reduction in the incidence of CHD. The effect of partial ileal bypass surgery has been studied in patients who had experienced a myocardial infarction and were hypercholesterolemic (POSCH study). This surgical procedure improved blood lipids and reduced morbidity caused by CHD. In the Scandinavian Simvastatin Survival Study (4S study), patients with CHD and hypercholesterolemia were randomized to receive the HMG-CoA reductase inhibitor simvastatin or placebo. After a 4-year follow-up period, both morbidity and mortality were significantly reduced in the treatment group. This secondary prevention study was followed by a primary prevention study using pravastatin in men with hypercholesterolemia. This study (WOSCOPS study) randomized men without evidence of CHD to treatment with the HMG-CoA reductase inhibitor pravastatin or to placebo and followed them for 4.9 years. Treatment with the drug significantly reduced the incidence of myocardial infarction and death from cardiovascular causes. In the Air Force/Texas Coronary Atherosclerosis Prevention Study, a primary prevention study, subjects with low levels of LDL cholesterol and HDL cholesterol showed a reduced risk of CHD with statins. The Helsinki Heart Study and the Veterans Affairs-HDL Intervention Study used fibrate drugs in patients with low LDL cholesterol and showed impressive increases in HDL cholesterol and reductions in CHD risk. A 1% increase in HDL was equivalent to a 3% decrease in CHD risk.

Studies such as the Cholesterol Lowering Atherosclerosis Study, in which patients were allocated to drug therapy or placebo, used coronary angiography to follow the effect of drugs on disease. A small reduction in cholesterol results in a disproportionately larger reduction in cardiovascular events.

These studies show that it is possible to arrest progress of the disease and, in some cases, bring about regression of atherosclerosis. The extent to which this happens seems to depend on the underlying disease and the degree of cholesterol lowering.

Atherosclerosis has a complex and multifactorial etiology characterized by inflammation. Clinical markers of inflammation include C-reactive protein, modified LDL, homocysteine, lipoprotein (a), and fibrinogen, which are emerging risk factors and may give prognostic information for patient management. Folate may be beneficial by reducing plasma homocysteine, enhancing endothelial nitric oxide, and showing antiinflammatory properties. Other antiinflammatory agents, such as IL-10, may be of benefit.

Classification of Hyperlipidemia

There are a number of classification systems available. In 1967, Fredrickson, Levy, and Lees introduced the first classification as a method of reporting that lipoproteins were raised. The World Health Organization adopted this classification (Table 3).

In 1987, the European Atherosclerosis Society recommended a five-group classification of primary hyperlipidemia (Table 4), and the National Cholesterol Education Program Adult Treatment Panel III published guidelines in 2002 for normal and elevated lipid levels (Table 5).

Clinically, the most important step is to determine if the lipid abnormality is primary or secondary to another condition. Table 6 shows the lipid changes seen in some common conditions. In practice, it is often easiest to classify lipid abnormalities into three

Table 3 Fredrickson/WHO classification of hyperlipoproteinemia

Type	Lipids increased	Lipoprotein increased
I	Triacylglycerol	Chylomicrons
II-a	Cholesterol	LDL
II-b	Cholesterol and triacylglycerol	LDL and VLDL
III	Cholesterol and triacylglycerol	Chylomicron remnants and IDL
IV	Triacylglycerol	VLDL
V	Cholesterol and triacylglycerol	Chylomicrons and VLDL

Table 4 European Atherosclerosis Society classification of hyperlipoproteinemia

Group	Total cholesterol (mmol/l)	Triacylglycerols (mmol/l)
Normal	<5.2	<2.3
A (mild hypercholesterolemia)	5.2–6.5	and <2.3
B (moderate hypercholesterolemia)	6.5–7.8	and <2.3
C (isolated hypertriglyceridemia)	<5.2	and 2.3–5.6
D (combined hyperlipidemia)	5.2–7.8	and 2.3–5.6
E (severe hypercholesterolemia and/or hypertriglyceridemia)	>7.8	and/or >5.6

Table 5 Adult Treatment Panel III levels for blood lipids

Classification	Total cholesterol (mmol/l)	LDL cholesterol (mmol/l)	Triacylglycerols (mmol/l)
Normal	<5.2	<2.59	<1.7
Above optimal	—	2.6–3.3	—
Borderline high	5.2–6.2	3.4–4.1	1.8–2.2
High	>6.2	4.2–4.8	2.3–5.6
Very high	—	>4.9	>5.6

Table 6 Lipid changes in some common conditions

Condition	Total cholesterol	HDL cholesterol	Triacylglycerol
Diabetes mellitus	Normal or ↑	↓	↑
Hypothyroidism	↑	↑	Can be ↑
Chronic renal failure	Normal or ↑	↓	↑
Nephrotic syndrome	↑	Often ↓	Often ↑
Cholestasis[a]	↑	↓	Can be ↑

[a]An abnormal lipoprotein called LpX is present.

categories: raised total cholesterol, raised triacylglycerol, mixed hyperlipidemia.

It is becoming clear that certain lipoprotein patterns are particularly atherogenic. Elevated IDL with increased small, dense LDL particles and low HDL is one such pattern. Classifications based on these patterns may emerge.

Causes of Hypercholesterolemia

Serum cholesterol at birth does not exceed 2.5 mmol/l and is rarely above 4.0 mmol/l in children. The values for adults are given in **Table 5**. A raised cholesterol level, with little or no elevation of triacylglycerol, is usually a result of raised LDL level. Occasionally, a raised HDL level is responsible for high cholesterol, as seen in the familial condition of primary hyper-α-lipoproteinemia. Secondary causes given in **Table 6** include hypothyroidism, nephrotic syndrome, some cases of diabetes mellitus, and cholestasis. Primary causes include polygenic familial hypercholesterolemia, in which several gene abnormalities together with environmental effects serve to raise serum cholesterol. Several genetic loci contribute to increased plasma LDL levels, but there are five specific monogenic disorders that increase LDL: familial hypercholesterolemia (LDL receptor gene), familial ligand-defective apoB-100 (apoB gene), autosomal recessive hypercholesterolemia (ARH gene), sitosterolen (ABCG5 or ABCG8 genes), and cholesterol 7α-hydroxylase deficiency (CYP7A1 gene).

Much less common, but more clearly defined, are the two autosomal conditions of familial combined hyperlipidemia (FCH) and monogenic familial hypercholesterolemia (FH). In FCH, there appears to be an increase in apoB production and thus an increase in serum LDL. Serum VLDL levels are raised in one-third of these subjects with an associated triacylglycerol increase, one-third show increases in LDL, and one-third show increases in LDL and VLDL. Monogenic FH is caused by a defect in the LDL receptor (LDLR). The consequent reduced LDL uptake by cells, particularly in the liver, results in raised LDL and cholesterol levels. There are 683 mutations in the LDLR gene. Of these, 58.9% are missense mutations, 21.1% are minor rearrangements, 13.5% are major rearrangements, and 6.6% are splice site mutations. The majority of mutations are found in two functional domains of the LDLR, the ligand binding domain (42%) and the epidermal growth factor precursor-like domain (47%).

Predominant hypertriglyceridemia may result from raised VLDL or chylomicron levels. Secondary causes include excess alcohol ingestion, obesity and excess carbohydrate intake, diabetes mellitus, renal failure, and pancreatitis. Primary hypertriglyceridemia can be a result of familial combined hypertriglyceridemia, familial endogenous hypertriglyceridemia, or hyperchylomicronemia.

Familial endogenous hypertriglyceridemia results from increased hepatic triacylglycerol production with increased VLDL production. It is associated with obesity, glucose intolerance, and hyperuricemia. Hyperchylomicronemia is a result of inherited or acquired impairment of lipoprotein lipase activity.

Reduced insulin levels in diabetes mellitus impair the activity of lipoprotein lipase, and hyperchylomicronemia can occur. Inherited deficiency of the lipase enzyme is rarely seen, as is deficiency of the apolipoprotein (apoC-II) required to activate the enzyme.

Mixed hyperlipidemia is often a secondary condition. Primary causes include familial combined hyperlipidemia and type III hyperlipidemia (dys-β-lipoproteinemia or broad β disease). Type III hyperlipidemia is associated with the apoE 2/2 phenotype, resulting in impaired recognition of apoE by hepatic receptors and an accumulation of IDL.

Dyslipoproteinemia is a central feature of the metabolic syndrome, which is associated with accelerated atherosclerosis. Visceral obesity, dyslipidemia, insulin resistance, hypertension, and a proinflammatory and prothrombotic state are the main characteristics of this condition. It has been defined by the World Health Organization and the National Cholesterol Education Programme. The worldwide increase in levels of obesity in the developed world may presage an increase in CHD.

Dietary Effects

Principles of Treatment

Treatment of hyperlipidemia is part of the management of CHD risk. This encompasses lifestyle changes, such as stopping smoking, increasing exercise, and modifying diet, as well as management of hypertension. Diet is the cornerstone of treating hyperlipidemia, best delivered by qualified dieticians, involving the whole family.

The main aims of diet are to correct excess calorie intake and to reduce the cholesterol and saturated fat content. Patients with hyperlipidemia can expect to see benefits from diet after 6 weeks and are reviewed every 4 months.

Diet can reduce total cholesterol 8–12%, with 60–80% of this change attributed to reductions in saturated fatty acid intake. The remaining change comes from reduced dietary cholesterol and changes in the intake of fiber and monounsaturated and polyunsaturated fatty acids. Dietary modification may not be successful in some primary hyperlipidemias. The Diet and Reinfarction Trial and the Mediterranean Diet Study in postmyocardial infarction survivors showed that dietary modification, not necessarily accompanied by plasma cholesterol lowering, can improve short-term prognosis.

Fat Most of the saturated fats in the diet come from just four fatty acids: lauric acid (C12:0), myristic acid (C14:0), palmitic acid (C16:0), and stearic acid (C18:0). The first three fatty acids reduce LDL receptor activity, raising LDL and total cholesterol by approximately 0.25 mmol/l per 10 g of saturated

fat ingested. Watts and coworkers showed that total dietary fat (mainly saturated) increases hepatic VLDL-apoB secretion, so decreasing total fat intake should decrease hepatic apoB secretion.

Monounsaturates are being recommended more often. The most common is oleic acid (C18:1), found in the Mediterranean diet as olive oil. Animal fats are rich in monounsaturates but are also rich in saturated fats. The *trans* isomers of monounsaturates may raise total and LDL cholesterol and are best avoided.

In both type I and type V hyperlipidemia, the dietary management is to reduce fat intake to 20–40 g/day. Medium-chain triacylglycerols are used and fish oils can be tried, but the mainstay of therapy is reduced fat intake. Dietary β-sitosterol can block cholesterol absorption to a limited extent but is not used therapeutically.

Carbohydrate and calories Obesity is a common cause of hypertriglyceridemia due to raised VLDL levels in the obese subject. This may be because of an increase in insulin resistance resulting from obesity with concomitant hyperinsulinemia and elevation in hepatic VLDL synthesis. Some hypertriglyceridemic patients experience a further increase in triacylglycerol levels with an increase in carbohydrate intake, known as carbohydrate induction. This situation is accompanied by an increase in serum insulin levels. With weight reduction, the hypertryglyceridemia reduces and HDL cholesterol increases after 24 months.

Mild alcohol ingestion increases HDL cholesterol. Excess alcohol ingestion can precipitate hypertriglyceridemia of a type IV phenotype due to increased hepatic synthesis and secretion that, in subjects who cannot clear triacylglycerols efficiently, can progress to a type V phenotype. Serum LDL levels are usually low in alcoholics, although in some individuals they can be elevated.

Protein Changes in dietary protein intake have minimal effects on lipid levels. Vegetarians have lower serum lipids than nonvegetarians, but it is not clear how much of this is the result of a change from animal to vegetable protein.

Fiber Soluble fiber such as oat bran and guar lower cholesterol levels, perhaps by reducing bile acid absorption.

Recommendations

The National Food Survey 1999 showed that the total amount of fat in the British diet decreased from 93 g/day in the1980s to 75 g/day in 1998 and so fat now contributes approximately 40% of calories, of which 15–20% comes from saturated fat. Cholesterol intake in the diet is approximately 500 mg/day. The American Heart Association (AHA) has recommended a two-step approach to dietary change, outlined in **Table 7**, and European recommendations for the diet of the population are shown in **Table 8**. The central approach of dietary

Table 7 American Heart Association dietary recommendations

Nutrient	Recommendations (% of total calories)	
	AHA step 1	AHA step 2
Total fat	<30	<30
Fatty acids		
Saturated fat	<10	<7
Polyunsaturated fatty acid	<10	<10
Monounsaturated fatty acids	10–15	10–15
Carbohydrates	50–60	50–60
Protein	10–20	10–20
Cholesterol	<300 mg/day	<200 mg/day
Reduce total calories to achieve and maintain desirable weight		

From Denke MA (1994) Diet and lifestye modification and its relationship to atherosclerosis. *Medical Clinics of North America: Lipid* Disorders **78**: 197–223.

Table 8 Intermediate and ultimate nutrient goals for Europe

	Intermediate goals		Ultimate goal
	General population	Cardiovascular high-risk group	
Percentage of total energy[a] derived from			
Complex carbohydrates[b]	>40	>45	45–55
Protein	12–13	12–13	12–13
Sugar	10	10	10
Total fat	35	30	20–30
Saturated fat	15	10	10
P:S ratio[c]	≥0.5	≥1.0	≥1.0
Cholesterol (mg/day)	<300	<300	<300
Fiber (g/day)	30	>30	>30
Salt (g/day)	7–8	5	5

[a]All values given refer to alcohol-free total energy intake.
[b]The complex carbohydrate data are implications of the other recommendations.
[c]The ratio of polyunsaturated to saturated fatty acids.
From Pyorala K, De Backer G, Graham I, Poole-Wilson P, and Wood D (1994) Prevention of coronary heart disease in clinical practice. Recommedations of the Task Force of the European Society of Cardiology, European Atherosclerosis Society and the European Society of Hypertension. *European Heart Journal* **15**: 1300–1331.

therapy is to reduce cholesterol-raising fatty foods, reduce cholesterol intake, and achieve a desirable body weight. The AHA step 1 diet can reduce total cholesterol by 0.5–1.0 mmol/l and the step 2 diet can provide a further 0.2–0.4 mmol/l reduction. Saturated fat in the diet is best replaced by increasing complex carbohydrates, with modest increases in monounsaturated and ω-6 polyunsaturated fatty acids. Increased fish oil intake giving additional ω-3 fatty acids will reduce triacylglycerol levels (but increase LDL cholesterol in certain patients).

Although a low-fat, high-carbohydrate, energy-deficient diet may be used for weight reduction in obese subjects, increasing evidence suggests that increased carbohydrate may not be desirable. Recently, a low-carbohydrate, high-protein, high-fat diet (the Atkins diet) has become popular. Although current studies are promising, the long-term effects of this diet are unknown and it is not currently recommended. Fresh fruit, vegetables, and fiber are encouraged.

See also: **Cholesterol**: Sources, Absorption, Function and Metabolism; Factors Determining Blood Levels. **Dietary Fiber**: Physiological Effects and Effects on Absorption; Potential Role in Etiology of Disease; Role in Nutritional Management of Disease. **Fats and Oils. Fatty Acids**: Metabolism; Monounsaturated; Omega-3 Polyunsaturated; Omega-6 Polyunsaturated; Saturated; *Trans* Fatty Acids. **Hyperlipidemia**: Overview. **Lipids**: Chemistry and Classification; Composition and Role of Phospholipids. **Vitamin E**: Metabolism and Requirements; Physiology and Health Effects.

Further Reading

De Backer G, Ambrosioni E, Borch-Johnsen K *et al.* (2003) European guidelines on cardiovascular disease prevention in clinical practice. Third Joint Task Force of European and Other Societies on Cardiovascular Disease in Clinical Practice. *European Journal of Cardiovascular Prevention and Rehabilitation* 10(supplement 1): S1–S78.

Denke MA (1994) Diet and lifestyle modification and its relationship to atherosclerosis. *Medical Clinics of North America: Lipid Disorders* 78: 197–223.

Durrington PN (2004) *Hyperlipidaemia: Diagnosis and Management.* London: Hodder Arnold.

Ginsberg HN (1994) Lipoprotein metabolism and its relationship to atherosclerosis. *Medical Clinics of North America: Lipid Disorders* 78: 1–20.

Grundy SM (1992) Etiologies and treatment of hyperlipidemia. In: Willerson JT (ed.) *Treatment of Heart Disease*, pp. 4.1–4.79. London: Gower Medical.

Marais AD (2004) Familial hypercholesterolaemia. *Clinical and Biochemical Reviews* 25: 49–68.

National Cholesterol Education Program (2002) *Third Report of the Expert Panel on Detection, Evaluation and Treatment of High Blood Cholesterol in Adults (Adult Treatment Panel III)*, NIH Publication No. 02-5215. Bethesda, MD: National Heart, Lung and Blood Institute.

Pyorala K, De Backer G, Graham I, Poole-Wilson P, and Wood D (1994) Prevention of coronary heart disease in clinical practice. Recommendations of the Task Force of the European Society of Cardiology, European Atherosclerosis Society and the European Society of Hypertension. *European Heart Journal* **15**: 1300–1331.

Scandinavian Simvastatin Survival Study Group (1994) Randomised trial of cholesterol lowering in 4444 patients with coronary heart disease: The Scandinavian Simvastatin Survival Study (4S). *Lancet* **344**: 1383–1389.

Shepherd J, Cobbe SM, Ford I *et al.* (1995) Prevention of coronary heart disease with pravastatin in men with hypercholesterolaemia. *New England Journal of Medicine* **333**: 1301–1307.

Steinberg D, Parthasarathy S, Carew TE, Khoo JC, and Witztum JL (1989) Beyond cholesterol. Modifications of low-density lipoproteins that increase its atherogenicity. *New England Journal of Medicine* **320**: 915–924.

Sullivan DR, Celermajer DS, Le Couteur DG, and Lam CWK (2004) The vascular implications of post-prandial lipoprotein metabolism. *Clinical and Biochemical Reviews* **25**: 19–30.

Watts GF and Burnett JR (2004) HDL revisited: New opportunities for managing dyslipoproteinaemia and cardiovascular disease. *Clinical and Biochemical Reviews* **25**: 7–18.

Watts GF, Moroz P, and Barrett PHR (2000) Kinetics of very-low-density lipoprotein apolipoprotein B-100 in normolipidaemic subjects: Pooled analysis of stable-isotope studies. *Metabolism* **49**: 1204–1210.

Nutritional Management

A H Lichtenstein, Tufts University, Boston, MA, USA

Introduction

There is a wide range of dietary approaches purported to decrease the risk of developing cardiovascular disease (CVD). Some were first identified early in the twentieth century while others have been recognized more recently. None are without controversy as to their absolute and relative efficacy. Some of this controversy is more likely attributable to biological variation among individuals (e.g., genetics, gender), interaction among putative dietary factors (e.g., per cent of energy as fat relative to carbohydrate), and differences in environmental factors (e.g., body weight, level of physical activity) than actual differences in whether they are effective modalities or not. This chapter will present current trends in dietary approaches to the prevention and management of CVD.

Surrogate Markers of CVD Risk

It is difficult, if not impossible, to directly assess the effect of any dietary intervention on CVD risk because the natural course of the disease frequently is as long or longer than the productive research life span of the scientists designing and implementing the studies. Hence, most dietary interventions aimed at reducing CVD risk are evaluated on the basis of surrogate markers of disease. However, as with dietary variables thought to be efficacious in decreasing CVD risk, the number of surrogate markers purported to be predictive of CVD has likewise multiplied in the past two decades. The relative importance of each has yet to be sorted out.

Traditionally, total cholesterol, high-density lipoprotein (HDL) cholesterol, and triacylglycerol (triglyceride) levels were measured directly. Low-density lipoprotein (LDL) levels were calculated using the 'Friedewald formula' (LDL cholesterol = total cholesterol − HDL cholesterol − (triglyceride/5)). Reliable automated direct assays for LDL cholesterol are now available and obviate the need for this calculation. Also potentially important in estimating changes in CVD risk as a function of dietary intervention are changes in the levels of lipoprotein (a) (Lp(a)), homocysteine, C-reactive protein (and other markers of inflammation), LDL particle size, hematologic factors, apolipoprotein genotypes, insulin and glucose levels, HDL subspecies, and remnant-like particles. No doubt in the near future the relative importance of each will be clarified and others will emerge.

Dietary Lipid: Approaches to the Prevention and Management of CVD

Level of Dietary Fat

Dietary fat serves as a major energy source for humans. One gram of fat contributes 9 cal, a little more than twice that contributed by protein or carbohydrate ($4\,\mathrm{cal\,g^{-1}}$) and somewhat more than that contributed by alcohol ($7\,\mathrm{cal\,g^{-1}}$). When considering the importance of the level of dietary fat with respect to CVD prevention and management there are two major factors to consider; the impact on plasma lipoprotein profiles and body weight. The potential relationship with body weight is important because of secondary effects on plasma lipids, blood pressure, dyslipidemia, and type 2 diabetes, all potential risk factors for CVD.

With respect to the effect of the level of dietary fat on plasma lipoprotein profiles, the focus is usually on triglyceride and HDL cholesterol levels or total cholesterol to HDL cholesterol ratios. Evidence indicates that when body weight is maintained at a constant level, decreasing the total fat content of the diet, expressed as a per cent of total energy, and replacing it with carbohydrate results in an increase in triglyceride levels, decrease in HDL cholesterol levels, and a less favorable (higher) total cholesterol/HDL cholesterol ratio. Low HDL cholesterol levels are an independent risk factor for CVD. Low fat diets are of particular concern in diabetic or overweight individuals who tend to have low HDL cholesterol levels.

With respect to the effect of the level of dietary fat on body weight two reviews of the long-term data published on the relationship between per cent of energy from fat and body weight have concluded that even a relatively large downward shift in dietary fat intake (approximately 10% of energy) resulted in only modest weight loss of 1.0 kg over a 12-month period in normal weight subjects and 3 kg in overweight or obese subjects. Some evidence suggests that dietary fiber content may be a mitigating factor. That is, substituting fruits, vegetables, and whole grains for fat instead of fat-free cookies, cakes, and snack foods may be more efficacious in promoting weight loss within the context of low-fat diets. The area of dietary fat and obesity is clearly complex. However, it is important to note that in those long-term studies where patients achieved a drastic reduction in dietary fat intake, in no case was weight gain reported.

Type of Fat

Studies done in the mid-1960s demonstrated that changes in the dietary fatty acid profiles altered plasma total cholesterol levels in most individuals.

As analytical techniques became more sophisticated, data on lipid, lipoprotein, and apolipoprotein levels routinely became available. Although many studies have confirmed these early observations, inconsistencies among the more recent results are not rare. These inconsistencies, when they do occur, are attributable to differences among the experimental diets, such as the magnitude or type of dietary perturbation, length of study period, habituation to nutrient intakes prior to the start of the study period, and the background diet on which the dietary variable was superimposed, as well as differences among experimental subjects, such as in age, sex, genetics, efficiency of cholesterol absorption, and initial blood lipid concentrations.

Saturated Fatty Acids

Early evidence demonstrated that the consumption of foods relatively high in saturated fatty acids (SFAs) increased plasma total cholesterol levels and that not all SFAs had identical effects. Subsequent work confirmed the hypercholesterolemic effect of SFAs, demonstrated that SFA intake results in an increase in both LDL and HDL cholesterol levels, and reaffirmed that not all SFAs have the same effect. Short-chain fatty acids (6:0 to 10:0) and stearic acid (18:0) produce little or no change in blood cholesterol levels, whereas SFAs with intermediate chain lengths (lauric (12:0) to palmitic (16:0) acids) appear to be the most potent in increasing blood cholesterol levels (**Table 1**). It has been postulated that stearic acid (18:0) is not absorbed or is rapidly converted to oleic acid (18:1), and for this reason has a relatively neutral effect on blood cholesterol levels. The underlying mechanism by which fatty

Table 1 Dietary fatty acids

Code	Common name	Formula
Saturated		
12:0	Lauric acid	$CH_3(CH_2)_{10}COOH$
14:0	Myristic acid	$CH_3(CH_2)_{12}COOH$
16:0	Palmitic acid	$CH_3(CH_2)_{14}COOH$
18:0	Stearic acid	$CH_3(CH_2)_{16}COOH$
Monounsaturated		
16:1n-7 *cis*	Palmitoleic acid	$CH_3(CH_2)_5CH{=}(c)CH(CH_2)_7COOH$
18:1n-9 *cis*	Oleic acid	$CH_3(CH_2)_7CH{=}(c)CH(CH_2)_7COOH$
18:1n-9 *trans*	Elaidic acid	$CH_3(CH_2)_7CH{=}(t)CH(CH_2)_7COOH$
Polyunsaturated		
18:2n-6,9 all *cis*	Linoleic acid	$CH_3(CH_2)_4CH{=}(c)CHCH_2CH{=}(c)CH(CH_2)_7COOH$
18:3n-3,6,9 all *cis*	α-Linolenic acid	$CH_3CH_2CH{=}(c)CHCH_2CH{=}(c)CHCH_2CH{=}(c)CH(CH_2)_7COOH$
18:3n-6,9,12 all *cis*	γ-Linolenic acid	$CH_3(CH_2)_4CH{=}(c)CHCH_2CH{=}(c)CHCH_2CH{=}(c)CH(CH_2)_4COOH$
20:4n-6,9,12,15 all *cis*	Arachidonic acid	$CH_3(CH_2)_4CH{=}(c)CHCH_2CH{=}(c)CHCH_2CH{=}(c)CHCH_2CH{=}(c)CH(CH_2)_3COOH$
20:5n-3,6,9,12,15 all *cis*	Eicosapentenoic acid	$CH_3(CH_2CH{=}(c)CH)_5(CH_2)_3COOH$
22:6n-3,6,9,12,15,18 all *cis*	Docosahexenoic acid	$CH_3(CH_2CH{=}(c)CH)_6(CH_2)_2COOH$

acids with 10 or fewer carbon atoms have different effects from those with 12–16 carbons is unknown.

When SFAs displace carbohydrate in the diet, total cholesterol levels increase (**Figure 1**). SFAs tend to be solid at room temperature. Notable exceptions are the tropical oils (palm, palm kernel, and coconut), which are liquid at room temperature because they have high levels of short-chain SFAs. Efforts to reduce dietary SFA intakes should include use of lean meat, the trimming of excess fat and skin from poultry, limiting portion size, and the substituting of non-fat and low-fat dairy products for their full-fat counterparts. The judicious use of ingredient listings and nutrient labels on processed foods will also help achieve the goal of reducing the SFA intakes.

Unsaturated Fatty Acids

Unsaturated fatty acids are fatty acids that contain one or more double bonds in the acyl chain. As the name implies, monounsaturated fatty acids (MUFAs) have one double bond and polyunsaturated fatty acids (PUFAs) have two or more double bonds. The majority of double bonds in fatty acids occurring in food are in the *cis* configuration, that is, the hydrogen atoms attached to the carbons forming the double bond are on the same side of the acyl chain. Alternatively, some double bonds occur in the *trans* configuration, that is, the hydrogen atoms attached to the carbons forming the double bond are on the opposite side of the acyl chain. This part of the discussion of unsaturated fatty acids will be restricted to those containing *cis* double bonds.

Relative to SFAs, MUFAs and PUFAs lower both LDL and HDL cholesterol levels. The absolute magnitude of the change is greater for LDL cholesterol than HDL cholesterol. Most of the data suggest that MUFAs have a slightly smaller effect than PUFAs in lowering both LDL and HDL cholesterol levels so that the change in the total cholesterol/HDL

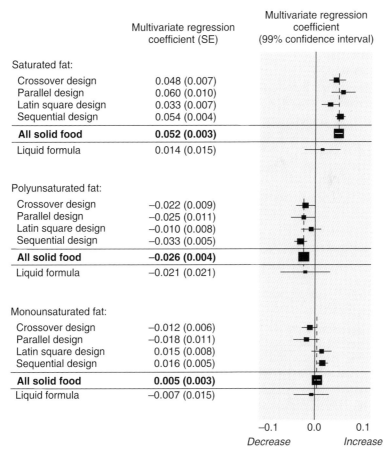

	Multivariate regression coefficient (SE)	Multivariate regression coefficient (99% confidence interval)
Saturated fat:		
Crossover design	0.048 (0.007)	
Parallel design	0.060 (0.010)	
Latin square design	0.033 (0.007)	
Sequential design	0.054 (0.004)	
All solid food	**0.052 (0.003)**	
Liquid formula	0.014 (0.015)	
Polyunsaturated fat:		
Crossover design	−0.022 (0.009)	
Parallel design	−0.025 (0.011)	
Latin square design	−0.010 (0.008)	
Sequential design	−0.033 (0.005)	
All solid food	**−0.026 (0.004)**	
Liquid formula	−0.021 (0.021)	
Monounsaturated fat:		
Crossover design	−0.012 (0.006)	
Parallel design	−0.018 (0.011)	
Latin square design	0.015 (0.008)	
Sequential design	0.016 (0.005)	
All solid food	**0.005 (0.003)**	
Liquid formula	−0.007 (0.015)	

−0.1   0.0   0.1
Decrease   *Increase*

Change in total blood cholesterol
(mmol l⁻¹ per 1% increase in total calories)

Figure 1 Change in total cholesterol when each fatty acid class displaces carbohydrate from the diet. (Reproduced from Clarke R, Frost C, Collins R, Appleby P, and Peto R (1997) Dietary lipids and blood cholesterol: quantitative meta-analysis of metabolic ward studies. *British Medical Journal* **314**: 112–117.)

cholesterol ratio (decrease) is similar. Because of the changes in plasma lipids and lipoproteins caused when unsaturated fat displaces SFAs from the diet, such a shift should be encouraged in the prevention and management of CVD.

MUFAs The major MUFA in the diet is oleic acid (18:1) (**Table 1**). Vegetable oils high in MUFAs include canola (rapeseed) and olive oils. Fat from meats are also relatively high in MUFAs but unlike vegetable oils, they also contain relatively high levels of SFA, hence would not be recommended as good sources of MUFAs. When MUFAs displace carbohydrate in the diet, there is little effect on total cholesterol levels (**Figure 1**). When MUFAs displace SFA in the diet, total cholesterol levels tend to decrease.

PUFAs There is a wider range of PUFAs than MUFAs in the diet. Dietary PUFAs vary on the basis of chain length, degree of saturation (number of double bonds), and position of the double bond(s) (positional isomers). Two positional isomers of interest with respect to diet and CVD risk are n-6 and n-3 (**Table 1**). The distinction is made on the basis of the location of the first double bond counting from the methyl end of the fatty acyl chain (as opposed to the carboxyl end). If the first double bond is six carbons from the methyl end, the fatty acid is classified as an n-6 fatty acid. If the first double bond is three carbons from the methyl end the fatty acid is classified as an n-3 fatty acid. When PUFAs displace carbohydrate in the diet, total cholesterol levels decrease (**Figure 1**). Vegetable oils high in PUFA include soy bean, corn, sunflower, and safflower oils. The major n-6 PUFA in the diet is linoleic acid (18:2n-6); other n-6 PUFAs, such as γ-linolenic acid (18:3 n-6) and arachidonic acid (20:4n-6), occur in smaller amounts but are important biologically.

n-3 fatty acids Quantitatively, the major n-3 PUFA in the diet is α-linolenic acid (18:3n-3). Major dietary sources include soy bean and canola oils. Two other n-3 PUFAs are eicosapentenoic acid (EPA, 20:5n-3) and docosahexenoic acid (DHA, 22:6n-3) and are sometimes referred to as very long-chain n-3 fatty acids (**Table 1**). The major source of these fatty acids is marine oils found in fish. Dietary intakes of very long-chain n-3 fatty acids are associated with decreased risk of heart disease and stroke (**Figure 2**). Interventions studies have substantiated these findings. The beneficial effects of EPA and DHA are attributed to decreased ventricular fibrillation resulting in decreased sudden death, and decreased triglyceride levels, platelet aggregation, and blood pressure.

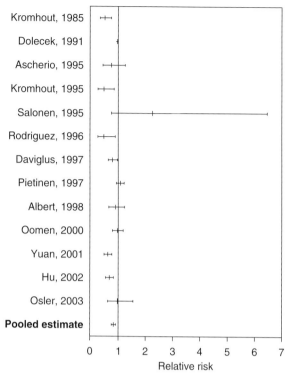

Figure 2 Mean relative risk of coronary heart disease for those consuming any amount of fish versus those reporting none. (Reproduced from Whelton SP, He J, Whelton PK, and Muntner P (2004) Meta-analysis of observational studies on fish intake and coronary heart disease. *American Journal of Cardiology* **93**: 1119–1123.)

Trans-Fatty Acids

Trans-fatty acids, by definition, contain at least one double bond in the *trans* configuration (**Figure 3**). Dietary *trans*-fatty acids occur naturally in meat and dairy products as a result of anaerobic bacterial fermentation in ruminant animals. *Trans*-fatty acids are also introduced into the diet as a result of the consumption of hydrogenated vegetable or fish oils. Hydrogenation results in a number of changes in the fatty acyl chain: the conversion of *cis* to *trans* double bonds, the saturation of double bonds, and the migration of double bonds along the acyl chain, resulting in multiple positional isomers. Oils are primarily hydrogenated to increase viscosity (change a liquid oil into a semiliquid or solid) and extend shelf life (decrease susceptibility to oxidation). The major source of dietary *trans*-fatty acids worldwide is from hydrogenated fat, primarily in products made from this, such as commercially fried foods and baked goods.

Since the early 1990s attention has been focused on the effects of *trans*-fatty acids on specific lipoprotein fractions. The findings of this work have suggested that, similar to saturated fatty acids,

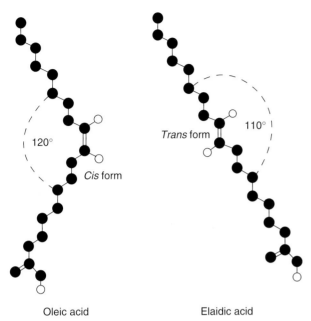

Oleic acid   Elaidic acid

Figure 3 Geometric isomers of 18:1n-9 (oleic and elaidic acids).

trans-fatty acids result in increased LDL cholesterol levels. In contrast to saturated fatty acids, they do not raise HDL cholesterol levels. The changes result in a less favorable LDL cholesterol:HDL cholesterol ratio, with respect to CVD risk (**Figure 4**). A trend towards increased triglyceride levels is frequently reported. Some research has also suggested that *trans*-fatty acids may increase Lp(a) levels. Levels of Lp(a) tend to be positively correlated with risk of developing CVD. However, at this time it appears that the magnitude of increase in Lp(a) levels

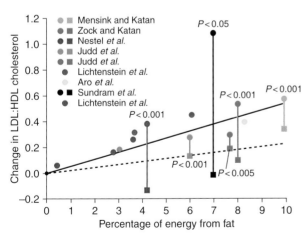

Figure 4 Change in LDL:HDL cholesterol ratio in response to *trans*-fatty acids (solid line) and saturated fatty acids (dashed line). (Reproduced from Ascherio A, Katan MB, Zock PL, Stampfer MJ, and Willett WC (1999) *Trans* fatty acids and coronary heart disease. *New England Journal of Medicine* **340**: 1994–1998.)

reported is not within the physiological range that would be predicted to increase CVD risk.

Recent estimates from 14 Western European countries report *trans*-fatty acid intakes ranging from 0.8% (Greece) to 1.9% (Iceland) of energy in women and 0.5% (Greece and Italy) to 2.1% (Iceland) of energy in men. Data collected in the US and Canada suggest average *trans*-fatty acid intakes ranging from 1% to 2.5% of energy. By way of contrast, estimates of saturated fat intake range from 10% to 19% per cent of energy.

Dietary Cholesterol

The observation that dietary cholesterol increased blood cholesterol levels and was associated with the development of arteriosclerosis was originally made early in the 20th century in rabbits. In humans, a positive correlation has been repeatedly observed between dietary cholesterol and both blood cholesterol levels and CVD risk, although relative to SFA, the effect is modest. Whether the increase in plasma cholesterol levels induced by dietary cholesterol is linear or curvilinear, or whether there is a break point or threshold/ceiling relationship beyond which individuals are no longer responsive, remains to be determined. With few exceptions, dietary cholesterol is present in foods of animal origin. Therefore, restricting saturated fat intake is likely to result in a decrease in dietary cholesterol.

Other Dietary Approaches for the Prevention and Management of CVD

Very Low-Fat/High-Carbohydrate Diet and High-Protein/Low-Carbohydrate Diet

When considering diets very low in fat and high in carbohydrates ('very low-fat' diets), it is important to separate the effects of the composition of the diet from confounding factors associated with intentional weight loss. For the purposes of this discussion, a very low-fat diet will be defined as less than 15% of energy as fat. Consumption of a very low-fat diet without a decrease in energy intake frequently decreases blood total, LDL, and HDL cholesterol levels and increases the total cholesterol:HDL cholesterol ratio (less favorable) and triglyceride levels. A mitigating factor may be the type of carbohydrate providing the bulk of the dietary energy: complex (whole grains, fruits, and vegetables) or simple (fat-free cookies and ice cream). The reason for this later observation has yet to be investigated. Notwithstanding these considerations, for this reason moderate fat intakes, ranging from <30% to 25 to 35% of energy as fat, are currently recommended to optimize lipoprotein profiles with respect to decreasing CVD risk.

Current interest in the area of weight loss is centered on high-protein/low-carbohydrate (high protein) diets. Recently, high-protein diets were shown to result in significantly more weight loss than standard reduced energy diets and were accompanied by more favorable blood lipid profiles (lower triglyceride, higher HDL cholesterol levels). However, by 1 year the advantage in terms of weight loss attributed to the high-protein diet did not persist (**Table 2**). The major concern with high-protein diets is that in the absence of steady weight loss the higher intakes of saturated fat and cholesterol can ultimately have an adverse effect on LDL cholesterol levels. Ongoing work will most likely resolve some of these issues.

Fiber

Dietary soluble fiber, primarily β-glucan, has been reported to have a modest independent effect on decreasing blood total and LDL cholesterol levels. A meta-analysis concluded that 3 g of soluble fiber (equivalent of three servings of oatmeal) reduced both total and LDL cholesterol levels approximately $0.13 \, \text{mmol} \, l^{-1}$ (**Figure 5**). Most evidence suggests that soluble fiber exerts its hypocholesterolemic effect by binding bile acids and cholesterol in the intestine, resulting in an increased fecal loss and altered colonic metabolism of bile acids. The fermentation of fiber polysaccharides in the colon yields short-chain fatty acids. Some evidence suggests that these compounds may have hypocholesterolemic effects via alterations in hepatic metabolism. At this time there is no evidence to suggest that insoluble fiber has an effect on blood lipid levels.

Soy Protein

The potential relationship between soy protein and the risk of developing CVD has a long history dating back to the 1940s. Despite this relatively protracted lead-time attempts at more precisely defining this relationship have been slow in coming and somewhat inconsistent. Renewed interest developed in the relationship between soy protein and blood lipid levels after a meta-analysis was published in the mid-1990s suggesting that soy protein resulted in significant reductions in total and LDL cholesterol levels, with the most pronounced effect in hypercholesterolemic individuals. Changes in HDL cholesterol levels were not significant. Whether the effect on total and LDL cholesterol levels was attributable to the soy protein *per se* or other soybean

derived factor(s), the most likely being the constitutive isoflavones, had yet to be determined. Since then a number of well-controlled studies have re-examined the effect of soy protein and/or isoflavones on blood lipid levels in humans. The results of more recent studies are variable. Declines in LDL cholesterol levels attributable to the substitution of 25–50 g of soy protein for animal protein range from null to small (3–6%) in normocholesterolemic and hypercholesterolemic individuals. Changes in HDL cholesterol levels were highly variable, ranging from −15% to +7%. Soy-derived isoflavones do not appear to have an independent effect on blood lipid levels. On the basis of the most recent data it can be concluded that, although helpful when used to displace products containing animal (saturated) fat from the diet, despite the current claims, individuals should be cautioned against an overreliance on the casual use of soy protein containing foods or the use of isolated isoflavones to control serum lipid levels.

Plant Sterols

Sterols compare for a group of compounds that are essential constituents of cell membranes in animals and plants. Cholesterol is the major sterol of mammalian cells. Phytosterols, such as beta-sitosterol, campesterol, and stigmasterol, are the major sterols of plant cells. In humans, plant sterols are not synthesized, are poorly absorbed, and appear to interfere with cholesterol absorption. It is this later property that has been exploited in the use of these compounds as blood cholesterol-lowering agents. Maximal LDL cholesterol lowering attributable to plant sterols occurs at a dose of about $2 \, \text{g day}^{-1}$ (**Figure 6**). Although a relatively wide range of responses has been reported, the majority of work suggests an expected LDL cholesterol lowering of about 10% in hypercholesterolemic subjects. Plant sterol-enriched margarines and other foods are currently available in some countries. Few side effects of plant sterols have been reported with the exception of decreased levels of circulating carotenoids; the long-term effect of this is unclear at this time but should continue to be monitored carefully.

Antioxidant Nutrients

Considerable interest had been generated in the potential benefit of dietary supplementation with vitamin E and other antioxidant nutrients in reducing CVD risk. Support for this hypothesis came from two sources. First from the epidemiological observations suggesting that vitamin E supplement use was associated with decreased risk of CVD.

Table 2 Summary mean outcomes

| | Carbohydrates in diet (g day^{-1}) | | | | | | | |
| | Lower (≤60) | | | | Higher (>60) | | | |
	No. of diets	No. of participants	Summary mean change (SD)	95% CI	No. of diets	No. of participants	Summary mean change (SD)	95% CI
Weight change (kg)								
All studies, all participants	34	668	−16.9 (0.2)	−16.6, −17.3	130	2092	−1.9 (0.2)	−1.6, −2.2
RCT and R-Cross only	7	132	−3.6 (1.2)	−1.2, −6.0	75	1122	−2.1 (0.3)	−1.6, −2.7
Caloric content of the diet (kcal day^{-1})								
<1500	18	614	−17.5 (0.2)	−17.1, −17.8	45	870	−3.1 (0.4)	−2.4, −3.8
≥1500	16	53	−5.7 (0.2)	−5.4, −6.0	84	1222	−1.5 (0.2)	−1.2, −1.9
Diet duration (days)								
<15	14	72	−13.6 (0.1)	−13.5, −13.8	25	198	−1.5 (0.2)	−1.1, −1.8
16–60	9	142	−5.3 (0.6)	−4.2, −6.4	52	827	−3.5 (0.4)	−2.9, −4.3
>60	10	447	−2.4 (2.1)	+1.8, −6.5	45	968	−1.1 (0.6)	−.01, −2.3
Participant age (years)								
<40	22	426	−17.7 (0.2)	−17.4, −18.1	59	642	−1.4 (0.2)	−1.0, −1.8
≥40	12	242	−5.0 (0.6)	−3.8, −6.2	62	1231	−2.9 (0.3)	−2.4, −3.5
Baseline weight (kg)								
<70	3	22	−19.6 (0.2)	−19.2, −20.0	19	230	−3.2 (0.6)	−1.9, −4.4
70–100	13	365	−0.8 (1.6)	+2.4, −4.0	77	1357	−2.4 (0.4)	−1.3, −0.4
>100	7	138	−6.6 (0.7)	−5.2, −8.0	18	301	−8.1 (0.8)	−6.5, −9.7
BMI (kg/m^{-2}) in all studies, all participants	1	113	−1.4 (4.6)	+7.6, −10.3	27	739	−0.4 (0.4)	+0.3, −1.1
Body fat (%) in all studies, all participants	5	66	−1.0 (5.6)	+4.0, −6.0	27	536	−1.0 (0.6)	+0.1, −2.1

Adapted from Bravata DM, Sanders L, Huang J, Krumholz HM, Olkin I, and Gardner CD (2003) Efficacy and safety of low-carbohydrate diets: a systematic review. *JAMA* **289**: 1837–1850.

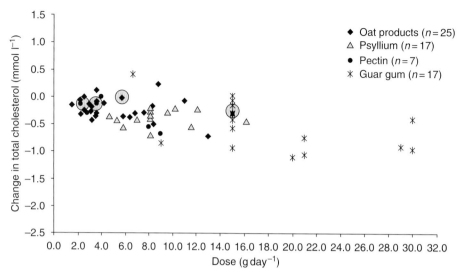

Figure 5 Relationship between fiber intake and change in total cholesterol levels. (Reproduced from Brown L, Rosner B, Willett WW, and Sacks FM (1999) Cholesterol-lowering effects of dietary fiber: a meta-analysis. *American Journal of Clinical Nutrition* **69**: 30–42.)

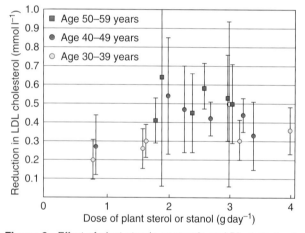

Figure 6 Effect of plant sterols or stanols on LDL cholesterol levels. (Reproduced from Law M (2000) Plant sterol and stanol margarines and health. British Medical Journal **320**: 861–864.)

Second from the *in vitro* work demonstrating that vitamin E in LDL was correlated with decreased susceptibility of the lipoprotein particle to oxidation and that in cell culture oxidized LDL resulted in foam cell formation. A number of recent intervention studies have failed to demonstrate a benefit of vitamin E or other antioxidant vitamins. At this time the data do not support a recommendation to use antioxidant vitamins for the prevention or management of CVD.

Conclusions

The relationship between diet and blood lipid levels has clearly been established. Current data support

dietary recommendations to decrease CVD risk that include restrictions in saturated and *trans*-fatty acids, and cholesterol and to include a source of long-chain n-3 fatty acids. Other dietary approaches to prevent and manage CVD include consuming fiber-rich diets such as that founds in fruits, vegetables, and whole grains. Attainment or maintenance of optimal body weight should be emphasized. All individuals should be encouraged to engage in physical activity daily. These recommendations are the culmination of nearly a century of work. They have evolved slowly. No doubt this evolution, frequently accompanied by debate, will continue into the future. It is important for nutrition scientists to implement current recommendations aimed at optimizing blood lipid levels and favorably affecting newer surrogate markers of CVD risk, and to reassess these recommendations as new findings emerge.

See also: **Antioxidants**: Diet and Antioxidant Defense; Observational Studies; Intervention Studies. **Cholesterol**: Sources, Absorption, Function and Metabolism; Factors Determining Blood Levels. **Dietary Fiber**: Physiological Effects and Effects on Absorption; Potential Role in Etiology of Disease; Role in Nutritional Management of Disease. **Fats and Oils**. **Fatty Acids**: Monounsaturated; Omega-3 Polyunsaturated; Omega-6 Polyunsaturated; Saturated. **Hyperlipidemia**: Overview. **Lipids**: Chemistry and Classification; Composition and Role of Phospholipids. **Lipoproteins**.

Further Reading

Expert Panel on Detection Evaluation and Treatment of High Blood Cholesterol in Adults (2001) Executive Summary of The Third Report of The National Cholesterol Education Program (NCEP) Expert Panel on Detection, Evaluation, And Treatment of High Blood Cholesterol In Adults (Adult Treatment Panel III). *Journal of the American Medical Association* **285**: 2486–2497.

Krauss RM, Eckel RH, Howard B *et al.* (2000) AHA Dietary Guidelines: revision 2000: A statement for healthcare professionals from the Nutrition Committee of the American Heart Association. *Circulation* **102**: 2284–2299.

Brown L, Rosner B, Willett WW, and Sacks FM (1999) Cholesterol-lowering effects of dietary fiber: a meta-analysis. *American Journal of Clinical Nutrition* **69**: 30–42.

Willett WC (1998) Is dietary fat a major determinant of body fat? *American Journal of Clinical Nutrition* **67**: 556S–562S.

Yao M and Roberts SB (2001) Dietary energy density and weight regulation. *Nutrition Reviews* **59**: 247–58.

Kris-Etherton P, Lichtenstein AH, Howard B, and Steinberg D, W JL (2004) Antioxidant vitamin supplements and cardiovascular disease. *Circulation* **110**: 637–641.

Kris-Etherton PM, Harris WS, and Appel LJ (2002) Fish consumption, fish oil, omega-3 fatty acids, and cardiovascular disease. *Circulation* **106**: 2747–57.

Ascherio A, Katan MB, Zock PL, Stampfer MJ, and Willett WC (1999) *Trans* fatty acids and coronary heart disease. *Journal of Medicine* **340**: 1994–1998. New England.

2005 US Dietary Guidelines http://WWW.health.gov/dietaryguidelines/dga2005/document/

HYPERTENSION

Contents
Etiology
Dietary Factors
Nutritional Management

Etiology

T Morgan, University of Melbourne, Melbourne, VIC, Australia
H Brunner, Centre Hospitalier Universitaire Vaudois, Lausanne, Switzerland

Blood pressure (BP) is determined by cardiac output (CO) and total peripheral resistance (TPR):

$$BP = CO \times TPR$$

These variables are controlled in turn by the activity of the autonomic nervous system, regulated by a variety of nuclei in the brain. There is a complex interaction between plasma volume, blood pressure, and a variety of humoral and neural mechanisms that determine blood pressure.

Blood pressure is not, however, a static value. It varies markedly in response to a variety of stimuli. Change of posture activates a variety of controls which keep the pressure relatively constant. Physical and mental activity may be associated with alterations in blood pressure, and there is a marked fall in blood pressure during sleep. Thus, there is no such value as a normal blood pressure based on a single measurement, as blood pressure needs to be related to the circumstances under which it is measured.

Likewise, there is no single blood pressure level that means a person is hypertensive. The present convention is that a blood pressure greater than 140 mmHg systolic or 90 mmHg diastolic on clinic recording makes a person hypertensive. Recently the JNC VII report has stated that patients with a blood pressure >120/80 are prehypertensive. However, blood pressure has a marked circadian variation (**Figure 1**), and an individual could have a blood pressure of

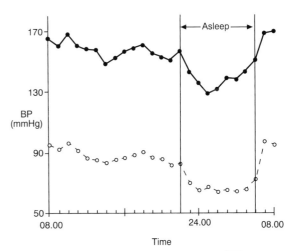

Figure 1 Hourly ambulatory blood pressure (BP) measurements in a 58-year-old man with borderline hypertension. Solid circles, systolic pressure; open circles, diastolic pressure.

150/90 mmHg at 09:00 h and be classified as hypertensive, while at 14:00 h it might be 137/85 mmHg and would be classified as normotensive. Thus in a normal person blood pressure may vary markedly during a day associated with reactive events, but in some people the baseline blood pressure eventually rises to a level that is defined as 'hypertension.' In this person with hypertension there will be fluctuations in blood pressure associated with the same controls as in normal people, but the fluctuations may be exaggerated, leading to high blood pressure levels.

At different times of the day blood pressure is regulated by different systems. Thus, during the day the cardiovascular sympathetics activated by the baroreceptors are important controls of blood pressure. When asleep the cardiovascular sympathetics turn off and blood pressure then appears to be maintained more by the renin angiotensin system. The variability in the activity of systems controlling blood pressure means that in hypertensive patients the response to drugs that act on these systems may have a circadian variation.

The etiology of essential hypertension is unknown; however, the condition is believed to result from an interaction of environmental and genetic factors. Environmental factors are undoubtedly of major importance, because in certain communities hypertension is virtually nonexistent; however, when such a community alters its life style, hypertension becomes common and may exist in 30% of the population. Not all people develop hypertension, and the ones who do are determined by their genetic composition (**Figure 2**). Investigations are under way to attempt to determine which individuals are more likely to develop hypertension and its complications, so that life style and environmental alterations can be initiated to prevent the disease occurring in such people. Certain specific genetic abnormalities have been identified and these cases are then removed from the classification of essential hypertension. It is of interest that the disorders that have been found in general alter sodium handling by the body. These have been either abnormalities in channels or transporters in the nephron that alter sodium excretion, or alternatively defects in circulating hormones that regulate the activity of the renal transporters. Hypertension is not seen in hunter-gatherer communities where sodium intake is low and potassium intake is high, and thus the genetic abnormality is not expressed phenotypically even though the genotype is probably present.

In established hypertension the defect is an increased peripheral resistance rather than an increased cardiac output. However, in people with minor blood pressure elevations and prehypertensive people cardiac output is increased, and it has been postulated that increased cardiac output in response to the retention of sodium

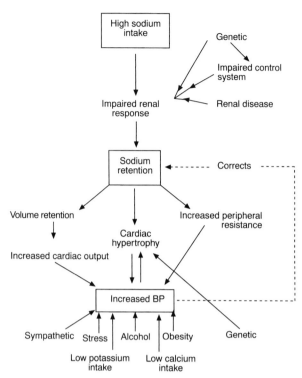

Figure 2 The interrelationships between sodium intake, renal function, hormonal control systems, and genetic inheritance in the etiology of hypertension and cardiac hypertrophy. BP, blood pressure.

is the initial hemodynamic change that leads to hypertension (**Figure 2**). However, experimentally hypertension can be produced without a stage of increased cardiac output, and increased peripheral resistance can result without an antecedent high cardiac output. It is likely that there is heterogeneity in the way people respond. The concept of an increased cardiac output leading to hypertension has been extensively developed by Guyton in a variety of computer and experimental models. However, in carefully conducted studies in which blood volume was measured in hypertensive patients, blood volume was decreased rather than increased, making this theory probably not applicable to all people. The relationship with sodium is also complicated. In young hypertensive subjects there is a better inverse correlation with total body potassium rather than a direct correlation with total body sodium content. In older people the correlation with body sodium content becomes more pronounced. The lack of a direct correlation between body sodium and hypertension in the young casts doubt on the absoluteness of the link between sodium and hypertension, and clearly potassium has an important effect modulating the response.

It has been suggested that the prime defect leading to increased peripheral resistance is the presence of a circulating factor that inhibits (Na^+-K^+)-ATPase

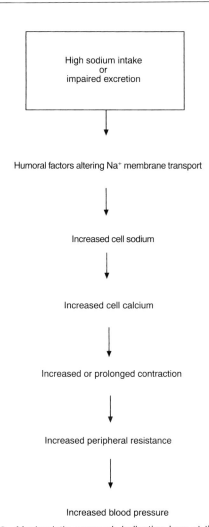

Figure 3 Mechanistic approach indicating how at the cellular level a high sodium intake may initiate the series of events leading to increased peripheral resistance and a high blood pressure.

activity, thereby increasing the sodium content of cells (**Figure 3**). This increased sodium content decreases the rate at which calcium can be removed from the cell by the Na^+-Ca^{2+} countertransport. In skeletal and cardiac muscle cells the contractile response is triggered by a small influx of Ca^{2+} that releases Ca^{2+} from the endoplasmic reticulum. The response is terminated by reuptake of Ca^{2+} into the endoplasmic reticulum and thus the Na^+-Ca^{2+} countertransport is not of critical importance, though in all cells the basal level and total content of calcium may be increased. In smooth muscle cells, including the arteriolar (resistance vessels) cells, contraction is initiated by entry of calcium across the cell membrane. If there is a defect in calcium removal by the Na^+-Ca^{2+} countertransport contraction will be prolonged, and if the basal level of cellular calcium is higher contraction may be more intense. Thus, peripheral resistance rises and hypertension results. All the physiological factors to support the above have been identified. However, despite intensive research it is unclear if a true circulating physiological factor capable of inhibiting $(Na^+$-$K^+)$-ATPase has been identified. Claims have been made for an ouabain-like factor in plasma and the hypothalamus, but there is skepticism whether this is the important physiological variable. In hypertensive patients cell sodium levels are elevated. This elevation need not necessarily be due to inhibition of $(Na^+$-$K^+)$-ATPase but could result from an increased entry of sodium into the cell down its electrochemical gradient by a variety of channels or transporters. There is evidence that abnormalities of these exist and are more prevalent in hypertensive people. There is also evidence that the rate of entry of Na^+ can be increased by a high sodium intake and that a circulating but unidentified factor may be increased. The signal for release of such a factor is unclear and does not appear to be plasma sodium concentration and probably not total plasma volume. It may be modulated by the kidney and related to 'turnover' of sodium.

The body can control plasma sodium concentration (by antidiuretic hormone) and plasma volume and total body sodium within well-defined limits, despite large variations (20–400 mmol) in daily sodium chloride intake. This control involves a variety of humoral factors (**Table 1**). Renin-angiotensin, aldosterone, atrial natriuretic peptide, sympathetic activity, and other variables are all altered by changes in sodium chloride and/or potassium intake. The capacity of these systems to respond maintains blood pressure in the 'normal' range. It is only when this capacity is exceeded that blood pressure becomes elevated. The increase in blood pressure will also correct the body sodium because the kidney has a sensitive 'pressure natriuresis response'. Thus, in most people as blood pressure rises sodium is excreted; this self-correction ensures that blood pressure does not rise to excessive levels. It has been suggested that in addition to high sodium intake and abnormalities of sodium handling by cells there must be a defect in the pressure natriuresis response. This could be due to

Table 1 Factors altering sodium balance

Variable	Site of action
Increases Na$^+$ retention	
Angiotensin II	Proximal tubule
	Increases aldosterone
Aldosterone	Distal nephron
Sympathetic	Proximal tubule
	Hemodynamics
Increases Na$^+$ excretion	
Atrial peptide	Proximal tubule
	Distal nephron
Parathyroid hormone	Proximal nephron
Natriuretic hormone (?)	Loop of Henle, plus others
Elevated blood pressure	Hemodynamics

excessive amounts of circulating hormones (aldosterone) or defective control systems in the kidney. The pressure natriuresis response may also be defective owing to reduction in nephron number following developmental problems or disease, or associated with the aging process. An association has been found between the weight of children at birth and subsequent development of hypertension and cardiovascular disease. The low birthweight could be due to defective nutritional intake of the mother or to diseases that affect fetal and placental growth. It has been suggested that the total nephron number is reduced, and that this alters sodium handling and causes hypertension.

Much research has focused on the importance of dietary sodium chloride, but there needs to be an associated genetic defect which may be a subtle defect in the systems controlling sodium excretion. Thus, the defect may be an inability of the renin–angiotensin–aldosterone system to suppress adequately or appropriately for that level of sodium intake. There is evidence from twin studies that the suppressibility of renin secretion is genetically determined and thus in some people there are inappropriate levels of angiotensin II for their level of sodium intake, resulting in hypertension. There are changes in secretion or response of renin, aldosterone, adrenaline, sympathetic activity, atrial peptide, and nitric oxide with increase in sodium intake. In most cases these responses are appropriate and prevent the unfettered rise in blood pressure. However, the ability to respond may be exceeded and blood pressure then rises.

Hemodynamics

As discussed above, it is unlikely that all people go through an increased cardiac output stage. Well-established hypertensive patients have high peripheral resistance and a normal cardiac output, but there are exceptions. The hypertension process itself causes significant alterations in hemodynamics affecting both the heart and the blood vessels, and reversal of these effects may be as important as reducing blood pressure (**Figure 4**).

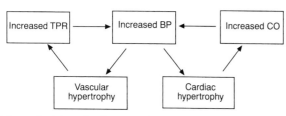

Figure 4 Interaction between the various parameters that control blood pressure, showing how they set up a positive feedback leading to worsening blood pressure. BP, blood pressure; CO, cardiac output; TPR, total peripheral resistance.

Early in the hypertensive process there is an increase in the thickness of the arteriolar muscle wall. This is probably a compensatory process which returns the wall tension to normal. Contrary to expectations, compliance of larger arteries is normal or increased in young hypertensive patients. However, the thickening of the resistance vessels, depending on the way it takes place, has certain consequences, and for a similar degree of muscle contraction there is a greater increase in vascular tone and thus peripheral resistance rises more, leading to a higher blood pressure, greater wall tension, and a further increase in vessel thickness. This is a positive feedback response and a vicious cycle may result (**Figure 4**). In the early hypertensive process the systolic and diastolic blood pressures rise more or less in parallel. However, in the older hypertensive patient the pulse pressure widens, due probably to increased stiffness of the arteries. This increased stiffness, which is associated with a loss of elastin and an increase in collagen, has important effects on the heart.

The endothelium of blood vessels is a major regulator of vascular tone and an important mechanism is the production of nitric oxide. If nitric oxide is removed, peripheral resistance rises and hypertension results. However, it is unlikely that defects in nitric oxide production are the cause of high blood pressure. In fact in early hypertension the nitric oxide production may be increased as a compensatory event modulating the rise in pressure, and this may explain why dynamic compliance is normal (**Figure 5**). However, when hypertension is established and there is vessel disease the nitric oxide response and endothelial control become impaired. This is probably an important factor leading to stiffness of the arteries and atherosclerosis.

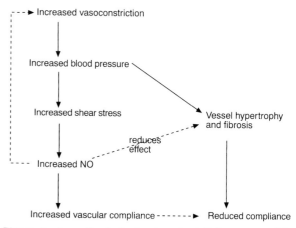

Figure 5 An outline indicating how the initial response of the endothelium is to prevent the rise of blood pressure by releasing nitric oxide (NO). This increases vessel compliance, reducing the adverse effects. If this system's capacity is exceeded the arterial damage process is accelerated. The dotted lines represent negative feedback attempting to restore the status quo.

Table 2 Factors determining extent of reflection and site where the reflected wave meets the flow wave

Poor arterial compliance	Increased pulse wave velocity
	Reflected wave closer to heart
Arterial branch points	Reflective site
Peripheral resistance	Increased reflection

The stiffness of blood vessels in older hypertensive patients has a number of important consequences. The pulse wave velocity is increased and thus reflected waves arrive back at the heart while the ventricle is still contracting, thereby augmenting the central systolic pressure (**Table 2**). In normotensive people the place at which the reflected wave and the oncoming flow meet is near the brachial artery, and thus central systolic pressure is lower than brachial artery systolic pressure (**Figure 6**). This increased central systolic blood pressure means that the heart contracts against a greater load and thus performs more work, leading to hypertrophy greater than might be predicted from the brachial artery pressure. The extent of the augmentation due to the pressure wave depends upon the degree of reflection, which is controlled in part by the peripheral resistance. The site at which augmentation

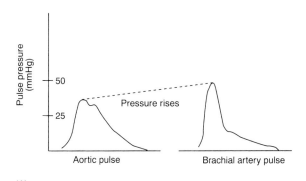

(A)

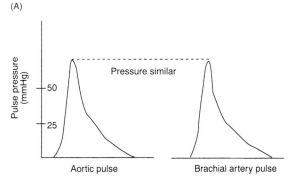

(B)

Figure 6 The central aortic and brachial artery pulse wave forms in normotensive (A) and hypertensive (B) subjects. In (B) the heart pumps blood out against a higher pressure leading to cardiac hypertrophy. See O'Rourke (1995) for discussion of how central aortic pressure is higher than brachial artery pressure due to reflected waves.

is highest depends on the pulse wave velocity. The deterioration in the elastic properties of the large blood vessels with loss of elastin and more collagen leads to increased pulse pressure, increased augmentation of central systolic pressure and a decrease in the peripheral diastolic pressure, all of which are common in the elderly hypertensive patient.

The Heart

In hypertensive patients the left ventricle is frequently enlarged and this is associated with an increased risk of cardiovascular death. When assessed by electrocardiography left ventricular hypertrophy (LVH) is relatively uncommon, but if assessed by echocardiography LVH is present in up to 50% of mild hypertensive patients and in adolescents not classified as hypertensive, but in the upper 10 percentile of blood pressure there is a 10–15% prevalence of LVH (**Table 3**). The cause of the LVH is not certain (**Table 4**). There is a better correlation with 24 h blood pressure than with clinic values, but the r value is about 0.14 indicating considerable variability. It is possible that acute elevations of blood pressure sustained for 1–2 h may have a potent effect by increasing wall stress and activating the processes that lead to myocyte hypertrophy. This may be of particular importance if it occurs at a time when plasma levels of potential growth factors such as angiotensin II and growth hormone are elevated. These hormones are elevated during sleep and thus blood pressure elevation at that time may be particularly detrimental. This is supported by observations that people who do not have the usual night-time (sleep) fall in blood pressure are more likely to have cardiac and renal complications. There is a significant genetic influence on cardiac hypertrophy and it has been proposed that cardiac enlargement may be antecedent to and the cause of hypertension. High blood pressure can undoubtedly cause cardiac enlargement, but independent of blood pressure elevation angiotensin II and salt can probably enlarge the heart.

The strongest predictor in some studies of cardiac size was the salt intake. In animals a high salt intake

Table 3 Prevalence of left ventricular hypertrophy

Subjects	Prevalence (%)
Normotensive	1–2
Adolescent, upper 10%	10–15
Borderline hypertensive	
by echo	20–50
by ECG	3–5
Severe hypertensive	90

ECG, electrocardiogram; echo, echocardiogram.

Table 4 Factors affecting cardiac hypertrophy

Factors leading to hypertrophy	Factors reducing or preventing hypertrophy
24 h cardiac work	Nitric oxide
Ventricular wall stress	Bradykinin
Sodium intake	
Sympathetic activity	
Angiotensin II	
Insulin-like growth factor	
Growth hormone	
Genotype	

can cause cardiac hypertrophy and a low salt intake allows resolution. The increased size of the heart is a response that decreases the wall stress of the ventricle and is a compensatory phenomenon. The cardiac hypertrophy with hypertension is concentric in nature, with sarcomeres laid down in the myocytes in parallel (**Figure 7**). The increased thickness of the myocytes together with associated fibrosis of the interstitium means that the oxygen diffusion pathway is increased and this may lead to precipitation of arrhythmias and sudden death. In cardiac hypertrophy associated with exercise the sarcomeres are laid down in series, and with this 'eccentric' hypertrophy there is no increased mortality.

In addition to cardiac hypertrophy in hypertensive patients there is significant impairment of diastolic relaxation. This may result from poor oxygen delivery to the mitochondria and thus a retarded reuptake of calcium into cell organelles. Thus, there is a dynamic aspect to diastolic dysfunction which may be reversible. However, in addition the laying down of fibrous tissue in the heart contributes to stiffness and poor diastolic filling. The poor diastolic function may occur prior to any increase in cardiac size. The poor diastolic filling due to reduction in left ventricular compliance may explain the subnormal stroke volume seen in hypertensive patients during exercise. In these circumstances the increased pulse rate means that there is insufficient time for a stiff left ventricle to fill adequately.

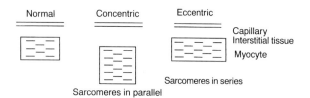

Figure 7 The diffusion distance in normal and eccentric hypertrophy is not increased. In concentric hypertrophy there is often associated fibrosis; this leads to a longer extracellular diffusion distance as well as a longer intercellular pathway. Thus, oxygen delivery to mitochondria is poor, the reuptake of calcium (an energy-dependent process) is sluggish, and 'functional' relaxation is slow, leading to impaired diastolic filling.

Early in the development of hypertension in spontaneously hypertensive rats and in humans total peripheral resistance is elevated. In rats changes in the resistance vessels are seen early. In borderline and mild hypertension in humans there may be little increase in total peripheral resistance at rest, but the total peripheral resistance does not fall to normal levels during conditions when maximal vasodilatation would be expected (e.g., exercise, heating, autonomic blockade). This probably indicates that structural changes occur early in the disease and the failure to dilate adequately may in part explain the excess rise in blood pressure seen in hypertensive patients during exercise.

Increased peripheral resistance is not evenly distributed across all regional vascular beds and the resistance in the kidney frequently appears to be increased, resulting in a reduction of about 10% in renal blood flow. In contrast, in prehypertensive people an increase has been reported in renal blood flow. Whether this has any pathogenic significance is not known. However, the reduced blood flow could result from activation of the tubuloglomerular feedback response due to altered sodium reabsorption in the proximal tubule.

The coronary flow in hypertensive patients is of importance. These people already may have an increased oxygen demand. The flow at rest is usually normal but even in patients with no evidence of coronary artery disease the flow reserve is impaired. In normal people the coronary artery rapidly dilates to meet the increased oxygen demand but in hypertensive patients this dilation is sluggish and does not reach the same maximal flow. The reason is complex and is possibly a combination of structural change and an impaired endothelial response.

The Sympathetic Nervous System

Many investigators have postulated that hypertension may result from impaired central control and this is mediated via the sympathetic nervous system. The increased cardiac output and heart rate seen in many people with early or incipient essential hypertension could be explained by excess sympathetic activity. However, it has been difficult to demonstrate that there is increased sympathetic activity because many of the techniques are relatively crude. It has been reported that plasma noradrenaline levels correlate with cardiac index and peripheral resistance in mildly hypertensive patients. It is difficult to know if increased sympathetic activity is primary, but in adolescents who later develop hypertension there is an increased blood pressure rise associated with mental or physical stress, which supports the concept of a dysregulatory neurogenic component. Sympathetic activity may also be altered by changes in sodium or potassium intake, and thus the 'prime' cause of hypertension remains to be elucidated.

Renal Function

There are undoubtedly subtle abnormalities in renal function in most hypertensive people. It is unclear if this is a cause or effect of hypertension. In spontaneous hypertensive rats (SHR) early in life the proximal tubule cells are very responsive to angiotensin II and this could cause sodium retention and initiate the development of the hypertensive process. However, in mature rats the responsiveness to angiotensin II of the proximal tubule is lost.

In hypertensive patients there is a reduced renal blood and plasma flow associated with an increased filtration fraction and hence a normal glomerular filtration rate. These changes would result in an increased fractional absorption of sodium by the proximal tubule and potential difficulty in excreting sodium by a pressure natriuresis. The pressure natriuresis curve is shifted with less sodium being excreted for a given pressure at rest, but exaggerated when pressure is acutely increased. It is not clear what is cause or effect, but it is tempting to assume that resetting of the pressure natriuresis response takes place, because if it operated normally the increased pressure should cause salt loss and correct the hypertensive process.

In some but not all people blood pressure falls with sodium restriction. Patients with salt-sensitive hypertension tend not to have a nocturnal fall in blood pressure; they have a greater prevalence of cardiac hypertrophy, microalbuminuria, and a worse prognosis.

Conclusions

Hypertension is not a disease but a sign of some underlying disturbance in the usual control systems for blood pressure. It is thus difficult to have a single description of the physiology of essential hypertension as it will depend upon the cause. There are, however, certain features common to many people. In people with certain (at present unknown) abnormalities in their genotype, exposure to a high-sodium, low-potassium diet together with other alterations in their life style leads to an elevation in blood pressure. In some people there is an initial stage of high cardiac output, but when hypertension is established peripheral resistance is elevated and is the explanation for the high blood pressure. The genetic abnormalities may relate to impairment of the control systems for excreting sodium chloride or a deficit in the ability of the kidney to excrete sodium. There are associated abnormalities in the sympathetic nervous system and the central regulation of blood pressure. When blood pressure is elevated a series of compensatory events are activated, particularly cardiac and vascular hypertrophy, which are initially appropriate responses but lead to the creation of a positive feedback loop which eventually becomes a vicious cycle leading to malignant hypertension.

Essential hypertension in some ways is a misnomer. It is caused by alterations in nutrition and life style in people with a susceptible genotype. The challenge is to identify such people and remove the appropriate environmental factor.

See also: **Coronary Heart Disease**: Hemostatic Factors; Lipid Theory. **Hypertension**: Nutritional Management. **Potassium**. **Sodium**: Physiology.

Further Reading

Avolio AP, Deng FQ, Li WQ *et al.* (1986) Improved arterial distensibility in normotensive subjects on a low salt diet. *Arteriosclerosis* **6**: 166–169.

Barker DJ, Winter PD, Osmond C, Margetts B, and Simmonds SJ (1989) Weight in infancy and death from ischaemic heart disease. *Lancet* ii(8663): 577–580.

Dampney RAL (1994) Functional organisation of central pathways regulating the cardiovascular system. *Physiological Reviews* **74**: 323.

Draaijer P, Kool MJ, Maessen JM *et al.* (1993) Vascular distensibility and compliance in salt-hypertensive and salt-resistant borderline hypertension. *Journal of Hypertension* **11**: 199–1207.

Folkow B (1982) Physiological aspects of primary hypertension. *Physiological Reviews* **62**: 347–504.

Guyton A (1980) *Arterial Pressure and Hypertension.* Philadelphia: WB Saunders.

Hayoz D, Rutschmann B, Perrett F *et al.* (1992) Conduit artery compliance and distensibility are not necessarily reduced in hypertension. *Hypertension* **20**: 1–6.

Lund-Johansen P and Omvik P (1990) Haemodynamic patterns of untreated hypertensive disease. In: Laragh J and Brenner BM (eds.) *Hypertension: Pathophysiology, Diagnosis and Management*, pp. 305–327. New York: Raven Press.

Morgan TO and Anderson A (2003) Different drug classes have variable effects on blood pressure depending on the time of day. *American Journal of Hypotension* **16**: 46–50.

Morgan T, Aubert J-F, and Brunner H (2001) Interaction between sodium intake, angiotensin II and blood pressure as a cause of cardiac hypertrophy. *American Journal of Hypertension* **14**(9): 914–920.

Morgan TO, Brunner HR, Aubert J-F, Wang Q, Griffiths C, and Delbridge L (2000) Cardiac hypertrophy depends upon sleep blood pressure: A study in rats. *Journal of Hypertension* **18**: 445–451.

O'Rourke M (1995) Mechanical principles in arterial disease. *Hypertension* **26**: 2–9.

Dietary Factors

L J Appel, Johns Hopkins University, Baltimore, MD, USA

Worldwide, elevated blood pressure is an extraordinarily common and important risk factor for cardiovascular and kidney diseases. As blood pressure rises, so does the risk of these diseases (**Figure 1**). The relationship is strong, consistent, continuous, independent, and etiologically relevant. Accordingly, the adverse consequences of elevated blood pressure are not just restricted to individuals with hypertension (a systolic blood pressure ≥140 mmHg or a diastolic blood pressure ≥90 mmHg). Those with prehypertension, namely, a systolic blood pressure of 120–139 mmHg or diastolic blood pressure of 80–89 mmHg, have a high probability of developing hypertension and carry an excess risk of cardiovascular disease compared to those with a normal blood pressure (systolic blood pressure <120 mmHg and diastolic blood pressure <90 mmHg). In fact, almost one-third of blood pressure-related deaths from coronary heart disease occur in individuals with blood pressure in the nonhypertensive range.

In Western countries and most economically developing countries, systolic blood pressure rises with age. As a consequence, the lifetime risk of developing hypertension is extremely high, approximately 90% among US adults older than age 50 years. However, the rise in blood pressure with age is not inevitable. There are numerous isolated populations in which the rise in blood pressure is blunted or even flat. These populations are typically characterized by extremely low intakes of salt, relatively high intakes of potassium, and a lean body habitus.

Lifestyle modification, which includes dietary changes and increased physical activity, has important roles in both nonhypertensive and hypertensive individuals. In nonhypertensive individuals, including those with prehypertension, lifestyle modifications have the potential to prevent hypertension, reduce blood pressure, and thereby lower the risk of blood pressure-related cardiovascular disease. Even an apparently small reduction in blood pressure, if applied to an entire population, could have an enormous beneficial impact. It has been estimated that a 3 mmHg reduction in systolic blood pressure could lead to an 8% reduction in stroke mortality and a 5% reduction in mortality from coronary heart disease (**Figure 2**). In hypertensive individuals, lifestyle modifications can serve as initial

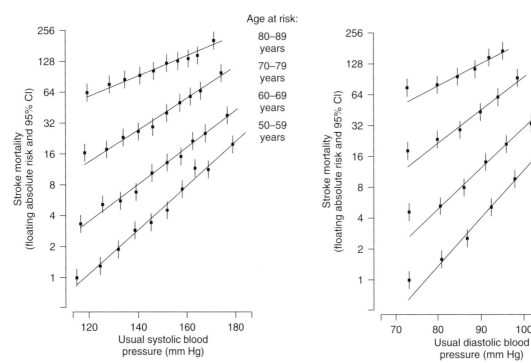

A: Systolic blood pressure

B: Diastolic blood pressure

Figure 1 Stroke mortality rate by decade of age versus systolic blood pressure (A) and diastolic blood pressure (B): meta-analysis of 61 prospective studies with 2.7 million person-years. (Reprinted with permission from Lewington S, Clarke R, Qizilbash N, Peto R, and Collins R (2002) Prospective Studies Collaboration. Age-specific relevance of usual blood pressure to vascular mortality: a meta-analysis of individual data for one million adults in 61 prospective studies. *Lancet* **360**: 1903–13.

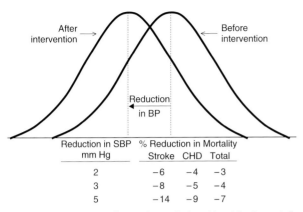

Reduction in SBP mm Hg	% Reduction in Mortality		
	Stroke	CHD	Total
2	−6	−4	−3
3	−8	−5	−4
5	−14	−9	−7

Figure 2 Estimated effects of populationwide shifts in systolic blood pressure (SBP) on mortality. (Reprinted with permission from Stamler R (1991) Implication of the INTERSALT study *Hypertension* **17**: I-16–I-20.)

treatment before the start of drug therapy and as an adjunct to medication in people already on antihypertensive drug therapy. In hypertensive individuals with medication-controlled blood pressure, lifestyle therapies can facilitate drug step-down and potentially drug withdrawal in individuals who sustain lifestyle changes.

Dietary Factors That Lower Blood Pressure

Weight Loss

On average, as weight increases, so does blood pressure. The importance of this relationship is reinforced by the high and increasing prevalence of overweight and obesity throughout the world. With rare exception, clinical trials have documented that weight loss lowers blood pressure. Importantly, reductions in blood pressure occur before and without attainment of a desirable body weight. In one meta-analysis that aggregated results across 25 trials, mean systolic and diastolic blood pressure reductions from an average weight loss of 5.1 kg were 4.4 and 3.6 mmHg, respectively. Greater weight loss leads to greater blood pressure reduction.

Additional trials have documented that modest weight loss can prevent hypertension by approximately 20% among overweight, prehypertensive individuals and can facilitate medication step-down and drug withdrawal. Lifestyle intervention trials have uniformly achieved short-term weight loss, primary through a reduction in total caloric intake. In some instances, substantial weight loss has also been sustained over 3 or more years.

In aggregate, available evidence strongly supports weight reduction, ideally attainment of a body mass index less than 25 kg/m², as an effective approach to prevent and treat hypertension. Weight reduction can also prevent diabetes and control lipids. Hence, the

beneficial effects of weight reduction in preventing cardiovascular–renal disease should be substantial. Finally, in view of the well-recognized challenges of maintaining weight loss, efforts to prevent weight gain among those with a normal body weight are critical.

Reduced Salt Intake

On average, as dietary salt (sodium chloride) intake rises, so does blood pressure.[1] To date, more than 50 randomized trials have tested the effects of salt on blood pressure, including several dose–response trials. Approximately 10 meta-analyses have aggregated data across these trials. In a recent meta-analysis that focused on moderate reductions in salt intake, a reduced sodium intake of 1.8 g/day (77 mmol/day) led to average systolic/diastolic blood pressure reductions of 5.2/3.7 mmHg in hypertensives and 1.3/1.1 mmHg in nonhypertensives.

One of the most important dose–response trials is the DASH-Sodium trial, which tested the effects of three different salt intakes separately in two distinct diets—the DASH (Dietary Approaches to Stop Hypertension) diet and a control diet more typical of what Americans eat. As displayed in **Figure 3**, the rise in blood pressure with higher salt intake was evident in both diets. Of note, the blood pressure response to salt intake was nonlinear. Specifically, decreasing salt intake caused a greater lowering of blood pressure when the starting sodium intake was less than 2.3 g/day (100 mmol/day) than when it was above this level.

The blood pressure response to changes in salt intake is heterogeneous. Despite the use of the terms 'salt sensitive' and 'salt resistant' to classify individuals in research studies, the change in blood pressure in response to a change in salt intake is not binary. Instead, the change in blood pressure from a reduced salt intake has a continuous distribution, with individuals having greater or lesser degrees of blood pressure reduction. Genetic factors influence the response to salt reduction. Concomitant diet also modifies the effects of salt on blood pressure. The rise in blood pressure for a given increase in salt intake is blunted in the setting of either the DASH diet or a high potassium intake (**Figure 3**). In general, the effects of salt on blood pressure tend to be greater in blacks, middle-aged and older people, and individuals with hypertension, diabetics, or chronic kidney disease. Although it is possible to identify groups that tend to be salt sensitive, it is impossible, given currently available diagnostic tools, to identify individuals who are salt sensitive.

---

[1]In view of the format of published data and of dietary recommendations, data are presented as g/day (mmol/day) of sodium rather than g/day of salt.

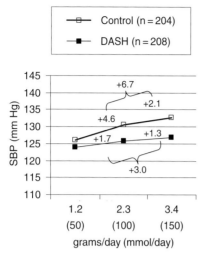

Figure 3 Mean systolic blood pressure (SBP) change in the DASH-Sodium trial from salt reduction in two diets and from the DASH diet at three salt levels. (Adapted with permission from Sacks FM, Svetkey LP, Vollmer WM *et al.* (2001) A clinical trial of the effects on blood pressure of reduced dietary sodium and the DASH dietary pattern (The DASH-Sodium Trial). *New England Journal of Medicine* **344**: 3–10.)

In addition to lowering blood pressure, clinical trials have documented that a reduced salt intake can prevent hypertension by approximately 20% (with or without concomitant weight loss) and can lower blood pressure in the setting of antihypertensive medication. Evidence from observational studies suggests that a reduced salt intake can blunt the age-related rise in systolic blood pressure (**Figure 4**) and can potentially prevent atherosclerotic cardiovascular events and heart failure. A reduced salt intake may also reduce the risk of left ventricular hypertrophy, osteoporosis, and gastric cancer.

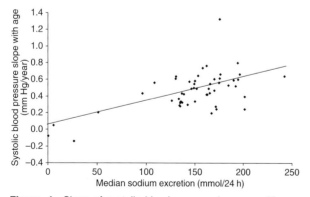

Figure 4 Slope of systolic blood pressure increase with age plotted by median sodium excretion in 52 communities worldwide: results from INTERSALT. (Adapted with permission from Rose G, Stamler J, Stamler R *et al.* (1988) INTERSALT: An international study of electrolyte excretion and blood pressure. Results for 24 hour urinary sodium and potassium excretion. *British Medical Journal* **297**: 319–328.)

Still, the effects of salt on health have been debated. Some have argued that the increases in plasma renin activity and perhaps insulin resistance that occur as a result of a reduced salt intake mitigate the beneficial effects of salt reduction on blood pressure. However, in contrast to blood pressure, the clinical relevance of increased plasma renin activity is uncertain, especially because antihypertensive medications that raise plasma renin levels actually lower cardiovascular disease risk. It has also been argued that a reduced salt intake has little or no effect on blood pressure in many individuals and that other aspects of diet (e.g., increased potassium intake or adoption of a mineral-rich diet) mitigate the harmful effects of salt on blood pressure. Although one cannot guarantee that all individuals will achieve a lower blood pressure from salt reduction, the fraction of individuals who will benefit is substantial.

In view of the progressive dose–response relationship between salt intake and blood pressure, it is difficult to set specific levels for dietary recommendations. Recently, an Institute of Medicine committee set 1.5 g/day (65 mmol/day) of sodium as an adequate intake level and 2.3 g/day (100 mmol/day) as an upper limit. Western-type diets that provide 1.5 g/day (65 mmol/day) have been shown to provide adequate levels of other nutrients. This level of salt intake also allows for excess sweat salt loss among unacclimatized individuals who become physically active or who become exposed to high temperatures. Numerous policymaking organizations have recommended an upper limit of 2.3 g/day (100 mmol/day) for sodium intake.

In most Western counties, average intake of sodium is high, greatly exceeding 2.3 g/day (100 mmol/day). In the United States, the median intake of sodium from foods, not including salt added at the table, varies by age and, according to a recent survey, ranges from 3.1 to 4.7 g/day (135 to 204 mmol/day) in adult men and 2.3 to 3.1 g/day (100 to 135 mmol/day) in adult women. Worldwide, there is greater variation in sodium intake, ranging from an estimated mean intake of 0.02 g/day (1.0 mmol/day) in Yanomamo Indians to more than 10.3 g/day (450 mmol/day) in northern Japanese.

In aggregate, available data strongly support current populationwide recommendations to lower salt intake. To reduce salt intake, consumers should choose foods low in salt and limit the amount of salt added to food. However, even motivated individuals find it difficult to reduce salt intake because more than 75% of consumed salt comes from processed foods (**Figure 5**). Hence, any meaningful strategy to reduce salt intake must involve the efforts of food manufacturers, who should reduce the amount of salt added during food processing.

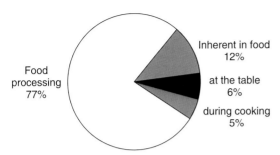

Figure 5   Sources of dietary sodium. (Data from Mattes RD and Donnelly D (1991) Relative contributions of dietary sodium sources *Journal of the American College of Nutrition* **10**: 383–393.)

Increased Potassium intake

High levels of potassium intake are associated with reduced blood pressure. Observational data have been reasonably consistent in documenting this inverse relationship, whereas data from individual trials have been less consistent. However, three meta-analyses of these trials have each documented a significant inverse relationship between potassium intake and blood pressure in nonhypertensive and hypertensive individuals. In one meta-analysis, average net systolic/diastolic blood pressure reductions from increased potassium intake were 4.4/2.4 mmHg. Available studies have documented greater blood pressure reductions from potassium in African Americans compared to non-African Americans. A high potassium intake has been shown to blunt the rise in blood pressure in response to increased salt intake. Potassium has greater blood pressure lowering in the context of a higher salt intake and lesser blood pressure reduction in the setting of a lower salt intake. Conversely, the blood pressure reduction from a reduced salt intake is greatest when potassium intake is low. These data are consistent with subadditive effects of reduced salt intake and increased potassium intake on blood pressure.

Most trials that tested the effects of potassium on blood pressure used pill supplements, typically potassium chloride. However, in foods, the conjugate anions associated with potassium are mainly citrate and other bicarbonate precursors. The latter is important because other potential benefits of foods rich in potassium (i.e., reduced risk of kidney stones and reduced bone turnover) likely result from effects of the conjugate anion. Because a high dietary intake of potassium can be achieved through diet rather than pills and because potassium derived from foods also comes with a variety of other nutrients, the preferred strategy to increase potassium intake is to consume foods, such as fruits and vegetables, rather than supplements.

On the basis of available data, an Institute of Medicine committee set an Adequate Intake for potassium of 4.7 g/day (120 mmol/day) for adults. This level of dietary intake should maintain lower blood pressure levels, reduce the adverse effects of salt on blood pressure, reduce the risk of kidney stones, and possibly decrease bone loss. Currently, dietary intake of potassium is considerably lower than this level. In recent surveys, the median intake of potassium by adults in the United States was approximately 2.9–3.2 g/day (74–82 mmol/day) for men and 2.1–2.3 g/day (54–59 mmol/day) for women. Because African Americans have a relatively low intake of potassium and a high prevalence of elevated blood pressure and salt sensitivity, this subgroup of the population would especially benefit from an increased potassium intake.

In the generally healthy population with normal kidney function, a potassium intake from foods higher than 4.7 g/day (120 mmol/day) poses no potential for increased risk because excess potassium is readily excreted in the urine. However, in individuals whose urinary potassium excretion is impaired, a potassium intake of less than 4.7 g/day (120 mmol/day) is appropriate because of adverse cardiac effects (arrhythmias) from hyperkalemia. Common drugs that impair potassium excretion are angiotensin converting enzyme inhibitors, angiotensin receptor blockers, and potassium-sparing diuretics. Medical conditions associated with impaired potassium excretion include diabetes, chronic renal insufficiency, end stage renal disease, severe heart failure, and adrenal insufficiency. Elderly individuals are at increased risk of hyperkalemia because they often have one or more of these conditions or take one or more of the medications that impair potassium excretion.

Moderation of Alcohol Intake

The relationship between alcohol intake and blood pressure is direct and progressive, particularly at an alcohol intake above approximately two drinks per day (~1 oz. or ~28 g of ethanol per day). A meta-analysis of 15 trials reported that decreased consumption of alcohol (median reduction in self-reported alcohol consumption of 76%) lowered systolic and diastolic blood pressure by 3.3 and 2.0 mmHg, respectively. In nonhypertensives and hypertensives, blood pressure reductions were similar. In aggregate, evidence supports moderation of alcohol intake (among those who drink) as an effective approach to lower blood pressure. It is recommended that alcohol consumption be limited to no more than 1 oz. (30 ml) of ethanol (e.g., 24 oz. (720 ml) beer, 10 oz. (300 ml) wine, or 2 oz. (60 ml) 100-proof whiskey) per day in most men and to no more than 0.5 oz. (15 ml) ethanol per day in women and lighter weight people.

Whole Dietary Patterns

Vegetarian diets Vegetarian diets have been associated with low blood pressure. In observational studies, vegetarians also experience a markedly lower, age-related rise in blood pressure. Aspects of a vegetarian lifestyle that might affect blood pressure include nondietary factors (e.g., physical activity), established dietary risk factors (e.g., salt, potassium, weight, and alcohol), and other aspects of a vegetarian diet (e.g., high fiber and no meat). To a very limited extent, observational studies have controlled for the well-established determinants of blood pressure. Hence, it is unclear whether blood pressure reductions result from established dietary risk factors that affect blood pressure or from other aspects of a vegetarian diet.

The DASH diet The DASH trial tested whether modification of whole dietary patterns might affect blood pressure. In this trial, participants were randomized to eat one of three diets: (i) a control diet, (ii) a diet rich in 'fruits and vegetables' but otherwise similar to control, or (iii) the DASH diet. The DASH diet emphasizes fruits, vegetables, and low-fat dairy products; includes whole grains, poultry, fish, and nuts; and is reduced in fats, red meat, sweets, and sugar-containing beverages. Accordingly, it is rich in potassium, magnesium, calcium, and fiber and reduced in total fat, saturated fat, and cholesterol; it is also slightly increased in protein.

Among all participants, the DASH diet significantly lowered mean systolic blood pressure by 5.5 mmHg and mean diastolic blood pressure by 3.0 mmHg. The fruits and vegetables diet also reduced blood pressure but to a lesser extent—approximately half of the effect of the DASH diet. The effect was relatively rapid; the full effect was apparent after 2 weeks (**Figure 6**). In subgroup analyses, the DASH diet significantly lowered blood pressure in all major subgroups (men, women, African Americans, non-African Americans, hypertensives, and nonhypertensives). However, the effects of the DASH diet were especially prominent in African Americans, who experienced net systolic/diastolic blood pressure reductions of 6.9/3.7 mmHg, and hypertensive individuals, who experienced net blood pressure reductions of 11.6/5.3 mmHg.

Results from the DASH trial have important clinical and public health implications. The effect of the DASH diet in hypertensive individuals was similar in magnitude to that of drug monotherapy. From a public

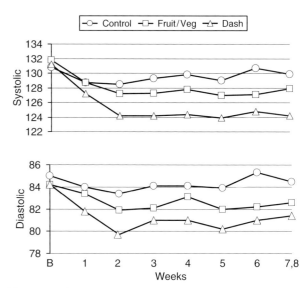

Figure 6 Blood pressure by week during the DASH feeding study in three diets (control diet, fruits and vegetables diet, and DASH diet). (Adapted with permission from Appel LJ, Moore TJ, Obarzanek E *et al.* (1997) The effect of dietary patterns on blood pressure: Results from the Dietary Approaches to Stop Hypertension (DASH) clinical trial. *New England Journal of Medicine* **336**: 1117–1124.)

health perspective, the DASH diet could potentially shift the population distribution of blood pressure downward, thereby reducing the risk of blood pressure-related cardiovascular disease (**Figure 2**).

Fish Oil Supplementation

High-dose, omega-3 polyunsaturated fatty acid (commonly termed 'fish oil') supplements can lower blood pressure in hypertensive individuals. In a meta-analysis of trials, average systolic and diastolic blood pressure reductions in hypertensive individuals were 5.5 and 3.5 mmHg, respectively. The effect of fish oil appears to be dose dependent, with blood pressure reductions only occurring at relatively high doses, namely 3 g/day or more. In nonhypertensive individuals, blood pressure reductions were nonsignificant and small. Side effects, including belching and a fishy taste, are common. In view of the side effect profile and the high dose required to lower blood pressure, fish oil supplements are not routinely recommended.

Dietary Factors with Limited or Uncertain Effect on Blood Pressure

Fiber

Evidence from observational studies and several clinical trials suggests that increased fiber intake may reduce blood pressure. A meta-analysis documented that supplemental fiber (average increase of 14 g/day) was associated with net systolic/diastolic reductions of 1.6/2.0 mmHg, respectively. Still, high-quality epidemiologic studies and clinical trials are needed before one can recommend increased fiber intake as a means to lower blood pressure.

Calcium and Magnesium

Evidence that increased calcium intake might lower blood pressure comes from a variety of sources, including animal studies, observational studies, clinical trials, and meta-analyses. Meta-analyses of trials documented modest reductions in systolic and diastolic blood pressure of 0.89–1.44 and 0.18–0.84 mmHg, respectively, with calcium supplementation (400–2000 mg/day). There is also evidence that calcium intake may affect the blood pressure response to salt. Overall, data are insufficient to recommend supplemental calcium alone as a means to lower blood pressure.

The body of evidence implicating magnesium as a major determinant of blood pressure is inconsistent. In observational studies, often cross-sectional in design, a common finding is an inverse association of dietary magnesium with blood pressure. However, in pooled analyses of clinical trials, there is no clear effect of magnesium intake on blood pressure. Hence, data are insufficient to recommend increased magnesium intake alone as a means to lower blood pressure.

Fats (Other Than Fish Oil) and Cholesterol

Numerous studies, including both observational studies and clinical trials, have examined the effects of fat intake on blood pressure. Overall, there is no apparent effect of saturated fat and n-6 polyunsaturated fat intake on blood pressure. Although a few trials suggest that an increased intake of monounsaturated fat may lower blood pressure, evidence is insufficient to make recommendations. Likewise, few studies have examined the effect of dietary cholesterol intake on blood pressure. Hence, although modification of dietary fat and cholesterol intake can be recommended as a means to prevent and treat hyperlipidemia and dyslipidemia, evidence is insufficient to recommend these changes alone as a means to lower blood pressure.

Protein Intake

A large and generally consistent body of evidence from observational studies has documented that higher protein intake, particularly protein from plant-based sources, is associated with lower blood pressure. In contrast to the large volume of evidence from observational studies, comparatively few trials have examined the effects of protein intake on blood pressure. Recent trials have tested the effects of soy-based interventions on blood pressure. In several but not all of these trials, soy supplementation reduced blood pressure. Although it is reasonable to speculate that an increased intake of protein from plant sources can lower blood pressure, this hypothesis has not been adequately tested in a clinical trial of sufficient size and rigor.

Vitamin C

Laboratory studies, depletion–repletion studies, and epidemiological studies suggest that increased vitamin C intake or status is associated with lower blood pressure. However, few trials have addressed this issue, and results of these trials have been inconsistent. Overall, it remains unclear whether an increased intake of vitamin C lowers blood pressure.

Gene–Diet Interactions

A rapidly increasing body of evidence indicates that genetic factors affect blood pressure levels and the blood pressure response to dietary changes. Most of the evidence relates to genetic factors that influence the blood pressure response to salt. Several genotypes that influence blood pressure have been identified. Most of these genotypes influence the renin–angiotensin–aldosterone axis or renal salt handling.

Special Populations

Children

Elevated blood pressure begins well before adulthood, during the first two decades of life and perhaps earlier during gestation. Numerous observational studies have documented that blood pressure tracks with age from childhood into the adult years. Hence, efforts to reduce blood pressure and to prevent the age-related rise in blood pressure in childhood are prudent.

Direct empiric evidence from rigorous, well-controlled trials in children and adolescents is sparse. There is some direct evidence from studies conducted in children that the dietary determinants of blood pressure in children and adults are similar. In this setting, the effect of diet on blood pressure in children and adolescents is, in large part, extrapolated from studies of adults. Such extrapolations are reasonable because elevated blood pressure is a chronic condition resulting from the insidious rise in blood pressure throughout childhood and adulthood.

Pregnant Women

Hypertension during pregnancy is a constellation of diverse clinical conditions, some of which can be extremely serious. Of substantial concern are preeclampsia and eclampsia. Both are multisystem disorders that are manifest by the onset of hypertension and proteinuria during the second half of pregnancy. Convulsions occur in the setting of eclampsia but not preeclampsia. The cause of these disorders is unknown. Several dietary interventions, including salt restriction, fish oil supplementation, and calcium supplementation, have been tested as a means to prevent preeclampsia, but none is considered effective. Although a meta-analysis of small trials suggested that calcium supplementation has some benefit in high-risk women, a large trial of calcium supplementation documented no benefit, either overall or in high-risk subgroups.

Older People

Because of the age-related rise in systolic blood pressure and because of the high prevalence of blood pressure-related cardiovascular disease in middle-aged and older people, dietary strategies should be especially beneficial as adults age. It is well documented that older people can make and sustain dietary changes, specifically weight loss and dietary salt reduction. Furthermore, salt sensitivity increases as individuals age. Lastly, because of the high attributable risk associated with elevated blood pressure in older people, the beneficial effects of dietary changes on blood pressure should translate into substantial reductions in cardiovascular risk in this age group.

Populations Defined by Race/Ethnicity or Geography

Worldwide, there is substantial variation in blood pressure among populations. In certain primitive societies, such as the Yanomamo Indians in Brazil, blood pressure does not rise with age, and hypertension is absent. In rural Africa and southern China, the prevalence of hypertension is less than 20%. Among urbanized populations, the prevalence of hypertension is high, especially among African Americans, a population in which the prevalence of hypertension approaches 40%. Other groups, such as Australian Aborigines, Eastern Europeans, and Russians, also have a high prevalence of hypertension.

Understanding the causes of geographic variation is difficult. However, migration studies provide strong evidence that modifiable environmental factors (e.g., diet and physical activity) rather than genetic factors or geographic factors account for this variation. Furthermore, as noted previously, trials have documented that compared to non-African Americans, African Americans achieve greater blood pressure reduction from several nonpharmacologic therapies, specifically a reduced salt intake, increased potassium intake, and the DASH diet. The potential benefits of these dietary therapies is amplified because US survey data indicate that African Americans consume less potassium than non-African Americans. On average, salt intake is high and similar in African Americans and non-African Americans. Hence, changes in diet should provide a means to reduce racial and perhaps geographic disparities in blood pressure.

Conclusion

In view of the continuing epidemic of blood pressure-related cardiovascular disease, efforts to reduce blood pressure in both nonhypertensive and hypertensive individuals are warranted. Such efforts will require individuals to change behavior and society to make substantial environmental changes. The current challenge to health care providers, researchers, government officials, and the general public is to develop and implement effective clinical and public health strategies that lead to sustained dietary changes among individuals and more broadly among populations.

See also: **Alcohol**: Absorption, Metabolism and Physiological Effects; Disease Risk and Beneficial Effects. **Ascorbic Acid**: Physiology, Dietary Sources and Requirements; Deficiency States. **Calcium**. **Fish**. **Hypertension**: Etiology; Nutritional Management. **Magnesium**. **Obesity**: Complications. **Older People**: Physiological Changes. **Potassium**. **Pregnancy**: Energy Requirements and Metabolic Adaptations. **Sodium**: Physiology; Salt Intake and Health. **Vegetarian Diets**.

Further Reading

Appel LJ, Moore TJ, Obarzanek E *et al.* (1997) The effect of dietary patterns on blood pressure: Results from the Dietary Approaches to Stop Hypertension (DASH) clinical trial. *New England Journal of Medicine* **336**: 1117–1124.

Chobanian AV, Bakris GL, Black HR *et al.* (2003) National High Blood Pressure Education Program Coordinating Committee.

Seventh report of the Joint National Committee on Prevention, Detection, Evaluation, and Treatment of High Blood Pressure. *Hypertension* **42**: 1206–1252.

Institute of Medicine (2004) *Dietary Reference Intakes for Water, Potassium, Sodium, Chloride and Sulfate*. Washington, DC: National Academy of Sciences.

Izzo JL and Black HR (eds.) (2003) *Hypertension Primer: The Essentials of High Blood Pressure*, 3rd edn. Washington, DC: American Heart Association.

Krauss RM, Eckel RH, Howard B *et al.* (2000) AHA dietary guidelines: Revision 2000: A statement for healthcare professionals from the nutrition committee of the American Heart Association. *Circulation* **102**: 2284–2299.

Lewington S, Clarke R, Qizilbash N, Peto R, and Collins R (2002) Age-specific relevance of usual blood pressure to vascular mortality: A meta-analysis of individual data for one million adults in 61 prospective studies. *Lancet* **360**: 1903–1913.

Rose G, Stamler J, Stamler R *et al.* (1988) INTERSALT: An international study of electrolyte excretion and blood pressure. Results for 24 hour urinary sodium and potassium excretion. *British Medical Journal* **297**: 319–328.

Sacks FM, Svetkey LP, Vollmer WM *et al.* (2001) A clinical trial of the effects on blood pressure of reduced dietary sodium and the DASH dietary pattern (The DASH-Sodium Trial). *New England Journal of Medicine* **344**: 3–10.

Simons-Morton DG and Obarzanek E (1997) Diet and blood pressure in children and adolescents. *Pediatric Nephrology* **11**: 244–249.

Stamler J, Stamler R, and Neaton JD (1993) Blood pressure, systolic and diastolic, and cardiovascular risks: U.S. population data. *Archives of Internal Medicine* **153**: 598–615.

Vasan RS, Beiser A, Seshadri S *et al.* (2002) Residual life-time risk for developing hypertension in middle-aged women and men: The Framingham Heart Study. *Journal of the American Medical Association* **287**: 1003–1010.

Whelton PK, He J, Appel LJ *et al.* (2002) Primary prevention of hypertension. Clinical and public health advisory from the National High Blood Pressure Education Program. *Journal of the American Medical Association* **288**: 1882–1888.

Whelton PK, He J, and Louis GT (eds.) (2003) *Lifestyle Modification for the Prevention and Treatment of Hypertension*. New York: Marcel Dekker.

older people, occurring in two-thirds of those older than 65 years of age—a population that is often untreated. The lifetime risk of developing hypertension for middle-aged and elderly individuals is 90%.

Recently, new guidelines suggest that the previous values of 120 mmHg/80 mmHg should not be considered normal. The revised categories are shown in **Table 1**. The recommendations for management of hypertension include lifestyle modification for all categories (even normal), with drugs not routinely promoted until the patient presents with at least stage 1 hypertension or other compelling indications.

The most definitive trials directed toward the nutritional management of hypertension are the DASH (Dietary Approaches to Stop Hypertension) and DASH-Sodium trials. DASH focused on establishing dietary patterns that would lower blood pressure while keeping sodium content constant. DASH-Sodium was designed to test the effects of varying levels of sodium in conjunction with the DASH diet in order to determine whether lowering sodium intake would have additional beneficial effects. Both trials were metabolic feeding trials, and each enrolled more than 400 participants at four sites in the United States. As a follow-up to the DASH and DASH-Sodium trials, essentially the same group of investigators conducted the PREMIER trial to test whether individuals could lower blood pressure by implementing established guidelines for treating hypertension and included the DASH diet in addition to the established recommendations. PREMIER used a lifestyle counseling approach and randomized more than 800 subjects to one of three treatment arms: advice only, established recommendations, and established recommendations plus DASH.

Nutritional Management

C M Champagne, Pennington Biomedical Research Center, Baton Rouge, LA, USA

Hypertension or high blood pressure affects more than 25% of adult Americans (50 million) and Canadians, and the rate of hypertension is reportedly as much as 60% higher in some European countries. African Americans typically have higher rates of hypertension compared to whites. Hypertension is also more common among

Table 1 Classification of blood pressure for adults 18 years of age or older

Category	Systolic blood pressure (mmHg)	Diastolic blood pressure (mmHg)
Normal or desirable	<120	<80
Prehypertensive	120–139	80–89
Stage 1 hypertension	140–159	90–99
Stage 2 hypertension	≥160	≥100

U.S. Dept of Health and Human Services, National Institutes of Health, National Heart, Lung and Blood Institute. The Seventh Report of the Joint National Committee on Prevention, Detection, Evaluation, and Treatment of High Blood Pressure. NIH Publication No. 04-5230, August 2004.

Recommended Lifestyle Modifications

Traditionally, the following lifestyle modifications have been recommended for the treatment of hypertension:

Lose weight, if one is overweight.
Reduce intake of salt, sodium, and foods containing them as much as possible.
Increase physical activity.
Limit intake of alcohol.
Stop smoking.
Control stress.

The established recommendations for lifestyle modification used in one arm of the PREMIER clinical trial were weight loss, increasing physical activity, reducing sodium intake, limiting alcohol consumption, and reducing total and saturated fat intake to that of an American Heart Association step 1 diet with 30% of energy from total and 10% from saturated fat. A second arm in PREMIER included essentially the same lifestyle modifications but a lower fat diet comparable to an American Heart Association step 2 diet with 25% of energy from total and 7% from saturated fat and also adherence to the DASH diet (emphasizing consumption of fruits, vegetables, and low-fat dairy products).

Nutritional Considerations

Reduction of Sodium Intake

Sodium reduction typically results in lower blood pressure in industrialized societies. Current guidelines in the United States suggest reducing the daily intake of sodium to approximately 100 mmol, or approximately 2.4 g of sodium or less per day.

The DASH-Sodium trial demonstrated that reduction of sodium intake from 100 to 50 mmol per day (approximately 1.5 g) significantly reduced blood pressure in individuals following either the common US diet or the DASH diet. In addition, TOHP2 (phase 2 of the Trials of Hypertension Prevention) and TONE (Trials of Nonpharmacologic Interventions in the Elderly) documented that reducing sodium can either prevent hypertension or facilitate hypertension control. It should also be noted that salt sensitivity increases with age, so those who demonstrate this sensitivity should maintain a reduced salt diet.

Consumers should either eliminate or limit salt added to foods in cooking and at the table as a means of reducing sodium intake. Nutrition facts labels require sodium content to be listed so that consumers can be more prudent about their diets. The amount of sodium in processed food, such as convenience foods (e.g., boxed products one would prepare at home), soups, and processed meats (e.g., sausage, ham, and other meat products), is often alarming. If there is not a nutrition label on a processed food product, one should assume sodium content is high. Canned products generally contain more sodium than fresh or frozen items, unless a product is specifically labeled as 'no salt added.' The consumption of fresh, unprocessed foods should be promoted.

Moderation of Alcohol Intake

The relationship between high consumption of alcohol (typically three or more drinks per day) and elevated blood pressure has been shown in numerous epidemiologic studies. A drink is defined as 12 oz. of beer, 5 oz. of wine, or 1.5 oz. of distilled spirits. Most evidence indicates that alcohol should be limited to two drinks per day for men and one drink per day for women. Ideally, daily alcohol consumption should be avoided. Whenever possible, alcohol, if consumed, should be done so with meals.

Consumption of a DASH Diet (Increasing Potassium, Magnesium, Calcium, and Fiber Intakes by Increasing Intakes of Fruits, Vegetables, and Low-Fat Dairy Foods)

The contribution of minerals, particularly potassium, magnesium, and calcium, and fiber was identified by contributions from fruits, vegetables, low-fat dairy products, whole grains, and nuts in the DASH eating plan. The DASH diet effectively used these components through an ideal dietary pattern to lower blood pressure.

Increased intakes of potassium have been associated with lower blood pressure. A meta-analysis of several trials suggested that 60–120 mmol per day of supplemental potassium reduces systolic and diastolic blood pressure by 4.4 and 2.5 mmHg, respectively, in hypertensive individuals. In normotensive individuals, systolic and diastolic blood pressure was reduced by 1.8 and 1.0 mmHg, respectively. Dietary intake of potassium can be easily achieved through consumption of various foods.

The DASH diet, while promoting dietary patterns, was developed very carefully with particular attention paid to the use of specific foods within categories that contribute more to the intakes of desired nutrients. As an example, consider the rank-ordered listing of potassium content of fruits and fruit juices presented in **Tables 2** and **3**. Dried fruits typically have the highest potassium content, followed by raw fruits and frozen fruits. Canned fruit products generally do not contain as high potassium content as other forms. There is less potassium contained in fruit juices and generally the

Table 2 Fruits, ranked by potassium content (mg/100 g)

Fruit	K (mg)
Dried	
Apricots, dehydrated (low moisture)	1850
Bananas, dehydrated, or banana powder	1491
Peaches (low moisture)	1351
Apricots	1162
Litchis	1110
Prunes (low moisture)	1058
Peaches	996
Currants, zante	892
Persimmons, Japanese	802
Raisins	746–825
Plums (prunes)	732
Dates, medjool	696
Figs	680
Longans	658
Dates, deglet noor	656
Apples (low moisture)	640
Pears	533
Jujube	531
Apples	450
Raw	
Tamarinds	628
Plantains	499
Breadfruit	490
Avocados	485
Durian, raw or frozen	436
Custardapple (bullock's heart)	382
Bananas	358
Passion-fruit, (granadilla), purple	348
Sapotes (marmalade plum)	344
Currants, European black	322
Kiwi fruit, (Chinese gooseberries)	312
Persimmons, native	310
Abiyuch	304
Jackfruit	303
Rhubarb	288
Guavas, common	284
Elderberries	280
Soursop	278
Currants, red and white	275
Cherimoya	269
Melons, cantaloupe	267
Longans	266
Loquats	266
Carissa (natal-plum)	260
Apricots	259
Pomegranates	259
Papayas	257
Jujube	250
Sugar apples (sweetsop)	247
Figs	232
Melons, honeydew	228
Cherries, sweet	222
Prickly pears	220
Pummelo	216
Roselle	208
Nectarines	201
Gooseberries	198
Quinces	197
Crabapples	194
Mulberries	194

Sapodilla	193
Grapes	191
Peaches	190
Kumquats	186
Melons, casaba	182
Cherries, sour, red	173
Litchis	171
Oranges	166–196
Carambola (starfruit)	163
Blackberries	162
Persimmons, Japanese	161
Plums	157
Tangerines (mandarin oranges)	157
Mangos	156
Feijoa	155
Strawberries	153
Raspberries	151
Acerola, (West Indian cherry)	146
Lemons	138–145
Rowal	131
Grapefruit	127–150
Rose apples	123
Pears, asian	121
Pears	119
Limes	117
Pineapple	115–125
Watermelon	112
Apples, with skin	107
Pitanga, (surinam cherry)	103
Apples, without skin	90
Cranberries	85
Java plum (jambolan)	79
Blueberries	77
Mammy apple (mamey)	47
Oheloberries	38
Fruits, frozen	
Strawberries	148
Loganberries	145
Boysenberries	139
Cherries, sour, red	124
Raspberries, red	114
Rhubarb	108

From U.S. Department of Agriculture, Agricultural Research Service (2003) *USDA National Nutrient Database for Standard Reference*, Release 16. Available at www.nal.usda.gov/fnic/foodcomp.

fresh forms of the juices have incrementally more than the processed forms. Fruits and juices in general contain some magnesium, another mineral of interest to the DASH investigators. Most fruits contain 2–30 mg of magnesium per 100 grams, but dried fruits contain much more (30–90 mg) and the amounts vary greatly. Fruit juices contain less than 20 mg of magnesium per 100 grams, with most containing less than 10 mg. Fiber content of fruit ranges from approximately 7 to 14 g of fiber for dried fruits on a per 100 gram basis and between 1 and 5 g for other fruits per 100 grams. Generally, fruit juices contribute less than 1 g of dietary fiber per 100 grams, but high-pulp varieties of juices provide slightly more dietary fiber.

Table 3 Fruit juices, ranked by potassium content (mg/100 g)

Fruit juice	K (mg)
Passion fruit juice, fresh	278
Prune juice, canned	276
Orange juice, fresh	200
Orange juice, from concentrate	190
Tangerine juice, fresh or canned	178
Orange juice, canned	175
Grapefruit juice, white or pink, fresh or canned	162
Pineapple juice, canned or from concentrate	134
Grape juice, canned or bottled, unsweetened	132
Apple juice, from frozen concentrate, unsweetened	126
Lemon juice, fresh	124
Apple juice, canned or bottled, unsweetened	119
Apricot nectar	114
Lime juice, fresh	109
Lemon juice, canned or bottled	102
Acerola juice, fresh	97
Cranberry juice, unsweetened	77
Lime juice, canned or bottled	75
Peach nectar	40
Papaya nectar	31
Grape juice, from frozen concentrate, sweetened	21
Pear nectar	13

From U.S. Department of Agriculture, Agricultural Research Service (2003) *USDA National Nutrient Database for Standard Reference*, Release 16. Available at www.nal.usda.gov/fnic/foodcomp.

Table 4 contains a rank-ordered listing of vegetables (including beans) by content of potassium. Magnesium content is also shown. The data are presented for vegetables and beans in the raw form generally. It is important to remember that many fresh forms are concentrated in terms of weight when cooked, especially spinach and other greens, and it is thus possible to obtain a higher mineral content from cooked vegetables (especially in the case of potassium). The magnesium content differs less from the fresh to the cooked state for most vegetables and beans. Most vegetables contain approximately 1–3 g of dietary fiber per

Table 4 Potassium and magnesium content of vegetables (including beans), rank ordered by potassium content (mg/100 g; presented for raw vegetables unless otherwise specified)

Vegetable	K (mg)	Mg (mg)
Tomatoes, sun-dried	3427	194
Palm hearts	1806	10
Arrowhead	922	51
Yam	816	21
Beet greens	762	70
Lemon grass (citronella)	723	60
Butterbur (fuki)	655	14
Taro leaves	648	45
Epazote	633	121
Soybeans, green	620	65
Amaranth leaves	611	55
Cress, garden	606	38
Taro, tahitian	606	47
Yautia (tannier)	598	24
Taro	591	33
Winged bean tuber	586	24
Waterchestnuts, Chinese (matai)	584	22
Wasabi, root	568	69
Chrysanthemum, garland	567	32
Chrysanthemum leaves	567	32
Jute, potherb	559	64
Spinach	558	79
Lotus root	556	23
Parsley	554	50
Pigeonpeas, immature seeds	552	68
Bamboo shoots	533	3
Coriander (cilantro) leaves	521	26
Sweetpotato leaves	518	61
Mushroom, oyster	516	20
Vinespinach (basella)	510	65
Purslane	494	68
Fireweed, leaves	494	156
Mushrooms, portabella	484	11
Soybeans, mature seeds	484	72
Borage	470	52
Lima beans, immature seeds	467	58
Horseradish tree, pods	461	45
Corn salad	459	13
Squash, zucchini, baby	459	33
Cowpeas, leafy tips	455	43
Potatoes, red, flesh and skin	455	22
Arrowroot	454	25
Lambsquarters	452	34
Kale, scotch	450	88
Mustard spinach (tendergreen)	449	11
Mushrooms, brown, Italian or Crimini	448	9
Kale	447	34
Pumpkin leaves	436	38
Cowpeas (blackeyes), immature seeds	431	51
Jerusalem artichokes	429	17
Potato, flesh and skin	421	23
Chicory greens	420	30
Mountain yam, Hawaii	418	12
Potatoes, russet, flesh and skin	417	23
Ginger root, raw	415	43
Fennel, bulb, raw	414	17
Potatoes, skin	413	23
Potatoes, white, flesh and skin	407	21
Garlic	401	25
Cardoon	400	42
Dandelion greens	397	36
Dock	390	103
Brussels sprouts	389	23
Peas, mature seeds, sprouted	381	56
Mushrooms, enoki	381	16
Salsify (vegetable oyster)	380	23
Chard, Swiss	379	81
Parsnips	375	29
Artichokes (globe or French)	370	60
Fiddlehead ferns	370	34
Arugula	369	47
Seaweed, laver	356	2
Mustard greens	354	32
Squash, winter, butternut	352	34

Continued

Table 4 Continued

Vegetable	K (mg)	Mg (mg)
Kohlrabi	350	19
Squash, winter, all varieties	350	14
Pumpkin	340	12
Eppaw	340	32
Peppers, hot chili, green	340	25
Horseradish tree leafy tips	337	147
Rutabagas	337	23
Sweet potato	337	25
Shallots	334	21
Taro shoots	332	8
Beans, fava, in pod	332	33
Celtuce	330	28
Watercress	330	21
Beets	325	23
Broccoli, leaves	325	25
Broccoli, flower clusters	325	25
Broccoli, stalks	325	25
Lentils, sprouted	322	37
Peppers, hot chili, red	322	23
Carrots	320	12
Squash, winter, hubbard	320	19
Broccoli	316	21
Endive	314	15
Mushrooms	314	9
Swamp cabbage (skunk cabbage)	312	71
Burdock root	308	38
Beans, navy, mature seeds	307	101
Beans, pinto, mature seeds	307	53
Pepper, Serrano	305	22
Cauliflower	303	15
Okra	303	57
Radicchio	302	13
Celeriac	300	20
Cauliflower, green	300	20
Balsam pear (bitter gourd), pods	296	17
Chives	296	42
Turnip greens	296	31
Chicory roots	290	22
Radishes, white icicle	280	9
Onions, spring or scallions	276	20
Grape leaves	272	95
Cassava	271	21
Corn, sweet, yellow or white	270	37
Tomatillos	268	20
Squash, summer, all varieties	262	17
Celery	260	11
Tomatoes, yellow	258	12
Nopales	257	52
Pepper, banana	256	17
Cabbage, Chinese (pak-choi)	252	19
Hyacinth beans, immature seeds	252	40
Broadbeans, immature seeds	250	38
Broccoli, frozen	250	16
Lettuce, cos or romaine	247	14
Cabbage	246	15
Peas, green	244	33
Cabbage, red	243	16
Pokeberry shoots (poke)	242	18
Yardlong bean	240	44
Cabbage, Chinese (pe-tsai)	238	13
Lettuce, butterhead	238	13
Tomatoes, red, ripe	237	11

Carrots, baby	237	10
Radishes	233	10
Cabbage, savoy	230	28
Eggplant	230	14
Radishes, oriental	227	16
Seaweed, agar	226	67
Winged beans, immature seeds	223	34
Cowpeas, young pods with seeds	215	58
Peppers, jalapeno	215	19
Onions, welsh	212	23
Squash, summer	212	21
Tomatoes, orange	212	8
Peppers, sweet, yellow	212	12
Chicory, witloof	211	10
Peppers, sweet, red	211	12
Beans, snap, green	209	25
Beans, snap, yellow	209	25
Tomatoes, green	204	10
Asparagus	202	14
Peppers, Hungarian	202	16
Peas, edible, podded	200	24
Broccoli raab	196	22
Turnips	191	11
Beans, kidney, mature seeds	187	21
Lettuce, red leaf	187	12
Sesbania flower	184	12
Poi	183	24
Squash, summer, scallop	182	23
Leeks (bulb and lower leaf portion)	180	28
Winged bean leaves	176	8
Peppers, sweet, green	175	10
Pumpkin flowers	173	24
Lettuce, iceberg	152	8
Gourd, white flowered (calabash)	150	11
Yambean (jicama)	150	12
Mung beans, mature seeds	149	21
Cucumber, with peel	147	13
Onions	144	10
Gourd, dishcloth (towelgourd)	139	14
Cucumber, peeled	136	12
New Zealand spinach	130	39
Seaweed, spirulina	127	19
Chayote, fruit	125	12
Onions, sweet	119	9
Squash, winter, spaghetti	108	12
Seaweed, kelp, raw	89	121
Radish seeds, sprouted, raw	86	44
Alfalfa seeds, sprouted, raw	79	27
Seaweed, irishmoss, raw	63	144
Seaweed, wakame, raw	50	107
Jew's ear (pepeao), raw	43	25

Data source: U.S. Department of Agriculture, Agricultural Research Service. 2003. USDA National Nutrient Database for Standard Reference, Release 16. Nutrient Data Laboratory Home Page, http://www.nal.usda.gov/fnic/foodcomp.

100 grams; beans and legumes offer approximately 5 g of dietary fiber, and some dried vegetables offer more than double this amount.

Nuts were also an important part of the DASH diet, contributing potassium, magnesium, fiber, and protein. They contain fat, mostly monounsaturated, and thereby contribute energy to the diet. **Table 5**

Table 5 Potassium, magnesium, and fiber content of nuts and seeds per 100 grams, ranked by potassium content

Description	K (mg)	Mg (mg)	Fiber (g)
Nuts			
Pistachio nuts, dry roasted	1042	120	10.3
Pistachio nuts, raw	1025	121	10.3
Ginkgo nuts, dried	998	53	9.3
Chestnuts, European, dried, unpeeled	986	74	11.7
Almonds, dry roasted	746	286	11.8
Almonds	728	275	11.8
Almonds, oil roasted	699	274	10.5
Almonds, blanched	687	275	10.4
Hazelnuts or filberts	680	163	9.7
Cashew nuts, raw	660	292	3.3
Brazil nuts, dried, unblanched	659	376	7.5
Hazelnuts or filberts, blanched	658	160	11.0
Cashew nuts, oil roasted	632	273	3.3
Pine nuts, pinyon, dried	628	234	10.7
Pine nuts, pignolia, dried	597	251	3.7
Chestnuts, European, roasted	592	33	5.1
Cashew nuts, dry roasted	565	260	3.0
Walnuts, black, dried	523	201	6.8
Chestnuts, European, raw, unpeeled	518	32	8.1
Ginkgo nuts, raw	510	27	9.3
Walnuts, English	441	158	6.7
Hickorynuts, dried	436	173	6.4
Pecans, dry roasted	424	132	9.4
Butternuts, dried	421	237	4.7
Pecans	410	121	9.6
Pecans, oil roasted	392	121	9.5
Macadamia nuts, raw	368	130	8.6
Macadamia nuts, dry roasted	363	118	8.0
Ginkgo nuts, canned	180	16	9.3
Seeds			
Breadnuttree seeds, dried	2011	115	14.9
Cottonseed kernels, roasted (glandless)	1350	440	5.5
Breadfruit seeds, roasted	1082	62	6.0
Breadfruit seeds, raw	941	54	5.2
Sunflower seed kernels, dry roasted	850	129	9.0
Pumpkin and squash seed kernels, dried	807	535	3.9
Pumpkin and squash seed kernels, roasted	806	534	3.9
Sunflower seed kernels, dried	689	354	10.5
Flaxseed	681	362	27.9
Sunflower seed kernels	491	129	11.5
Sunflower seed kernels, oil roasted	483	127	6.8
Sesame seeds, whole, dried	468	351	11.8
Sesame seed kernels, dried (decorticated)	407	347	12.7
Sesame seed kernels, toasted	406	346	16.9

From U.S. Department of Agriculture, Agricultural Research Service (2003) *USDA National Nutrient Database for Standard Reference*, Release 16. Available at www.nal.usda.gov/fnic/foodcomp.

includes the potassium, magnesium, and fiber content of some common nuts and seeds. Although this is presented based on a rank-ordered content of potassium, it is easy to see that some nuts and seeds are a significant source of magnesium and dietary fiber and their consumption was therefore encouraged in the DASH diet.

Low-fat dairy products were also an important part of the DASH diets. These were used primarily to increase the calcium content of the diets from a low content of approximately 450 mg on the control and fruit and vegetable diets to approximately 1250 mg on the DASH diet at the 2000 kcal (8368 kJ) level. Calcium has frequently been reported to have an inverse relationship with blood pressure, but studies utilizing supplemental calcium have been inconsistent. With supplements, effects on blood pressure reduction have been negligible. Nonetheless, the blood pressure lowering effect of the DASH diet has been suggested to be in part related to the calcium content of the diet. It should be noted that the DASH diet also was lower in fat and higher in protein, and therefore it is not easily attributable to one factor alone but rather a combination of several factors, as depicted in **Figure 1**.

The final point regarding composition of the DASH diet is that it included specific food choices. The diet contained whole grains, poultry, and fish (in addition to the fruits, vegetables, low-fat dairy, and nuts previously mentioned). Although it was reduced in total and saturated fat, it was also reduced in meats, sweets, and sugar-containing beverages. Food was consumed as an overall pattern in which it is quite possible that the interaction between food items is as important as the specific foods in reducing blood pressure. Thus, the DASH diet contained dietary patterns promoted by the National Institutes of Health, National Heart, Lung, and Blood Institute. The dietary patterns of DASH are presented at three energy levels in **Table 6**.

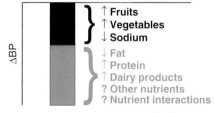

Figure 1 Assessing the effects of the DASH-Sodium diet on blood pressure. The figure depicts the fact that there is some certainty associated with the increases in fruits and vegetables and reduction in sodium. The gray areas represent the other components of the diet and the possible contribution of each, alone or in combination with other factors.

Table 6 Food group servings for the DASH diet at three energy levels

Food group	Daily servings (except as noted)		
	1600 kcal or 6694 kJ	2000 kcal or 8368 kJ	3100 kcal or 12970 kJ
Grains and grain products	6	7–8	12–13
Vegetables	3–4	4–5	6
Fruits	4	4–5	6
Low-fat or fat-free dairy foods	2–3	2–3	3–4
Meats, poultry, fish	1–2	2 or less	2–3
Nuts, seeds, dry beans	3 per week	4–5 per week	1
Fats and oils	2	2–3	4
Sweets	0	5 per week	2

Dietary Protein Consumption

Results of meta-analyses from several investigators indicate an inverse association between dietary protein and blood pressure levels. However, data have not been conclusive. The DASH diet contained approximately 18% of energy from protein compared to 15% of energy from protein in the other diets tested. Because of the addition of low-fat dairy foods and the reduced emphasis on high-fat meats, it can be assumed that this elevation in protein was brought about by foods that contributed protein from perceived beneficial sources. This is an area of dietary intake that requires more research.

Fish Oil Supplementation

Studies suggest that an intake of fish oil at a level of approximately 4 g per day reduces systolic blood pressure by approximately 1.7–2.1 mmHg and diastolic blood pressure by 1.5–1.6 mmHg. These effects tend to be larger in individuals older than 45 years of age and in populations with blood pressure readings greater than 140/90 mmHg. Generally, there have been differences associated with fish oil capsules compared to naturally occurring sources of EPA and DHA from fatty fish, again indicating dietary pattern rather than consumption of individual items may be crucial. The DASH diet had a relatively high fish content (compared to animal meats) and this may be yet one more factor contributing to the lowering of blood pressure in individuals on the DASH diet.

The American Heart Association recommends eating two servings of fish per week and emphasizes that the choice should be a fatty fish (such as salmon, herring, or mackerel). Not all fish have the same content of omega-3 fatty acids. **Table 7** provides a listing of amounts of combined EPA/DHA in fish and other seafood sources and the amount of consumption (in ounces of product) necessary to provide a 4-g intake. Descriptors include common raw and canned products, but the intakes given are rough estimates due to potential variability in oil content within species, season, and diet. Cooking methods and other preparation techniques may affect the final concentrations in raw fish.

Other Fatty Acid Effects

Monounsaturated fatty acids, particularly olive oil, may help lower blood pressure. Olive oil has typically been associated with the popularized Mediterranean diet, which has been promoted as a treatment for cardiovascular disease. Other oils (e.g., canola and peanut oil) have a high monounsaturated fat content. Nuts, which are part of the DASH diet, contain significant amounts of monounsaturated fats and fit well in the Mediterranean diet.

Caffeine

Although a link between caffeine consumption (particularly coffee) and hypertension may exist, effects of coffee drinking on blood pressure appear to be dependent on the time of consumption and subsequent determination of blood pressure values. Generally, a role for caffeine intake and development of hypertension is not believed to be significant.

Weight Reduction

Obesity and overweight are considered independent risk factors for cardiovascular disease and are closely associated with hypertension. This linkage was demonstrated in the 1960s by the Framingham Heart Study investigators in the United States. Obesity in the industrialized world has been increasing at epidemic proportions. The relationship between increasing body weight and increasing blood pressure has been termed obesity hypertension, and treatment requires consideration of physiologic changes related to this disorder. Although efforts have been under way in the United States to reduce overweight and obesity, it is estimated that the age-adjusted prevalence of overweight and obesity (body mass index (BMI) ≥ 25.0) among adults aged 20 or older is 64%; for those considered obese (BMI ≥ 30.0) it is 30%. During a 25-year period in the United States, this reflects approximately a 36% increase in the combined levels of overweight and obesity and essentially a doubling of obesity rates.

Table 7 Eicosapentaenoic (EPA, 20:5 n-3) and docosahexaenoic (DHA, 22:6 n-3) acid in fish/seafood (per 100 grams) and the amount of consumption (in ounces) required to provide ~4 g of EPA + DHA per day (ranked in order of content)

Fish/seafood	EPA (g)	DHA (g)	EPA + DHA (g)	Oz. to provide ~4 g EPA + DHA
Fish, caviar, black and red, granular	2.74	3.80	6.54	2.2
Fish, mackerel, salted	1.62	2.97	4.58	3.1
Fish, roe, mixed species, cooked	1.26	1.75	3.01	4.7
Fish, shad, American, raw	1.09	1.32	2.41	5.9
Fish, roe, mixed species, raw	0.98	1.36	2.35	6.0
Fish, mackerel, Atlantic, raw	0.90	1.40	2.30	6.1
Fish, anchovy, European, canned in oil	0.76	1.29	2.06	6.9
Fish, salmon, chinook, raw	1.01	0.94	1.95	7.2
Fish, salmon, Atlantic, farmed, raw	0.62	1.29	1.91	7.4
Fish, herring, Pacific, raw	0.97	0.69	1.66	8.5
Fish, salmon, pink, canned	0.85	0.81	1.65	8.5
Fish, herring, Atlantic, raw	0.71	0.86	1.57	9.0
Fish, anchovy, European, raw	0.54	0.91	1.45	9.7
Fish, mackerel, Pacific and jack, raw	0.51	0.93	1.44	9.8
Fish, salmon, Atlantic, wild, raw	0.32	1.12	1.44	9.8
Fish, sablefish, raw	0.68	0.72	1.40	10.1
Fish, mackerel, spanish, raw	0.33	1.01	1.34	10.5
Fish, whitefish, mixed species, raw	0.32	0.94	1.26	11.2
Fish, salmon, coho, farmed, raw	0.39	0.82	1.21	11.7
Fish, salmon, chum, canned	0.47	0.70	1.18	12.0
Fish, tuna, fresh, bluefin, raw	0.28	0.89	1.17	12.0
Fish, salmon, sockeye, raw	0.52	0.65	1.17	12.0
Fish, salmon, sockeye, canned	0.49	0.66	1.16	12.2
Fish, salmon, coho, wild, raw	0.43	0.66	1.09	13.0
Fish, salmon, pink, raw	0.42	0.59	1.01	14.0
Fish, sardine, Atlantic, canned in oil	0.47	0.51	0.98	14.4
Fish, trout, rainbow, farmed, raw	0.26	0.67	0.93	15.2
Fish, halibut, Greenland, raw	0.53	0.39	0.92	15.4
Fish, tuna, white, canned in water	0.23	0.63	0.86	16.4
Fish, shark, mixed species, raw	0.32	0.53	0.84	16.7
Fish, bluefish, raw	0.25	0.52	0.77	18.3
Fish, bass, striped, raw	0.17	0.59	0.75	18.7
Fish, trout, mixed species, raw	0.20	0.53	0.73	19.3
Fish, smelt, rainbow, raw	0.28	0.42	0.69	20.4
Mollusks, oyster, Pacific, raw	0.44	0.25	0.69	20.5
Fish, swordfish, raw	0.11	0.53	0.64	22.1
Fish, spot, raw	0.22	0.41	0.63	22.4
Fish, salmon, chum, raw	0.23	0.39	0.63	22.5
Fish, wolffish, Atlantic, raw	0.31	0.32	0.62	22.6
Fish, bass, freshwater, mixed species, raw	0.24	0.36	0.60	23.7
Fish, sea bass, mixed species, raw	0.16	0.43	0.60	23.7
Fish, trout, rainbow, wild, raw	0.17	0.42	0.59	24.0
Fish, pompano, florida, raw	0.18	0.39	0.57	24.8
Mollusks, oyster, eastern, wild, raw	0.27	0.29	0.56	25.2
Fish, drum, freshwater, raw	0.23	0.29	0.52	27.3
Mollusks, squid, mixed species, raw	0.15	0.34	0.49	28.9
Crustaceans, shrimp, mixed species, raw	0.26	0.22	0.48	29.4
Fish, sucker, white, raw	0.19	0.29	0.48	29.5
Mollusks, mussel, blue, raw	0.19	0.25	0.44	32.0
Fish, tilefish, raw	0.09	0.35	0.43	32.8
Fish, pollock, Atlantic, raw	0.07	0.35	0.42	33.5
Mollusks, oyster, eastern, farmed, raw	0.19	0.20	0.39	36.1
Fish, pollock, walleye, raw	0.15	0.22	0.37	37.9
Fish, seatrout, mixed species, raw	0.17	0.21	0.37	37.9
Crustaceans, crab, queen, raw	0.26	0.11	0.37	37.9
Fish, catfish, channel, wild, raw	0.13	0.23	0.36	38.8
Fish, halibut, Atlantic and Pacific, raw	0.07	0.29	0.36	38.9
Crustaceans, crab, blue, canned	0.19	0.17	0.36	38.9
Fish, carp, raw	0.24	0.11	0.35	40.1
Fish, cisco, raw	0.10	0.26	0.35	40.1

Continued

Table 7 Continued

Fish/seafood	EPA (g)	DHA (g)	EPA + DHA (g)	Oz. to provide ~4 g EPA + DHA
Fish, rockfish, Pacific, raw	0.14	0.20	0.35	40.9
Fish, mullet, striped, raw	0.22	0.11	0.33	43.4
Crustaceans, crab, blue, raw	0.17	0.15	0.32	44.1
Fish, mackerel, king, raw	0.14	0.18	0.31	45.1
Fish, pike, walleye, raw	0.09	0.23	0.31	45.4
Fish, snapper, mixed species, raw	0.05	0.26	0.31	45.4
Crustaceans, crab, dungeness, raw	0.22	0.09	0.31	46.0
Fish, ocean perch, Atlantic, raw	0.08	0.21	0.29	48.5
Fish, sturgeon, mixed species, raw	0.19	0.09	0.29	49.2
Fish, catfish, channel, farmed, raw	0.07	0.21	0.27	51.5
Fish, tuna, light, canned in water	0.05	0.22	0.27	52.3
Fish, sheepshead, raw	0.14	0.12	0.26	54.1
Fish, tuna, fresh, skipjack, raw	0.07	0.19	0.26	55.1
Fish, perch, mixed species, raw	0.08	0.17	0.25	55.8
Fish, grouper, mixed species, raw	0.03	0.22	0.25	57.1
Fish, whiting, mixed species, raw	0.09	0.13	0.22	63.0
Fish, croaker, Atlantic, raw	0.12	0.10	0.22	64.1
Fish, tuna, fresh, yellowfin, raw	0.04	0.18	0.22	64.7
Fish, cod, Pacific, raw	0.08	0.14	0.22	65.6
Fish, flatfish (flounder and sole species), raw	0.09	0.11	0.20	70.9
Mollusks, scallop, mixed species, raw	0.09	0.11	0.20	71.3
Fish, haddock, raw	0.06	0.13	0.19	76.3
Fish, cod, Atlantic, raw	0.06	0.12	0.18	76.7
Fish, burbot, raw	0.07	0.10	0.17	85.0
Mollusks, octopus, common, raw	0.08	0.08	0.16	89.9
Fish, eel, mixed species, raw	0.08	0.06	0.15	96.0
Crustaceans, crayfish, farmed, raw	0.12	0.03	0.14	98.0
Mollusks, clam, mixed species, raw	0.07	0.07	0.14	99.4
Crustaceans, crayfish, wild, raw	0.10	0.04	0.14	99.4
Mollusks, snail, raw	0.12	0.00	0.12	118.6
Fish, sunfish, pumpkin seed, raw	0.04	0.07	0.11	129.4
Fish, dolphinfish, raw	0.02	0.09	0.11	130.6
Fish, pike, northern, raw	0.03	0.07	0.11	131.9
Mollusks, cuttlefish, mixed species, raw	0.04	0.07	0.11	134.4
Turtle, green, raw	0.02	0.03	0.06	252.0
Mollusks, abalone, mixed species, raw	0.05	0.00	0.05	287.9
Frog legs, raw	0.01	0.02	0.03	415.0

From U.S. Department of Agriculture, Agricultural Research Service (2003) *USDA National Nutrient Database for Standard Reference*, Release 16. Available at www.nal.usda.gov/fnic/foodcomp.

The increase in obesity is seen in all ethnic, gender, and age groups. This problem is not confined to the average American; the US military reported that more than 50% of military personnel were overweight and more than 6% were obese in the late 1990s, despite high physical activity levels due to the rigors of basic training and regular field exercises. For the military, this reflects a trend that mirrors what is happening in the general population.

Globally, more than 1 billion adults are classified as overweight and approximately 300 million as clinically obese, ranging from less than 5% in China, Japan, and some African nations to more than 75% in urban Samoa. Alarmingly, this epidemic has spread to children, with 17.6 million children younger than 5 years of age estimated to be overweight worldwide. Data from the United States indicate that 15% of children and adolescents 6–19 years of age are overweight, a figure at least three times higher than that reported in the period from 1960 to 1970. Overweight children are at risk of becoming overweight adults but, more important, are likely to experience chronic health problems (including hypertension) associated typically with only adult obesity.

The World Health Organization has recommended an integrated, multifaceted, population approach be implemented to bring about effective weight management for those at risk of overweight and obesity. The key elements for developing such an environmental support include the following:

• Availability and access to a variety of low-fat, high-fiber foods
• Opportunities for physical activities

- Promotion of healthy behavior to encourage, motivate, and enable individuals to lose weight by
  Eating more fruits, vegetables, nuts, and whole grains
  Engaging in moderate physical activity for at least 30 minutes a day
  Reducing the amounts of fat and sugar in the diet
  Changing from a diet containing saturated animal fats to one emphasizing unsaturated vegetable oils
- Proper training of clinical personnel to ensure effective support for those trying to lose weight or avoid further weight gain

Obviously, it is essential to maintain a healthy body weight and thus necessary to keep a focus on energy intake in an effort to prevent overweight. Regarding hypertension, weight reduction appears to be the most promising answer in terms of potential impact on lowering blood pressure. Losing as few as 4.5 kg, or 10 pounds, of body weight can reduce blood pressure. Adopting healthy eating patterns yields additional benefits.

Strategies for Implementing Nutritional Changes to Control Blood Pressure

Self-Monitoring

A strategy undeniably praised for weight control is self-monitoring of one's food intake. Although a difficult undertaking for most individuals, the success of this technique is impressive, as evidenced by the successful long-term weight loss maintainers in the National Weight Control Registry.

The self-monitoring technique has been used to help people comply with other lifestyle recommendations (e.g., to increase physical activity by recording physical activity minutes). In the PREMIER clinical trial, participants in the 'established plus DASH' arm were required to monitor intake of energy, sodium, total fat, and saturated fat and servings of fruit, vegetables, and dairy to determine their compliance with the intervention. Those participants in the 'established' arm only recorded energy, sodium, and total fat intake. Most people find these recordings difficult but readily admit that they are successful in documenting dietary compliance if taken seriously.

Although a time-consuming and difficult task, successful diet compliers continue this behavior change strategy over the long term. Those who discontinue this technique often revert back to their old habits and relapse.

Working with a Dietetics Professional

Dietitians in North America and abroad typically have to meet national standards set by professional organizations such as the American Dietetic Association and the Canadian Dietetic Association. As such, these individuals are called 'registered dietitian' or other titles used only by those who have met these standards. Although one does not necessarily need to work with a professional, for some it is often easier to implement change when they can clear up confusing and often conflicting information by working with a dietitian who can provide credible nutrition information. Dietitians are taught to interpret the science into meaningful terms for the consumer. In addition, a well-trained professional will be equipped with a knowledge of motivational and behavior strategies to help effect change.

There are many important aspects of behavior change that are taught to the hypertensive client. Making lifestyle changes gradually so that one adjusts to one change before making another change is important. One should strive for short-term, attainable goals. Getting off track is not uncommon, but identifying what triggered the sidetrack and getting back on track are equally important. One should understand that slips are inevitable; it takes time to get used to the changes. In essence, lifestyle change is a long-term process, but it is worthwhile for good health.

Conclusions

Ultimately, blood pressure control will mandate lifestyle changes, even if hypertensive medications are prescribed. Most important, body weight has to be a key focus and the goal should be to work toward an ideal body weight and avoid gaining weight during the aging process. In addition to diet, physical activity factors into this scenario, and one should strive to be more physically active and less sedentary as one grows older. Diet, as described previously, plays a key role in blood pressure control. Increasing fruits, vegetables, and dairy products in the diet and reducing sodium should be the first objective. This will increase potassium, magnesium, and calcium by natural sources as much as possible. Increasing whole grains, nuts, and legumes will also improve mineral and fiber content of the diet. One should focus less on red meat; instead, one should choose fatty fish to increase consumption of omega-3 fatty acids. If one drinks alcohol, one should do so in moderation. These simple, but often difficult to accomplish, strategies will help to lower blood pressure and improve risk against cardiovascular disease.

See also: **Alcohol**: Effects of Consumption on Diet and Nutritional Status. **Caffeine. Fats and Oils. Fish. Fruits and Vegetables. Hypertension**: Etiology; Dietary Factors. **Magnesium. Nuts and Seeds. Potassium. Protein**: Synthesis and Turnover; Requirements and Role in Diet. **Sodium**: Physiology; Salt Intake and Health. **Weight Management**: Approaches. **World Health Organization**.

Further Reading

Appel LJ, Champagne CM, Harsha DW *et al.* Writing Group of the PREMIER Collaborative Research Group (2003) Effects of comprehensive lifestyle modification on blood pressure control: Main results of the PREMIER clinical trial. *Journal of the American Medical Association* **289**: 2083–2093.

Appel LJ, Moore TJ, Obarzanek E *et al.* for the DASH Collaborative Research Group (1997) A clinical trial of the effects of dietary patterns on blood pressure. *New England Journal of Medicine* **336**: 1117–1124.

Blumenthal JA, Sherwood A, Gullette ECD *et al.* (2002) Biobehavioral approaches to the treatment of essential hypertension. *Journal of Consulting and Clinical Psychology* **70**: 569–589.

Chobanian AV, Bakris GL, Black HR *et al.* and the National High Blood Pressure Education Program Coordinating Committee (2003) The seventh report of the Joint National Committee on Prevention, Detection, Evaluation, and Treatment of High Blood Pressure: The JNC 7 report. *Journal of the American Medical Association* **289**: 2560–2572.

Ferrara LA, Raimondi S, d'Episcopa L *et al.* (2000) Olive oil and reduced need for anti-hypertensive medications. *Archives of Internal Medicine* **160**: 837–842.

Geleijnse JM, Giltay EJ, Grobbee DE *et al.* (2002) Blood pressure response to fish oil supplementation: Metaregression analysis of randomized trials. *Journal of Hypertension* **20**: 1493–1499.

Klag MJ, Wang NY, Meoni LA *et al.* (2002) Coffee intake and risk of hypertension: The Johns Hopkins precursors study. *Archives of Internal Medicine* **162**: 657–662.

Lindquist CH and Bray RM (2001) Trends in overweight and physical activity among U.S. military personnel, 1995–1998. *Preventive Medicine* **32**: 57–65.

Rosenthal T, Shamiss A, and Holtzman E (2001) Dietary electrolytes and hypertension in the elderly. *International Urology and Nephrology* **33**: 575–582.

Sacks FM, Svetkey LP, Vollmer WM *et al.* for the DASH-Sodium Collaborative Research Group (2001) Effects on blood pressure of reduced dietary sodium and the Dietary Approaches to Stop Hypertension (DASH) diet. *New England Journal of Medicine* **344**: 3–10.

Suter PM, Sierro C, and Vetter W (2002) Nutritional factors in the control of blood pressure and hypertension. *Nutrition in Clinical Care* **5**: 9–19.

Trials of Hypertension Prevention Collaborative Research Group (1997) Effects of weight loss and sodium reduction intervention on blood pressure and hypertension incidence in overweight people with high-normal blood pressure. The Trials of Hypertension Prevention, Phase II. *Archives of Internal Medicine* **157**: 657–667.

U.S. Department of Health and Human Services, National Institutes of Health and National Heart, Lung, and Blood Institute (1998) *Clinical Guidelines on the Identification, Evaluation, and Treatment of Overweight and Obesity in Adults: The Evidence Report*, NIH Publication No. 98-4083. Bethesda, Md.: National Institutes of Health.

U.S. Department of Health and Human Services, National Institutes of Health and National Heart, Lung, and Blood Institute (2003) *Facts about the DASH Eating Plan*, NIH Publication No. 03-4082. Bethesda, Md.: National Institutes of Health.

Vasan RS, Beiser A, Seshadri S *et al.* (2002) Residual lifetime risk for developing hypertension in middle-aged women and men: The Framingham Heart Study. *Journal of the American Medical Association* **287**: 1003–1010.

Whelton PK, Appel LJ, Espeland MA *et al.* for the TONE Collaborative Research Group (1998) Sodium reduction and weight loss in the treatment of hypertension in older persons: A randomized, controlled trial of nonpharmacologic interventions in the elderly (TONE). *Journal of the American Medical Association* **279**: 839–846.

Wing RR and Hill JO (2001) Successful weight loss maintenance. *Annual Review of Nutrition* **21**: 323–341.

Wofford MR, Davis MM, Harkins G *et al.* (2002) Therapeutic considerations in the treatment of obesity hypertension. *Journal of Clinical Hypertension* **4**: 189–196.

Wolf-Maier K, Cooper RS, Banegas JR *et al.* (2003) Hypertension prevalence and blood pressure levels in 6 European countries, Canada, and the United States. *Journal of the American Medical Association* **289**: 2363–2369.

World Health Organization (2003) *Diet, Nutrition and the Prevention of Chronic Diseases: Report of a Joint WHO/FAO Expert Consultation*, WHO Technical Report Series 916. Geneva: WHO.

Zimmerman E and Wylie-Rosett J (2003) Nutrition therapy for hypertension. *Current Diabetes Reports* **3**: 404–411.

HYPOGLYCEMIA

V Marks, University of Surrey, Guildford, UK

Introduction

Hypoglycemia is defined as a blood glucose concentration of $2.2\,\mathrm{mmol\,l^{-1}}$ (plasma glucose concentration of $2.5\,\mathrm{mmol\,l^{-1}}$) or less. Its definition is necessarily arbitrary and owes its importance to the fact that hypoglycemia (literally low blood glucose) of this severity produces brain dysfunction by depriving its neurons of glucose.

Hypoglycemia is not a disease but a manifestation of it. It has, however, come to have a totally different meaning amongst certain sections of the population that has very little to do with blood glucose concentration but a lot to do with their feelings of well being, discomfort, and attitudes to life but, above all, with the role of diet in the achievement and maintenance of good health. And whilst no discussion of the dietary treatment of hypoglycemia can be meaningful without reference to this concept – referred to, for want of a better term, as nonhypoglycemia, – hypoglycemia will, throughout this article, be used only to describe a measured low blood glucose concentration.

Brain Function and Hypoglycemia

The brain malfunction to which hypoglycemia gives rise will be referred to as neuroglycopenia.

The brain is often thought of as being incapable of using metabolites other than glucose as a source of energy. This is untrue. It has been known for more than 30 years to be able, under certain circumstances including prolonged fasting, to utilize the 'ketone bodies,' β-hydroxybutyrate and aceto-acetate. Under these circumstances the need for glucose and its supply through gluconeogenesis is drastically reduced. The survival value of this ability is immense as it permits fat stores rather than structural muscle and other tissue proteins to be utilized for maintenance of vital processes under these stressful conditions. Only when fat stores have become completely exhausted and plasma ketone levels fallen to below normal fasting levels does the brain's demand for glucose rise above the ability of gluconeogenesis to provide it. Only at this point does hypoglycemia intervene and portend death from starvation or inanition (see later).

The Blood Glucose Concentration

Failure to appreciate the differences between arterial and venous blood glucose is a major cause of the confusion that has surrounded the recognition and diagnosis of hypoglycemia and been responsible for nonhypoglycaemia becoming a common diagnosis amongst those whom Singer and coworkers refer to as, the folk sector.

In the fasting subject the concentration of glucose in arterial and venous blood is virtually identical but may differ by as much as $2.5 \, \text{mmol} \, \text{l}^{-1}$ following ingestion of a carbohydrate-rich meal. Because it is arterial blood glucose that determines glucose supply to the brain, regulates the secretion of insulin and other hormones, and is itself homeostatically controlled, it is necessary to define hypoglycemia in terms of glucose in arterial (or more realistically free flowing capillary) than in venous blood.

Mechanism of Hypoglycemia Glucose Pool in Fasting Subjects

Glucose is confined within the body to the extracellular fluid where it is referred to as the glucose pool: detailed discussion of its regulation is outside the scope of this article except to stress that it reflects the concentration of glucose in the blood. This remains remarkably constant despite huge changes in the rates of delivery and utilization of glucose, by meals and exercise (and fasting), respectively, and is described as glucose homeostasis (**Figure 1**). The main but far from sole regulator is insulin.

Insulin Release in Response to Eating and Fasting

Evidence for a 'cephalic phase' of insulin secretion in humans is scanty and conflicting. Most observers have found a minimal, if any, response to the prospect of eating, or the reality of drinking, a noncalorigenic sweet drink except in some obese individuals.

After a carbohydrate-containing meal, glucose derived from food enters the portal vein. From here it is conveyed to the liver where much of it is extracted and converted to glycogen. What remains unabsorbed passes into the systemic circulation, producing small and variable rises in arterial, capillary, and, initially, venous blood glucose concentrations. The modest rise in arterial blood glucose concentration perfusing the pancreas, augmented by nervous stimuli and insulinotrophic hormones, collectively called incretins, released from the gut in response to meals containing carbohydrate and/or fats, leads to the secretion of insulin in greater amounts than is occasioned by the rise in blood glucose concentration alone.

In the postprandial period, as the blood glucose concentration fall towards its homeostatically controlled level, insulin secretion declines to a level that is just sufficient to suppress unbridled lipolysis. Absence of this constitutive insulin secretion in patients with type 1 diabetes is the cause of diabetic ketoacidosis.

The Role of the Liver in Glucose Homeostasis

The liver, under the influence of insulin reaching it in high concentration in the portal vein after ingestion of a meal, switches from being a net exporter to net importer of glucose from the glucose pool. Any insulin not extracted and degraded by the liver passes through the heart and lungs to reach peripheral tissues, notably muscle, adipose tissue, and skin, where, providing the concentration of insulin in blood is sufficiently high, it promotes glucose uptake.

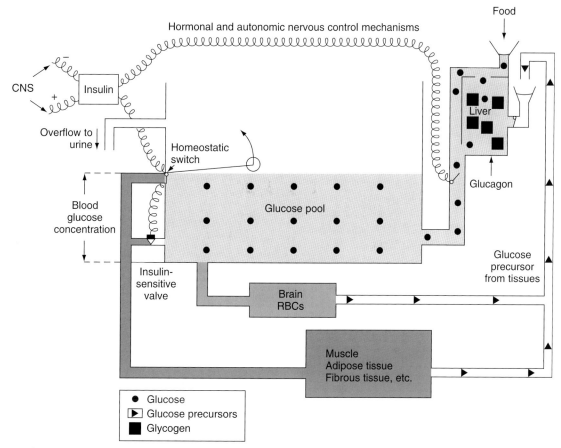

Figure 1 Schematic representation of homeostatic control of blood glucose level and mechanism of hypoglycemia. Hypoglycemia results whenever inflow of glucose from the gut and/or liver fails to meet the outflow of glucose from the glucose pool, which consists of glucose dissolved in the extracellular water only. Imbalance arises from: (1) excessive outflow into the tissues due to insulin (or very rarely IGF-II) overproduction or activity; or (2) in the fasting state, an inability of the liver to liberate or produce glucose at a rate sufficient to meet the non-insulin-dependent, and obligatory, requirements of the brain and red blood cells for glucose.

Except in disease, the glucose pool, amounting to just 5–15 g, rarely expands by more than 100% even after ingestion of a meal providing up to 300 g of carbohydrate as starch or glucose. Nor does it shrink to less than 4 g even after many days of fasting.

Entry of glucose into the glucose pool is limited by the rate at which it can be absorbed from the intestine. This is normally in the region of 25–50 g h^{-1}. In people with normal glucose tolerance, venous blood glucose levels generally return to overnight fasting values within 2 h of eating a meal regardless of how much carbohydrate it contains. Arterial blood glucose levels take somewhat longer to return to preingestion levels but they too are always within the normal fasting range by 3 h, even though the evidence provided by measurement of the gut hormones Glucose-Dependent Insulinotrophic Peptide (GIP), the main incretin, indicate that absorption of large meals continues for much longer. Absorption of a 200-g liquid glucose meal by normal healthy subjects, for example, is still incomplete after 5 h

even though both their venous and arterial blood glucose levels have long since returned to normal.

The outflow of glucose into the tissues, on the other hand, depends upon many factors; the two most important are the plasma insulin concentration and the blood concentration itself. Under maximum insulin stimulation – and at 'normal' blood glucose levels – glucose can disappear from the glucose pool at a rate of up to 40–50 g h^{-1} but these conditions are rarely encountered except experimentally or in cases of gross insulin overdose.

Onset of insulin action is almost instantaneous and persists for as long as insulin remains bound to insulin receptors. This is generally slightly longer than insulin levels in the blood themselves remain elevated. In other words glucose continues to enter insulin-dependent cells for up to 30 min after plasma insulin levels have returned to 'fasting' levels. During this time the glucose pool may shrink sufficiently to produce hypoglycemia unless replenished by glucose continuing to enter from the intestine (or experimentally/therapeutically by intravenous infusion) or from the liver, once it has switched from the glycogenic to glycogenolytic mode.

Small, and always temporary, imbalances between the rate at which insulin action declines and glucose enters the glucose pool can occur in healthy subjects after ingestion of a large dose of glucose in solution on an empty stomach, but is rare following the ingestion of an ordinary mixed meal.

A slight delay in stimulating insulin release in response to a meal is the earliest and most characteristic abnormality observed in patients with non-insulin-dependent diabetes mellitus (NIDDM) who may secrete more insulin in total than people of comparable age, though not of body mass index. They are, however, generally insulin resistant, which explains why, despite the larger amounts of insulin secreted in response to meals in the early stages of their illness, they do not suffer from meal-induced hypoglycemia.

Hypoglycemic Syndromes

Brain Malfunction from Hypoglycemia

The brain ordinarily requires a regular and plentiful supply of glucose, which gets to it from the blood by active transport utilizing the glucose transporter protein GLUT 1. Reduction of supply to below critical limits causes the brain to malfunction and this manifests itself subjectively as symptoms and objectively as neurological deficit. The blood glucose level at which impairment occurs varies. Symptoms are unusual at blood glucose levels above $3.0 \, \mathrm{mmol \, l^{-1}}$ except in diabetic and elderly subjects in whom they may occur at higher levels. Objective evidence of cerebral impairment can however often be discerned by an investigator at blood glucose levels around $3.5-4 \, \mathrm{mmol \, l^{-1}}$.

Causes of neuroglycopenia other than hypoglycemia, i.e., normoglycemic neuroglycopenia, are currently thought to be rare but include congenital or acquired reduction in GLUT 1. The possibility that such defects are more common than currently supposed and are responsible for some cases of 'nonhypoglycemia' cannot be dismissed at the present time, and would help explain why, under research conditions, some people diagnosed with this condition appear to develop symptoms at higher blood glucose levels than control subjects.

Neuroglycopenic Syndromes

Four more or less distinct neuroglycopenic syndromes (one of which is so rare that it will not be considered further here) can be recognized. They are not mutually exclusive, nor do they depend upon the ultimate cause of the hypoglycemia.

Acute Neuroglycopenia

This syndrome comprises a collection of vague symptoms such as feelings of alternating hot and cold, feeling unwell, anxiety, panic, inner trembling, unnatural feelings, blurring of vision, and palpitations, any or all of which may be accompanied by objective signs of facial flushing, sweating, tachycardia, and unsteadiness of gait. There is no particular order in which these features occur, nor are they constant. Nevertheless, patients on insulin therapy for diabetes, in whom they are common, rely upon them to warn of more severe neuroglycopenic impairment culminating in loss of consciousness. These patients can be taught to abort progression of symptoms by eating carbohydrate.

Many of the features of acute neuroglycopenia resemble those produced by adrenaline and consequently are often referred to as adrenergic.

Subacute Neuroglycopenia

This syndrome is more insidious and may go completely unrecognized unless or until the patient loses consciousness. Often, however, there is loss of spontaneous activity, impairment of cognitive function and the onset of somnolence that is more discernible to the bystander than to the patient and which, when it occurs *de novo* in an insulin-treated diabetic, is often referred to as 'hypoglycemia unawareness.'

Acute can proceed to subacute neuroglycopenia and both can progress to stupor or coma unless relieved by food or injection of glucagon. Even when this is not done, however, full recovery, under the influence of endogenous counter-regulatory mechanisms, is almost invariable and is the reason why treatment with insulin is so safe despite the potential dangers of hypoglycemia.

Chronic Neuroglycopenia

The third syndrome is exceedingly rare. It occurs only when the blood glucose concentration remains low, either due to the presence of an insulin-secreting tumor of the pancreas or overzealous treatment of diabetes with insulin for weeks or months on end. It is characterized by mental dysfunction resembling clinical depression, schizophrenia, or dementia, the symptoms of which are not relieved by restoring the blood glucose level to normal. Partial recovery may, however, take place over the ensuing months or years if the cause of the hypoglycemia is remedied.

This condition might be confused with 'nonhypoglycaemia' were it not for the fact that the blood glucose concentration is invariably low ($<3.0 \, \text{mmol} \, l^{-1}$) while the patient is fasting, does not rise normally in response to food, and evidence of underlying disease can always be found.

Diagnosis

Causes of Hypoglycemia

There is something in the region of 100 causes of hypoglycemia but all, apart from exogenous (or iatrogenic) insulin overdose, are uncommon. Some of the most important causes of recurrent hypoglycemia are listed and briefly described in **Table 1**. Simultaneous occurrence of symptoms, a measured low blood glucose concentration, and relief from intravenous glucose are a sine qua non for diagnosis. Differentiation is seldom simple and always rests heavily upon the results of laboratory data of which measurements of plasma insulin and C-peptide are the most important.

Endocrinological and other anatomico-pathological causes of hypoglycemia will not be considered further. Nor will iatrogenic or toxic causes, of which alcohol-induced fasting hypoglycemia is easily the most common. Instead, attention will be given to those conditions (including 'nonhypoglycaemia') that have a mainly or exclusively dietary etiology and which respond partially or completely to dietary measures.

Spontaneous Reactive Hypoglycemia

Within a year of the discovery of insulin, and the symptoms to which hypoglycemia can give rise, Seale Harris, an American physician, had proposed that spontaneous overproduction of endogenous insulin might produce a similar condition. Confirmation of this hypothesis soon followed. The seminal work of Whipple on the diagnosis of insulinoma and of Conn on diet-induced postprandial reactive hypoglycemia, both in 1936, distinguished between fast-induced (fasting) hypoglycemia and that which occurred only in response to feeding. The latter, reactive or postprandial hypoglycemia, could be reproduced by oral administration of large doses of glucose in solution and this became the standard criterion for its diagnosis – the 5-h glucose tolerance test.

Glucose Load Test

The observation that in a substantial percentage of normal healthy people glucose taken in solution on an empty stomach produces a rebound fall in venous blood glucose levels to below fasting levels was made soon after blood glucose measurements became possible and before the discovery of insulin. It attracted little attention at the time being considered to have only curiosity value and little pathological significance.

The situation changed dramatically during the early 1950s and, subsequently, particularly in the US, with the appearance of books written for lay consumption attributing a vast array of common symptoms to hypoglycemia, whether the blood glucose concentration was low at the time or not. Belief in the importance and prevalence of 'hypoglycemia' grew amongst fashionable medical practitioners and the general public alike to such an extent that, by the early 1970s, alarm bells began to ring amongst consumer action groups and the scientific medical community.

With the passage of time the original, well-defined syndrome of postprandial reactive hypoglycemia had become so distorted, and the criteria for its diagnosis so blurred, that anyone with vague symptoms could be, and often was, described as suffering from 'hypoglycemia,' without anyone bothering to measure their blood glucose concentration.

Not until a consensus 'Statement on 'Post Prandial' or 'Reactive' Hypoglycemia' was issued by the Third International Symposium on Hypoglycemia and generally recognized by medical practitioners throughout the world did scientific criteria for the diagnosis of reactive hypoglycemia gain universal acceptance and its purported incidence declined dramatically.

Definition

It is now accepted that some people exhibit, in the course of their everyday life, symptoms similar to those caused by acute neuroglycopenia and may, if accompanied by a capillary or arterialized venous blood glucose concentration of $2.8–2.5 \, \text{mmol} \, l^{-1}$ or less, justify description as being of postprandial reactive hypoglycemic origin. Reactive hypoglycemia may itself be a consequence of any one of a large number of well-recognized but generally uncommon conditions that can also produce fast-induced hypoglycemia, and it is only after they have been excluded by appropriate laboratory investigations that a diagnosis of functional or dietary reactive hypoglycemia is justified.

Specifically, the prolonged oral glucose load (tolerance) test is now deemed inappropriate for the diagnosis of postprandial or reactive hypoglycemia since the incidence of false-positive results with this test is so high as to make it meaningless, especially if, as is so often the case, venous rather than arterial blood is sampled.

Table 1 The main causes of non-iatrogenic hypoglycemia

Description	Mechanism	Diagnostic criteria	Dietary considerations
Fasting hypoglycemia			
Insulin-secreting tumor (insulinoma) and nesidioblastosis	Abnormal B cells with failure to suppress insulin secretion in response to hypoglycemia	Inappropriate high plasma insulin ($>30\,pmol\,l^{-1}$) and C-peptide ($>100\,pmol\,l^{-1}$) concentrations in presence of hypoglycemia (BG $<2.2\,mmol\,l^{-1}$); Suppressed β-hydroxybutyrate levels ($<500\,\mu mol\,l^{-1}$)	High-carbohydrate intake orally or intravenously until curative surgical ablation or effective hyperglycemic therapy with diazoxide plus chlorothiazide can be instituted
Non-Islet cell tumor hypoglycemia (NICTH)	Abnormal tumor cells secreting big IGF-II	Low plasma insulin & C-peptide levels; low plasma IGF-I, normal or raised IGF-II levels; abnormal IGF-I:IGF-II ratio. Suppressed β-hydroxybutyrate levels ($<500\,\mu mol\,l^{-1}$)	High-carbohydrate intake orally or intravenously until curative surgical ablation of effective hyperglycemic therapy with growth hormone &/or prednisone can be instituted
Endocrine disease, e.g., Hypopituitarism, Addison's disease	Reduced availability of diabetogenic or hypoglycemia counterregulatory hormones	Clinical features of primary disease with subnormal levels of appropriate counter-regulatory hormones, e.g., cortisol, growth hormone. Appropriately raised β-hyroxybutyrate levels ($>500\,\mu mol\,l^{-1}$) during hypoglycemia	High-carbohydrate intake orally or intravenously until effective hormone replacement therapy has been established
Glycogen storage disease	Inability to release glucose from liver during fasting	Usually present in childhood; low blood glucose, high β-hydroxybutyrate levels, low insulin and C-peptide; high lactate; impaired or absent glucose response to glucagon	Avoid fasting: a constant intake of slowly absorbed carbohydrate may be required day and night in infants
Disorders of mitochondrial β-oxidation	Defective utilization of fat as fuel in tissues: compensatory increase in glucose utilization	Occurs in infancy; low glucose, low insulin & C-peptide, high FFA, normal lactate, low β-hydroxybutyrate, increased urinary organic acids. Hypocarnitinemia in some cases	Avoid fasting; frequent high-carbohydrate, low-fat feeding
Fasting alcohol-induced hypoglycemia	Alcohol impaired hepatic gluconeogenesis	Low blood glucose, raised blood alcohol, lactate and usually β-hydroxybutyrate: low plasma insulin and C-peptide	Avoid drinking alcohol whilst fasting or whilst on a low-energy diet
Idiopathic ketotic hypoglycemia of childhood	Varied: but always due to exhaustion of hepatic glycogen stores faster than cerebral adaptation to ketosis can occur	Low blood glucose; high plasma fatty acids and β-hydroxybutyrate; low insulin and C-peptide	High-carbohydrate feeding; avoidance of prolonged abstinence from food particularly during intercurrent illness, especially infections
Stimulative hypoglycemia			
Inborn errors of metabolism, e.g., hereditary fructose intolerance, galactosemia	Impaired release of glucose from liver in response to hepatotoxicity of food constituent	Hypoglycemia evoked by ingestion of foods containing appropriate noxious stimulus: galactose in galactosemia; fructose in hereditary fructose intolerance and fructose 1-6 bisphosphatase deficiency	Avoid foods containing provocative sugars, e.g., fructose, galactose as appropriate
Autoimmune insulin syndrome	Delayed release of insulin from antibody binding after all of meal has been absorbed	Profound hypoglycemia from 3 to 12 hs after last eating; total plasma insulin high; C-peptide high, normal or low proinsulin normal or high. Antibodies to insulin present. Common in Japan, infrequent elsewhere	Frequent small mixed meals, low in rapidly absorbed carbohydrate; rich in dietary fiber

Continued

Table 1 Continued

Description	Mechanism	Diagnostic criteria	Dietary considerations
Postgastrectomy and rapid gastric empying	Accelerated deposition of nutrients in duodenum and increased release of insulinotrophic hormones, e.g., GIP, GLP-1	Normal blood glucose during fasting; hypoglycemia only follows 1–3 hs after eating. History of gastrectomy or objective evidence of rapid gastric emptying. Exaggerated insulinemic response to food	Frequent small mixed meals rich in dietary fiber. May benefit from treatment with acabose or miglitol (α-glucosidase inhibitors)
Idiopathic reactive or functional hypoglycemia	Unknown: probably heterogeneous including increased insulin sensitivity, lowered cerebral threshold to neuroglycopenia	Hypoglycemia 3–5 hs after eating. Normal blood glucose during fasting: low capillary (arterial) blood glucose during spontaneous symptomatic neuroglycopenic episodes (<3 mmol l^{-1}). All other objective tests of glucose homeostasis normal (including GIP and GLP-1 responses to food). Exclude noninsulinoma pancreatogenic hypoglycemia by intra-arterial calcium test	Frequent small mixed meals low in absorbed carbohydrates; rich in soluble dietary fiber. May benefit from treatment with acabose or miglitol (α-glucosidase inhibitors)

The Postprandial Syndrome

Typically, the patient is a normal-weight woman of 20–50 years whose main complaint is of vague feelings of distress occurring predominantly mid morning, about 11.00 a.m.–12.00 noon, but occasionally mid afternoon or evening and never before breakfast. In between attacks, characterized by feeling of faintness, anxiety, nervousness, irritability, inner trembling, rapid heart beat, headache, and sweatiness, either alone or in combination, they may be completely well. More often they describe themselves as suffering from increased tiredness, lacking in zest for life, and apathetic much, or all, of the time: symptoms often associated with depression or chronic alcohol abuse.

Patients seldom notice any fixed relationship to food unless, as so often happens nowadays, they have diagnosed themselves, on the basis of articles they may have read, as suffering from 'hypoglycemia.' Almost without exception they reject the possibility that their symptoms might have a contributory, or even large, psychogenic element.

Symptoms wax and wane during middle life but often remit completely for years or may never recur. They are not progressive and never cause severe neurological dysfunction such as coma, psychosis, or dementia. Hypoglycemia cannot be demonstrated during spontaneous symptomatic episodes in most people with the postprandial syndrome and some other explanation should be sought for them.

Differential Diagnosis

Studies using finger-prick blood sampling during spontaneous symptomatic episodes have shown that only a very small proportion of sufferers from the postprandial syndrome have hypoglycemia at the relevant time. Of those who do, a substantial proportion have an identifiable cause for it. The commonest is partial gastrectomy and rapid gastric emptying from any cause, in the West, and the autoimmune insulin syndrome in the Far East, i.e., Japan. Other more rare causes include insulinoma, the newly described condition of noninsulinoma pancreatogenic hypoglycemia, and abnormalities of GLP-1 secretion.

In some people reactive hypoglycemia occurs only in response to a specific dietary indiscretion: for example, ingestion of large amounts of gin (alcohol) and tonic (sugar and quinine) on an empty stomach. A hard core of subjects remains for whom no satisfactory pathogenic mechanism can be identified. Only in them is it justified to describe them as suffering from (idiopathic or functional) reactive hypoglycemia (**Figure 2**).

Dietary Management

Treatment of Attacks

Because of their short duration and modest severity, acute spontaneous neuroglycopenic episodes require no specific treatment beyond ingestion of a rapidly assimilable form of carbohydrate (e.g., a lump of sugar), exactly as for iatrogenic hypoglycemia.

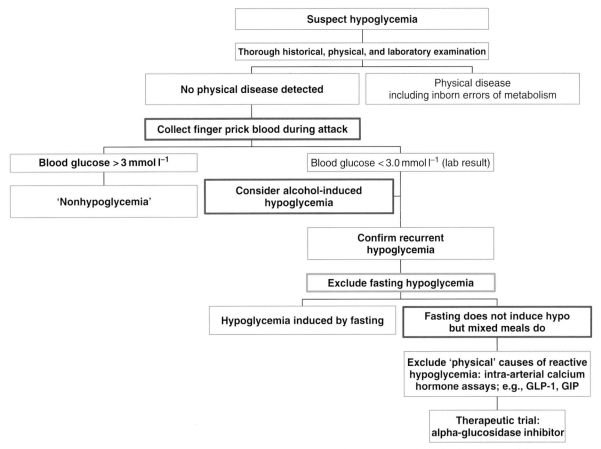

Figure 2 Investigation of reactive hypoglycemia. Steps in the diagnosis of reactive hypoglycemia of unknown etiology.

There is no evidence that this ever produces rebound hypoglycemia and should it do so the grounds for making a diagnosis of essential reactive hypoglycemia should be reviewed.

Prevention

Dietary prevention of reactive hypoglycemia, whether of the 'idiopathic', alimentary variety, or secondary to some other disease, is based on the premise that it is caused by imbalance between the timing and amount of insulin secreted in response to the ingestion of a meal and disposal of the glucose derived from it. Evidence for this supposition is small and disputed but provides the best explanation for the apparent breakdown in glucose homeostasis in patients with idiopathic reactive hypoglycemia.

Frequent small meals containing only modest amounts of sugars (glucose and sucrose) and refined starches but rich in poorly absorbed complex carbohydrates and containing dietary fiber have replaced the diets rich in proteins (and fats) previously advocated, but evidence of their unique efficacy is lacking. Avoidance of drinks rich in sucrose or glucose, especially with alcohol, may be helpful in subjects who are highly susceptible to this combination. There is no evidence that confectionery eaten in moderation is uniquely detrimental, though excessive use should be discouraged on general health grounds.

The long-term outcome of such dietary advice in patients in whom strict criteria for diagnosis were adopted are not available and most published studies on the subject have drawn attention to the need for supplementary pharmacological methods in order to achieve a satisfactory therapeutic outcome.

Pharmaceutical agents that have been used include guar, acarbose, and miglitol, all of which slow glucose absorption and decrease the insulinemic response to food, while others including phenytoin and propranolol do not. Paradoxically, diazoxide, which inhibits insulin secretion by direct action, has not been found effective except in patients with proven endogenous hyperinsulinism.

Nonhypoglycemia

No account of dietetic treatment of hypoglycemia would be complete without a brief description of 'nonhypoglycemia', which has been described as a controversial illness and epidemic in the US. Clinically, the illness is indistinguishable from (idiopathic) reactive hypoglycemia, except that the blood glucose level is never pathologically low during symptomatic episodes. Moreover, although transient 'turns' are often a major feature of the illness, only rarely, if ever, does the patient consider their health, between turns, as normal.

The attribution of these patients' illness to hypoglycemia had its origins in the early 1950s with the appearance, in the US, of a book by Drs Abrahams and Pezet entitled 'Body, Mind and Sugar.' Other American practitioners, notably John Tintera, founder of the Hypoglycemia Foundation Inc., Stephen Gyland, Harry Saltzer and, others, including the medical writer Carlton Fredericks, publicized the concept. This led to 'hypoglycemia' being held, by a large section of the public, responsible for such diverse diseases as coronary artery disease, allergy, asthma, rheumatic fever, susceptibility to viral infections, epilepsy, gastric ulcer, alcoholism, suicide, and even homicide, as well as for a whole galaxy of symptoms in their own right. 'Hypoglycemia' was treated as though it were a disease entity and asserted by its advocates to be 'one of the most common illnesses in the United States' and that because of it 'thousands of Americans have forgotten, or perhaps never known, what it is like to feel completely healthy.' Diagnosis of 'nonhypoglycemia' generally depends upon the results of the 6-h oral glucose tolerance test, using venous blood, although some have dispensed even with this discredited formality in favor of just purely clinical criteria.

The appearance in the *New England Journal of Medicine* of an article entitled "Nonhypoglycemia is an epidemic condition" first drew international attention to the illness in 1974. It had previously been almost unknown outside the US and Australia, though known to a few fashionable medical practitioners in Britain.

Many patients with 'nonhypoglycemia' undoubtedly derive some benefit, probably through a powerful placebo effect, from severely restrictive dietary regimes. Although differing in details most of the diets emphasize the purported specifically detrimental effects of sugar (sucrose), salt, alcohol, and caffeine.

While the cause of illness in people with 'nonhypoglycemia' remains unknown, and is unlikely to be the same in all cases, in a tiny proportion it is due to caffeine intoxication, which can be confirmed by a dietary history and, above all, by measurement of plasma caffeine levels. Such patients do benefit specifically from reducing their intake of caffeinated beverages, though not necessarily from avoiding them

completely. Ironically, and probably significantly, caffeine restores hypoglycemia awareness to diabetic patients on insulin who have become insensitive to it. The possibility exists, therefore, that a combination of reasonable or normal caffeine intake occurring in combination with the normal rebound in arterial blood glucose to just below fasting levels that sometimes occurs 3–5 h after a meal in someone with an unusually low threshold for neuroglycopenia, might precipitate symptoms. This explanation must, however, be considered no more than speculative.

On the other hand such diverse illnesses as hyperventilation, panic attacks, unadmitted alcohol or drug abuse, and genuine food intolerances are all established as capable of producing the 'nonhypoglyacemia' syndrome and should always be considered in the differential diagnosis.

Exercise-Induced Hypoglycemia

Previously only associated with marathon running, hypoglycemia is now recognized to be comparatively common in inadequately trained individuals undertaking strenuous exercise. Consumption of rapidly absorbed carbohydrate prior to taking exercise may encourage its appearance whilst consumption of slowly absorbed, low glycemic index foods may prevent it as does appropriate training.

Hepatic and Renal Failure

Considering the importance of the liver and kidney in the maintenance of blood glucose levels hypoglycemia is remarkably rare in both liver and kidney disease. In liver disease hypoglycemia is virtually confined to patients with acute toxic hepatic necrosis, whether due to overwhelming viral infection or specific hepatotoxins such as poisonous mushrooms, unripe akee fruit, and paracetamol in excess. Its appearance always portends an extremely poor prognosis. The association of hypoglycemia with primary cancer of the liver is comparatively common and due to overexpression and secretion of aberrant, or big IGF-II, and is not, as was once supposed, due to nonspecific destruction of hepatic tissue. Hypoglycemia is very rarely due to hepatic secondaries except from IGF-II secreting tumors.

Kidney failure is one of the commoner causes of hypoglycemia in nondiabetic hospital inpatients and does not carry as grave a prognostic significance as in patients with liver disease. It generally responds to appropriate dietary and other supportive treatments for end-stage kidney disease.

Inborn Errors of Metabolism

Hypoglycemia is a manifestation of many inborn errors of metabolism (see **Table 1**) especially in children but also occasionally in adults. It is particularly important in some varieties of liver glycogen storage diseases, especially types I and III, and in disorders of fatty acid metabolism in which it is often the presenting symptom.

Type I liver glycogen storage disease is due to a defect in glucose-6-phosphatase activity and produces a severe form of fasting hypoglycemia. Fortunately, this responds to dietary therapy in the form of continuous feeding with slowly absorbed starch solution through a nasal or gastrostomy tube, especially during the night when the body normally has to resort to glycogenolysis to maintain the supply of glucose to the brain. Hypoglycemia in untreated type I patients produces hypoinsulinemia and high to very high plasma ketone levels. Children with abnormalities of fatty acid metabolism, on the other hand, are characterized by hypoglycemia, hypoinsulinemia, and hypoketonemia. As with children with liver glycogen disease, treatment is to ensure that they are constantly supplied with carbohydrates and are never fasting for more than a very short period.

Starvation

Although average fasting blood glucose levels are lower in victims of famine than in well-fed populations, overt hypoglycemia is rare. Even in patients suffering from kwashiorkor, hypoglycemia is uncommon and is usually associated with infection, hypothermia, and coma. Patients with anorexia nervosa develop hypoglycemia only as an agonal phenomenon and its appearance generally portends imminent death. The characteristic clinical biochemistry findings are of low or undetectably low plasma insulin, proinsulin, C-peptide, and IGF-1 levels, grossly depressed plasma nonesterified fatty acids (NEFA) and β-hydroxybutyrate, and elevated growth hormone and cortisol levels. Relief of hypoglycemia by re-feeding is the only measure carrying any chance of preventing death, but it is rarely successful.

Hypoglycemia in the Elderly Sick

The high incidence of hypoglycemia in sick elderly patients has become apparent from the use of routine blood glucose measurements. The cause is seldom attributable to any of the well-recognized causes of hypoglycemia found in younger fitter people. It is probably due to chronic malnutrition that is so common in the elderly sick, compounded by coincident disease but which is not of itself sufficiently severe to produce hypoglycemia.

Conclusions

Symptoms due to documented spontaneous hypoglycemia are an unusual consequence of many different rare diseases and are sometimes the primary reason for a patient seeking medical help. In a minority of patients no pathological cause can be found to account for the hypoglycemia and no specific curative or palliative therapy can be instituted. Amongst these are a group of patients who only experience neuroglycopenic symptoms 2–5 h after eating a meal. They may benefit from eating small, frequent, slowly absorbed carbohydrate-rich meals. Usually, however, they also need addition of an α-glucosidase inhibitor to their diet.

Patients with self-diagnosed hypoglycemia in whom blood glucose levels are never pathologically low in everyday life and do not have any other known cause for their symptoms may also derive some benefit from a high-fiber, high complex carbohydrate diet, but how much of this is due to a placebo rather than specific dietary effect is still unknown.

See also: **Aging**. **Cancer**: Epidemiology and Associations Between Diet and Cancer; Epidemiology of Gastrointestinal Cancers Other Than Colorectal Cancers. **Diabetes Mellitus**: Etiology and Epidemiology; Classification and Chemical Pathology; Dietary Management. **Exercise**: Beneficial Effects; Diet and Exercise. **Famine**. **Fatty Acids**: Metabolism. **Glucose**: Chemistry and Dietary Sources; Metabolism and Maintenance of Blood Glucose Level; Glucose Tolerance. **Liver Disorders**. **Starvation and Fasting**.

Further Reading

Brun JF, Dumortier M, Fedou C, and Mercier J (2001) Exercise hypoglycemia in non-diabetic subjects. *Diabetes and Metabolism* **27**: 92–106.

Brun JF, Fedou C, and Mercier J (2000) Postprandial reactive hypoglycemia. *Diabetes and Metabolism* **26**: 337–351.

Editorial (1974) Low blood sugar: Fact and Fiction. *Consumer Reports USA* **36**: 444–446.

Fonseca V, Ball S, Marks V, and Havard CWH (1991) Hypoglycaemia associated with anorexia nervosa. *Postgraduate Medical Journal* **67**: 460–461.

Hojlund K, Hansen T, Lajer M, Henriksen JE, Levin K, Lindholm J, Pedersen O, and Beck-Nielsen H (2004) A novel syndrome of autosomal-dominant hypersinsulinemic hypoglycemia linked to a mutation in the human insulin receptor gene. *Diabetes* **53**: 1592–1598.

Kerr D, Sherwin RS, Pavalkis F, Fayad PB, Sikorski L, Rife F, Tamborlane WV, and During MJ (1993) Effect of caffeine on the recognition of and the responses to hypoglycemia in humans. *Annals of Internal Medicine* **119**: 799–804.

Klepper J and Voit T (2002) Facilitated glucose transporter protein type 1 (GLUT 1) deficiency syndrome: impaired glucose transport into brain – a review. *European Journal of Pediatrics* **161**: 295–304.

Lefebvre PJ, Andreani D, Marks V, and Creutzfeldt W (1988) Statement on postprandial hypoglycemia. *Diabetes Care* **11**: 439–440.

Marks V (1976) The measurement of blood glucose and the definition of hypoglycemia. In: Andreani D, Lefebvre PJ, and Marks V (eds.) *Hypoglycemia. Proceedings of the European Symposium, Rome. Hormone and Metabolic Research*, pp. 1–6. Suppl 6 Stuttgart: Georg Thieme.

Marks V (1987) Functional hypoglycaemia: fact or fancy. In: Andreani D, Marks V, and Lefebvre PJ (eds.) *Hypoglycaemia: Serono Symposia Publications*, vol. 38, pp. 1–17. New York: Raven Press.

Marks V (2003) Hypoglycaemia. In: Warrell DA, Cox TM, Firth JD, and Benz EJ (eds.) *Oxford Textbook of Medicine*, 4th edn, vol. 2, pp. 362–369. Oxford: Oxford University Press.

Mori S and Ito H (1988) Hypoglycemia in the Elderly. *Japanese Journal of Medicine* **27**: 160–166.

Palardy J, Havrankova J, Lepage R, Matte R, Belanger R, D'Amour P, and Ste-Marie L-G (1989) Blood glucose measurements during symptomatic episodes in patients with suspected postprandial hypoglycemia. *New England Journal of Medicine* **321**: 1421–1425.

Peter S (2003) Acabose and idiopathic hypoglycemia. *Hormone Research* **60**: 166–167.

Service FJ (1989) Hypoglycemia and the postprandial syndrome. *New England Journal of Medicine* **321**: 1472–1473.

Service FJ, Natt N, Thompson GB, Grant CS, van Heerden JA, Andrews JC, Lorenz E, Terzic A, and Lloyd RV (1999) Non-insulinoma pancreatogenous hypoglycemia: a novel syndrome of hyperinsulinemic hypoglycemia in adults independent of mutations in Kir6.2 and SUR1 genes. *The Journal of Clinical Endocrinology and Metabolism* **84**: 1582–1589.

Shilo S, Berezovsky S, Friedlander Y, and Sonnenblick M (1998) Hypoglycemia in hospitalized non-diabetic older patients. *Journal of the American Geriatric Society* **46**: 978–982.

Singer M, Arnold C, Fitzgerald M, Madden L, and Voight von Legat C (1984) Hypoglycemia: a controversial illness in US society. *Medical Anthropology* **8**: 1–35.

Snorgaard O, Lassen LH, Rosenfalck AM, and Binder C (1991) Glycaemic thresholds for hypoglycaemic symptoms, impairment of cognitive function, and release of counterregulatory hormones in subjects with functional hypoglycaemia. *Journal of Internal Medicine* **229**: 343–350.

Tamburrano G, Leonetti F, Sbraccia P, Giaccari A, Locuratolo N, and Lala A (1989) Increased insulin sensitivity in patients with idiopathic reactive hypoglycemia. *Journal of Clinical Endocrinology and Metabolism* **69**: 885–890.

Teale JD, Wark G, and Marks V (2002) The biochemical investigation of cases of hypoglycaemia: an assessment of the clinical effectiveness of analytical services. *Journal of Clinical Pathology* **55**: 503–507.

Yager J and Young RT (1974) Sounding board: non-hypoglycemia is an epidemic condition. *New England Journal of Medicine* **291**: 907–908.

ISBN 0-12-150110-8